Chobits
ちょびっツ

◄ BOOK 1 ►

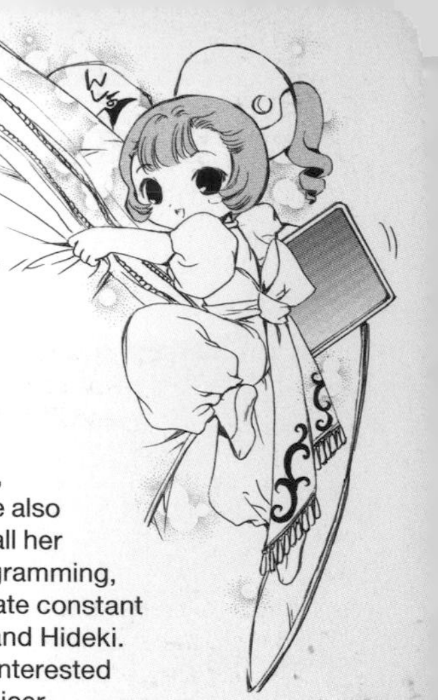

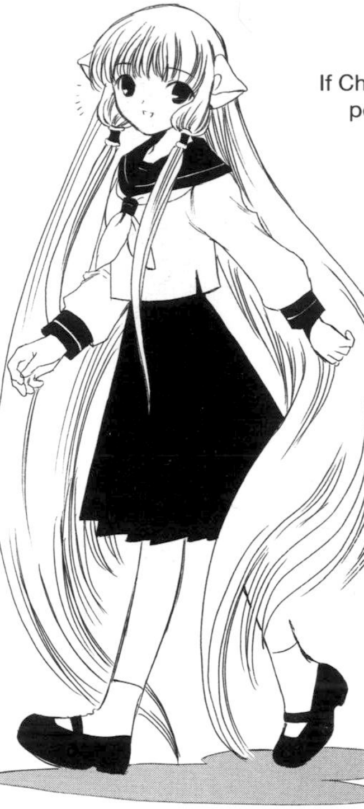

Sumomo
If Chi is a desktop-sized persocom, Sumomo is a laptop version! Shimbo is very fond of the sprightly Sumomo.

Chi
Even for a persocom, Chi is charming. She also seems to have lost all her memories and programming, which tends to create constant trouble for herself and Hideki. A lot of people are interested in Chi . . . some for nicer reasons than others. Chi, like Yumi (below) often gets the cute-sounding *-chan* added to her name when people address her.

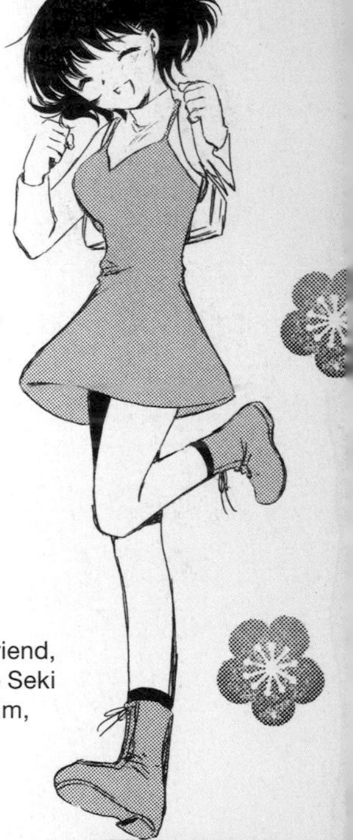

Yumi Omura
Bouncy high-school student Yumi also works at Club Pleasure. She tends to call Motosuwa *sempai*, meaning “senior,” because he’s been there longer than her.

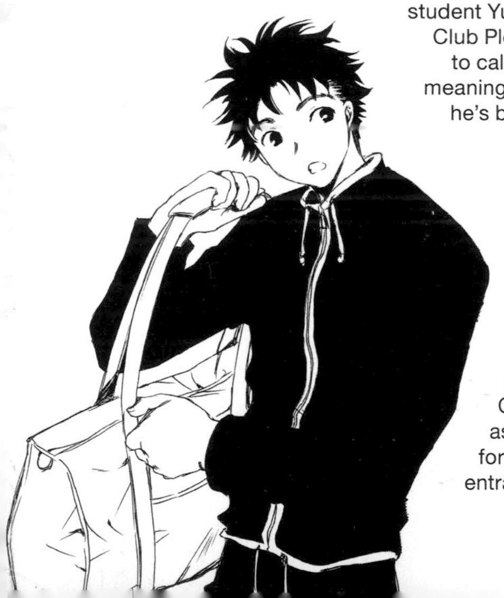

Hiromu Shimbo
Motosuwa’s best friend, Shimbo attends the Seki Cram School with him, as both are studying for their college-entrance exams.

SOME OF THE CHARACTERS IN *CHOBITS* BOOK 1

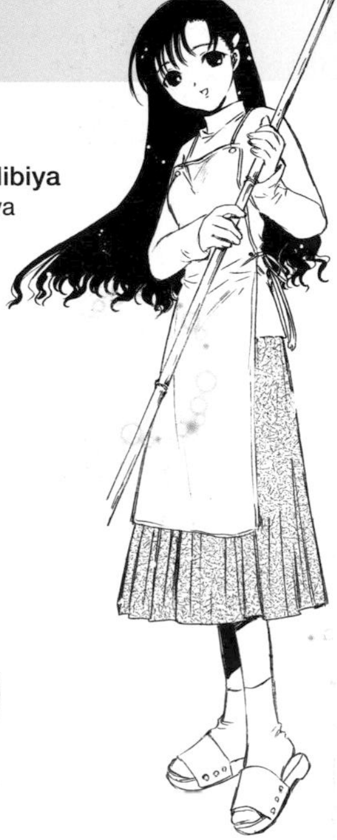

Chitose Hibiya

Motosuwa's landlady, the kind and lovely Ms. Hibiya helps him out with gifts of much-needed food, and Chi with gifts of much-needed clothes.

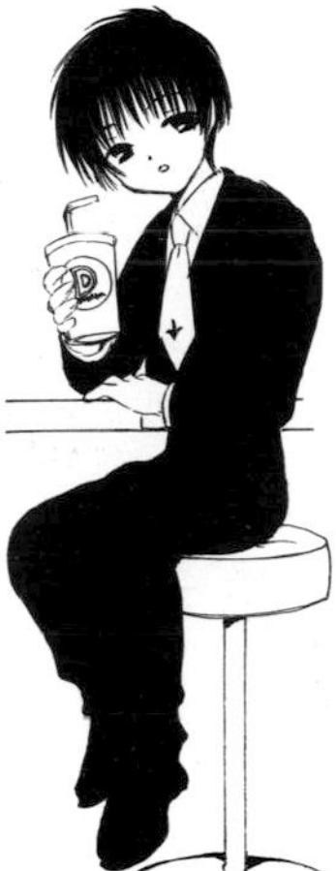

Minoru Kokubunji

Rich, reserved, aristocratic . . . and he's only in the sixth grade. Kokubunji is an expert on persocoms and custom-builds them. He tends to refer to Motosuwa by the polite Motosuwa-*san*, but perhaps because of his age (and resentment), Motosuwa calls him by the more familiar Minoru-*kun*.

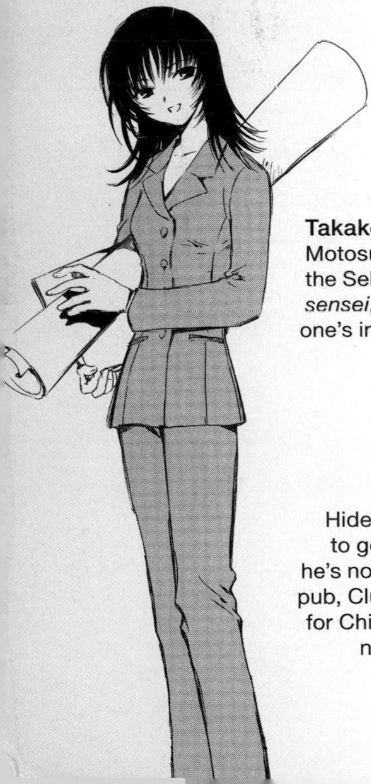

Takako Shimizu

Motosuwa and Shimbo's teacher at the Seki Cram School. She's often called *sensei*, a common way of addressing one's instructor.

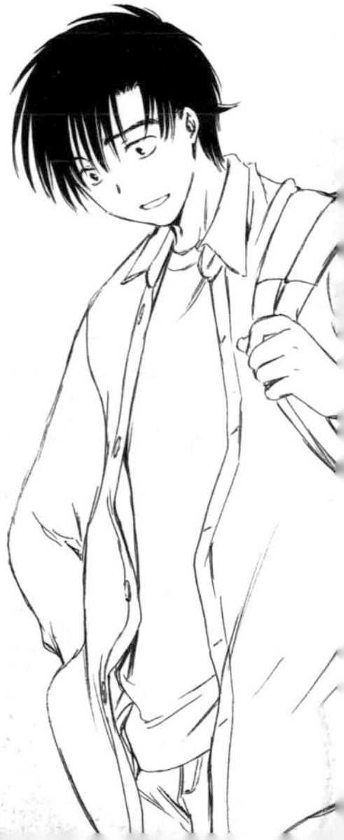

Hideki Motosuwa

A farm boy who's moved to Tokyo, Hideki's struggling in the big city—both to get by and to get into college. When he's not studying, he's got a job at a local pub, Club Pleasure. Most people—except for Chi!—call him by his last name, as last names are more commonly used than first ones in Japan.

CLAMP

SATSUKI IGARASHI
MOKONA
TSUBAKI NEKOI
NANASE OHKAWA

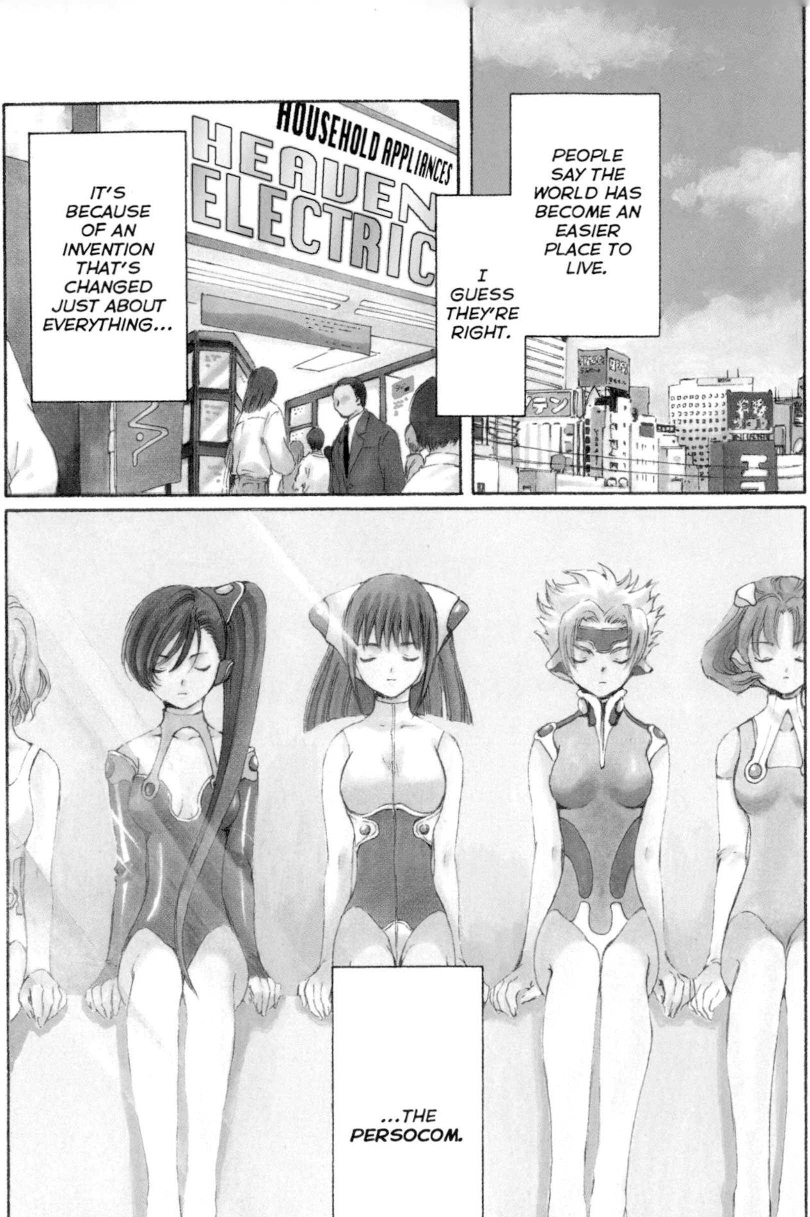
PEOPLE SAY THE WORLD HAS BECOME AN EASIER PLACE TO LIVE.
I GUESS THEY'RE RIGHT.
HOUSEHOLD APPLIANCES
HEAVEN ELECTRIC
IT'S BECAUSE OF AN INVENTION THAT'S CHANGED JUST ABOUT EVERYTHING...
...THE PERSOCOM.

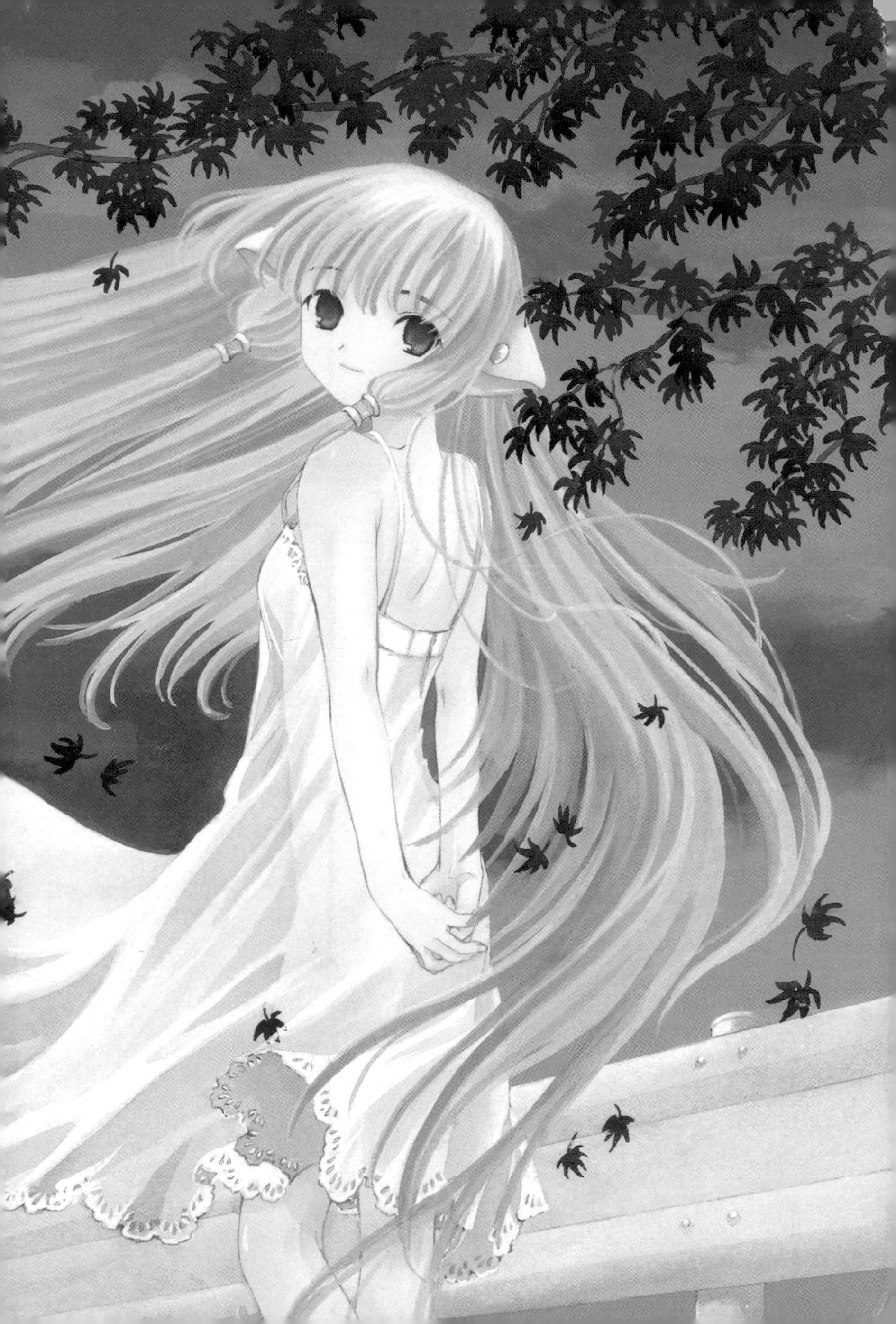

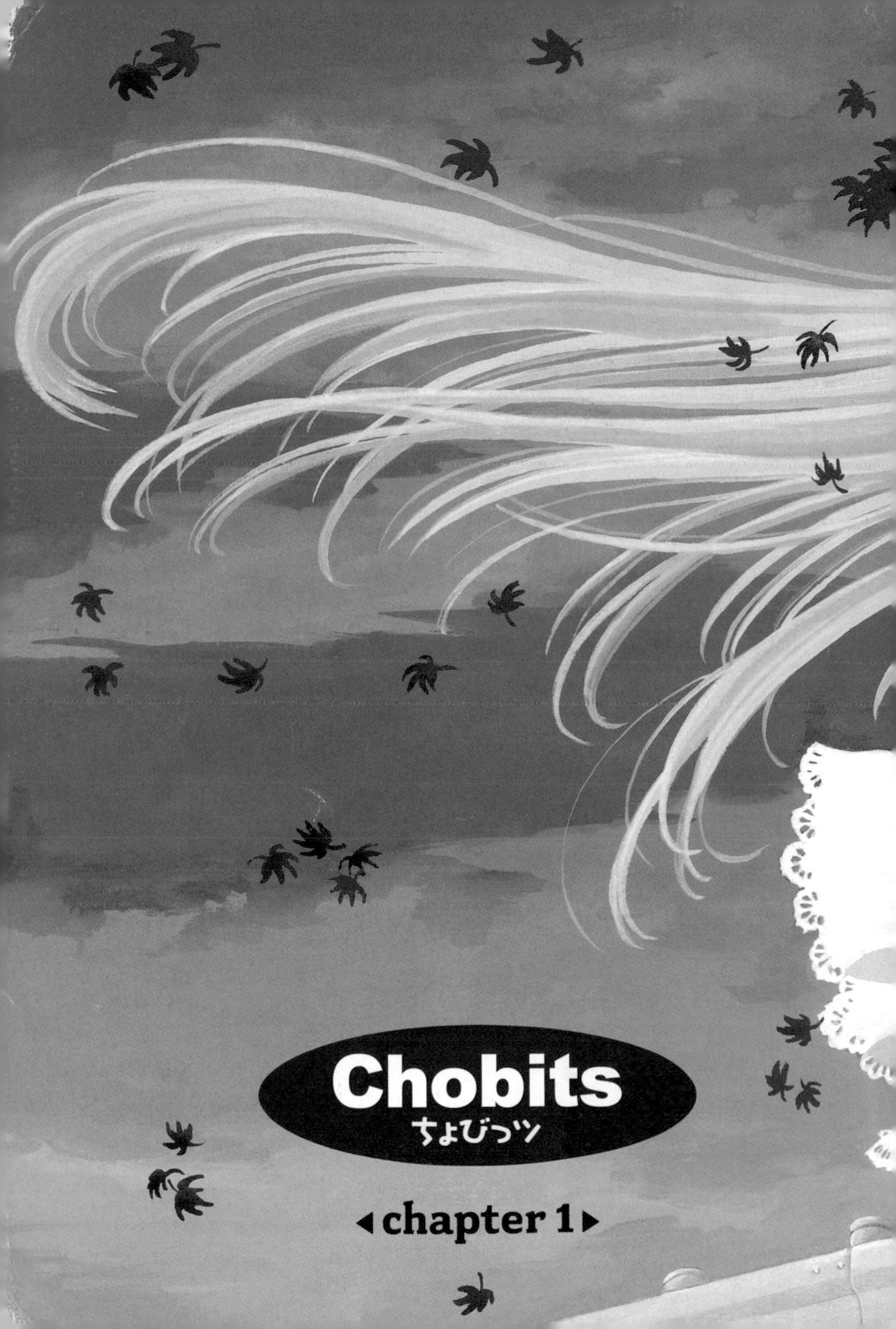
Chobits
ちょびっツ
chapter 1

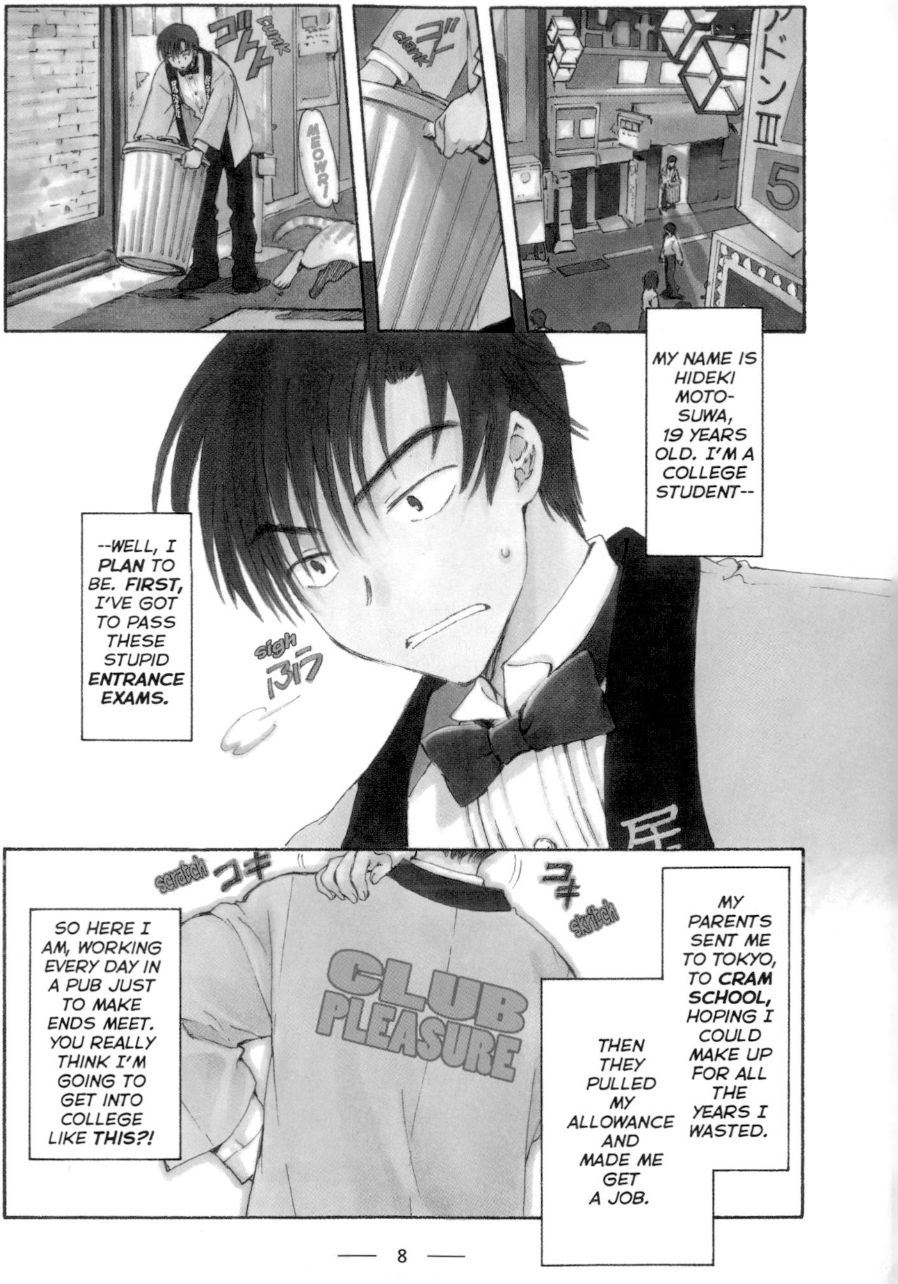
clank
clunk
MEOWR!
MY NAME IS HIDEKI MOTO-SUWA, 19 YEARS OLD. I'M A COLLEGE STUDENT--
--WELL, I **PLAN** TO BE. **FIRST,** I'VE GOT TO PASS THESE STUPID **ENTRANCE EXAMS.**
sigh
MY PARENTS SENT ME TO TOKYO, TO **CRAM SCHOOL,** HOPING I COULD MAKE UP FOR ALL THE YEARS I WASTED.
THEN THEY PULLED MY ALLOWANCE AND MADE ME GET A JOB.
skritch
scratch
CLUB PLEASURE
SO HERE I AM, WORKING EVERY DAY IN A PUB JUST TO MAKE ENDS MEET. YOU REALLY THINK I'M GOING TO GET INTO COLLEGE LIKE **THIS?!**

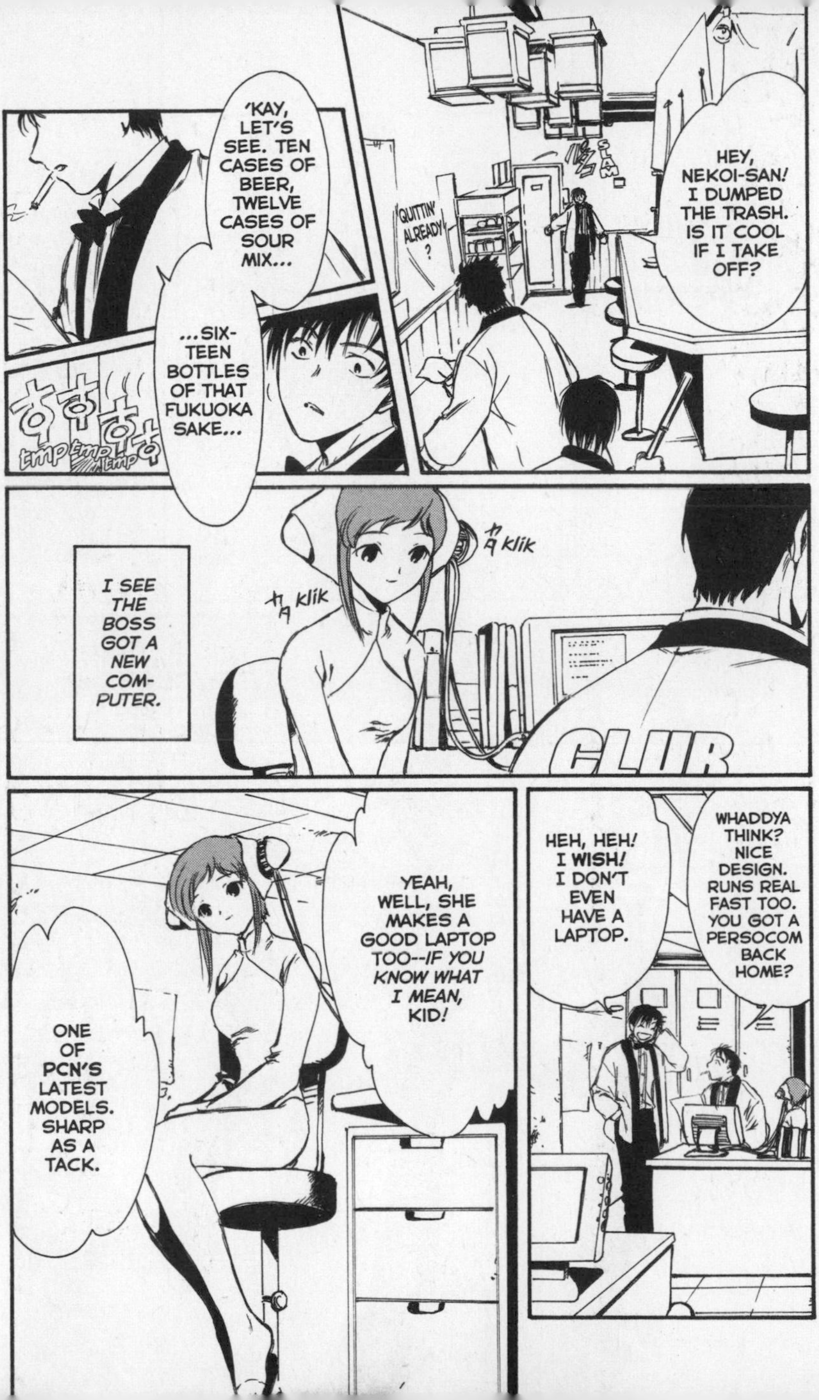
HEY, NEKOI-SAN! I DUMPED THE TRASH. IS IT COOL IF I TAKE OFF?
SLAM
QUITTIN' ALREADY?
'KAY, LET'S SEE. TEN CASES OF BEER, TWELVE CASES OF SOUR MIX...
...SIX-TEEN BOTTLES OF THAT FUKUOKA SAKE...
tmp tmp tmp
klik
klik
I SEE THE BOSS GOT A NEW COMPUTER.
CLUB
WHADDYA THINK? NICE DESIGN. RUNS REAL FAST TOO. YOU GOT A PERSOCOM BACK HOME?
HEH, HEH! I WISH! I DON'T EVEN HAVE A LAPTOP.
YEAH, WELL, SHE MAKES A GOOD LAPTOP TOO--IF YOU KNOW WHAT I MEAN, KID!
ONE OF PCN'S LATEST MODELS. SHARP AS A TACK.

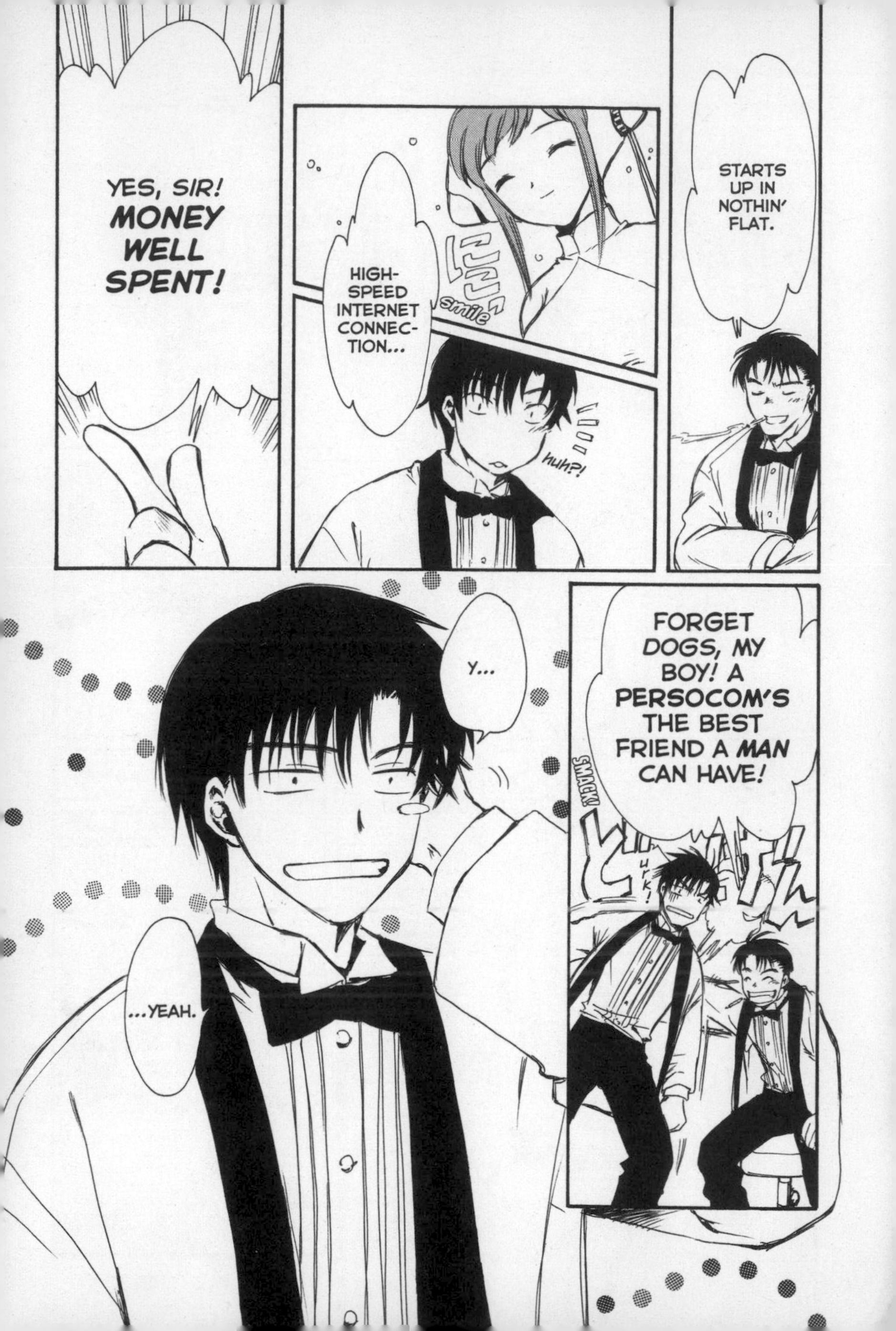
STARTS UP IN NOTHIN' FLAT.
smile
HIGH-SPEED INTERNET CONNECTION...
huh?!
YES, SIR! MONEY WELL SPENT!
FORGET DOGS, MY BOY! A PERSOCOM'S THE BEST FRIEND A MAN CAN HAVE!
SMACK!
urk!
Y...
...YEAH.

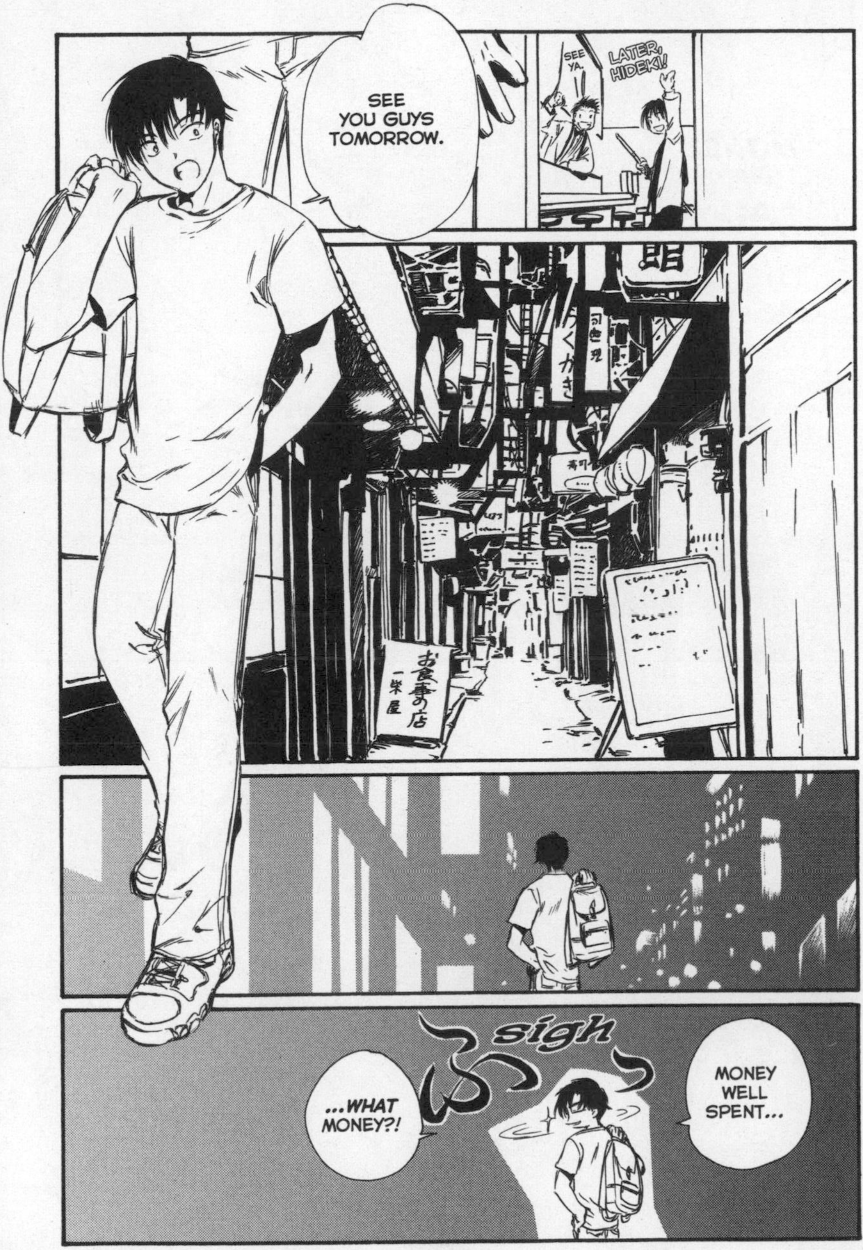
LATER, HIDEKI!
SEE YA.
SEE YOU GUYS TOMORROW.
sigh
MONEY WELL SPENT...
...WHAT MONEY?!

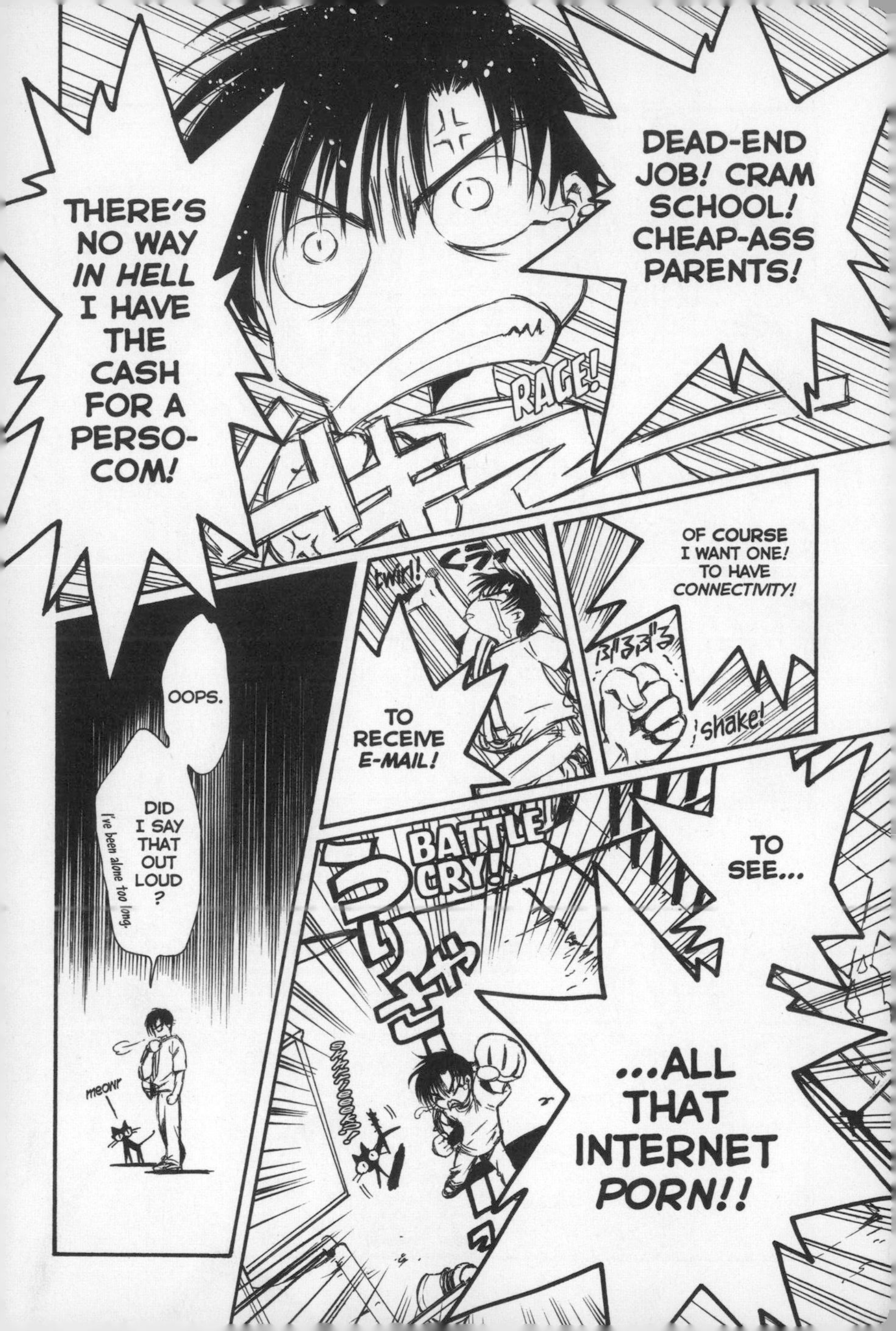
DEAD-END JOB! CRAM SCHOOL! CHEAP-ASS PARENTS!
RAGE!
THERE'S NO WAY IN HELL I HAVE THE CASH FOR A PERSO-COM!
OF COURSE I WANT ONE! TO HAVE CONNECTIVITY!
shake!
twirl!
TO RECEIVE E-MAIL!
TO SEE...
BATTLE CRY!
...ALL THAT INTERNET PORN!!
OOPS.
DID I SAY THAT OUT LOUD?
I've been alone too long.
meowr

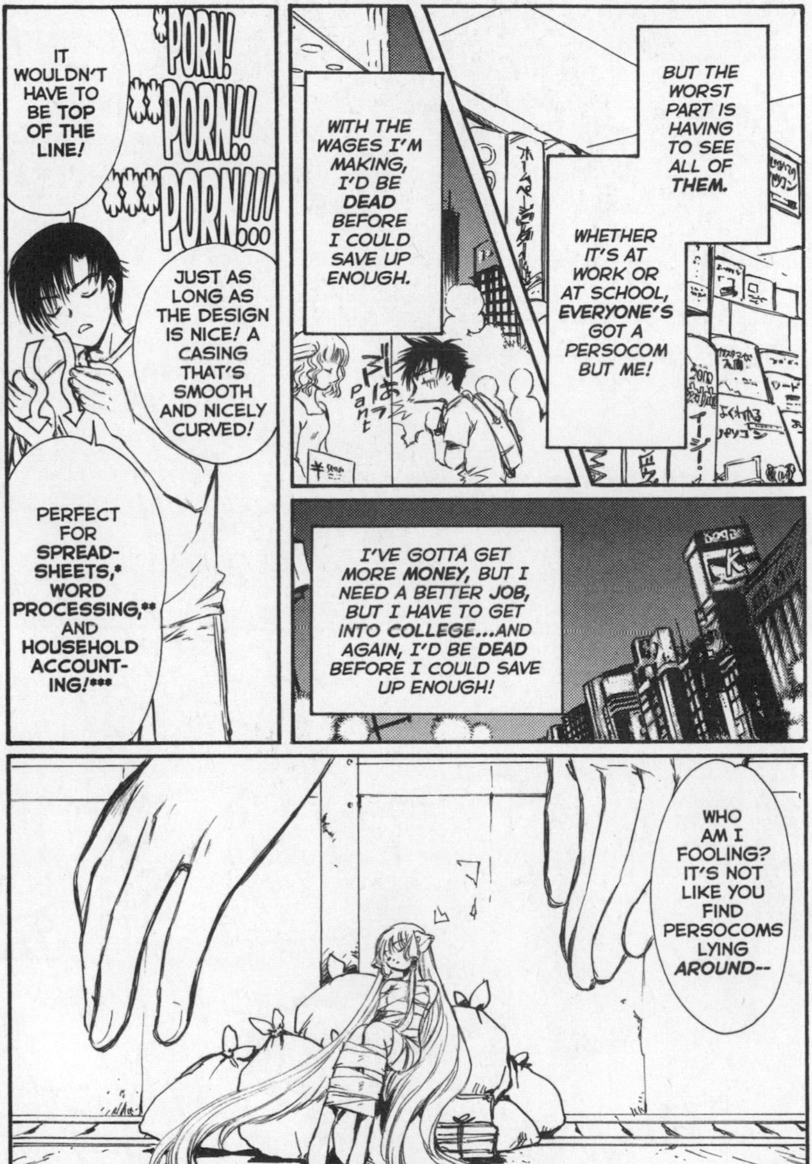
BUT THE WORST PART IS HAVING TO SEE ALL OF THEM.
WHETHER IT'S AT WORK OR AT SCHOOL, EVERYONE'S GOT A PERSOCOM BUT ME!
WITH THE WAGES I'M MAKING, I'D BE DEAD BEFORE I COULD SAVE UP ENOUGH.
I'VE GOTTA GET MORE MONEY, BUT I NEED A BETTER JOB, BUT I HAVE TO GET INTO COLLEGE...AND AGAIN, I'D BE DEAD BEFORE I COULD SAVE UP ENOUGH!
*PORN! **PORN!! ***PORN!!!
IT WOULDN'T HAVE TO BE TOP OF THE LINE!
JUST AS LONG AS THE DESIGN IS NICE! A CASING THAT'S SMOOTH AND NICELY CURVED!
PERFECT FOR SPREADSHEETS,* WORD PROCESSING,** AND HOUSEHOLD ACCOUNTING!***
WHO AM I FOOLING? IT'S NOT LIKE YOU FIND PERSOCOMS LYING AROUND--

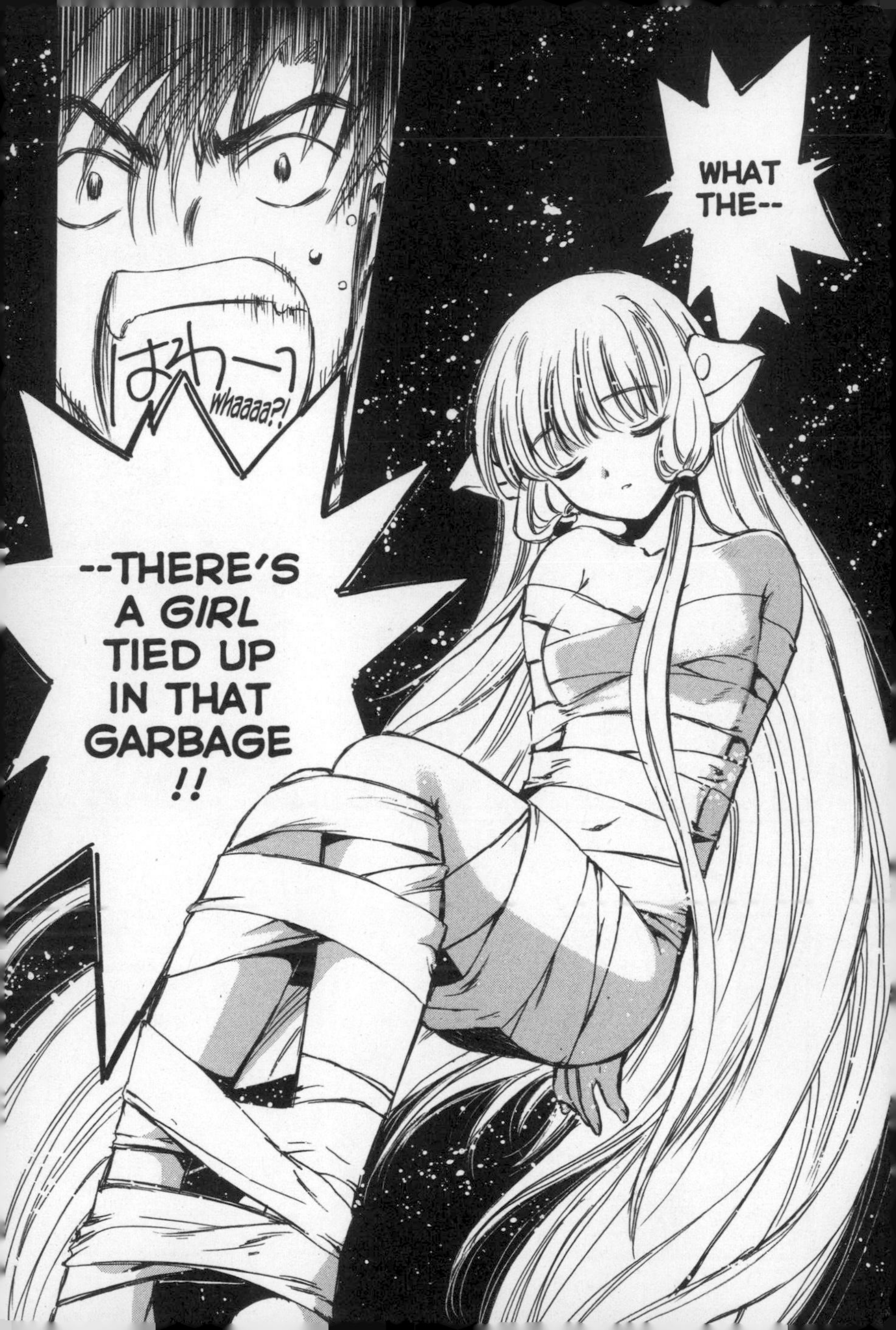
WHAT THE--
はわー
whaaaa?!
--THERE'S A GIRL TIED UP IN THAT GARBAGE !!

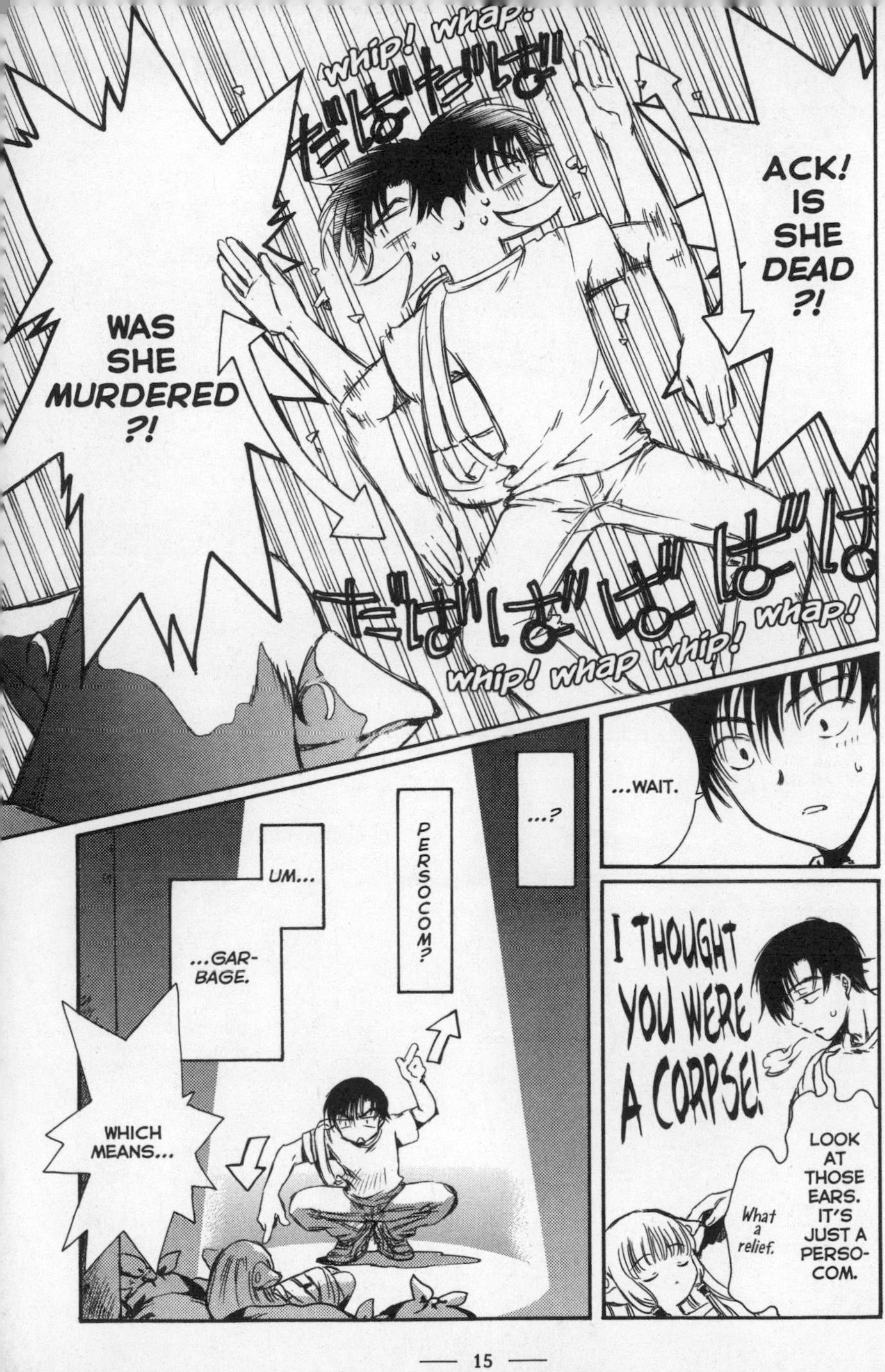
whip! whap!
ACK! IS SHE DEAD?!
WAS SHE MURDERED?!
whip! whap whip! whap!
...WAIT.
I THOUGHT YOU WERE A CORPSE!
LOOK AT THOSE EARS. IT'S JUST A PERSO-COM.
What a relief.
...?
PERSOCOM?
UM...
...GAR-BAGE.
WHICH MEANS...

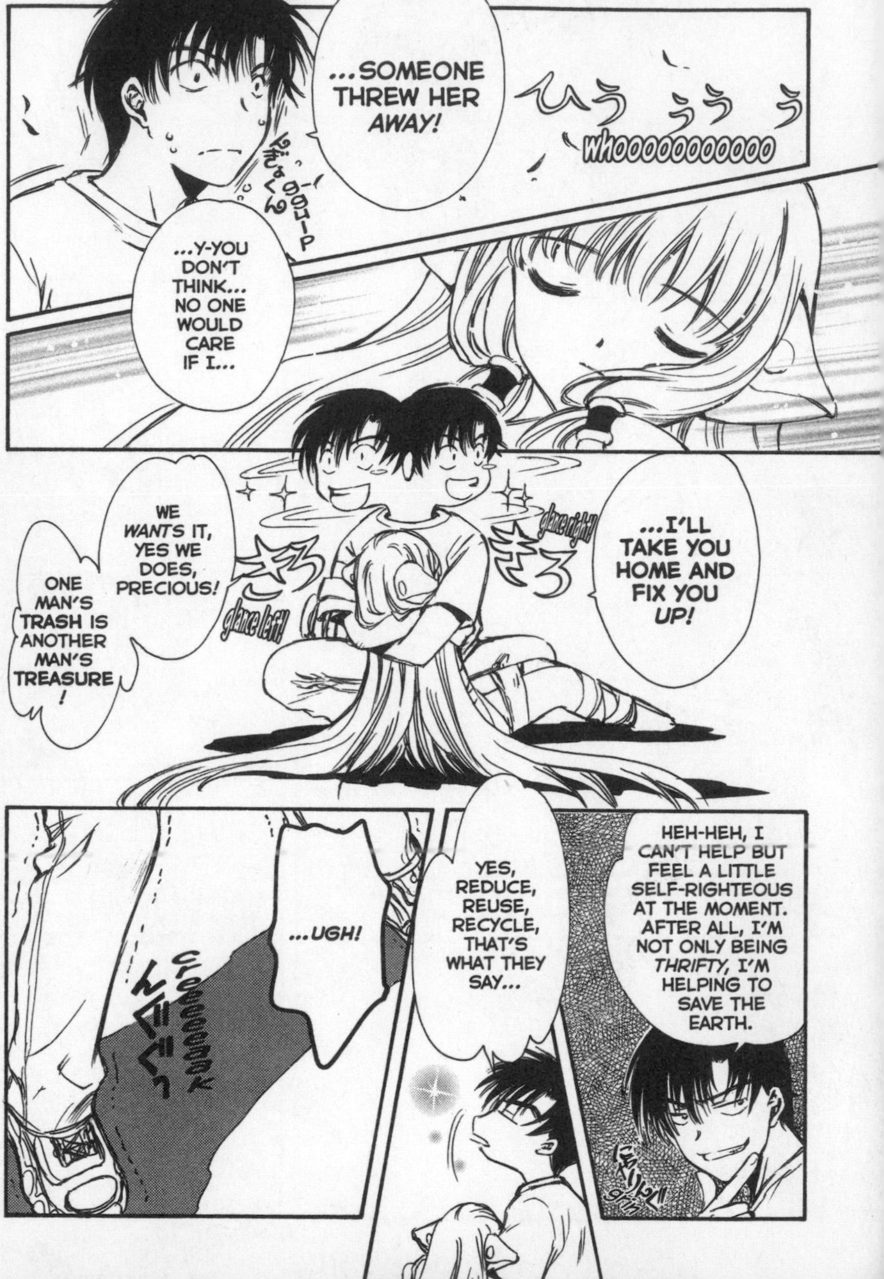

ひう ううう
whoooooooooo
...SOMEONE THREW HER AWAY!
ぎょくん
g-ggulp
...Y-YOU DON'T THINK... NO ONE WOULD CARE IF I...
...I'LL TAKE YOU HOME AND FIX YOU UP!
きろ
glance right
きろ
glance left
WE WANTS IT, YES WE DOES, PRECIOUS!
ONE MAN'S TRASH IS ANOTHER MAN'S TREASURE!
HEH-HEH, I CAN'T HELP BUT FEEL A LITTLE SELF-RIGHTEOUS AT THE MOMENT. AFTER ALL, I'M NOT ONLY BEING THRIFTY, I'M HELPING TO SAVE THE EARTH.
にやり
grin
YES, REDUCE, REUSE, RECYCLE, THAT'S WHAT THEY SAY...
...UGH!
creeeeeeeak

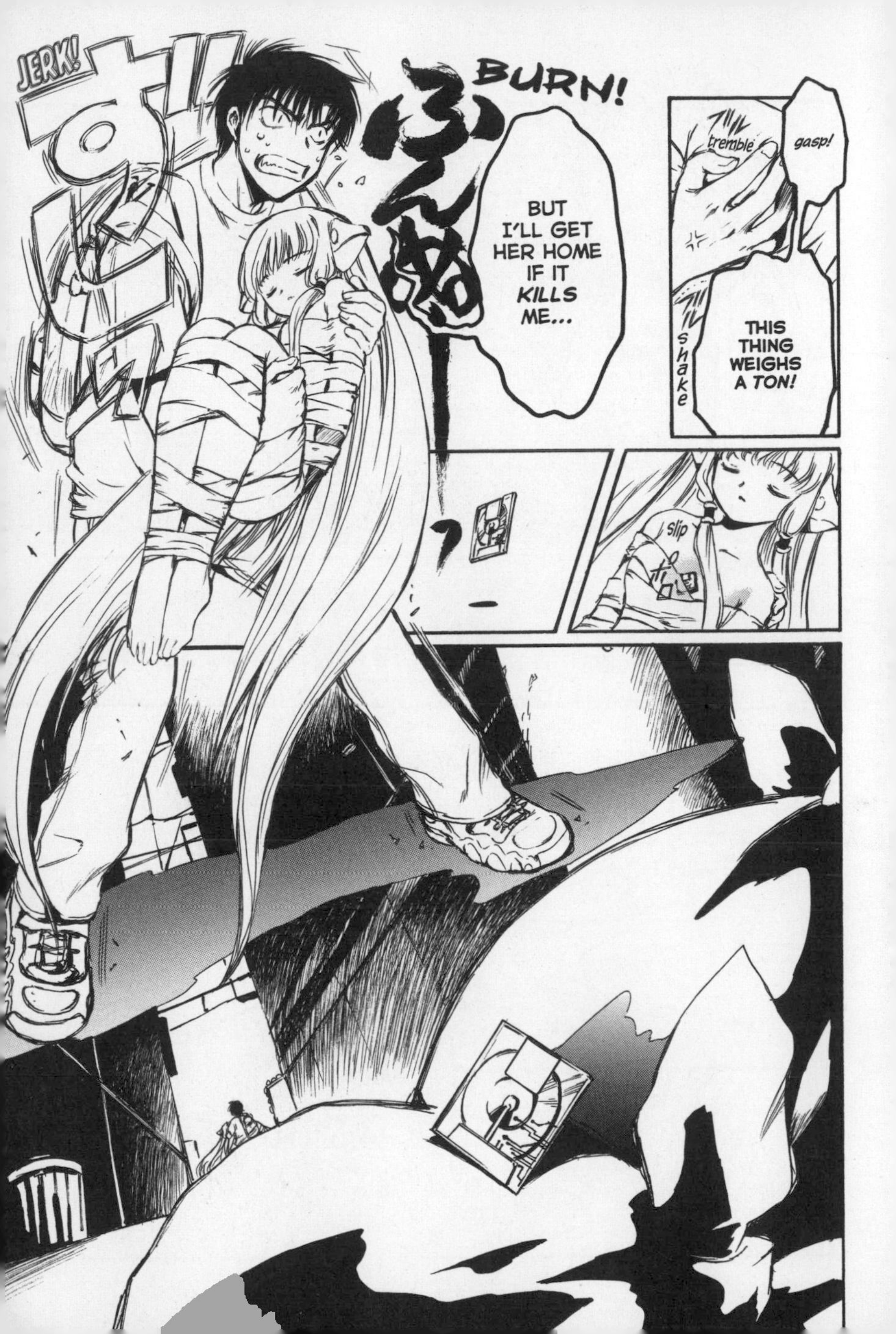
gasp!
tremble
shake
THIS THING WEIGHS A TON!
slip
BURN!
BUT I'LL GET HER HOME IF IT KILLS ME...
JERK!

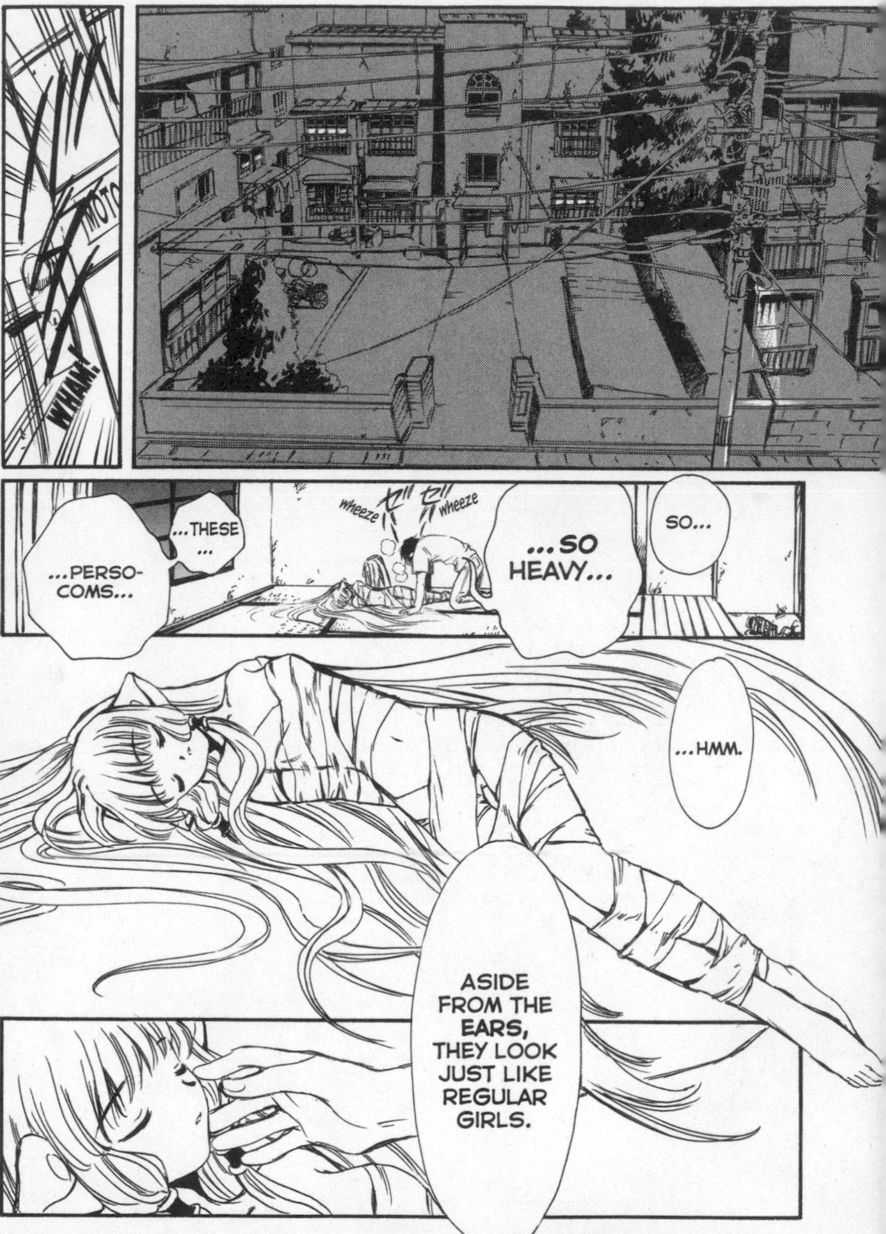
MOTO
WHAM!
SO...
...SO HEAVY...
wheeze
wheeze
...THESE ...
...PERSO-COMS...
...HMM.
ASIDE FROM THE EARS, THEY LOOK JUST LIKE REGULAR GIRLS.

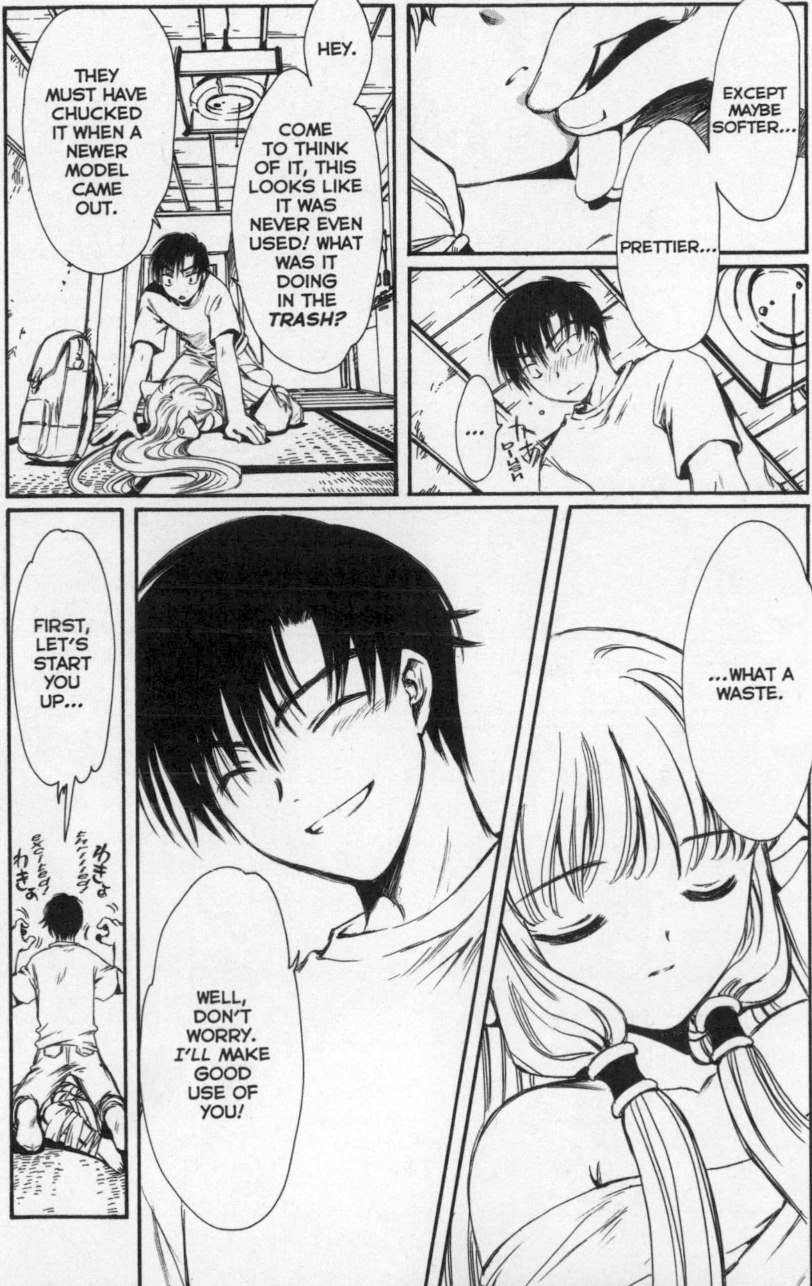
EXCEPT MAYBE SOFTER...
PRETTIER...
...
blush
HEY.
COME TO THINK OF IT, THIS LOOKS LIKE IT WAS NEVER EVEN USED! WHAT WAS IT DOING IN THE *TRASH?*
THEY MUST HAVE CHUCKED IT WHEN A NEWER MODEL CAME OUT.
...WHAT A WASTE.
WELL, DON'T WORRY. *I'LL* MAKE GOOD USE OF YOU!
FIRST, LET'S START YOU UP...
excited! excited!

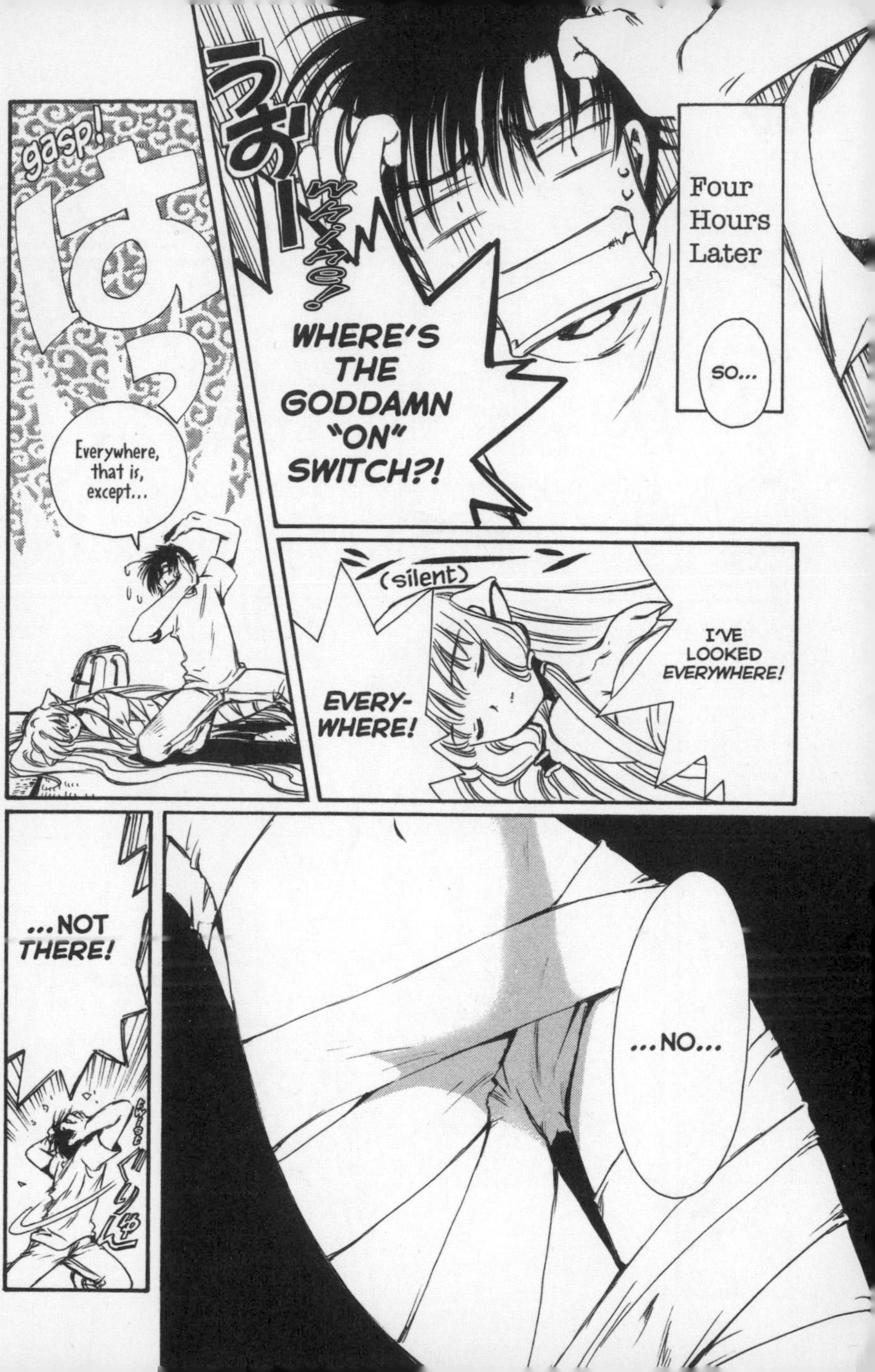
Four Hours Later
so...
うおー
whine!
WHERE'S THE GODDAMN "ON" SWITCH?!
I'VE LOOKED EVERYWHERE!
(silent)
EVERY-WHERE!
gasp!
はっ
Everywhere, that is, except...
...NO...
...NOT THERE!

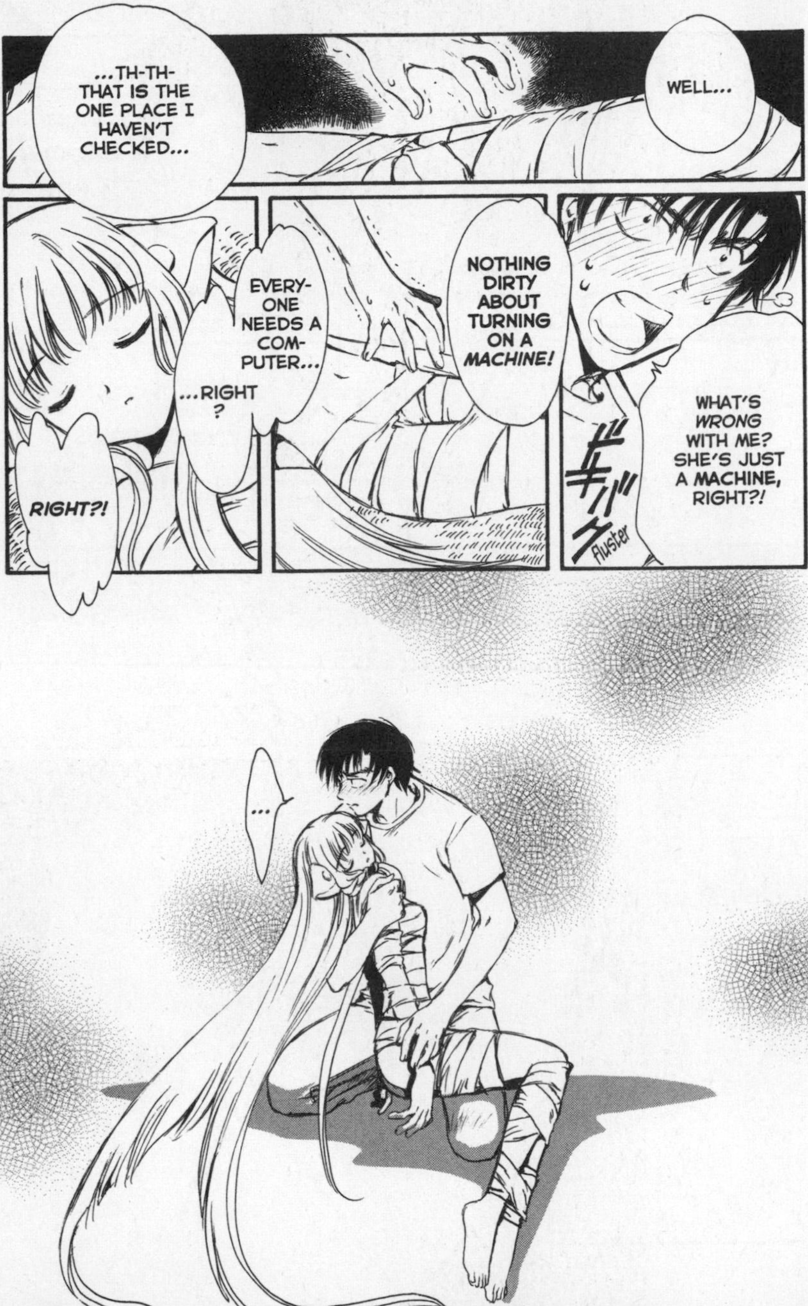
WELL...
...TH-TH-THAT IS THE ONE PLACE I HAVEN'T CHECKED...
Fluster
WHAT'S *WRONG* WITH ME? SHE'S JUST A MACHINE, RIGHT?!
NOTHING DIRTY ABOUT TURNING ON A *MACHINE!*
EVERY-ONE NEEDS A COM-PUTER...
...RIGHT?
RIGHT?!
...

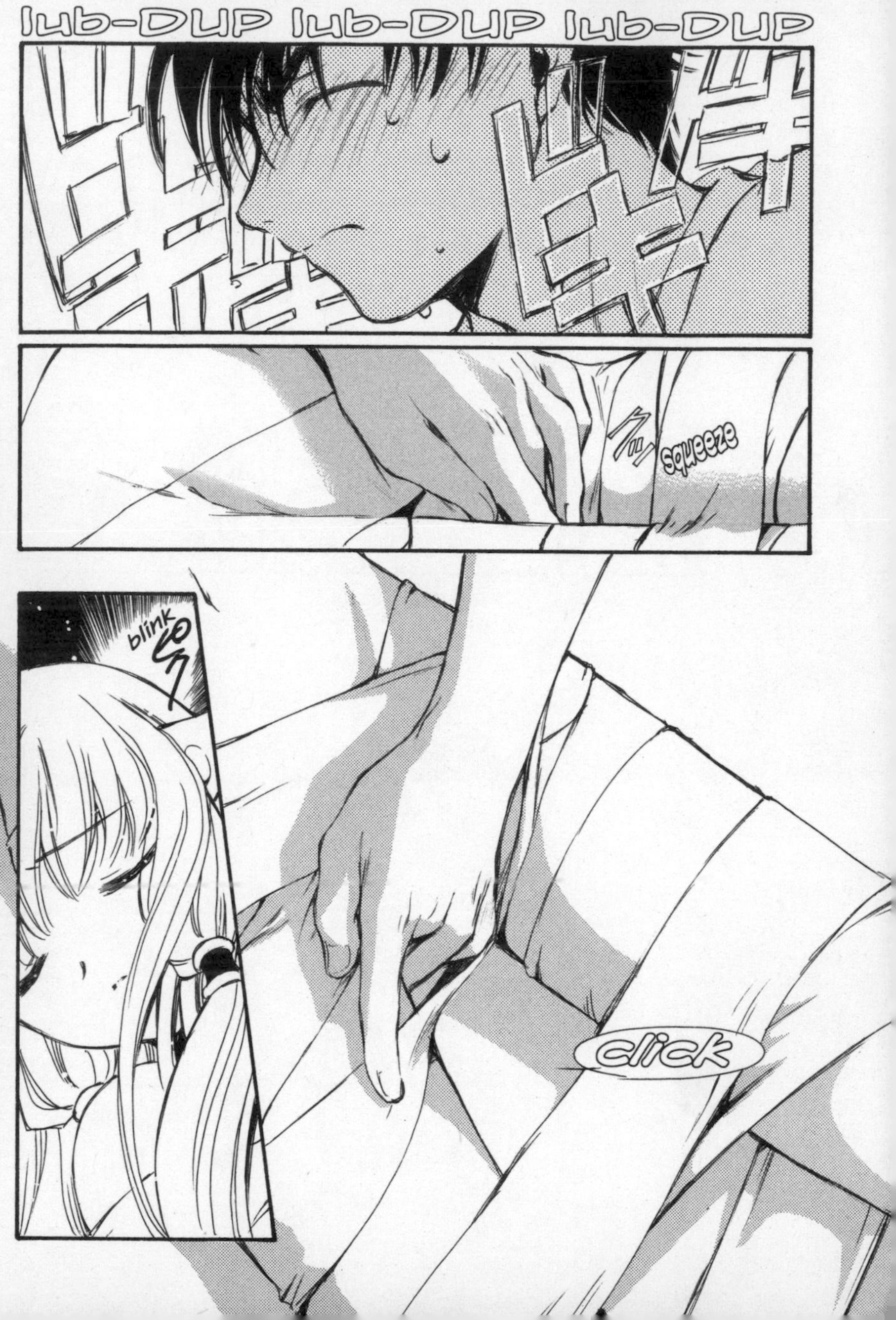
lub-DUP lub-DUP lub-DUP
squeeze
blink
click

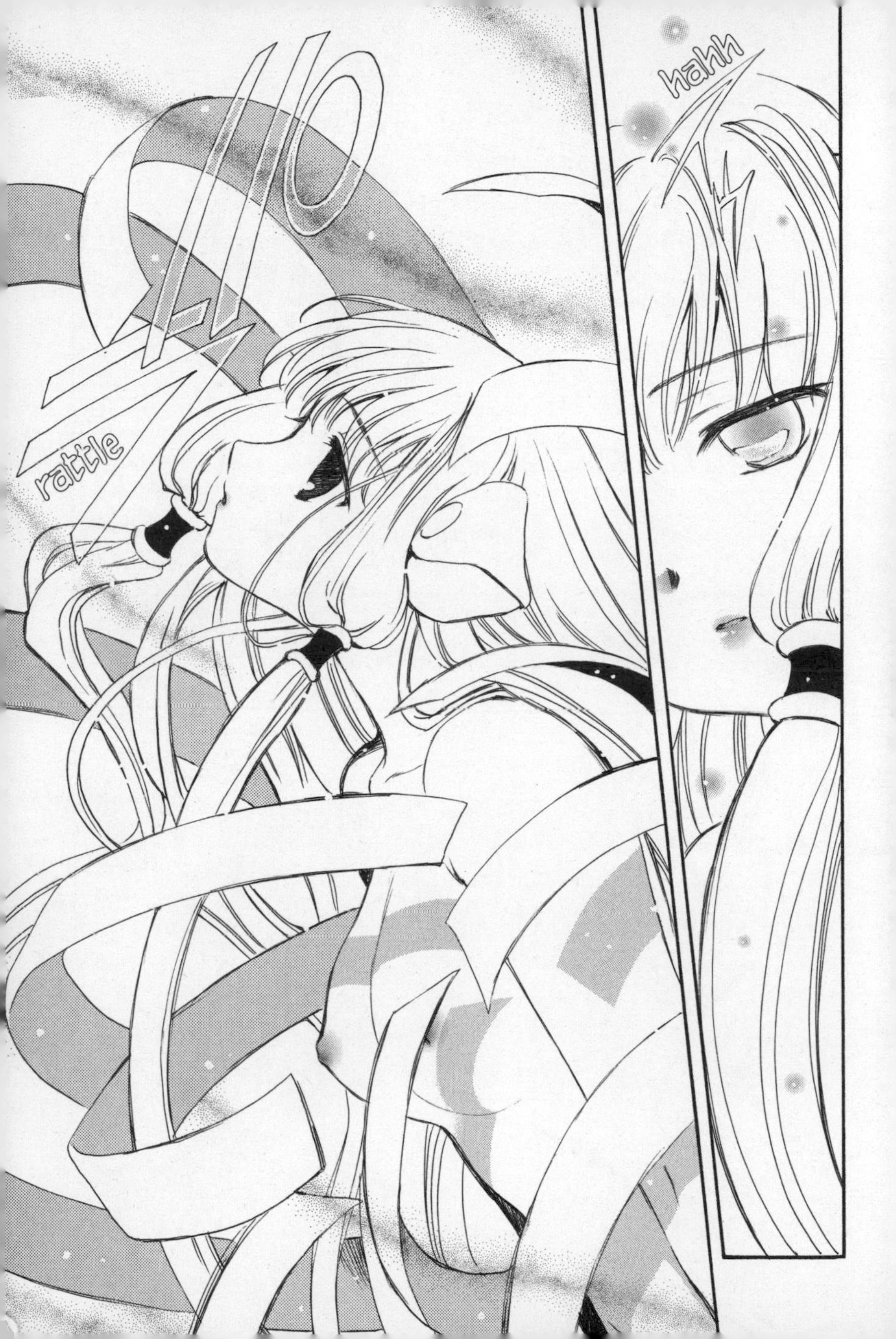
hahh
rattle

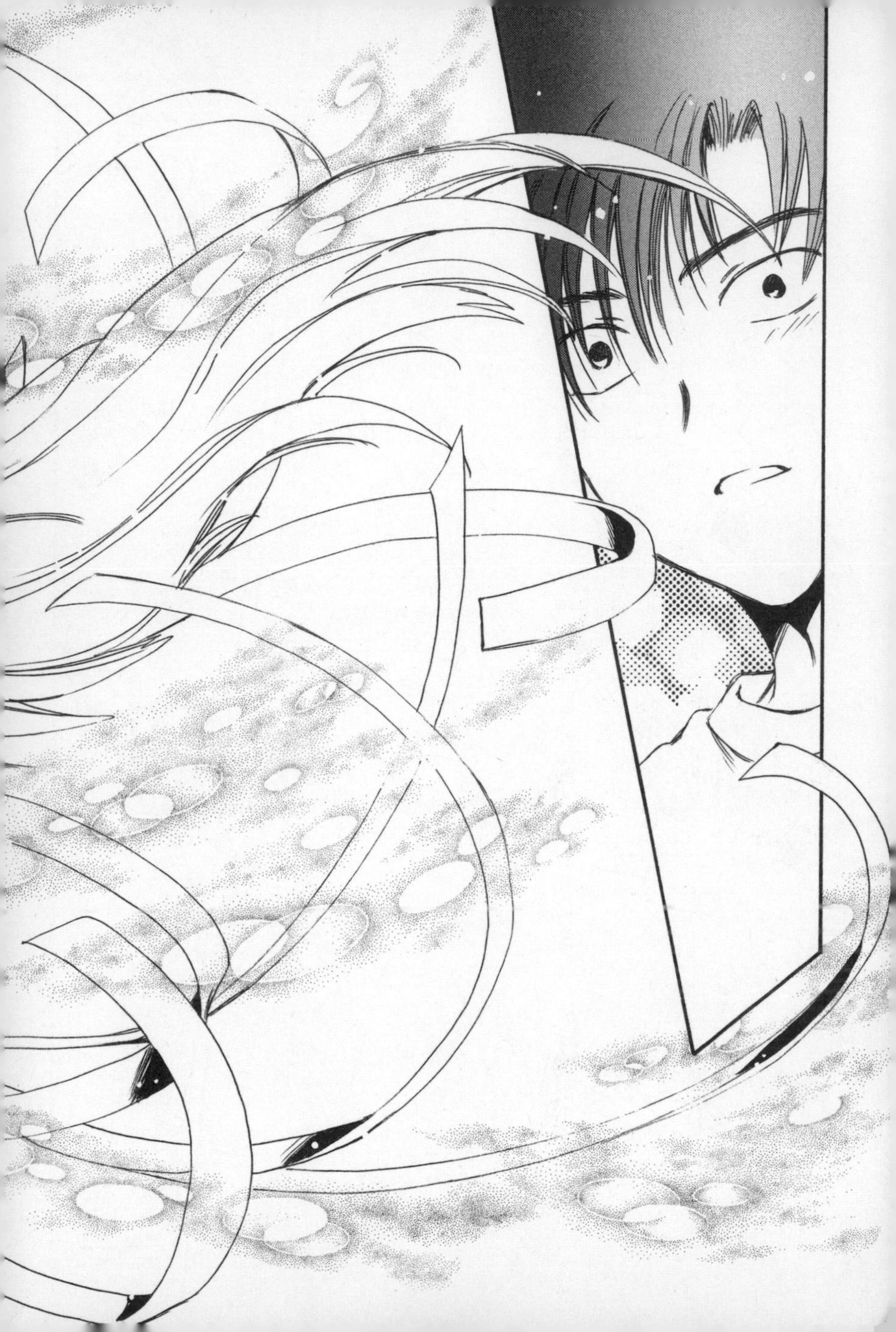

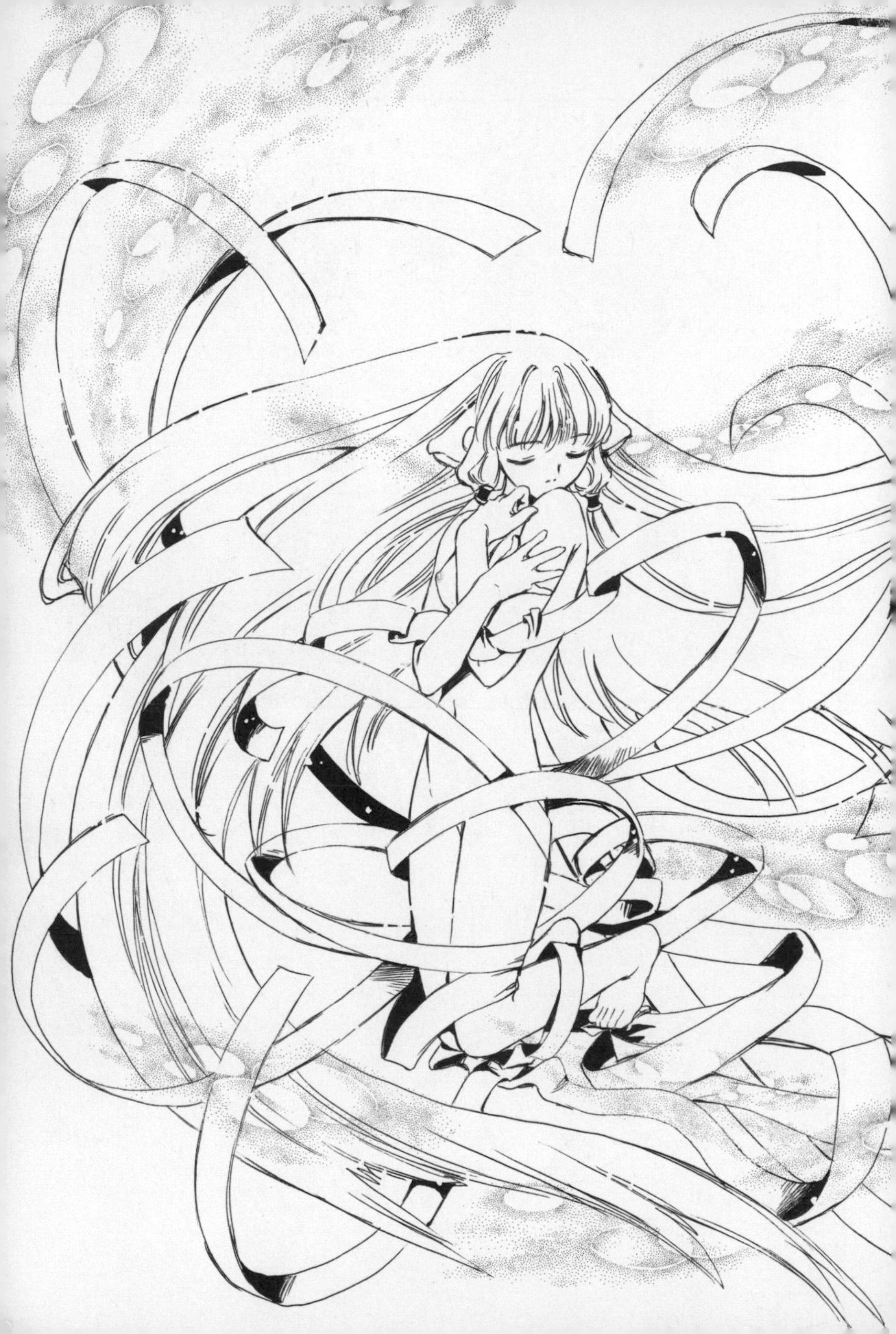

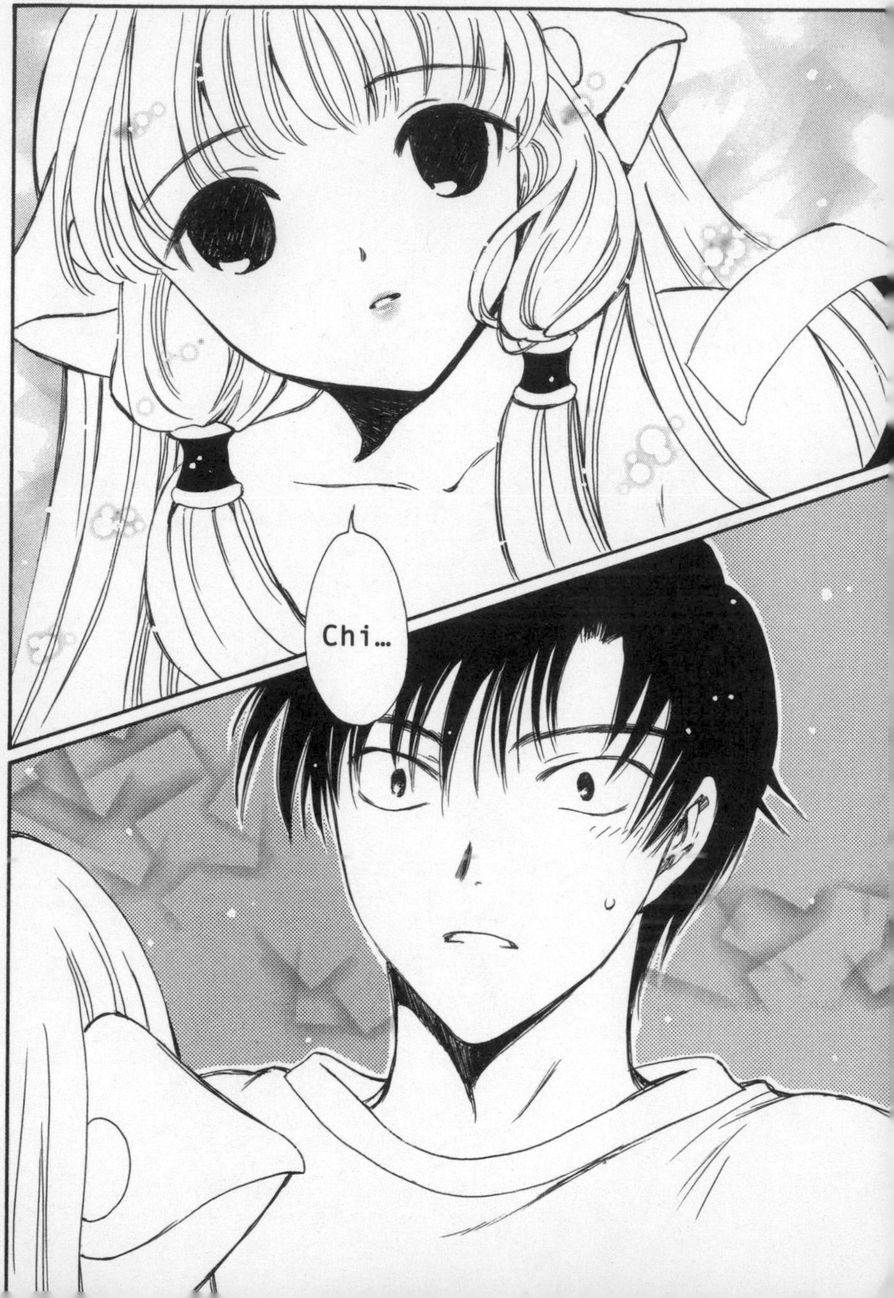
Chi...

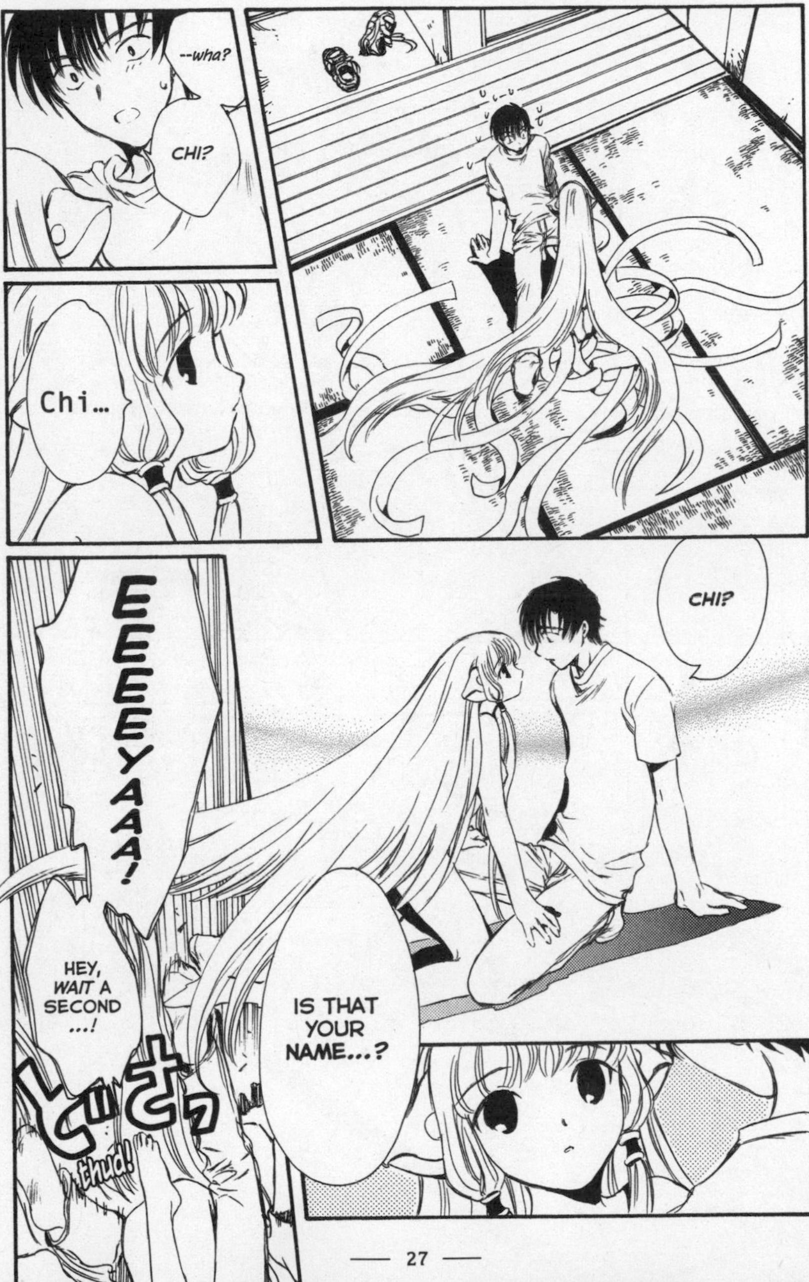
--wha?
CHI?
Chi…
CHI?
IS THAT YOUR NAME...?
EEEEEYAAA!
HEY, WAIT A SECOND ...!
どさっ
thud!

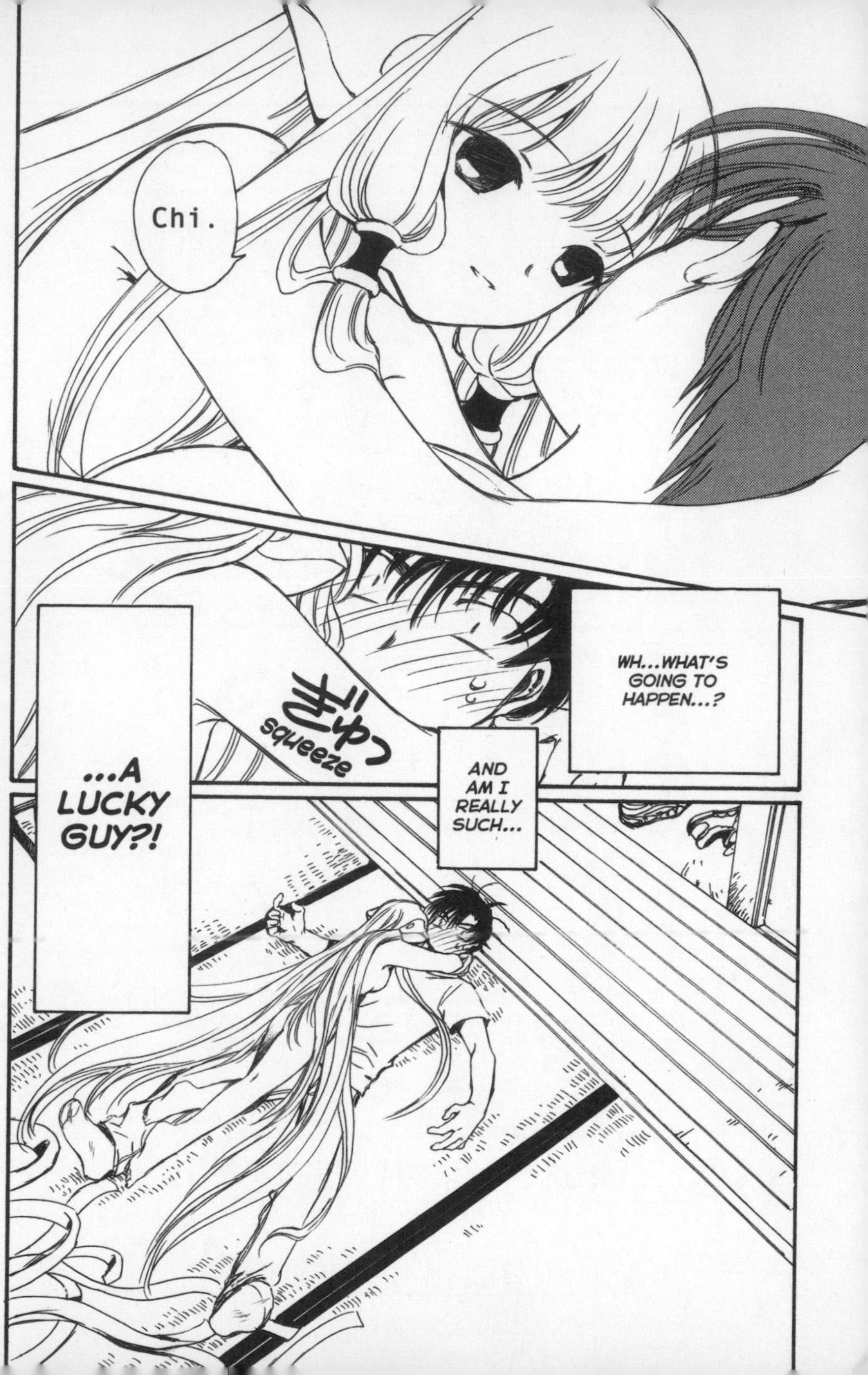
Chi.
WH...WHAT'S GOING TO HAPPEN...?
ぎゅっ squeeze
AND AM I REALLY SUCH...
...A LUCKY GUY?!

Chobits
ちょびっツ

◀chapter 2▶

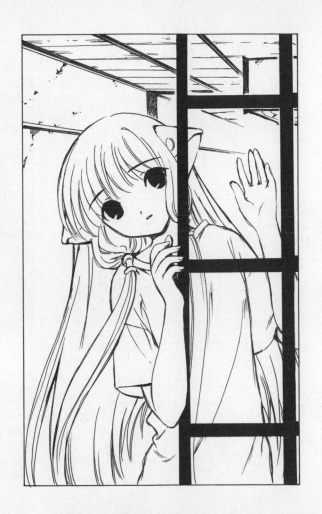

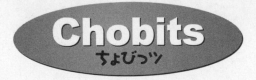

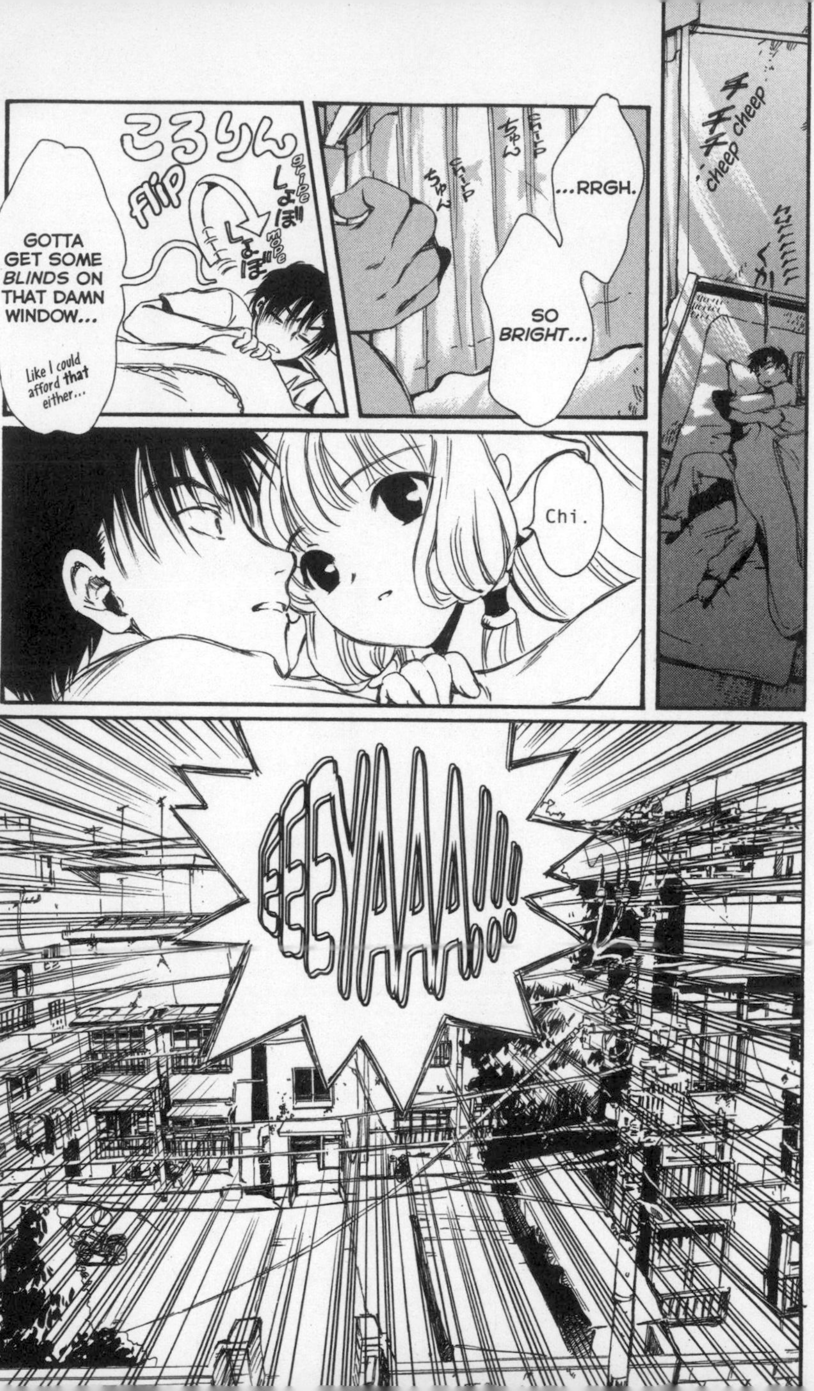
チチチ
cheep cheep
CHIRP
ちゅん
CHIRP
ちゅん
...RRGH.
SO BRIGHT...
ころりん
flip
しょぼ
gripe
しょぼ
mope
GOTTA GET SOME BLINDS ON THAT DAMN WINDOW...
Like I could afford that either...
Chi.
EEEYAAA!!!

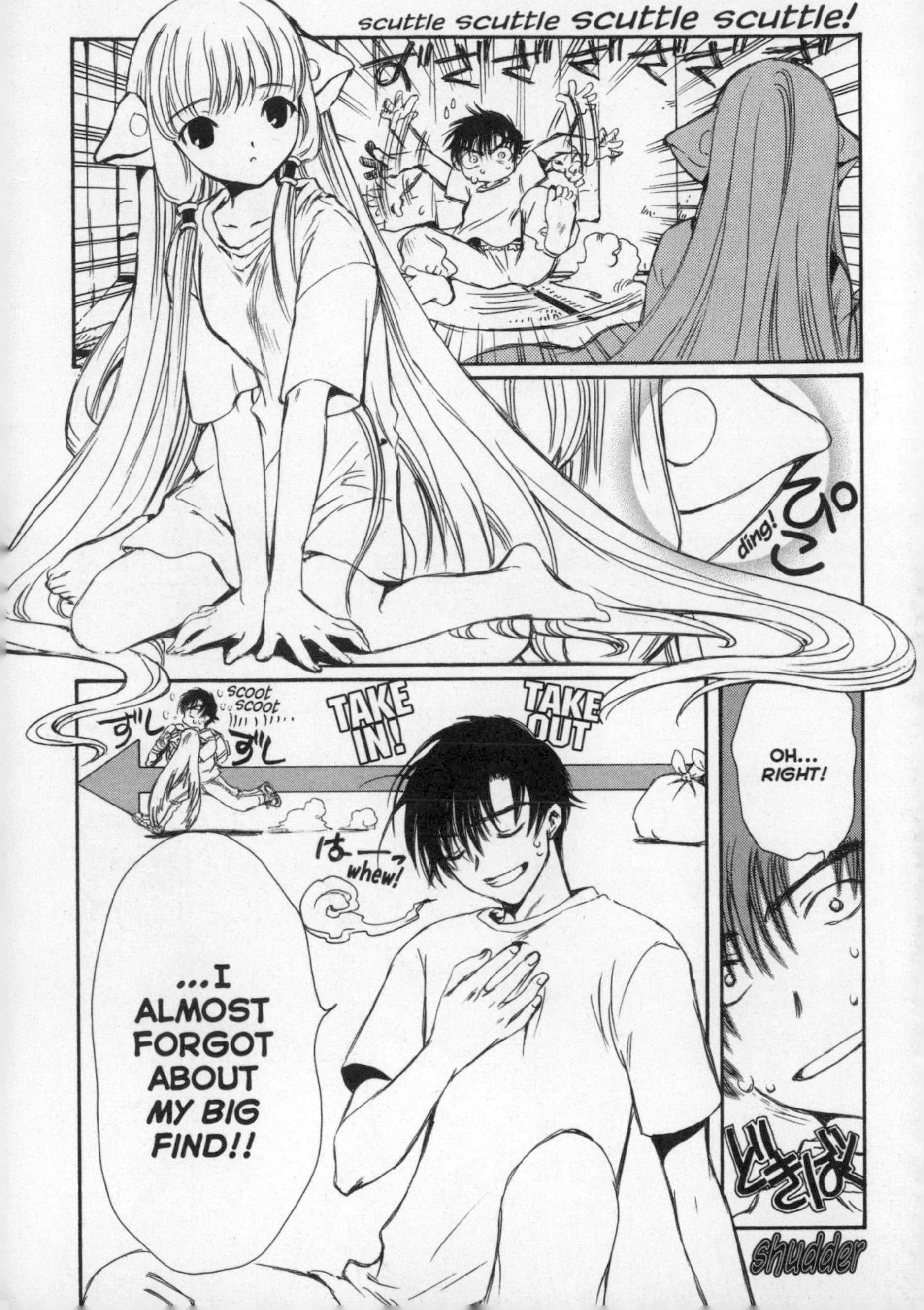
scuttle scuttle scuttle scuttle!
ずざざざざざざ
ぴこ
ding!
OH... RIGHT!
どきぱ
shudder
TAKE OUT
TAKE IN!
ずしずし
scoot scoot
はー
whew!
...I ALMOST FORGOT ABOUT MY BIG FIND!!

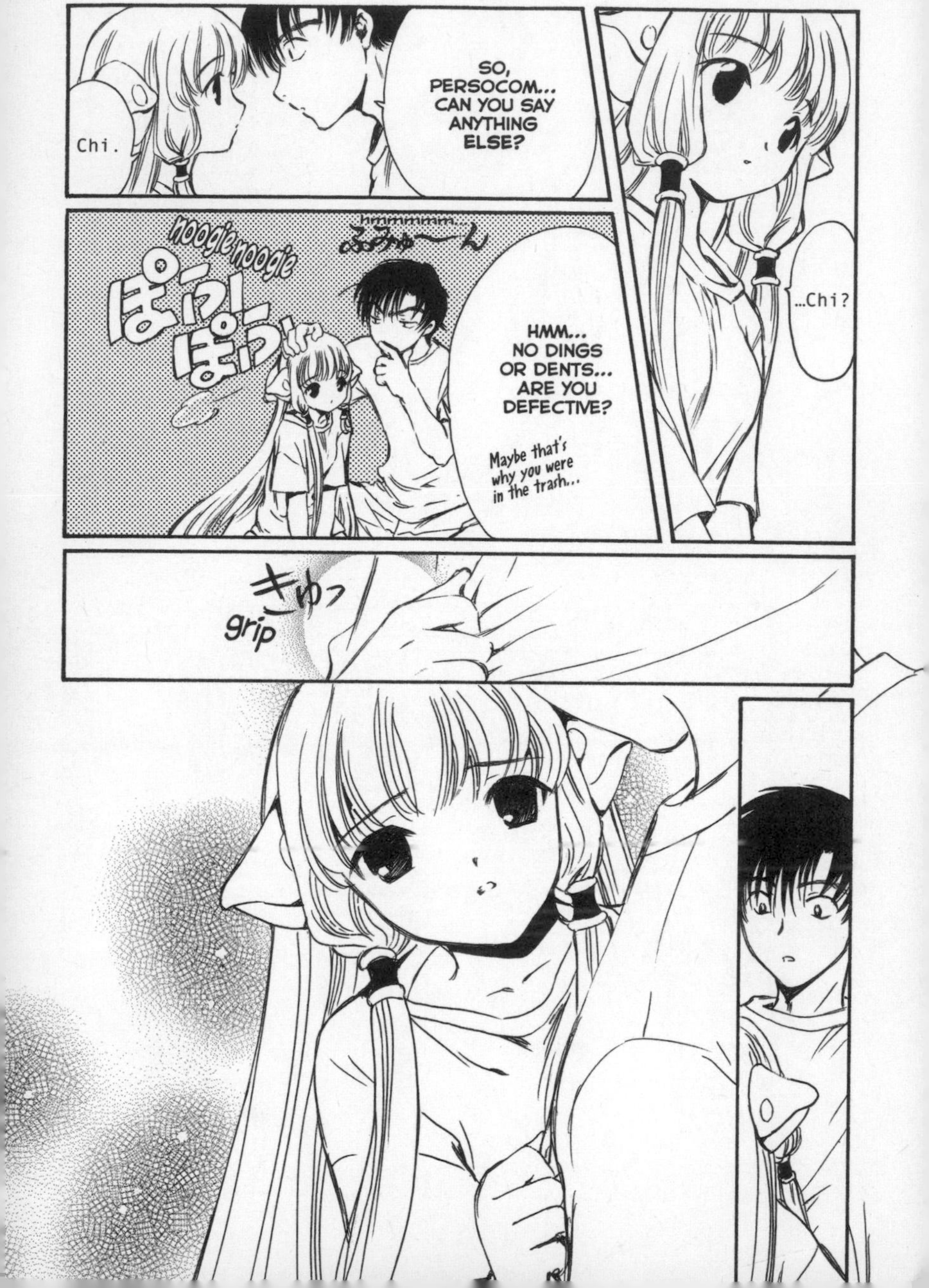

...Chi?
SO, PERSOCOM... CAN YOU SAY ANYTHING ELSE?
Chi.
ふみゅ〜ん
hmmmmmm
HMM... NO DINGS OR DENTS... ARE YOU DEFECTIVE?
Maybe that's why you were in the trash...
noogie noogie
ぽふ！ぽふ！
きゅっ
grip

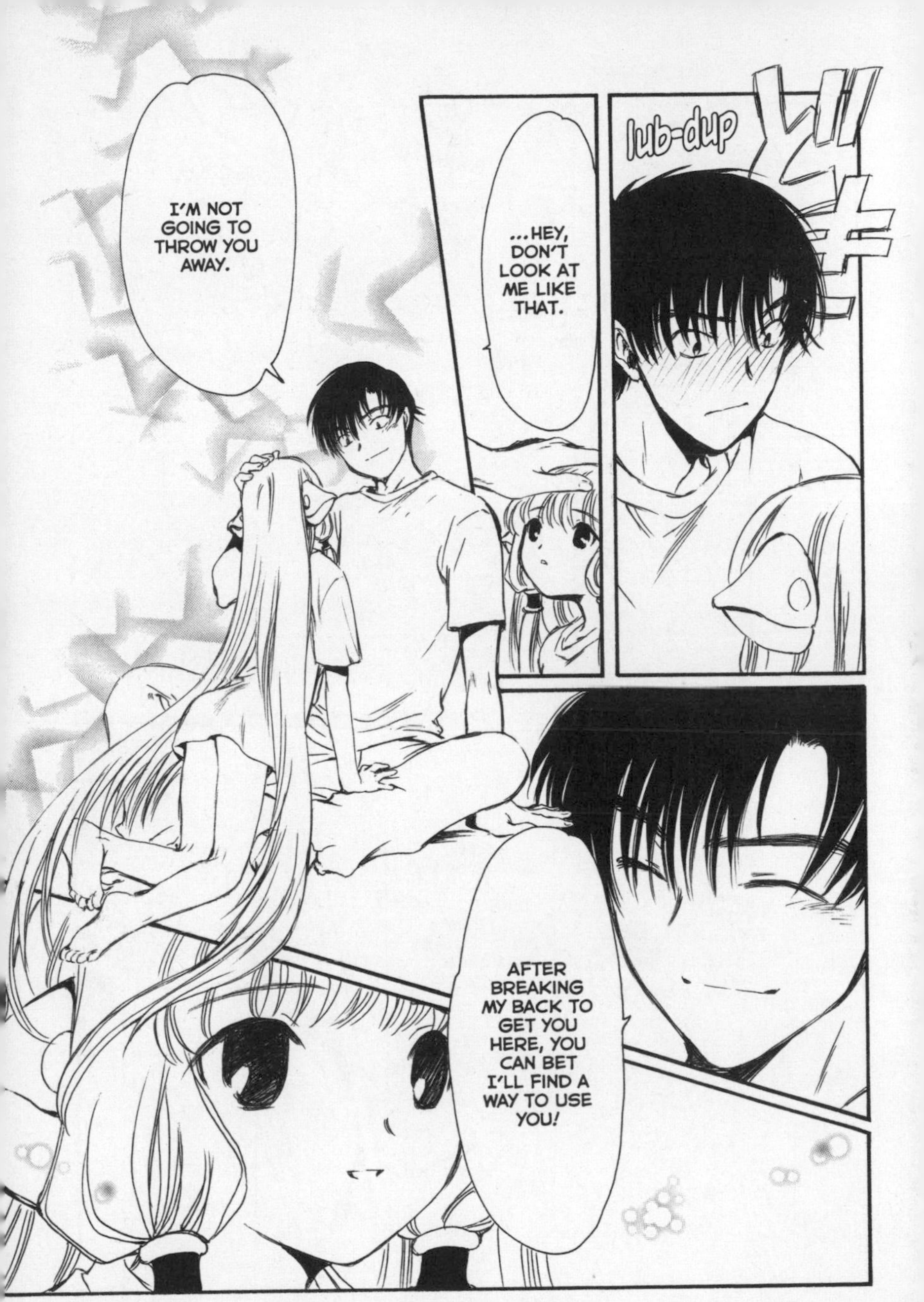
lub-dup
...HEY, DON'T LOOK AT ME LIKE THAT.
I'M NOT GOING TO THROW YOU AWAY.
AFTER BREAKING MY BACK TO GET YOU HERE, YOU CAN BET I'LL FIND A WAY TO USE YOU!

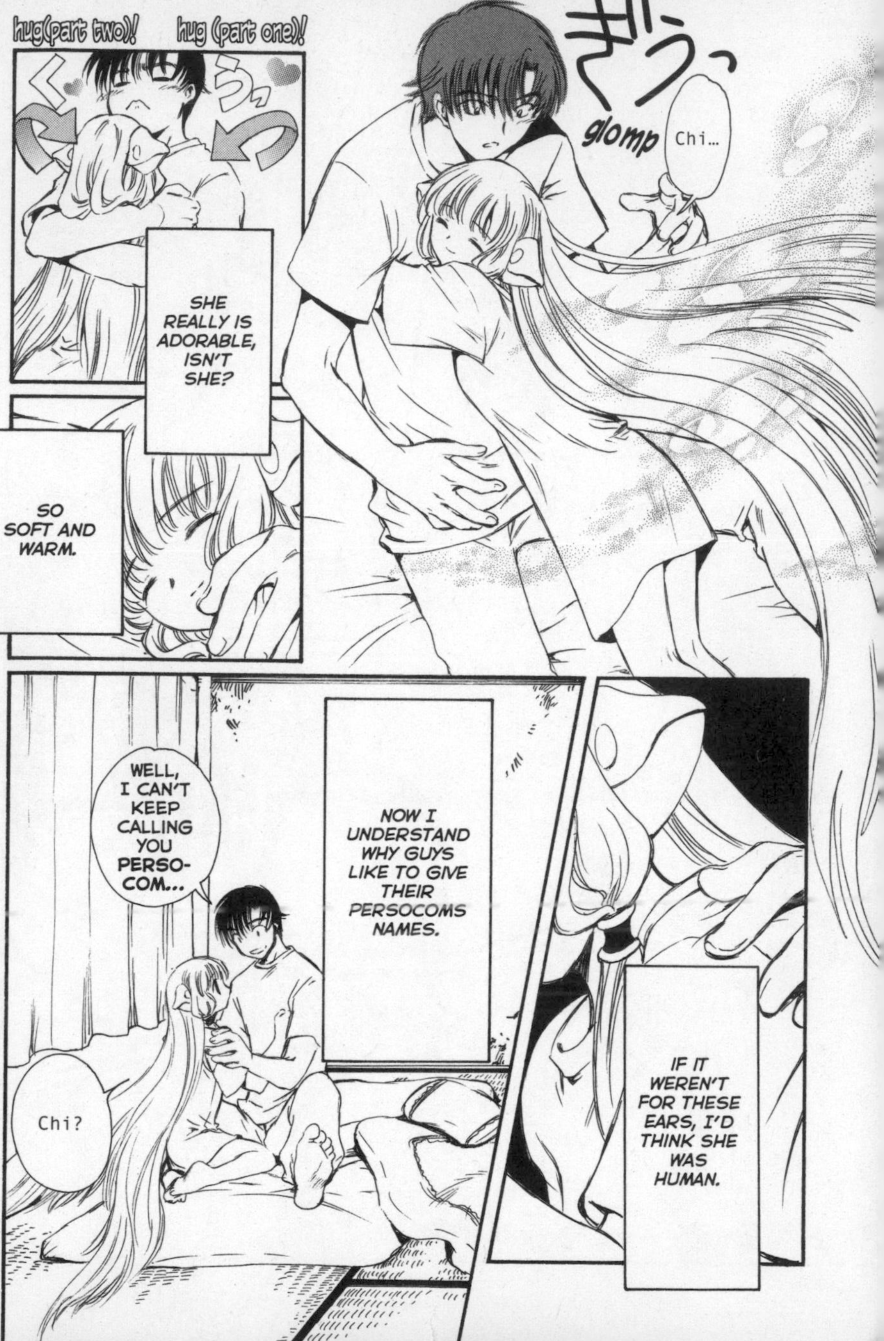

ぎうっ
glomp
Chi…
SHE REALLY IS ADORABLE, ISN'T SHE?
hug (part one)!
hug(part two)!
くっ
うっ
SO SOFT AND WARM.
IF IT WEREN'T FOR THESE EARS, I'D THINK SHE WAS HUMAN.
NOW I UNDERSTAND WHY GUYS LIKE TO GIVE THEIR PERSOCOMS NAMES.
WELL, I CAN'T KEEP CALLING YOU PERSO-COM...
Chi?

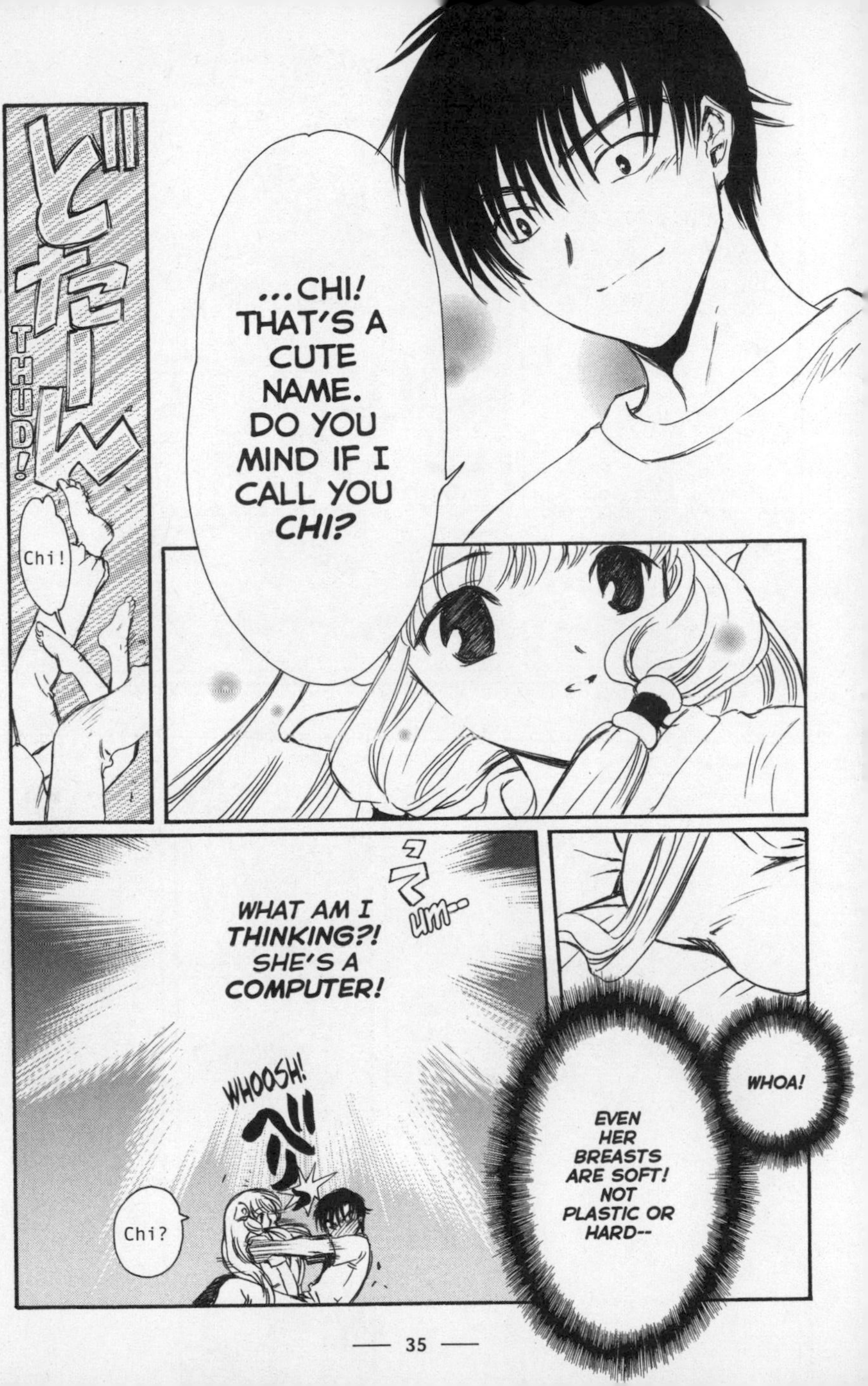
...CHI! THAT'S A CUTE NAME. DO YOU MIND IF I CALL YOU CHI?
THUD!
Chi!
WHOA!
EVEN HER BREASTS ARE SOFT! NOT PLASTIC OR HARD--
UM--
WHAT AM I THINKING?! SHE'S A COMPUTER!
WHOOSH!
Chi?

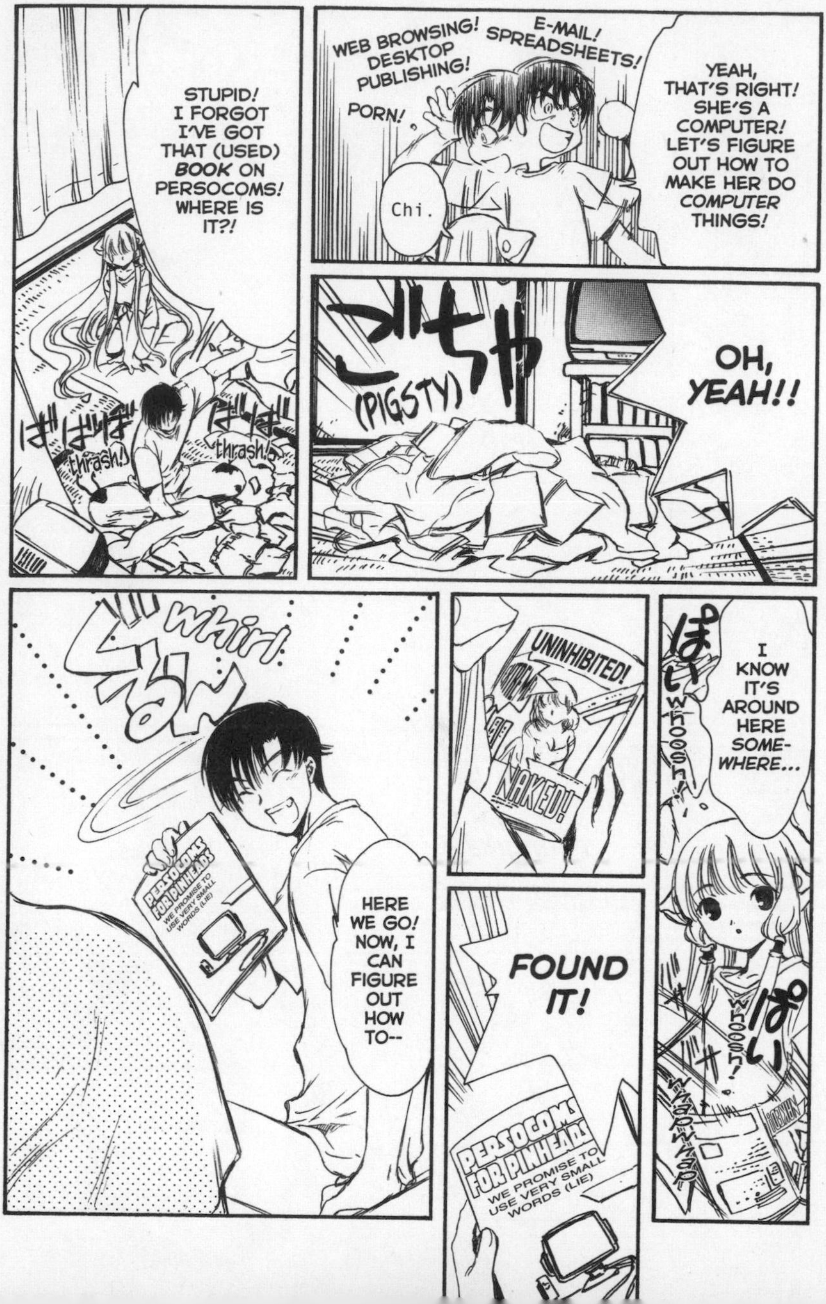
YEAH, THAT'S RIGHT! SHE'S A COMPUTER! LET'S FIGURE OUT HOW TO MAKE HER DO COMPUTER THINGS!
E-MAIL! SPREADSHEETS!
WEB BROWSING! DESKTOP PUBLISHING!
PORN!
Chi.
OH, YEAH!!
ごちゃ
(PIGSTY)
STUPID! I FORGOT I'VE GOT THAT (USED) BOOK ON PERSOCOMS! WHERE IS IT?!
ばばば
thrash!
ばばば
thrash!
I KNOW IT'S AROUND HERE SOMEWHERE...
ぱい
whoosh!
ぱい
whoosh!
UNINHIBITED!
NAKED!
FOUND IT!
PERSOCOMS FOR PINHEADS
WE PROMISE TO USE VERY SMALL WORDS (LIE)
くるん
whirl!
PERSOCOMS FOR PINHEADS
WE PROMISE TO USE VERY SMALL WORDS (LIE)
HERE WE GO! NOW, I CAN FIGURE OUT HOW TO--

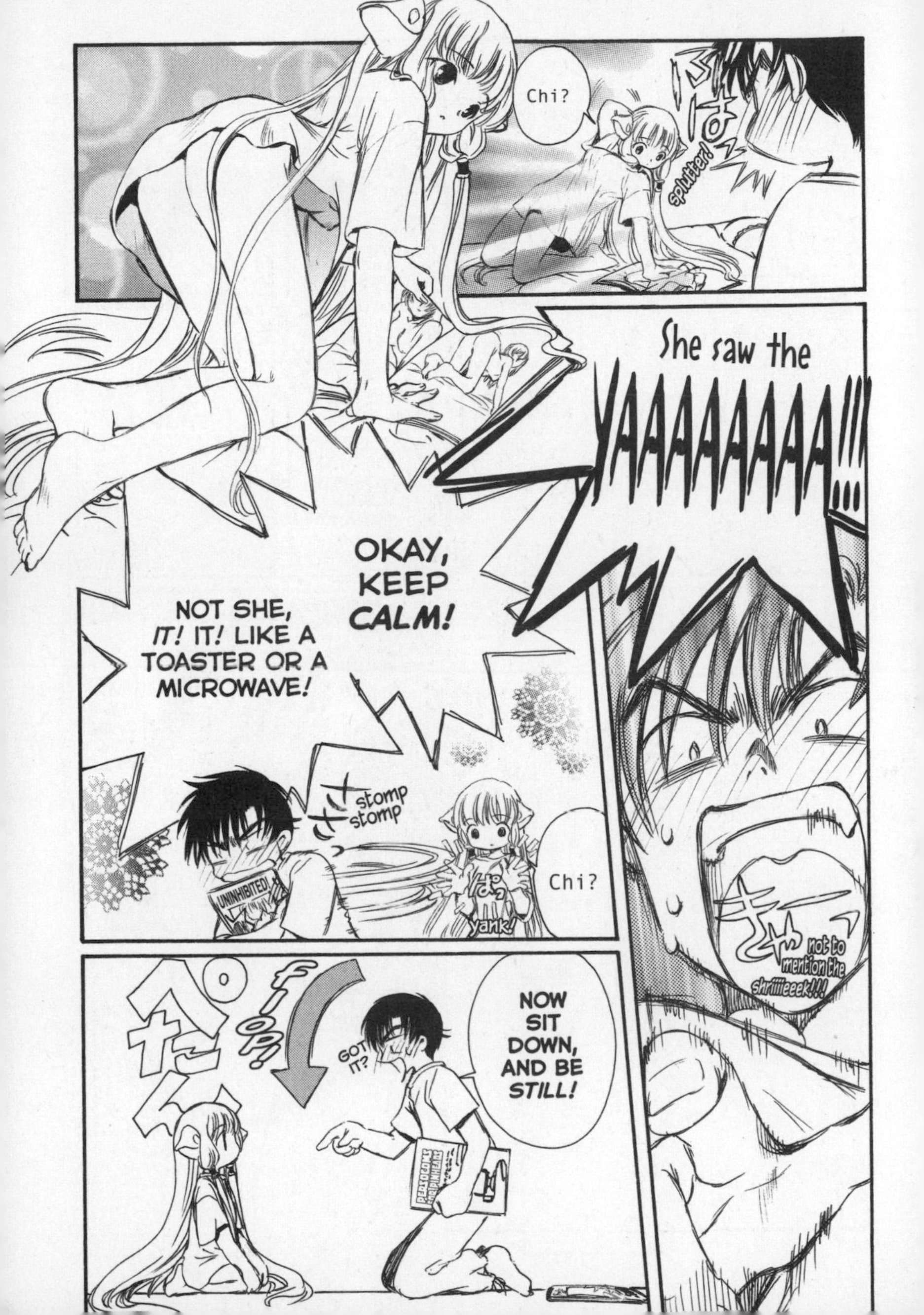
ぶはっ
splutter!
Chi?
She saw the
YAAAAAAA!!!
きゃー
not to mention the shriiiieek!!!
OKAY, KEEP CALM!
NOT SHE, IT! IT! LIKE A TOASTER OR A MICROWAVE!
Chi?
ぱっ
yank!
stomp stomp
UNINHIBITED!
NOW SIT DOWN, AND BE STILL!
GOT IT?
f-lop!
ぺたん

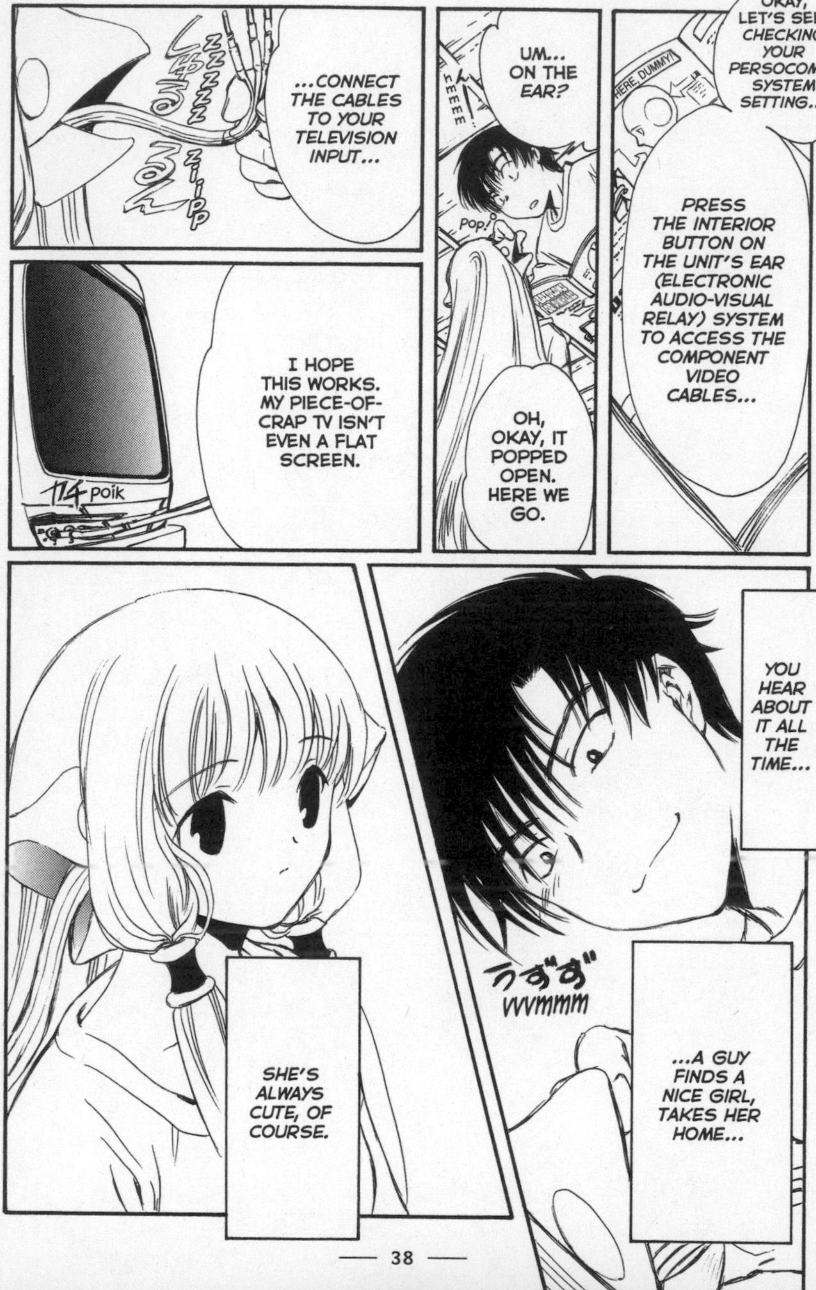
OKAY, LET'S SEE. CHECKING YOUR PERSOCOM'S SYSTEM SETTING...
HERE, DUMMY!
PRESS THE INTERIOR BUTTON ON THE UNIT'S EAR (ELECTRONIC AUDIO-VISUAL RELAY) SYSTEM TO ACCESS THE COMPONENT VIDEO CABLES...
UM... ON THE EAR?
hmmmm
Pop!
OH, OKAY, IT POPPED OPEN. HERE WE GO.
...CONNECT THE CABLES TO YOUR TELEVISION INPUT...
zzzzz
ziipp
I HOPE THIS WORKS. MY PIECE-OF-CRAP TV ISN'T EVEN A FLAT SCREEN.
poik
YOU HEAR ABOUT IT ALL THE TIME...
vvvmmm
...A GUY FINDS A NICE GIRL, TAKES HER HOME...
SHE'S ALWAYS CUTE, OF COURSE.

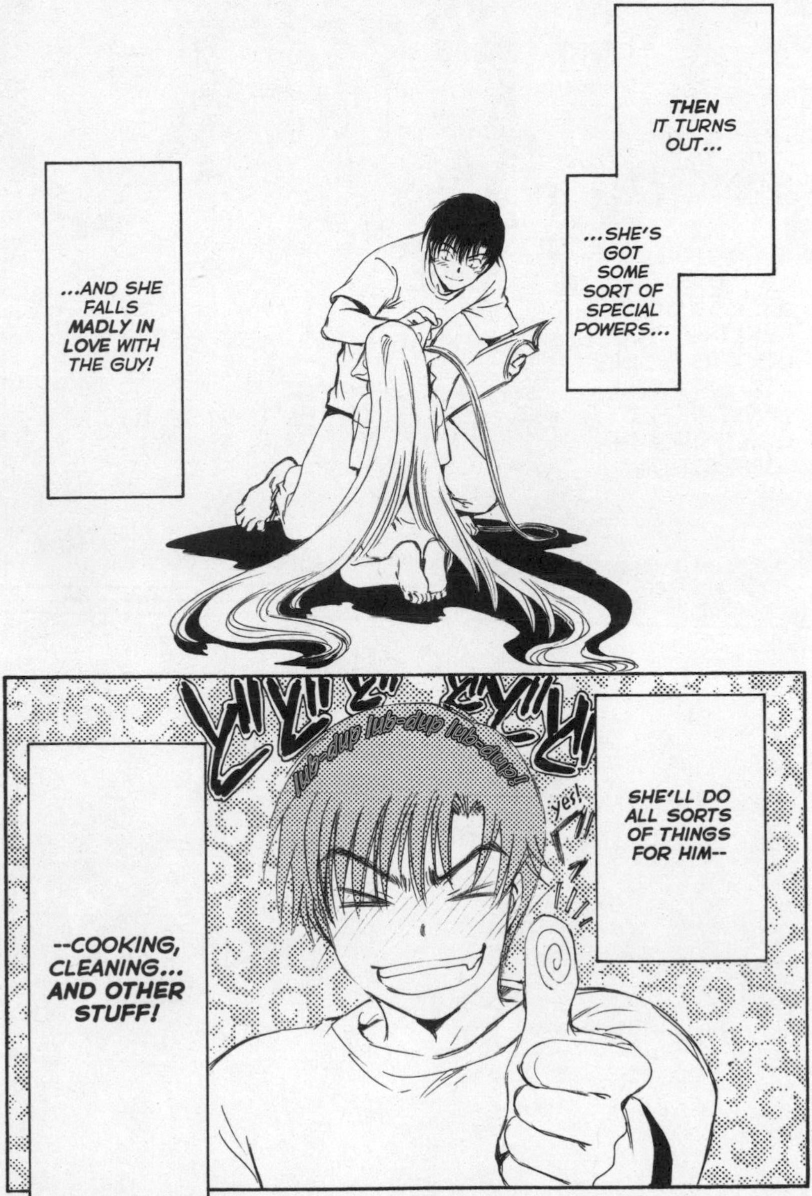
THEN IT TURNS OUT...
...SHE'S GOT SOME SORT OF SPECIAL POWERS...
...AND SHE FALLS MADLY IN LOVE WITH THE GUY!
SHE'LL DO ALL SORTS OF THINGS FOR HIM--
lub-dup lub-dup lub-dup lub-dup!
yes!
--COOKING, CLEANING... AND OTHER STUFF!

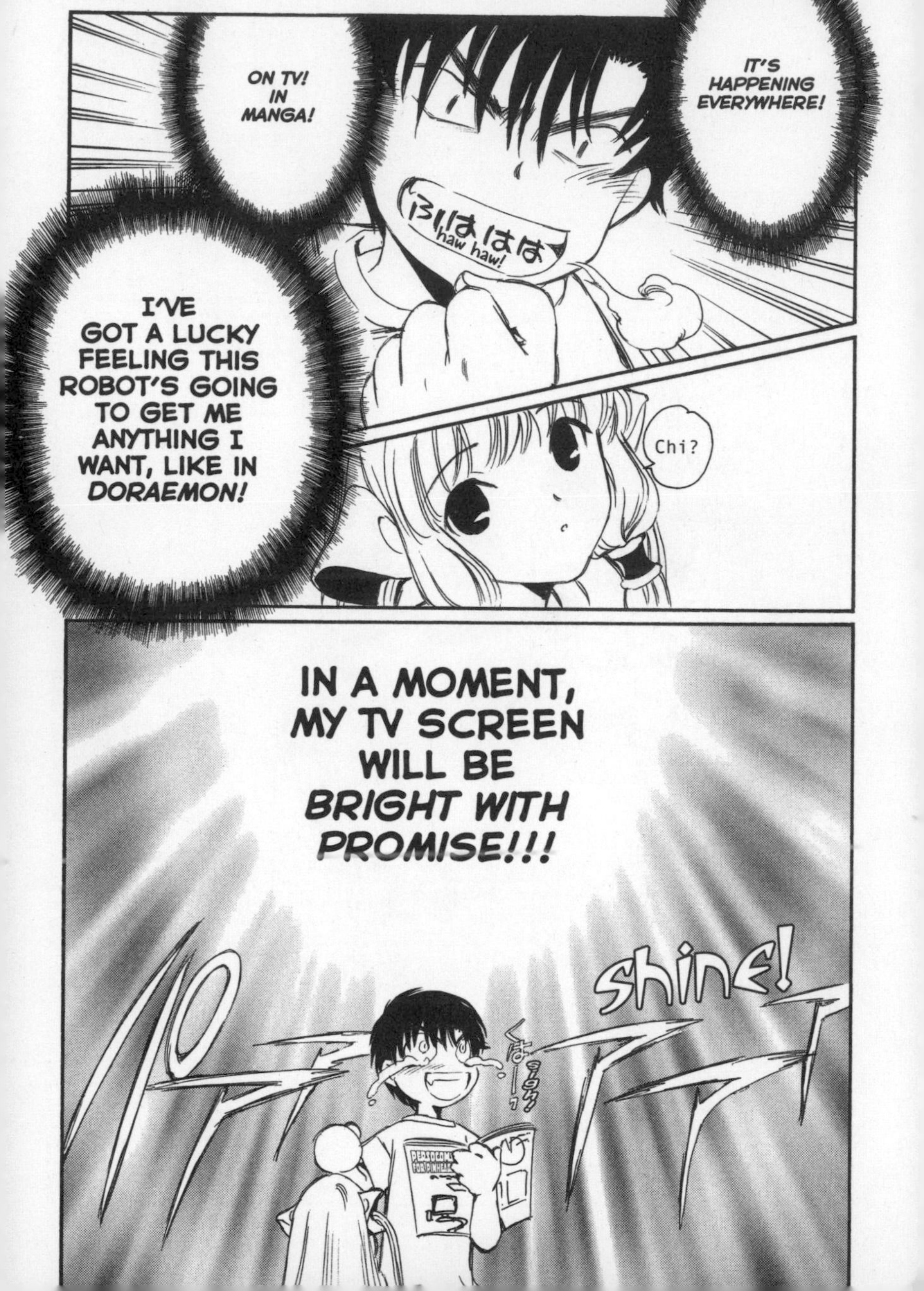
IT'S HAPPENING EVERYWHERE!
ON TV! IN MANGA!
ふははは
haw haw!
I'VE GOT A LUCKY FEELING THIS ROBOT'S GOING TO GET ME ANYTHING I WANT, LIKE IN DORAEMON!
Chi?
IN A MOMENT, MY TV SCREEN WILL BE BRIGHT WITH PROMISE!!!
shine!

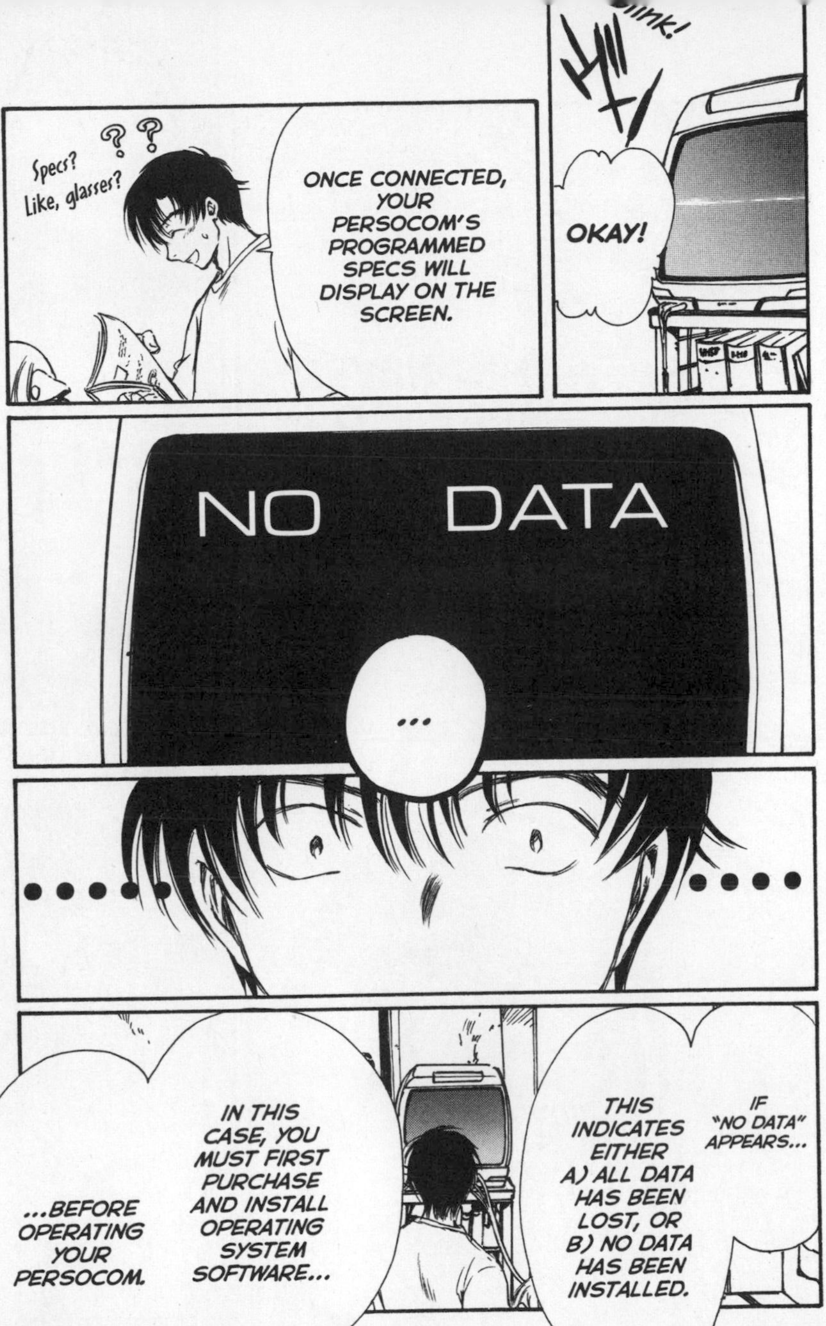

ink!
OKAY!
ONCE CONNECTED, YOUR PERSOCOM'S PROGRAMMED SPECS WILL DISPLAY ON THE SCREEN.
Specs? Like, glasses?
NO DATA
...
IF "NO DATA" APPEARS...
THIS INDICATES EITHER A) ALL DATA HAS BEEN LOST, OR B) NO DATA HAS BEEN INSTALLED.
IN THIS CASE, YOU MUST FIRST PURCHASE AND INSTALL OPERATING SYSTEM SOFTWARE...
...BEFORE OPERATING YOUR PERSOCOM.

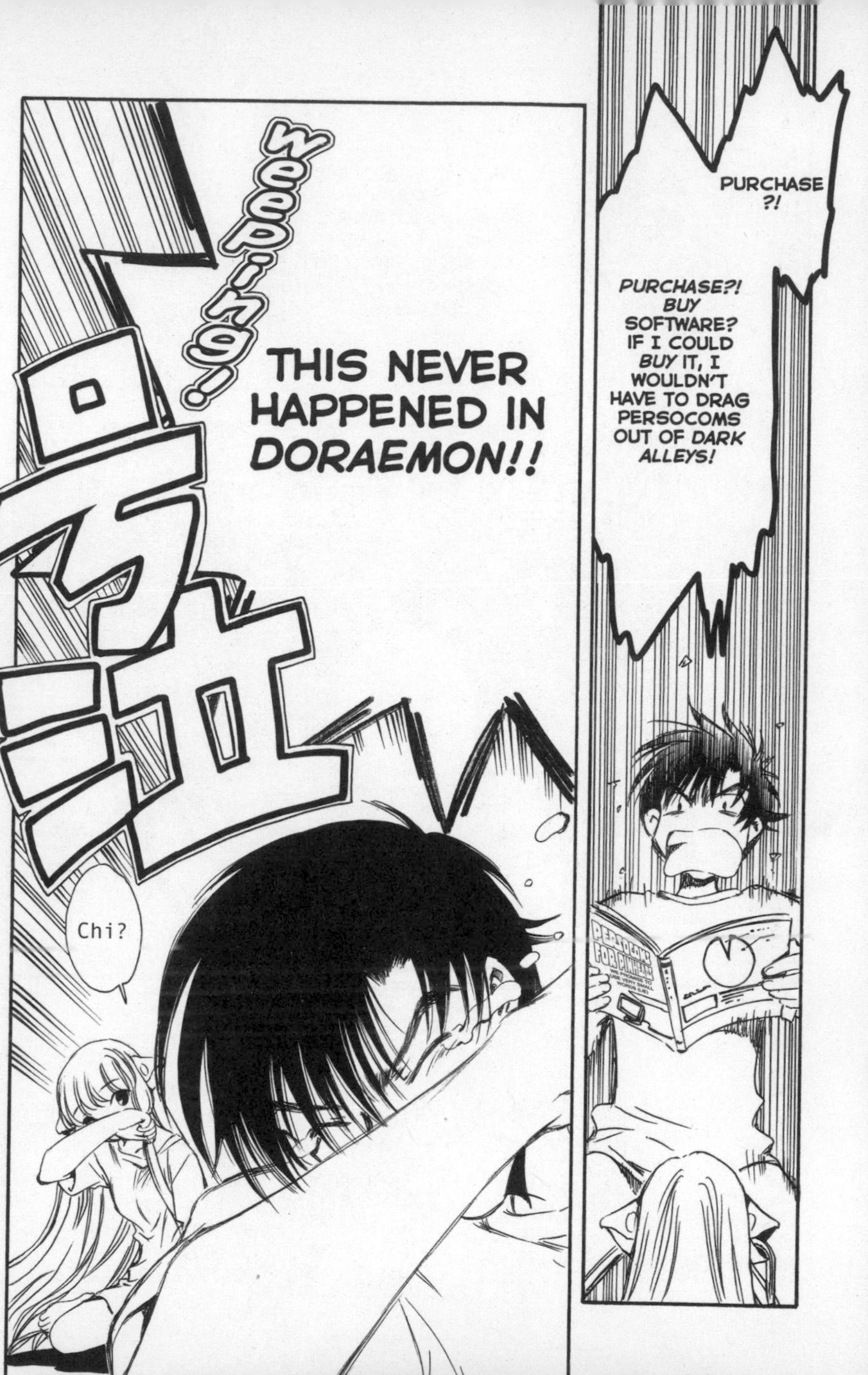

PURCHASE ?!
PURCHASE?! BUY SOFTWARE? IF I COULD BUY IT, I WOULDN'T HAVE TO DRAG PERSOCOMS OUT OF DARK ALLEYS!
PERSOCOMS FOR PINHEADS
weeping!
THIS NEVER HAPPENED IN DORAEMON!!
Chi?

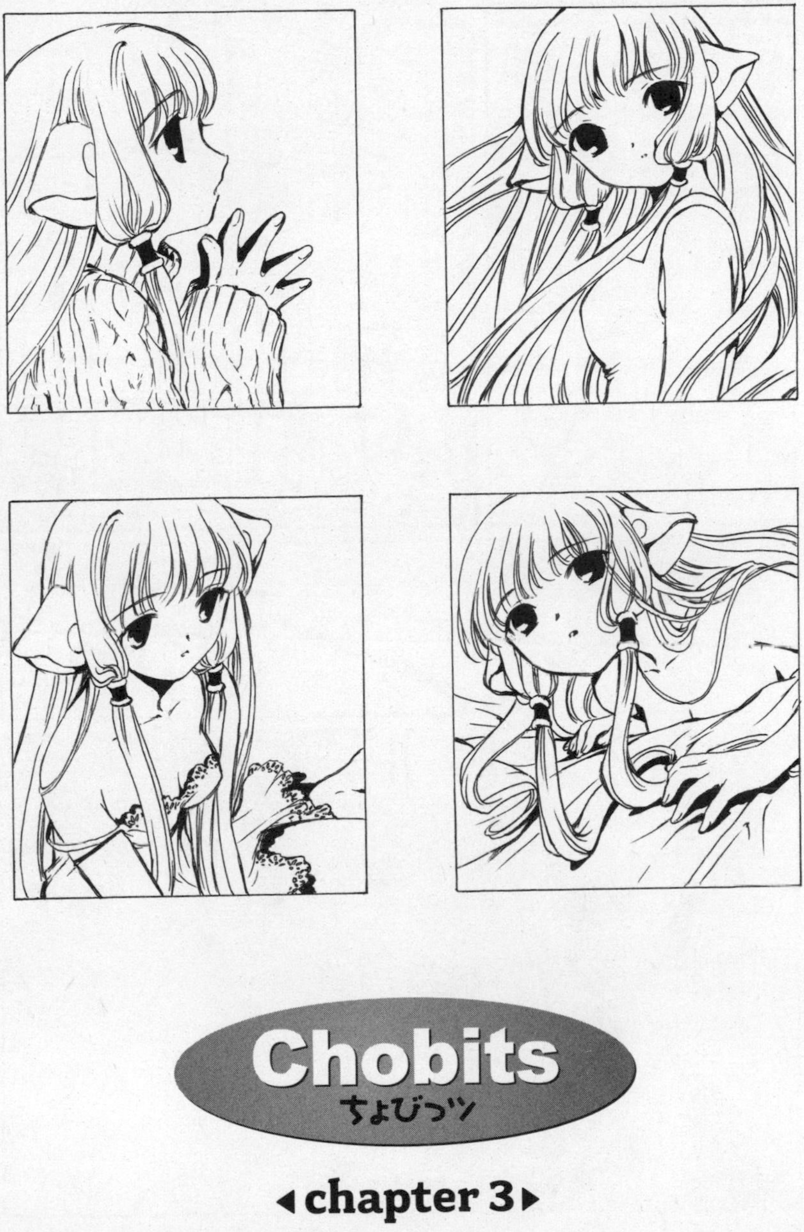

Chobits
ちょびっツ

◂chapter 3▸

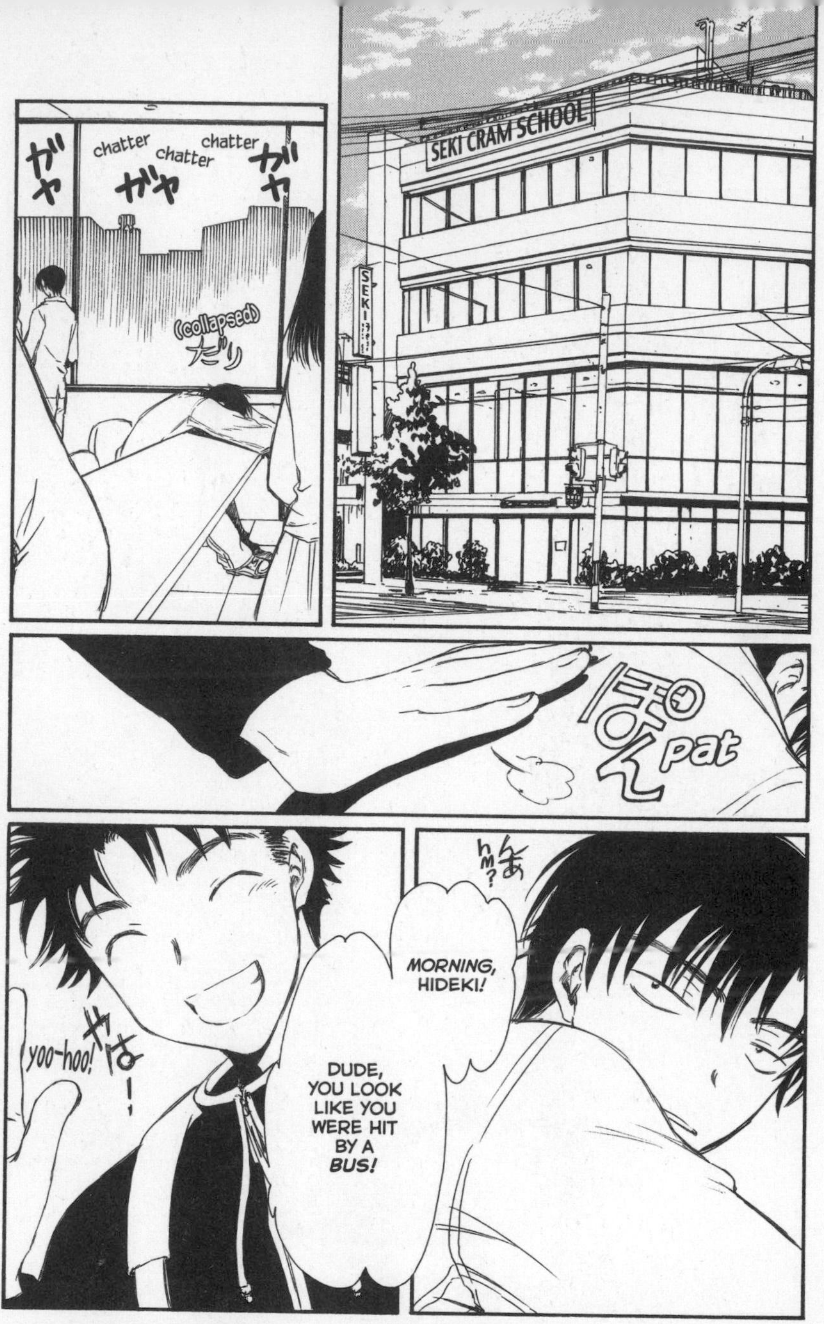
SEKI CRAM SCHOOL
SEKI
ガヤ
chatter
ガヤ
chatter
ガヤ
chatter
(collapsed)
だり
ぽん
pat
んあ
hm?
MORNING, HIDEKI!
DUDE, YOU LOOK LIKE YOU WERE HIT BY A *BUS!*
やは!
yoo-hoo!

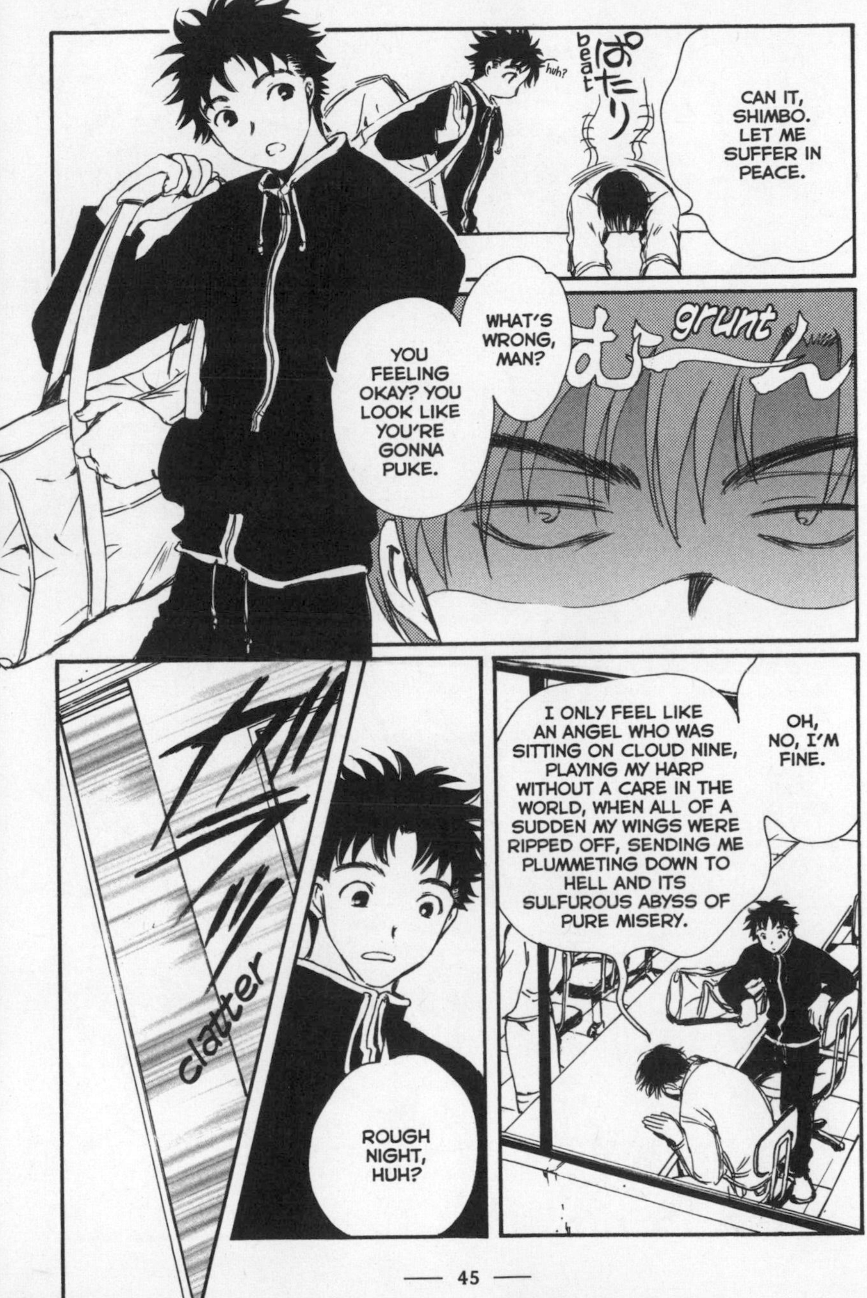
CAN IT, SHIMBO. LET ME SUFFER IN PEACE.
ぱたり
beat
huh?
grunt
WHAT'S WRONG, MAN?
YOU FEELING OKAY? YOU LOOK LIKE YOU'RE GONNA PUKE.
OH, NO, I'M FINE.
I ONLY FEEL LIKE AN ANGEL WHO WAS SITTING ON CLOUD NINE, PLAYING MY HARP WITHOUT A CARE IN THE WORLD, WHEN ALL OF A SUDDEN MY WINGS WERE RIPPED OFF, SENDING ME PLUMMETING DOWN TO HELL AND ITS SULFUROUS ABYSS OF PURE MISERY.
clatter
ROUGH NIGHT, HUH?

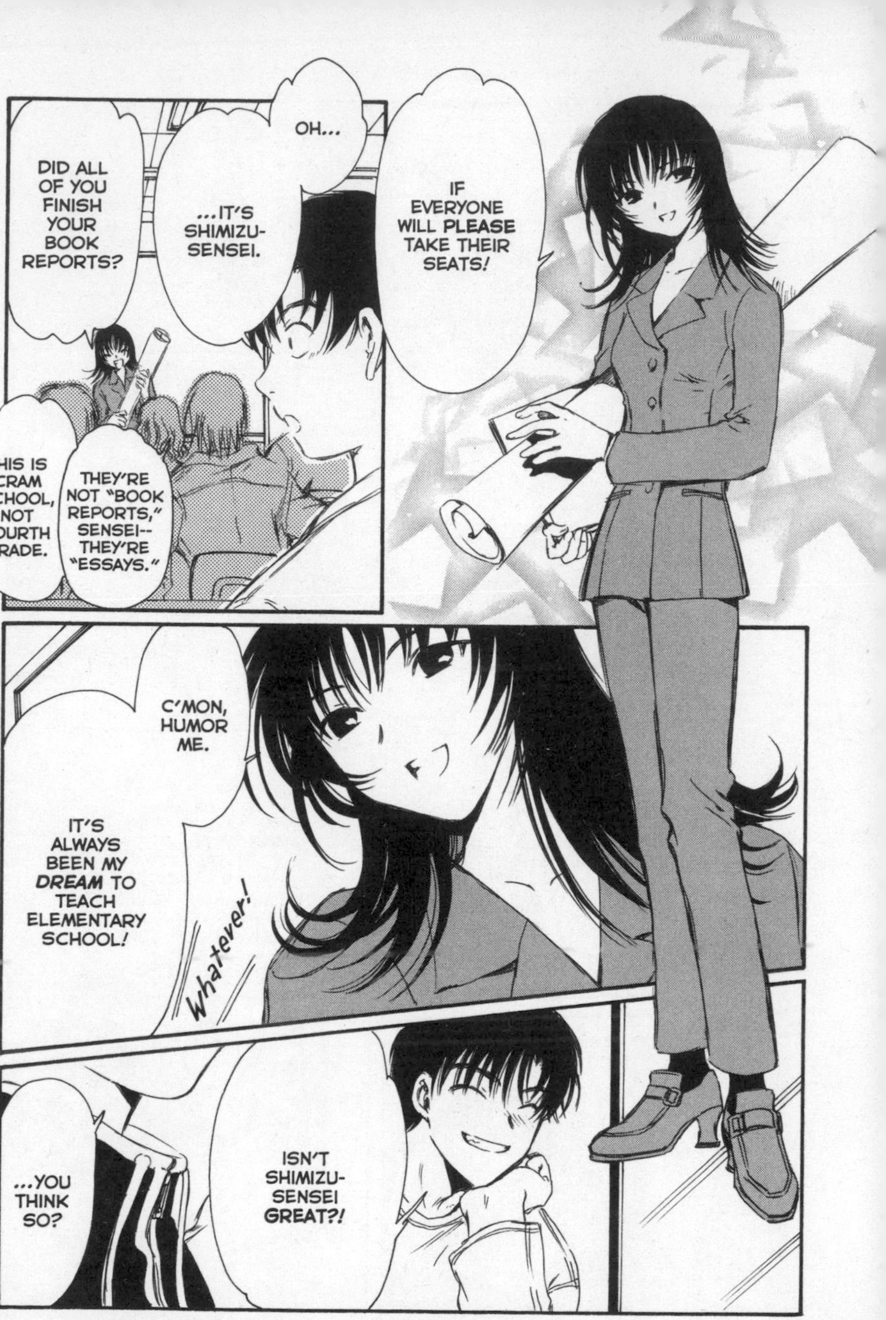
IF EVERYONE WILL **PLEASE** TAKE THEIR SEATS!
OH...
...IT'S SHIMIZU-SENSEI.
DID ALL OF YOU FINISH YOUR BOOK REPORTS?
THEY'RE NOT "BOOK REPORTS," SENSEI--THEY'RE "ESSAYS."
THIS IS CRAM SCHOOL, NOT FOURTH GRADE.
C'MON, HUMOR ME.
IT'S ALWAYS BEEN MY ***DREAM*** TO TEACH ELEMENTARY SCHOOL!
Whatever!
ISN'T SHIMIZU-SENSEI **GREAT?!**
...YOU THINK SO?

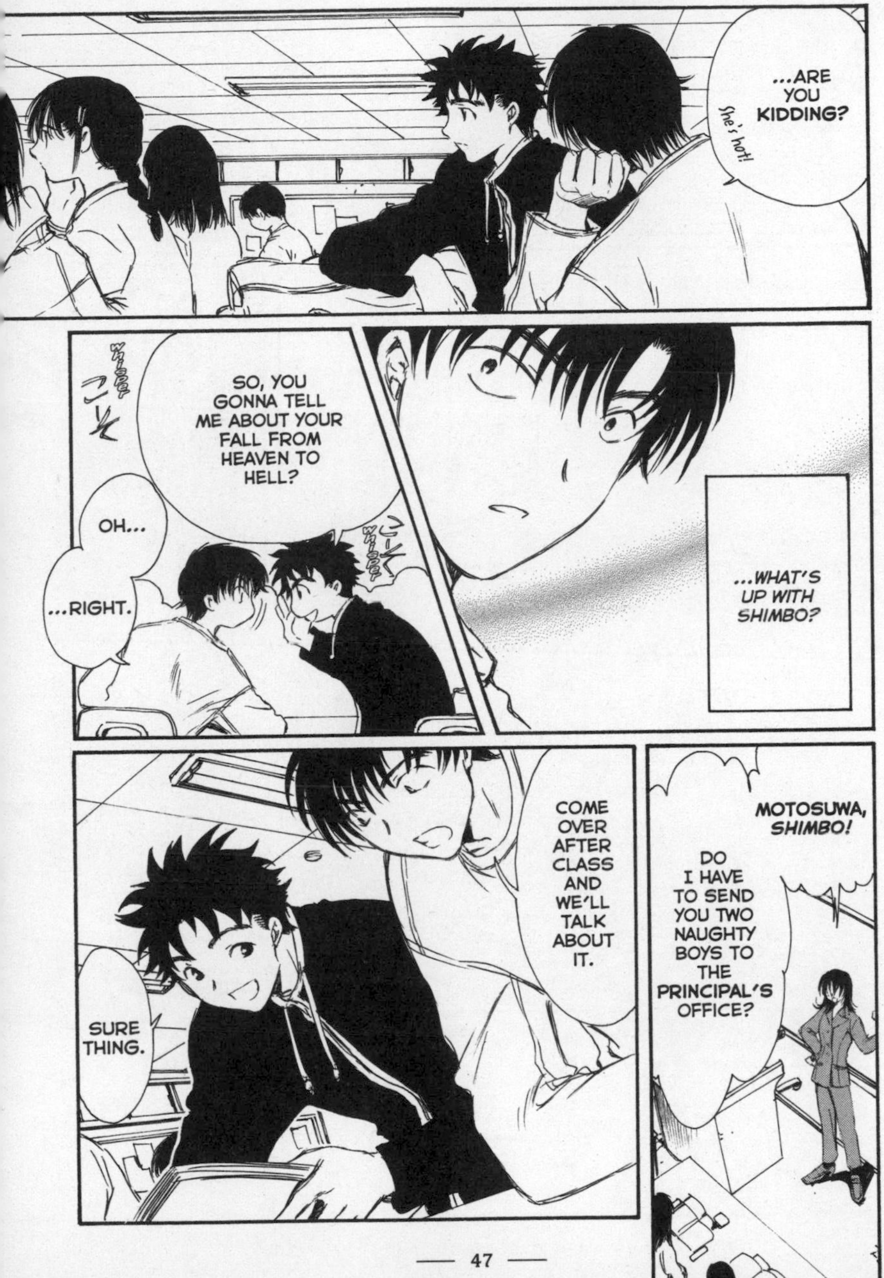
...ARE YOU KIDDING?
She's hot!
...WHAT'S UP WITH SHIMBO?
WHISPER
SO, YOU GONNA TELL ME ABOUT YOUR FALL FROM HEAVEN TO HELL?
WHISPER
OH...
...RIGHT.
MOTOSUWA, SHIMBO!
DO I HAVE TO SEND YOU TWO NAUGHTY BOYS TO THE PRINCIPAL'S OFFICE?
COME OVER AFTER CLASS AND WE'LL TALK ABOUT IT.
SURE THING.

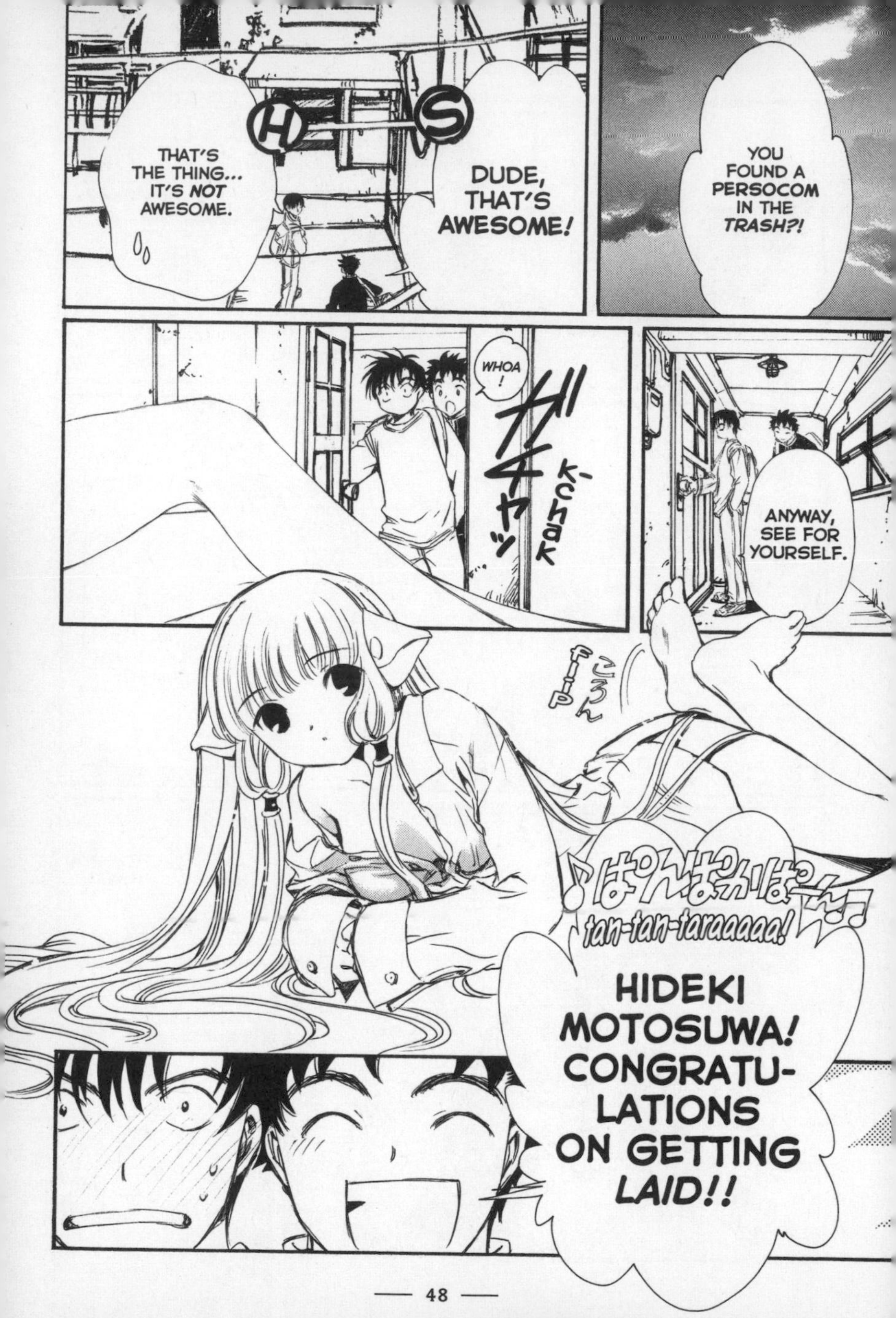
YOU FOUND A PERSOCOM IN THE TRASH?!
S
H
DUDE, THAT'S AWESOME!
THAT'S THE THING... IT'S NOT AWESOME.
ANYWAY, SEE FOR YOURSELF.
WHOA!
ガチャッ
k-chak
ころん
flip
♪ぱんぱかぱーん♪
tan-tan-taraaaaa!
HIDEKI MOTOSUWA! CONGRATU-LATIONS ON GETTING LAID!!

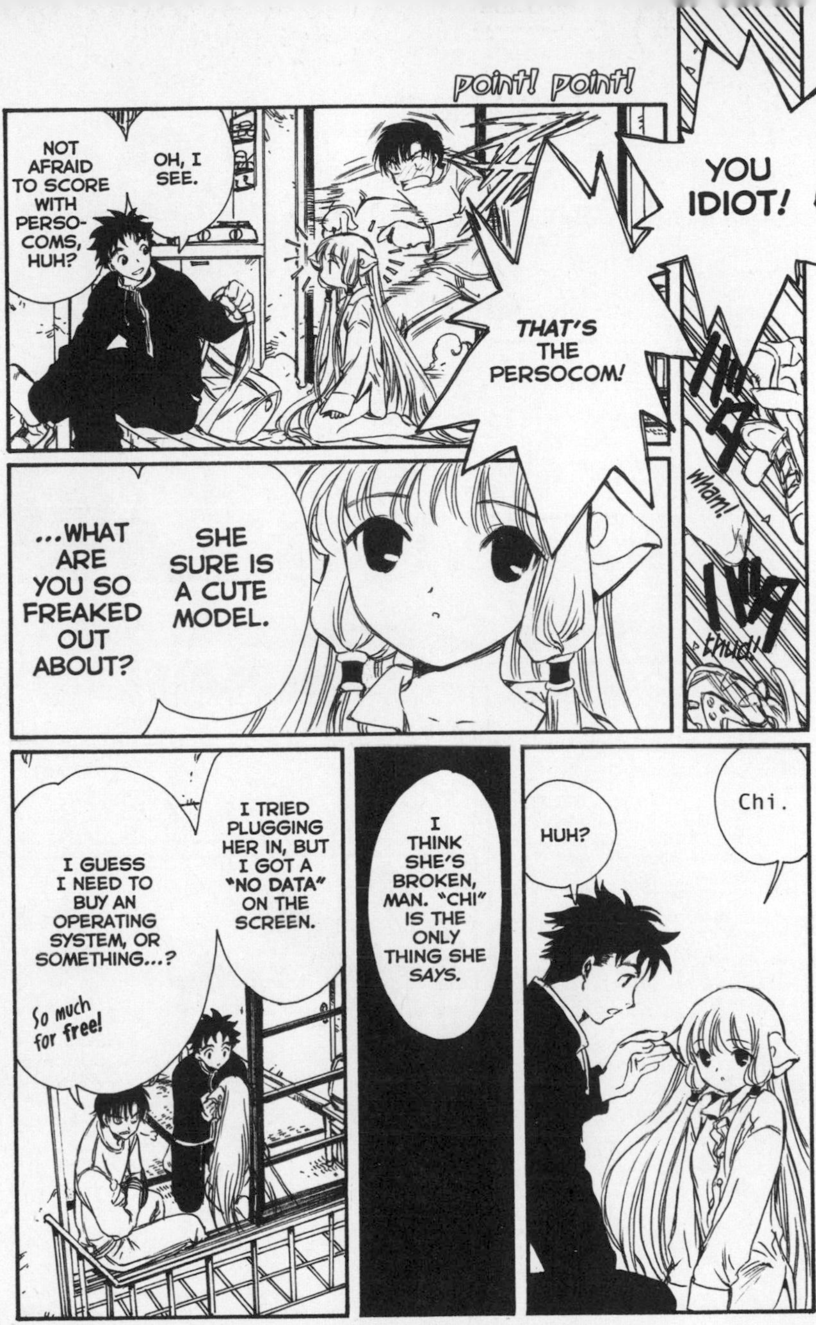
point! point!
YOU IDIOT!
wham!
thud!
THAT'S THE PERSOCOM!
OH, I SEE.
NOT AFRAID TO SCORE WITH PERSOCOMS, HUH?
SHE SURE IS A CUTE MODEL.
...WHAT ARE YOU SO FREAKED OUT ABOUT?
Chi.
HUH?
I THINK SHE'S BROKEN, MAN. "CHI" IS THE ONLY THING SHE SAYS.
I TRIED PLUGGING HER IN, BUT I GOT A "NO DATA" ON THE SCREEN.
I GUESS I NEED TO BUY AN OPERATING SYSTEM, OR SOMETHING...?
So much for free!

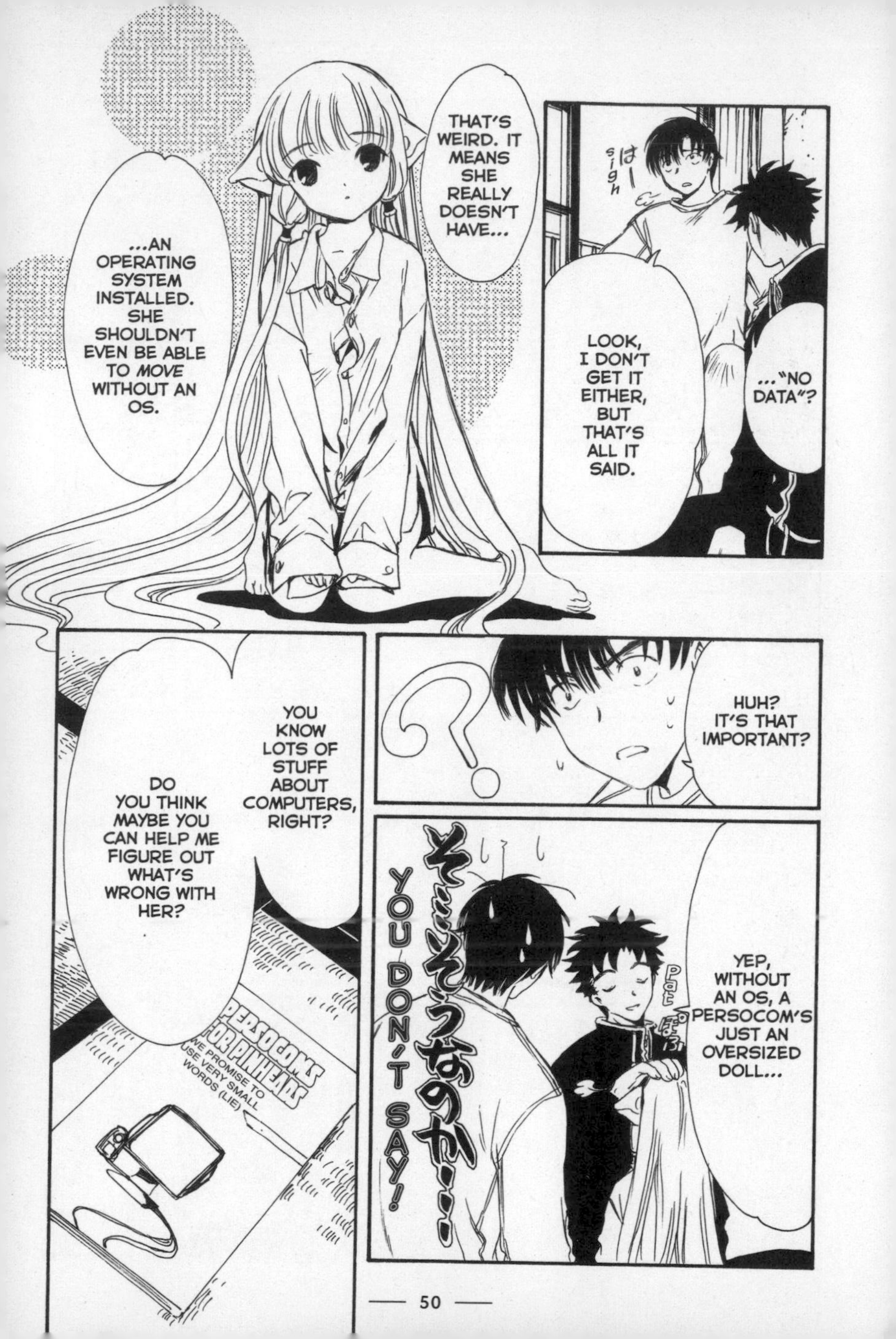
はー
sigh
..."NO DATA"?
LOOK, I DON'T GET IT EITHER, BUT THAT'S ALL IT SAID.
THAT'S WEIRD. IT MEANS SHE REALLY DOESN'T HAVE...
...AN OPERATING SYSTEM INSTALLED. SHE SHOULDN'T EVEN BE ABLE TO *MOVE* WITHOUT AN OS.
HUH? IT'S THAT IMPORTANT?
YEP, WITHOUT AN OS, A PERSOCOM'S JUST AN OVERSIZED DOLL...
pat
YOU DON'T SAY!
YOU KNOW LOTS OF STUFF ABOUT COMPUTERS, RIGHT?
DO YOU THINK MAYBE YOU CAN HELP ME FIGURE OUT WHAT'S WRONG WITH HER?
PERSOCOMS FOR PINHEADS
WE PROMISE TO USE VERY SMALL WORDS (LIE)

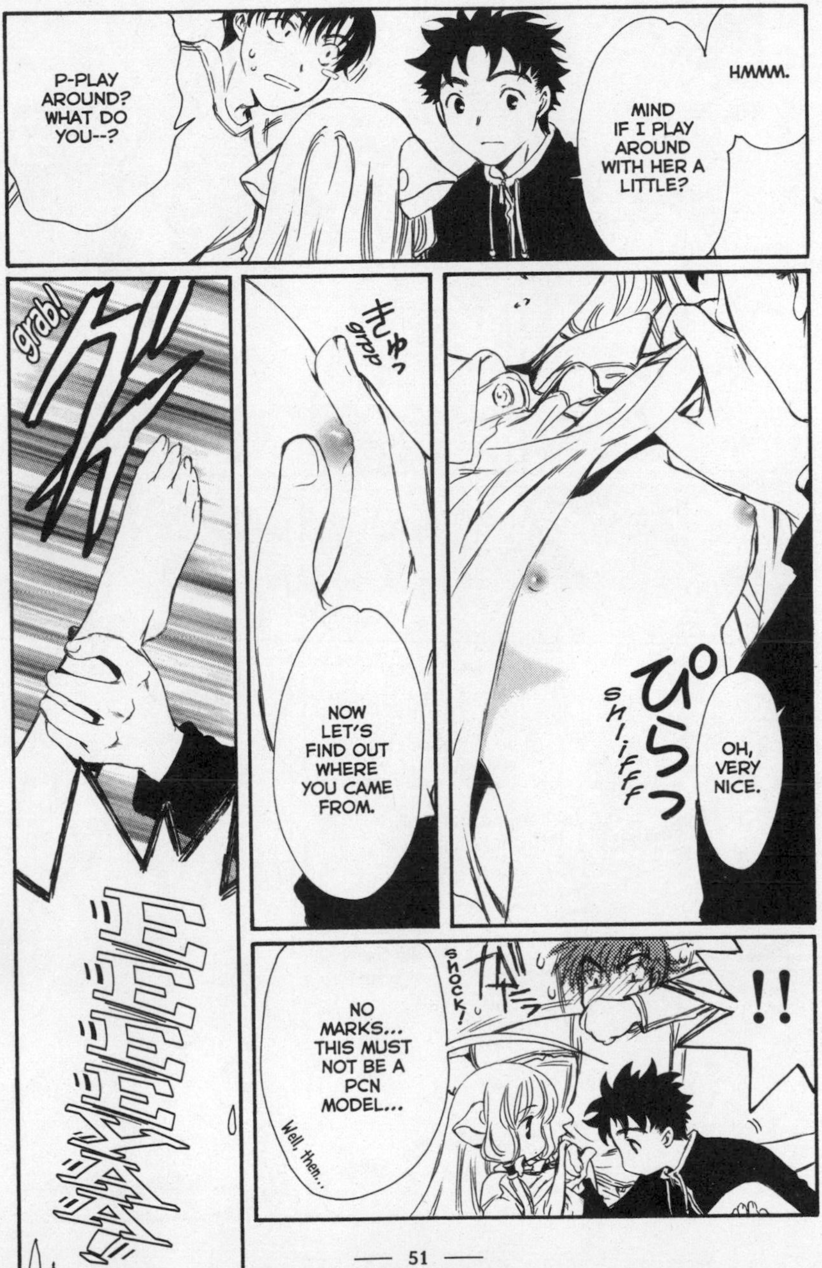
HMMM.
MIND IF I PLAY AROUND WITH HER A LITTLE?
P-PLAY AROUND? WHAT DO YOU--?
ぴらっ
shriffff
OH, VERY NICE.
きゅっ
grip
NOW LET'S FIND OUT WHERE YOU CAME FROM.
!!
SHOCK!
NO MARKS... THIS MUST NOT BE A PCN MODEL...
Well, then...
grab!

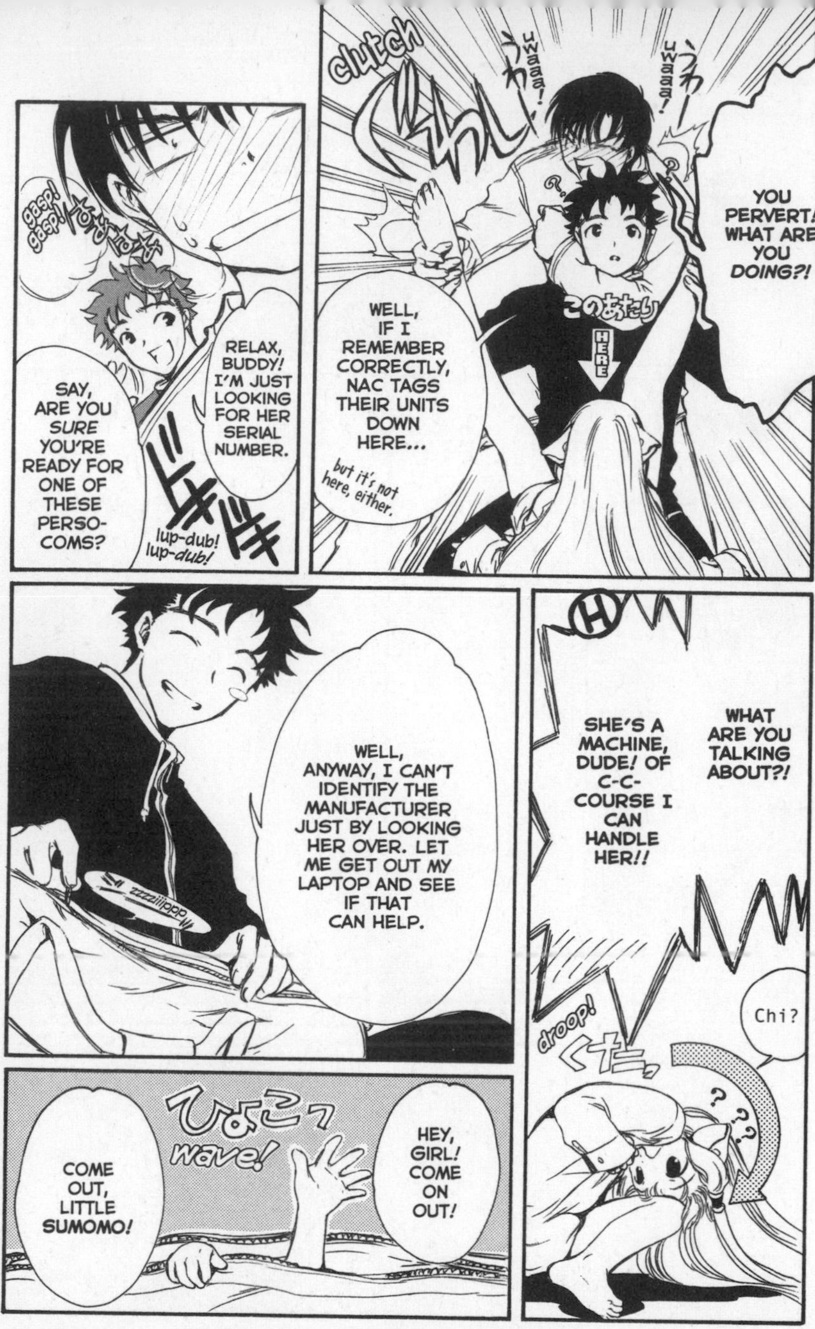
clutch
uwaaa!
uwaaa!
YOU PERVERT! WHAT ARE YOU DOING?!
このあたり
HERE
WELL, IF I REMEMBER CORRECTLY, NAC TAGS THEIR UNITS DOWN HERE...
but it's not here, either.
gasp! gasp!
RELAX, BUDDY! I'M JUST LOOKING FOR HER SERIAL NUMBER.
SAY, ARE YOU SURE YOU'RE READY FOR ONE OF THESE PERSO-COMS?
lup-dub! lup-dub!
WHAT ARE YOU TALKING ABOUT?!
SHE'S A MACHINE, DUDE! OF C-C-COURSE I CAN HANDLE HER!!
droop!
Chi?
WELL, ANYWAY, I CAN'T IDENTIFY THE MANUFACTURER JUST BY LOOKING HER OVER. LET ME GET OUT MY LAPTOP AND SEE IF THAT CAN HELP.
zzzziiiip
HEY, GIRL! COME ON OUT!
wave!
COME OUT, LITTLE SUMOMO!

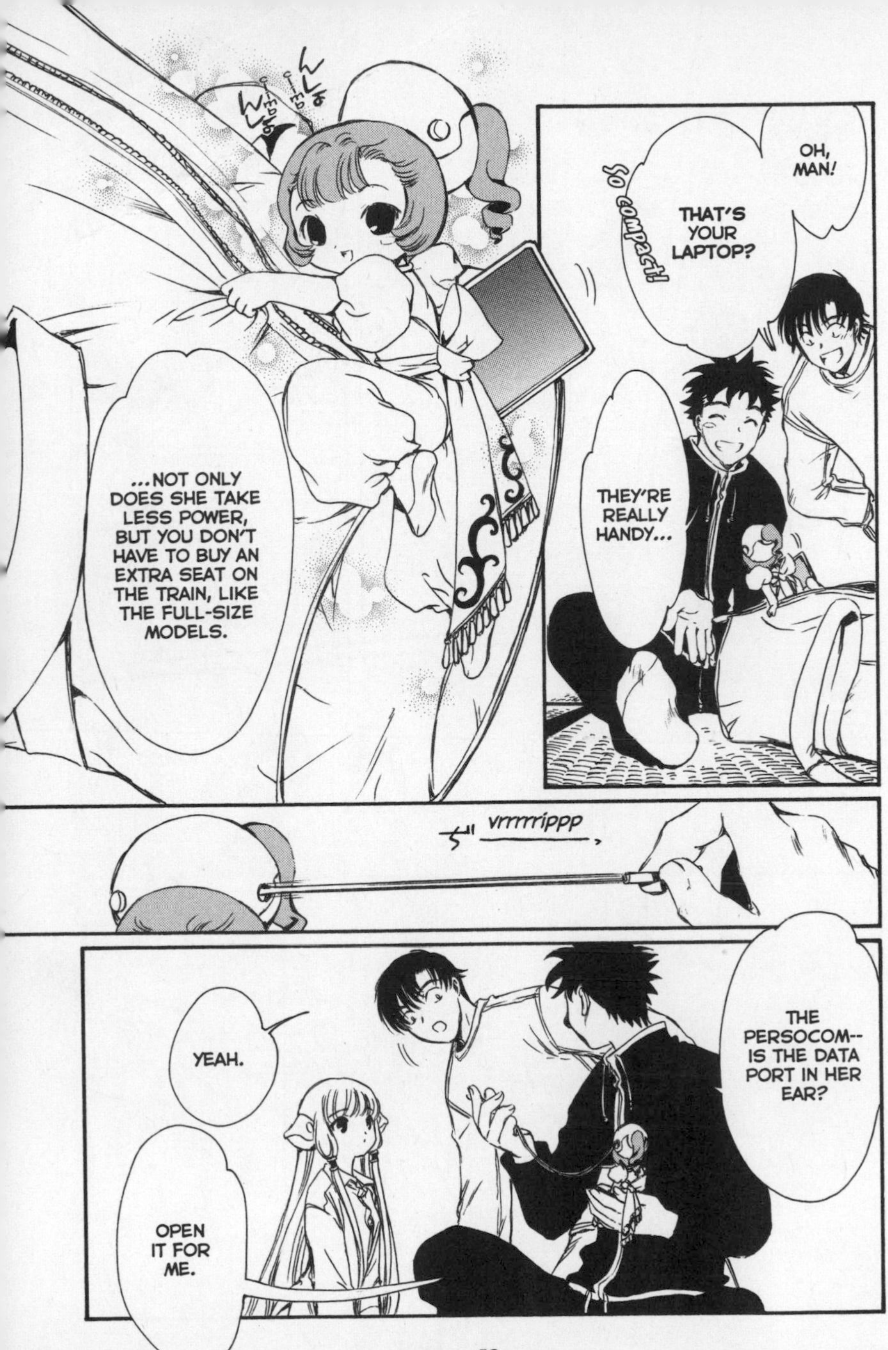
OH, MAN!
THAT'S YOUR LAPTOP?
SO COMPACT!
THEY'RE REALLY HANDY...
んしょ
んしょ
...NOT ONLY DOES SHE TAKE LESS POWER, BUT YOU DON'T HAVE TO BUY AN EXTRA SEAT ON THE TRAIN, LIKE THE FULL-SIZE MODELS.
ぢ vrrrrripp
THE PERSOCOM-- IS THE DATA PORT IN HER EAR?
YEAH.
OPEN IT FOR ME.

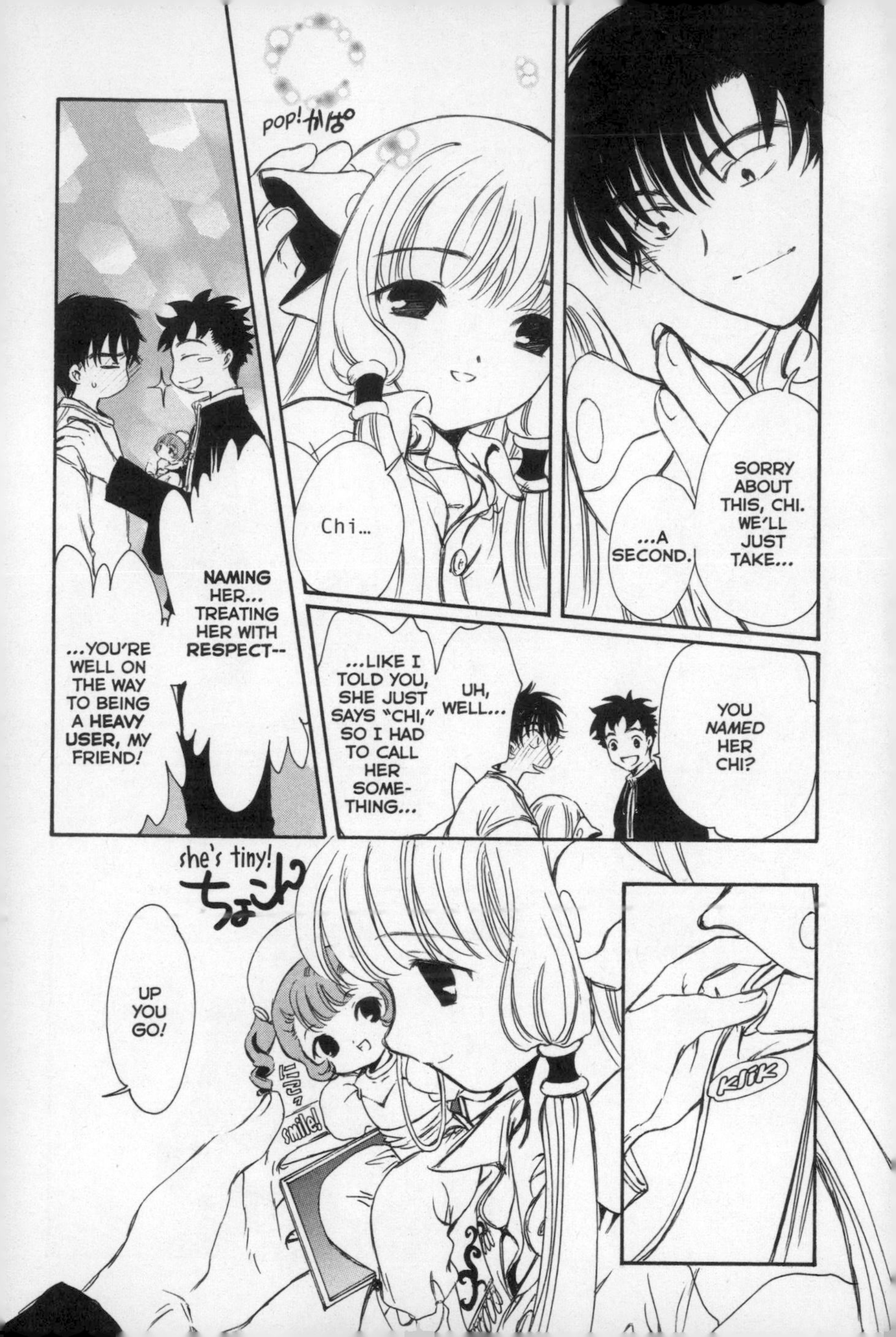

SORRY ABOUT THIS, CHI. WE'LL JUST TAKE...
...A SECOND.
pop! かぱ
Chi...
YOU *NAMED* HER CHI?
UH, WELL...
...LIKE I TOLD YOU, SHE JUST SAYS "CHI," SO I HAD TO CALL HER SOMETHING...
NAMING HER... TREATING HER WITH RESPECT--
...YOU'RE WELL ON THE WAY TO BEING A HEAVY USER, MY FRIEND!
klik
she's tiny! ちょこん
UP YOU GO!
ニコッ
smile!

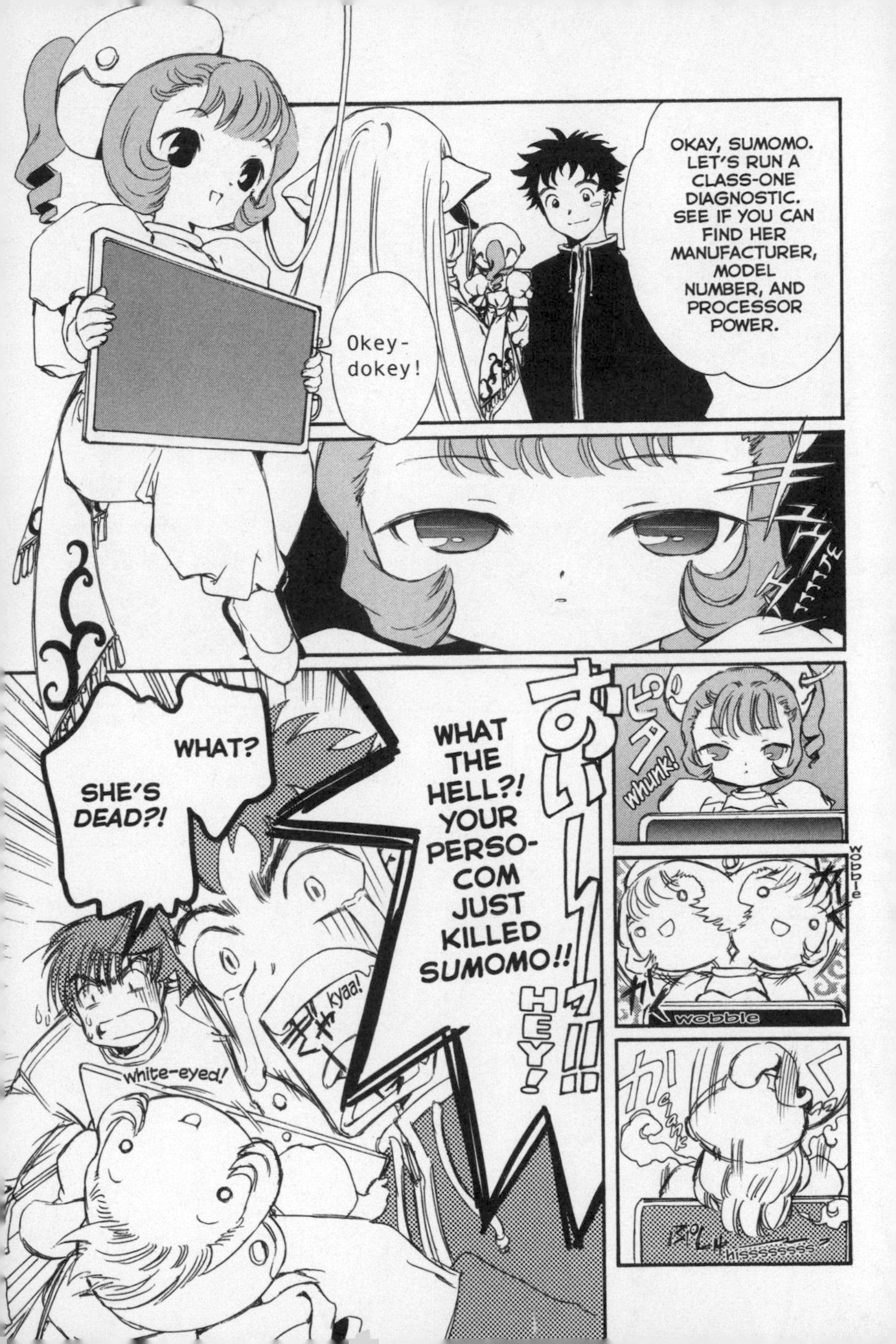

OKAY, SUMOMO. LET'S RUN A CLASS-ONE DIAGNOSTIC. SEE IF YOU CAN FIND HER MANUFACTURER, MODEL NUMBER, AND PROCESSOR POWER.
Okey-dokey!
whunk!
wobble
wobble
clank
hissssssss
WHAT THE HELL?! YOUR PERSO-COM JUST KILLED SUMOMO!!
HEY!
WHAT?
SHE'S DEAD?!
kyaa!
white-eyed!

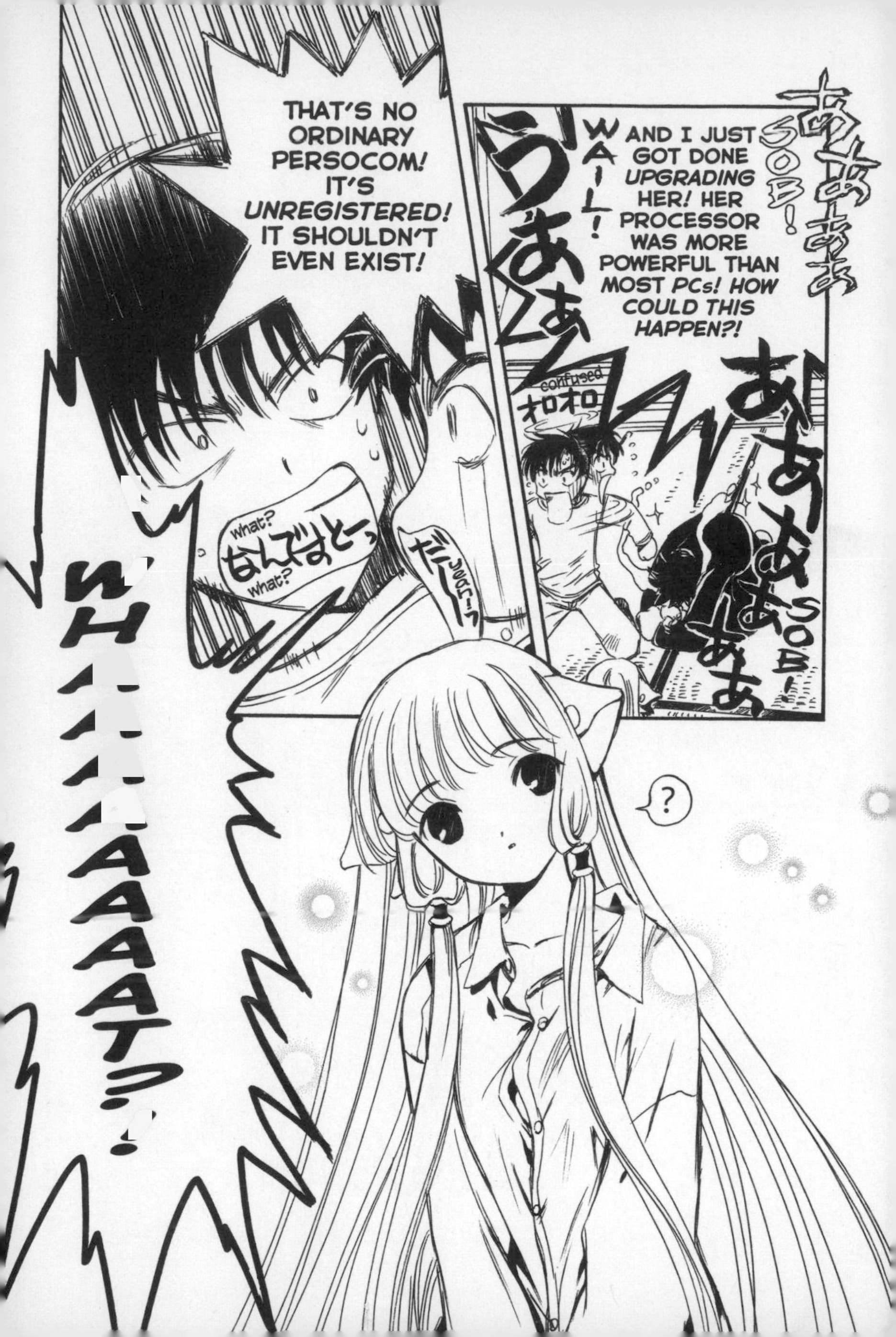
SOB!
WAIL!
AND I JUST GOT DONE UPGRADING HER! HER PROCESSOR WAS MORE POWERFUL THAN MOST PCs! HOW COULD THIS HAPPEN?!
confused
オロオロ
SOB!
THAT'S NO ORDINARY PERSOCOM! IT'S UNREGISTERED! IT SHOULDN'T EVEN EXIST!
WHAAAAAAAT?!
what?
なんですとー
what?
だー
yeah!?
?

Chobits
ちょびっツ

◀ chapter 4 ▶

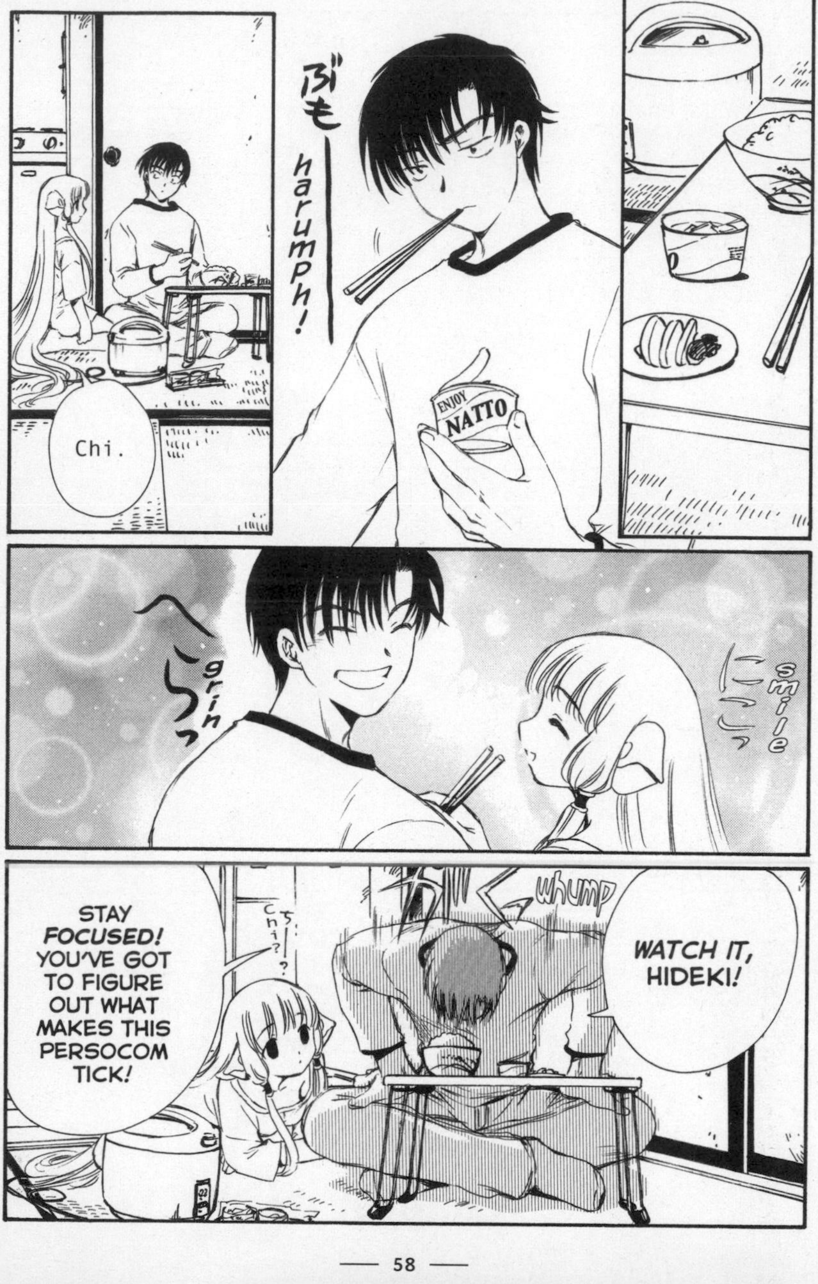
ぶも
harumph!
ENJOY NATTO
Chi.
smile
grin
WATCH IT, HIDEKI!
whump
ちー??
Chi??
STAY FOCUSED! YOU'VE GOT TO FIGURE OUT WHAT MAKES THIS PERSOCOM TICK!

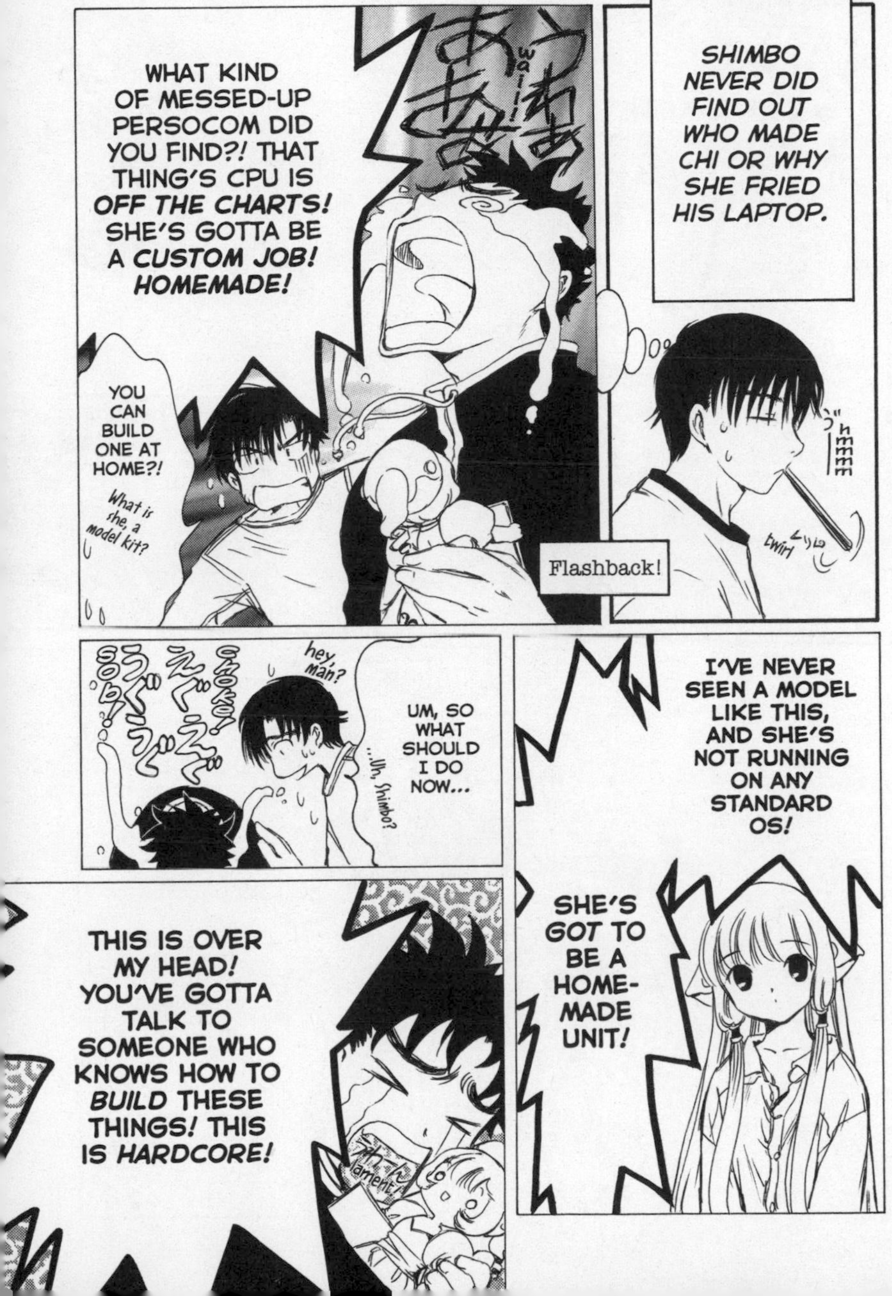
SHIMBO NEVER DID FIND OUT WHO MADE CHI OR WHY SHE FRIED HIS LAPTOP.
hmmm
twirl
Flashback!
WHAT KIND OF MESSED-UP PERSOCOM DID YOU FIND?! THAT THING'S CPU IS *OFF THE CHARTS!* SHE'S GOTTA BE A *CUSTOM JOB! HOMEMADE!*
YOU CAN BUILD ONE AT HOME?!
What is she, a model kit?
I'VE NEVER SEEN A MODEL LIKE THIS, AND SHE'S NOT RUNNING ON ANY STANDARD OS!
SHE'S *GOT* TO BE A HOME-MADE UNIT!
hey, man?
UM, SO WHAT SHOULD I DO NOW...
...Uh, Shimbo?
THIS IS OVER MY HEAD! YOU'VE GOTTA TALK TO SOMEONE WHO KNOWS HOW TO *BUILD* THESE THINGS! THIS IS *HARDCORE!*
lament!

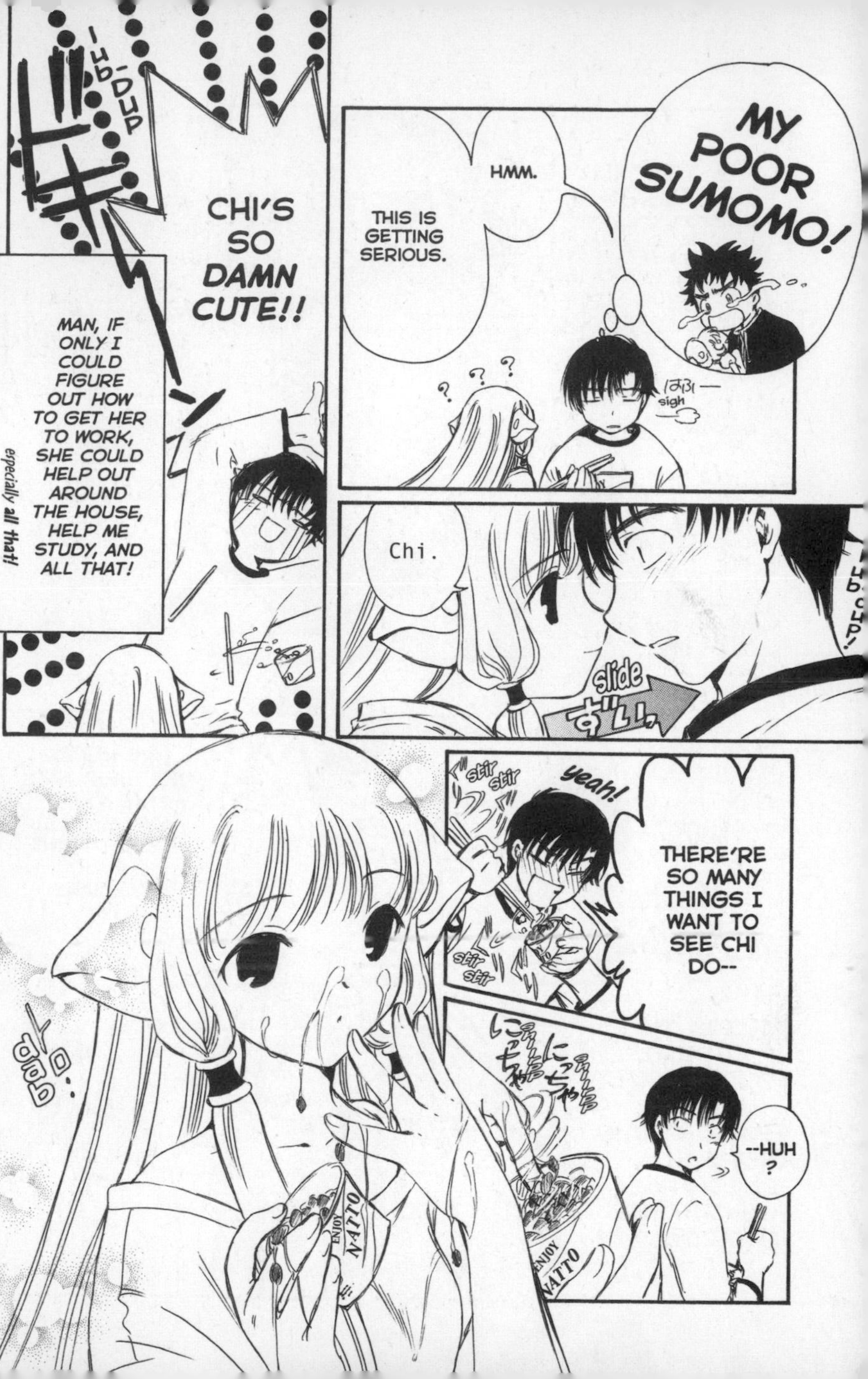

MY POOR SUMOMO!
HMM.
THIS IS GETTING SERIOUS.
sigh
Chi.
lub-dup!
slide
lub-DUP
CHI'S SO DAMN CUTE!!
MAN, IF ONLY I COULD FIGURE OUT HOW TO GET HER TO WORK, SHE COULD HELP OUT AROUND THE HOUSE, HELP ME STUDY, AND ALL THAT!
especially all that!
yeah!
stir stir
THERE'RE SO MANY THINGS I WANT TO SEE CHI DO--
stir stir
--HUH?
ENJOY NATTO
drip..
ENJOY NATTO

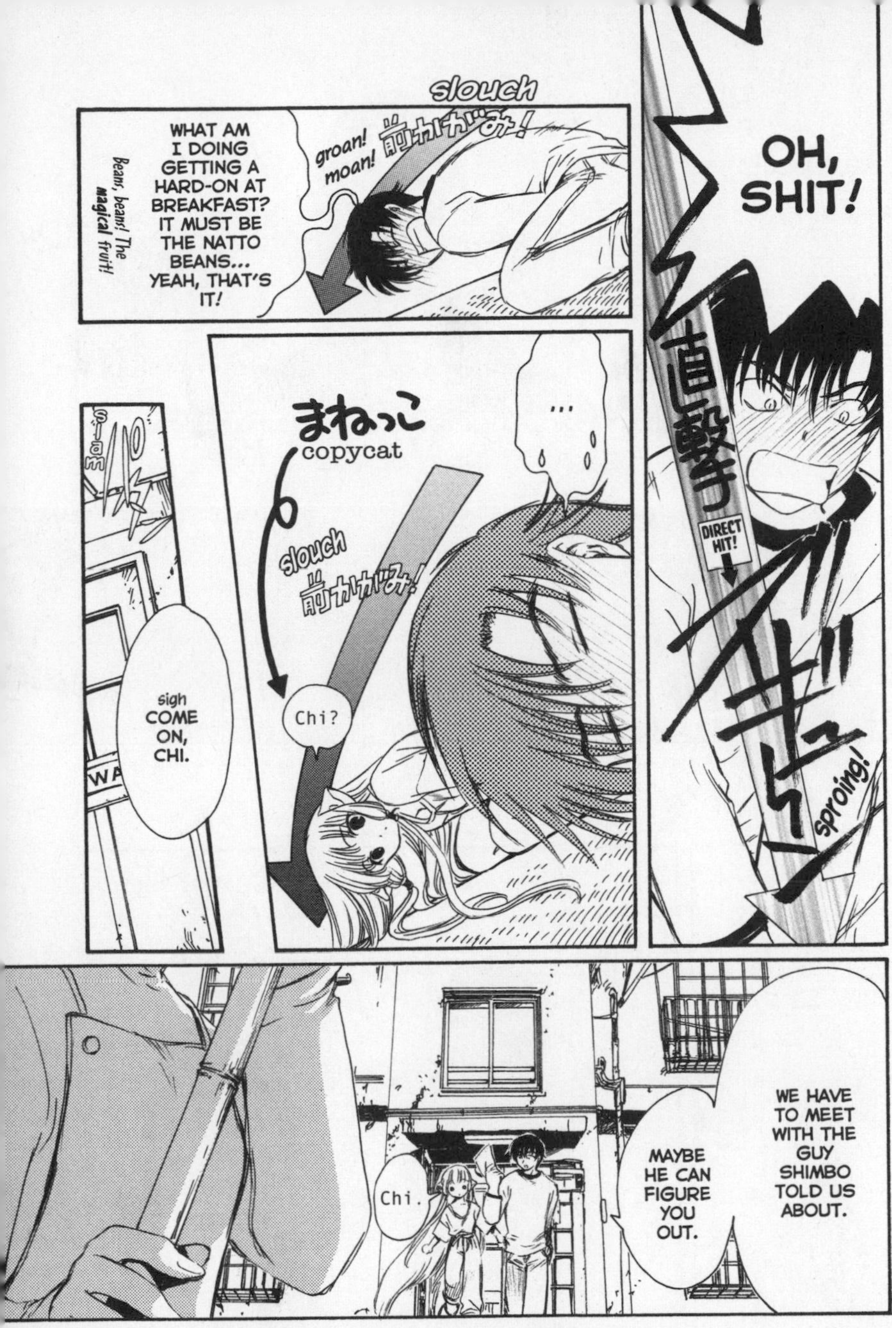
OH, SHIT!
直撃
DIRECT HIT!
sproing!
slouch
前かがみ!
groan! moan!
WHAT AM I DOING GETTING A HARD-ON AT BREAKFAST? IT MUST BE THE NATTO BEANS... YEAH, THAT'S IT!
Beans, beans! The magical fruit!
...
まねっこ
copycat
slouch
前かがみ!
Chi?
slam
sigh
COME ON, CHI.
WE HAVE TO MEET WITH THE GUY SHIMBO TOLD US ABOUT.
MAYBE HE CAN FIGURE YOU OUT.
Chi.

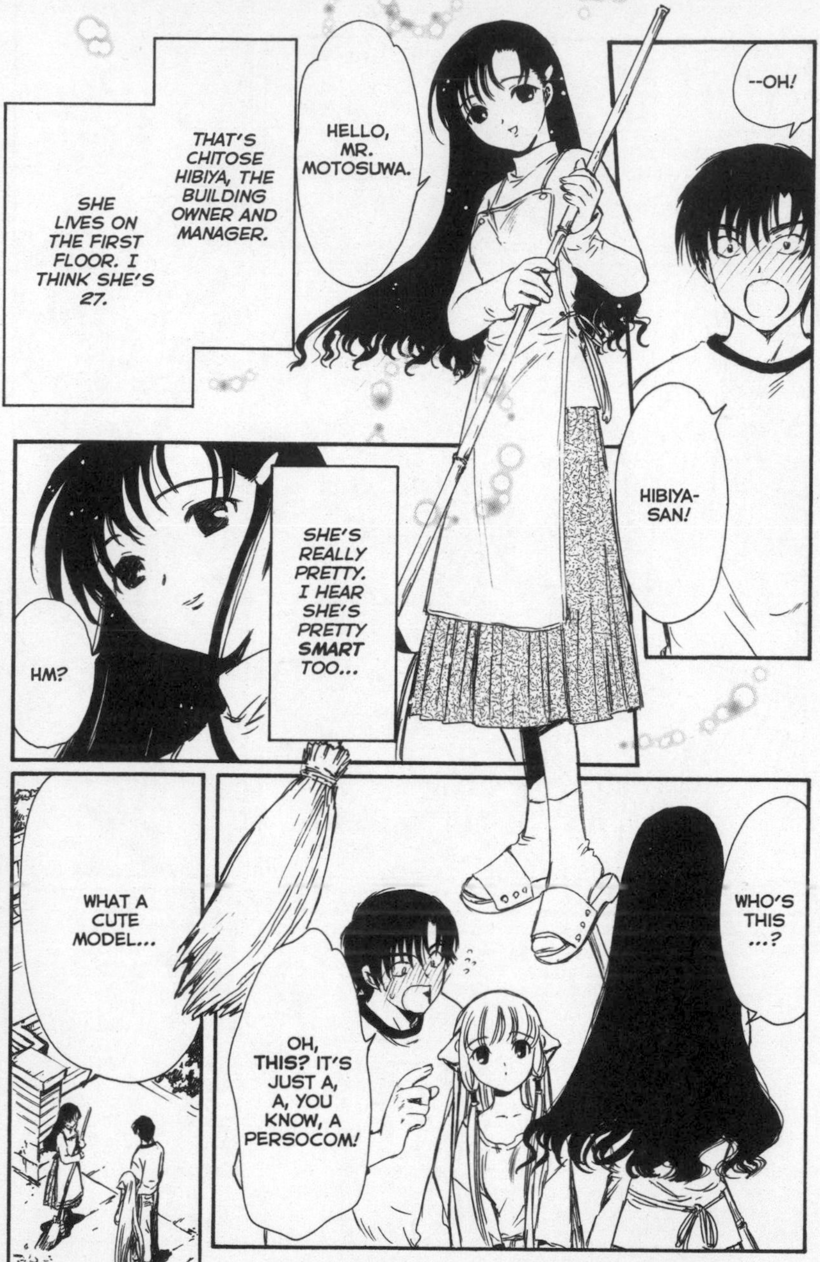
--OH!
HELLO, MR. MOTOSUWA.
HIBIYA-SAN!
THAT'S CHITOSE HIBIYA, THE BUILDING OWNER AND MANAGER.
SHE LIVES ON THE FIRST FLOOR. I THINK SHE'S 27.
SHE'S REALLY PRETTY. I HEAR SHE'S PRETTY SMART TOO...
HM?
WHO'S THIS ...?
OH, THIS? IT'S JUST A, A, YOU KNOW, A PERSOCOM!
WHAT A CUTE MODEL...

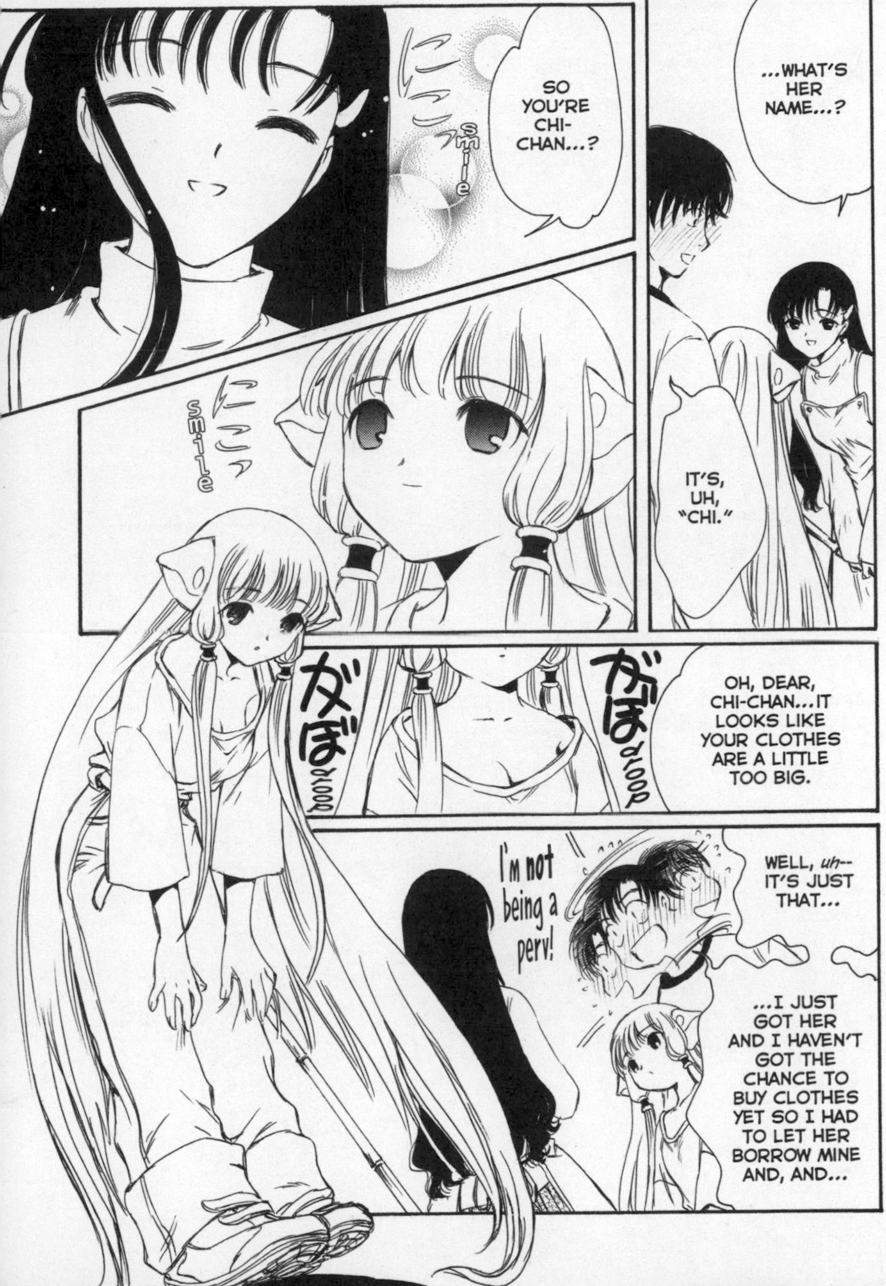
...WHAT'S HER NAME...?
IT'S, UH, "CHI."
にっこっ
smile
SO YOU'RE CHI-CHAN...?
にこっ
smile
OH, DEAR, CHI-CHAN...IT LOOKS LIKE YOUR CLOTHES ARE A LITTLE TOO BIG.
がぼ
がぼ
WELL, uh-- IT'S JUST THAT...
I'm not being a perv!
...I JUST GOT HER AND I HAVEN'T GOT THE CHANCE TO BUY CLOTHES YET SO I HAD TO LET HER BORROW MINE AND, AND...

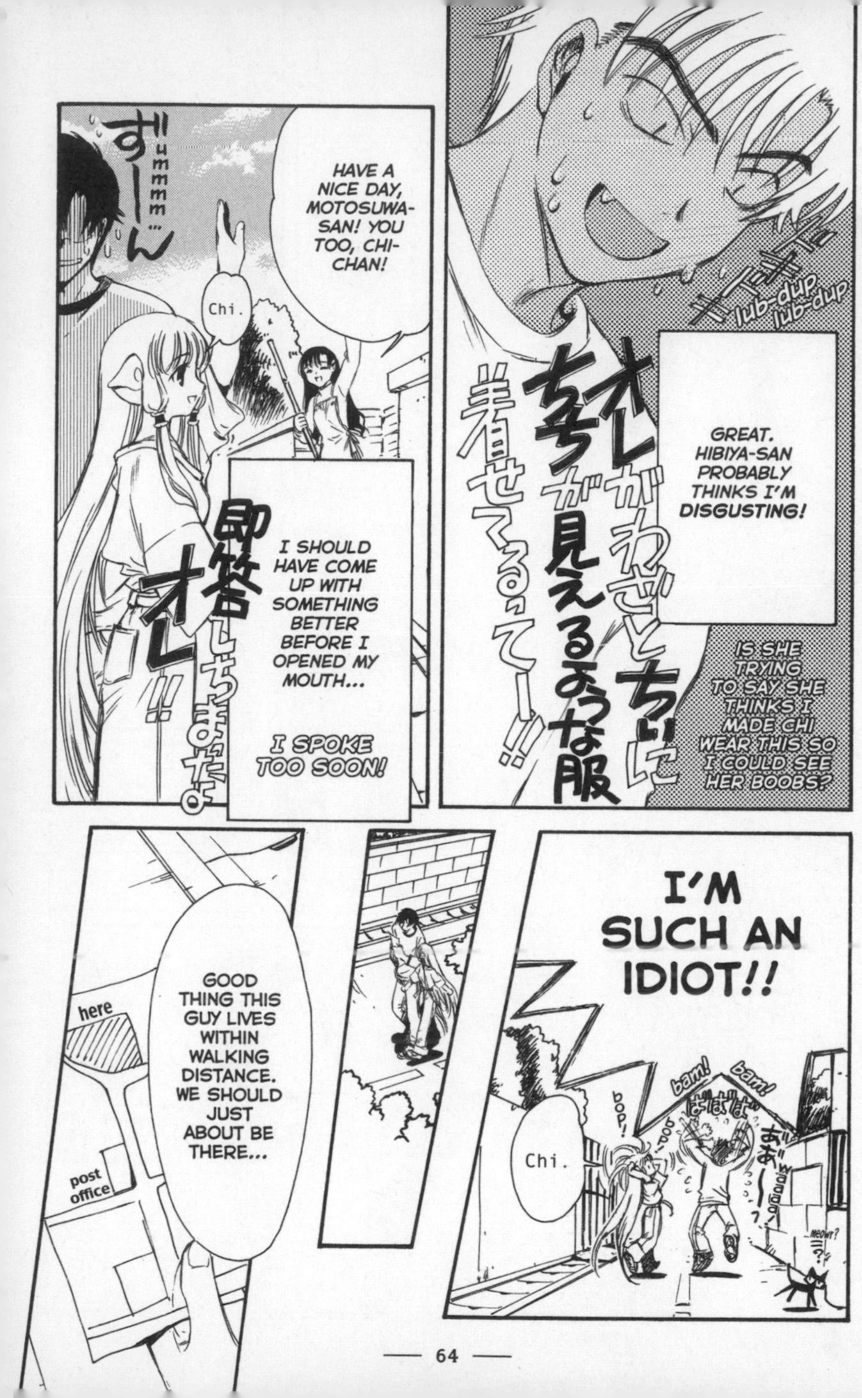
lub-dup lub-dup
オレがわざとちぃにちちが見えるような服着せてるって—!!
GREAT. HIBIYA-SAN PROBABLY THINKS I'M DISGUSTING!
IS SHE TRYING TO SAY SHE THINKS I MADE CHI WEAR THIS SO I COULD SEE HER BOOBS?
すーん
ummmm...
HAVE A NICE DAY, MOTOSUWA-SAN! YOU TOO, CHI-CHAN!
Chi.
即答しちまったよ。オレ!!
I SHOULD HAVE COME UP WITH SOMETHING BETTER BEFORE I OPENED MY MOUTH...
I SPOKE TOO SOON!
I'M SUCH AN IDIOT!!
Chi.
bop! bop!
bam! bam!
ばばば
meowr?
GOOD THING THIS GUY LIVES WITHIN WALKING DISTANCE. WE SHOULD JUST ABOUT BE THERE...
here
post office

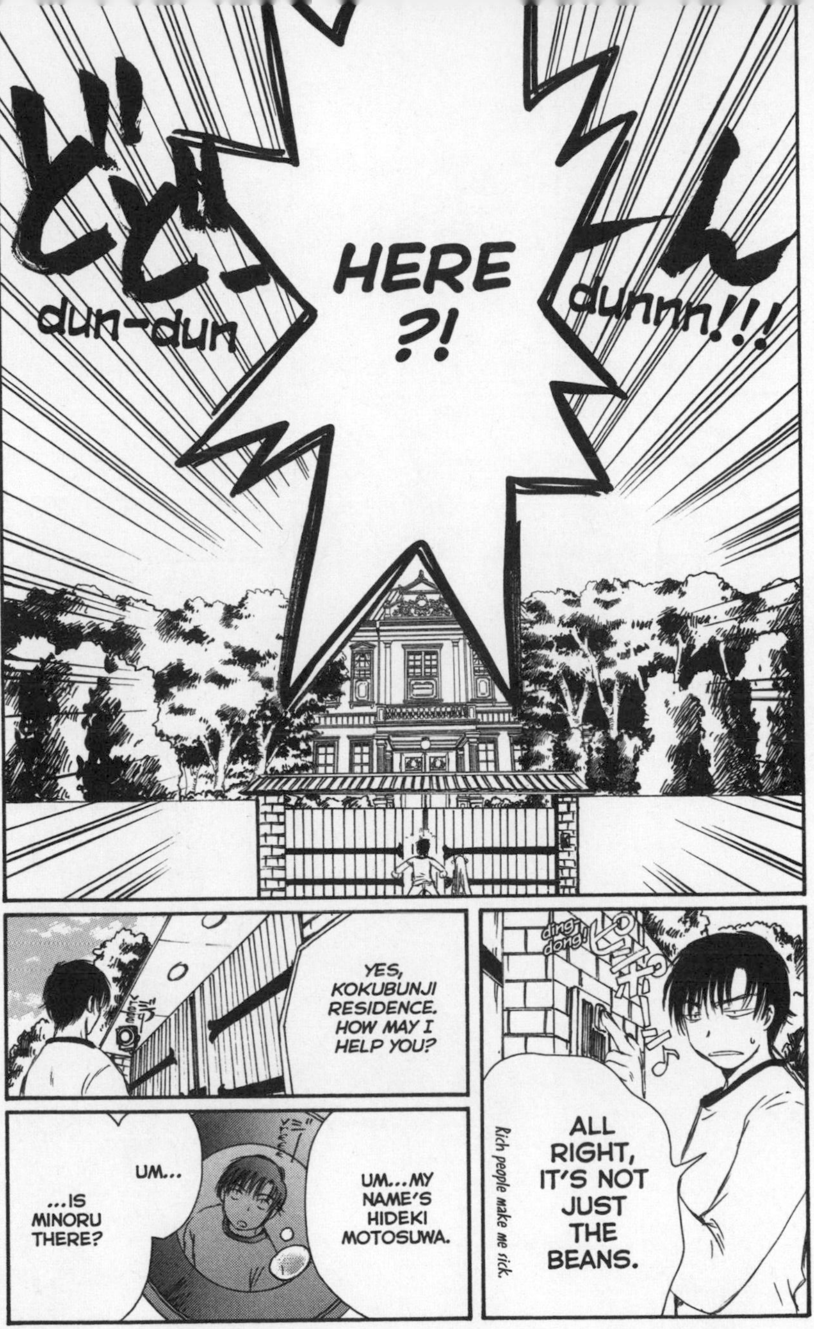

dun-dun
HERE ?!
dunnn!!!
ding-dong!
Rich people make me sick.
ALL RIGHT, IT'S NOT JUST THE BEANS.
YES, KOKUBUNJI RESIDENCE. HOW MAY I HELP YOU?
UM...MY NAME'S HIDEKI MOTOSUWA.
UM...
...IS MINORU THERE?

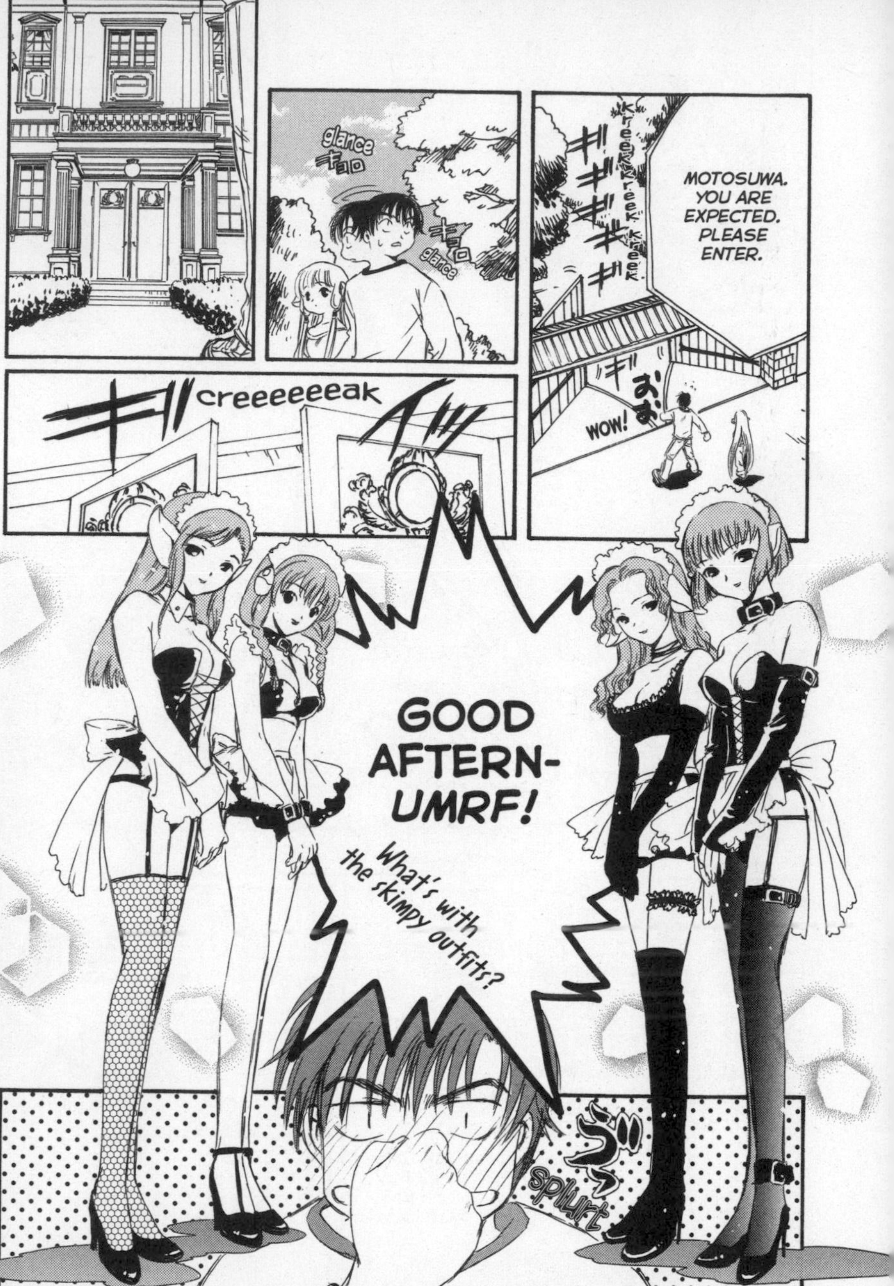
kreek kreek kreek
MOTOSUWA. YOU ARE EXPECTED. PLEASE ENTER.
WOW!
glance
glance
creeeeeeak
GOOD AFTERN-UMRF!
What's with the skimpy outfits?
splurt

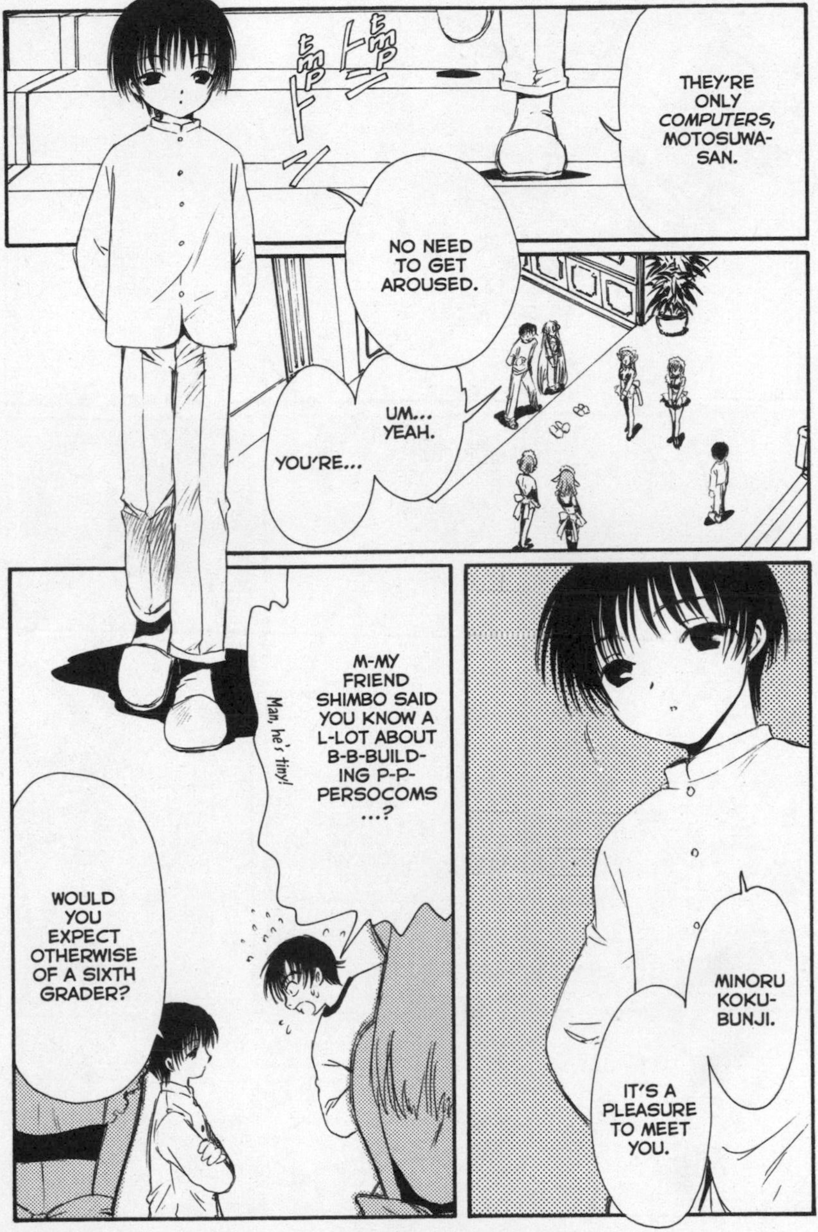
THEY'RE ONLY COMPUTERS, MOTOSUWA-SAN.
tmp tmp
NO NEED TO GET AROUSED.
UM... YEAH.
YOU'RE...
MINORU KOKU-BUNJI.
IT'S A PLEASURE TO MEET YOU.
M-MY FRIEND SHIMBO SAID YOU KNOW A L-LOT ABOUT B-B-BUILD-ING P-P-PERSOCOMS ...?
Man, he's tiny!
WOULD YOU EXPECT OTHERWISE OF A SIXTH GRADER?

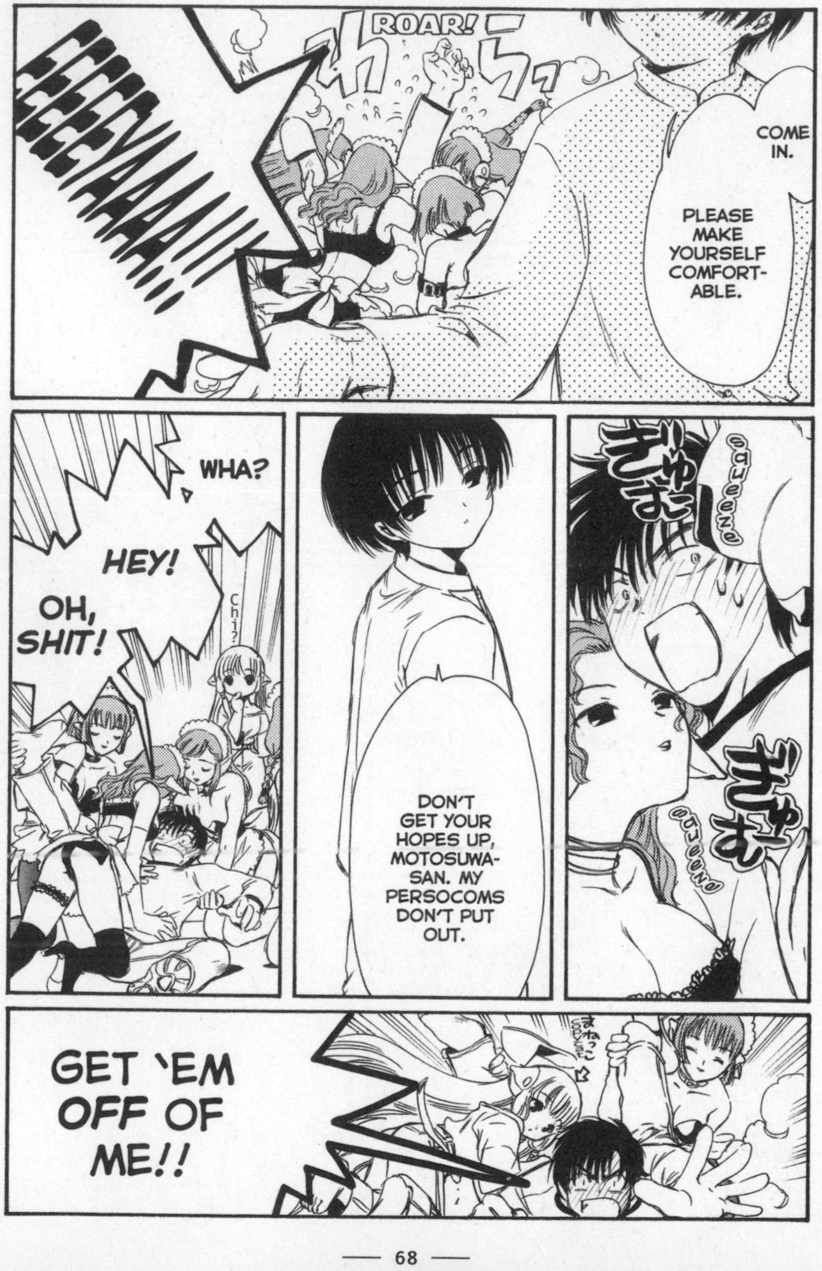
COME IN.
PLEASE MAKE YOURSELF COMFORTABLE.
ROAR!
わらっ
EEEEEYAAAA!!!
ぎゅむっ
squeeze
ぎゅむ
squeeze
DON'T GET YOUR HOPES UP, MOTOSUWA-SAN. MY PERSOCOMS DON'T PUT OUT.
WHA?
HEY!
Chi?
OH, SHIT!
GET 'EM OFF OF ME!!

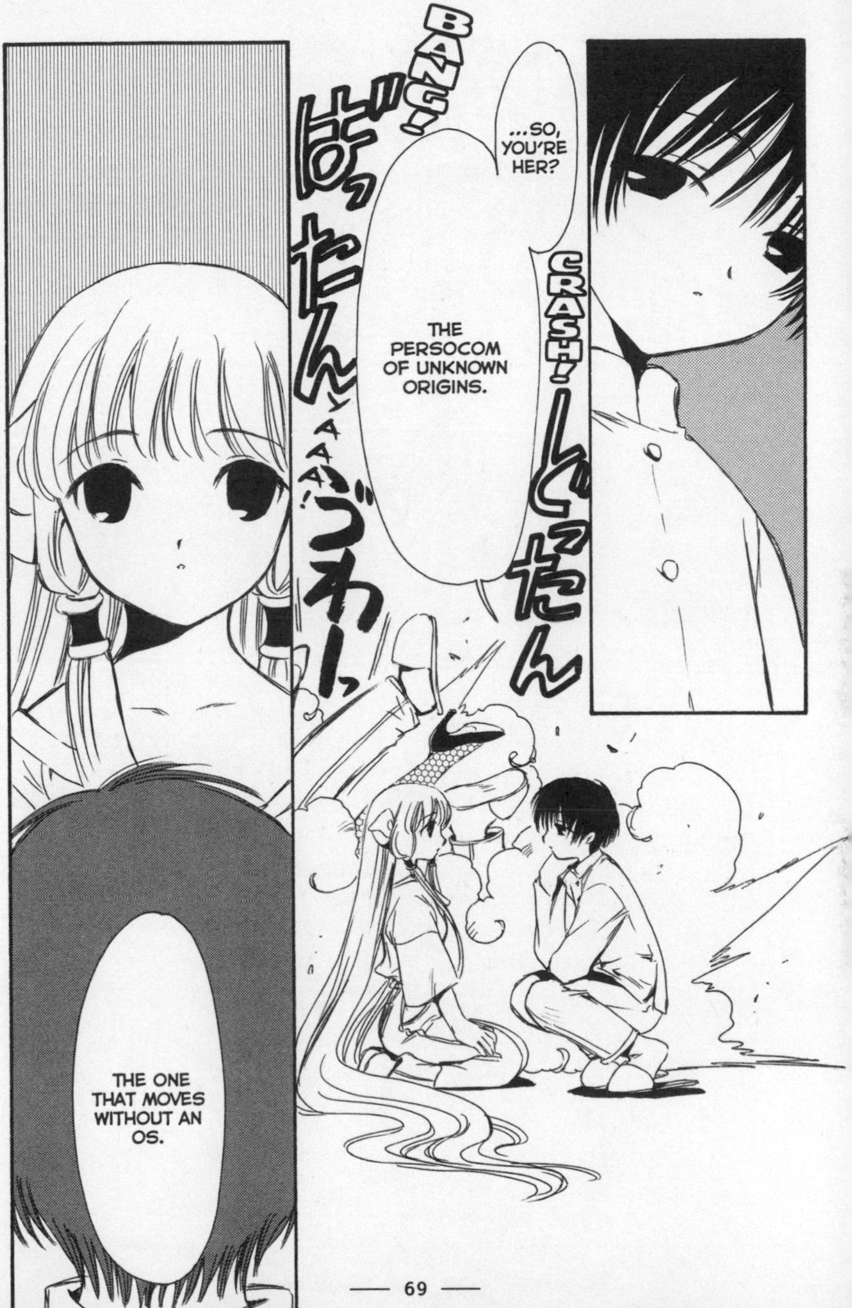
...SO, YOU'RE HER?
BANG!
CRASH!
YAAAA!
THE PERSOCOM OF UNKNOWN ORIGINS.
THE ONE THAT MOVES WITHOUT AN OS.

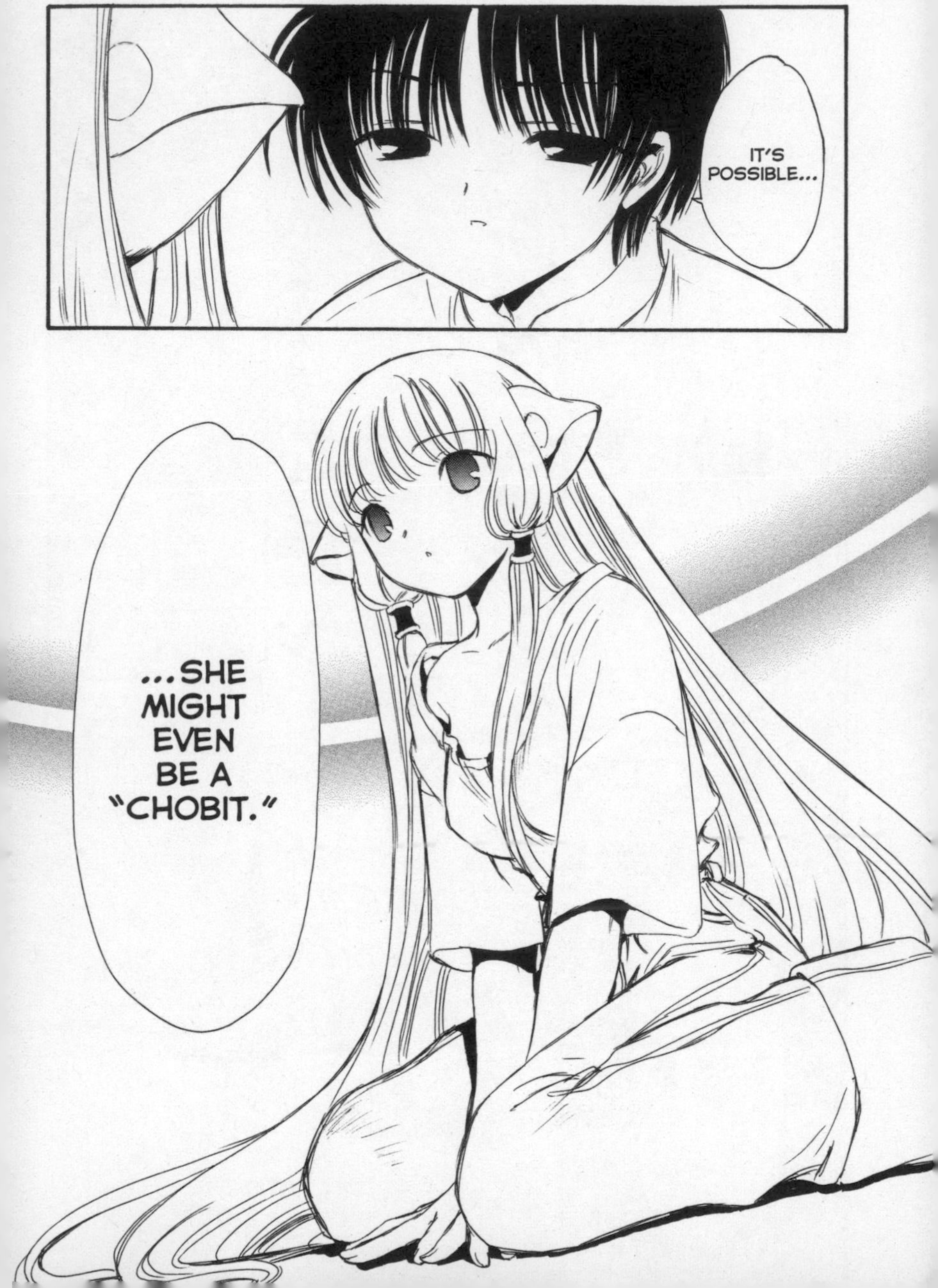
IT'S POSSIBLE...
...SHE MIGHT EVEN BE A "CHOBIT."

Chobits

ちょびっツ

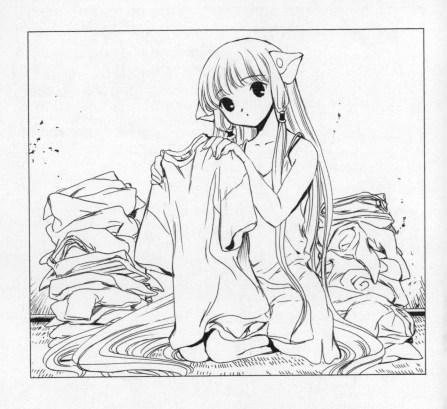

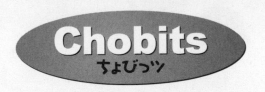

◂chapter 5▸

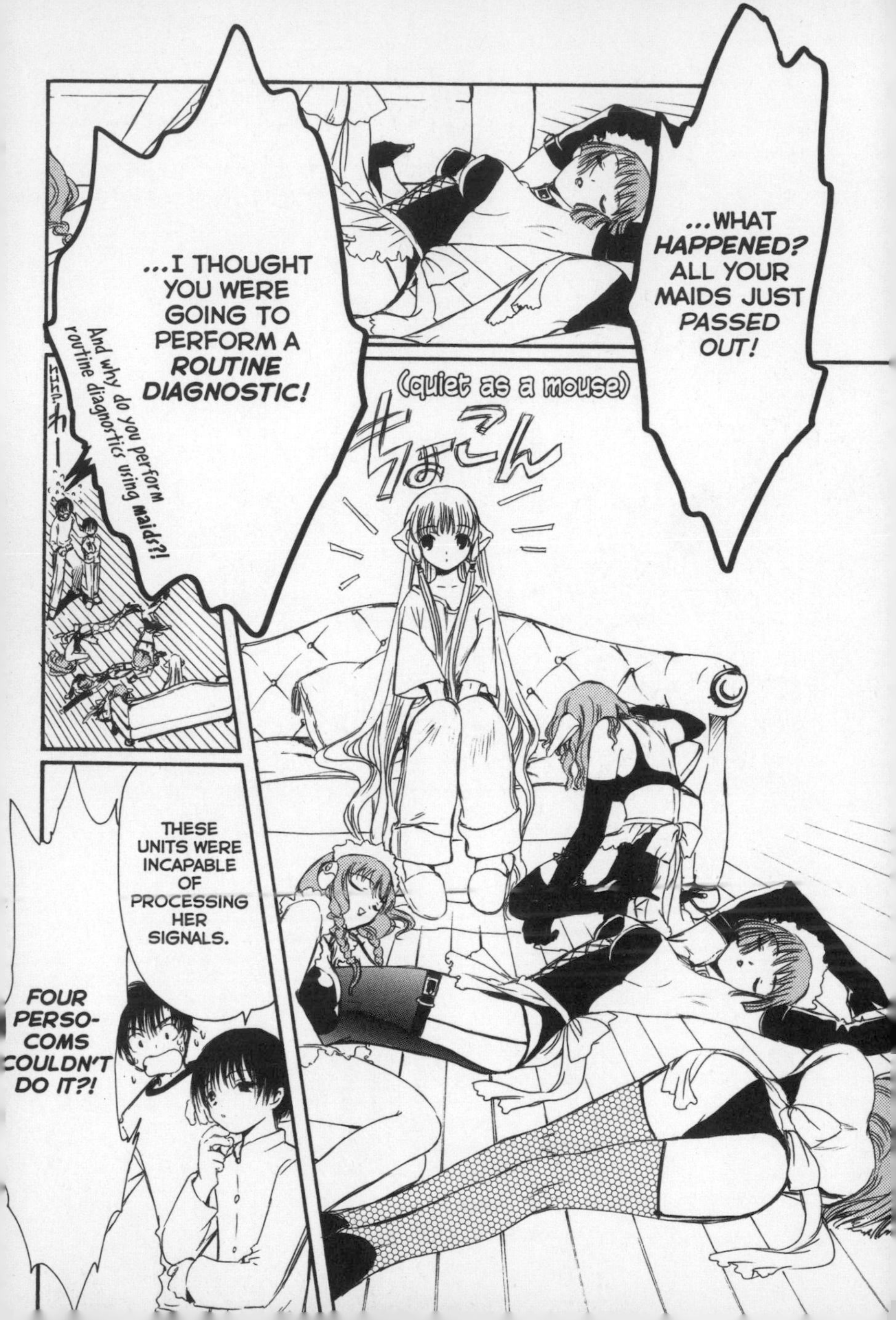
...WHAT HAPPENED? ALL YOUR MAIDS JUST PASSED OUT!
...I THOUGHT YOU WERE GOING TO PERFORM A ROUTINE DIAGNOSTIC!
(quiet as a mouse)
ちょこん
And why do you perform routine diagnostics using maids?!
わー
THESE UNITS WERE INCAPABLE OF PROCESSING HER SIGNALS.
FOUR PERSO-COMS COULDN'T DO IT?!

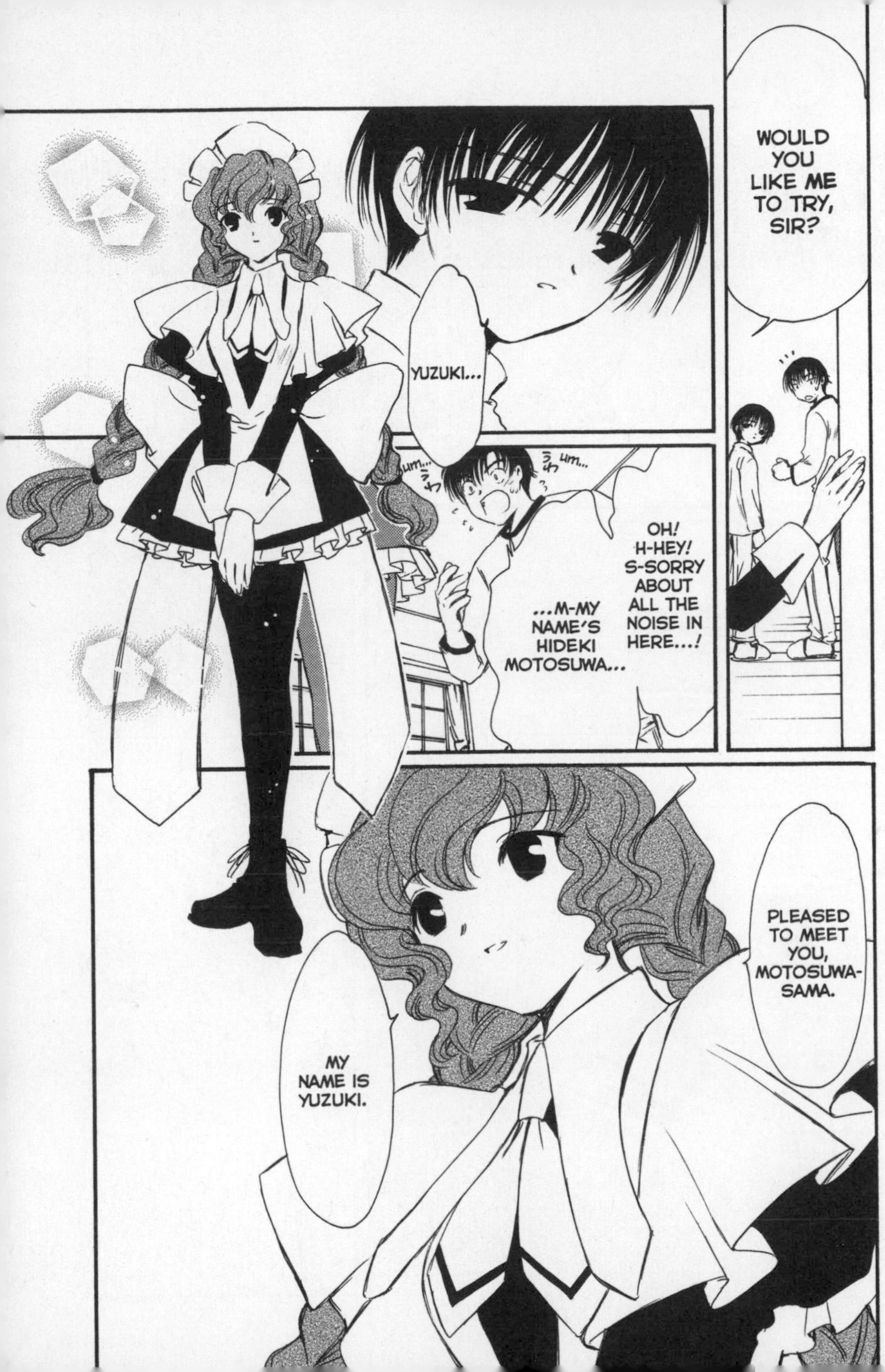
WOULD YOU LIKE ME TO TRY, SIR?
YUZUKI...
um...
um...
OH! H-HEY! S-SORRY ABOUT ALL THE NOISE IN HERE...!
...M-MY NAME'S HIDEKI MOTOSUWA...
PLEASED TO MEET YOU, MOTOSUWA-SAMA.
MY NAME IS YUZUKI.

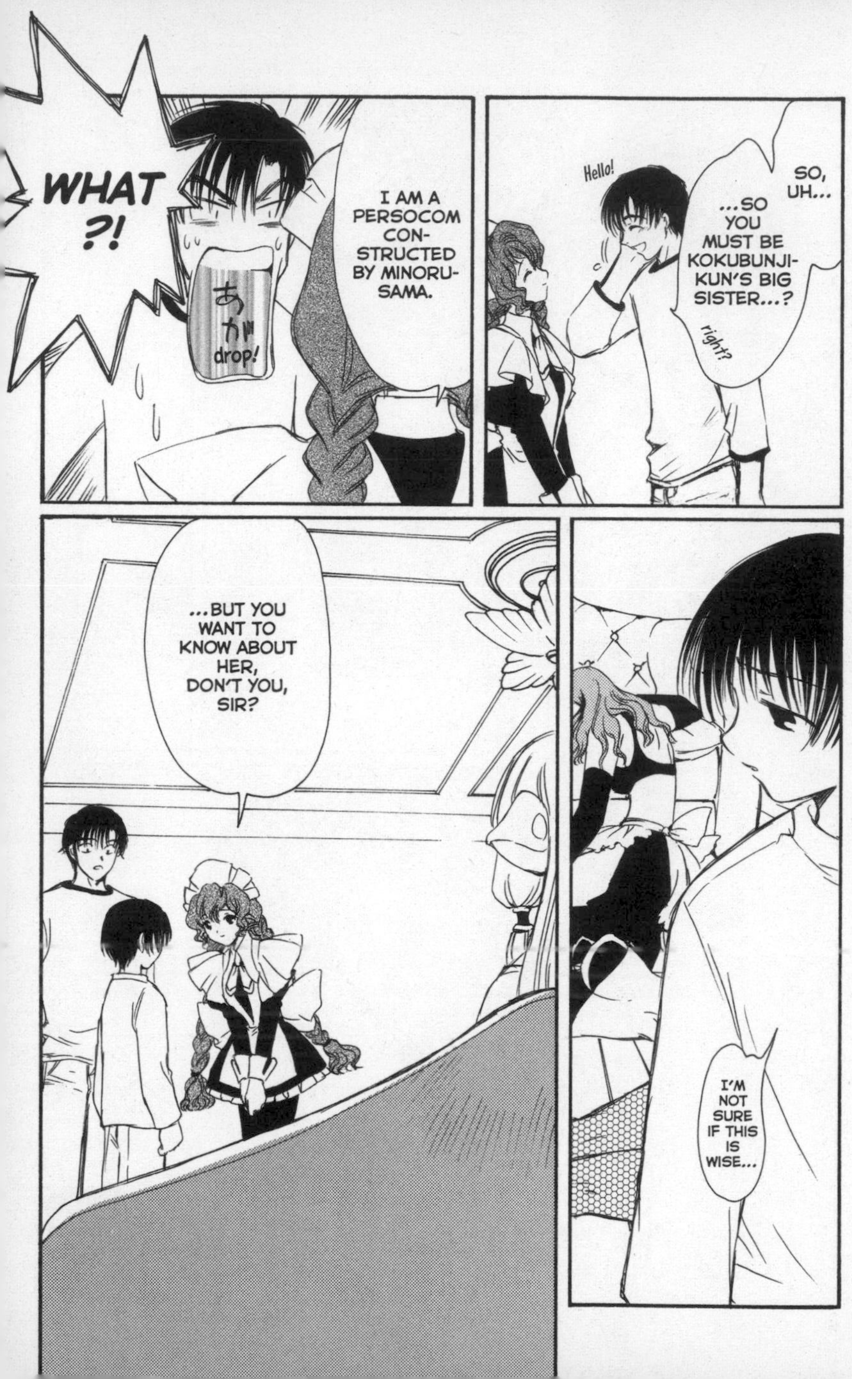
SO, UH...
...SO YOU MUST BE KOKUBUNJI-KUN'S BIG SISTER...?
Hello!
right?
I AM A PERSOCOM CON-STRUCTED BY MINORU-SAMA.
WHAT ?!
あが drop!
I'M NOT SURE IF THIS IS WISE...
...BUT YOU WANT TO KNOW ABOUT HER, DON'T YOU, SIR?

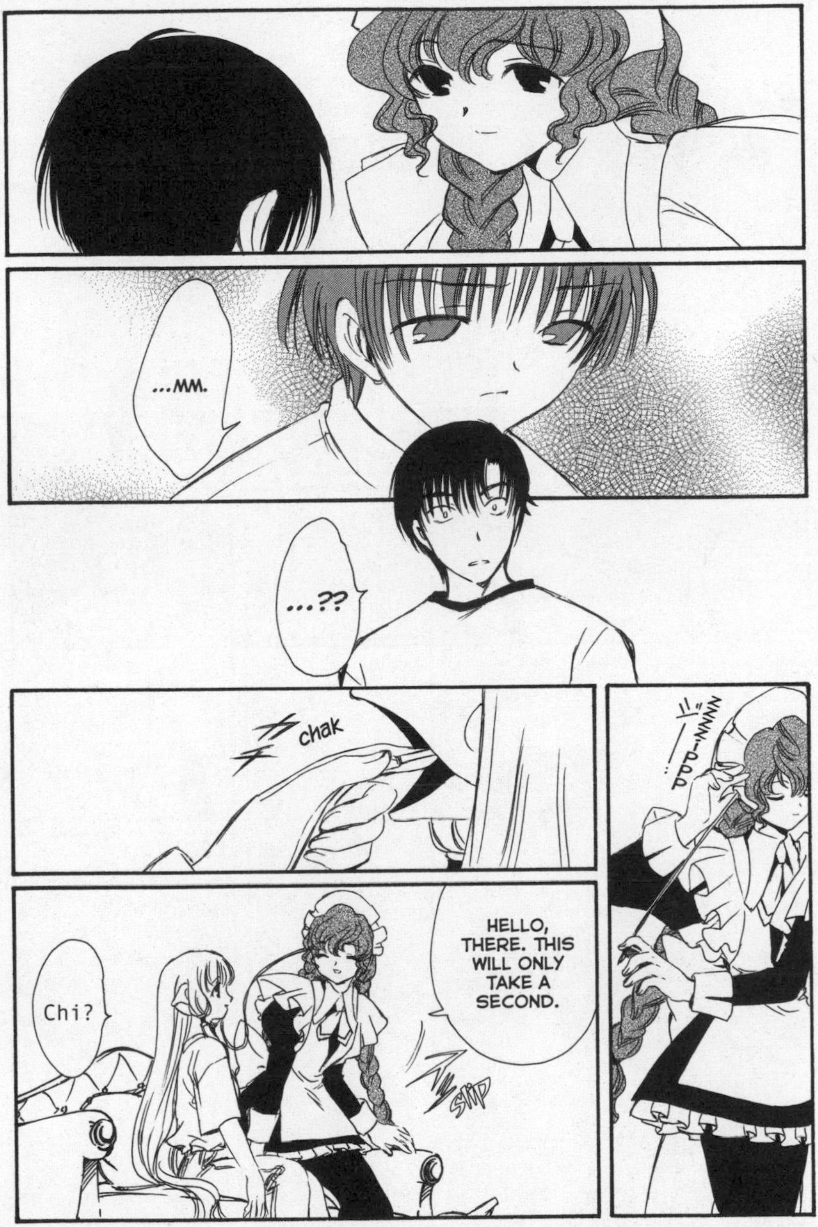
...MM.
...??
ZZZZ-IPPP
chak
HELLO, THERE. THIS WILL ONLY TAKE A SECOND.
slip
Chi?

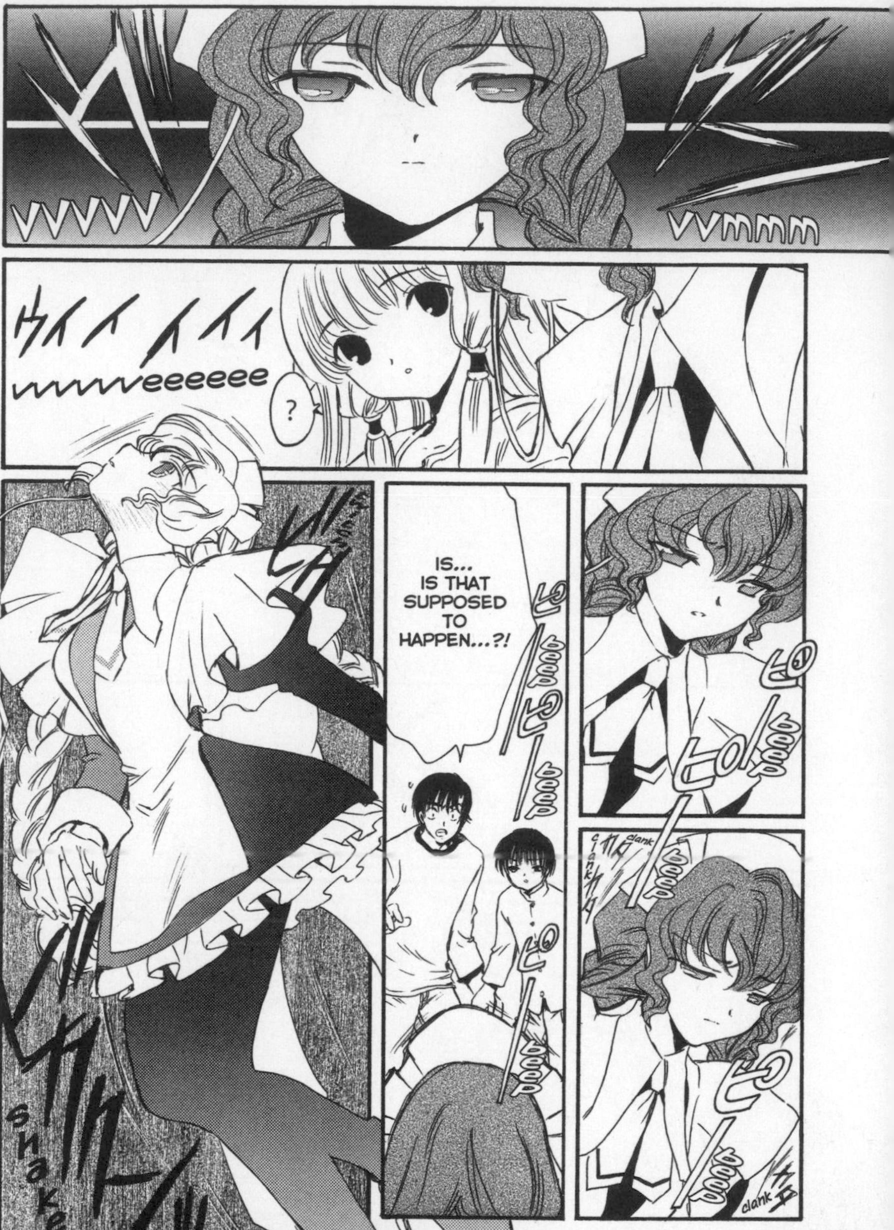
vvmmm
VVVVV
ウイイイイイ
wwwveeeeee
?
beep
beep
IS... IS THAT SUPPOSED TO HAPPEN...?!
beep
beep
clank
clank
beep
beep
clank
shake

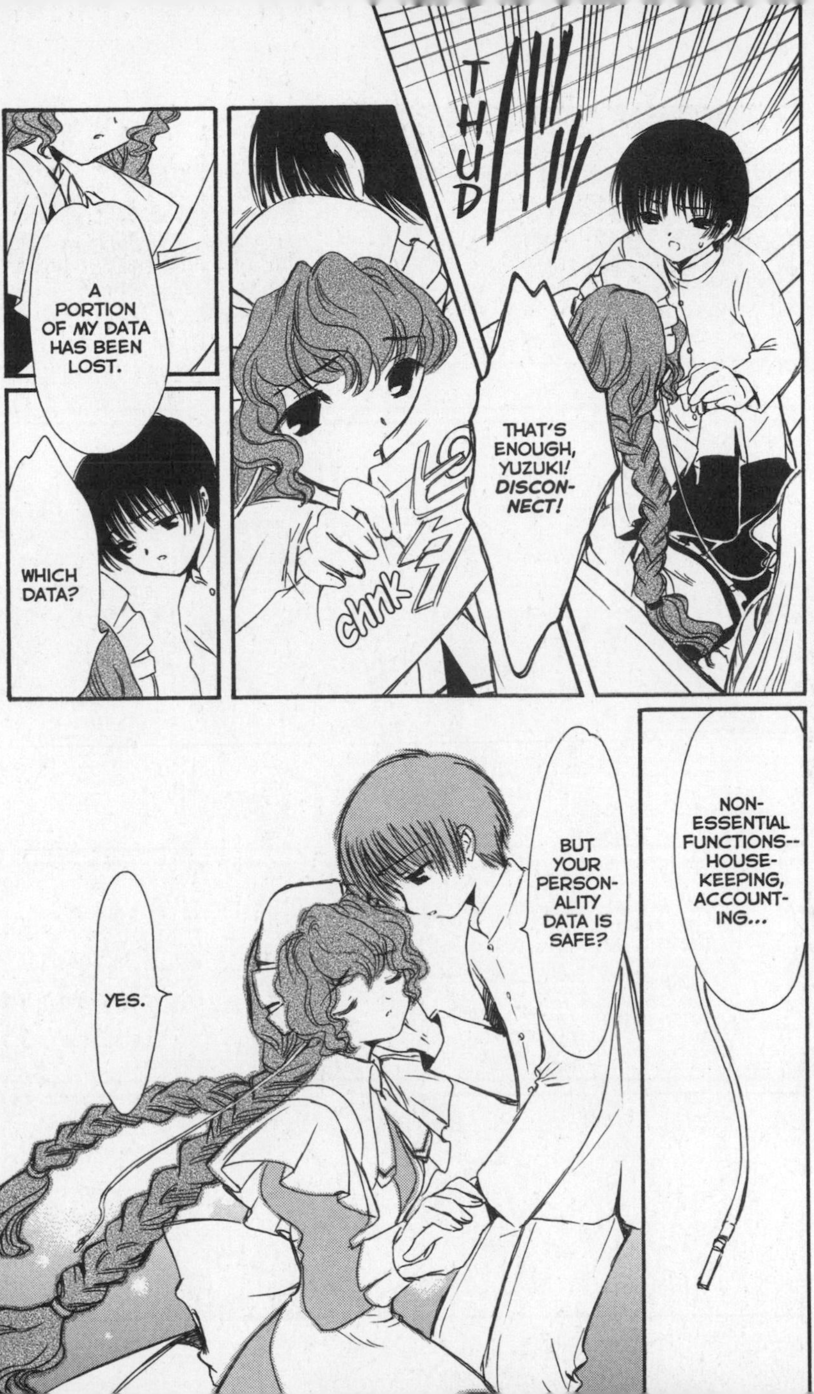
THUD
THAT'S ENOUGH, YUZUKI! DISCONNECT!
chnk
A PORTION OF MY DATA HAS BEEN LOST.
WHICH DATA?
NON-ESSENTIAL FUNCTIONS--HOUSE-KEEPING, ACCOUNT-ING...
BUT YOUR PERSON-ALITY DATA IS SAFE?
YES.

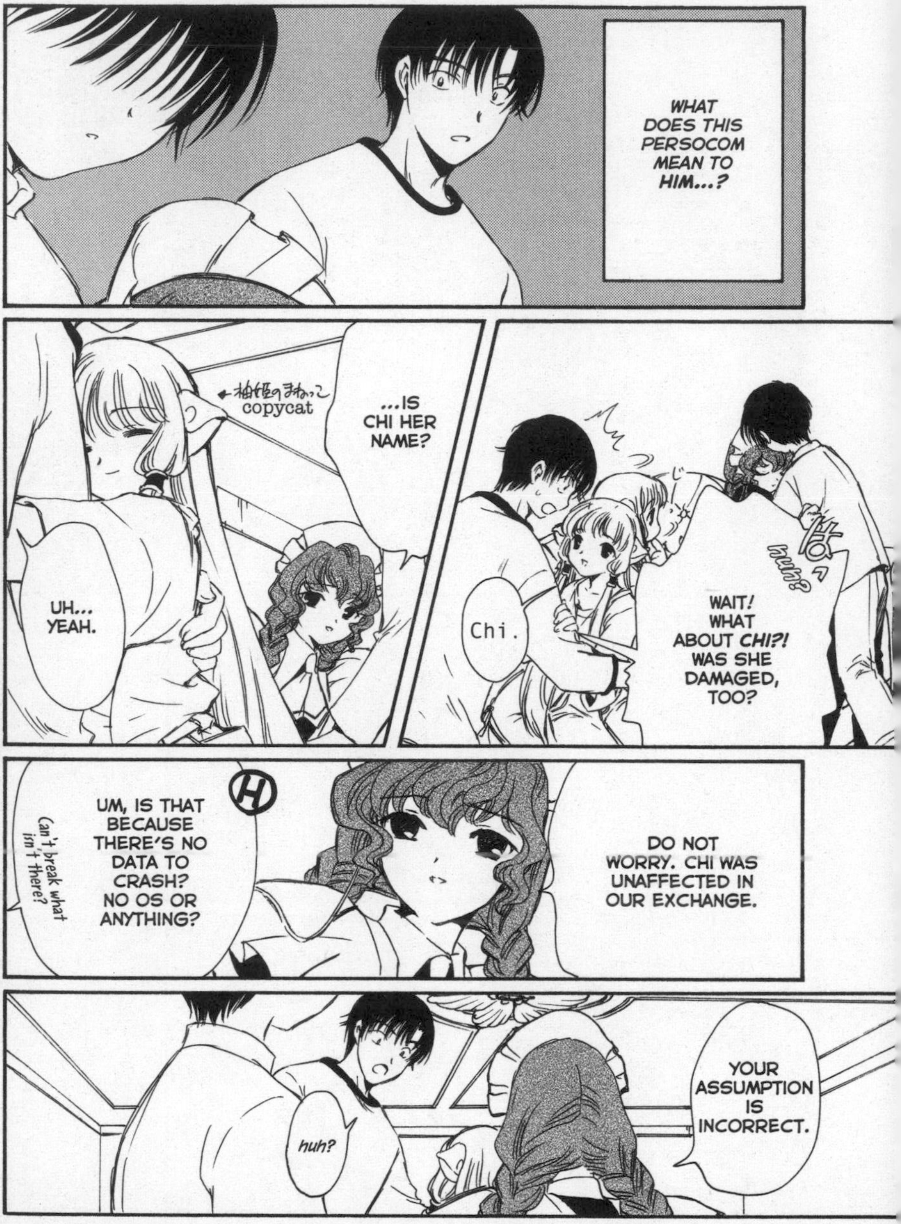
WHAT DOES THIS PERSOCOM MEAN TO HIM...?
WAIT! WHAT ABOUT CHI?! WAS SHE DAMAGED, TOO?
huh?
Chi.
...IS CHI HER NAME?
←柚姫のまねっこ
copycat
UH... YEAH.
DO NOT WORRY. CHI WAS UNAFFECTED IN OUR EXCHANGE.
UM, IS THAT BECAUSE THERE'S NO DATA TO CRASH? NO OS OR ANYTHING?
Can't break what isn't there?
YOUR ASSUMPTION IS INCORRECT.
huh?

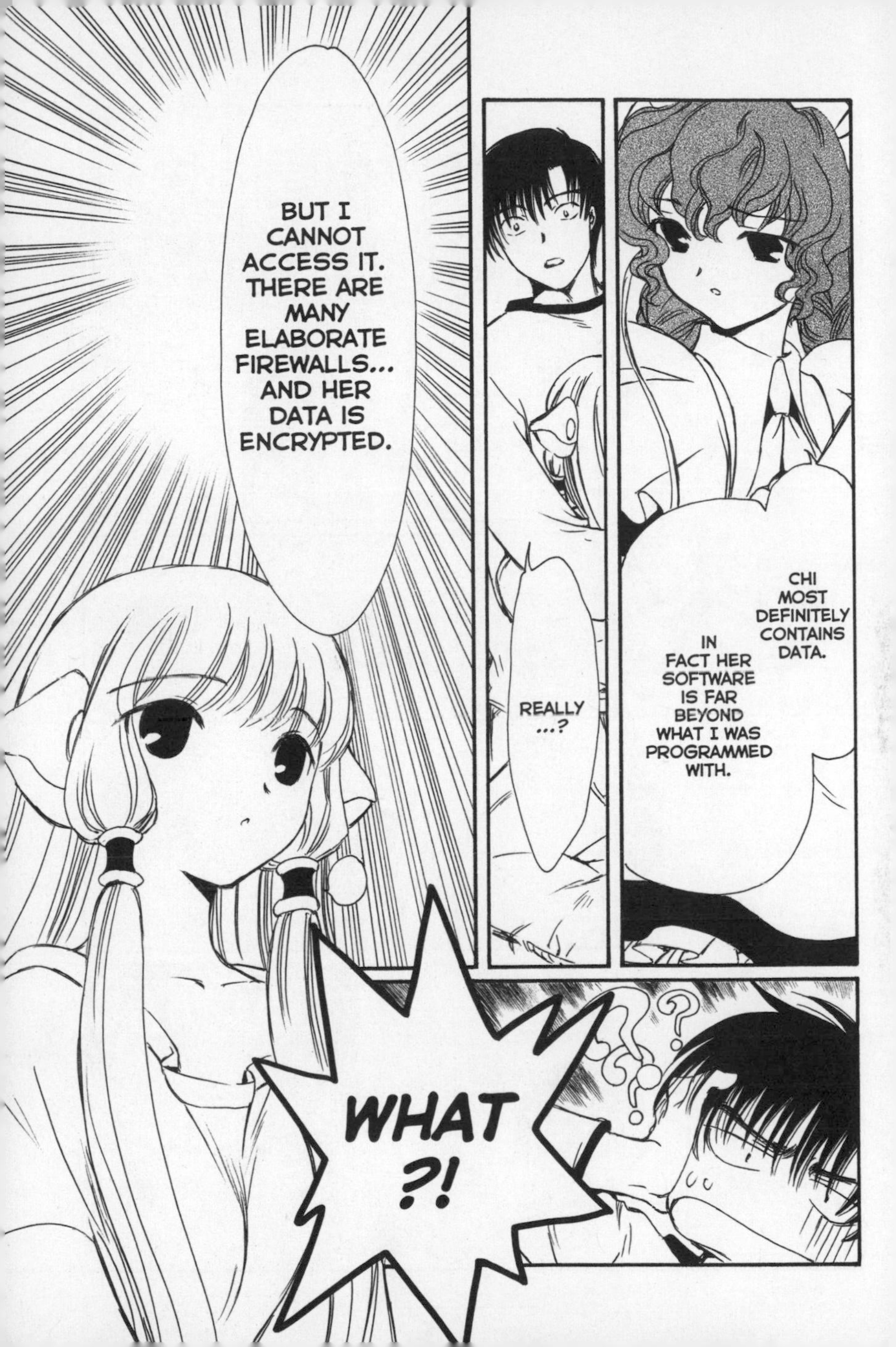
CHI MOST DEFINITELY CONTAINS DATA.
IN FACT HER SOFTWARE IS FAR BEYOND WHAT I WAS PROGRAMMED WITH.
REALLY ...?
BUT I CANNOT ACCESS IT. THERE ARE MANY ELABORATE FIREWALLS... AND HER DATA IS ENCRYPTED.
WHAT ?!

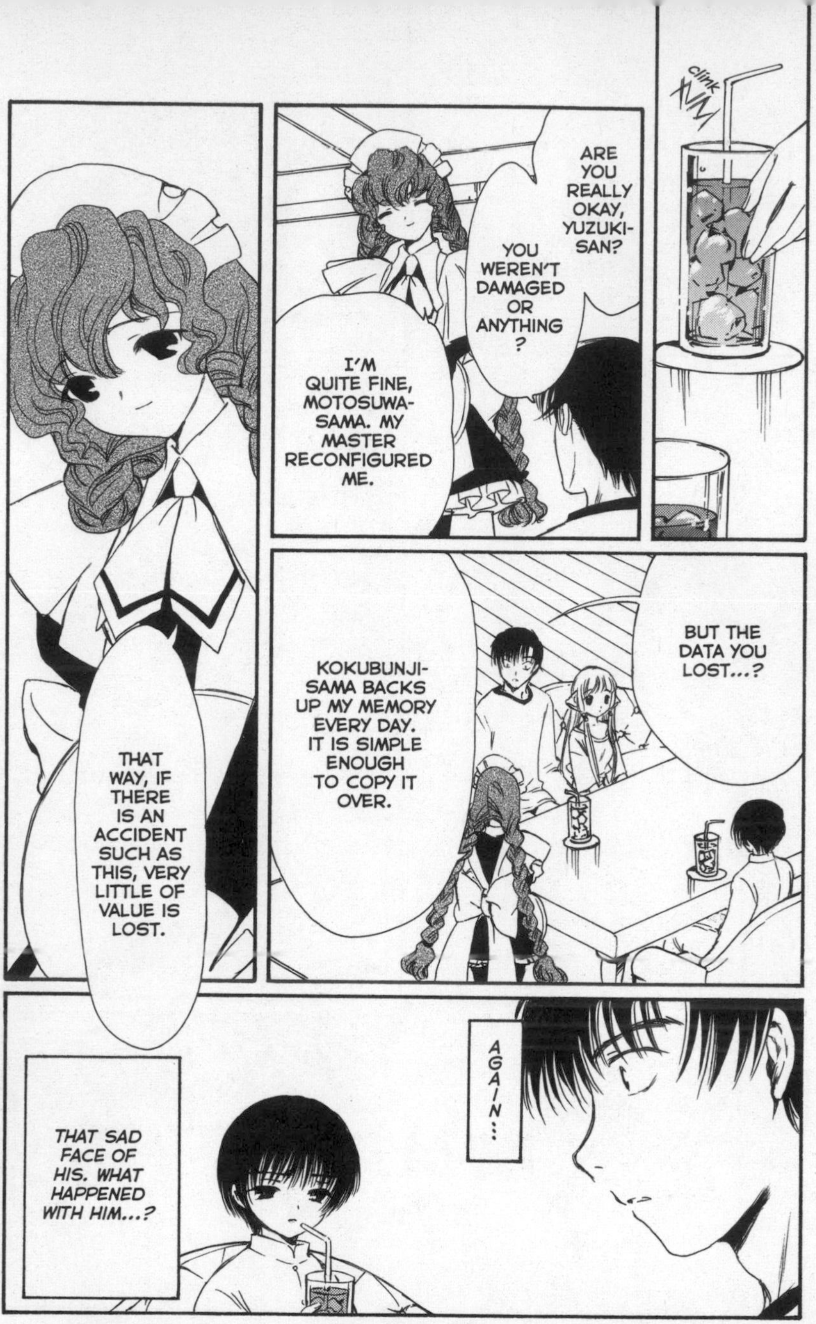
clink
ARE YOU REALLY OKAY, YUZUKI-SAN?
YOU WEREN'T DAMAGED OR ANYTHING?
I'M QUITE FINE, MOTOSUWA-SAMA. MY MASTER RECONFIGURED ME.
BUT THE DATA YOU LOST...?
KOKUBUNJI-SAMA BACKS UP MY MEMORY EVERY DAY. IT IS SIMPLE ENOUGH TO COPY IT OVER.
THAT WAY, IF THERE IS AN ACCIDENT SUCH AS THIS, VERY LITTLE OF VALUE IS LOST.
AGAIN...
THAT SAD FACE OF HIS. WHAT HAPPENED WITH HIM...?

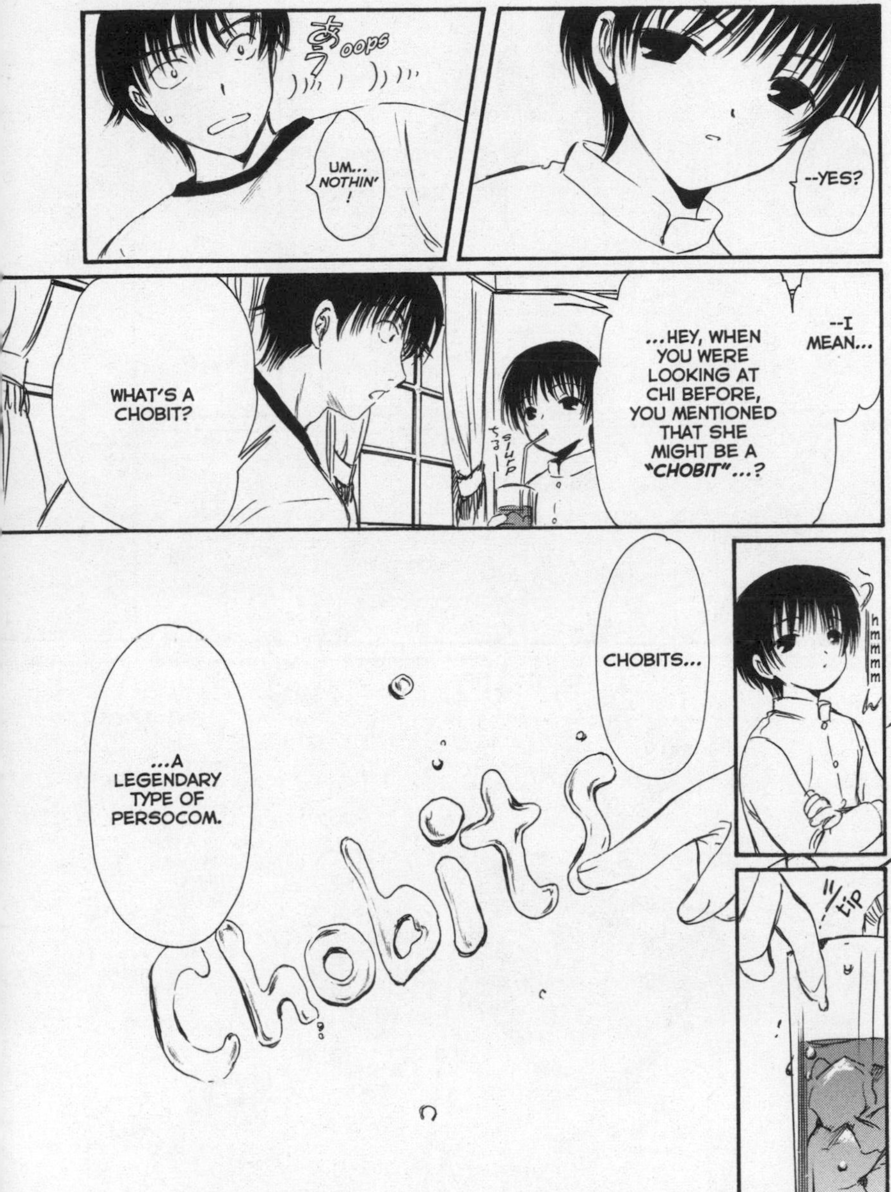
--YES?
oops
UM... NOTHIN'!
--I MEAN...
...HEY, WHEN YOU WERE LOOKING AT CHI BEFORE, YOU MENTIONED THAT SHE MIGHT BE A "CHOBIT"...?
slurp
WHAT'S A CHOBIT?
hmmmm
tip
CHOBITS...
...A LEGENDARY TYPE OF PERSOCOM.
Chobits

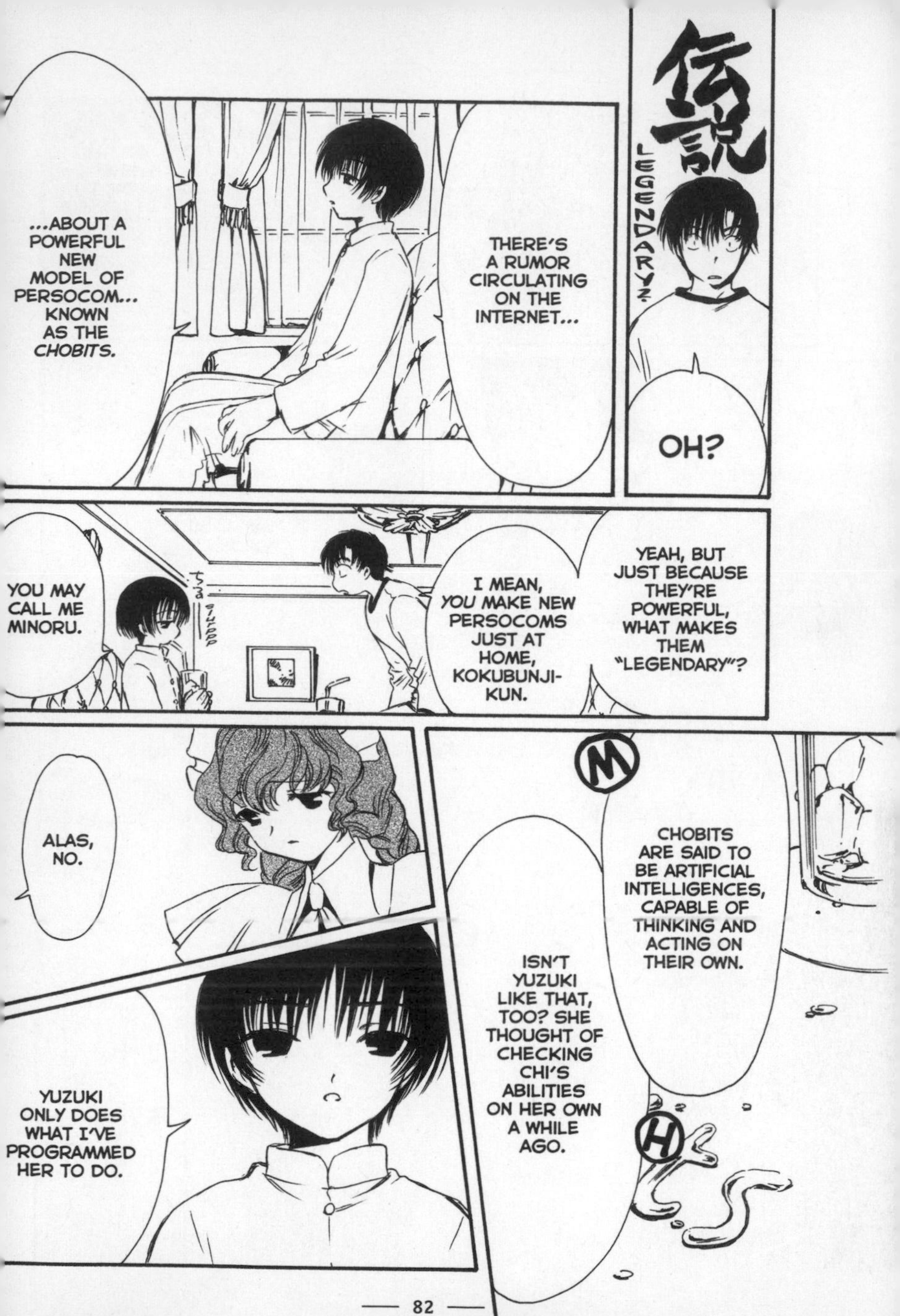
伝説
LEGENDARY?
OH?
THERE'S A RUMOR CIRCULATING ON THE INTERNET...
...ABOUT A POWERFUL NEW MODEL OF PERSOCOM... KNOWN AS THE *CHOBITS*.
YEAH, BUT JUST BECAUSE THEY'RE POWERFUL, WHAT MAKES THEM "LEGENDARY"?
I MEAN, *YOU* MAKE NEW PERSOCOMS JUST AT HOME, KOKUBUNJI-KUN.
ちゅる
SLURPP
YOU MAY CALL ME MINORU.
M
CHOBITS ARE SAID TO BE ARTIFICIAL INTELLIGENCES, CAPABLE OF THINKING AND ACTING ON THEIR OWN.
ISN'T YUZUKI LIKE THAT, TOO? SHE THOUGHT OF CHECKING CHI'S ABILITIES ON HER OWN A WHILE AGO.
H
ALAS, NO.
YUZUKI ONLY DOES WHAT I'VE PROGRAMMED HER TO DO.

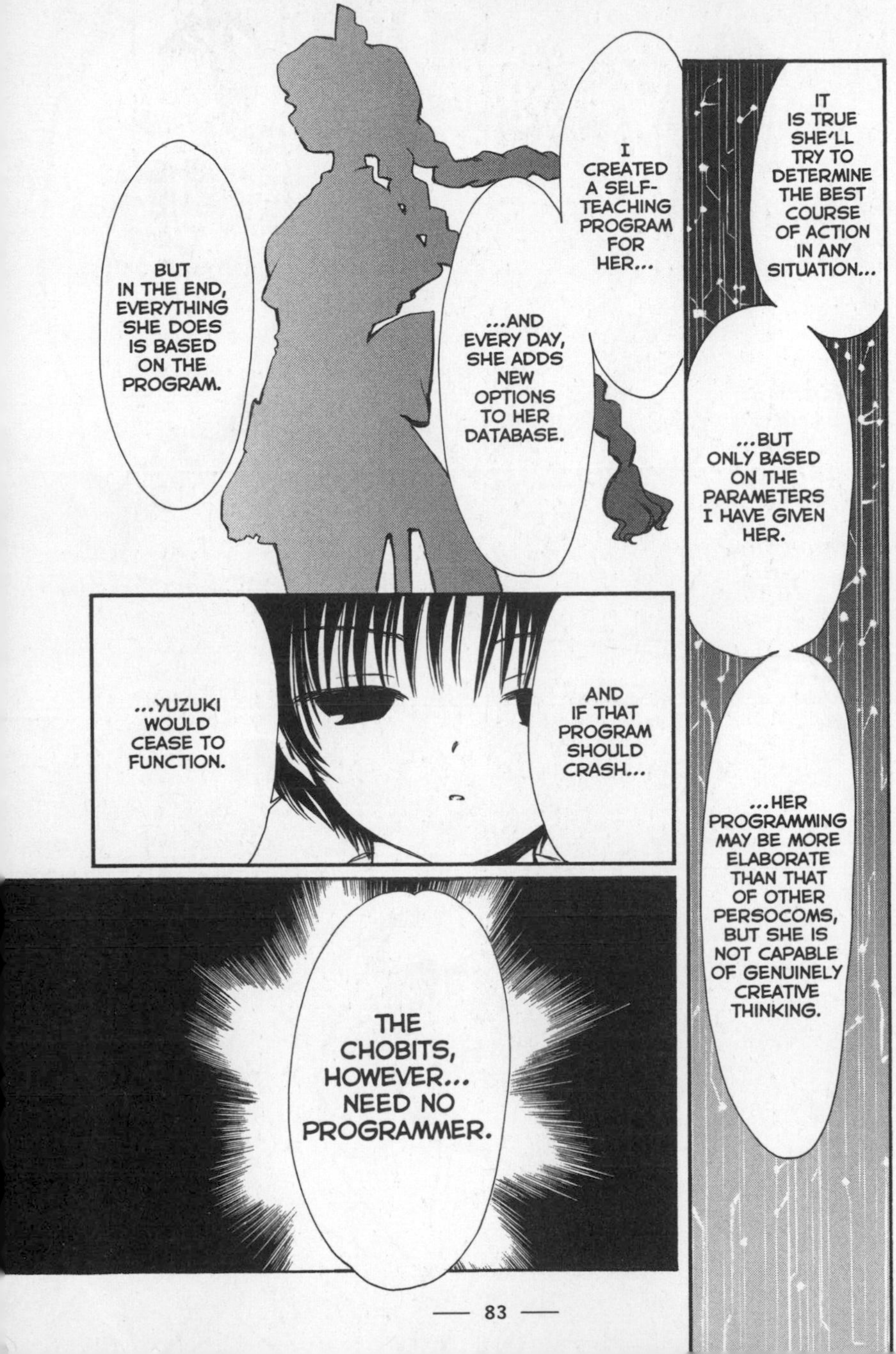
IT IS TRUE SHE'LL TRY TO DETERMINE THE BEST COURSE OF ACTION IN ANY SITUATION...
...BUT ONLY BASED ON THE PARAMETERS I HAVE GIVEN HER.
...HER PROGRAMMING MAY BE MORE ELABORATE THAN THAT OF OTHER PERSOCOMS, BUT SHE IS NOT CAPABLE OF GENUINELY CREATIVE THINKING.
I CREATED A SELF-TEACHING PROGRAM FOR HER...
...AND EVERY DAY, SHE ADDS NEW OPTIONS TO HER DATABASE.
BUT IN THE END, EVERYTHING SHE DOES IS BASED ON THE PROGRAM.
AND IF THAT PROGRAM SHOULD CRASH...
...YUZUKI WOULD CEASE TO FUNCTION.
THE CHOBITS, HOWEVER... NEED NO PROGRAMMER.

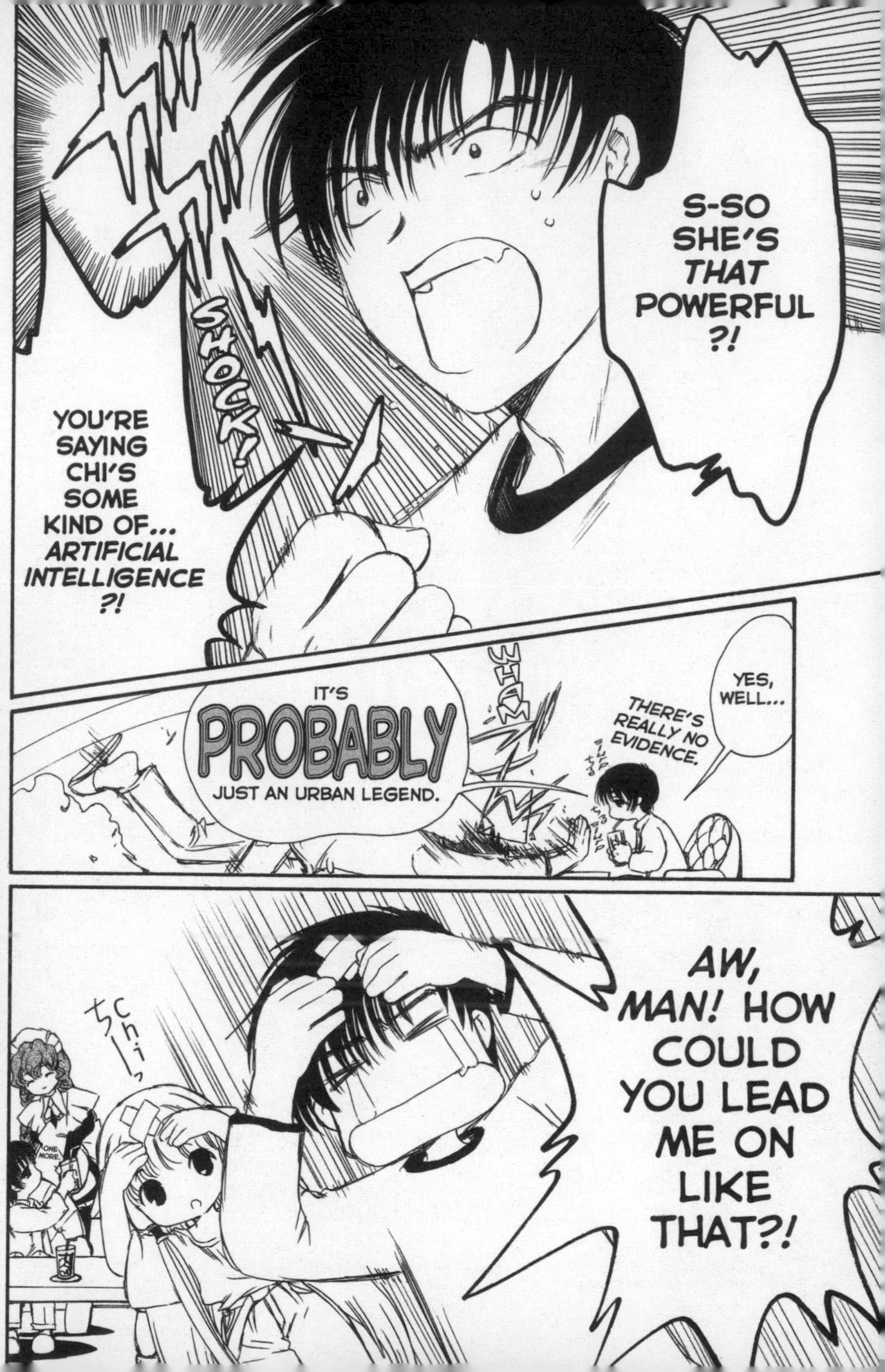
S-SO SHE'S THAT POWERFUL ?!
SHOCK!
YOU'RE SAYING CHI'S SOME KIND OF... ARTIFICIAL INTELLIGENCE ?!
YES, WELL...
THERE'S REALLY NO EVIDENCE.
WHAM
IT'S PROBABLY JUST AN URBAN LEGEND.
AW, MAN! HOW COULD YOU LEAD ME ON LIKE THAT?!
chi
ONE MORE.

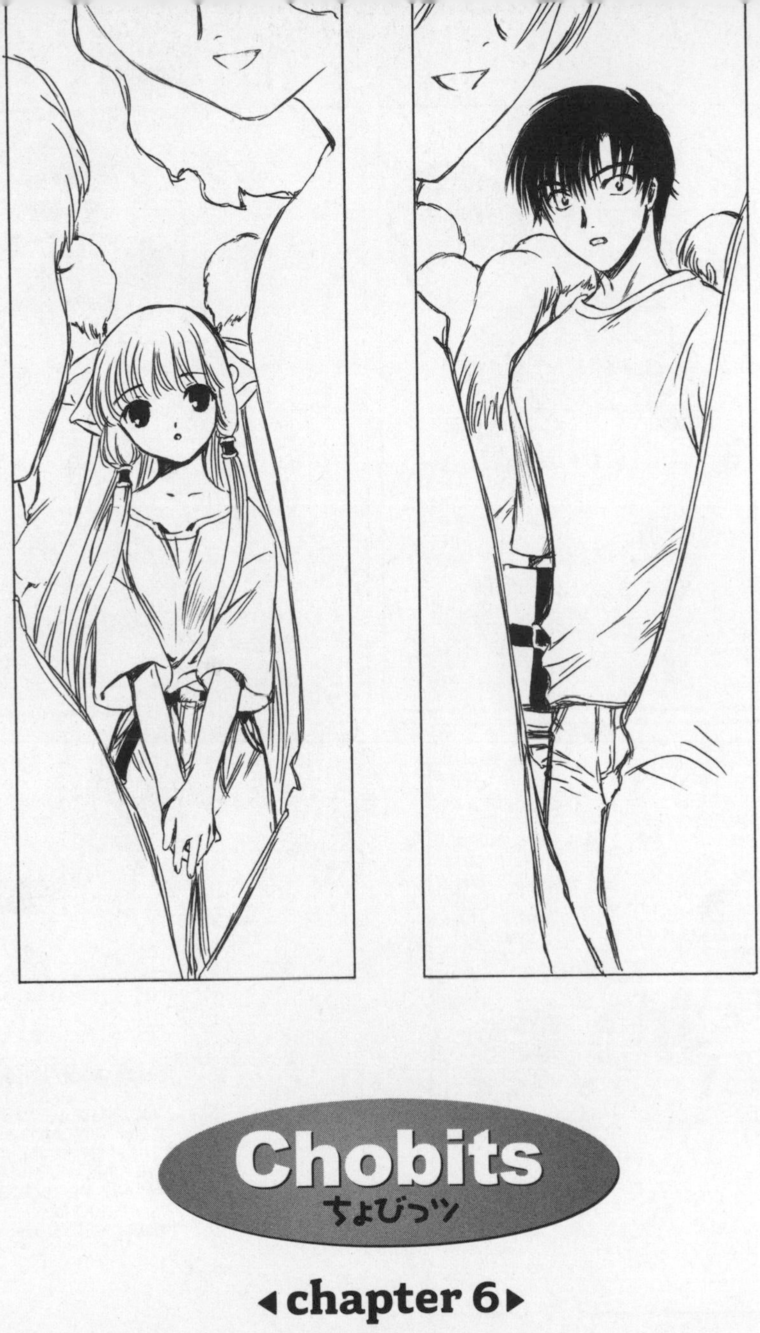

Chobits

ちょびっツ

◂chapter 6▸

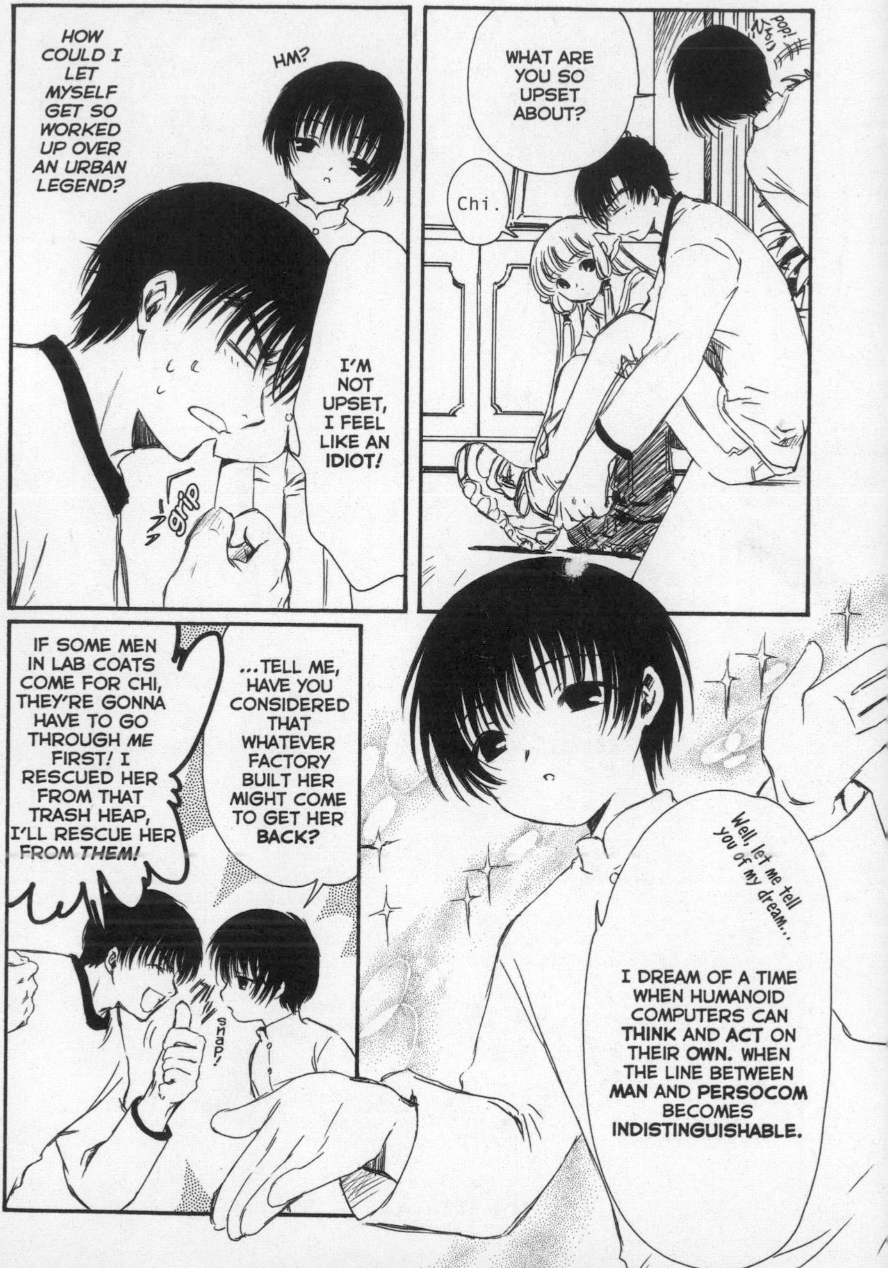
POP!
WHAT ARE YOU SO UPSET ABOUT?
Chi.
HOW COULD I LET MYSELF GET SO WORKED UP OVER AN URBAN LEGEND?
HM?
I'M NOT UPSET, I FEEL LIKE AN IDIOT!
grip
Well, let me tell you of my dream...
I DREAM OF A TIME WHEN HUMANOID COMPUTERS CAN THINK AND ACT ON THEIR OWN. WHEN THE LINE BETWEEN MAN AND PERSOCOM BECOMES INDISTINGUISHABLE.
...TELL ME, HAVE YOU CONSIDERED THAT WHATEVER FACTORY BUILT HER MIGHT COME TO GET HER BACK?
IF SOME MEN IN LAB COATS COME FOR CHI, THEY'RE GONNA HAVE TO GO THROUGH ME FIRST! I RESCUED HER FROM THAT TRASH HEAP, I'LL RESCUE HER FROM THEM!
snap!

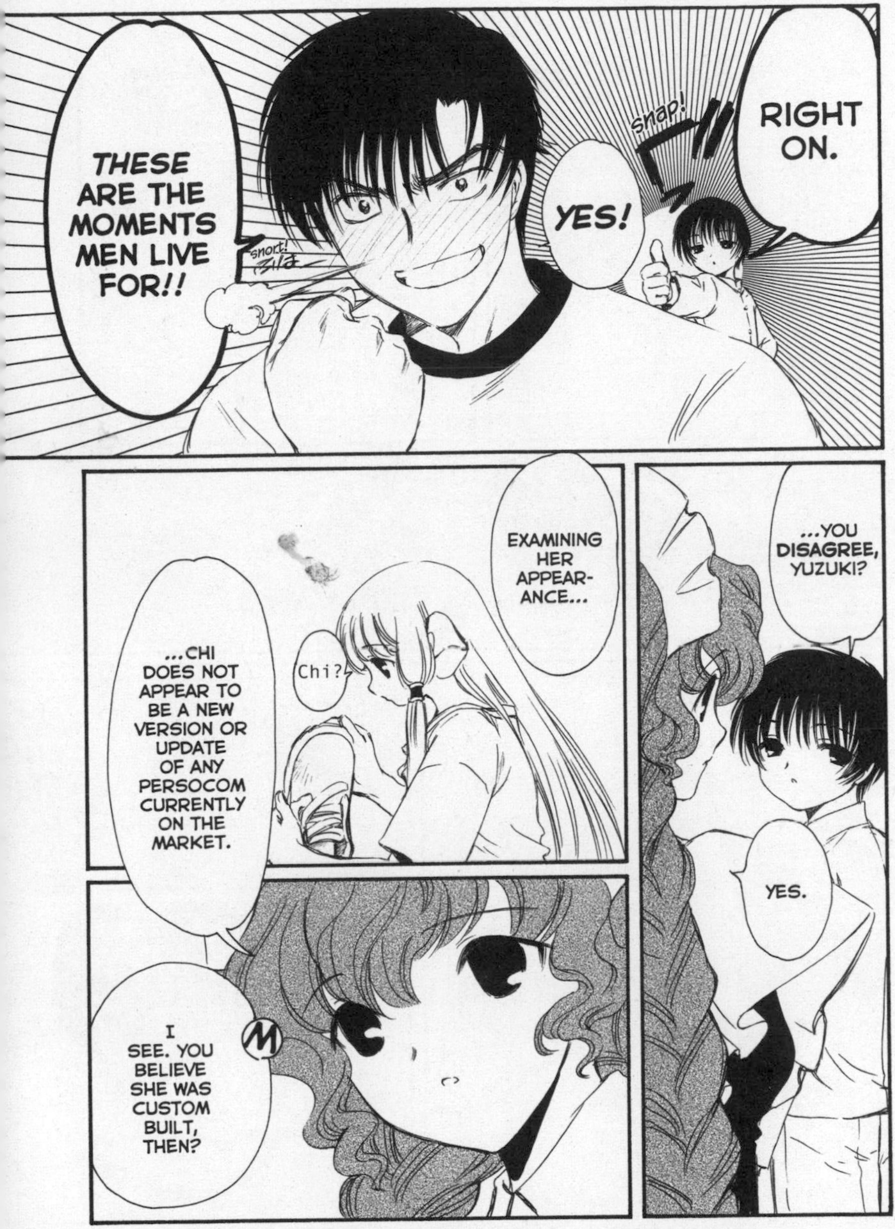
RIGHT ON.
snap!
YES!
snort!
THESE ARE THE MOMENTS MEN LIVE FOR!!
...YOU DISAGREE, YUZUKI?
YES.
EXAMINING HER APPEARANCE...
Chi?
...CHI DOES NOT APPEAR TO BE A NEW VERSION OR UPDATE OF ANY PERSOCOM CURRENTLY ON THE MARKET.
I SEE. YOU BELIEVE SHE WAS CUSTOM BUILT, THEN?

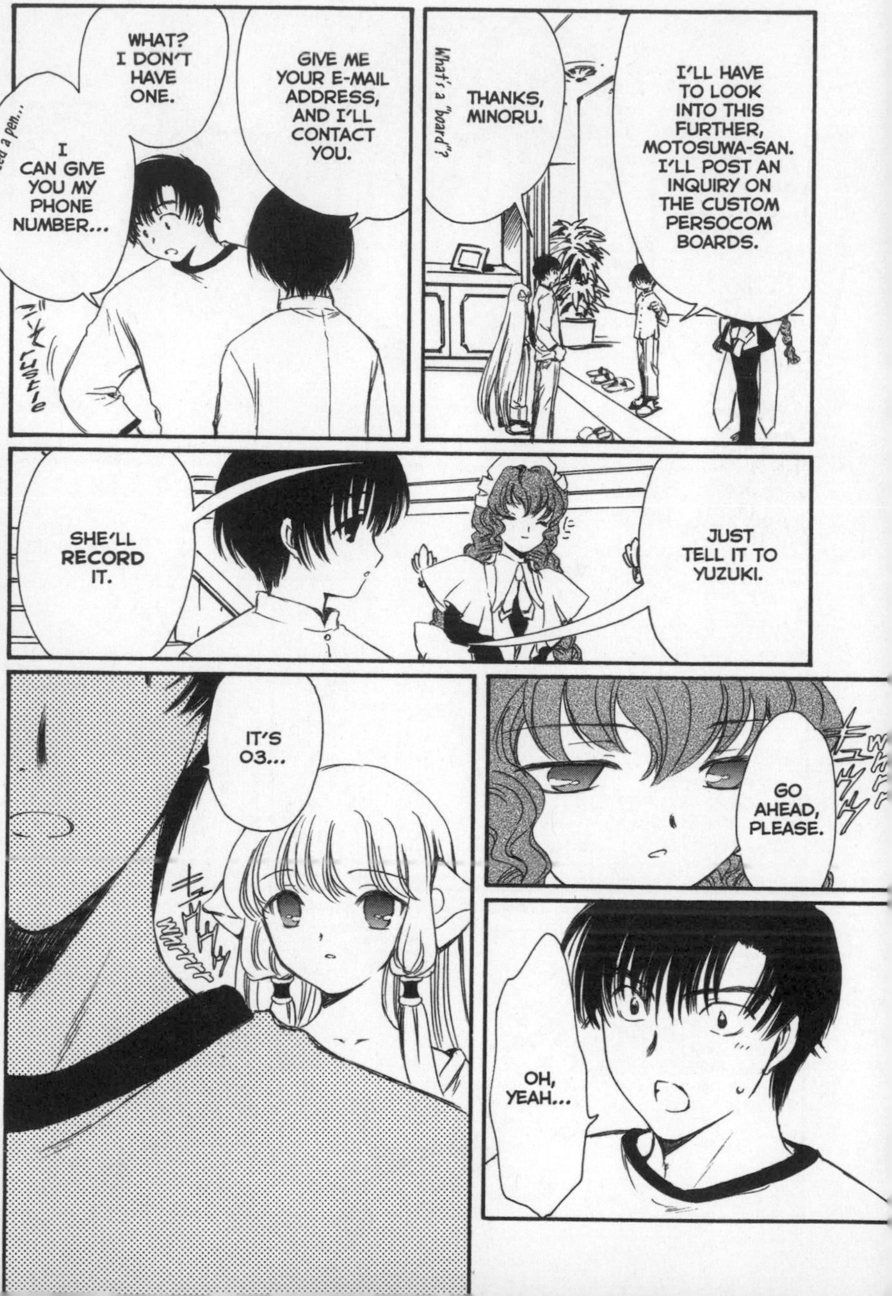
I'LL HAVE TO LOOK INTO THIS FURTHER, MOTOSUWA-SAN. I'LL POST AN INQUIRY ON THE CUSTOM PERSOCOM BOARDS.
THANKS, MINORU.
What's a "board"?
GIVE ME YOUR E-MAIL ADDRESS, AND I'LL CONTACT YOU.
WHAT? I DON'T HAVE ONE.
I CAN GIVE YOU MY PHONE NUMBER...
Need a pen...
rustle
JUST TELL IT TO YUZUKI.
SHE'LL RECORD IT.
GO AHEAD, PLEASE.
OH, YEAH...
IT'S 03...

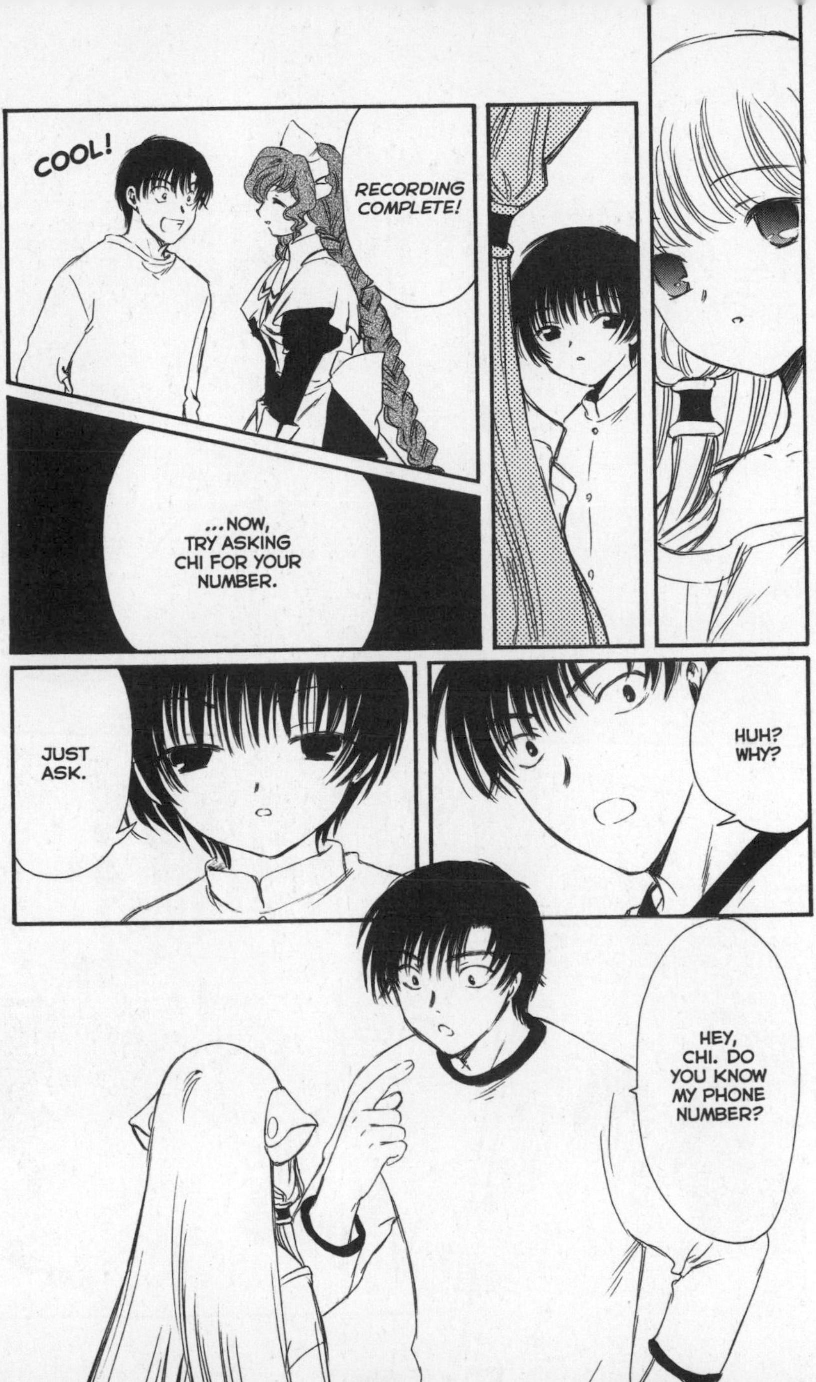
RECORDING COMPLETE!
COOL!
...NOW, TRY ASKING CHI FOR YOUR NUMBER.
HUH? WHY?
JUST ASK.
HEY, CHI. DO YOU KNOW MY PHONE NUMBER?

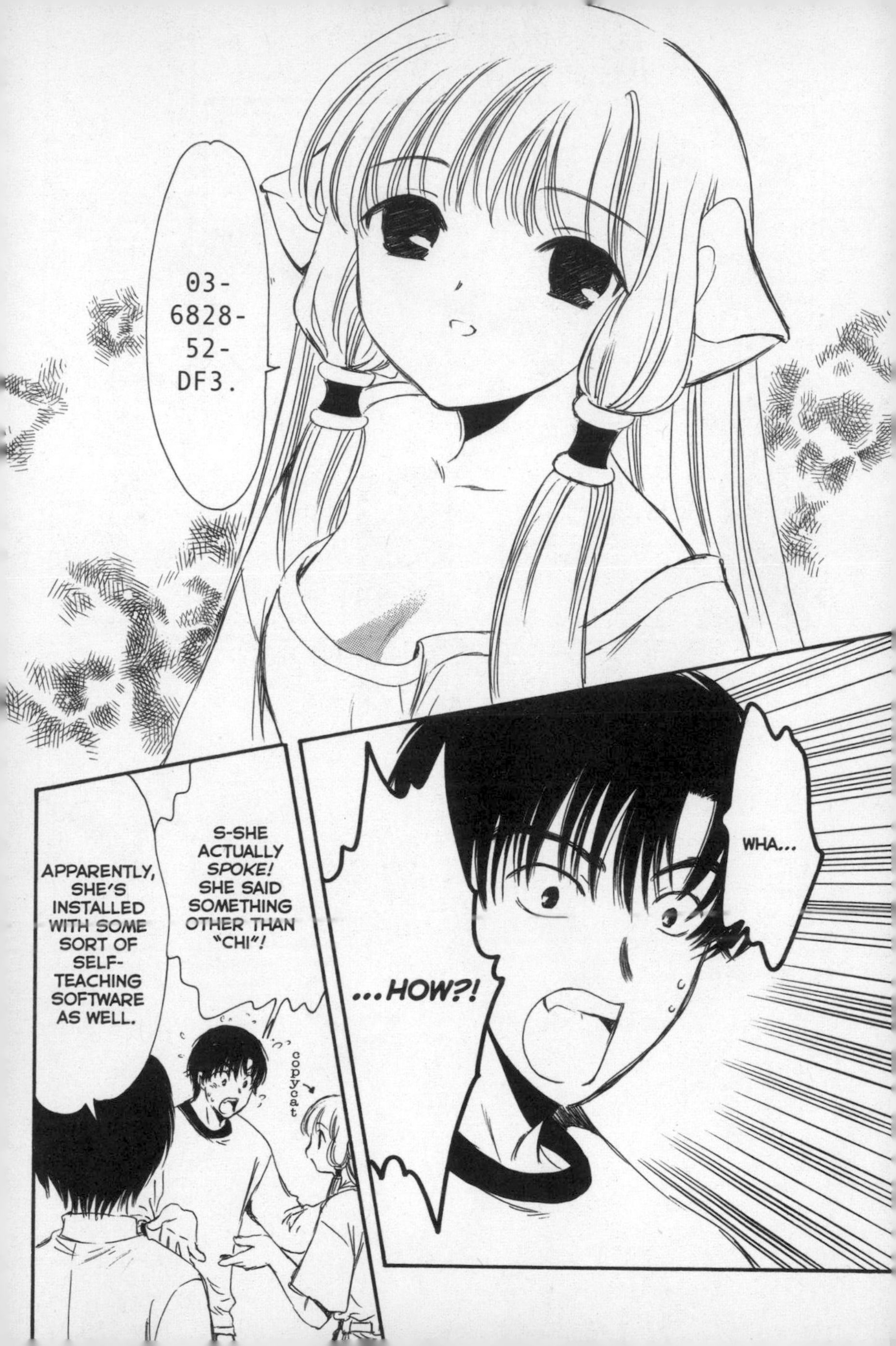
03-6828-52-DF3.
WHA...
...HOW?!
S-SHE ACTUALLY *SPOKE!* SHE SAID SOMETHING OTHER THAN "CHI"!
APPARENTLY, SHE'S INSTALLED WITH SOME SORT OF SELF-TEACHING SOFTWARE AS WELL.
copycat

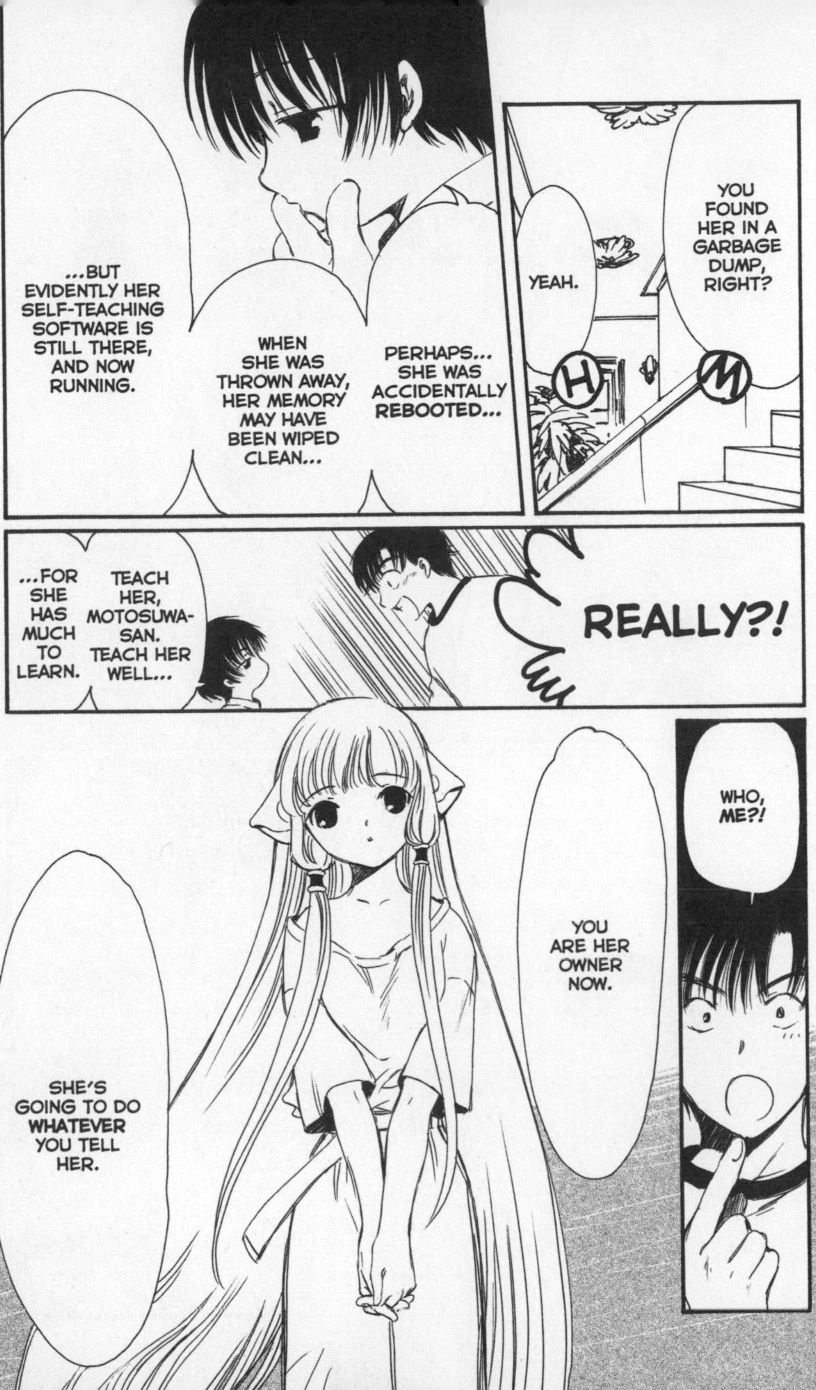
YOU FOUND HER IN A GARBAGE DUMP, RIGHT?
YEAH.
PERHAPS... SHE WAS ACCIDENTALLY REBOOTED...
WHEN SHE WAS THROWN AWAY, HER MEMORY MAY HAVE BEEN WIPED CLEAN...
...BUT EVIDENTLY HER SELF-TEACHING SOFTWARE IS STILL THERE, AND NOW RUNNING.
REALLY?!
TEACH HER, MOTOSUWA-SAN. TEACH HER WELL...
...FOR SHE HAS MUCH TO LEARN.
WHO, ME?!
YOU ARE HER OWNER NOW.
SHE'S GOING TO DO WHATEVER YOU TELL HER.

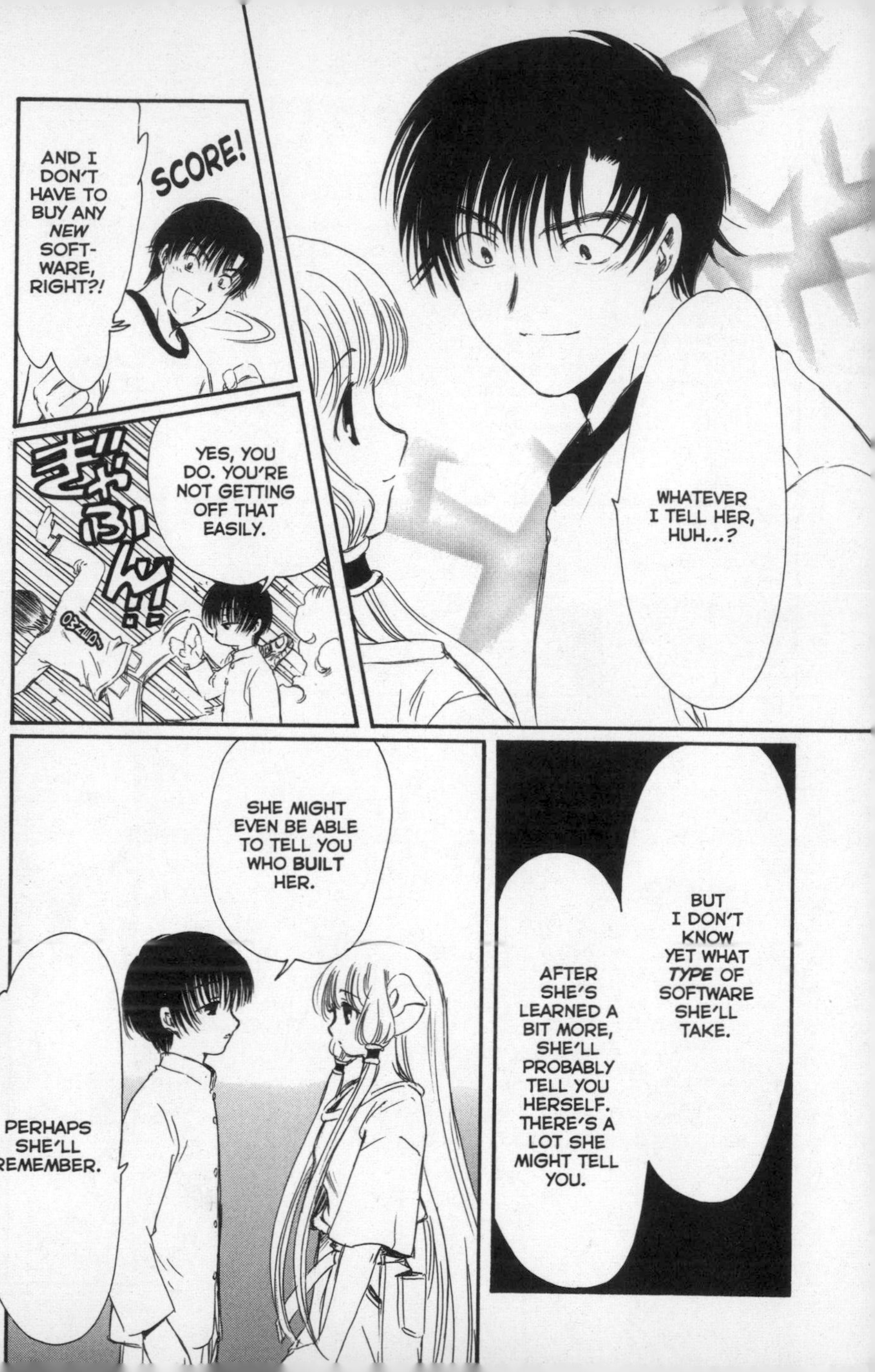
WHATEVER I TELL HER, HUH...?
AND I DON'T HAVE TO BUY ANY *NEW* SOFTWARE, RIGHT?!
SCORE!
YES, YOU DO. YOU'RE NOT GETTING OFF THAT EASILY.
ぎゃふん!!
BUT I DON'T KNOW YET WHAT *TYPE* OF SOFTWARE SHE'LL TAKE.
AFTER SHE'S LEARNED A BIT MORE, SHE'LL PROBABLY TELL YOU HERSELF. THERE'S A LOT SHE MIGHT TELL YOU.
SHE MIGHT EVEN BE ABLE TO TELL YOU WHO BUILT HER.
PERHAPS SHE'LL REMEMBER.

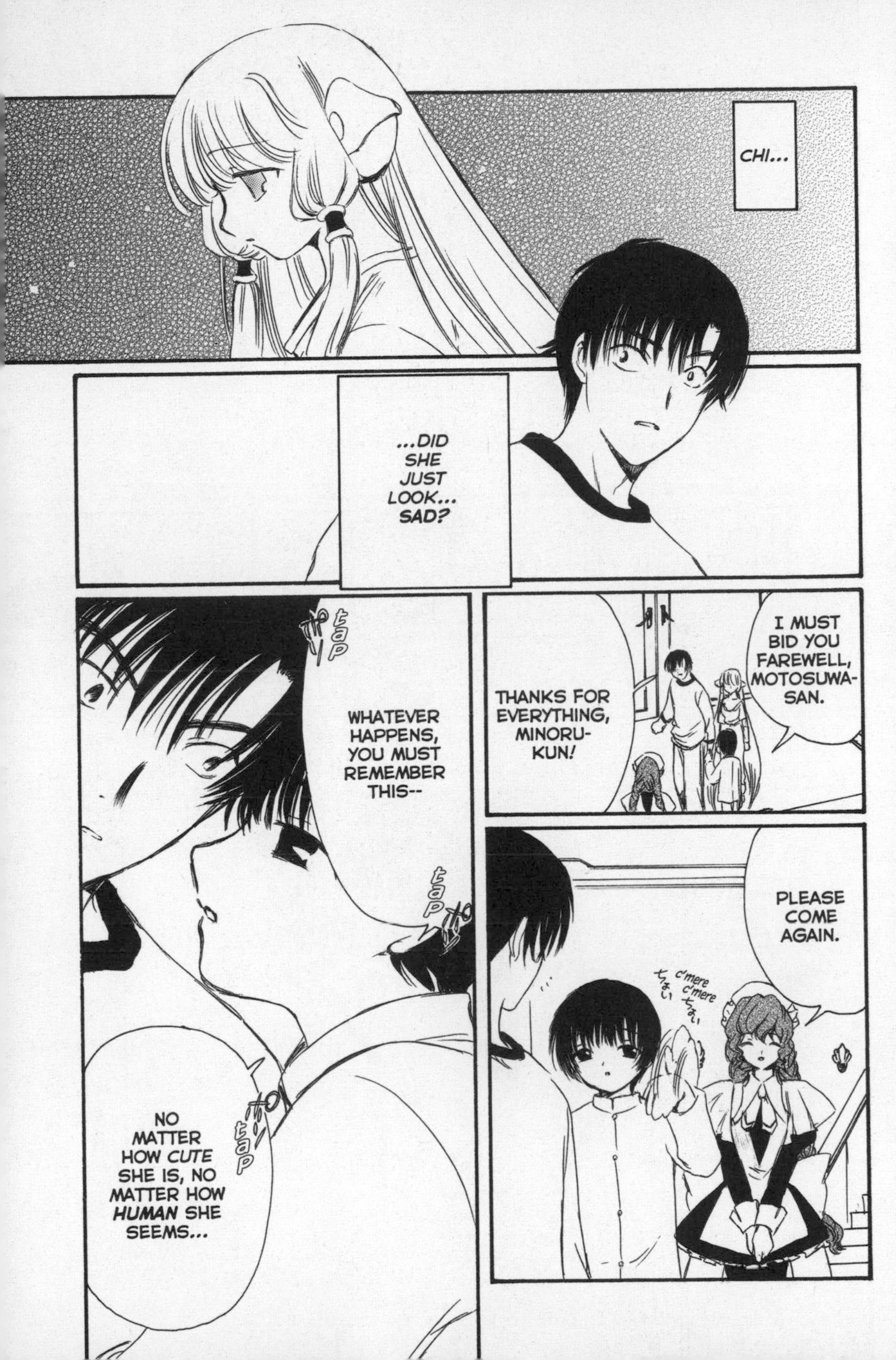
CHI...
...DID SHE JUST LOOK... SAD?
I MUST BID YOU FAREWELL, MOTOSUWA-SAN.
THANKS FOR EVERYTHING, MINORU-KUN!
PLEASE COME AGAIN.
c'mere c'mere
ちょい ちょい
tap
WHATEVER HAPPENS, YOU MUST REMEMBER THIS--
tap
tap
NO MATTER HOW CUTE SHE IS, NO MATTER HOW HUMAN SHE SEEMS...

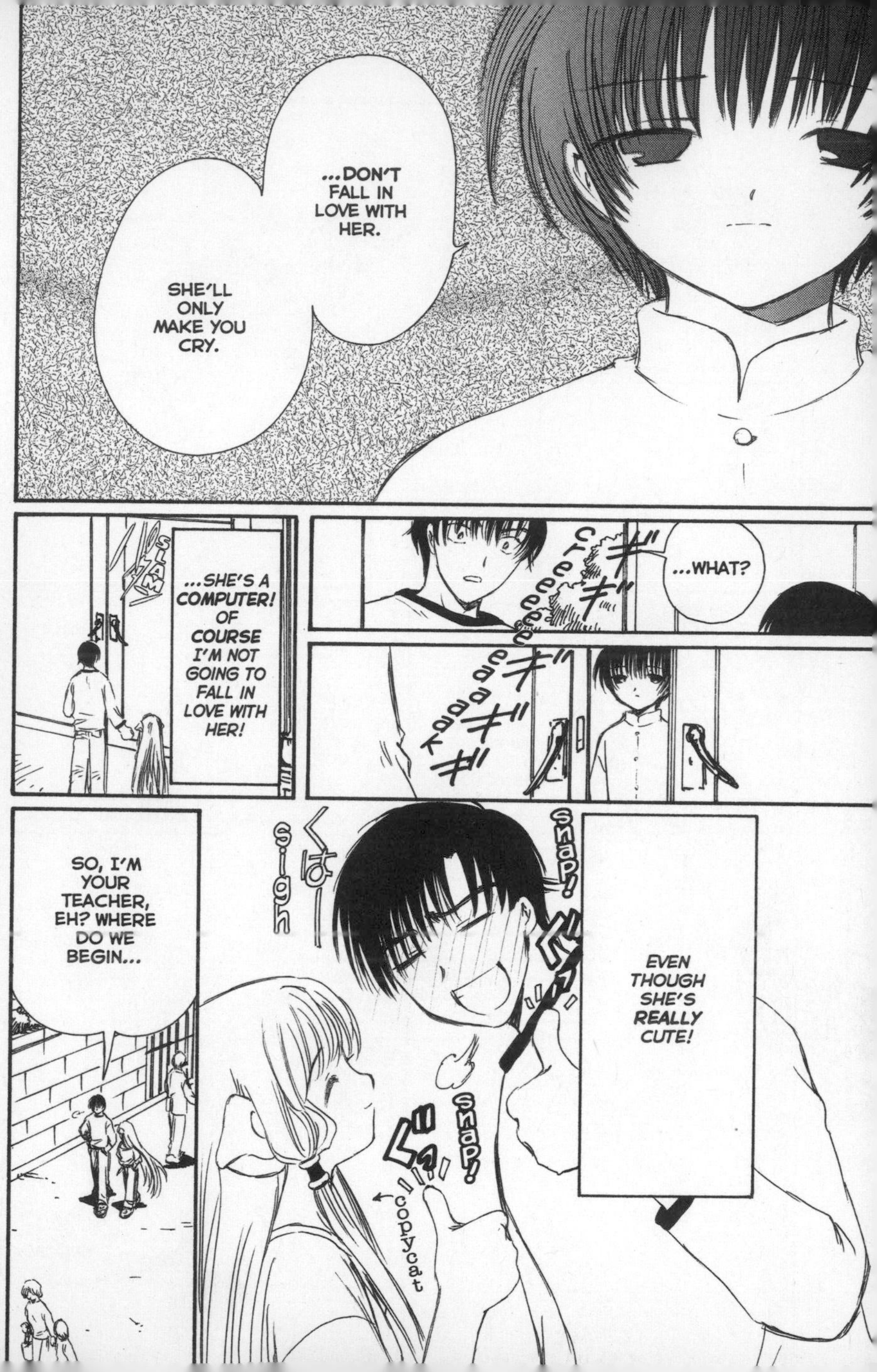
...DON'T FALL IN LOVE WITH HER.
SHE'LL ONLY MAKE YOU CRY.
creeeeeeeeeaaaak
...WHAT?
SLAM
...SHE'S A COMPUTER! OF COURSE I'M NOT GOING TO FALL IN LOVE WITH HER!
EVEN THOUGH SHE'S REALLY CUTE!
snap!
snap!
copycat
sigh
SO, I'M YOUR TEACHER, EH? WHERE DO WE BEGIN...

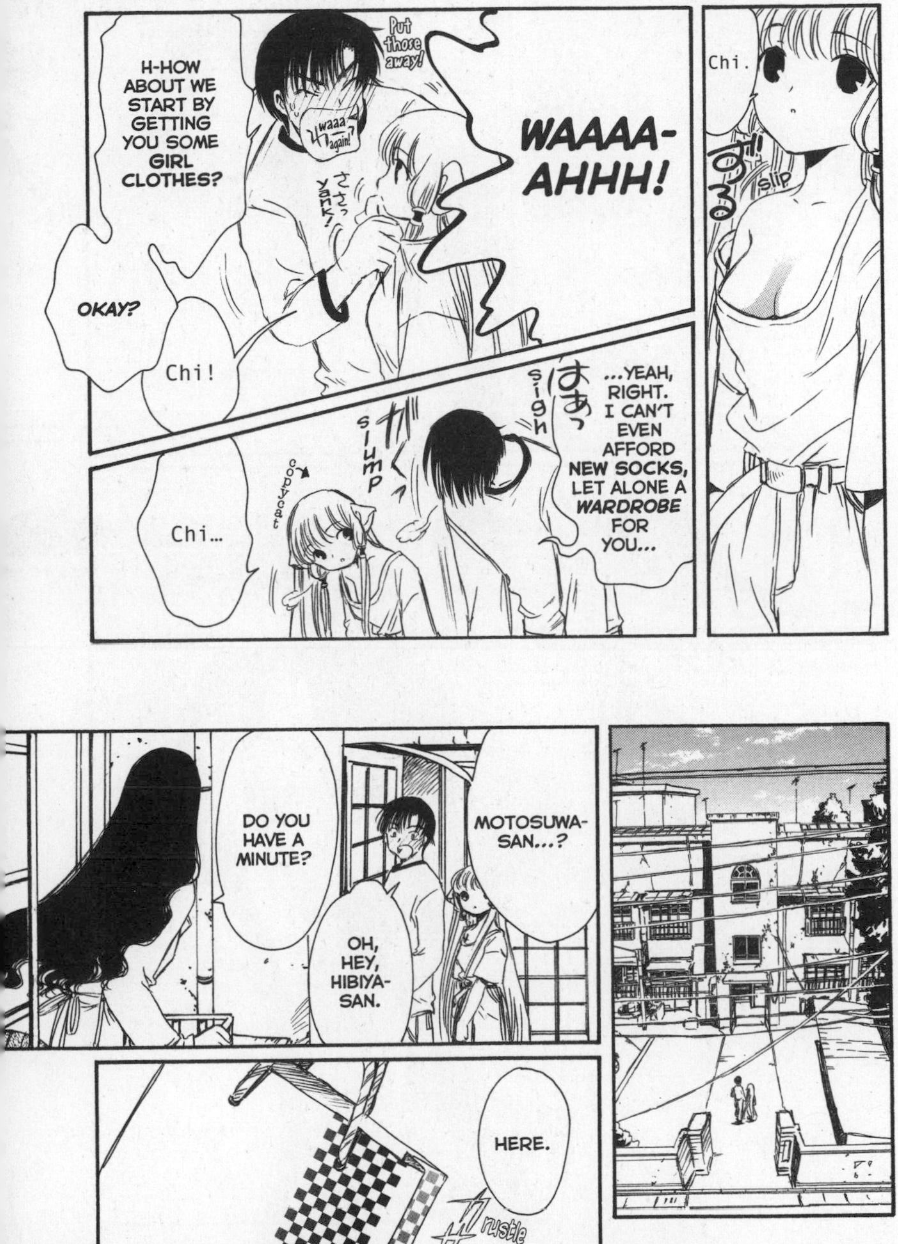

Chi.
ずるっ
slip
Put those away!
WAAAA-AHHH!
waaa again!
さっ
yank!
H-HOW ABOUT WE START BY GETTING YOU SOME GIRL CLOTHES?
OKAY?
Chi!
はあっ
sigh
...YEAH, RIGHT. I CAN'T EVEN AFFORD NEW SOCKS, LET ALONE A WARDROBE FOR YOU...
がくっ
slump
copycat
Chi...
MOTOSUWA-SAN...?
DO YOU HAVE A MINUTE?
OH, HEY, HIBIYA-SAN.
HERE.
rustle

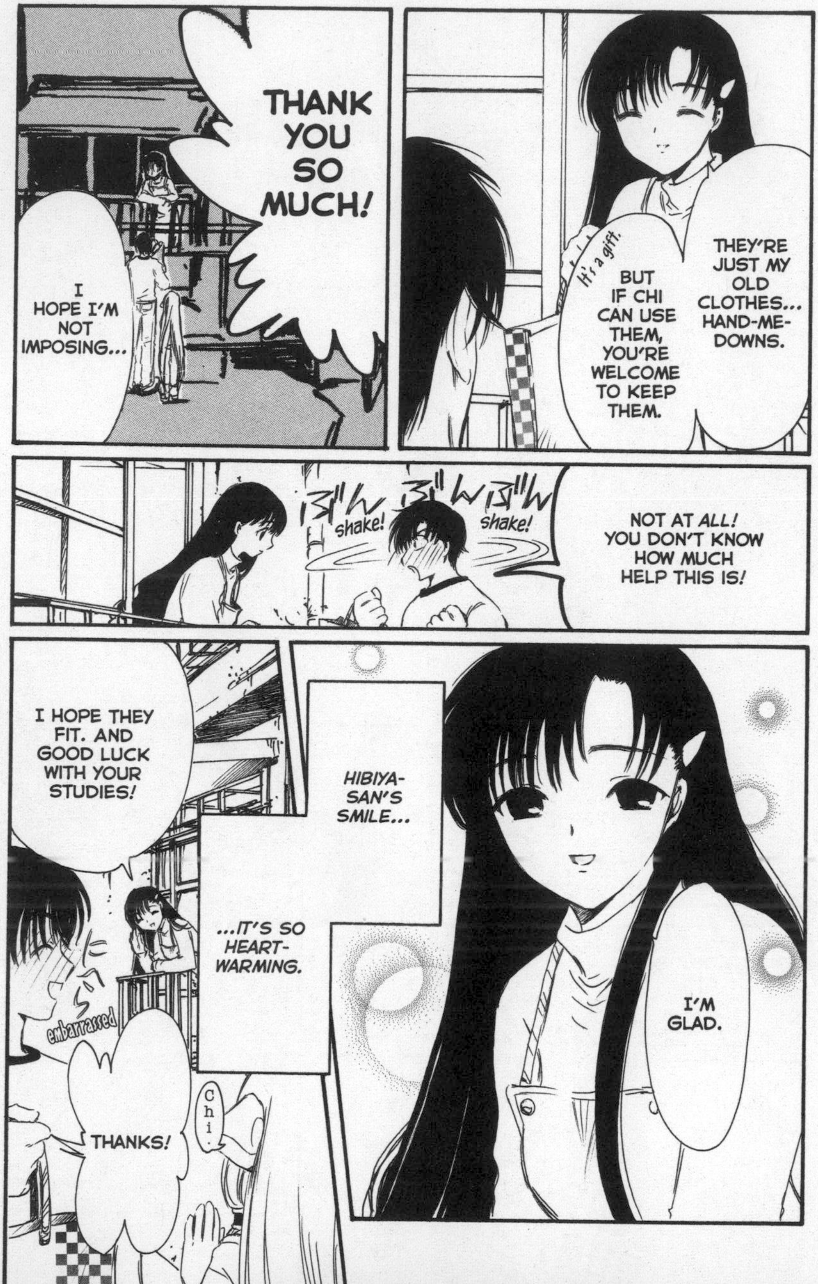
THEY'RE JUST MY OLD CLOTHES... HAND-ME-DOWNS.
BUT IF CHI CAN USE THEM, YOU'RE WELCOME TO KEEP THEM.
It's a gift.
THANK YOU SO MUCH!
I HOPE I'M NOT IMPOSING...
NOT AT ALL! YOU DON'T KNOW HOW MUCH HELP THIS IS!
ぶんぶんぶん
shake!
shake!
I'M GLAD.
HIBIYA-SAN'S SMILE...
...IT'S SO HEART-WARMING.
I HOPE THEY FIT. AND GOOD LUCK WITH YOUR STUDIES!
embarrassed
THANKS!
Chi.

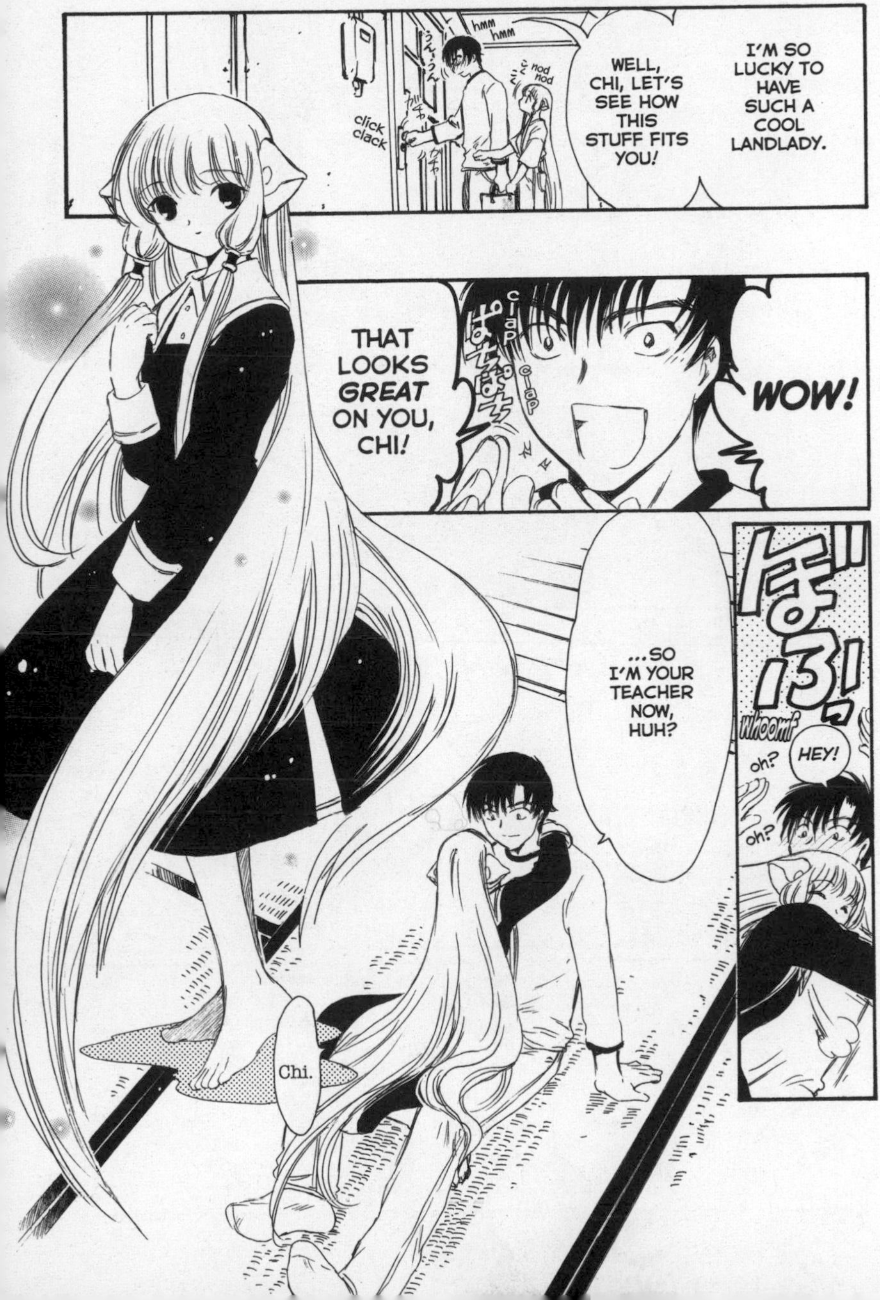
I'M SO LUCKY TO HAVE SUCH A COOL LANDLADY.
WELL, CHI, LET'S SEE HOW THIS STUFF FITS YOU!
hmm hmm
nod nod
click clack
WOW!
clap clap
THAT LOOKS GREAT ON YOU, CHI!
whoomf
HEY!
oh?
oh?
...SO I'M YOUR TEACHER NOW, HUH?
Chi.

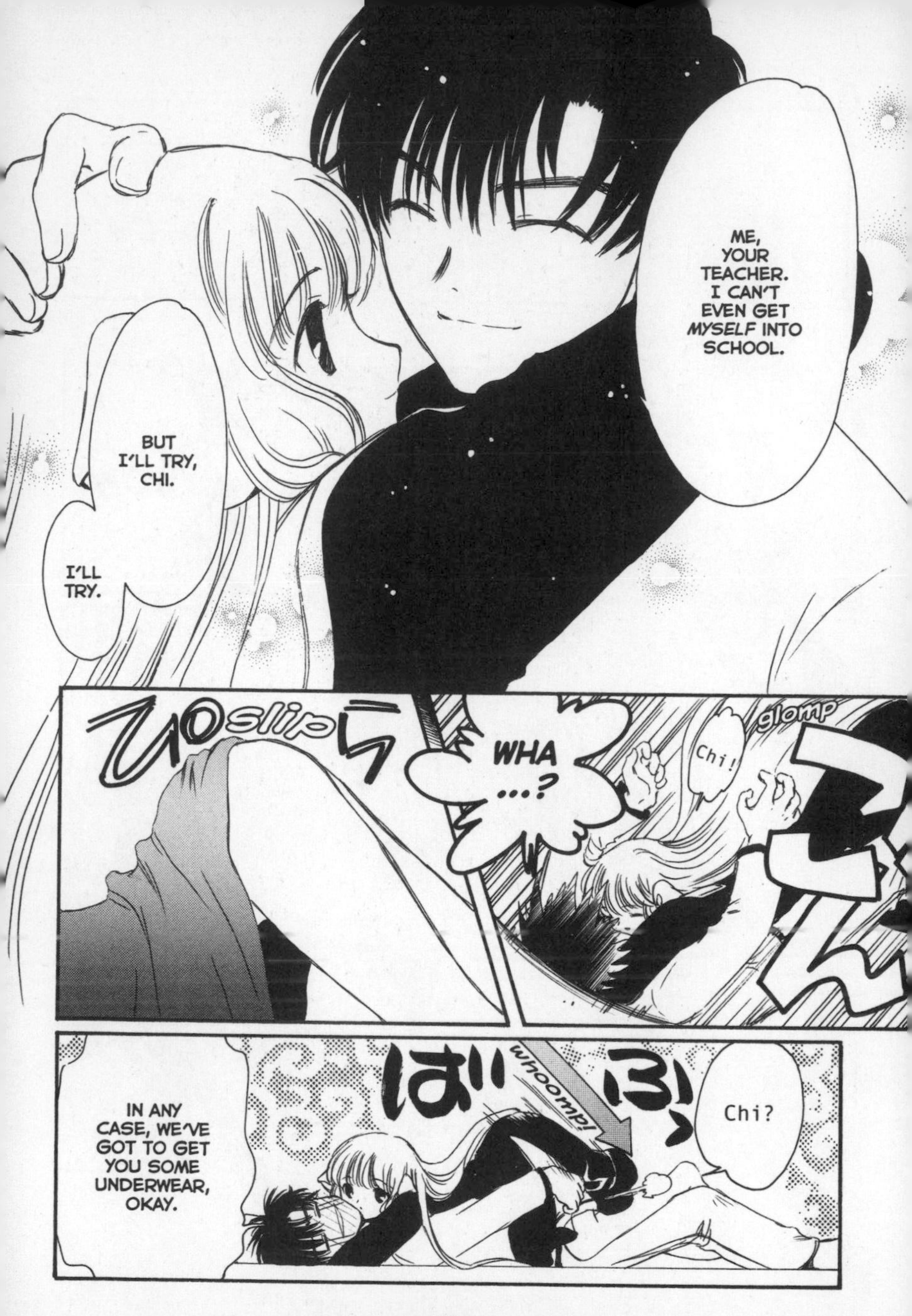
ME, YOUR TEACHER. I CAN'T EVEN GET *MYSELF* INTO SCHOOL.
BUT I'LL TRY, CHI.
I'LL TRY.
glomp
Chi!
WHA ...?
slip
whoomp!
Chi?
IN ANY CASE, WE'VE GOT TO GET YOU SOME UNDERWEAR, OKAY.

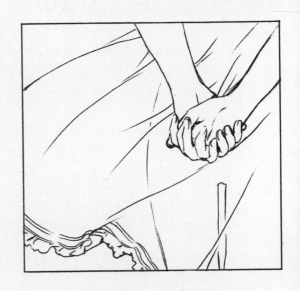

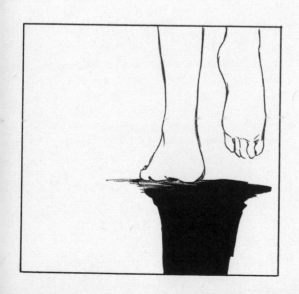

Chobits

ちょびっツ

◀ chapter 7 ▶

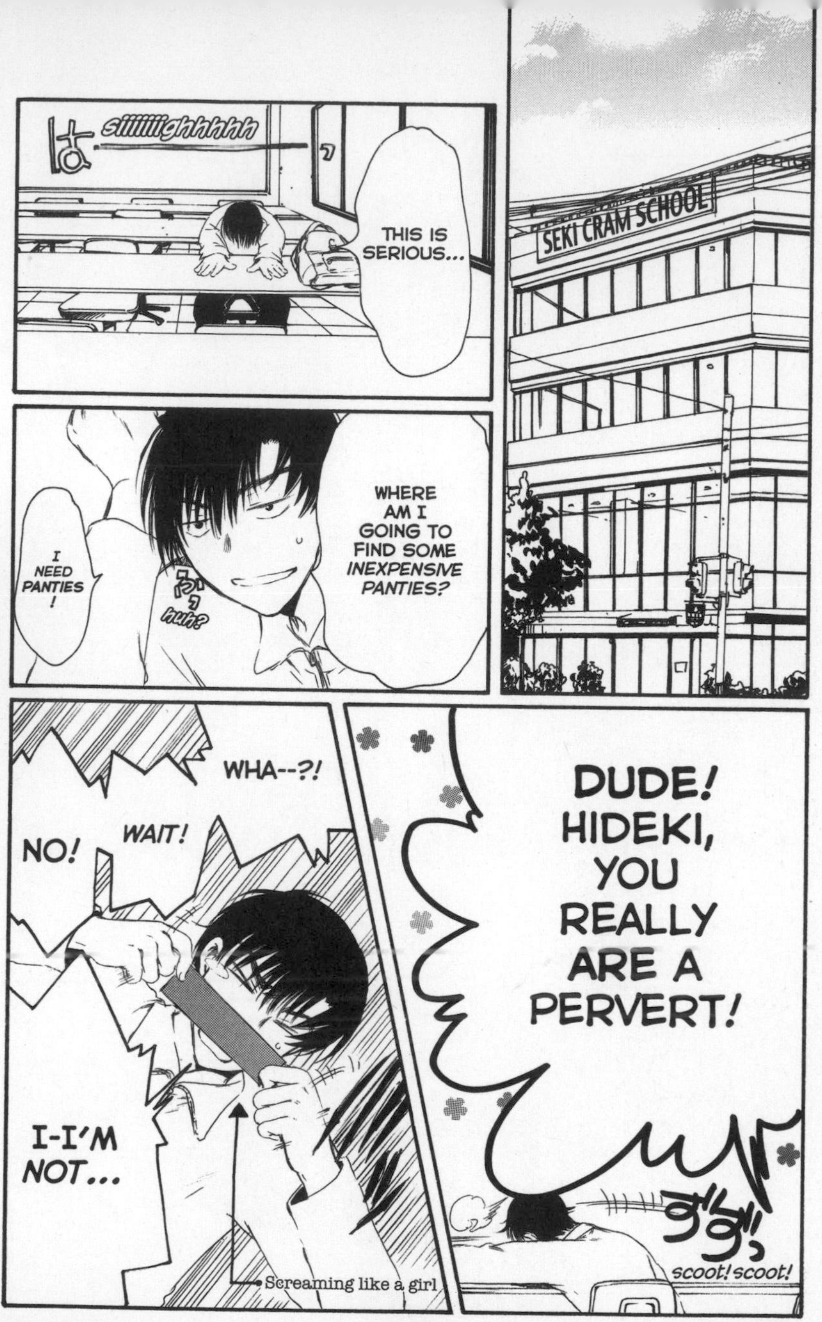
SEKI CRAM SCHOOL
は siiiiiiighhhhh
THIS IS SERIOUS...
WHERE AM I GOING TO FIND SOME INEXPENSIVE PANTIES?
わっ huh?
I NEED PANTIES!
DUDE! HIDEKI, YOU REALLY ARE A PERVERT!
scoot! scoot!
WHA--?!
WAIT!
NO!
I-I'M NOT...
Screaming like a girl

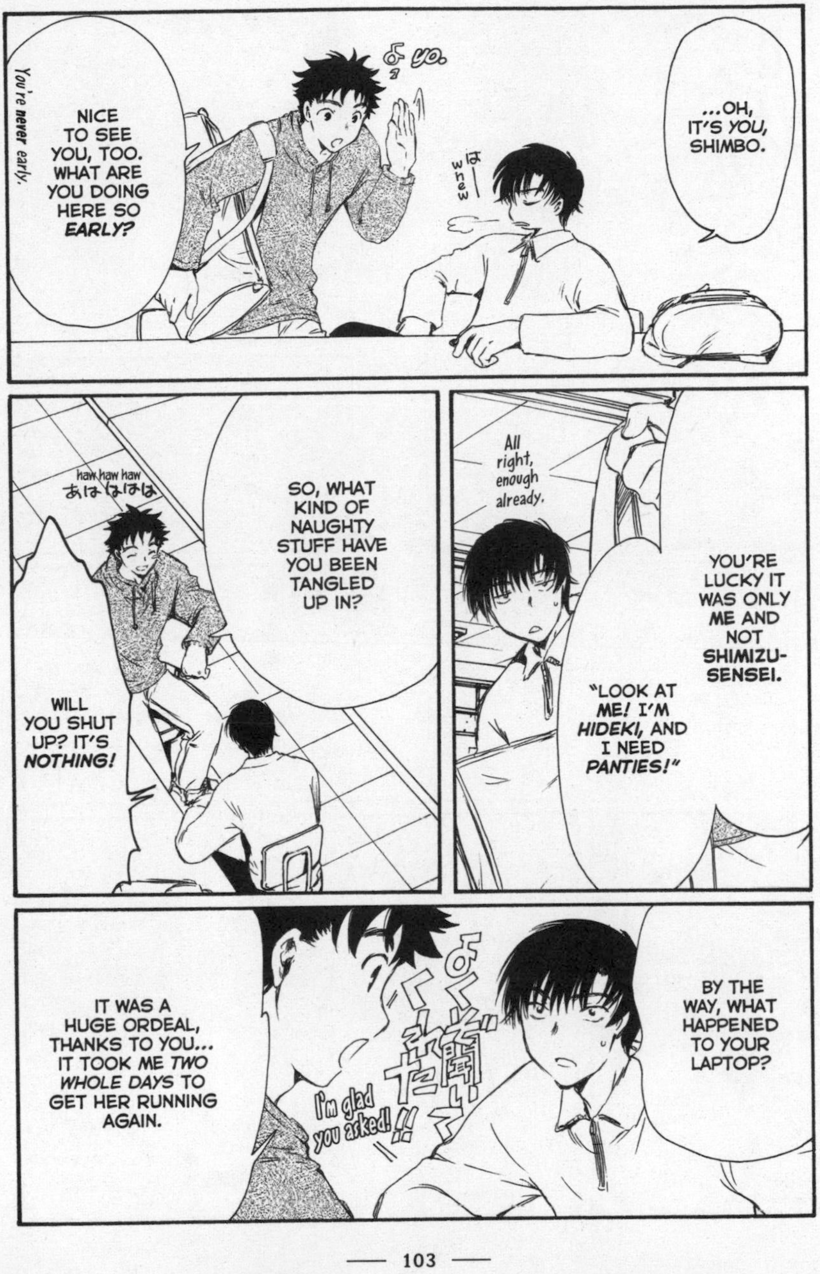
...OH, IT'S *YOU*, SHIMBO.
は— whew
よっ yo.
NICE TO SEE YOU, TOO. WHAT ARE YOU DOING HERE SO *EARLY?*
You're **never** early.
YOU'RE LUCKY IT WAS ONLY ME AND NOT SHIMIZU-SENSEI.
All right, enough already.
"LOOK AT *ME!* I'M *HIDEKI*, AND I NEED *PANTIES!*"
SO, WHAT KIND OF NAUGHTY STUFF HAVE YOU BEEN TANGLED UP IN?
haw haw haw あははは
WILL YOU SHUT UP? IT'S *NOTHING!*
BY THE WAY, WHAT HAPPENED TO YOUR LAPTOP?
よくぞ聞いてくれた!!
I'm glad you asked!!
IT WAS A HUGE ORDEAL, THANKS TO YOU... IT TOOK ME *TWO WHOLE DAYS* TO GET HER RUNNING AGAIN.

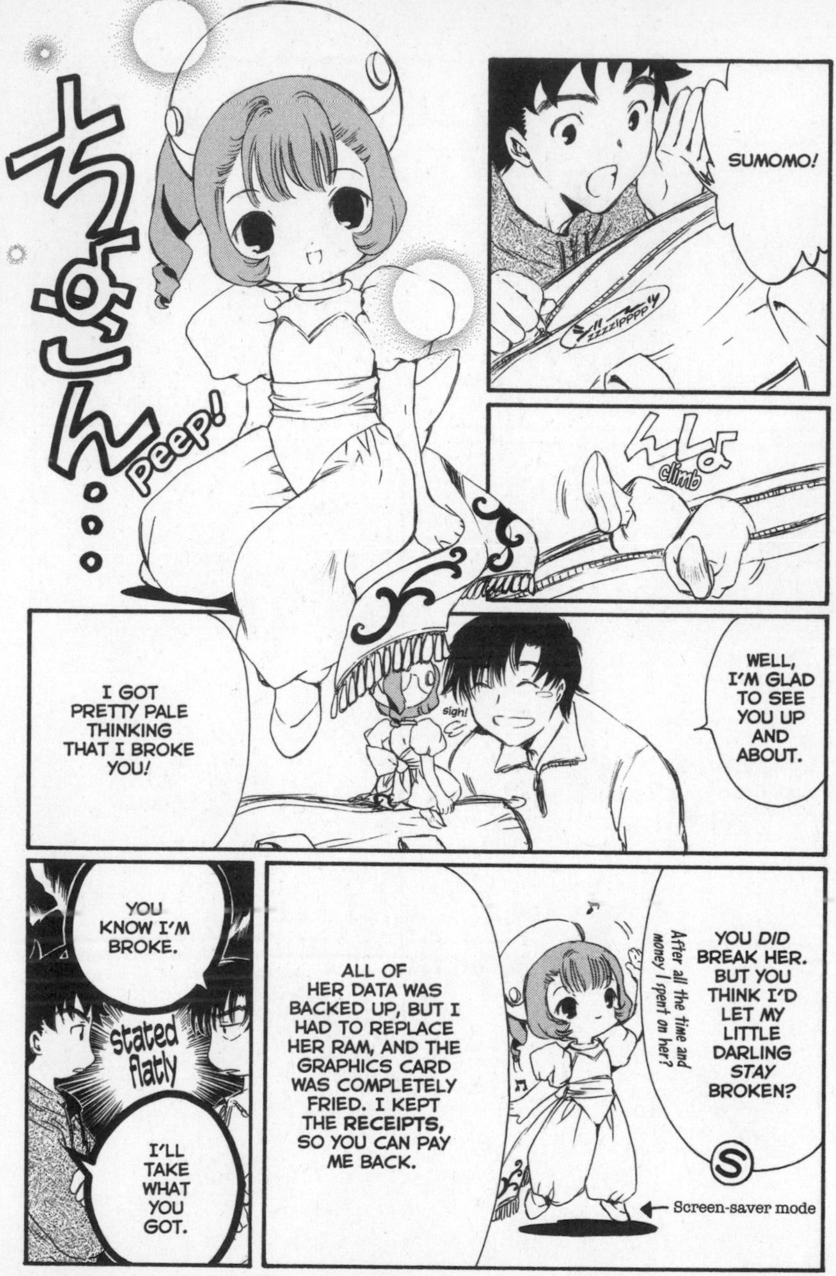
SUMOMO!
zzzzipppp
んしょ
climb
ちゅん...
peep!
WELL, I'M GLAD TO SEE YOU UP AND ABOUT.
sigh!
I GOT PRETTY PALE THINKING THAT I BROKE YOU!
YOU *DID* BREAK HER. BUT YOU THINK I'D LET MY LITTLE DARLING *STAY* BROKEN?
After all the time and money I spent on her?
ALL OF HER DATA WAS BACKED UP, BUT I HAD TO REPLACE HER RAM, AND THE GRAPHICS CARD WAS COMPLETELY FRIED. I KEPT THE RECEIPTS, SO YOU CAN PAY ME BACK.
S
Screen-saver mode
YOU KNOW I'M BROKE.
stated flatly
I'LL TAKE WHAT YOU GOT.

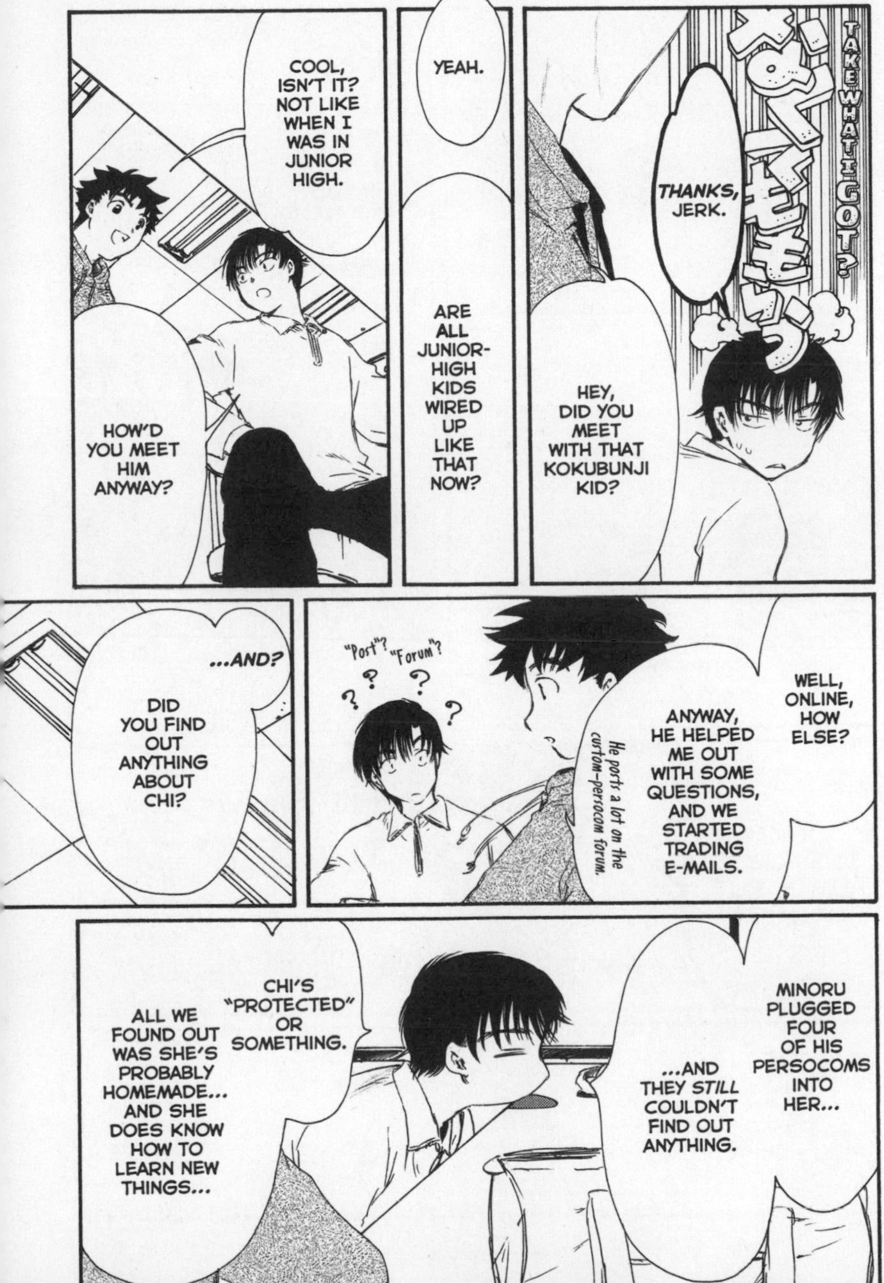
TAKE WHAT I GOT?
THANKS, JERK.
HEY, DID YOU MEET WITH THAT KOKUBUNJI KID?
YEAH.
ARE ALL JUNIOR-HIGH KIDS WIRED UP LIKE THAT NOW?
COOL, ISN'T IT? NOT LIKE WHEN I WAS IN JUNIOR HIGH.
HOW'D YOU MEET HIM ANYWAY?
WELL, ONLINE, HOW ELSE?
ANYWAY, HE HELPED ME OUT WITH SOME QUESTIONS, AND WE STARTED TRADING E-MAILS.
He posts a lot on the custom-persocom forum.
"Post"? "Forum"?
...AND?
DID YOU FIND OUT ANYTHING ABOUT CHI?
MINORU PLUGGED FOUR OF HIS PERSOCOMS INTO HER...
...AND THEY *STILL* COULDN'T FIND OUT ANYTHING.
CHI'S "PROTECTED" OR SOMETHING.
ALL WE FOUND OUT WAS SHE'S PROBABLY HOMEMADE... AND SHE DOES KNOW HOW TO LEARN NEW THINGS...

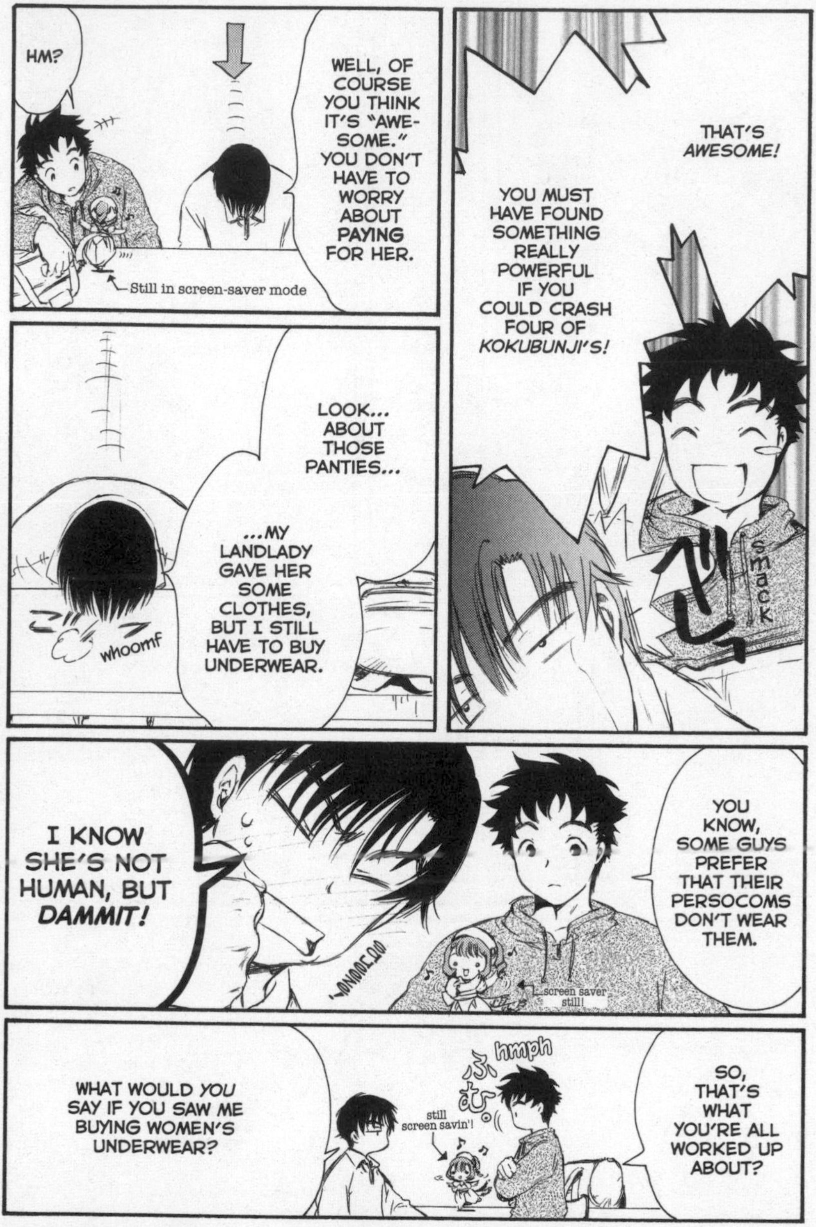
THAT'S *AWESOME!*
YOU MUST HAVE FOUND SOMETHING REALLY POWERFUL IF YOU COULD CRASH FOUR OF *KOKUBUNJI'S!*
smack
WELL, OF COURSE YOU THINK IT'S "AWE-SOME." YOU DON'T HAVE TO WORRY ABOUT PAYING FOR HER.
HM?
Still in screen-saver mode
LOOK... ABOUT THOSE PANTIES...
...MY LANDLADY GAVE HER SOME CLOTHES, BUT I STILL HAVE TO BUY UNDERWEAR.
whoomf
YOU KNOW, SOME GUYS PREFER THAT THEIR PERSOCOMS DON'T WEAR THEM.
I KNOW SHE'S NOT HUMAN, BUT *DAMMIT!*
screen saver still!
SO, THAT'S WHAT YOU'RE ALL WORKED UP ABOUT?
hmph
still screen savin'!
WHAT WOULD *YOU* SAY IF YOU SAW ME BUYING WOMEN'S UNDERWEAR?

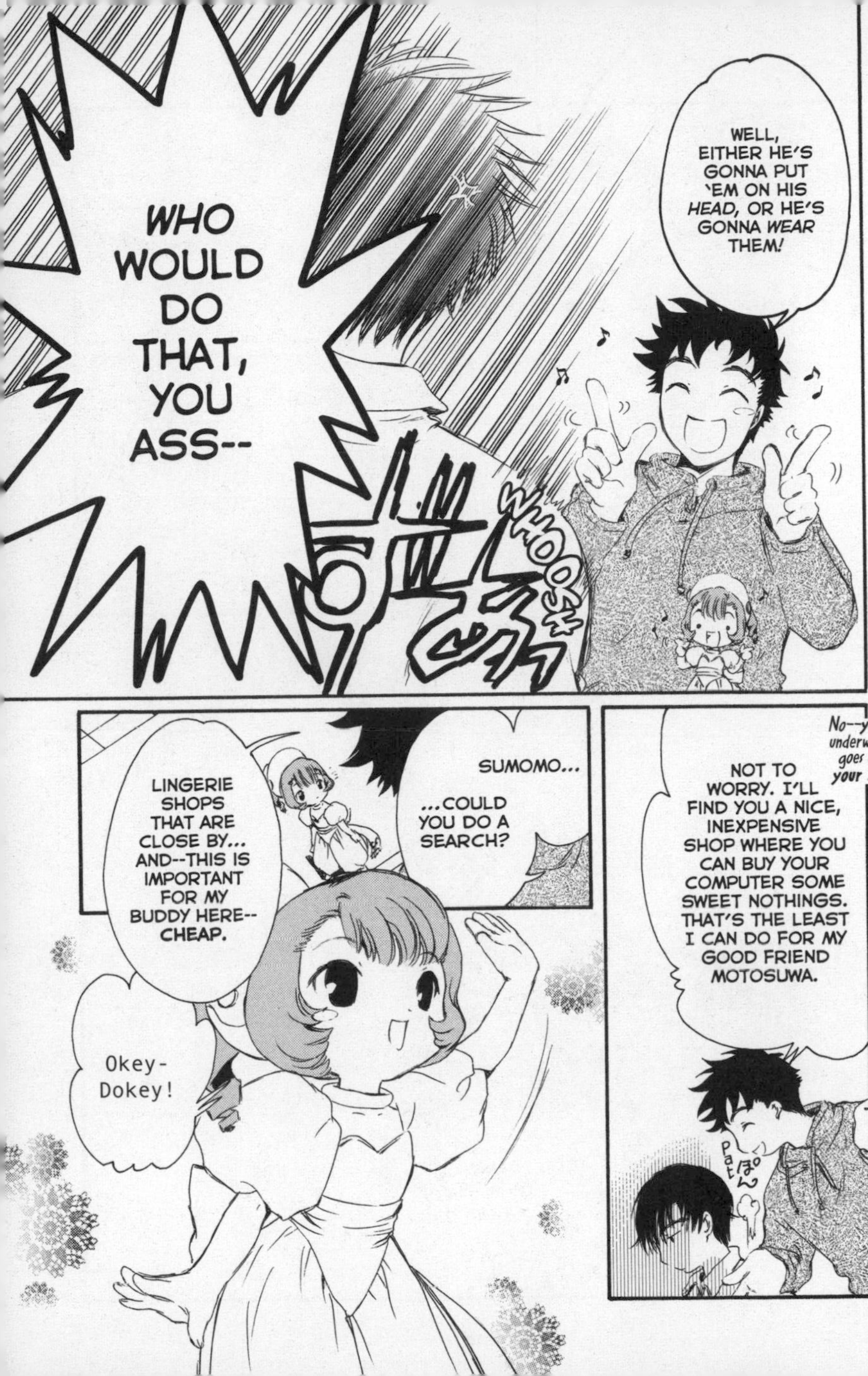
WELL, EITHER HE'S GONNA PUT 'EM ON HIS *HEAD*, OR HE'S GONNA *WEAR* THEM!
WHO WOULD DO THAT, YOU ASS--
WHOOSH
NOT TO WORRY. I'LL FIND YOU A NICE, INEXPENSIVE SHOP WHERE YOU CAN BUY YOUR COMPUTER SOME SWEET NOTHINGS. THAT'S THE LEAST I CAN DO FOR MY GOOD FRIEND MOTOSUWA.
No--**your** underwear goes on **your** ass.
Pat
SUMOMO...
...COULD YOU DO A SEARCH?
LINGERIE SHOPS THAT ARE CLOSE BY... AND--THIS IS IMPORTANT FOR MY BUDDY HERE--CHEAP.
Okey-Dokey!

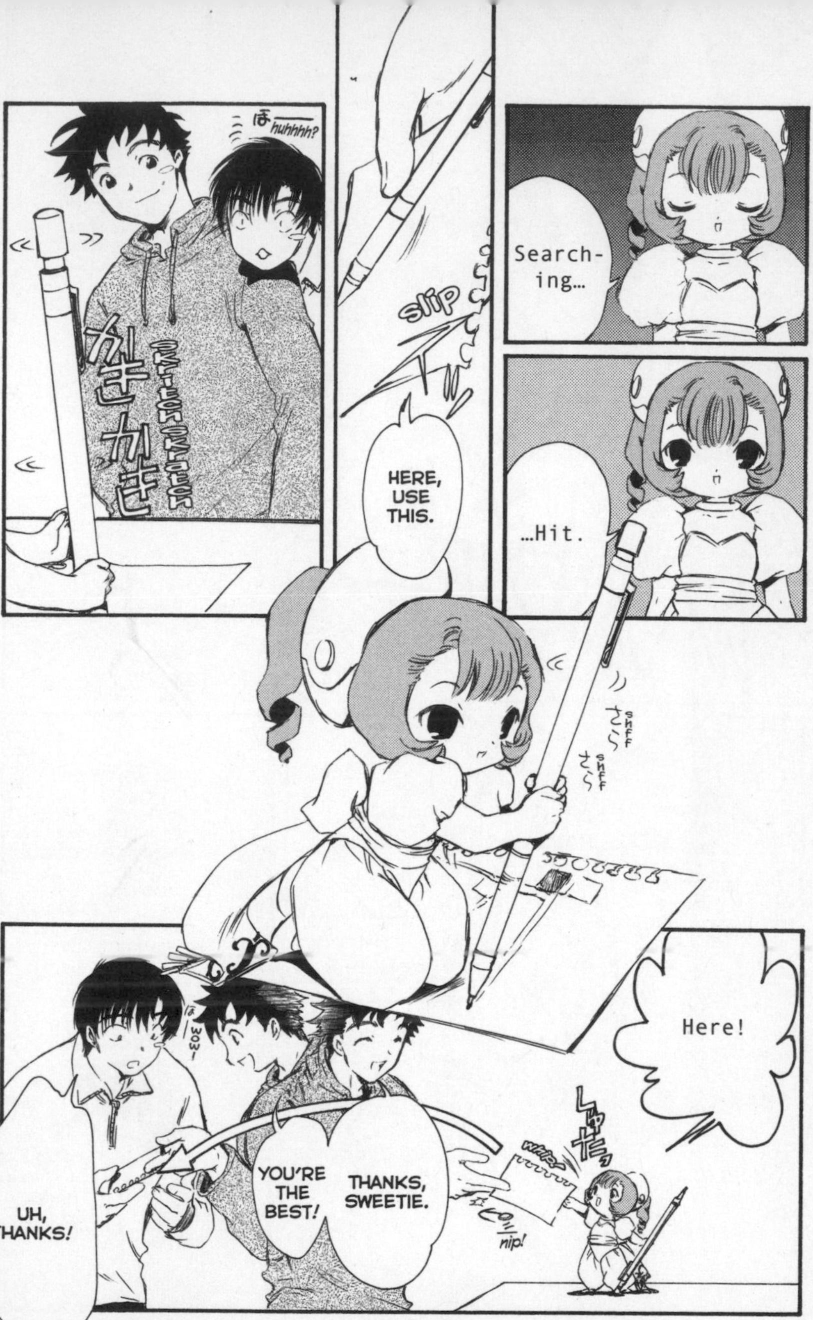
Search-
ing...
...Hit.
slip
HERE, USE THIS.
ほ— huhhhh?
かきかき
scritch scratch
さら shff
さら shff
Here!
しゅたっ
whip—
ピッ
nip!
THANKS, SWEETIE.
YOU'RE THE BEST!
ほ— WOW!
UH, THANKS!

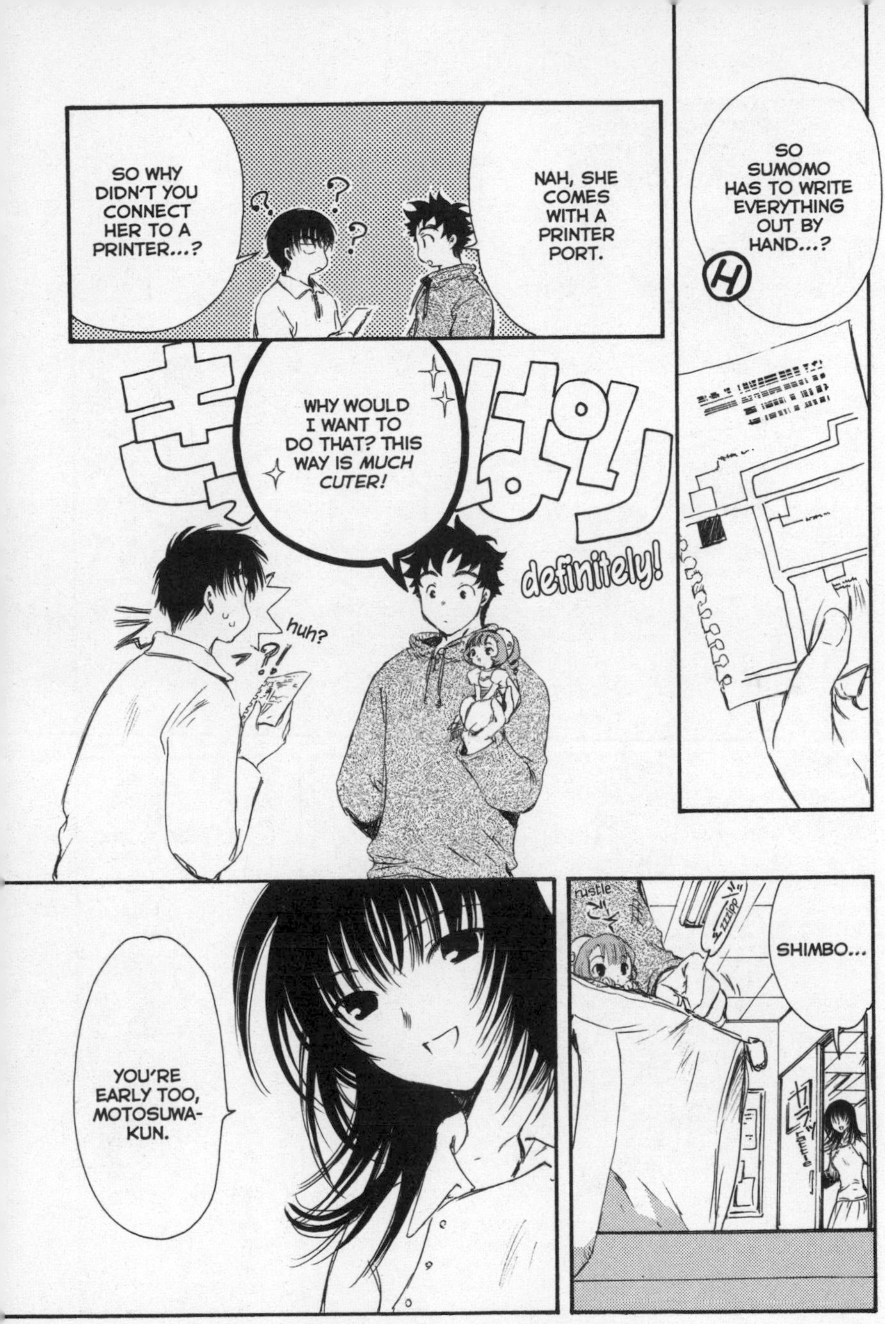

SO SUMOMO HAS TO WRITE EVERYTHING OUT BY HAND...?
H
SO WHY DIDN'T YOU CONNECT HER TO A PRINTER...?
NAH, SHE COMES WITH A PRINTER PORT.
WHY WOULD I WANT TO DO THAT? THIS WAY IS *MUCH* CUTER!
definitely!
huh?
?!
SHIMBO...
rustle
zzzipp
YOU'RE EARLY TOO, MOTOSUWA-KUN.

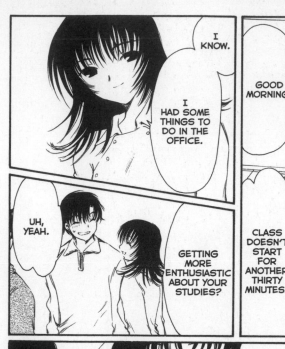

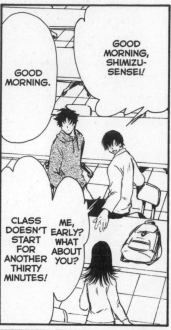

GOOD MORNING, SHIMIZU-SENSEI!
GOOD MORNING.
ME, EARLY? WHAT ABOUT YOU?
CLASS DOESN'T START FOR ANOTHER THIRTY MINUTES!
I KNOW.
I HAD SOME THINGS TO DO IN THE OFFICE.
GETTING MORE ENTHUSIASTIC ABOUT YOUR STUDIES?
UH, YEAH.
I HOPE YOU DID YOUR HOMEWORK. I'M GOING TO CALL ON YOU, MOTOSUWA-KUN.
For the entire first assignment!
WHAAAAT?!
C'MON, IT'LL BE GOOD FOR YOU.
wobble

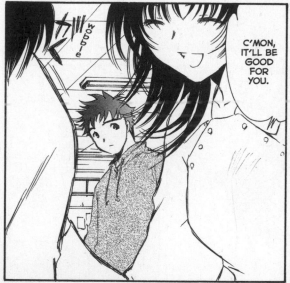

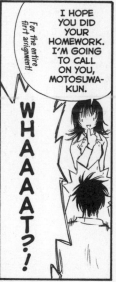

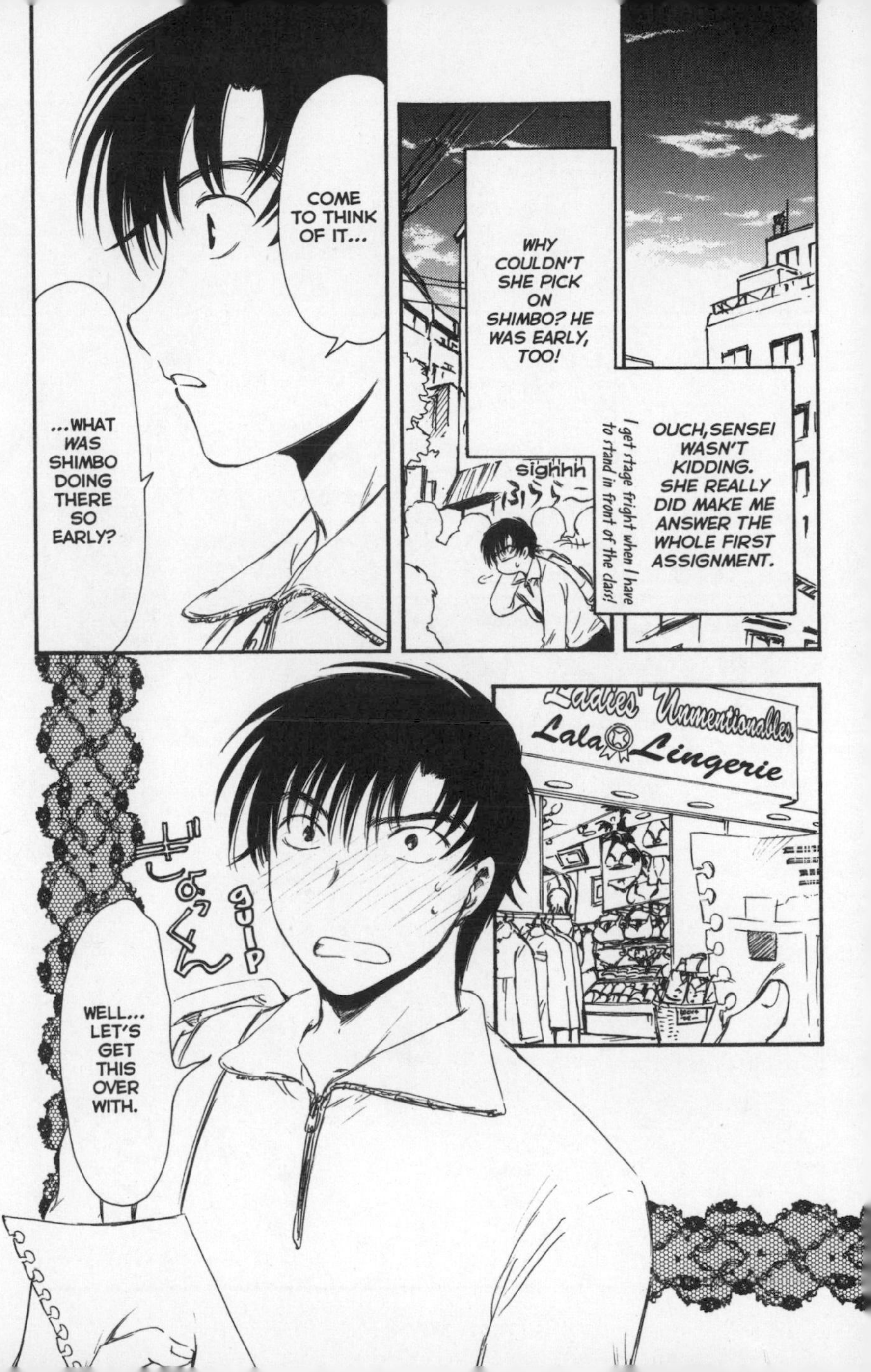
OUCH, SENSEI WASN'T KIDDING. SHE REALLY DID MAKE ME ANSWER THE WHOLE FIRST ASSIGNMENT.
I get stage fright when I have to stand in front of the class!
WHY COULDN'T SHE PICK ON SHIMBO? HE WAS EARLY, TOO!
sighhh
ふらら～
COME TO THINK OF IT...
...WHAT WAS SHIMBO DOING THERE SO EARLY?
Ladies' Unmentionables
Lala Lingerie
gulp
ぎゅっくん
WELL... LET'S GET THIS OVER WITH.

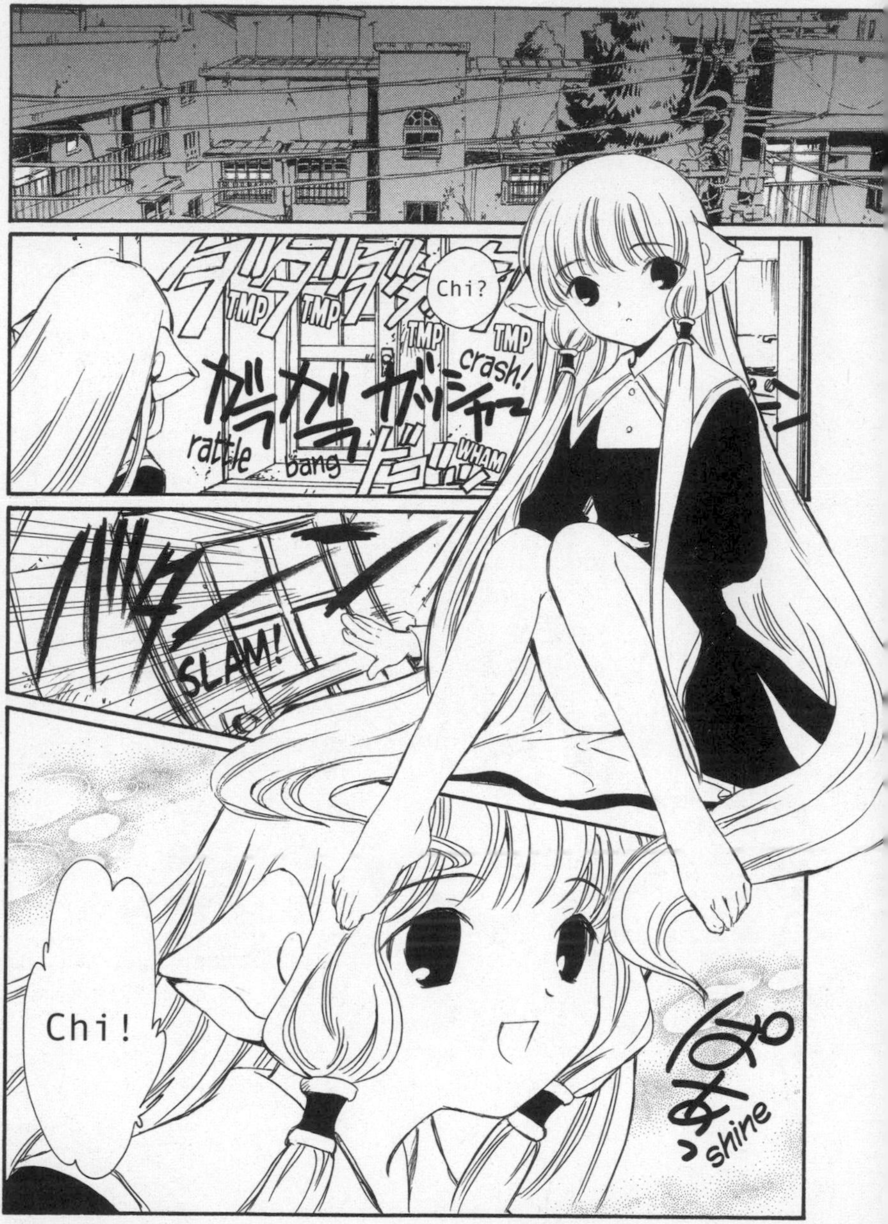
Chi?
TMP
TMP
TMP
TMP
crash!
WHAM
bang
rattle
SLAM!
shine
Chi!

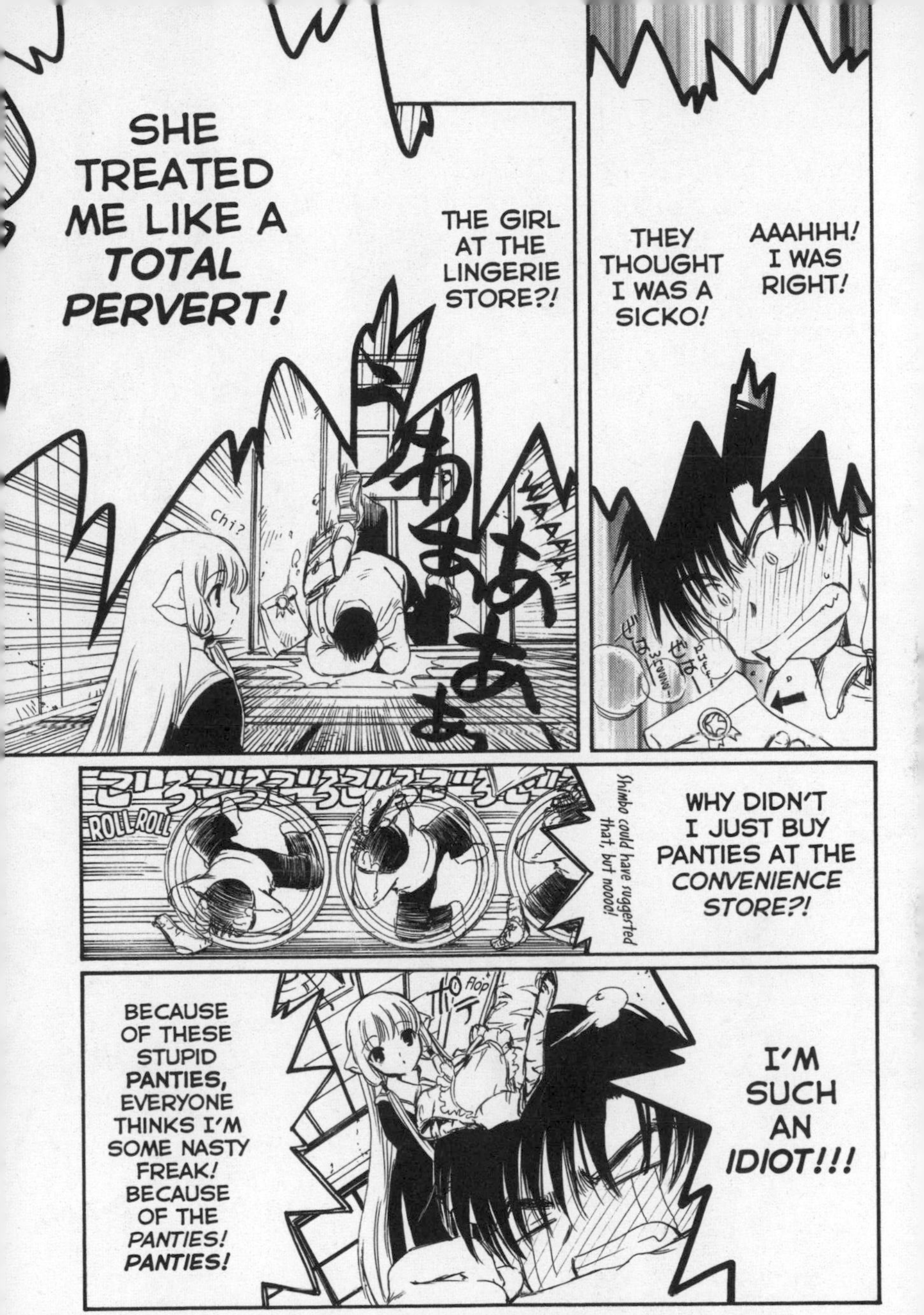
AAAHHH! I WAS RIGHT!
THEY THOUGHT I WAS A SICKO!
THE GIRL AT THE LINGERIE STORE?!
SHE TREATED ME LIKE A TOTAL PERVERT!
Chi?
WHY DIDN'T I JUST BUY PANTIES AT THE CONVENIENCE STORE?!
Shimbo could have suggested that, but noooo!
ROLL ROLL
I'M SUCH AN IDIOT!!!
Flop
BECAUSE OF THESE STUPID PANTIES, EVERYONE THINKS I'M SOME NASTY FREAK! BECAUSE OF THE PANTIES! PANTIES!

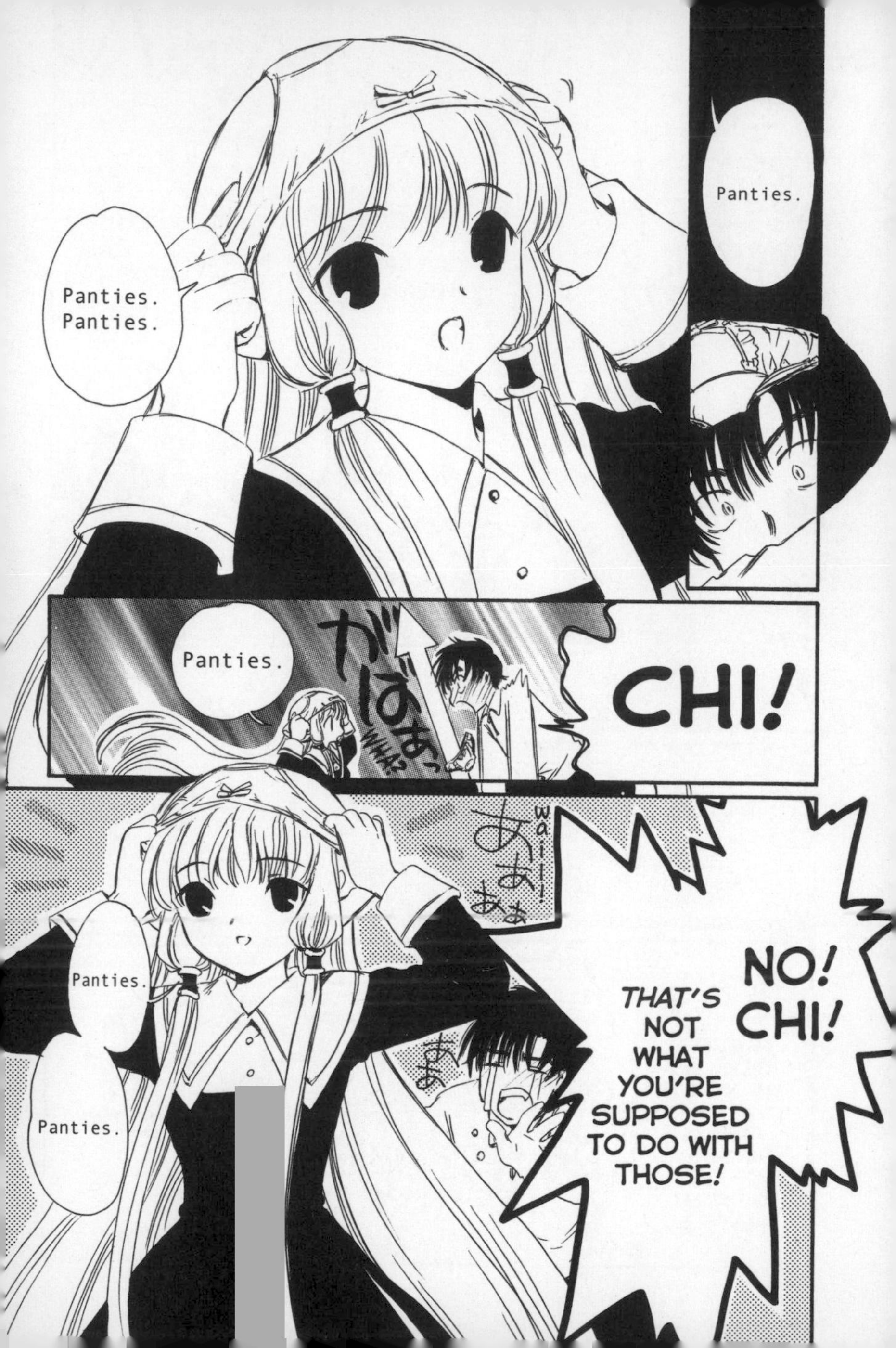
Panties.
Panties.
Panties.
CHI!
がばぁっ
Panties.
NO! CHI!
THAT'S NOT WHAT YOU'RE SUPPOSED TO DO WITH THOSE!
あああ
wail!
Panties.
Panties.

Chobits
ちょびっツ

◀ chapter 8 ▶

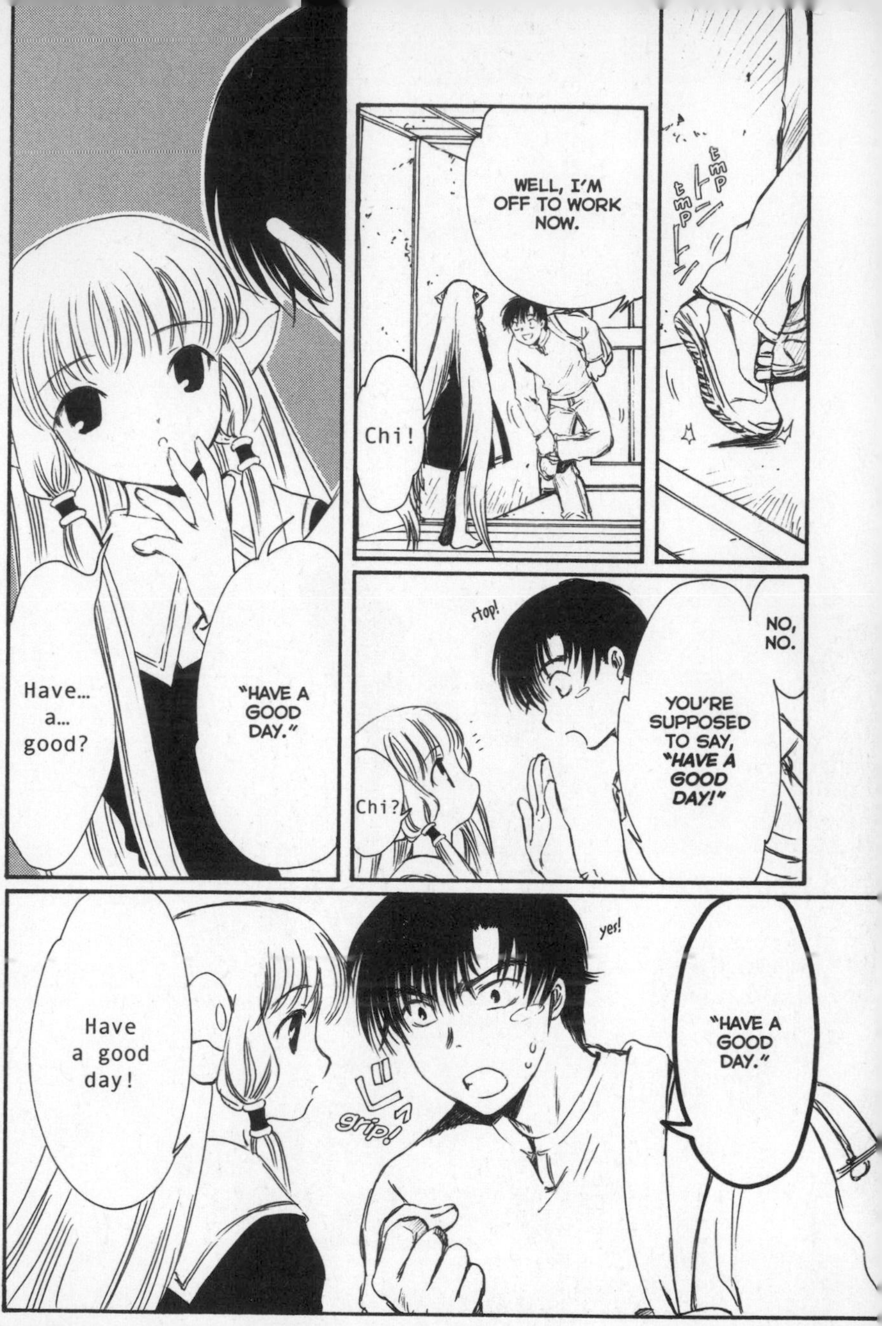
tmp
tmp
WELL, I'M OFF TO WORK NOW.
Chi!
NO, NO.
YOU'RE SUPPOSED TO SAY, "HAVE A GOOD DAY!"
stop!
Chi?
"HAVE A GOOD DAY."
Have... a... good?
"HAVE A GOOD DAY."
yes!
grip!
Have a good day!

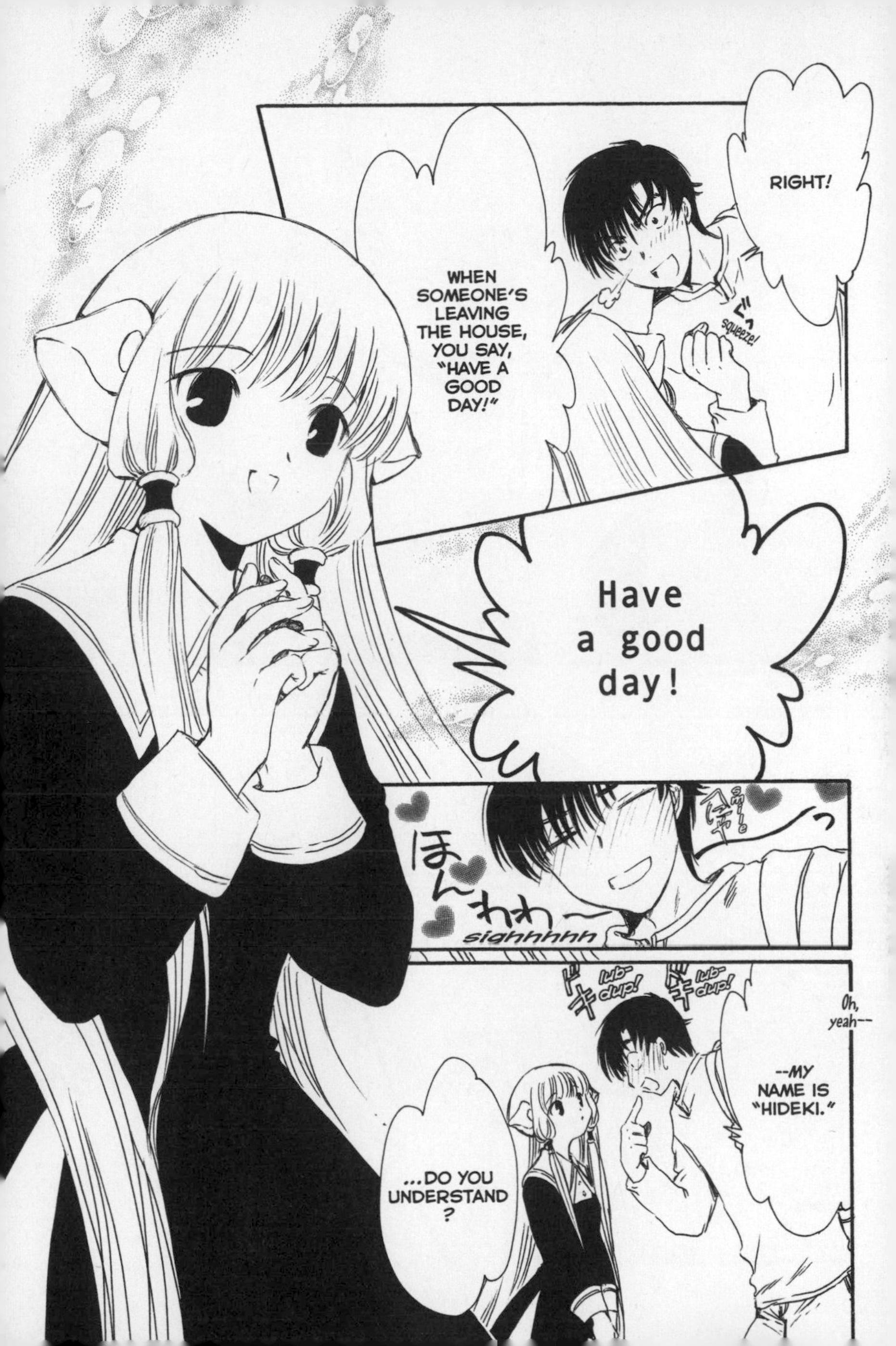
RIGHT!
WHEN SOMEONE'S LEAVING THE HOUSE, YOU SAY, "HAVE A GOOD DAY!"
squeeze!
Have a good day!
smile
ほんわわ~
sighhhhh
lub-dup!
lub-dup!
Oh, yeah--
--MY NAME IS "HIDEKI."
...DO YOU UNDERSTAND?

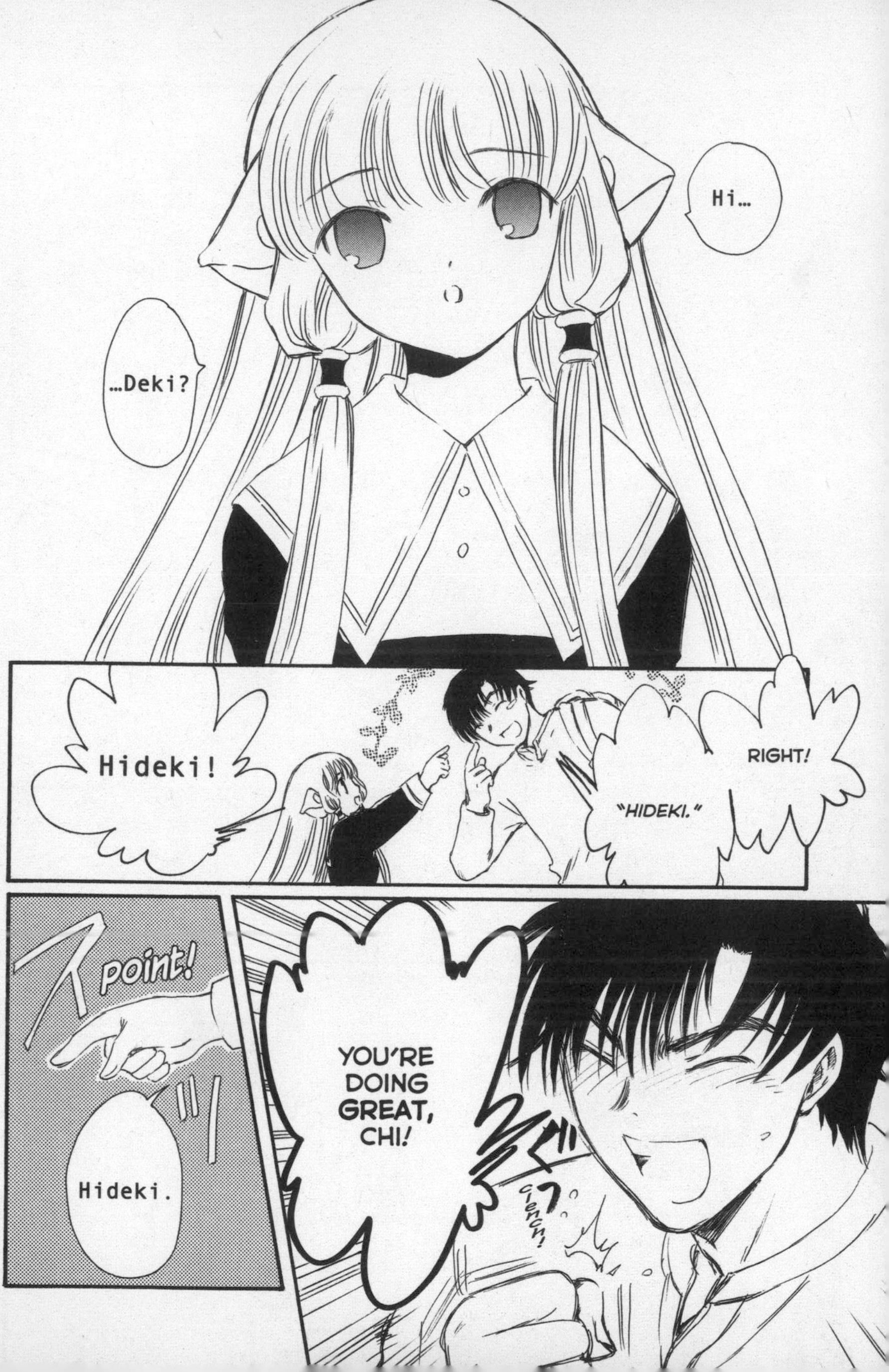
Hi…
…Deki?
RIGHT!
"HIDEKI."
Hideki!
YOU'RE DOING GREAT, CHI!
clench!
point!
Hideki.

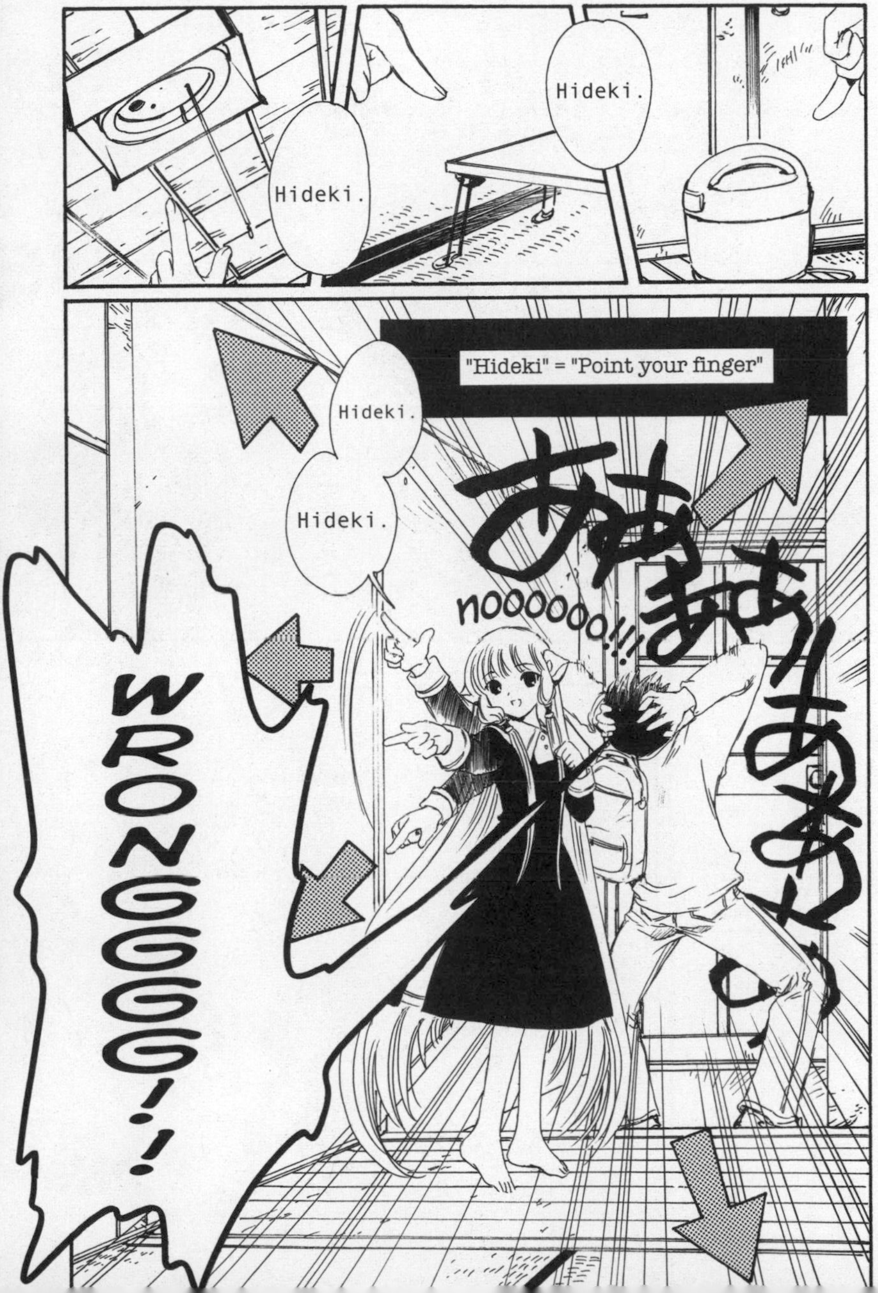
Hideki.
Hideki.
"Hideki" = "Point your finger"
Hideki.
Hideki.
noooooo!!!
WRONGGGG!!!

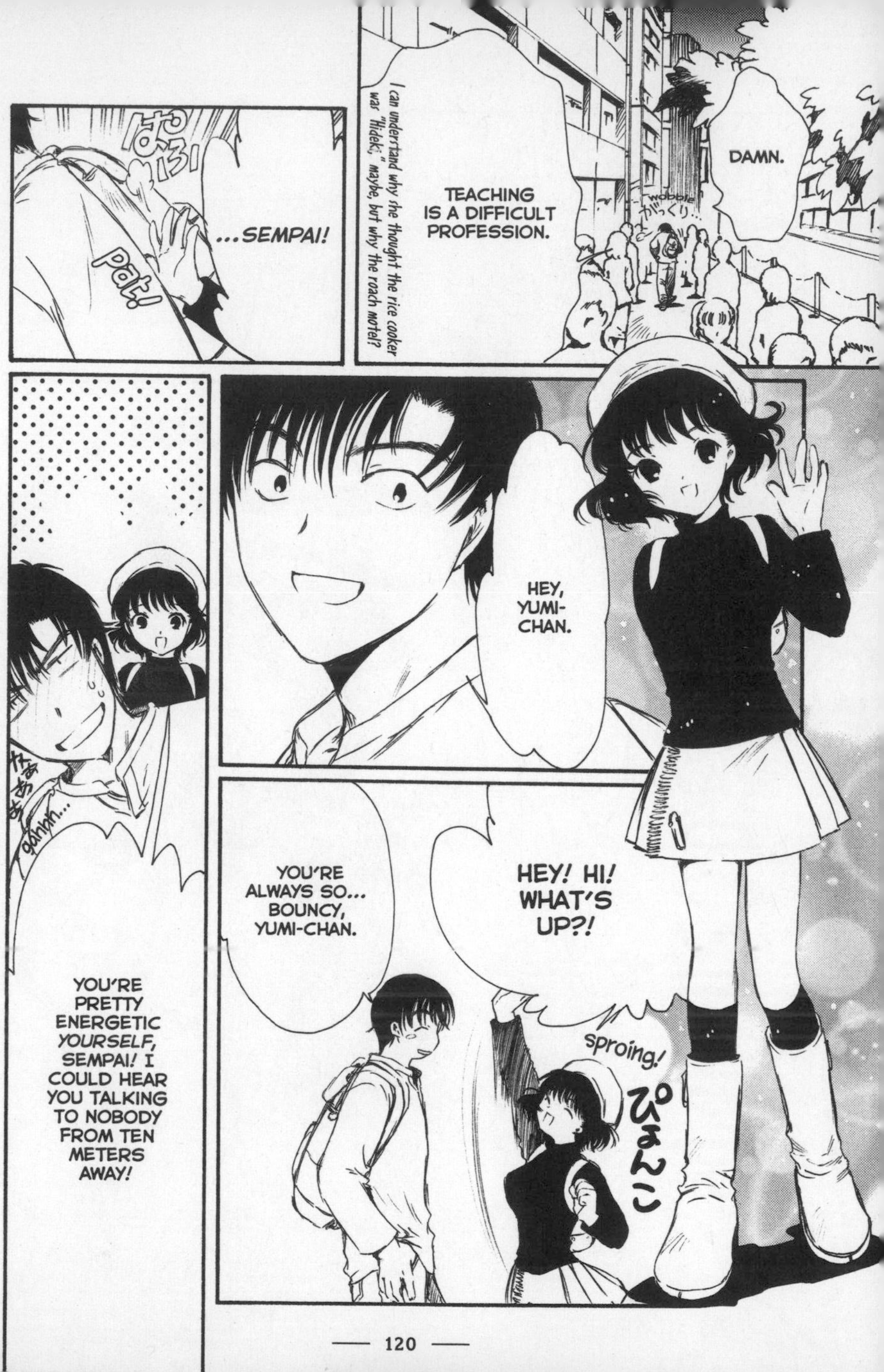
DAMN.
wobble
がっくり…
TEACHING IS A DIFFICULT PROFESSION.
I can understand why she thought the rice cooker was "Hideki," maybe, but why the roach motel?
はろ
...SEMPAI!
Pat!
HEY, YUMI-CHAN.
HEY! HI! WHAT'S UP?!
YOU'RE ALWAYS SO... BOUNCY, YUMI-CHAN.
Sproing!
ぴょんこ
aahhh...
YOU'RE PRETTY ENERGETIC *YOURSELF*, SEMPAI! I COULD HEAR YOU TALKING TO NOBODY FROM TEN METERS AWAY!

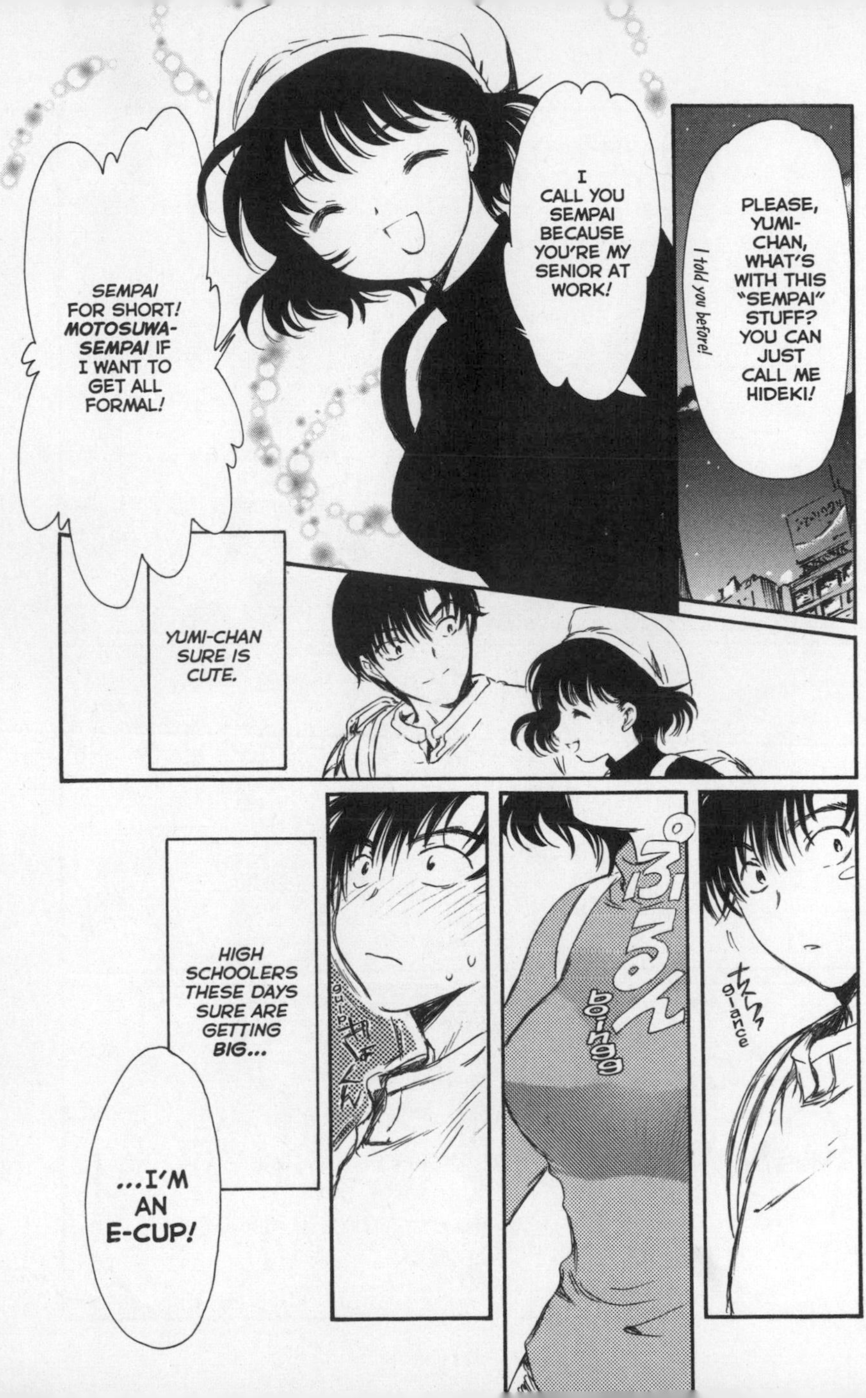
PLEASE, YUMI-CHAN, WHAT'S WITH THIS "SEMPAI" STUFF? YOU CAN JUST CALL ME HIDEKI!
I told you before!
I CALL YOU SEMPAI BECAUSE YOU'RE MY SENIOR AT WORK!
SEMPAI FOR SHORT! MOTOSUWA-SEMPAI IF I WANT TO GET ALL FORMAL!
YUMI-CHAN SURE IS CUTE.
glance
ぷるん
boing
gulp
HIGH SCHOOLERS THESE DAYS SURE ARE GETTING BIG...
...I'M AN E-CUP!

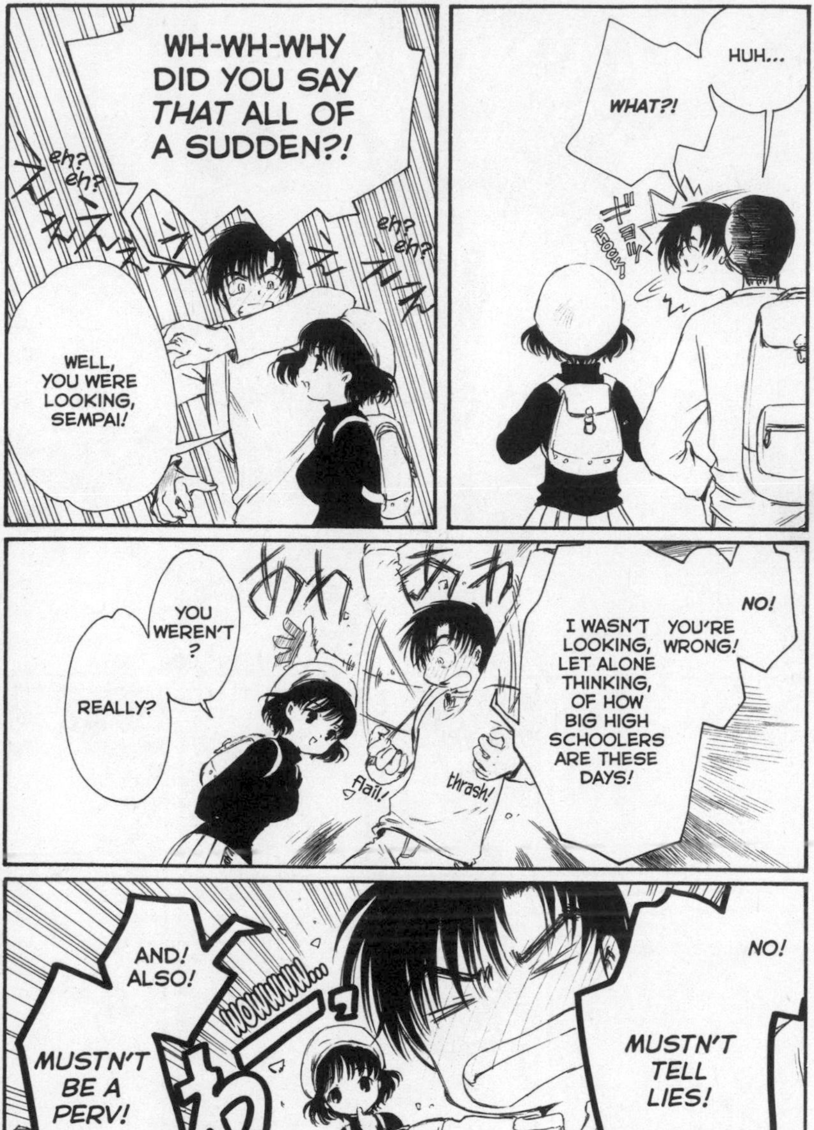
HUH...
WHAT?!
ギョッ
GASOOK!
WH-WH-WHY DID YOU SAY *THAT* ALL OF A SUDDEN?!
eh? eh?
eh? eh?
WELL, YOU WERE LOOKING, SEMPAI!
NO!
YOU'RE WRONG!
I WASN'T LOOKING, LET ALONE THINKING, OF HOW BIG HIGH SCHOOLERS ARE THESE DAYS!
あわ あわ
thrash!
flail!
YOU WEREN'T?
REALLY?
NO!
MUSTN'T TELL LIES!
わ
WOWWWW...
AND! ALSO!
MUSTN'T BE A PERV!

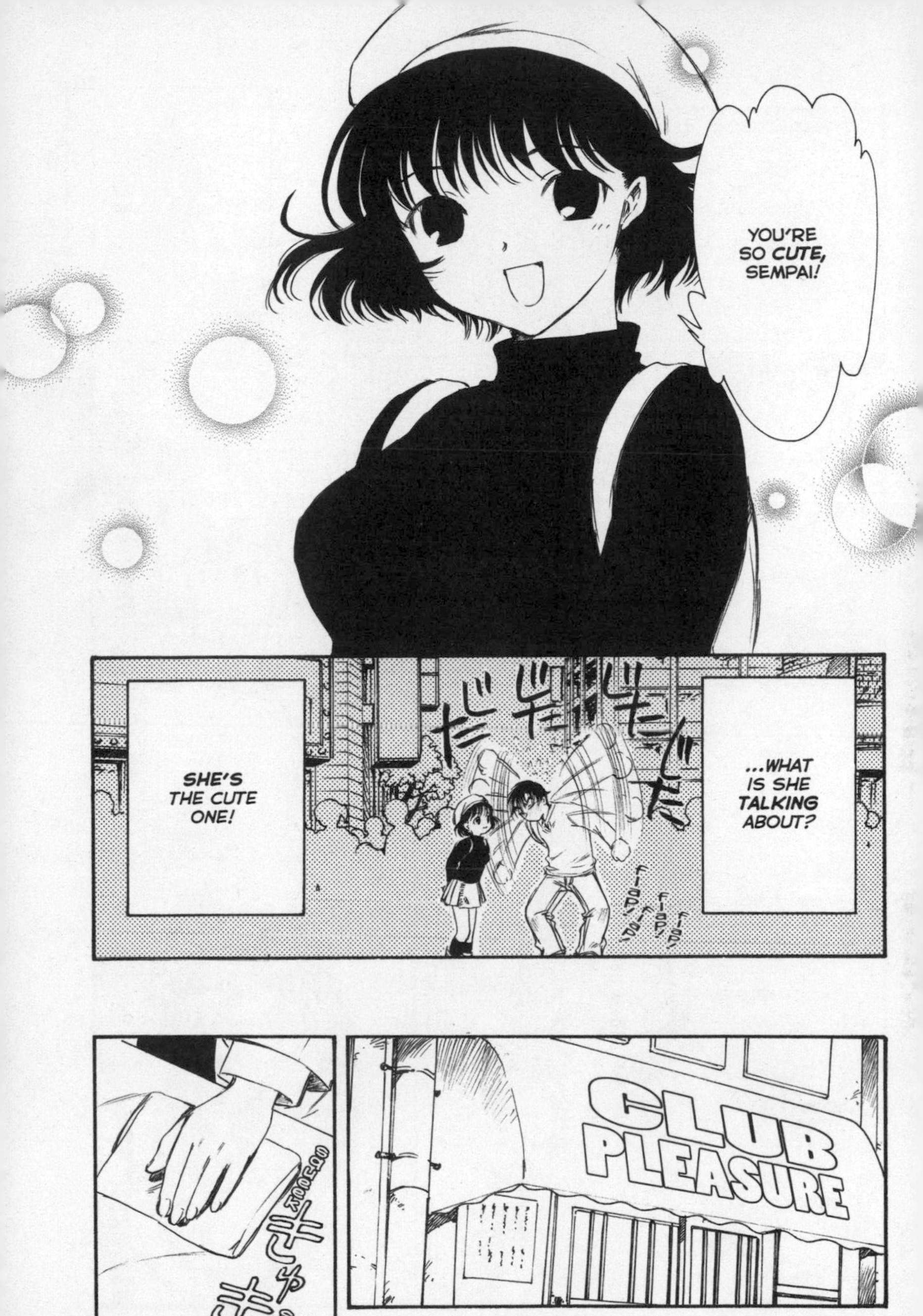
YOU'RE SO CUTE, SEMPAI!
...WHAT IS SHE TALKING ABOUT?
だだだだ
SHE'S THE CUTE ONE!
FLAP! FLAP! FLAP! FLAP!
CLUB PLEASURE
キュッキュッ

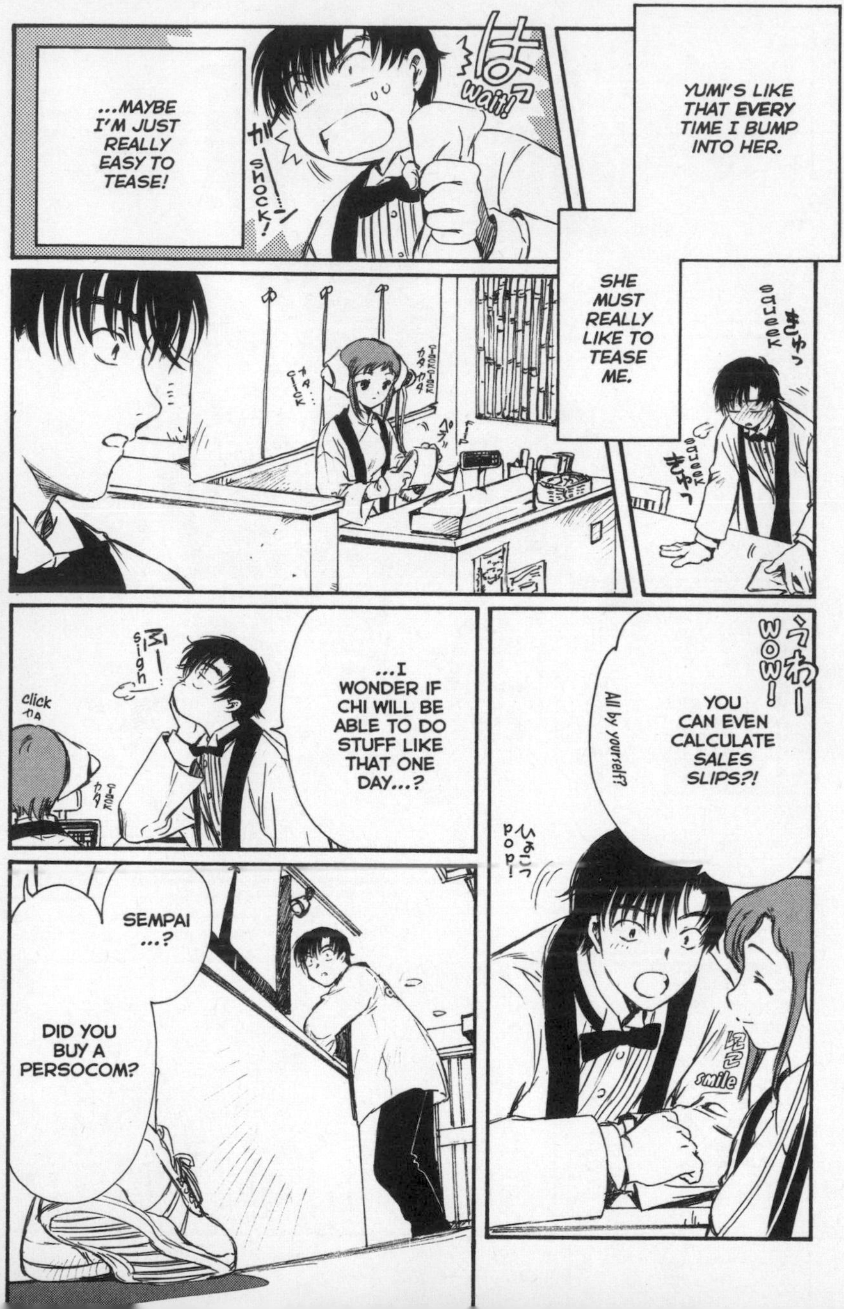
YUMI'S LIKE THAT EVERY TIME I BUMP INTO HER.
はっ
wait!
ガーン
SHOCK!
...MAYBE I'M JUST REALLY EASY TO TEASE!
SHE MUST REALLY LIKE TO TEASE ME.
きゅっ
squeek
きゅっ
squeek
カタカタ
click click
パラ
flip
カタ
click
うわー
WOW!
YOU CAN EVEN CALCULATE SALES SLIPS?!
All by yourself?
ひょこ
pop!
にこ
smile
ふー
sigh
...I WONDER IF CHI WILL BE ABLE TO DO STUFF LIKE THAT ONE DAY...?
click
カタ
click
カタ
SEMPAI ...?
DID YOU BUY A PERSOCOM?

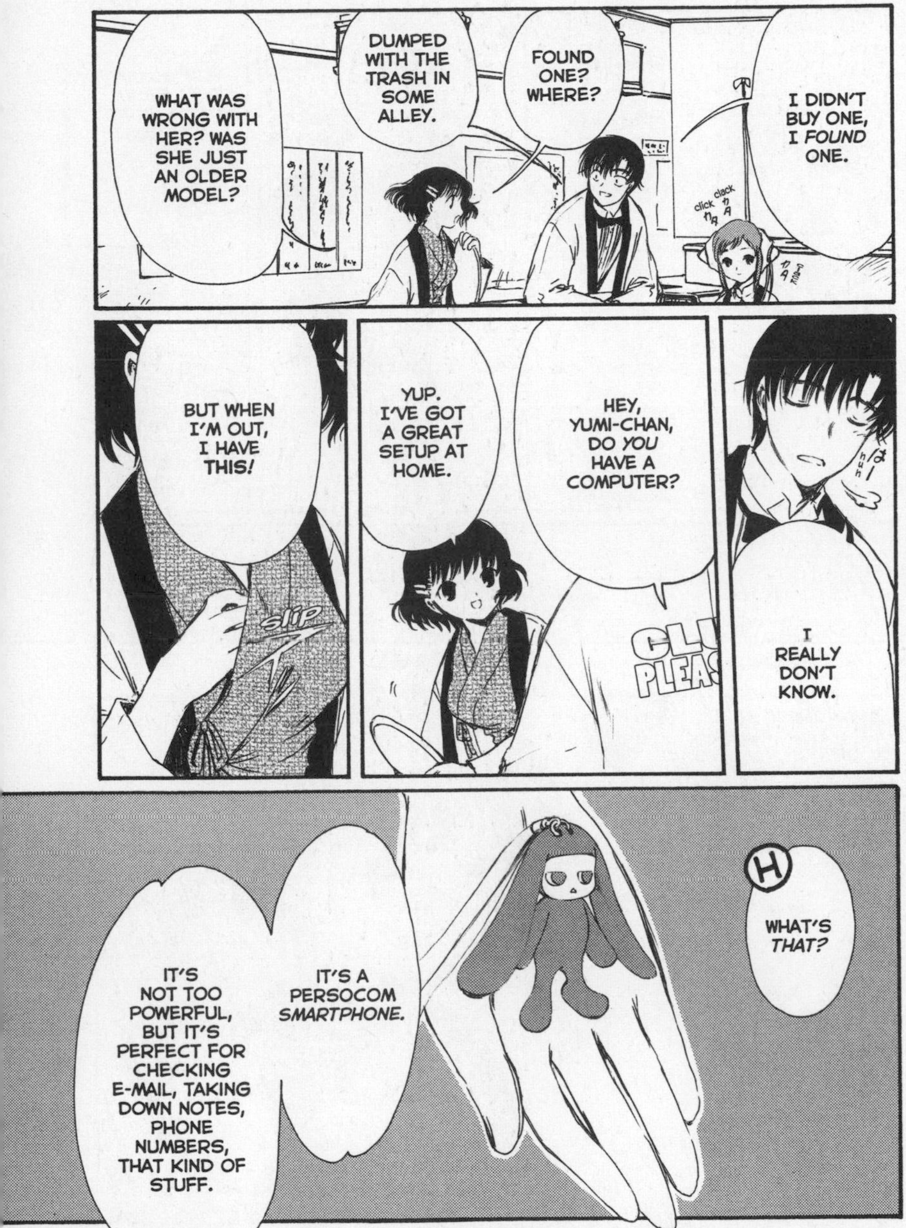
I DIDN'T BUY ONE, I *FOUND* ONE.
click clack
FOUND ONE? WHERE?
DUMPED WITH THE TRASH IN SOME ALLEY.
WHAT WAS WRONG WITH HER? WAS SHE JUST AN OLDER MODEL?
huh
I REALLY DON'T KNOW.
HEY, YUMI-CHAN, DO *YOU* HAVE A COMPUTER?
YUP. I'VE GOT A GREAT SETUP AT HOME.
BUT WHEN I'M OUT, I HAVE **THIS!**
slip
WHAT'S *THAT?*
IT'S A PERSOCOM *SMARTPHONE.*
IT'S NOT TOO POWERFUL, BUT IT'S PERFECT FOR CHECKING E-MAIL, TAKING DOWN NOTES, PHONE NUMBERS, THAT KIND OF STUFF.

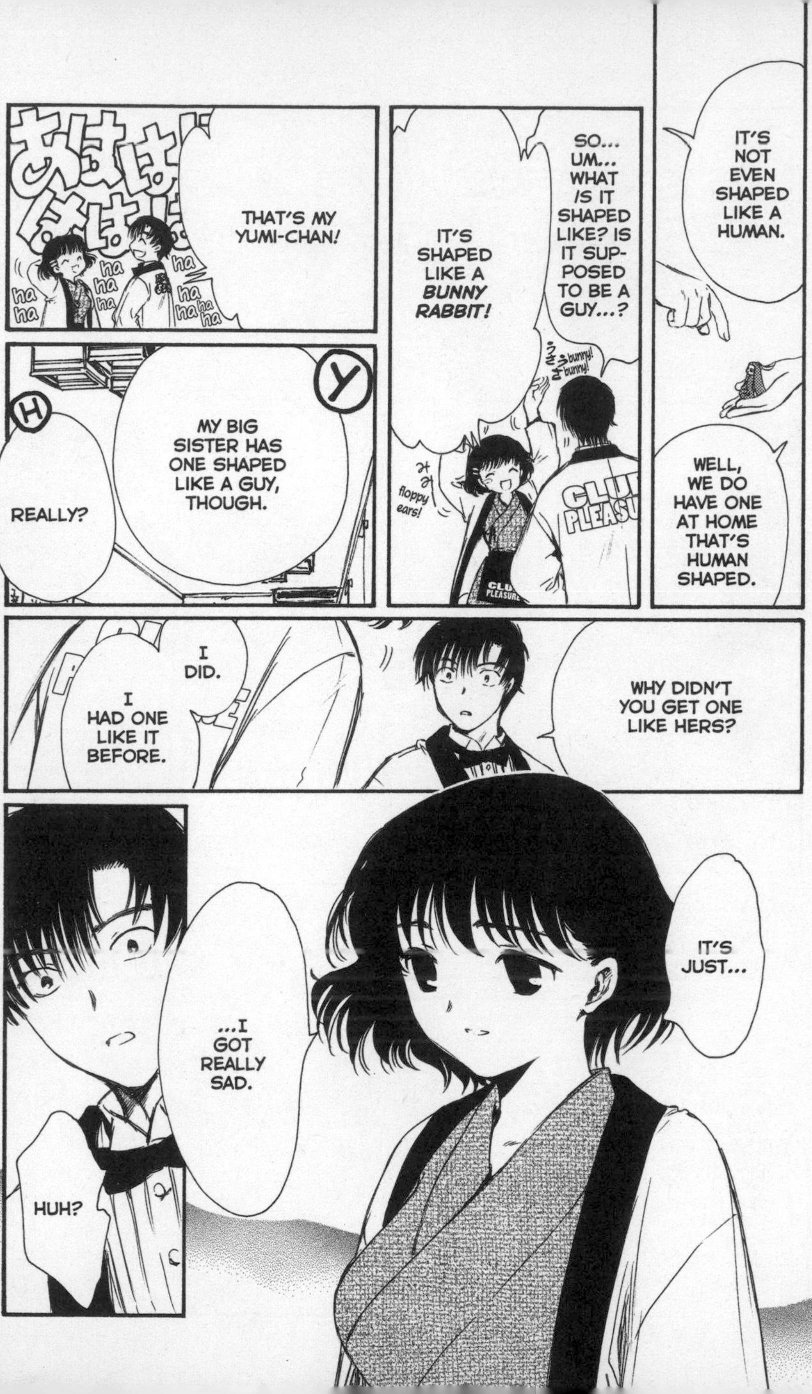
IT'S NOT EVEN SHAPED LIKE A HUMAN.
WELL, WE DO HAVE ONE AT HOME THAT'S HUMAN SHAPED.
SO... UM... WHAT *IS* IT SHAPED LIKE? IS IT SUPPOSED TO BE A GUY...?
IT'S SHAPED LIKE A *BUNNY RABBIT!*
bunny! bunny!
floppy ears!
THAT'S MY YUMI-CHAN!
ha ha ha ha ha ha ha ha ha ha
Y
MY BIG SISTER HAS ONE SHAPED LIKE A GUY, THOUGH.
H
REALLY?
WHY DIDN'T YOU GET ONE LIKE HERS?
I DID.
I HAD ONE LIKE IT BEFORE.
IT'S JUST...
...I GOT REALLY SAD.
HUH?

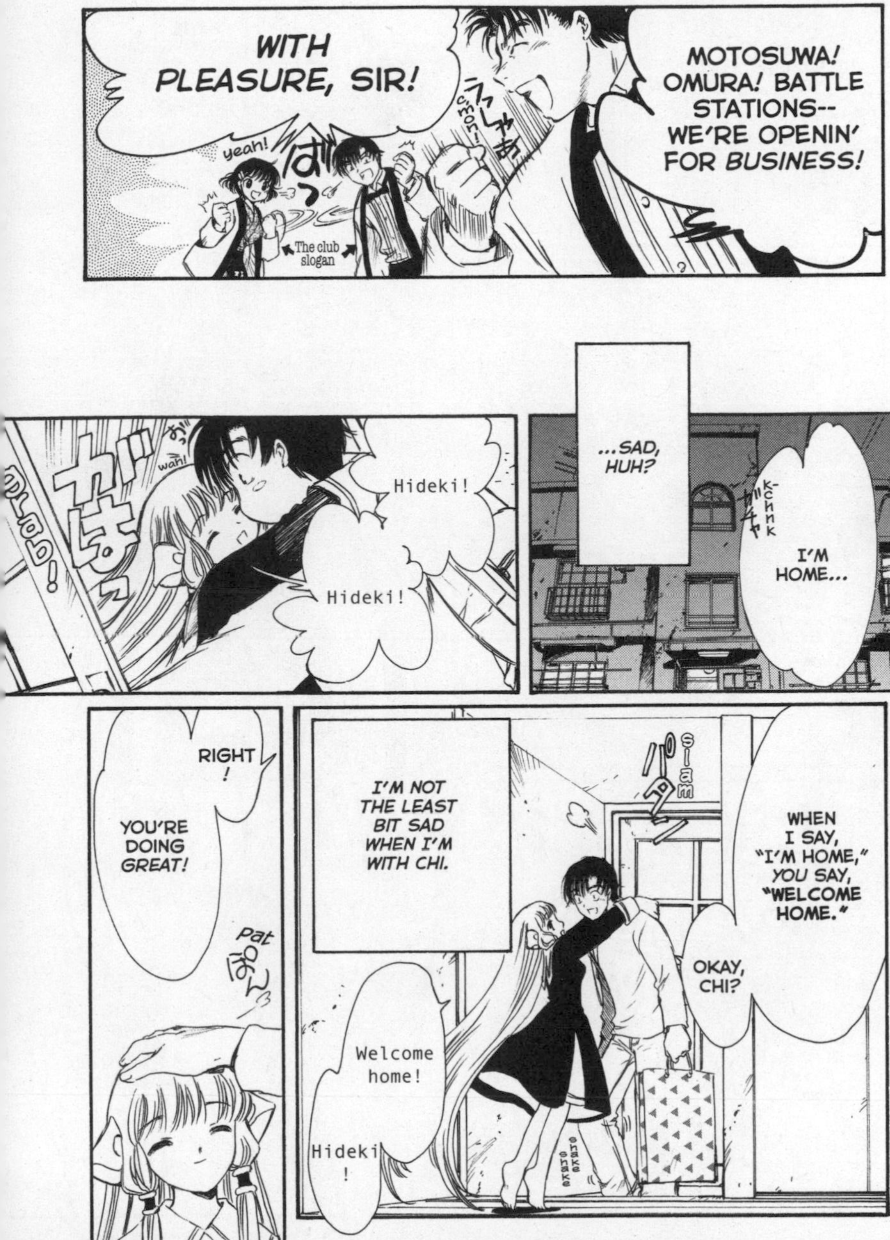
MOTOSUWA! OMURA! BATTLE STATIONS-- WE'RE OPENIN' FOR *BUSINESS!*
c'mon!
WITH PLEASURE, SIR!
yeah!
The club slogan
I'M HOME...
k-chnk
...SAD, HUH?
Hideki!
Hideki!
wah!
WHEN I SAY, "I'M HOME," *YOU* SAY, "WELCOME HOME."
OKAY, CHI?
slam
I'M NOT THE LEAST BIT SAD WHEN I'M WITH CHI.
Welcome home!
Hideki!
shake shake
RIGHT!
YOU'RE DOING GREAT!
Pat

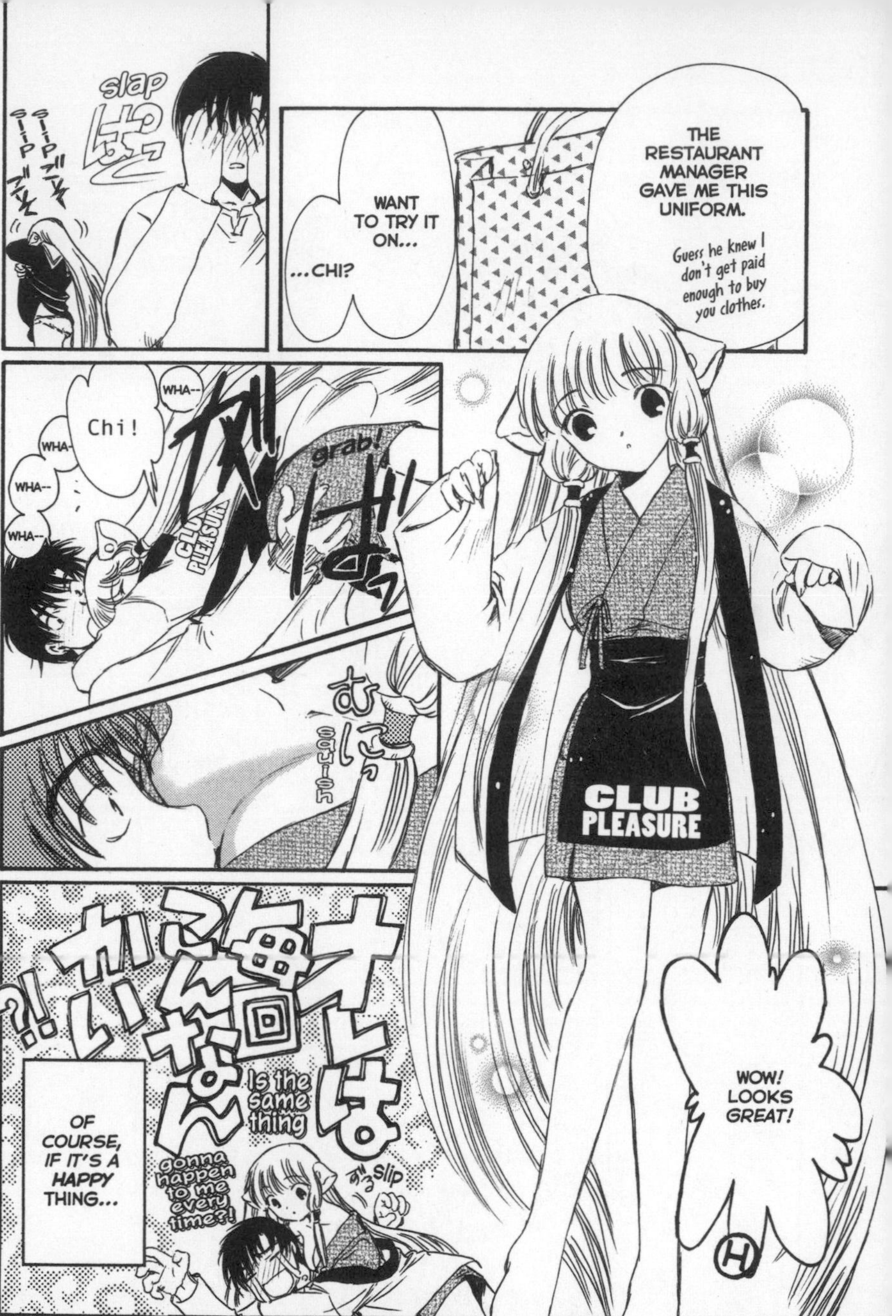

THE RESTAURANT MANAGER GAVE ME THIS UNIFORM.
Guess he knew I don't get paid enough to buy you clothes.
WANT TO TRY IT ON...
...CHI?
slap
slip
slip
CLUB PLEASURE
WOW! LOOKS GREAT!
H
Chi!
WHA--
WHA-
WHA--
WHA--
grab!
CLUB PLEASURE
squish
Is the same thing gonna happen to me every time?!
slip
OF COURSE, IF IT'S A HAPPY THING...

Chobits
ちょびっツ

◀ chapter 9 ▶

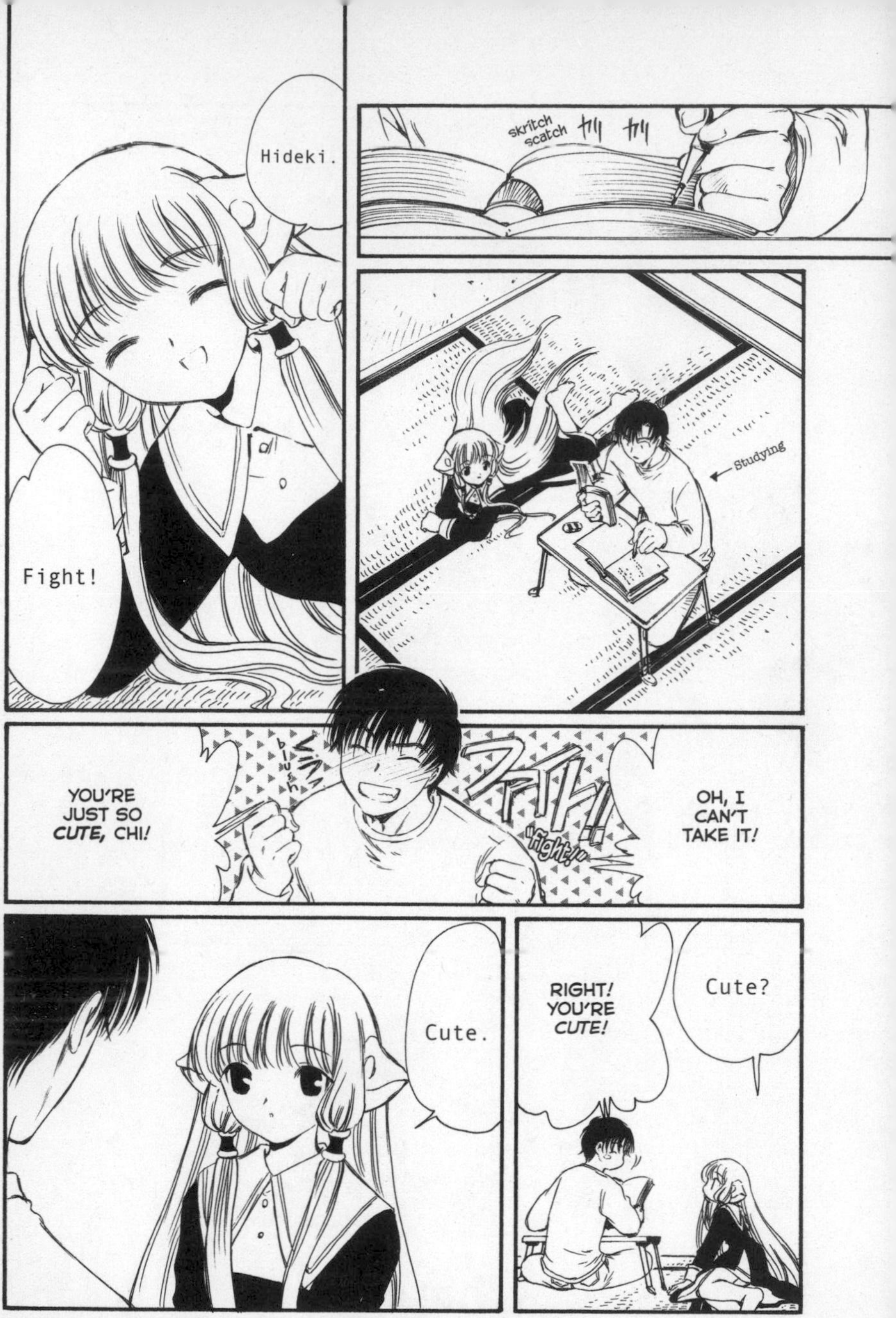
skritch scatch
カリ カリ
Studying
Hideki.
Fight!
OH, I CAN'T TAKE IT!
ファイト!!
"Fight!"
blush
YOU'RE JUST SO *CUTE,* CHI!
Cute?
RIGHT! YOU'RE *CUTE!*
Cute.

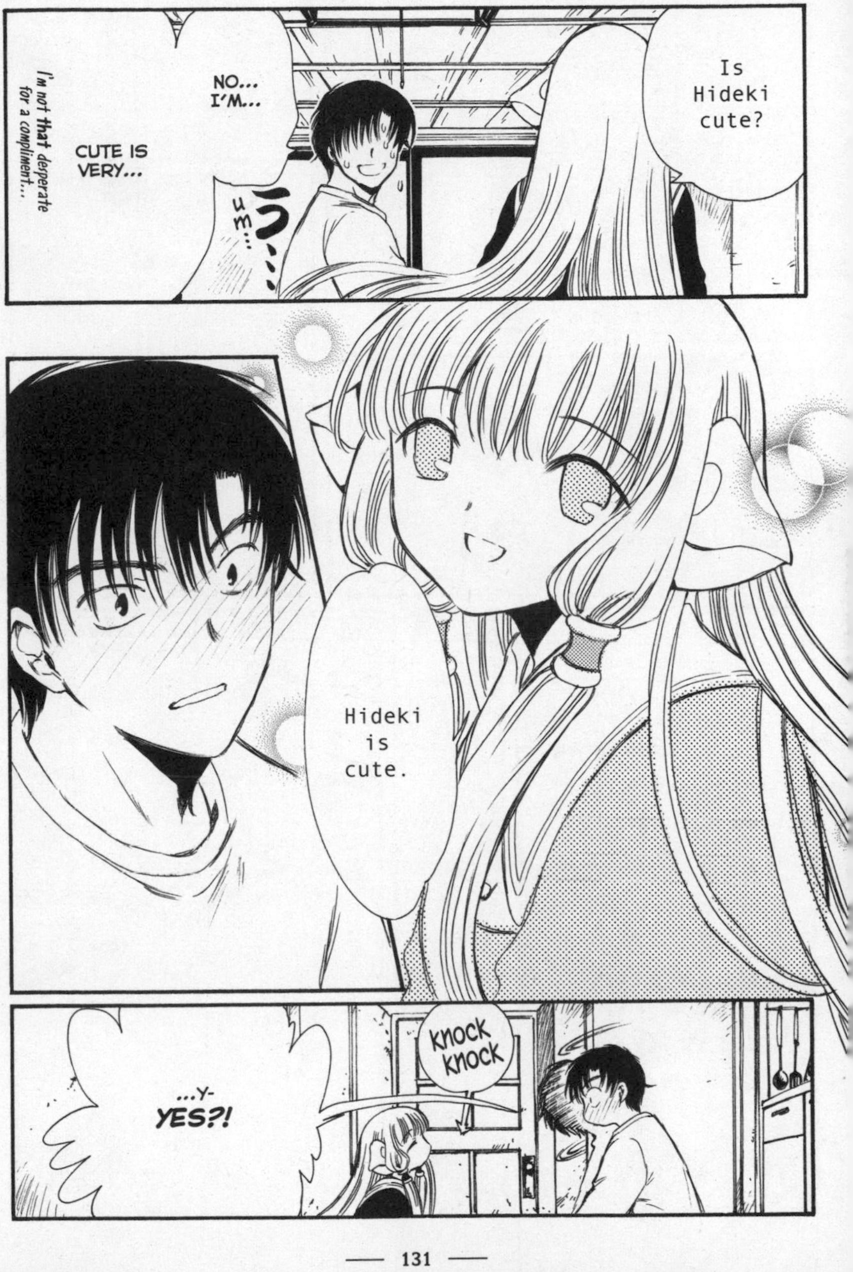

Is Hideki cute?
NO... I'M...
う...
um...
CUTE IS VERY...
I'm not that desperate for a compliment...
Hideki is cute.
knock knock
...Y- YES?!

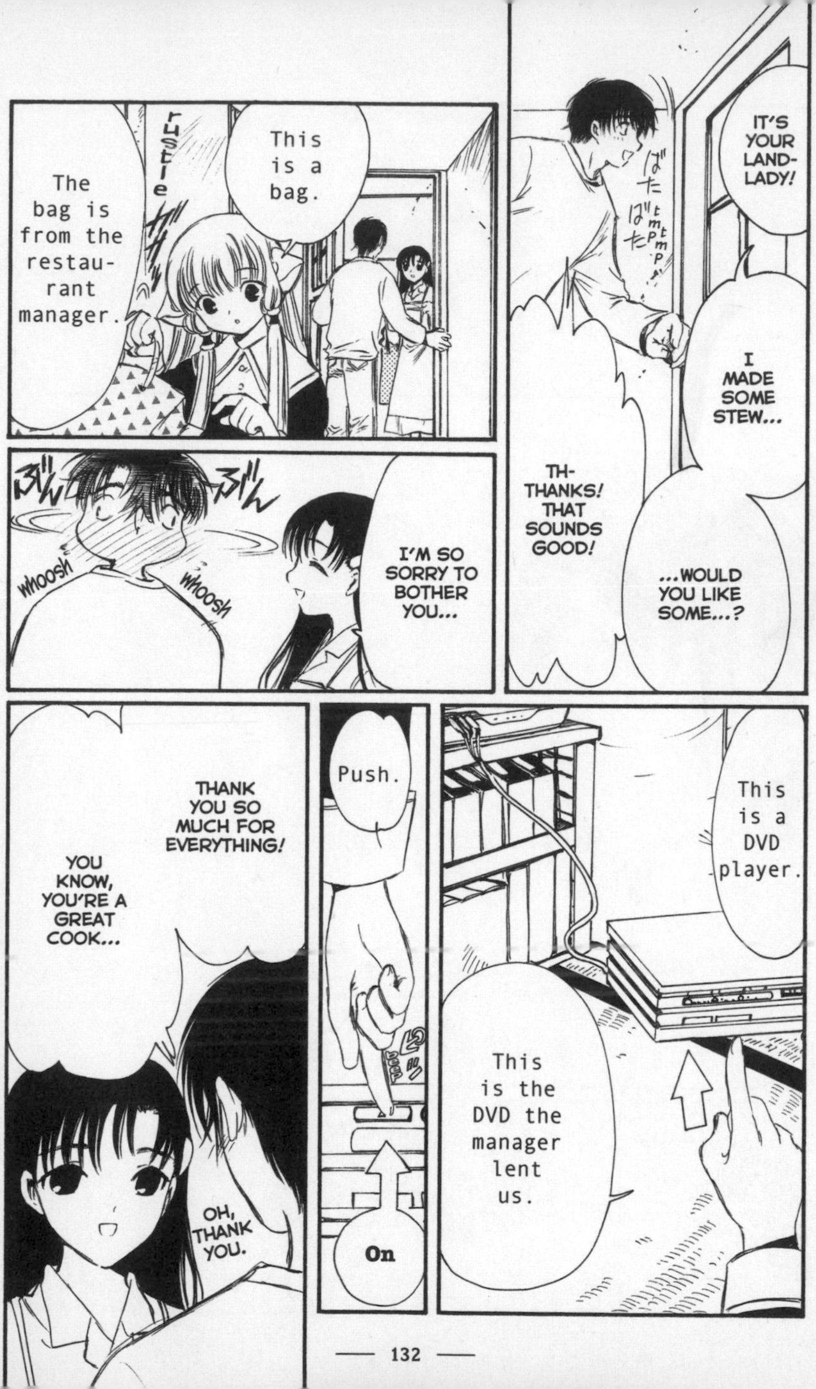
IT'S YOUR LAND-LADY!
ばたばた
tmp tmp
I MADE SOME STEW...
...WOULD YOU LIKE SOME...?
TH-THANKS! THAT SOUNDS GOOD!
This is a bag.
rustle
The bag is from the restau-rant manager.
I'M SO SORRY TO BOTHER YOU...
ぶん ぶん
whoosh
whoosh
This is a DVD player.
This is the DVD the manager lent us.
Push.
On
THANK YOU SO MUCH FOR EVERYTHING!
YOU KNOW, YOU'RE A GREAT COOK...
OH, THANK YOU.

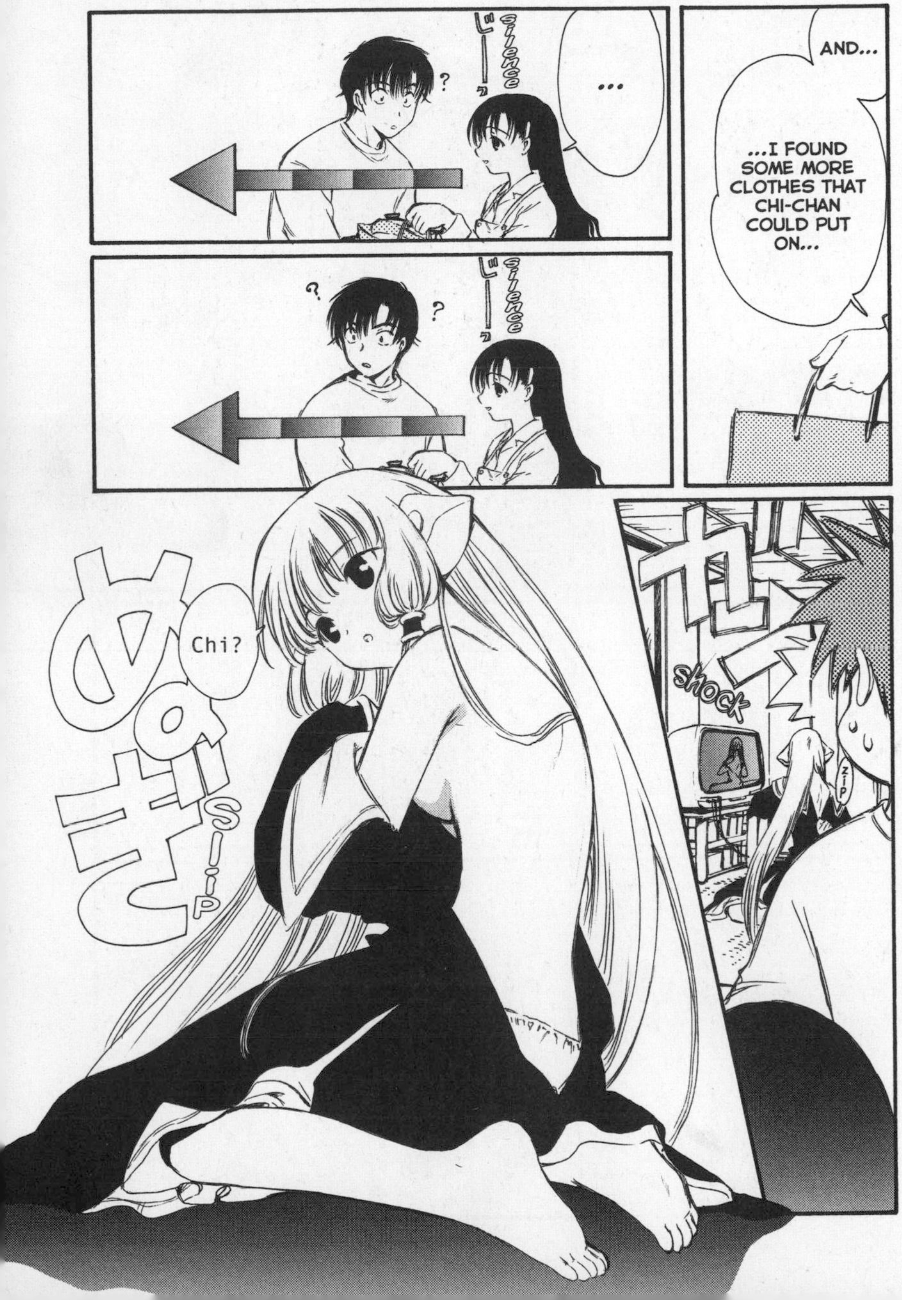
AND...
...I FOUND SOME MORE CLOTHES THAT CHI-CHAN COULD PUT ON...
silence
...
silence
shock
zip
Chi?
slip

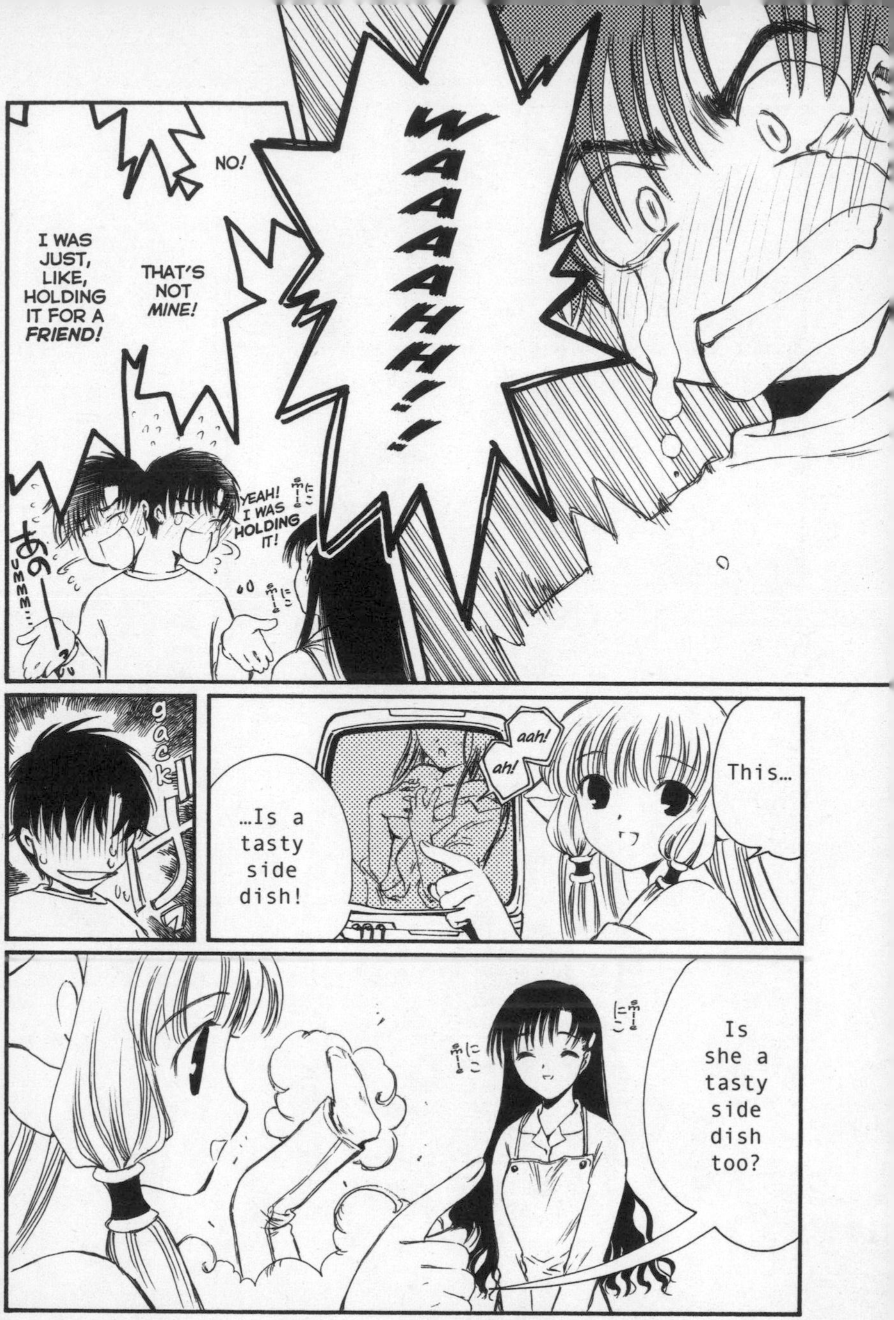
WAAAAHH!!!
NO!
THAT'S NOT MINE!
I WAS JUST, LIKE, HOLDING IT FOR A FRIEND!
YEAH! I WAS HOLDING IT!
にこ smile
にこ smile
あの UMMM...
This…
aah!
ah!
…Is a tasty side dish!
gack
Is she a tasty side dish too?
にこ smile
にこ smile

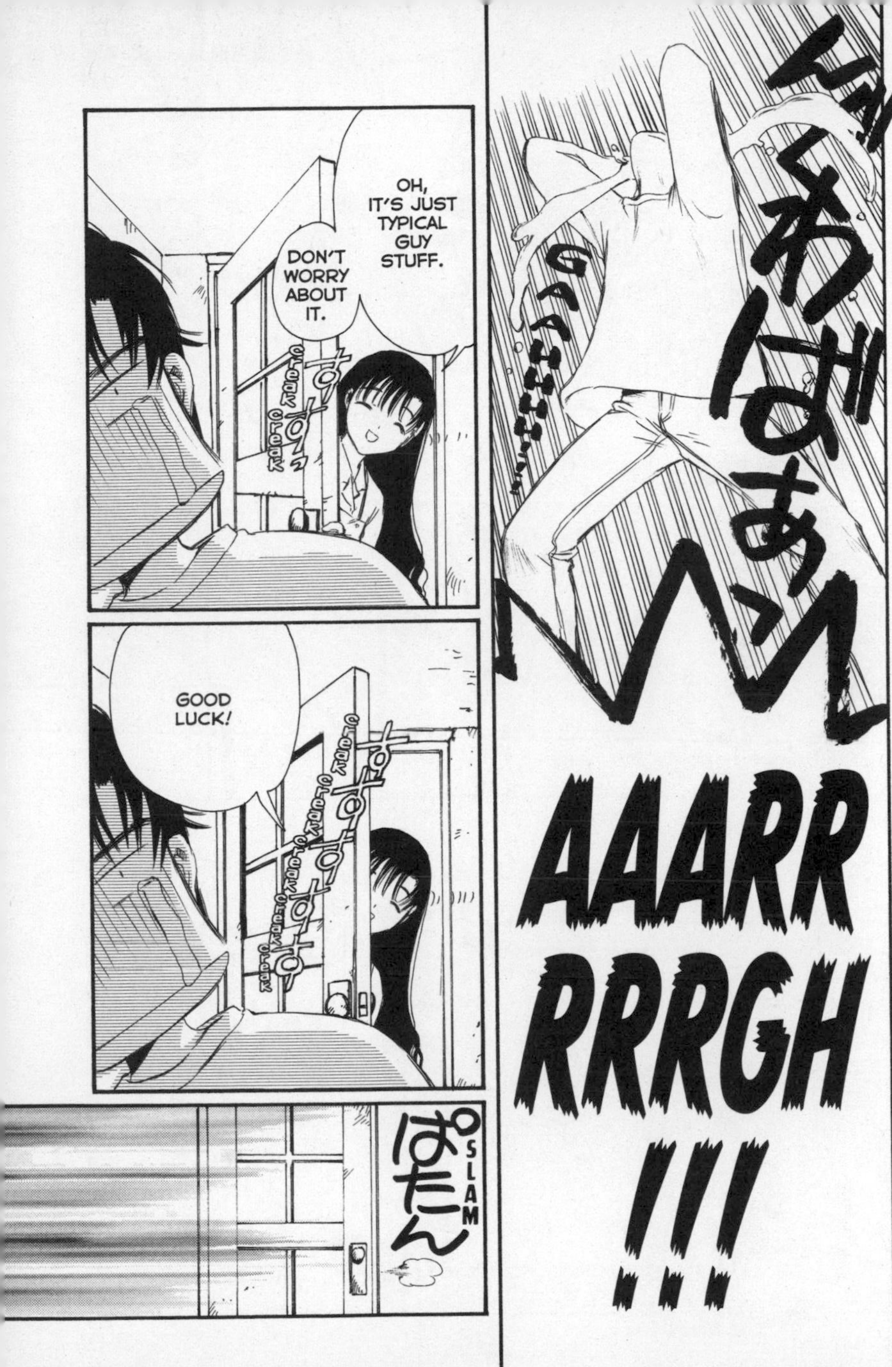
GAAHHHH...
AAARRRRRGH!!!
OH, IT'S JUST TYPICAL GUY STUFF.
DON'T WORRY ABOUT IT.
creak creak
GOOD LUCK!
creak creak creak creak
ぱたん
SLAM

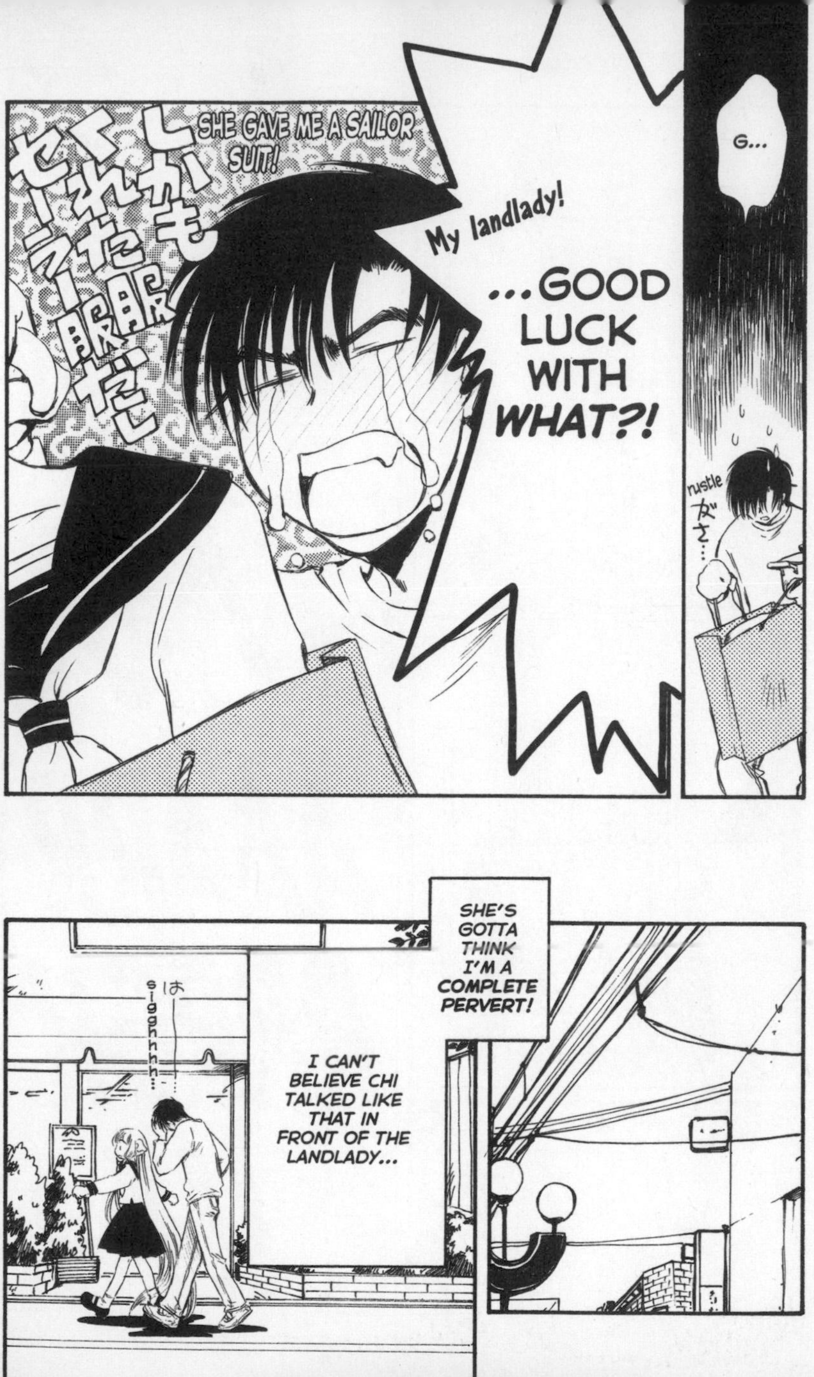
G...
rustle
がさ…
...GOOD LUCK WITH WHAT?!
My landlady!
SHE GAVE ME A SAILOR SUIT!
しかも
くれた服
セーラー服だし
SHE'S GOTTA THINK I'M A COMPLETE PERVERT!
I CAN'T BELIEVE CHI TALKED LIKE THAT IN FRONT OF THE LANDLADY...
sigghhh...
は

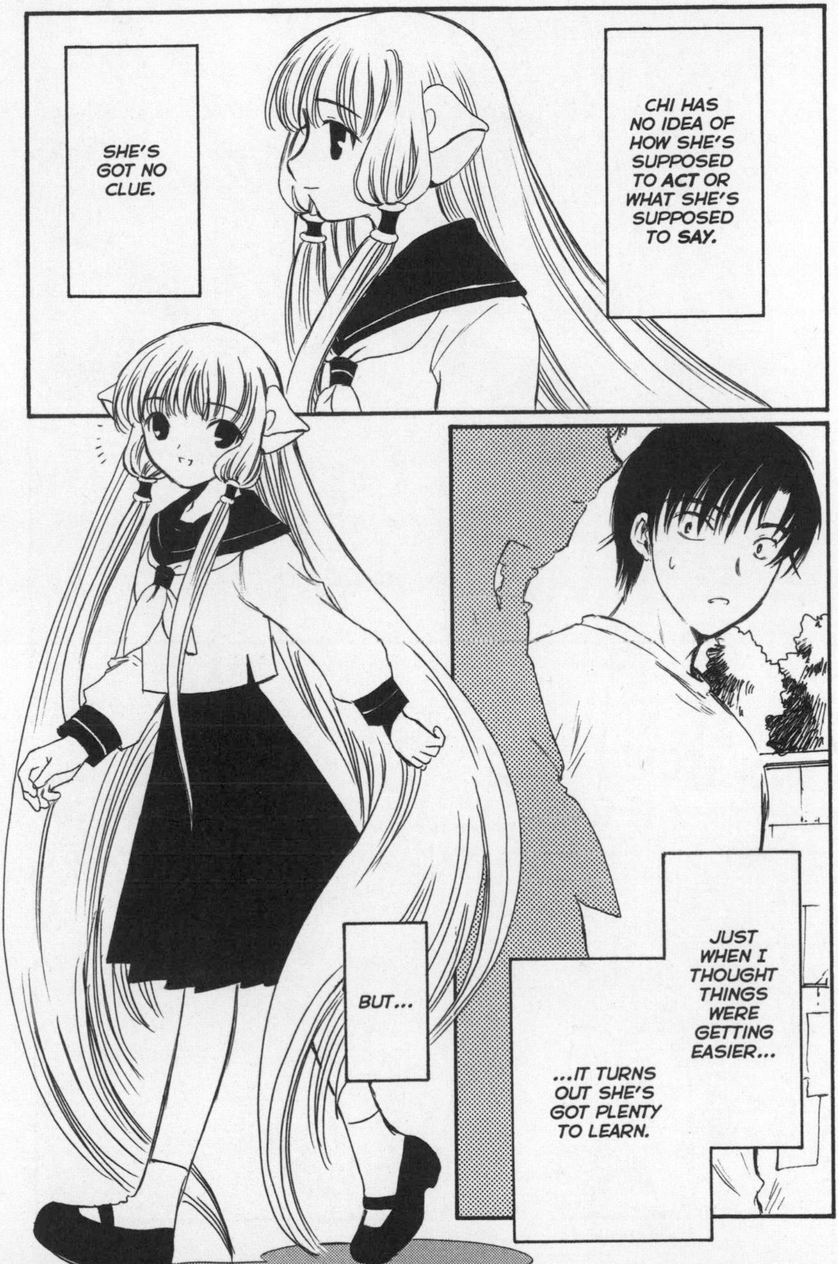
CHI HAS NO IDEA OF HOW SHE'S SUPPOSED TO ACT OR WHAT SHE'S SUPPOSED TO SAY.
SHE'S GOT NO CLUE.
JUST WHEN I THOUGHT THINGS WERE GETTING EASIER...
...IT TURNS OUT SHE'S GOT PLENTY TO LEARN.
BUT...

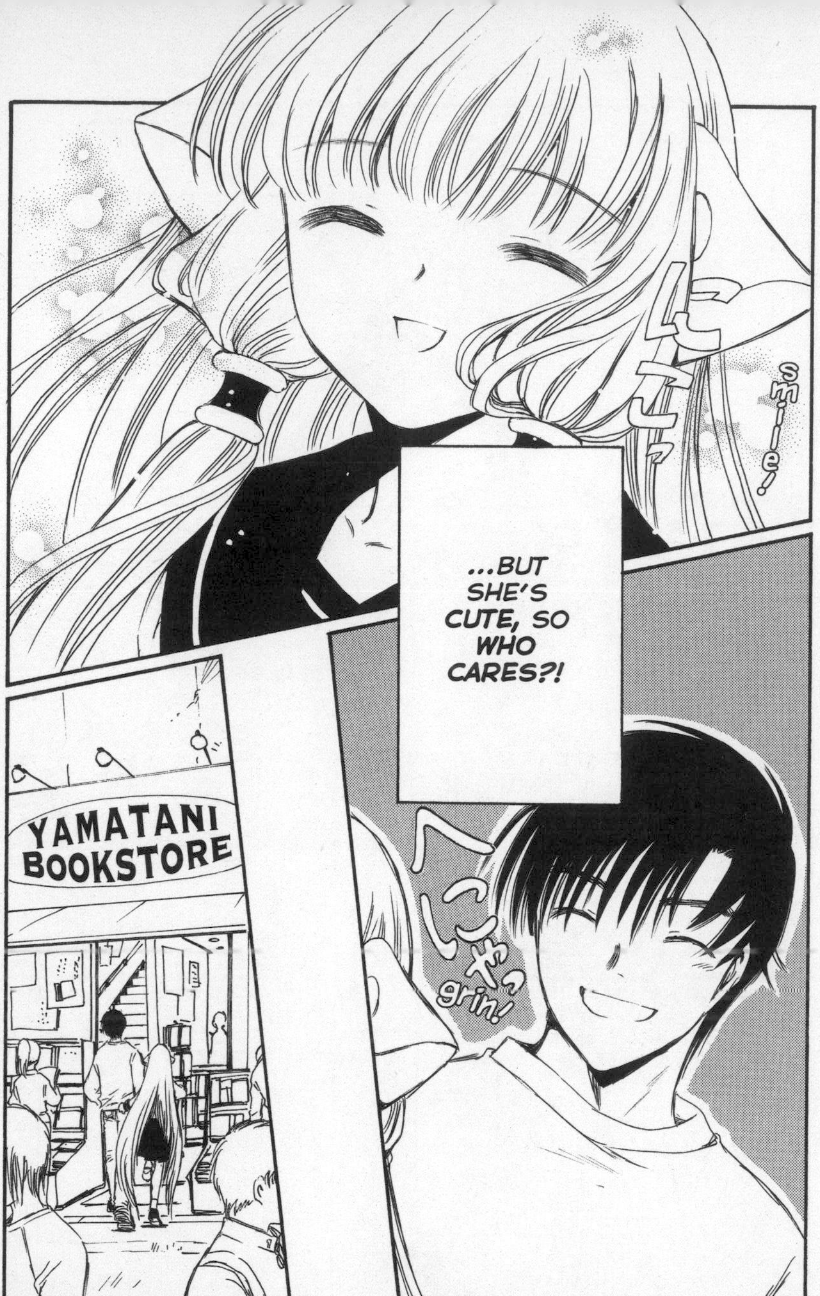
smile!
...BUT SHE'S CUTE, SO WHO CARES?!
grin!
YAMATANI BOOKSTORE

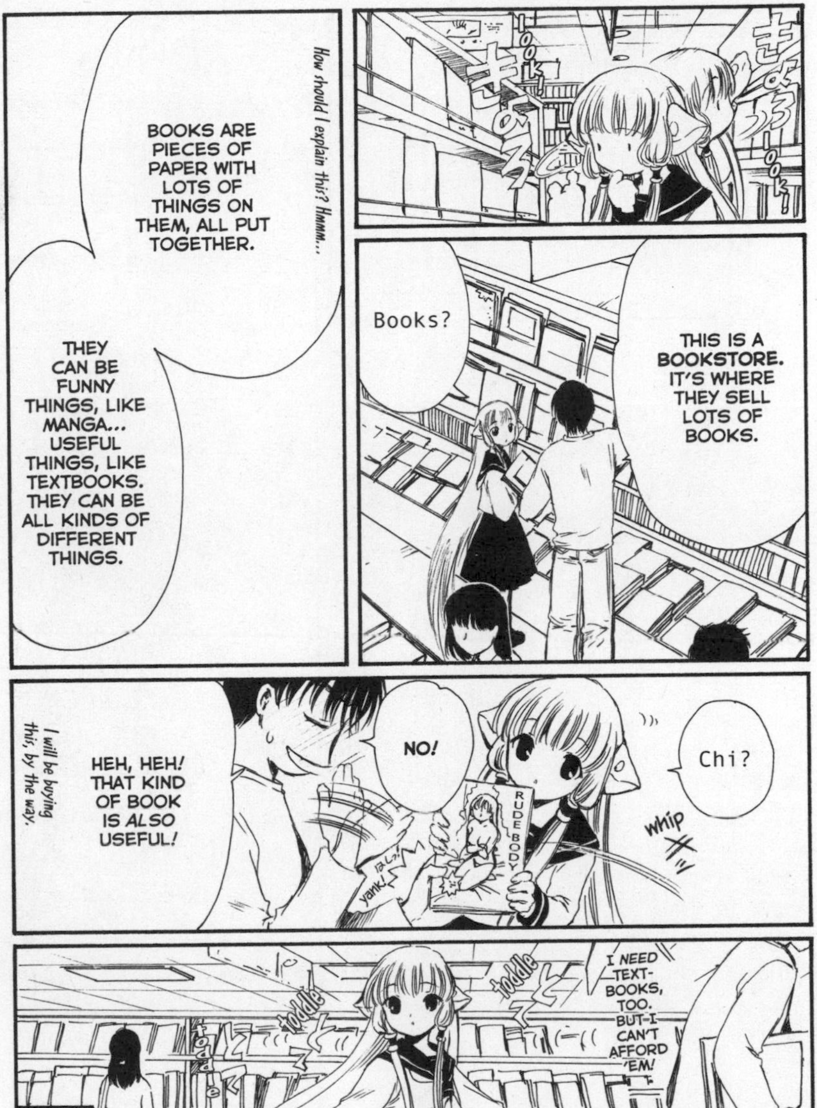

look!
look!
THIS IS A BOOKSTORE. IT'S WHERE THEY SELL LOTS OF BOOKS.
Books?
BOOKS ARE PIECES OF PAPER WITH LOTS OF THINGS ON THEM, ALL PUT TOGETHER.
How should I explain this? Hmmm...
THEY CAN BE FUNNY THINGS, LIKE MANGA... USEFUL THINGS, LIKE TEXTBOOKS. THEY CAN BE ALL KINDS OF DIFFERENT THINGS.
Chi?
whip
RUDE BODY
NO!
yank!
HEH, HEH! THAT KIND OF BOOK IS *ALSO* USEFUL!
I will be buying this, by the way.
I *NEED* TEXT-BOOKS, TOO. BUT I CAN'T AFFORD 'EM!
toddle
toddle
toddle

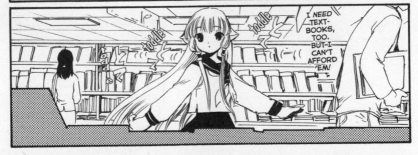

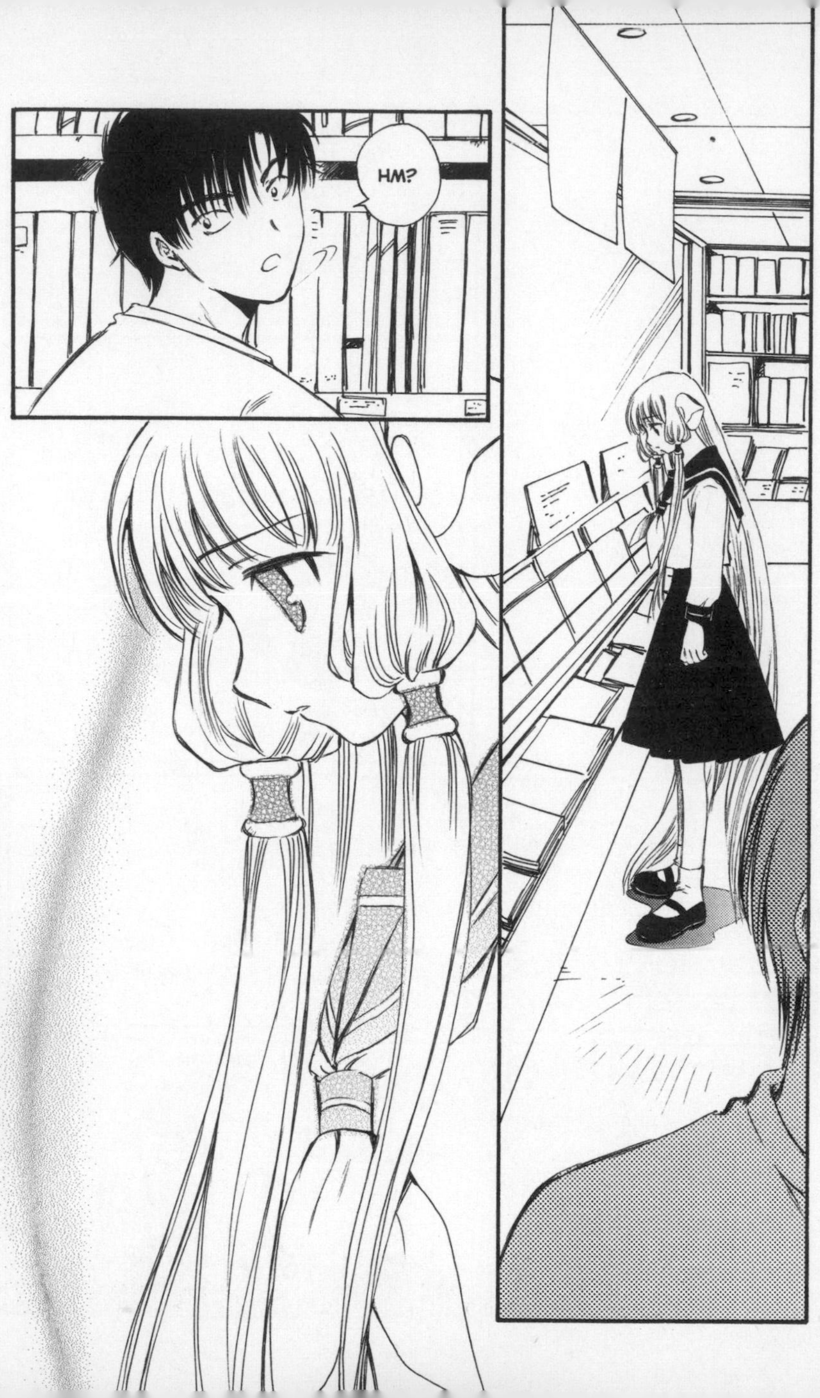
HM?

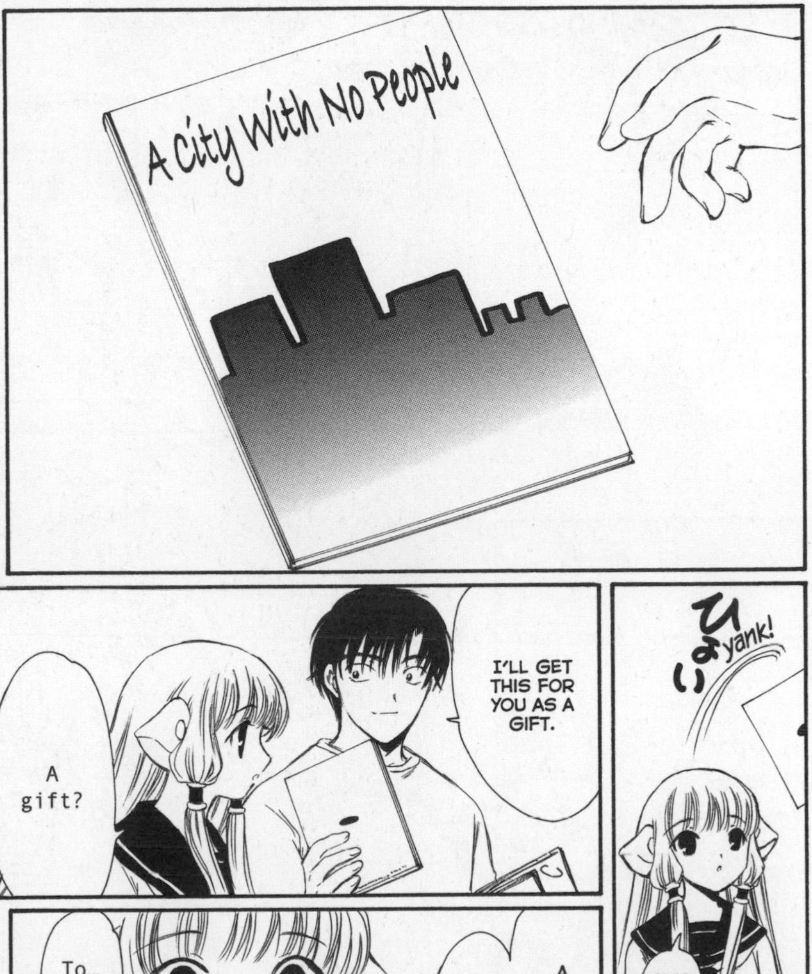
A City With No People
ひょい
yank!
Chi?
I'LL GET THIS FOR YOU AS A GIFT.
A gift?
A GIFT.
FROM ME TO YOU.
To...
...Chi?
A City With
RIGHT.

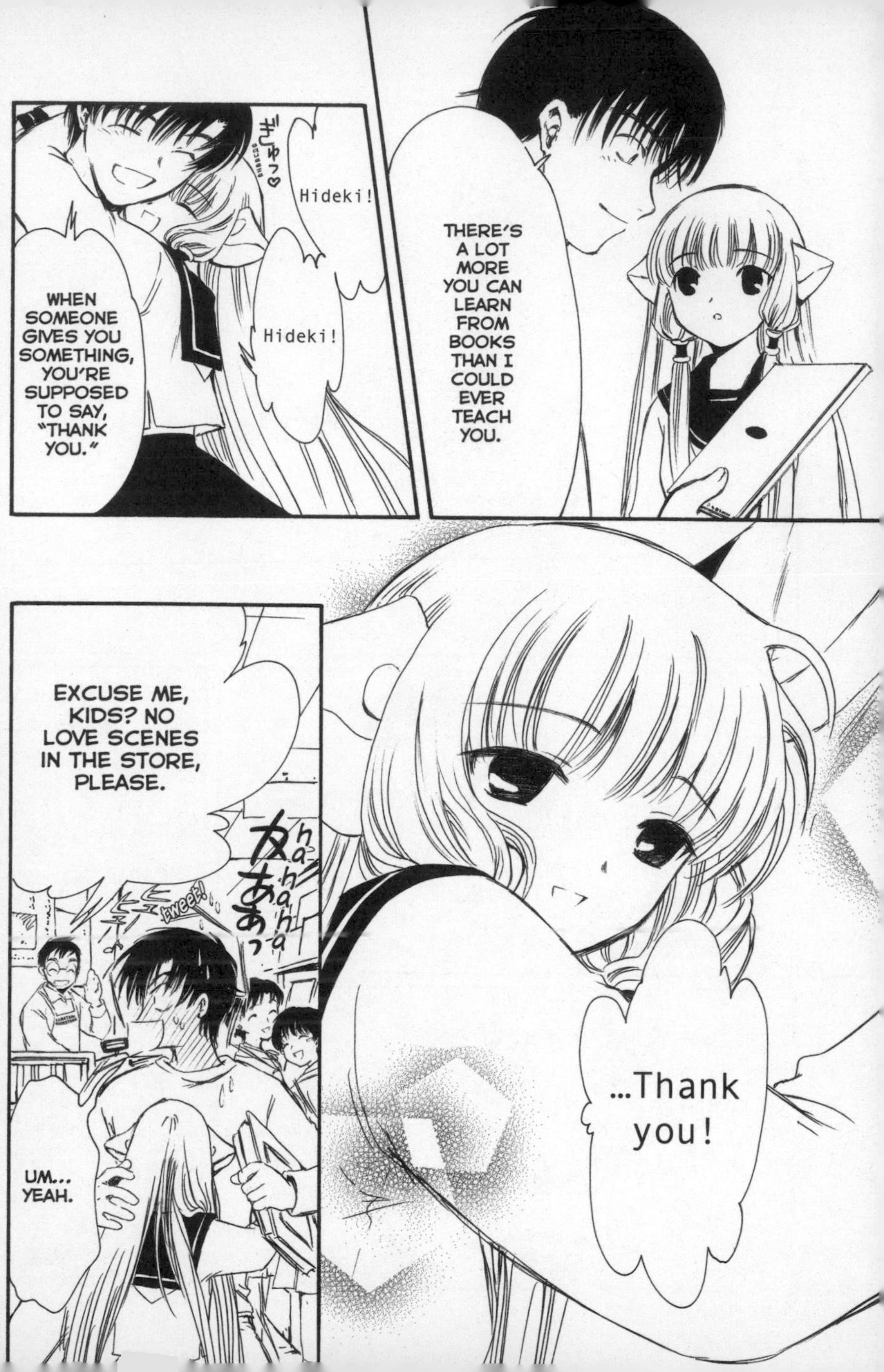
THERE'S A LOT MORE YOU CAN LEARN FROM BOOKS THAN I COULD EVER TEACH YOU.
Hideki!
Hideki!
WHEN SOMEONE GIVES YOU SOMETHING, YOU'RE SUPPOSED TO SAY, "THANK YOU."
...Thank you!
EXCUSE ME, KIDS? NO LOVE SCENES IN THE STORE, PLEASE.
tweet!
UM... YEAH.

Chobits

ちょびっツ

◀ **chapter 10** ▶

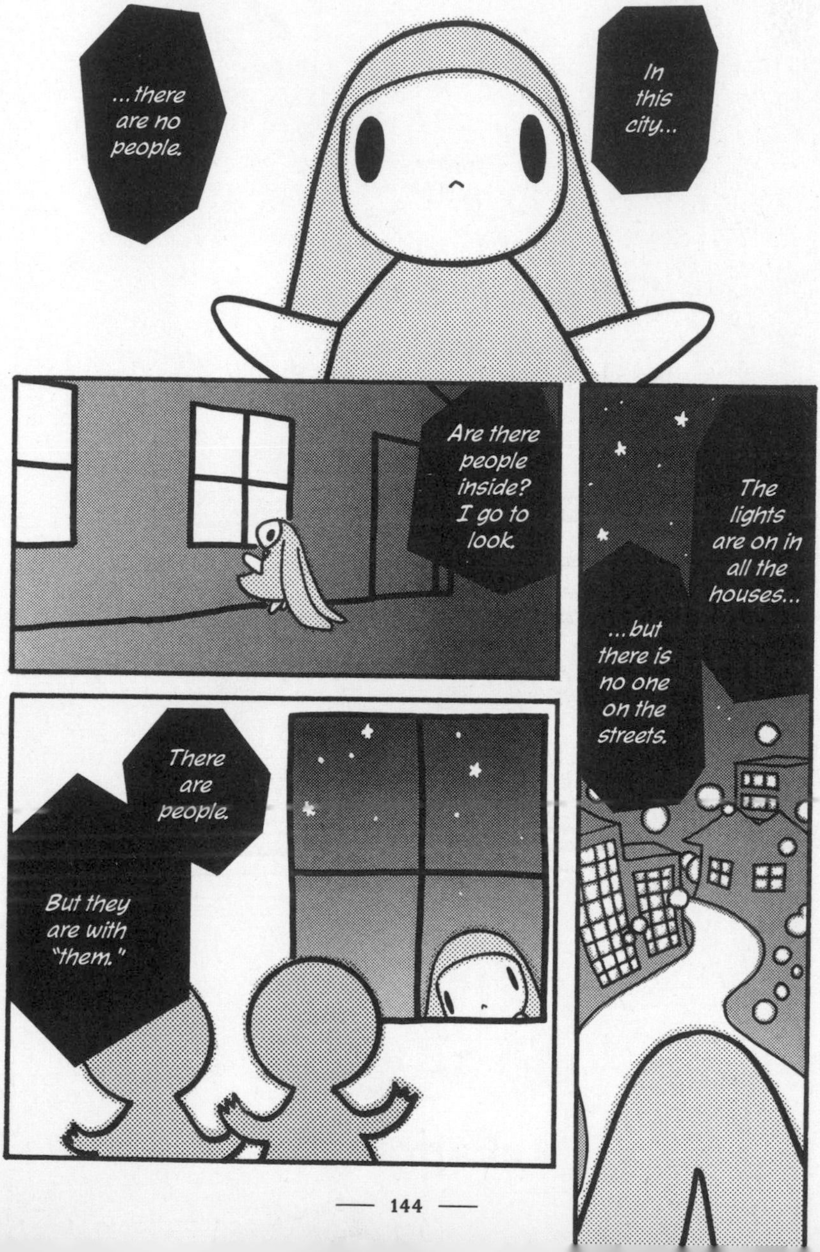
In this city...
...there are no people.
The lights are on in all the houses...
...but there is no one on the streets.
Are there people inside? I go to look.
There are people.
But they are with "them."

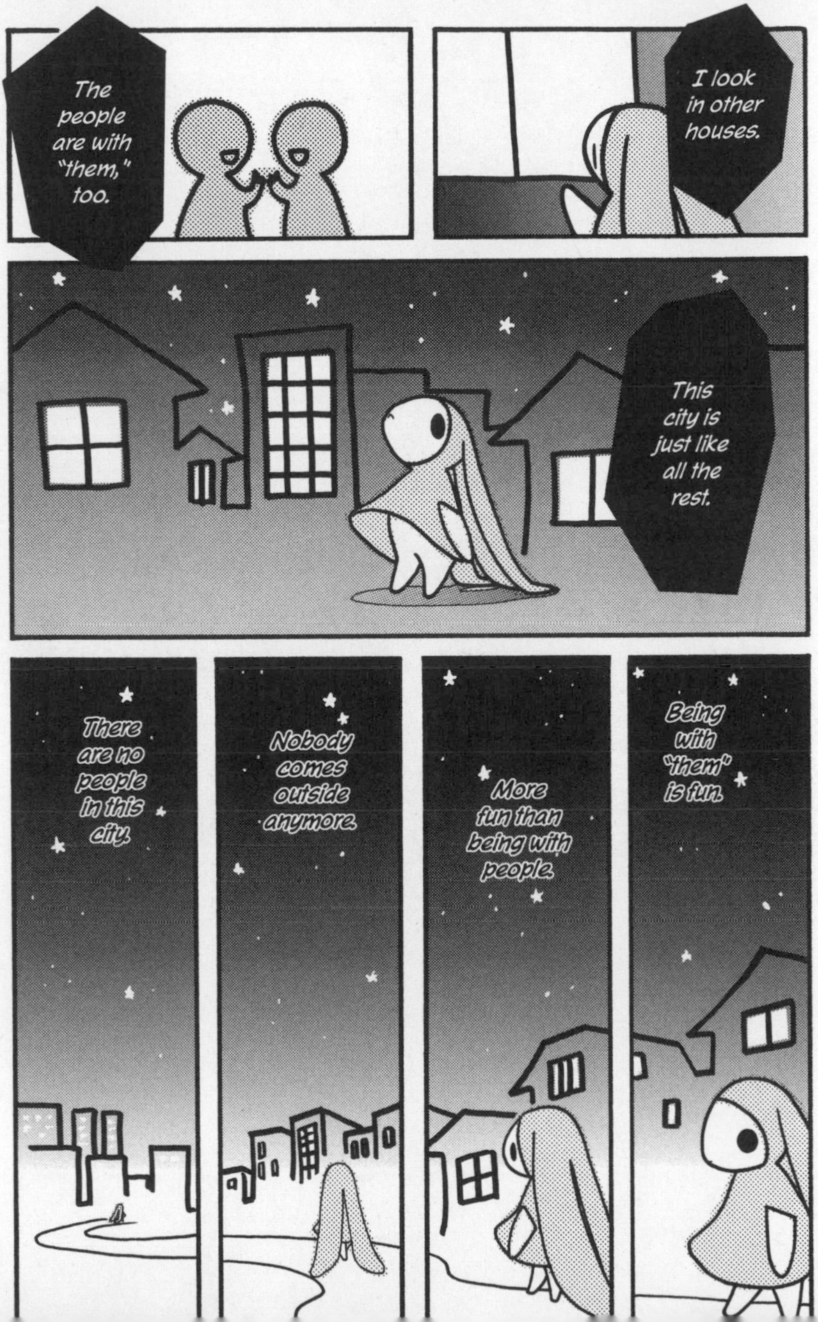
I look in other houses.
The people are with "them," too.
This city is just like all the rest.
Being with "them" is fun.
More fun than being with people.
Nobody comes outside anymore.
There are no people in this city.

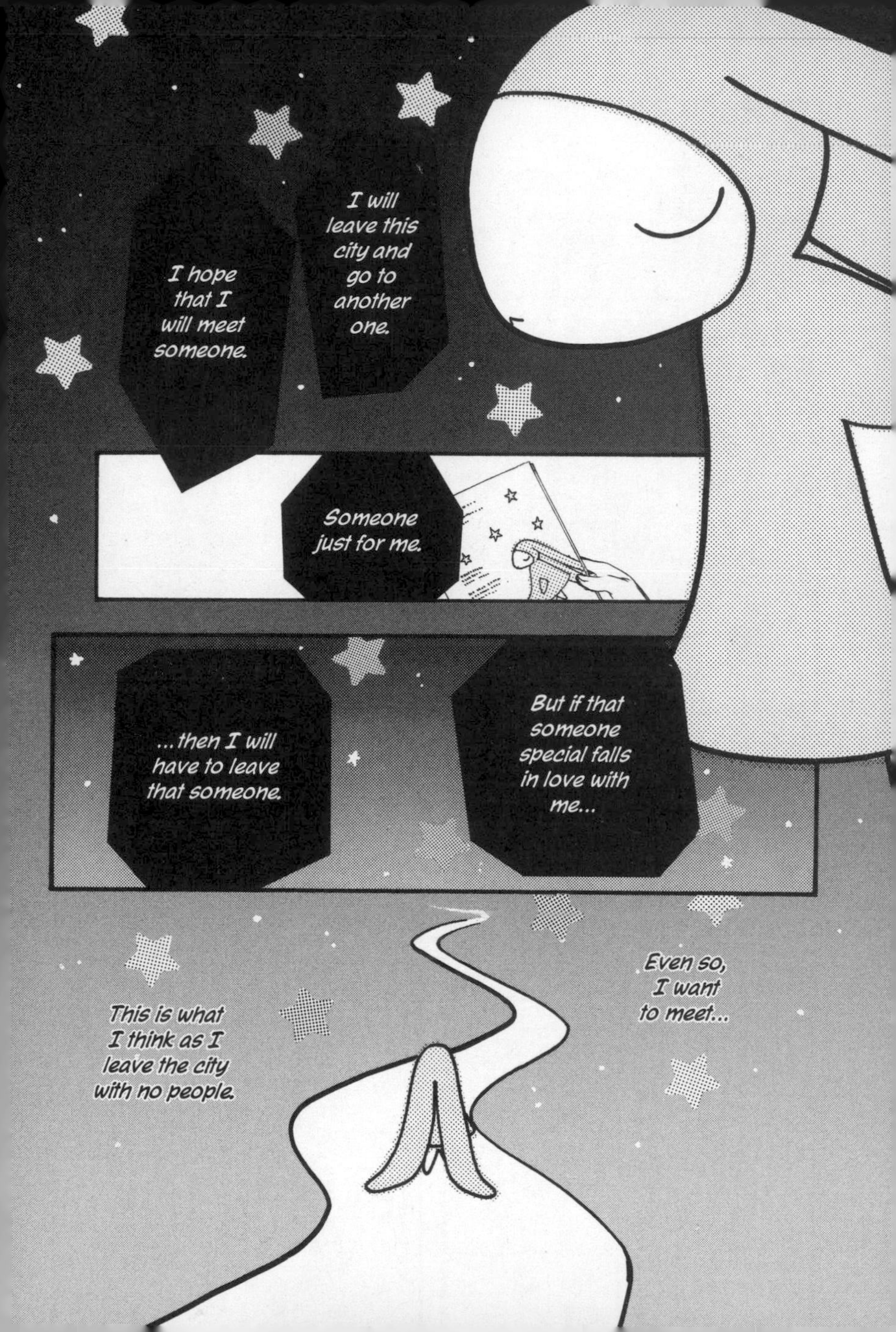
I will leave this city and go to another one.
I hope that I will meet someone.
Someone just for me.
But if that someone special falls in love with me...
...then I will have to leave that someone.
Even so, I want to meet...
This is what I think as I leave the city with no people.

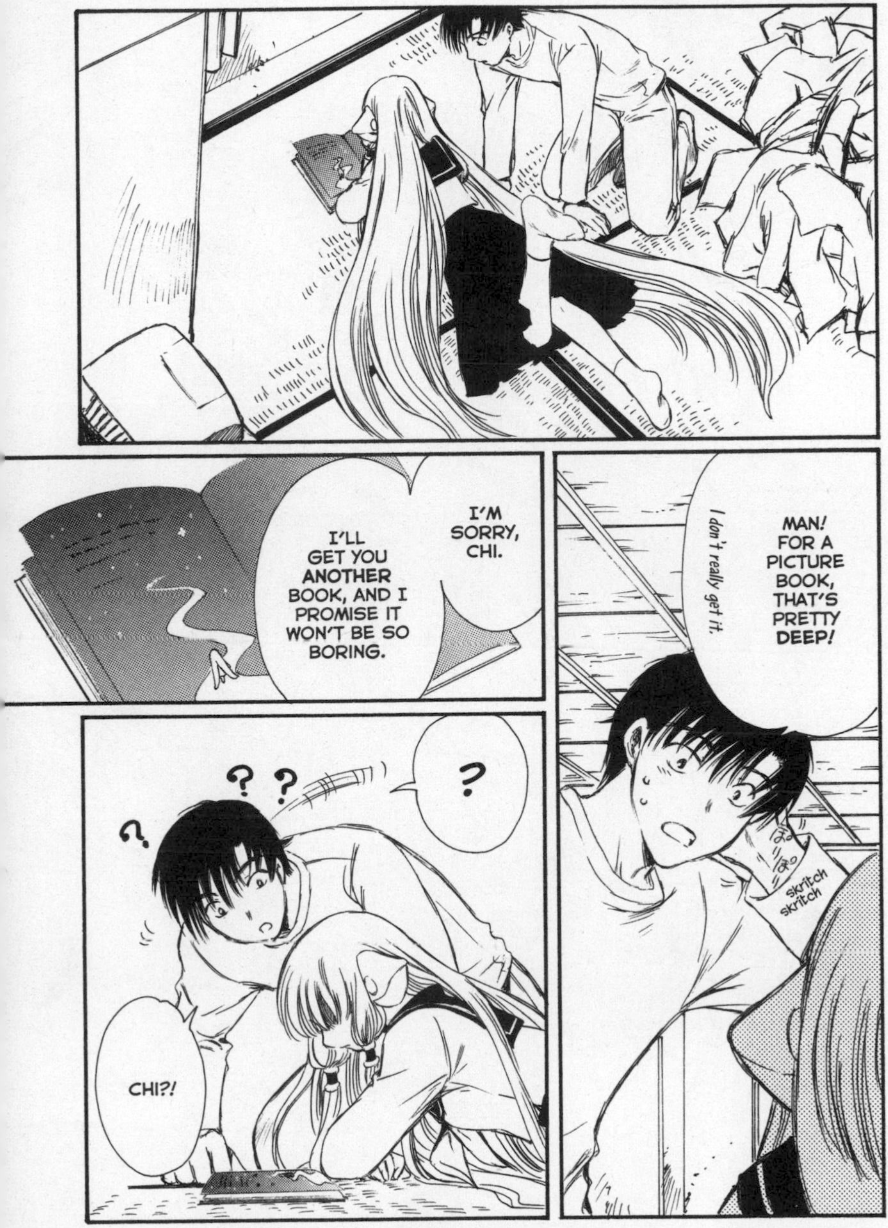
MAN! FOR A PICTURE BOOK, THAT'S PRETTY DEEP!
I don't really get it.
skritch skritch
I'M SORRY, CHI.
I'LL GET YOU ANOTHER BOOK, AND I PROMISE IT WON'T BE SO BORING.
?
CHI?!

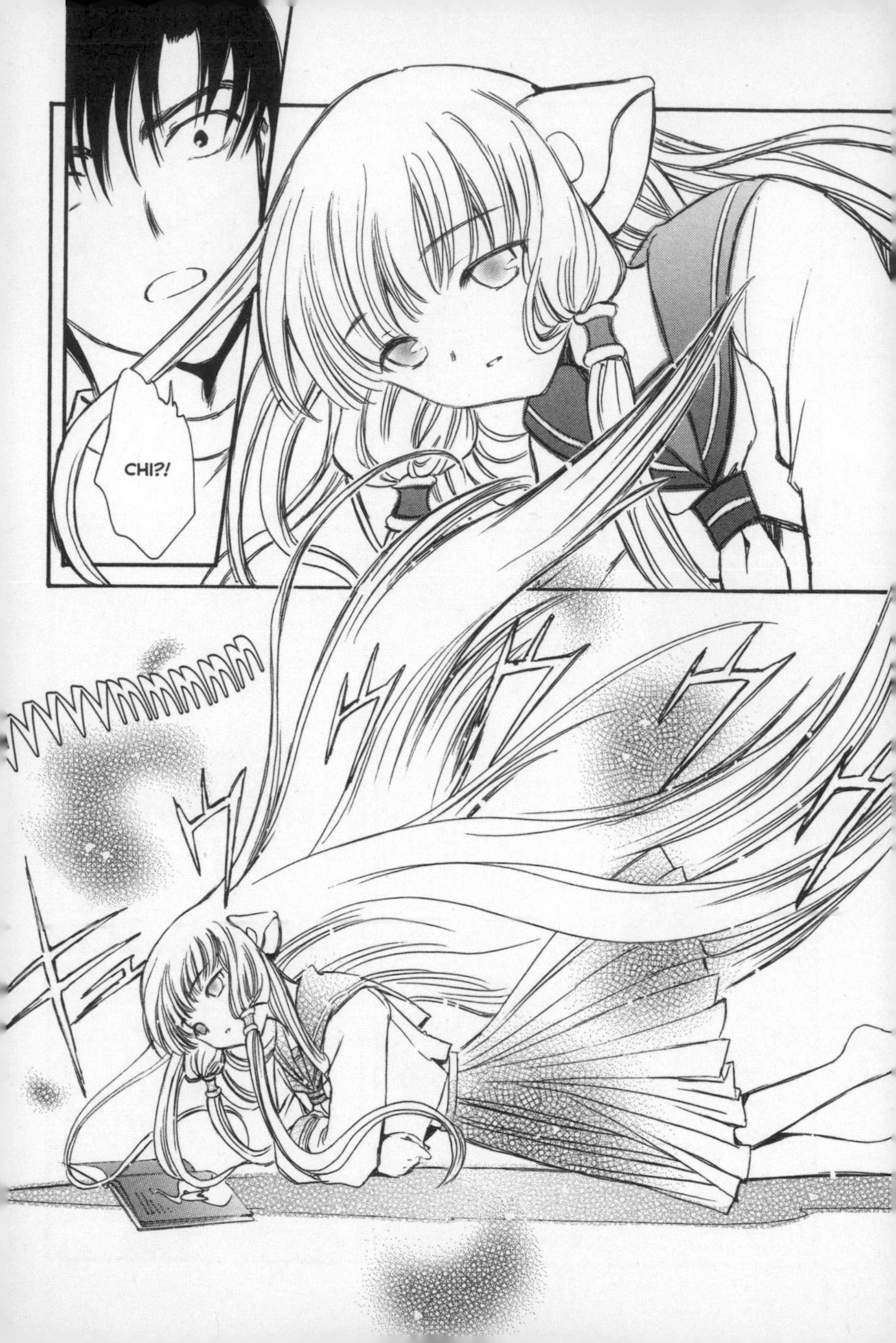
CHI?!
NNNNMMMMMM

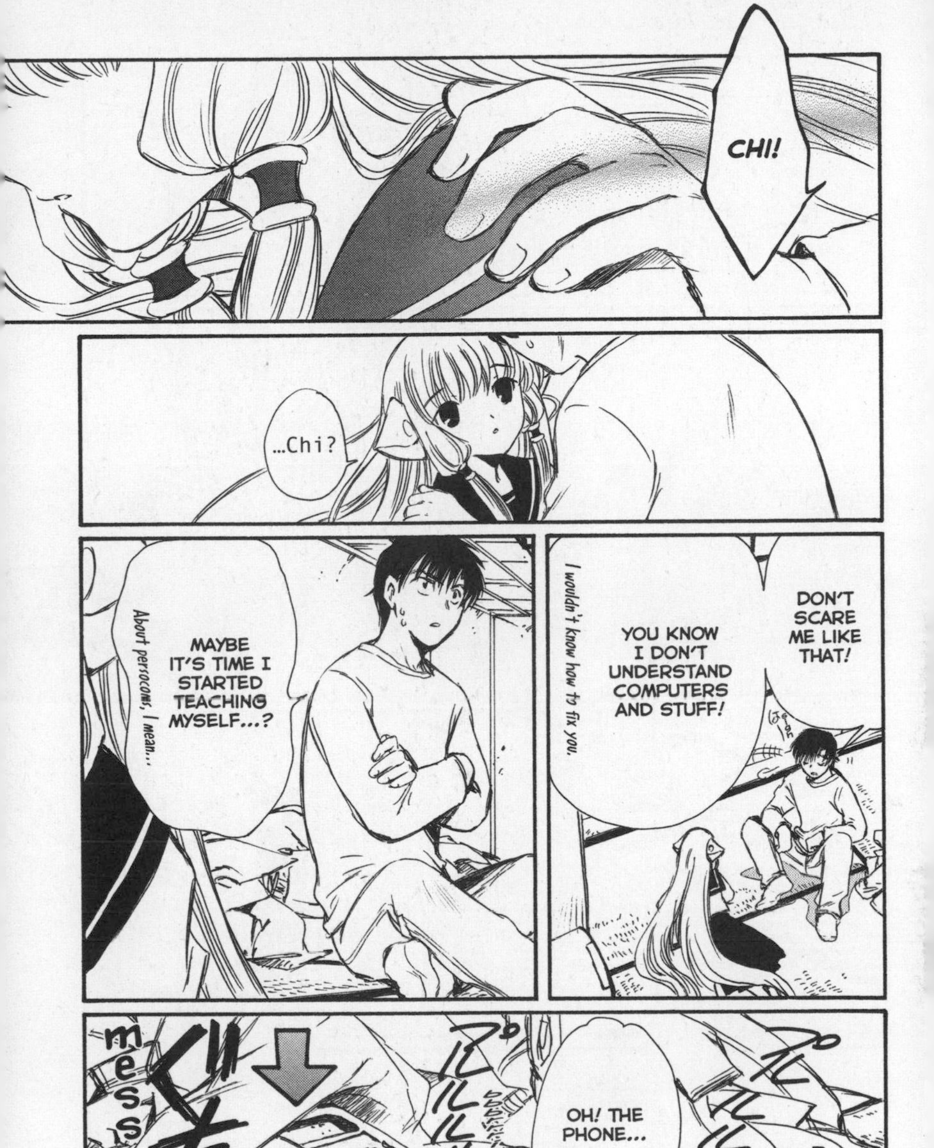

CHI!
...Chi?
DON'T SCARE ME LIKE THAT!
YOU KNOW I DON'T UNDERSTAND COMPUTERS AND STUFF!
I wouldn't know how to fix you.
MAYBE IT'S TIME I STARTED TEACHING MYSELF...?
About persocoms, I mean...
プルルル
OH! THE PHONE...
somewhere under there...
プルルル
mess

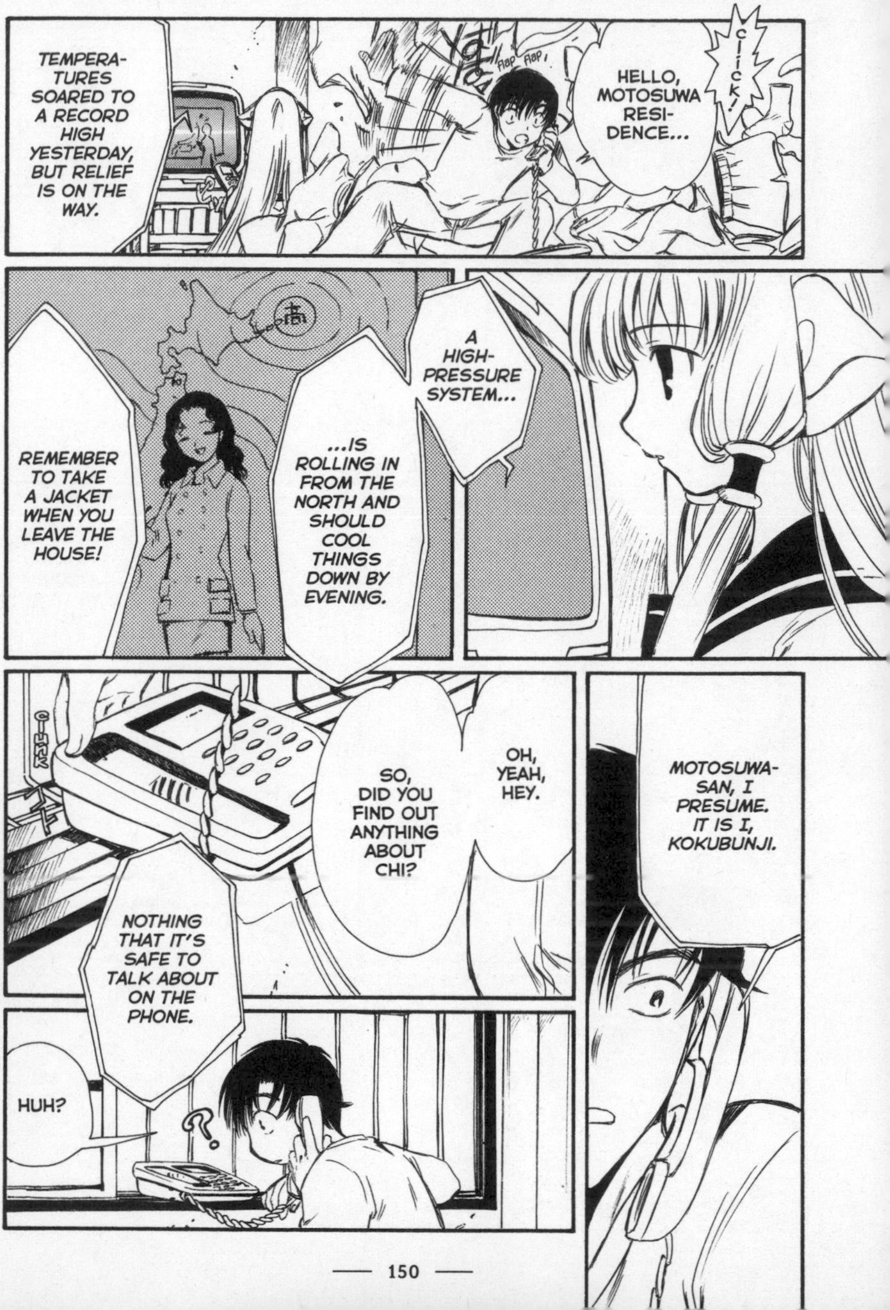
Click!
HELLO, MOTOSUWA RESI-DENCE...
Flap Flap
TEMPERA-TURES SOARED TO A RECORD HIGH YESTERDAY, BUT RELIEF IS ON THE WAY.
A HIGH-PRESSURE SYSTEM...
...IS ROLLING IN FROM THE NORTH AND SHOULD COOL THINGS DOWN BY EVENING.
REMEMBER TO TAKE A JACKET WHEN YOU LEAVE THE HOUSE!
MOTOSUWA-SAN, I PRESUME. IT IS I, KOKUBUNJI.
OH, YEAH, HEY.
SO, DID YOU FIND OUT ANYTHING ABOUT CHI?
NOTHING THAT IT'S SAFE TO TALK ABOUT ON THE PHONE.
HUH?

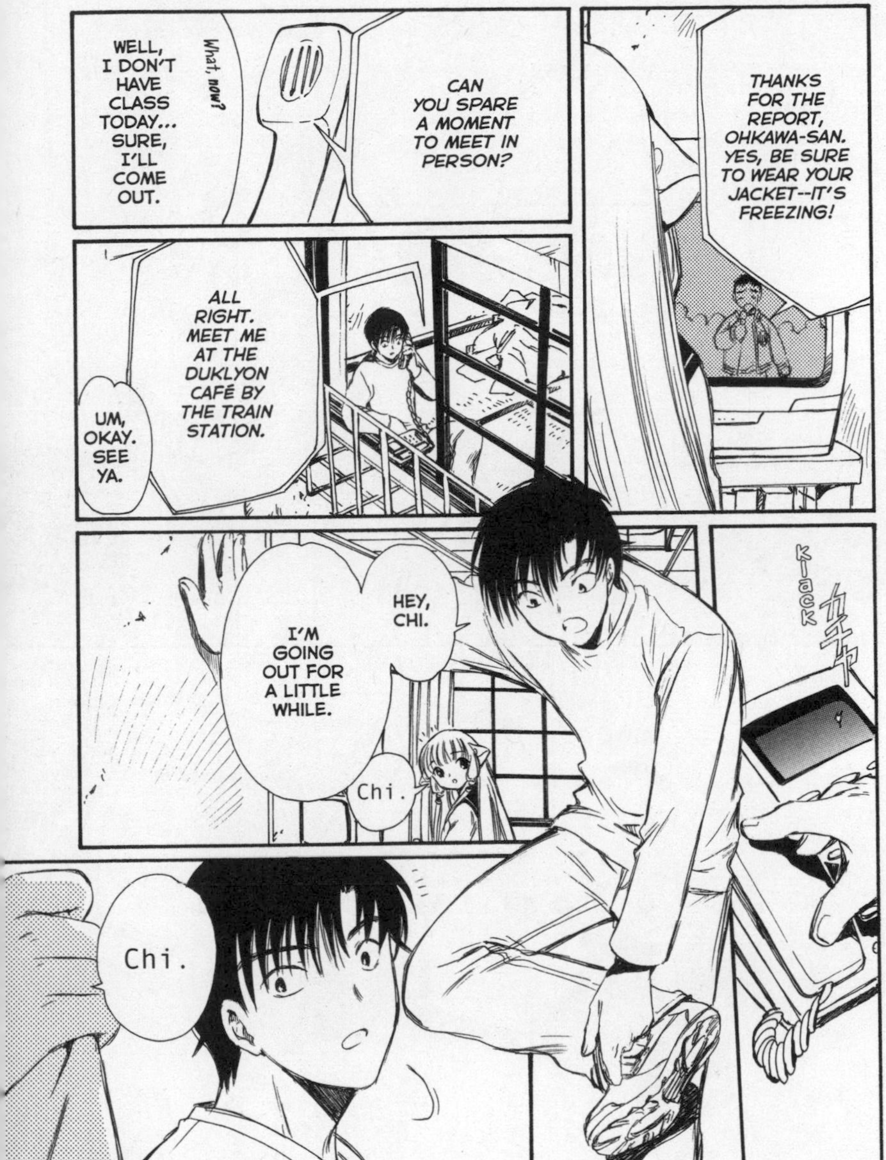
THANKS FOR THE REPORT, OHKAWA-SAN. YES, BE SURE TO WEAR YOUR JACKET--IT'S FREEZING!
CAN YOU SPARE A MOMENT TO MEET IN PERSON?
What, now?
WELL, I DON'T HAVE CLASS TODAY... SURE, I'LL COME OUT.
ALL RIGHT. MEET ME AT THE DUKLYON CAFÉ BY THE TRAIN STATION.
UM, OKAY. SEE YA.
klack
カチャ
HEY, CHI.
I'M GOING OUT FOR A LITTLE WHILE.
Chi.
Chi.

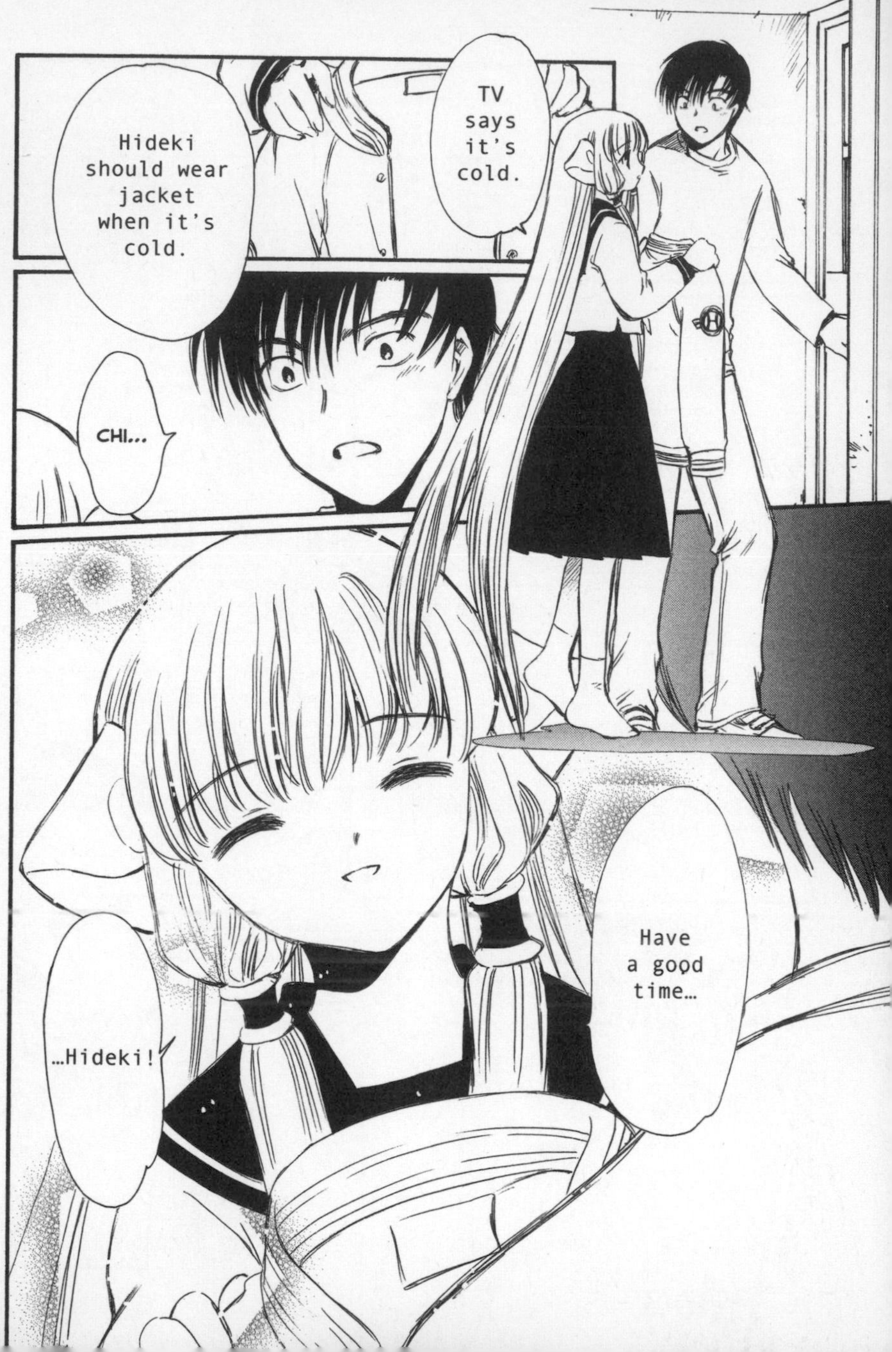
TV says it's cold.
Hideki should wear jacket when it's cold.
CHI...
Have a good time...
...Hideki!

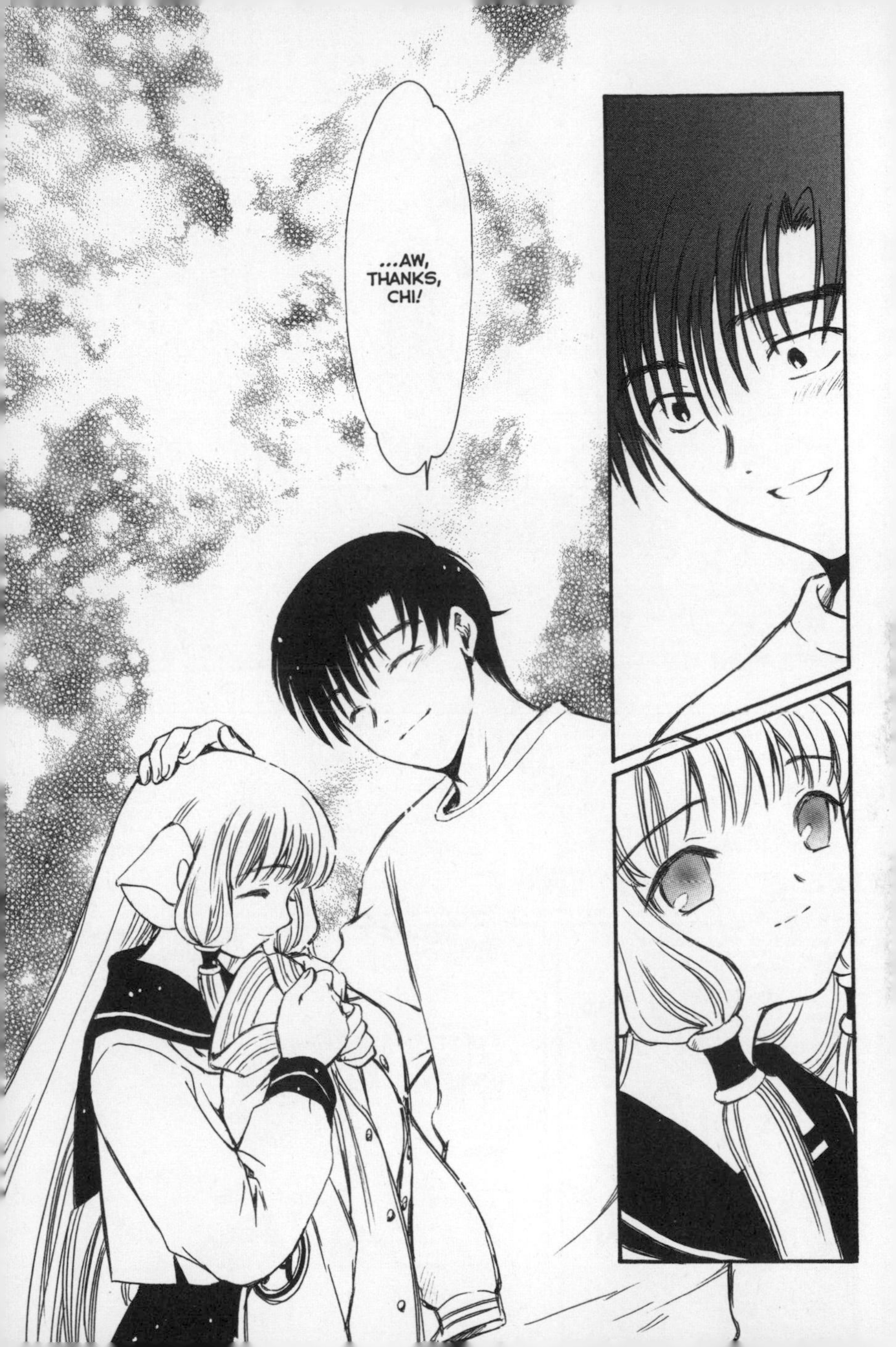
...AW, THANKS, CHI!

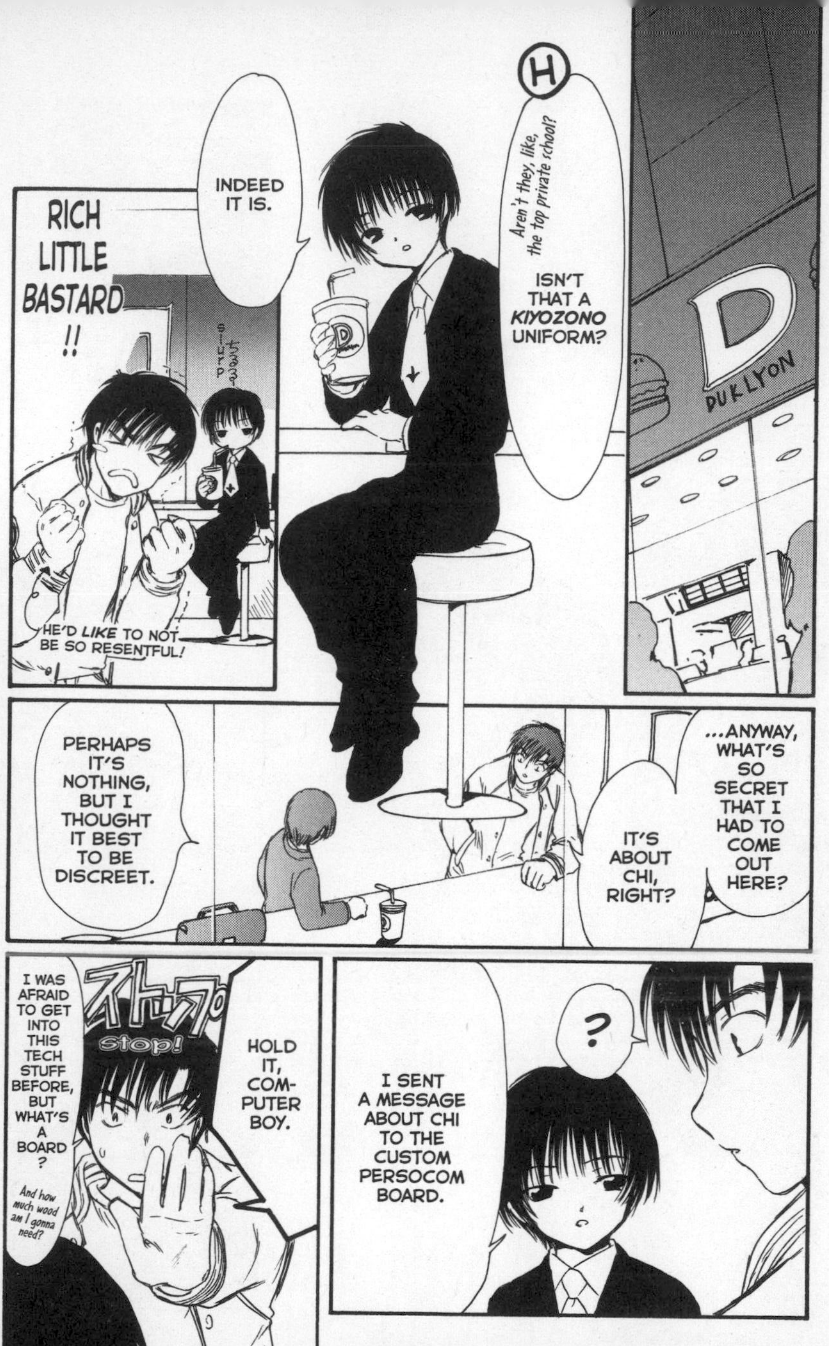
D
DUKLYON
H
Aren't they, like, the top private school?
ISN'T THAT A KIYOZONO UNIFORM?
INDEED IT IS.
RICH LITTLE BASTARD!!
ちゅるるー
slurp
HE'D LIKE TO NOT BE SO RESENTFUL!
...ANYWAY, WHAT'S SO SECRET THAT I HAD TO COME OUT HERE?
IT'S ABOUT CHI, RIGHT?
PERHAPS IT'S NOTHING, BUT I THOUGHT IT BEST TO BE DISCREET.
?
I SENT A MESSAGE ABOUT CHI TO THE CUSTOM PERSOCOM BOARD.
HOLD IT, COMPUTER BOY.
ストップ
stop!
I WAS AFRAID TO GET INTO THIS TECH STUFF BEFORE, BUT WHAT'S A BOARD?
And how much wood am I gonna need?

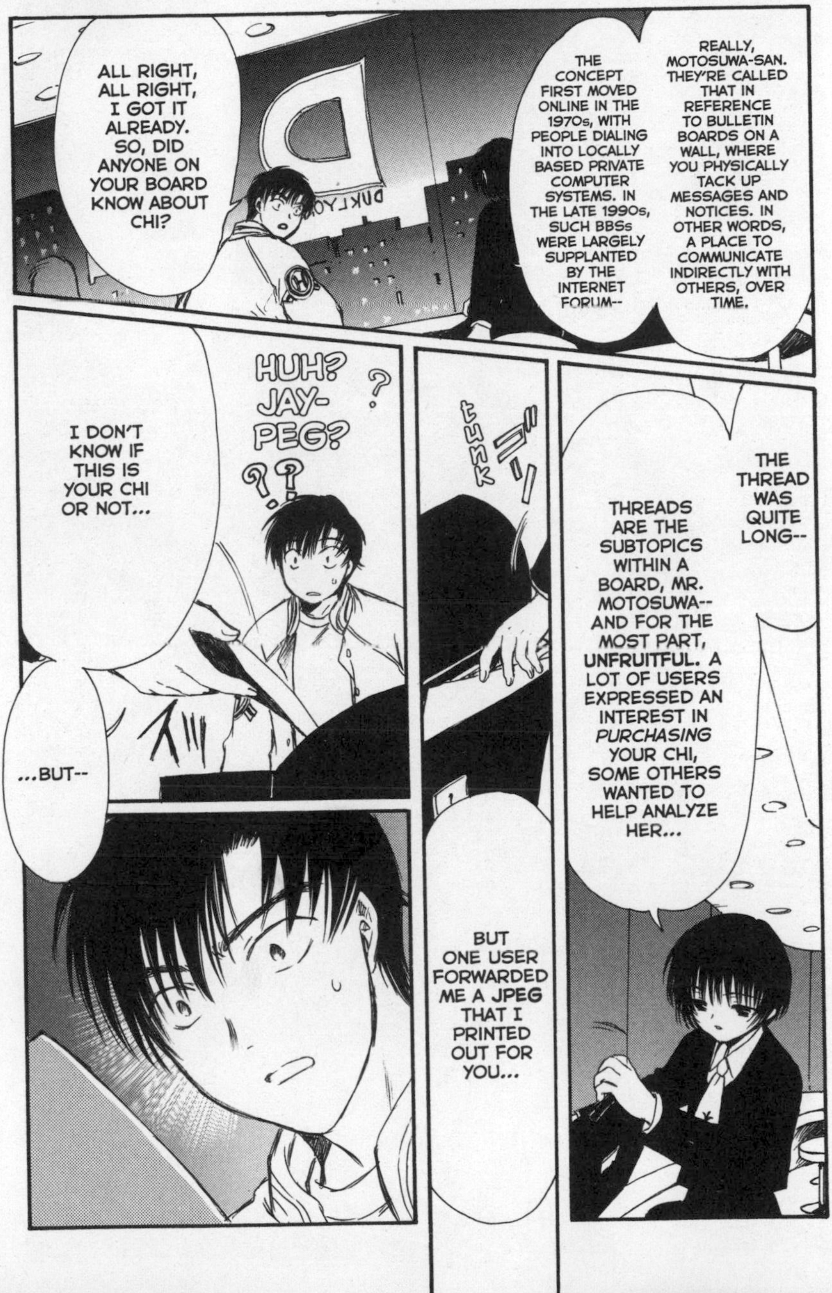
REALLY, MOTOSUWA-SAN. THEY'RE CALLED THAT IN REFERENCE TO BULLETIN BOARDS ON A WALL, WHERE YOU PHYSICALLY TACK UP MESSAGES AND NOTICES. IN OTHER WORDS, A PLACE TO COMMUNICATE INDIRECTLY WITH OTHERS, OVER TIME.
THE CONCEPT FIRST MOVED ONLINE IN THE 1970s, WITH PEOPLE DIALING INTO LOCALLY BASED PRIVATE COMPUTER SYSTEMS. IN THE LATE 1990s, SUCH BBSs WERE LARGELY SUPPLANTED BY THE INTERNET FORUM--
ALL RIGHT, ALL RIGHT, I GOT IT ALREADY. SO, DID ANYONE ON YOUR BOARD KNOW ABOUT CHI?
THE THREAD WAS QUITE LONG--
THREADS ARE THE SUBTOPICS WITHIN A BOARD, MR. MOTOSUWA-- AND FOR THE MOST PART, UNFRUITFUL. A LOT OF USERS EXPRESSED AN INTEREST IN PURCHASING YOUR CHI, SOME OTHERS WANTED TO HELP ANALYZE HER...
BUT ONE USER FORWARDED ME A JPEG THAT I PRINTED OUT FOR YOU...
tunk
HUH? JAY-PEG?
?
??
I DON'T KNOW IF THIS IS YOUR CHI OR NOT...
...BUT--

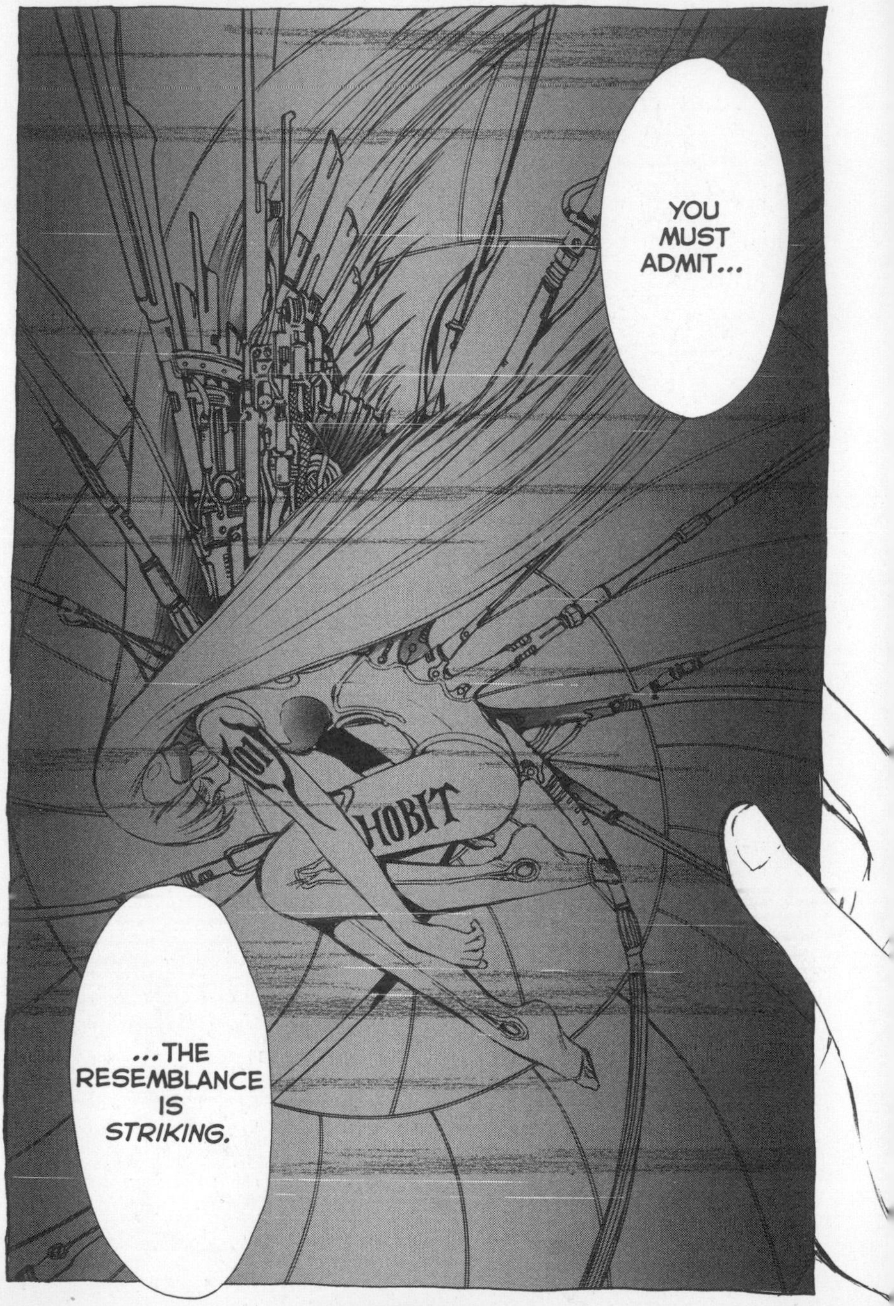
YOU MUST ADMIT...
...THE RESEMBLANCE IS STRIKING.
HOBIT

Chobits

ちょびっツ

◄ chapter 11 ►

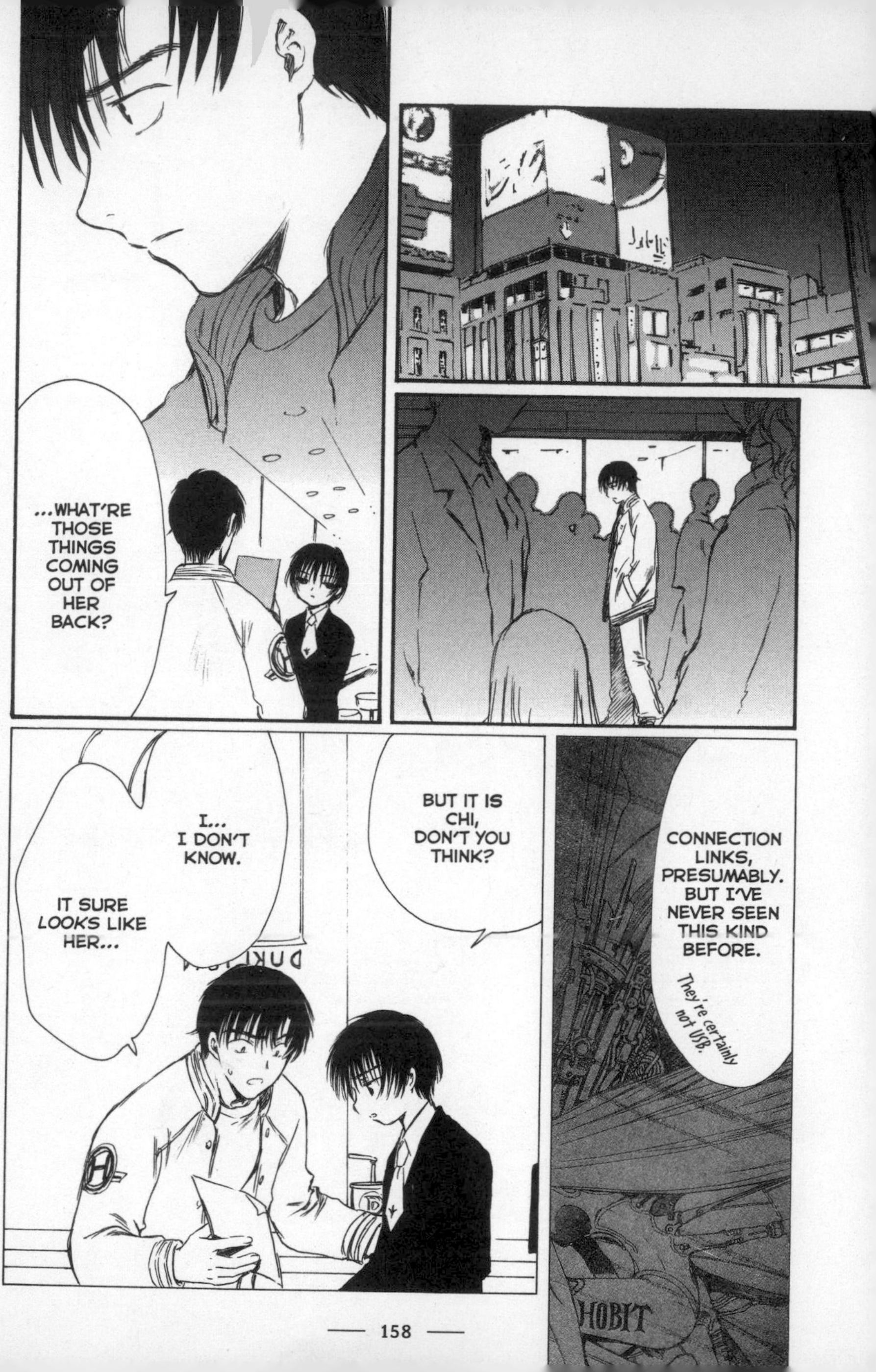
...WHAT'RE THOSE THINGS COMING OUT OF HER BACK?
CONNECTION LINKS, PRESUMABLY. BUT I'VE NEVER SEEN THIS KIND BEFORE.
They're certainly not USB.
HOBIT
BUT IT IS CHI, DON'T YOU THINK?
I... I DON'T KNOW.
IT SURE *LOOKS* LIKE HER...

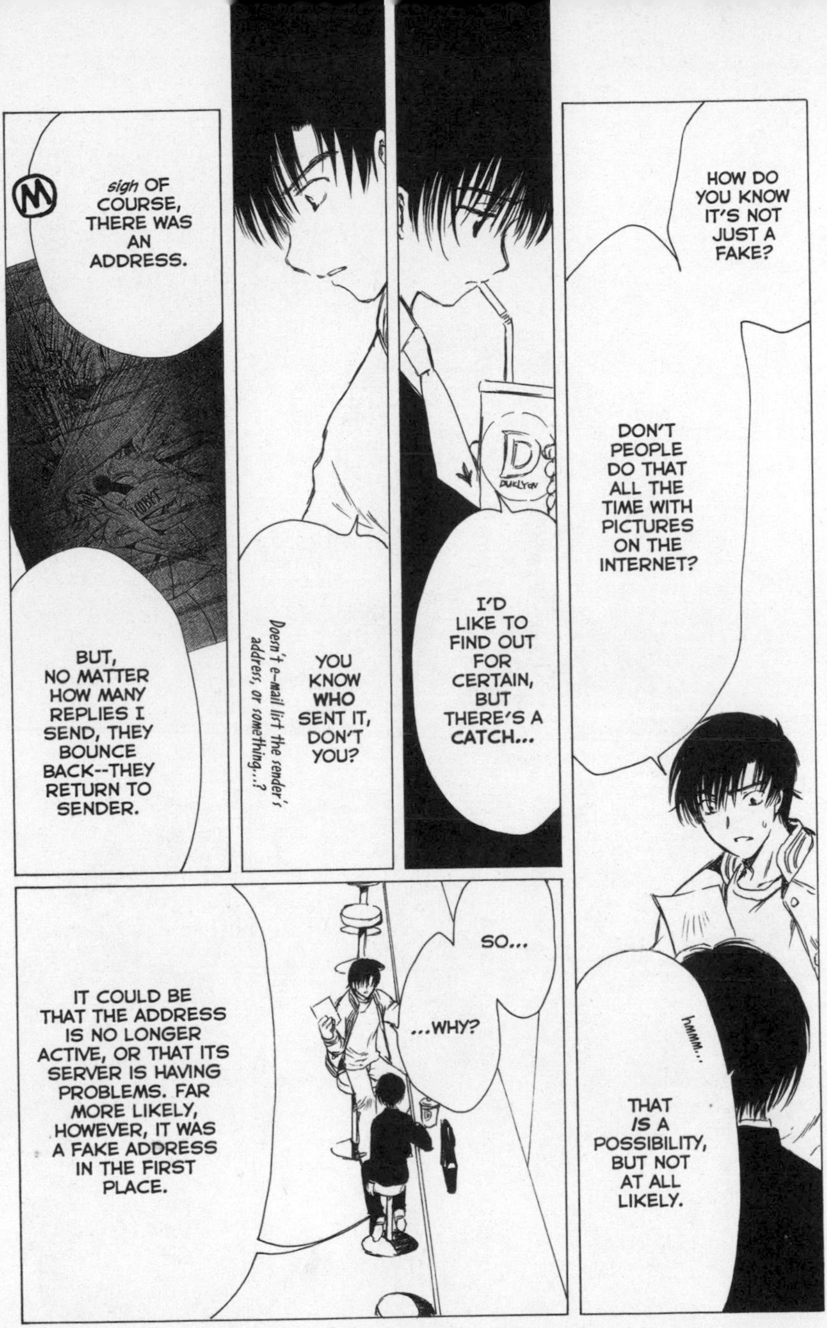
HOW DO YOU KNOW IT'S NOT JUST A FAKE?
DON'T PEOPLE DO THAT ALL THE TIME WITH PICTURES ON THE INTERNET?
hmmm...
THAT *IS* A POSSIBILITY, BUT NOT AT ALL LIKELY.
I'D LIKE TO FIND OUT FOR CERTAIN, BUT THERE'S A CATCH...
YOU KNOW WHO SENT IT, DON'T YOU?
Doesn't e-mail list the sender's address, or something...?
sigh OF COURSE, THERE WAS AN ADDRESS.
BUT, NO MATTER HOW MANY REPLIES I SEND, THEY BOUNCE BACK--THEY RETURN TO SENDER.
SO...
...WHY?
IT COULD BE THAT THE ADDRESS IS NO LONGER ACTIVE, OR THAT ITS SERVER IS HAVING PROBLEMS. FAR MORE LIKELY, HOWEVER, IT WAS A FAKE ADDRESS IN THE FIRST PLACE.

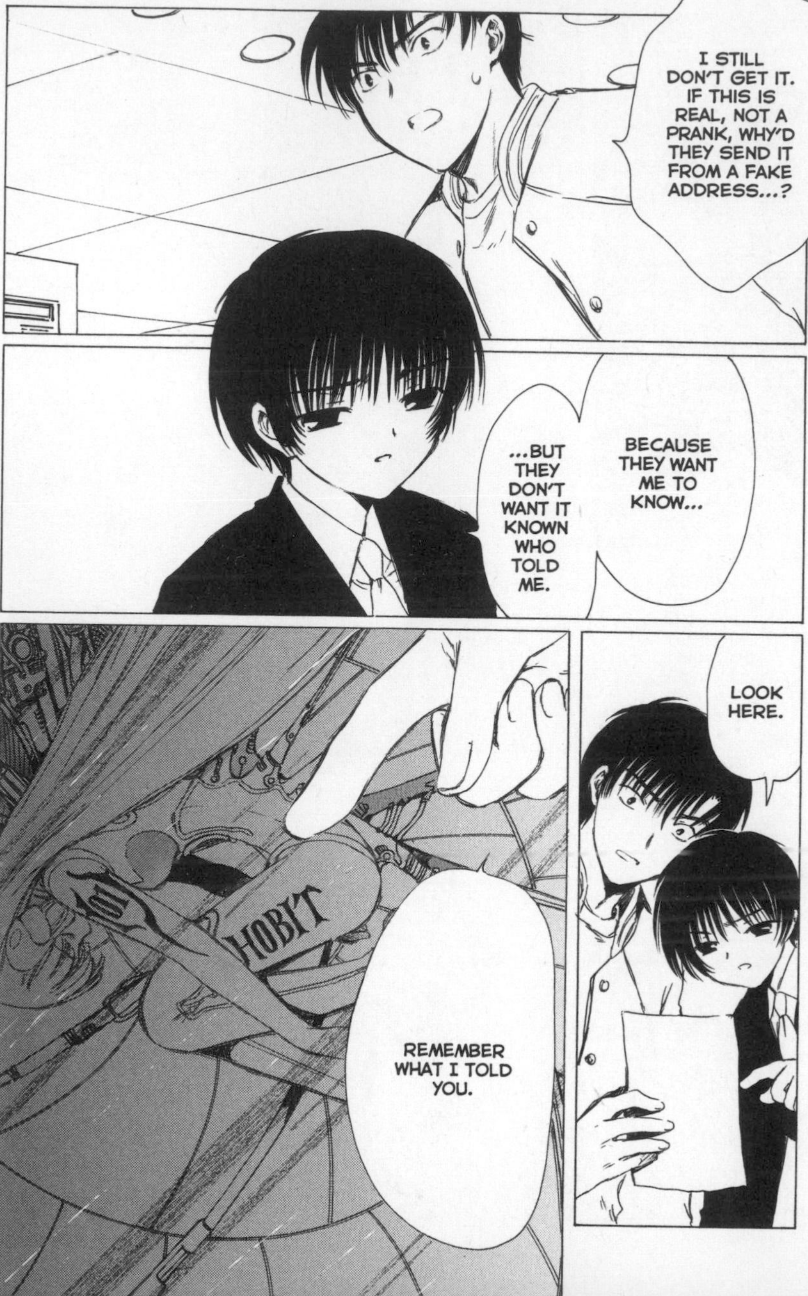
I STILL DON'T GET IT. IF THIS IS REAL, NOT A PRANK, WHY'D THEY SEND IT FROM A FAKE ADDRESS...?
BECAUSE THEY WANT ME TO KNOW...
...BUT THEY DON'T WANT IT KNOWN WHO TOLD ME.
LOOK HERE.
REMEMBER WHAT I TOLD YOU.
HOBIT

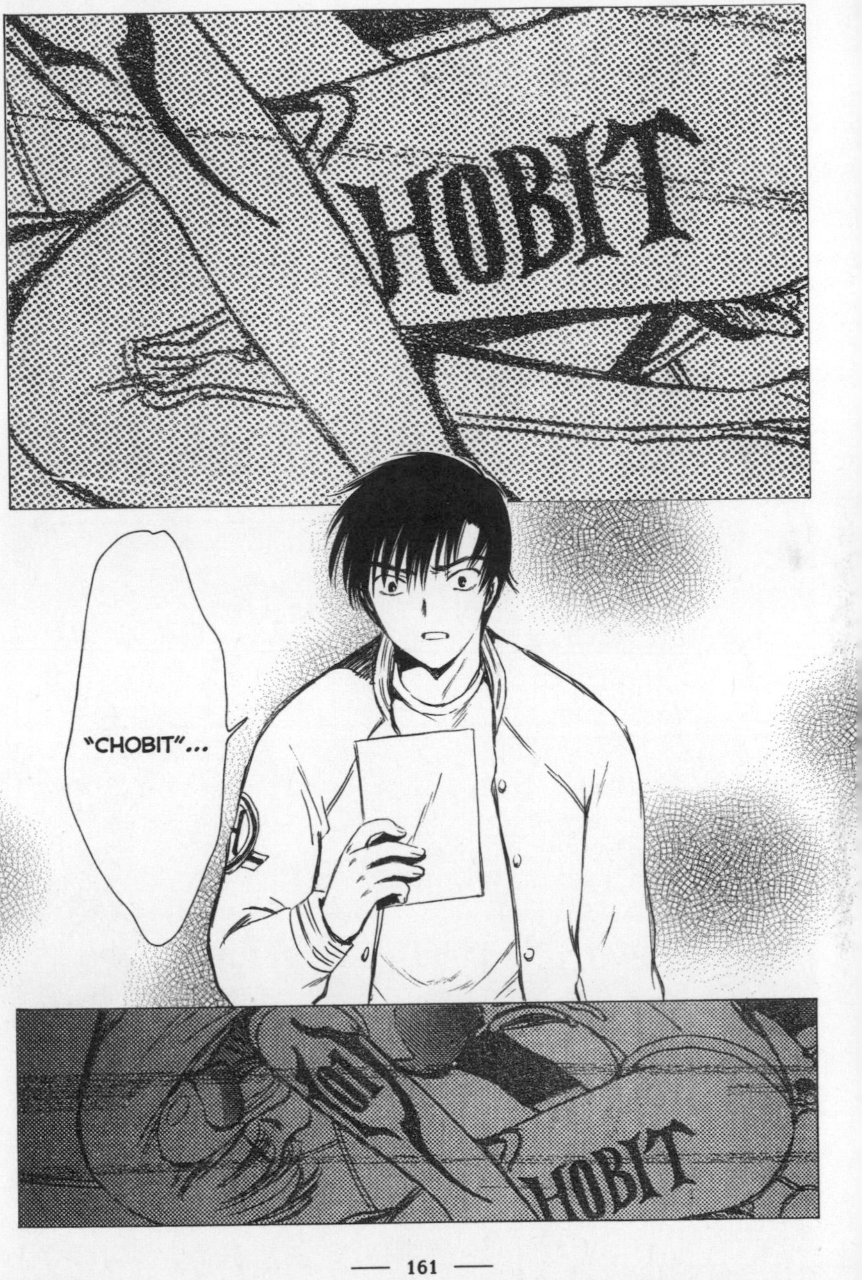
HOBIT
"CHOBIT"...
HOBIT

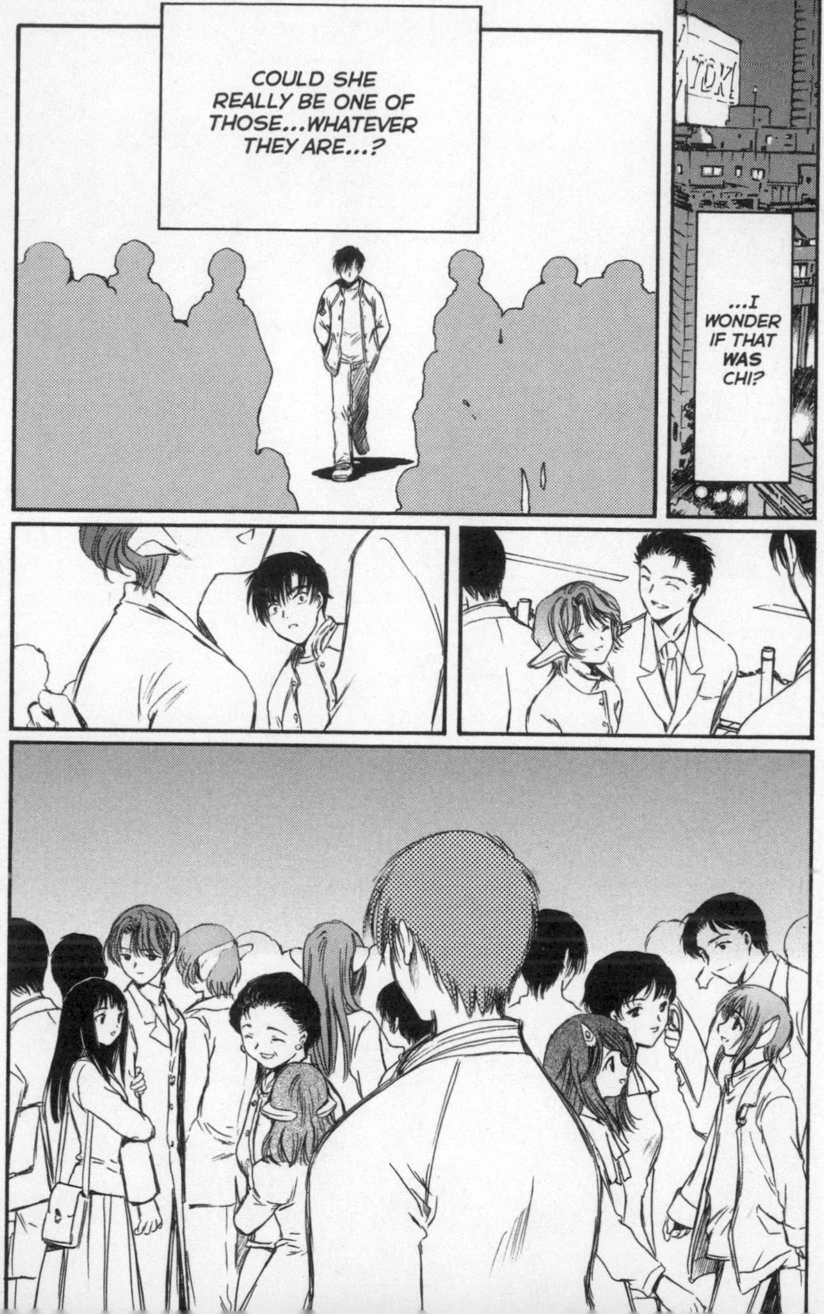
...I WONDER IF THAT WAS CHI?
COULD SHE REALLY BE ONE OF THOSE...WHATEVER THEY ARE...?

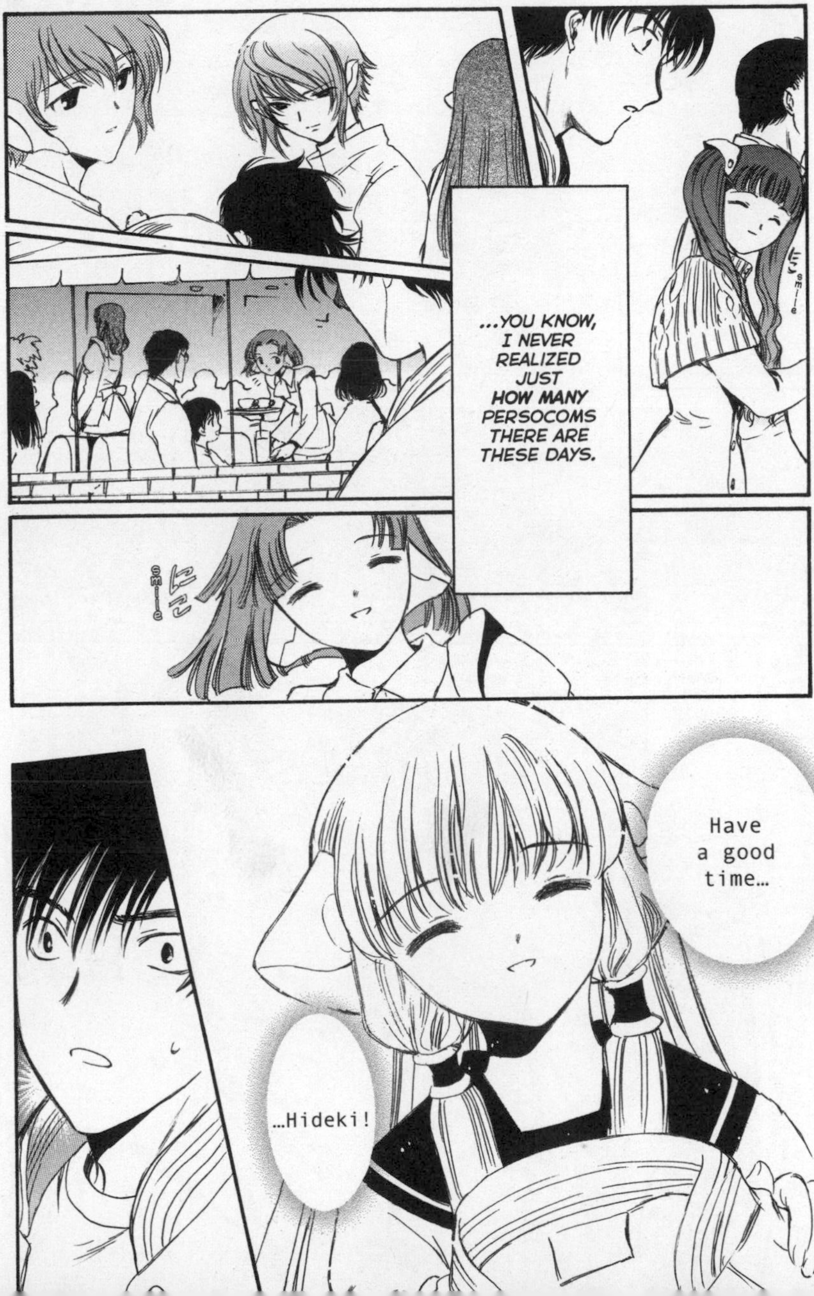
にこ smile
...YOU KNOW, I NEVER REALIZED JUST HOW MANY PERSOCOMS THERE ARE THESE DAYS.
にこ smile
Have a good time...
...Hideki!

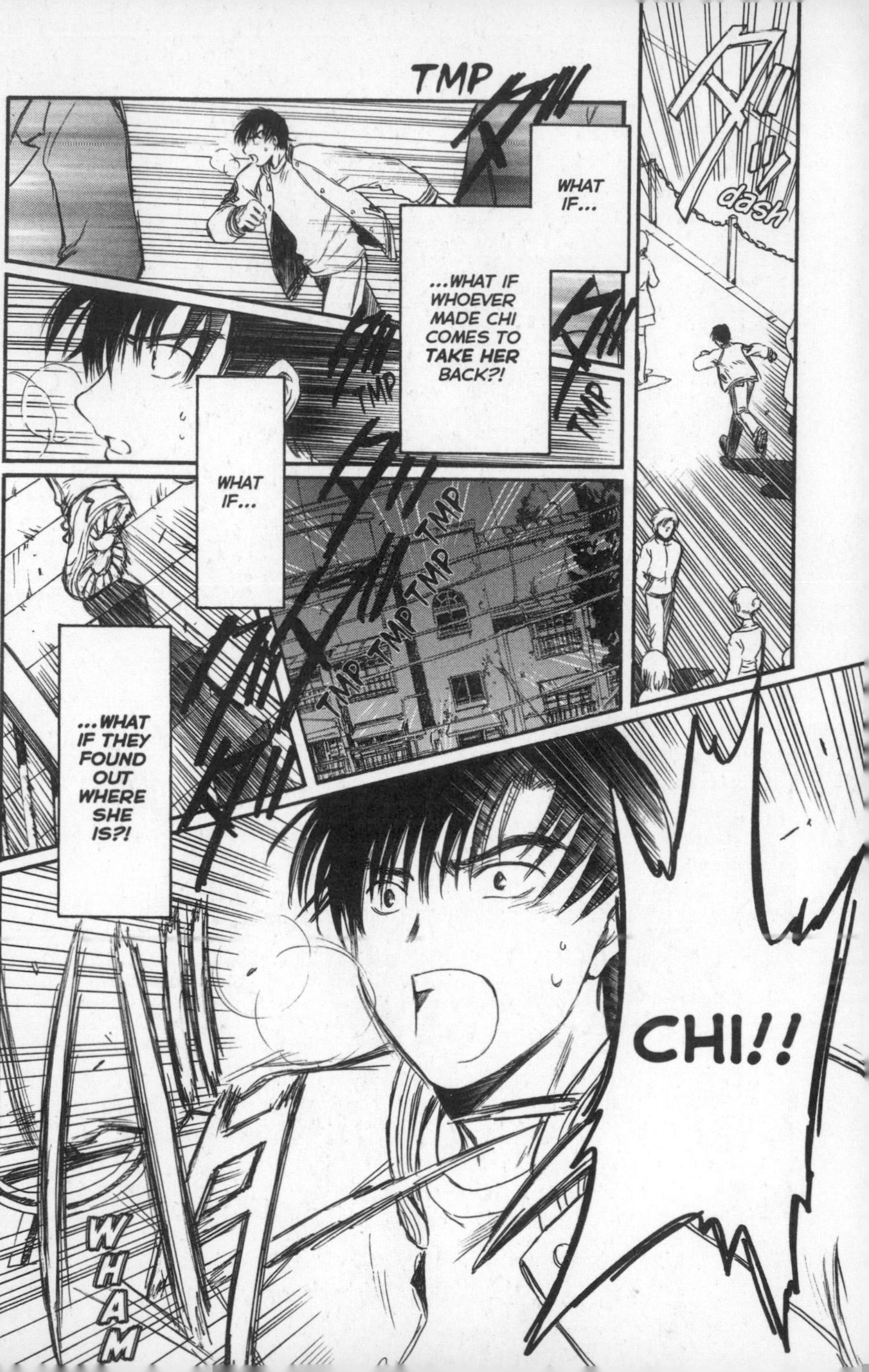
dash
TMP
WHAT IF...
...WHAT IF WHOEVER MADE CHI COMES TO TAKE HER BACK?!
TMP
TMP
WHAT IF...
TMP TMP TMP TMP TMP
...WHAT IF THEY FOUND OUT WHERE SHE IS?!
CHI!!
WHAM

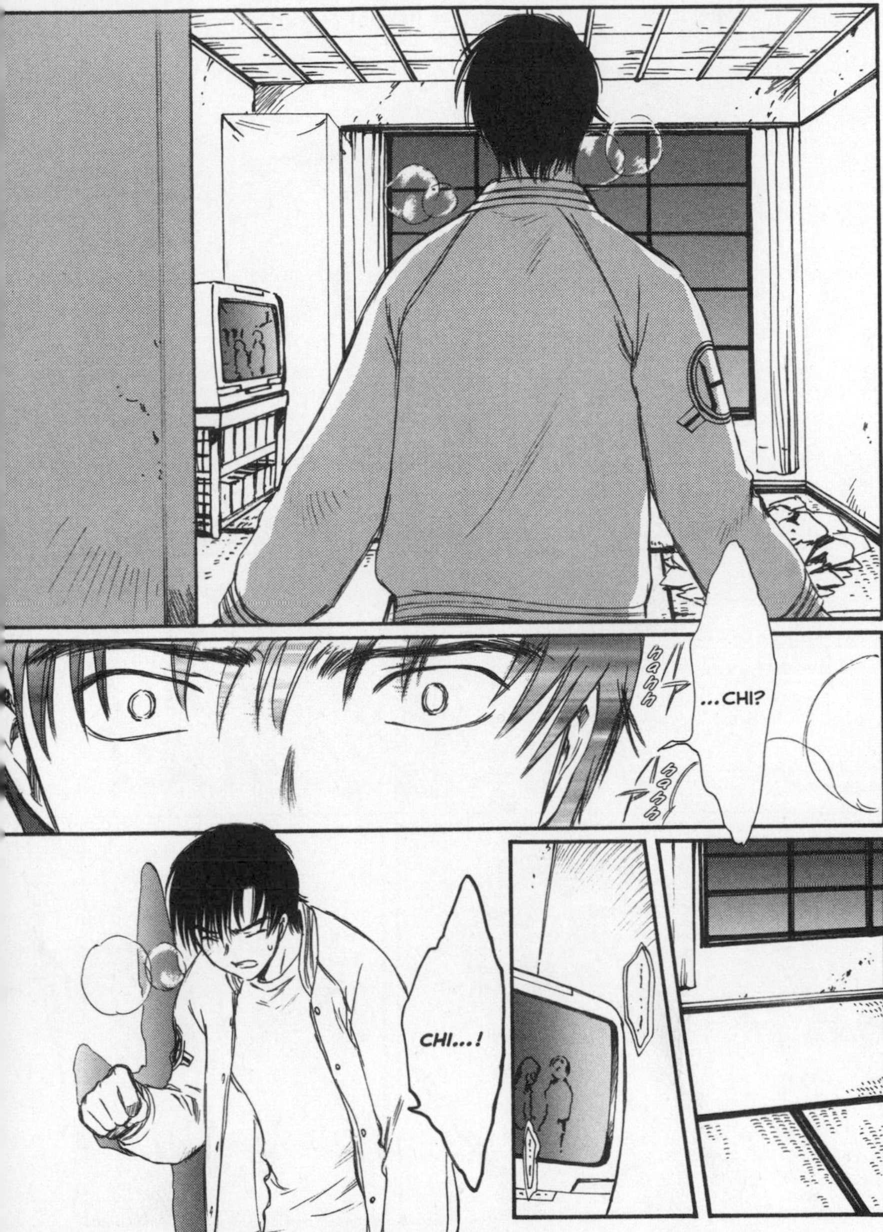
...CHI?
hahh
ハア
hahh
ハア
CHI...!

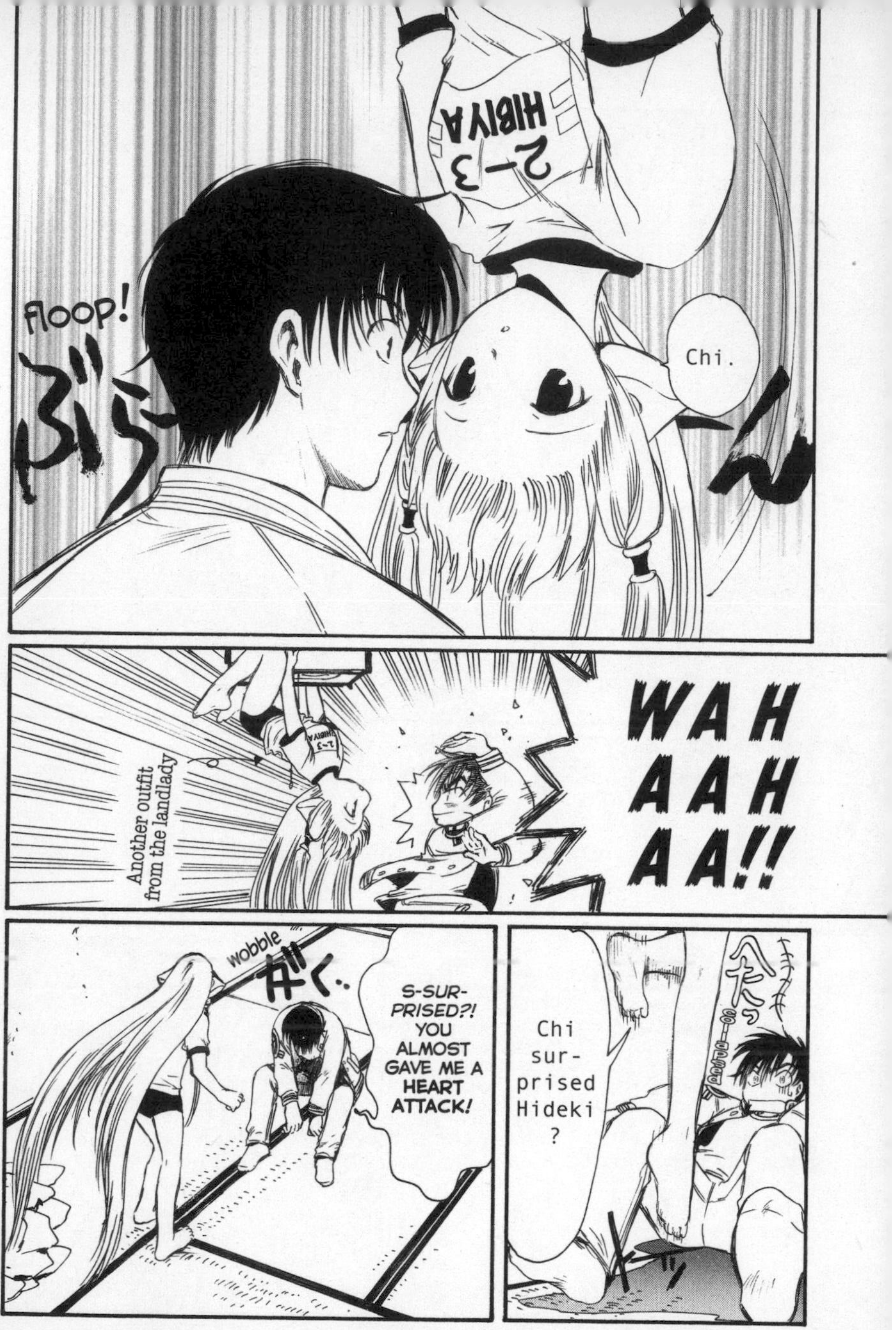

floop!
Chi.
WAH AAH AA!!
Another outfit from the landlady
Chi surprised Hideki?
S-SUR-PRISED?! YOU ALMOST GAVE ME A HEART ATTACK!
wobble

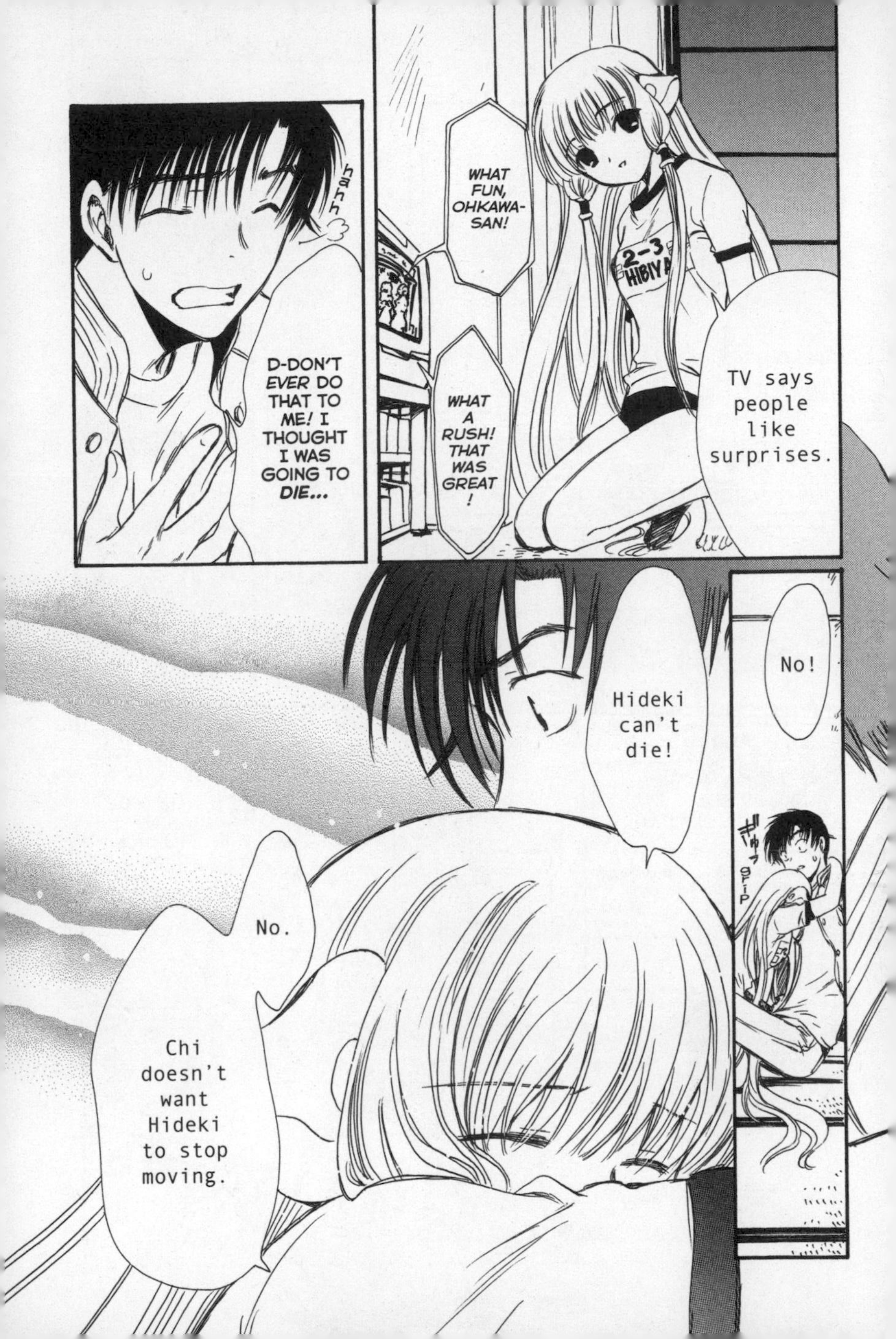
WHAT FUN, OHKAWA-SAN!
WHAT A RUSH! THAT WAS GREAT!
TV says people like surprises.
hahh
D-DON'T EVER DO THAT TO ME! I THOUGHT I WAS GOING TO DIE...
No!
grip
Hideki can't die!
No.
Chi doesn't want Hideki to stop moving.

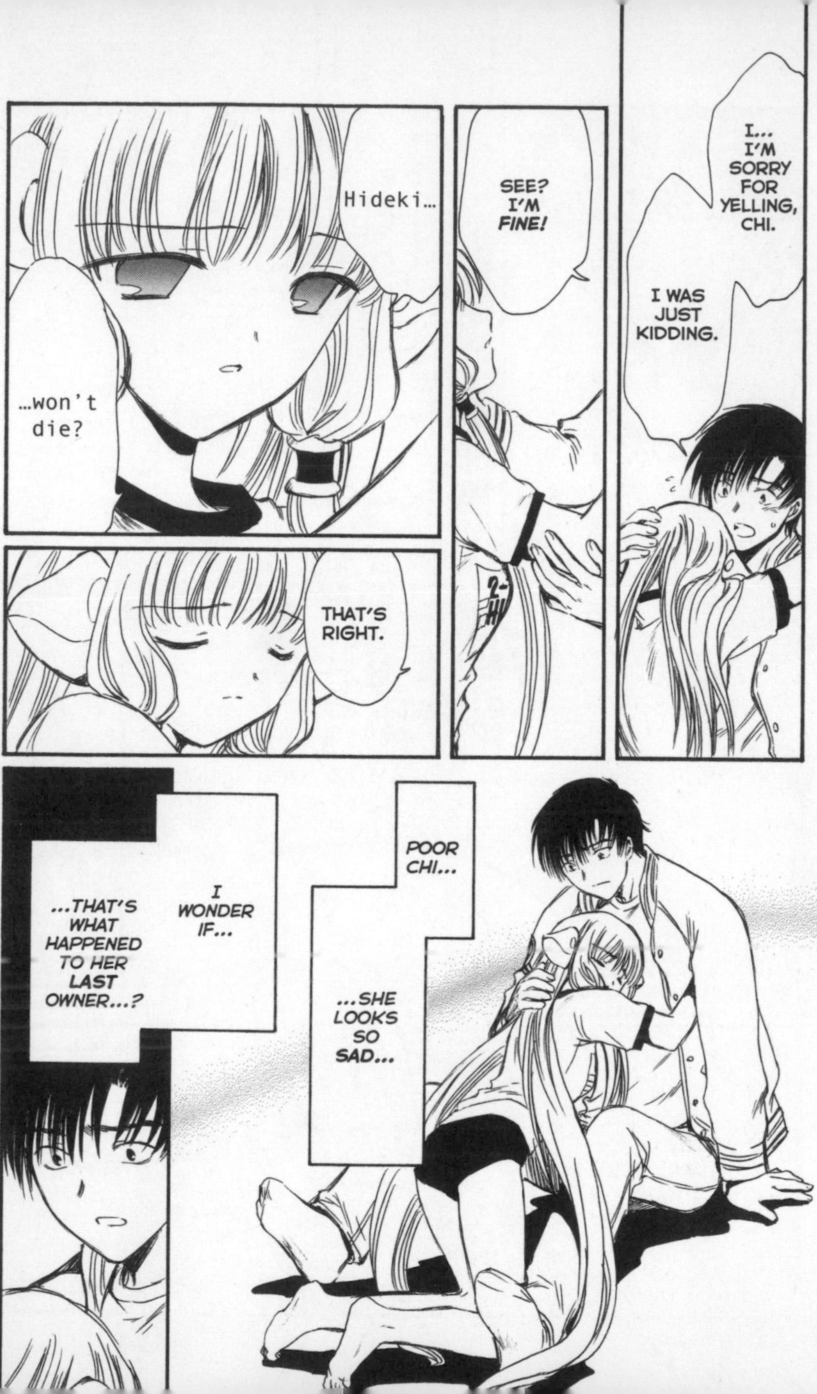
I... I'M SORRY FOR YELLING, CHI.
I WAS JUST KIDDING.
SEE? I'M *FINE!*
Hideki...
...won't die?
THAT'S RIGHT.
POOR CHI...
...SHE LOOKS SO SAD...
I WONDER IF...
...THAT'S WHAT HAPPENED TO HER LAST OWNER...?

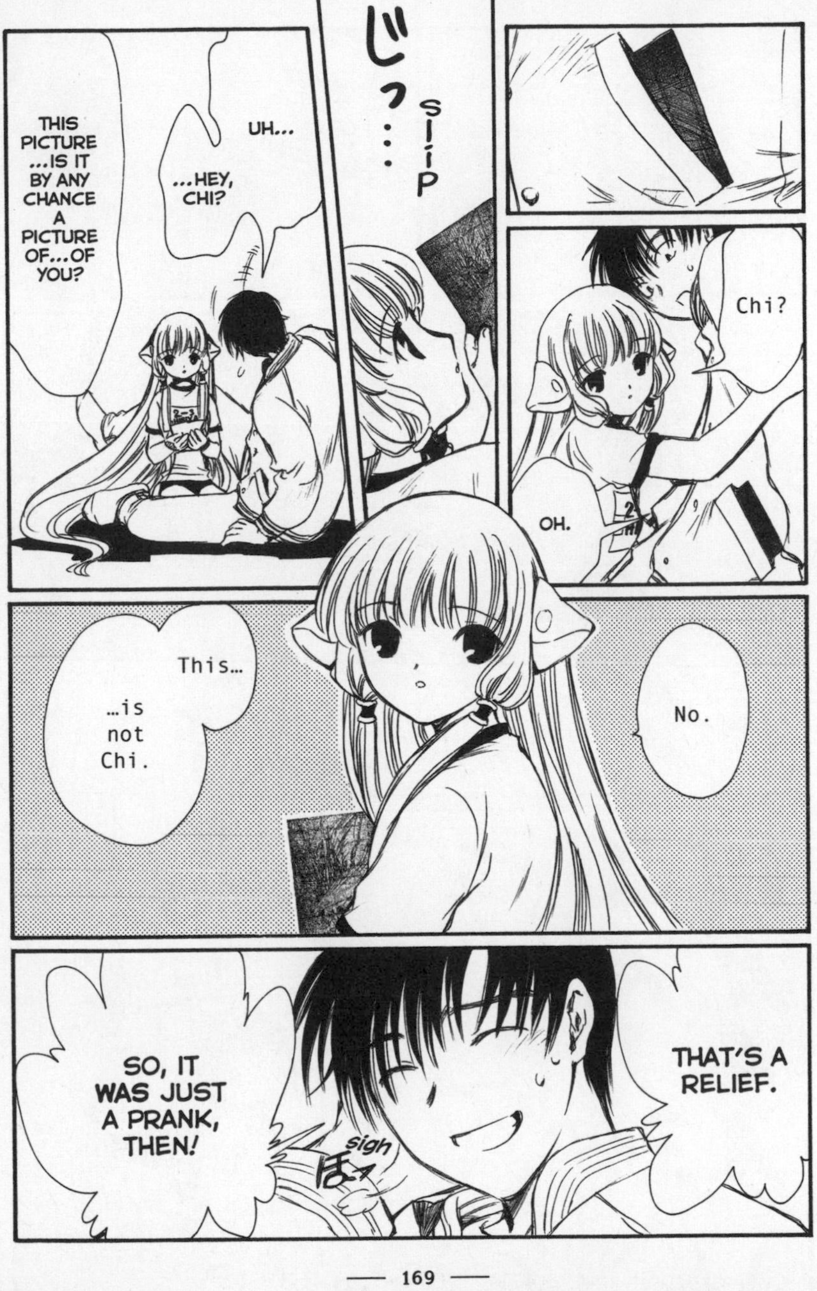

Chi?
OH.
じっ…
SIIP
UH…
…HEY, CHI?
THIS PICTURE …IS IT BY ANY CHANCE A PICTURE OF…OF YOU?
No.
This…
…is not Chi.
THAT'S A RELIEF.
SO, IT WAS JUST A PRANK, THEN!
ほっ
sigh

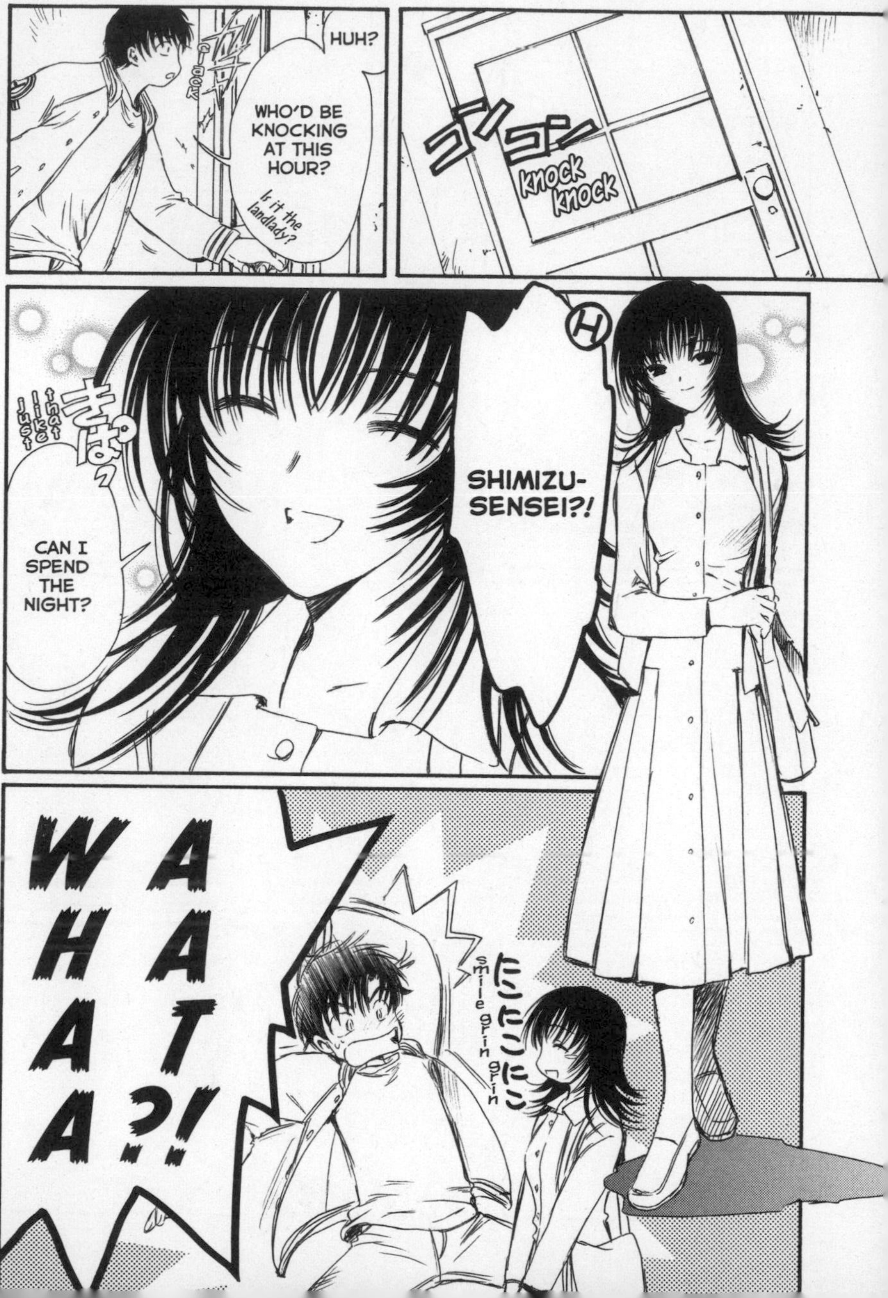

コンコン
knock knock
creak
HUH?
WHO'D BE KNOCKING AT THIS HOUR?
Is it the landlady?
SHIMIZU-SENSEI?!
きぱっ
just like that
CAN I SPEND THE NIGHT?
WHAAAAAT?!
にこにこ
smile grin grin

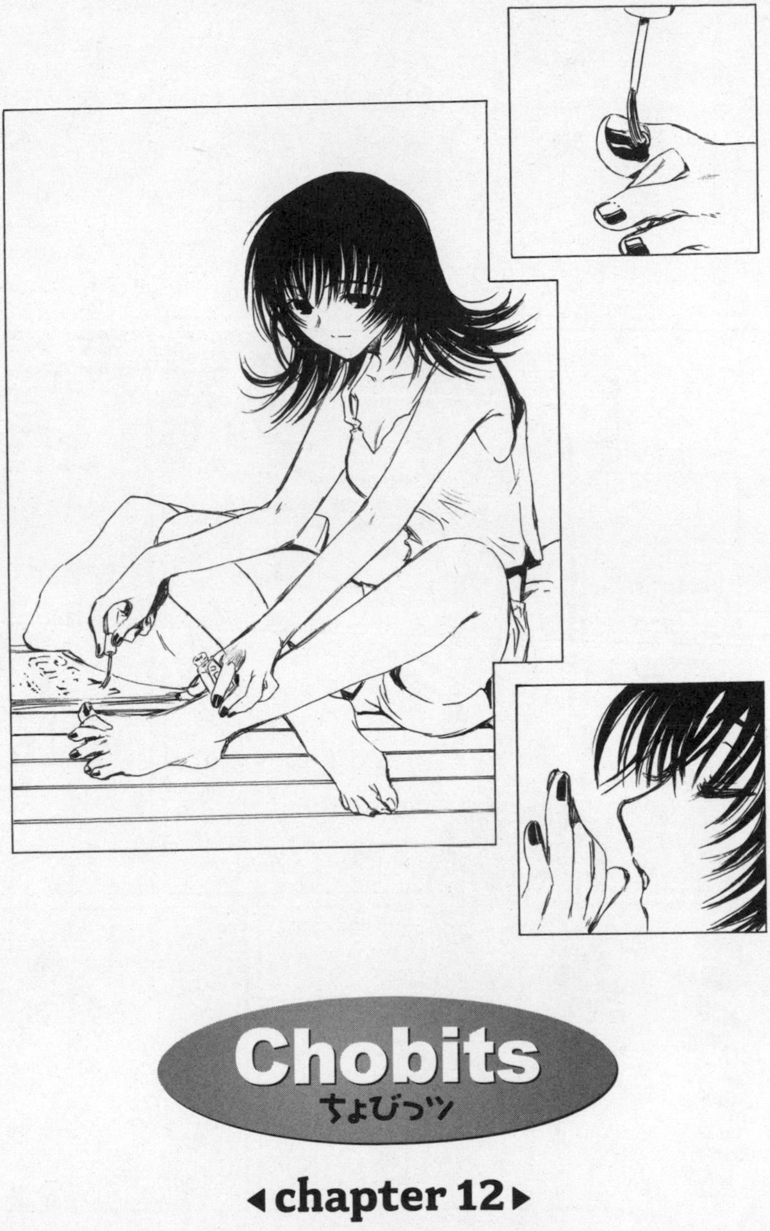

Chobits
ちょびっツ

◂chapter 12▸

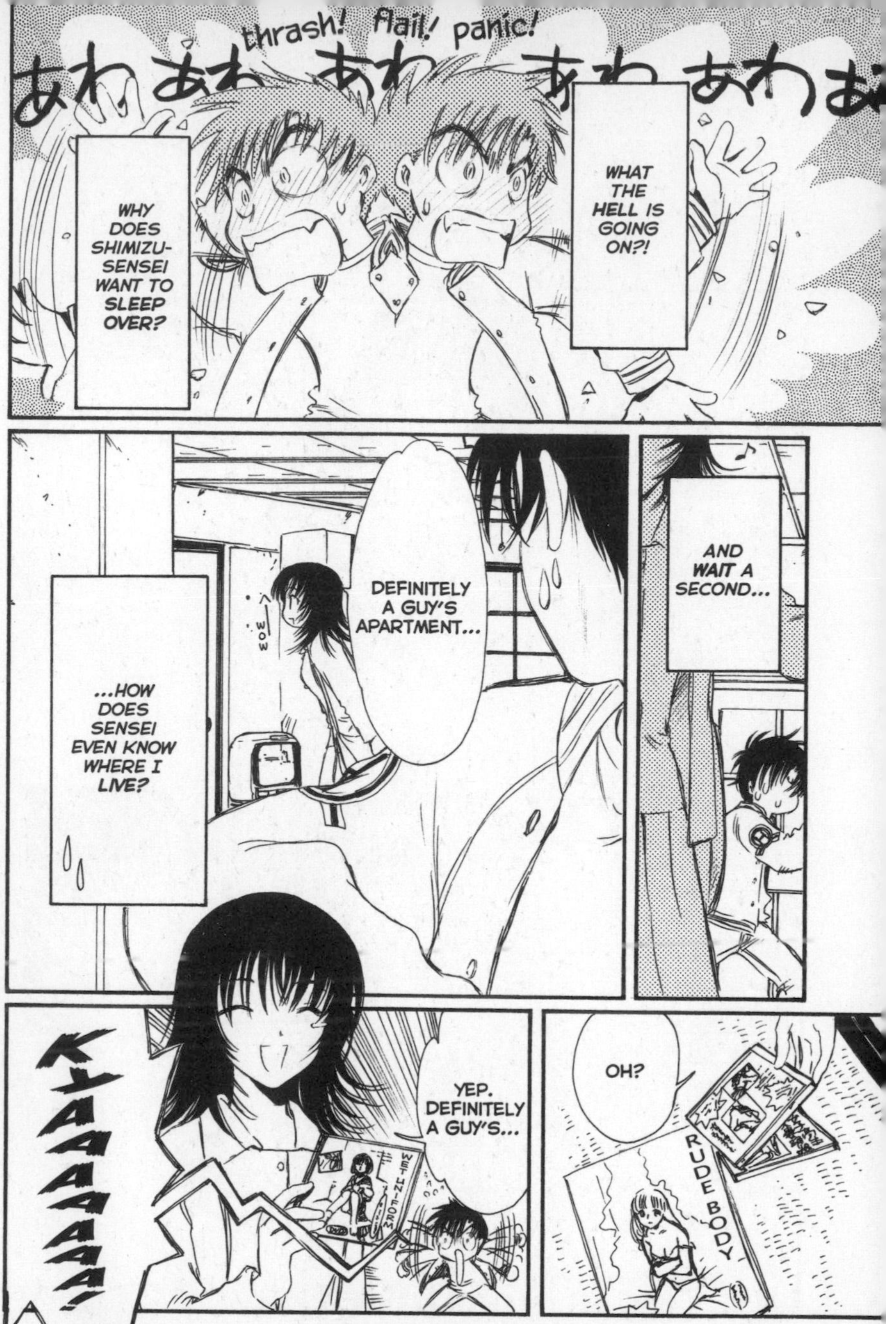
thrash! flail! panic!
あわあわ あわ あわ あわあわ
WHAT THE HELL IS GOING ON?!
WHY DOES SHIMIZU-SENSEI WANT TO SLEEP OVER?
AND WAIT A SECOND...
DEFINITELY A GUY'S APARTMENT...
WOW
...HOW DOES SENSEI EVEN KNOW WHERE I LIVE?
OH?
RUDE BODY
YEP. DEFINITELY A GUY'S...
WET UNIFORM
KYAAAAAAA!

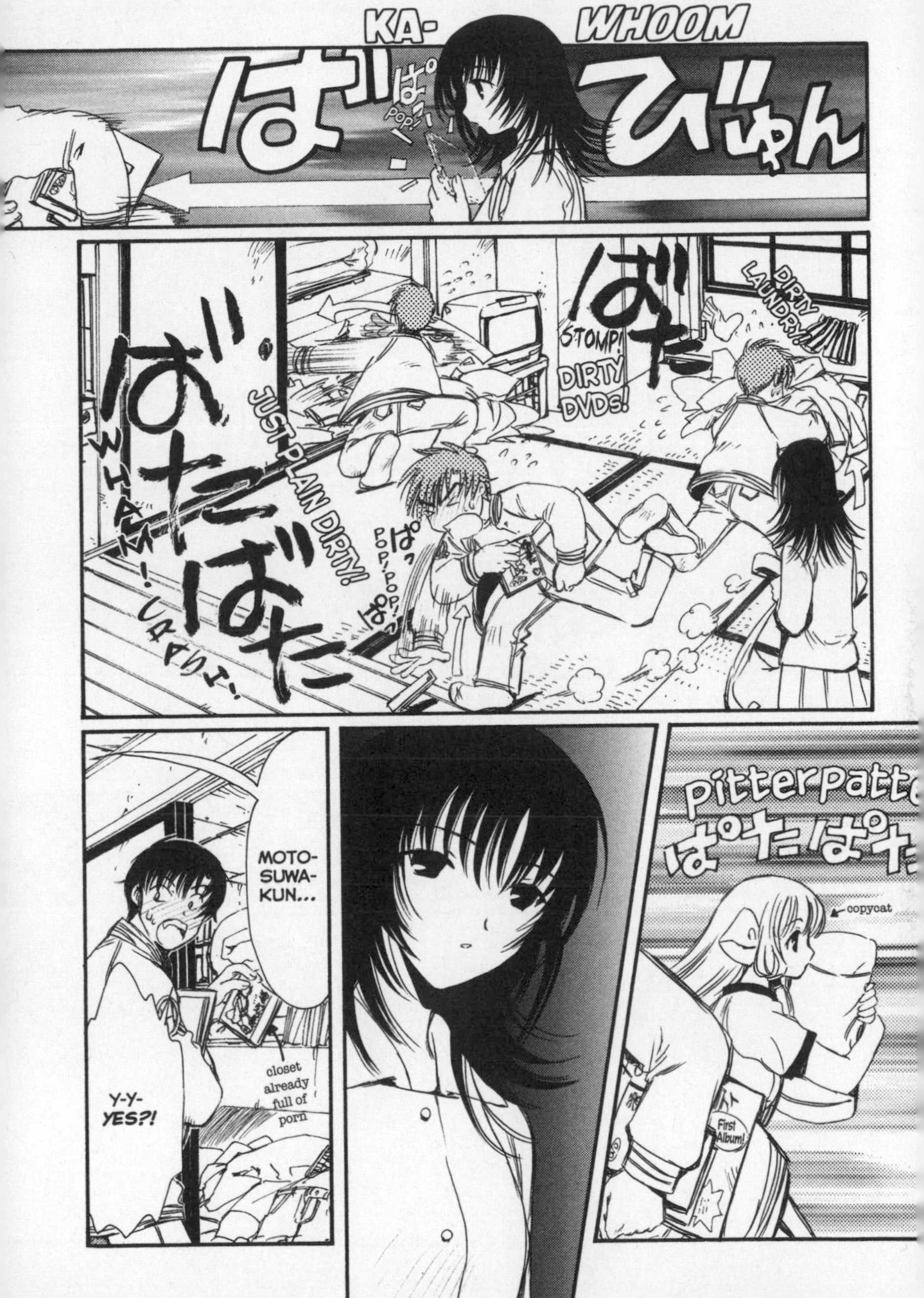
KA-
WHOOM
POP!
DIRTY LAUNDRY!
STOMP!
DIRTY DVDS!
JUST PLAIN DIRTY!
POP! POP!
WHAM!
pitterpatte
copycat
First Album!
MOTO-SUWA-KUN...
closet already full of porn
Y-Y-YES?!

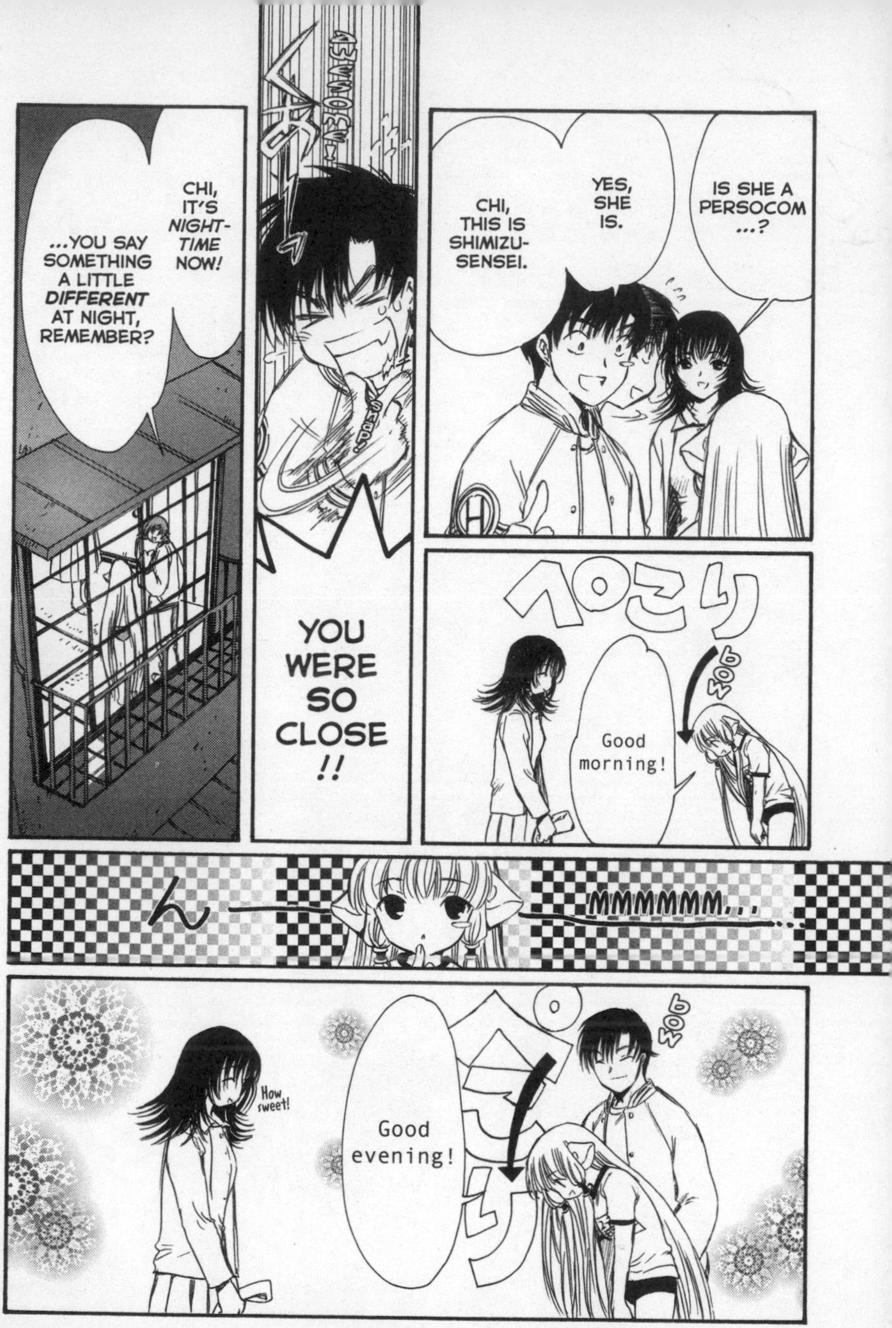
IS SHE A PERSOCOM ...?
YES, SHE IS.
CHI, THIS IS SHIMIZU-SENSEI.
へこり
BOW
Good morning!
SWOOSH!
SNAP!
YOU WERE SO CLOSE!!
CHI, IT'S NIGHT-TIME NOW!
...YOU SAY SOMETHING A LITTLE DIFFERENT AT NIGHT, REMEMBER?
ん——
MMMMMM...
BOW
Good evening!
How sweet!

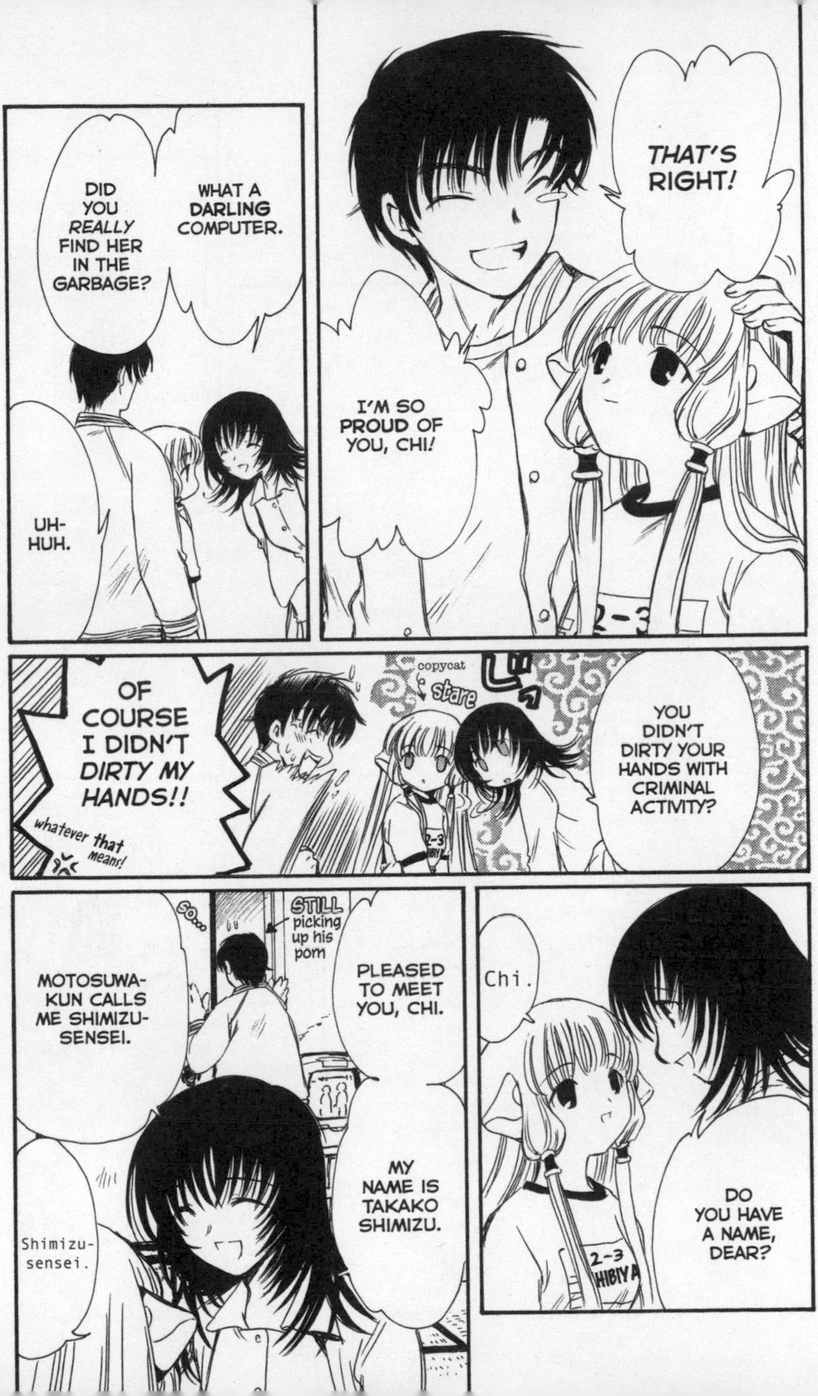
THAT'S RIGHT!
I'M SO PROUD OF YOU, CHI!
WHAT A DARLING COMPUTER.
DID YOU REALLY FIND HER IN THE GARBAGE?
UH-HUH.
YOU DIDN'T DIRTY YOUR HANDS WITH CRIMINAL ACTIVITY?
copycat
stare
OF COURSE I DIDN'T DIRTY MY HANDS!!
whatever that means!
DO YOU HAVE A NAME, DEAR?
Chi.
PLEASED TO MEET YOU, CHI.
MY NAME IS TAKAKO SHIMIZU.
STILL picking up his porn
SO...
MOTOSUWA-KUN CALLS ME SHIMIZU-SENSEI.
Shimizu-sensei.

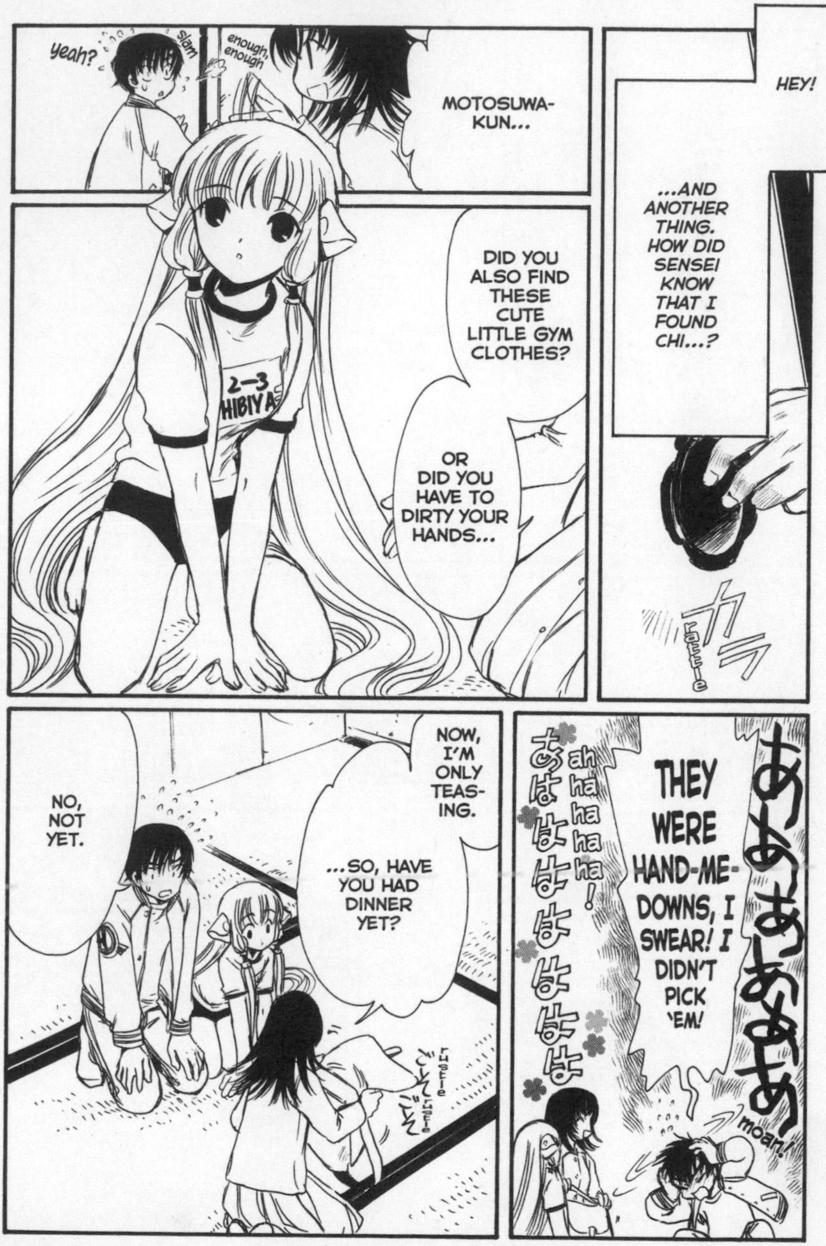

HEY!
...AND ANOTHER THING. HOW DID SENSEI KNOW THAT I FOUND CHI...?
カラ
rattle
MOTOSUWA-KUN...
yeah?
slam
enough, enough
DID YOU ALSO FIND THESE CUTE LITTLE GYM CLOTHES?
OR DID YOU HAVE TO DIRTY YOUR HANDS...
2-3 HIBIYA
THEY WERE HAND-ME-DOWNS, I SWEAR! I DIDN'T PICK 'EM!
moan!
ah ha ha ha ha!
あはははは
NOW, I'M ONLY TEAS-ING.
...SO, HAVE YOU HAD DINNER YET?
NO, NOT YET.
rustle
ごそごそ
rustle

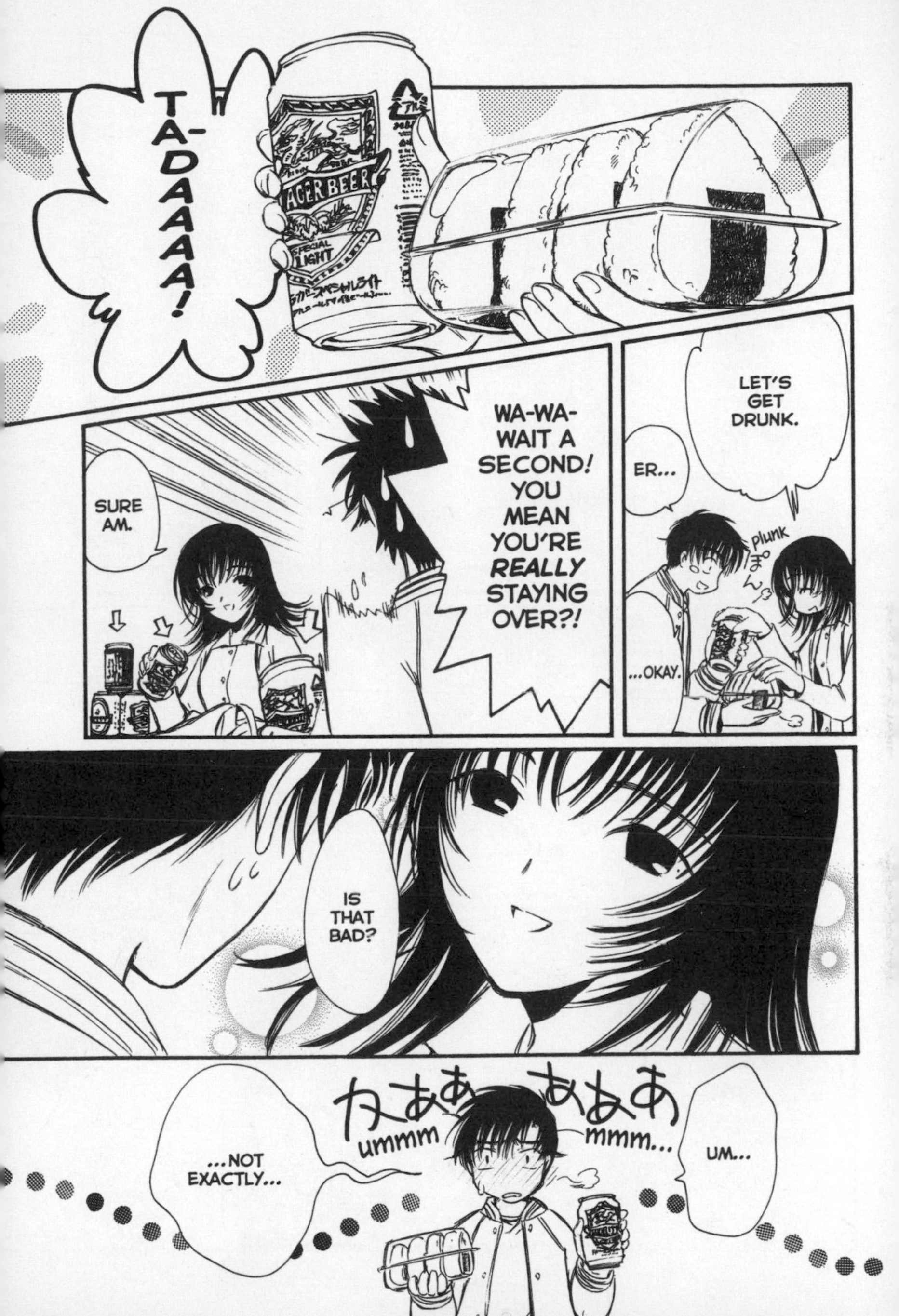
TA-DAAAAA!
LET'S GET DRUNK.
ER...
plunk
ぽん
...OKAY.
WA-WA-WAIT A SECOND! YOU MEAN YOU'RE REALLY STAYING OVER?!
SURE AM.
IS THAT BAD?
UM...
かあああ あああ
ummmm mmm...
...NOT EXACTLY...

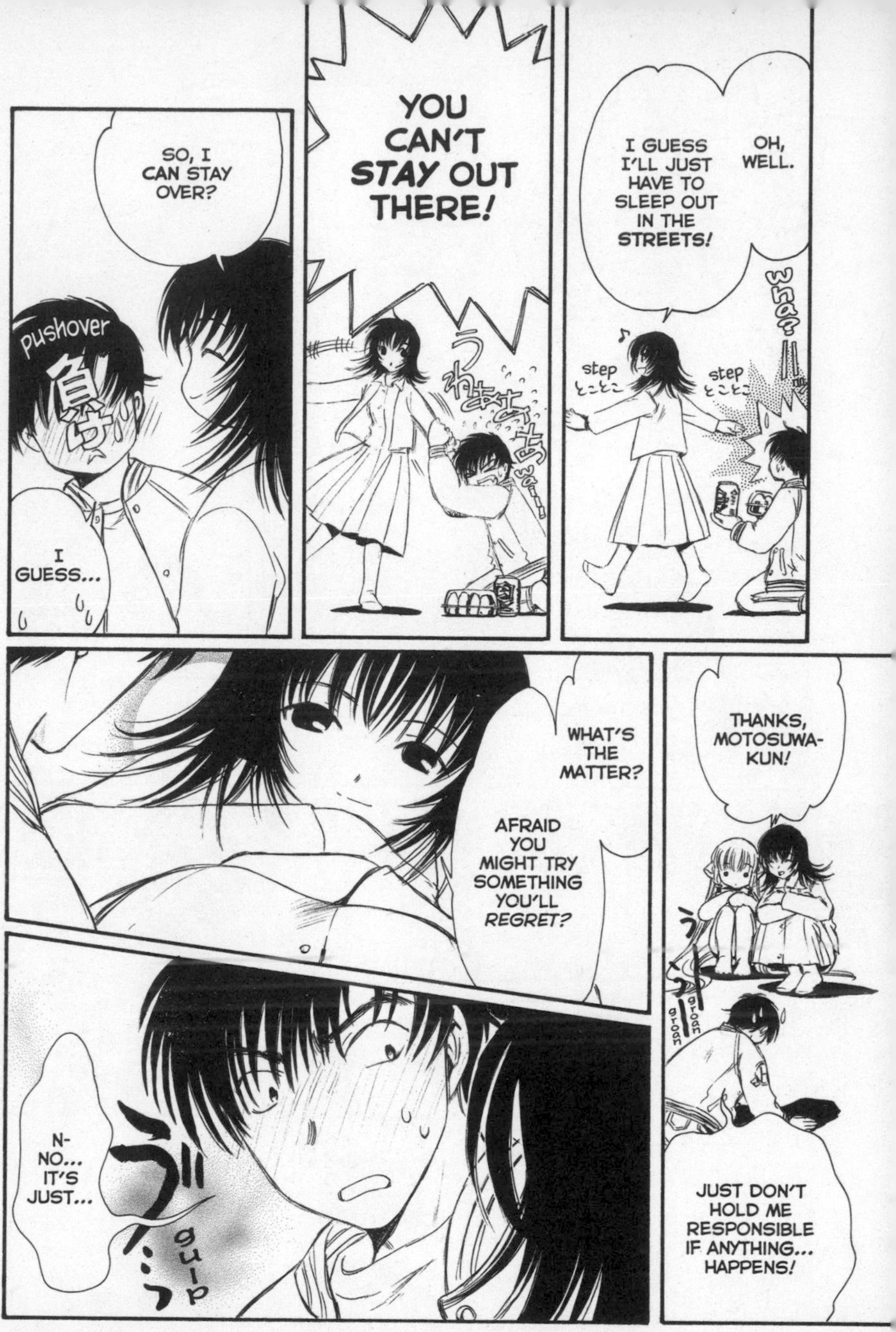
OH, WELL.
I GUESS I'LL JUST HAVE TO SLEEP OUT IN THE STREETS!
step とことこ
step とことこ
wha?!!
YOU CAN'T STAY OUT THERE!
SO, I CAN STAY OVER?
pushover
I GUESS...
THANKS, MOTOSUWA-KUN!
groan
groan
JUST DON'T HOLD ME RESPONSIBLE IF ANYTHING... HAPPENS!
WHAT'S THE MATTER?
AFRAID YOU MIGHT TRY SOMETHING YOU'LL REGRET?
N-NO... IT'S JUST...
gulp

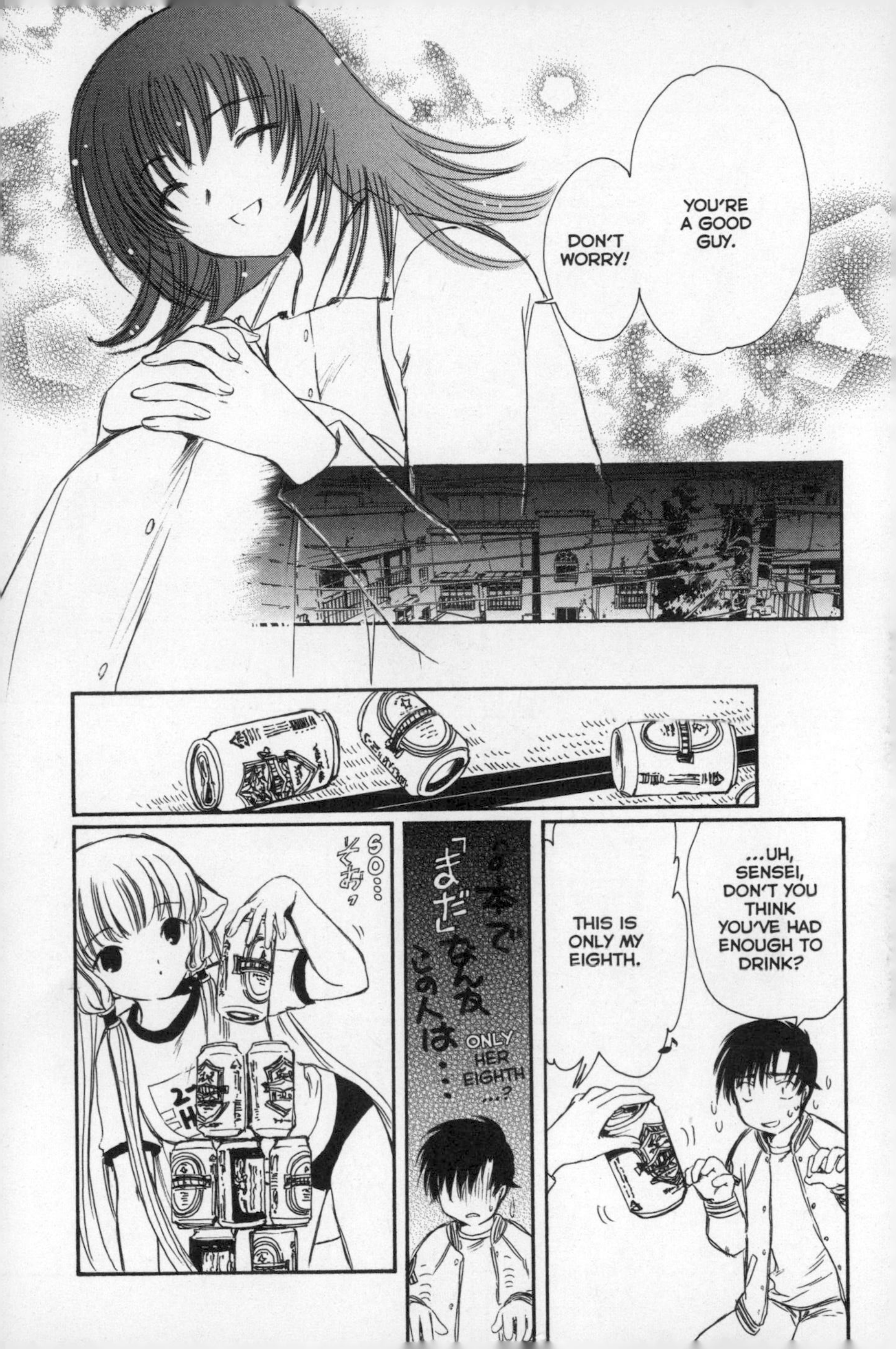
YOU'RE A GOOD GUY.
DON'T WORRY!
...UH, SENSEI, DON'T YOU THINK YOU'VE HAD ENOUGH TO DRINK?
THIS IS ONLY MY EIGHTH.
8本で「まだ」なんだこの人は・・・
ONLY HER EIGHTH ...?
SO...
そお

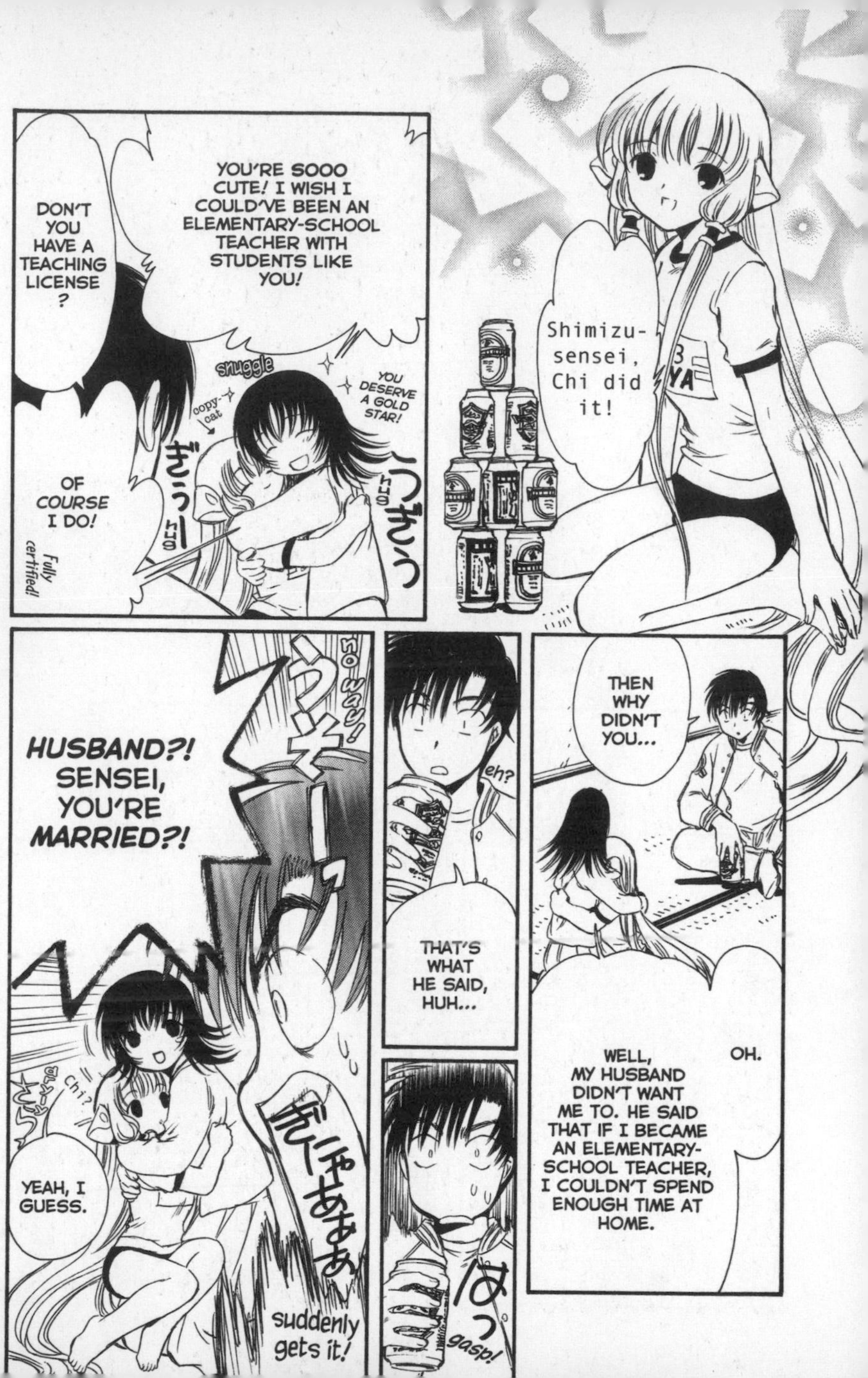
Shimizu-sensei, Chi did it!
YOU'RE SOOO CUTE! I WISH I COULD'VE BEEN AN ELEMENTARY-SCHOOL TEACHER WITH STUDENTS LIKE YOU!
DON'T YOU HAVE A TEACHING LICENSE?
YOU DESERVE A GOLD STAR!
snuggle
copy-cat
ぎゅう
hug
ぎゅう
hug
OF COURSE I DO!
Fully certified!
THEN WHY DIDN'T YOU...
OH.
WELL, MY HUSBAND DIDN'T WANT ME TO. HE SAID THAT IF I BECAME AN ELEMENTARY-SCHOOL TEACHER, I COULDN'T SPEND ENOUGH TIME AT HOME.
eh?
THAT'S WHAT HE SAID, HUH...
はっ
gasp!
no way!
HUSBAND?! SENSEI, YOU'RE MARRIED?!
suddenly gets it!
Chi?
YEAH, I GUESS.

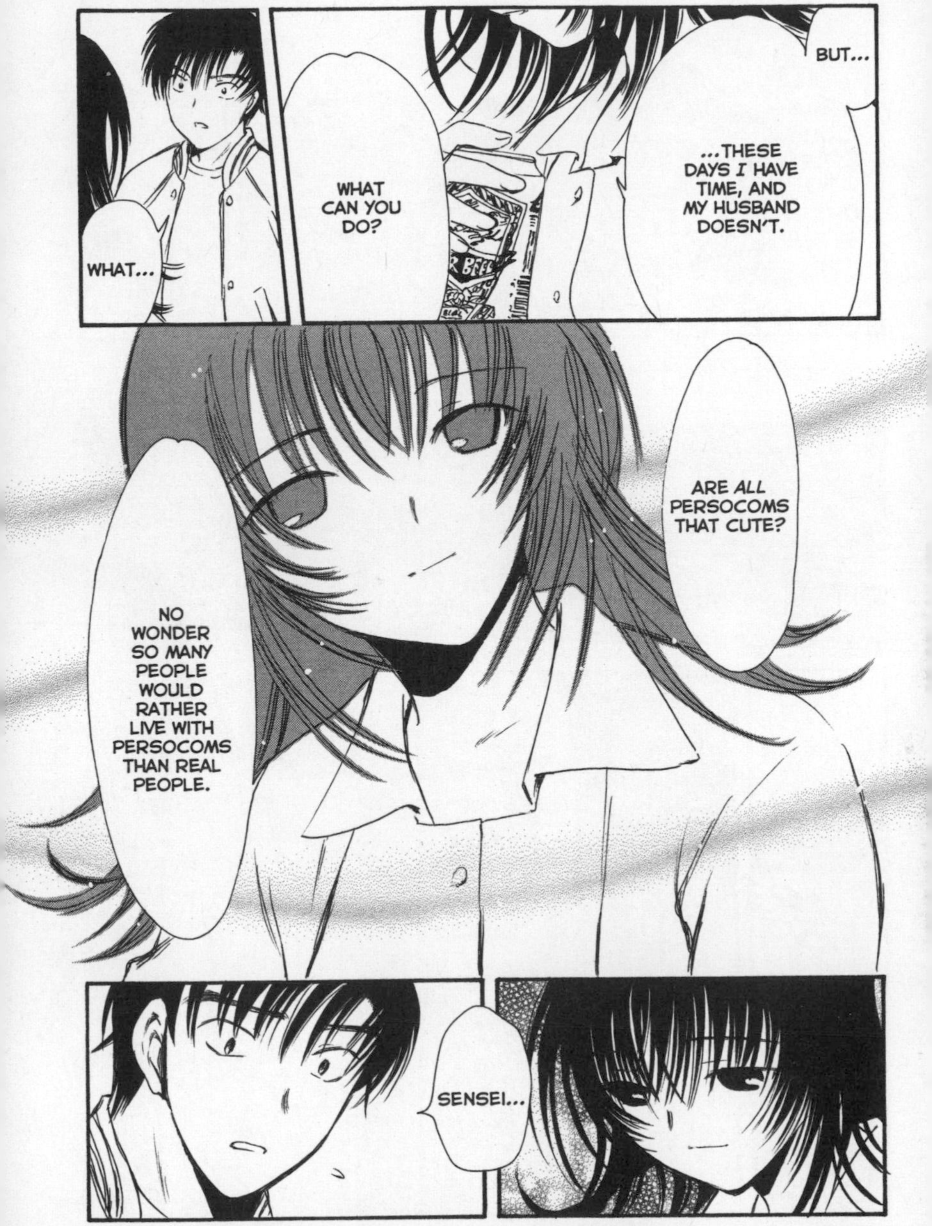
BUT...
...THESE DAYS I HAVE TIME, AND MY HUSBAND DOESN'T.
WHAT CAN YOU DO?
WHAT...
ARE *ALL* PERSOCOMS THAT CUTE?
NO WONDER SO MANY PEOPLE WOULD RATHER LIVE WITH PERSOCOMS THAN REAL PEOPLE.
SENSEI...

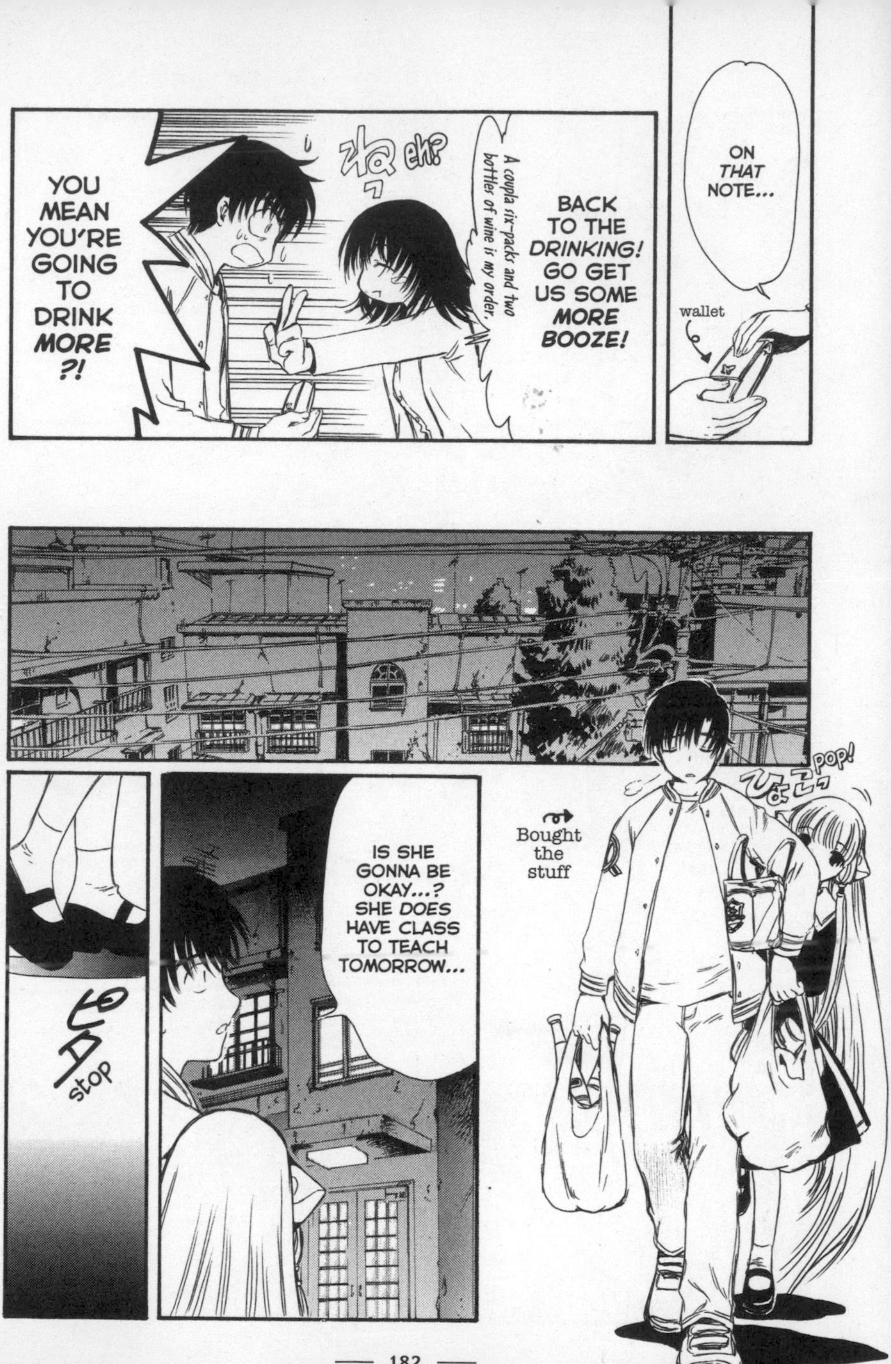
ON THAT NOTE...
wallet
BACK TO THE DRINKING! GO GET US SOME MORE BOOZE!
A coupla six-packs and two bottles of wine is my order.
eh?
YOU MEAN YOU'RE GOING TO DRINK MORE ?!
Bought the stuff
pop!
IS SHE GONNA BE OKAY...? SHE DOES HAVE CLASS TO TEACH TOMORROW...
stop

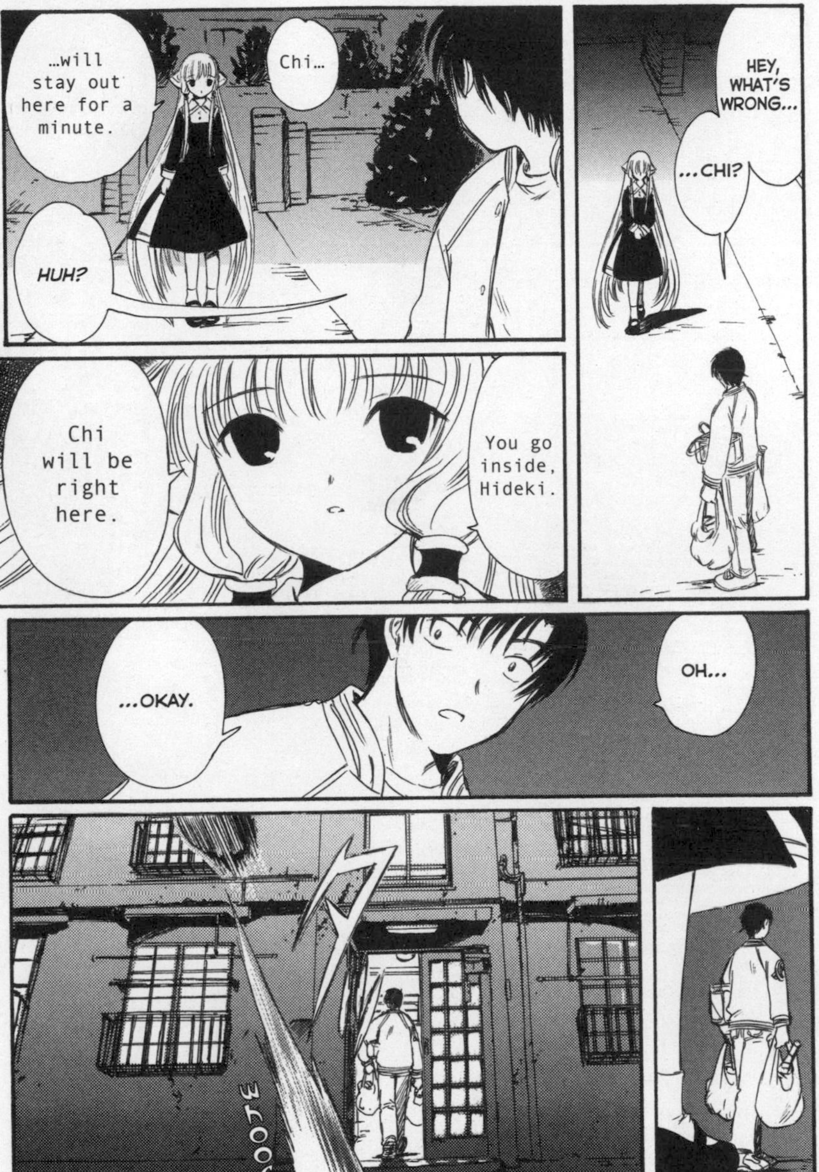
HEY, WHAT'S WRONG...
...CHI?
Chi...
...will stay out here for a minute.
HUH?
You go inside, Hideki.
Chi will be right here.
OH...
...OKAY.
WHOOSH

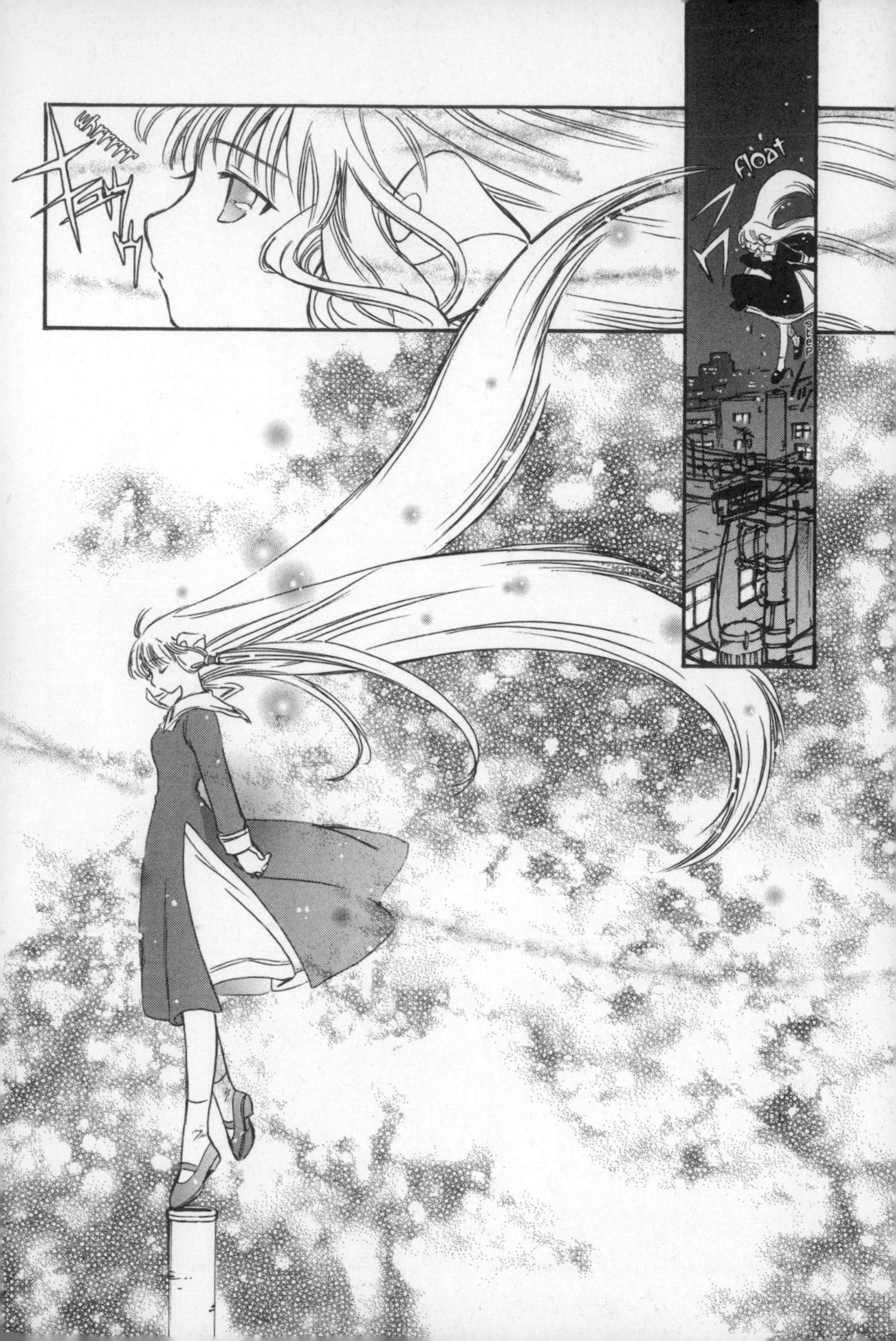
float
step
whrrrrr

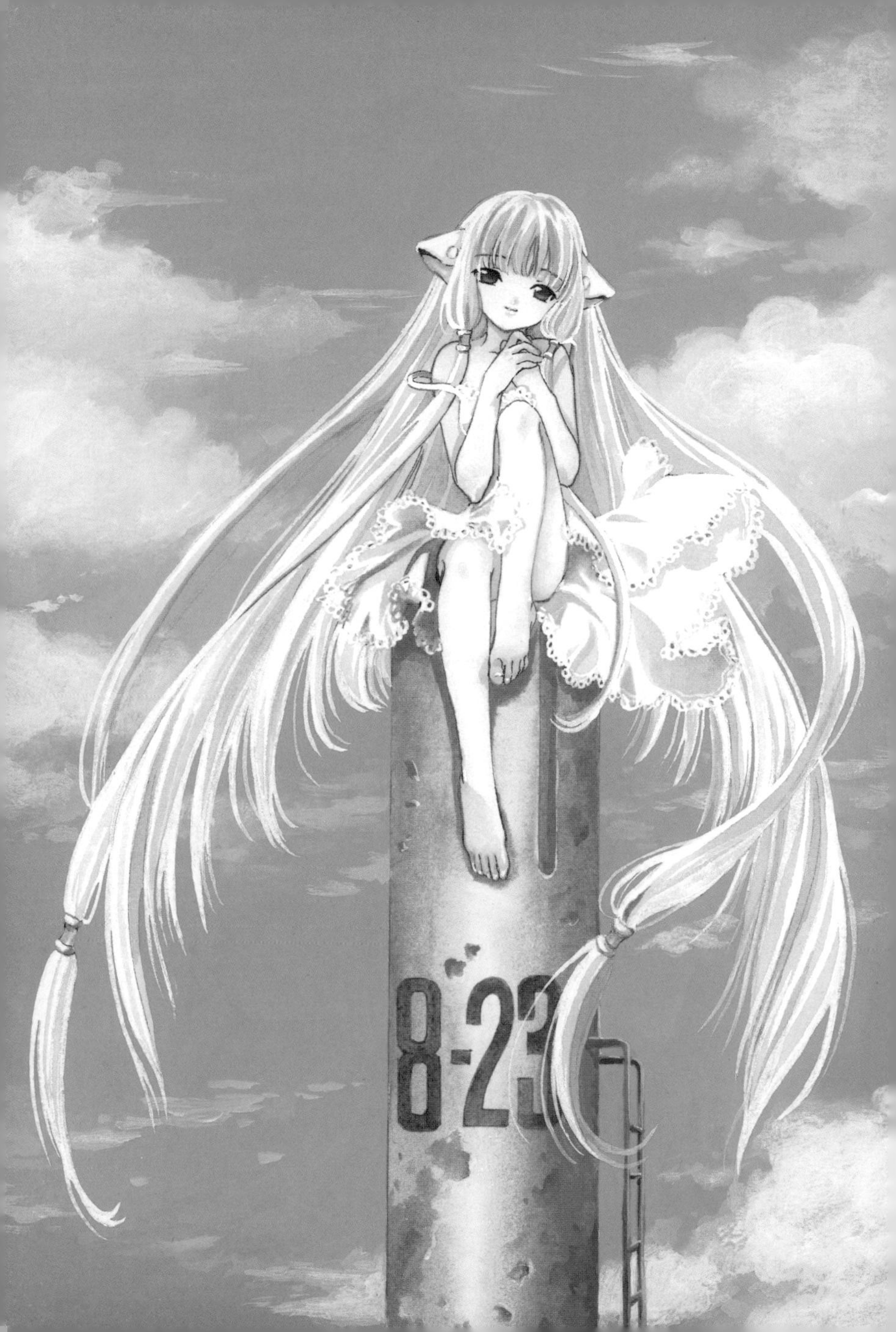
8-23

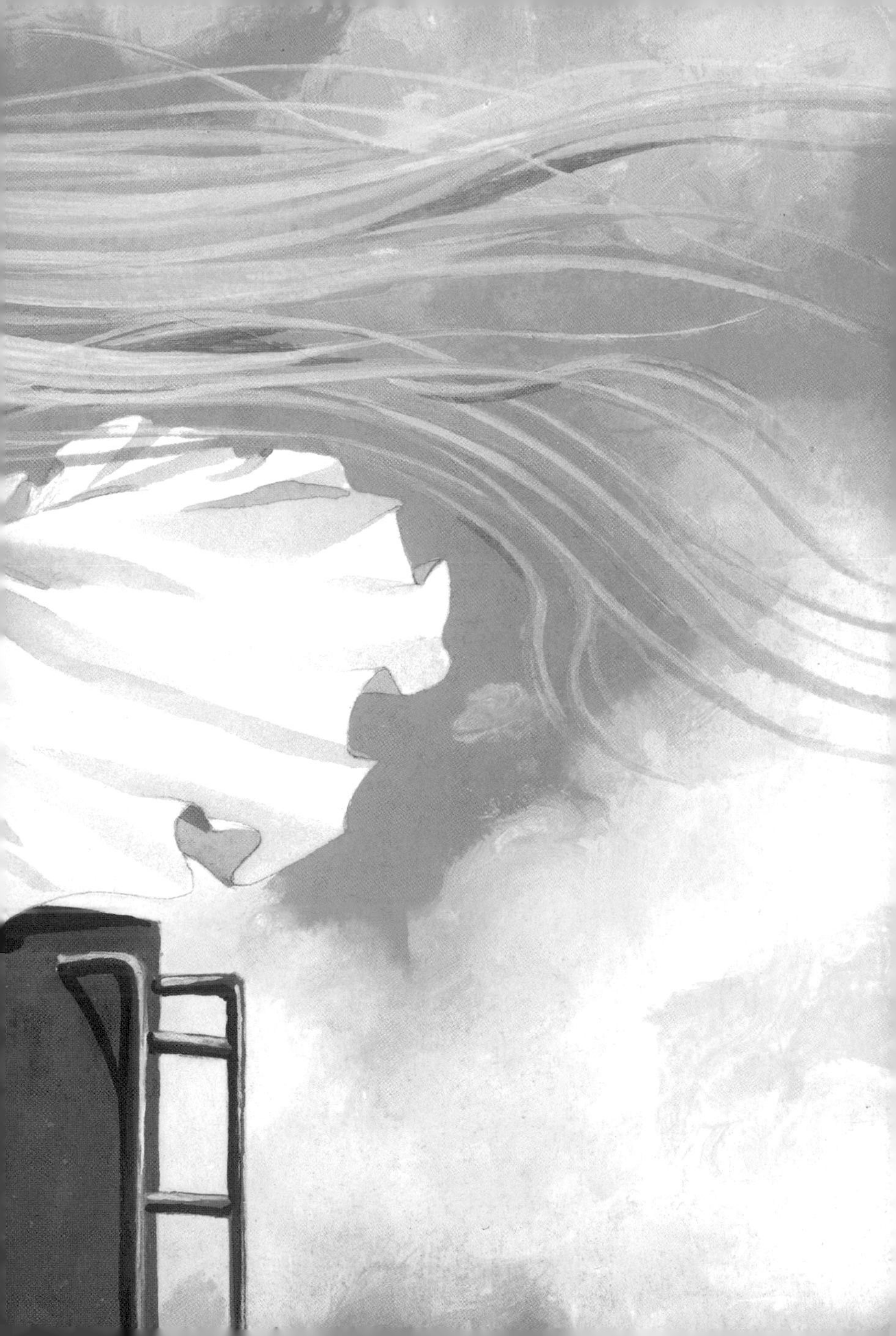

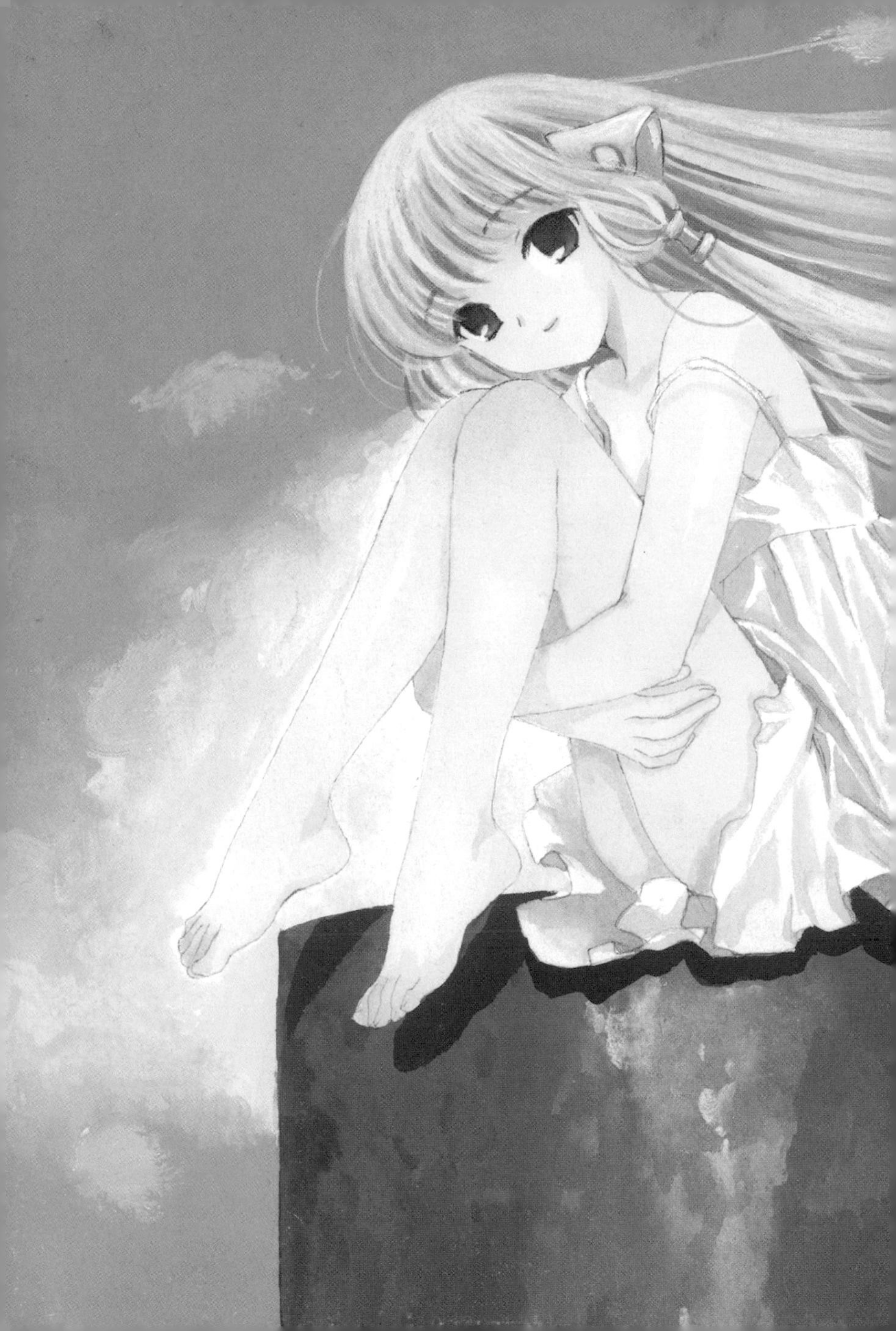

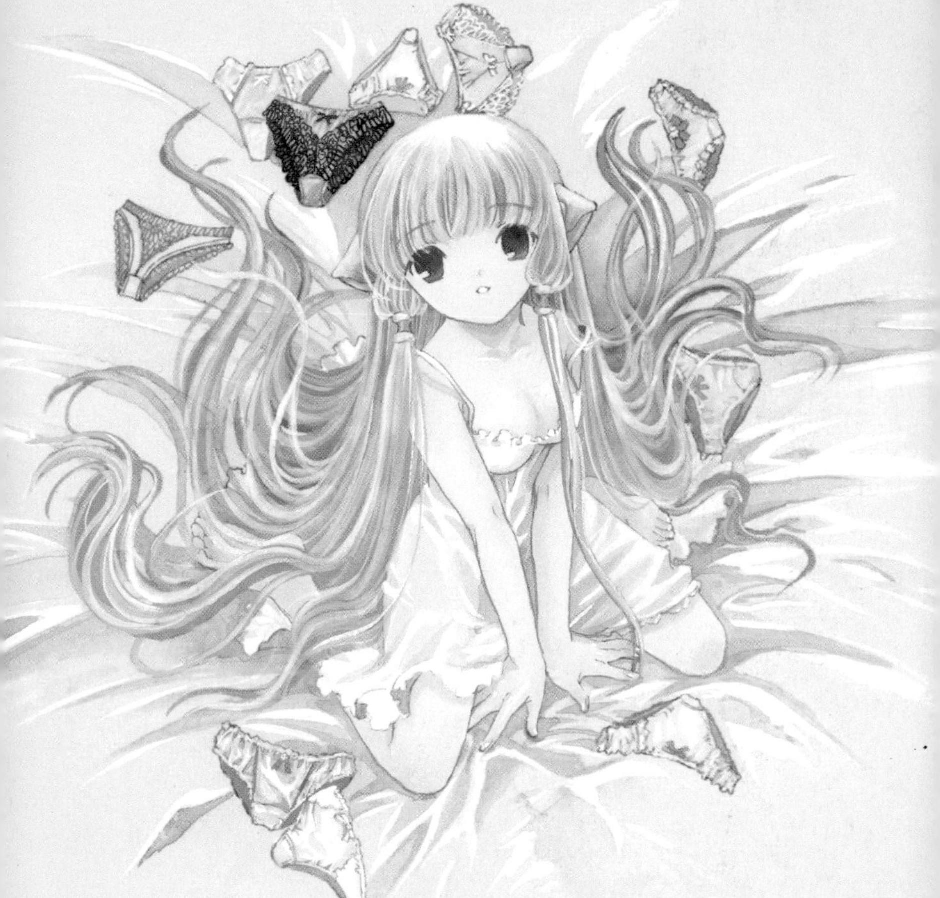

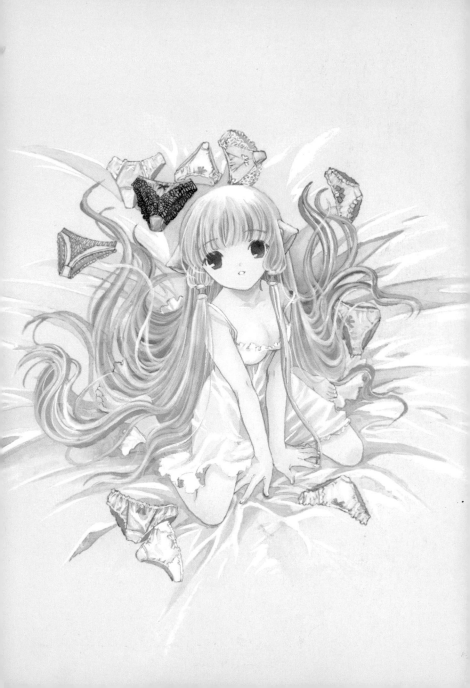

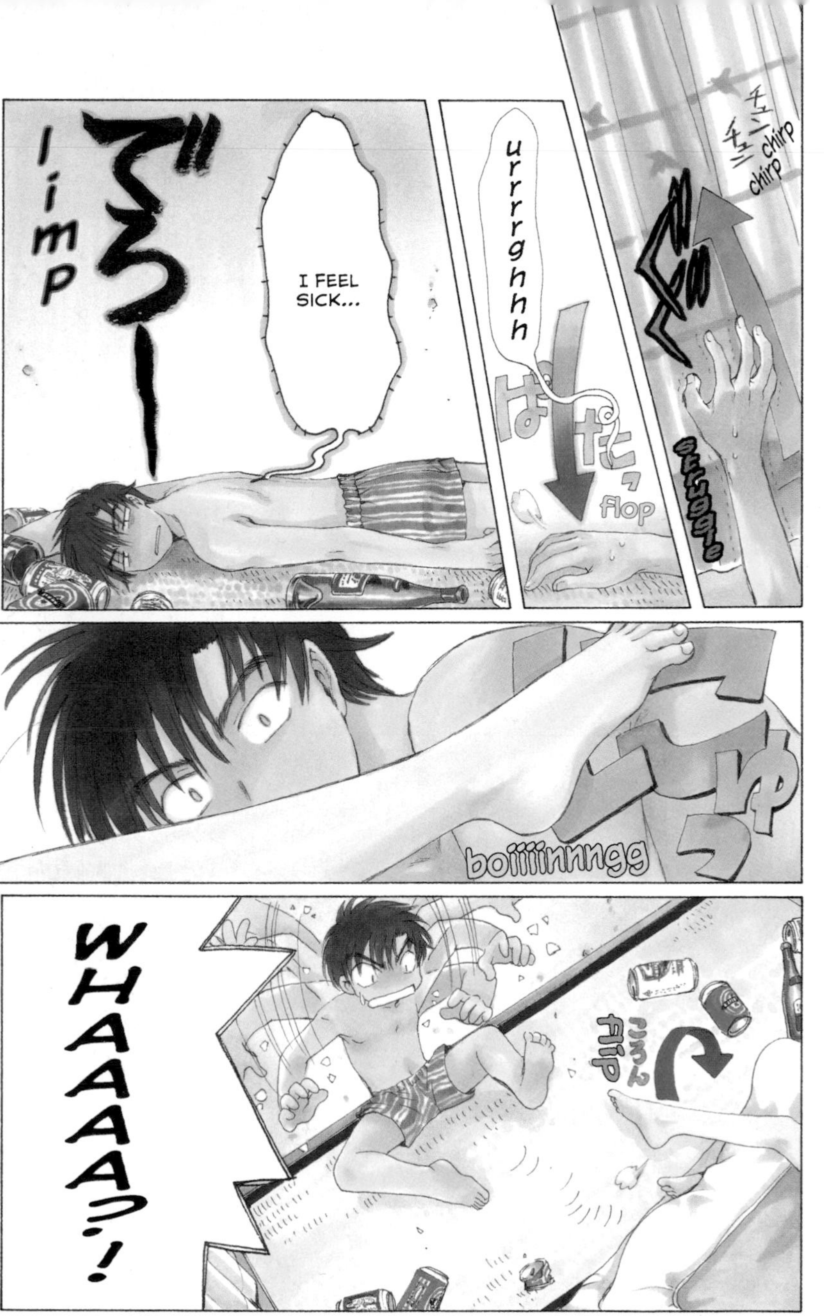
chirp chirp
struggle
urrrrghhh
flop
I FEEL SICK...
limp
boiiiinnngg
WHAAAA?!
ころん
tip

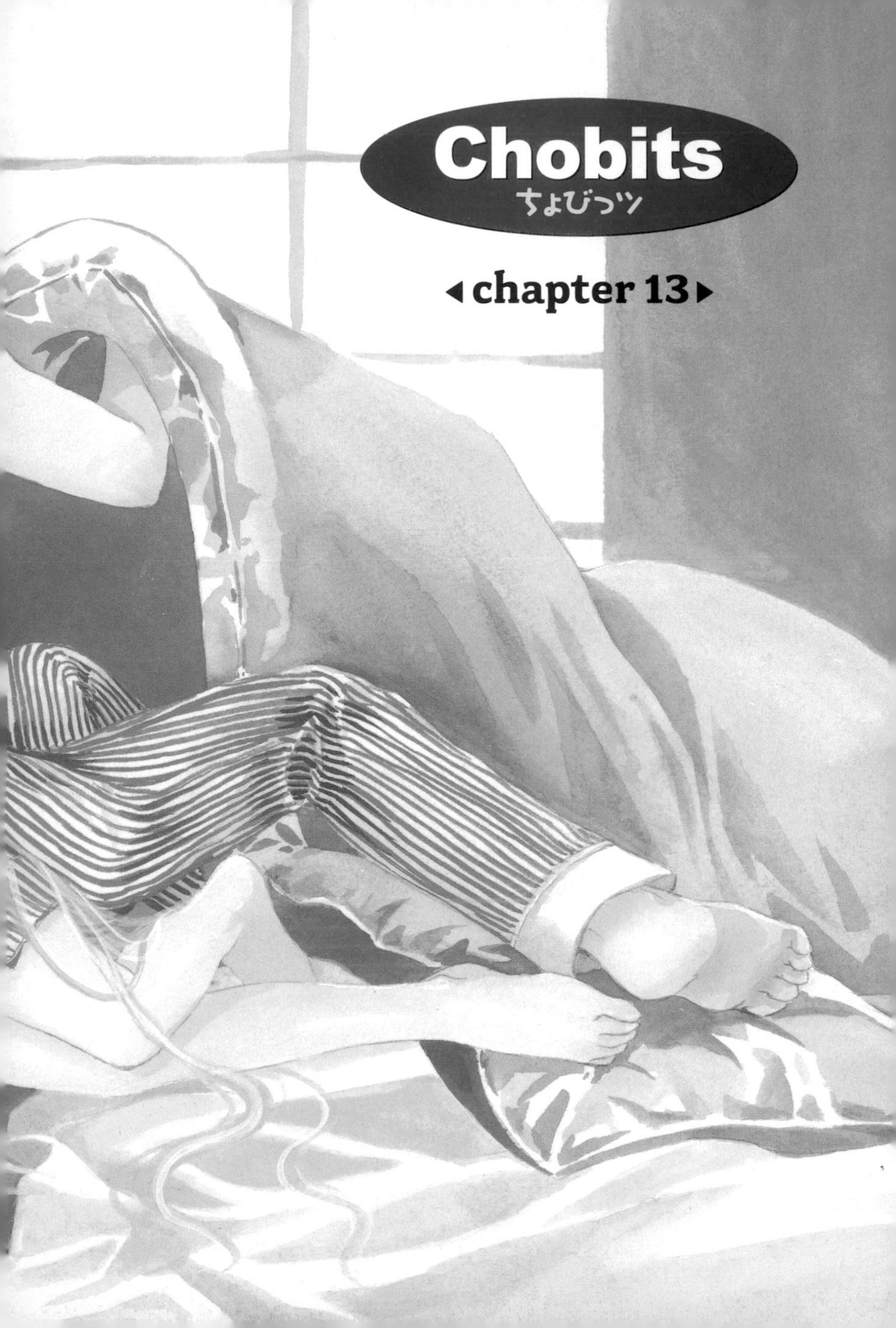
Chobits
ちょびっツ
chapter 13

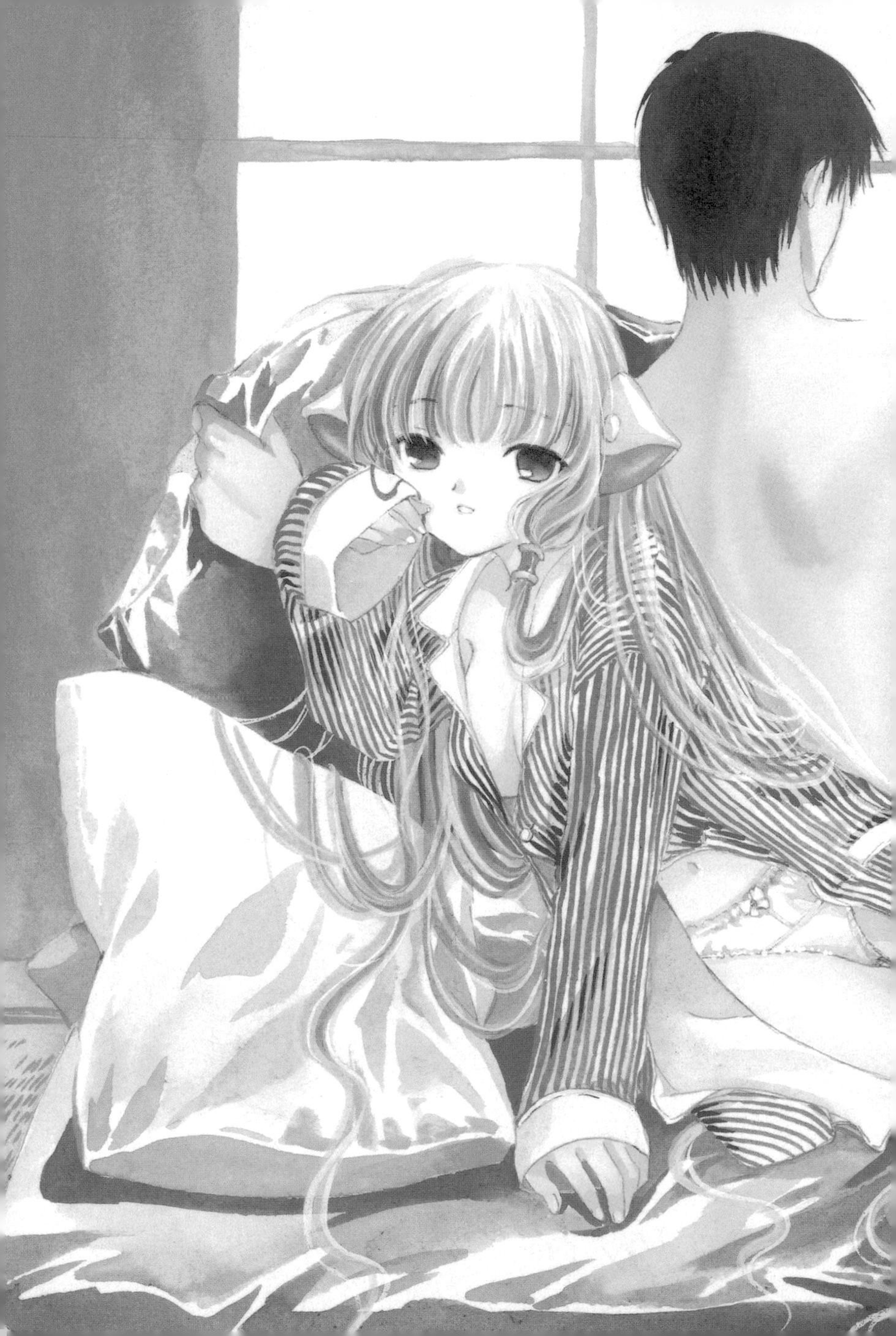

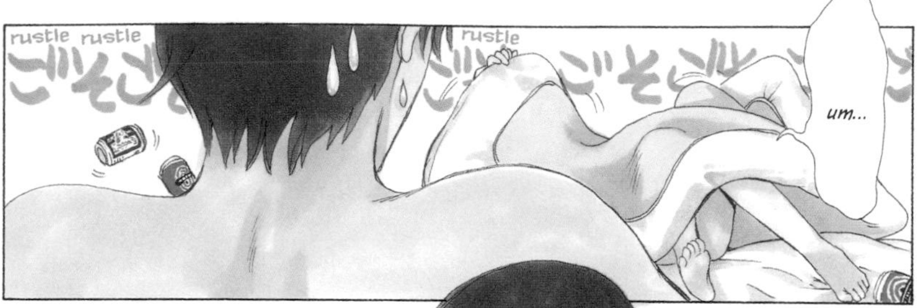
um...
rustle
rustle rustle

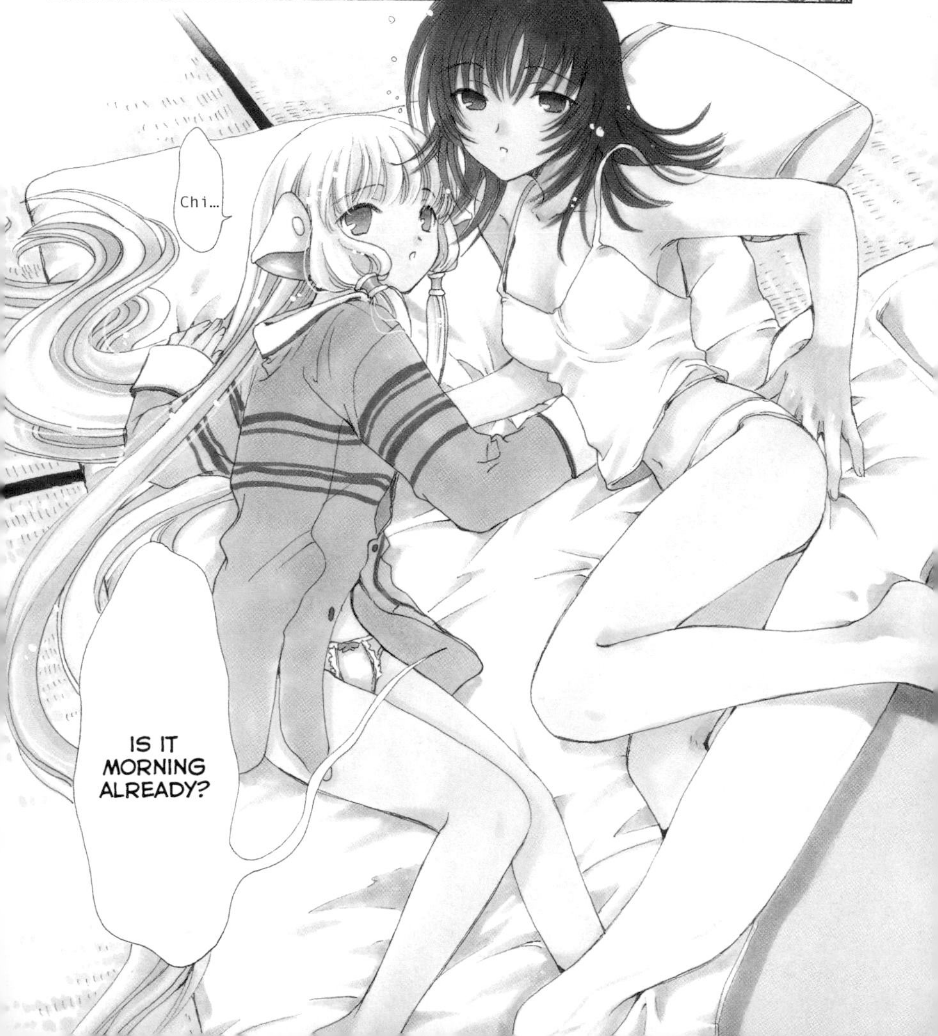
Chi...
IS IT MORNING ALREADY?

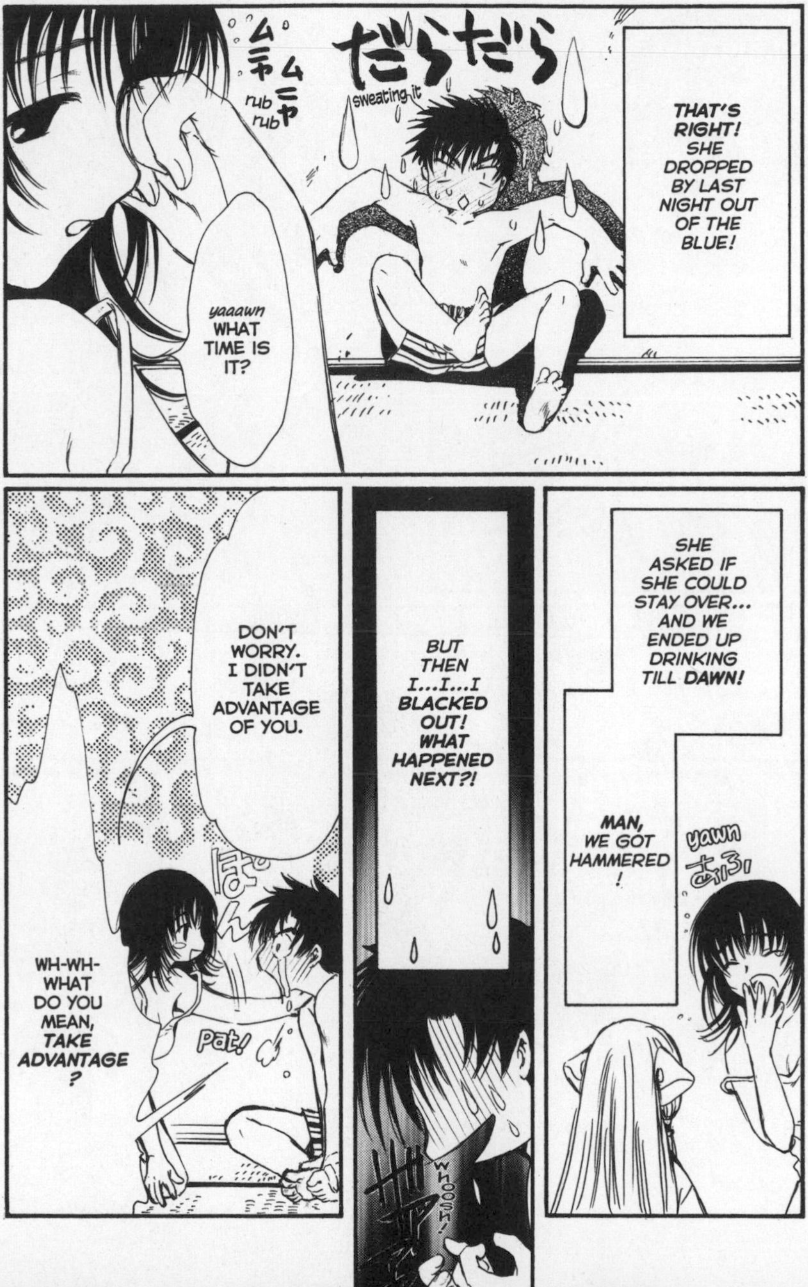
THAT'S RIGHT! SHE DROPPED BY LAST NIGHT OUT OF THE BLUE!
だらだら
sweating it
ムニャムニャ
rub rub
yaaawn WHAT TIME IS IT?
SHE ASKED IF SHE COULD STAY OVER... AND WE ENDED UP DRINKING TILL DAWN!
yawn
ふぁ
MAN, WE GOT HAMMERED!
BUT THEN I...I...I BLACKED OUT! WHAT HAPPENED NEXT?!
whoosh!
DON'T WORRY. I DIDN'T TAKE ADVANTAGE OF YOU.
ぽん
WH-WH-WHAT DO YOU MEAN, TAKE ADVANTAGE?
pat!

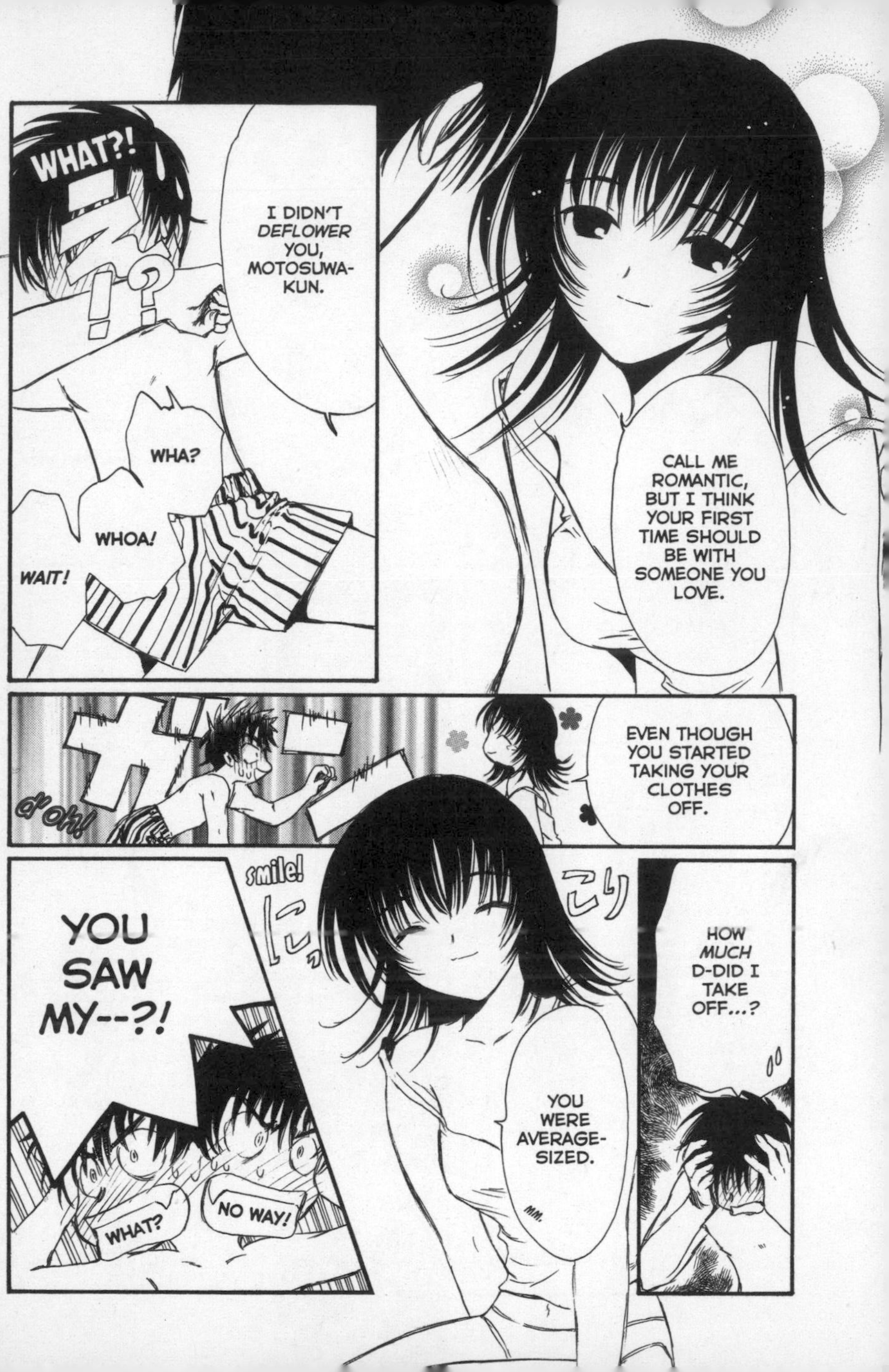
CALL ME ROMANTIC, BUT I THINK YOUR FIRST TIME SHOULD BE WITH SOMEONE YOU LOVE.
I DIDN'T *DEFLOWER* YOU, MOTOSUWA-KUN.
WHAT?!
WHA?
WHOA!
WAIT!
EVEN THOUGH YOU STARTED TAKING YOUR CLOTHES OFF.
d'oh!
HOW *MUCH* D-DID I TAKE OFF...?
smile!
YOU WERE AVERAGE-SIZED.
MM.
YOU SAW MY--?!
NO WAY!
WHAT?

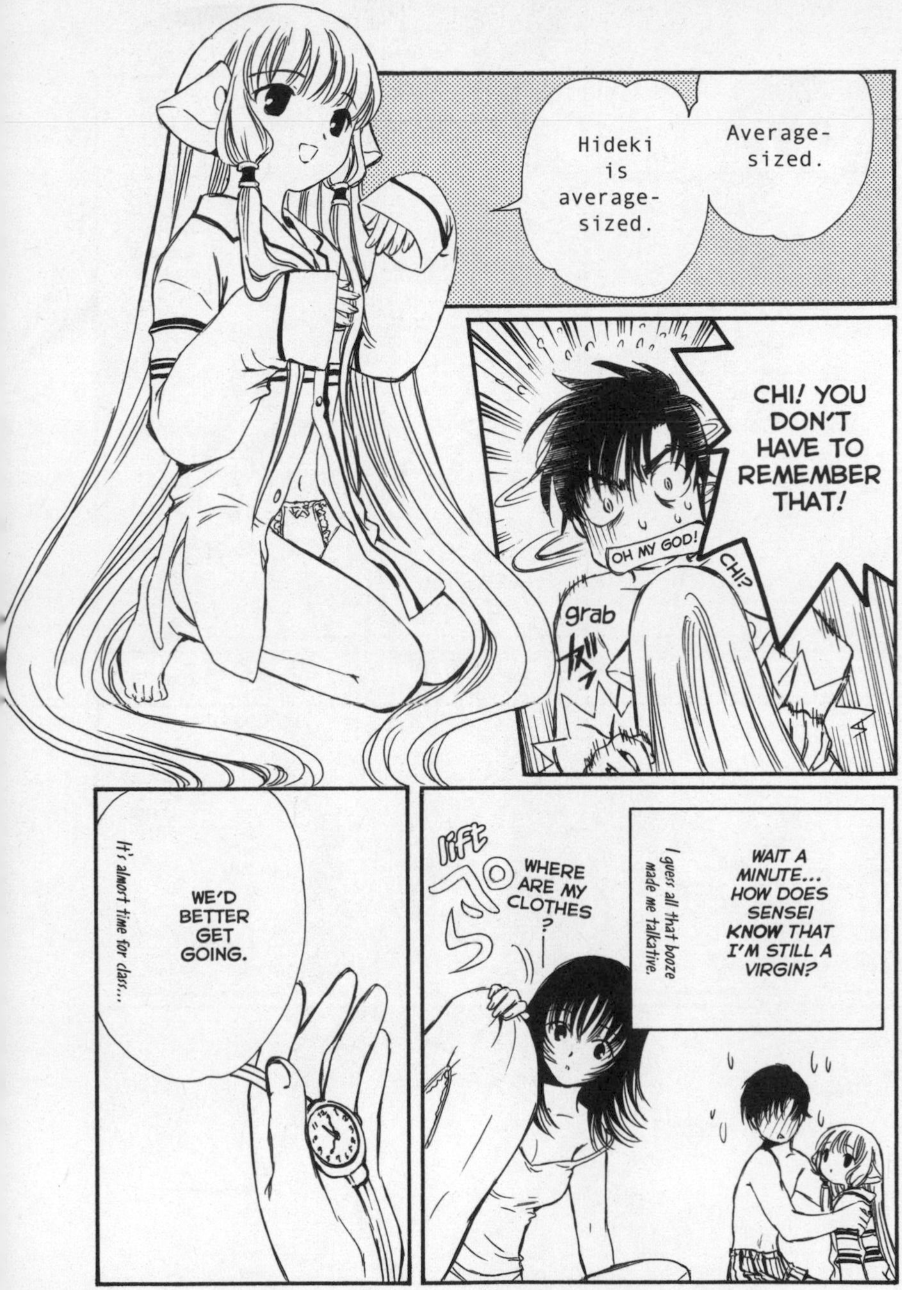
Average-sized.
Hideki is average-sized.
CHI! YOU DON'T HAVE TO REMEMBER THAT!
OH MY GOD!
CHI?
grab
WAIT A MINUTE... HOW DOES SENSEI KNOW THAT I'M STILL A VIRGIN?
I guess all that booze made me talkative.
WHERE ARE MY CLOTHES?
lift
WE'D BETTER GET GOING.
It's almost time for class...

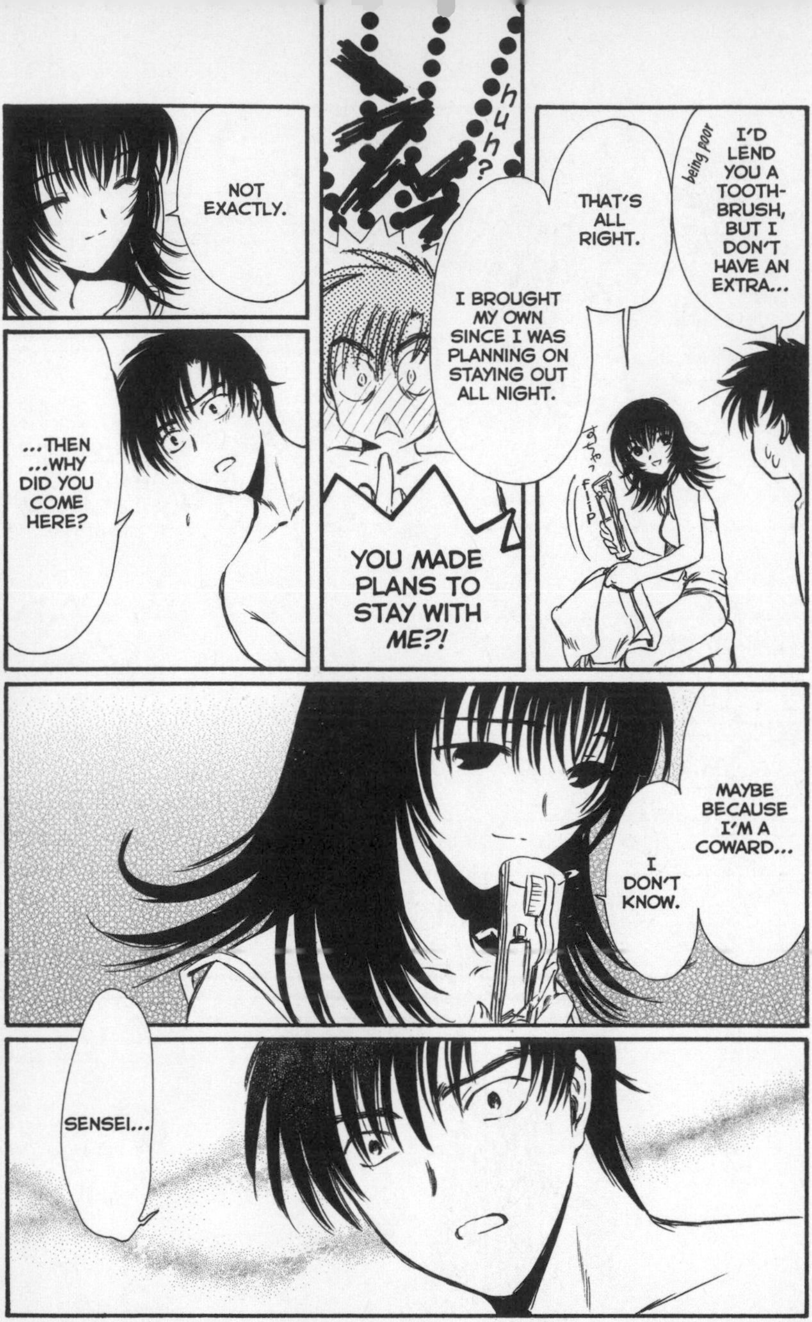
I'D LEND YOU A TOOTH-BRUSH, BUT I DON'T HAVE AN EXTRA...
being poor
THAT'S ALL RIGHT.
I BROUGHT MY OWN SINCE I WAS PLANNING ON STAYING OUT ALL NIGHT.
flip
huh?
YOU MADE PLANS TO STAY WITH *ME?!*
NOT EXACTLY.
...THEN ...WHY DID YOU COME HERE?
MAYBE BECAUSE I'M A COWARD...
I DON'T KNOW.
SENSEI...

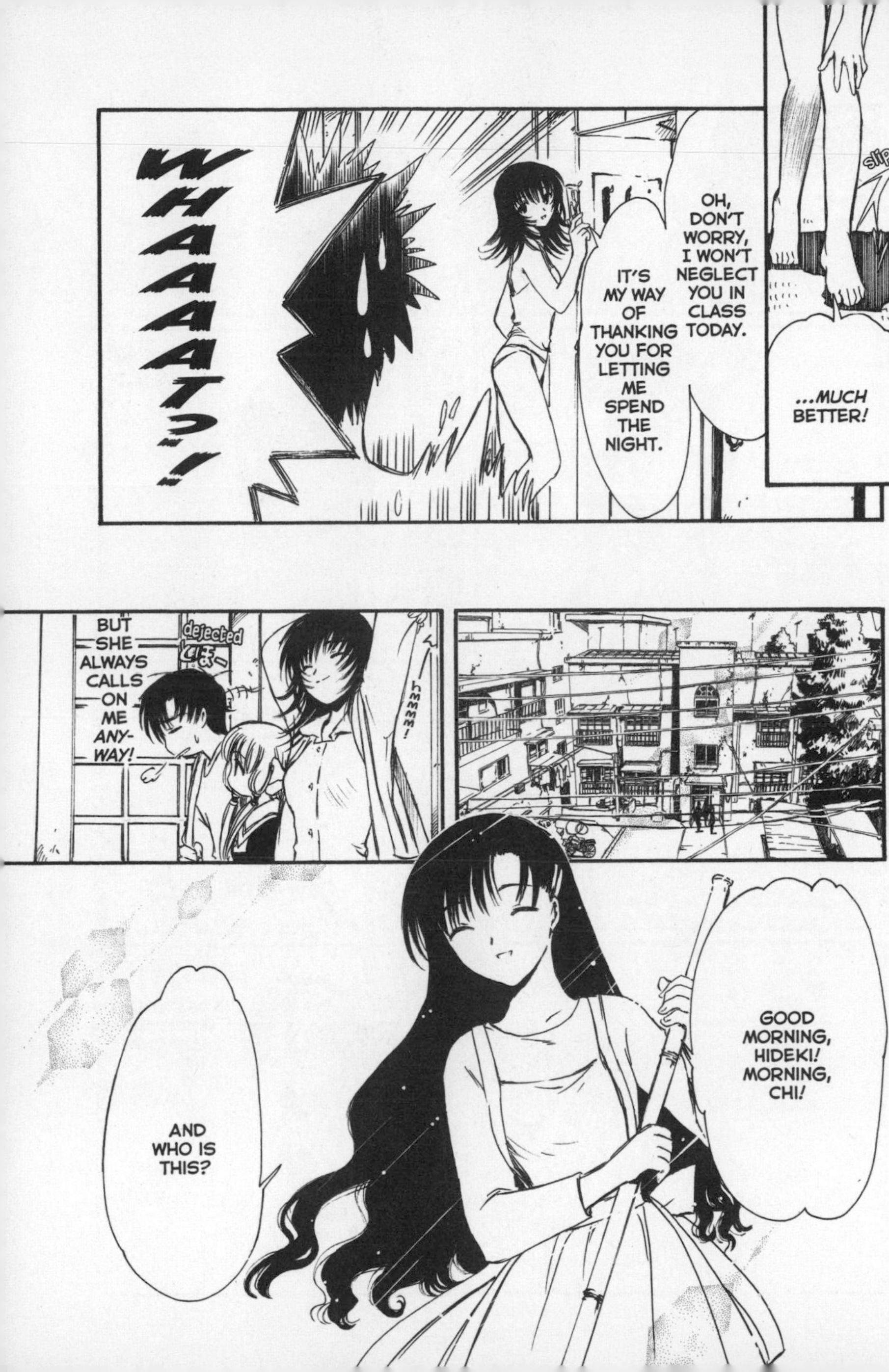
slip
...MUCH BETTER!
OH, DON'T WORRY, I WON'T NEGLECT YOU IN CLASS TODAY.
IT'S MY WAY OF THANKING YOU FOR LETTING ME SPEND THE NIGHT.
WHAAAAAT?!
hmmmm!
dejected
BUT SHE ALWAYS CALLS ON ME ANY-WAY!
GOOD MORNING, HIDEKI! MORNING, CHI!
AND WHO IS THIS?

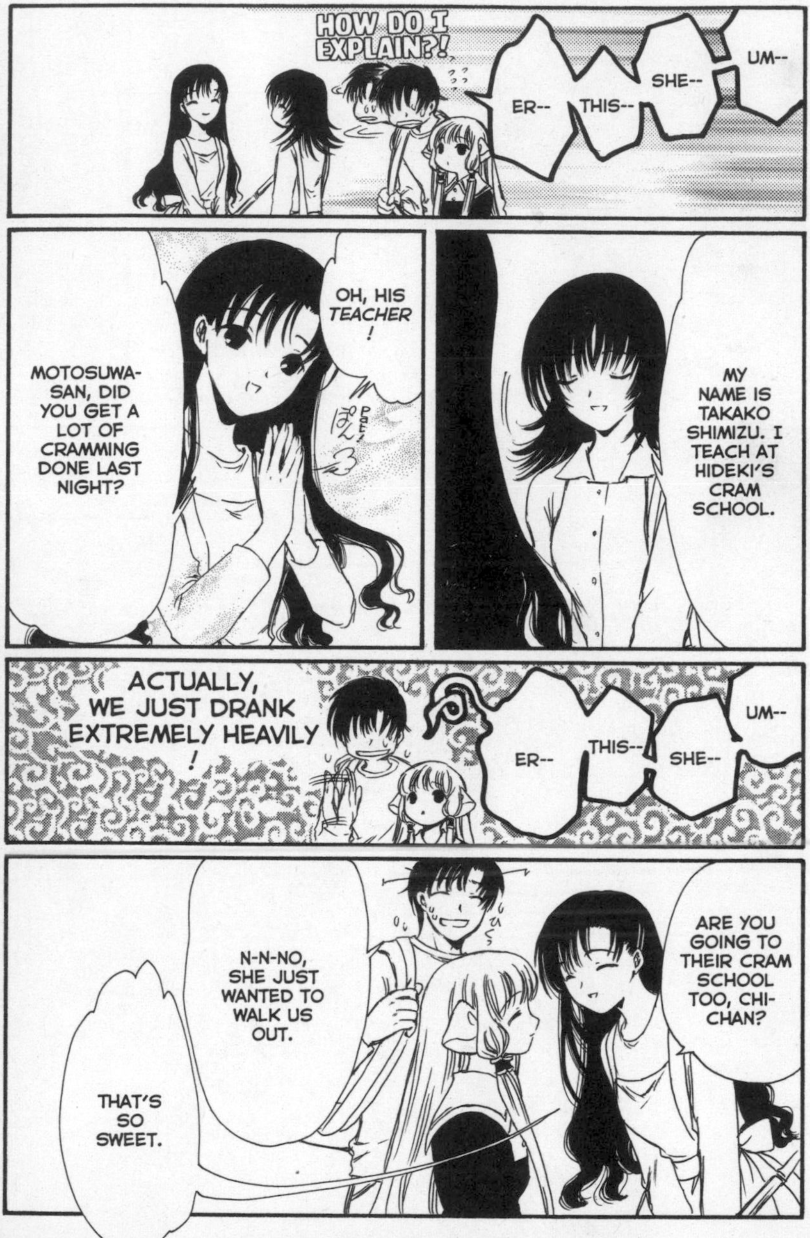
UM--
SHE--
THIS--
ER--
HOW DO I EXPLAIN?!
MY NAME IS TAKAKO SHIMIZU. I TEACH AT HIDEKI'S CRAM SCHOOL.
OH, HIS TEACHER!
ぽん Pat!
MOTOSUWA-SAN, DID YOU GET A LOT OF CRAMMING DONE LAST NIGHT?
UM--
SHE--
THIS--
ER--
ACTUALLY, WE JUST DRANK EXTREMELY HEAVILY!
ARE YOU GOING TO THEIR CRAM SCHOOL TOO, CHI-CHAN?
N-N-NO, SHE JUST WANTED TO WALK US OUT.
THAT'S SO SWEET.

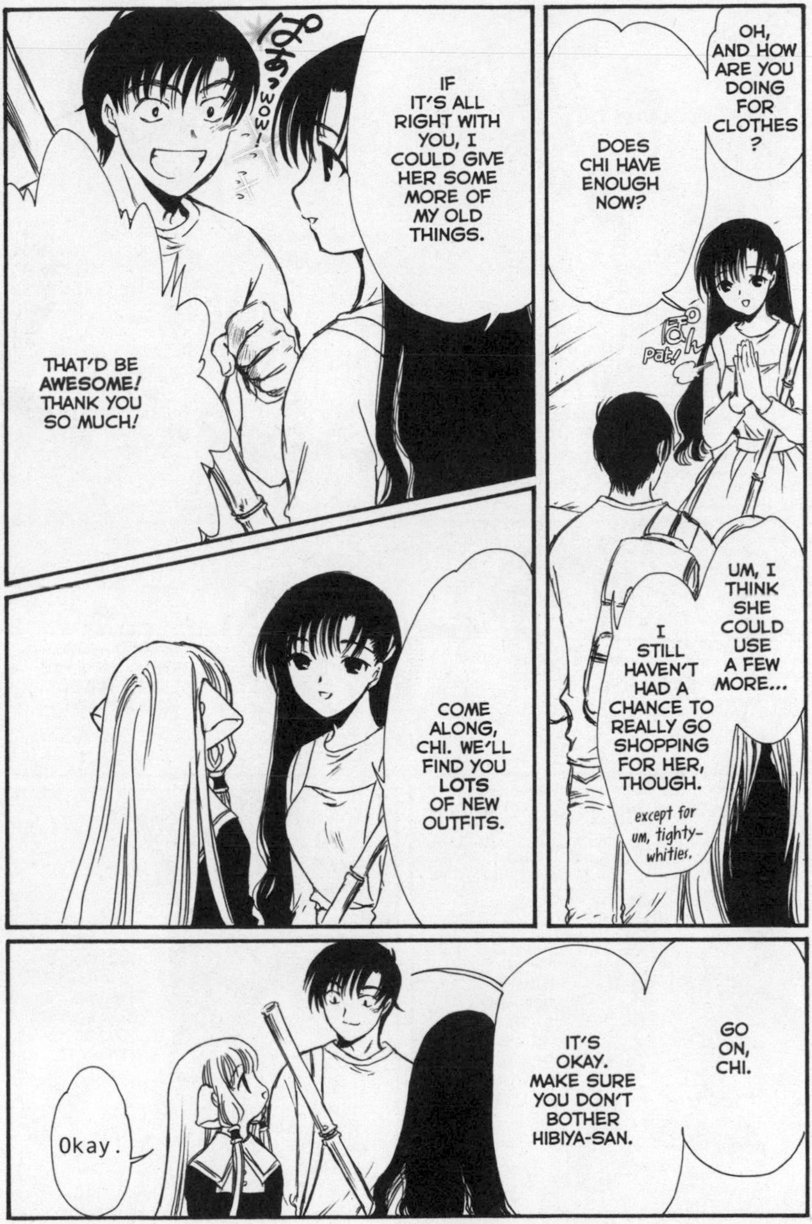
OH, AND HOW ARE YOU DOING FOR CLOTHES?
DOES CHI HAVE ENOUGH NOW?
ぽん pat!
UM, I THINK SHE COULD USE A FEW MORE...
I STILL HAVEN'T HAD A CHANCE TO REALLY GO SHOPPING FOR HER, THOUGH.
except for um, tighty-whities.
IF IT'S ALL RIGHT WITH YOU, I COULD GIVE HER SOME MORE OF MY OLD THINGS.
ぱあっ WOW!
THAT'D BE AWESOME! THANK YOU SO MUCH!
COME ALONG, CHI. WE'LL FIND YOU LOTS OF NEW OUTFITS.
GO ON, CHI.
IT'S OKAY. MAKE SURE YOU DON'T BOTHER HIBIYA-SAN.
Okay.

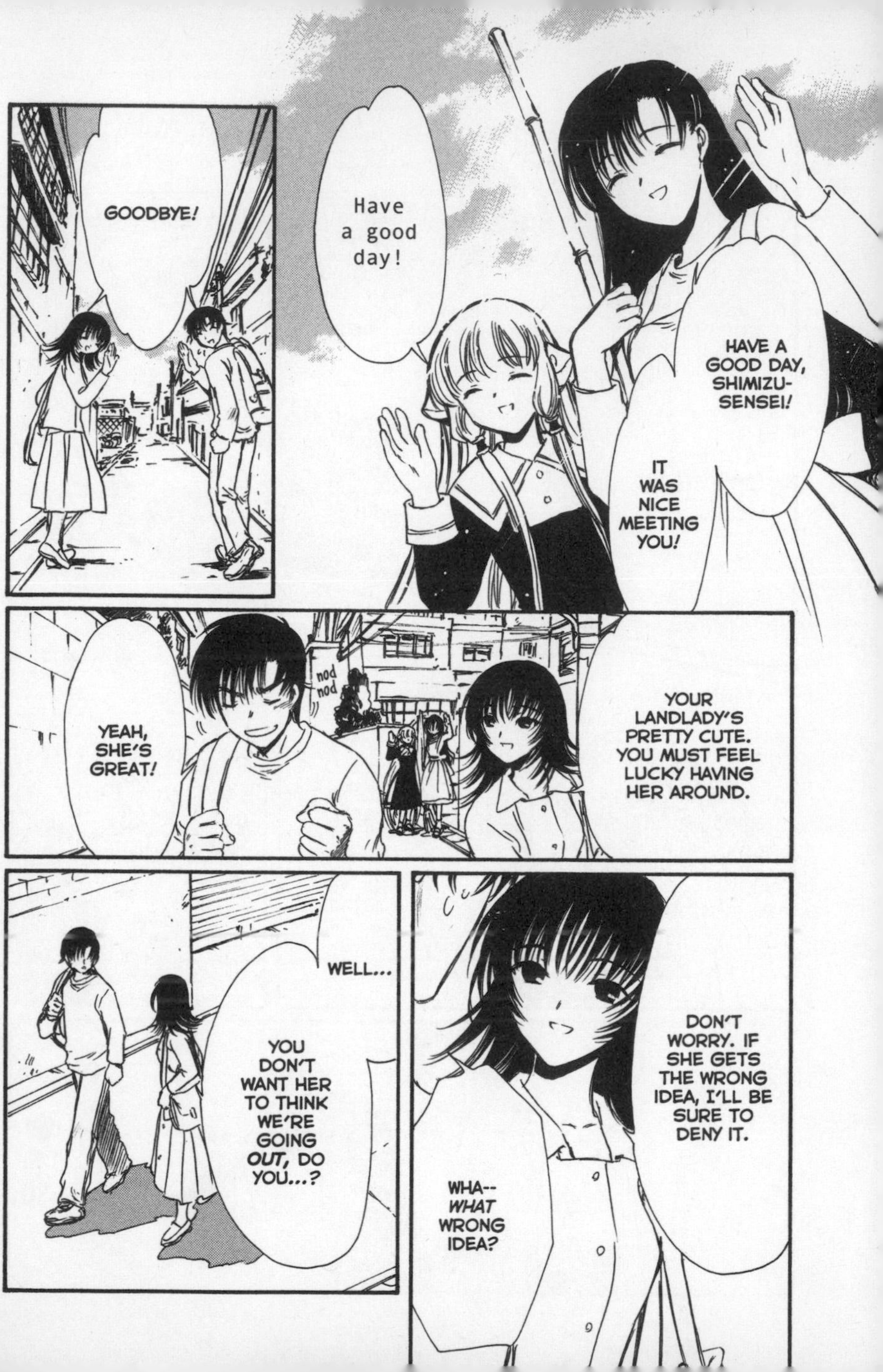
HAVE A GOOD DAY, SHIMIZU-SENSEI!
IT WAS NICE MEETING YOU!
Have a good day!
GOODBYE!
YOUR LANDLADY'S PRETTY CUTE. YOU MUST FEEL LUCKY HAVING HER AROUND.
nod nod
YEAH, SHE'S GREAT!
DON'T WORRY. IF SHE GETS THE WRONG IDEA, I'LL BE SURE TO DENY IT.
WHA-- *WHAT* WRONG IDEA?
WELL...
YOU DON'T WANT HER TO THINK WE'RE GOING *OUT*, DO YOU...?

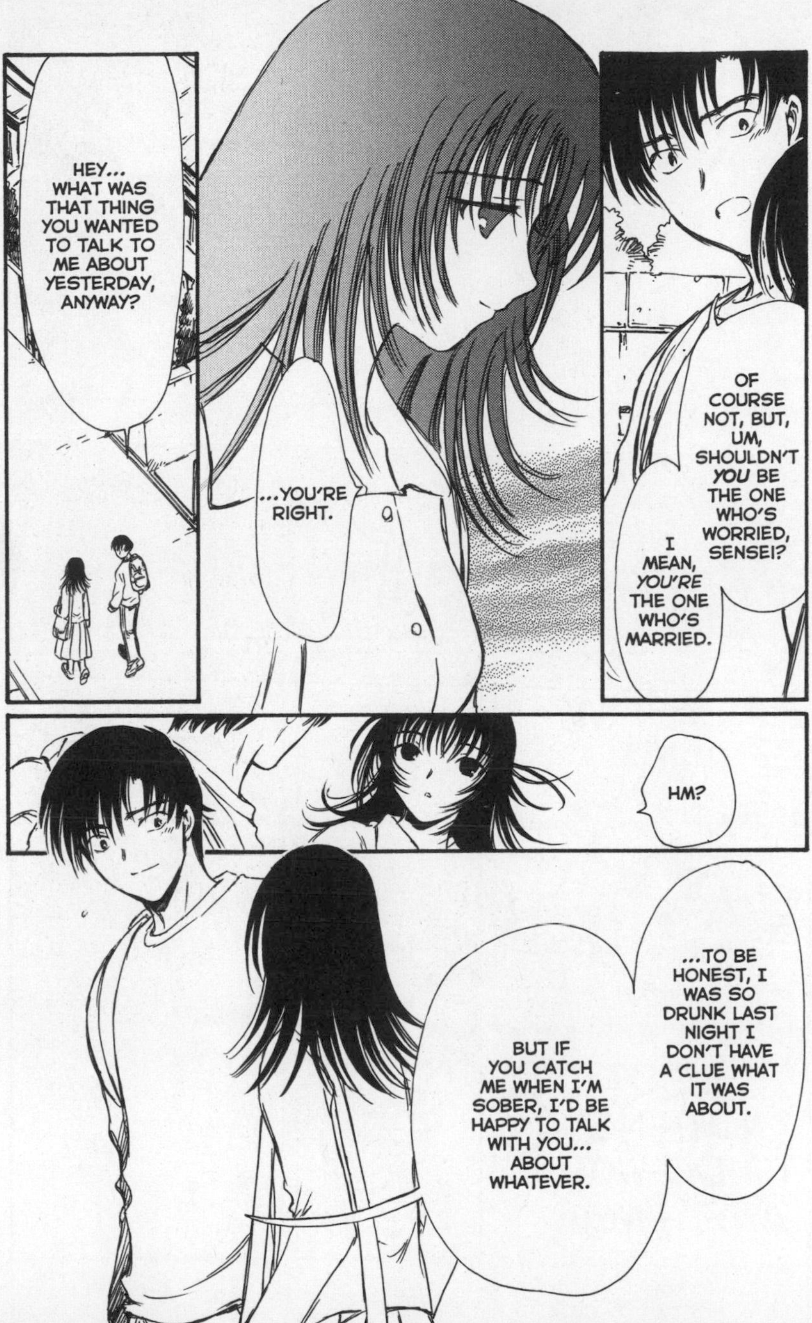
OF COURSE NOT, BUT, UM, SHOULDN'T *YOU* BE THE ONE WHO'S WORRIED, SENSEI?
I MEAN, *YOU'RE* THE ONE WHO'S MARRIED.
...YOU'RE RIGHT.
HEY... WHAT WAS THAT THING YOU WANTED TO TALK TO ME ABOUT YESTERDAY, ANYWAY?
HM?
...TO BE HONEST, I WAS SO DRUNK LAST NIGHT I DON'T HAVE A CLUE WHAT IT WAS ABOUT.
BUT IF YOU CATCH ME WHEN I'M SOBER, I'D BE HAPPY TO TALK WITH YOU... ABOUT WHATEVER.

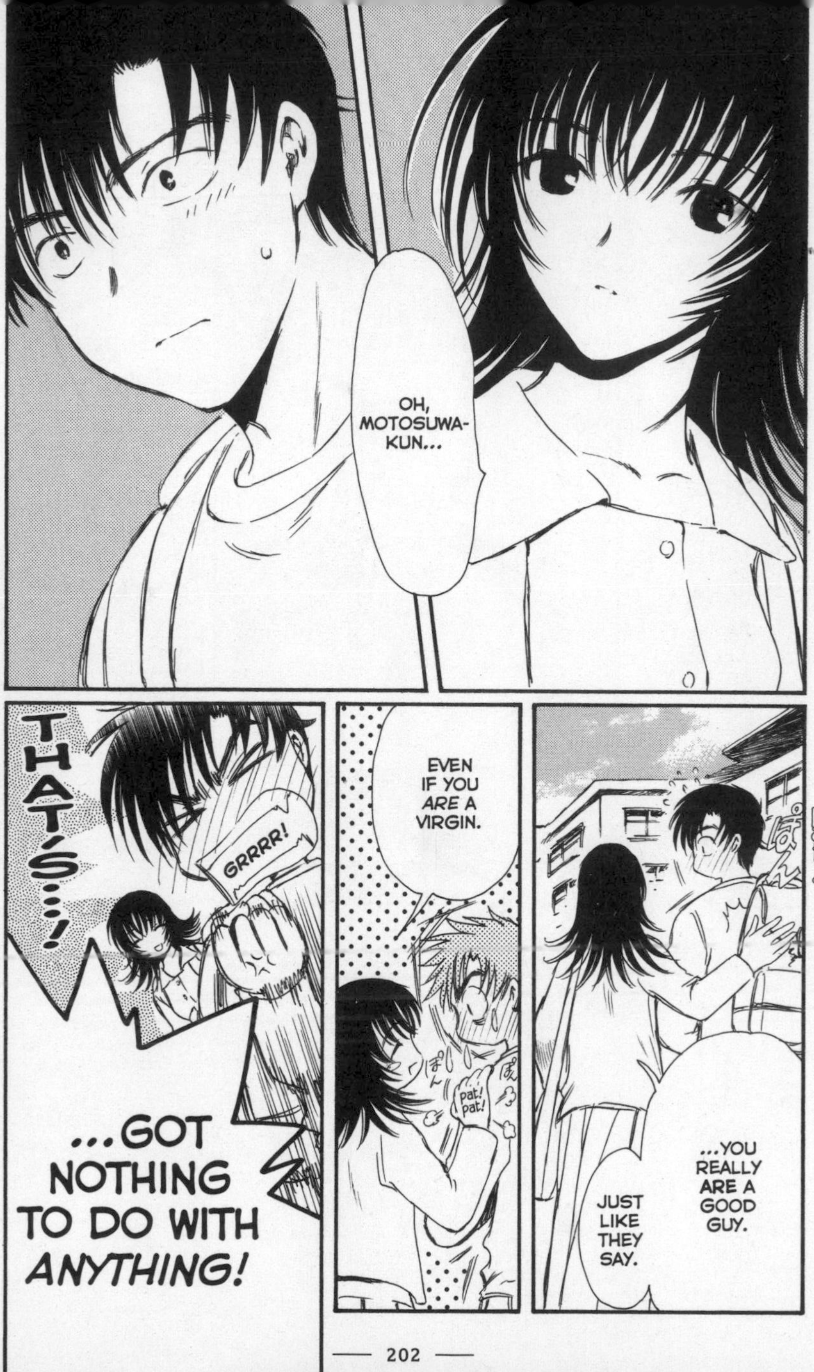
OH, MOTOSUWA-KUN...
Pat!
...YOU REALLY ARE A GOOD GUY.
JUST LIKE THEY SAY.
EVEN IF YOU ARE A VIRGIN.
pat! pat!
THAT'S...!
GRRRR!
...GOT NOTHING TO DO WITH ANYTHING!

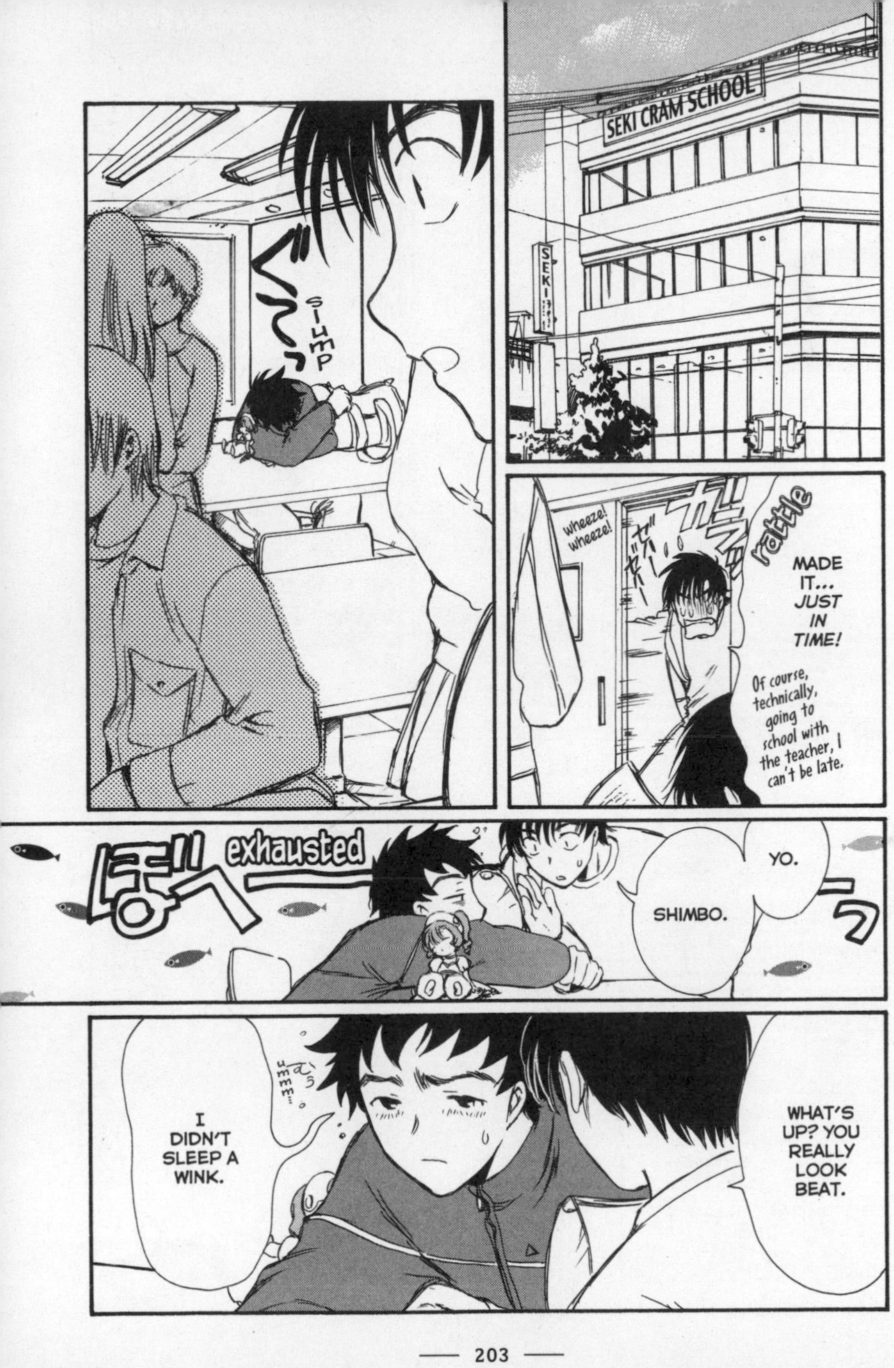
SEKI CRAM SCHOOL
SEKI
rattle
wheeze! wheeze!
MADE IT... JUST IN TIME!
Of course, technically, going to school with the teacher, I can't be late.
slump
exhausted
YO.
SHIMBO.
WHAT'S UP? YOU REALLY LOOK BEAT.
ummm...
I DIDN'T SLEEP A WINK.

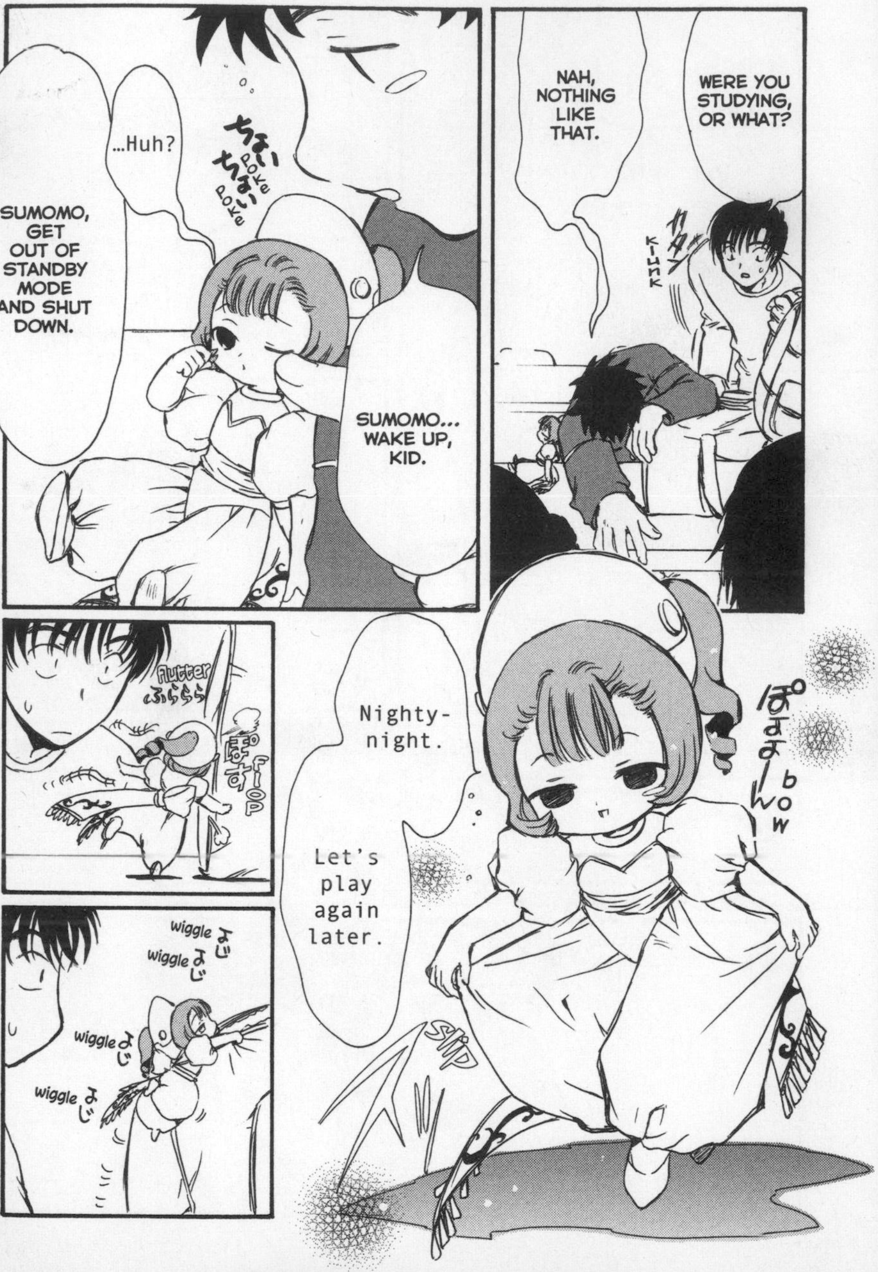
WERE YOU STUDYING, OR WHAT?
KLUNK
NAH, NOTHING LIKE THAT.
SUMOMO... WAKE UP, KID.
POKE POKE
...Huh?
SUMOMO, GET OUT OF STANDBY MODE AND SHUT DOWN.
Nighty-night.
Let's play again later.
bow
SLIP
flutter
flop
wiggle よじ
wiggle よじ
wiggle よじ
wiggle よじ

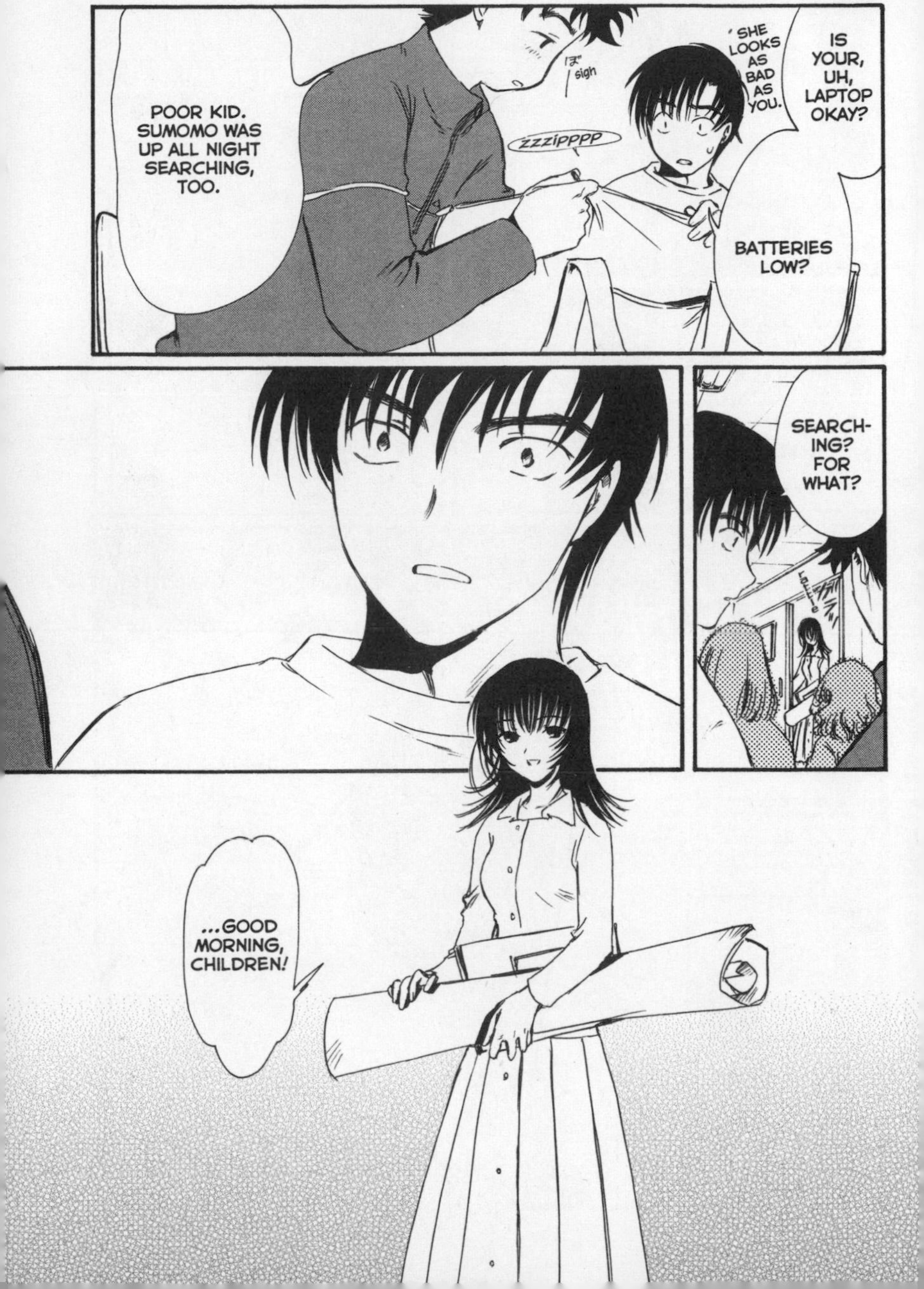
IS YOUR, UH, LAPTOP OKAY?
SHE LOOKS AS BAD AS YOU.
sigh
zzzipppp
BATTERIES LOW?
POOR KID. SUMOMO WAS UP ALL NIGHT SEARCHING, TOO.
SEARCHING? FOR WHAT?
...GOOD MORNING, CHILDREN!

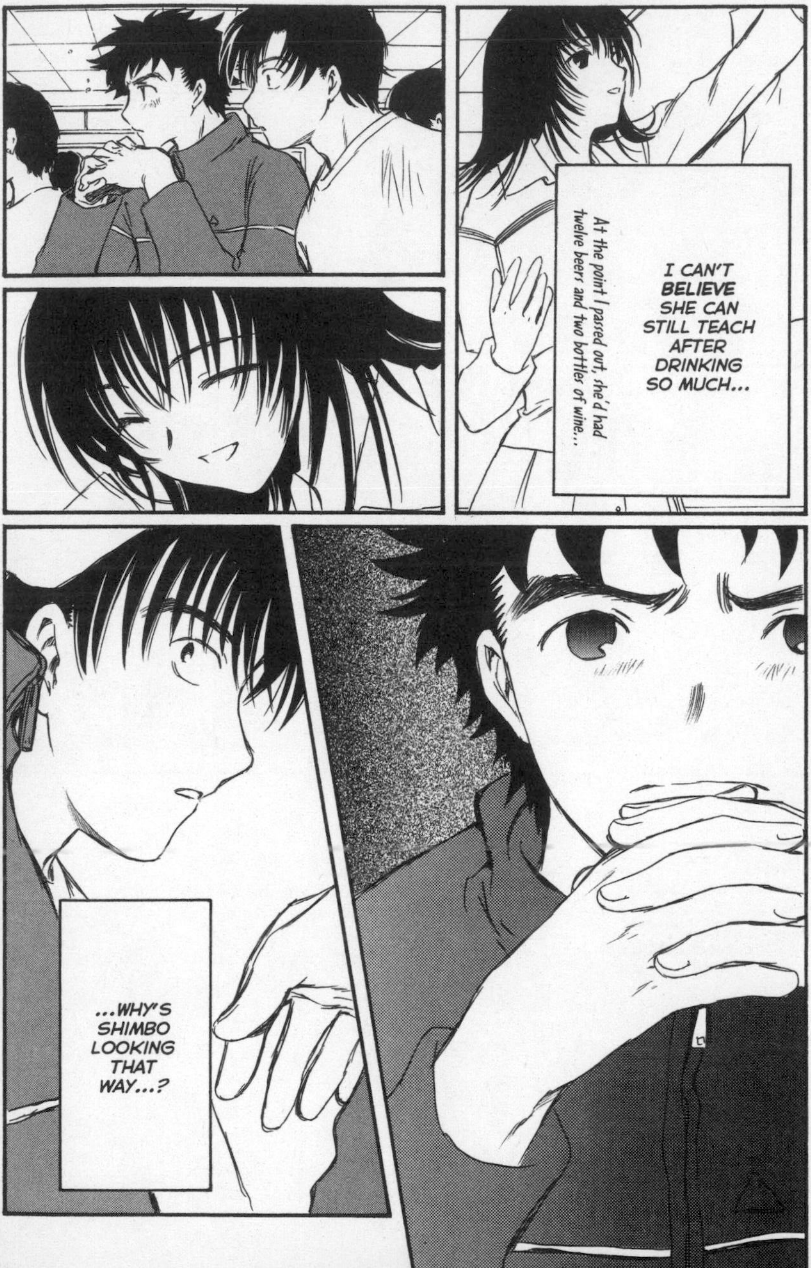
I CAN'T BELIEVE SHE CAN STILL TEACH AFTER DRINKING SO MUCH...
At the point I passed out, she'd had twelve beers and two bottles of wine...
...WHY'S SHIMBO LOOKING THAT WAY...?

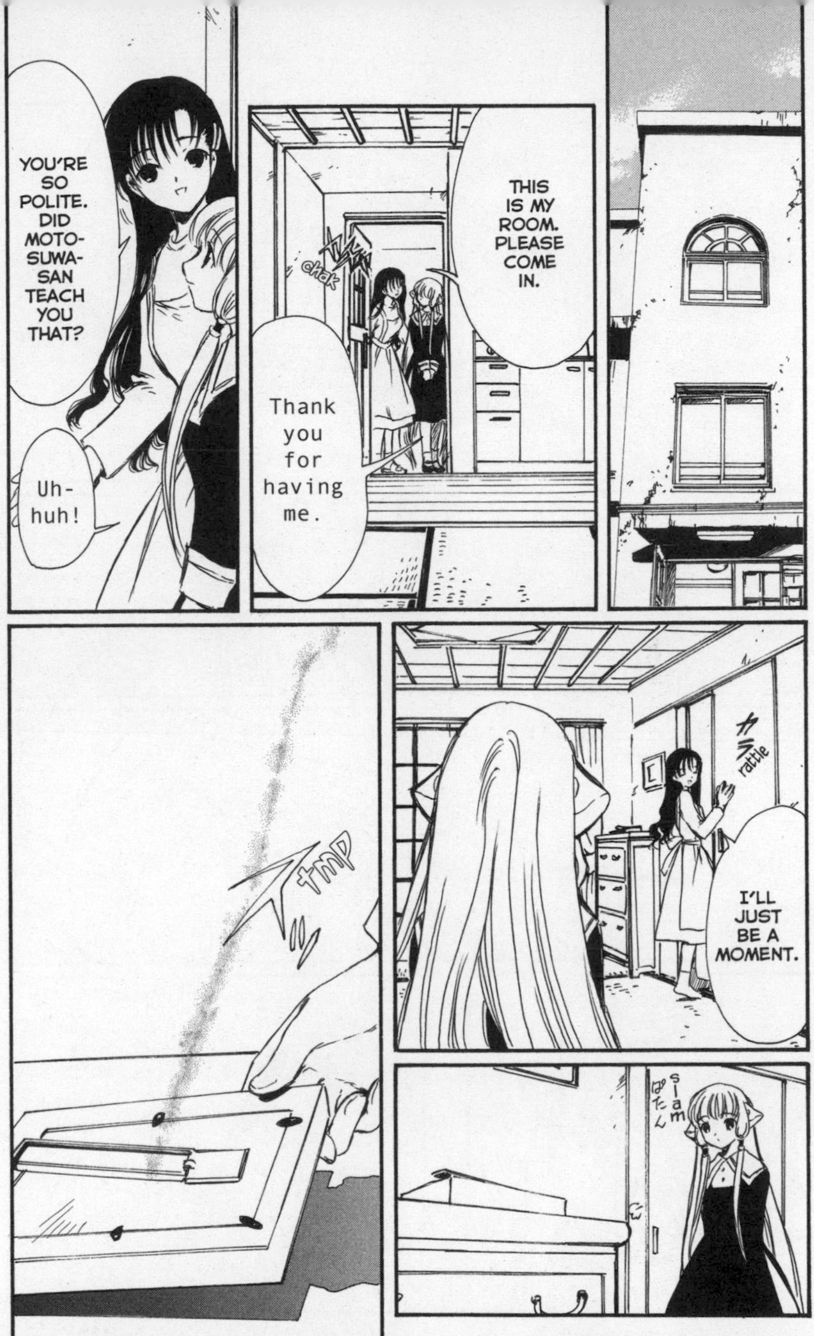
THIS IS MY ROOM. PLEASE COME IN.
chak
Thank you for having me.
YOU'RE SO POLITE. DID MOTO-SUWA-SAN TEACH YOU THAT?
Uh-huh!
カラ rattle
I'LL JUST BE A MOMENT.
ぱたん slam
tmp

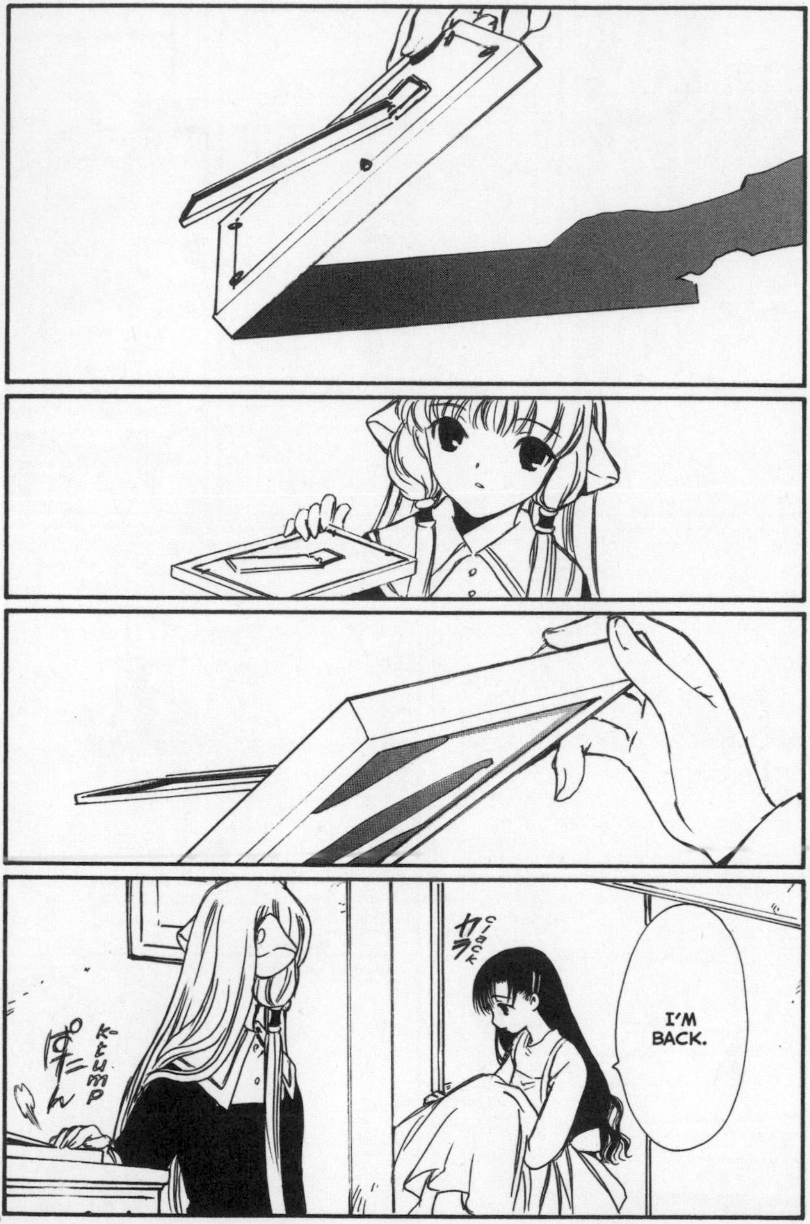
I'M BACK.
カラ
clack
ぽすーん
k-tump

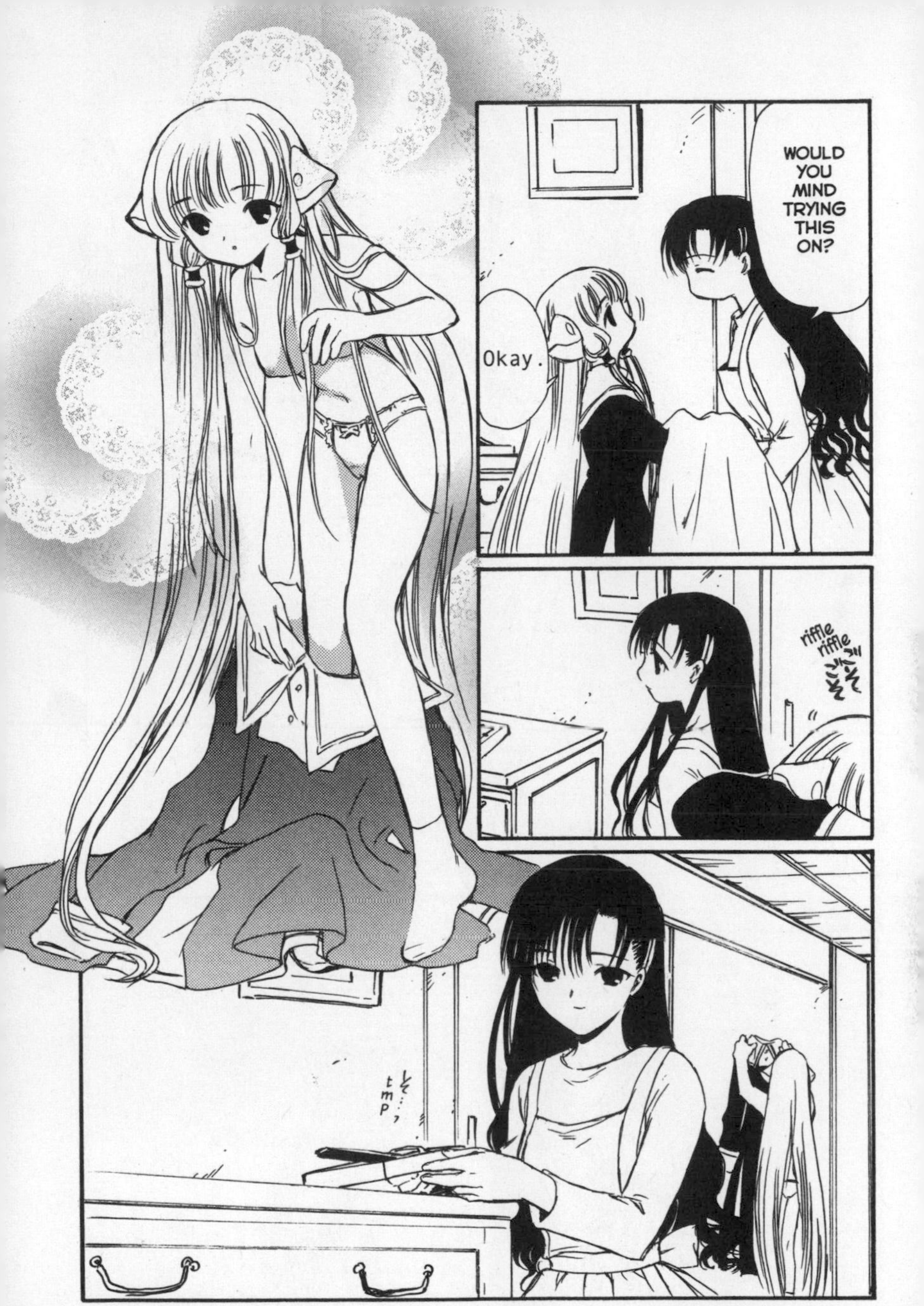
WOULD YOU MIND TRYING THIS ON?
Okay.
riffle riffle
tmp

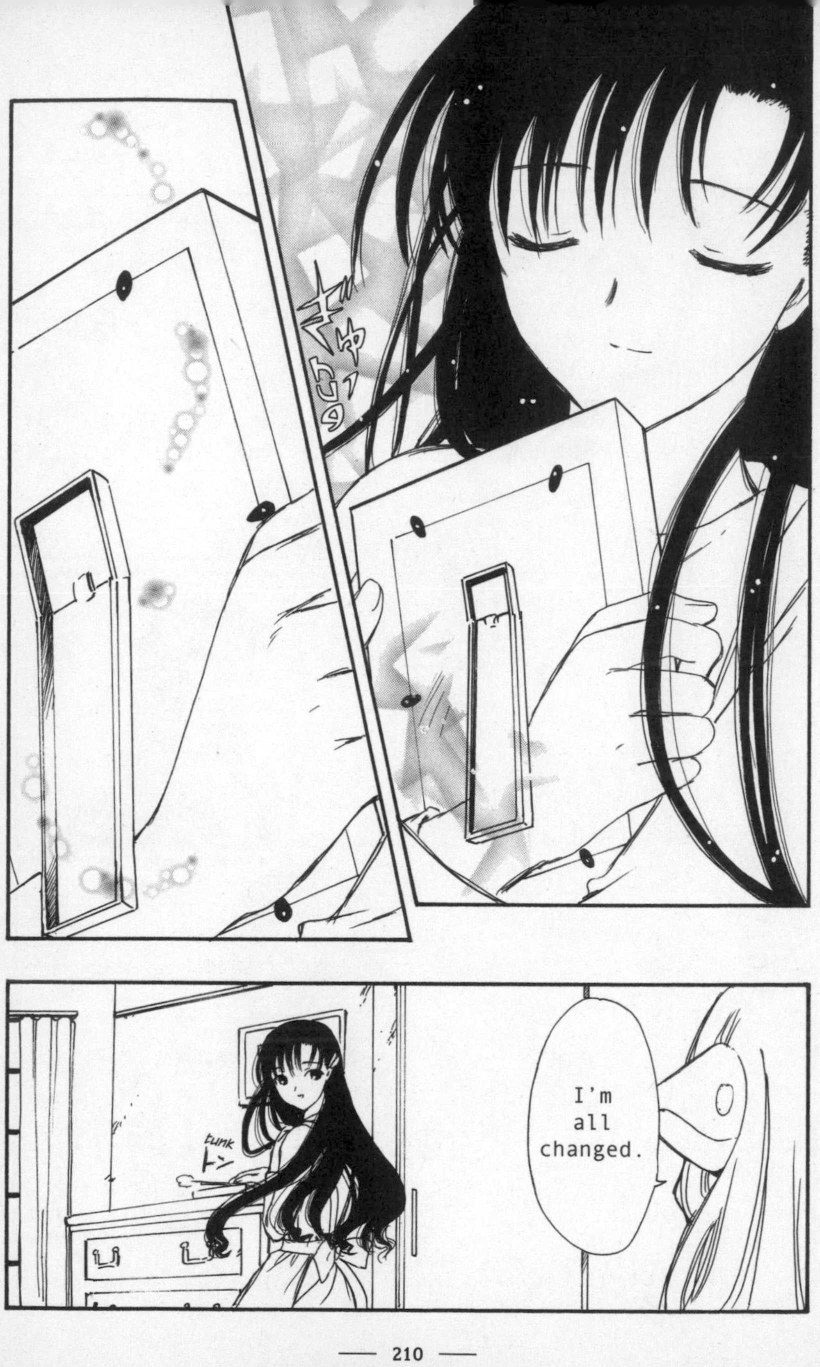
I'm all changed.
tunk
トン

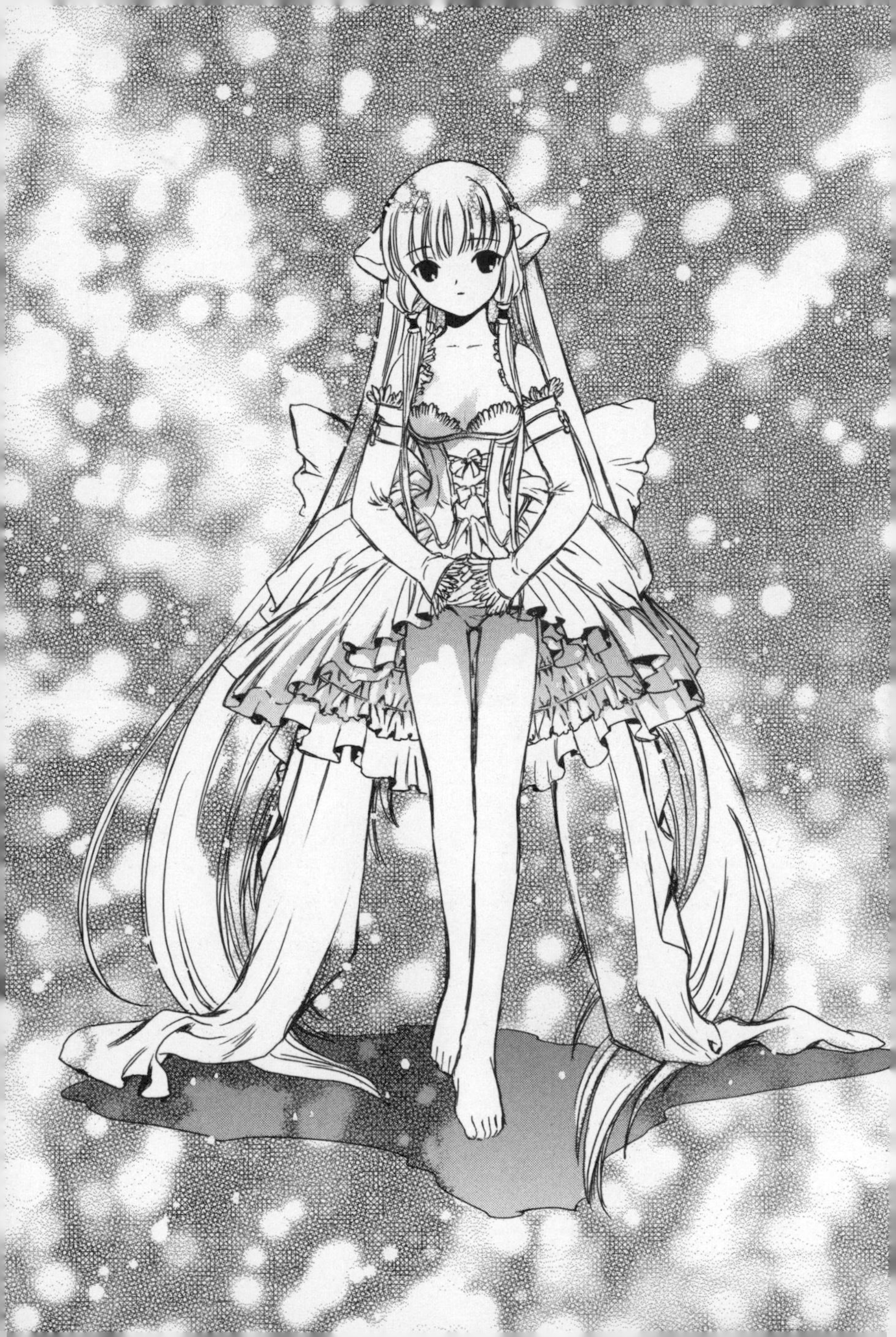

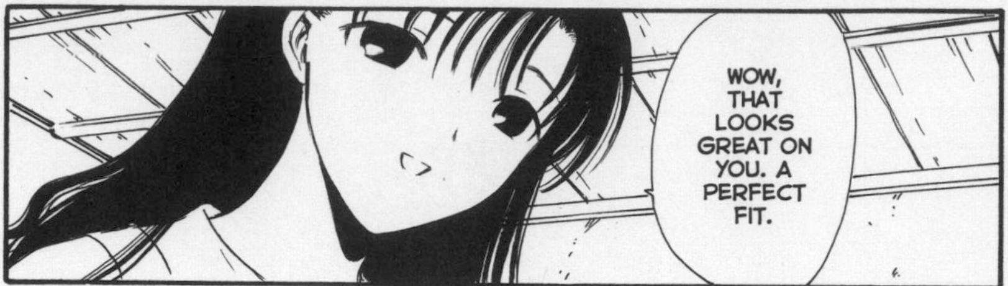
WOW, THAT LOOKS GREAT ON YOU. A PERFECT FIT.

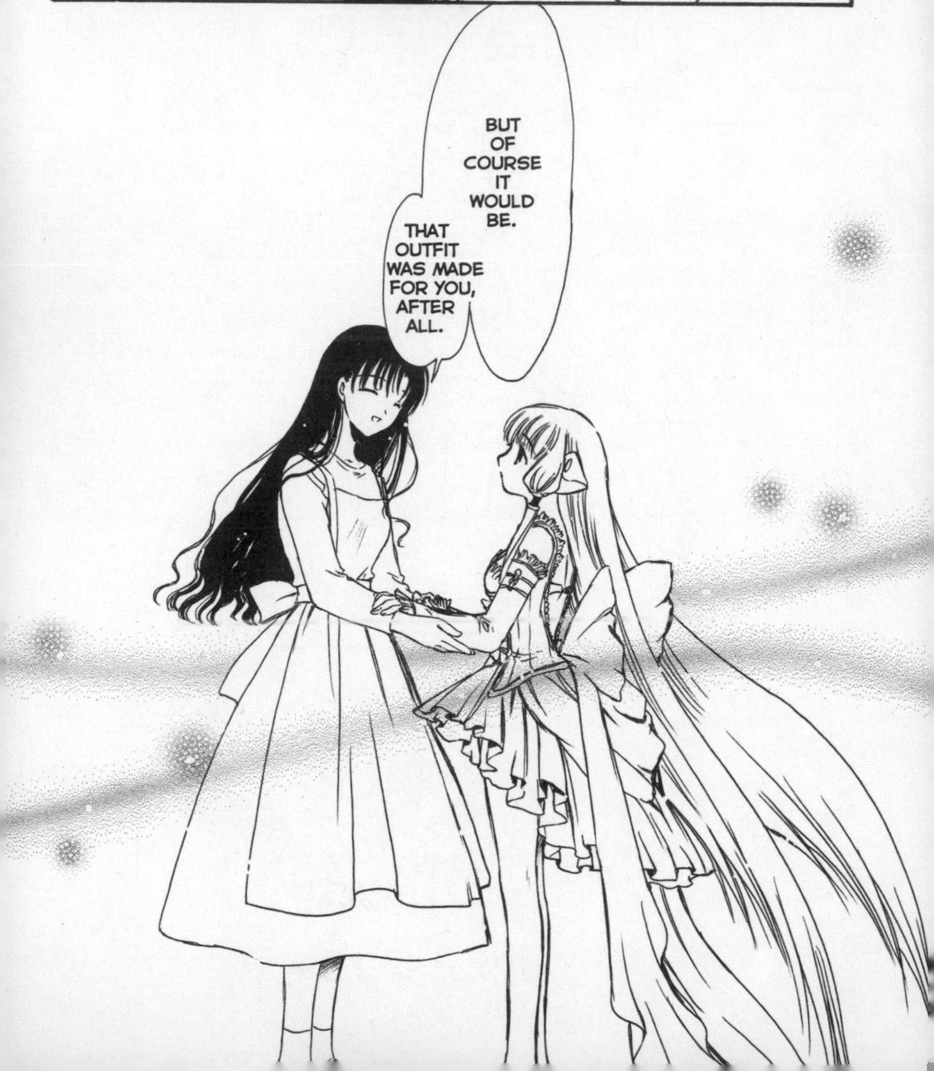
BUT OF COURSE IT WOULD BE.
THAT OUTFIT WAS MADE FOR YOU, AFTER ALL.

Chobits
ちょびっツ

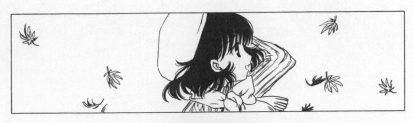

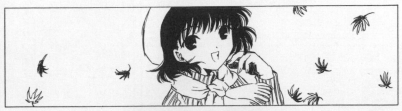

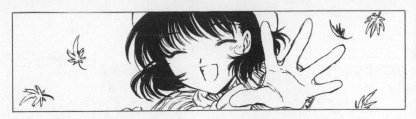

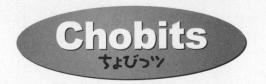

◂chapter 14▸

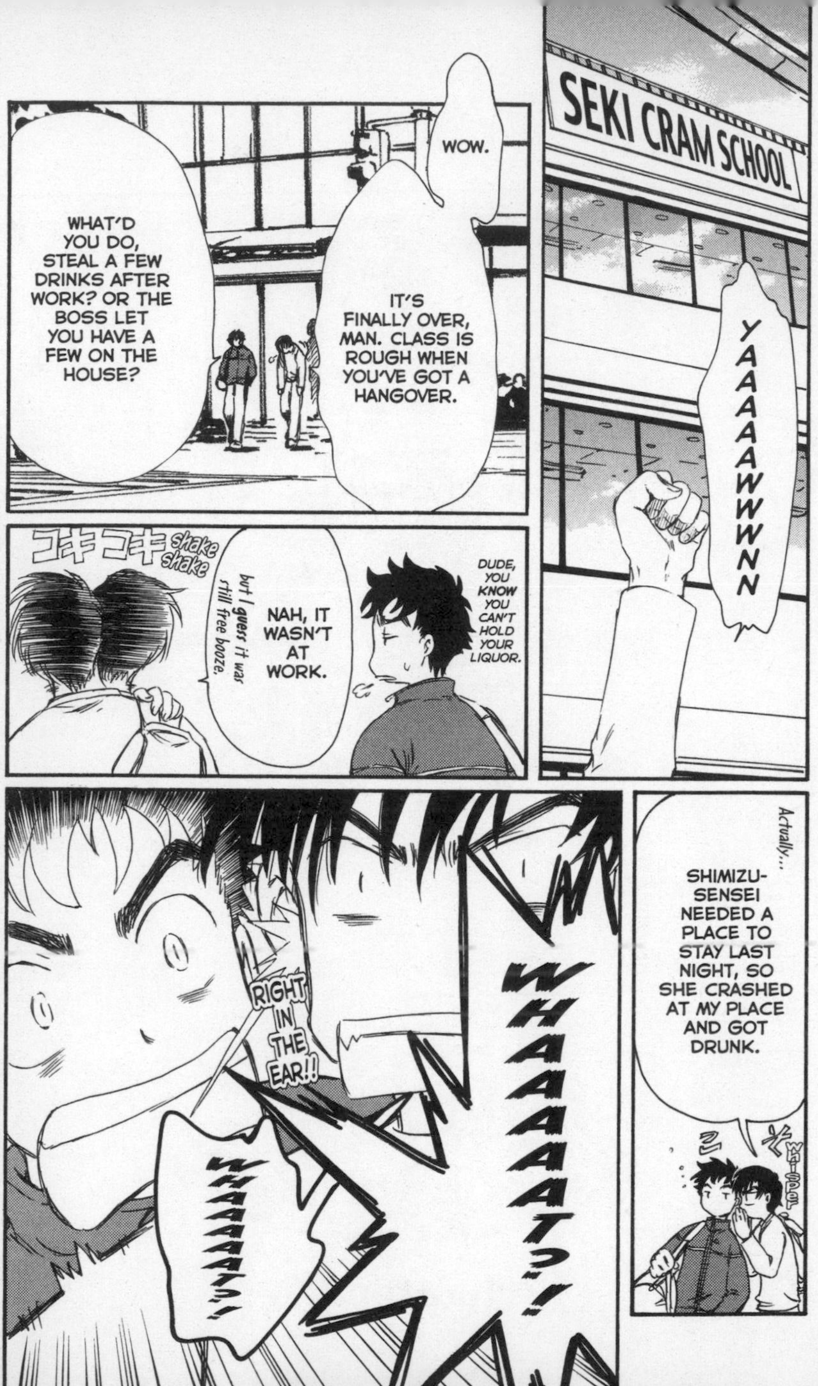
SEKI CRAM SCHOOL
YAAAAAAWWWNN
WOW.
IT'S FINALLY OVER, MAN. CLASS IS ROUGH WHEN YOU'VE GOT A HANGOVER.
WHAT'D YOU DO, STEAL A FEW DRINKS AFTER WORK? OR THE BOSS LET YOU HAVE A FEW ON THE HOUSE?
DUDE, YOU KNOW YOU CAN'T HOLD YOUR LIQUOR.
NAH, IT WASN'T AT WORK.
but I guess it was still free booze.
shake shake
Actually...
SHIMIZU-SENSEI NEEDED A PLACE TO STAY LAST NIGHT, SO SHE CRASHED AT MY PLACE AND GOT DRUNK.
WHAAAAAAT?!!
RIGHT IN THE EAR!!
WHAAAAAT?!

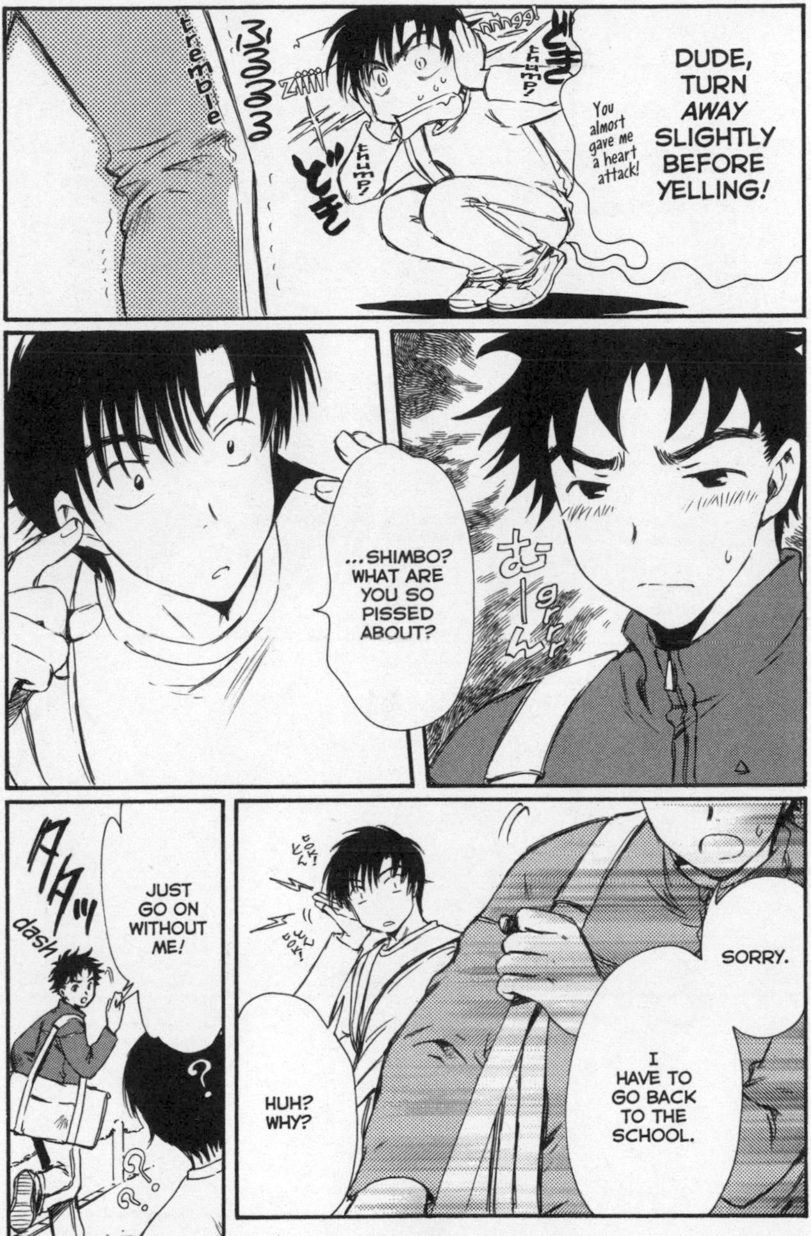
DUDE, TURN AWAY SLIGHTLY BEFORE YELLING!
You almost gave me a heart attack!
nnngg!
thump!
ziiiii
thump!
tremble
grrr
...SHIMBO? WHAT ARE YOU SO PISSED ABOUT?
SORRY.
I HAVE TO GO BACK TO THE SCHOOL.
HUH? WHY?
JUST GO ON WITHOUT ME!
dash

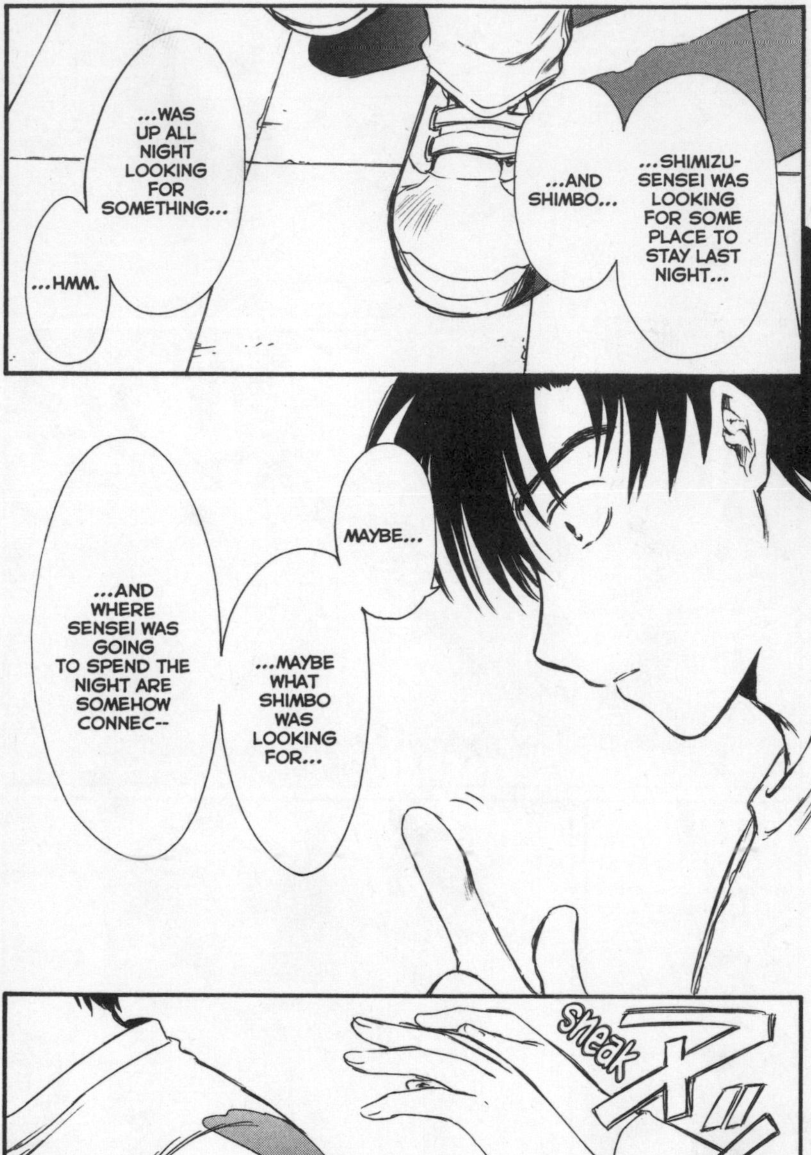
...SHIMIZU-SENSEI WAS LOOKING FOR SOME PLACE TO STAY LAST NIGHT...
...AND SHIMBO...
...WAS UP ALL NIGHT LOOKING FOR SOMETHING...
...HMM.
MAYBE...
...MAYBE WHAT SHIMBO WAS LOOKING FOR...
...AND WHERE SENSEI WAS GOING TO SPEND THE NIGHT ARE SOMEHOW CONNEC--
sneak

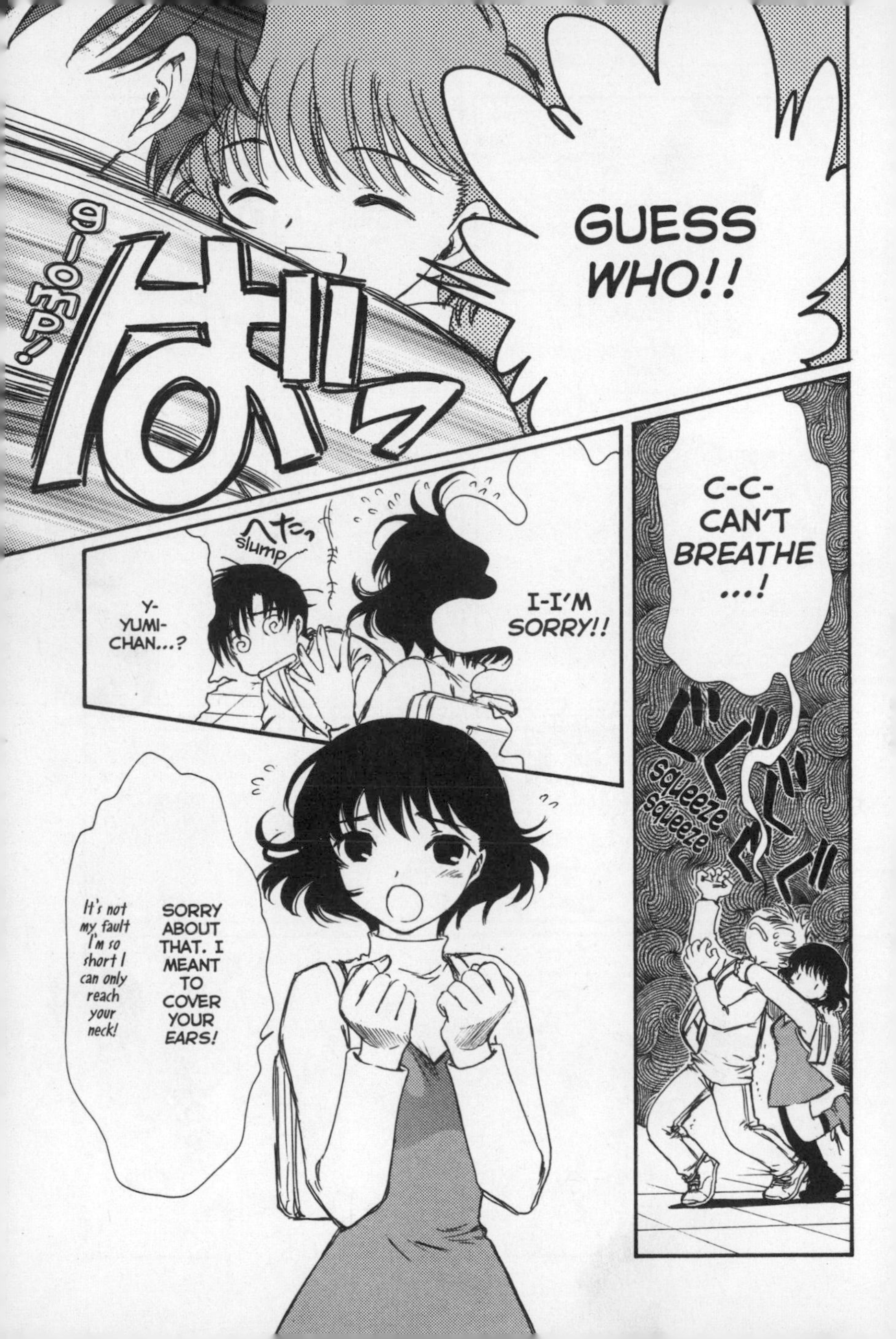
GUESS WHO!!
g-lomp!
C-C-CAN'T BREATHE ...!
squeeze squeeze
slump
I-I'M SORRY!!
Y-YUMI-CHAN...?
SORRY ABOUT THAT. I MEANT TO COVER YOUR EARS!
It's not my fault I'm so short I can only reach your neck!

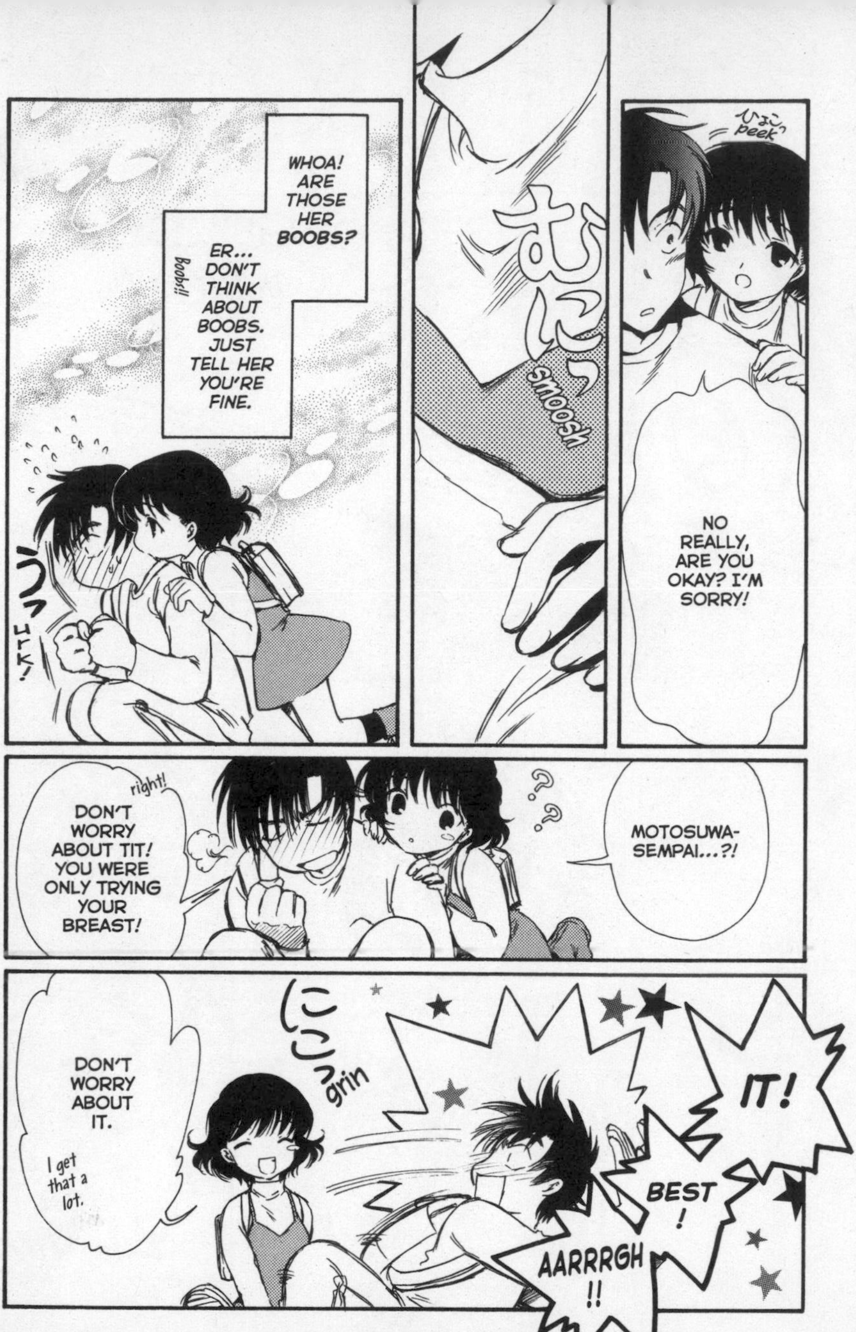
ひよこっ peek
NO REALLY, ARE YOU OKAY? I'M SORRY!
むにっ
smoosh
WHOA! ARE THOSE HER BOOBS?
ER... DON'T THINK ABOUT BOOBS. JUST TELL HER YOU'RE FINE.
Boobs!!
うっ
urk!
MOTOSUWA-SEMPAI...?!
right!
DON'T WORRY ABOUT TIT! YOU WERE ONLY TRYING YOUR BREAST!
IT!
BEST!
AARRRGH!!
にこっ
grin
DON'T WORRY ABOUT IT.
I get that a lot.

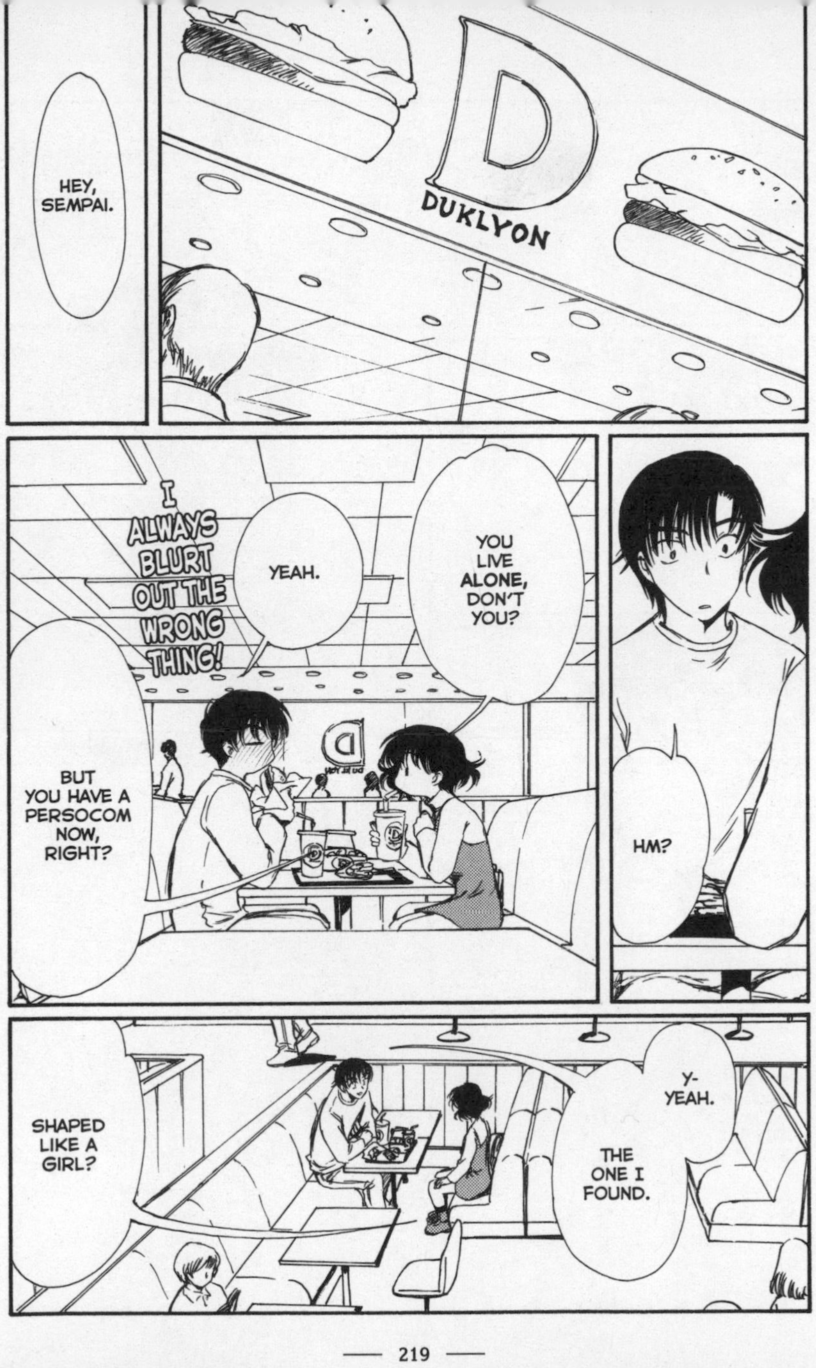
DUKLYON
HEY, SEMPAI.
HM?
YOU LIVE ALONE, DON'T YOU?
YEAH.
I ALWAYS BLURT OUT THE WRONG THING!
BUT YOU HAVE A PERSOCOM NOW, RIGHT?
SHAPED LIKE A GIRL?
Y-YEAH.
THE ONE I FOUND.

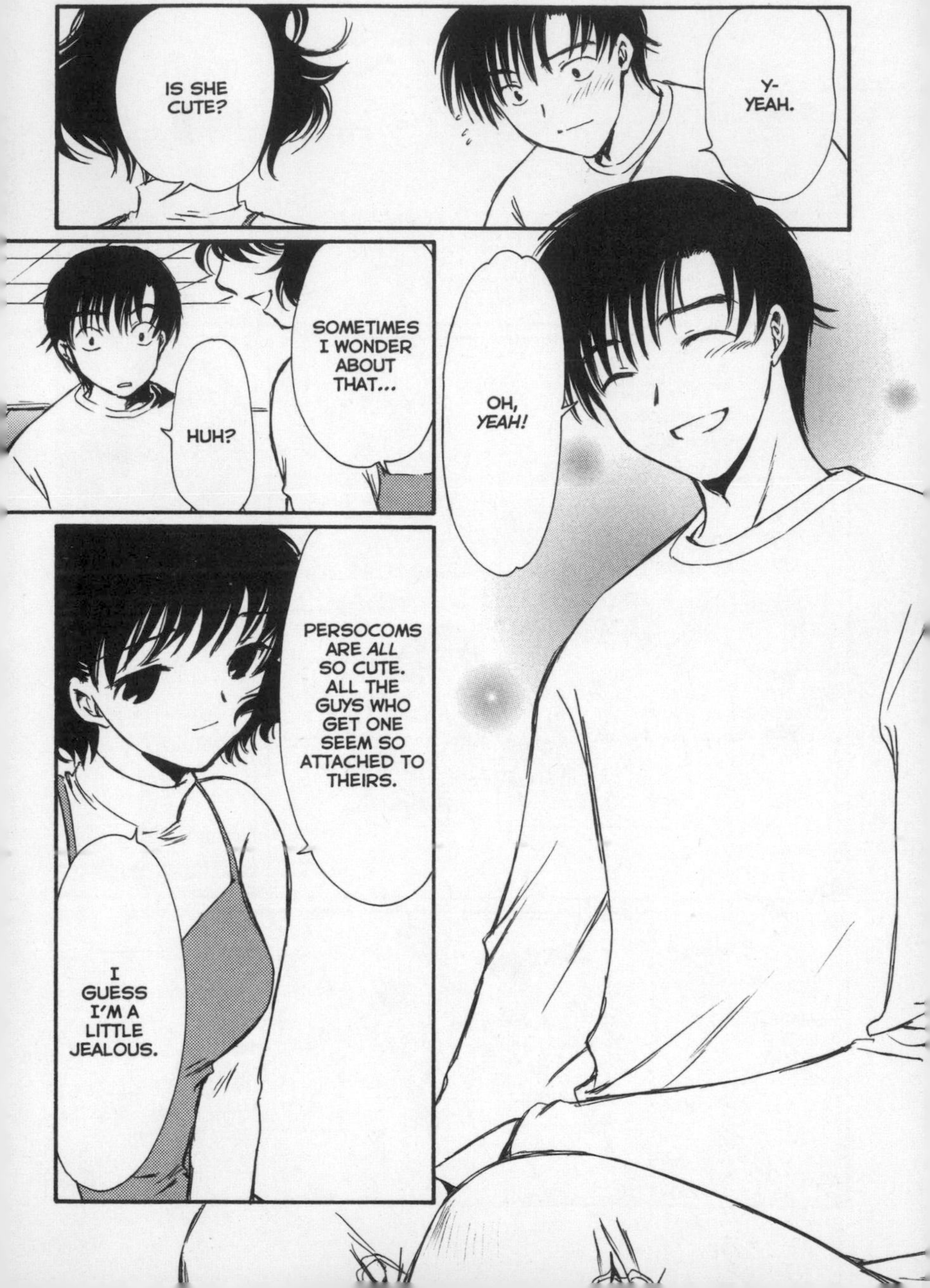
Y- YEAH.
IS SHE CUTE?
OH, YEAH!
SOMETIMES I WONDER ABOUT THAT...
HUH?
PERSOCOMS ARE ALL SO CUTE. ALL THE GUYS WHO GET ONE SEEM SO ATTACHED TO THEIRS.
I GUESS I'M A LITTLE JEALOUS.

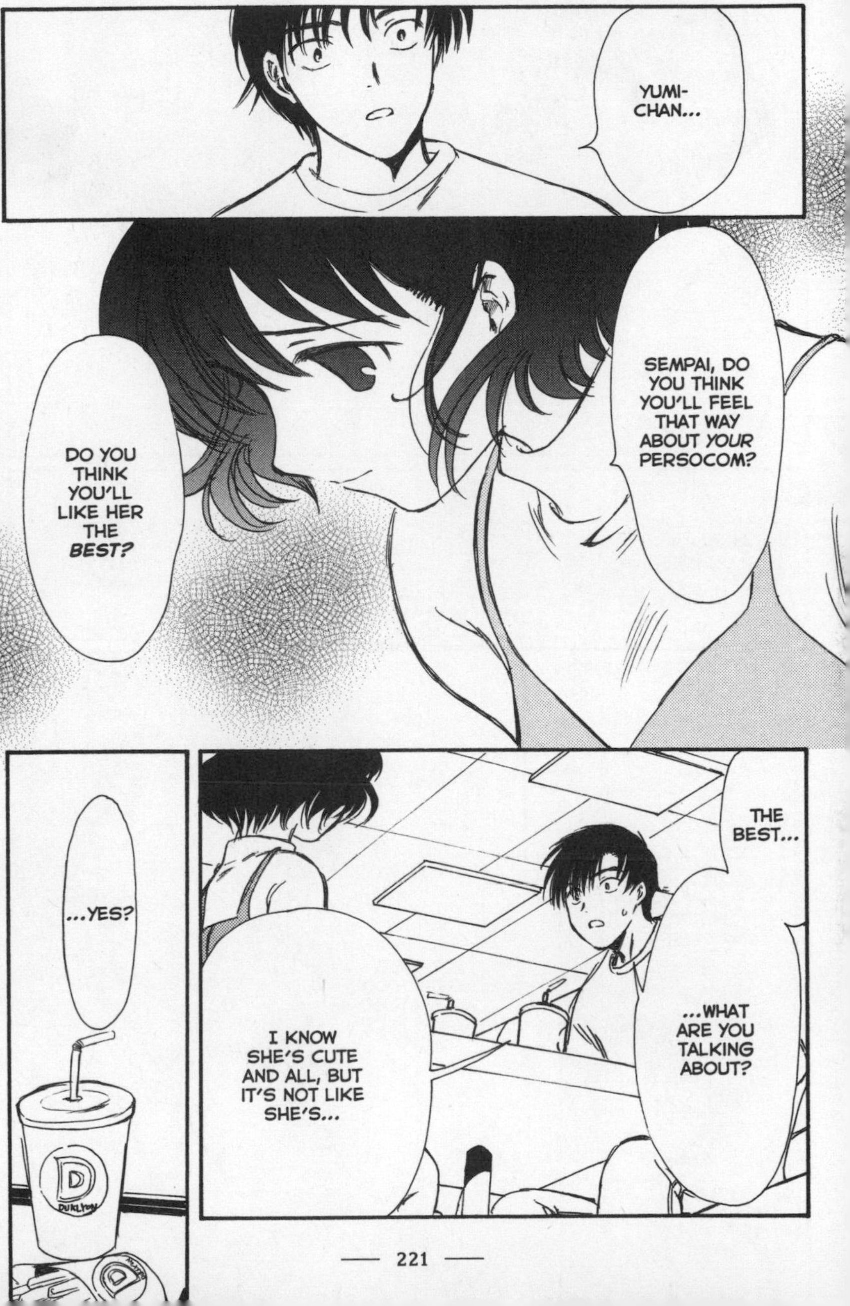
YUMI-CHAN...
SEMPAI, DO YOU THINK YOU'LL FEEL THAT WAY ABOUT *YOUR* PERSOCOM?
DO YOU THINK YOU'LL LIKE HER THE *BEST?*
THE BEST...
...WHAT ARE YOU TALKING ABOUT?
I KNOW SHE'S CUTE AND ALL, BUT IT'S NOT LIKE SHE'S...
...YES?

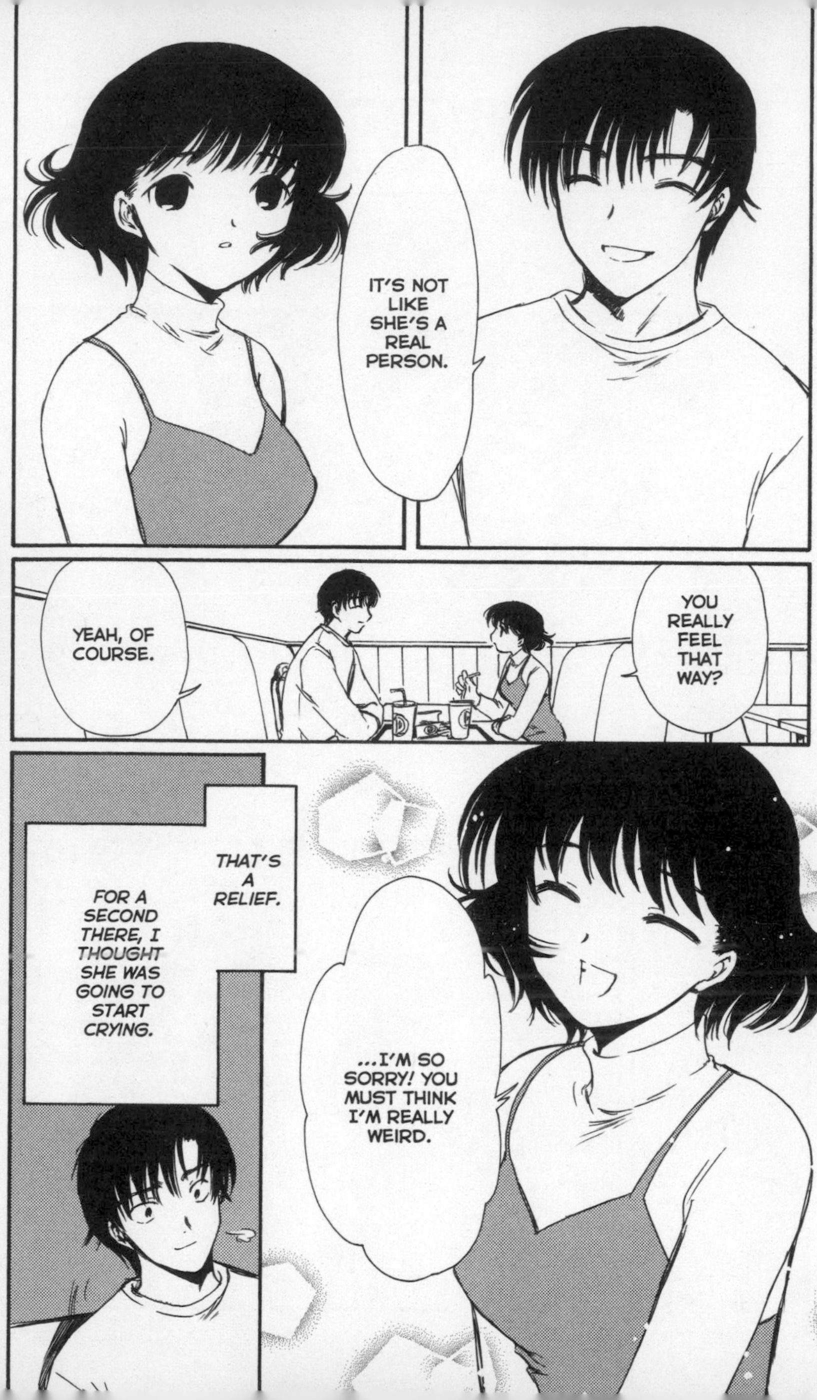
IT'S NOT LIKE SHE'S A REAL PERSON.
YOU REALLY FEEL THAT WAY?
YEAH, OF COURSE.
...I'M SO SORRY! YOU MUST THINK I'M REALLY WEIRD.
THAT'S A RELIEF.
FOR A SECOND THERE, I THOUGHT SHE WAS GOING TO START CRYING.

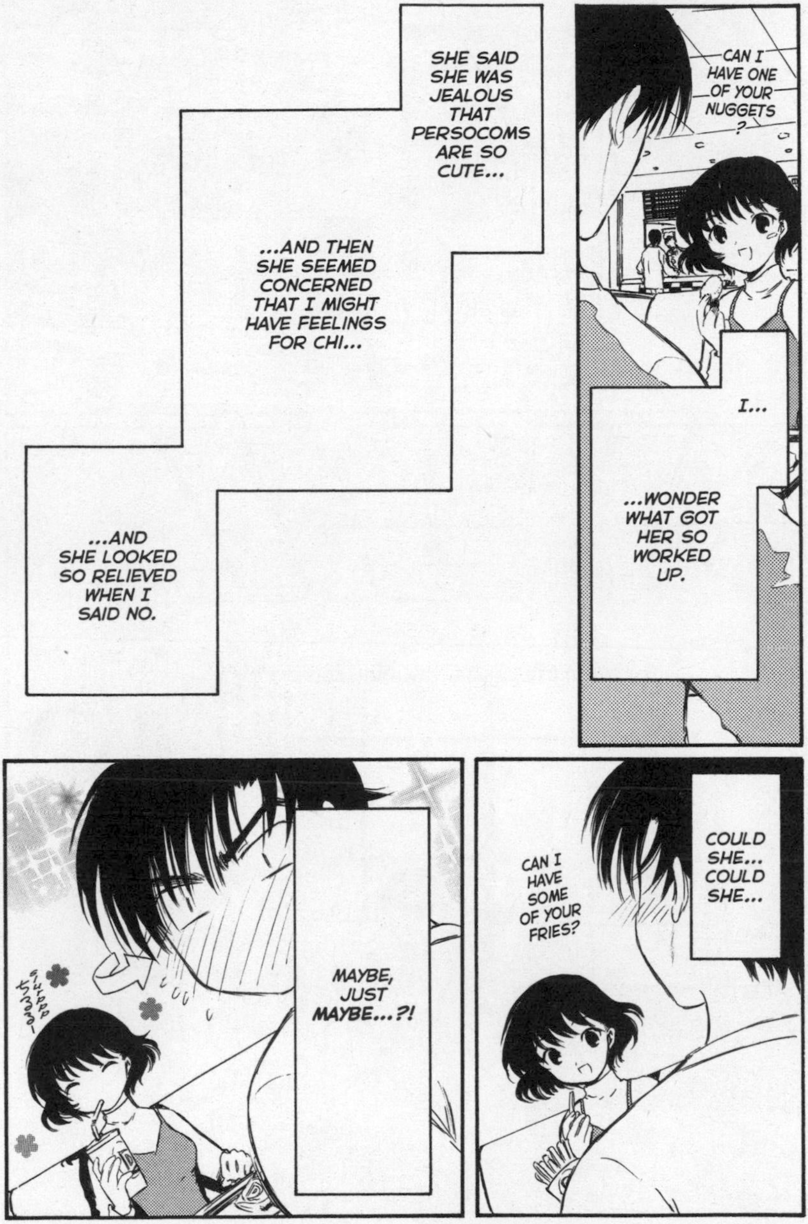

CAN I HAVE ONE OF YOUR NUGGETS?
I...
...WONDER WHAT GOT HER SO WORKED UP.
SHE SAID SHE WAS JEALOUS THAT PERSOCOMS ARE SO CUTE...
...AND THEN SHE SEEMED CONCERNED THAT I MIGHT HAVE FEELINGS FOR CHI...
...AND SHE LOOKED SO RELIEVED WHEN I SAID NO.
COULD SHE... COULD SHE...
CAN I HAVE SOME OF YOUR FRIES?
MAYBE, JUST MAYBE...?!
SLURPP

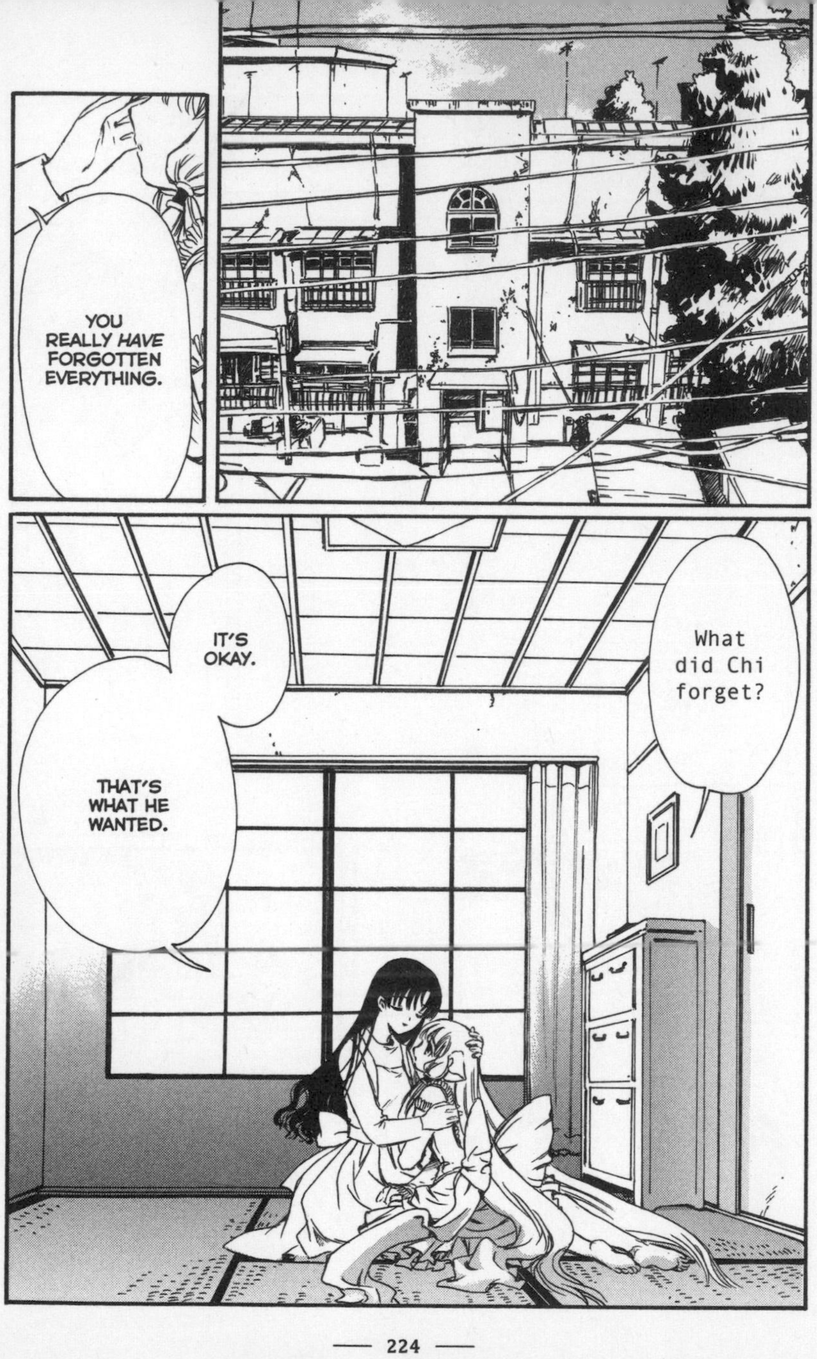
YOU REALLY *HAVE* FORGOTTEN EVERYTHING.
What did Chi forget?
IT'S OKAY.
THAT'S WHAT HE WANTED.

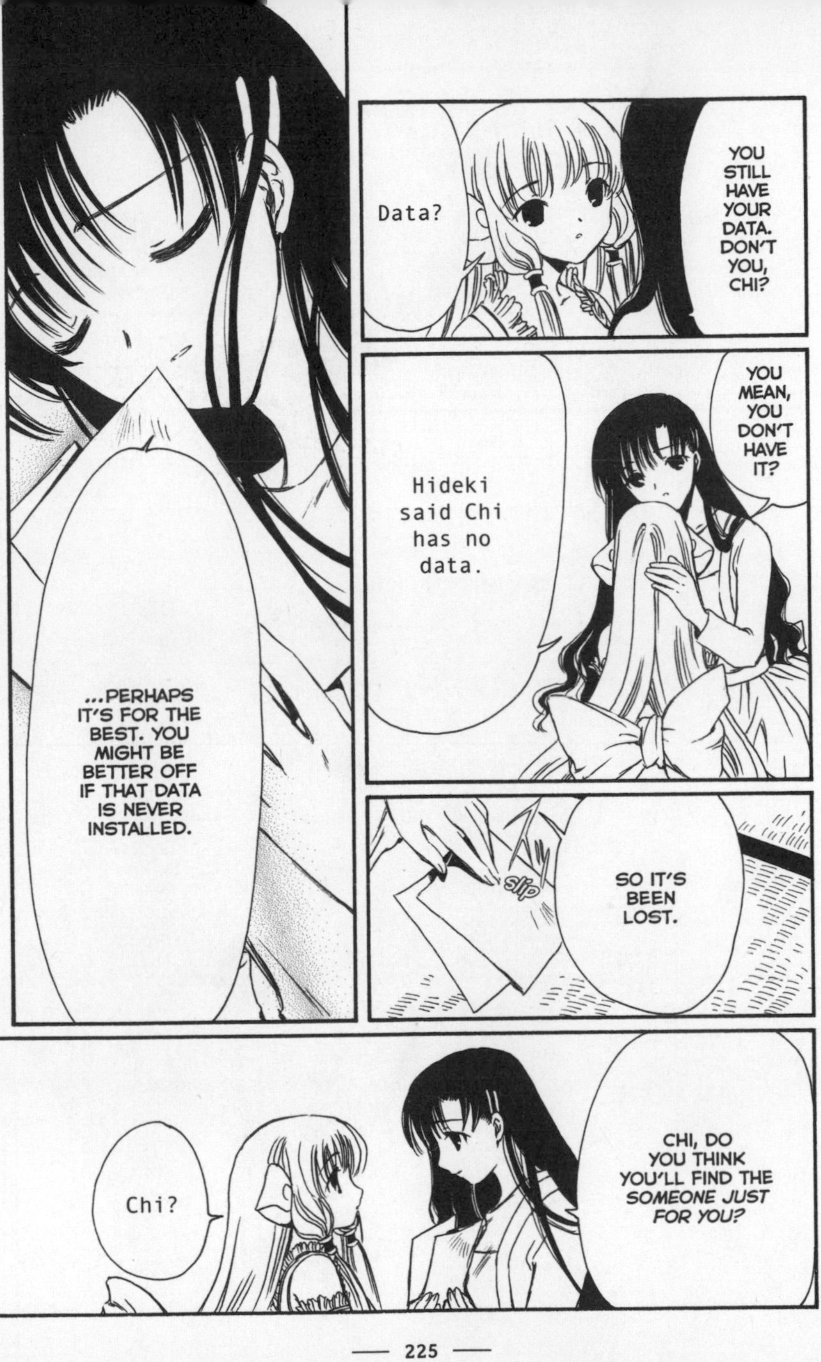
YOU STILL HAVE YOUR DATA. DON'T YOU, CHI?
Data?
YOU MEAN, YOU DON'T HAVE IT?
Hideki said Chi has no data.
SO IT'S BEEN LOST.
slip
...PERHAPS IT'S FOR THE BEST. YOU MIGHT BE BETTER OFF IF THAT DATA IS NEVER INSTALLED.
CHI, DO YOU THINK YOU'LL FIND THE *SOMEONE JUST FOR YOU?*
Chi?

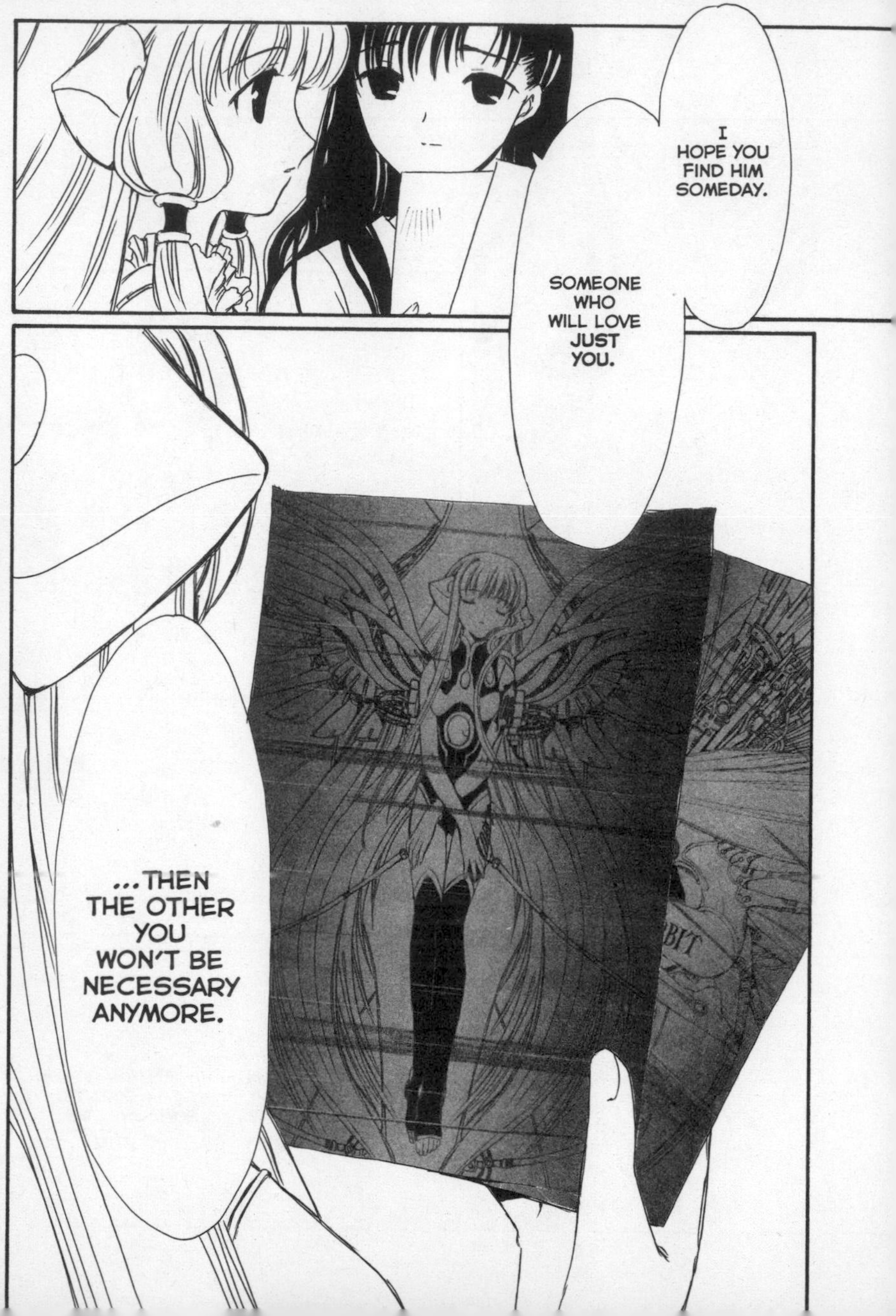
I HOPE YOU FIND HIM SOMEDAY.
SOMEONE WHO WILL LOVE JUST YOU.
...THEN THE OTHER YOU WON'T BE NECESSARY ANYMORE.

Chobits
ちょびっツ

◄ chapter 15 ►

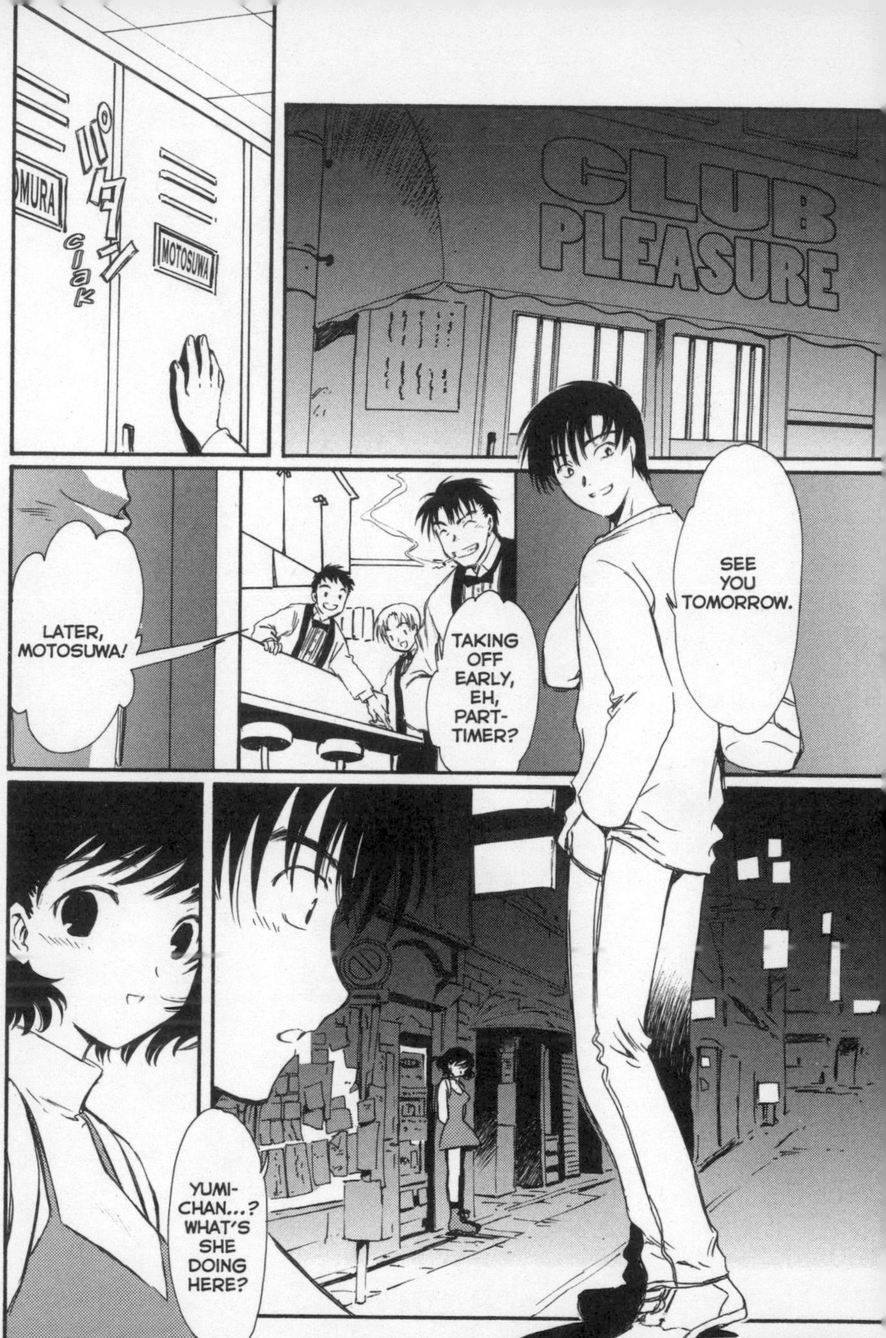
CLUB PLEASURE
MOTOSUWA
OMURA
パタン
clak
SEE YOU TOMORROW.
TAKING OFF EARLY, EH, PART-TIMER?
LATER, MOTOSUWA!
YUMI-CHAN...? WHAT'S SHE DOING HERE?

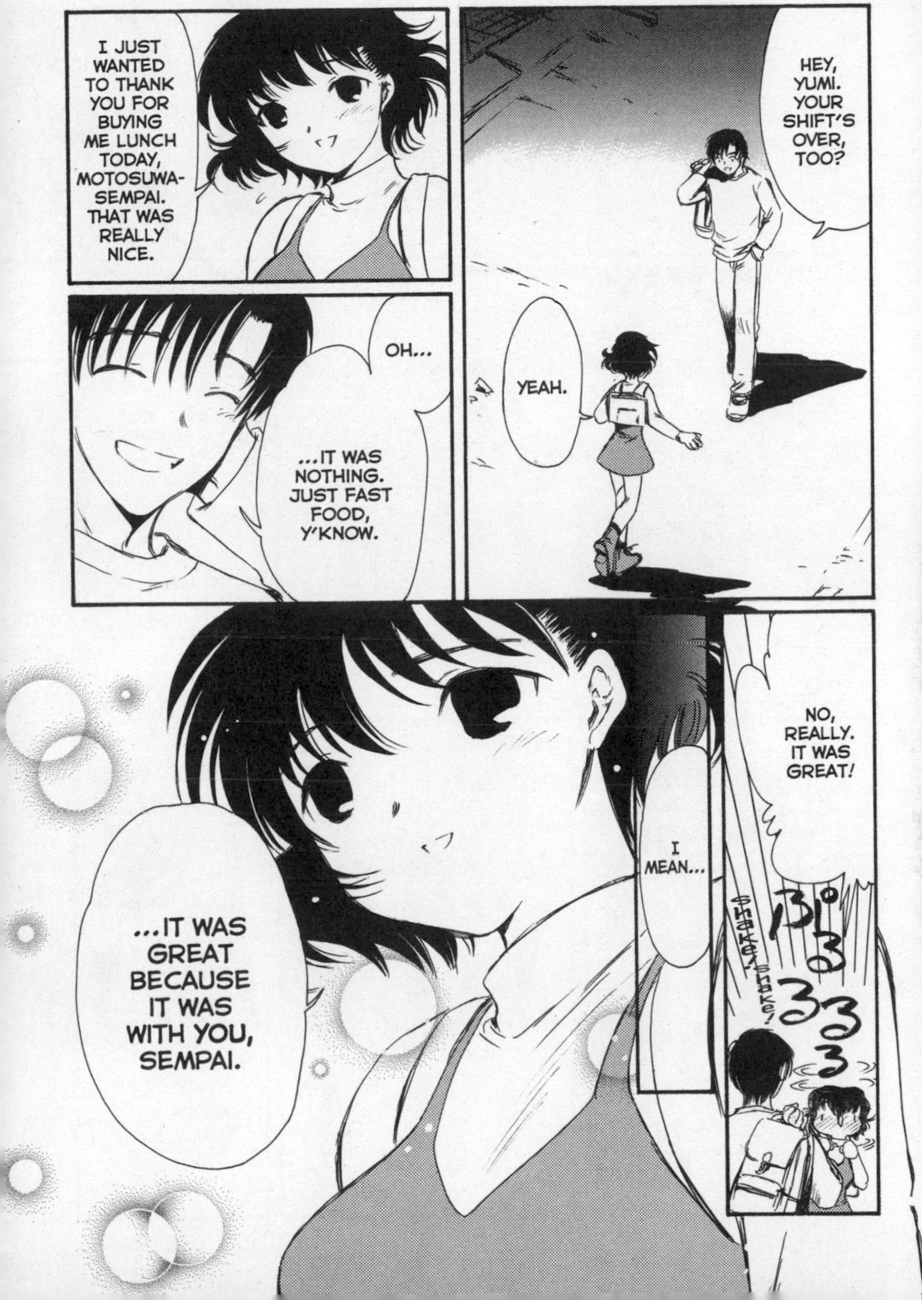
HEY, YUMI. YOUR SHIFT'S OVER, TOO?
YEAH.
I JUST WANTED TO THANK YOU FOR BUYING ME LUNCH TODAY, MOTOSUWA-SEMPAI. THAT WAS REALLY NICE.
OH...
...IT WAS NOTHING. JUST FAST FOOD, Y'KNOW.
NO, REALLY. IT WAS GREAT!
shake, shake!
I MEAN...
...IT WAS GREAT BECAUSE IT WAS WITH YOU, SEMPAI.

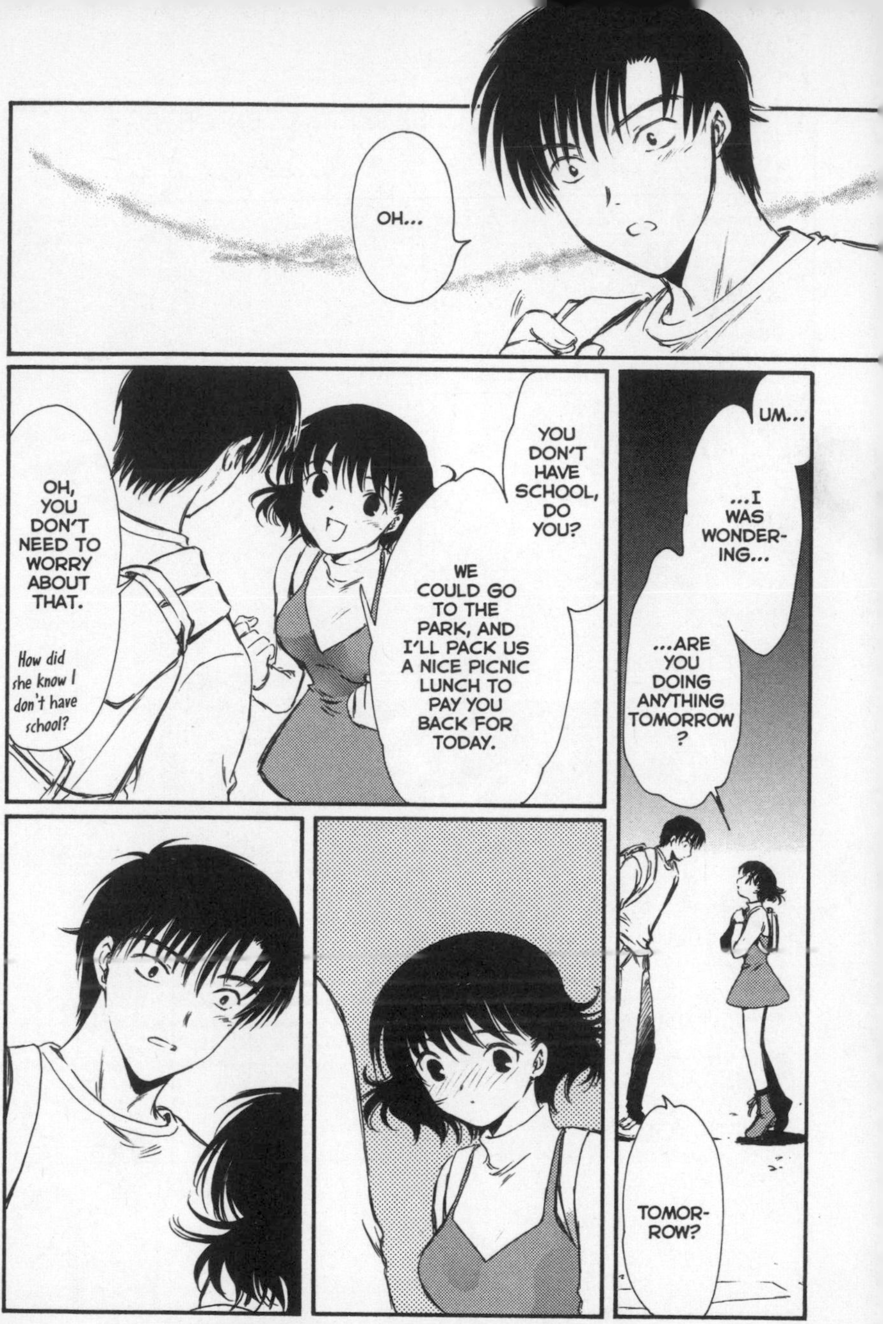
OH...
UM...
...I WAS WONDERING...
...ARE YOU DOING ANYTHING TOMORROW?
TOMORROW?
YOU DON'T HAVE SCHOOL, DO YOU?
WE COULD GO TO THE PARK, AND I'LL PACK US A NICE PICNIC LUNCH TO PAY YOU BACK FOR TODAY.
OH, YOU DON'T NEED TO WORRY ABOUT THAT.
How did she know I don't have school?

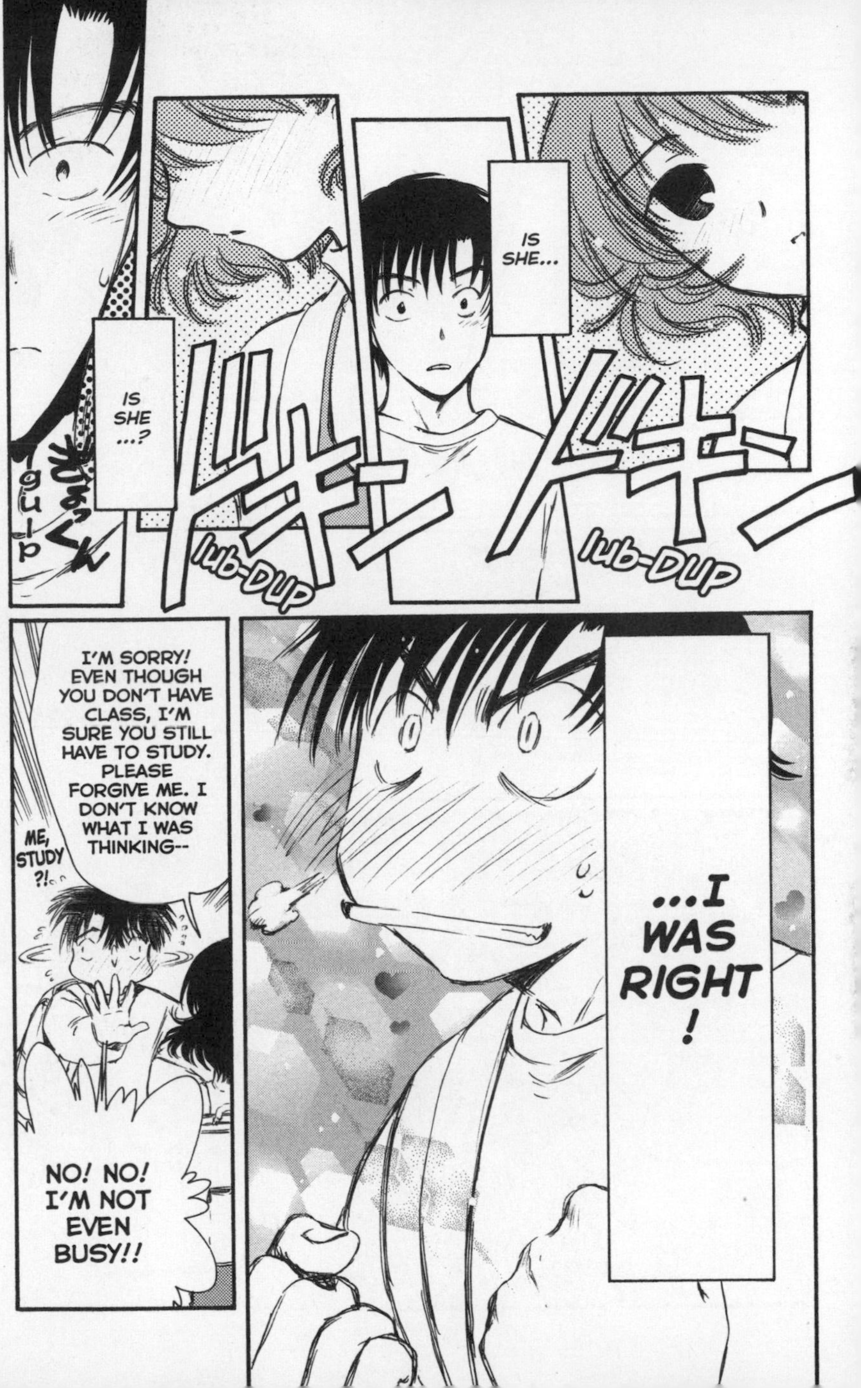
lub-DUP
IS SHE...
lub-DUP
IS SHE ...?
gulp
...I WAS RIGHT!
I'M SORRY! EVEN THOUGH YOU DON'T HAVE CLASS, I'M SURE YOU STILL HAVE TO STUDY. PLEASE FORGIVE ME. I DON'T KNOW WHAT I WAS THINKING--
ME, STUDY?!
NO! NO! I'M NOT EVEN BUSY!!

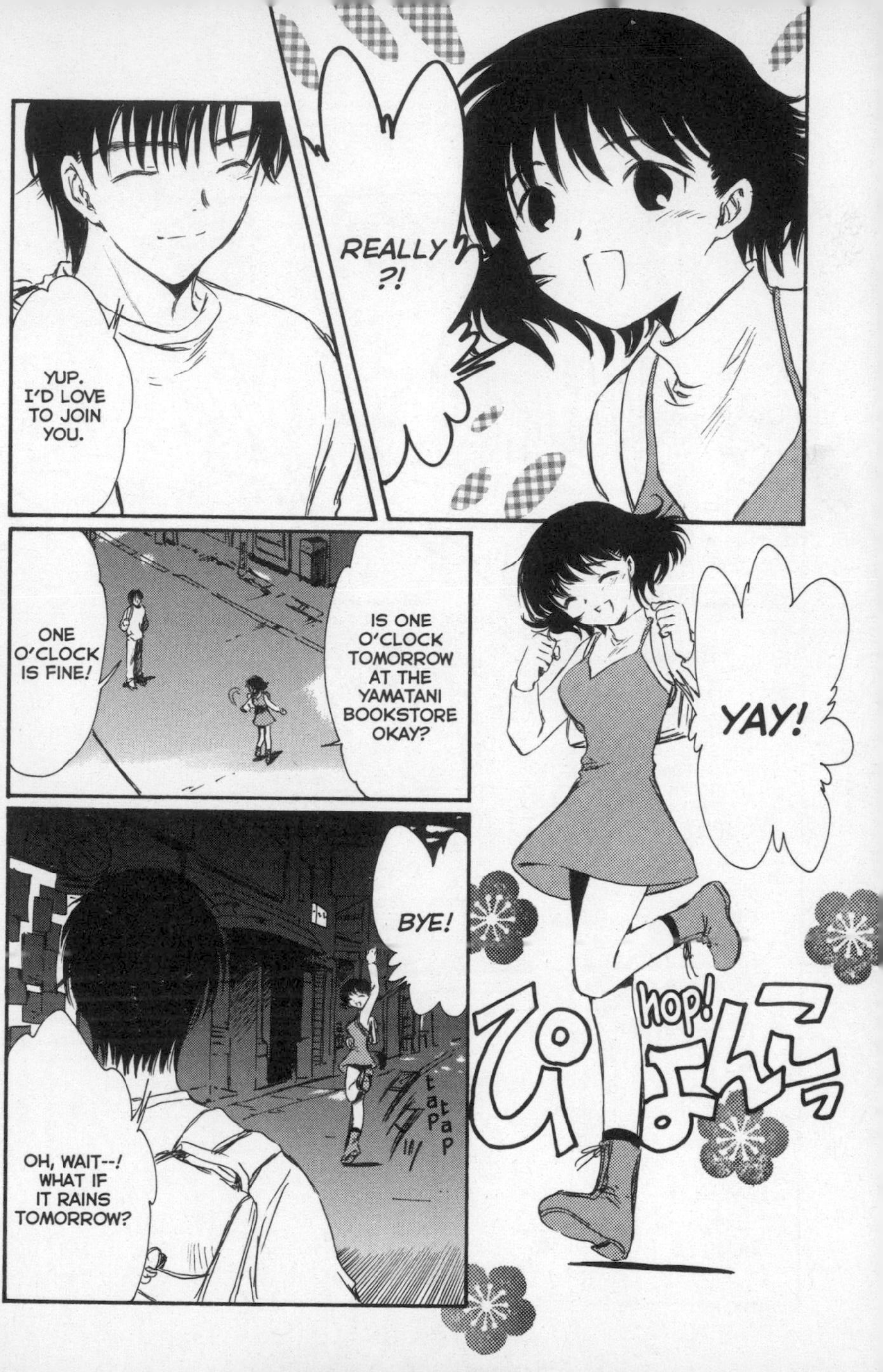

REALLY?!
YUP. I'D LOVE TO JOIN YOU.
YAY!
hop!
ぴょんこっ
IS ONE O'CLOCK TOMORROW AT THE YAMATANI BOOKSTORE OKAY?
ONE O'CLOCK IS FINE!
BYE!
tap tap
OH, WAIT--! WHAT IF IT RAINS TOMORROW?

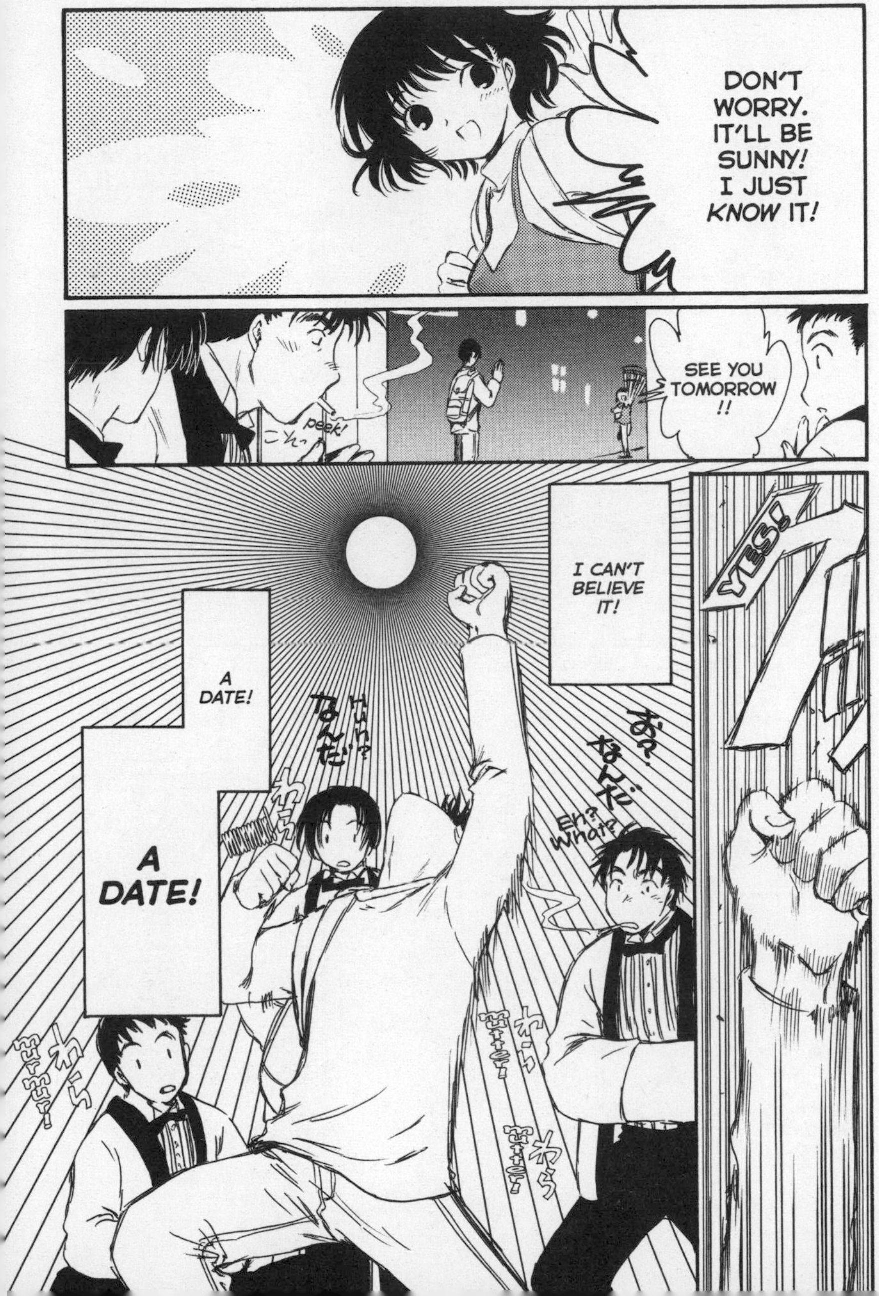
DON'T WORRY. IT'LL BE SUNNY! I JUST KNOW IT!
SEE YOU TOMORROW !!
こそっ
peek!
YES!
I CAN'T BELIEVE IT!
おっ? なんだ
Eh? What?
なんだ
Huh?
A DATE!
A DATE!
わら
わら
murmur!
わら
murmur!
わら
murmur!

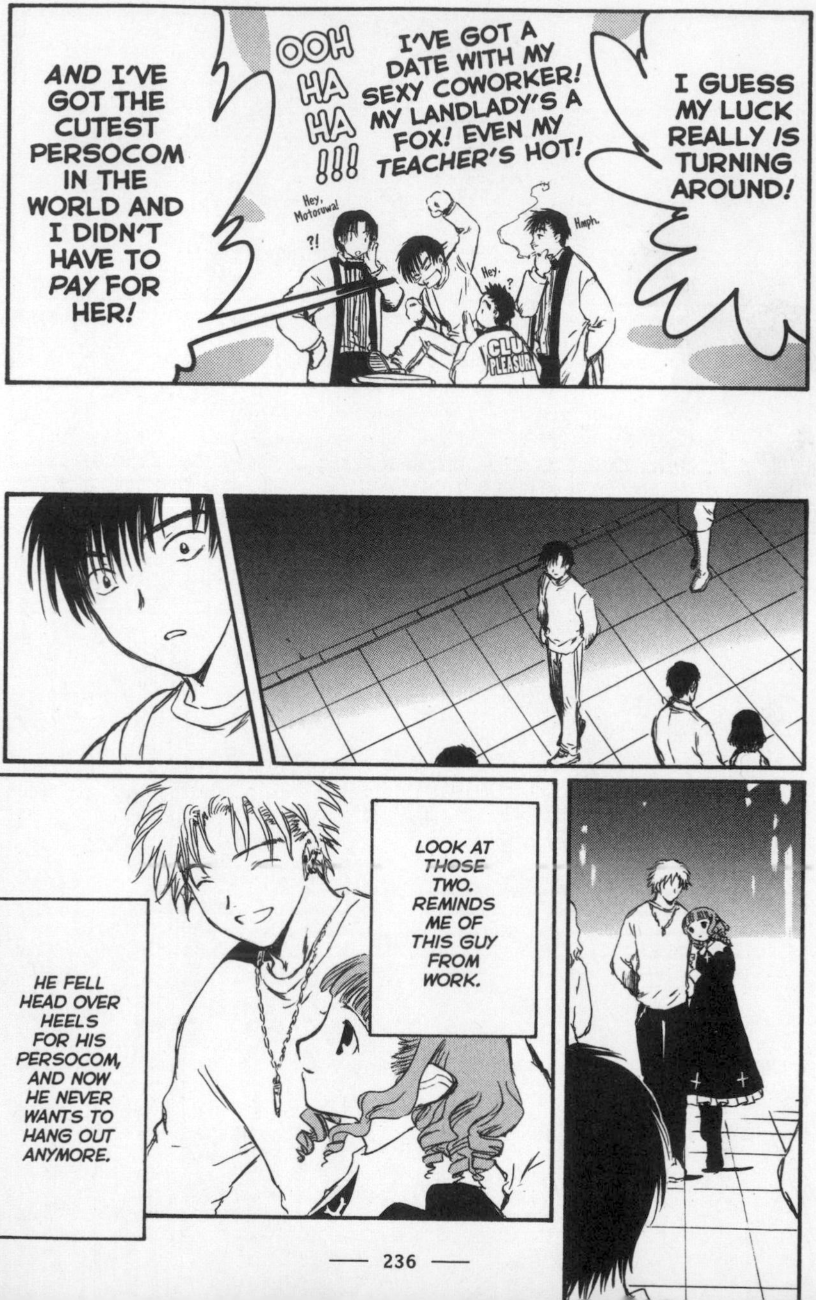
I GUESS MY LUCK REALLY *IS* TURNING AROUND!
Hmph.
Hey.
?
I'VE GOT A DATE WITH MY SEXY COWORKER! MY LANDLADY'S A FOX! EVEN MY TEACHER'S HOT!
OOH HA HA !!!
Hey, Motoruwa!
?!
AND I'VE GOT THE CUTEST PERSOCOM IN THE WORLD AND I DIDN'T HAVE TO *PAY* FOR HER!
LOOK AT THOSE TWO. REMINDS ME OF THIS GUY FROM WORK.
HE FELL HEAD OVER HEELS FOR HIS PERSOCOM, AND NOW HE NEVER WANTS TO HANG OUT ANYMORE.

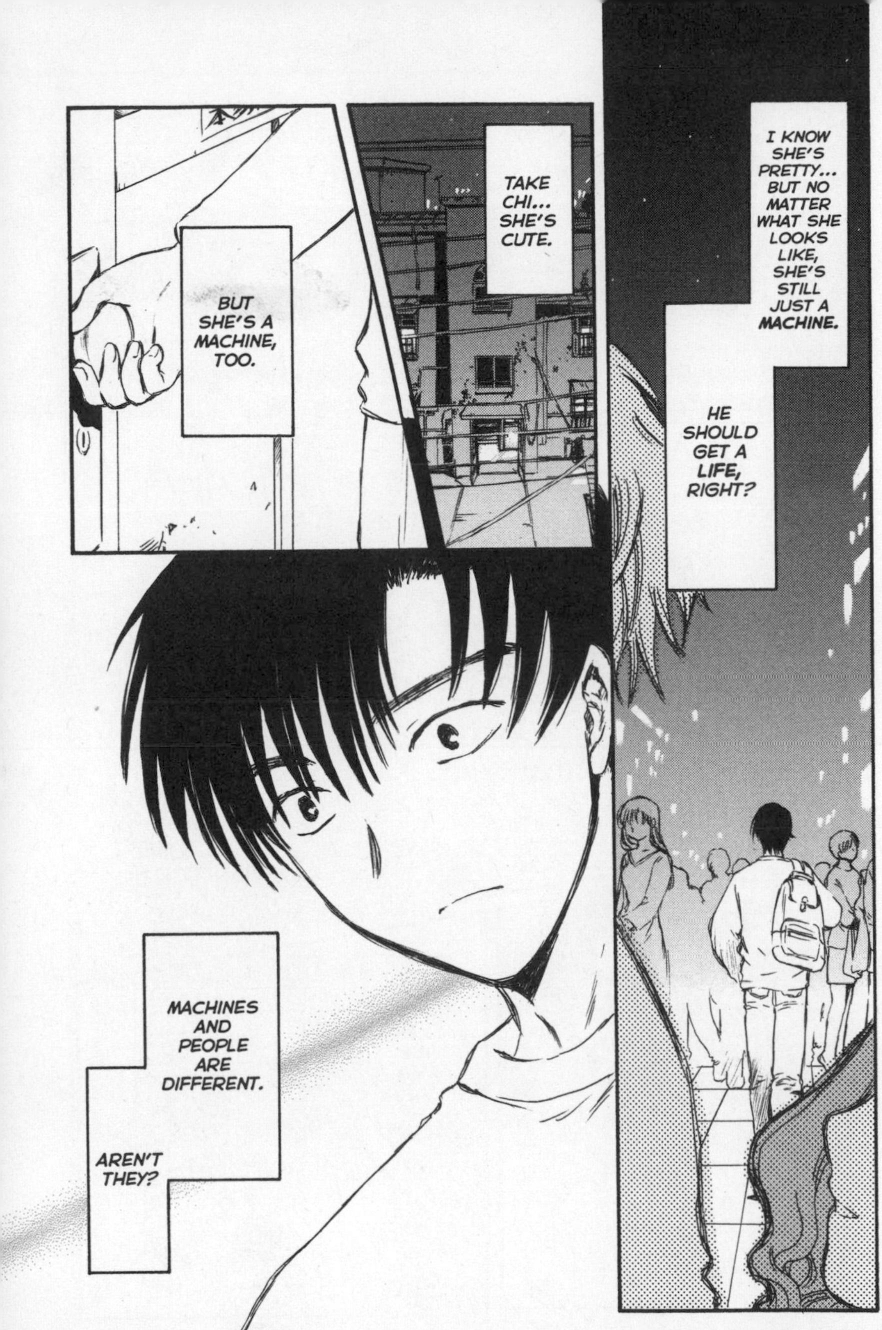
I KNOW SHE'S PRETTY... BUT NO MATTER WHAT SHE LOOKS LIKE, SHE'S STILL JUST A MACHINE.
HE SHOULD GET A LIFE, RIGHT?
TAKE CHI... SHE'S CUTE.
BUT SHE'S A MACHINE, TOO.
MACHINES AND PEOPLE ARE DIFFERENT.
AREN'T THEY?

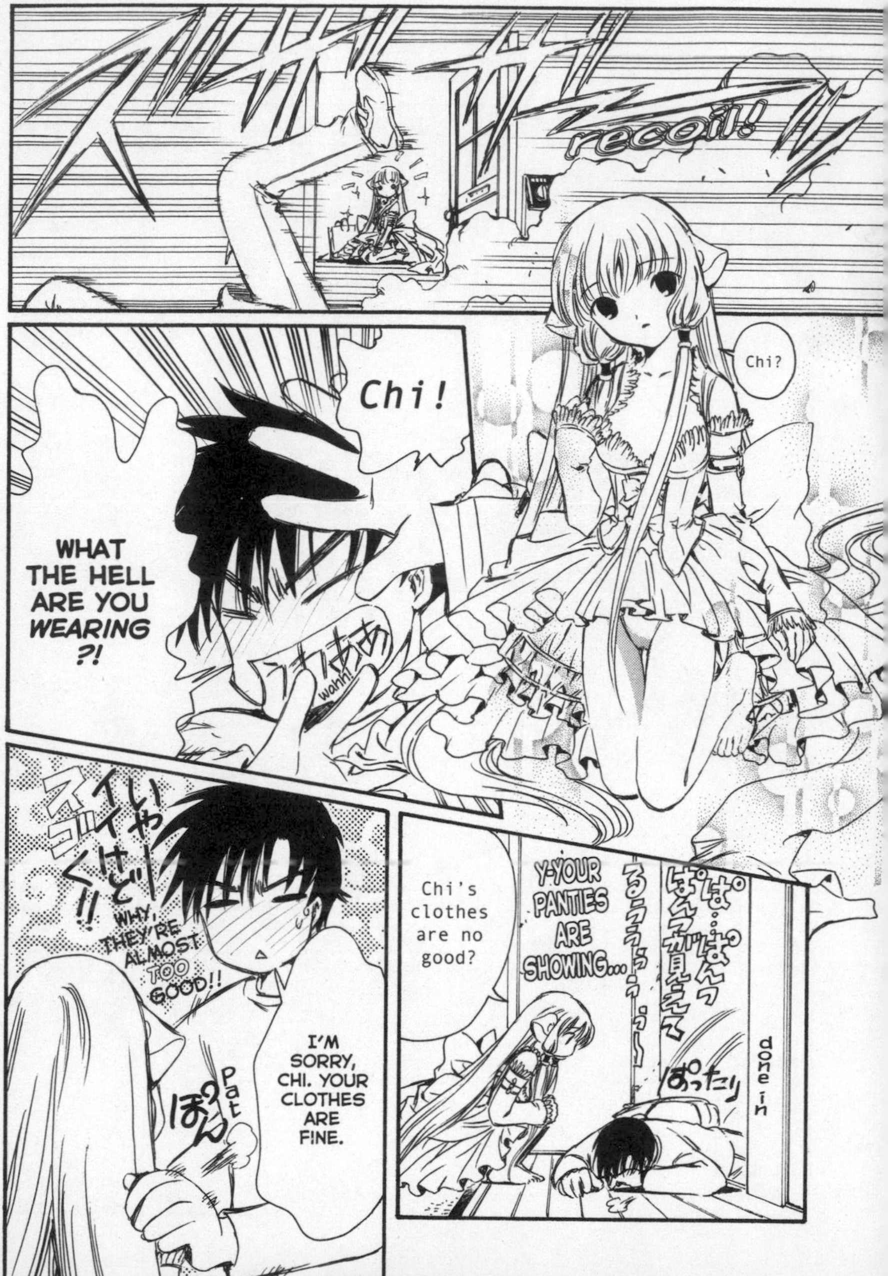
recoil!
Chi?
Chi!
WHAT THE HELL ARE YOU WEARING?!
うわああ
wahh!
ぱ…ぱんつが見えて
Y-YOUR PANTIES ARE SHOWING...
Chi's clothes are no good?
ぱったり
done in
いやーイイけどスゴく!!
WHY, THEY'RE ALMOST TOO GOOD!!
I'M SORRY, CHI. YOUR CLOTHES ARE FINE.
ぽん
Pat

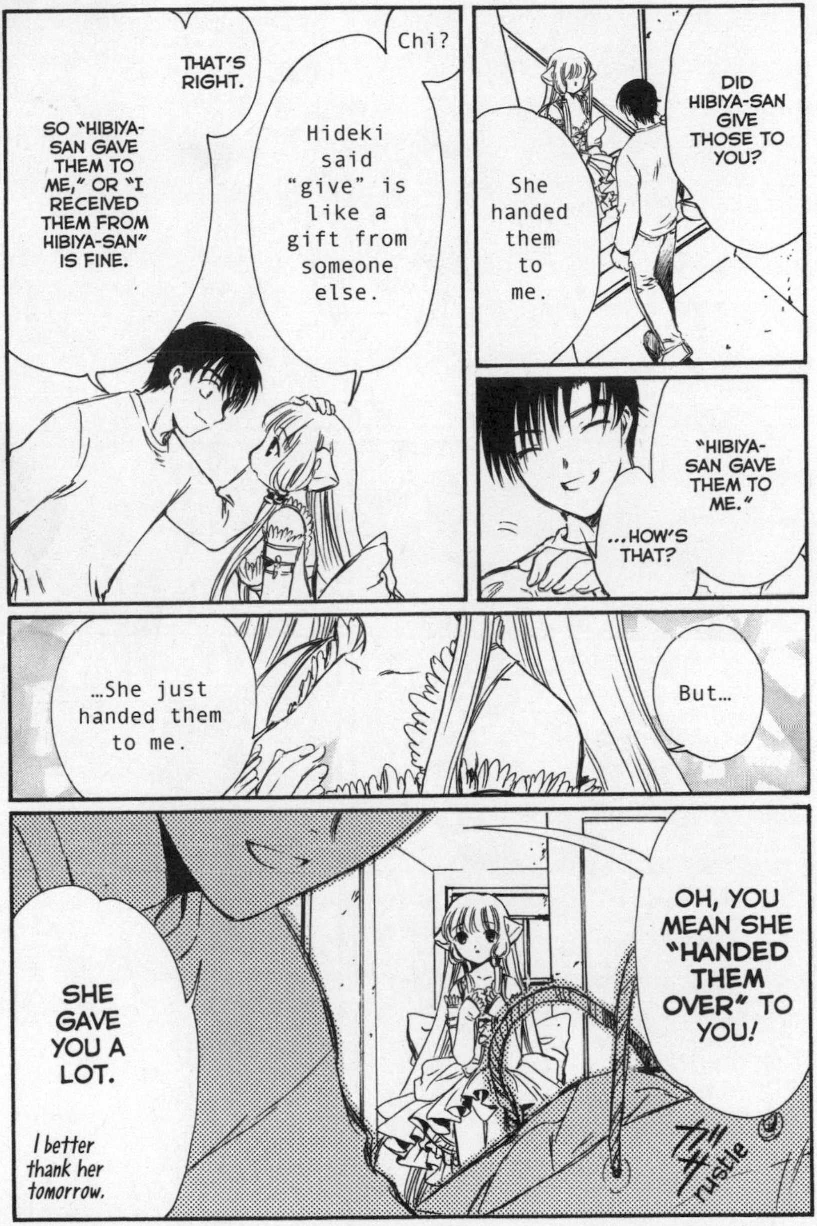
DID HIBIYA-SAN GIVE THOSE TO YOU?
She handed them to me.
"HIBIYA-SAN GAVE THEM TO ME."
...HOW'S THAT?
Chi?
Hideki said "give" is like a gift from someone else.
THAT'S RIGHT.
SO "HIBIYA-SAN GAVE THEM TO ME," OR "I RECEIVED THEM FROM HIBIYA-SAN" IS FINE.
But...
...She just handed them to me.
OH, YOU MEAN SHE "HANDED THEM OVER" TO YOU!
rustle
SHE GAVE YOU A LOT.
I better thank her tomorrow.

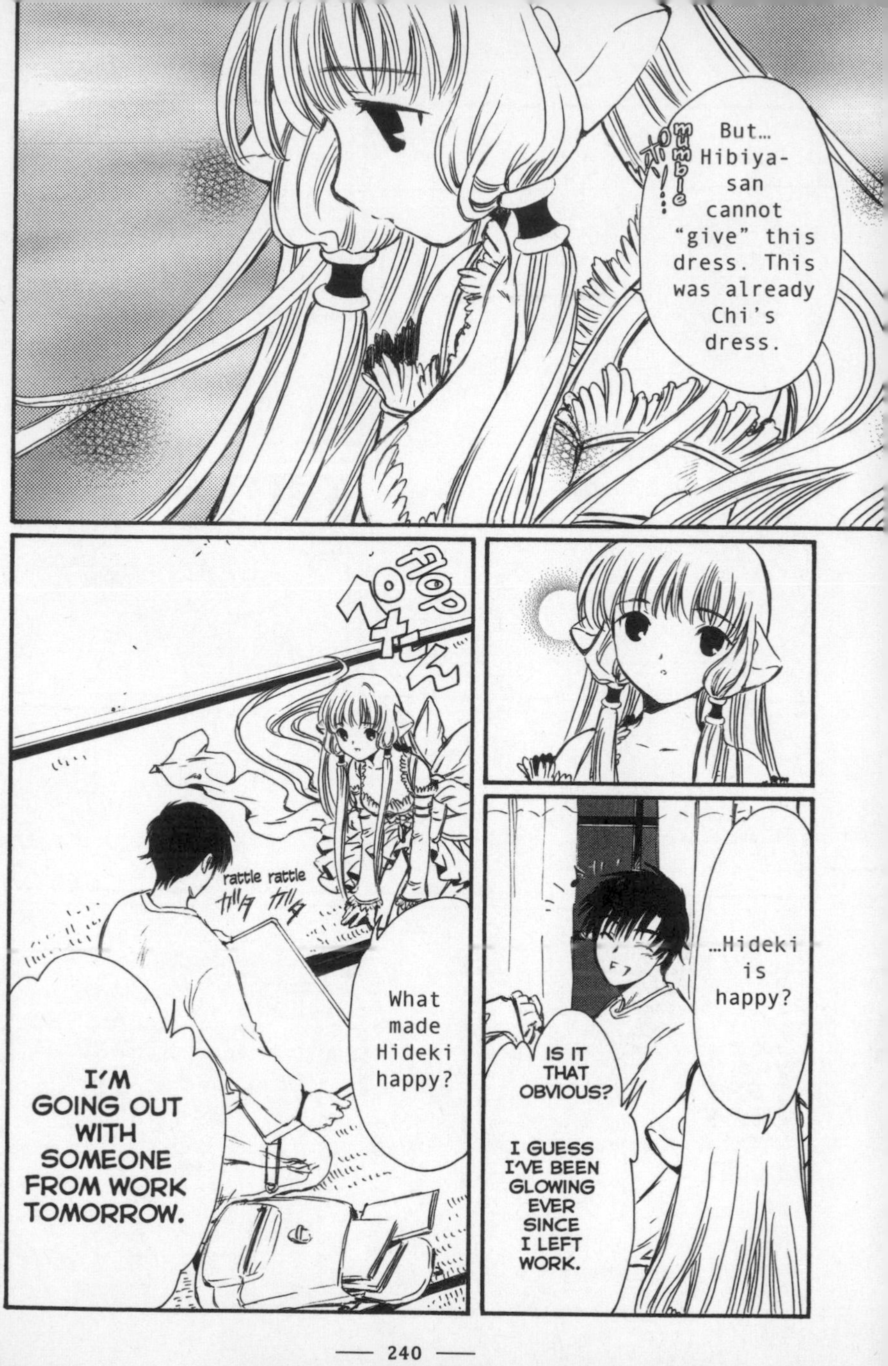
But… Hibiya-san cannot "give" this dress. This was already Chi's dress.
mumble
…Hideki is happy?
IS IT THAT OBVIOUS?
I GUESS I'VE BEEN GLOWING EVER SINCE I LEFT WORK.
plop
rattle rattle
What made Hideki happy?
I'M GOING OUT WITH SOMEONE FROM WORK TOMORROW.

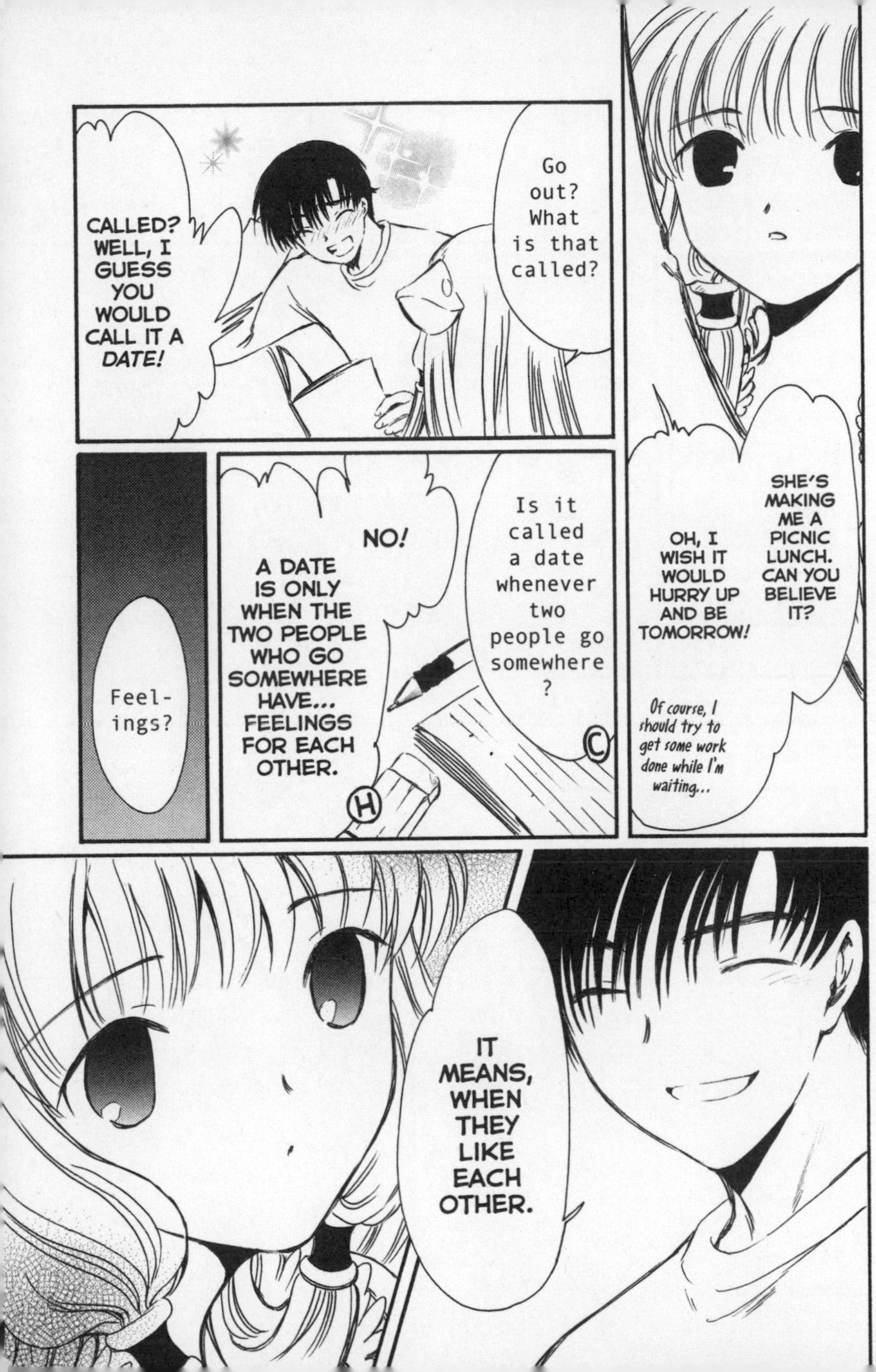
SHE'S MAKING ME A PICNIC LUNCH. CAN YOU BELIEVE IT?
OH, I WISH IT WOULD HURRY UP AND BE TOMORROW!
Of course, I should try to get some work done while I'm waiting...
Go out? What is that called?
CALLED? WELL, I GUESS YOU WOULD CALL IT A *DATE!*
Is it called a date whenever two people go somewhere?
NO! A DATE IS ONLY WHEN THE TWO PEOPLE WHO GO SOMEWHERE HAVE... FEELINGS FOR EACH OTHER.
Feel-ings?
IT MEANS, WHEN THEY LIKE EACH OTHER.

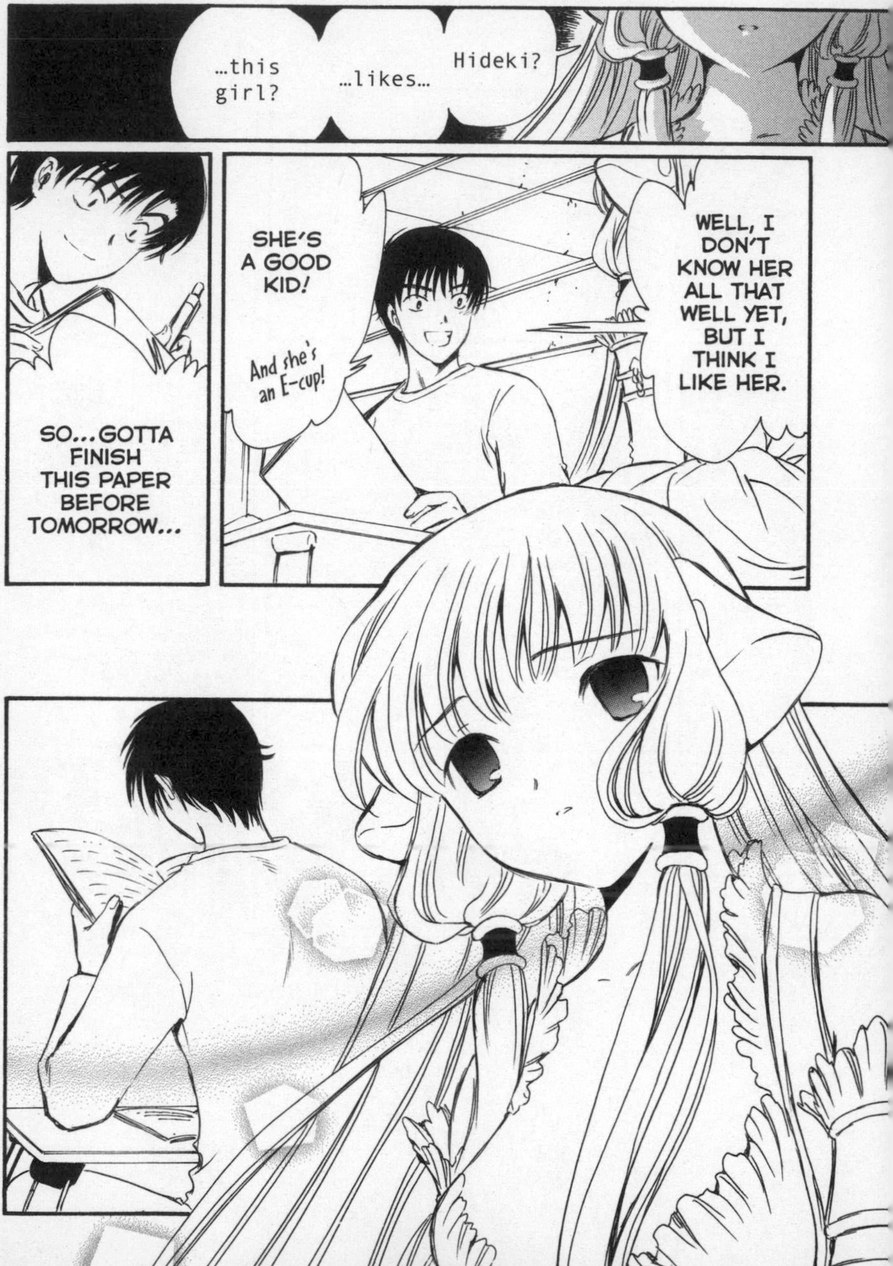
Hideki?
…likes…
…this girl?
WELL, I DON'T KNOW HER ALL THAT WELL YET, BUT I THINK I LIKE HER.
SHE'S A GOOD KID!
And she's an E-cup!
SO…GOTTA FINISH THIS PAPER BEFORE TOMORROW…

Chobits
ちょびっツ

◀ **chapter 16** ▶

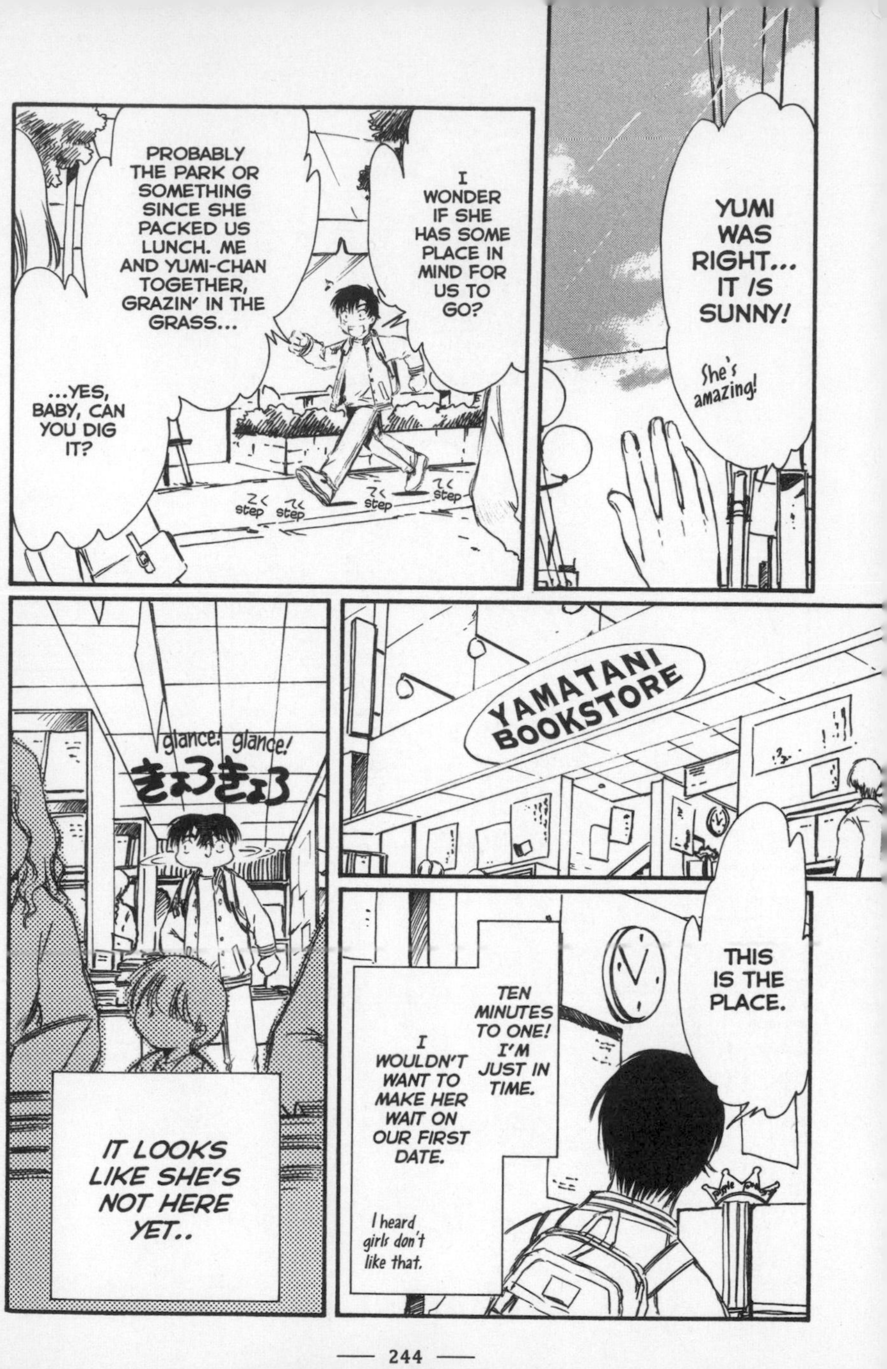
YUMI WAS RIGHT... IT IS SUNNY!
She's amazing!
I WONDER IF SHE HAS SOME PLACE IN MIND FOR US TO GO?
PROBABLY THE PARK OR SOMETHING SINCE SHE PACKED US LUNCH. ME AND YUMI-CHAN TOGETHER, GRAZIN' IN THE GRASS...
...YES, BABY, CAN YOU DIG IT?
てく step
てく step
てく step
てく step
YAMATANI BOOKSTORE
THIS IS THE PLACE.
TEN MINUTES TO ONE! I'M JUST IN TIME.
I WOULDN'T WANT TO MAKE HER WAIT ON OUR FIRST DATE.
I heard girls don't like that.
glance! glance!
きょろきょろ
IT LOOKS LIKE SHE'S NOT HERE YET..

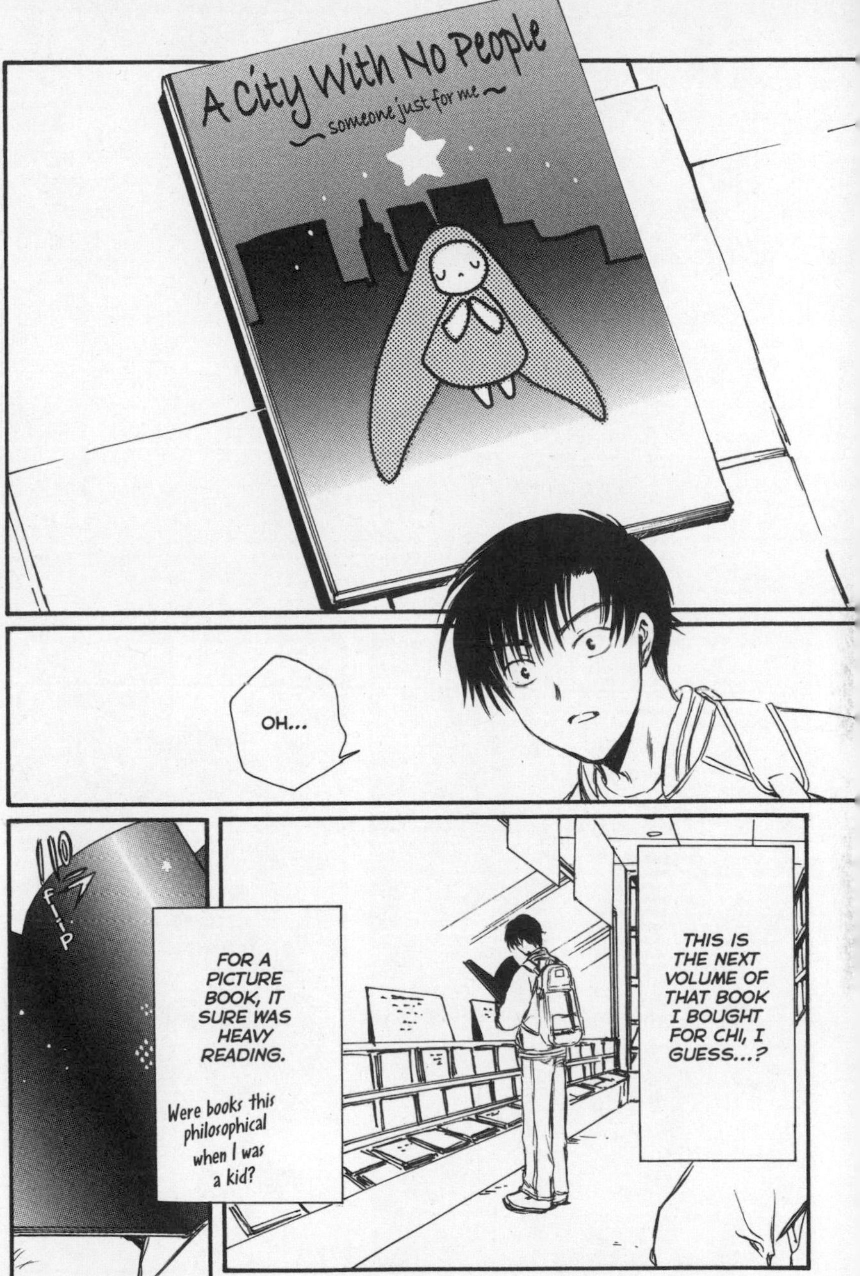
A City With No People
~someone just for me~
OH...
THIS IS THE NEXT VOLUME OF THAT BOOK I BOUGHT FOR CHI, I GUESS...?
FOR A PICTURE BOOK, IT SURE WAS HEAVY READING.
Were books this philosophical when I was a kid?
FLIP

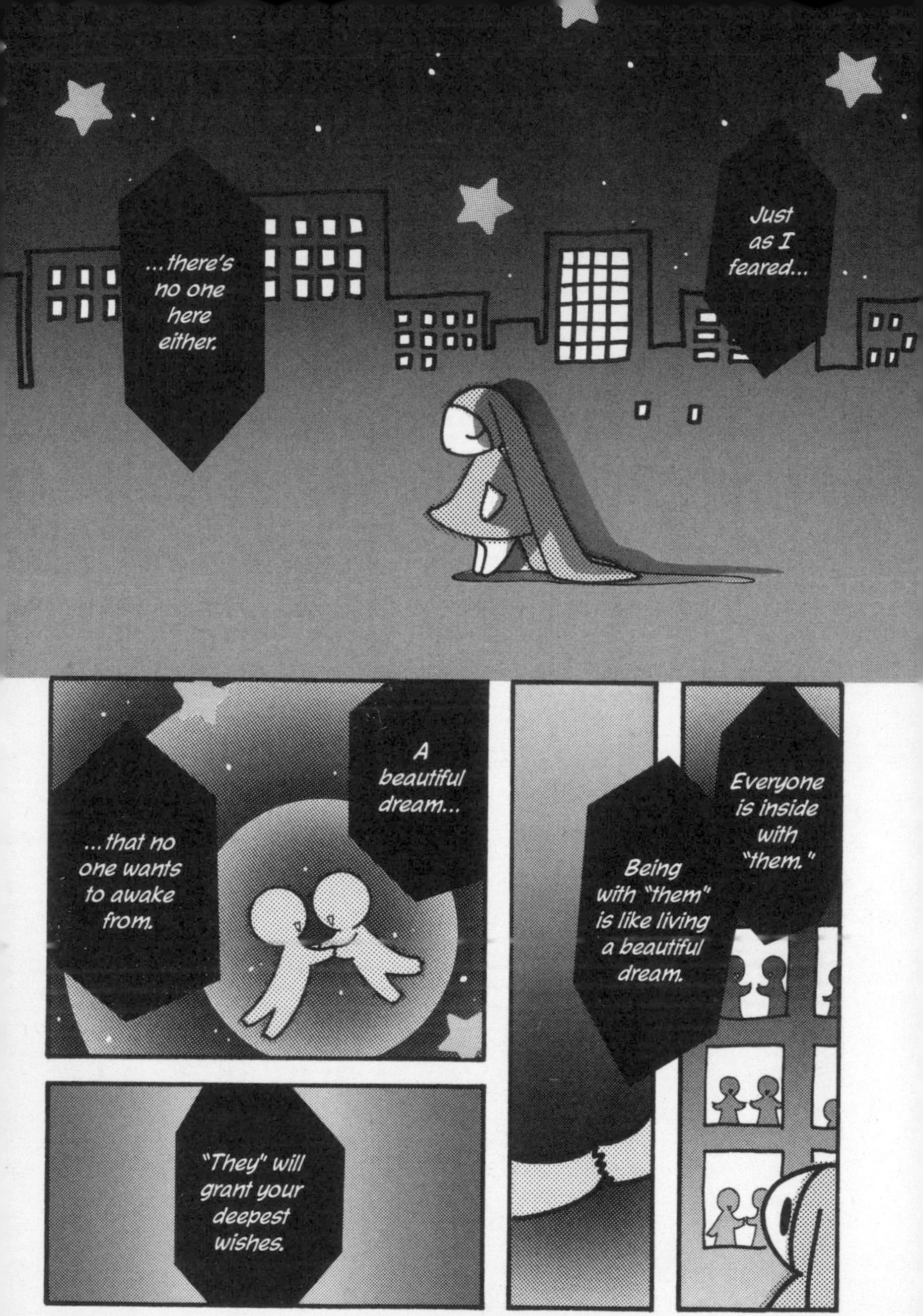
Just as I feared...
...there's no one here either.
Everyone is inside with "them."
Being with "them" is like living a beautiful dream.
A beautiful dream...
...that no one wants to awake from.
"They" will grant your deepest wishes.

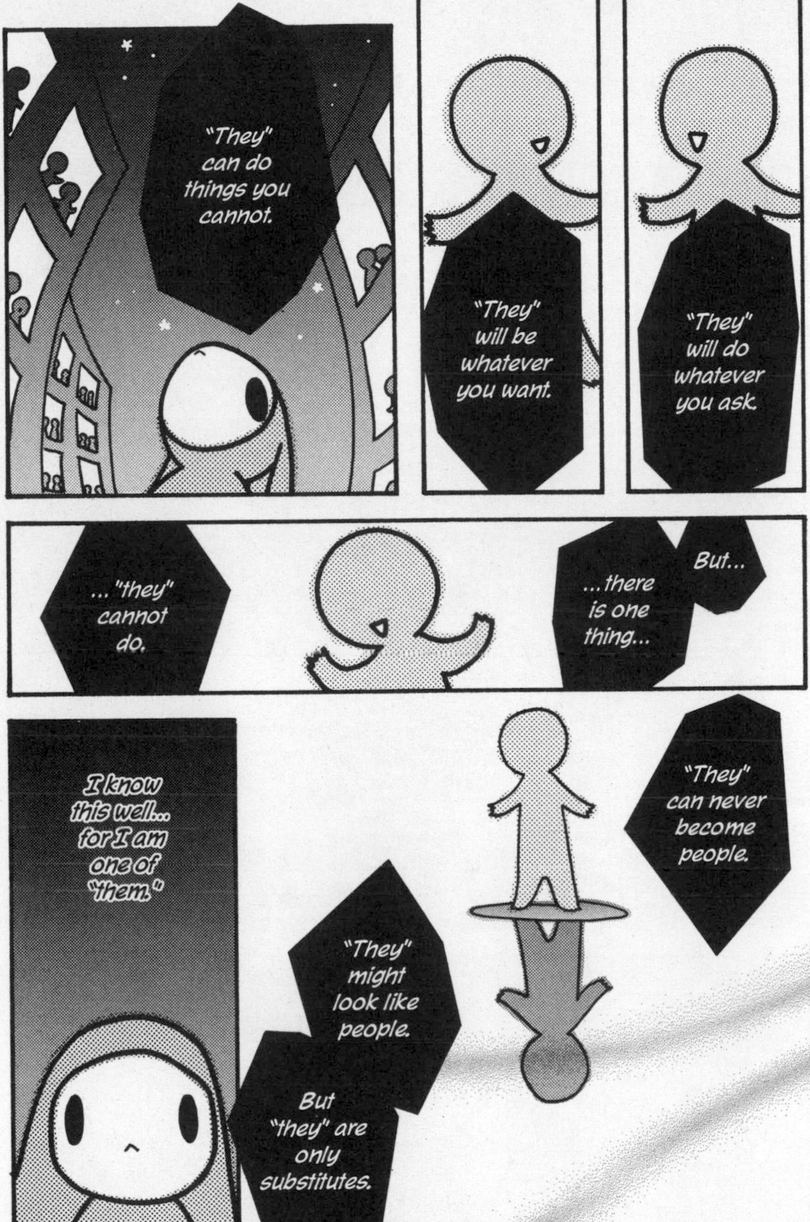
"They" will do whatever you ask.
"They" will be whatever you want.
"They" can do things you cannot.
But...
...there is one thing...
..."they" cannot do.
"They" can never become people.
"They" might look like people.
But "they" are only substitutes.
I know this well... for I am one of "them."

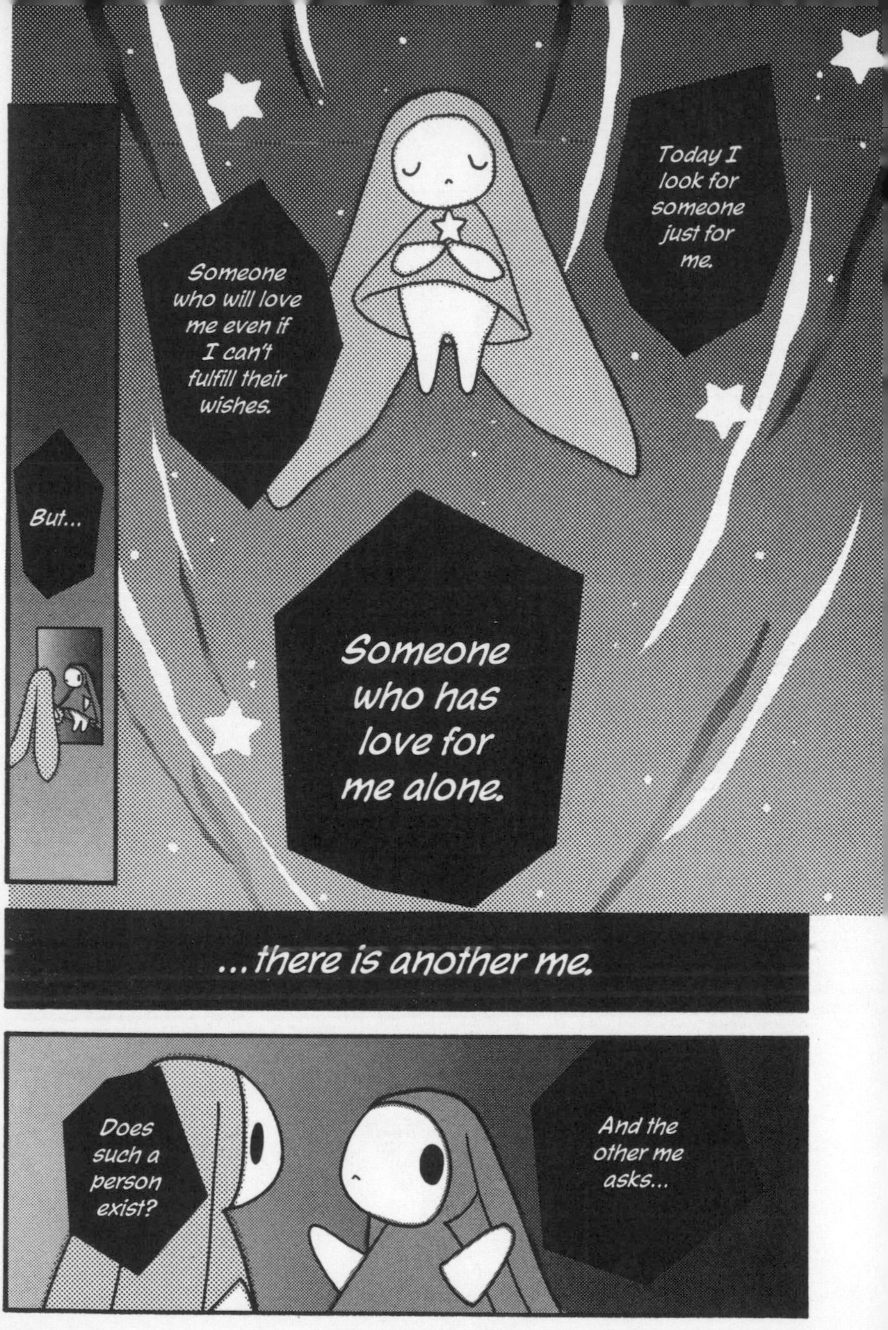
Today I look for someone just for me.
Someone who will love me even if I can't fulfill their wishes.
Someone who has love for me alone.
But...
...there is another me.
And the other me asks...
Does such a person exist?

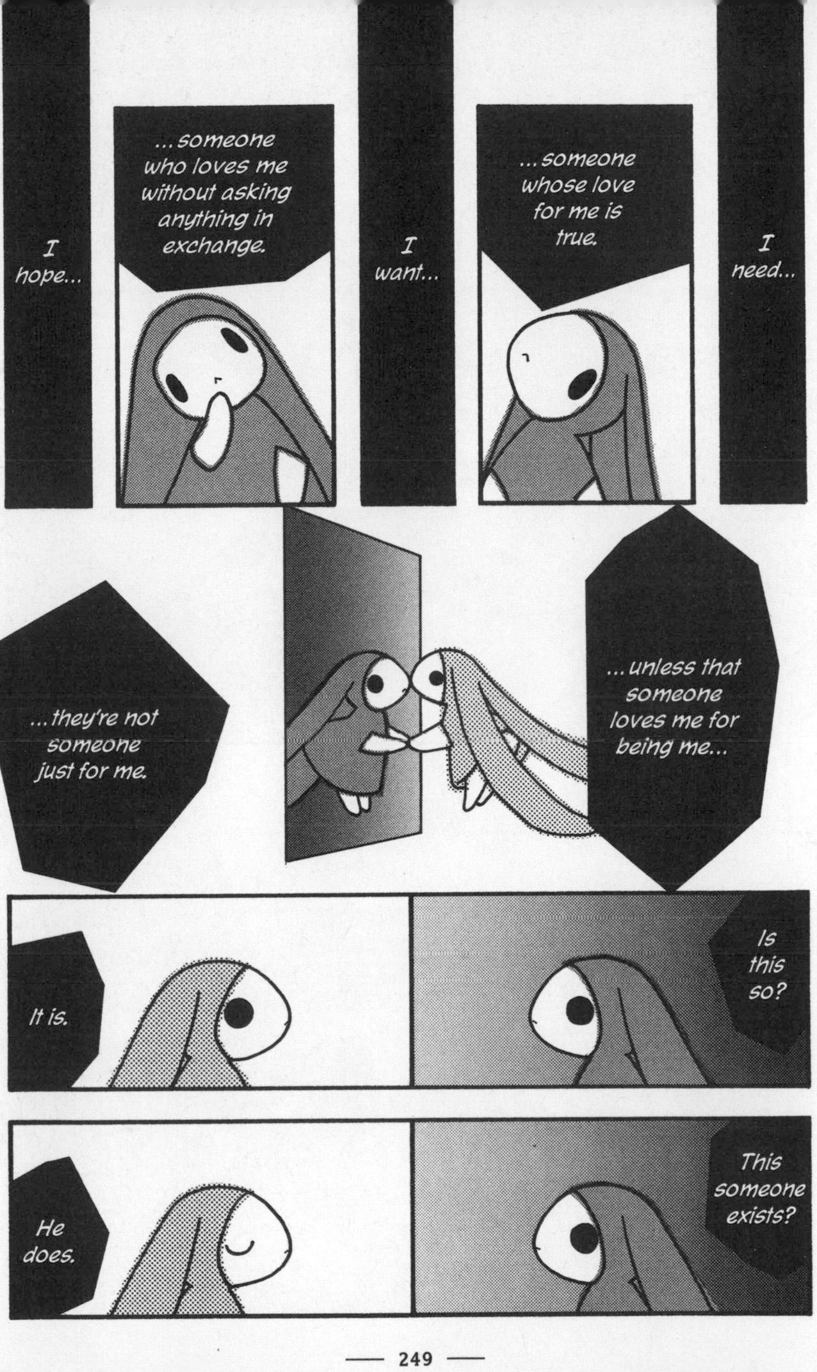
I need...
...someone whose love for me is true.
I want...
...someone who loves me without asking anything in exchange.
I hope...
...unless that someone loves me for being me...
...they're not someone just for me.
Is this so?
It is.
This someone exists?
He does.

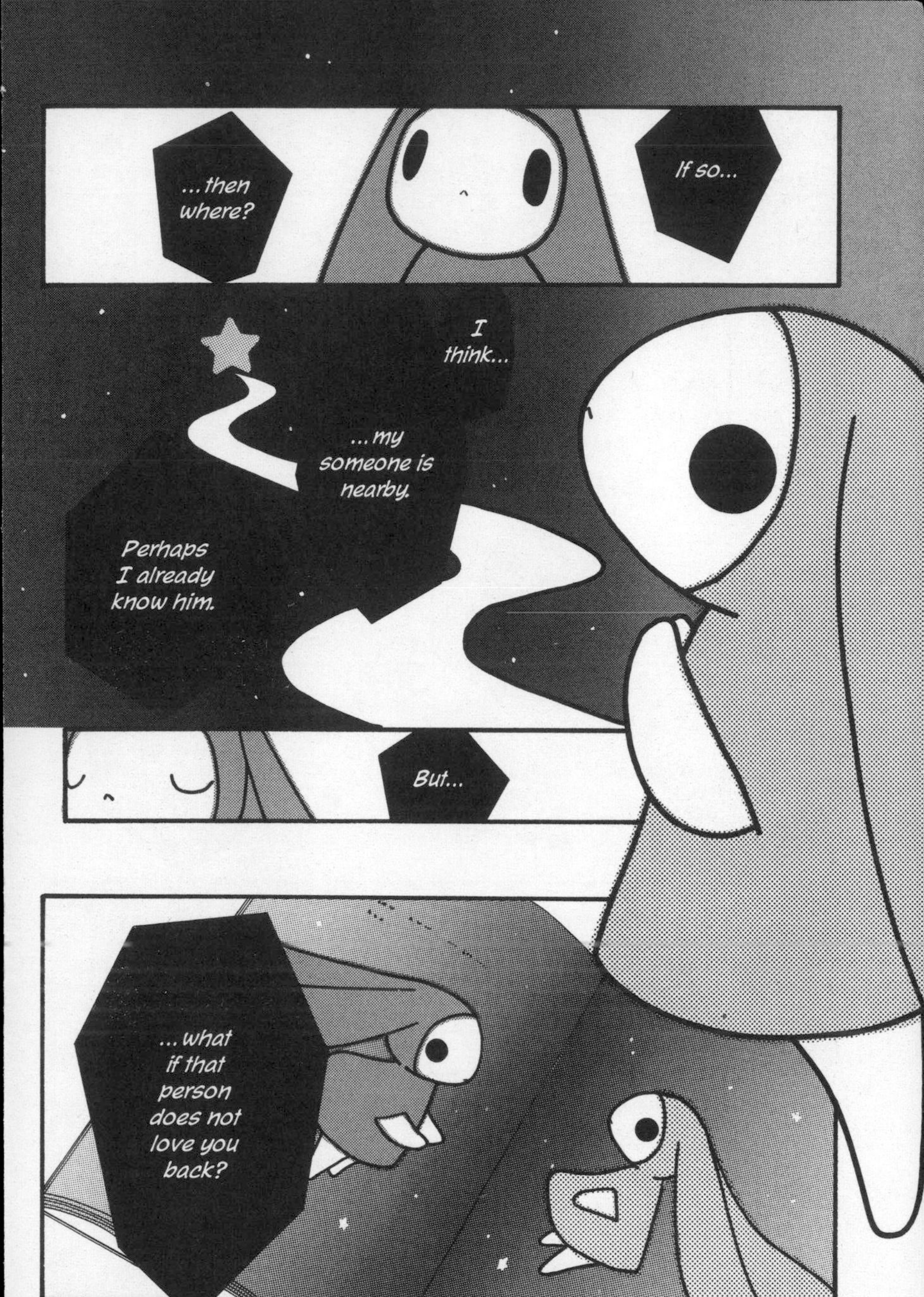
If so...
...then where?
I think...
...my someone is nearby.
Perhaps I already know him.
But...
...what if that person does not love you back?

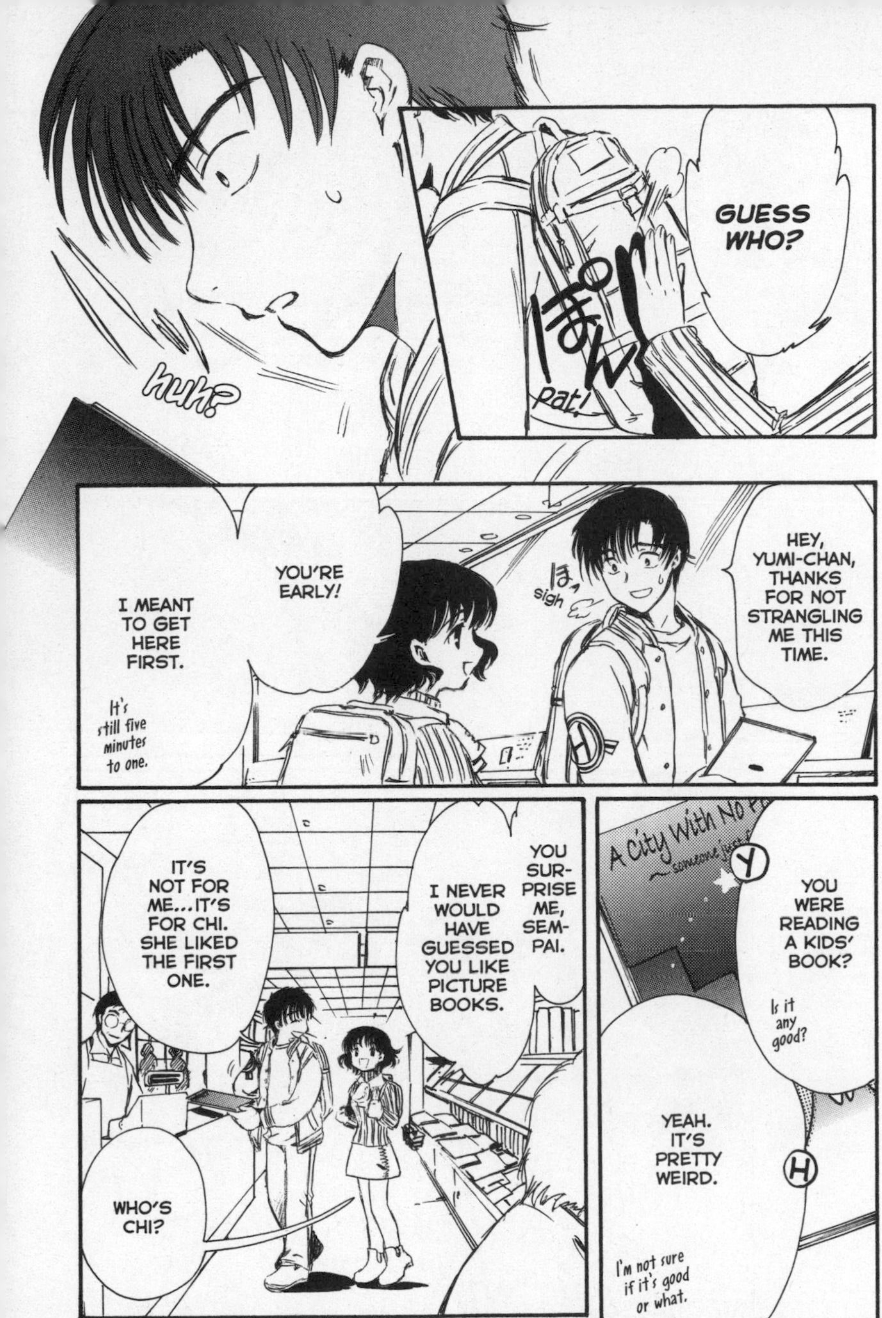
GUESS WHO?
ぽん
pat!
huh?
HEY, YUMI-CHAN, THANKS FOR NOT STRANGLING ME THIS TIME.
ほ,
sigh
YOU'RE EARLY!
I MEANT TO GET HERE FIRST.
It's still five minutes to one.
A City with No
YOU WERE READING A KIDS' BOOK?
Is it any good?
YEAH. IT'S PRETTY WEIRD.
I'm not sure if it's good or what.
YOU SUR-PRISE ME, SEM-PAI.
I NEVER WOULD HAVE GUESSED YOU LIKE PICTURE BOOKS.
IT'S NOT FOR ME...IT'S FOR CHI. SHE LIKED THE FIRST ONE.
WHO'S CHI?

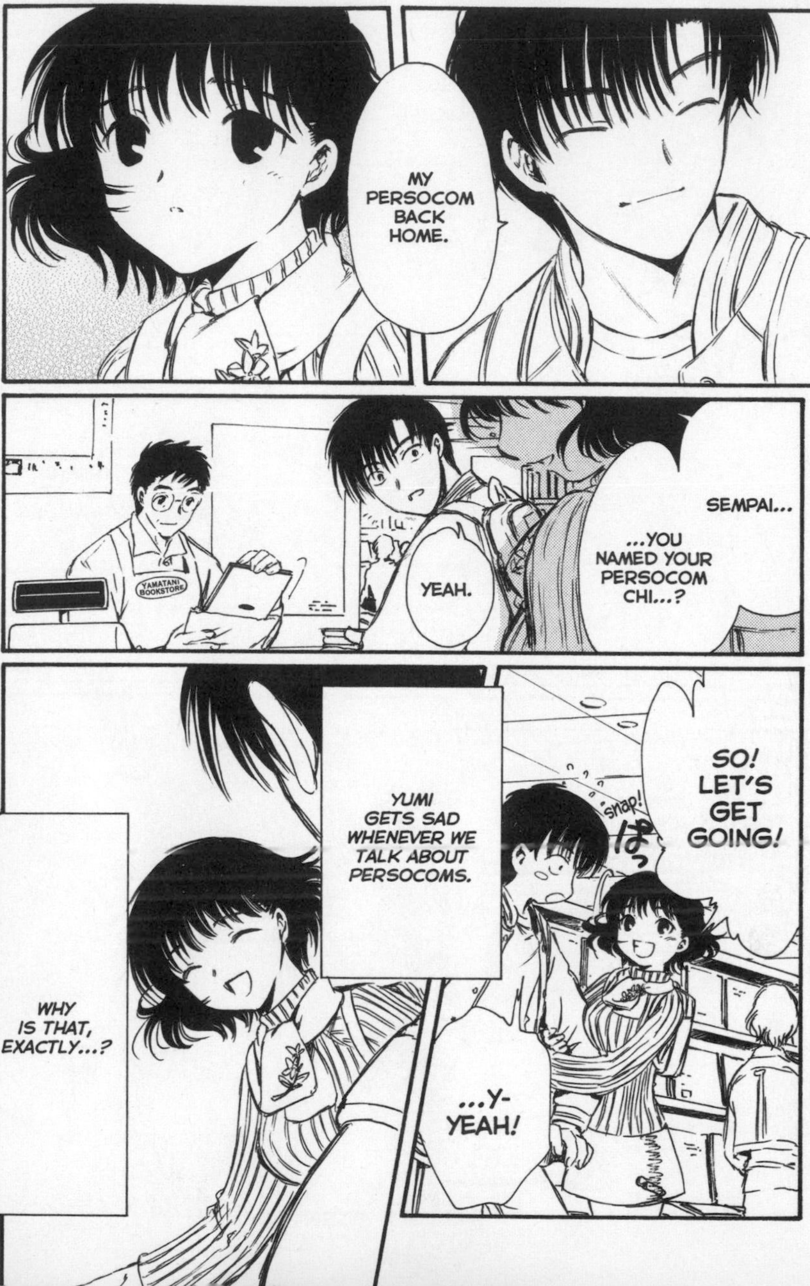
MY PERSOCOM BACK HOME.
SEMPAI...
...YOU NAMED YOUR PERSOCOM CHI...?
YEAH.
YAMATANI BOOKSTORE
SO! LET'S GET GOING!
snap!
ぱっ
...Y-YEAH!
YUMI GETS SAD WHENEVER WE TALK ABOUT PERSOCOMS.
WHY IS THAT, EXACTLY...?

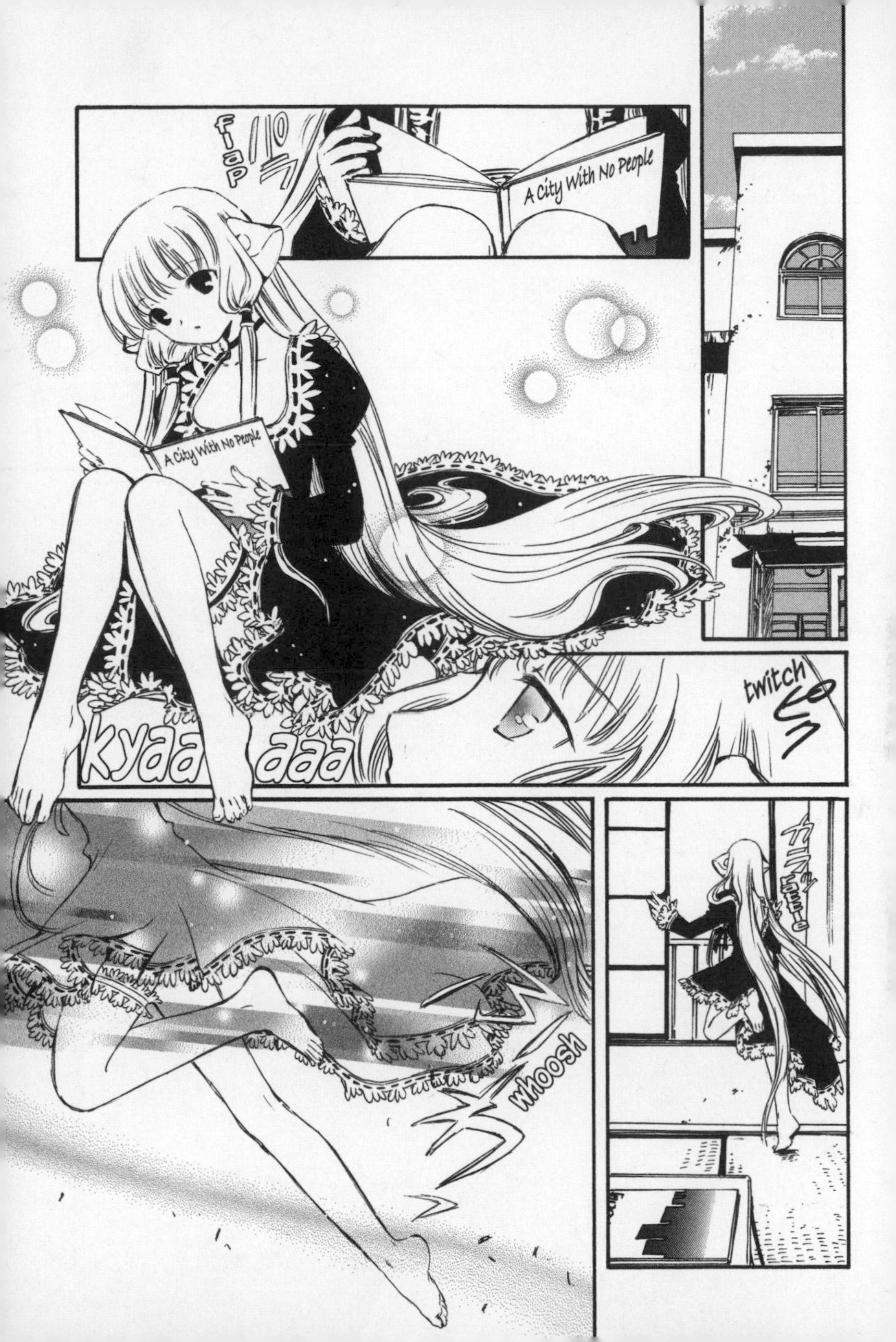
A City With No People
flap
A City With No People
twitch
kyaa aaa
whoosh

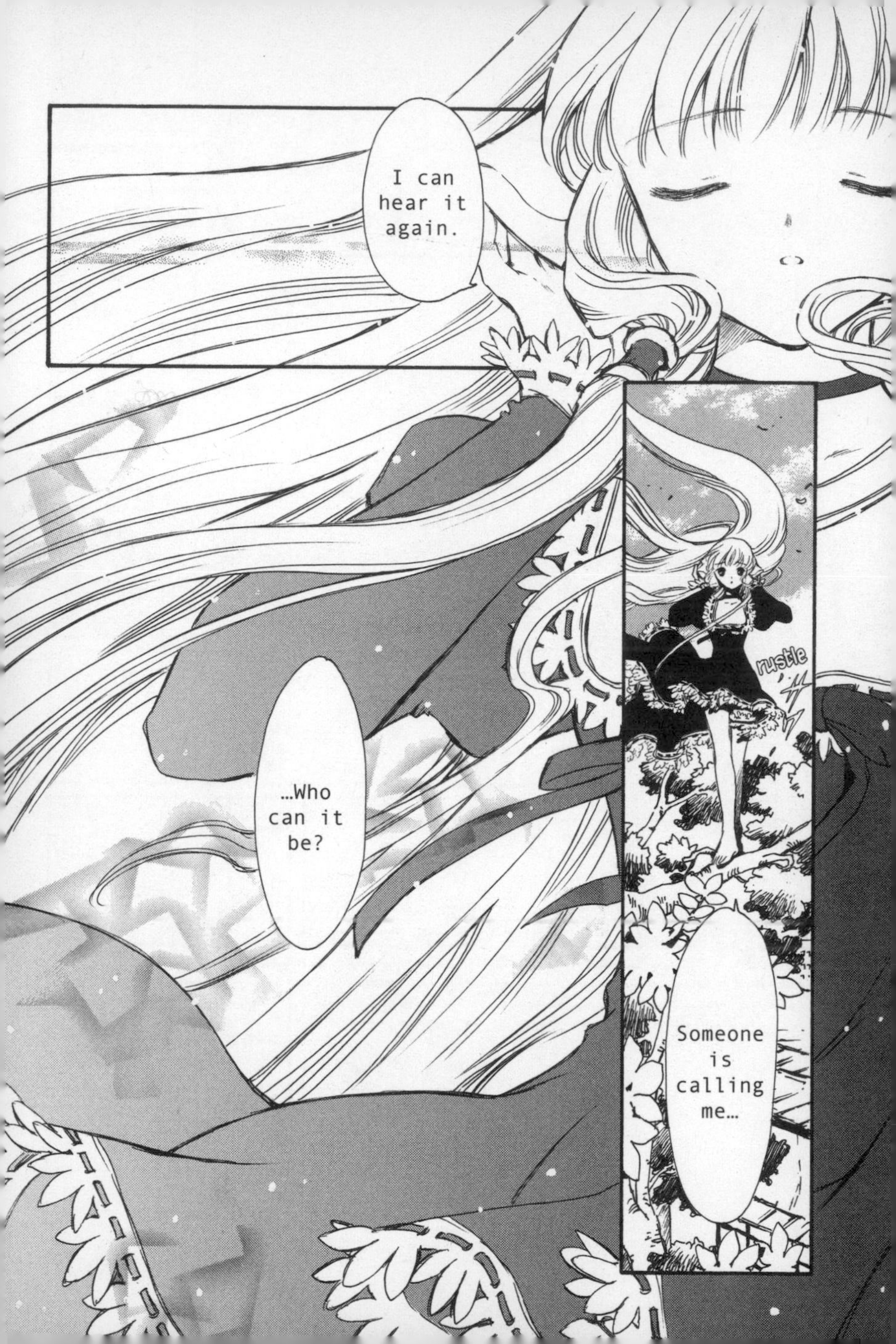
I can hear it again.
rustle
Someone is calling me…
…Who can it be?

Chobits
ちょびっツ

◀ **chapter 17** ▶

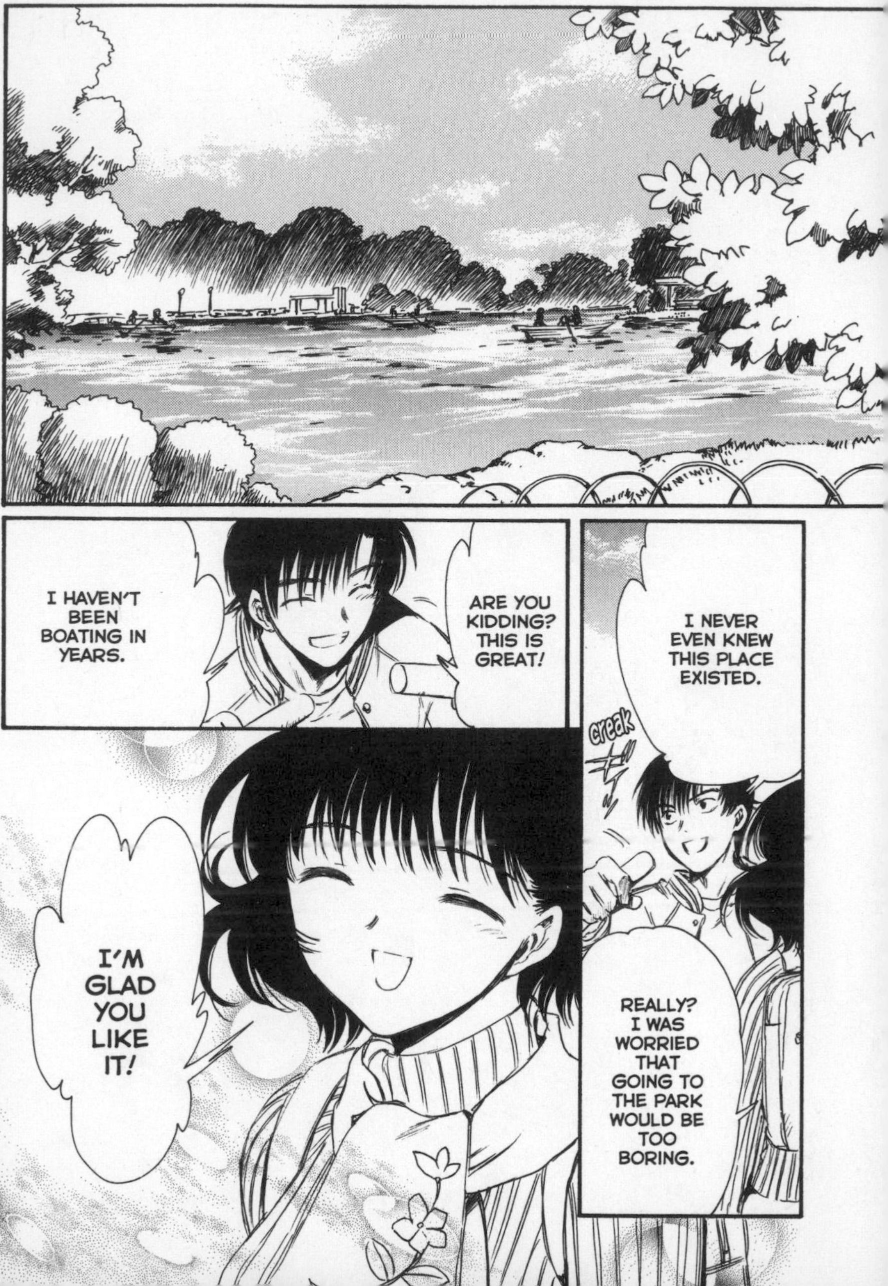

I NEVER EVEN KNEW THIS PLACE EXISTED.
creak
REALLY? I WAS WORRIED THAT GOING TO THE PARK WOULD BE TOO BORING.
ARE YOU KIDDING? THIS IS GREAT!
I HAVEN'T BEEN BOATING IN YEARS.
I'M GLAD YOU LIKE IT!

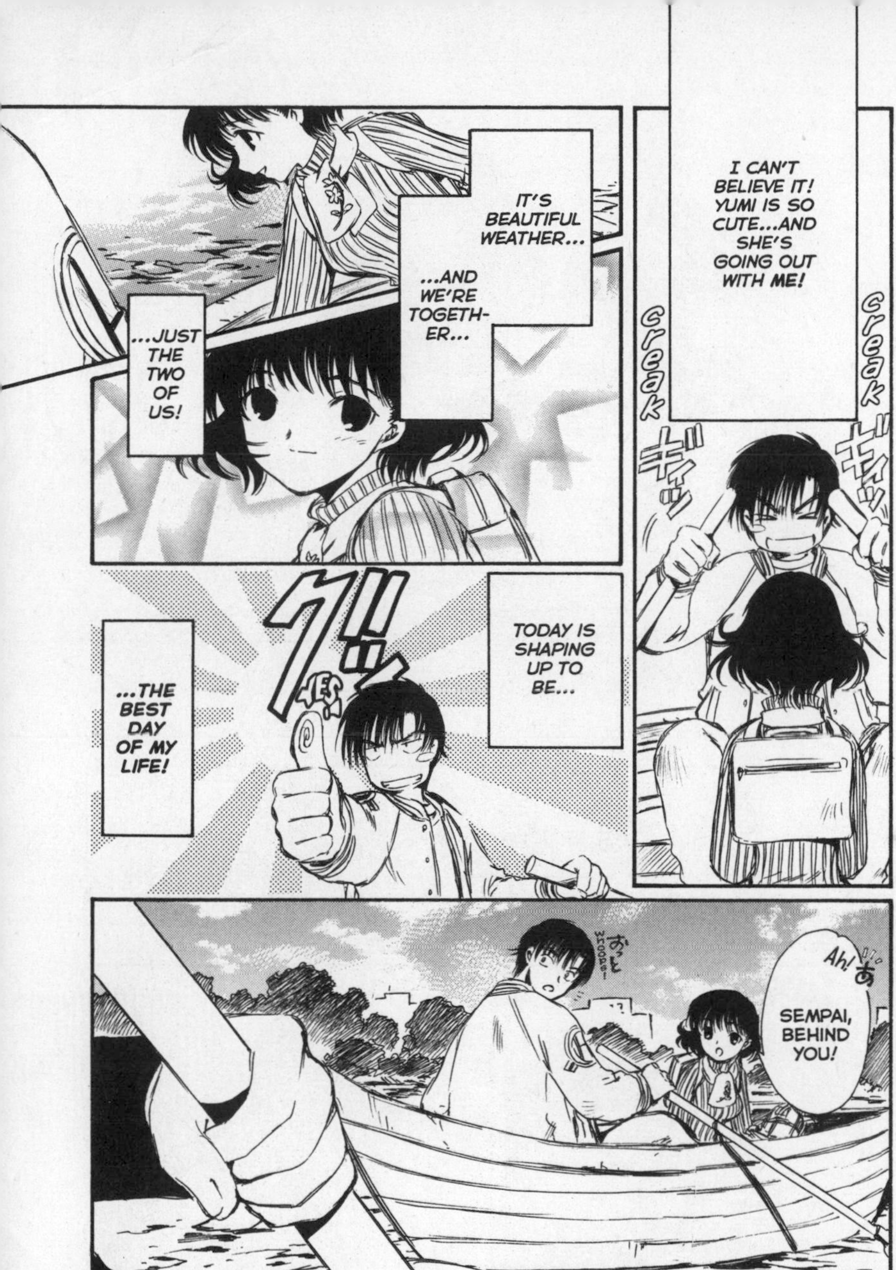
I CAN'T BELIEVE IT! YUMI IS SO CUTE...AND SHE'S GOING OUT WITH ME!
creak
ギィッ
creak
ギィッ
IT'S BEAUTIFUL WEATHER...
...AND WE'RE TOGETH-ER...
...JUST THE TWO OF US!
TODAY IS SHAPING UP TO BE...
グッ
YES
...THE BEST DAY OF MY LIFE!
Ah! あ
SEMPAI, BEHIND YOU!
おっと
whoops!

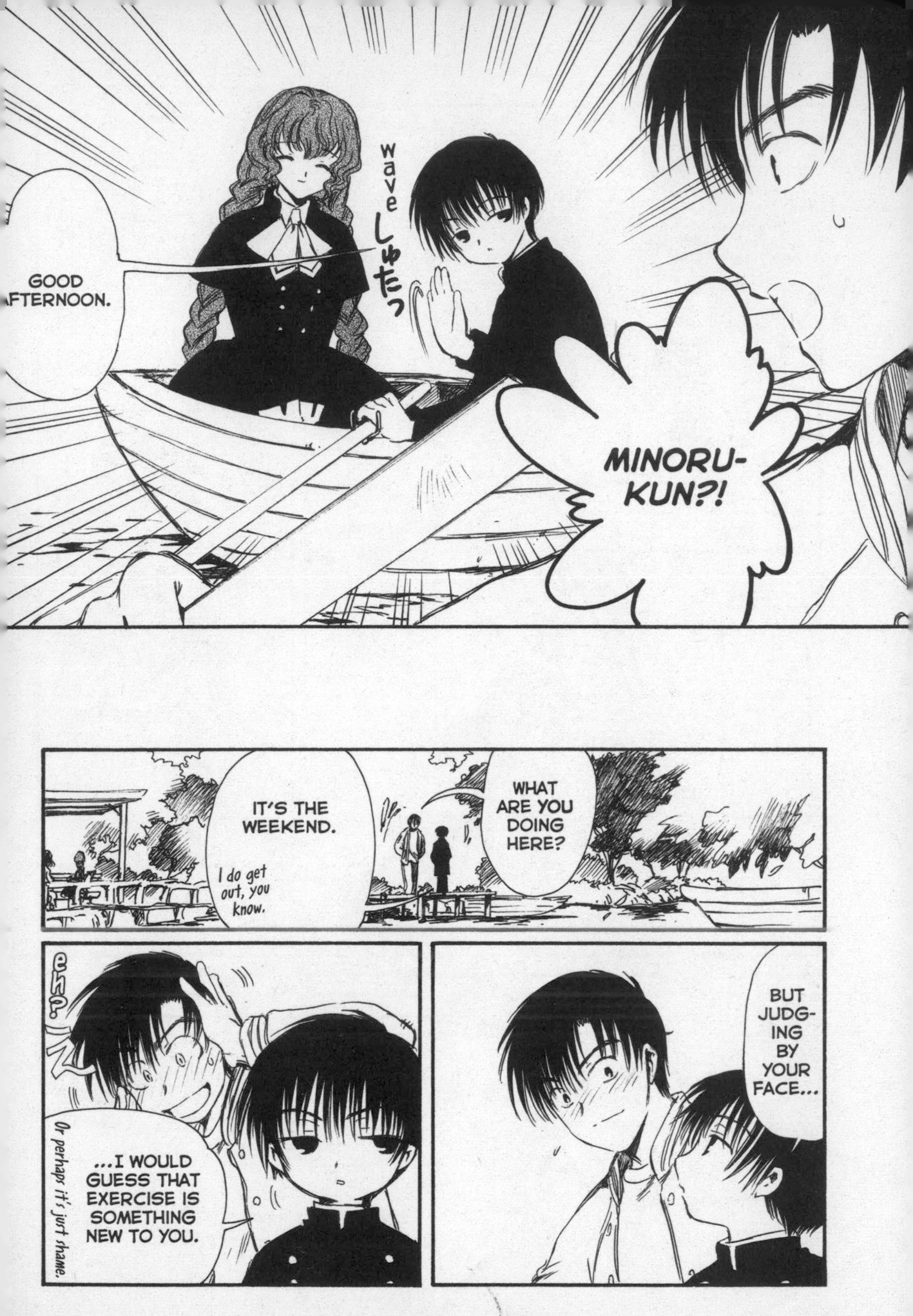
MINORU-KUN?!
wave しゅたっ
GOOD AFTERNOON.
WHAT ARE YOU DOING HERE?
IT'S THE WEEKEND.
I do get out, you know.
BUT JUDG-ING BY YOUR FACE...
eh?
...I WOULD GUESS THAT EXERCISE IS SOMETHING NEW TO YOU.
Or perhaps it's just shame.

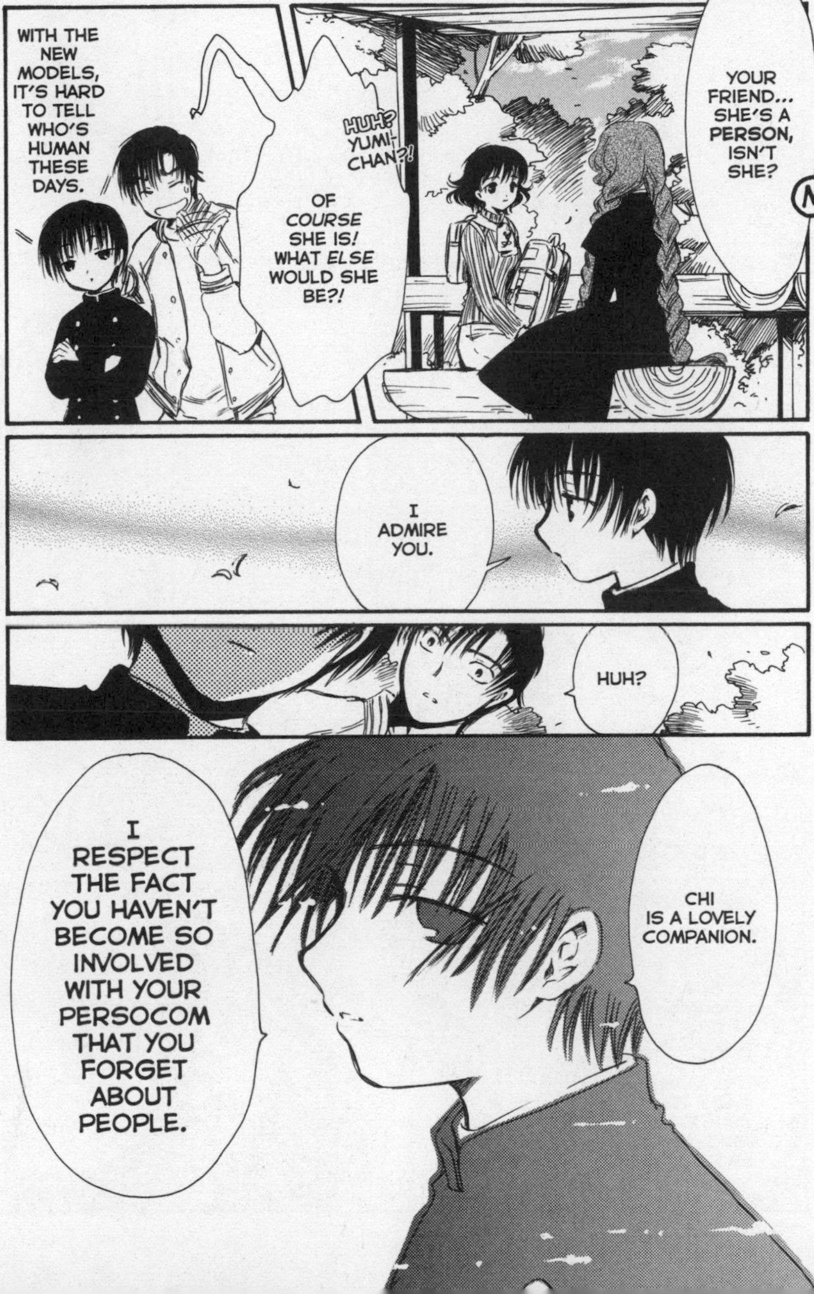
YOUR FRIEND... SHE'S A PERSON, ISN'T SHE?
HUH? YUMI-CHAN?!
OF COURSE SHE IS! WHAT ELSE WOULD SHE BE?!
WITH THE NEW MODELS, IT'S HARD TO TELL WHO'S HUMAN THESE DAYS.
I ADMIRE YOU.
HUH?
CHI IS A LOVELY COMPANION.
I RESPECT THE FACT YOU HAVEN'T BECOME SO INVOLVED WITH YOUR PERSOCOM THAT YOU FORGET ABOUT PEOPLE.

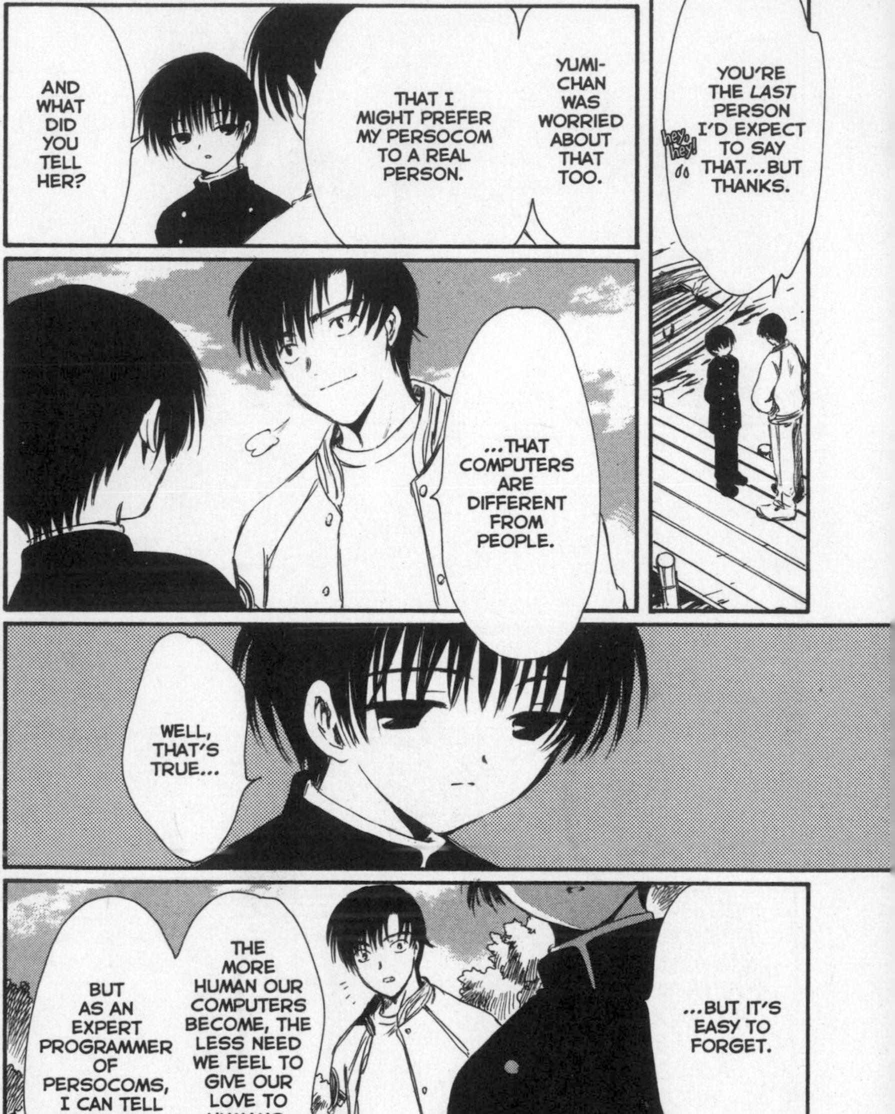
hey, hey!
YOU'RE THE *LAST* PERSON I'D EXPECT TO SAY THAT...BUT THANKS.
YUMI-CHAN WAS WORRIED ABOUT THAT TOO.
THAT I MIGHT PREFER MY PERSOCOM TO A REAL PERSON.
AND WHAT DID YOU TELL HER?
...THAT COMPUTERS ARE DIFFERENT FROM PEOPLE.
WELL, THAT'S TRUE...
...BUT IT'S EASY TO FORGET.
THE MORE HUMAN OUR COMPUTERS BECOME, THE LESS NEED WE FEEL TO GIVE OUR LOVE TO HUMANS.
BUT AS AN EXPERT PROGRAMMER OF PERSOCOMS, I CAN TELL YOU THIS... OUR LOVE IS WASTED ON THEM.

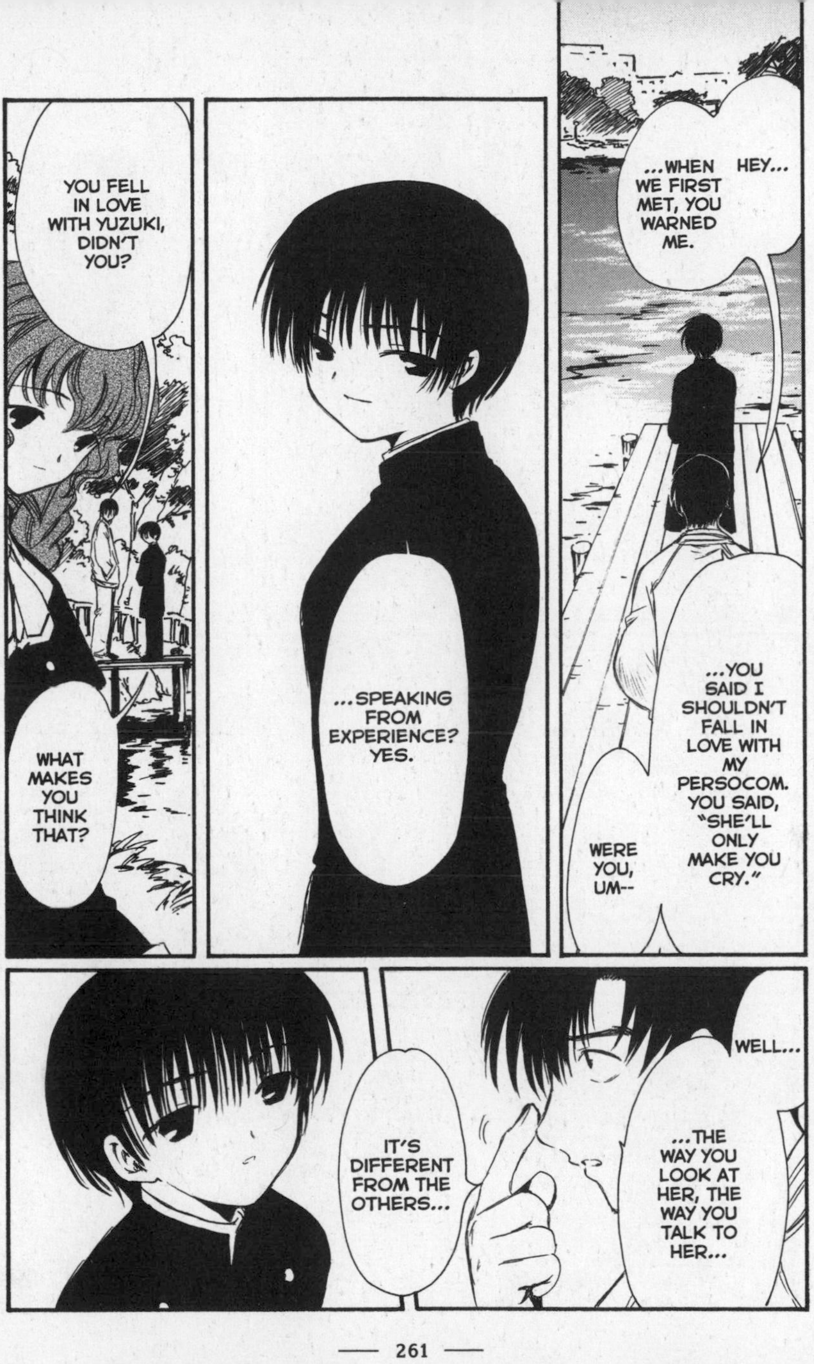
HEY...
...WHEN WE FIRST MET, YOU WARNED ME.
...YOU SAID I SHOULDN'T FALL IN LOVE WITH MY PERSOCOM. YOU SAID, "SHE'LL ONLY MAKE YOU CRY."
WERE YOU, UM--
...SPEAKING FROM EXPERIENCE? YES.
YOU FELL IN LOVE WITH YUZUKI, DIDN'T YOU?
WHAT MAKES YOU THINK THAT?
WELL...
...THE WAY YOU LOOK AT HER, THE WAY YOU TALK TO HER...
IT'S DIFFERENT FROM THE OTHERS...

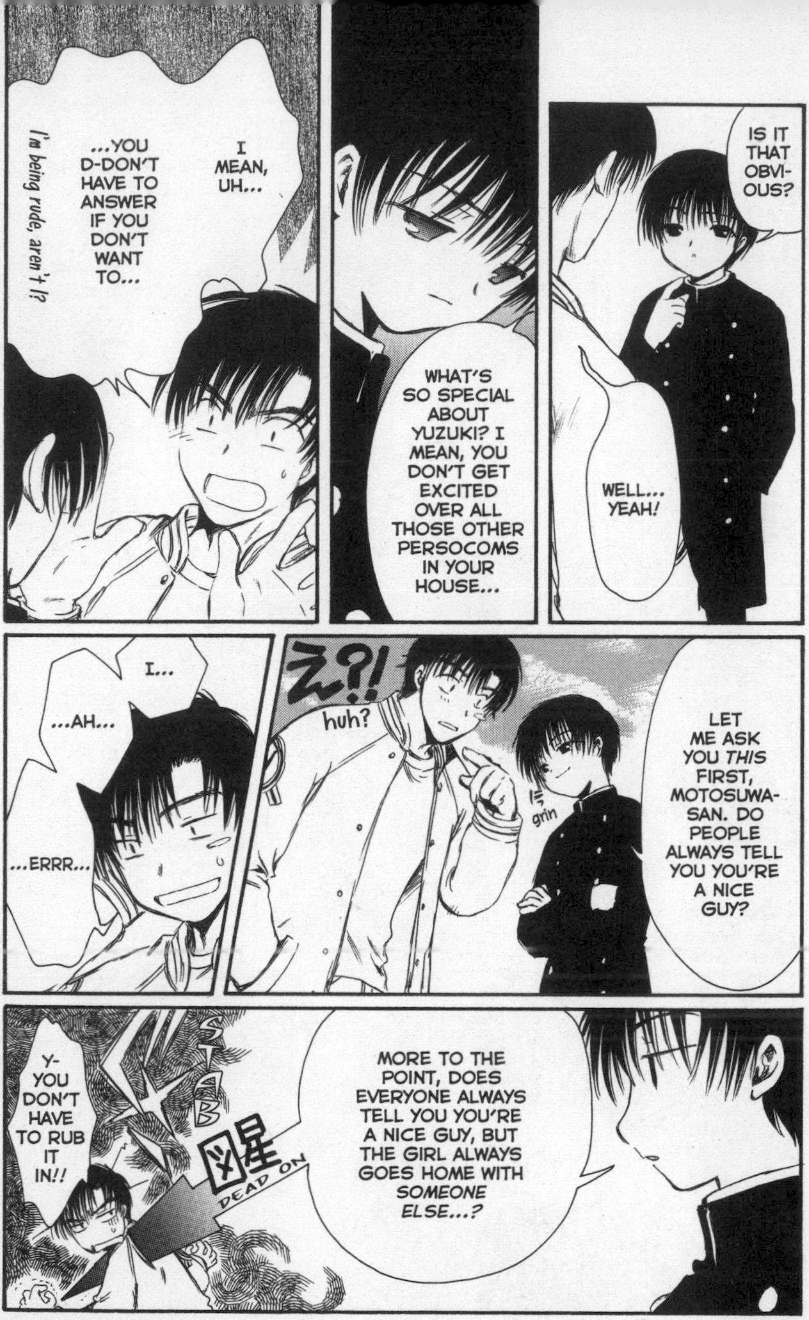
IS IT THAT OBVI-OUS?
WELL... YEAH!
WHAT'S SO SPECIAL ABOUT YUZUKI? I MEAN, YOU DON'T GET EXCITED OVER ALL THOSE OTHER PERSOCOMS IN YOUR HOUSE...
I MEAN, UH...
...YOU D-DON'T HAVE TO ANSWER IF YOU DON'T WANT TO...
I'm being rude, aren't I!?
LET ME ASK YOU *THIS* FIRST, MOTOSUWA-SAN. DO PEOPLE ALWAYS TELL YOU YOU'RE A NICE GUY?
grin
huh?
I...
...AH...
...ERRR...
MORE TO THE POINT, DOES EVERYONE ALWAYS TELL YOU YOU'RE A NICE GUY, BUT THE GIRL ALWAYS GOES HOME WITH *SOMEONE ELSE*...?
STAB
DEAD ON
Y-YOU DON'T HAVE TO RUB IT IN!!

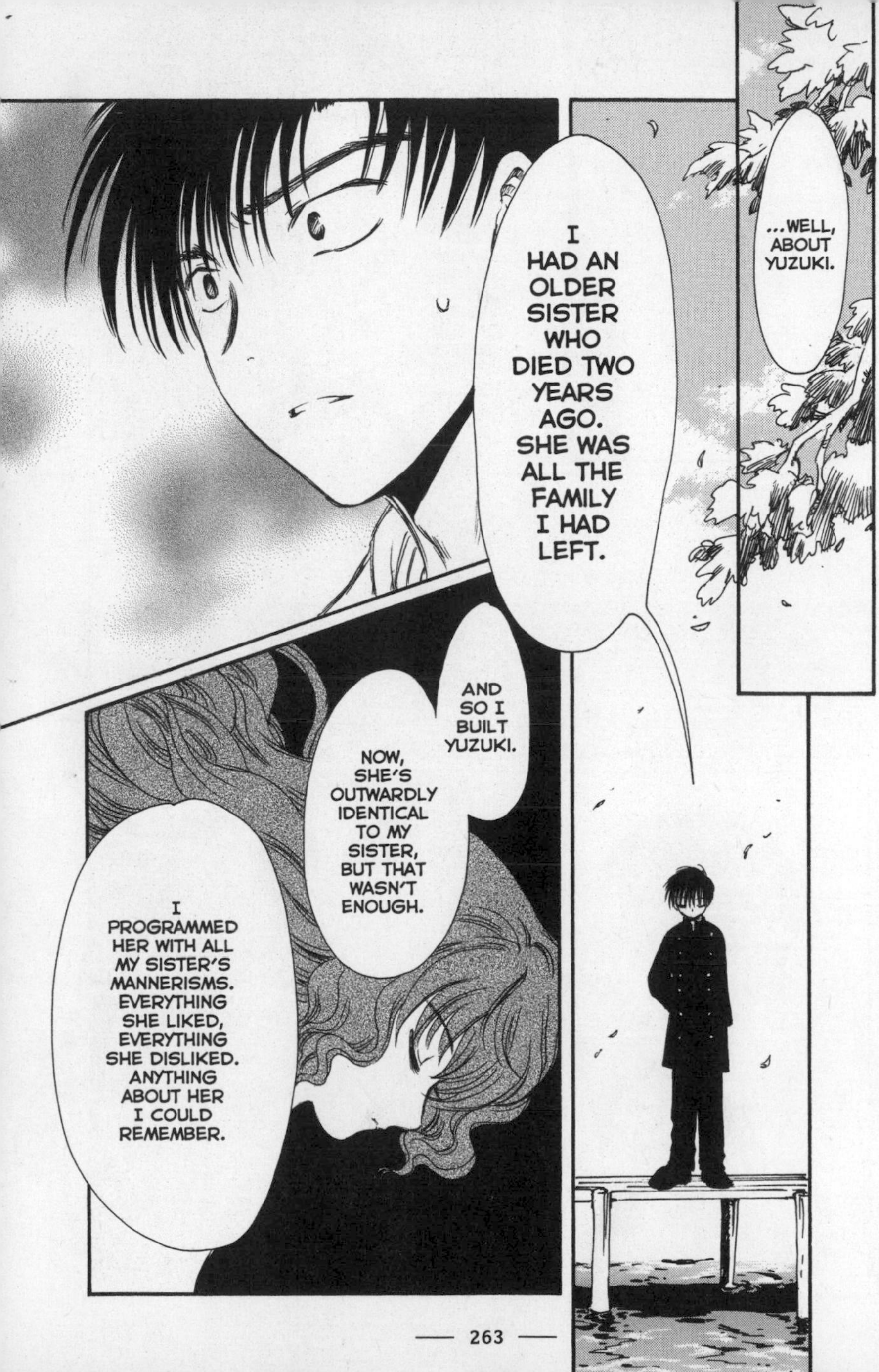
...WELL, ABOUT YUZUKI.
I HAD AN OLDER SISTER WHO DIED TWO YEARS AGO. SHE WAS ALL THE FAMILY I HAD LEFT.
AND SO I BUILT YUZUKI.
NOW, SHE'S OUTWARDLY IDENTICAL TO MY SISTER, BUT THAT WASN'T ENOUGH.
I PROGRAMMED HER WITH ALL MY SISTER'S MANNERISMS. EVERYTHING SHE LIKED, EVERYTHING SHE DISLIKED. ANYTHING ABOUT HER I COULD REMEMBER.

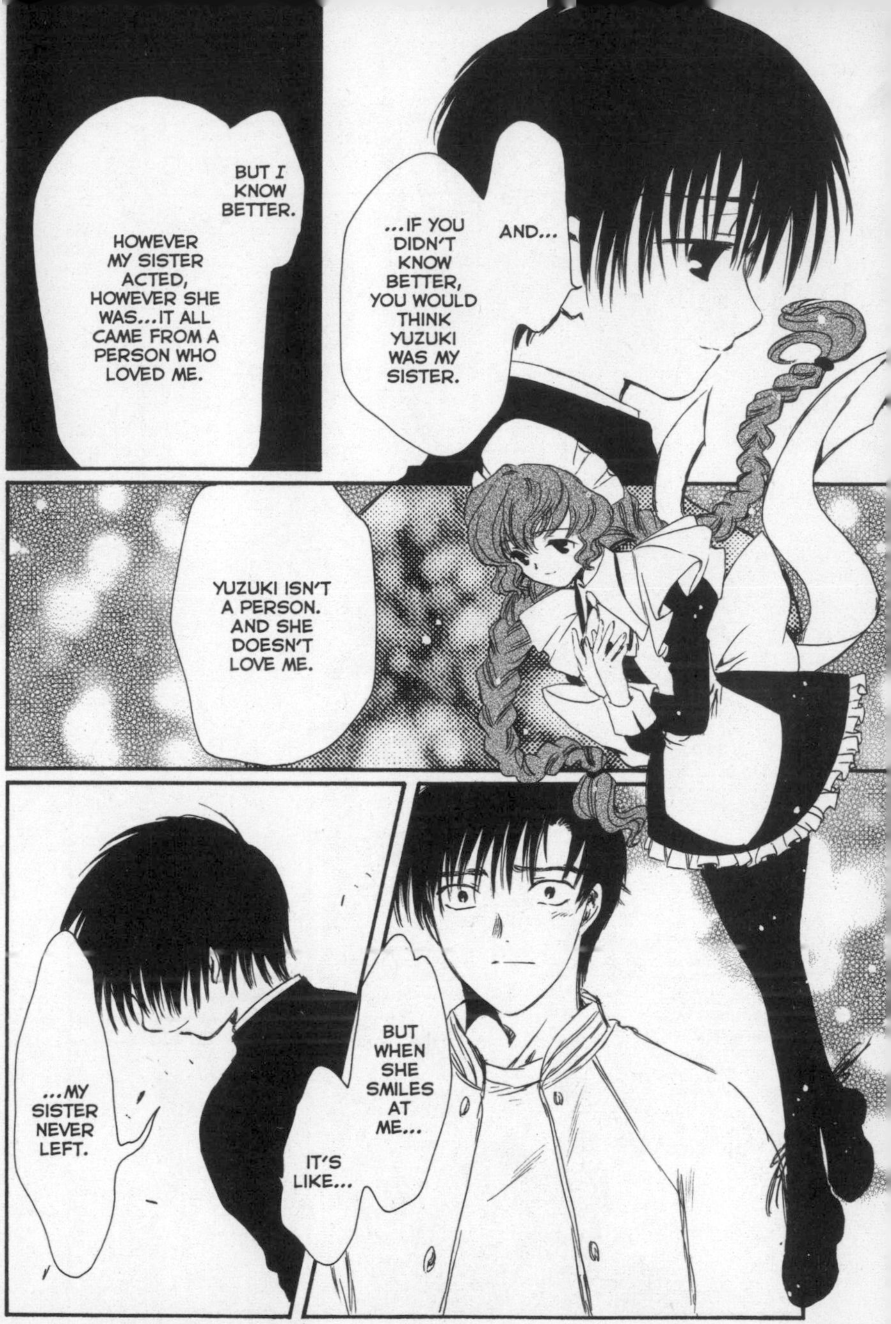
AND...
...IF YOU DIDN'T KNOW BETTER, YOU WOULD THINK YUZUKI WAS MY SISTER.
BUT I KNOW BETTER.
HOWEVER MY SISTER ACTED, HOWEVER SHE WAS...IT ALL CAME FROM A PERSON WHO LOVED ME.
YUZUKI ISN'T A PERSON. AND SHE DOESN'T LOVE ME.
BUT WHEN SHE SMILES AT ME...
IT'S LIKE...
...MY SISTER NEVER LEFT.

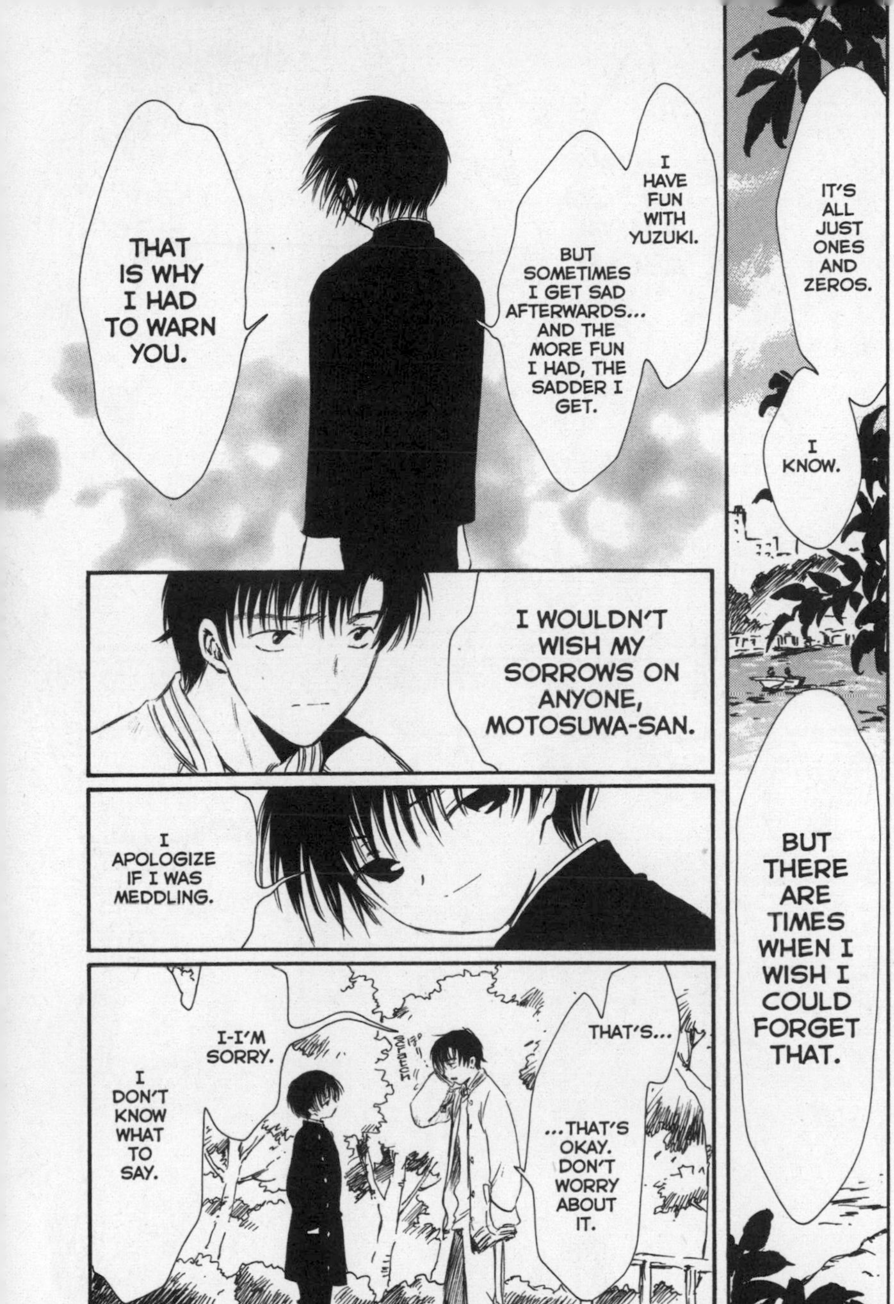
IT'S ALL JUST ONES AND ZEROS.
I KNOW.
BUT THERE ARE TIMES WHEN I WISH I COULD FORGET THAT.
I HAVE FUN WITH YUZUKI.
BUT SOMETIMES I GET SAD AFTERWARDS... AND THE MORE FUN I HAD, THE SADDER I GET.
THAT IS WHY I HAD TO WARN YOU.
I WOULDN'T WISH MY SORROWS ON ANYONE, MOTOSUWA-SAN.
I APOLOGIZE IF I WAS MEDDLING.
THAT'S...
...THAT'S OKAY. DON'T WORRY ABOUT IT.
I-I'M SORRY.
I DON'T KNOW WHAT TO SAY.

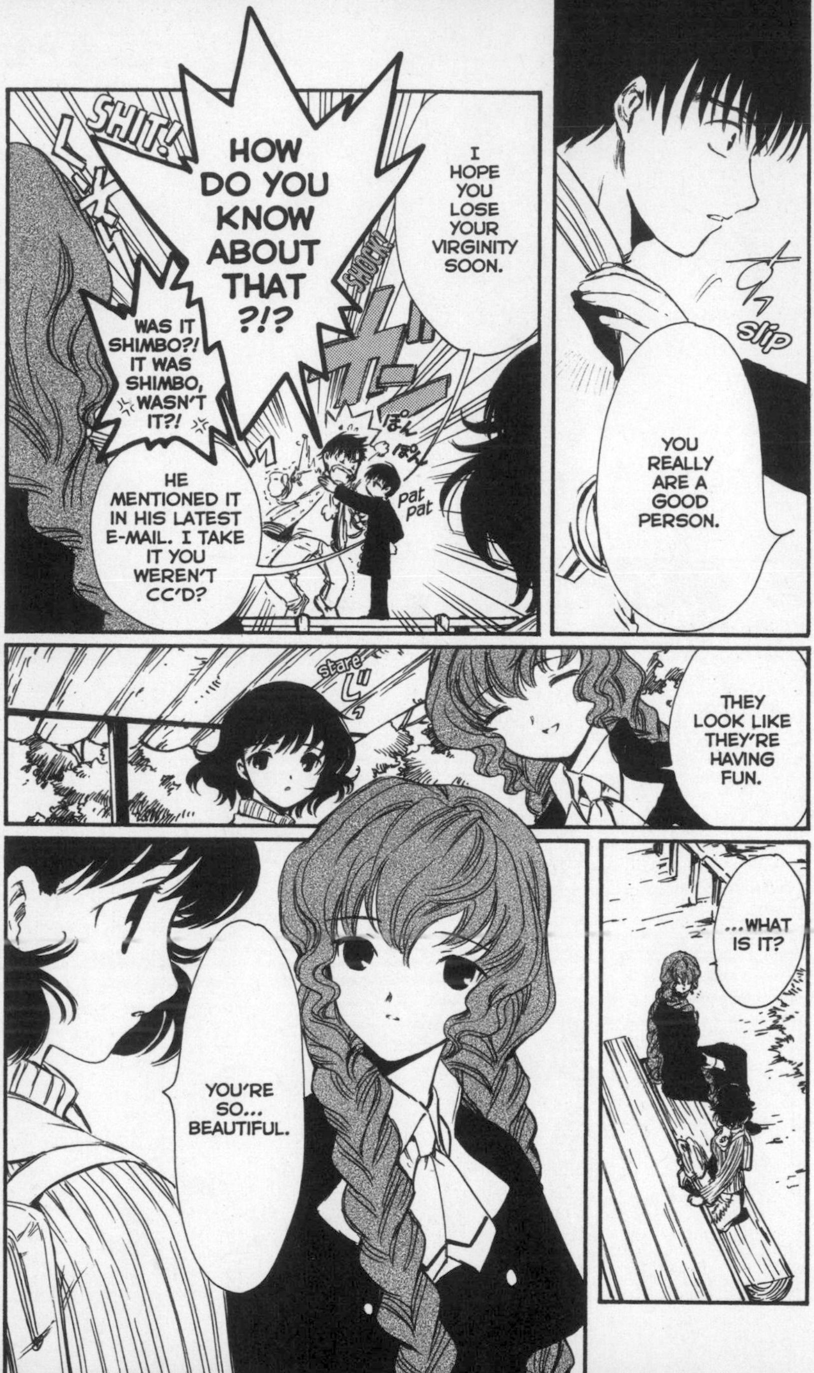
slip
YOU REALLY ARE A GOOD PERSON.
I HOPE YOU LOSE YOUR VIRGINITY SOON.
HOW DO YOU KNOW ABOUT THAT?!?
SHIT!
SHOCK!
WAS IT SHIMBO?! IT WAS SHIMBO, WASN'T IT?!
pat pat
HE MENTIONED IT IN HIS LATEST E-MAIL. I TAKE IT YOU WEREN'T CC'D?
THEY LOOK LIKE THEY'RE HAVING FUN.
stare
...WHAT IS IT?
YOU'RE SO... BEAUTIFUL.

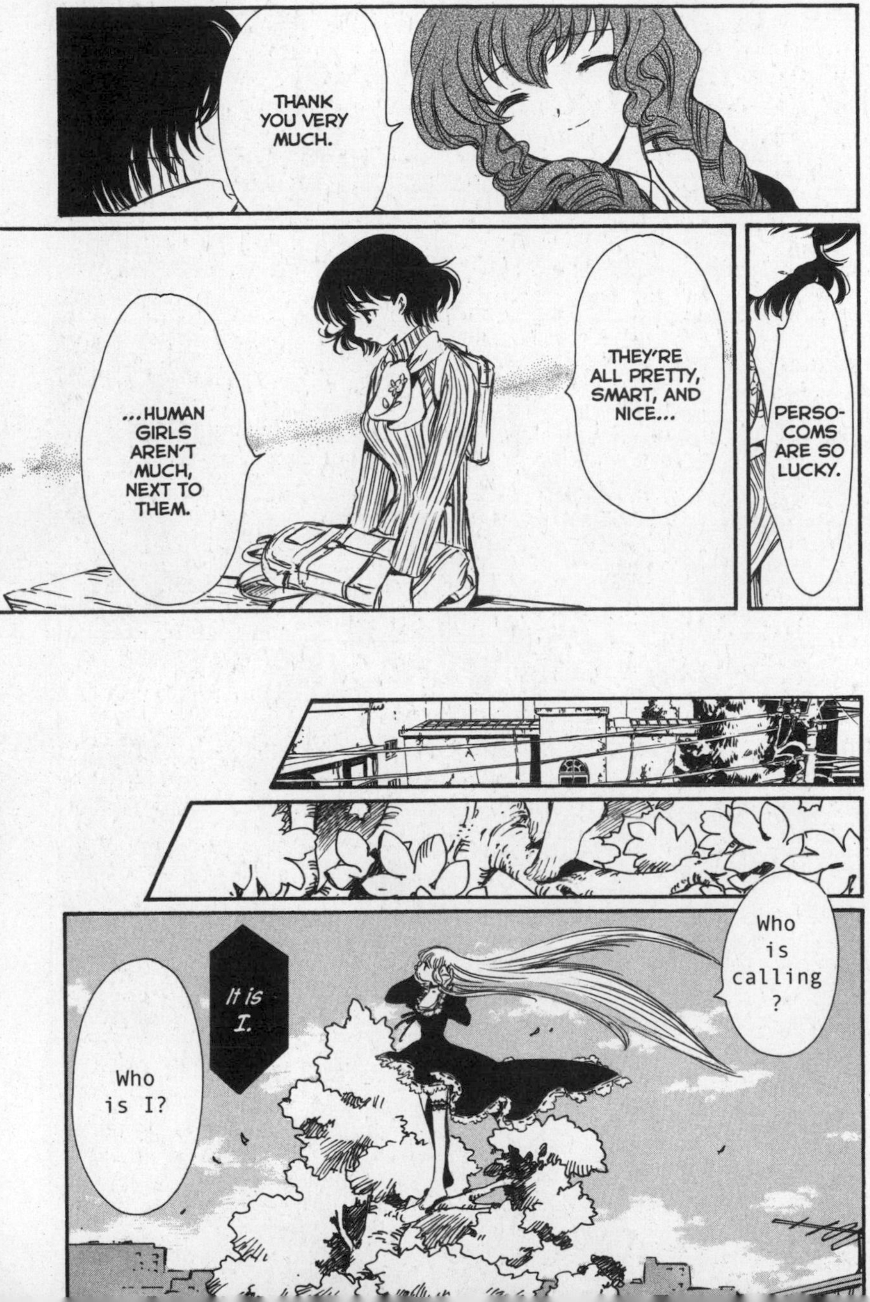
THANK YOU VERY MUCH.
PERSO-COMS ARE SO LUCKY.
THEY'RE ALL PRETTY, SMART, AND NICE...
...HUMAN GIRLS AREN'T MUCH, NEXT TO THEM.
Who is calling?
It is I.
Who is I?

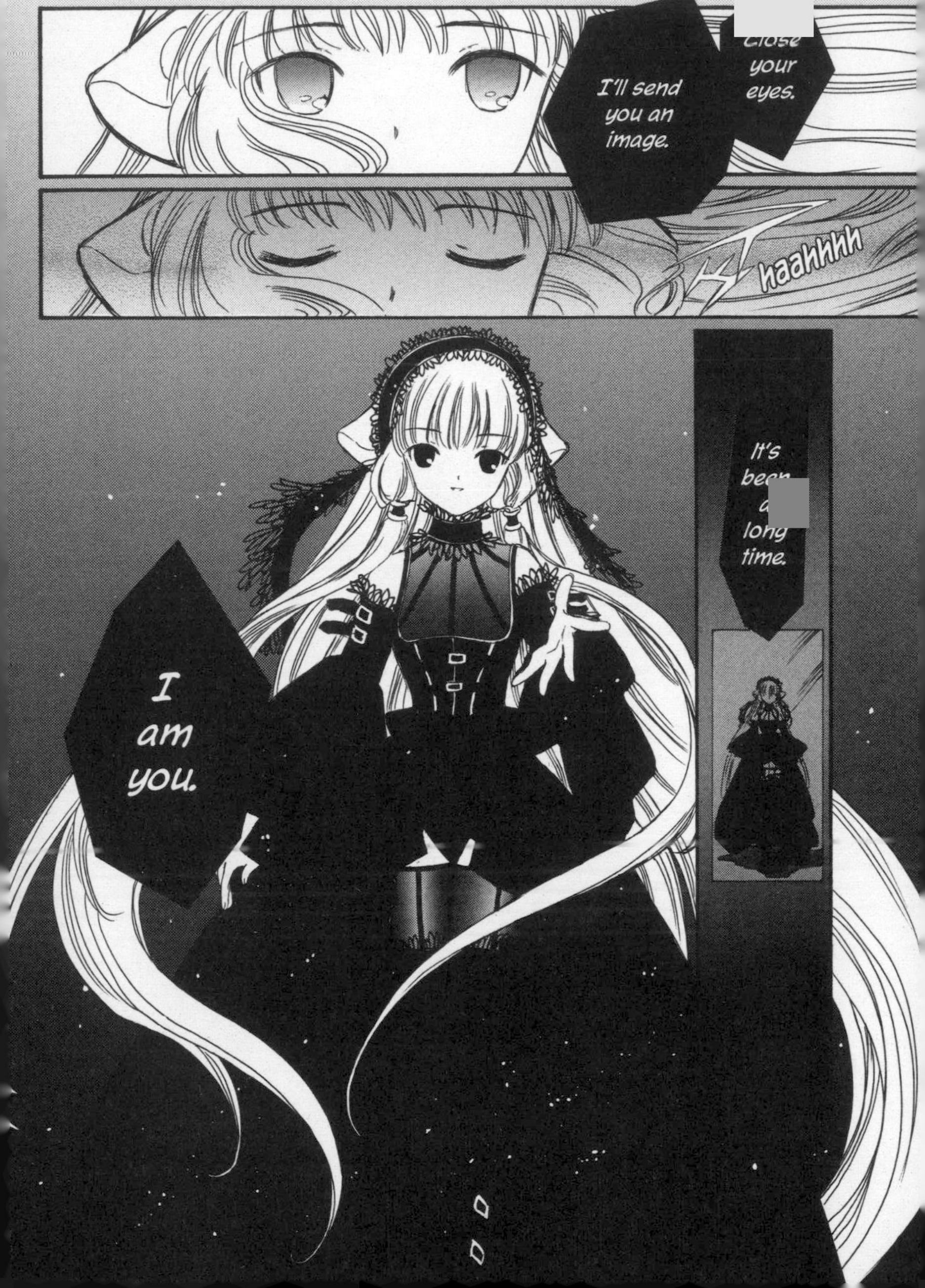
Close your eyes.
I'll send you an image.
haahhhh
It's been a long time.
I am you.

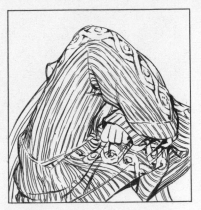

Chobits
ちょびっツ

◄ **chapter 18** ►

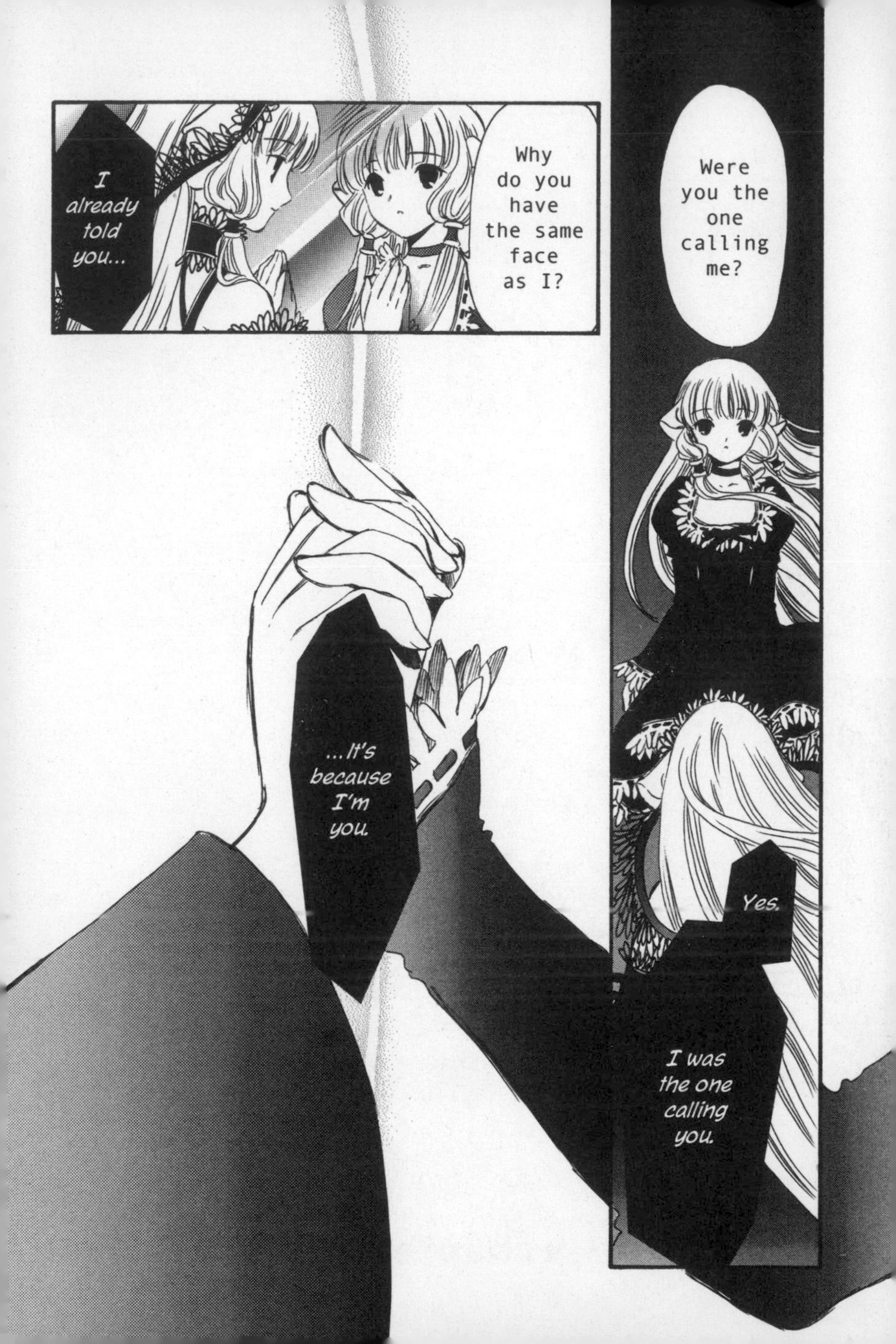
Were you the one calling me?
Yes.
I was the one calling you.
Why do you have the same face as I?
I already told you...
...It's because I'm you.

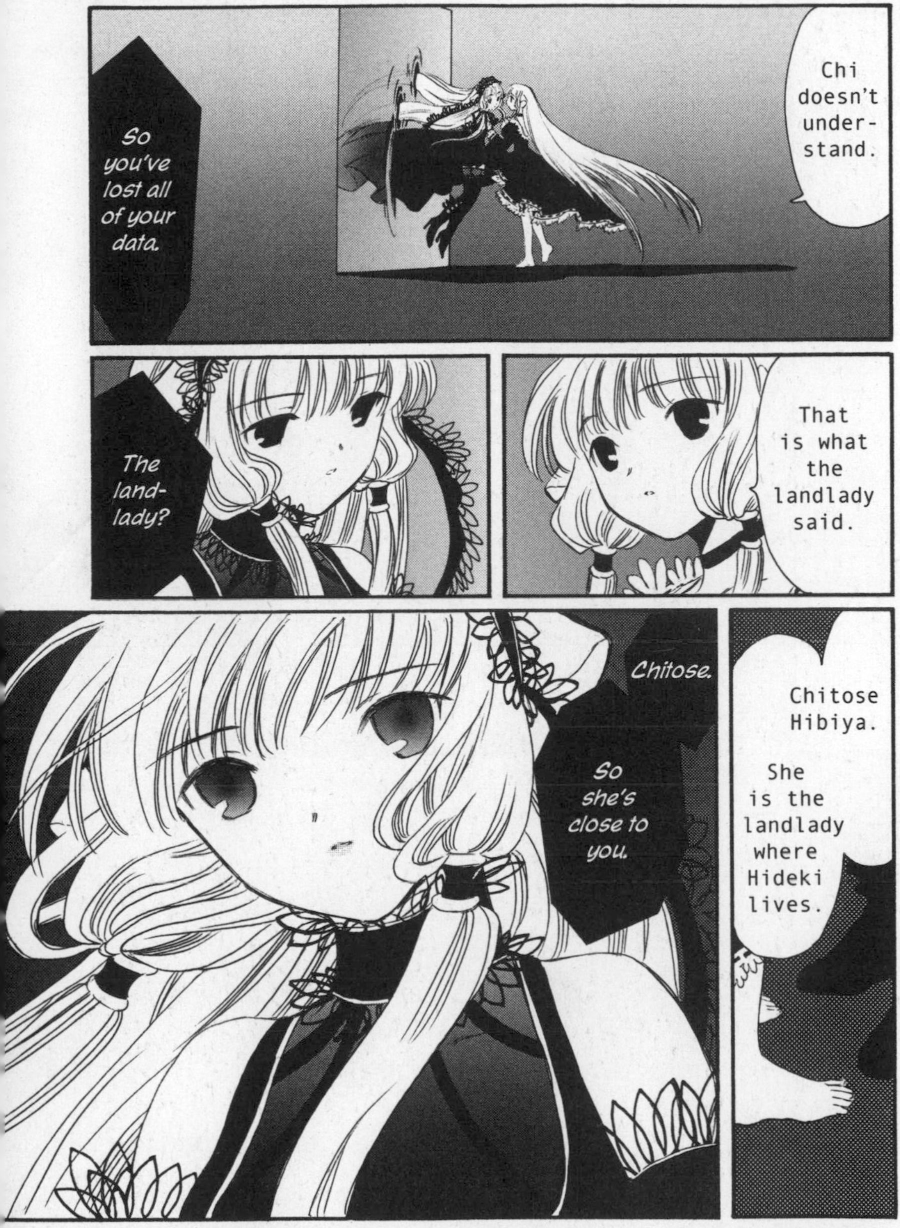

Chi doesn't understand.
So you've lost all of your data.
That is what the landlady said.
The landlady?
Chitose Hibiya.
She is the landlady where Hideki lives.
Chitose.
So she's close to you.

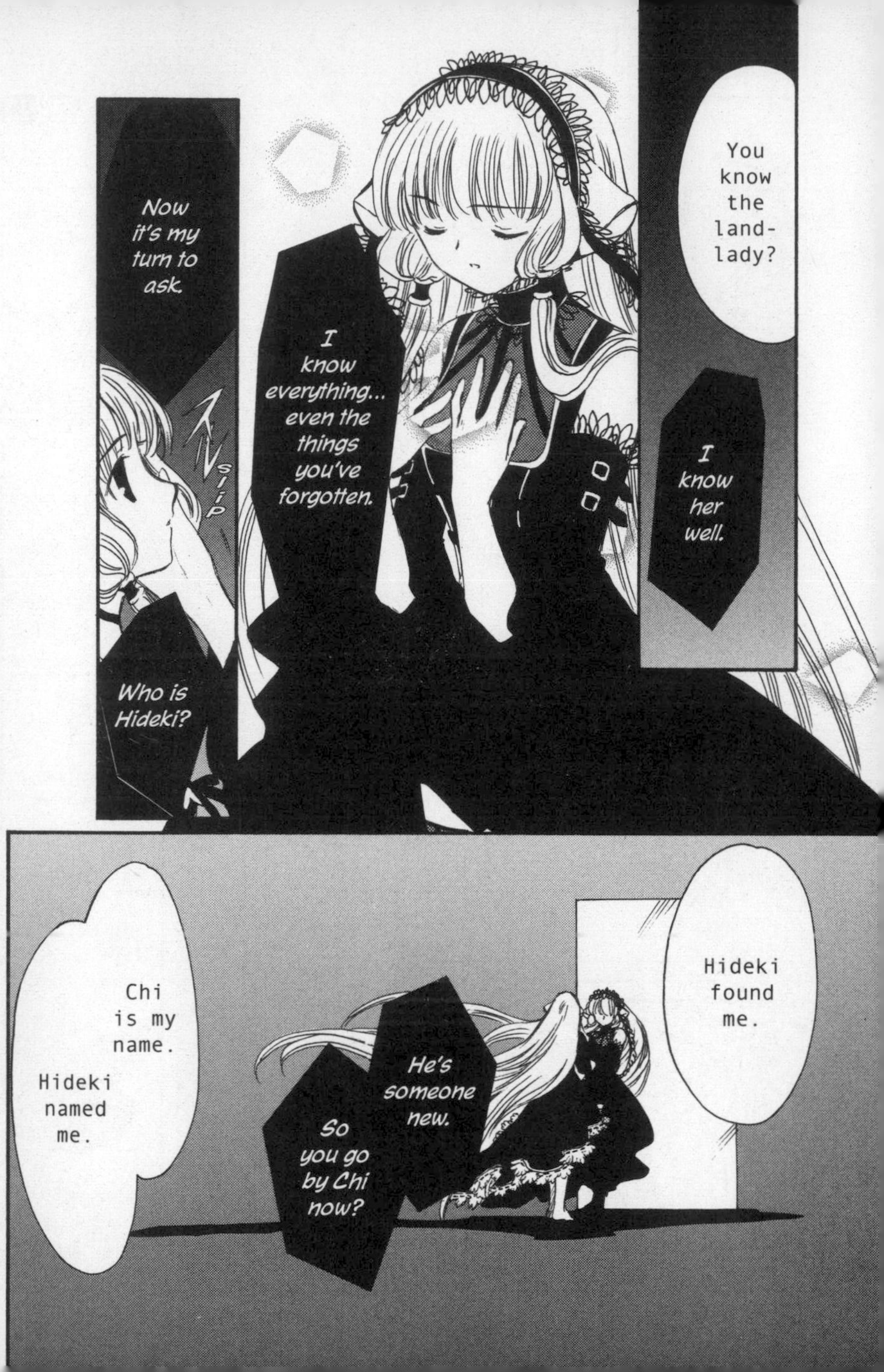
You know the land-lady?
I know her well.
I know everything... even the things you've forgotten.
Now it's my turn to ask.
slip
Who is Hideki?
Hideki found me.
He's someone new.
So you go by Chi now?
Chi is my name.
Hideki named me.

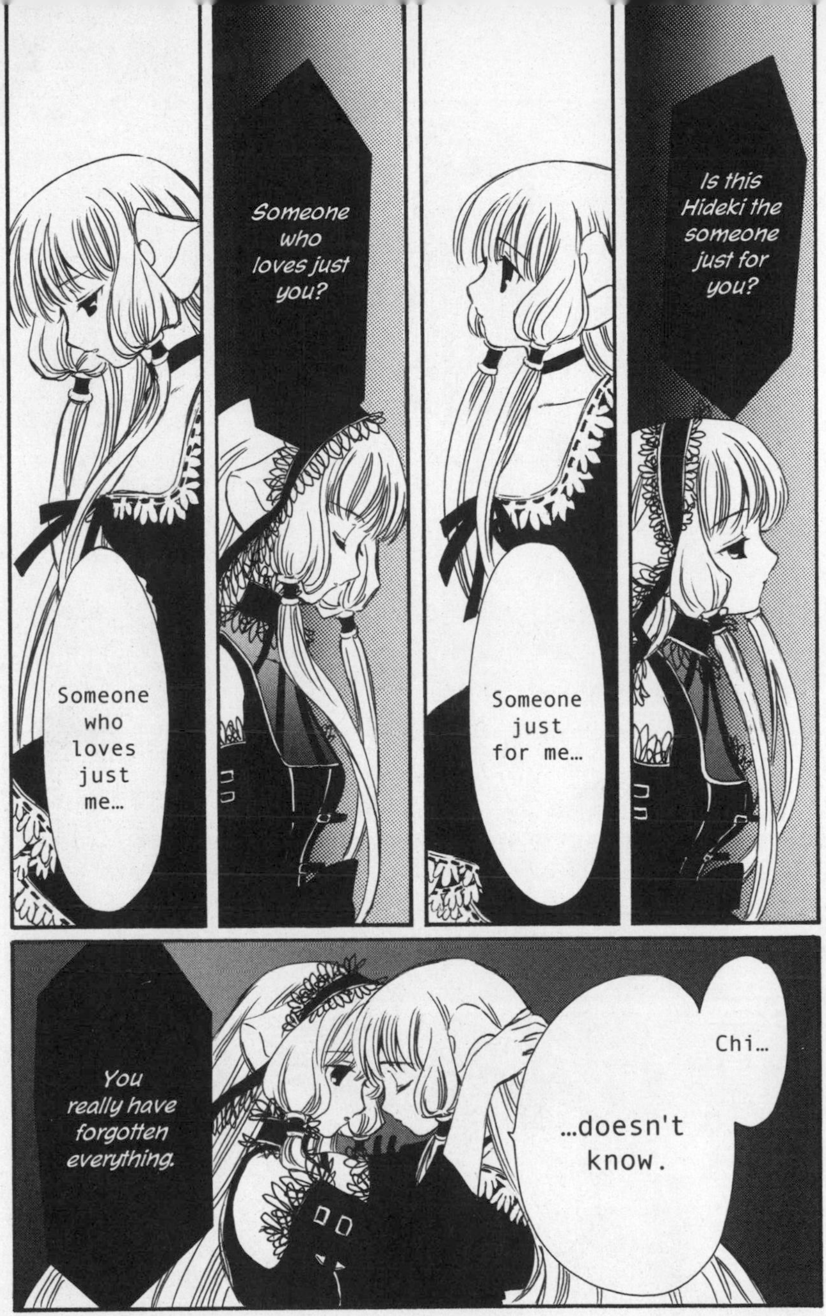
Is this Hideki the someone just for you?
Someone just for me...
Someone who loves just you?
Someone who loves just me...
Chi... ...doesn't know.
You really have forgotten everything.

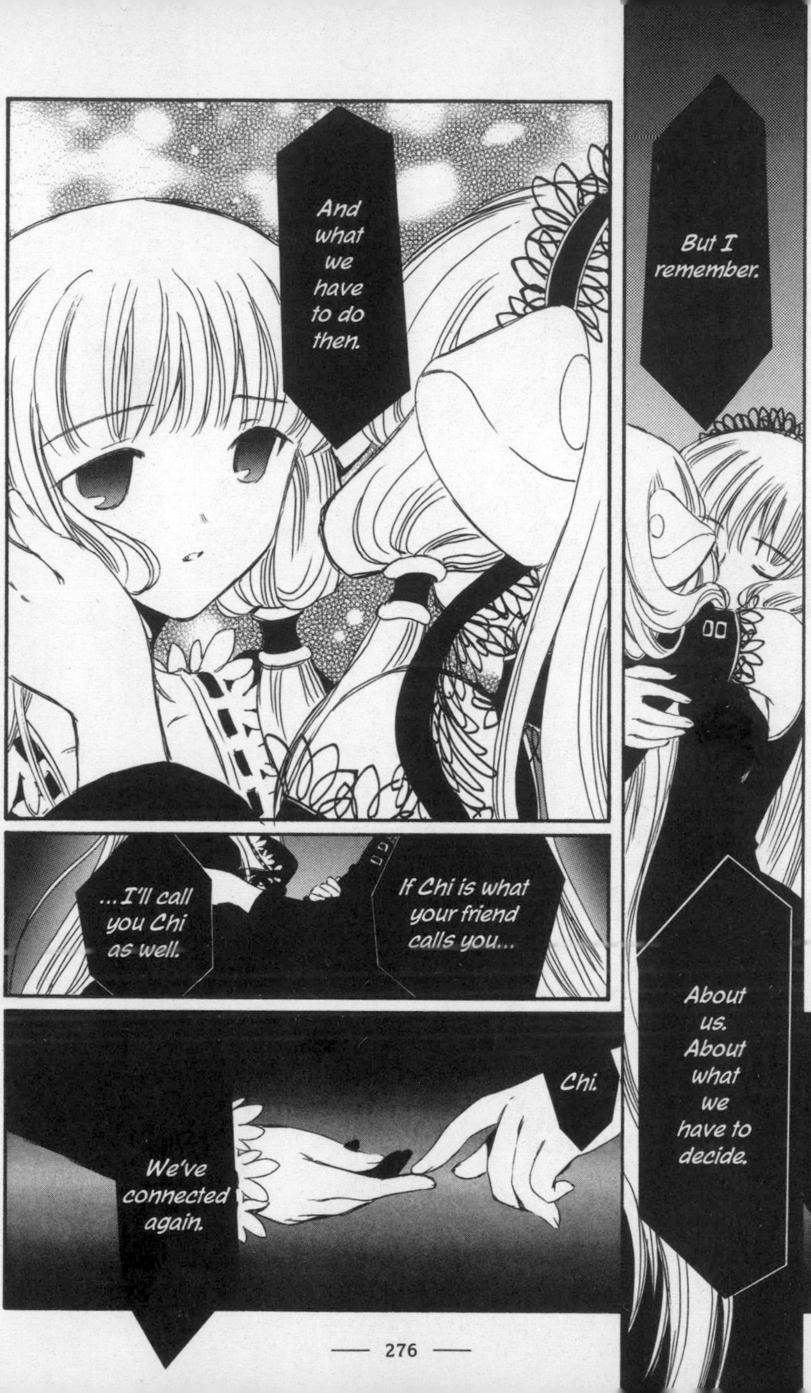

But I remember.
About us. About what we have to decide.
And what we have to do then.
If Chi is what your friend calls you...
...I'll call you Chi as well.
Chi.
We've connected again.

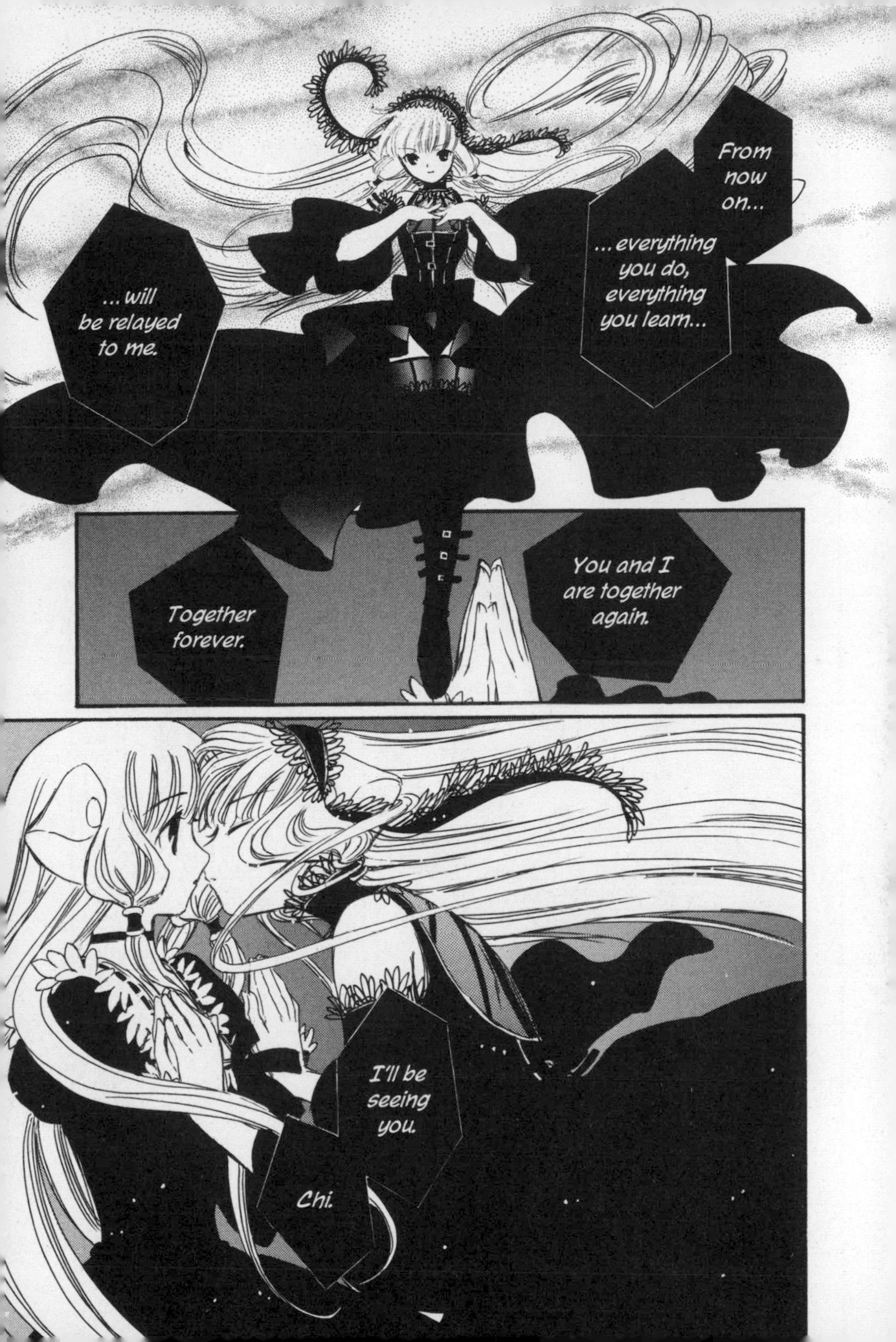
From now on...
...everything you do, everything you learn...
...will be relayed to me.
You and I are together again.
Together forever.
I'll be seeing you.
Chi.

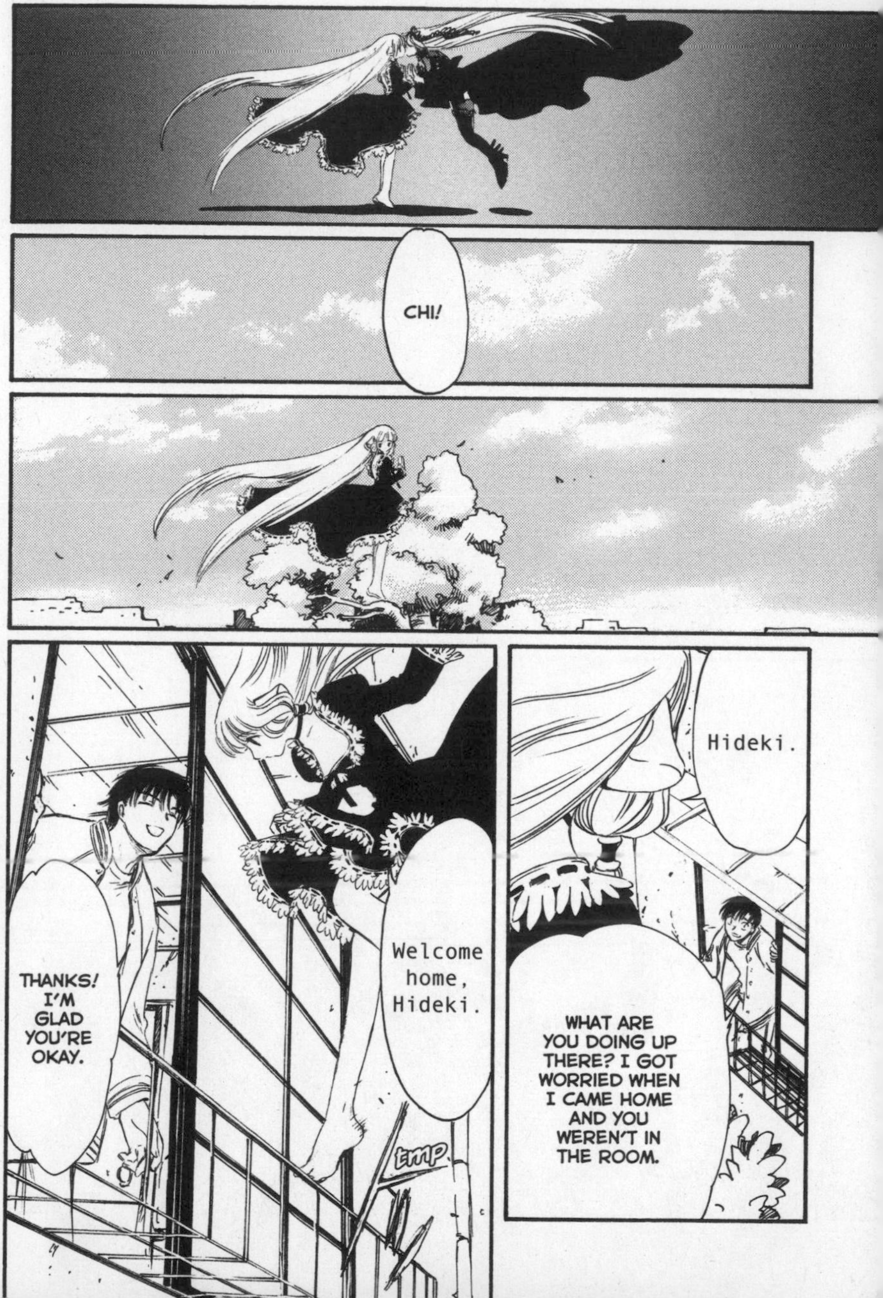
CHI!
Hideki.
WHAT ARE YOU DOING UP THERE? I GOT WORRIED WHEN I CAME HOME AND YOU WEREN'T IN THE ROOM.
Welcome home, Hideki.
tmp
THANKS! I'M GLAD YOU'RE OKAY.

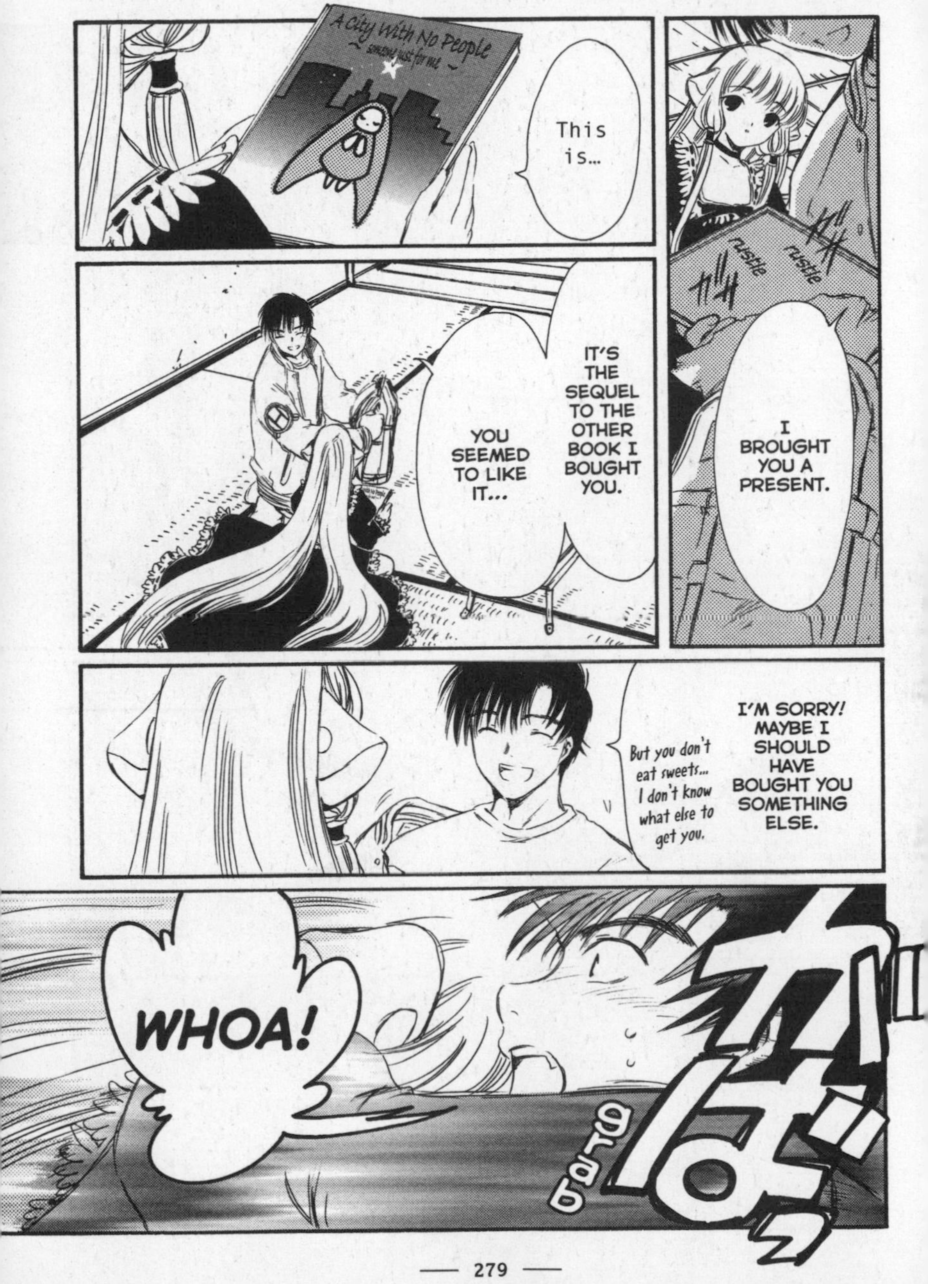
rustle
rustle
I BROUGHT YOU A PRESENT.
A City With No People
This is...
IT'S THE SEQUEL TO THE OTHER BOOK I BOUGHT YOU.
YOU SEEMED TO LIKE IT...
I'M SORRY! MAYBE I SHOULD HAVE BOUGHT YOU SOMETHING ELSE.
But you don't eat sweets... I don't know what else to get you.
grab
WHOA!

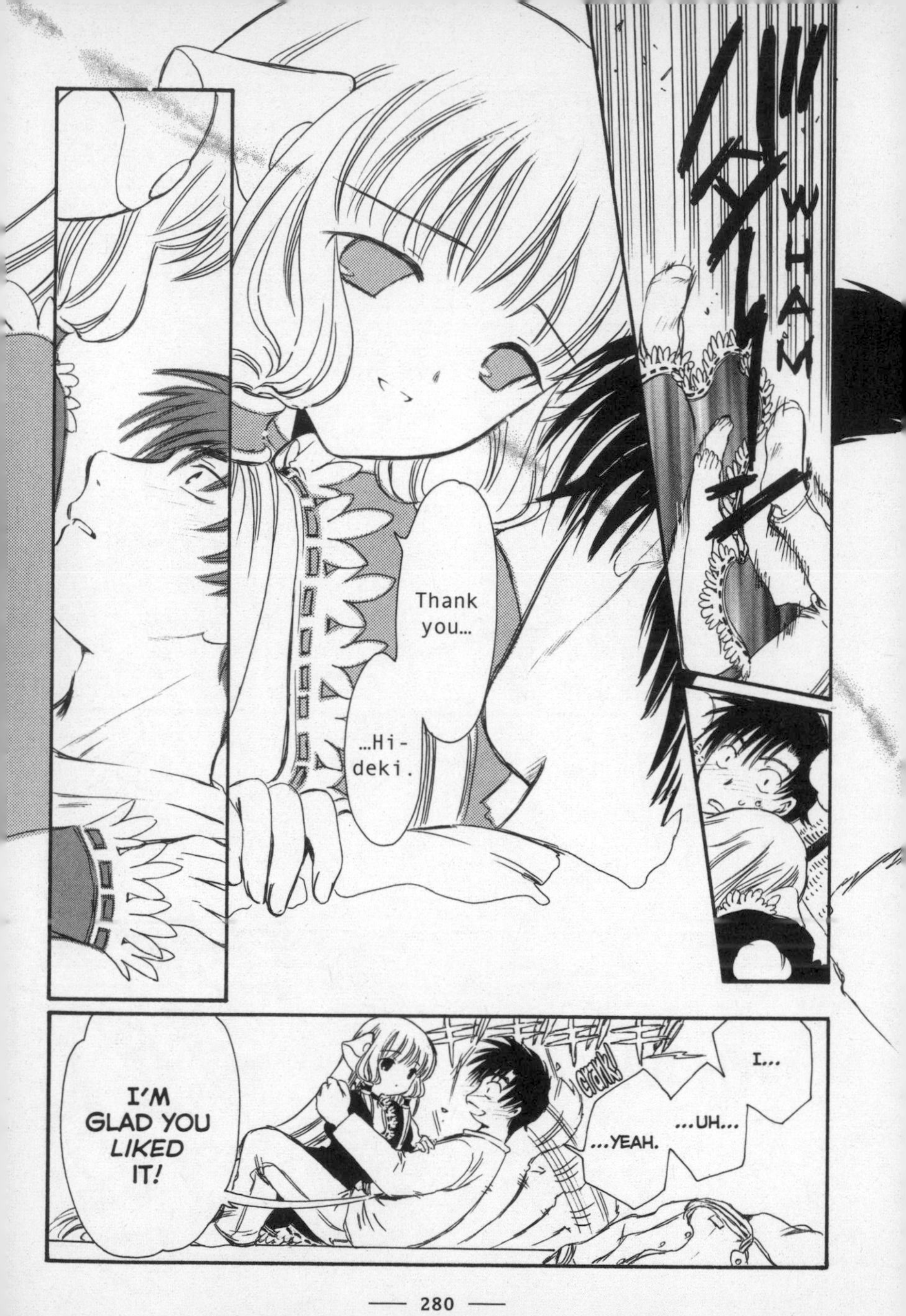
WHAM
Thank you...
...Hi-deki.
I...
crank!
...UH...
...YEAH.
I'M GLAD YOU LIKED IT!

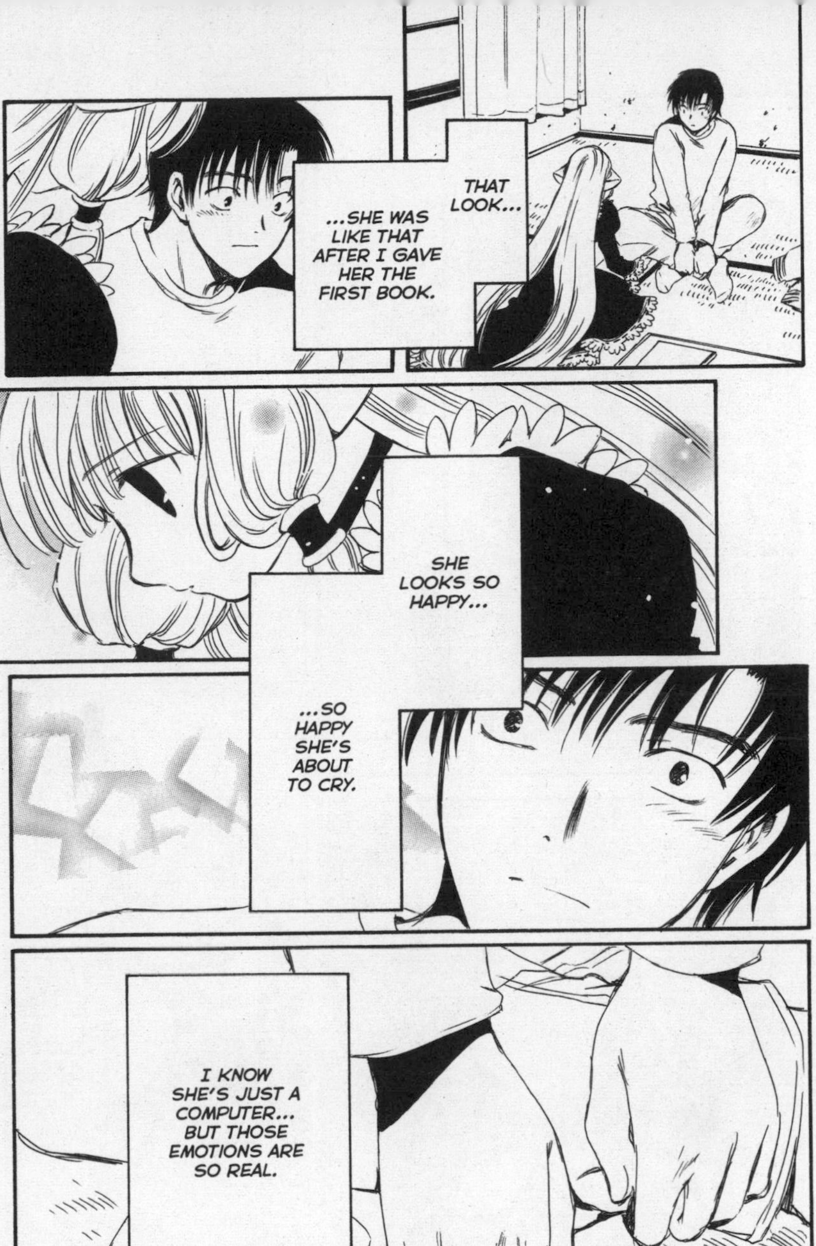
THAT LOOK...
...SHE WAS LIKE THAT AFTER I GAVE HER THE FIRST BOOK.
SHE LOOKS SO HAPPY...
...SO HAPPY SHE'S ABOUT TO CRY.
I KNOW SHE'S JUST A COMPUTER... BUT THOSE EMOTIONS ARE SO REAL.

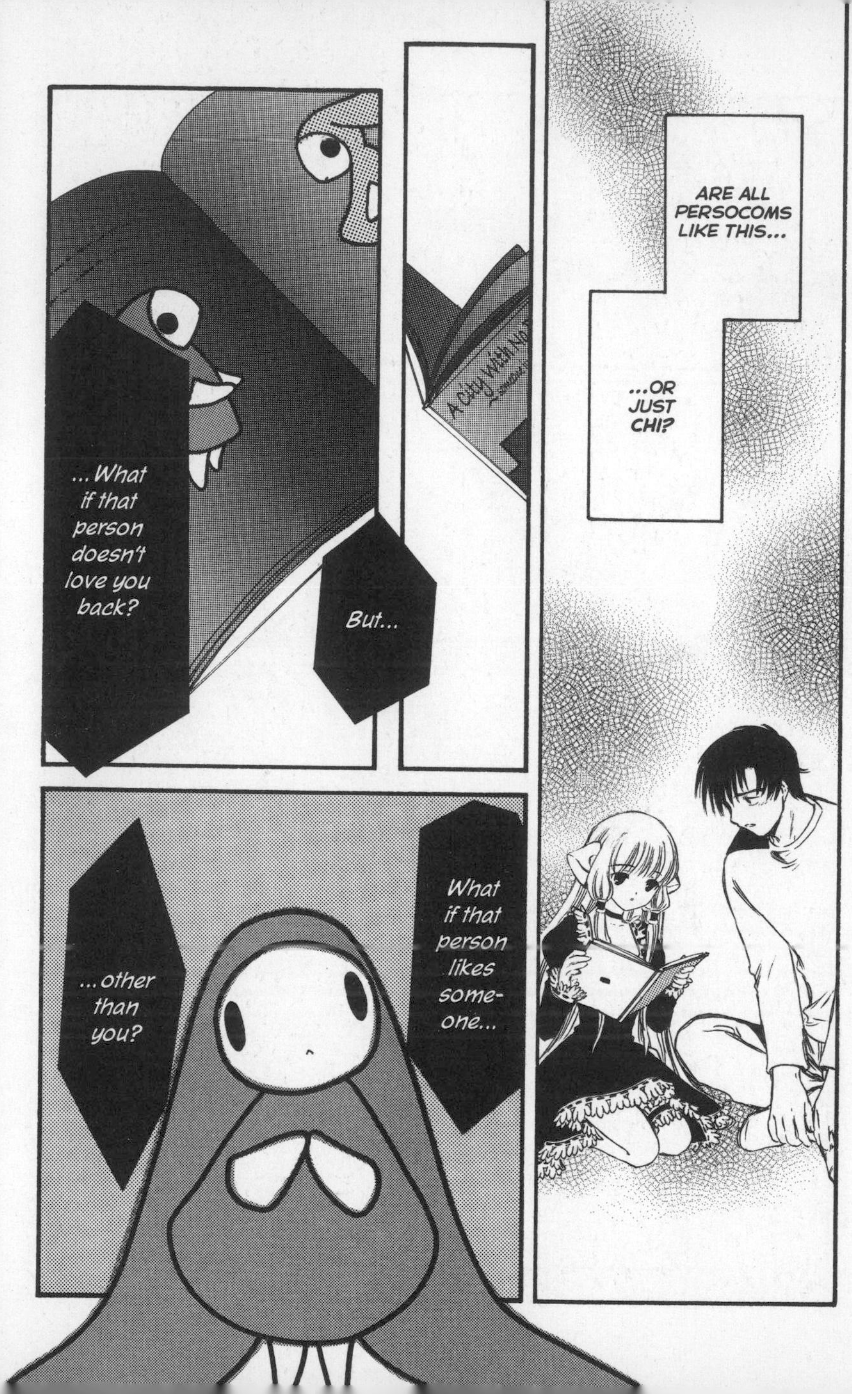
ARE ALL PERSOCOMS LIKE THIS...
...OR JUST CHI?
But...
...What if that person doesn't love you back?
What if that person likes some-one...
...other than you?

People aren't like "them." You can't erase their feelings.
People aren't easy to change.
I know.
But people do change.
Their feelings are dynamic.
Feelings of love are more resistant than other kinds.
What if he never loves you?

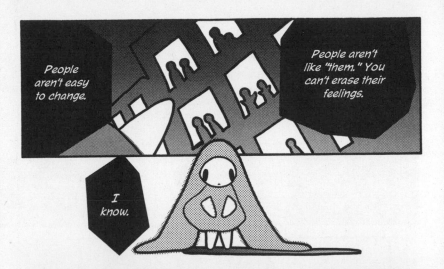

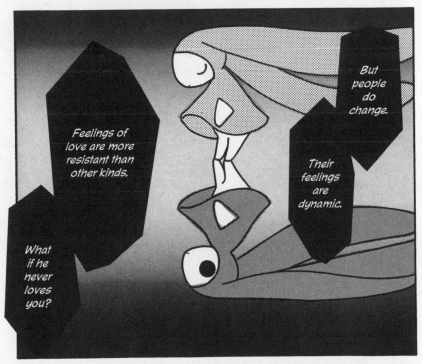

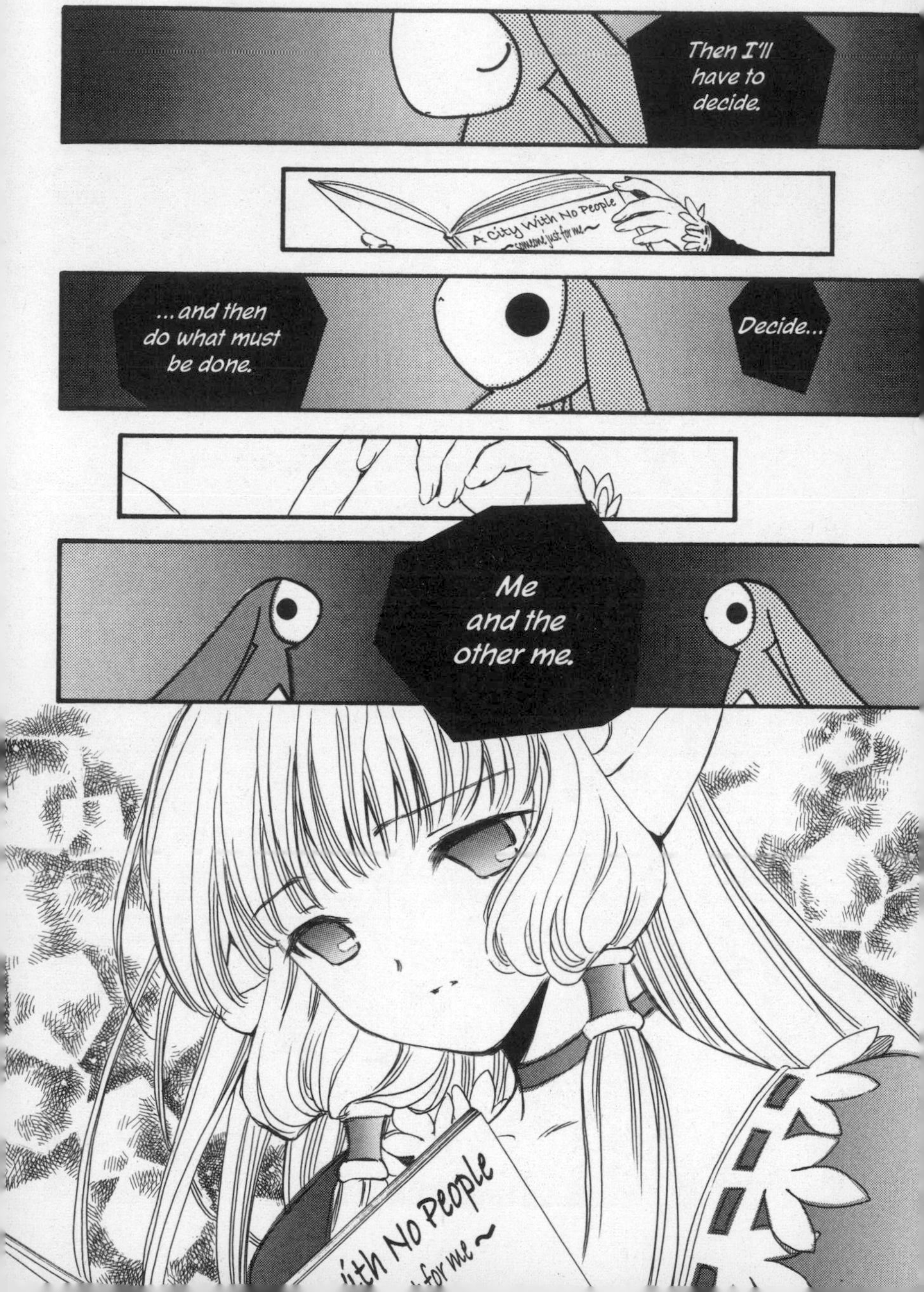
Then I'll have to decide.
A City With No People
~someone just for me~
Decide...
...and then do what must be done.
Me and the other me.
ith No People
for me ~

Chobits
ちょびっツ

◄ chapter 19 ►

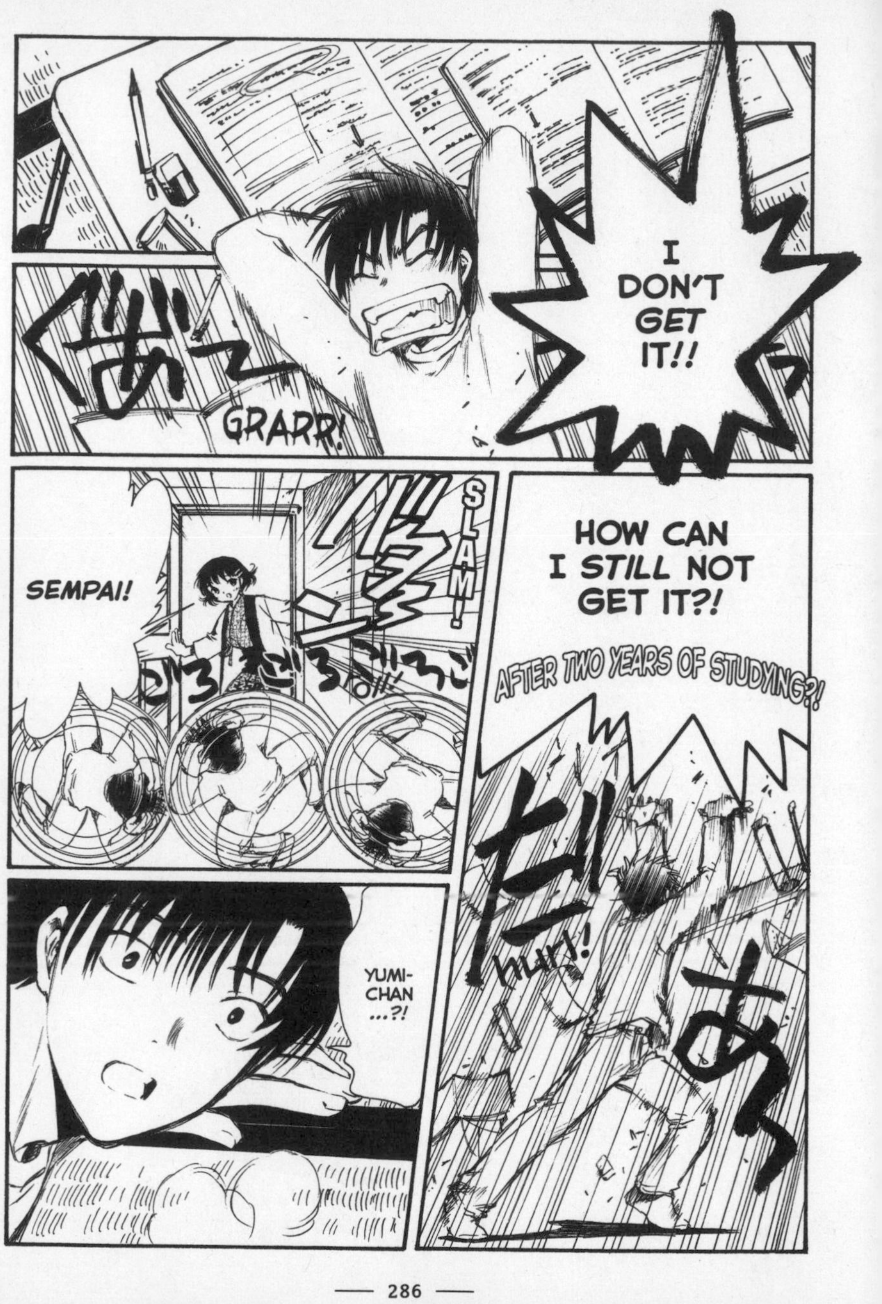
I DON'T GET IT!!
GRARR!
HOW CAN I *STILL* NOT GET IT?!
AFTER TWO YEARS OF STUDYING?!
hurl!
SLAM!
SEMPAI!
YUMI-CHAN ...?!

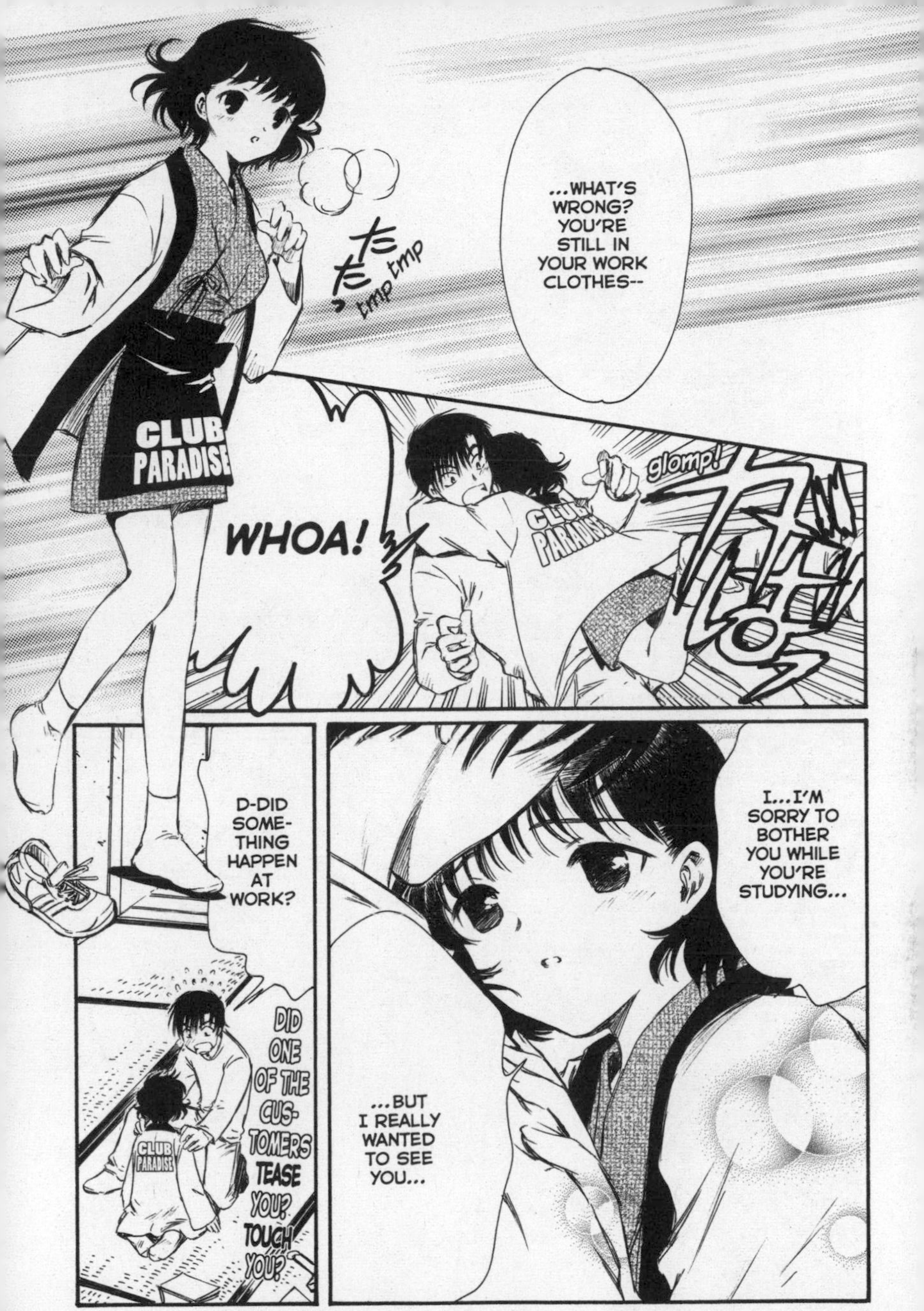
...WHAT'S WRONG? YOU'RE STILL IN YOUR WORK CLOTHES--
たた
tmp tmp
glomp!
WHOA!
CLUB PARADISE
I...I'M SORRY TO BOTHER YOU WHILE YOU'RE STUDYING...
...BUT I REALLY WANTED TO SEE YOU...
D-DID SOMETHING HAPPEN AT WORK?
DID ONE OF THE CUS-TOMERS TEASE YOU? TOUCH YOU?

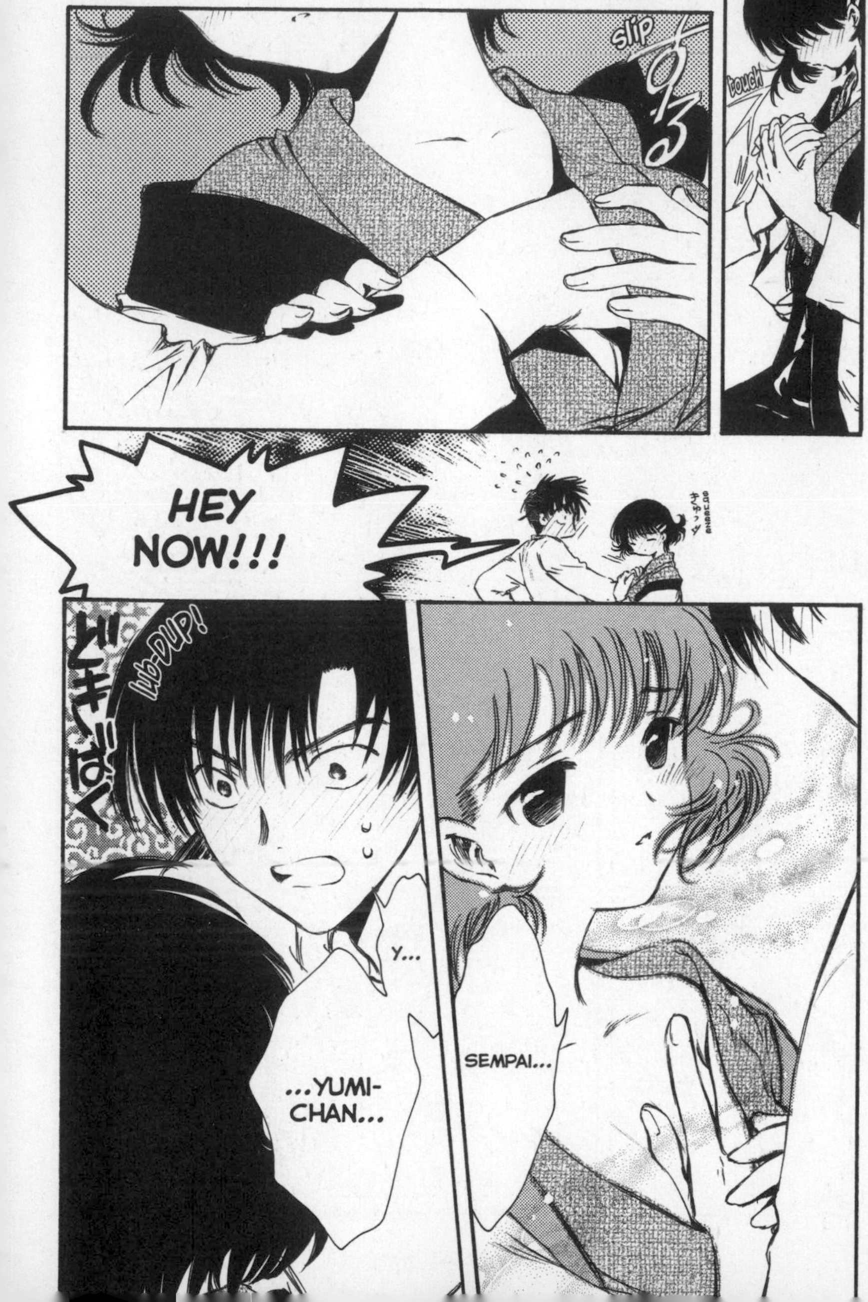
touch
slip
squeeze
HEY NOW!!!
SEMPAI...
lub-DUP!
Y...
...YUMI-CHAN...

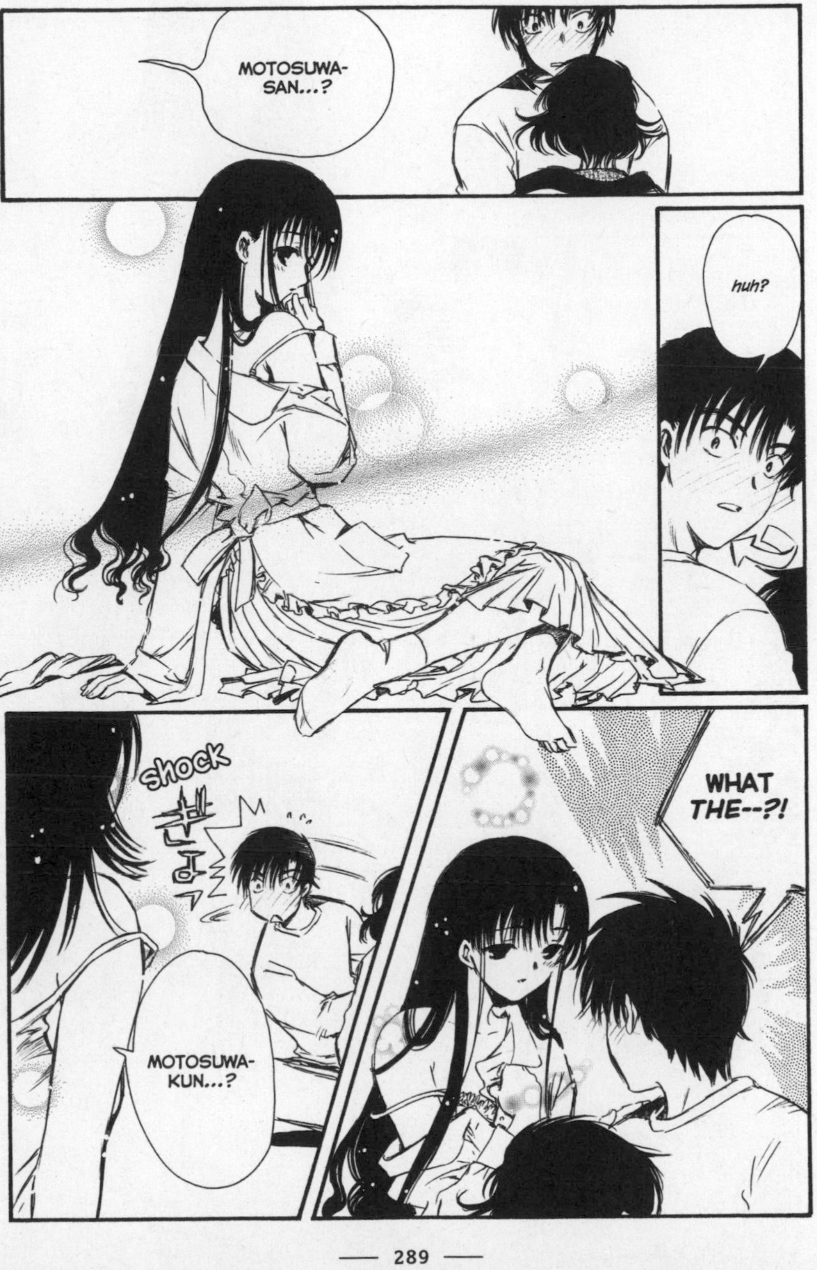
MOTOSUWA-SAN...?
huh?
WHAT THE--?!
shock
MOTOSUWA-KUN...?

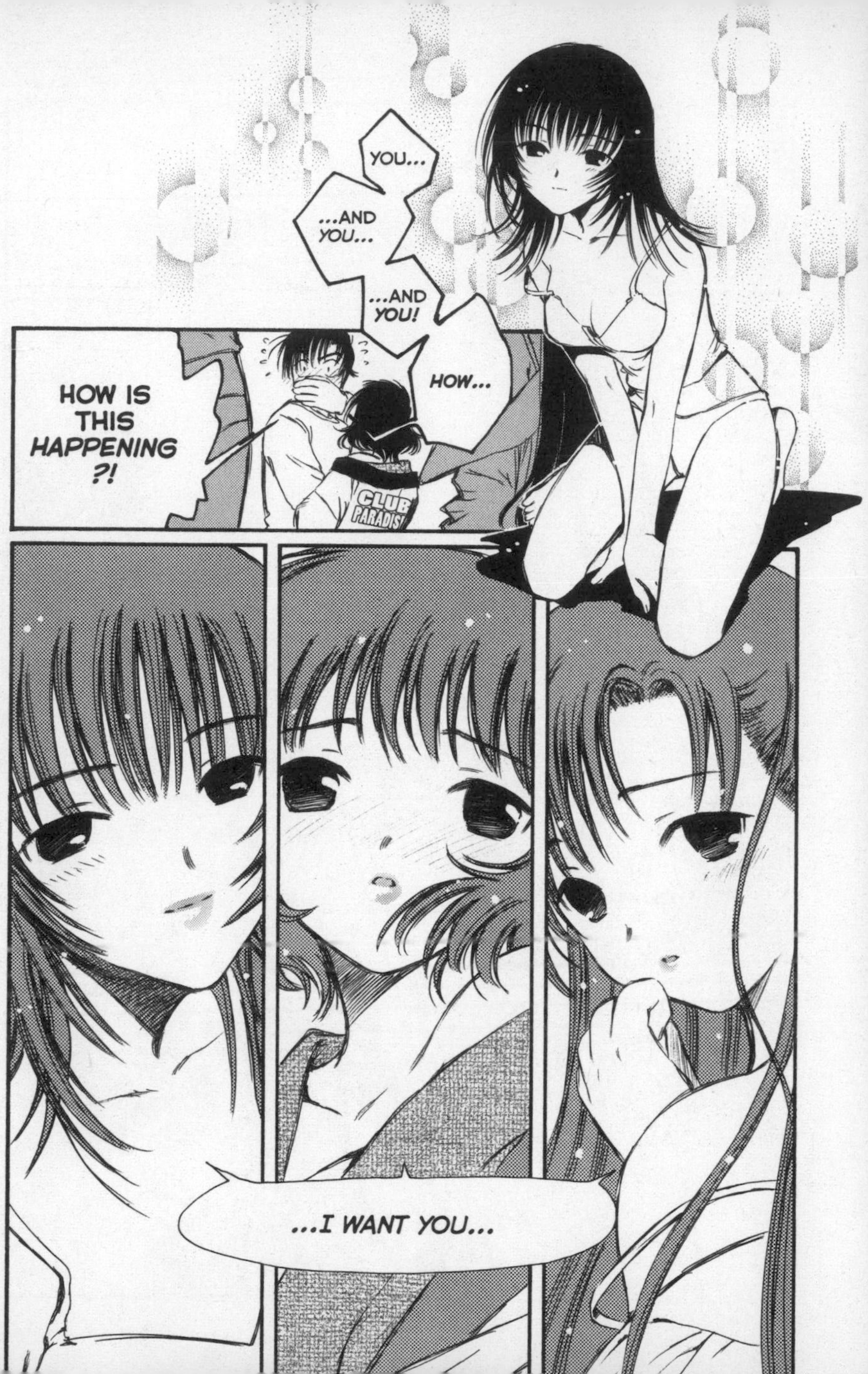

YOU...
...AND YOU...
...AND YOU!
HOW...
HOW IS THIS HAPPENING?!
CLUB PARADISE
...I WANT YOU...

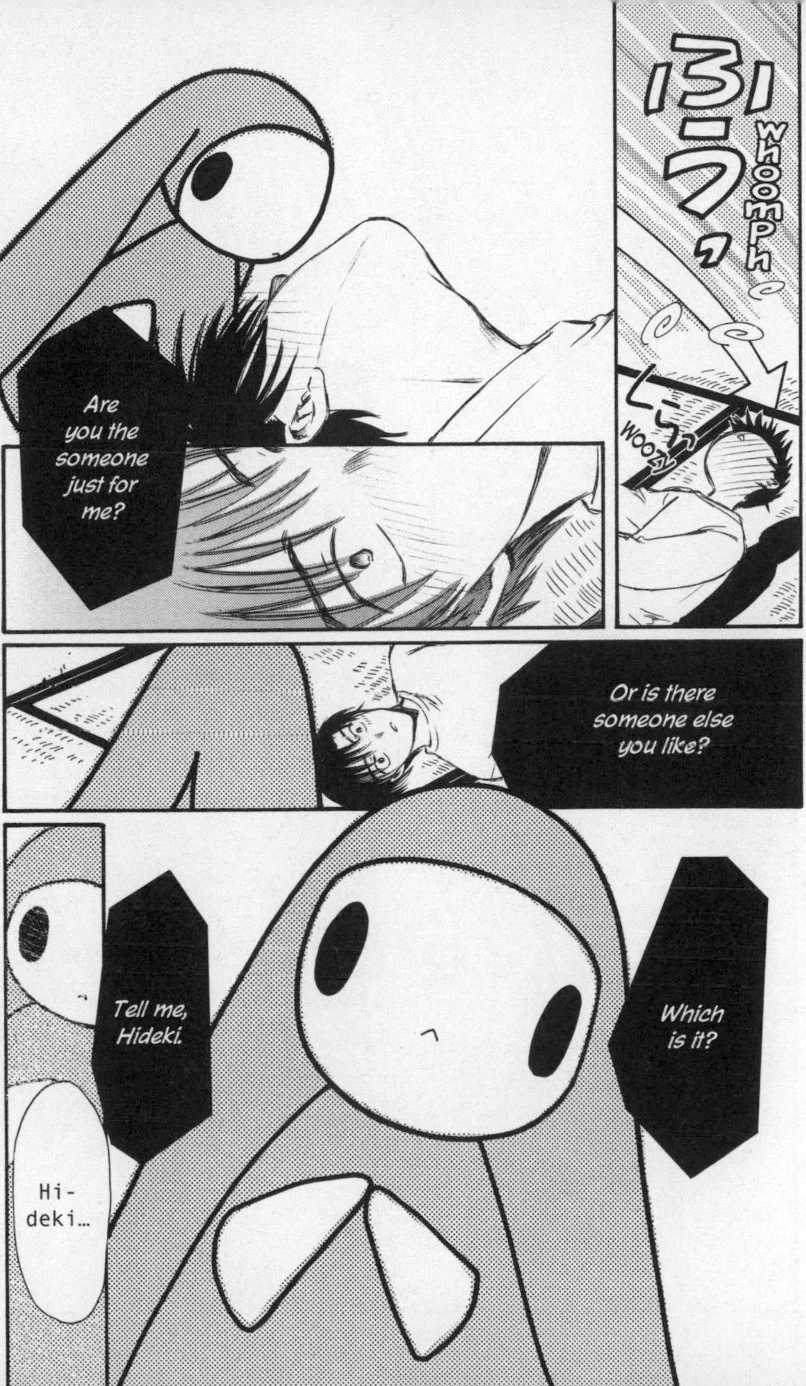
whoomph
WOOZY
Are you the someone just for me?
Or is there someone else you like?
Which is it?
Tell me, Hideki.
Hi-deki...

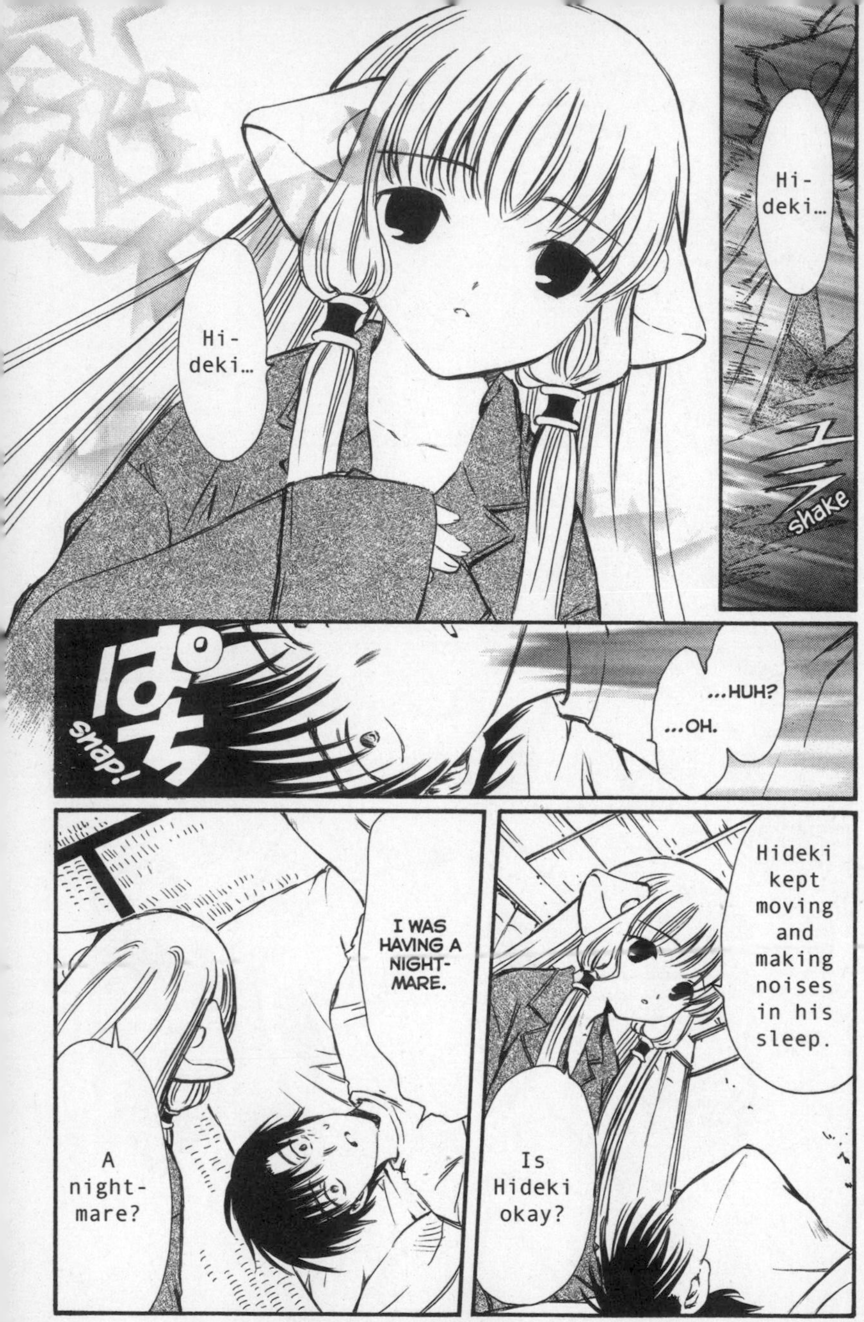
Hi-
deki…
shake
Hi-
deki…
ぱち
snap!
...HUH?
...OH.
Hideki
kept
moving
and
making
noises
in his
sleep.
Is
Hideki
okay?
I WAS
HAVING A
NIGHT-
MARE.
A
night-
mare?

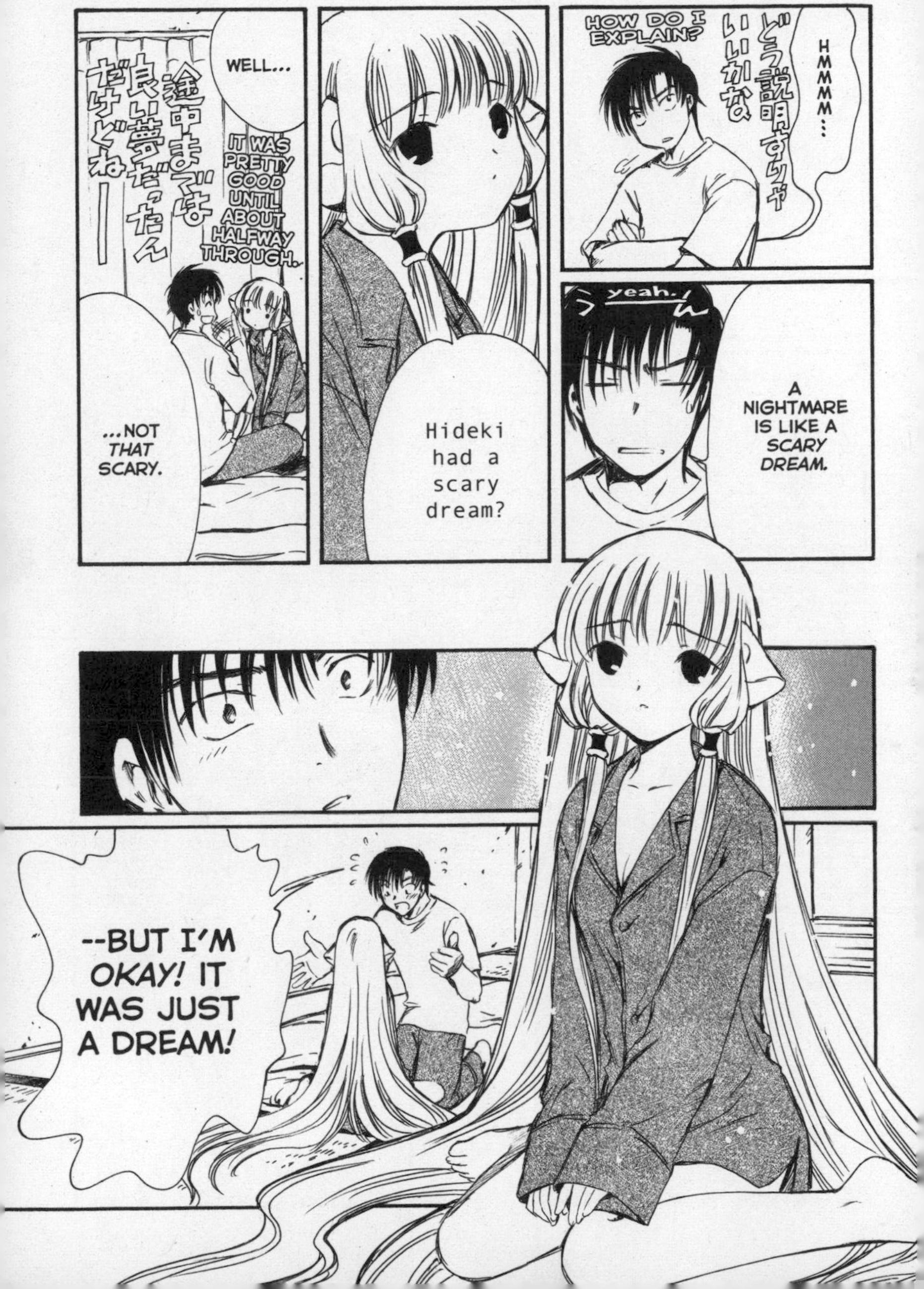
HMMMM...
どう説明すりゃいいかな
HOW DO I EXPLAIN?
うーん
yeah.
A NIGHTMARE IS LIKE A *SCARY DREAM.*
Hideki had a scary dream?
WELL...
途中までは良い夢だったんだけどねー
IT WAS PRETTY GOOD UNTIL ABOUT HALFWAY THROUGH.
...NOT *THAT* SCARY.
--BUT I'M *OKAY!* IT WAS JUST A DREAM!

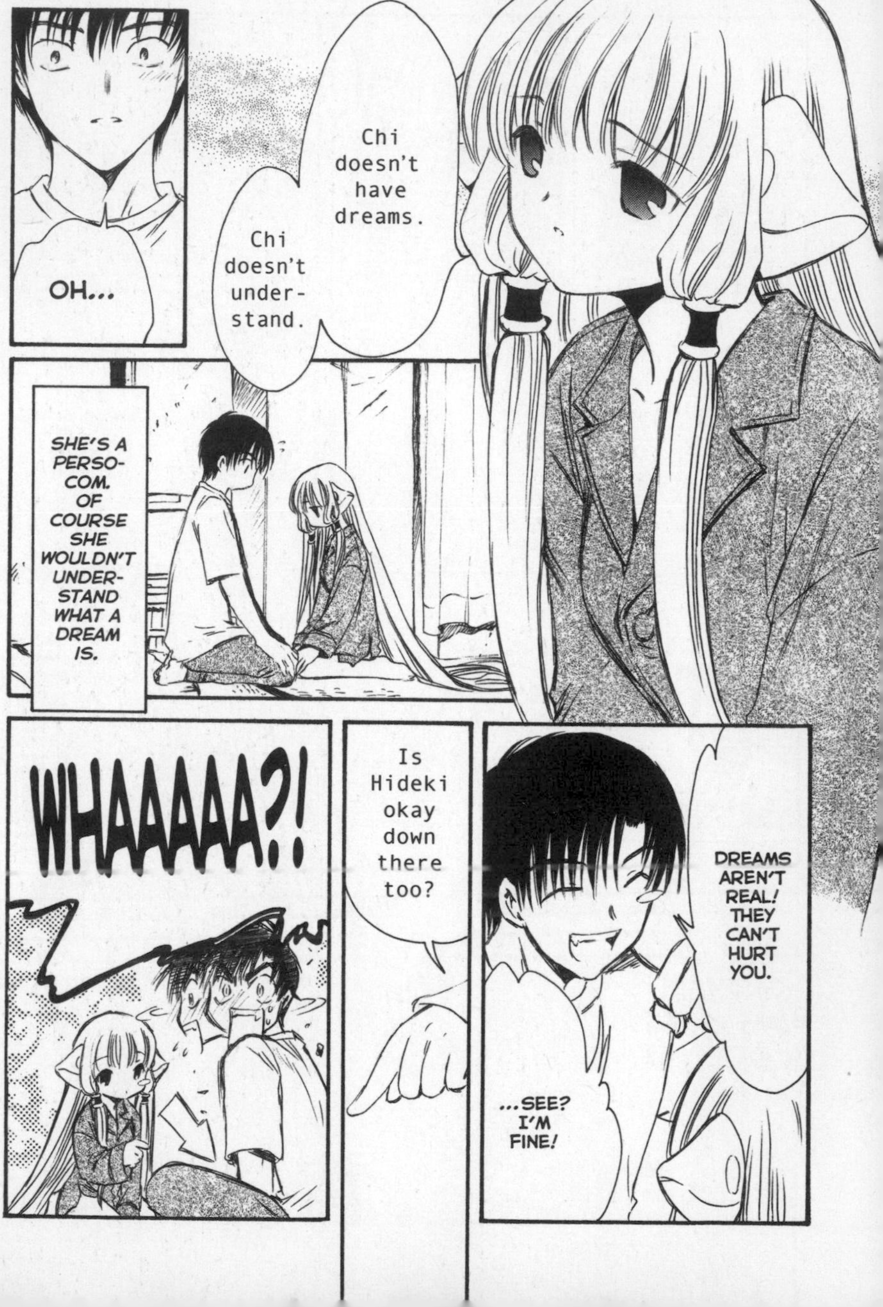

Chi doesn't have dreams.
Chi doesn't under-stand.
OH...
SHE'S A PERSO-COM. OF COURSE SHE WOULDN'T UNDER-STAND WHAT A DREAM IS.
DREAMS AREN'T REAL! THEY CAN'T HURT YOU.
...SEE? I'M FINE!
Is Hideki okay down there too?
WHAAAAA?!

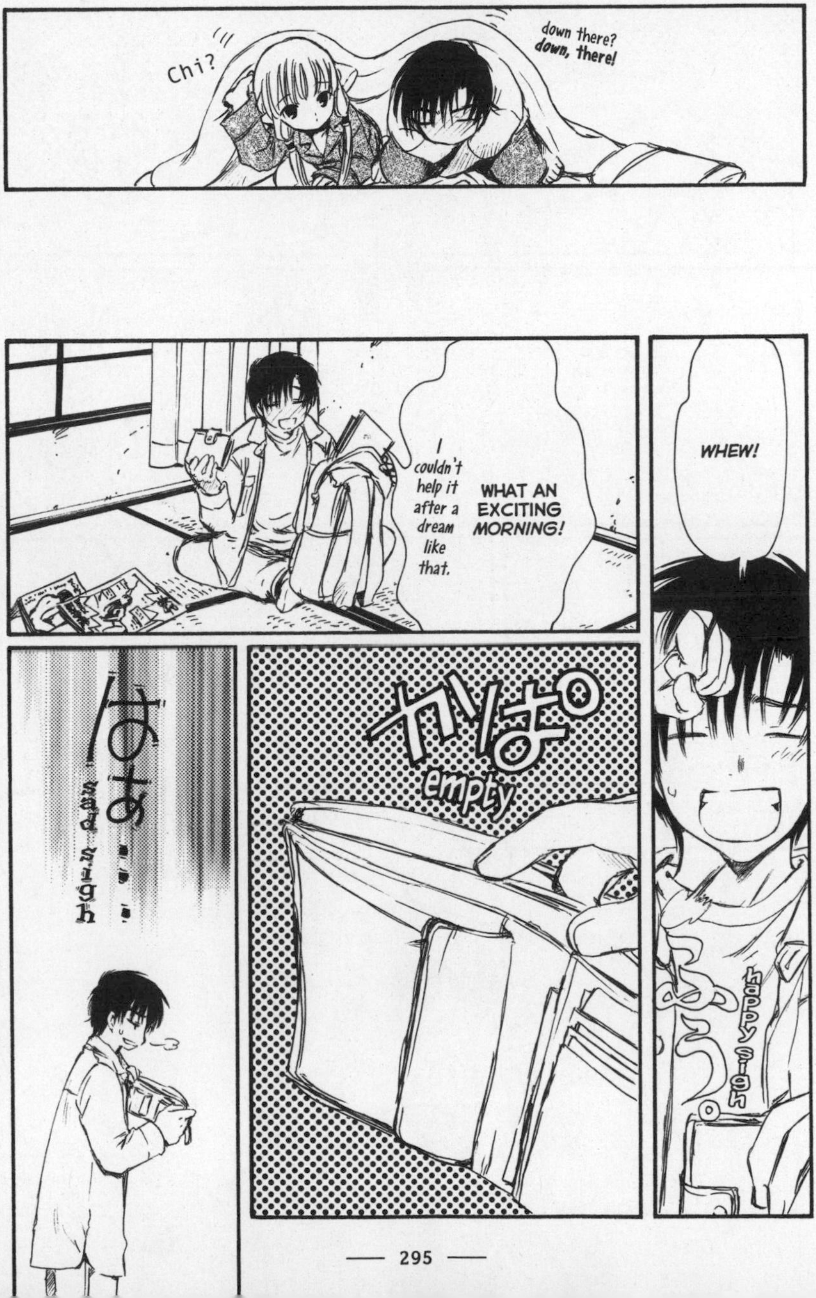
down there?
down, there!
Chi?
WHEW!
ふぅ。
happy sigh
WHAT AN EXCITING MORNING!
I couldn't help it after a dream like that.
かぽ
empty
はぁ……
sad sigh

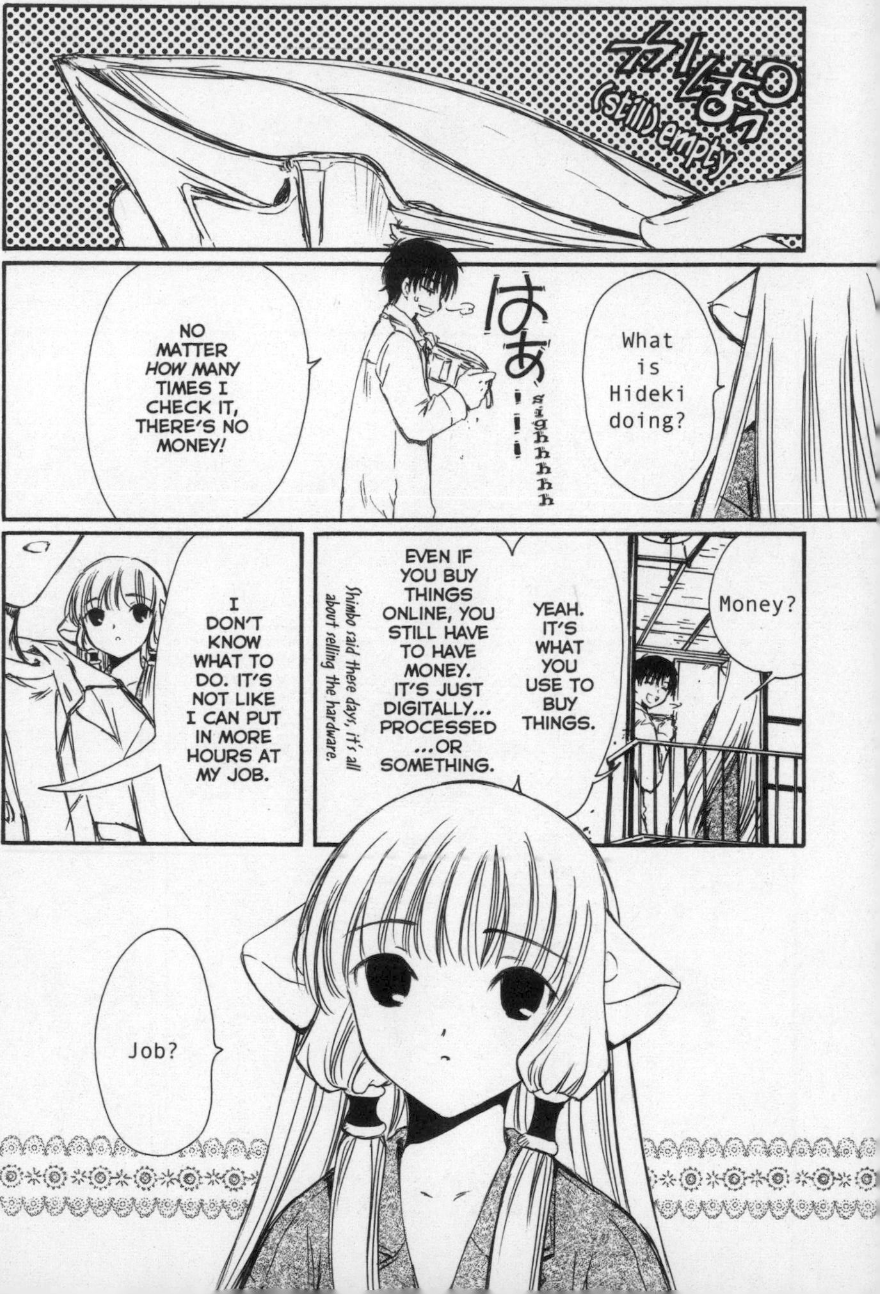
からっぽ
(still) empty
What is Hideki doing?
はぁ
sighhhhh
NO MATTER HOW MANY TIMES I CHECK IT, THERE'S NO MONEY!
Money?
YEAH. IT'S WHAT YOU USE TO BUY THINGS.
EVEN IF YOU BUY THINGS ONLINE, YOU STILL HAVE TO HAVE MONEY. IT'S JUST DIGITALLY... PROCESSED ...OR SOMETHING.
Shimbo said there days, it's all about selling the hardware.
I DON'T KNOW WHAT TO DO. IT'S NOT LIKE I CAN PUT IN MORE HOURS AT MY JOB.
Job?

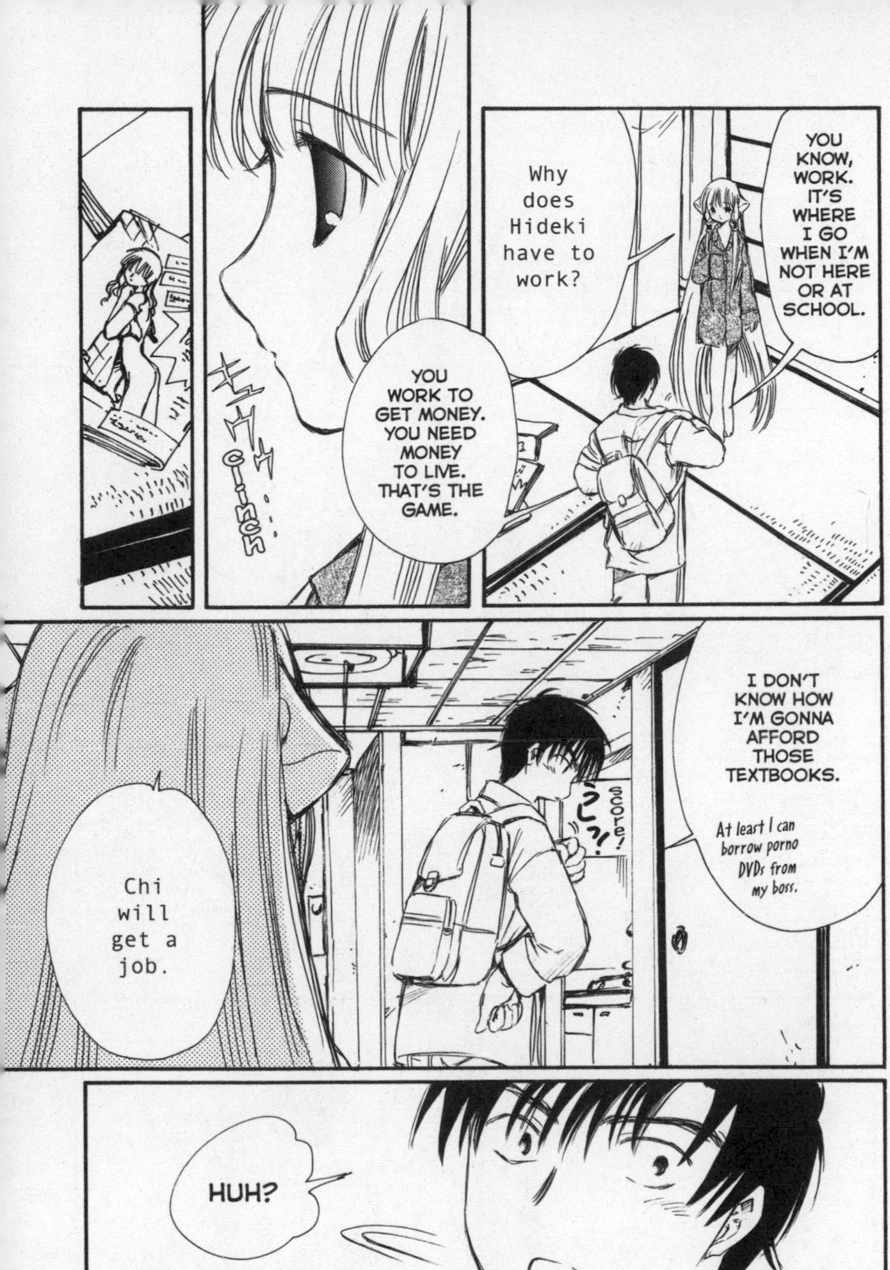
YOU KNOW, WORK. IT'S WHERE I GO WHEN I'M NOT HERE OR AT SCHOOL.
Why does Hideki have to work?
YOU WORK TO GET MONEY. YOU NEED MONEY TO LIVE. THAT'S THE GAME.
Clinch
I DON'T KNOW HOW I'M GONNA AFFORD THOSE TEXTBOOKS.
At least I can borrow porno DVDs from my boss.
score!
Chi will get a job.
HUH?

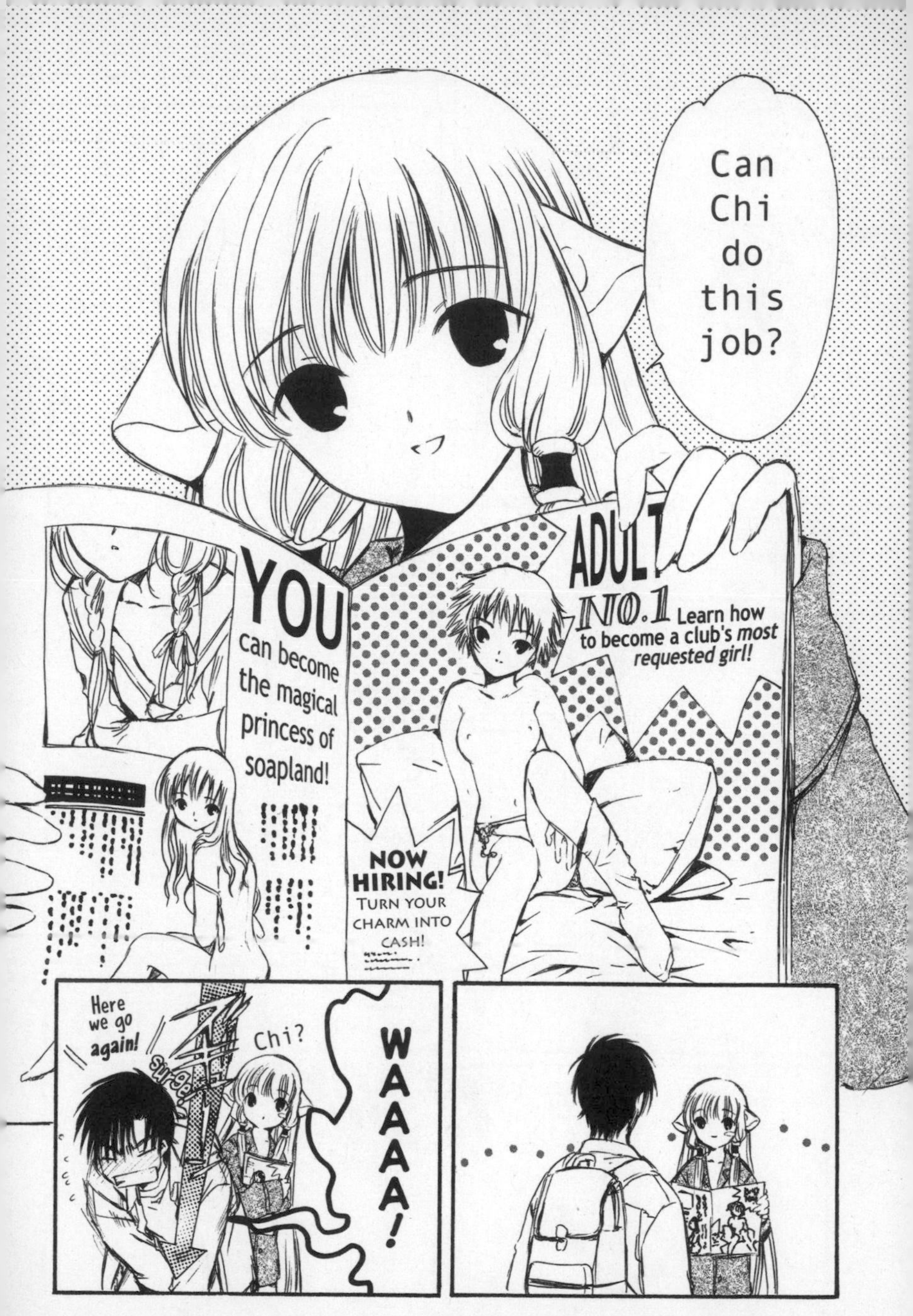

Can Chi do this job?
ADULT
NO.1 Learn how to become a club's *most requested girl!*
YOU can become the magical princess of soapland!
NOW HIRING! TURN YOUR CHARM INTO CASH!
WAAAA!
Chi?
surge
Here we go again!

Chobits
ちょびっツ

◀ **chapter 20** ▶

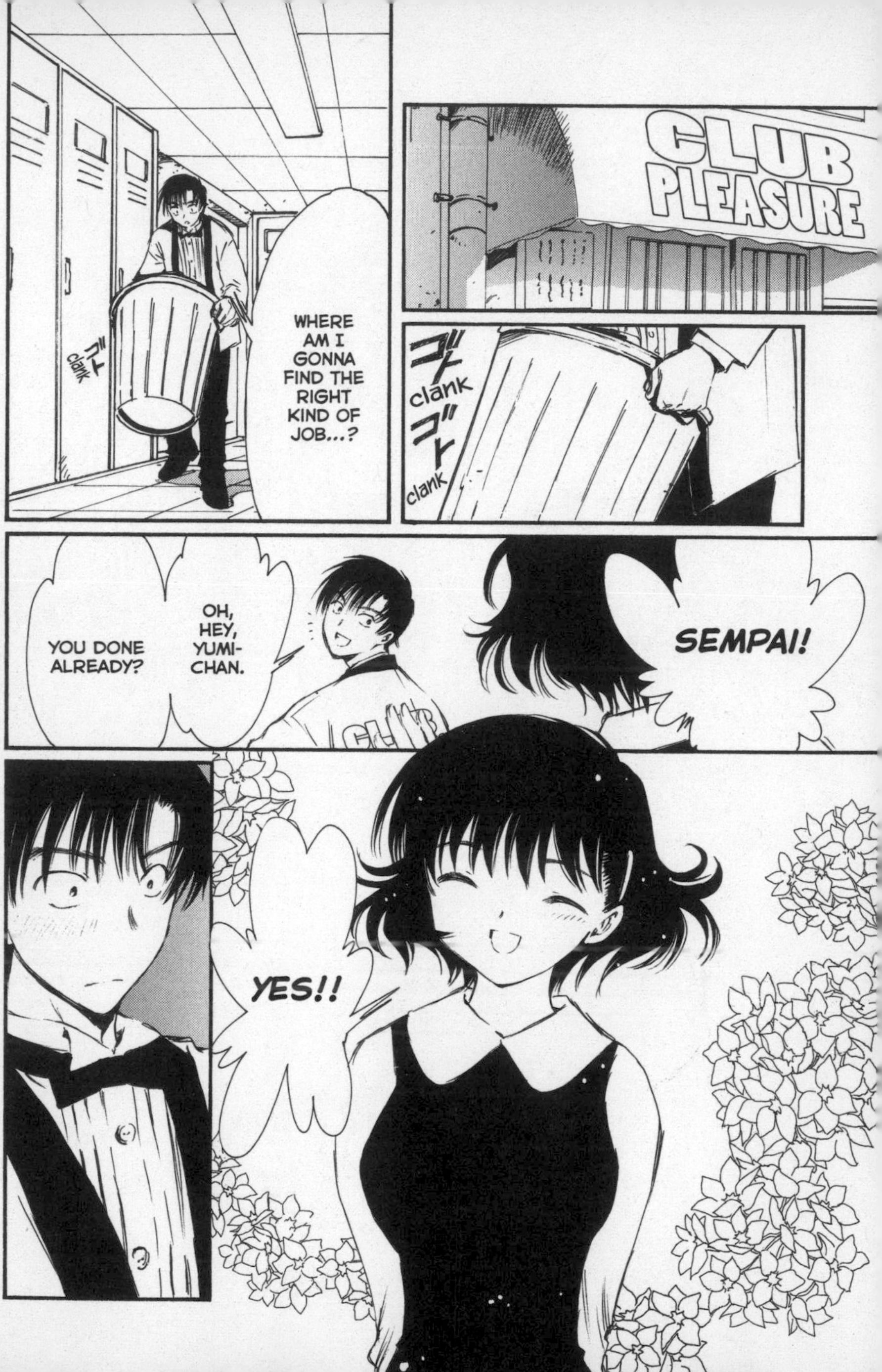

CLUB PLEASURE
ゴト clank
ゴト clank
ゴト clank
WHERE AM I GONNA FIND THE RIGHT KIND OF JOB...?
SEMPAI!
OH, HEY, YUMI-CHAN.
YOU DONE ALREADY?
YES!!

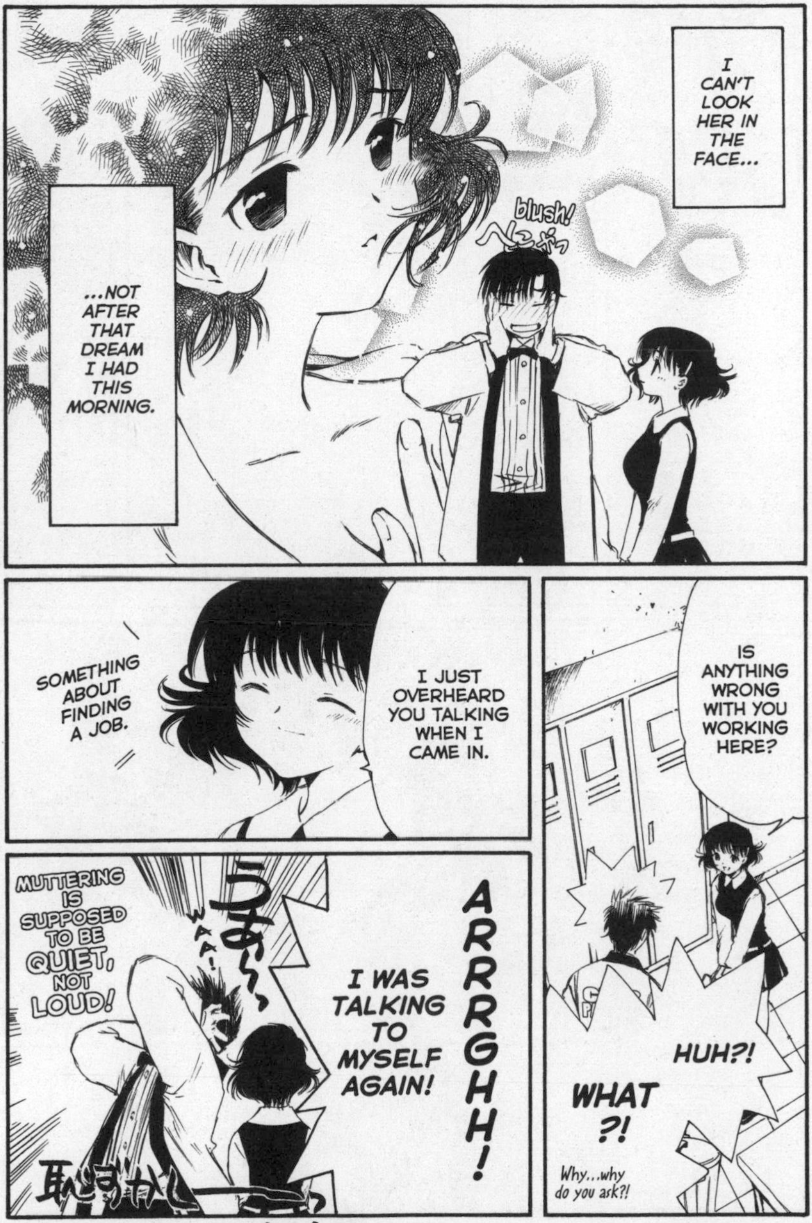
I CAN'T LOOK HER IN THE FACE...
blush!
...NOT AFTER THAT DREAM I HAD THIS MORNING.
IS ANYTHING WRONG WITH YOU WORKING HERE?
HUH?!
WHAT ?!
Why...why do you ask?!
I JUST OVERHEARD YOU TALKING WHEN I CAME IN.
SOMETHING ABOUT FINDING A JOB.
ARRRGHH!
I WAS TALKING TO MYSELF AGAIN!
WAA!
MUTTERING IS SUPPOSED TO BE QUIET, NOT LOUD!
how embarrassing!

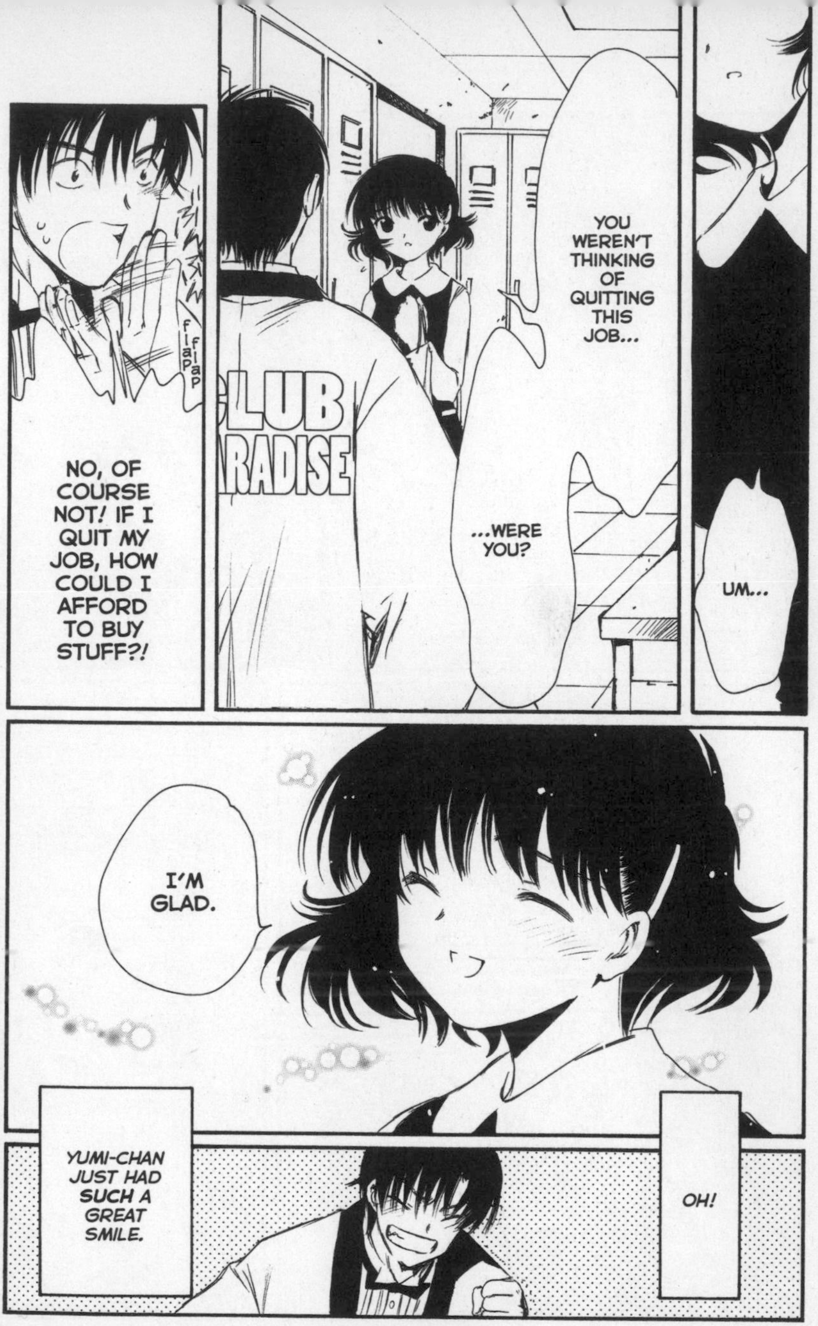
UM...
YOU WEREN'T THINKING OF QUITTING THIS JOB...
...WERE YOU?
CLUB
flap flap
NO, OF COURSE NOT! IF I QUIT MY JOB, HOW COULD I AFFORD TO BUY STUFF?!
I'M GLAD.
OH!
YUMI-CHAN JUST HAD SUCH A GREAT SMILE.

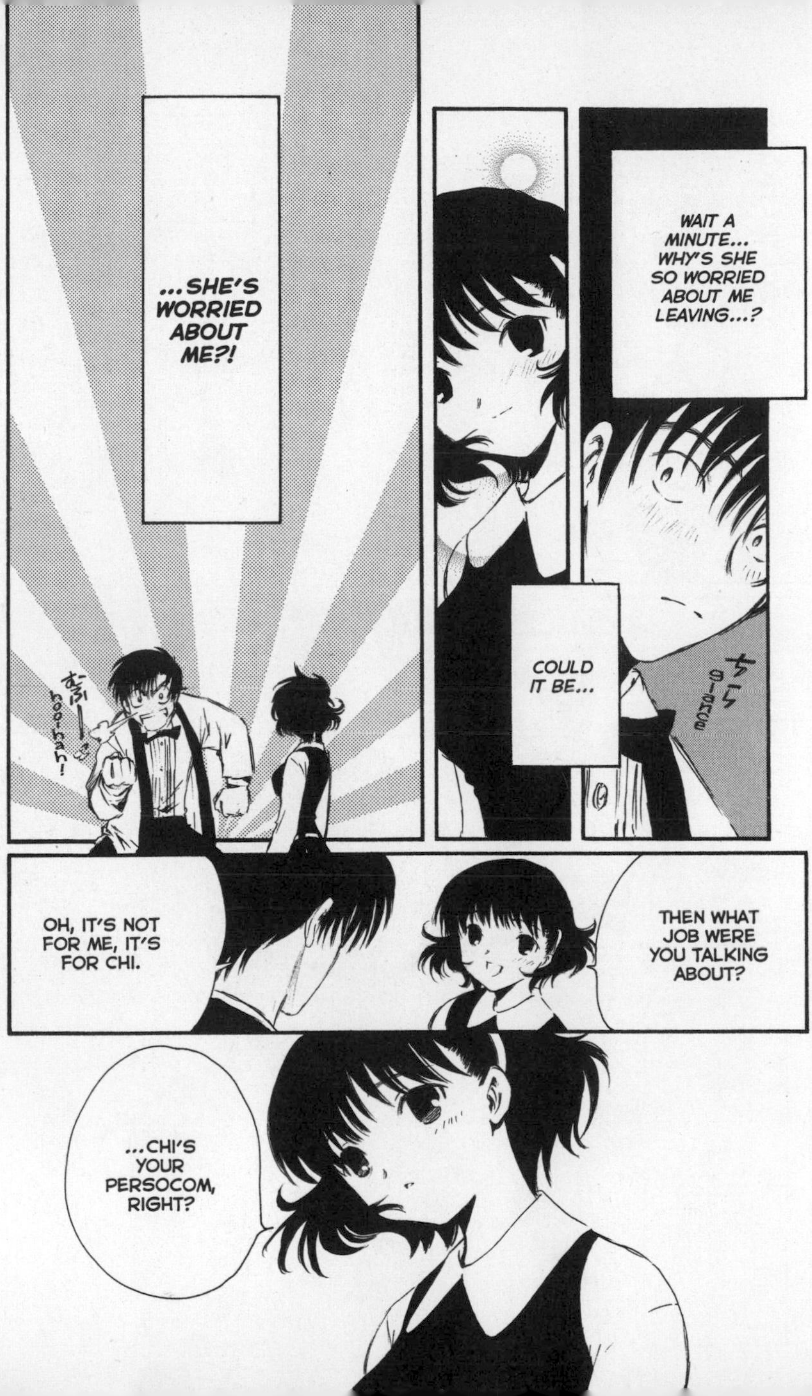
WAIT A MINUTE... WHY'S SHE SO WORRIED ABOUT ME LEAVING...?
COULD IT BE...
ちら
glance
...SHE'S WORRIED ABOUT ME?!
hoo-hah!
THEN WHAT JOB WERE YOU TALKING ABOUT?
OH, IT'S NOT FOR ME, IT'S FOR CHI.
...CHI'S YOUR PERSOCOM, RIGHT?

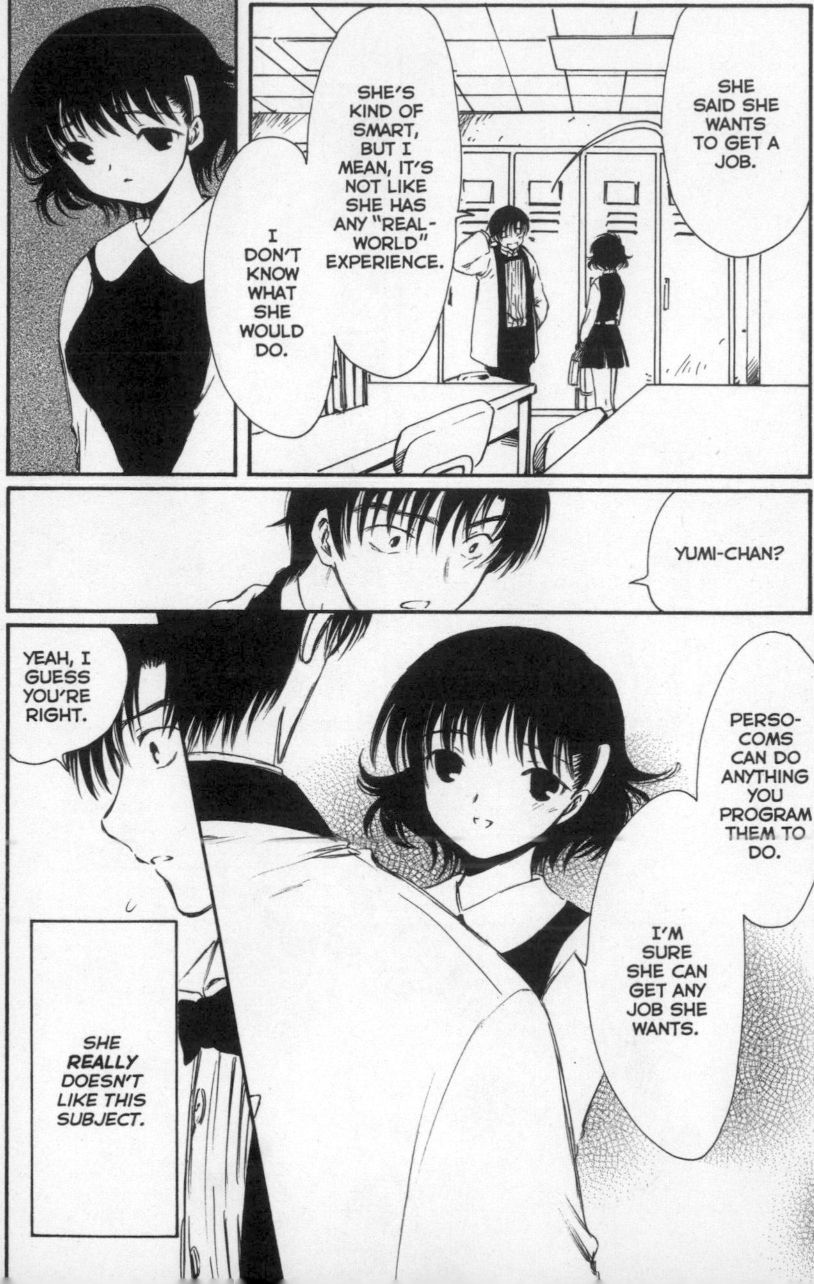
SHE SAID SHE WANTS TO GET A JOB.
SHE'S KIND OF SMART, BUT I MEAN, IT'S NOT LIKE SHE HAS ANY "REAL-WORLD" EXPERIENCE.
I DON'T KNOW WHAT SHE WOULD DO.
YUMI-CHAN?
PERSO-COMS CAN DO ANYTHING YOU PROGRAM THEM TO DO.
I'M SURE SHE CAN GET ANY JOB SHE WANTS.
YEAH, I GUESS YOU'RE RIGHT.
SHE *REALLY* DOESN'T LIKE THIS SUBJECT.

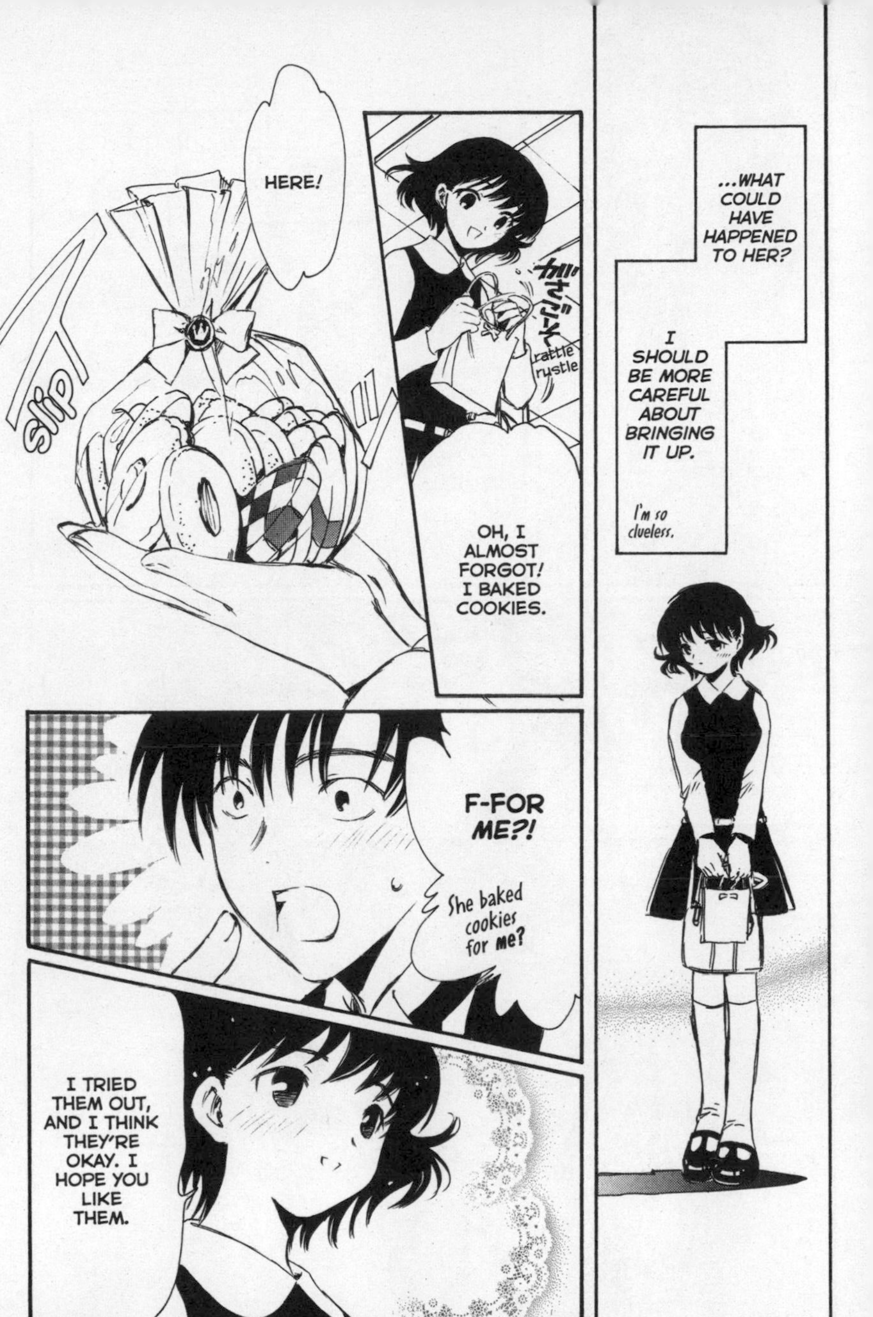
...WHAT COULD HAVE HAPPENED TO HER?
I SHOULD BE MORE CAREFUL ABOUT BRINGING IT UP.
I'm so clueless.
rattle rustle
OH, I ALMOST FORGOT! I BAKED COOKIES.
HERE!
slip
F-FOR ME?!
She baked cookies for me?
I TRIED THEM OUT, AND I THINK THEY'RE OKAY. I HOPE YOU LIKE THEM.

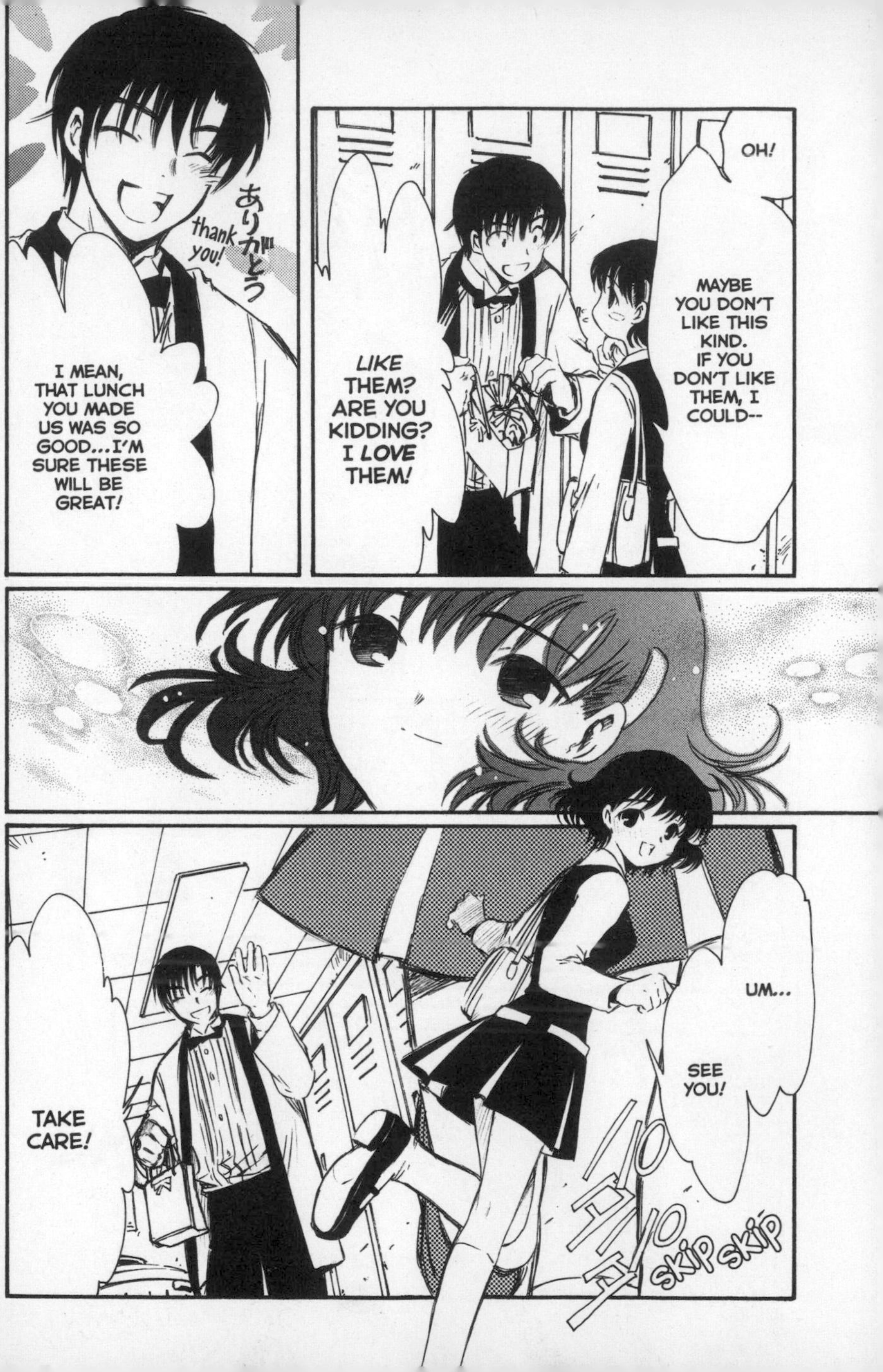
OH!
MAYBE YOU DON'T LIKE THIS KIND. IF YOU DON'T LIKE THEM, I COULD--
LIKE THEM? ARE YOU KIDDING? I LOVE THEM!
ありがとう
thank you!
I MEAN, THAT LUNCH YOU MADE US WAS SO GOOD...I'M SURE THESE WILL BE GREAT!
UM...
SEE YOU!
TAKE CARE!
skip skip

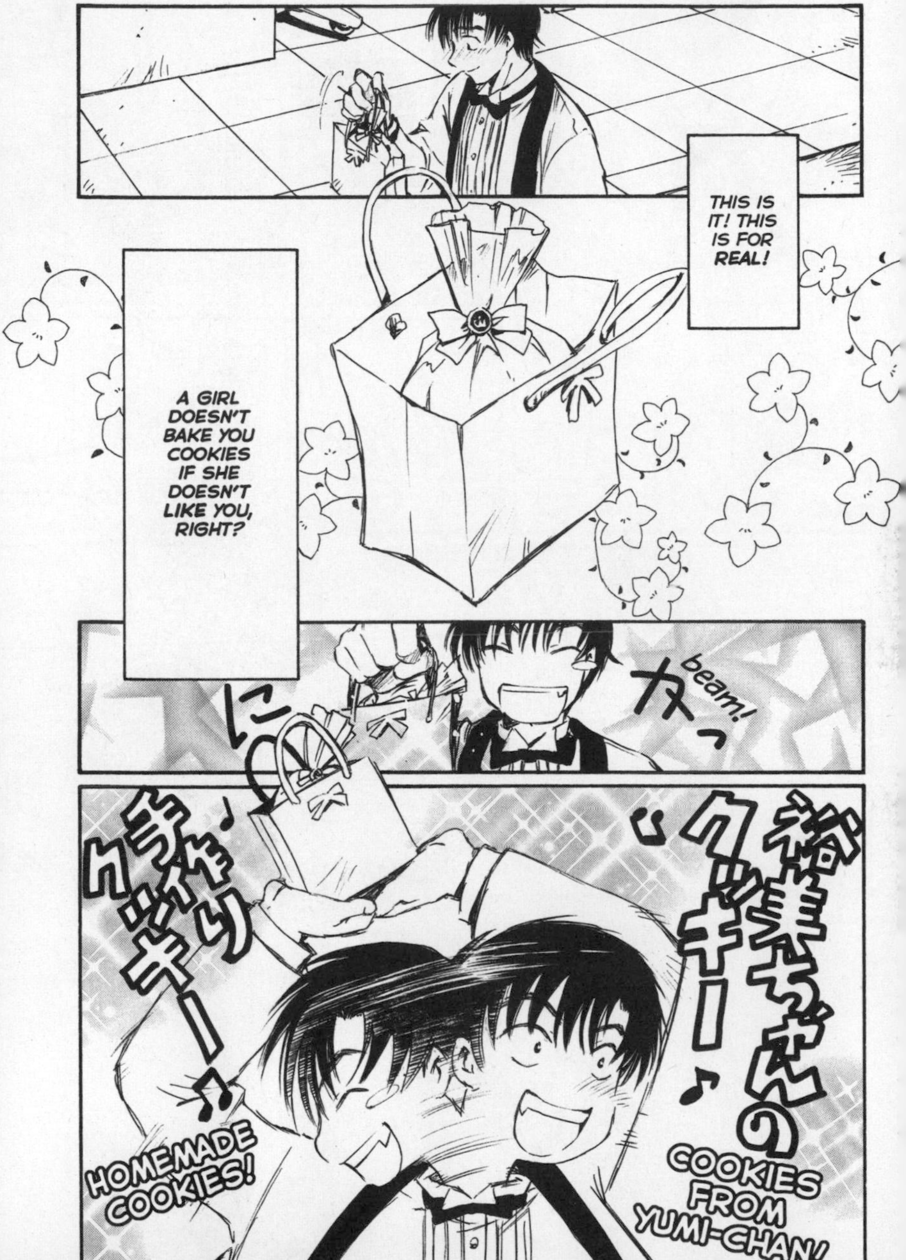
THIS IS IT! THIS IS FOR REAL!
A GIRL DOESN'T BAKE YOU COOKIES IF SHE DOESN'T LIKE YOU, RIGHT?
カッ
beam!
にっ
裕美ちゃんのクッキー♪
COOKIES FROM YUMI-CHAN!
手作りクッキー♪
HOMEMADE COOKIES!

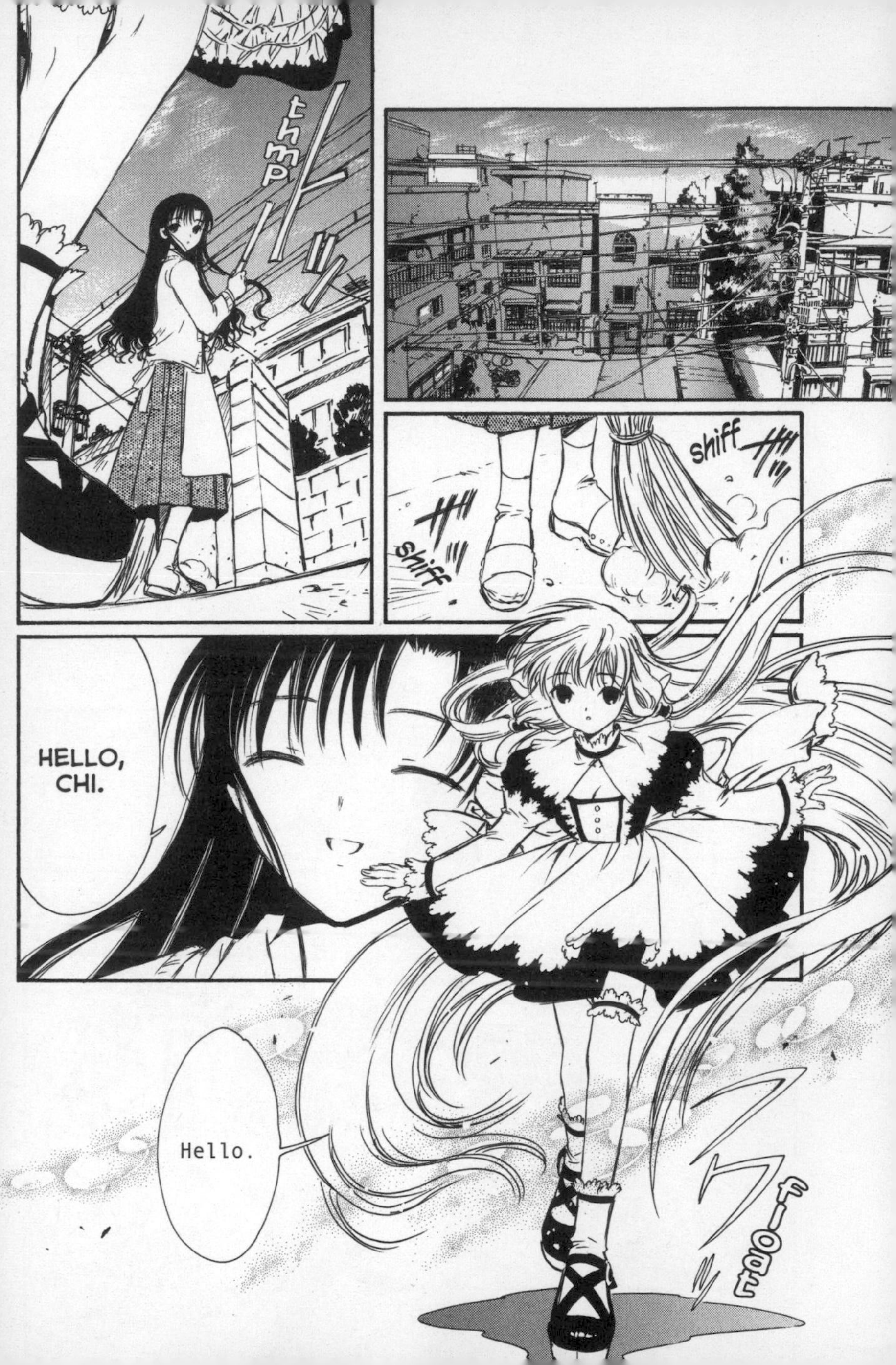
shiff
shiff
thmp
HELLO, CHI.
Hello.
float

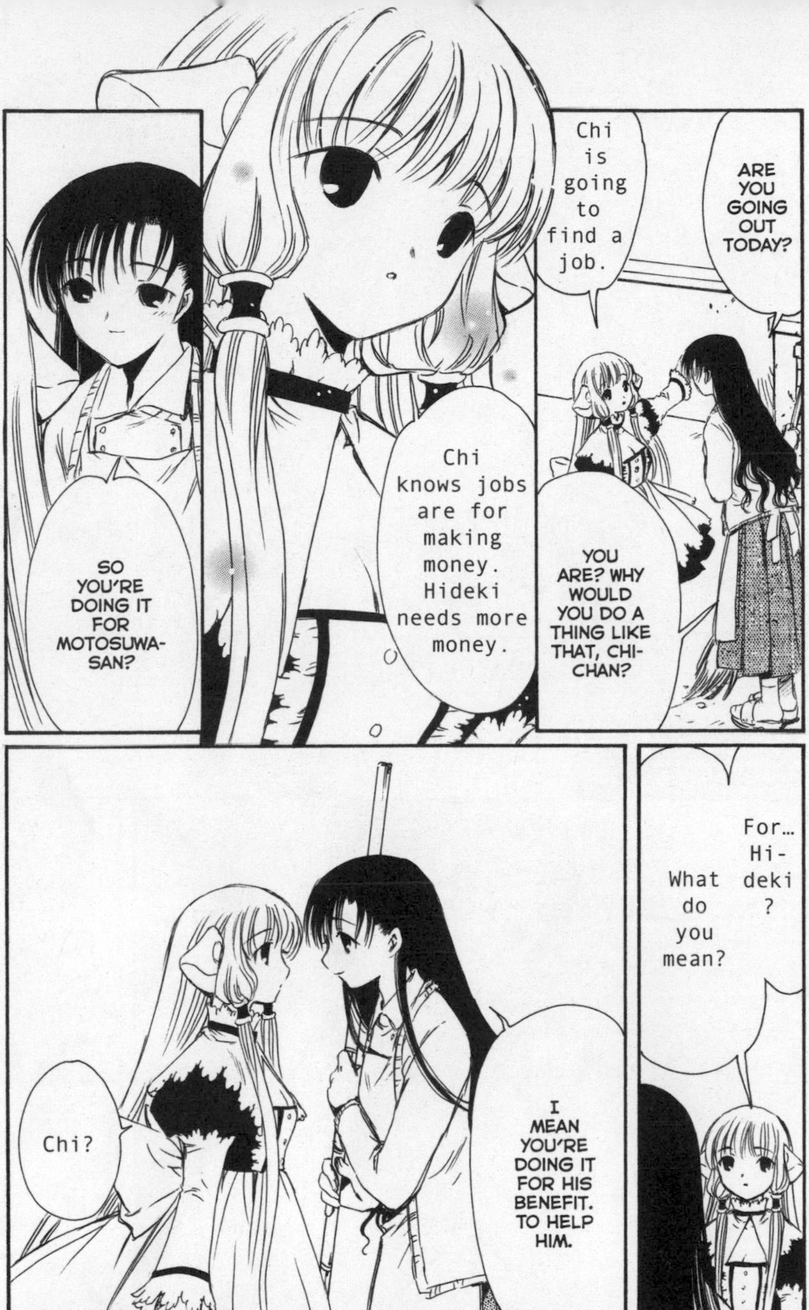
ARE YOU GOING OUT TODAY?
Chi is going to find a job.
YOU ARE? WHY WOULD YOU DO A THING LIKE THAT, CHI-CHAN?
Chi knows jobs are for making money. Hideki needs more money.
SO YOU'RE DOING IT FOR MOTOSUWA-SAN?
For… Hi-deki ?
What do you mean?
I MEAN YOU'RE DOING IT FOR HIS BENEFIT. TO HELP HIM.
Chi?

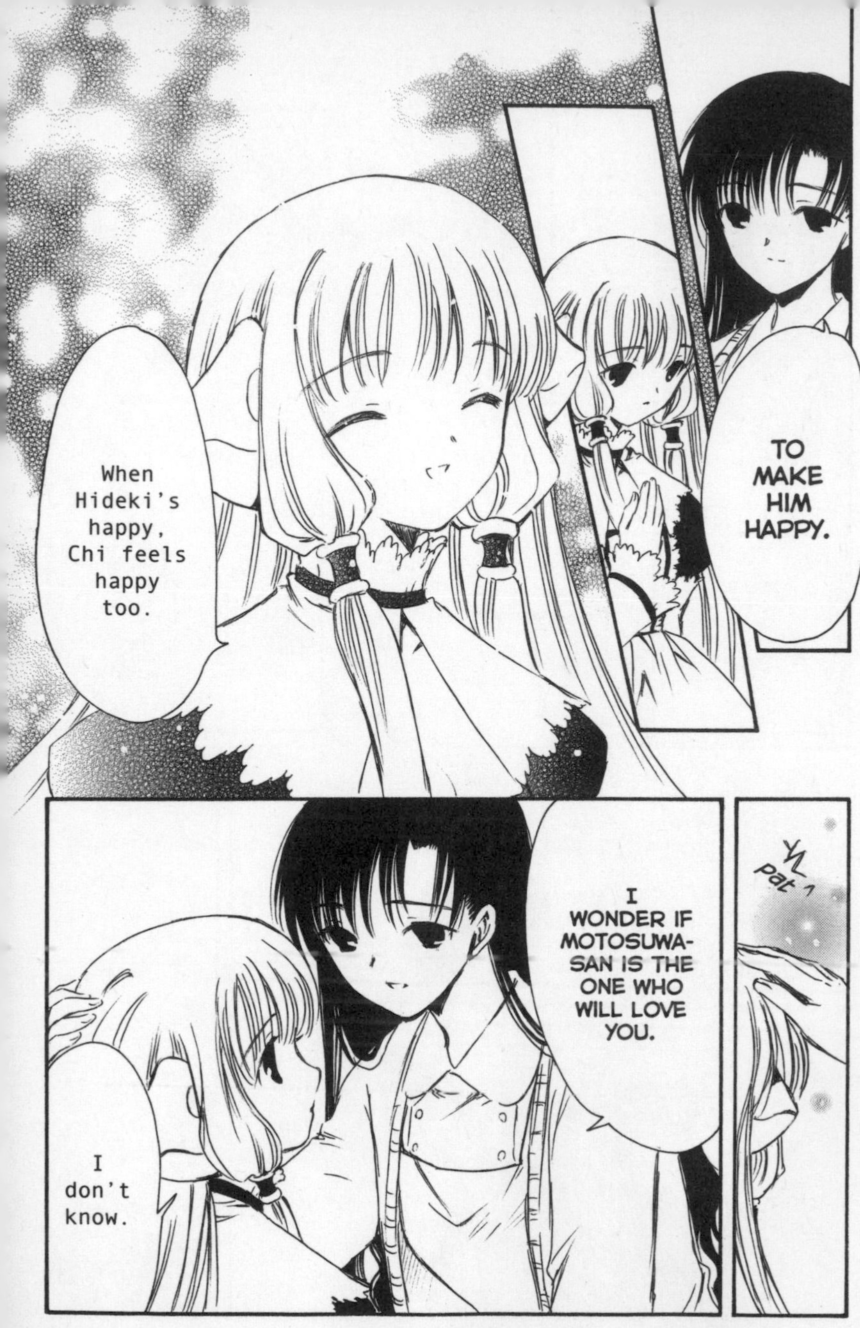
TO MAKE HIM HAPPY.
When Hideki's happy, Chi feels happy too.
pat
I WONDER IF MOTOSUWA-SAN IS THE ONE WHO WILL LOVE YOU.
I don't know.

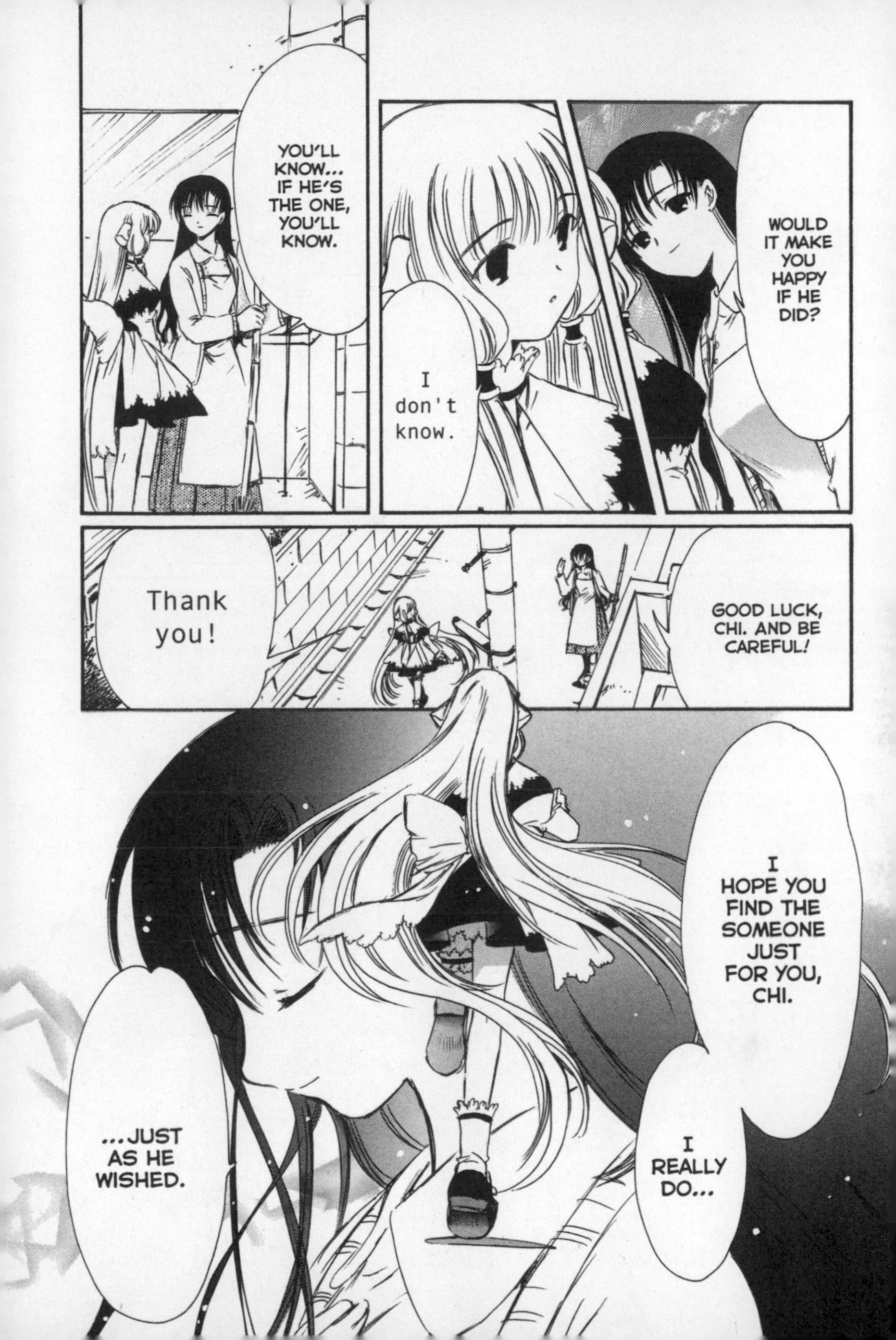
WOULD IT MAKE YOU HAPPY IF HE DID?
I don't know.
YOU'LL KNOW... IF HE'S THE ONE, YOU'LL KNOW.
GOOD LUCK, CHI. AND BE CAREFUL!
Thank you!
I HOPE YOU FIND THE SOMEONE JUST FOR YOU, CHI.
I REALLY DO...
...JUST AS HE WISHED.

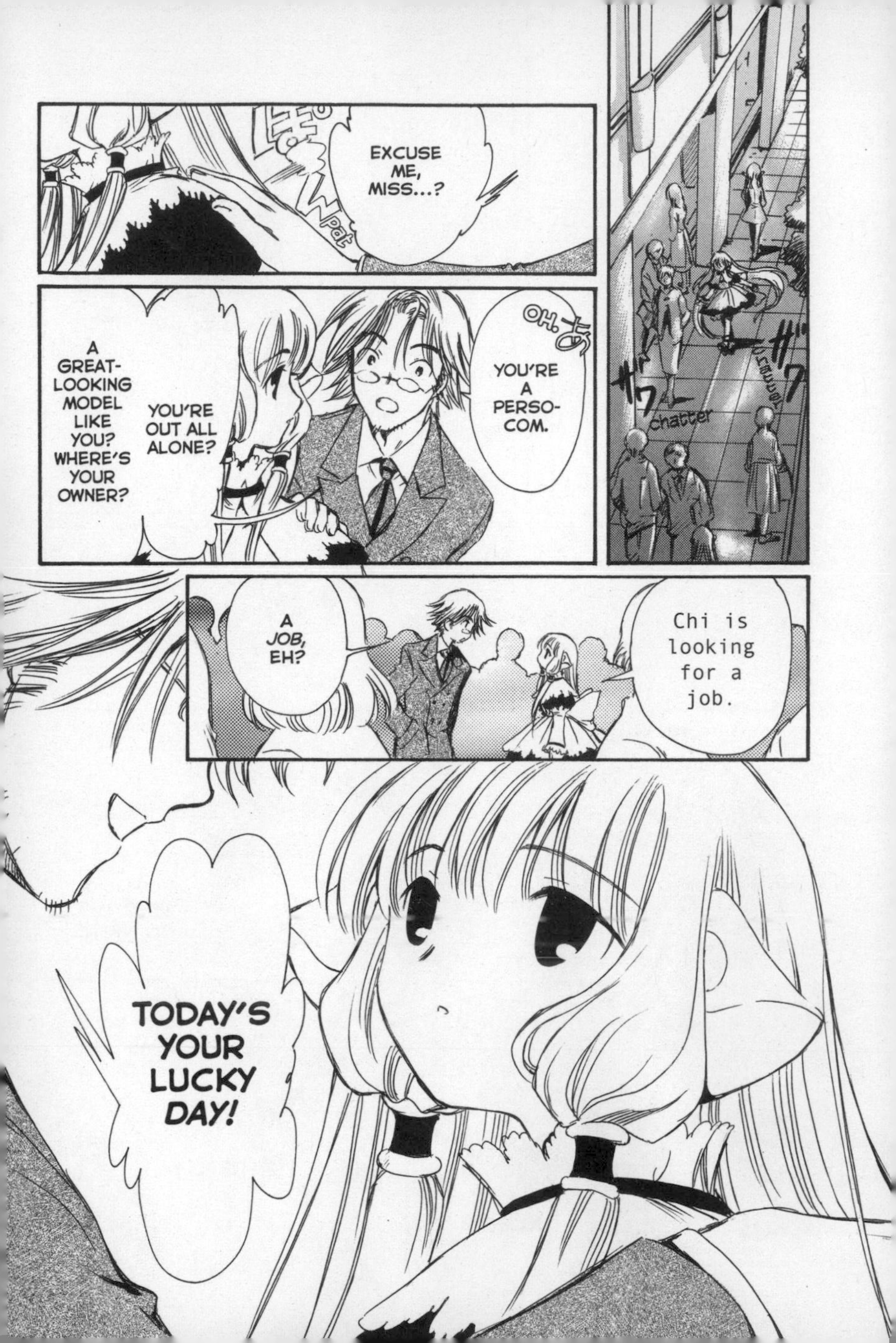
chatter
EXCUSE ME, MISS...?
pat
OH.
YOU'RE A PERSO-COM.
YOU'RE OUT ALL ALONE?
A GREAT-LOOKING MODEL LIKE YOU? WHERE'S YOUR OWNER?
Chi is looking for a job.
A JOB, EH?
TODAY'S YOUR LUCKY DAY!

◀ chapter 21 ▶

Chobits
ちょびっツ

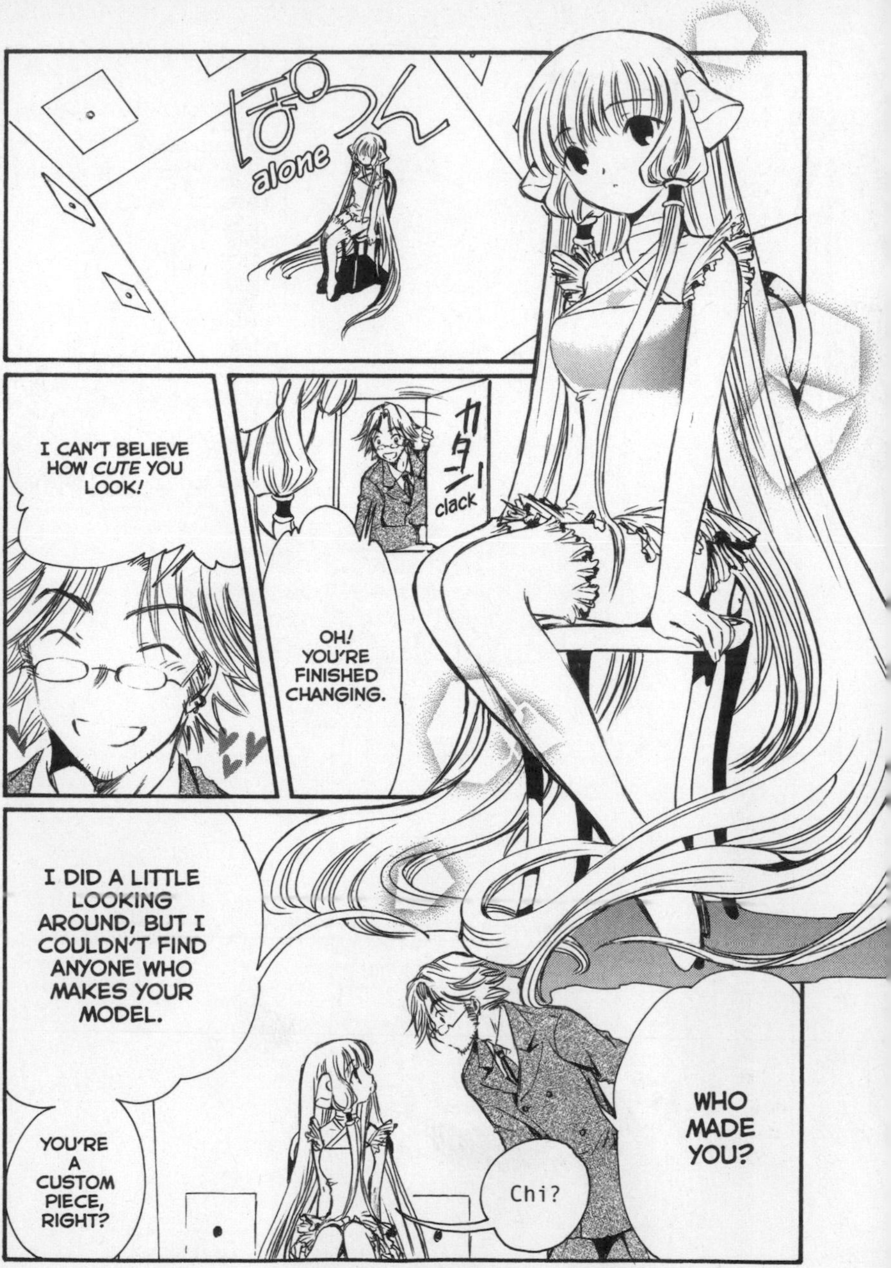
ぽつん
alone
カタン
clack
OH! YOU'RE FINISHED CHANGING.
I CAN'T BELIEVE HOW *CUTE* YOU LOOK!
I DID A LITTLE LOOKING AROUND, BUT I COULDN'T FIND ANYONE WHO MAKES YOUR MODEL.
YOU'RE A CUSTOM PIECE, RIGHT?
WHO MADE YOU?
Chi?

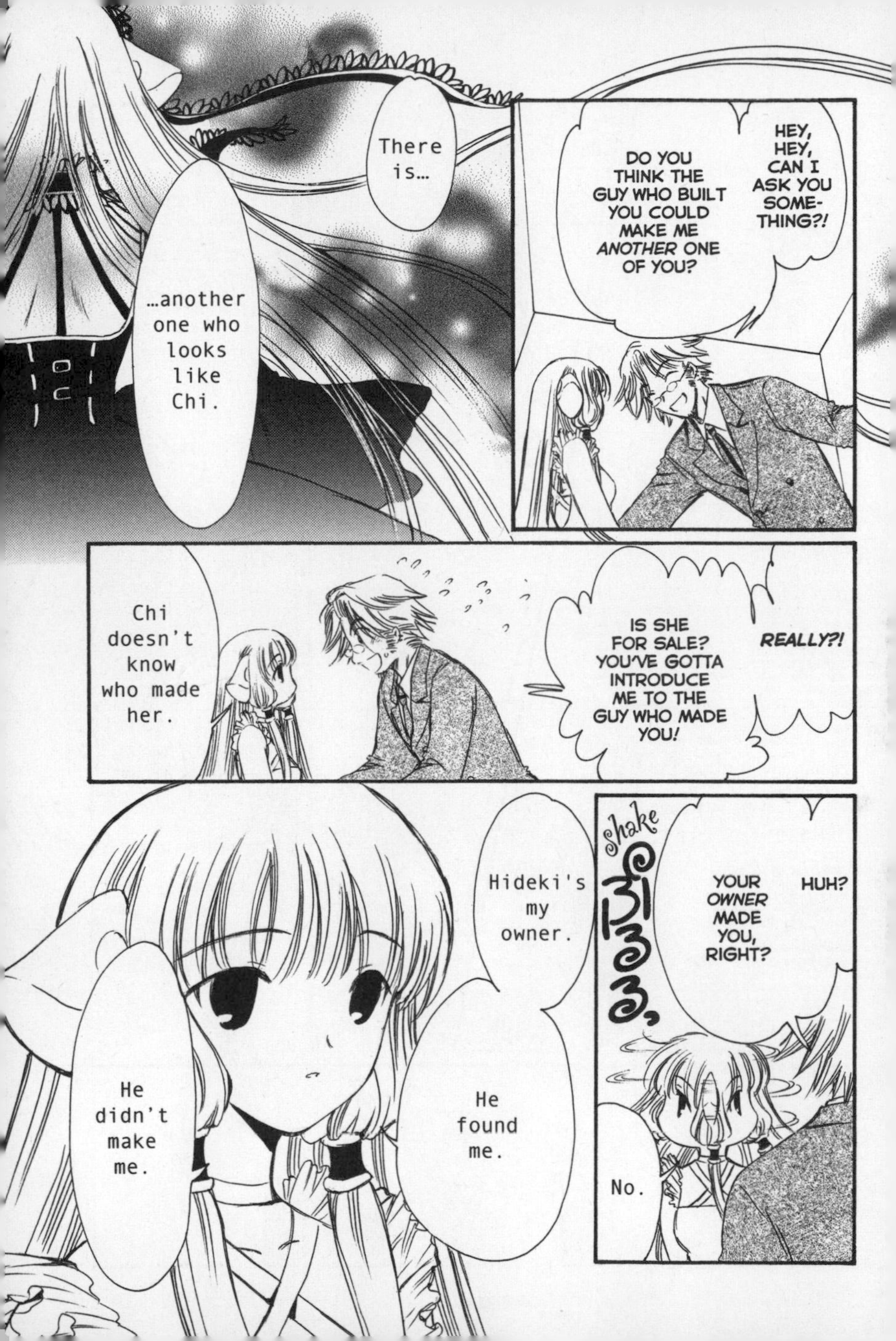
HEY, HEY, CAN I ASK YOU SOME-THING?!
DO YOU THINK THE GUY WHO BUILT YOU COULD MAKE ME *ANOTHER* ONE OF YOU?
There is...
...another one who looks like Chi.
REALLY?!
IS SHE FOR SALE? YOU'VE GOTTA INTRODUCE ME TO THE GUY WHO MADE *YOU!*
Chi doesn't know who made her.
HUH?
YOUR *OWNER* MADE YOU, RIGHT?
shake
No.
Hideki's my owner.
He found me.
He didn't make me.

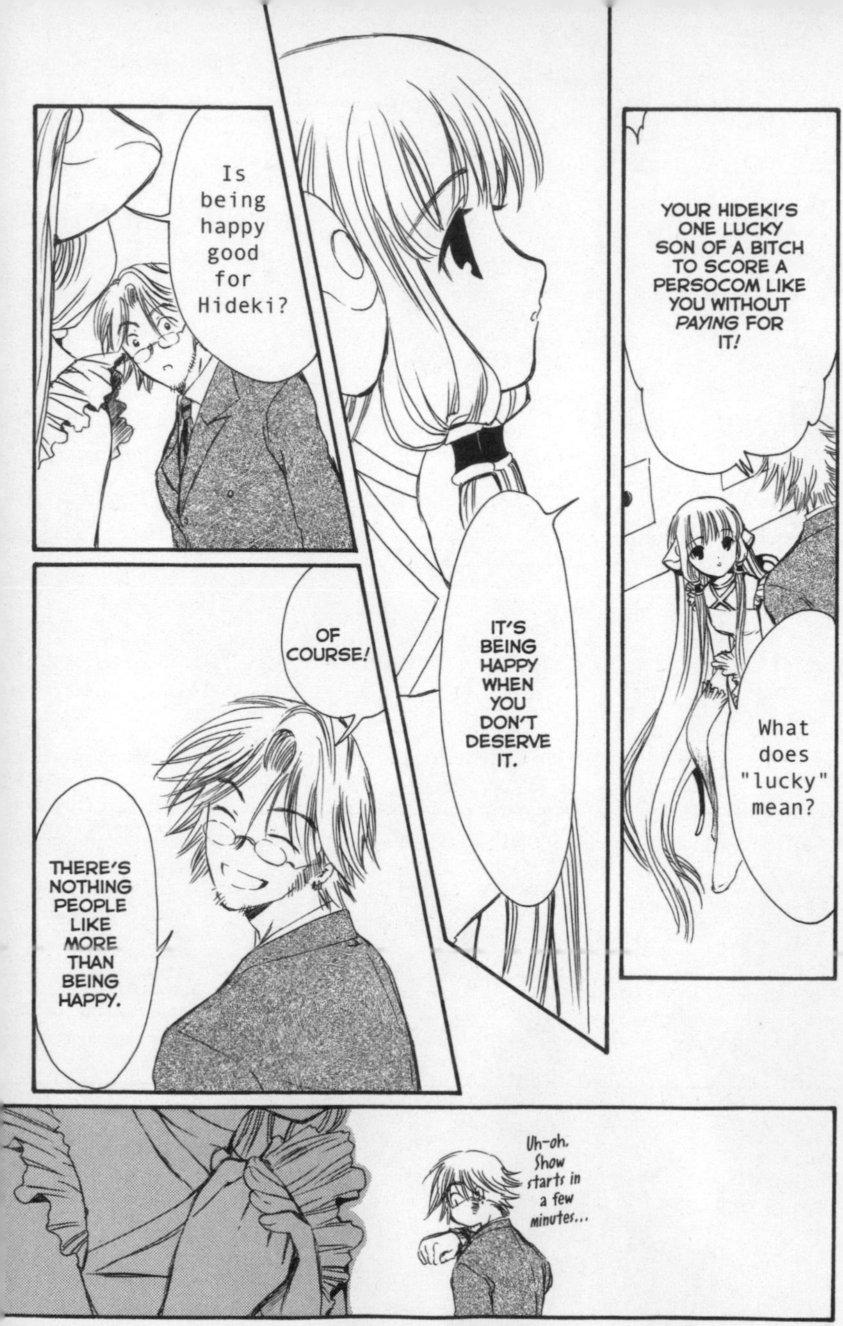
YOUR HIDEKI'S ONE LUCKY SON OF A BITCH TO SCORE A PERSOCOM LIKE YOU WITHOUT *PAYING* FOR IT!
What does "lucky" mean?
IT'S BEING HAPPY WHEN YOU DON'T DESERVE IT.
Is being happy good for Hideki?
OF COURSE!
THERE'S NOTHING PEOPLE LIKE MORE THAN BEING HAPPY.
Uh-oh. Show starts in a few minutes...

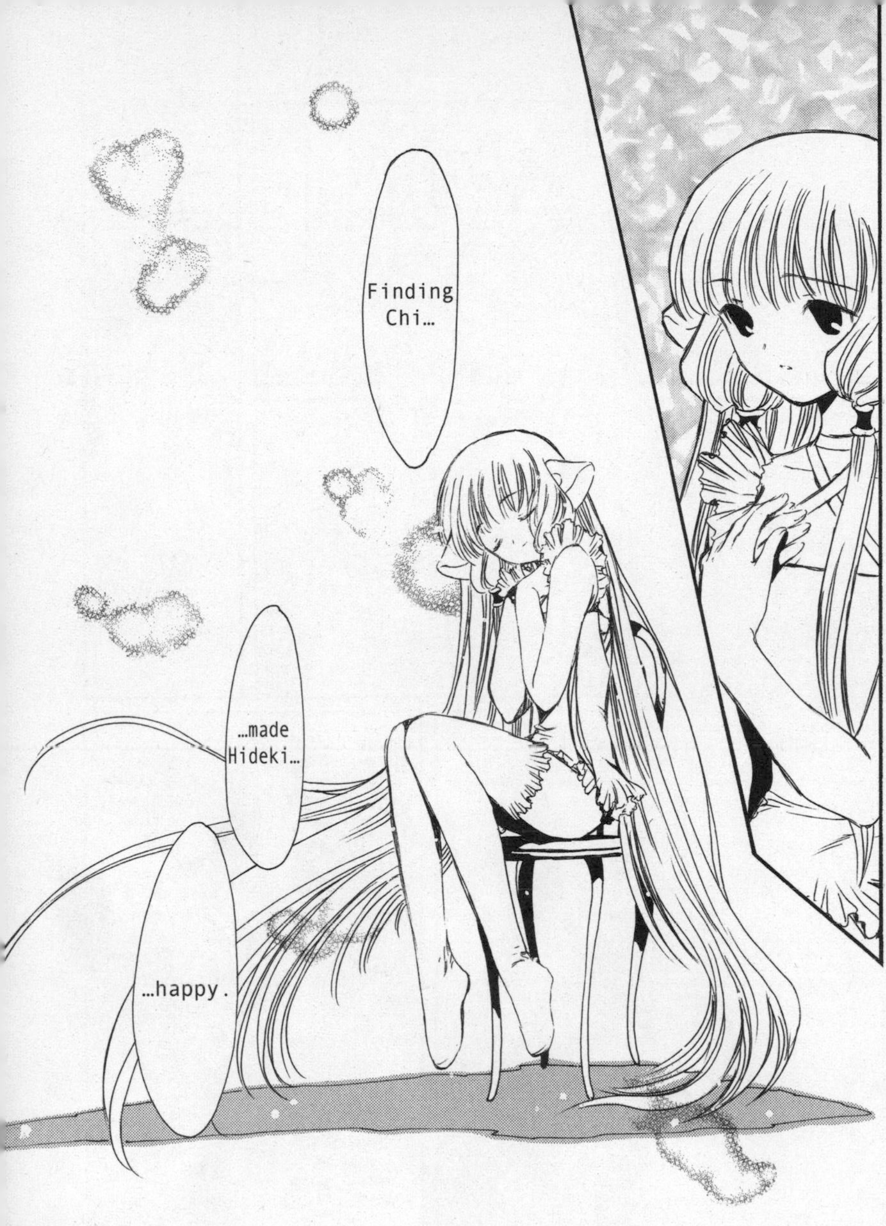
Finding Chi…
…made Hideki…
…happy.

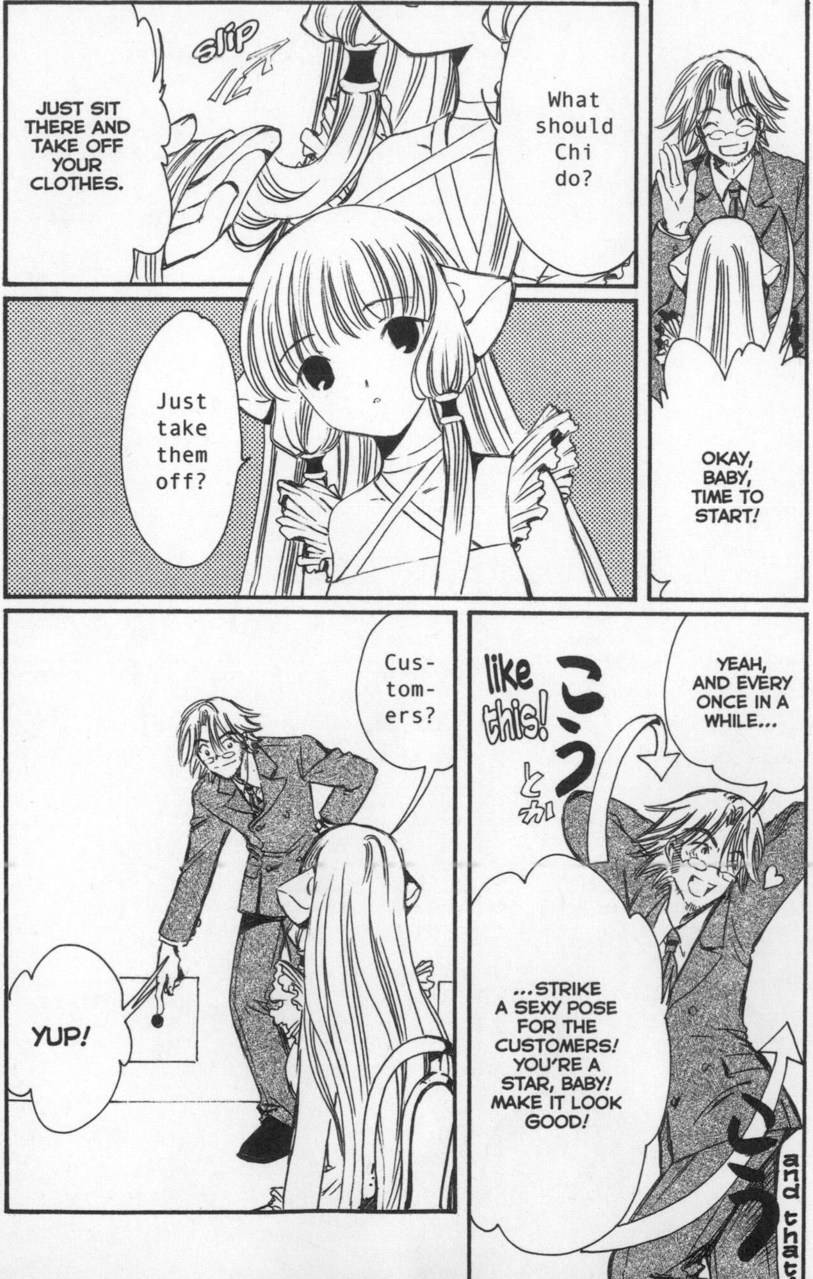
OKAY, BABY, TIME TO START!
What should Chi do?
slip
JUST SIT THERE AND TAKE OFF YOUR CLOTHES.
Just take them off?
YEAH, AND EVERY ONCE IN A WHILE...
like this!
...STRIKE A SEXY POSE FOR THE CUSTOMERS! YOU'RE A STAR, BABY! MAKE IT LOOK GOOD!
and that!
Cus-tom-ers?
YUP!

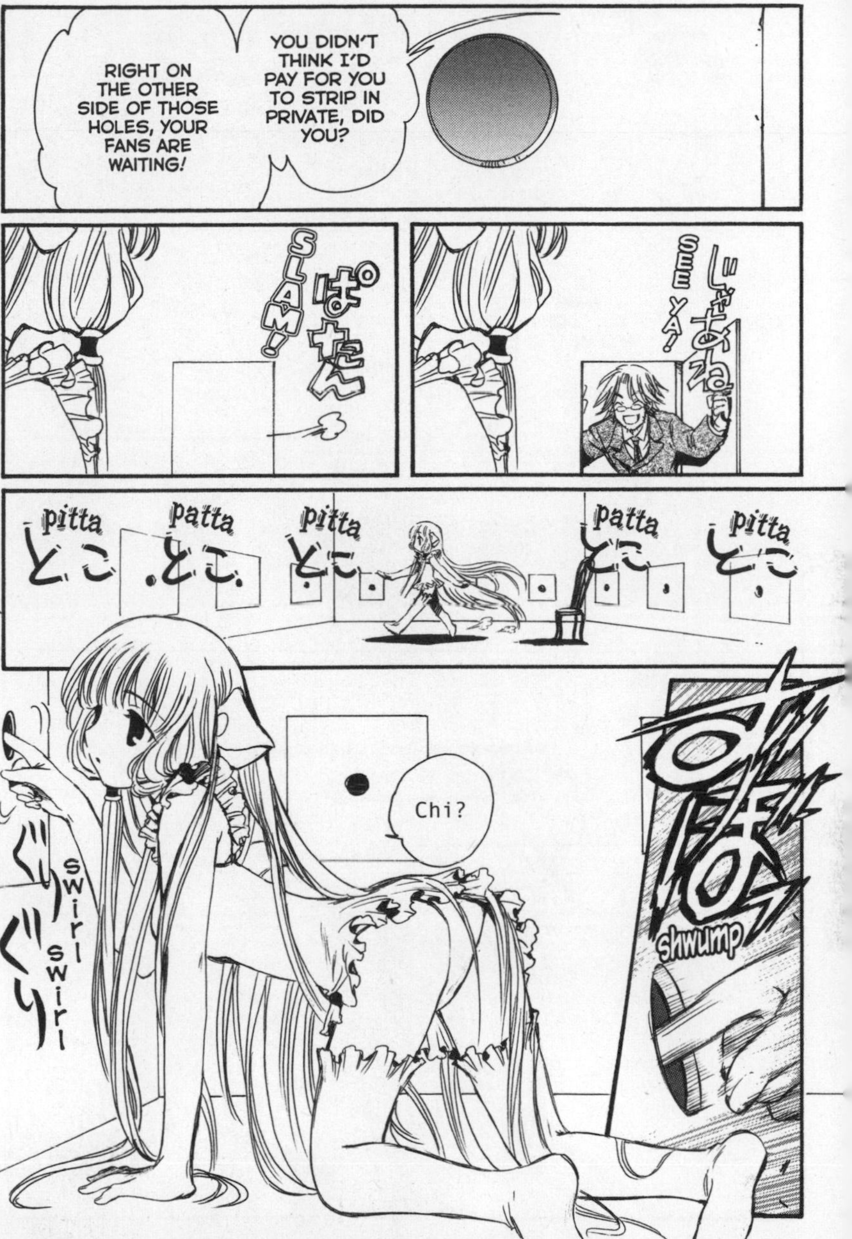
YOU DIDN'T THINK I'D PAY FOR YOU TO STRIP IN PRIVATE, DID YOU?
RIGHT ON THE OTHER SIDE OF THOSE HOLES, YOUR FANS ARE WAITING!
じゃあね
SEE YA!
ぱたん
SLAM!
どこ pitta
どこ patta
どこ pitta
どこ patta
どこ pitta
shwump
Chi?
ぐりぐり
swirl swirl

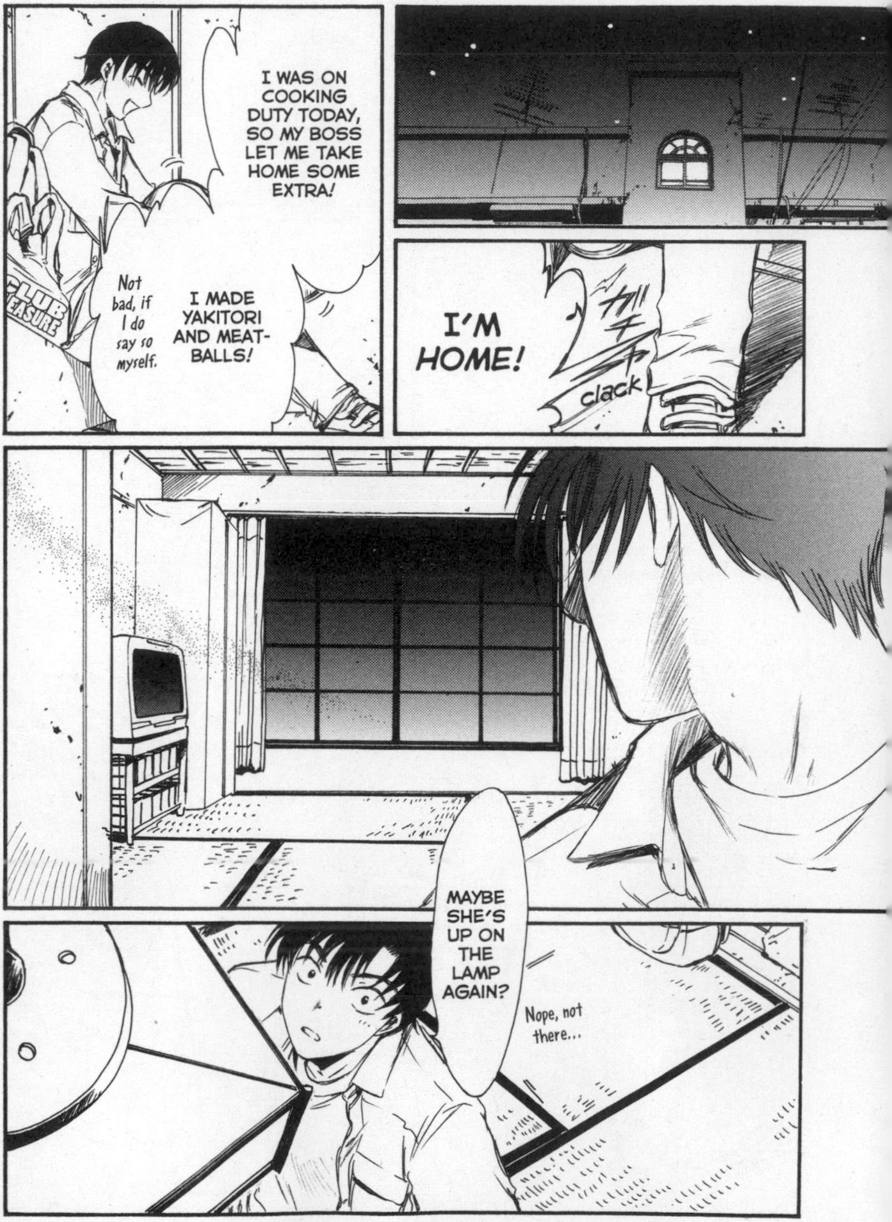
I'M HOME!
clack
I WAS ON COOKING DUTY TODAY, SO MY BOSS LET ME TAKE HOME SOME EXTRA!
I MADE YAKITORI AND MEAT-BALLS!
Not bad, if I do say so myself.
MAYBE SHE'S UP ON THE LAMP AGAIN?
Nope, not there...

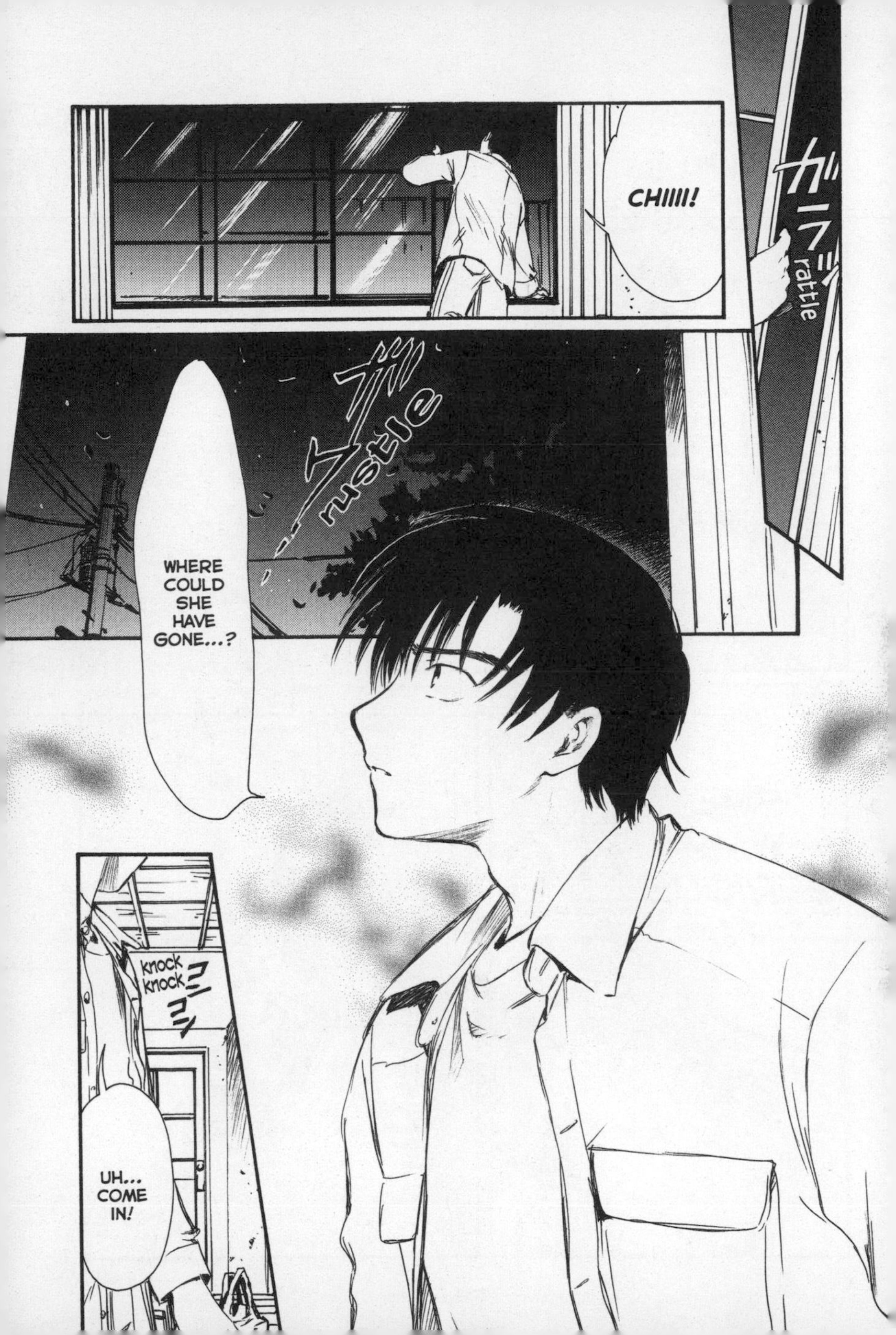
rattle
CHIIII!
rustle
WHERE COULD SHE HAVE GONE...?
knock knock
UH... COME IN!

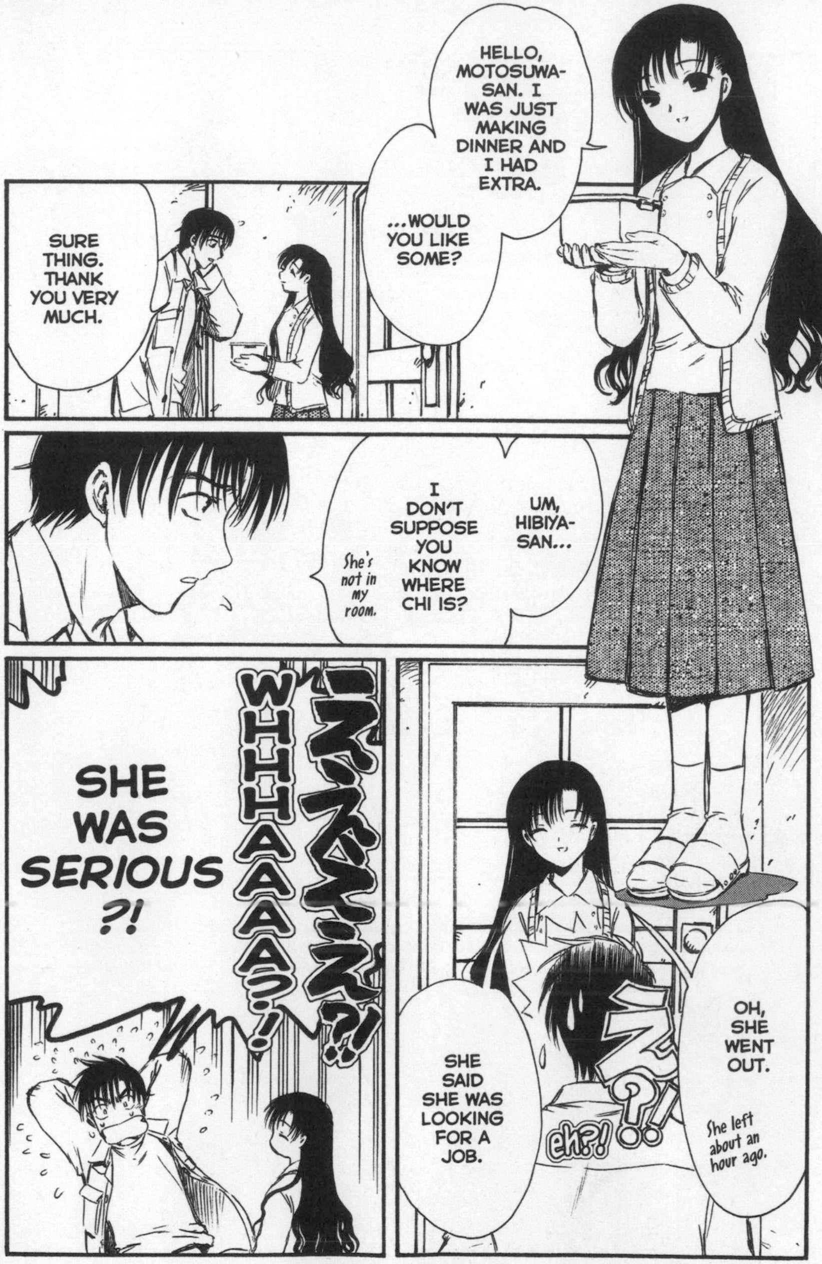
HELLO, MOTOSUWA-SAN. I WAS JUST MAKING DINNER AND I HAD EXTRA.
...WOULD YOU LIKE SOME?
SURE THING. THANK YOU VERY MUCH.
UM, HIBIYA-SAN...
I DON'T SUPPOSE YOU KNOW WHERE CHI IS?
She's not in my room.
OH, SHE WENT OUT.
She left about an hour ago.
SHE SAID SHE WAS LOOKING FOR A JOB.
eh?!
WHHHAAAAA?!
SHE WAS SERIOUS?!

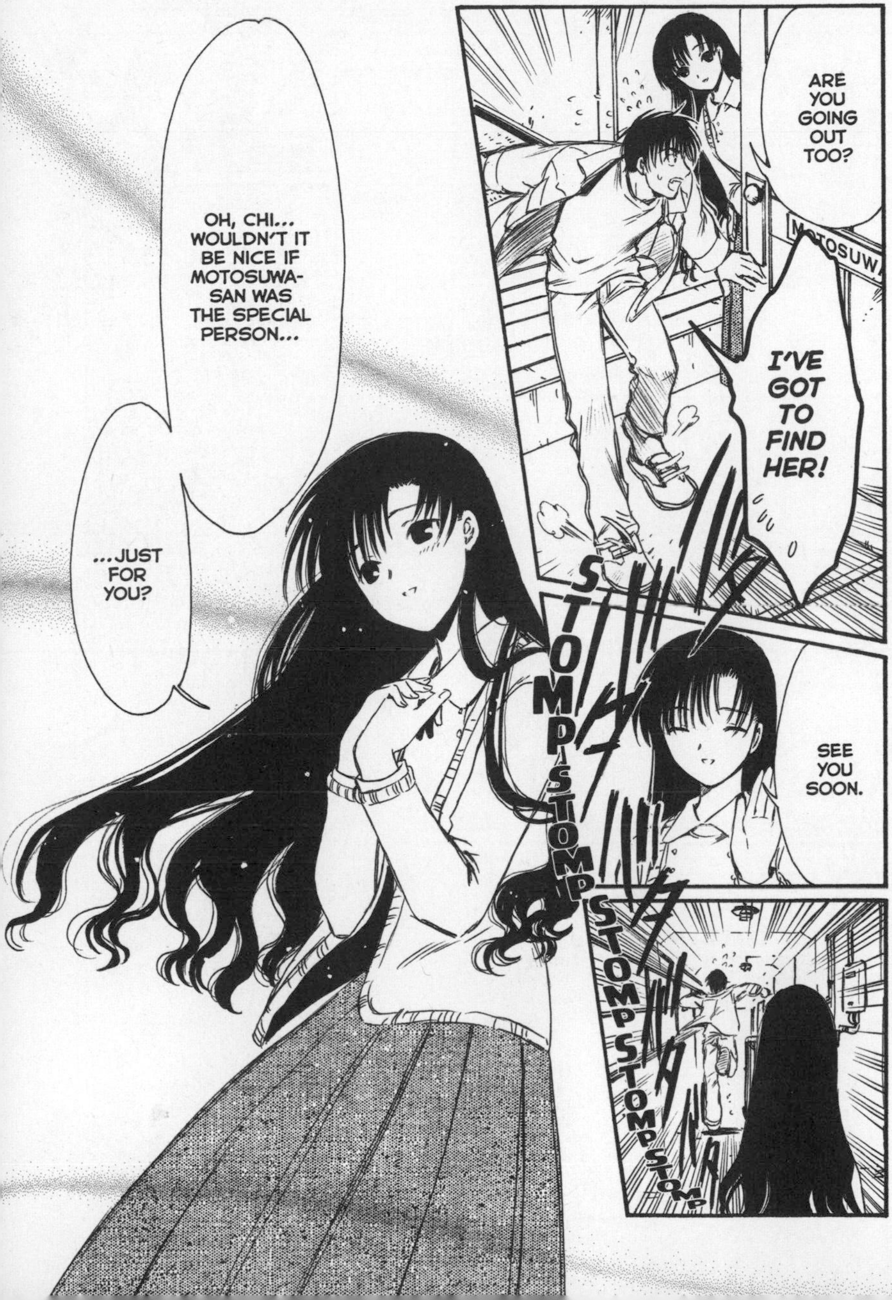

ARE YOU GOING OUT TOO?
I'VE GOT TO FIND HER!
STOMP STOMP STOMP
SEE YOU SOON.
STOMP STOMP STOMP
OH, CHI... WOULDN'T IT BE NICE IF MOTOSUWA-SAN WAS THE SPECIAL PERSON...
...JUST FOR YOU?

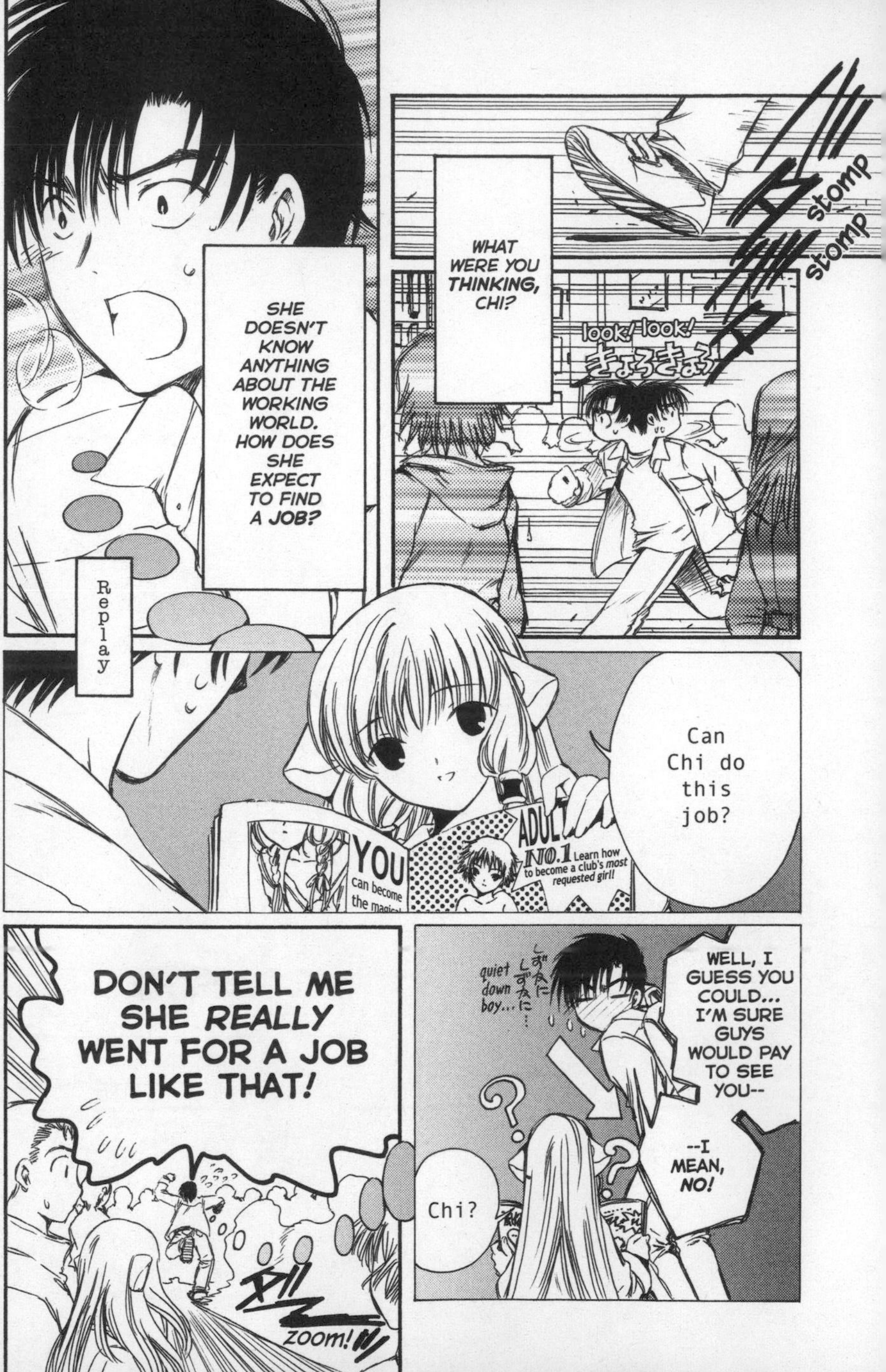
stomp stomp
WHAT WERE YOU THINKING, CHI?
look! look!
きょろきょろ
SHE DOESN'T KNOW ANYTHING ABOUT THE WORKING WORLD. HOW DOES SHE EXPECT TO FIND A JOB?
Replay
Can Chi do this job?
YOU can become the magical
NO.1 Learn how to become a club's most requested girl!
WELL, I GUESS YOU COULD... I'M SURE GUYS WOULD PAY TO SEE YOU--
--I MEAN, NO!
quiet down boy...
しずかにしずかに…
Chi?
DON'T TELL ME SHE REALLY WENT FOR A JOB LIKE THAT!
zoom!

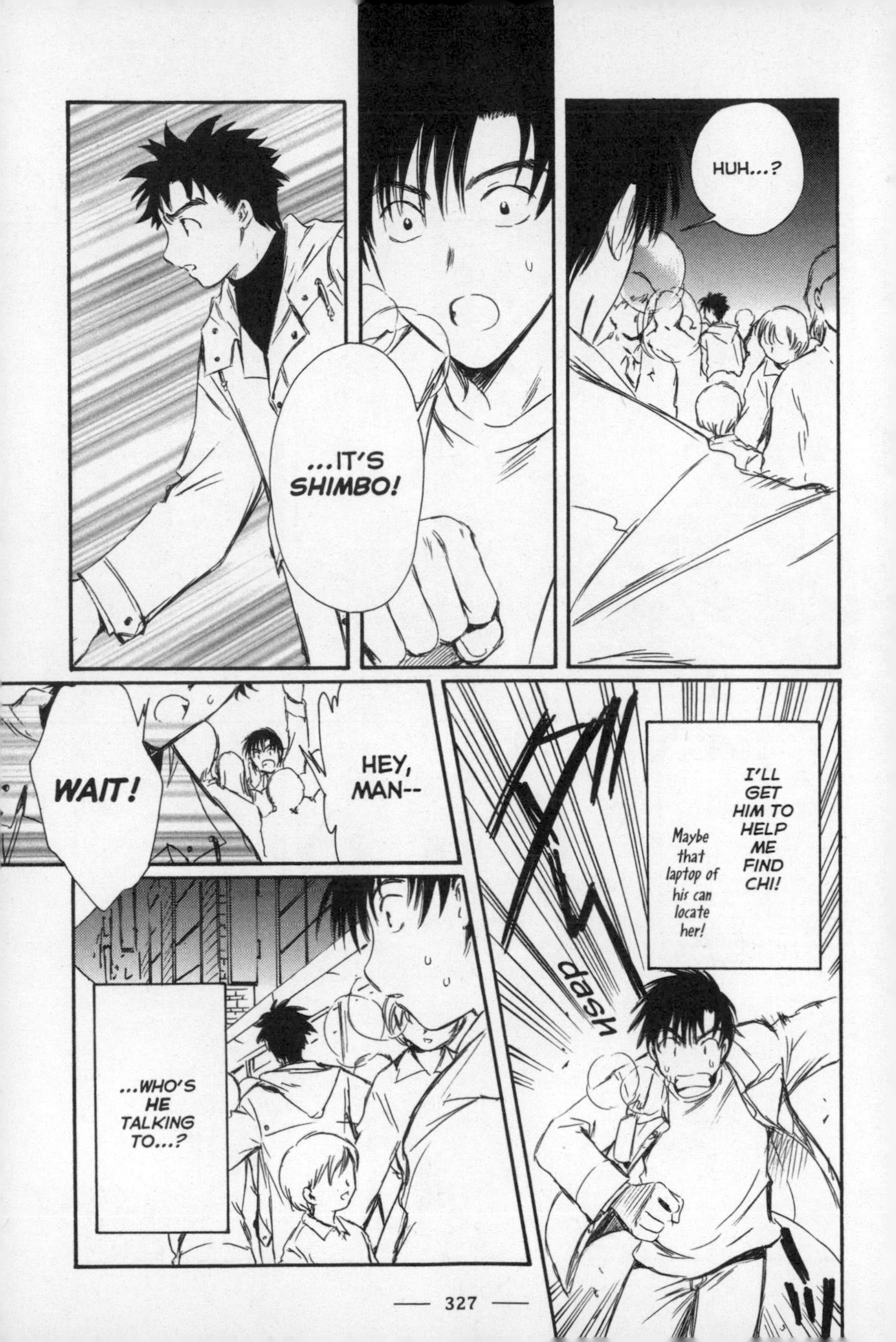
HUH...?
...IT'S SHIMBO!
I'LL GET HIM TO HELP ME FIND CHI!
Maybe that laptop of his can locate her!
dash
HEY, MAN--
WAIT!
...WHO'S HE TALKING TO...?

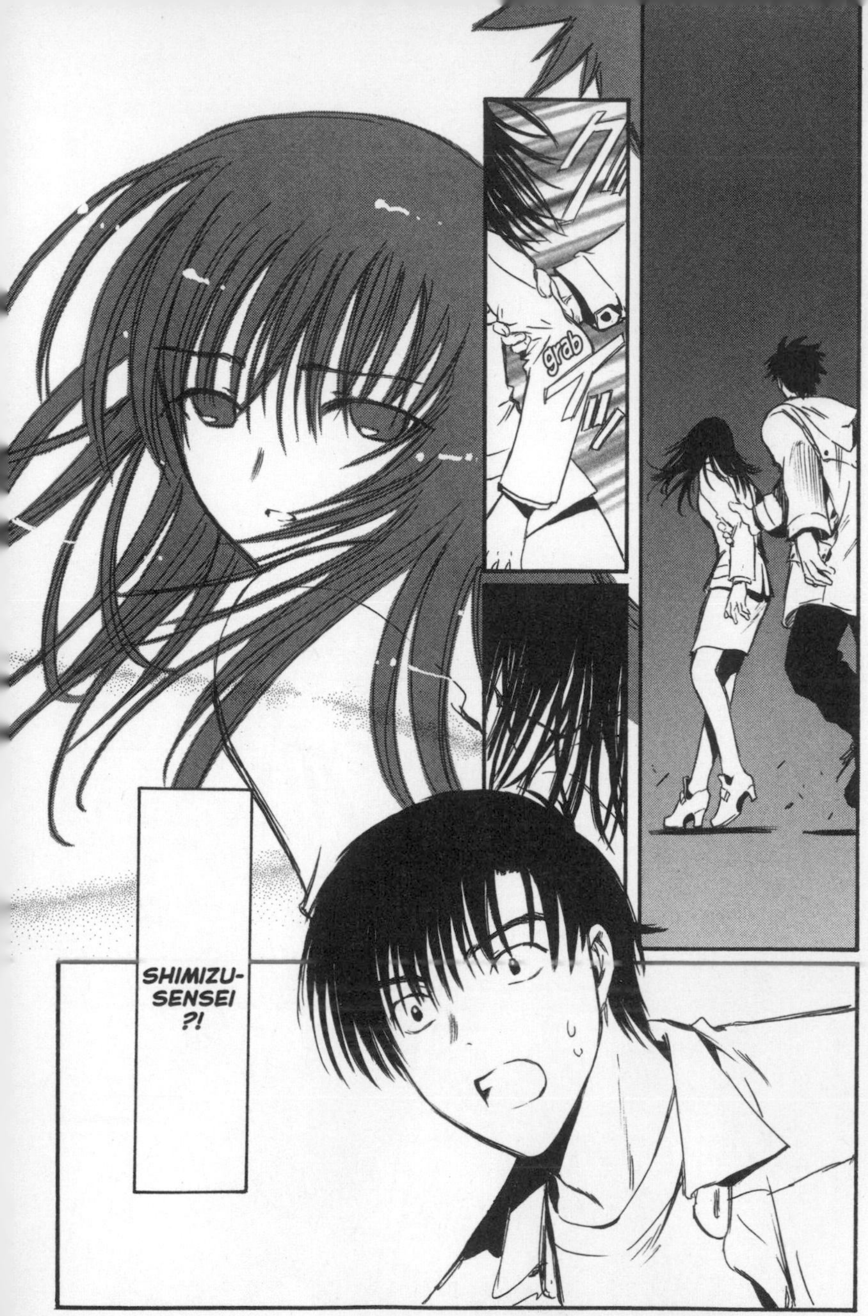
grab
SHIMIZU-SENSEI?!

Chobits
ちょびっツ

◀ **chapter 22** ▶

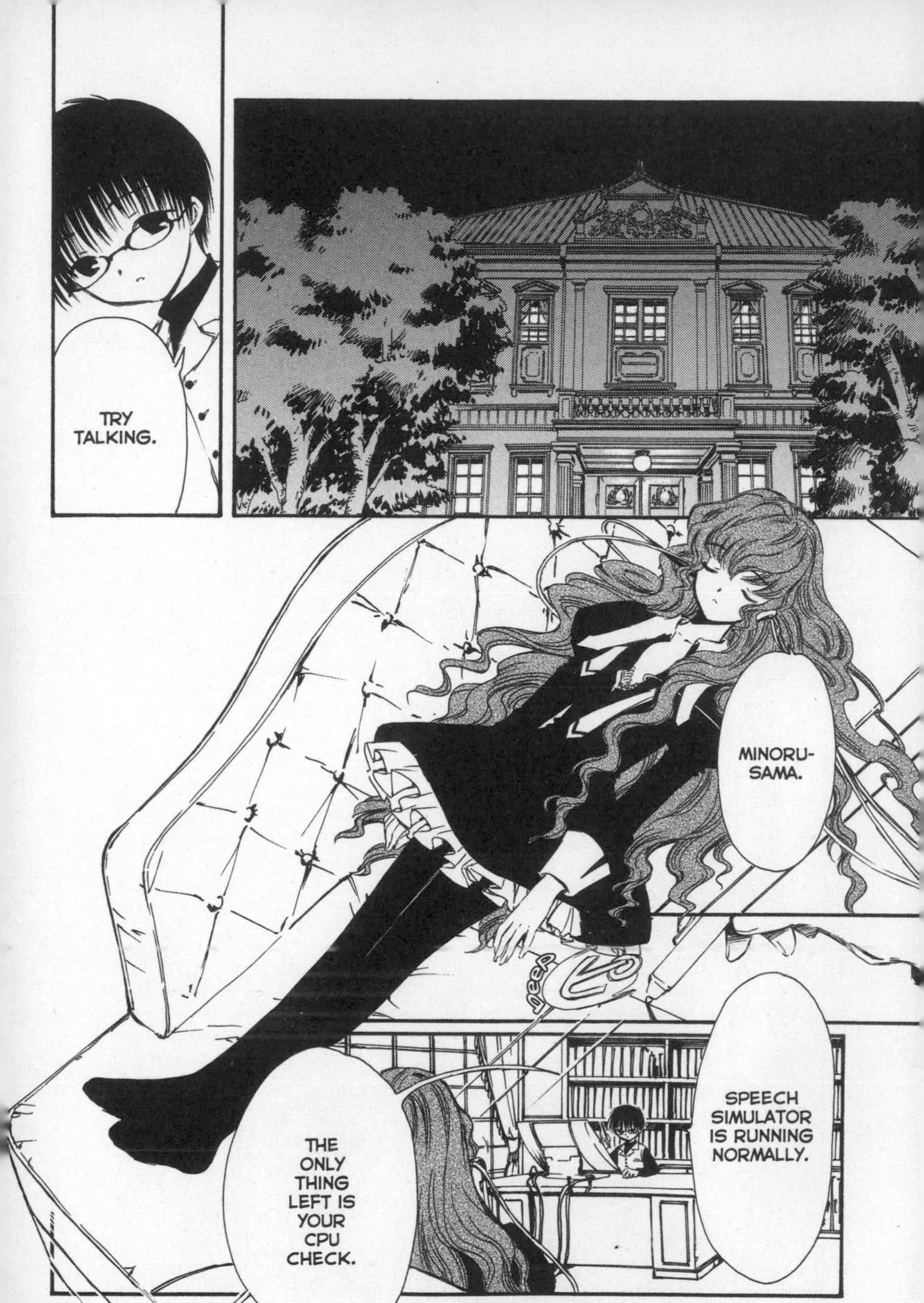
TRY TALKING.
MINORU-SAMA.
SPEECH SIMULATOR IS RUNNING NORMALLY.
THE ONLY THING LEFT IS YOUR CPU CHECK.

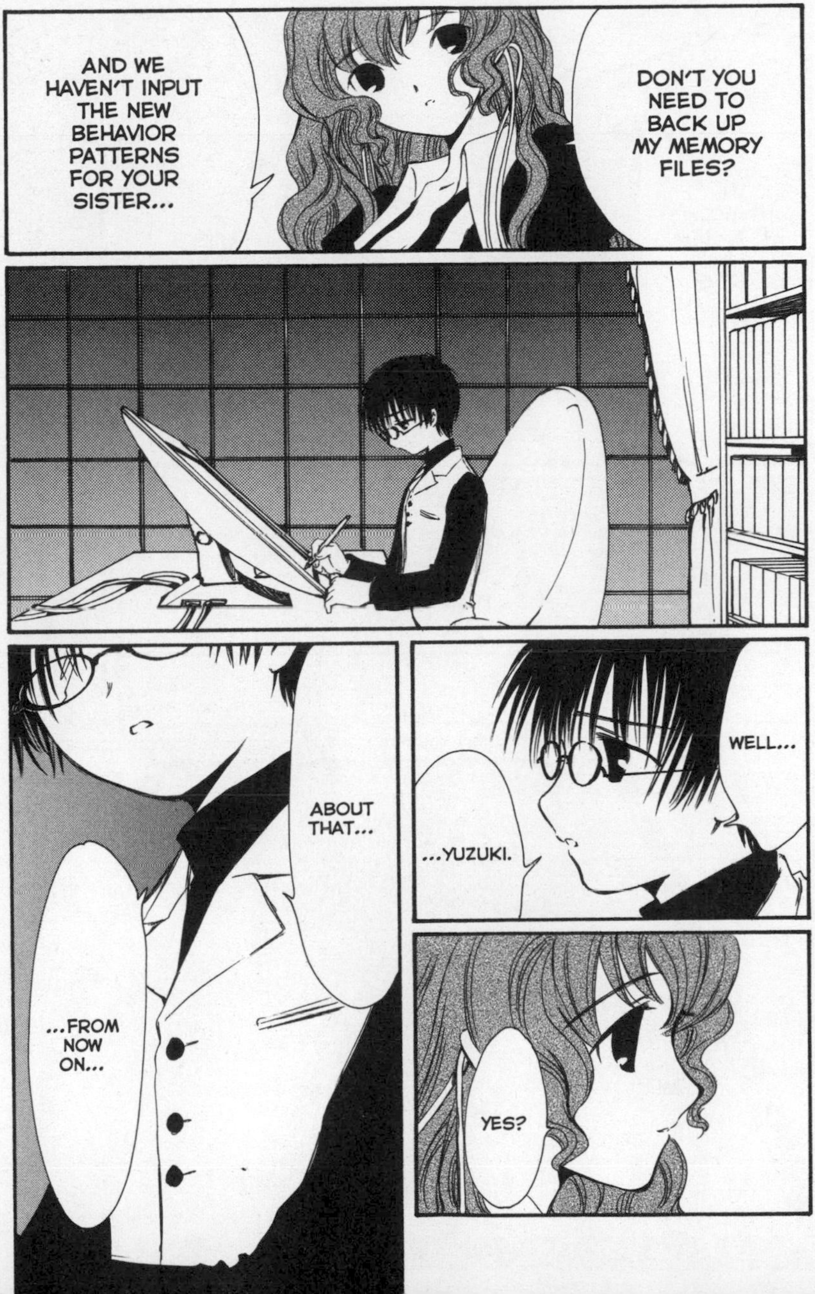
DON'T YOU NEED TO BACK UP MY MEMORY FILES?
AND WE HAVEN'T INPUT THE NEW BEHAVIOR PATTERNS FOR YOUR SISTER...
WELL...
...YUZUKI.
YES?
ABOUT THAT...
...FROM NOW ON...

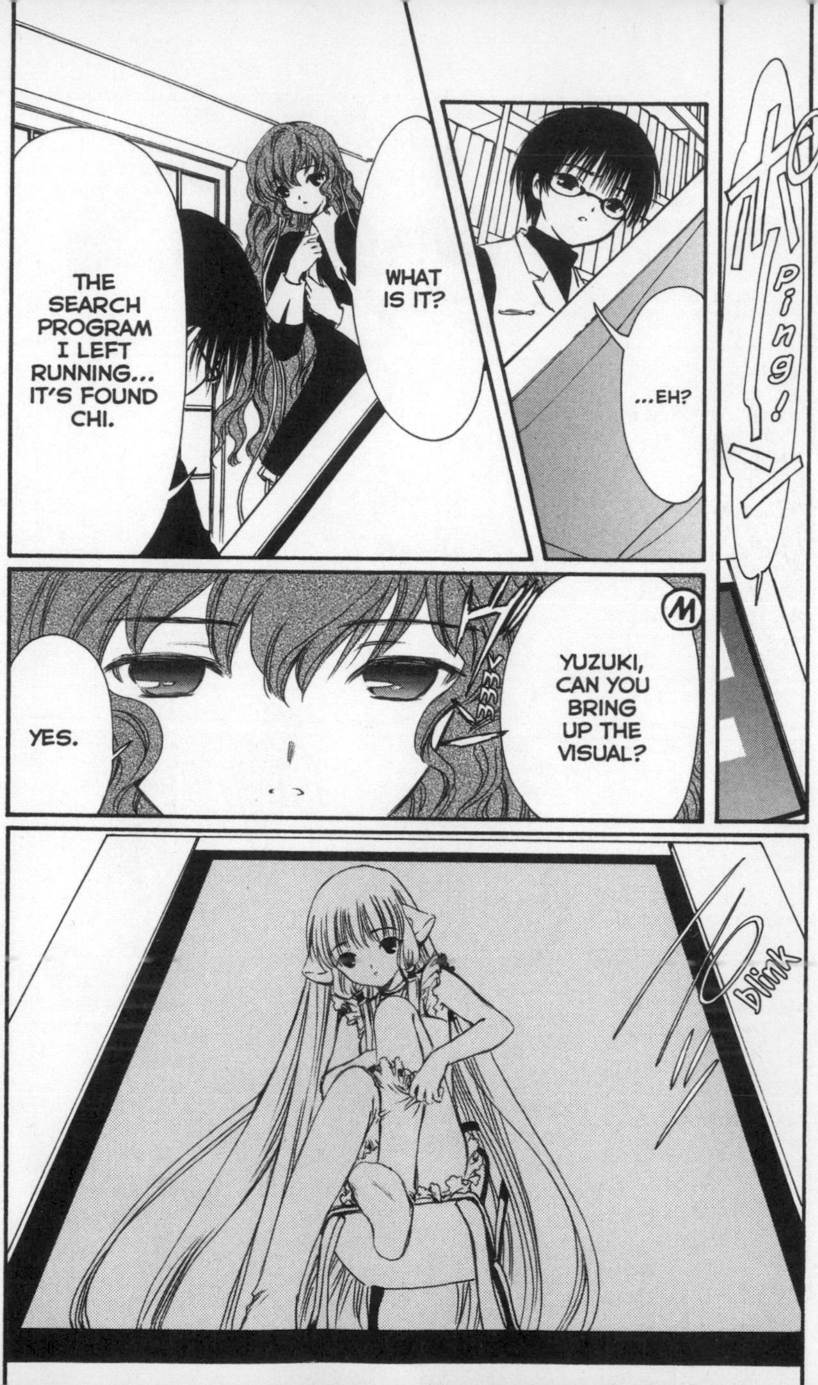
Ping!
...EH?
WHAT IS IT?
THE SEARCH PROGRAM I LEFT RUNNING... IT'S FOUND CHI.
YUZUKI, CAN YOU BRING UP THE VISUAL?
YES.
blink

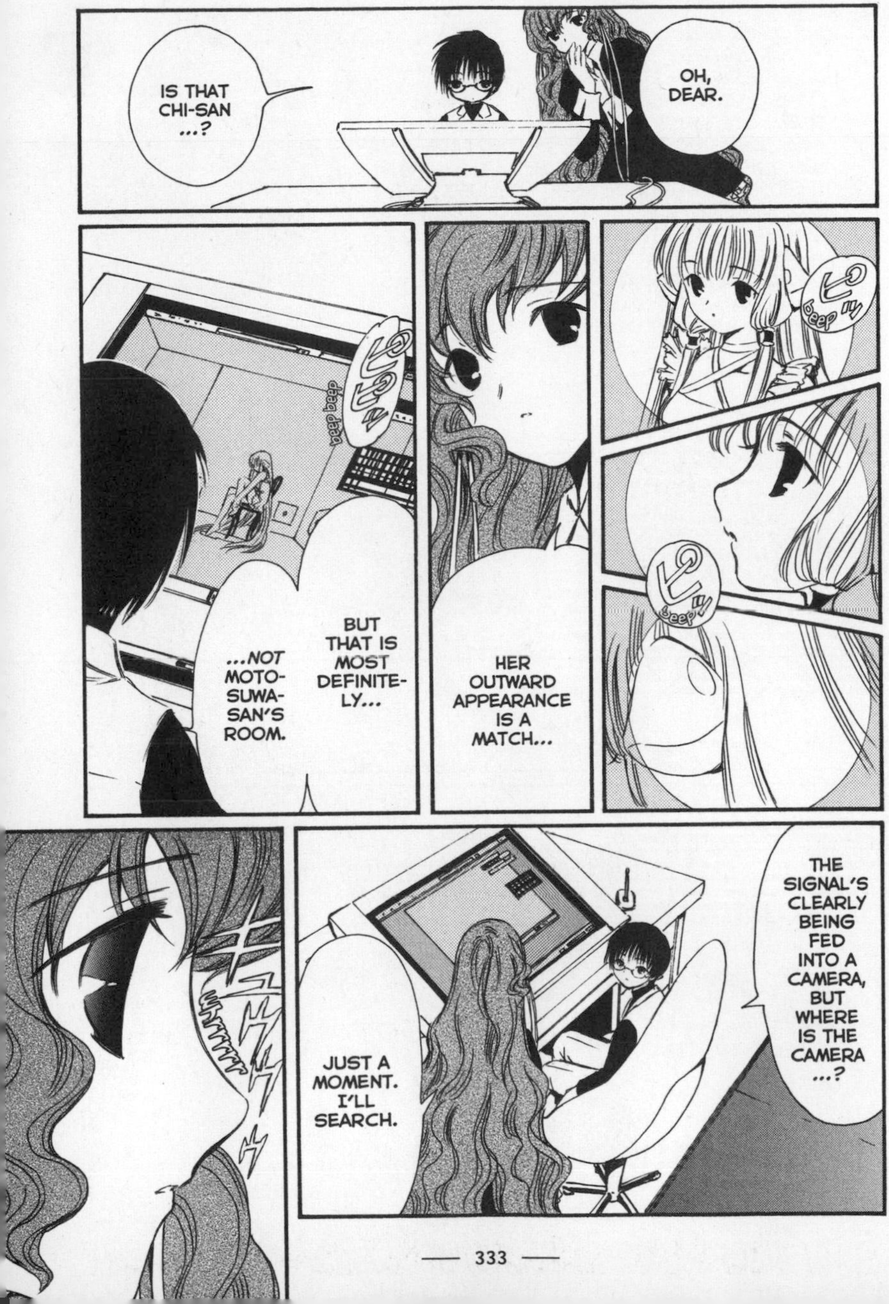
OH, DEAR.
IS THAT CHI-SAN ...?
beep
beep
HER OUTWARD APPEARANCE IS A MATCH...
beep beep
BUT THAT IS MOST DEFINITE-LY...
...NOT MOTO-SUWA-SAN'S ROOM.
THE SIGNAL'S CLEARLY BEING FED INTO A CAMERA, BUT WHERE IS THE CAMERA ...?
JUST A MOMENT. I'LL SEARCH.

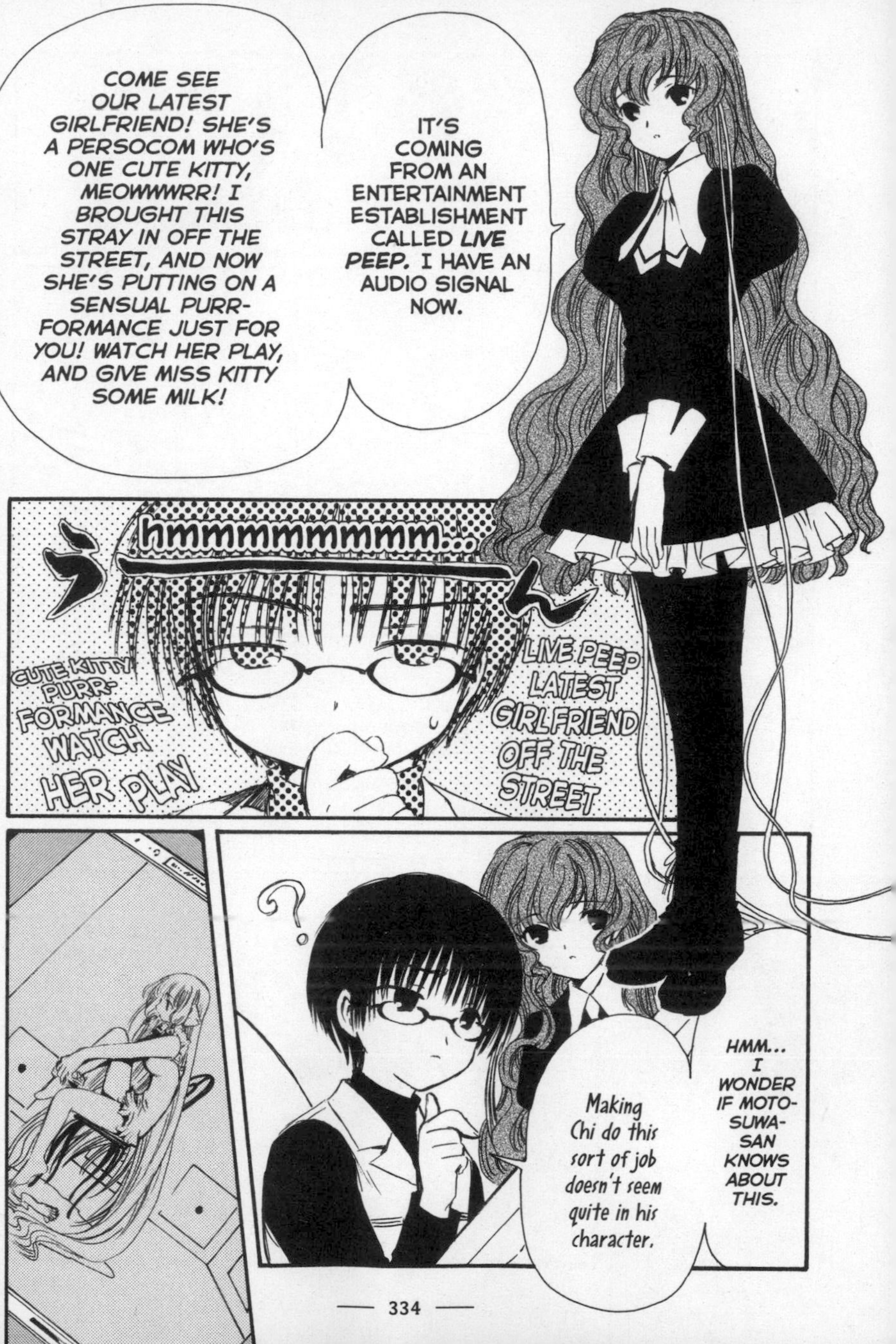
IT'S COMING FROM AN ENTERTAINMENT ESTABLISHMENT CALLED *LIVE PEEP.* I HAVE AN AUDIO SIGNAL NOW.
COME SEE OUR LATEST GIRLFRIEND! SHE'S A PERSOCOM WHO'S ONE CUTE KITTY, MEOWWWRR! I BROUGHT THIS STRAY IN OFF THE STREET, AND NOW SHE'S PUTTING ON A SENSUAL PURR-FORMANCE JUST FOR YOU! WATCH HER PLAY, AND GIVE MISS KITTY SOME MILK!
hmmmmmmmm...
LIVE PEEP LATEST GIRLFRIEND OFF THE STREET
CUTE KITTY PURR-FORMANCE WATCH HER PLAY
HMM... I WONDER IF MOTO-SUWA-SAN KNOWS ABOUT THIS.
Making Chi do this sort of job doesn't seem quite in his character.

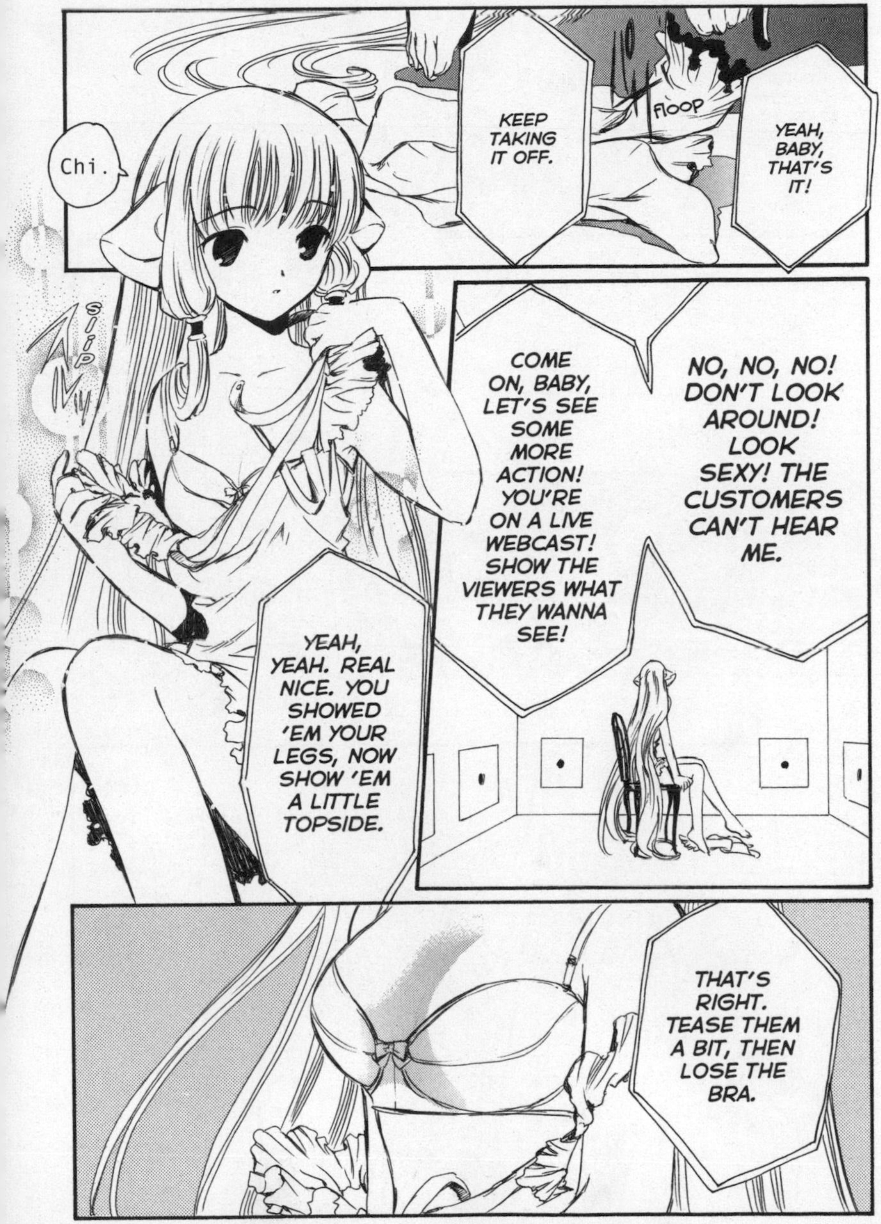
YEAH, BABY, THAT'S IT!
FLOOP
KEEP TAKING IT OFF.
Chi.
NO, NO, NO! DON'T LOOK AROUND! LOOK SEXY! THE CUSTOMERS CAN'T HEAR ME.
COME ON, BABY, LET'S SEE SOME MORE ACTION! YOU'RE ON A LIVE WEBCAST! SHOW THE VIEWERS WHAT THEY WANNA SEE!
SLIP
YEAH, YEAH. REAL NICE. YOU SHOWED 'EM YOUR LEGS, NOW SHOW 'EM A LITTLE TOPSIDE.
THAT'S RIGHT. TEASE THEM A BIT, THEN LOSE THE BRA.

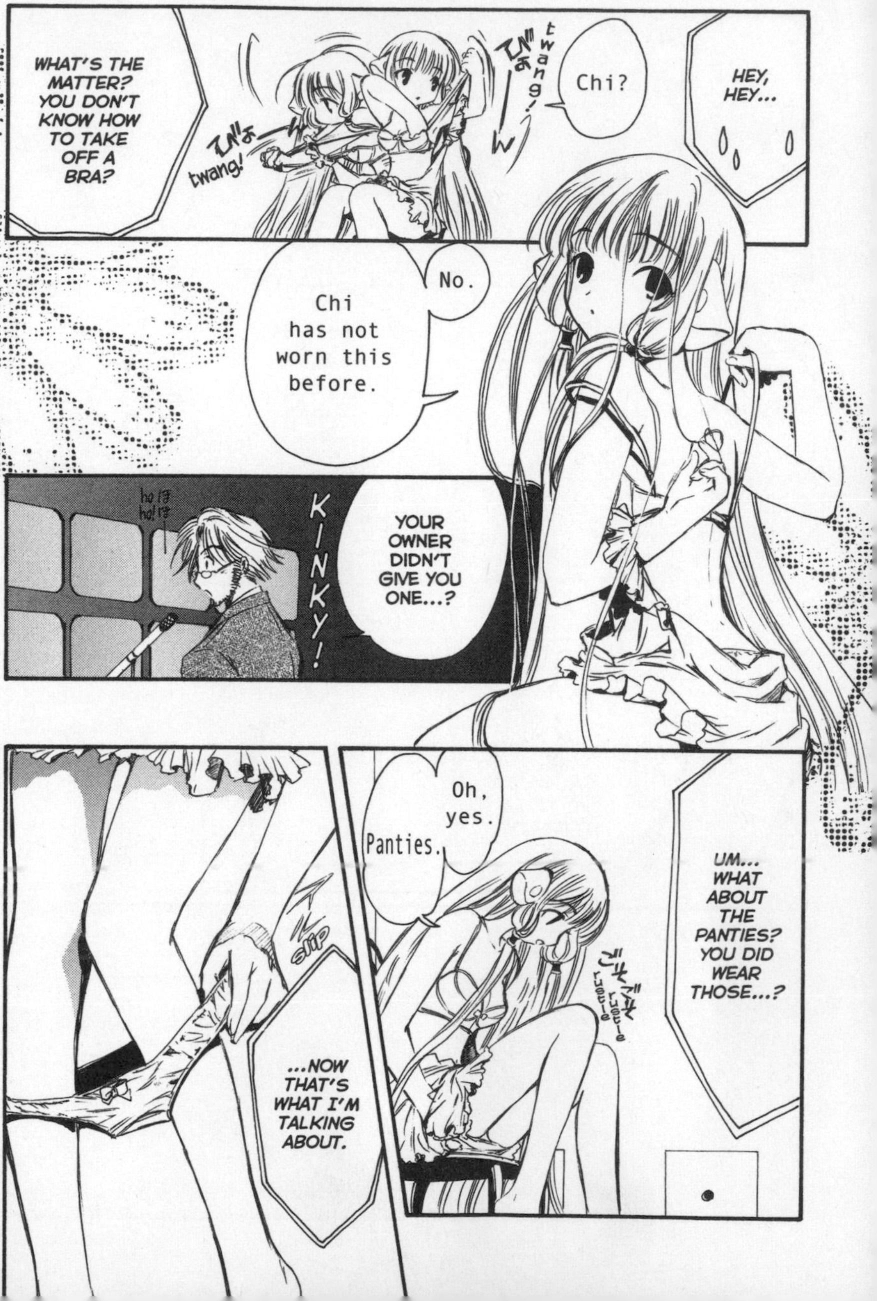
HEY, HEY...
Chi?
twang!
twang!
WHAT'S THE MATTER? YOU DON'T KNOW HOW TO TAKE OFF A BRA?
No.
Chi has not worn this before.
YOUR OWNER DIDN'T GIVE YOU ONE...?
KINKY!
ho ho!
UM... WHAT ABOUT THE PANTIES? YOU DID WEAR THOSE...?
Oh, yes.
Panties.
rustle rustle
slip
...NOW THAT'S WHAT I'M TALKING ABOUT.

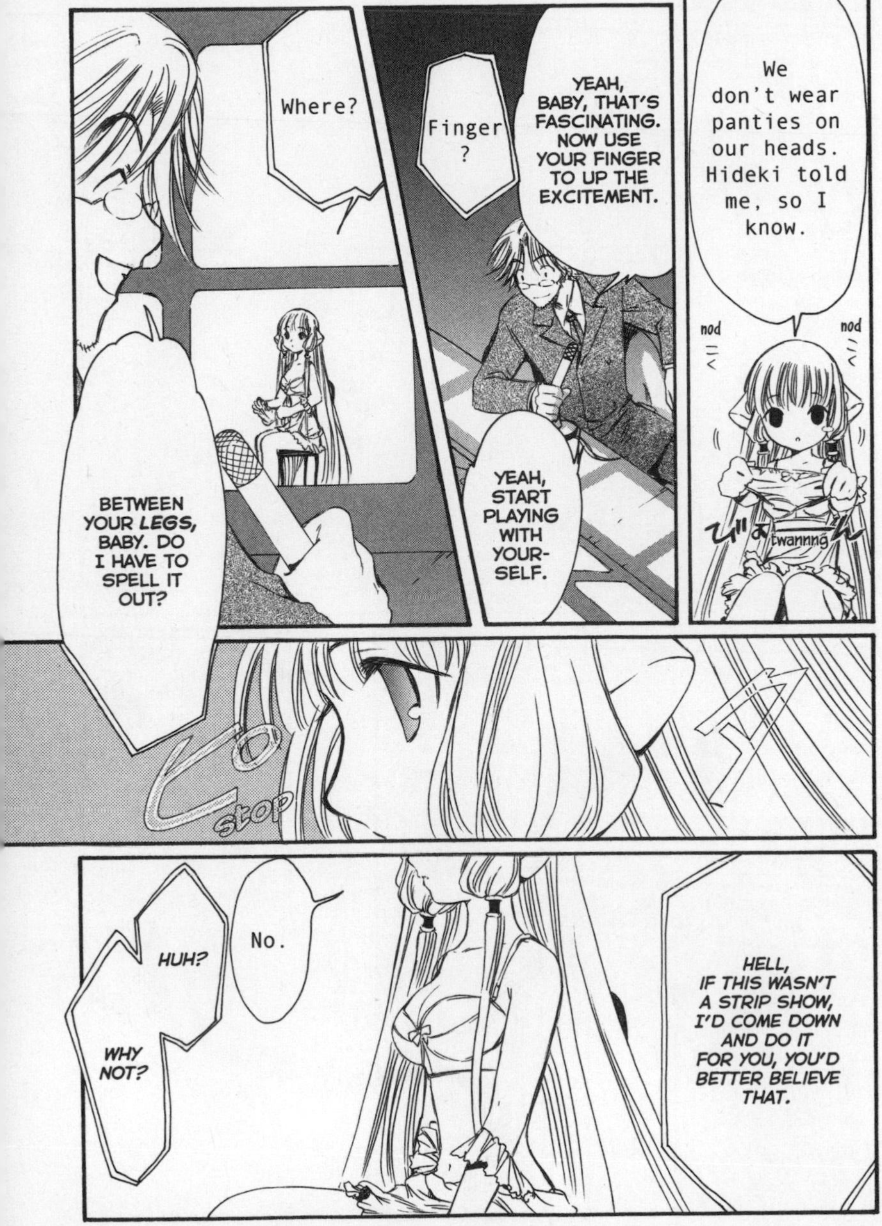
We don't wear panties on our heads. Hideki told me, so I know.
nod
nod
twanng
YEAH, BABY, THAT'S FASCINATING. NOW USE YOUR FINGER TO UP THE EXCITEMENT.
Finger?
YEAH, START PLAYING WITH YOURSELF.
Where?
BETWEEN YOUR *LEGS*, BABY. DO I HAVE TO SPELL IT OUT?
stop
HELL, IF THIS WASN'T A STRIP SHOW, I'D COME DOWN AND DO IT FOR YOU, YOU'D BETTER BELIEVE THAT.
No.
HUH?
WHY NOT?

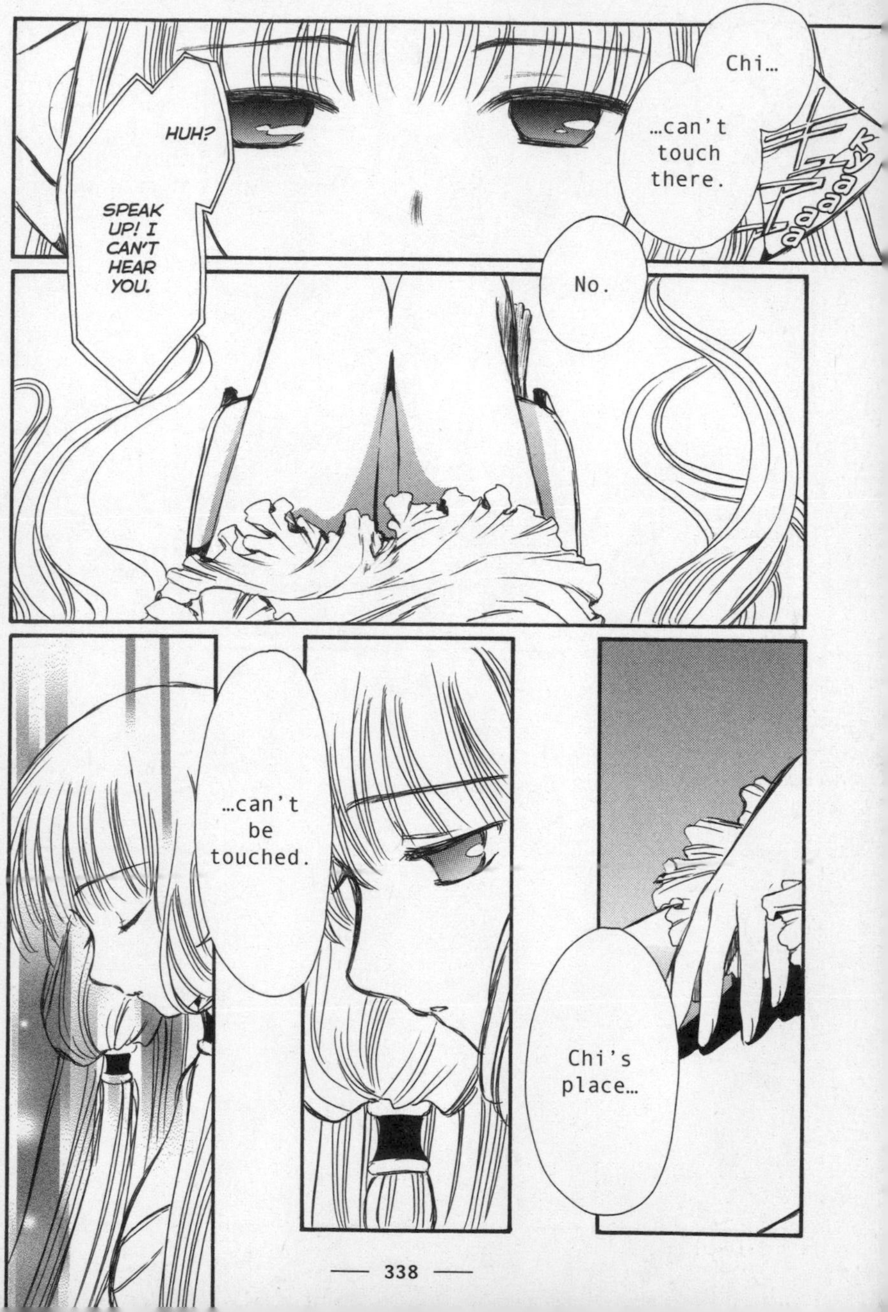
Chi…
…can't touch there.
HUH?
SPEAK UP! I CAN'T HEAR YOU.
No.
Chi's place…
…can't be touched.

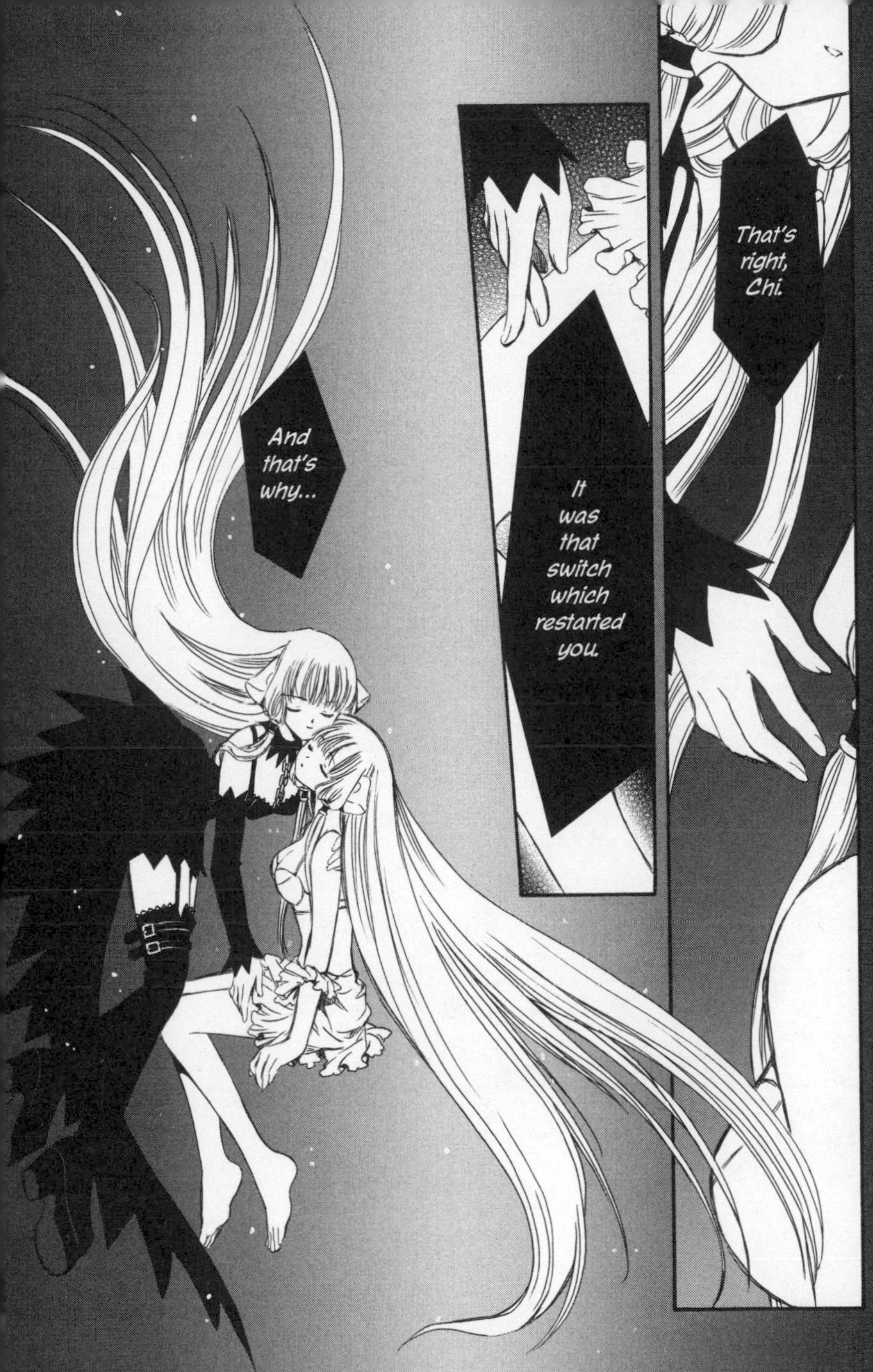
That's right, Chi.
It was that switch which restarted you.
And that's why...

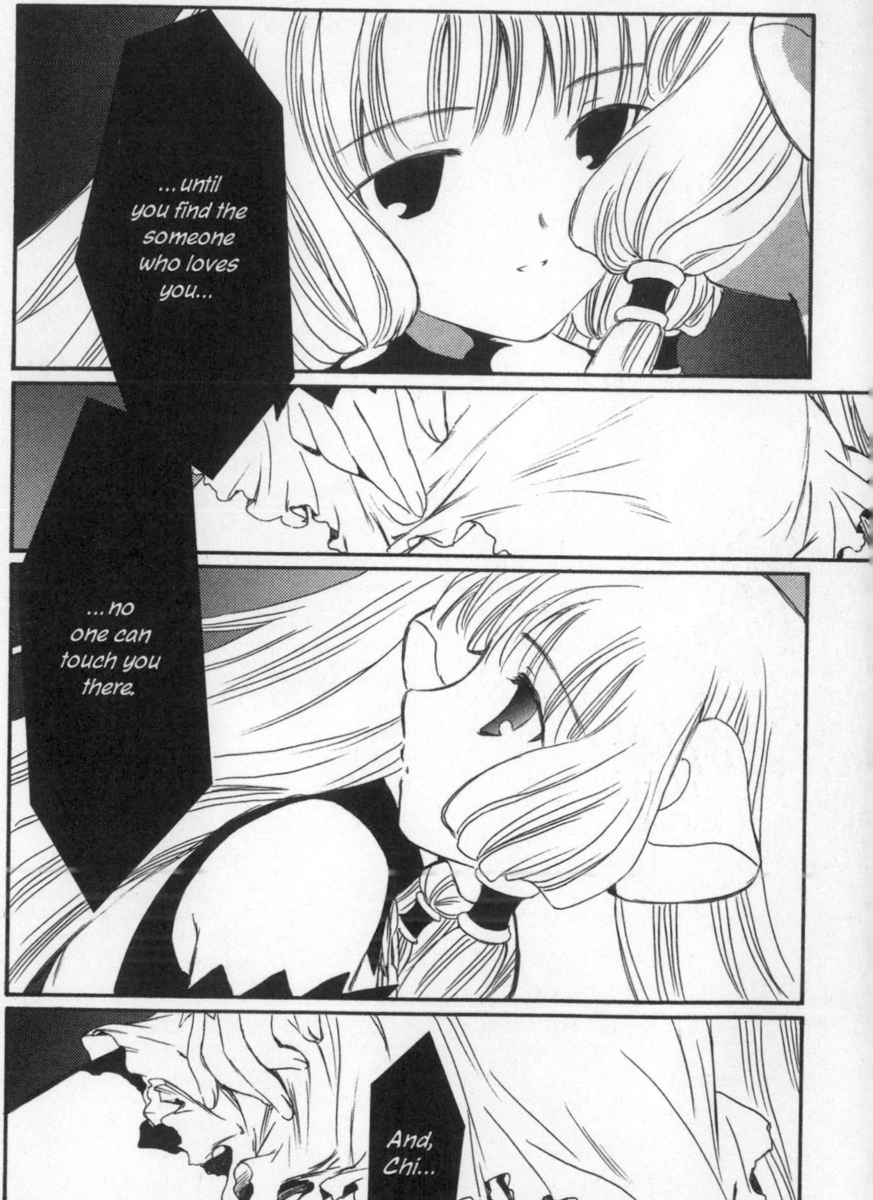
...until you find the someone who loves you...
...no one can touch you there.
And, Chi...

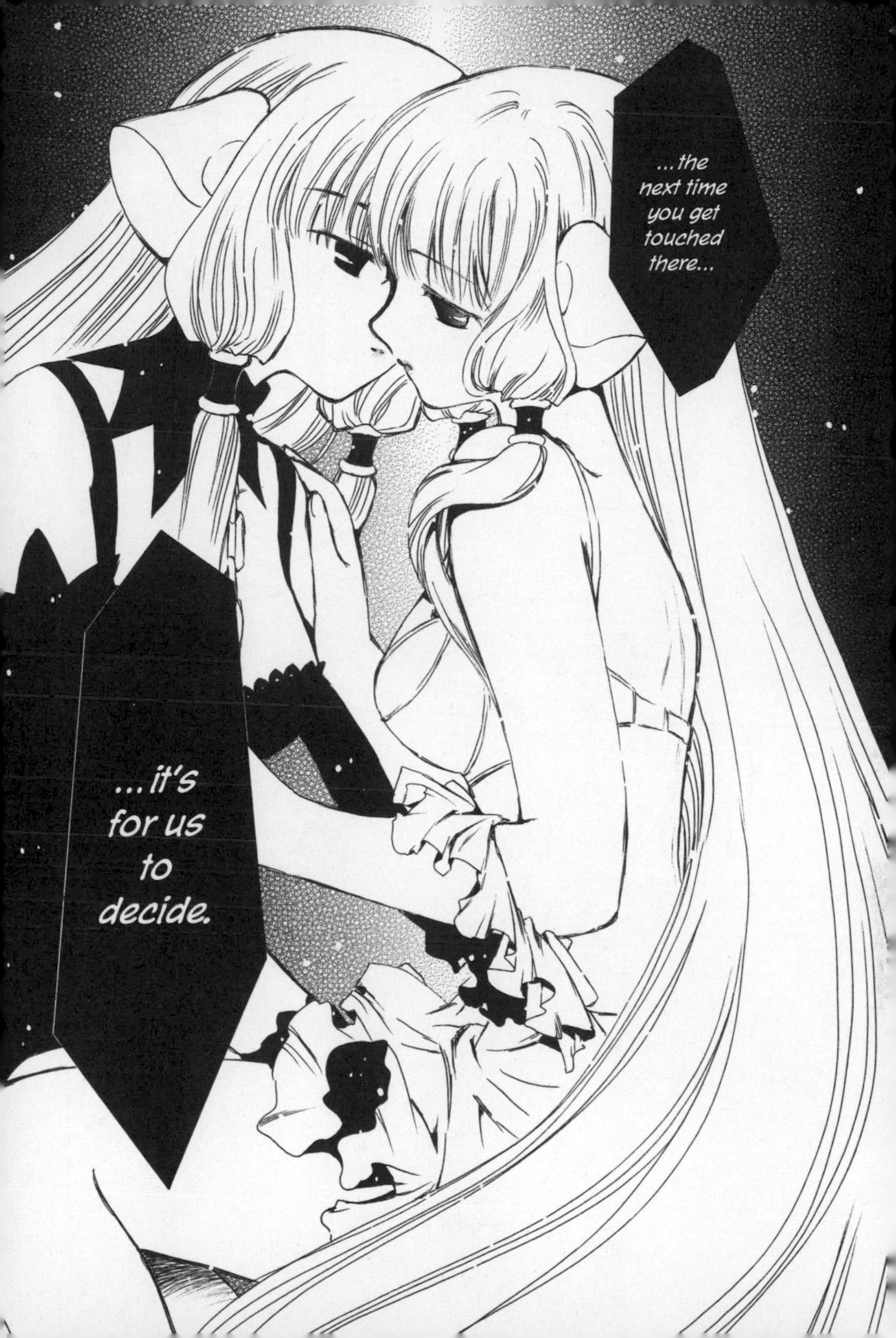
...the next time you get touched there...
...it's for us to decide.

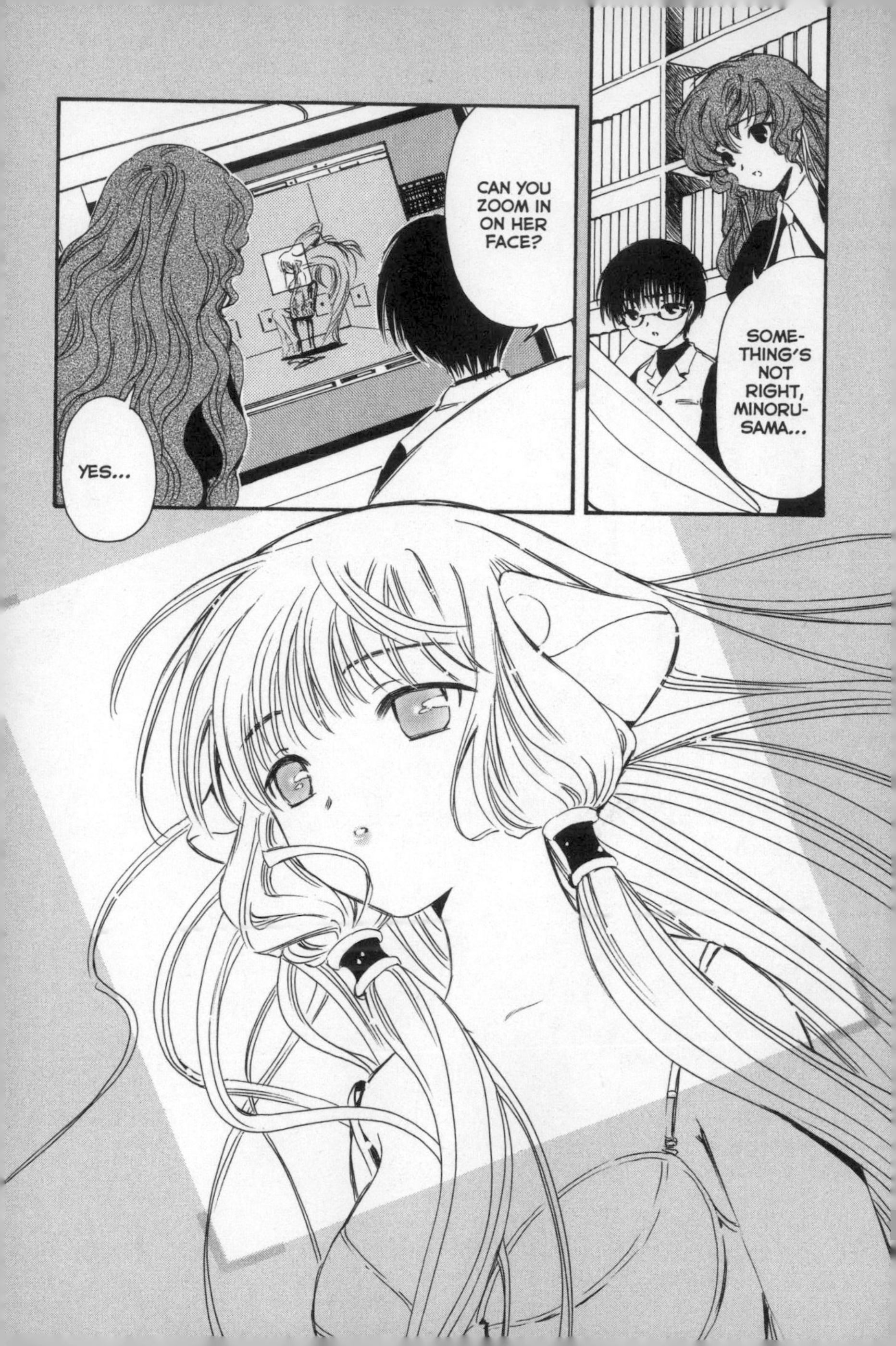
SOME-THING'S NOT RIGHT, MINORU-SAMA...
CAN YOU ZOOM IN ON HER FACE?
YES...

Chobits
ちょびっつ

◄ chapter 23 ►

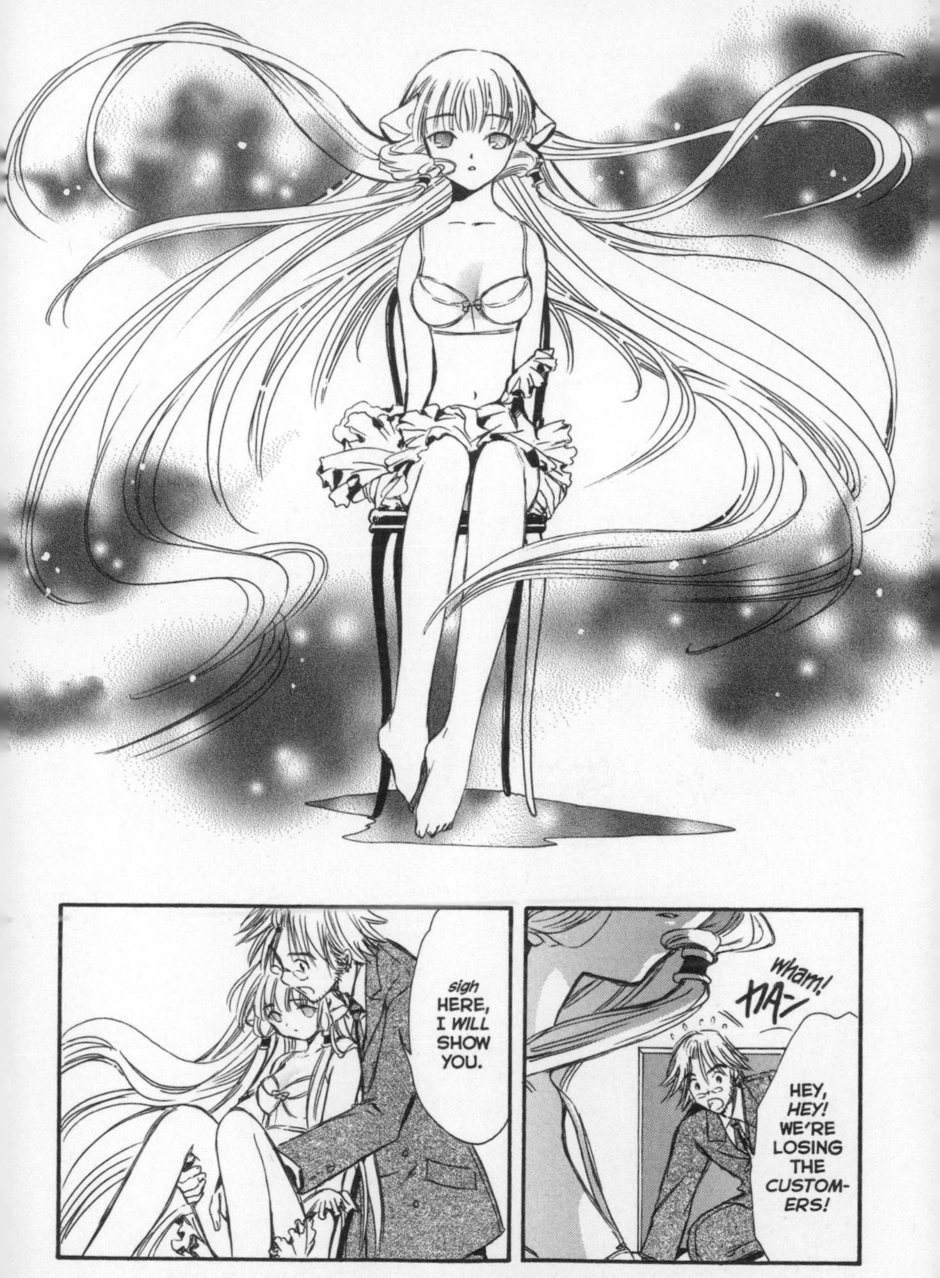
wham!
HEY, HEY! WE'RE LOSING THE CUSTOMERS!
sigh
HERE, I WILL SHOW YOU.

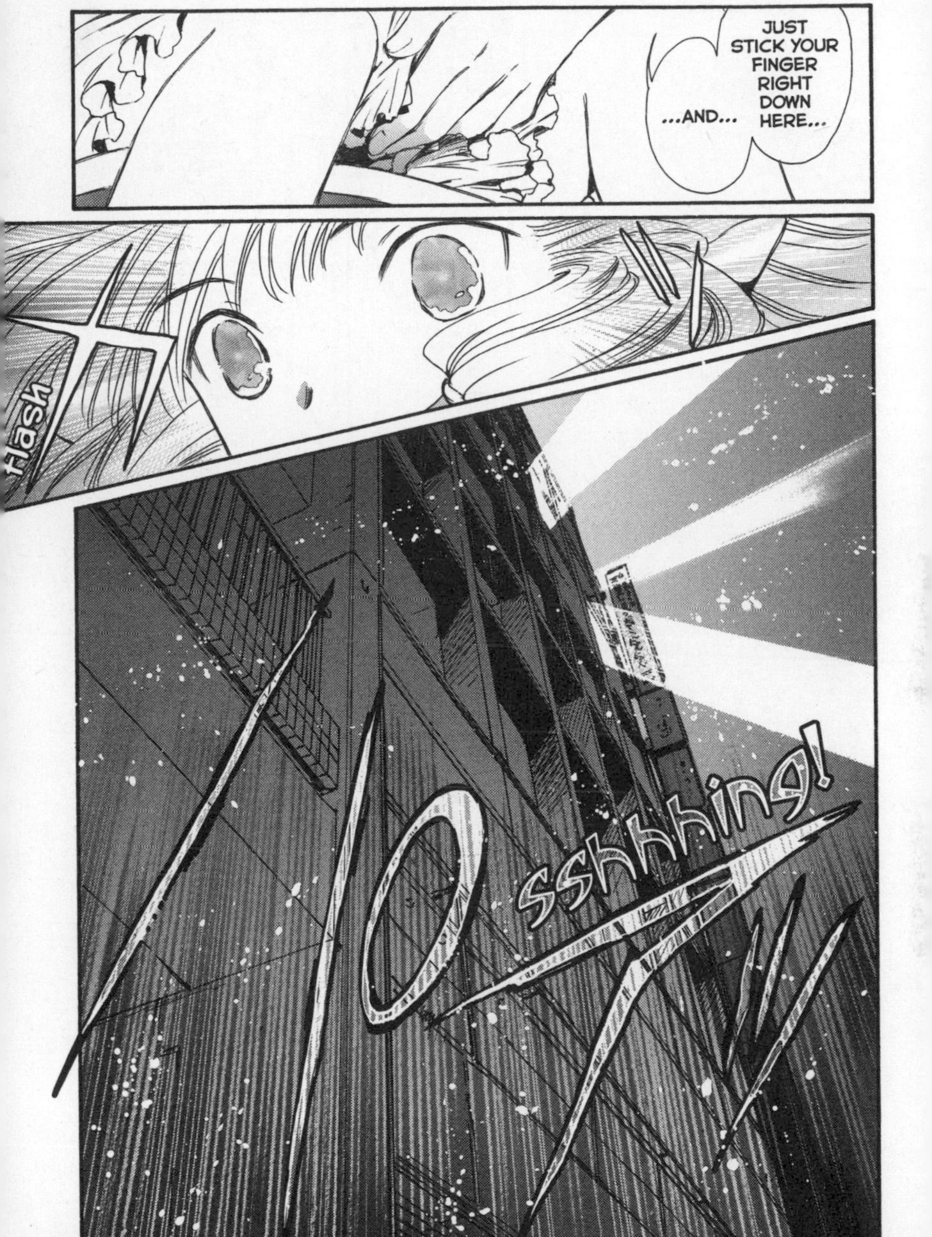
JUST STICK YOUR FINGER RIGHT DOWN HERE...
...AND...
flash
ssshhhing!

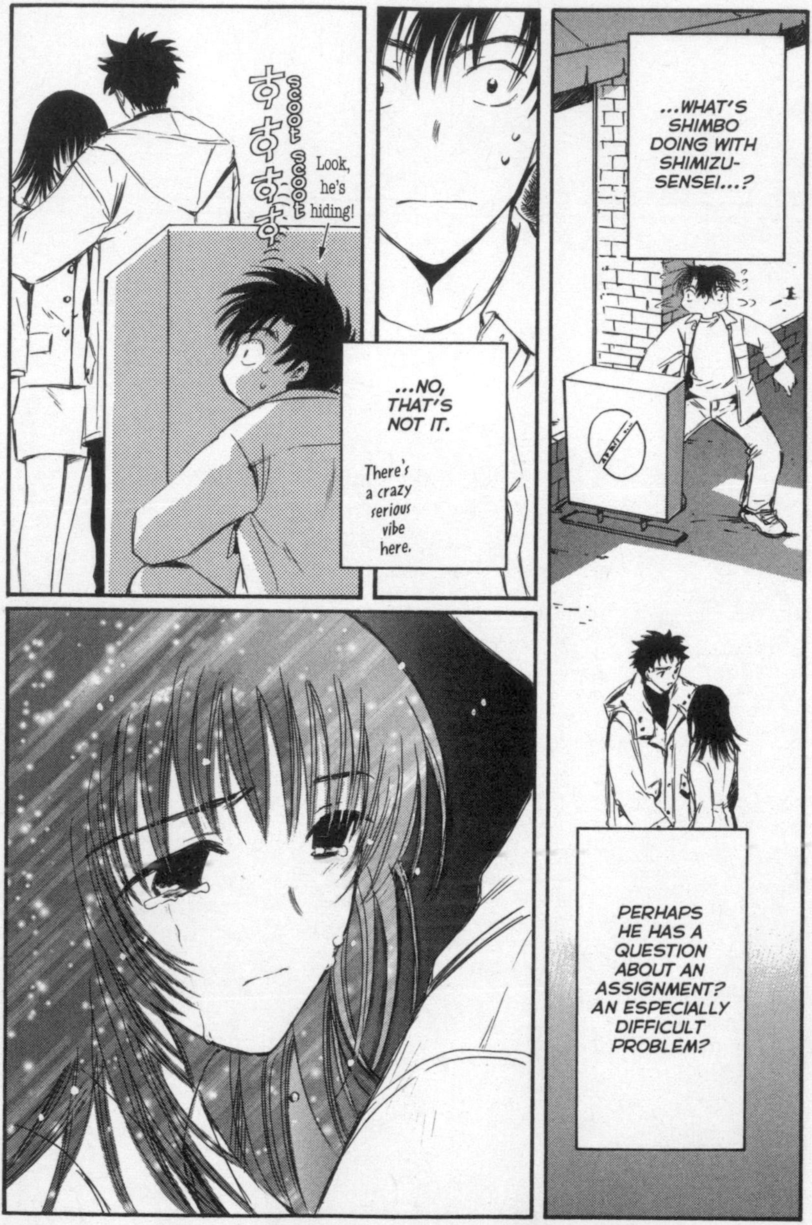
...WHAT'S SHIMBO DOING WITH SHIMIZU-SENSEI...?
PERHAPS HE HAS A QUESTION ABOUT AN ASSIGNMENT? AN ESPECIALLY DIFFICULT PROBLEM?
...NO, THAT'S NOT IT.
There's a crazy serious vibe here.
すすす
scoot scoot
Look, he's hiding!

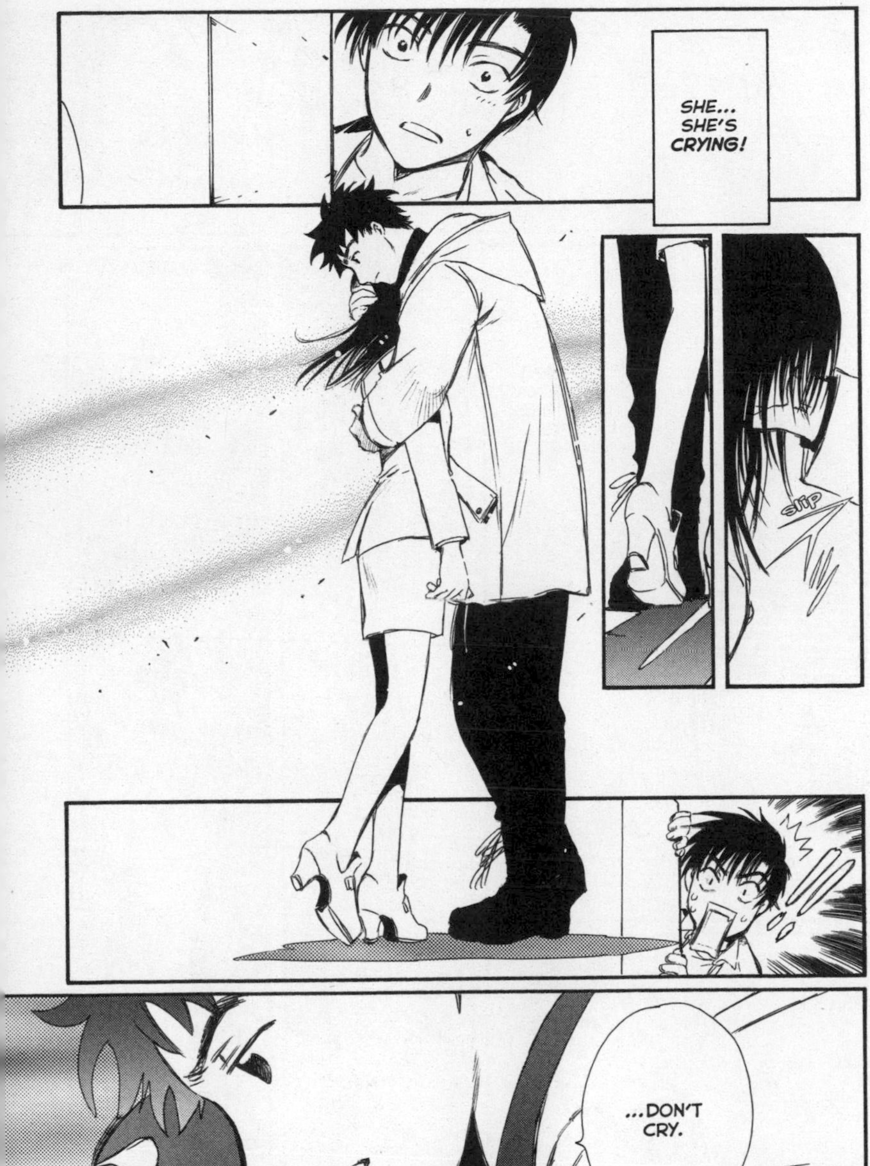
SHE... SHE'S CRYING!
slip
...DON'T CRY.

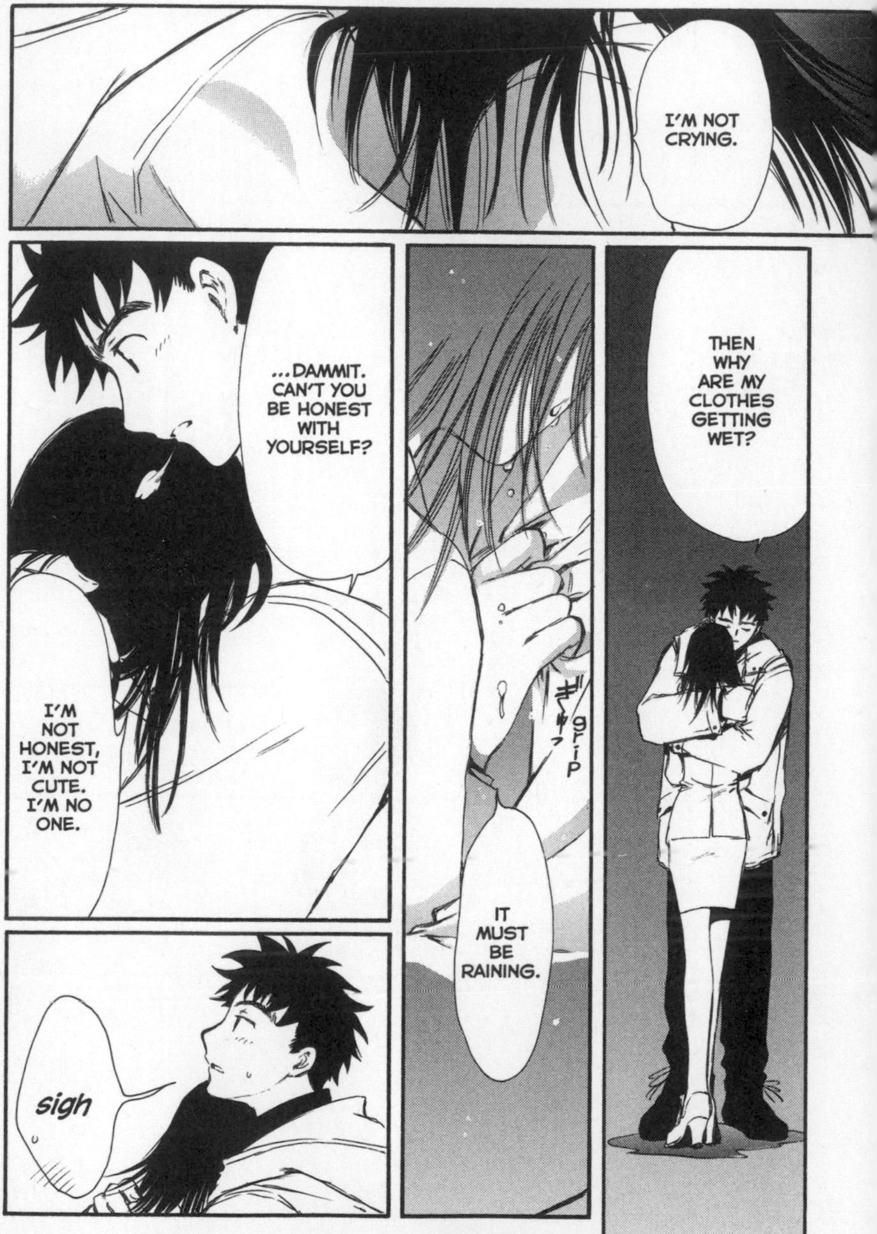
I'M NOT CRYING.
THEN WHY ARE MY CLOTHES GETTING WET?
grip
IT MUST BE RAINING.
...DAMMIT. CAN'T YOU BE HONEST WITH YOURSELF?
I'M NOT HONEST, I'M NOT CUTE. I'M NO ONE.
sigh

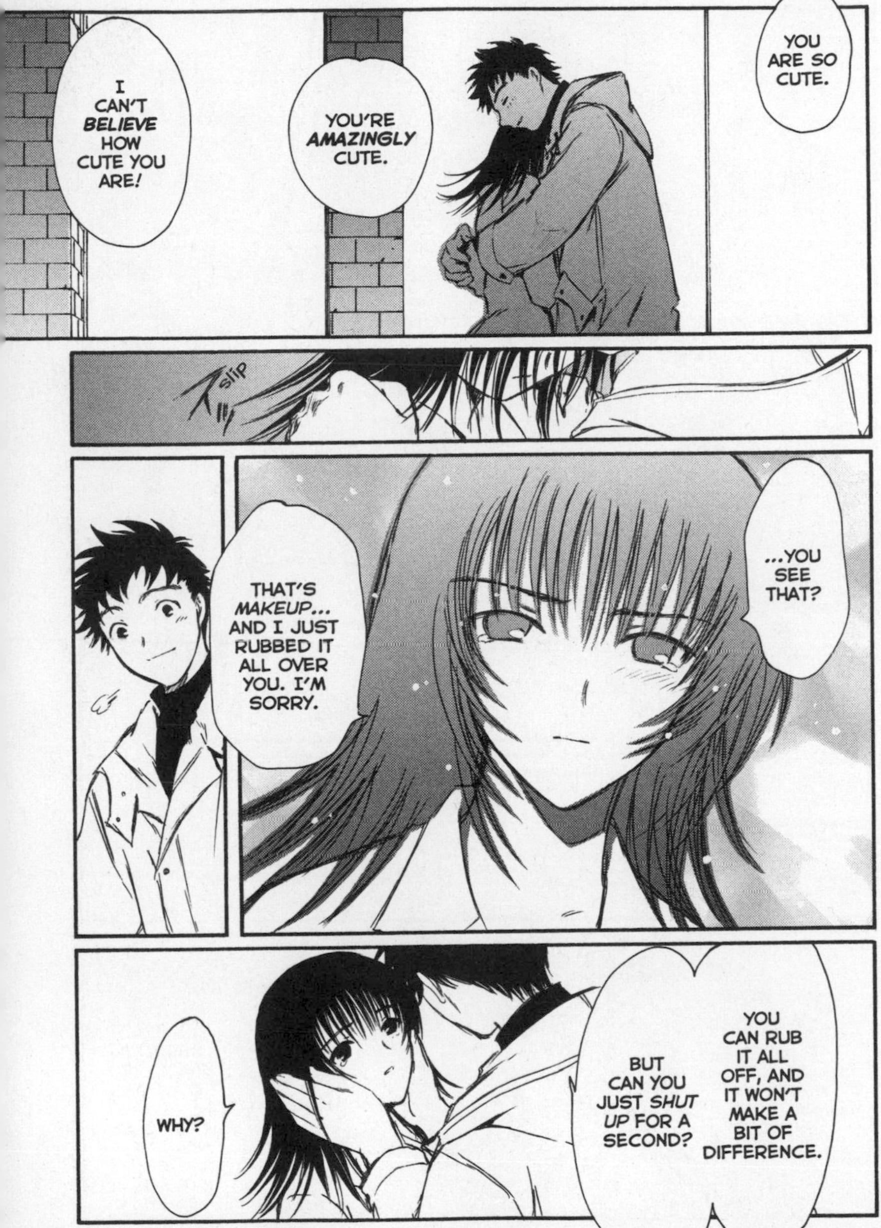
YOU ARE SO CUTE.
YOU'RE *AMAZINGLY* CUTE.
I CAN'T *BELIEVE* HOW CUTE YOU ARE!
slip
...YOU SEE THAT?
THAT'S *MAKEUP*... AND I JUST RUBBED IT ALL OVER YOU. I'M SORRY.
YOU CAN RUB IT ALL OFF, AND IT WON'T MAKE A BIT OF DIFFERENCE.
BUT CAN YOU JUST *SHUT UP* FOR A SECOND?
WHY?

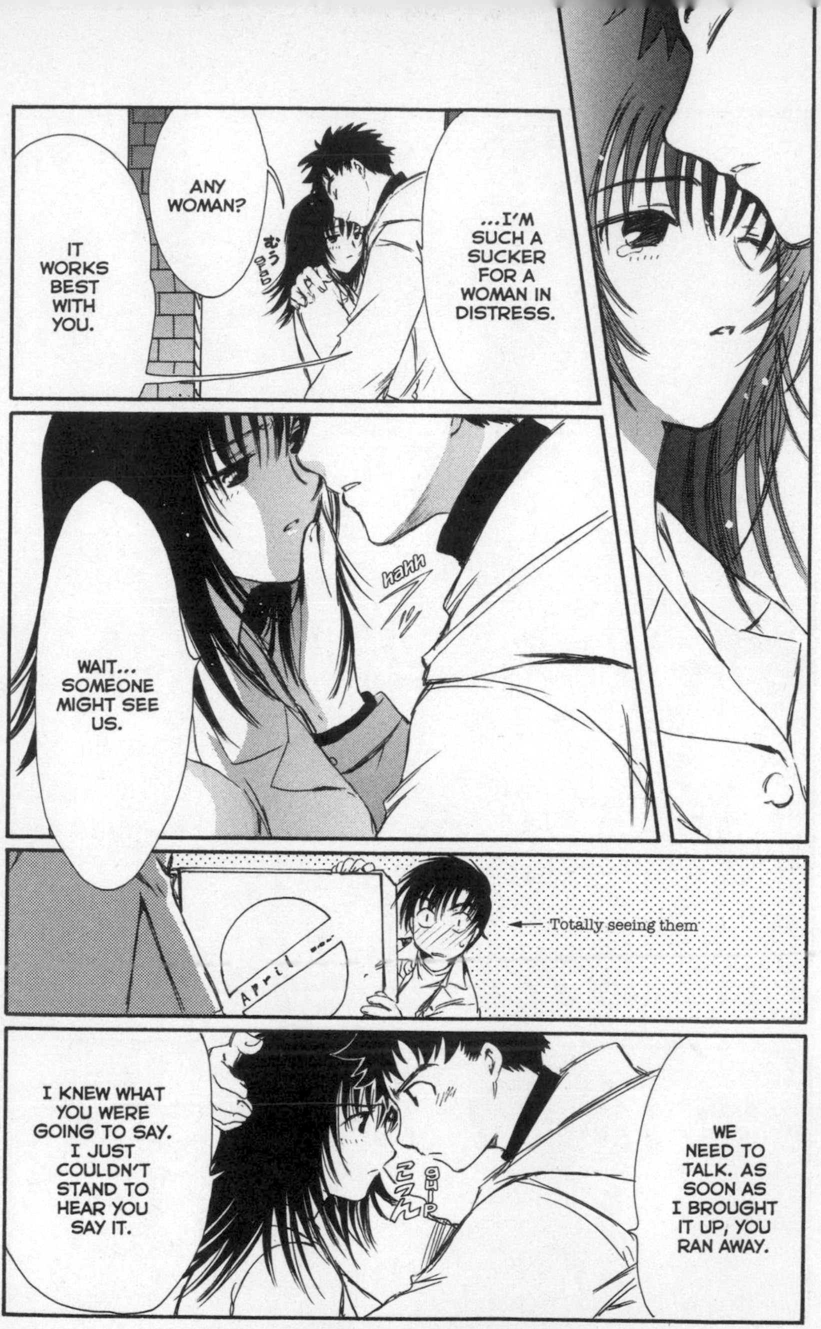
...I'M SUCH A SUCKER FOR A WOMAN IN DISTRESS.
ANY WOMAN?
むう
IT WORKS BEST WITH YOU.
hahh
WAIT... SOMEONE MIGHT SEE US.
April
Totally seeing them
WE NEED TO TALK. AS SOON AS I BROUGHT IT UP, YOU RAN AWAY.
gulp
ごくん
I KNEW WHAT YOU WERE GOING TO SAY. I JUST COULDN'T STAND TO HEAR YOU SAY IT.

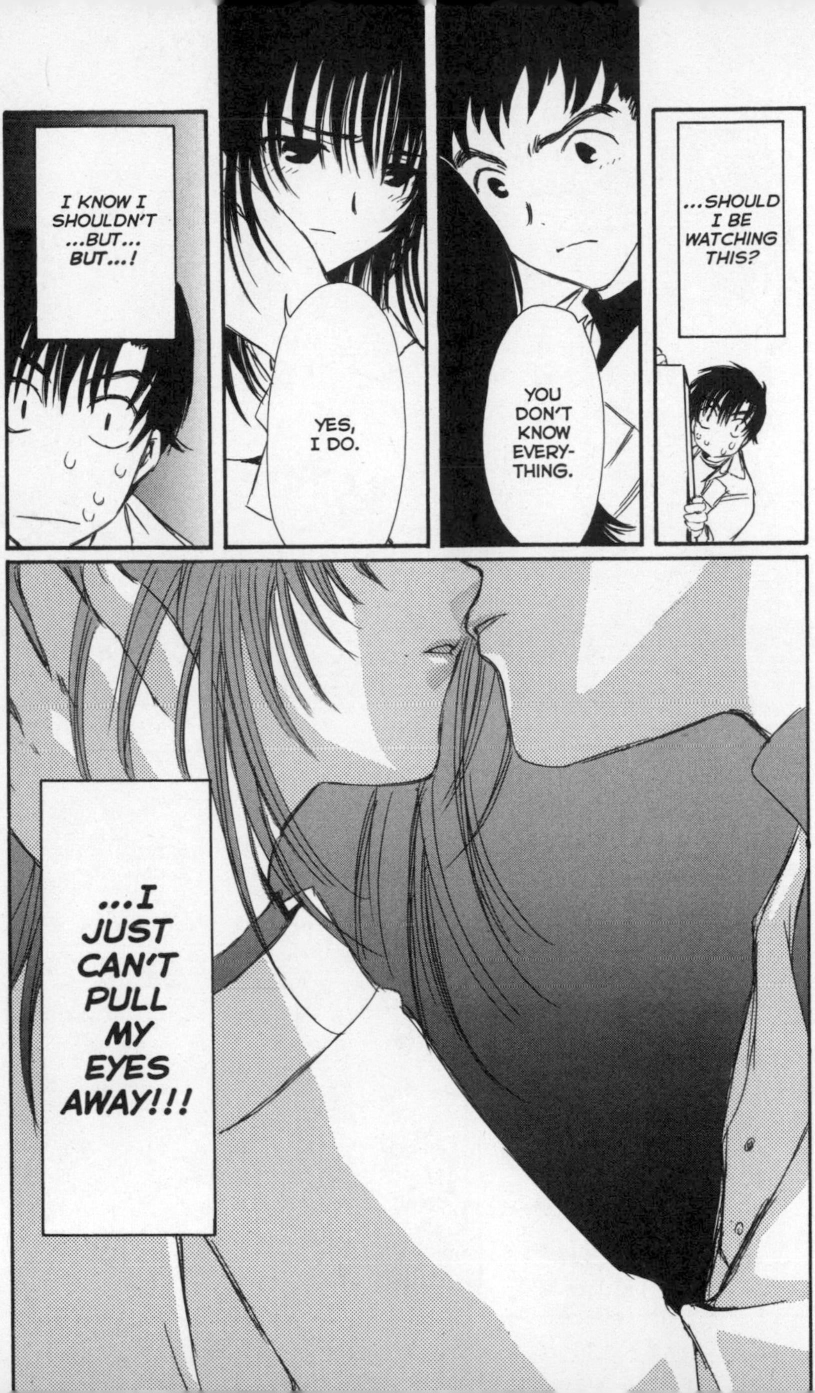
...SHOULD I BE WATCHING THIS?
YOU DON'T KNOW EVERY-THING.
YES, I DO.
I KNOW I SHOULDN'T ...BUT... BUT...!
...I JUST CAN'T PULL MY EYES AWAY!!!

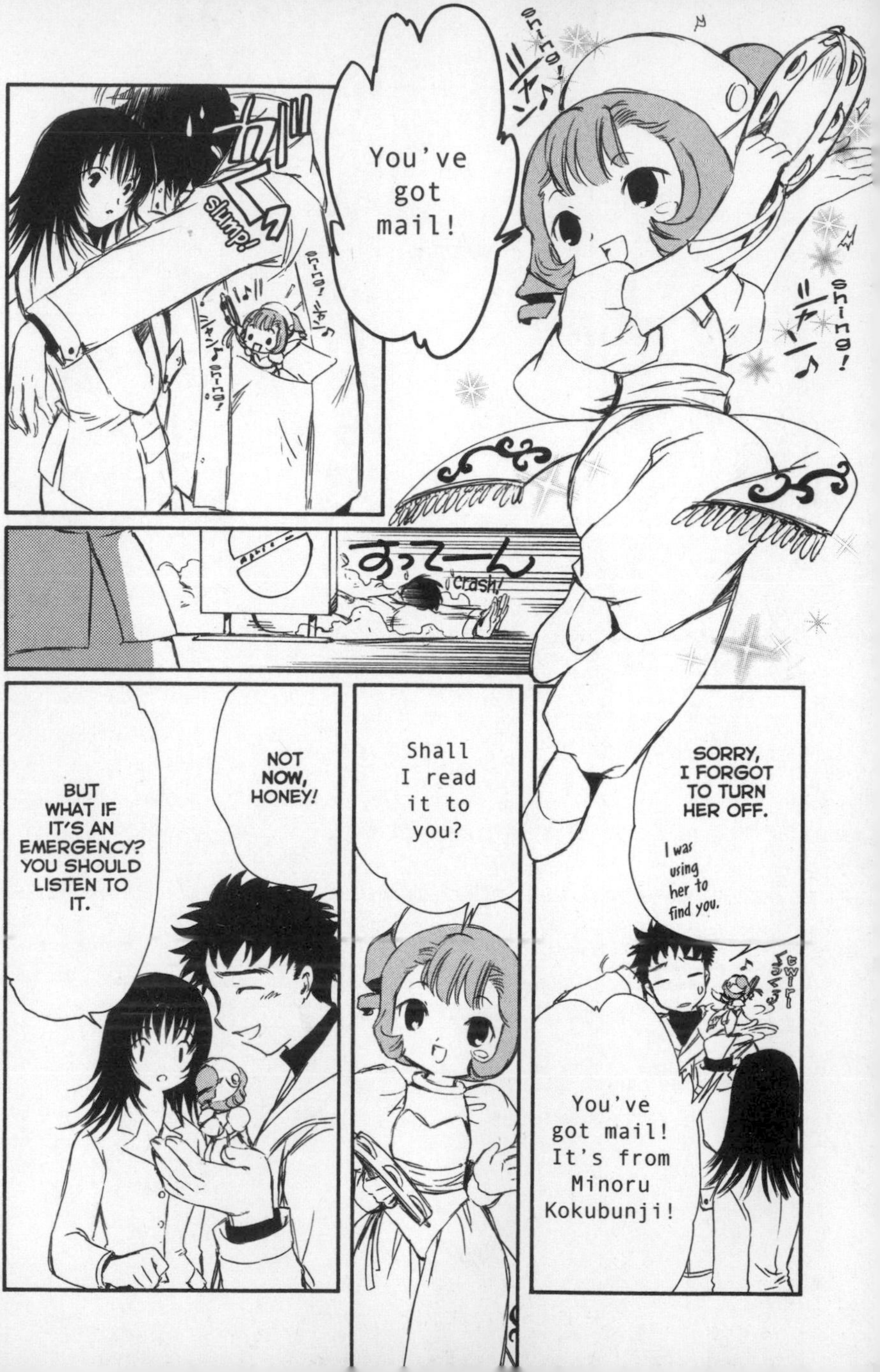
shing!
You've got mail!
shing!
slump!
shing! shing!
すってーん
crash!
SORRY, I FORGOT TO TURN HER OFF.
I was using her to find you.
swirl
You've got mail! It's from Minoru Kokubunji!
Shall I read it to you?
NOT NOW, HONEY!
BUT WHAT IF IT'S AN EMERGENCY? YOU SHOULD LISTEN TO IT.

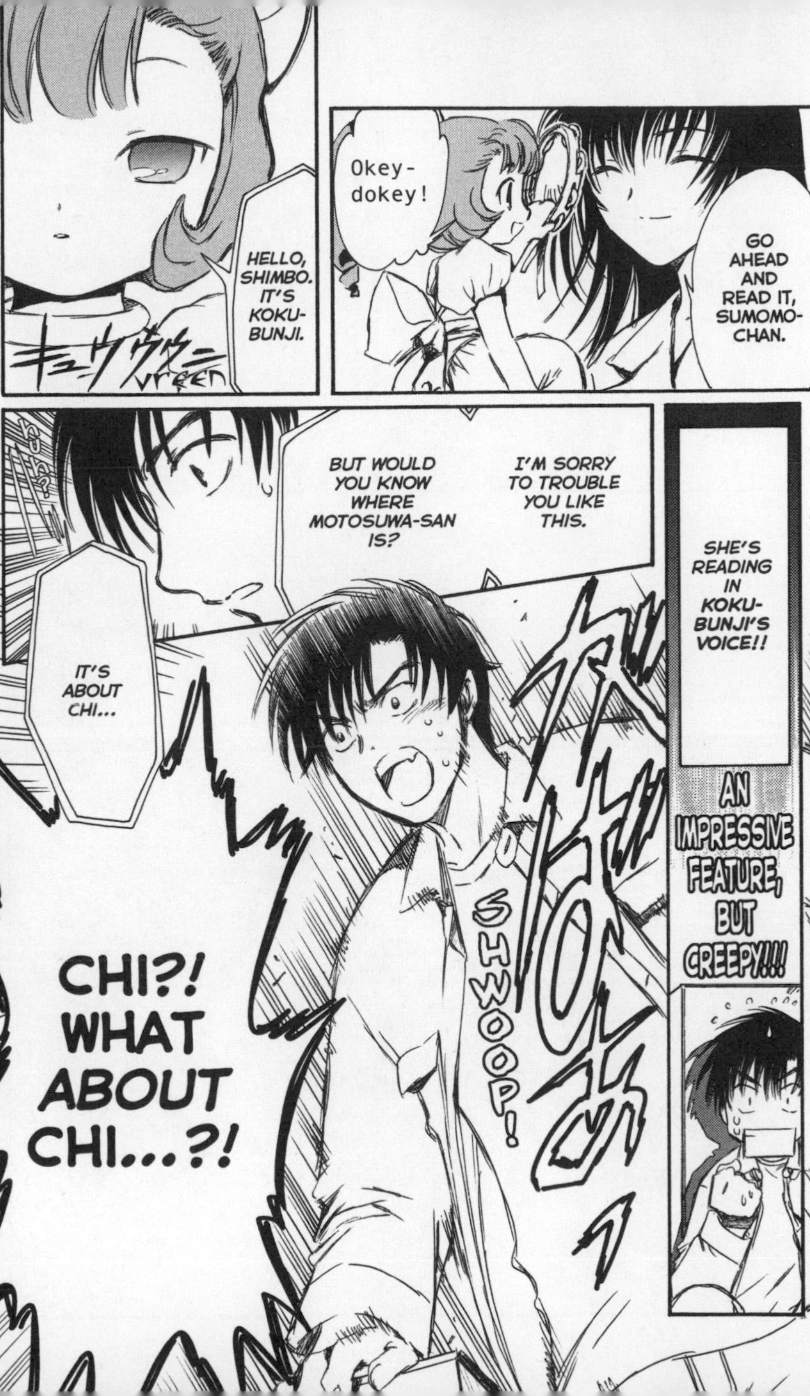
GO AHEAD AND READ IT, SUMOMO-CHAN.
Okey-dokey!
HELLO, SHIMBO. IT'S KOKU-BUNJI.
vreen
SHE'S READING IN KOKU-BUNJI'S VOICE!!
AN IMPRESSIVE FEATURE, BUT CREEPY!!!
I'M SORRY TO TROUBLE YOU LIKE THIS.
BUT WOULD YOU KNOW WHERE MOTOSUWA-SAN IS?
IT'S ABOUT CHI...
SHWOOP!
CHI?! WHAT ABOUT CHI...?!

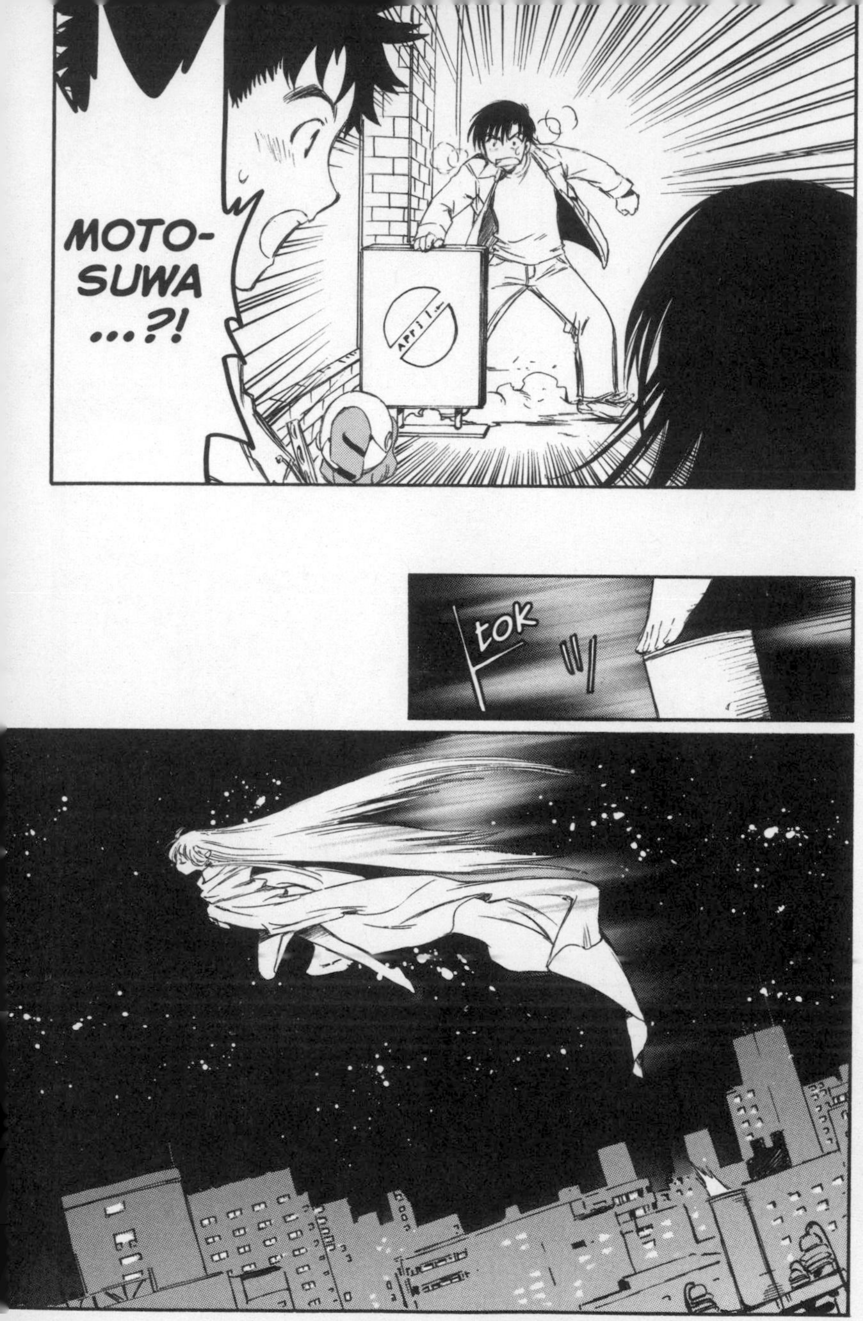
MOTO-SUWA ...?!
tok

Chobits
ちょびっツ

◄ **chapter 24** ►

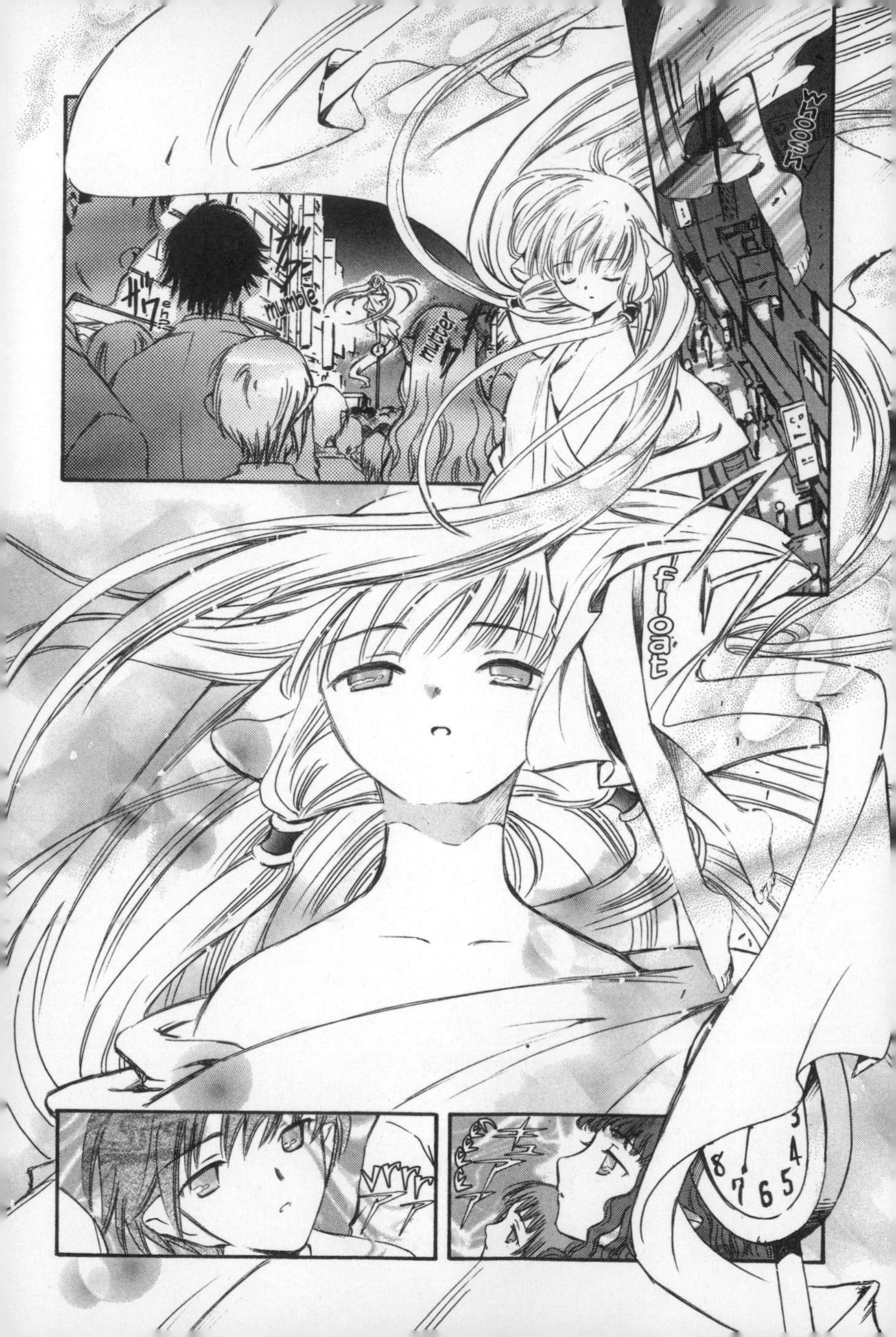
whoosh
eh?
mumble
mutter
float
vrrr

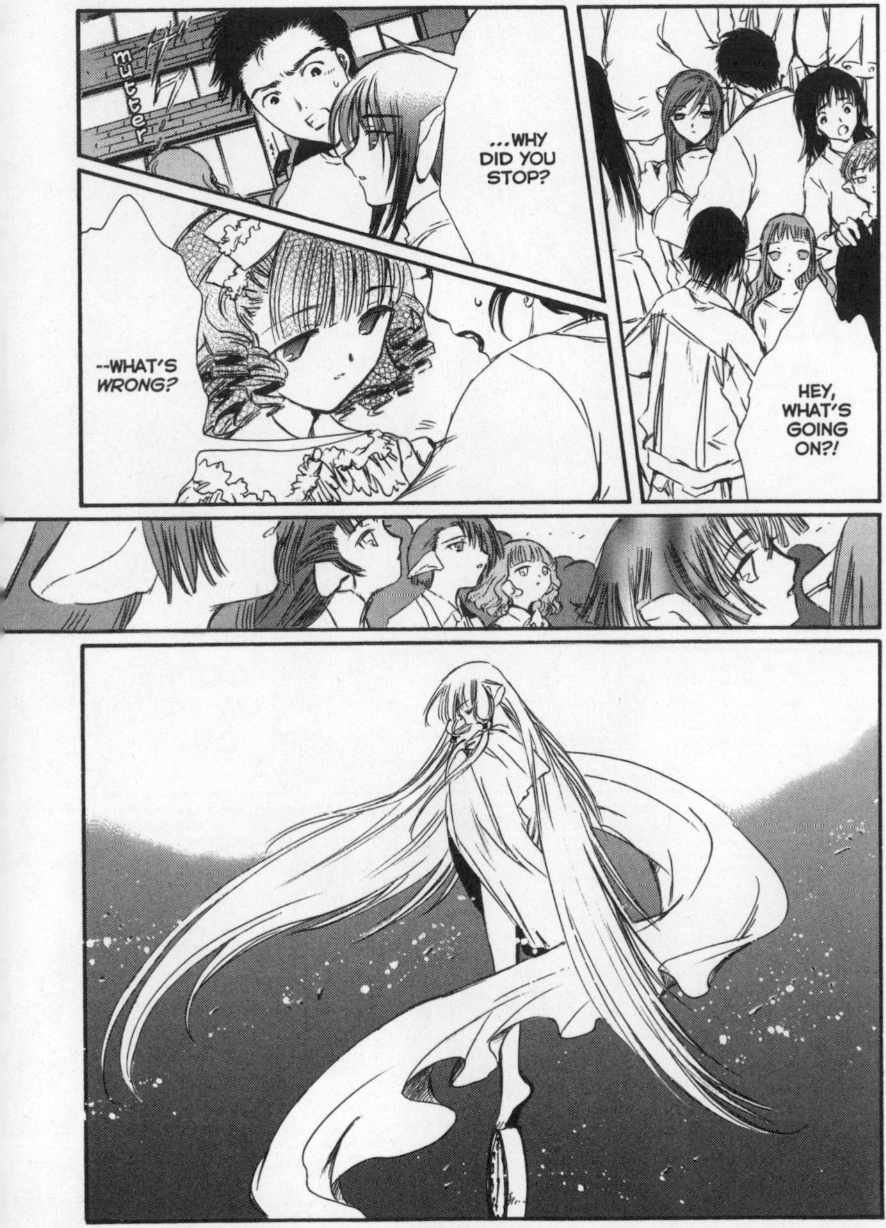
HEY, WHAT'S GOING ON?!
mutter
...WHY DID YOU STOP?
--WHAT'S WRONG?

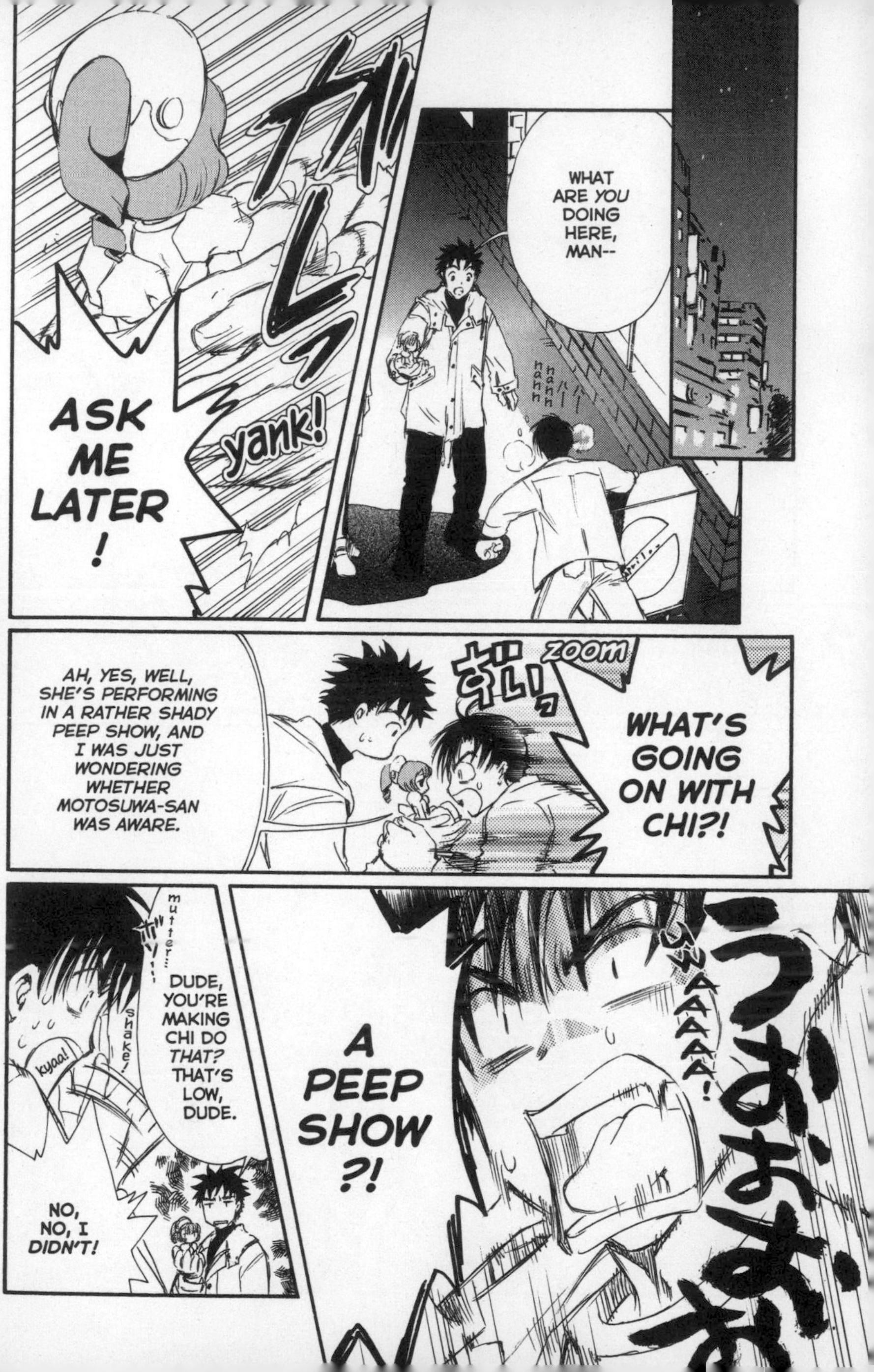
WHAT ARE *YOU* DOING HERE, MAN--
hann hann
yank!
ASK ME LATER!
zoom
WHAT'S GOING ON WITH CHI?!
AH, YES, WELL, SHE'S PERFORMING IN A RATHER SHADY PEEP SHOW, AND I WAS JUST WONDERING WHETHER MOTOSUWA-SAN WAS AWARE.
UWAAAAA!
A PEEP SHOW ?!
mutter
DUDE, YOU'RE MAKING CHI DO *THAT*? THAT'S LOW, DUDE.
shake!
kyaa!
NO, NO, I DIDN'T!

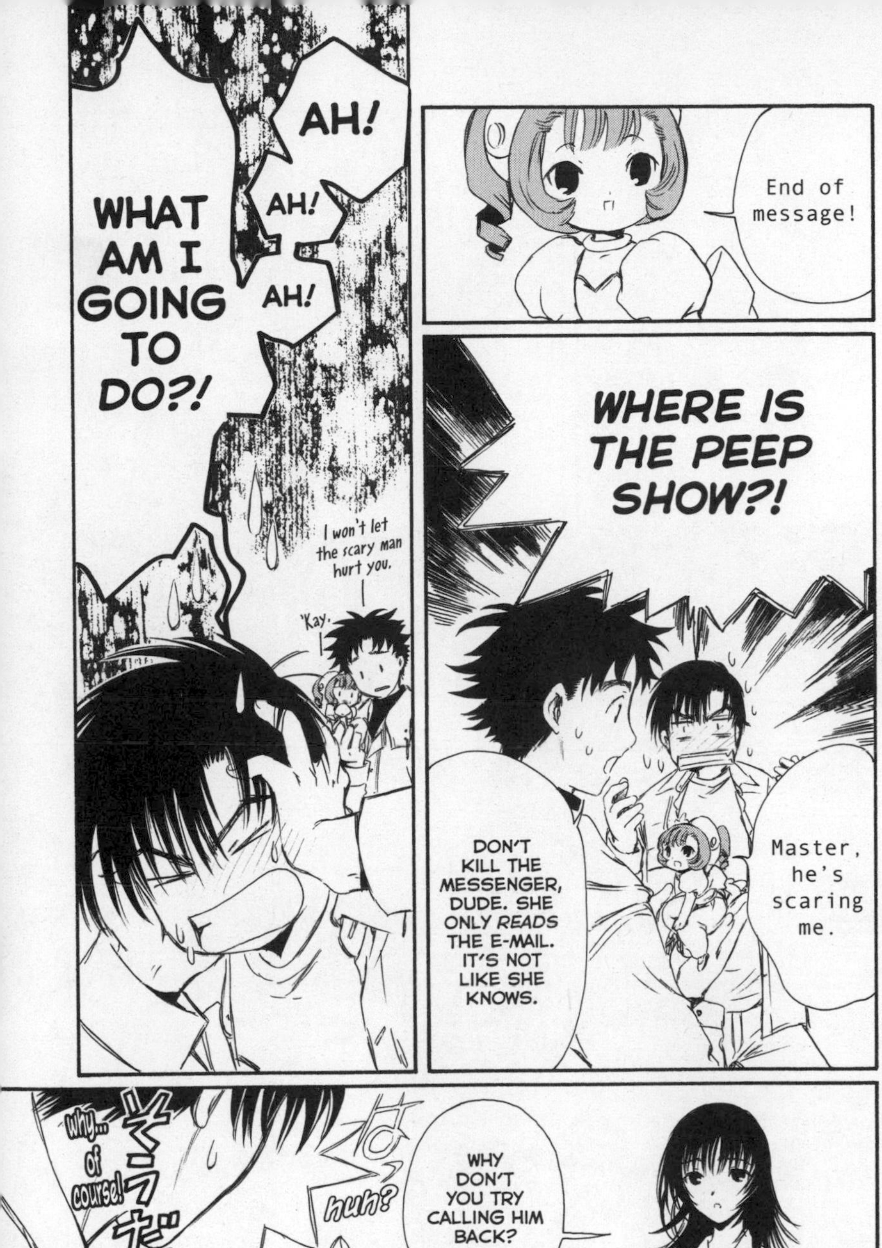

End of message!
WHERE IS THE PEEP SHOW?!
Master, he's scaring me.
DON'T KILL THE MESSENGER, DUDE. SHE ONLY *READS* THE E-MAIL. IT'S NOT LIKE SHE KNOWS.
AH!
AH!
AH!
WHAT AM I GOING TO *DO*?!
I won't let the scary man hurt you.
'Kay.
WHY DON'T YOU TRY CALLING HIM BACK?
huh?
why... of course!

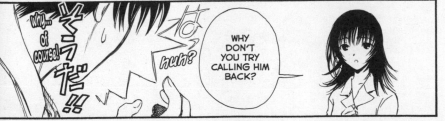

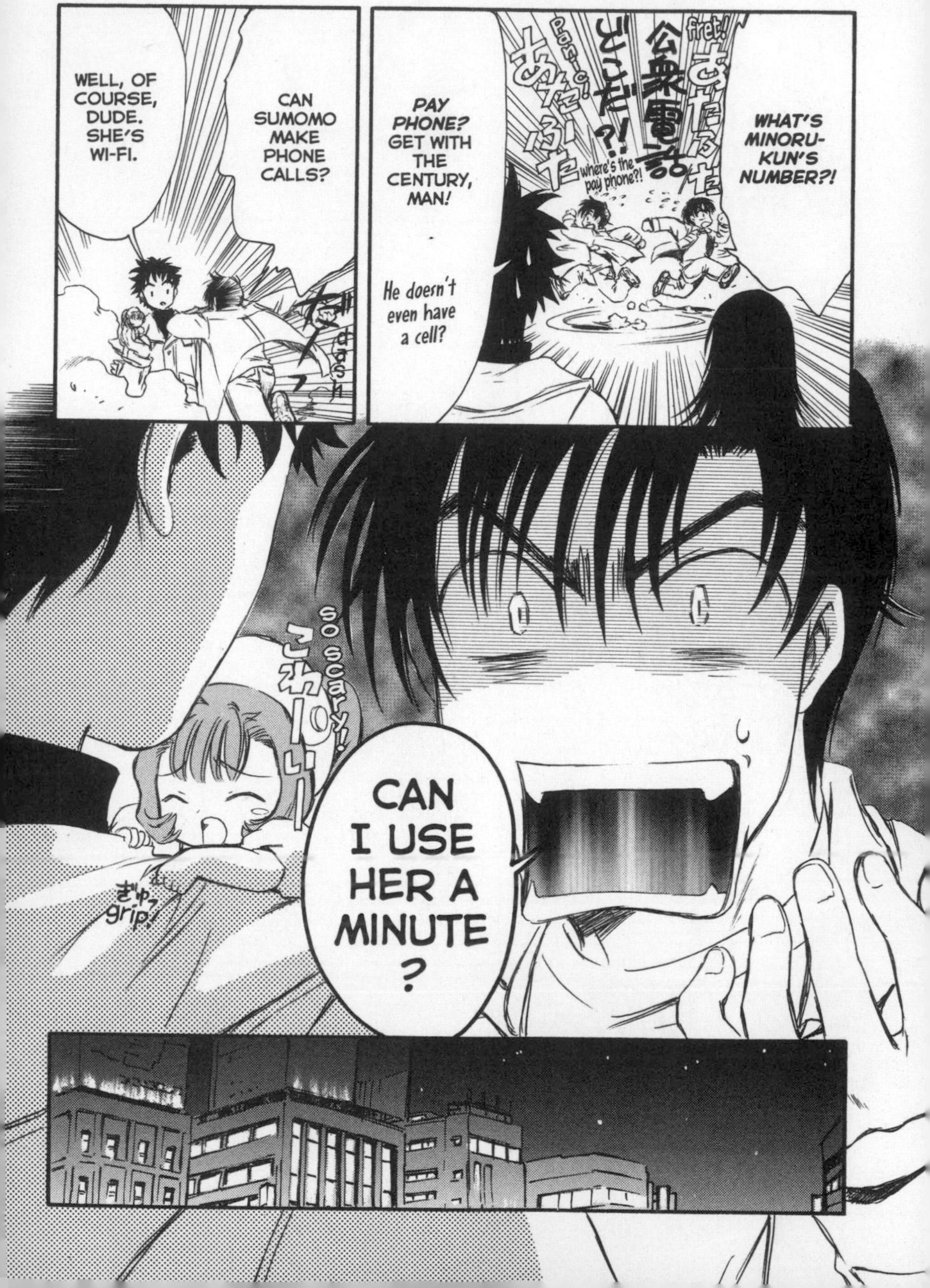

WHAT'S MINORU-KUN'S NUMBER?!
fret!
あたふた
公衆電話どこだ?!
where's the pay phone?!
panic!
あたふた
PAY PHONE? GET WITH THE CENTURY, MAN!
He doesn't even have a cell?
CAN SUMOMO MAKE PHONE CALLS?
WELL, OF COURSE, DUDE. SHE'S WI-FI.
dash
こわーい
so scary!
CAN I USE HER A MINUTE?
ぎゅっ
grip!

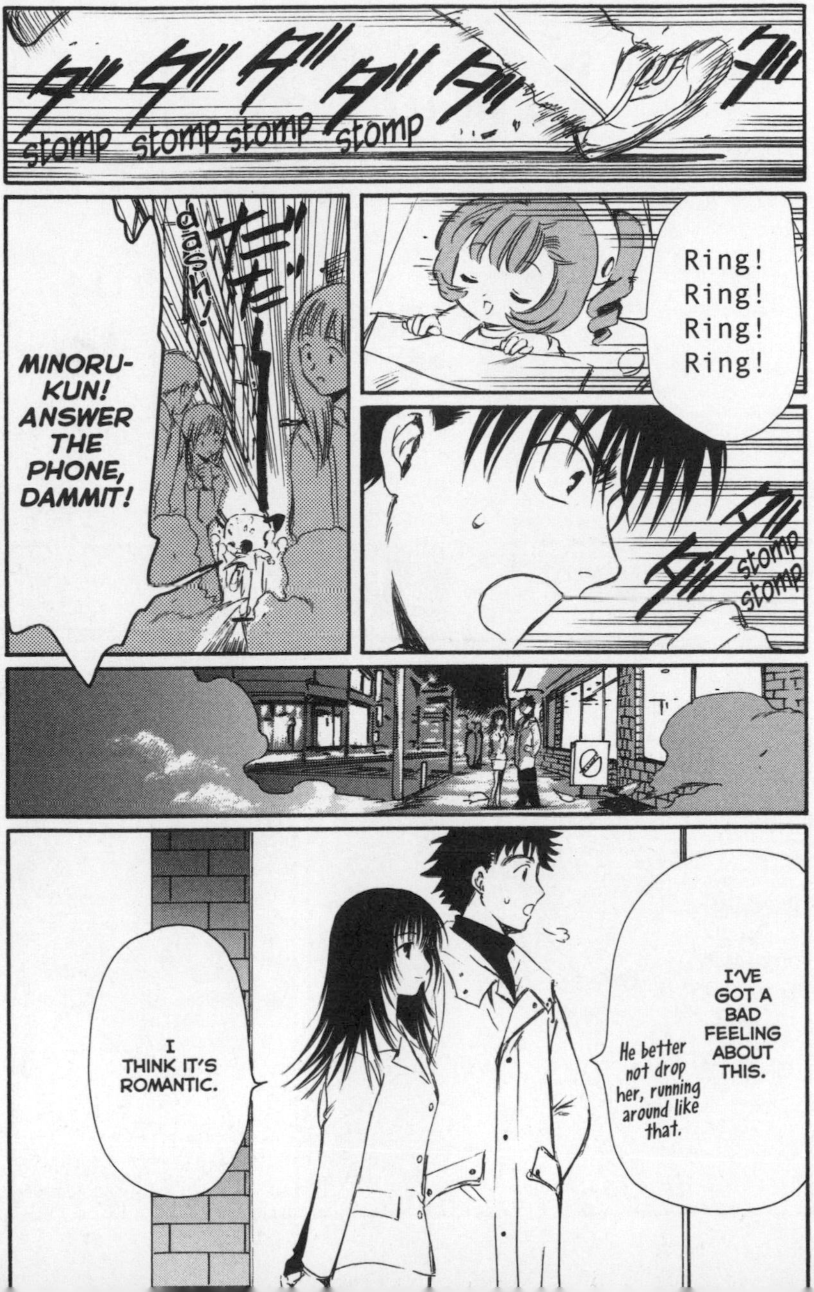
stomp stomp stomp stomp
Ring! Ring! Ring! Ring!
stomp stomp
dash!
MINORU-KUN! ANSWER THE PHONE, DAMMIT!
I'VE GOT A BAD FEELING ABOUT THIS.
He better not drop her, running around like that.
I THINK IT'S ROMANTIC.

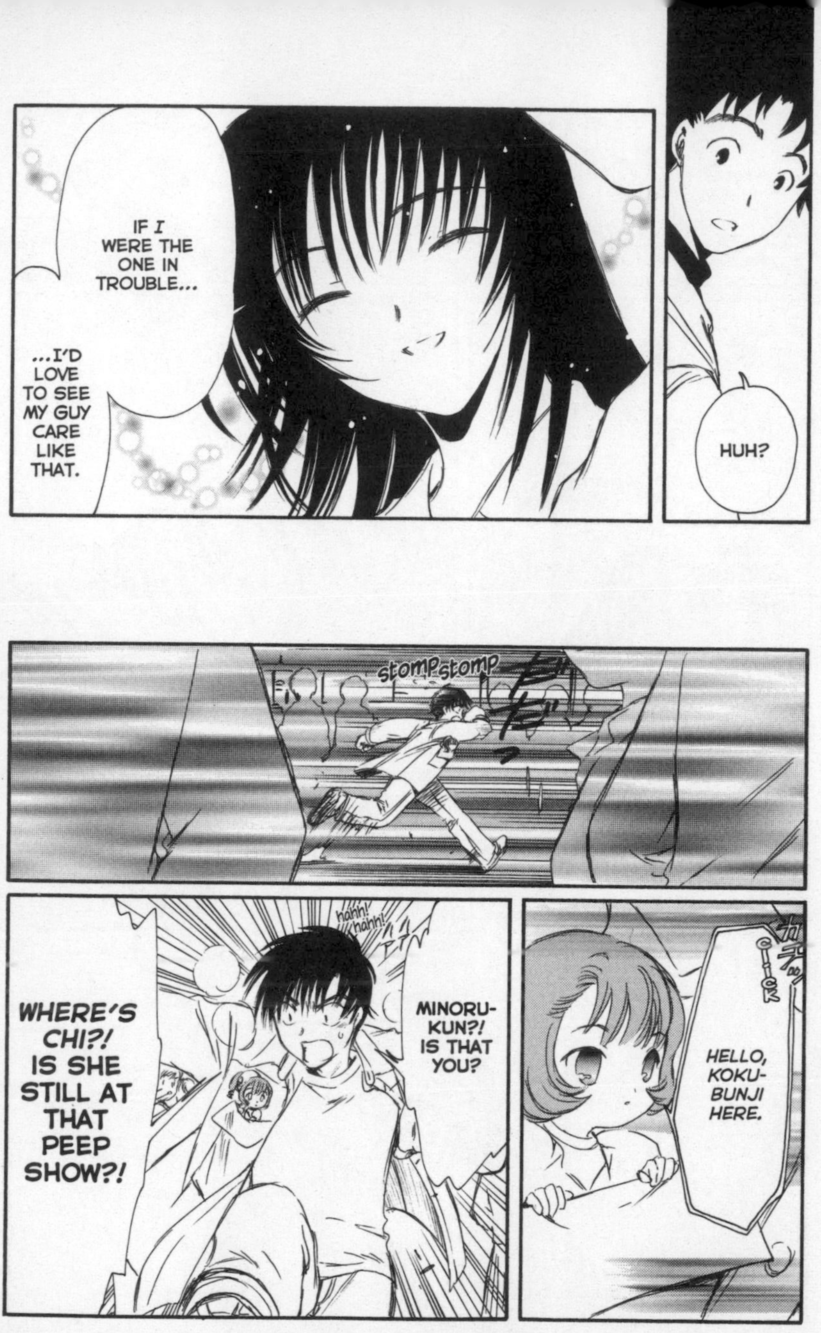
HUH?
IF I WERE THE ONE IN TROUBLE...
...I'D LOVE TO SEE MY GUY CARE LIKE THAT.
stomp stomp
click
HELLO, KOKUBUNJI HERE.
hahh! hahh!
MINORU-KUN?! IS THAT YOU?
WHERE'S CHI?! IS SHE STILL AT THAT PEEP SHOW?!

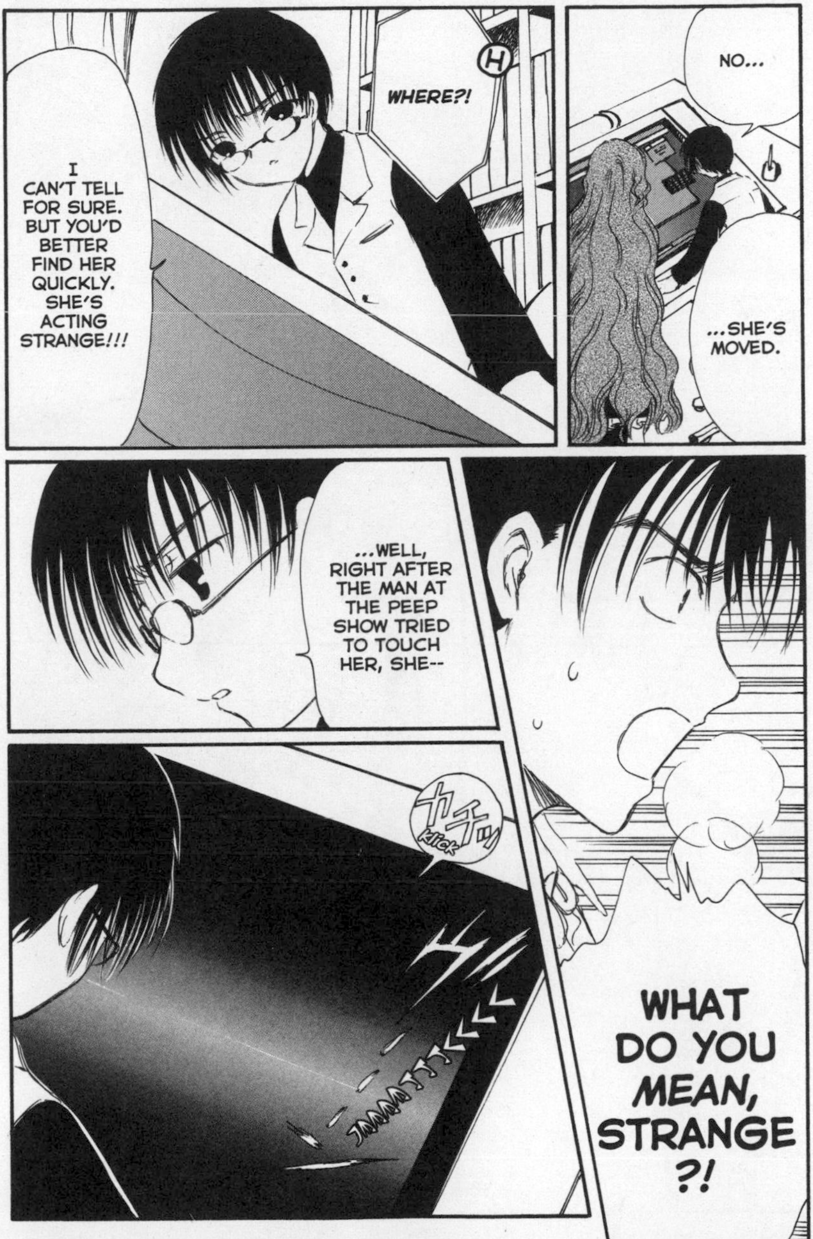
NO...
...SHE'S MOVED.
H
WHERE?!
I CAN'T TELL FOR SURE. BUT YOU'D BETTER FIND HER QUICKLY. SHE'S ACTING STRANGE!!!
WHAT DO YOU MEAN, STRANGE ?!
...WELL, RIGHT AFTER THE MAN AT THE PEEP SHOW TRIED TO TOUCH HER, SHE--
カチッ
klick

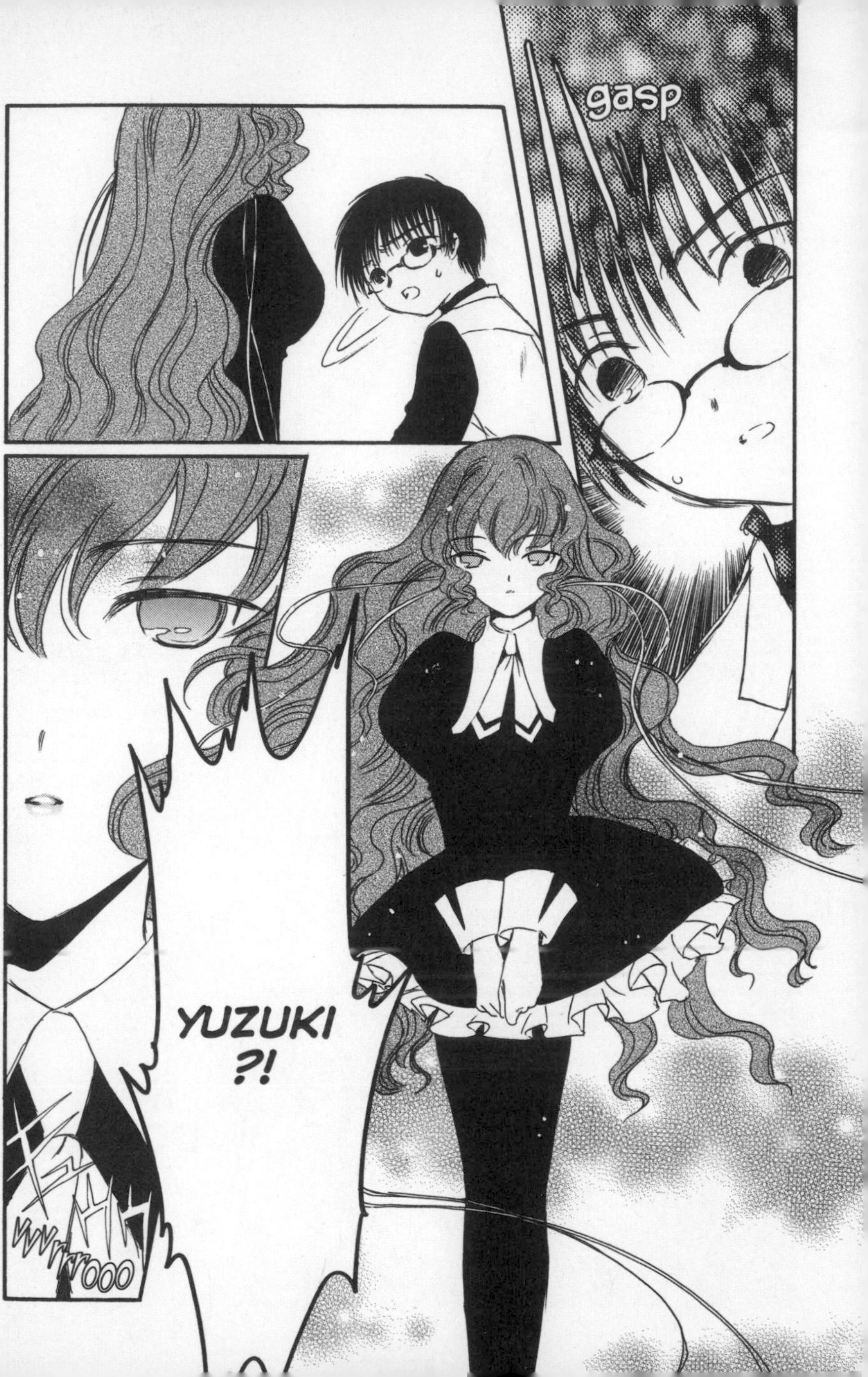
gasp
YUZUKI ?!
vvvrrrooo

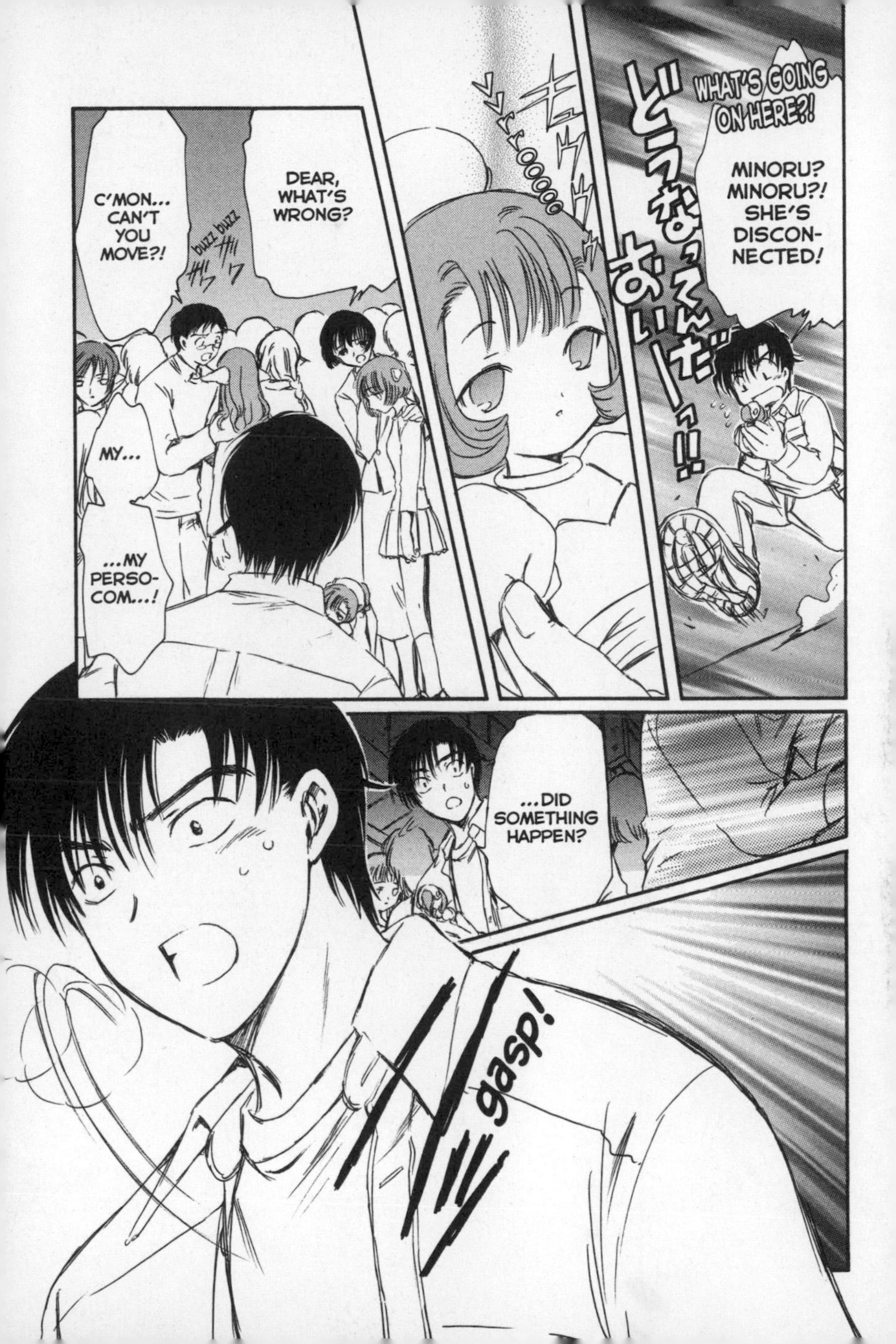
WHAT'S GOING ON HERE?!
どうなってんだ おいーっ!!
MINORU? MINORU?! SHE'S DISCONNECTED!
vvrrooooooo
DEAR, WHAT'S WRONG?
C'MON... CAN'T YOU MOVE?!
buzz buzz
MY...
...MY PERSOCOM...!
...DID SOMETHING HAPPEN?
gasp!

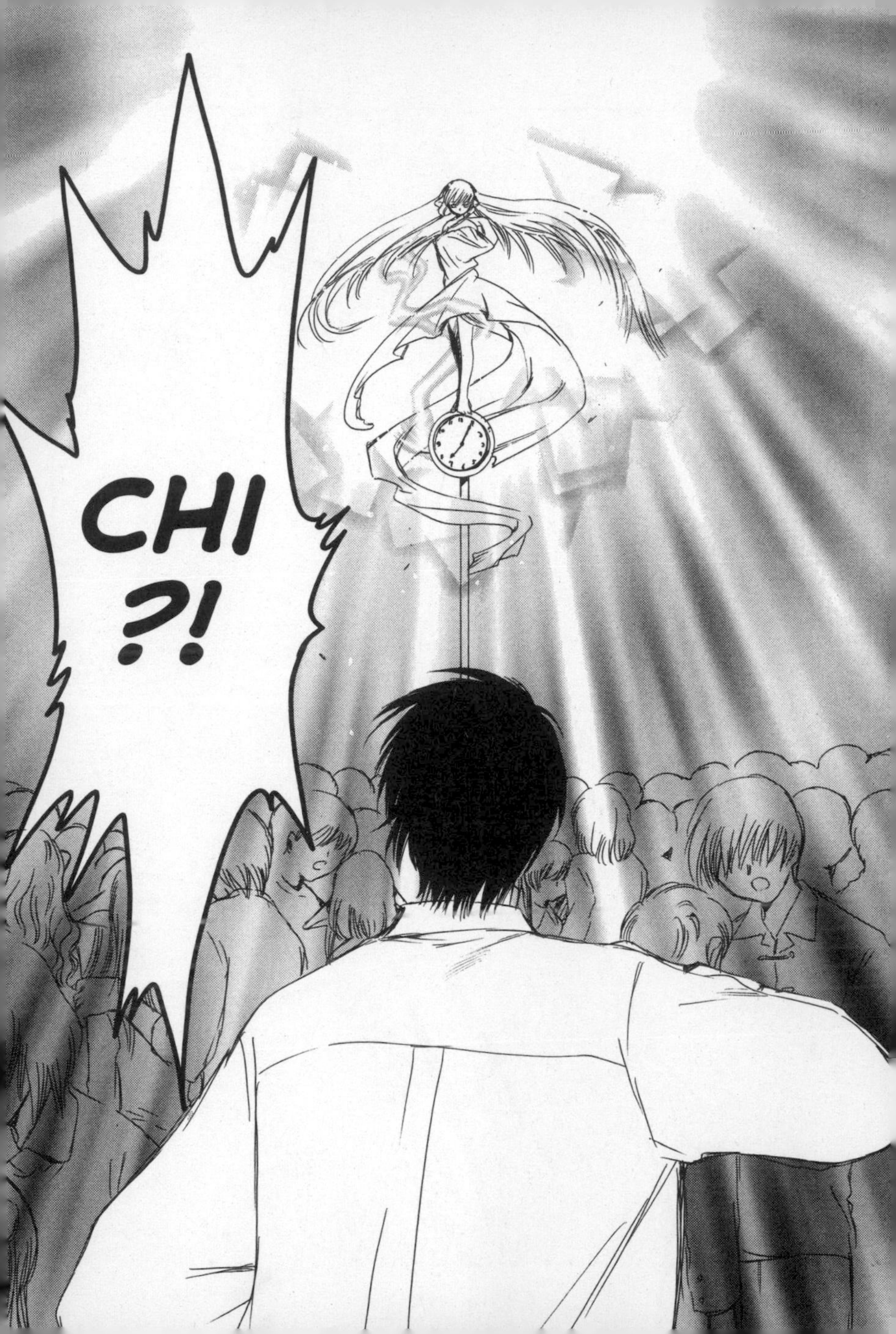
CHI ?!

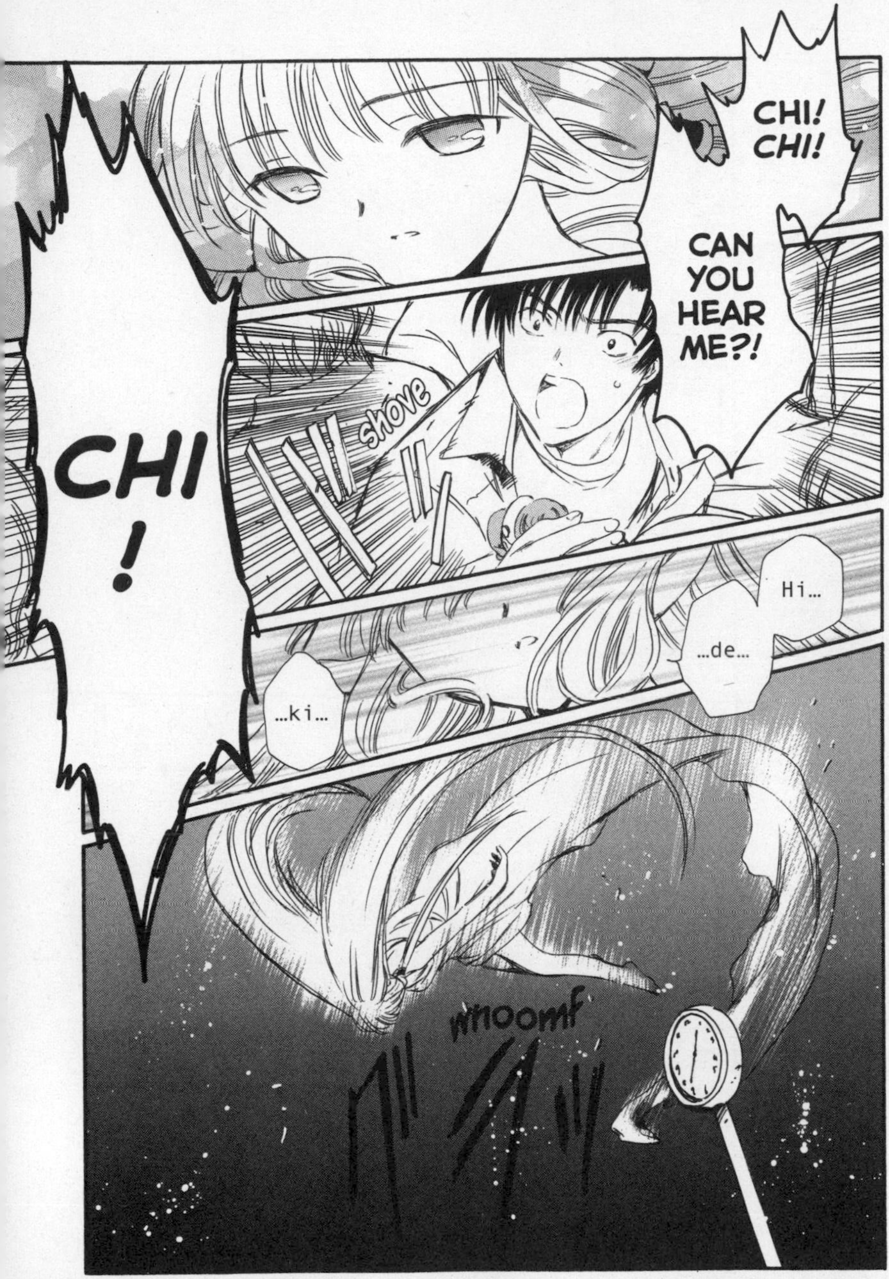
CHI! CHI!
CAN YOU HEAR ME?!
shove
Hi...
...de...
...ki...
wnoomf
CHI !

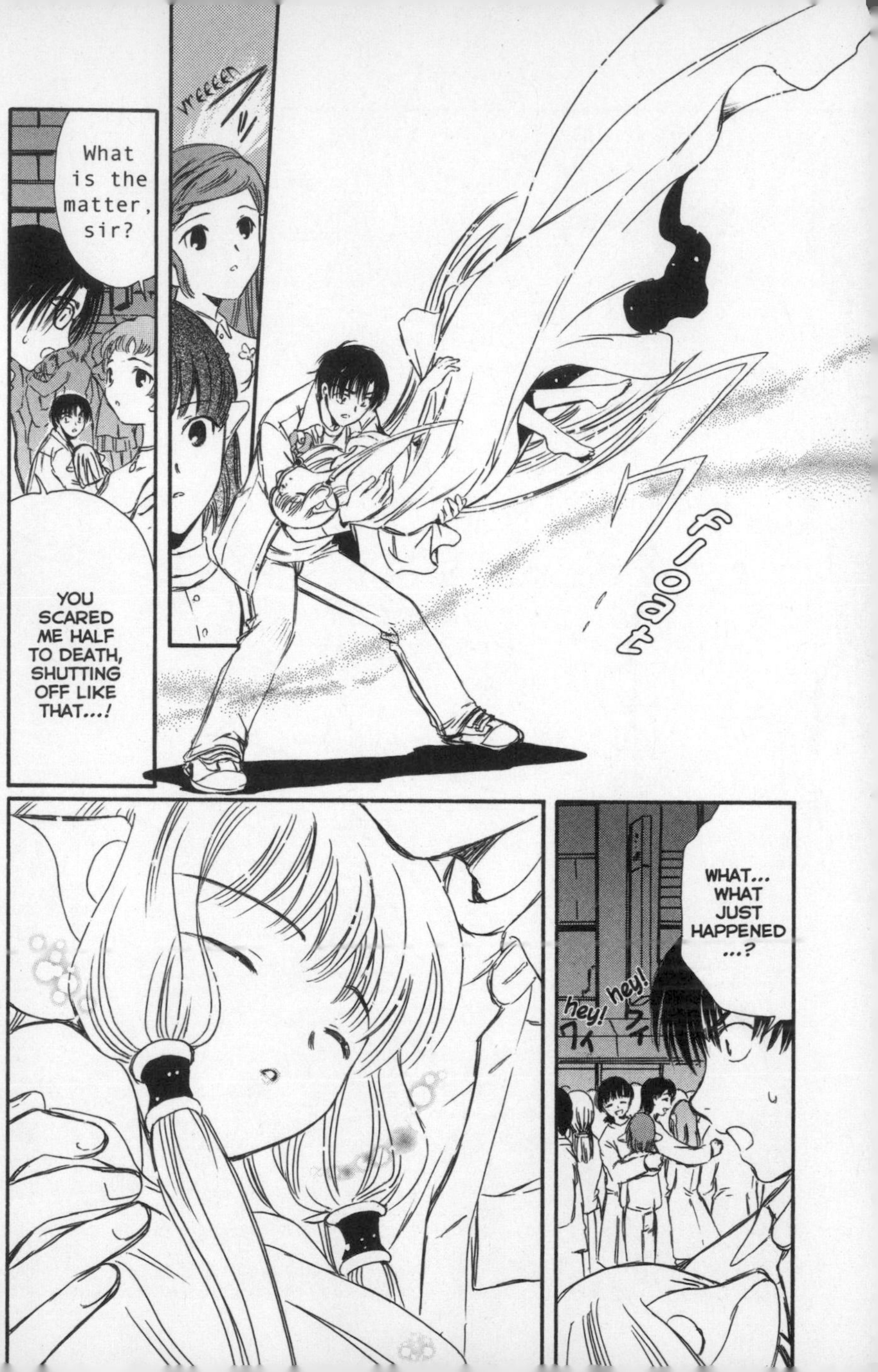
f-loat
vreeeen
What is the matter, sir?
YOU SCARED ME HALF TO DEATH, SHUTTING OFF LIKE THAT...!
WHAT... WHAT JUST HAPPENED ...?
hey!
hey!

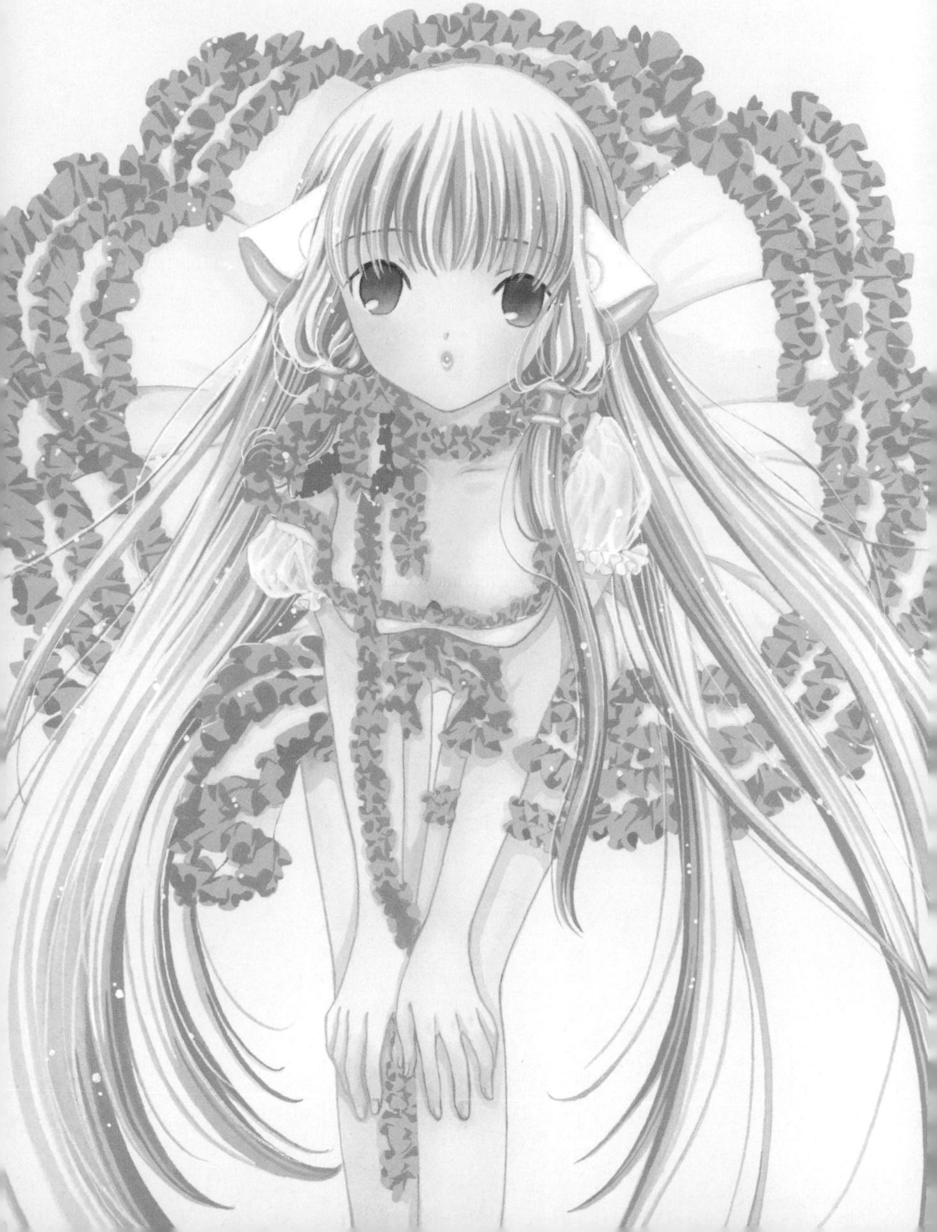

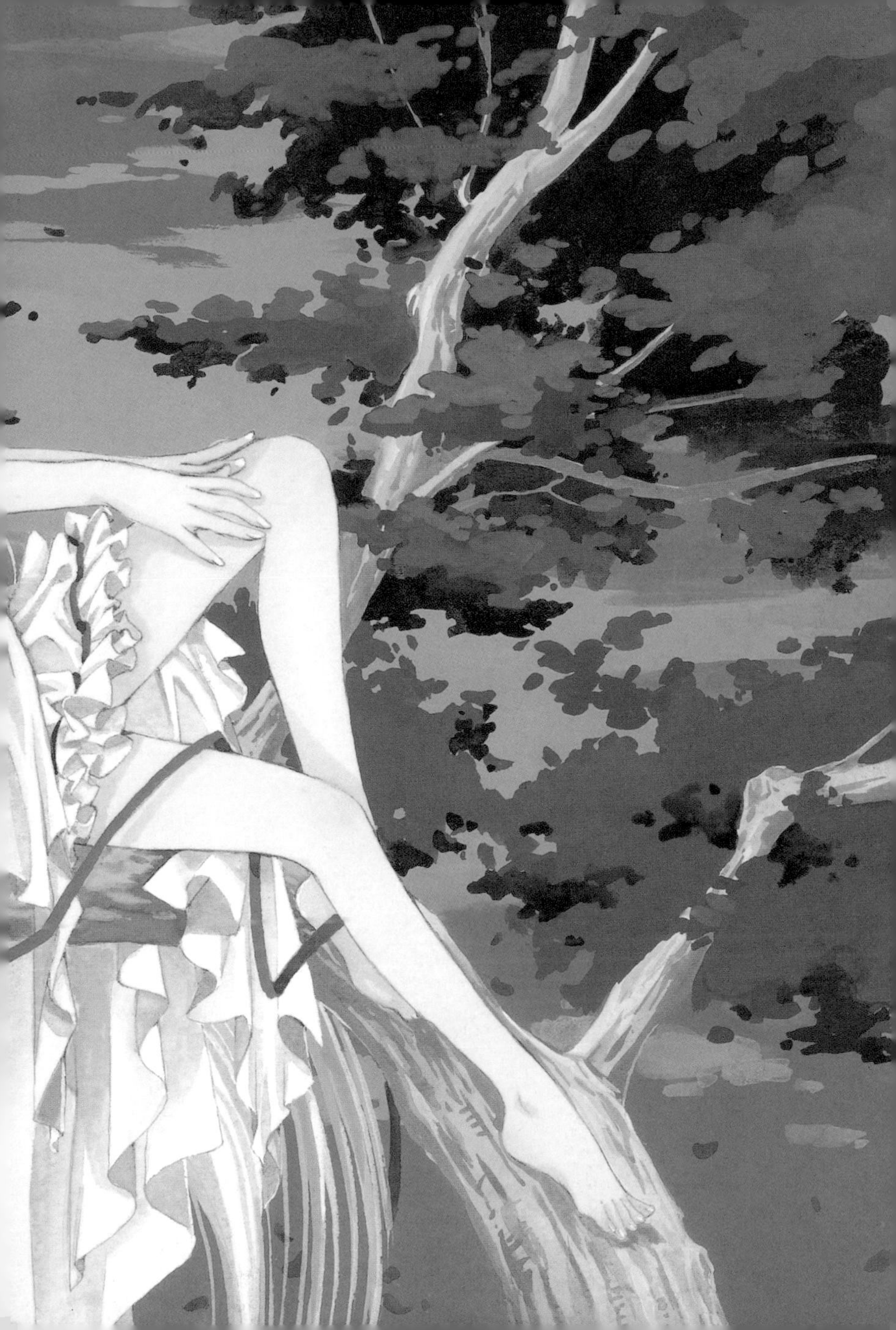

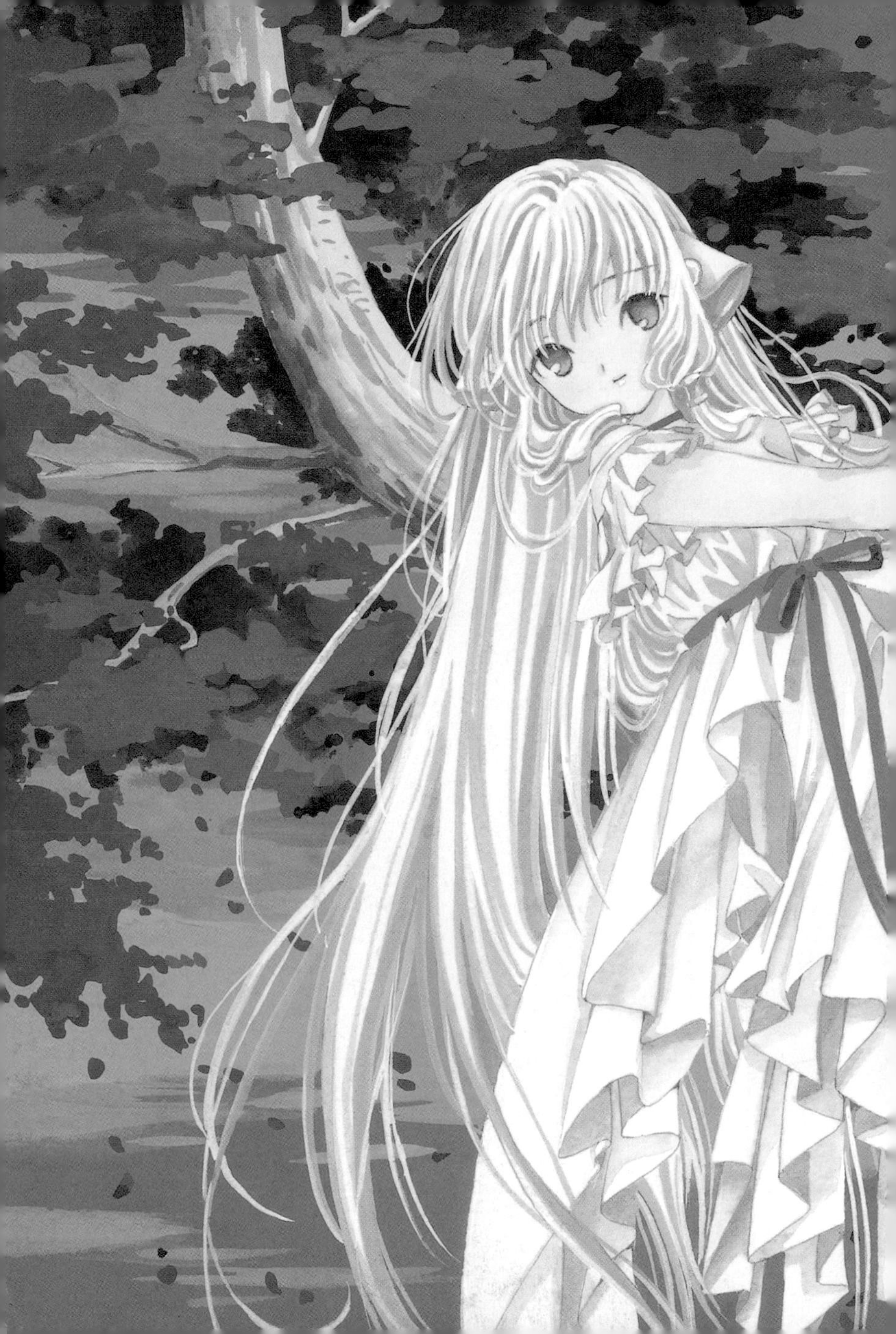

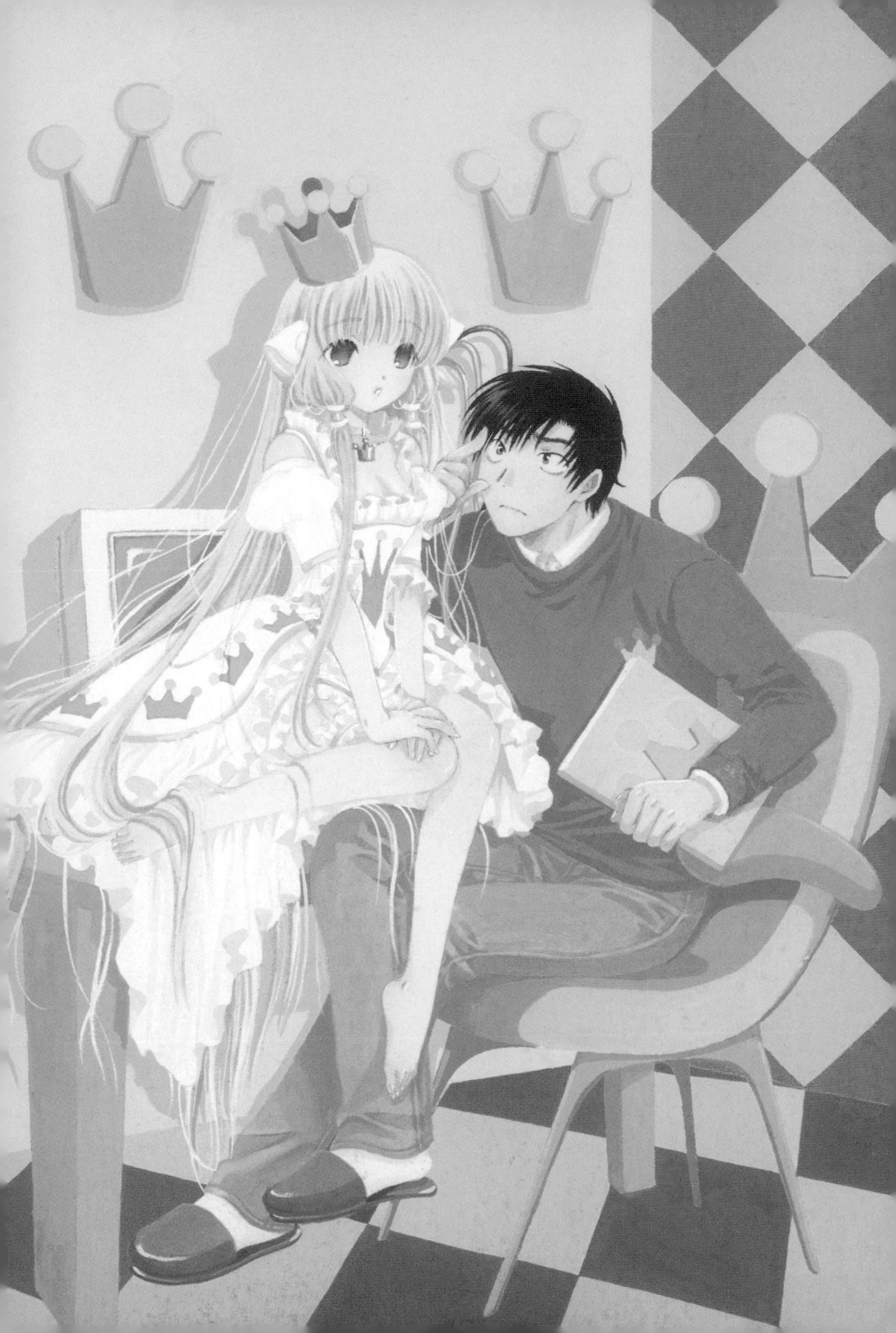

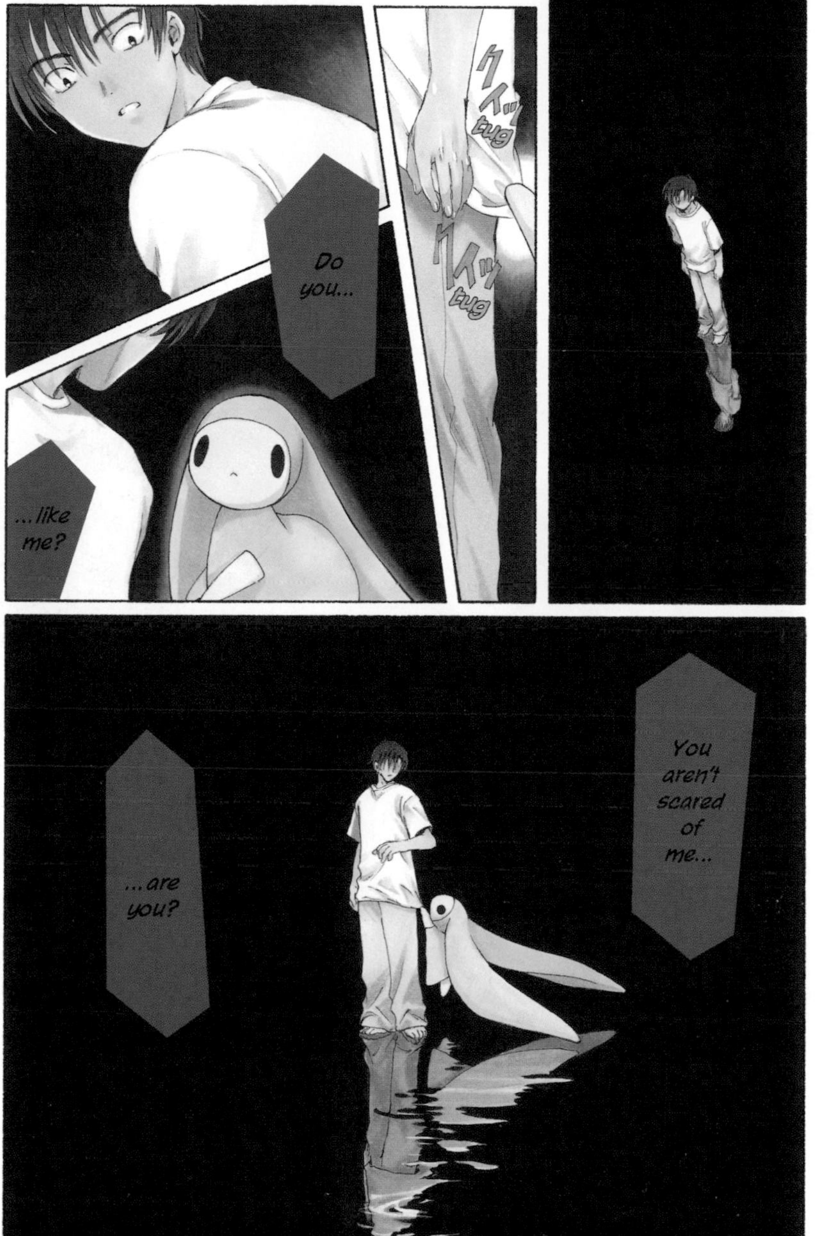
クイッ tug
クイッ tug
Do you...
...like me?
You aren't scared of me...
...are you?

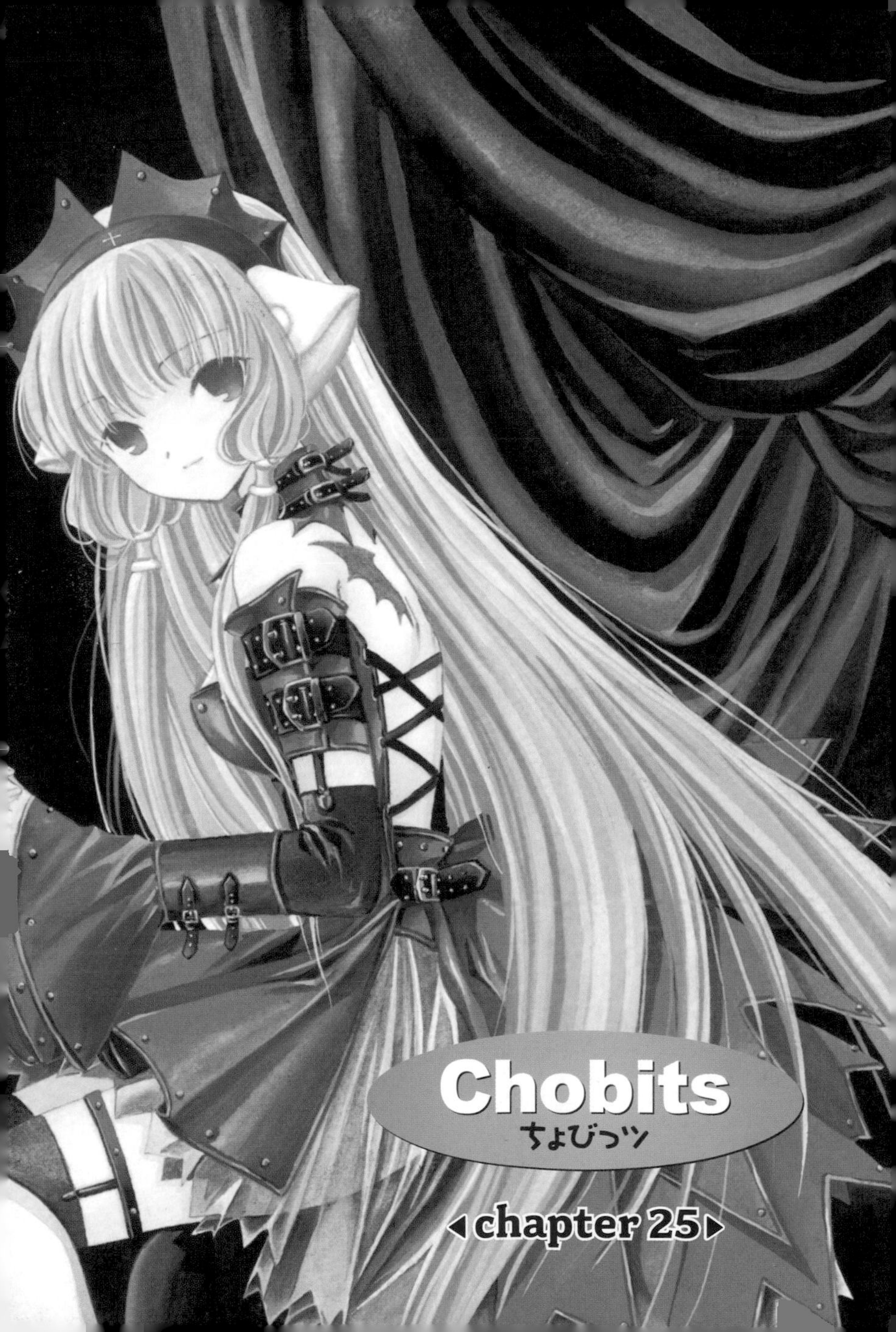
Chobits
ちょびっツ
chapter 25

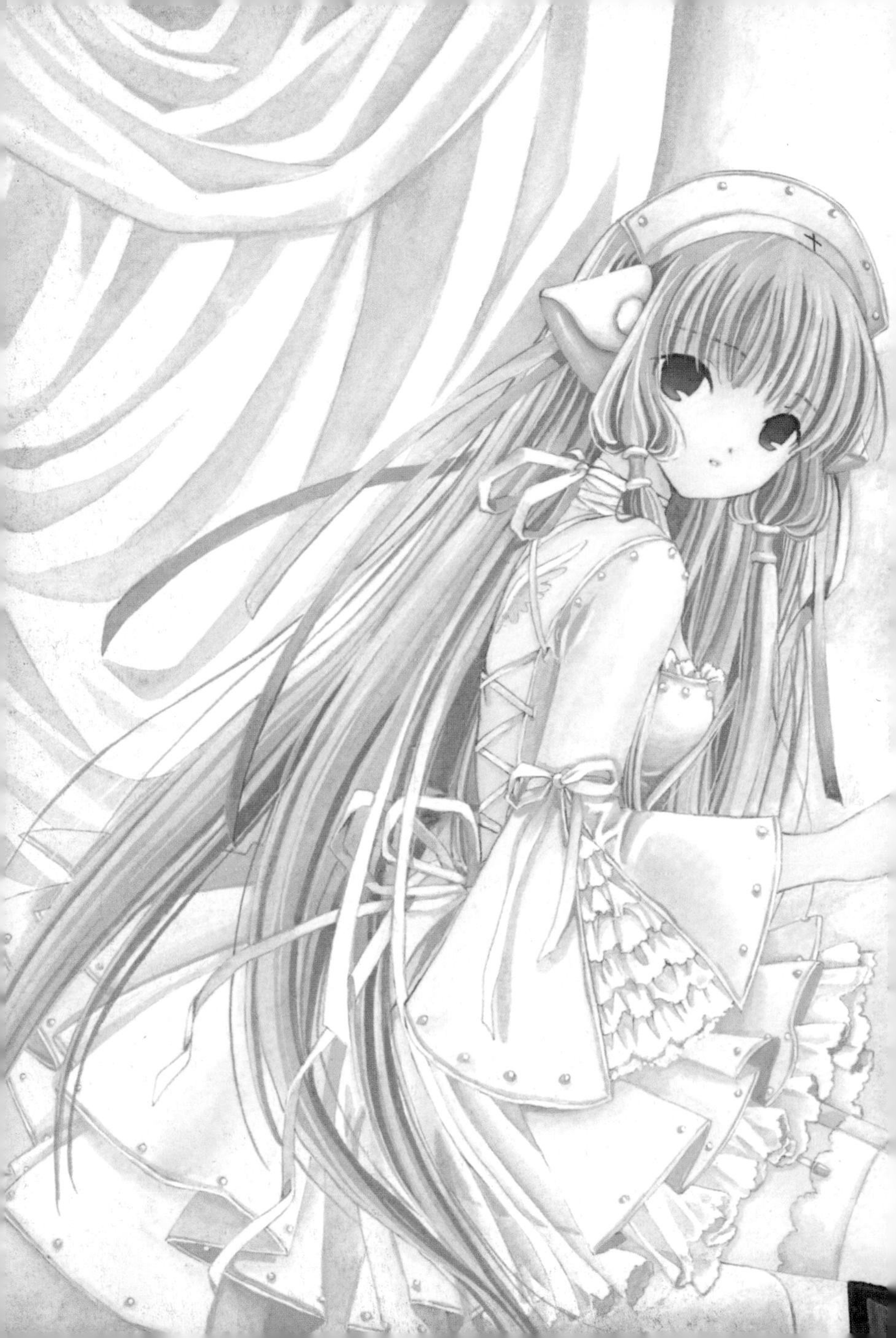

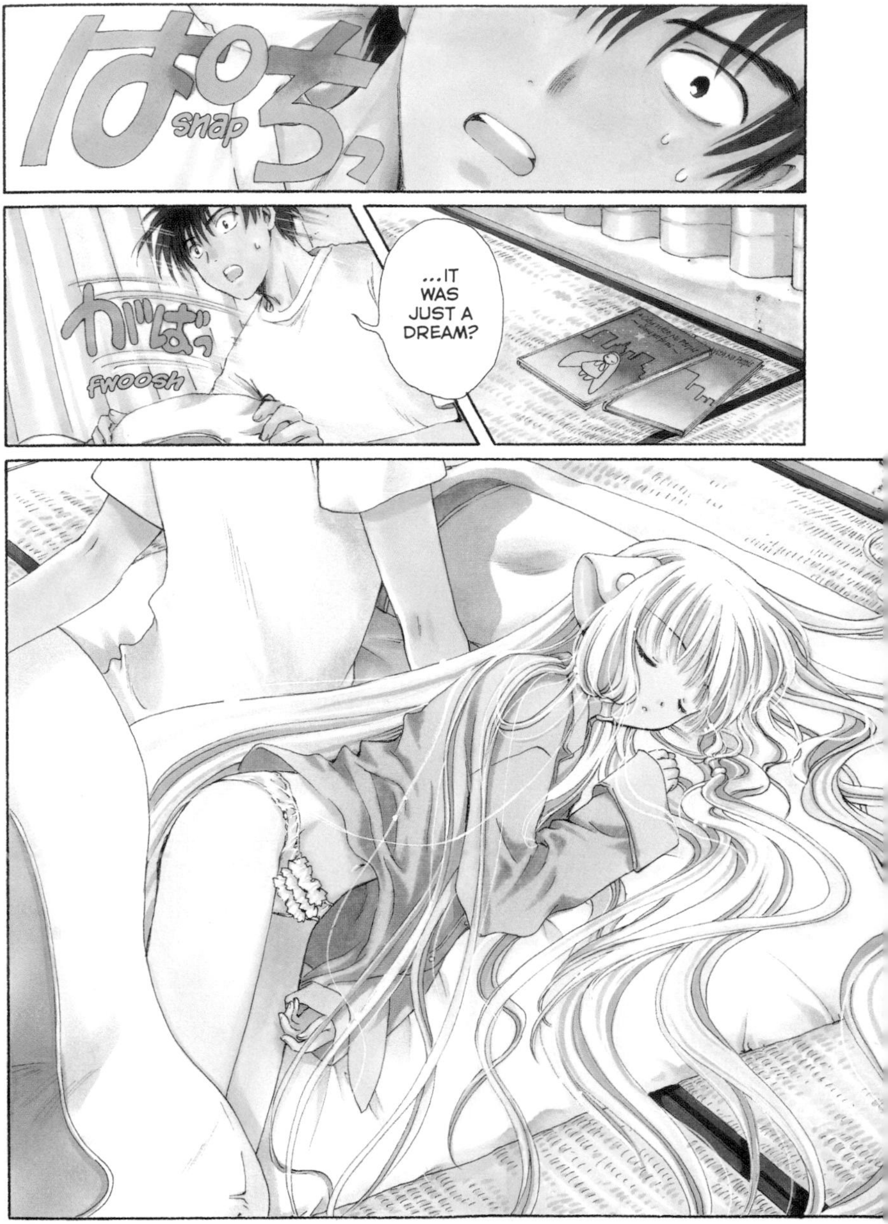
snap
...IT WAS JUST A DREAM?
fwoosh

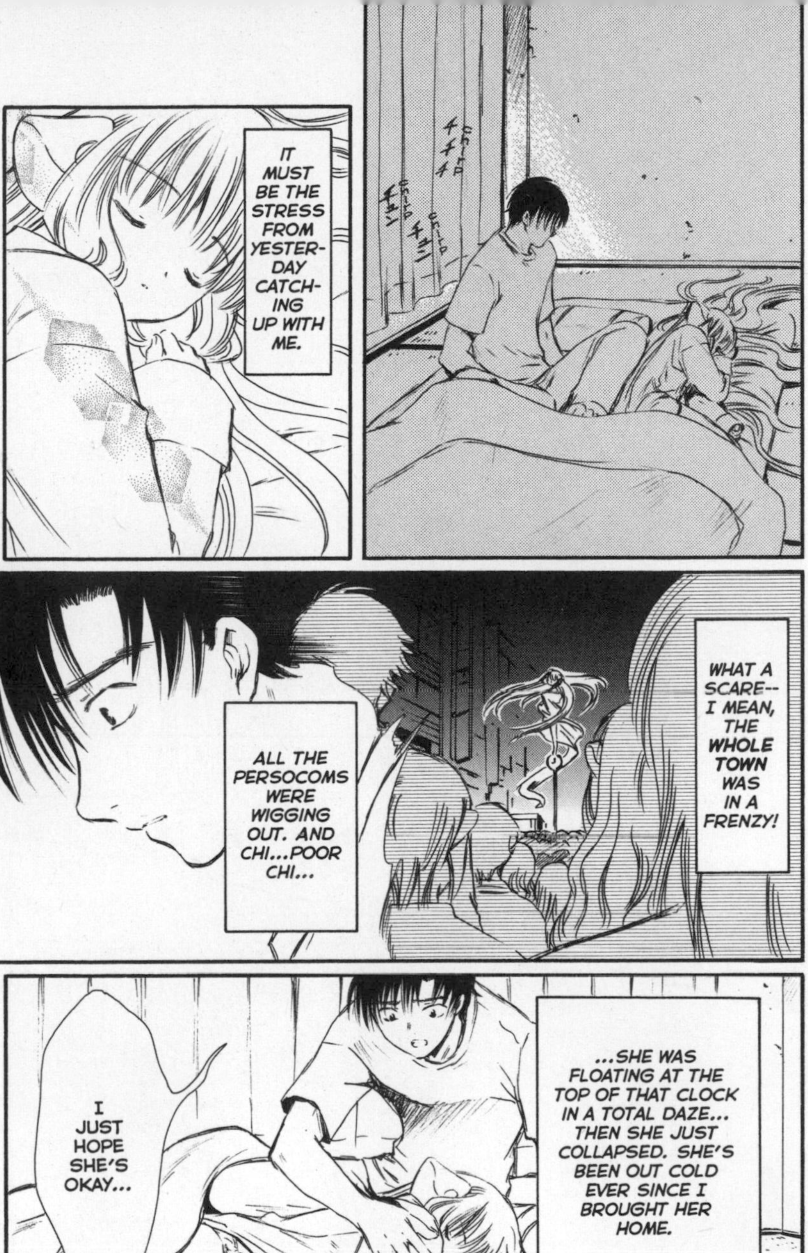
チチチ
CHIRP
CHIRP
チュン
CHIRP
チチ
IT MUST BE THE STRESS FROM YESTER-DAY CATCH-ING UP WITH ME.
WHAT A SCARE-- I MEAN, THE WHOLE TOWN WAS IN A FRENZY!
ALL THE PERSOCOMS WERE WIGGING OUT. AND CHI...POOR CHI...
...SHE WAS FLOATING AT THE TOP OF THAT CLOCK IN A TOTAL DAZE... THEN SHE JUST COLLAPSED. SHE'S BEEN OUT COLD EVER SINCE I BROUGHT HER HOME.
I JUST HOPE SHE'S OKAY...

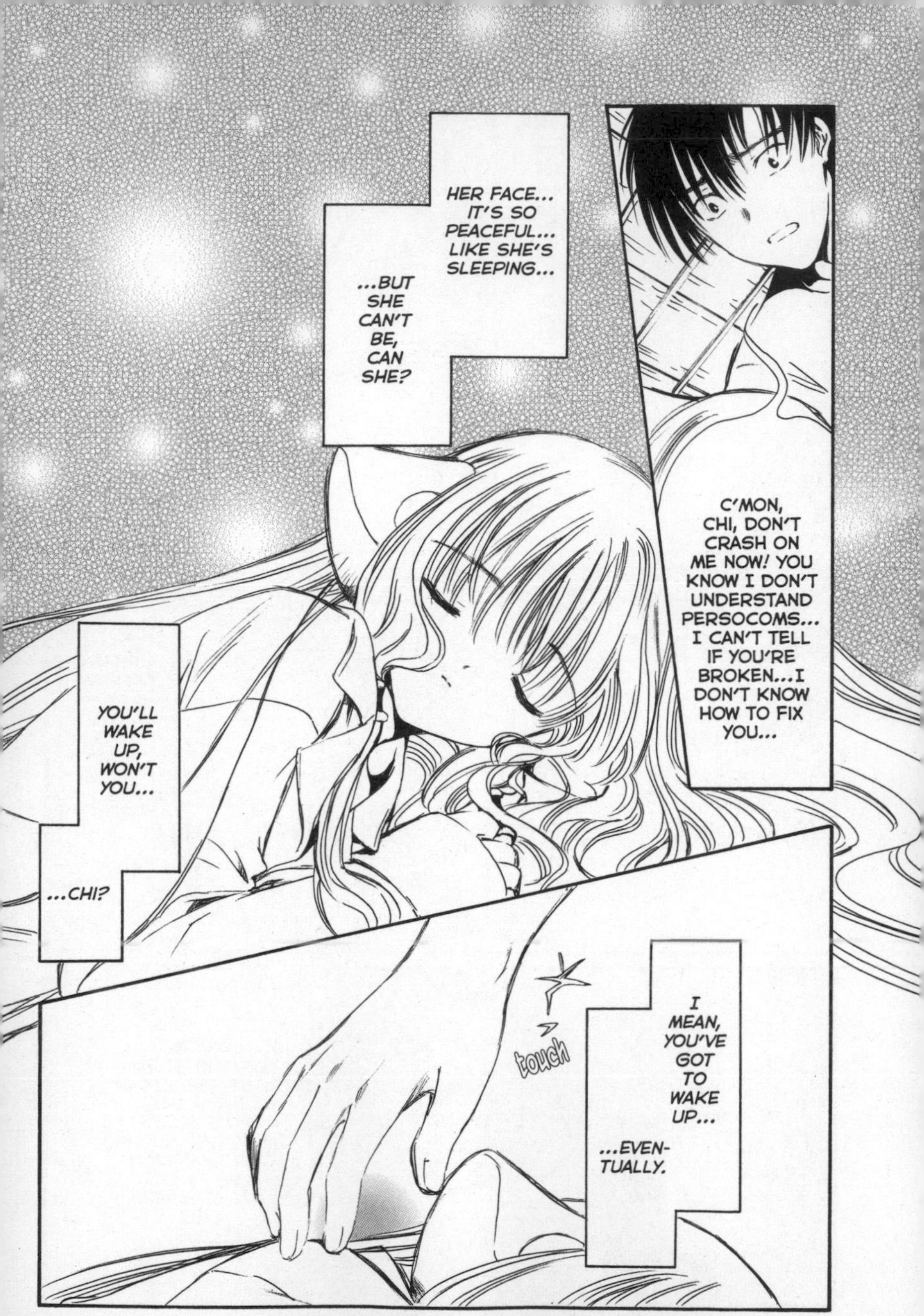
HER FACE... IT'S SO PEACEFUL... LIKE SHE'S SLEEPING...
...BUT SHE CAN'T BE, CAN SHE?
C'MON, CHI, DON'T CRASH ON ME NOW! YOU KNOW I DON'T UNDERSTAND PERSOCOMS... I CAN'T TELL IF YOU'RE BROKEN...I DON'T KNOW HOW TO FIX YOU...
YOU'LL WAKE UP, WON'T YOU...
...CHI?
I MEAN, YOU'VE GOT TO WAKE UP...
touch
...EVEN-TUALLY.

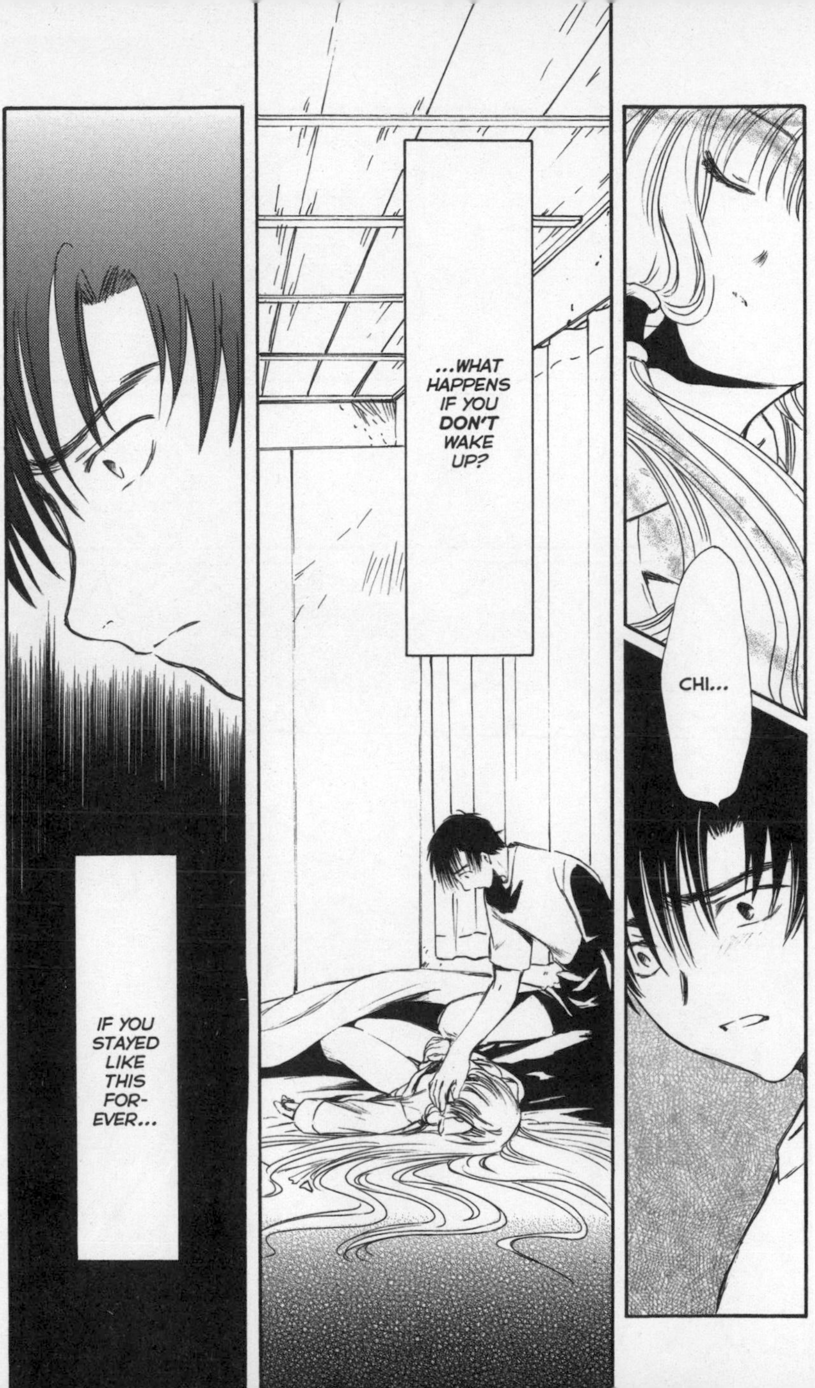
CHI...
...WHAT HAPPENS IF YOU DON'T WAKE UP?
IF YOU STAYED LIKE THIS FOR-EVER...

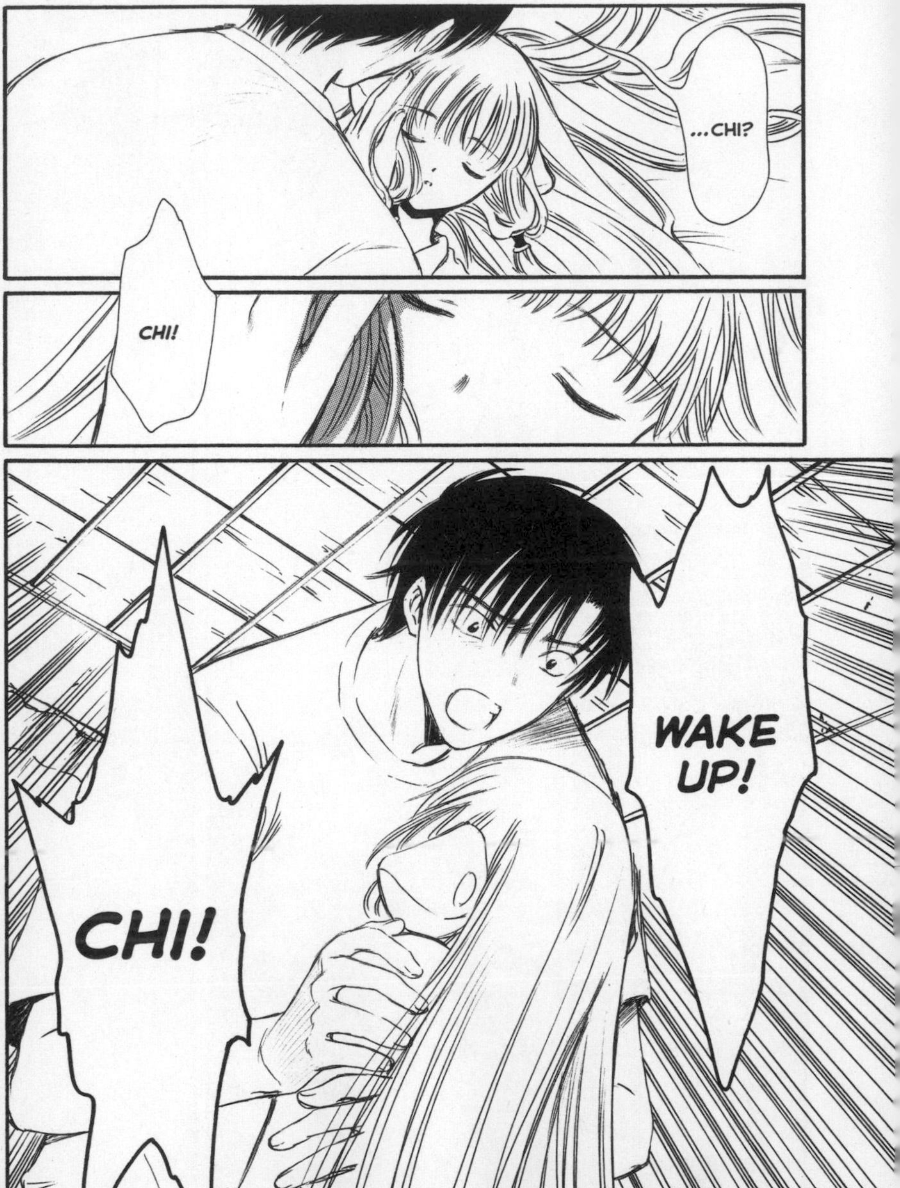
...CHI?
CHI!
WAKE UP!
CHI!

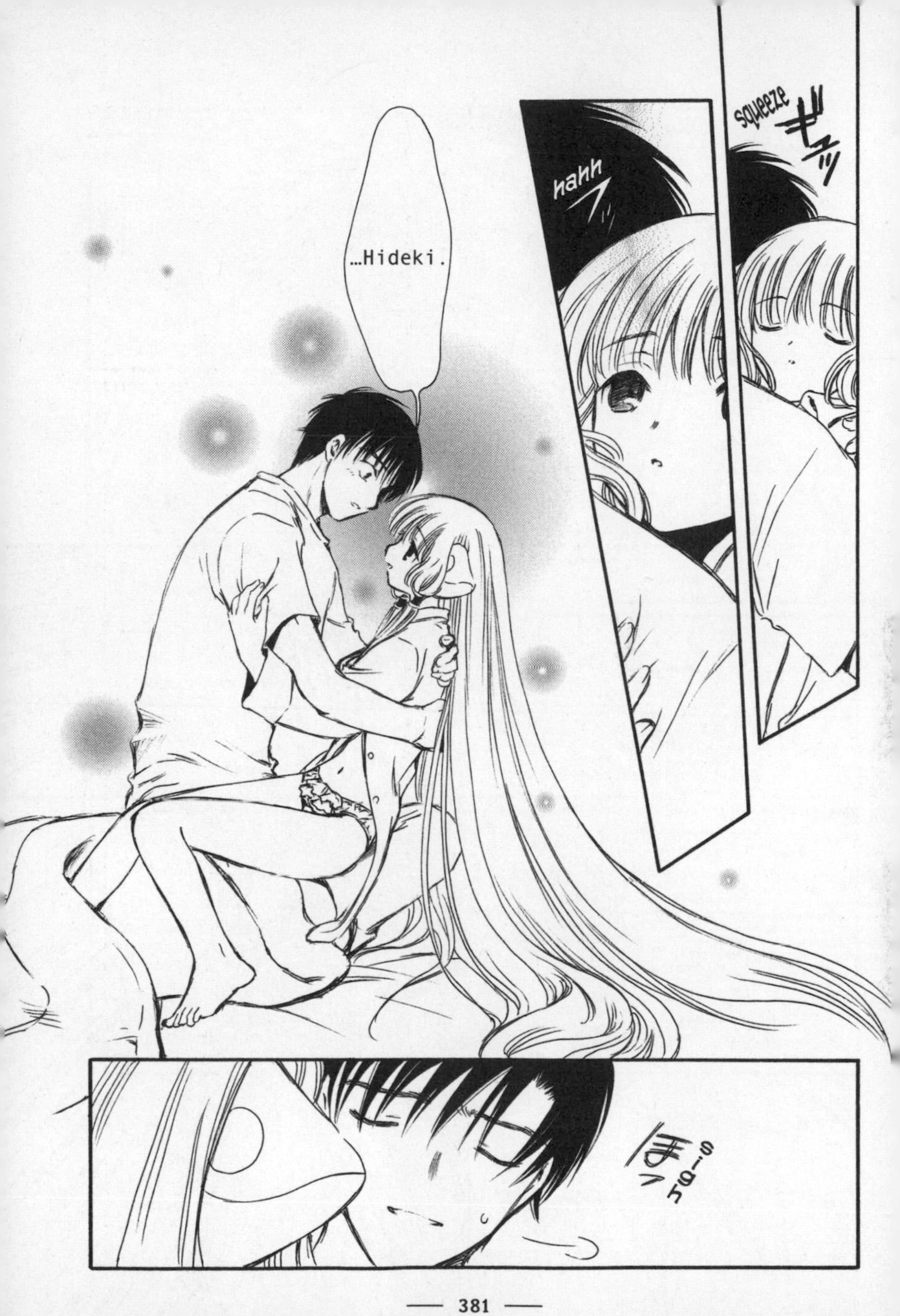
ギュッ
squeeze
hahn
...Hideki.
ほっ
sigh

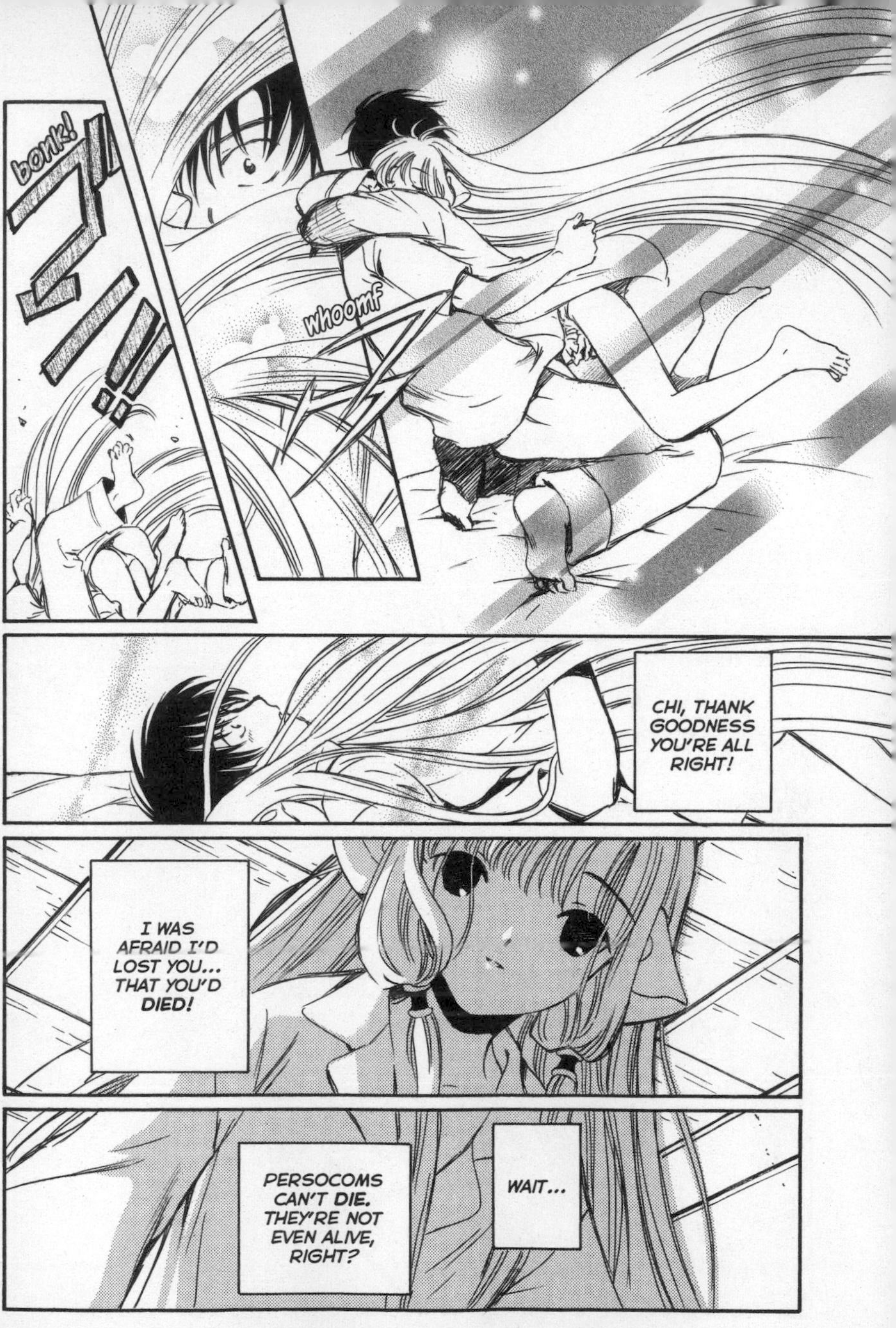
whoomf
bonk!
CHI, THANK GOODNESS YOU'RE ALL RIGHT!
I WAS AFRAID I'D LOST YOU... THAT YOU'D DIED!
WAIT...
PERSOCOMS CAN'T DIE. THEY'RE NOT EVEN ALIVE, RIGHT?

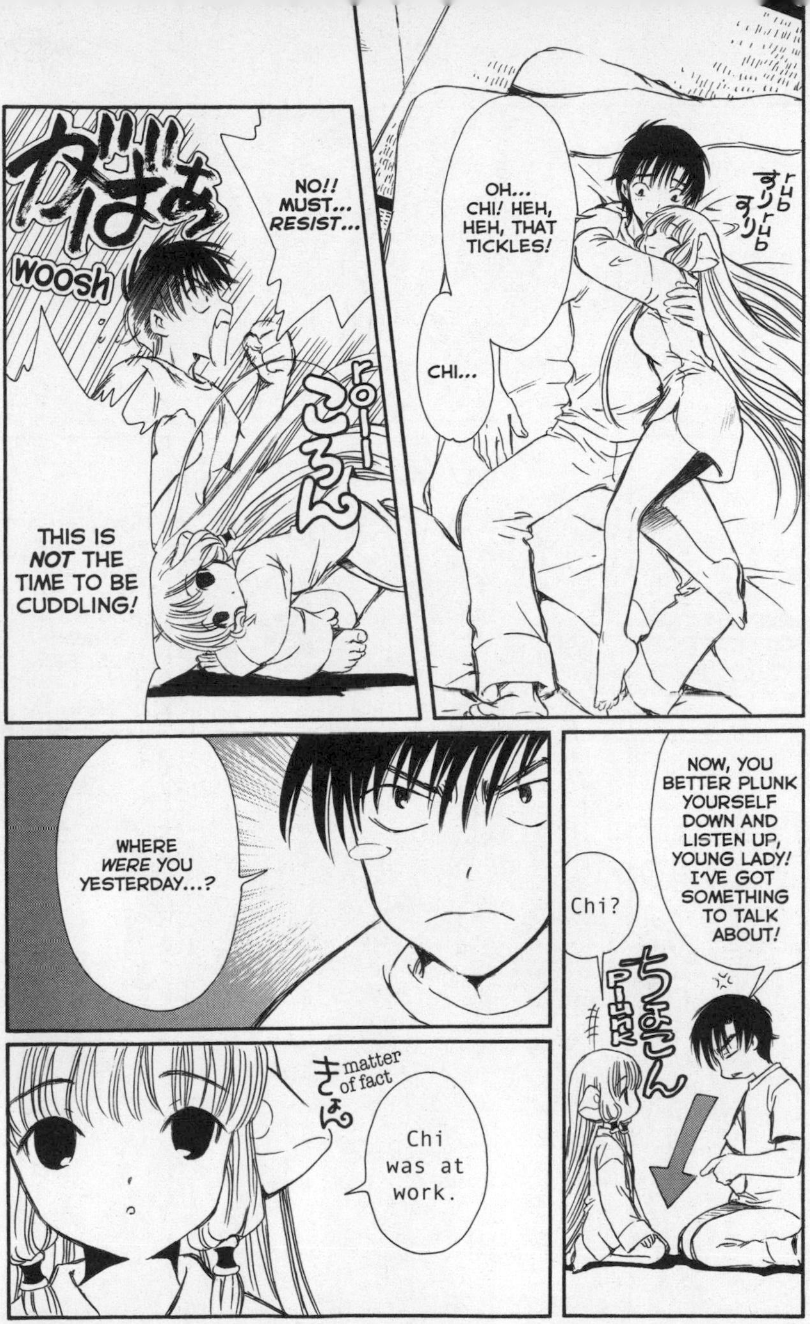
OH... CHI! HEH, HEH, THAT TICKLES!
CHI...
すりすり
rub rub
がばぁ
WOOSH
NO!! MUST... RESIST...
ころん
roll
THIS IS NOT THE TIME TO BE CUDDLING!
NOW, YOU BETTER PLUNK YOURSELF DOWN AND LISTEN UP, YOUNG LADY! I'VE GOT SOMETHING TO TALK ABOUT!
Chi?
ちょこん
PLUNK
WHERE WERE YOU YESTERDAY...?
きょん
matter of fact
Chi was at work.

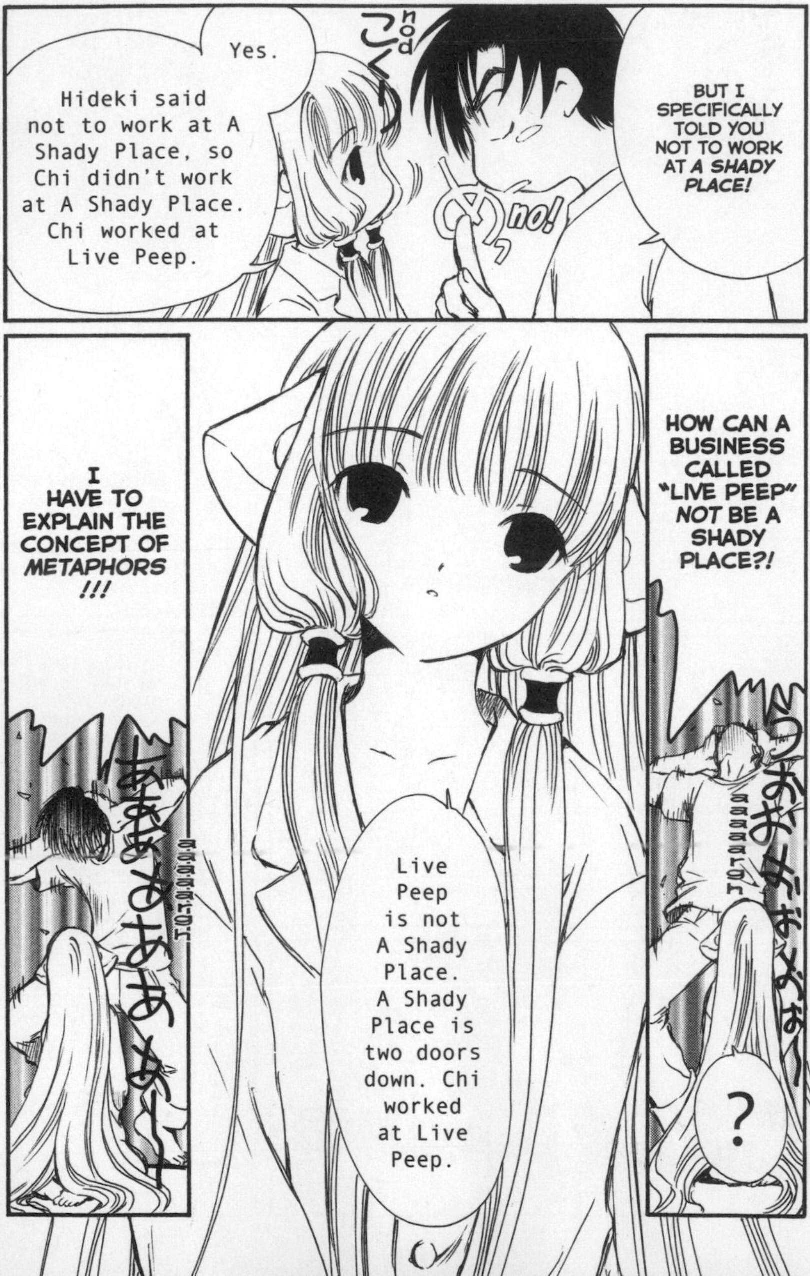
BUT I SPECIFICALLY TOLD YOU NOT TO WORK AT A SHADY PLACE!
no!
nod
Yes.
Hideki said not to work at A Shady Place, so Chi didn't work at A Shady Place. Chi worked at Live Peep.
HOW CAN A BUSINESS CALLED "LIVE PEEP" NOT BE A SHADY PLACE?!
aaaaargh
?
Live Peep is not A Shady Place. A Shady Place is two doors down. Chi worked at Live Peep.
I HAVE TO EXPLAIN THE CONCEPT OF METAPHORS!!!
aaaaargh

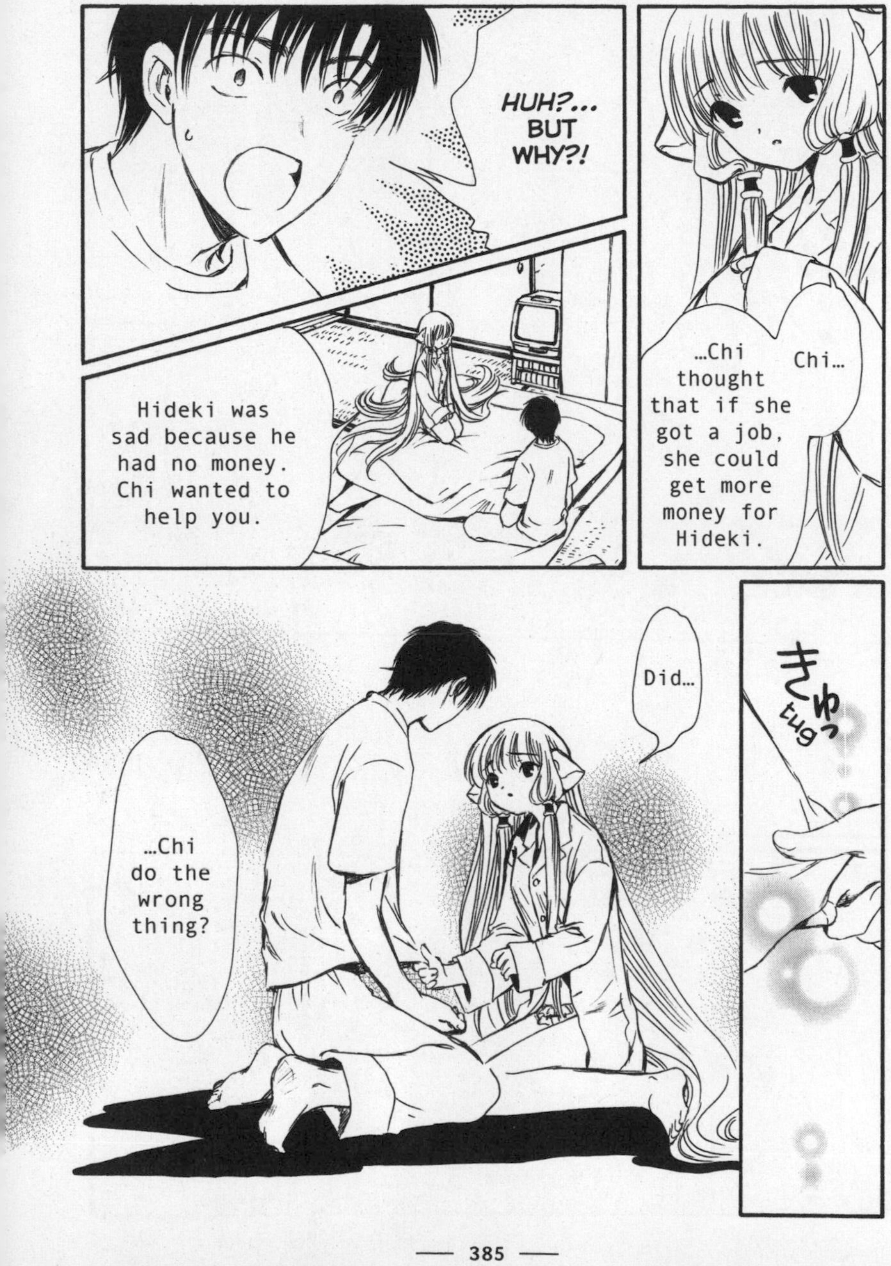
Chi…
…Chi thought that if she got a job, she could get more money for Hideki.
HUH?… BUT WHY?!
Hideki was sad because he had no money. Chi wanted to help you.
きゅっ tug
Did…
…Chi do the wrong thing?

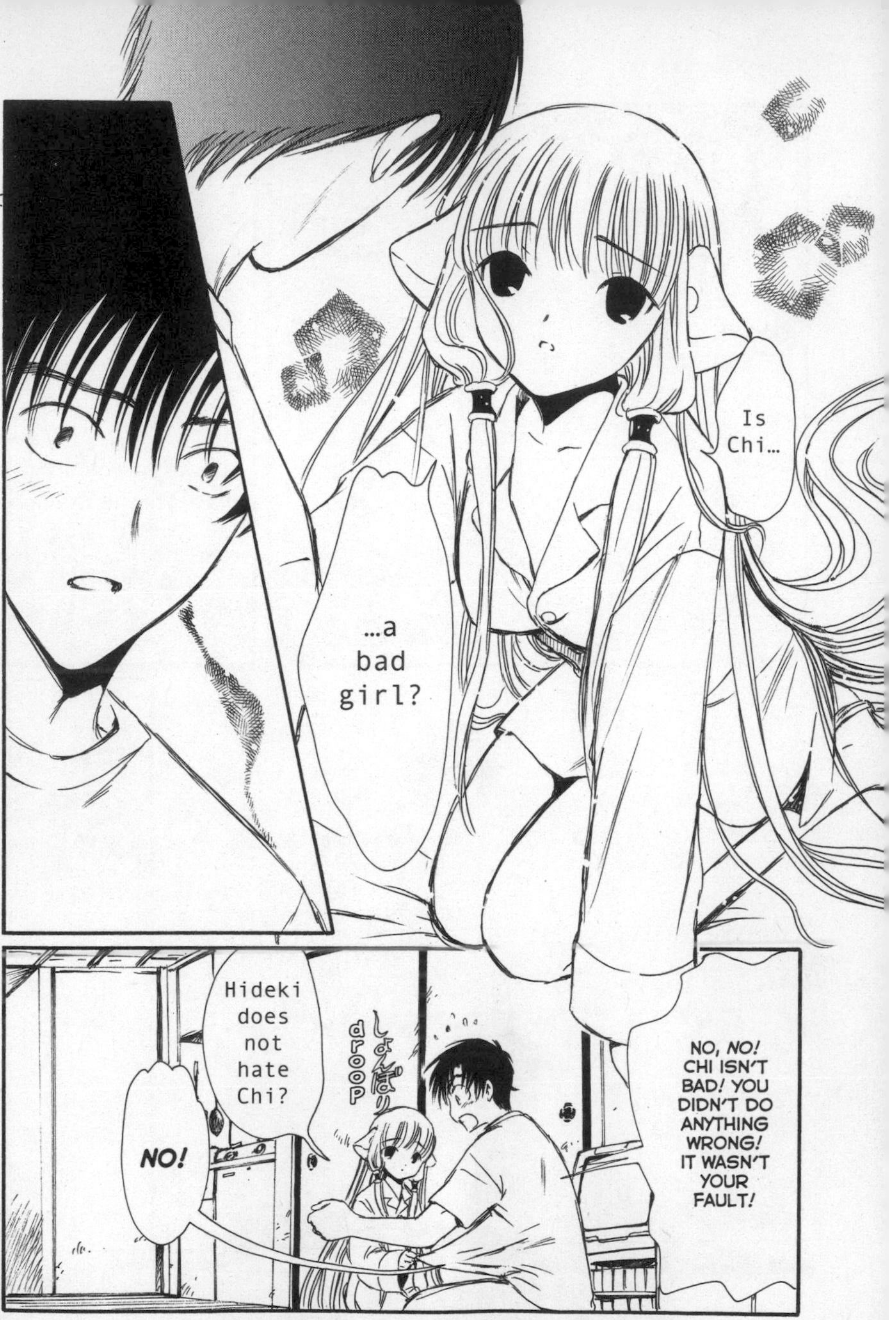
Is Chi...
...a bad girl?
NO, NO! CHI ISN'T BAD! YOU DIDN'T DO ANYTHING WRONG! IT WASN'T YOUR FAULT!
しょんぼり
droop
Hideki does not hate Chi?
NO!

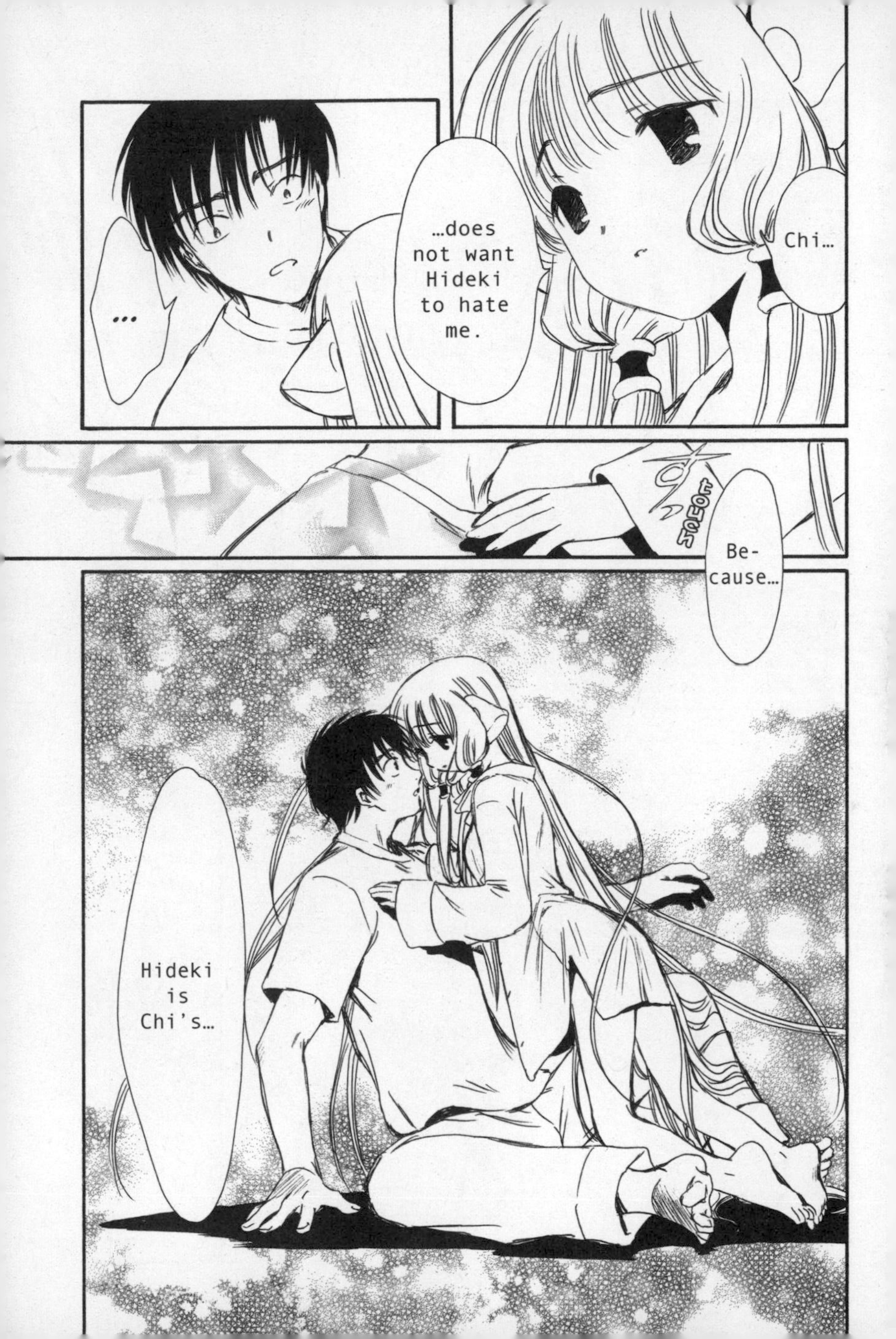
Chi…
…does not want Hideki to hate me.
…
touch
Be-cause…
Hideki is Chi's…

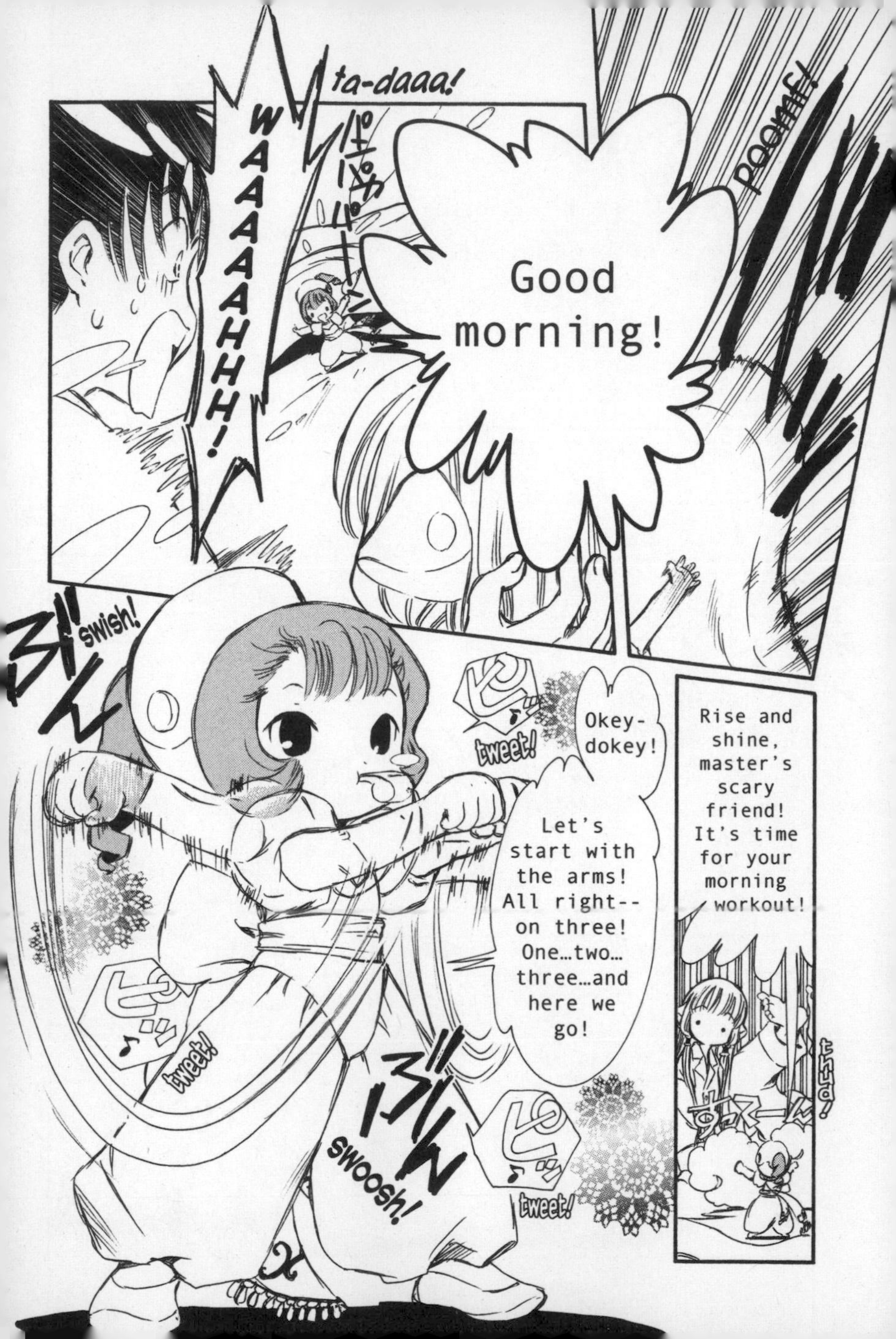
poomf!
Good morning!
ta-daaa!
WAAAAAAHHH!
Rise and shine, master's scary friend! It's time for your morning workout!
Okey-dokey!
tweet!
swish!
Let's start with the arms! All right--on three! One…two…three…and here we go!
tweet!
swoosh!
tweet!

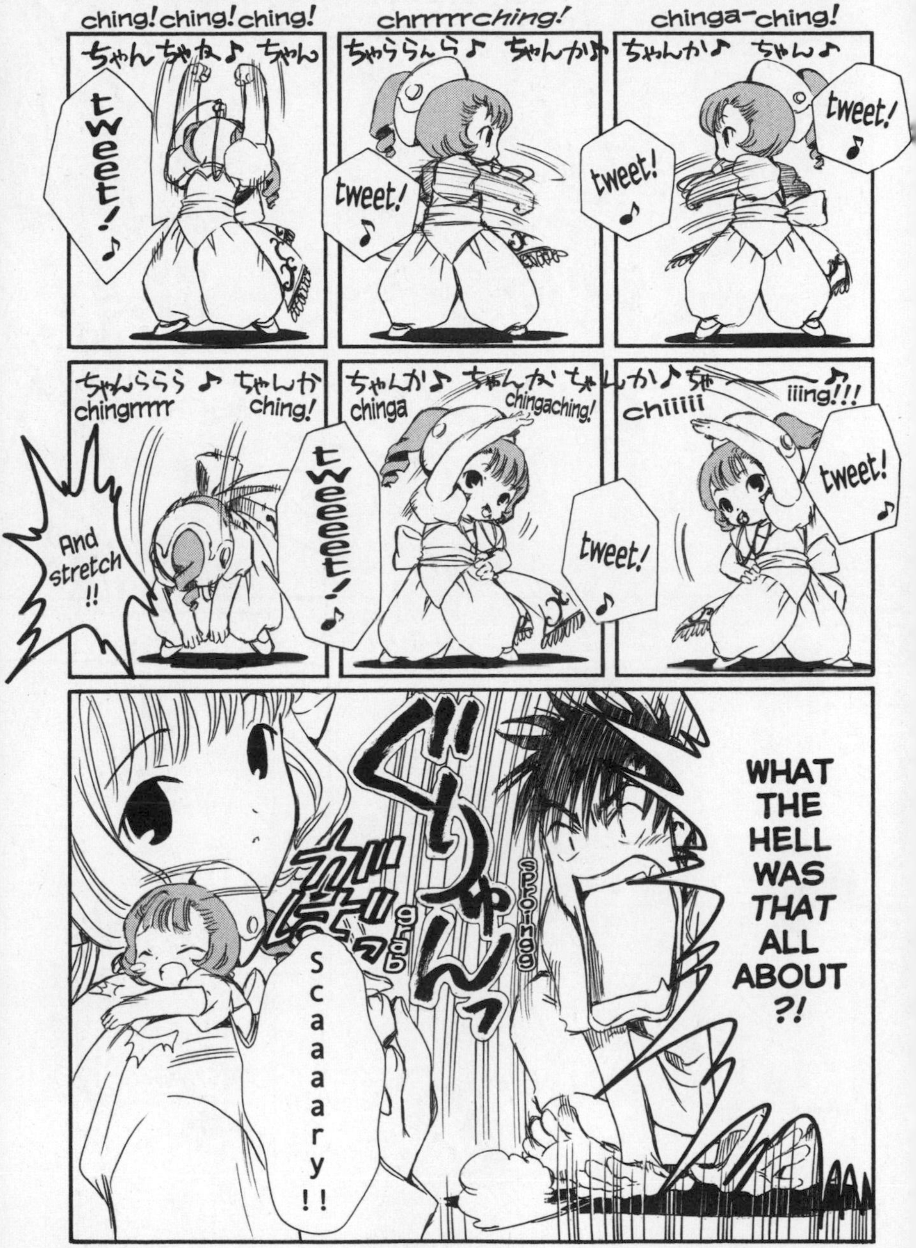
chinga-ching!
ちゃんか♪ ちゃん♪
tweet! ♪
tweet! ♪
chrrrrrching!
ちゃららんら♪ ちゃんか♪
tweet! ♪
ching! ching! ching!
ちゃんちゃね♪ ちゃん
tweet! ♪
chiiiii
iiing!!!
tweet! ♪
tweet! ♪
ちゃんか♪ ちゃんな ちゃんか♪ちゃ——♪
chinga
chingaching!
tweeeeet! ♪
ちゃんららら♪ ちゃんか
chingrrrrr
ching!
And stretch !!
WHAT THE HELL WAS THAT ALL ABOUT ?!
sproingg
ぐりゅんっ
grab
がしっ
Scaaaary!!

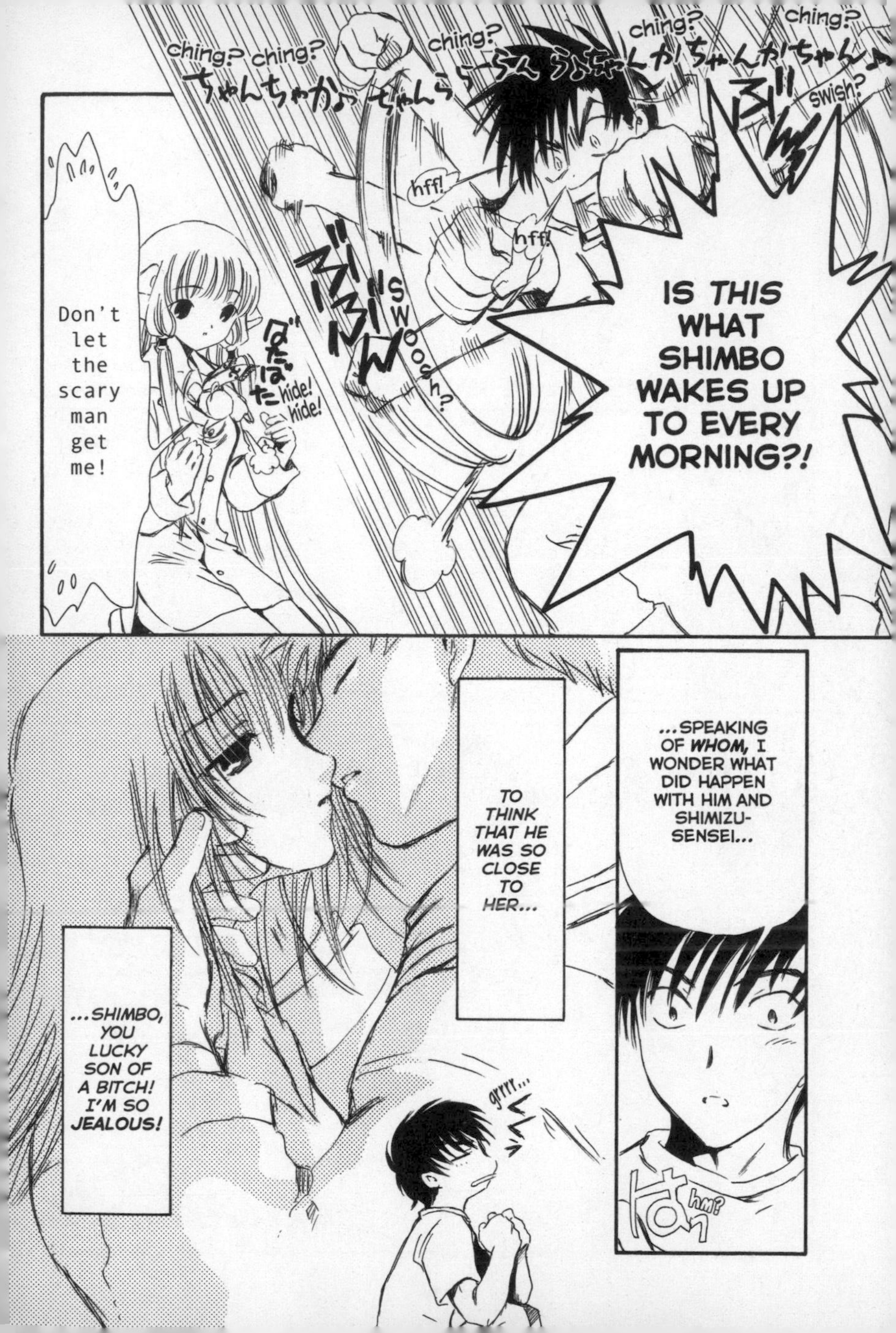
ching? ching? ching? ching? ching?
ちゃんちゃか♪ ちゃんら ら～らん ら♪ちゃんか! ちゃんか! ちゃん♪
ぶ swish?
hff!
hff!
IS THIS WHAT SHIMBO WAKES UP TO EVERY MORNING?!
ブーブーブン SWOOSH?
だばた hide! hide!
Don't let the scary man get me!
...SPEAKING OF WHOM, I WONDER WHAT DID HAPPEN WITH HIM AND SHIMIZU-SENSEI...
はっ hm?
TO THINK THAT HE WAS SO CLOSE TO HER...
...SHIMBO, YOU LUCKY SON OF A BITCH! I'M SO JEALOUS!
grrrr...

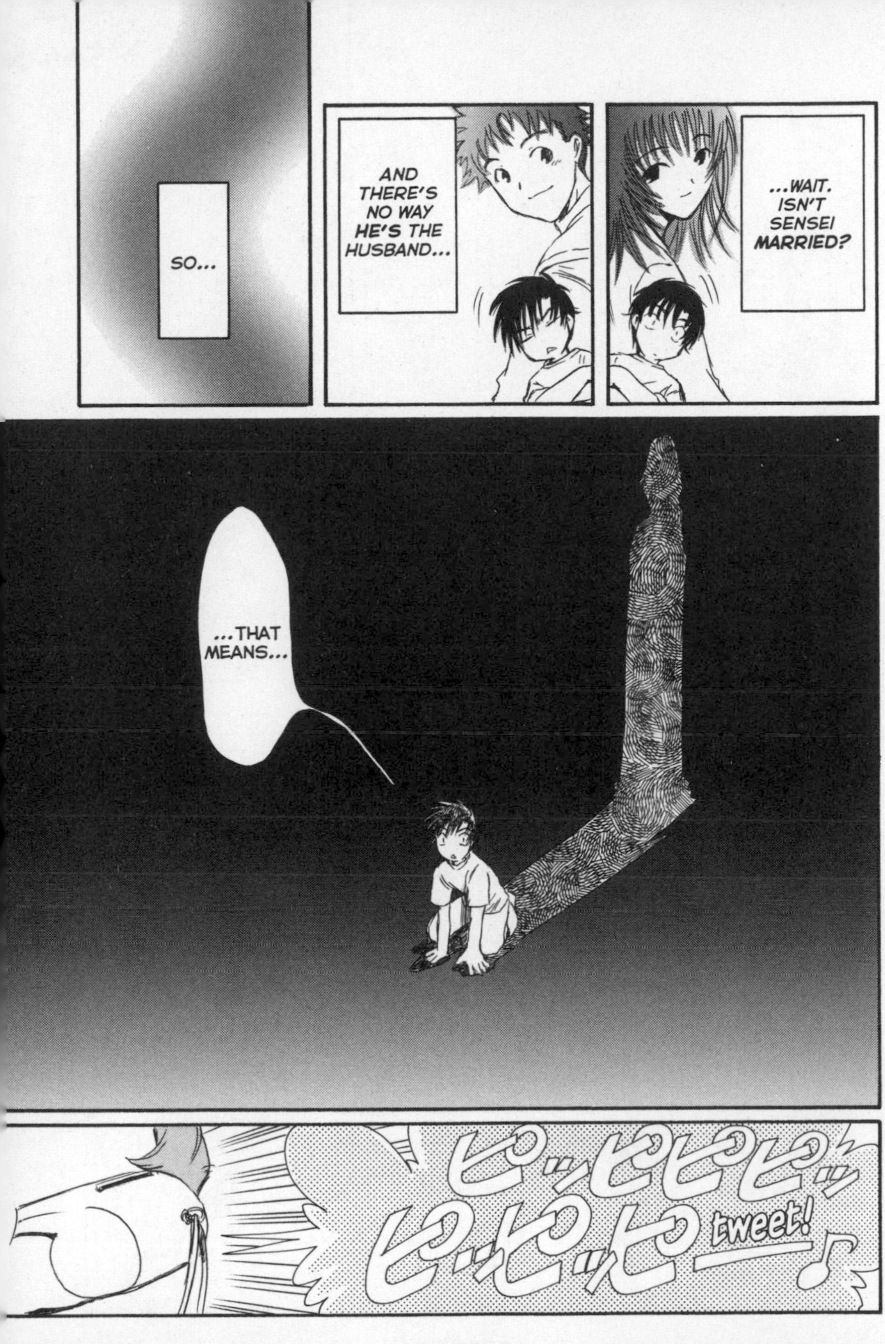
...WAIT. ISN'T SENSEI MARRIED?
AND THERE'S NO WAY HE'S THE HUSBAND...
SO...
...THAT MEANS...
ピッピピピッ
ピッピッピー
tweet!

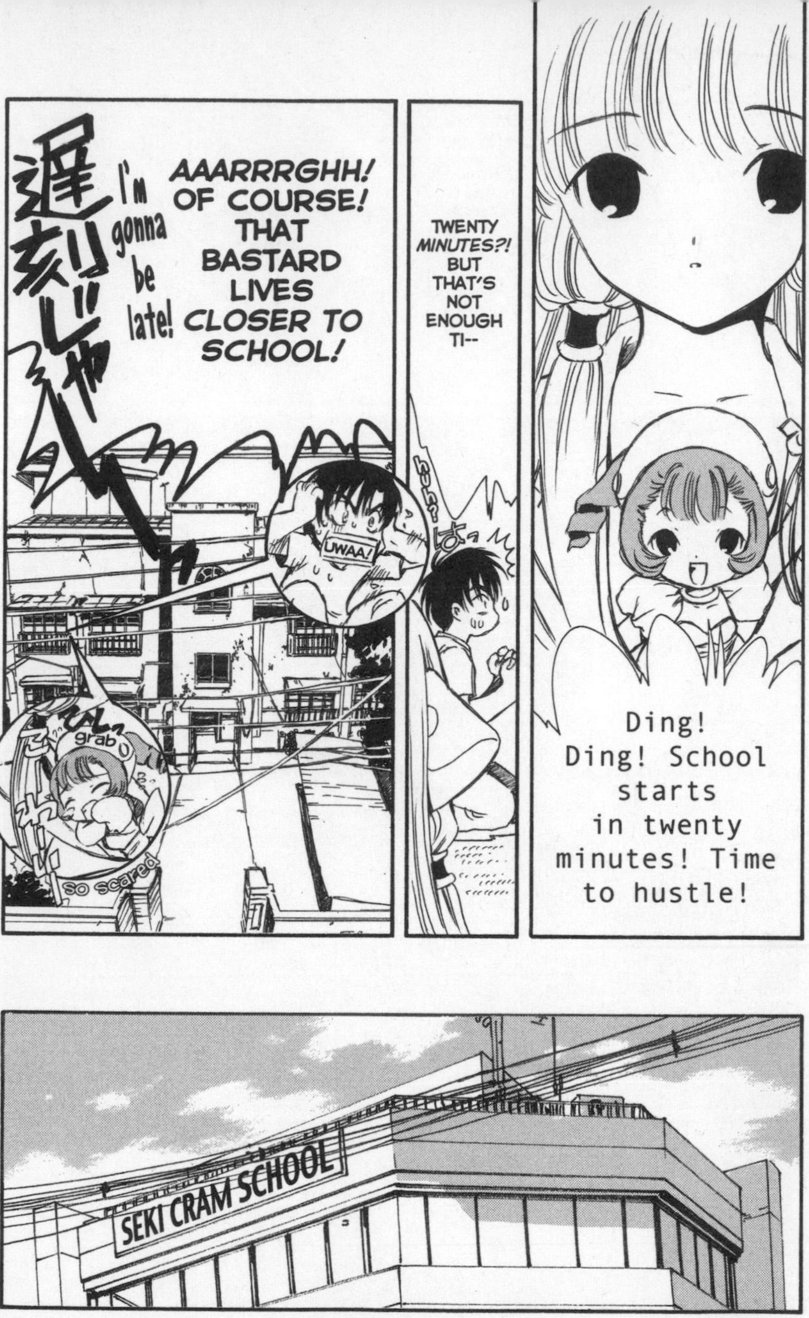

Ding! Ding! School starts in twenty minutes! Time to hustle!
huh?
TWENTY MINUTES?! BUT THAT'S NOT ENOUGH TI--
AAARRRGHH! OF COURSE! THAT BASTARD LIVES CLOSER TO SCHOOL!
I'm gonna be late!
UWAA!
grab
so scared
SEKI CRAM SCHOOL

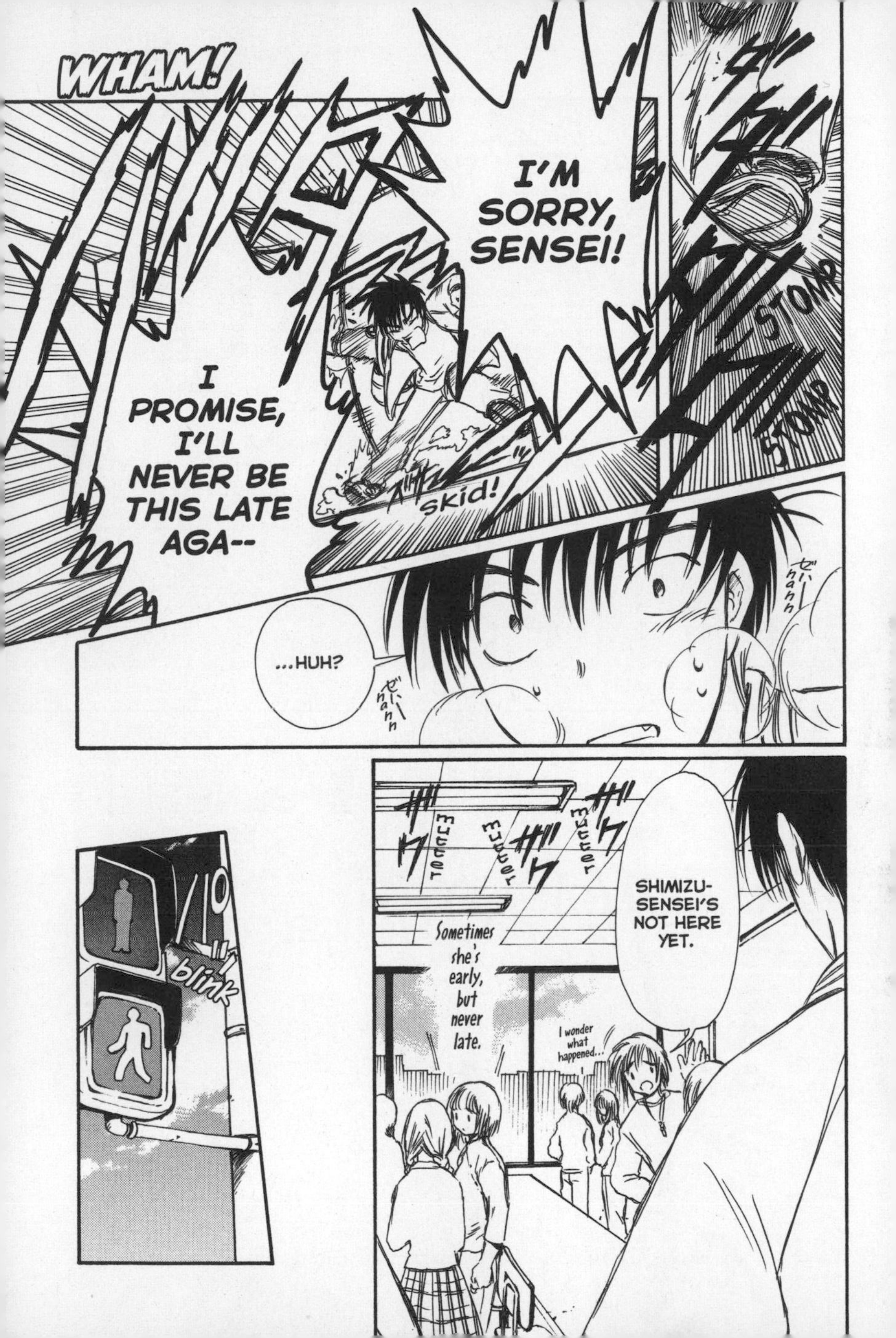
STOMP
STOMP
I'M SORRY, SENSEI!
I PROMISE, I'LL NEVER BE THIS LATE AGA--
skid!
WHAM!
hahn
...HUH?
hahn
SHIMIZU-SENSEI'S NOT HERE YET.
mutter
mutter
mutter
Sometimes she's early, but never late.
I wonder what happened...
blink

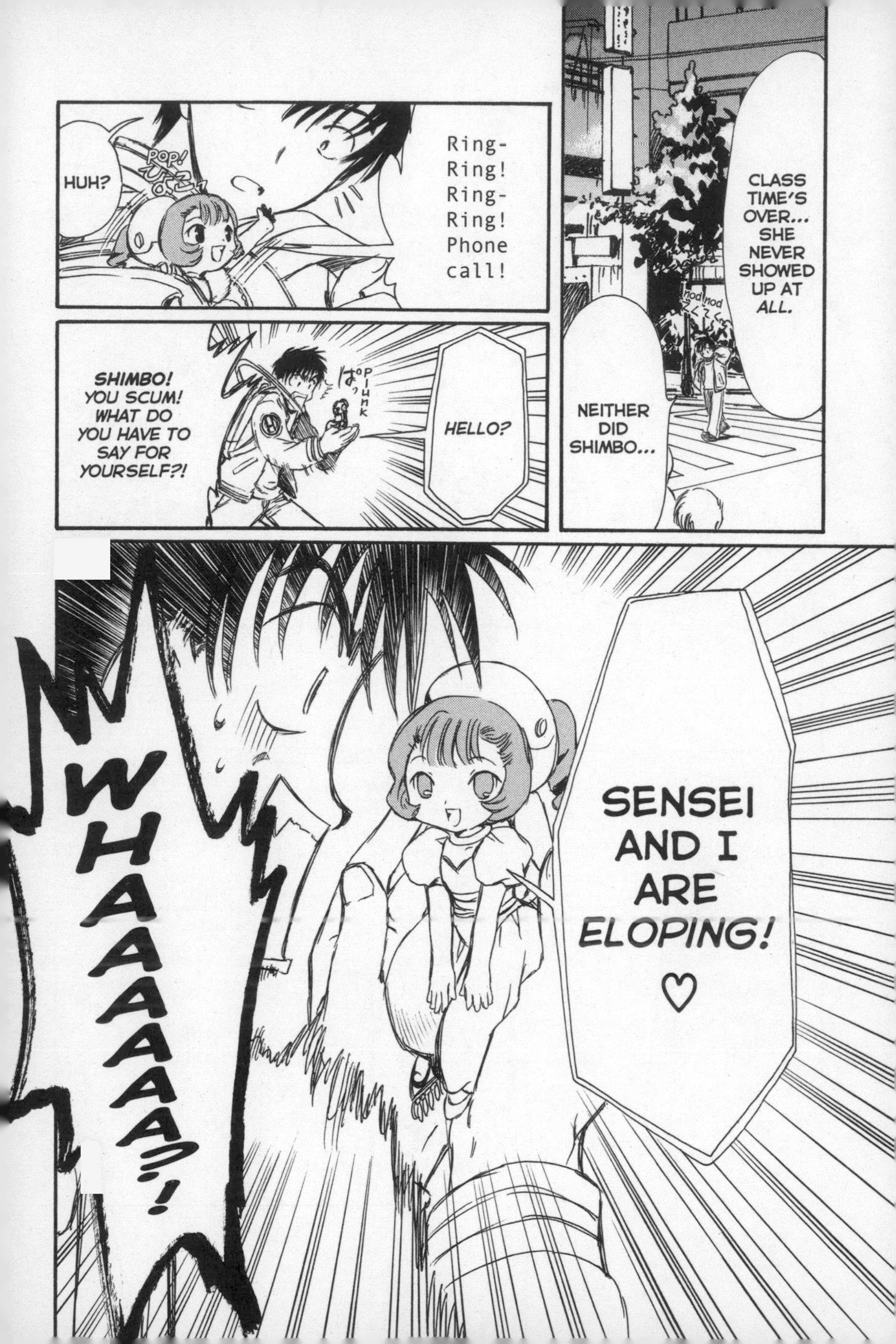
CLASS TIME'S OVER... SHE NEVER SHOWED UP AT ALL.
nod nod
NEITHER DID SHIMBO...
Ring-Ring! Ring-Ring! Phone call!
POP!
HUH?
HELLO?
PLINK
SHIMBO! YOU SCUM! WHAT DO YOU HAVE TO SAY FOR YOURSELF?!
SENSEI AND I ARE ELOPING! ♡
WHAAAAA?!

Chobits
ちょびっツ

◀ **chapter 26** ▶

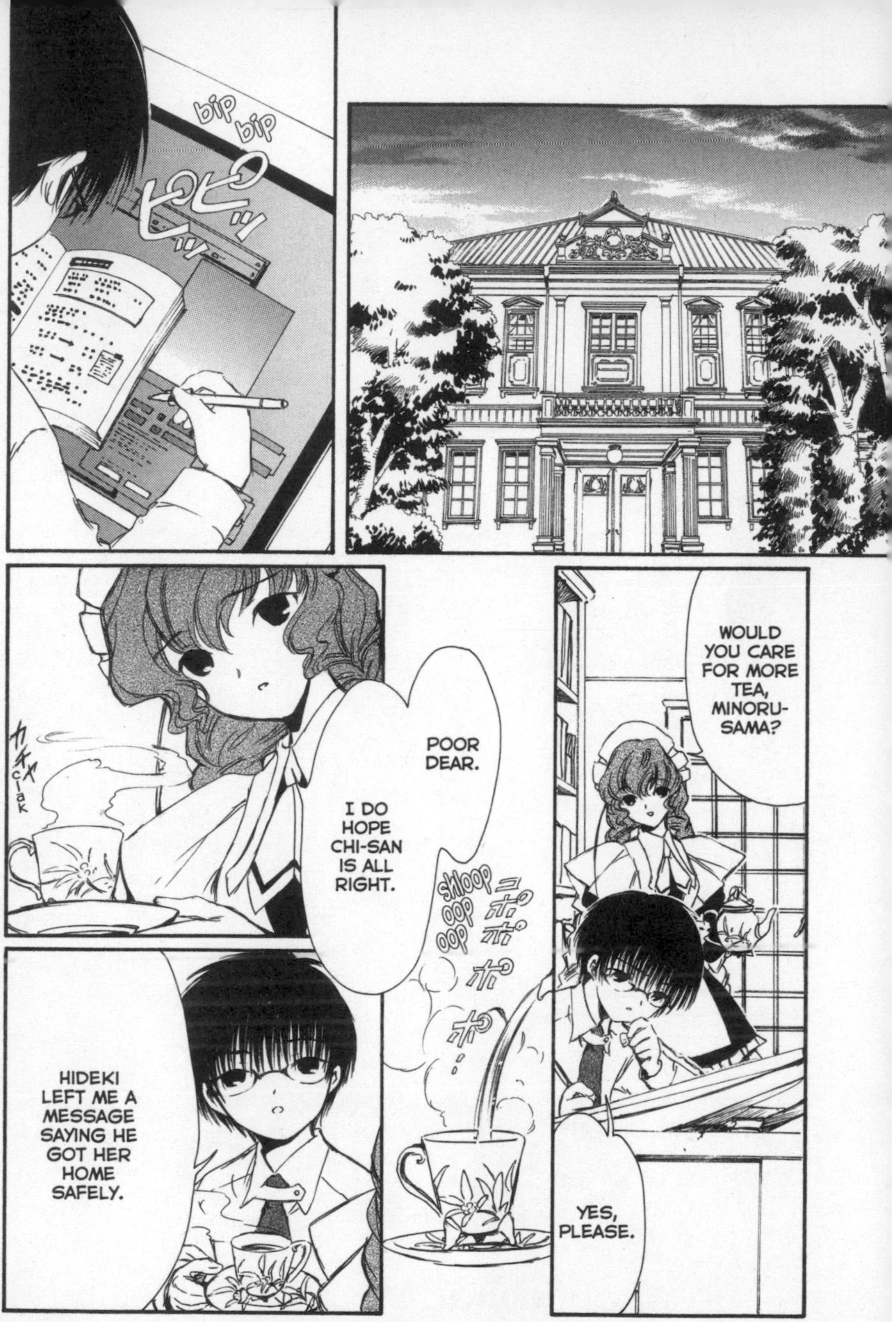
bip bip
ピピッ
ピッ
WOULD YOU CARE FOR MORE TEA, MINORU-SAMA?
shloop oop oop
コポポポポ
YES, PLEASE.
カチャ
clak
POOR DEAR.
I DO HOPE CHI-SAN IS ALL RIGHT.
HIDEKI LEFT ME A MESSAGE SAYING HE GOT HER HOME SAFELY.

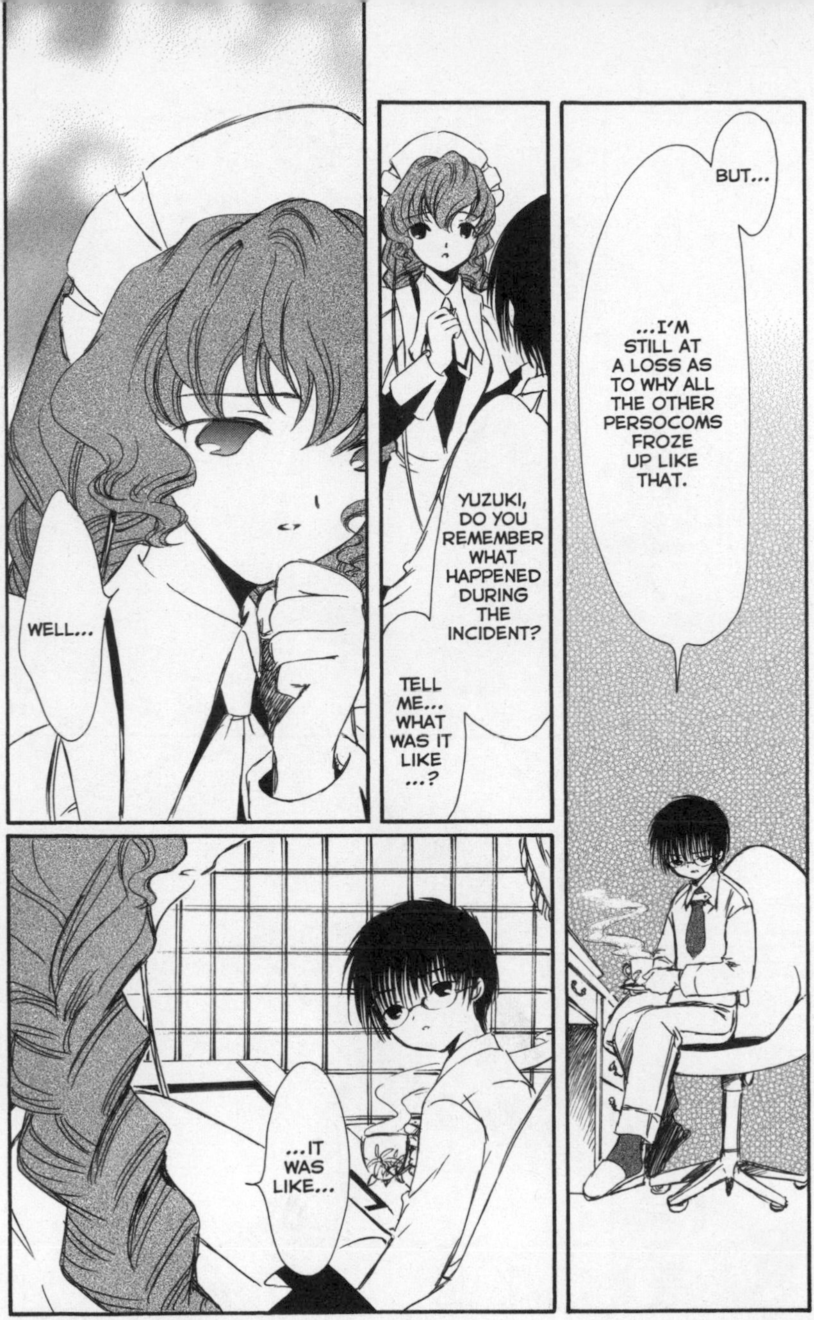

BUT...
...I'M STILL AT A LOSS AS TO WHY ALL THE OTHER PERSOCOMS FROZE UP LIKE THAT.
YUZUKI, DO YOU REMEMBER WHAT HAPPENED DURING THE INCIDENT?
TELL ME... WHAT WAS IT LIKE ...?
WELL...
...IT WAS LIKE...

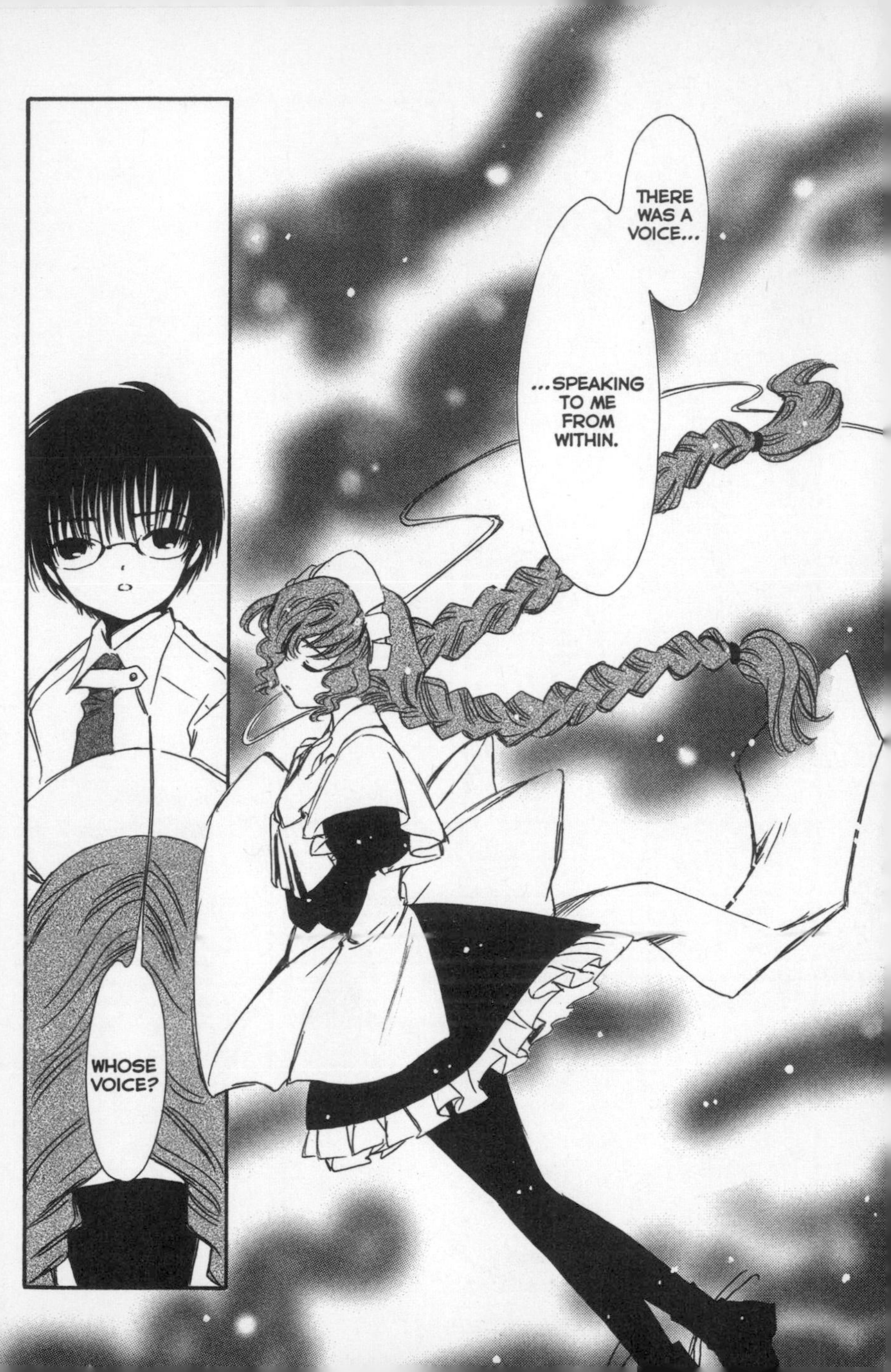
THERE WAS A VOICE...
...SPEAKING TO ME FROM WITHIN.
WHOSE VOICE?

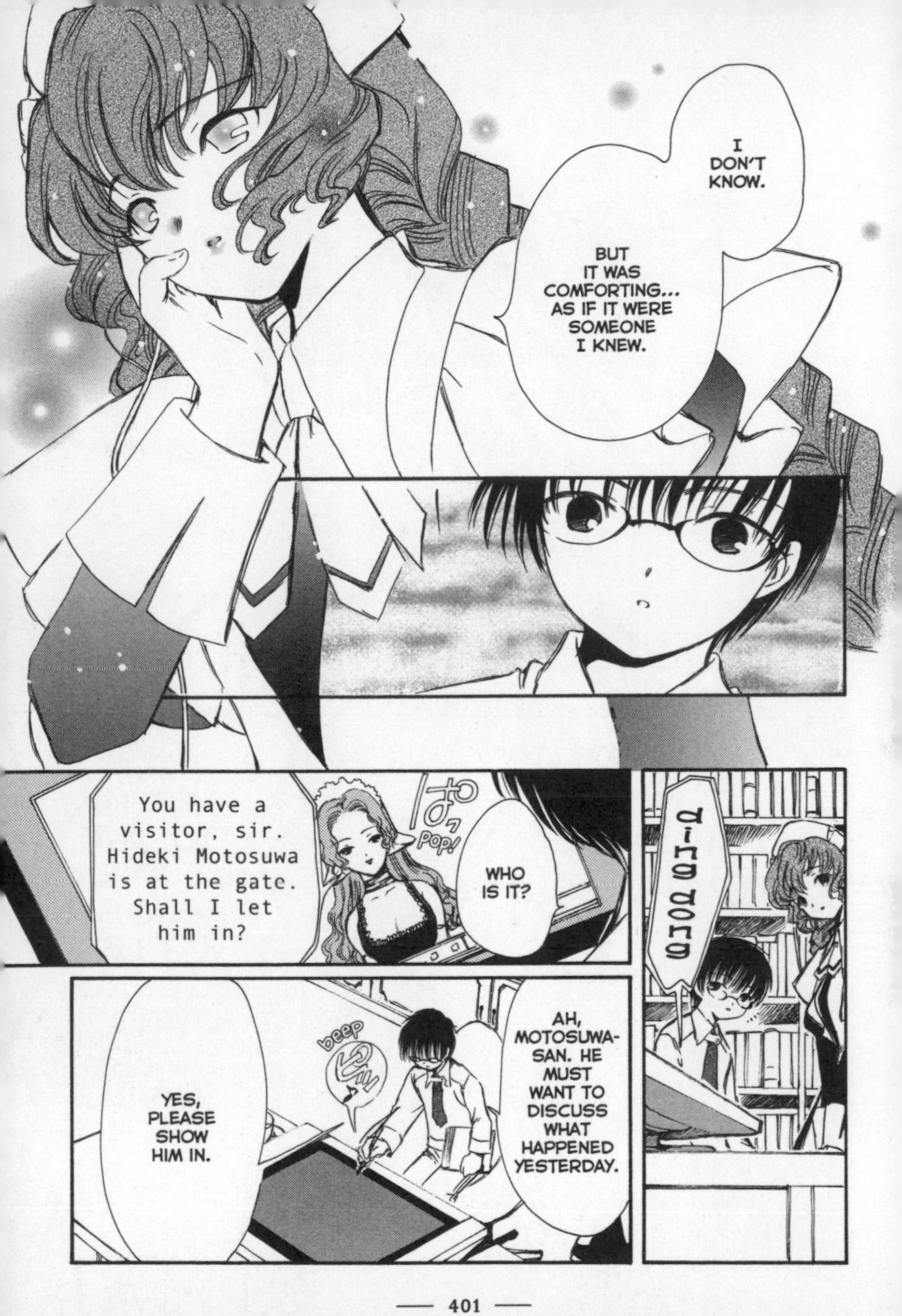
I DON'T KNOW.
BUT IT WAS COMFORTING... AS IF IT WERE SOMEONE I KNEW.
ding dong
WHO IS IT?
POP!
You have a visitor, sir. Hideki Motosuwa is at the gate. Shall I let him in?
AH, MOTOSUWA-SAN. HE MUST WANT TO DISCUSS WHAT HAPPENED YESTERDAY.
beep
YES, PLEASE SHOW HIM IN.

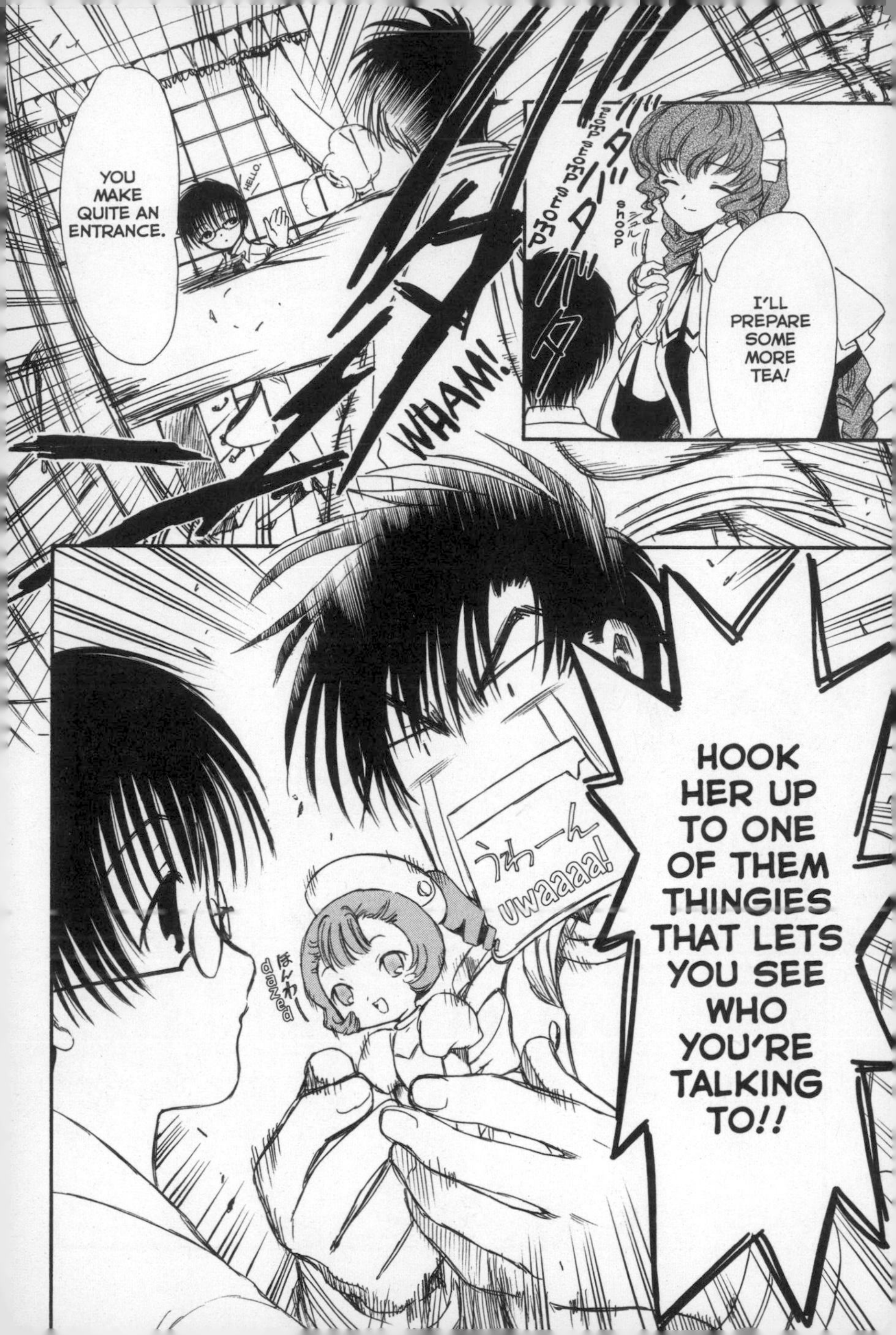

バタバタ
STOMP STOMP STOMP
シュル
shoop
I'LL PREPARE SOME MORE TEA!
WHAM!
HELLO.
YOU MAKE QUITE AN ENTRANCE.
HOOK HER UP TO ONE OF THEM THINGIES THAT LETS YOU SEE WHO YOU'RE TALKING TO!!
うわーん
uwaaaaa!
ほんわ～
dazed

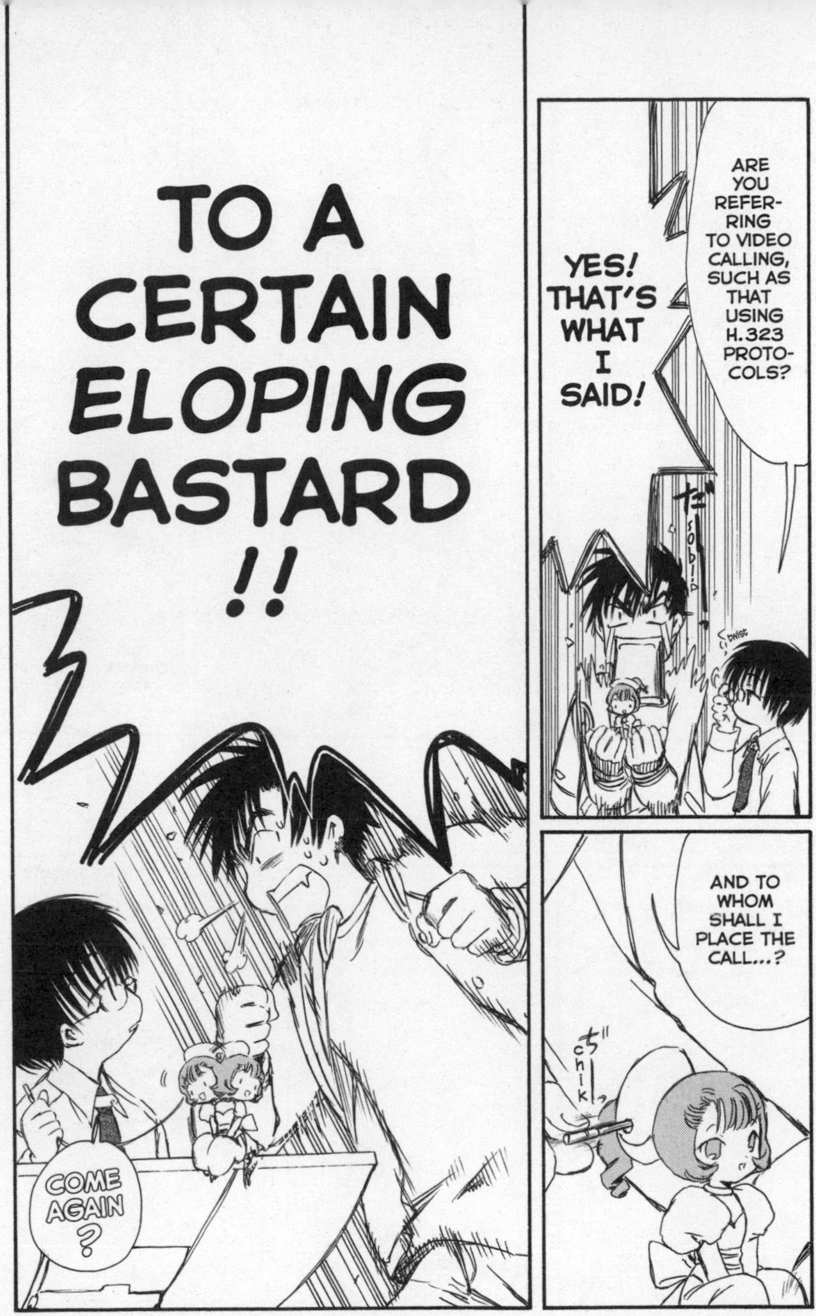
ARE YOU REFERRING TO VIDEO CALLING, SUCH AS THAT USING H.323 PROTOCOLS?
YES! THAT'S WHAT I SAID!
sobi!
twist
AND TO WHOM SHALL I PLACE THE CALL...?
chik
TO A CERTAIN *ELOPING* BASTARD!!
COME AGAIN?

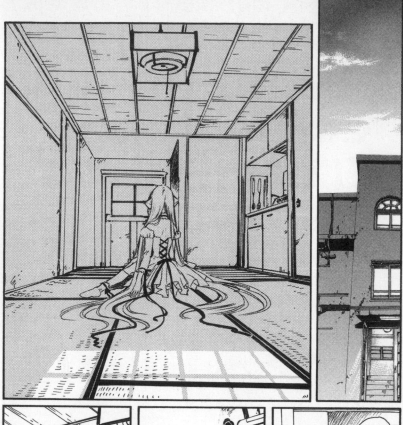

...then work.

...at school...

Hideki is...

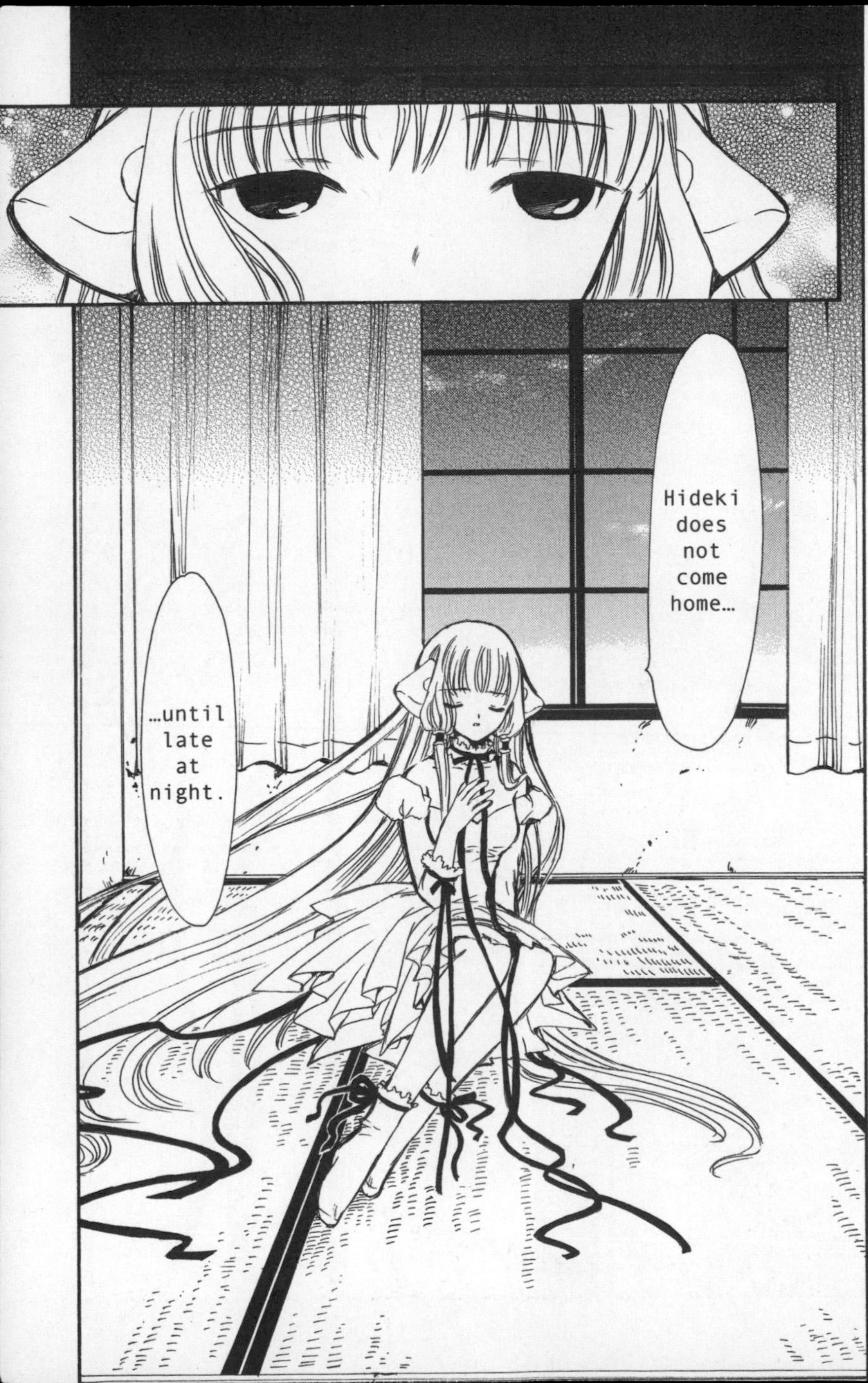
Hideki does not come home...
...until late at night.

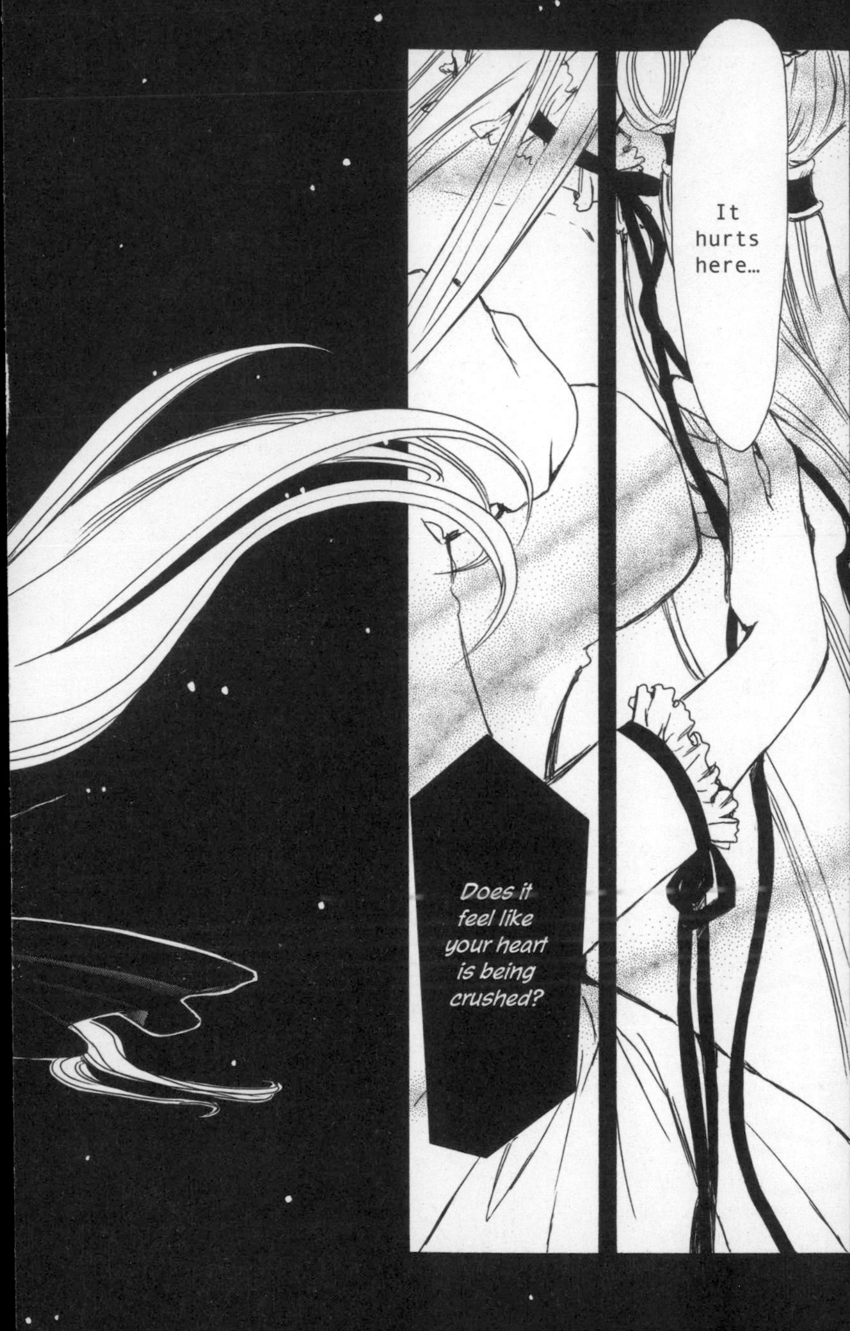
It hurts here...
Does it feel like your heart is being crushed?

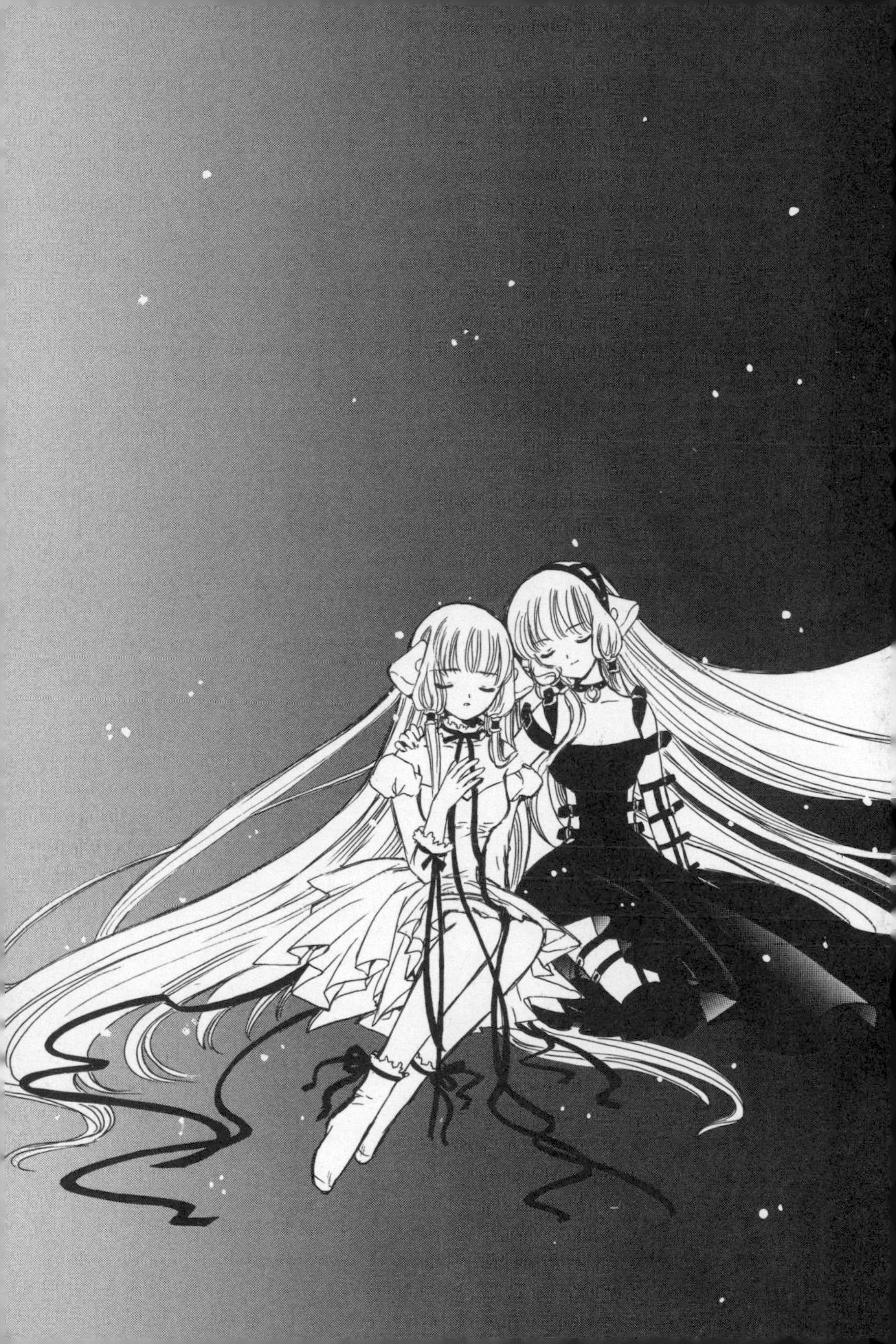

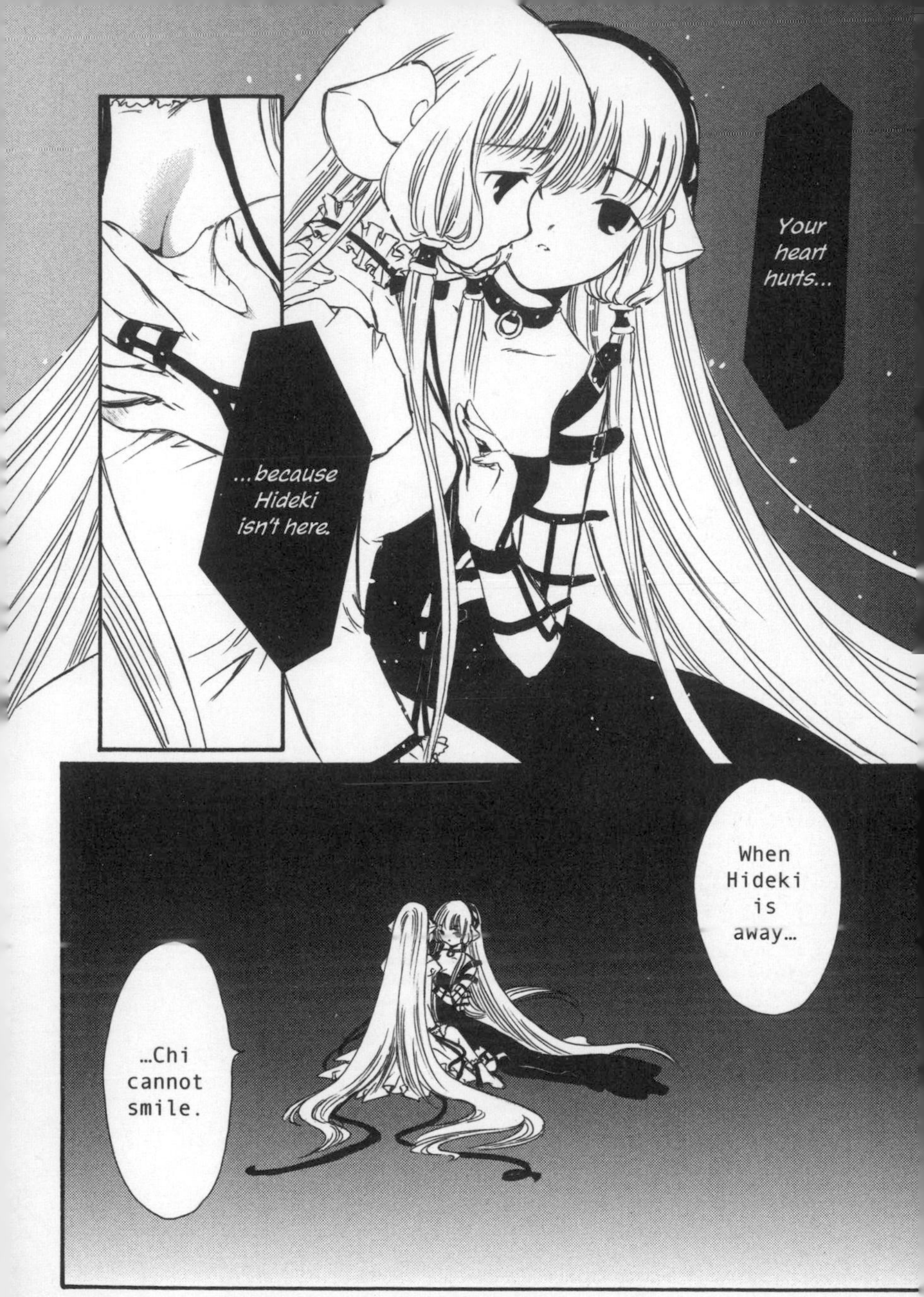
Your heart hurts...
...because Hideki isn't here.
When Hideki is away...
...Chi cannot smile.

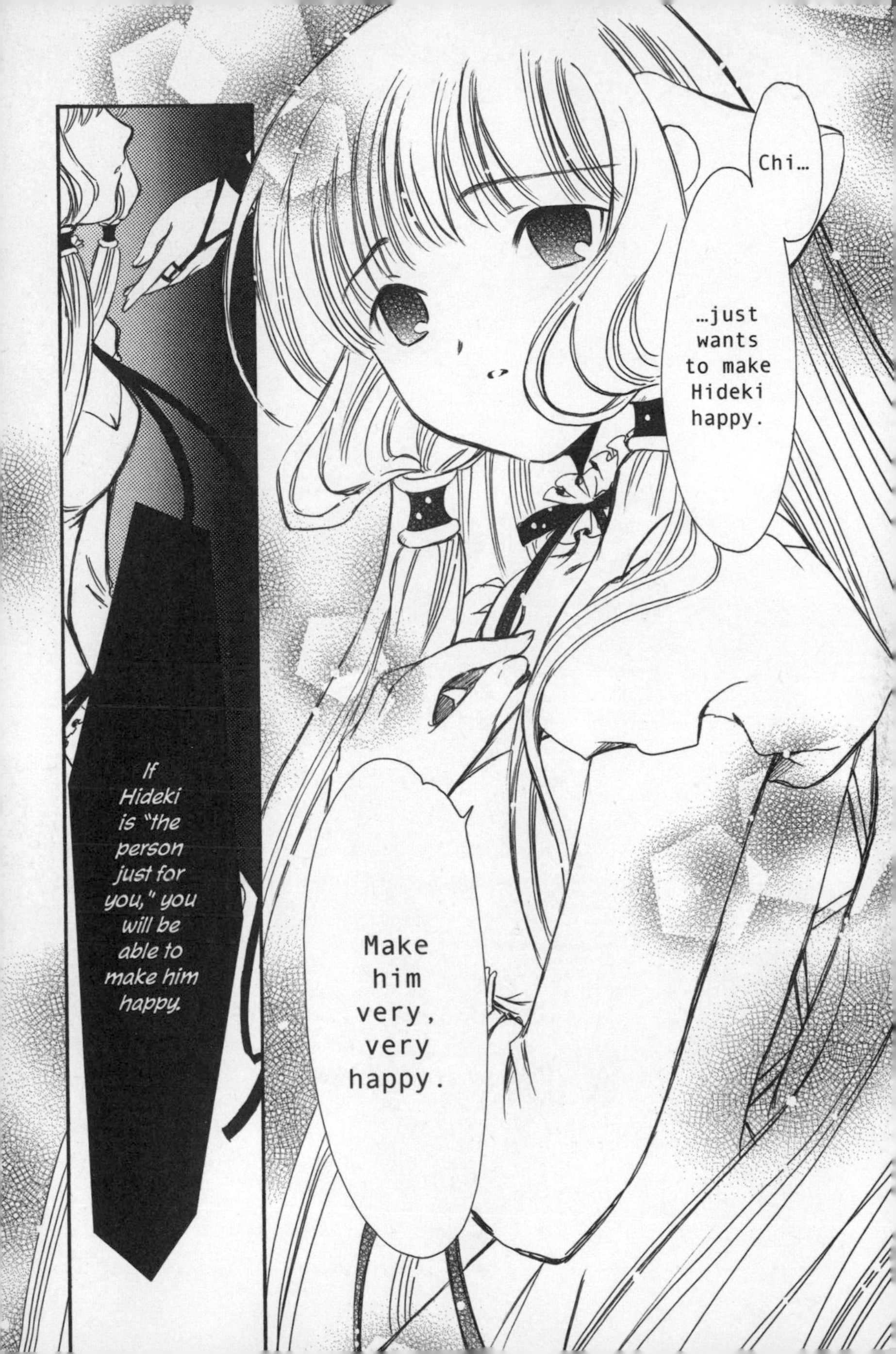
Chi…
…just wants to make Hideki happy.
Make him very, very happy.
If Hideki is "the person just for you," you will be able to make him happy.

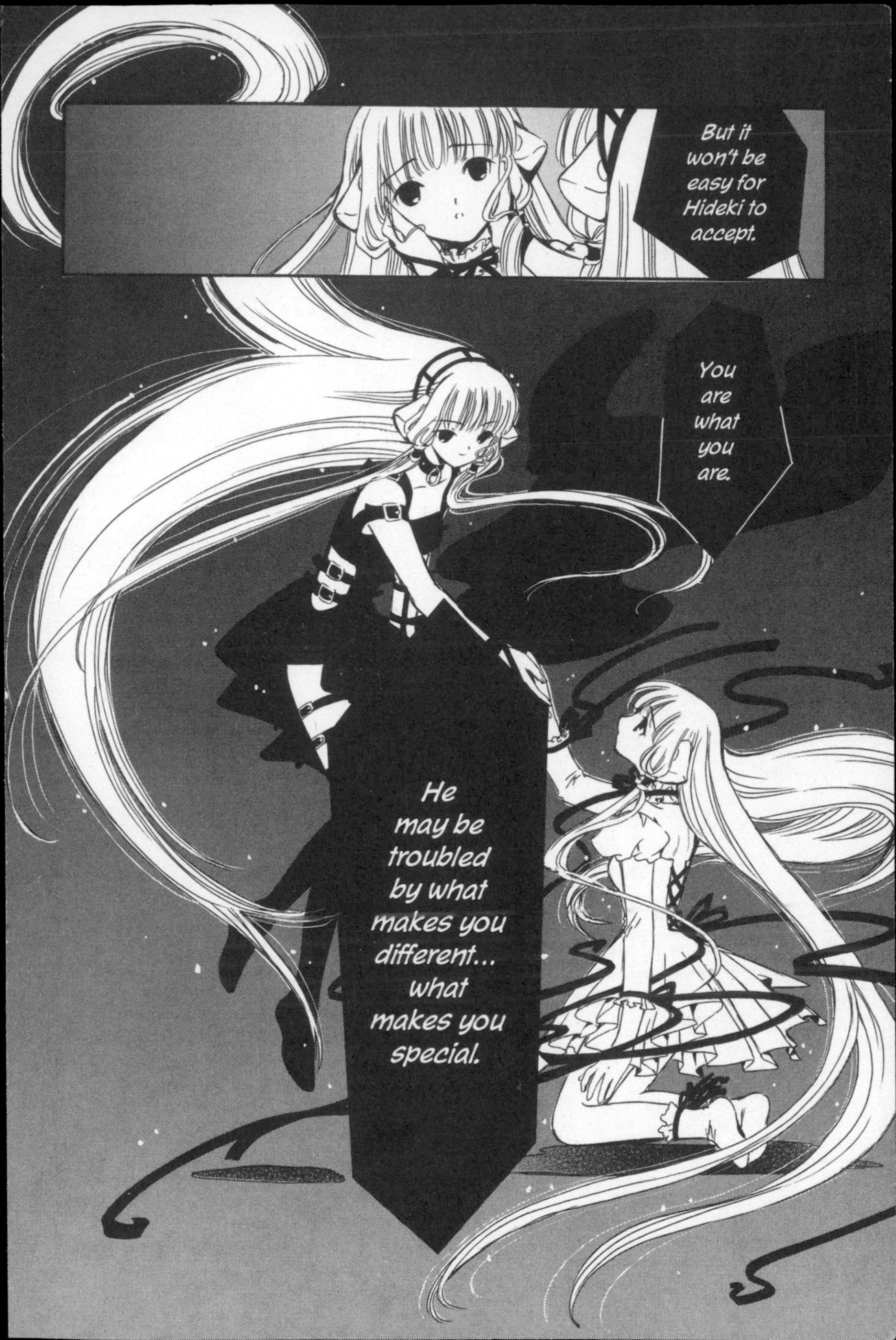
But it won't be easy for Hideki to accept.
You are what you are.
He may be troubled by what makes you different... what makes you special.

Chobits
ちょびっツ

◀ chapter 27 ▶

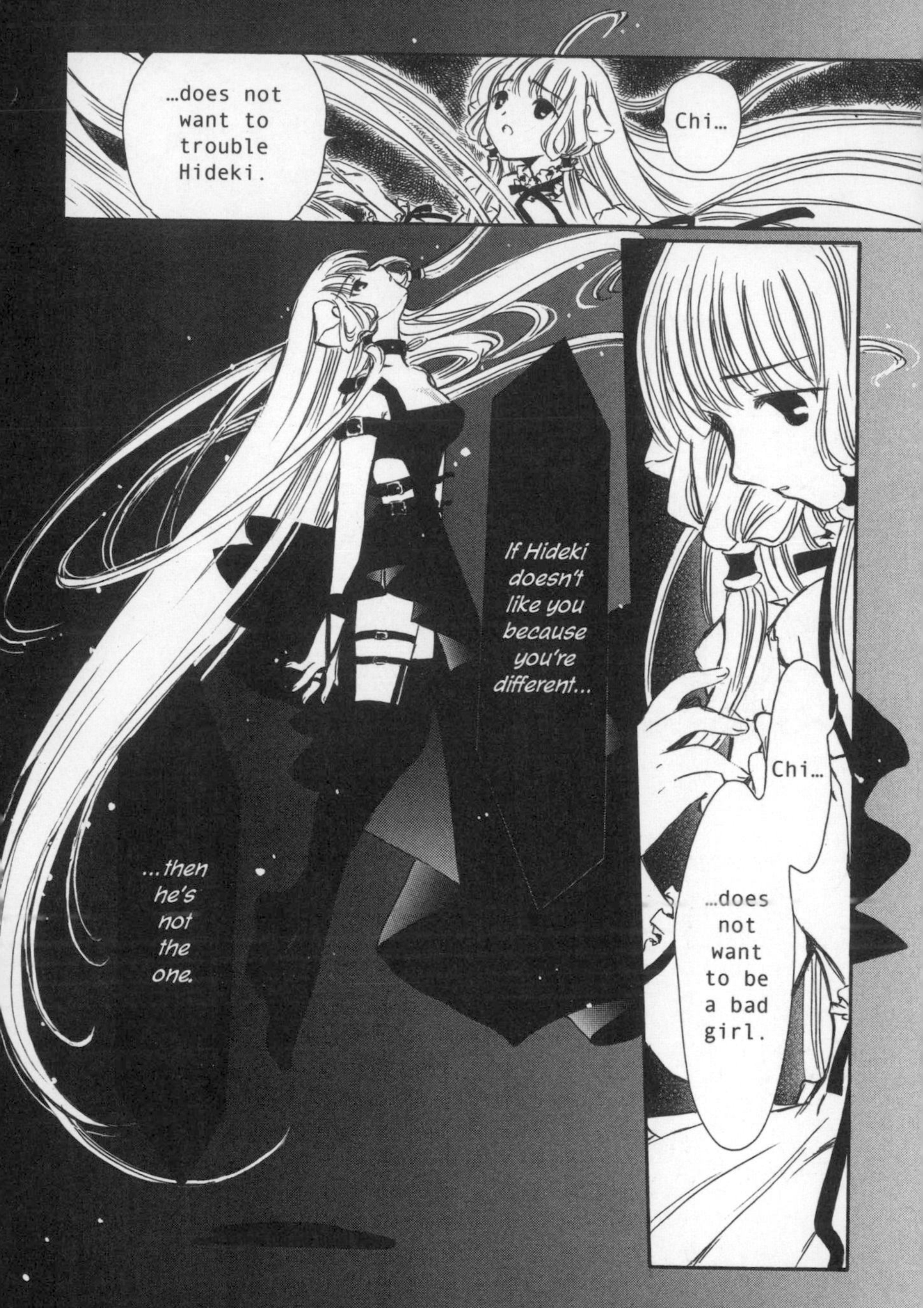
Chi…
…does not want to trouble Hideki.
Chi…
…does not want to be a bad girl.
If Hideki doesn't like you because you're different…
…then he's not the one.

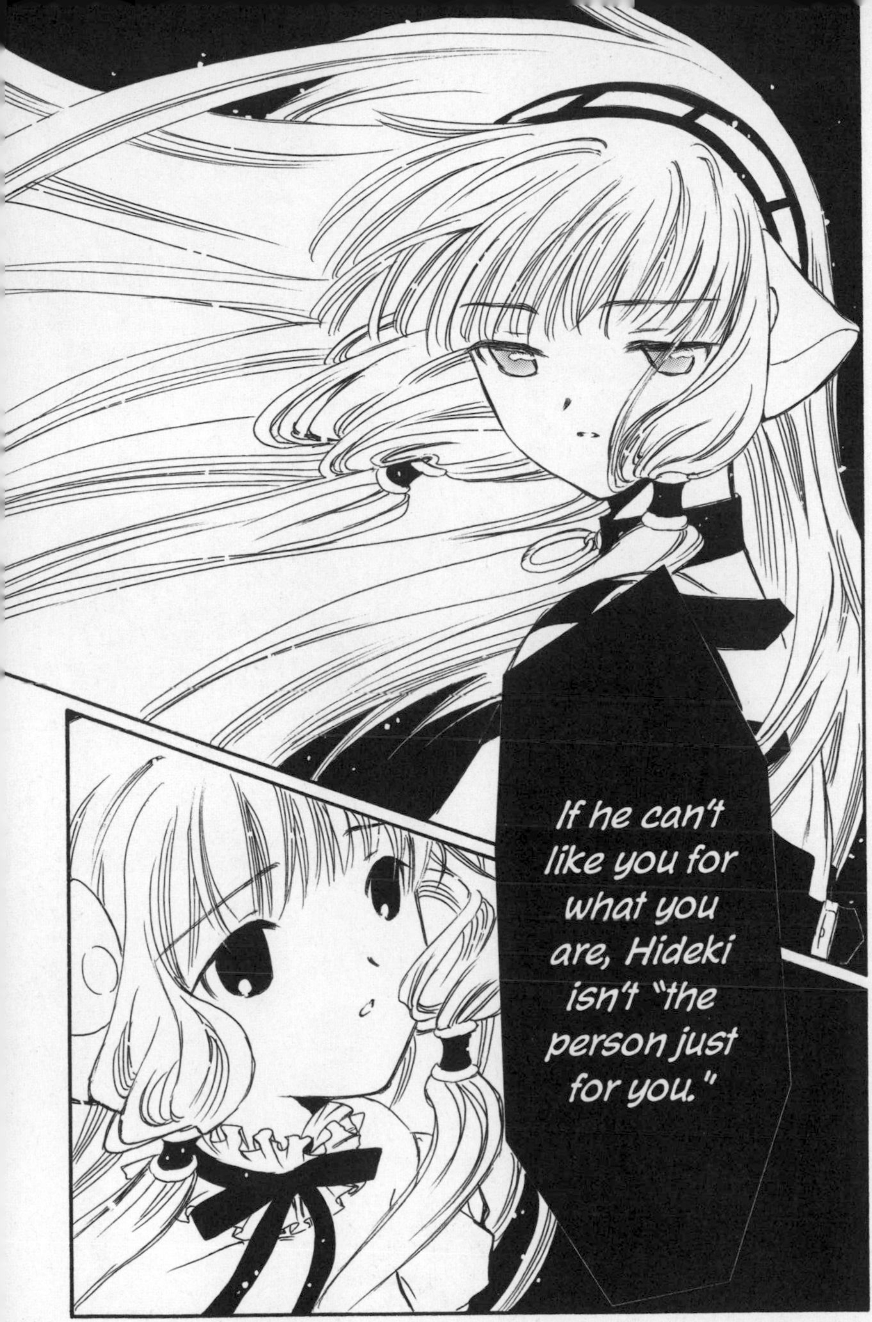
If he can't like you for what you are, Hideki isn't "the person just for you."

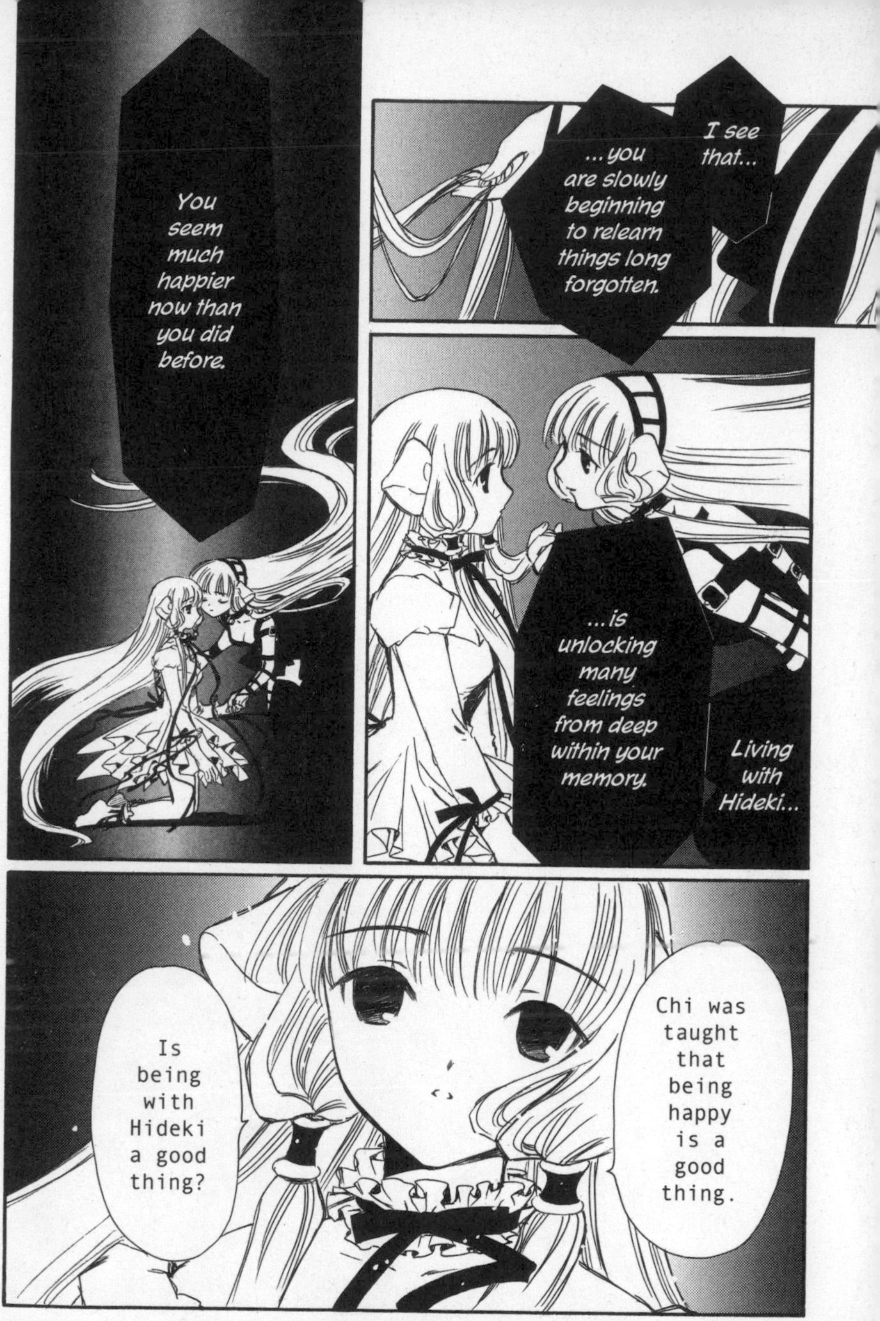
I see that...
...you are slowly beginning to relearn things long forgotten.
Living with Hideki...
...is unlocking many feelings from deep within your memory.
You seem much happier now than you did before.
Chi was taught that being happy is a good thing.
Is being with Hideki a good thing?

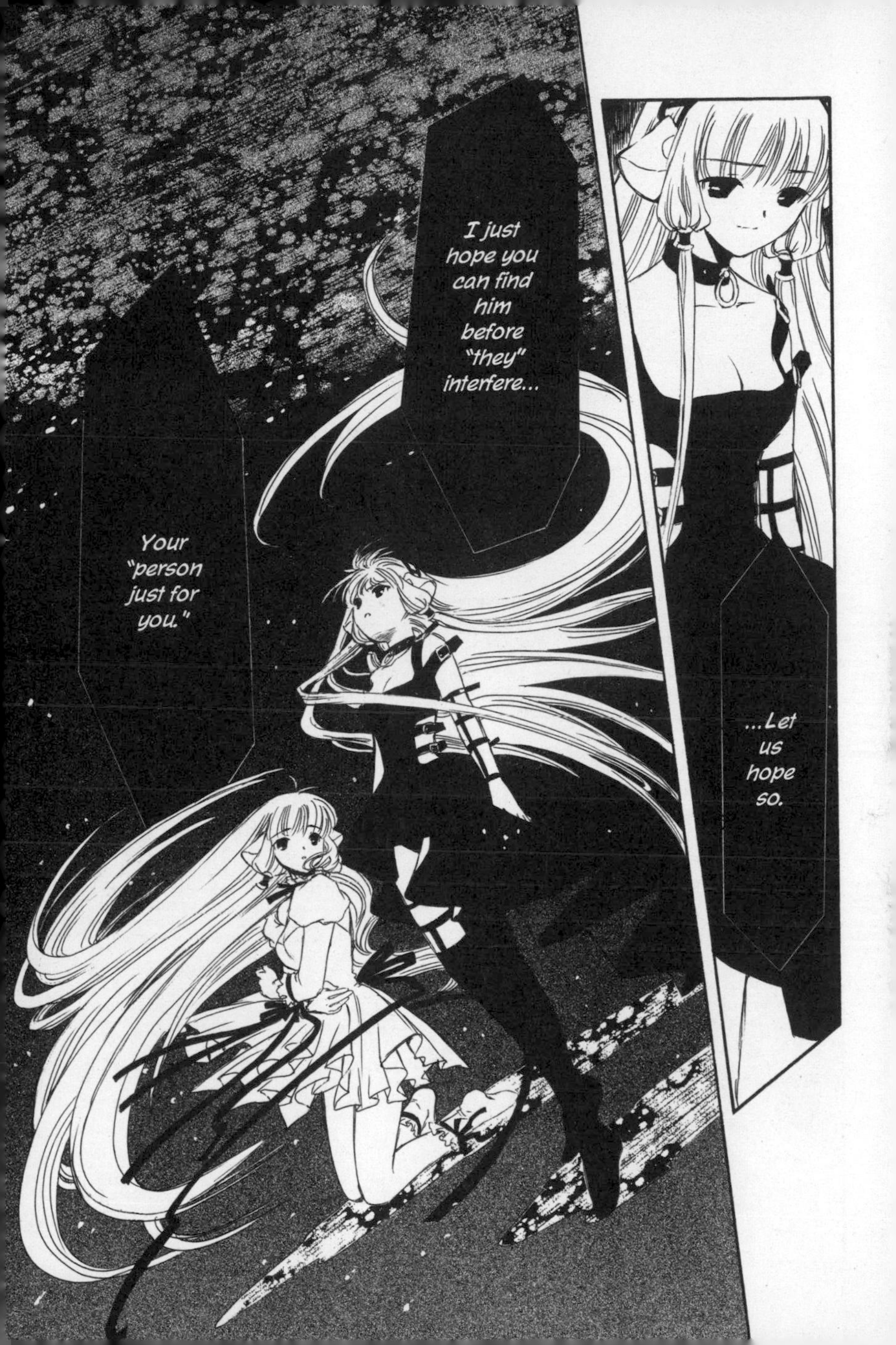
I just hope you can find him before "they" interfere...
Your "person just for you."
...Let us hope so.

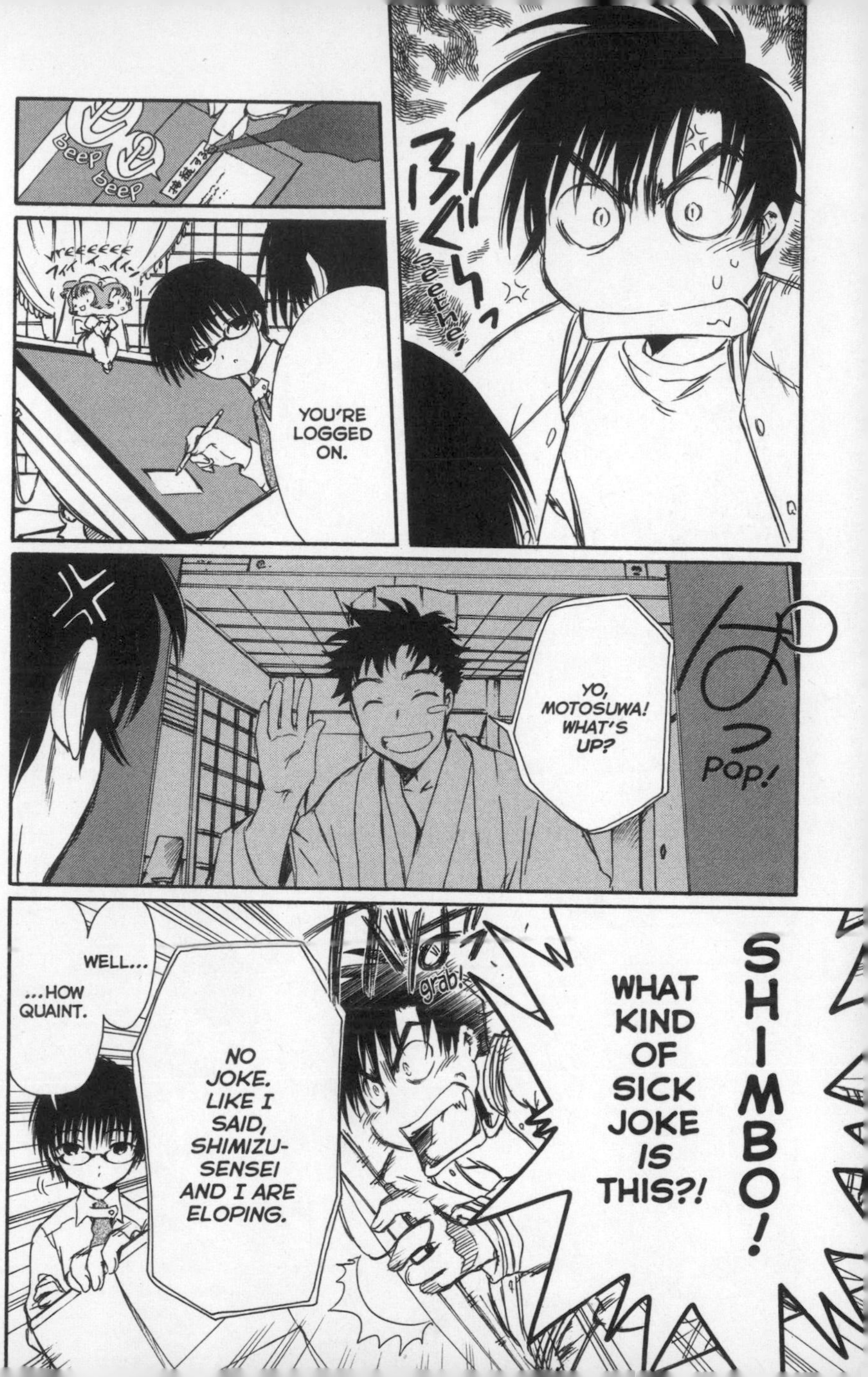
seethe!
beep beep
YOU'RE LOGGED ON.
Pop!
YO, MOTOSUWA! WHAT'S UP?
SHIMBO!
WHAT KIND OF SICK JOKE IS THIS?!
grab!
NO JOKE. LIKE I SAID, SHIMIZU-SENSEI AND I ARE ELOPING.
WELL...
...HOW QUAINT.

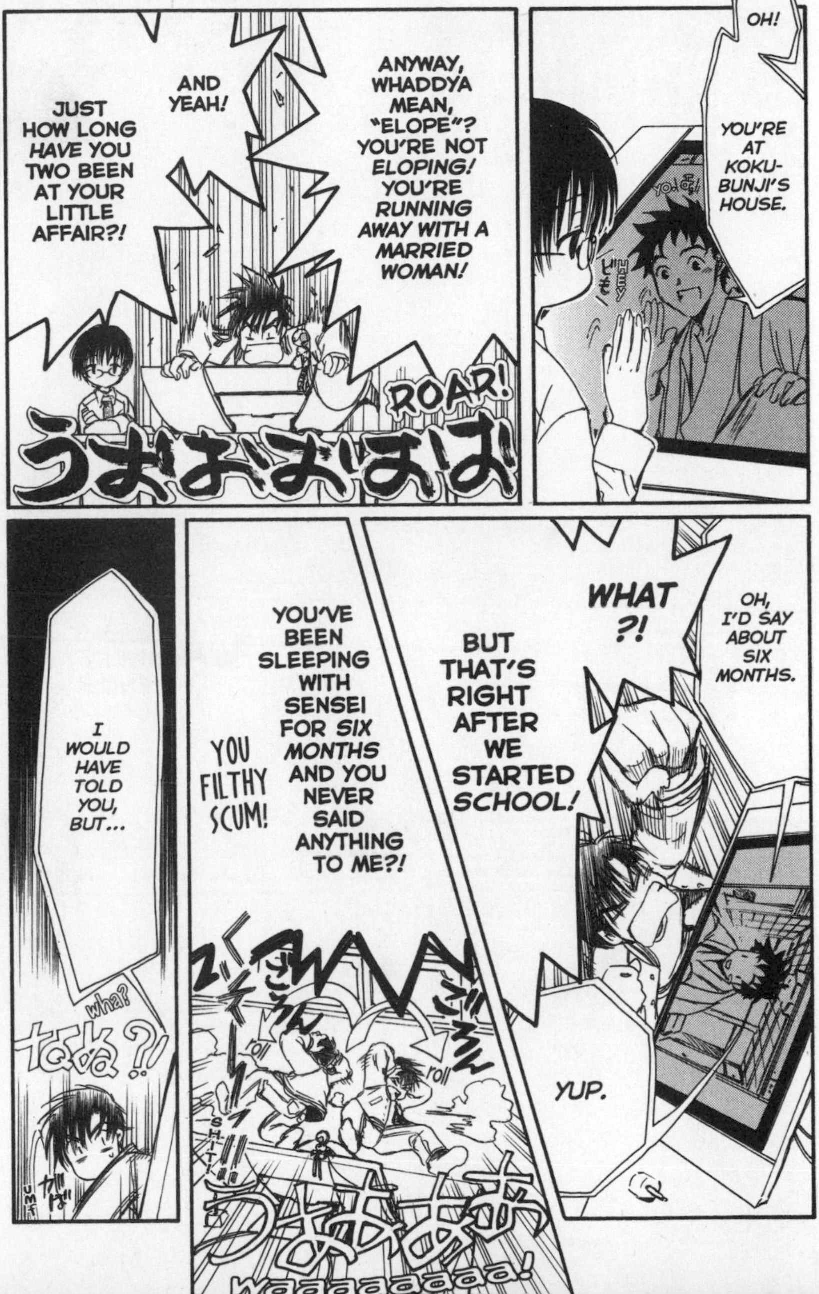
OH!
YOU'RE AT KOKU-BUNJI'S HOUSE.
HEY
ANYWAY, WHADDYA MEAN, "ELOPE"? YOU'RE NOT ELOPING! YOU'RE RUNNING AWAY WITH A MARRIED WOMAN!
AND YEAH!
JUST HOW LONG HAVE YOU TWO BEEN AT YOUR LITTLE AFFAIR?!
ROAR!
OH, I'D SAY ABOUT SIX MONTHS.
WHAT ?!
BUT THAT'S RIGHT AFTER WE STARTED SCHOOL!
YUP.
YOU'VE BEEN SLEEPING WITH SENSEI FOR SIX MONTHS AND YOU NEVER SAID ANYTHING TO ME?!
YOU FILTHY SCUM!
roll
roll
SHIT!
waaaaaaaaaa!
I WOULD HAVE TOLD YOU, BUT...
wha?
なぬ?!
UMF

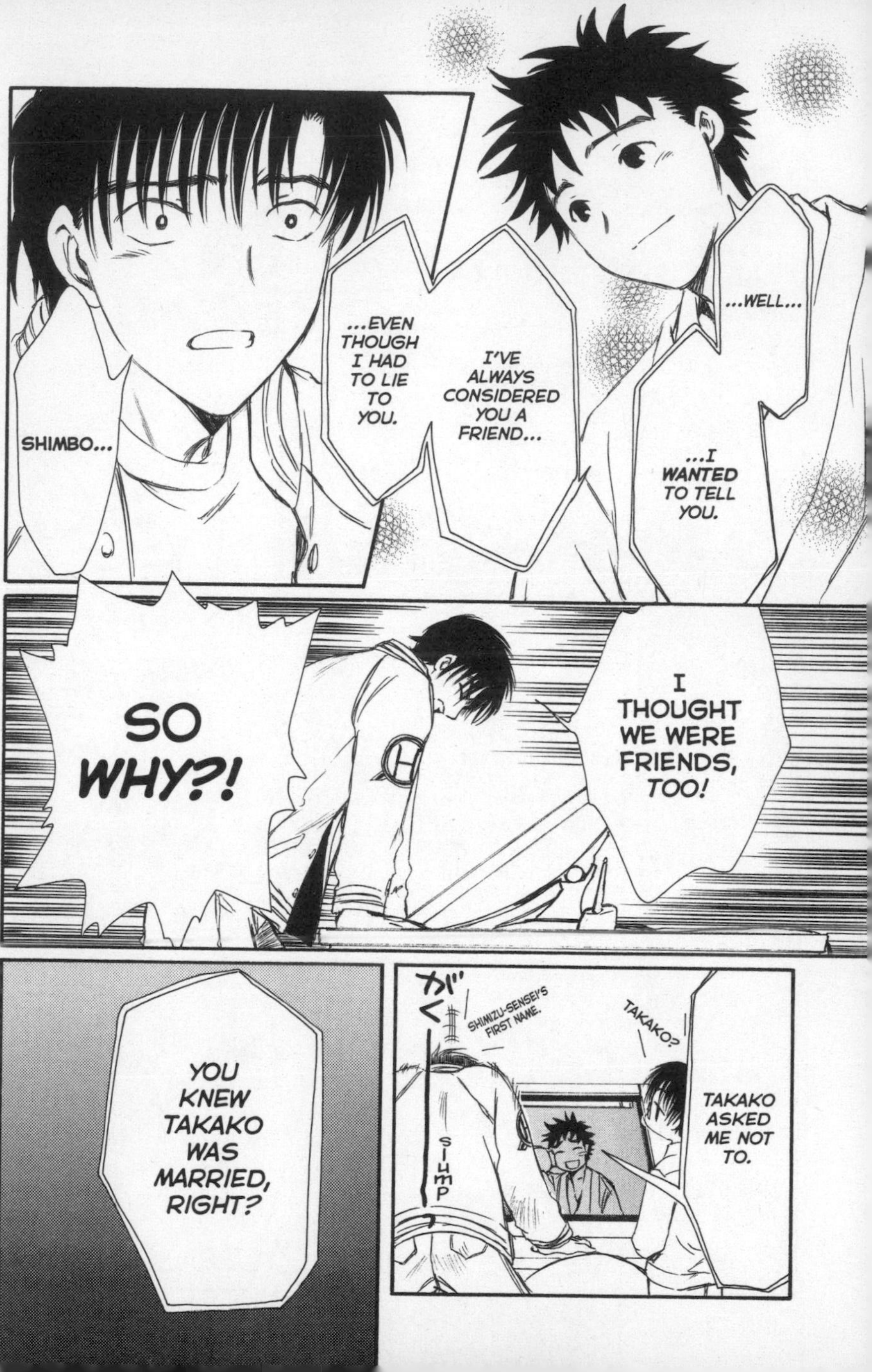
...WELL...
...I WANTED TO TELL YOU.
I'VE ALWAYS CONSIDERED YOU A FRIEND...
...EVEN THOUGH I HAD TO LIE TO YOU.
SHIMBO...
I THOUGHT WE WERE FRIENDS, TOO!
SO WHY?!
TAKAKO?
SHIMIZU-SENSEI'S FIRST NAME.
TAKAKO ASKED ME NOT TO.
がく
SLUMP
YOU KNEW TAKAKO WAS MARRIED, RIGHT?

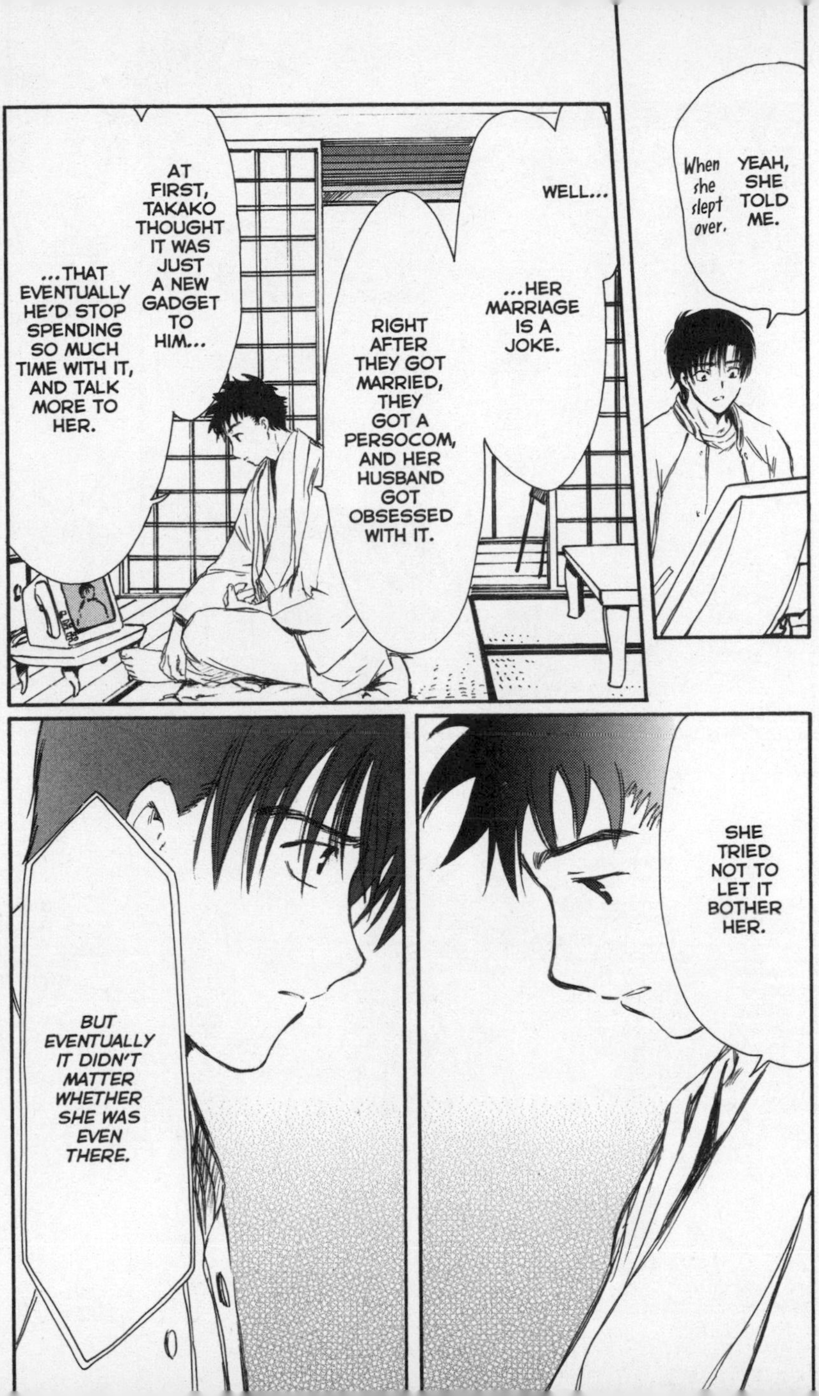
YEAH, SHE TOLD ME.
When she slept over.
WELL...
...HER MARRIAGE IS A JOKE.
RIGHT AFTER THEY GOT MARRIED, THEY GOT A PERSOCOM, AND HER HUSBAND GOT OBSESSED WITH IT.
AT FIRST, TAKAKO THOUGHT IT WAS JUST A NEW GADGET TO HIM...
...THAT EVENTUALLY HE'D STOP SPENDING SO MUCH TIME WITH IT, AND TALK MORE TO HER.
SHE TRIED NOT TO LET IT BOTHER HER.
BUT EVENTUALLY IT DIDN'T MATTER WHETHER SHE WAS EVEN THERE.

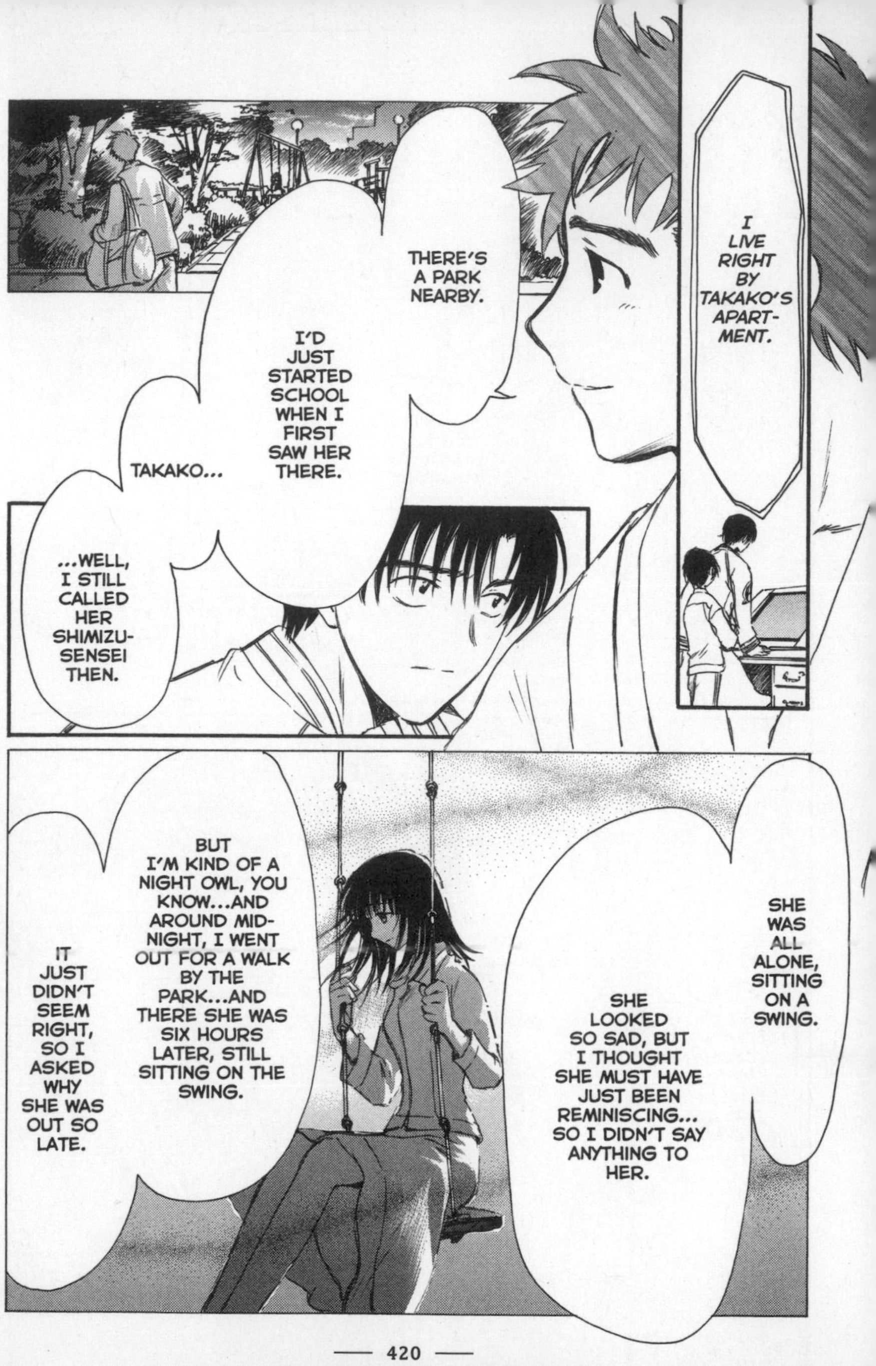
I LIVE RIGHT BY TAKAKO'S APART-MENT.
THERE'S A PARK NEARBY.
I'D JUST STARTED SCHOOL WHEN I FIRST SAW HER THERE.
TAKAKO...
...WELL, I STILL CALLED HER SHIMIZU-SENSEI THEN.
SHE WAS ALL ALONE, SITTING ON A SWING.
SHE LOOKED SO SAD, BUT I THOUGHT SHE MUST HAVE JUST BEEN REMINISCING... SO I DIDN'T SAY ANYTHING TO HER.
BUT I'M KIND OF A NIGHT OWL, YOU KNOW...AND AROUND MID-NIGHT, I WENT OUT FOR A WALK BY THE PARK...AND THERE SHE WAS SIX HOURS LATER, STILL SITTING ON THE SWING.
IT JUST DIDN'T SEEM RIGHT, SO I ASKED WHY SHE WAS OUT SO LATE.

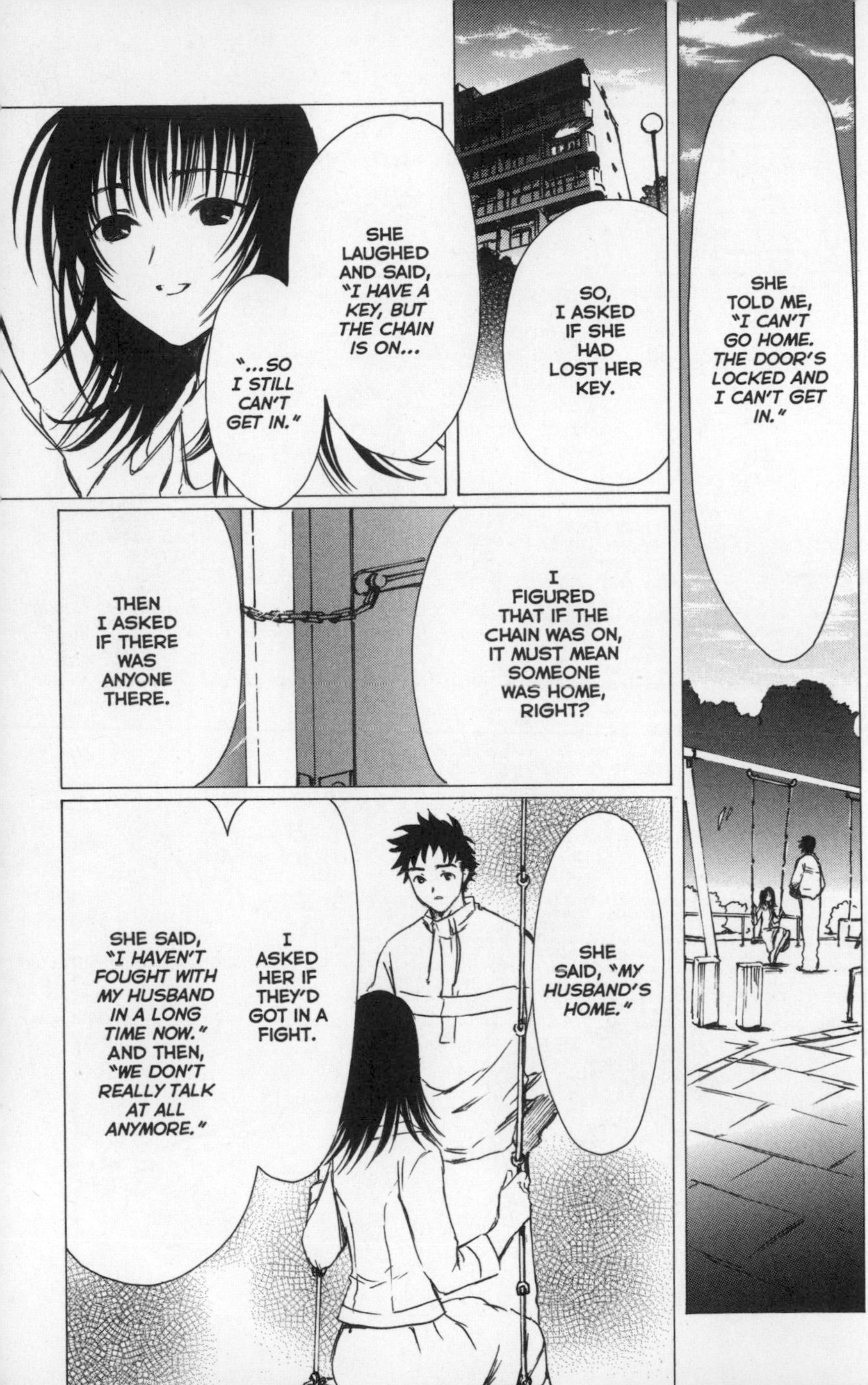
SHE TOLD ME, "I CAN'T GO HOME. THE DOOR'S LOCKED AND I CAN'T GET IN."
SO, I ASKED IF SHE HAD LOST HER KEY.
SHE LAUGHED AND SAID, "I HAVE A KEY, BUT THE CHAIN IS ON...
"...SO I STILL CAN'T GET IN."
I FIGURED THAT IF THE CHAIN WAS ON, IT MUST MEAN SOMEONE WAS HOME, RIGHT?
THEN I ASKED IF THERE WAS ANYONE THERE.
SHE SAID, "MY HUSBAND'S HOME."
I ASKED HER IF THEY'D GOT IN A FIGHT.
SHE SAID, "I HAVEN'T FOUGHT WITH MY HUSBAND IN A LONG TIME NOW." AND THEN, "WE DON'T REALLY TALK AT ALL ANYMORE."

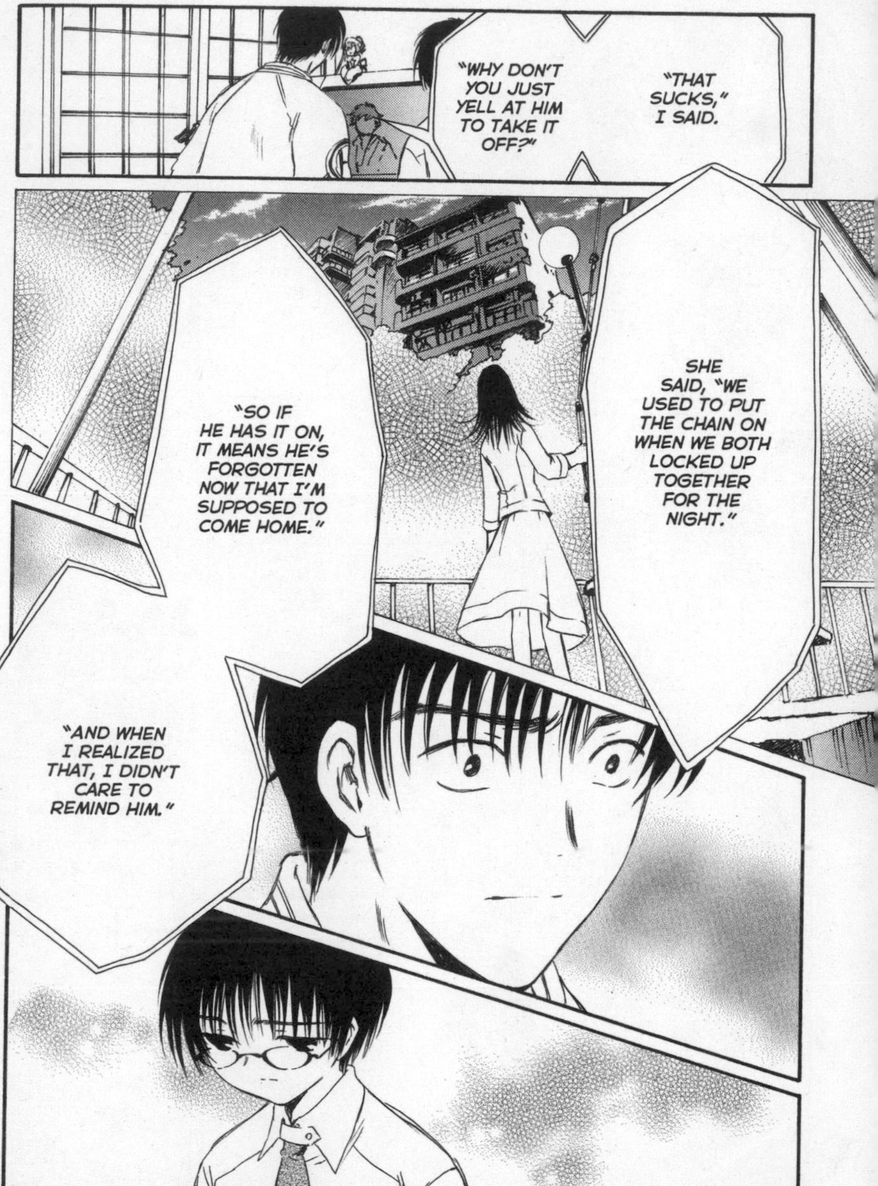
"THAT SUCKS," I SAID.
"WHY DON'T YOU JUST YELL AT HIM TO TAKE IT OFF?"
SHE SAID, "WE USED TO PUT THE CHAIN ON WHEN WE BOTH LOCKED UP TOGETHER FOR THE NIGHT."
"SO IF HE HAS IT ON, IT MEANS HE'S FORGOTTEN NOW THAT I'M SUPPOSED TO COME HOME."
"AND WHEN I REALIZED THAT, I DIDN'T CARE TO REMIND HIM."

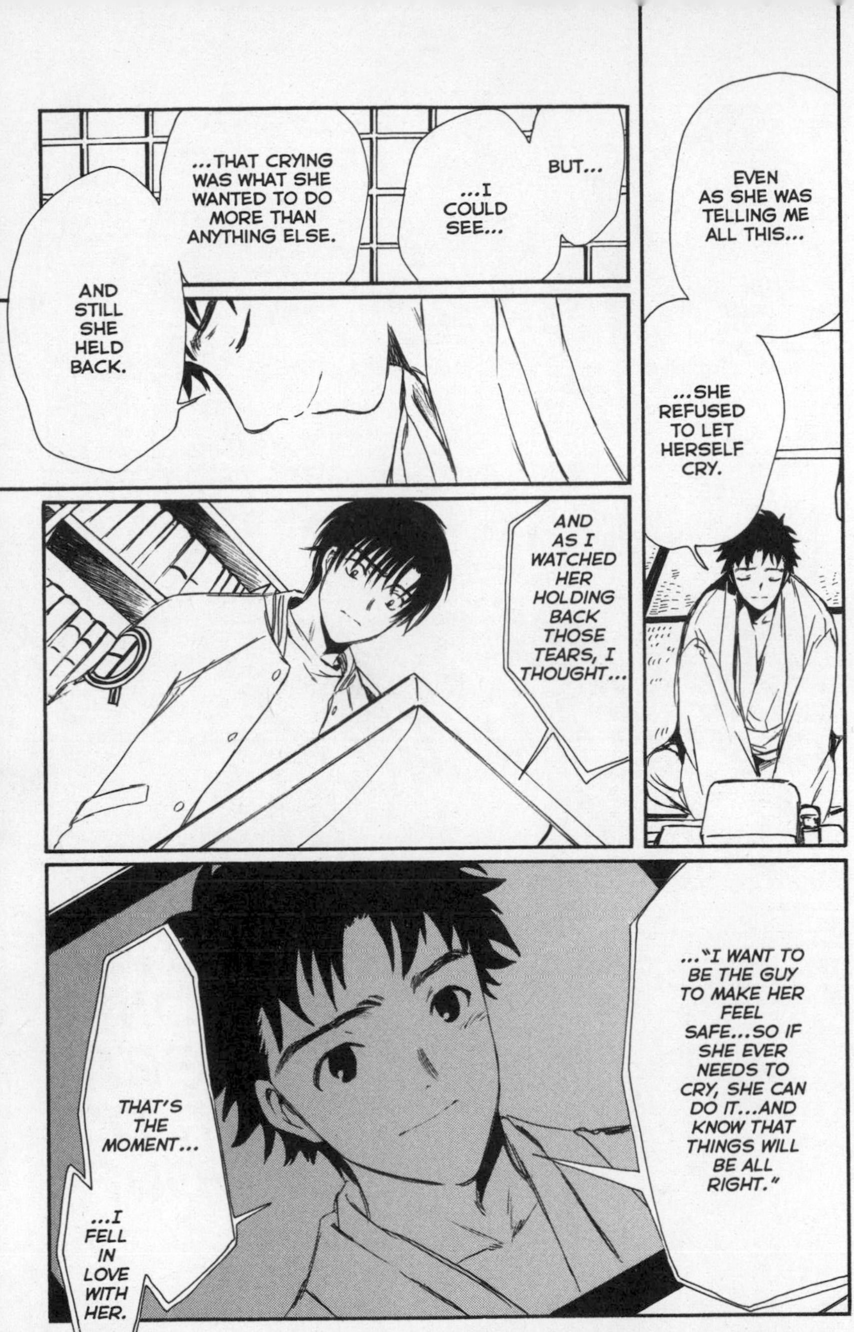
EVEN AS SHE WAS TELLING ME ALL THIS...
...SHE REFUSED TO LET HERSELF CRY.
BUT...
...I COULD SEE...
...THAT CRYING WAS WHAT SHE WANTED TO DO MORE THAN ANYTHING ELSE.
AND STILL SHE HELD BACK.
AND AS I WATCHED HER HOLDING BACK THOSE TEARS, I THOUGHT...
..."I WANT TO BE THE GUY TO MAKE HER FEEL SAFE...SO IF SHE EVER NEEDS TO CRY, SHE CAN DO IT...AND KNOW THAT THINGS WILL BE ALL RIGHT."
THAT'S THE MOMENT...
...I FELL IN LOVE WITH HER.

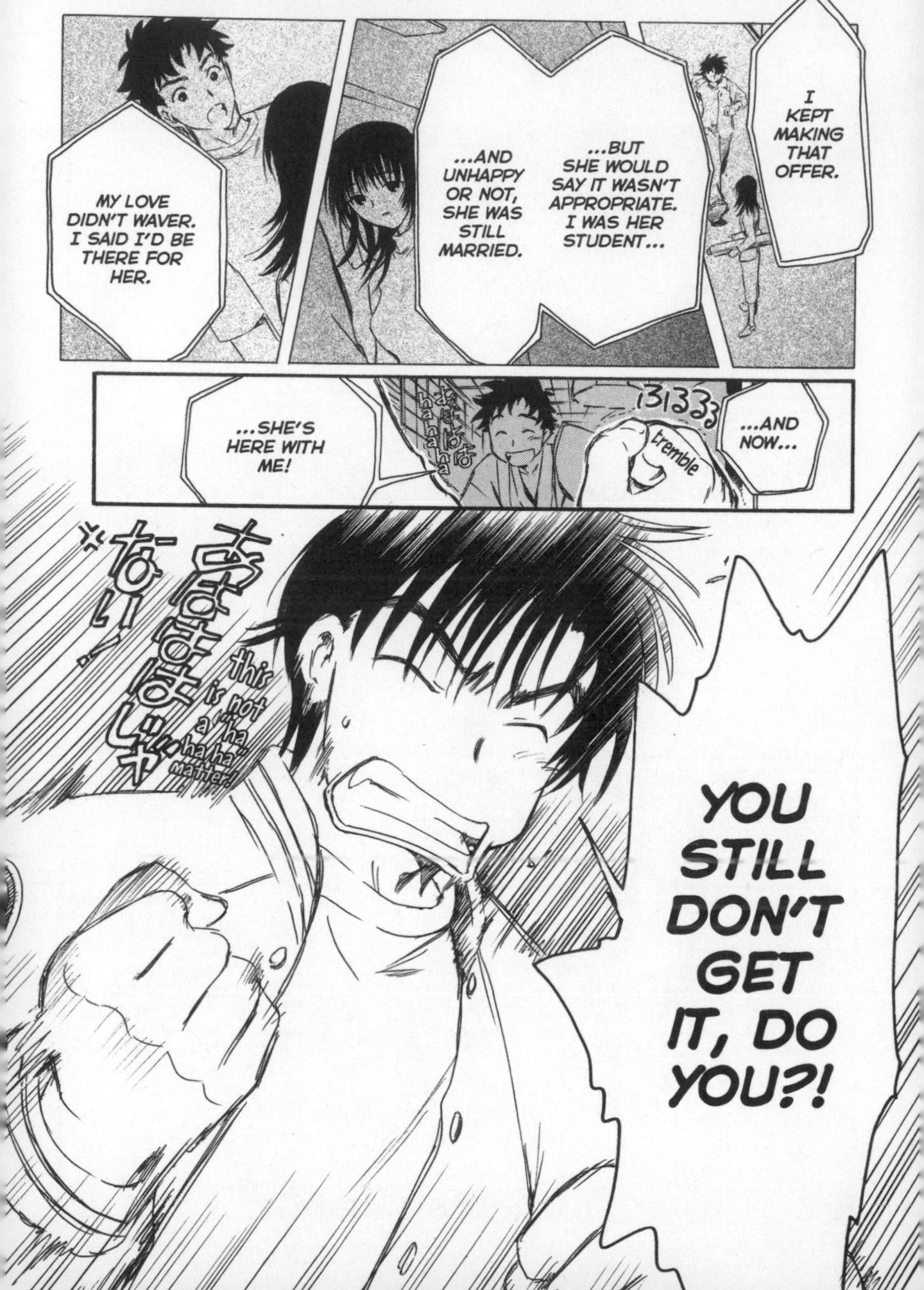
I KEPT MAKING THAT OFFER.
...BUT SHE WOULD SAY IT WASN'T APPROPRIATE. I WAS HER STUDENT...
...AND UNHAPPY OR NOT, SHE WAS STILL MARRIED.
MY LOVE DIDN'T WAVER. I SAID I'D BE THERE FOR HER.
...AND NOW...
ふるるるる
tremble
ははは
ha ha ha
...SHE'S HERE WITH ME!
YOU STILL DON'T GET IT, DO YOU?!
あはははじゃない!!
this is not a "ha ha ha" matter!

OMURA

Chobits
ちょびっツ

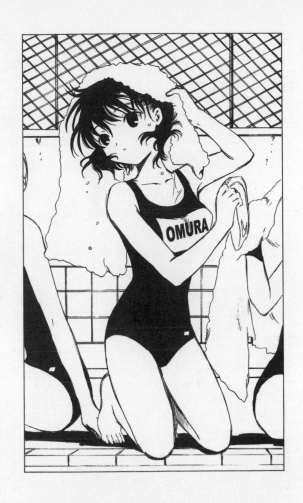

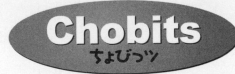

◂chapter 28▸

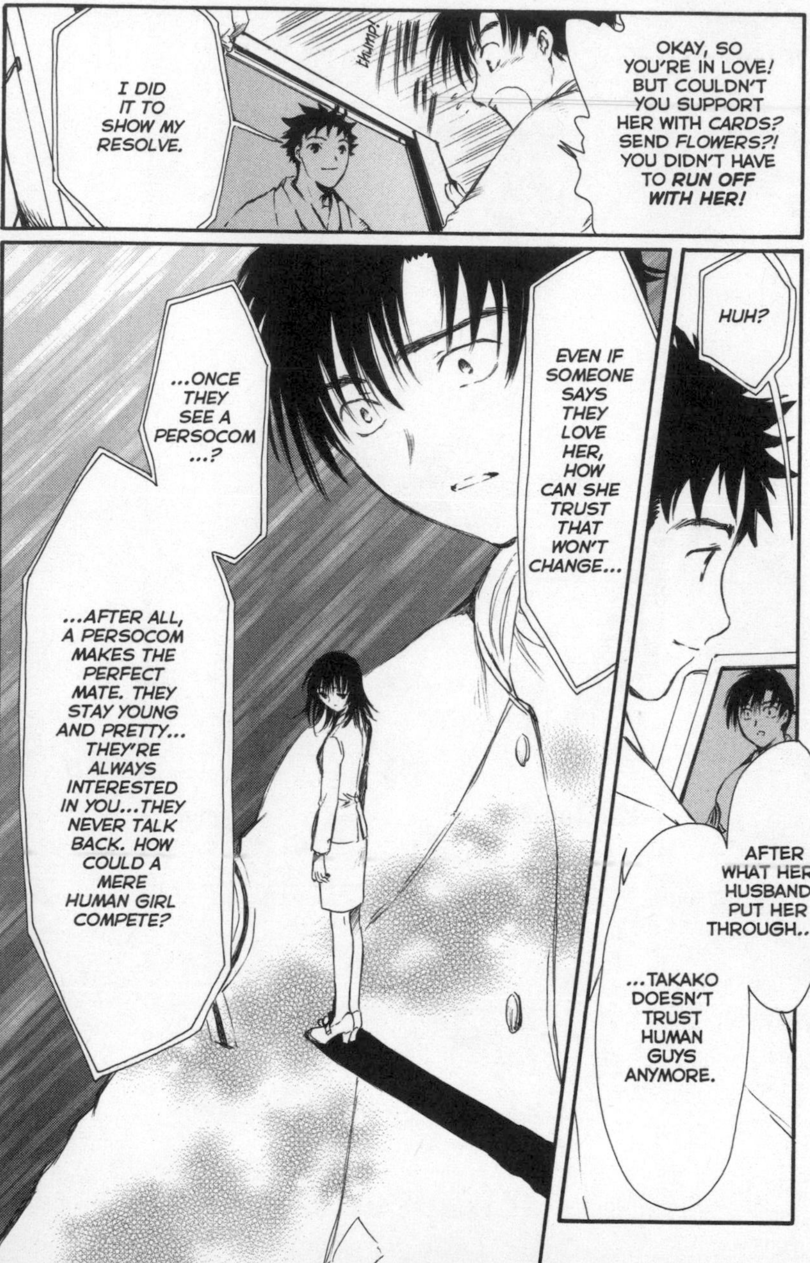
OKAY, SO YOU'RE IN LOVE! BUT COULDN'T YOU SUPPORT HER WITH CARDS? SEND FLOWERS?! YOU DIDN'T HAVE TO RUN OFF WITH HER!
thump!
I DID IT TO SHOW MY RESOLVE.
HUH?
AFTER WHAT HER HUSBAND PUT HER THROUGH...
...TAKAKO DOESN'T TRUST HUMAN GUYS ANYMORE.
EVEN IF SOMEONE SAYS THEY LOVE HER, HOW CAN SHE TRUST THAT WON'T CHANGE...
...ONCE THEY SEE A PERSOCOM...?
...AFTER ALL, A PERSOCOM MAKES THE PERFECT MATE. THEY STAY YOUNG AND PRETTY... THEY'RE ALWAYS INTERESTED IN YOU...THEY NEVER TALK BACK. HOW COULD A MERE HUMAN GIRL COMPETE?

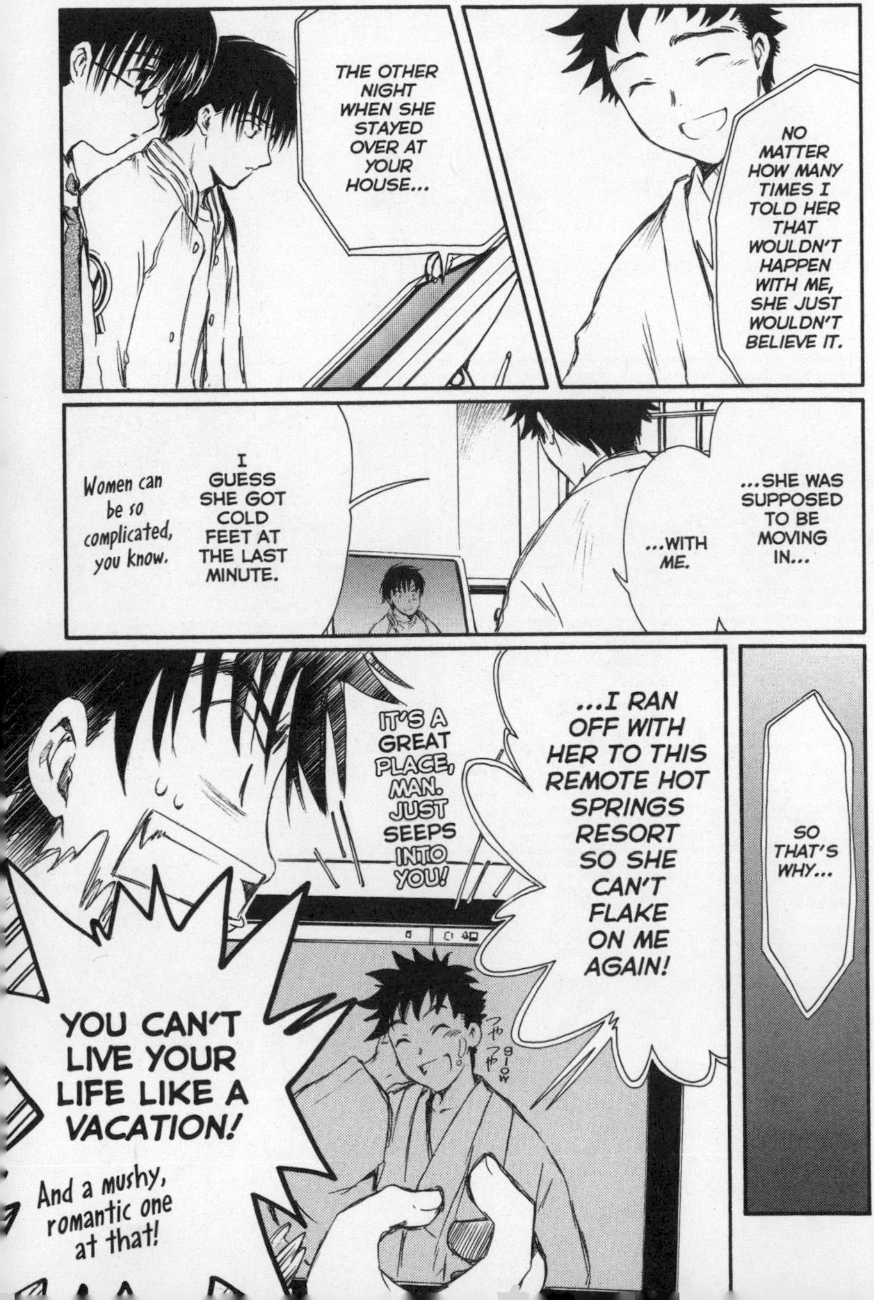
NO MATTER HOW MANY TIMES I TOLD HER THAT WOULDN'T HAPPEN WITH ME, SHE JUST WOULDN'T BELIEVE IT.
THE OTHER NIGHT WHEN SHE STAYED OVER AT YOUR HOUSE...
...SHE WAS SUPPOSED TO BE MOVING IN...
...WITH ME.
I GUESS SHE GOT COLD FEET AT THE LAST MINUTE.
Women can be so complicated, you know.
SO THAT'S WHY...
...I RAN OFF WITH HER TO THIS REMOTE HOT SPRINGS RESORT SO SHE CAN'T FLAKE ON ME AGAIN!
IT'S A GREAT PLACE, MAN. JUST SEEPS INTO YOU!
glow
YOU CAN'T LIVE YOUR LIFE LIKE A VACATION!
And a mushy, romantic one at that!

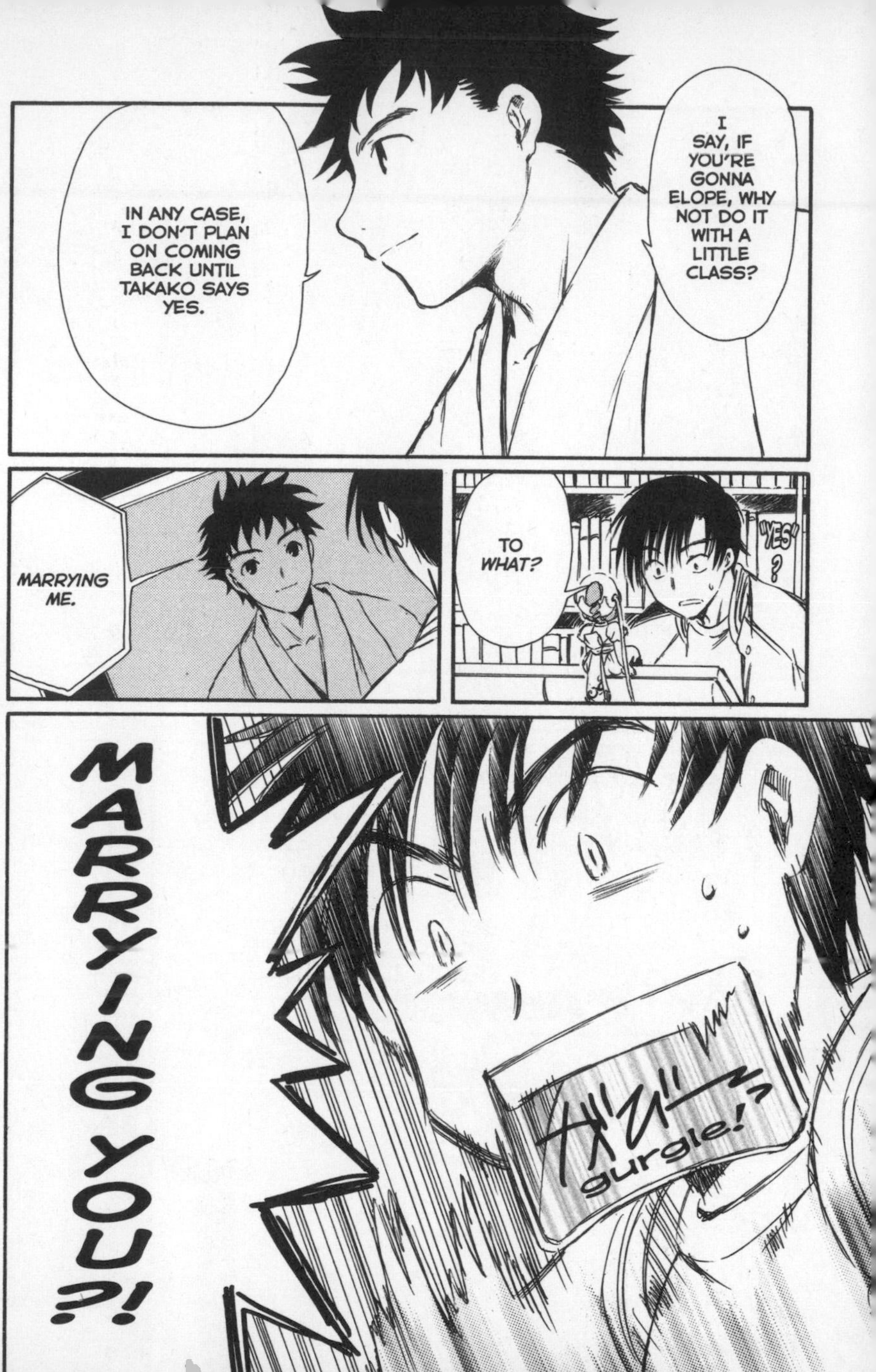
I SAY, IF YOU'RE GONNA ELOPE, WHY NOT DO IT WITH A LITTLE CLASS?
IN ANY CASE, I DON'T PLAN ON COMING BACK UNTIL TAKAKO SAYS YES.
"YES"?
TO WHAT?
MARRYING ME.
MARRYING YOU?!
gurgle!

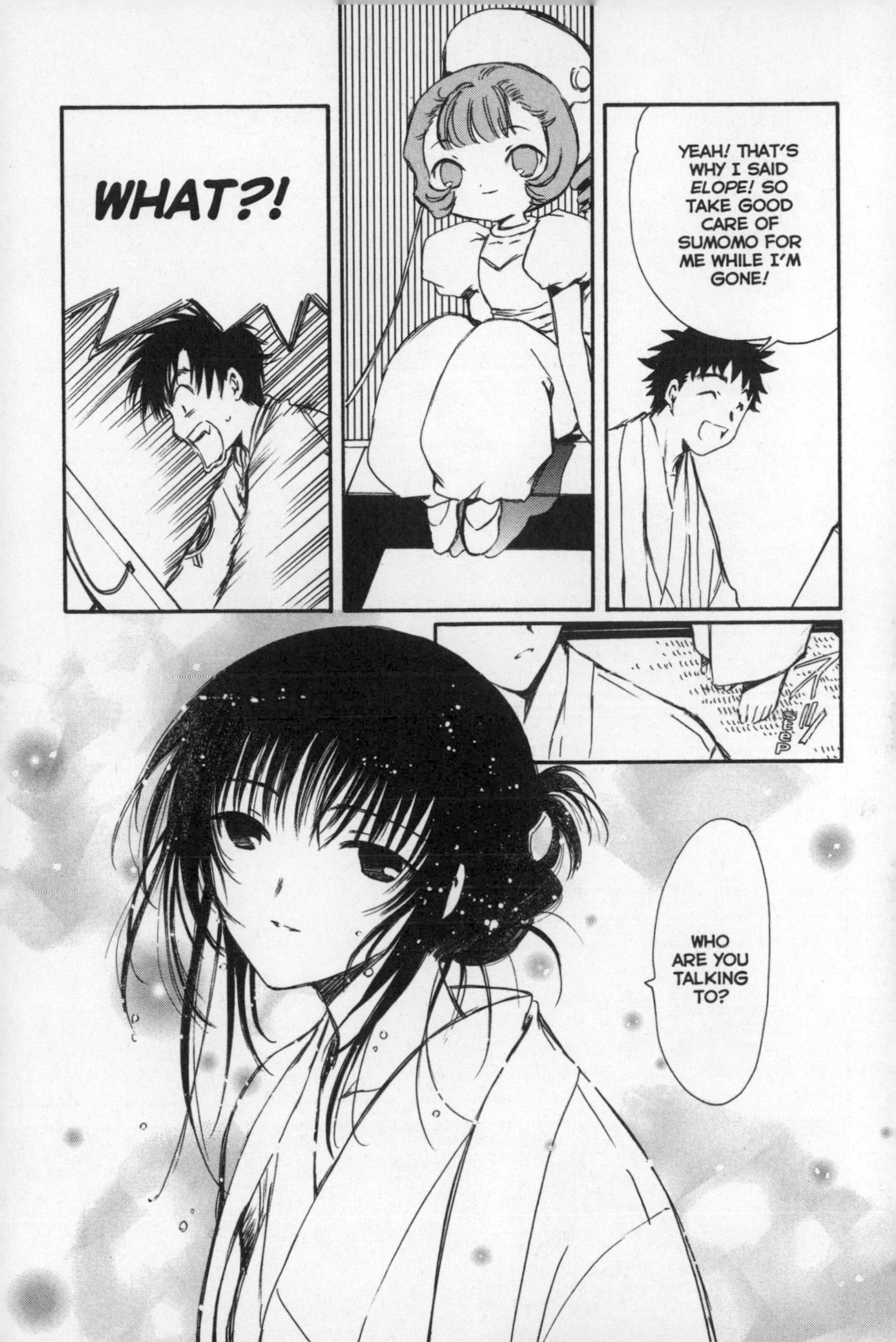
YEAH! THAT'S WHY I SAID *ELOPE!* SO TAKE GOOD CARE OF SUMOMO FOR ME WHILE I'M GONE!
WHAT?!
step
WHO ARE YOU TALKING TO?

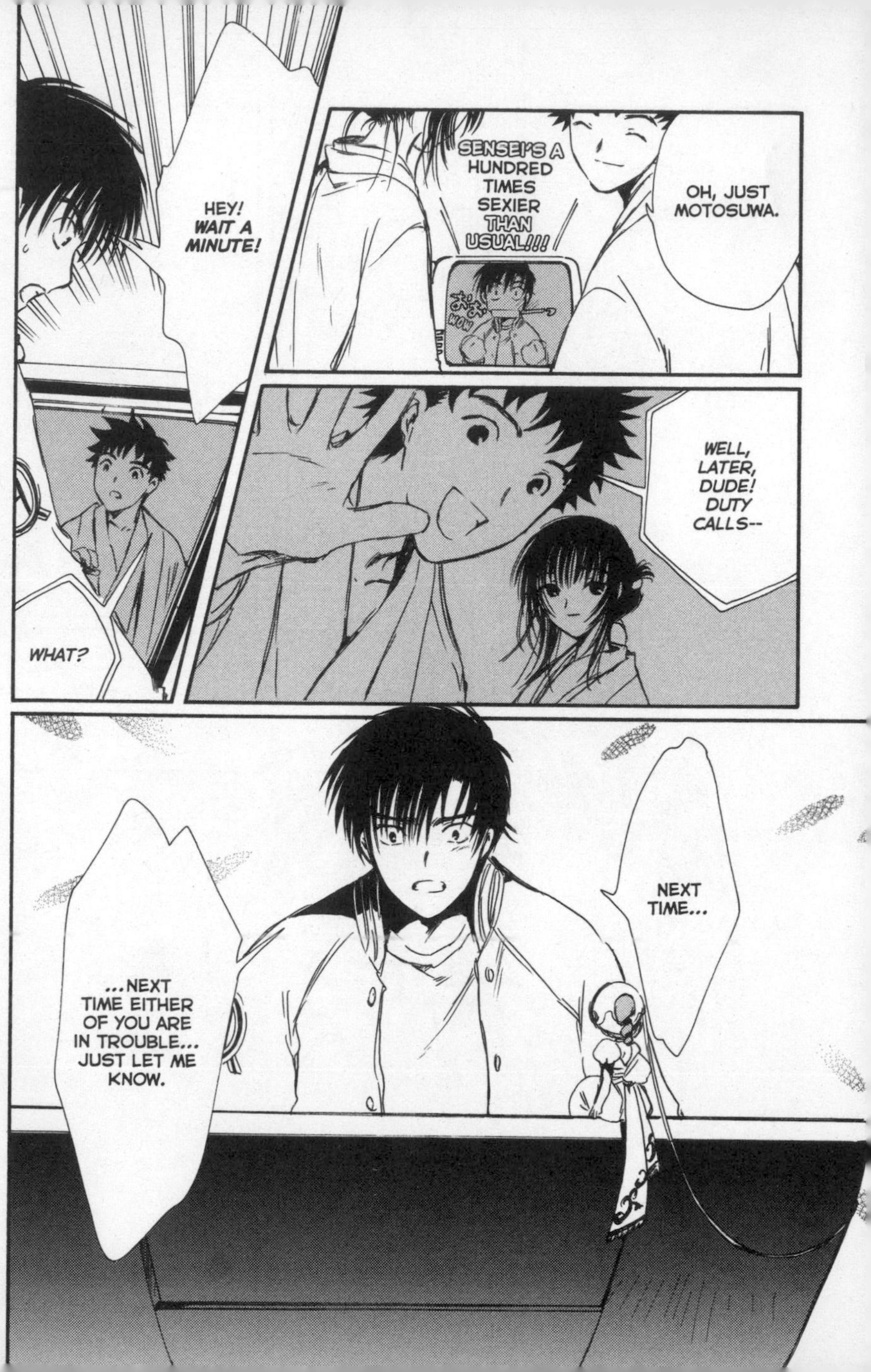
OH, JUST MOTOSUWA.
SENSEI'S A HUNDRED TIMES SEXIER THAN USUAL!!!
WOW
HEY! WAIT A MINUTE!
WELL, LATER, DUDE! DUTY CALLS--
WHAT?
NEXT TIME...
...NEXT TIME EITHER OF YOU ARE IN TROUBLE... JUST LET ME KNOW.

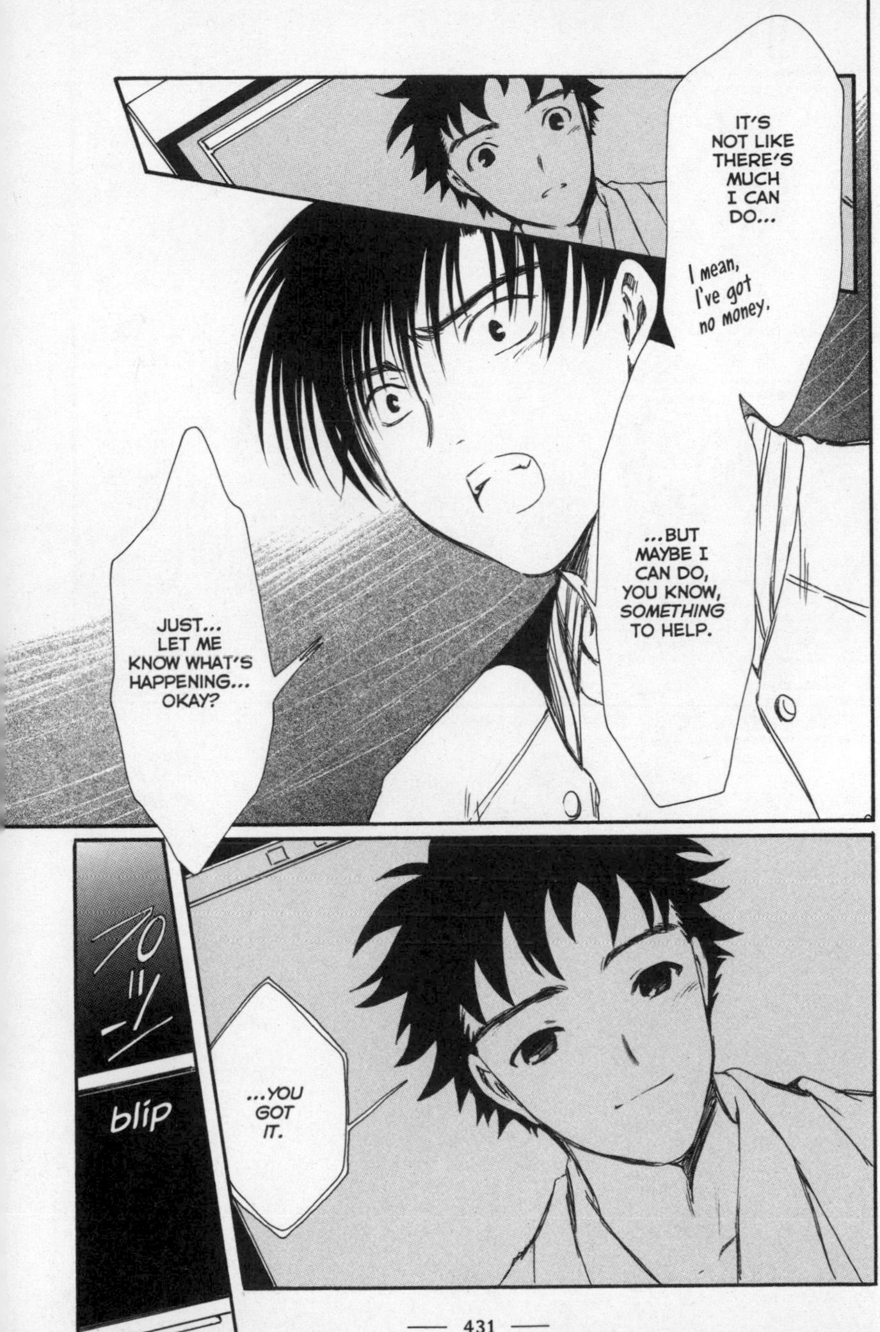
IT'S NOT LIKE THERE'S MUCH I CAN DO...
I mean, I've got no money.
...BUT MAYBE I CAN DO, YOU KNOW, *SOMETHING* TO HELP.
JUST... LET ME KNOW WHAT'S HAPPENING... OKAY?
...YOU GOT IT.
blip

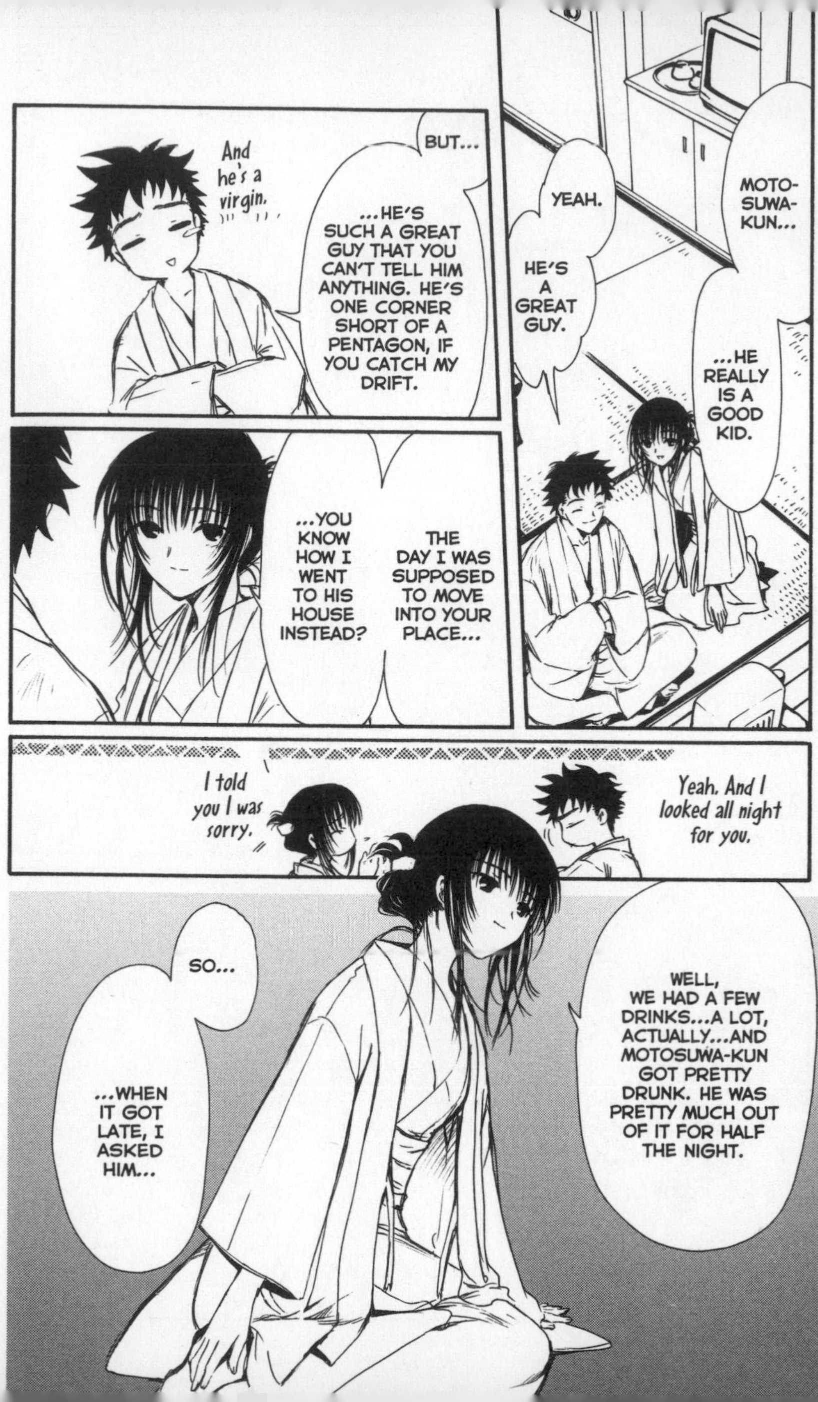
MOTO-SUWA-KUN...
...HE REALLY IS A GOOD KID.
YEAH.
HE'S A GREAT GUY.
BUT...
...HE'S SUCH A GREAT GUY THAT YOU CAN'T TELL HIM ANYTHING. HE'S ONE CORNER SHORT OF A PENTAGON, IF YOU CATCH MY DRIFT.
And he's a virgin.
THE DAY I WAS SUPPOSED TO MOVE INTO YOUR PLACE...
...YOU KNOW HOW I WENT TO HIS HOUSE INSTEAD?
Yeah. And I looked all night for you.
I told you I was sorry.
WELL, WE HAD A FEW DRINKS...A LOT, ACTUALLY...AND MOTOSUWA-KUN GOT PRETTY DRUNK. HE WAS PRETTY MUCH OUT OF IT FOR HALF THE NIGHT.
SO...
...WHEN IT GOT LATE, I ASKED HIM...

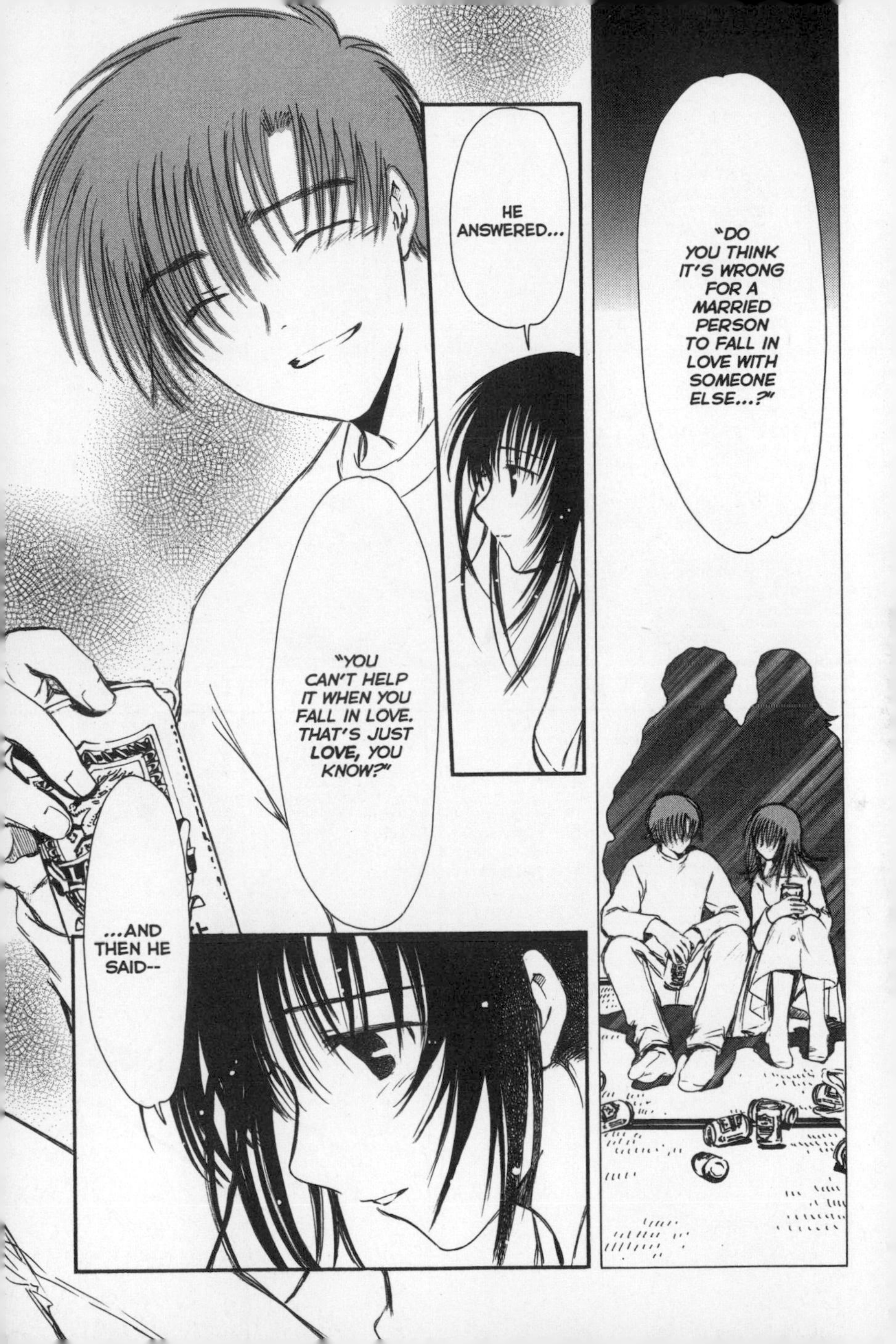
"DO YOU THINK IT'S WRONG FOR A MARRIED PERSON TO FALL IN LOVE WITH SOMEONE ELSE...?"
HE ANSWERED...
"YOU CAN'T HELP IT WHEN YOU FALL IN LOVE. THAT'S JUST LOVE, YOU KNOW?"
...AND THEN HE SAID--

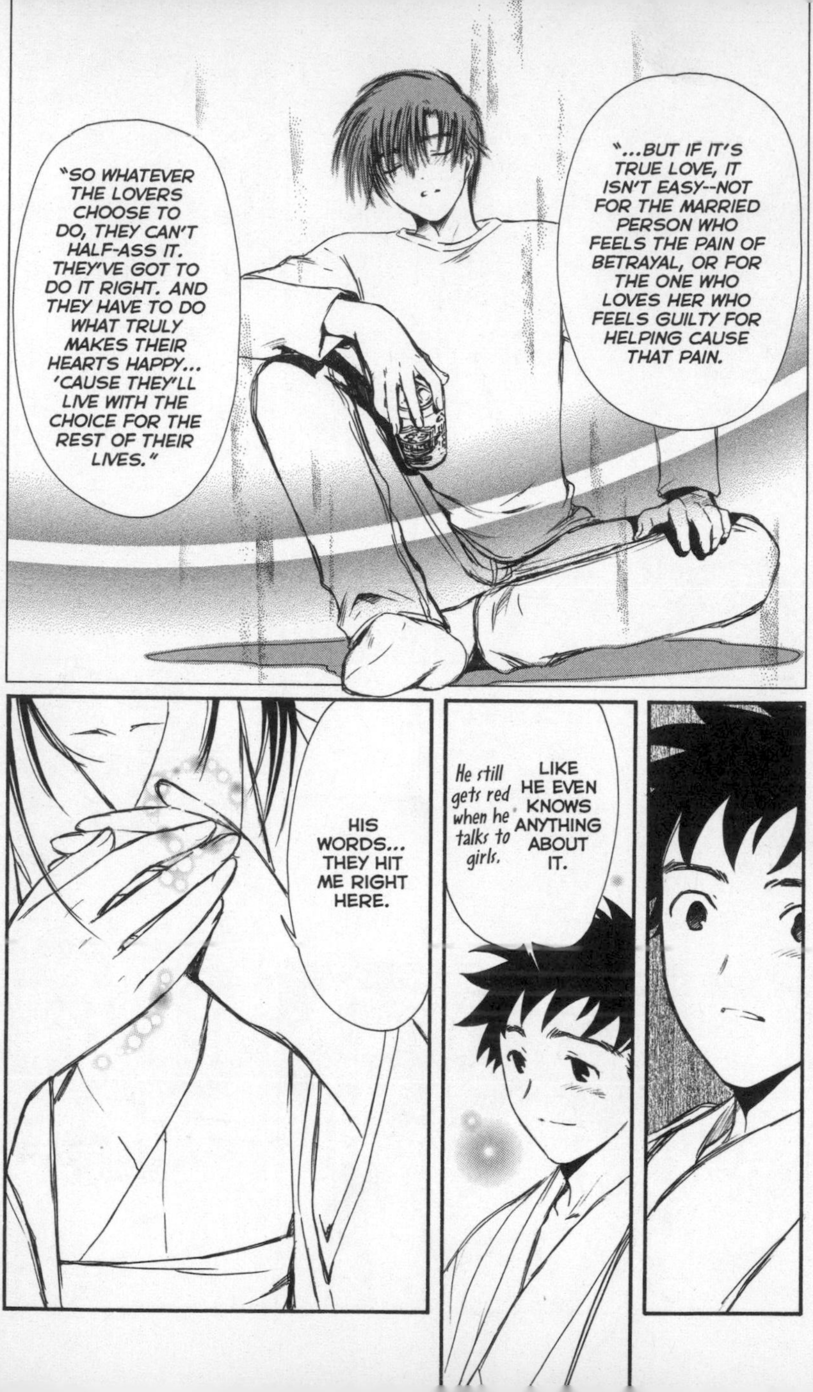
"...BUT IF IT'S TRUE LOVE, IT ISN'T EASY--NOT FOR THE MARRIED PERSON WHO FEELS THE PAIN OF BETRAYAL, OR FOR THE ONE WHO LOVES HER WHO FEELS GUILTY FOR HELPING CAUSE THAT PAIN.
"SO WHATEVER THE LOVERS CHOOSE TO DO, THEY CAN'T HALF-ASS IT. THEY'VE GOT TO DO IT RIGHT. AND THEY HAVE TO DO WHAT TRULY MAKES THEIR HEARTS HAPPY... 'CAUSE THEY'LL LIVE WITH THE CHOICE FOR THE REST OF THEIR LIVES."
LIKE HE EVEN KNOWS ANYTHING ABOUT IT.
He still gets red when he talks to girls.
HIS WORDS... THEY HIT ME RIGHT HERE.

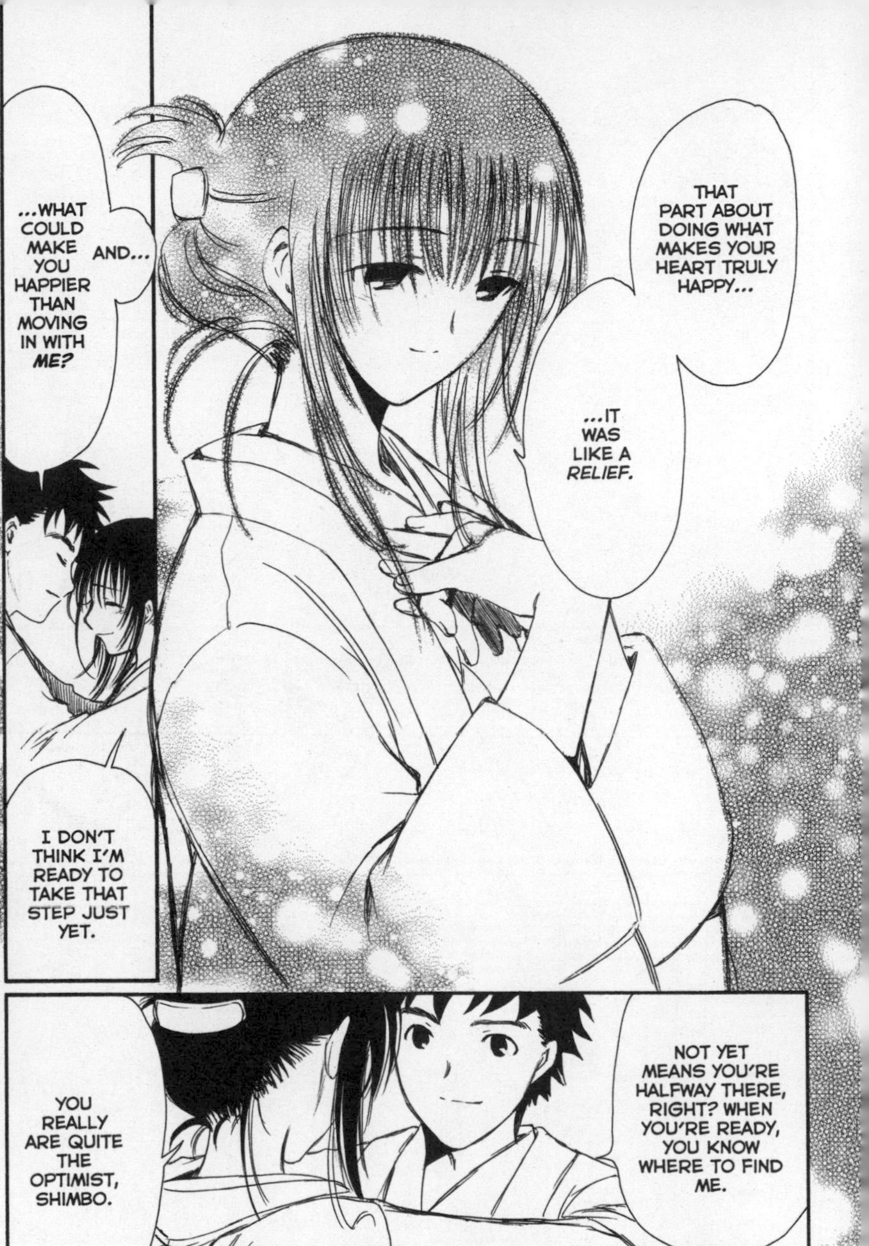
THAT PART ABOUT DOING WHAT MAKES YOUR HEART TRULY HAPPY...
...IT WAS LIKE A *RELIEF.*
AND...
...WHAT COULD MAKE YOU HAPPIER THAN MOVING IN WITH *ME?*
I DON'T THINK I'M READY TO TAKE THAT STEP JUST YET.
NOT YET MEANS YOU'RE HALFWAY THERE, RIGHT? WHEN YOU'RE READY, YOU KNOW WHERE TO FIND ME.
YOU REALLY ARE QUITE THE OPTIMIST, SHIMBO.

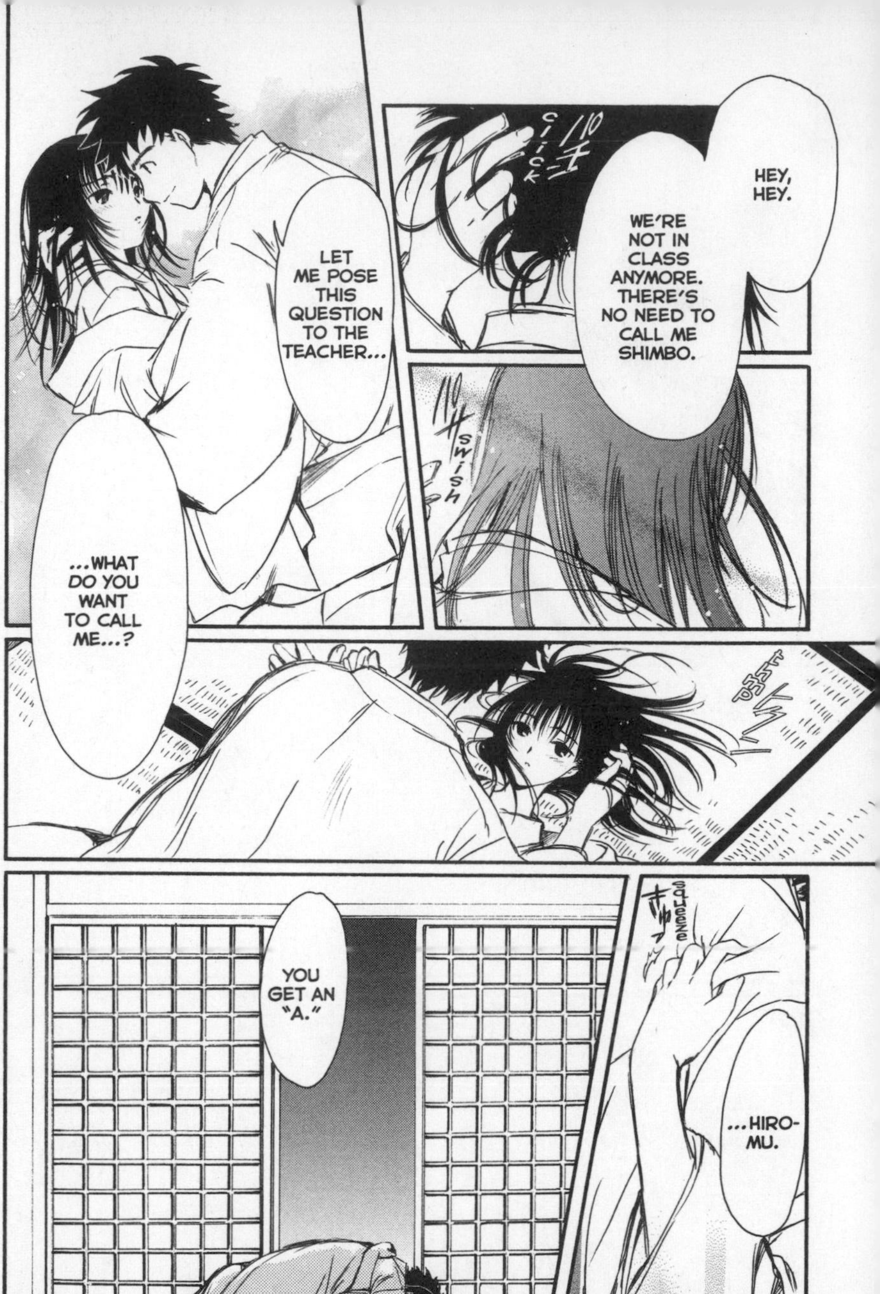
click
HEY, HEY.
WE'RE NOT IN CLASS ANYMORE. THERE'S NO NEED TO CALL ME SHIMBO.
swish
LET ME POSE THIS QUESTION TO THE TEACHER...
...WHAT DO YOU WANT TO CALL ME...?
flop
squeeze
...HIRO-MU.
YOU GET AN "A."

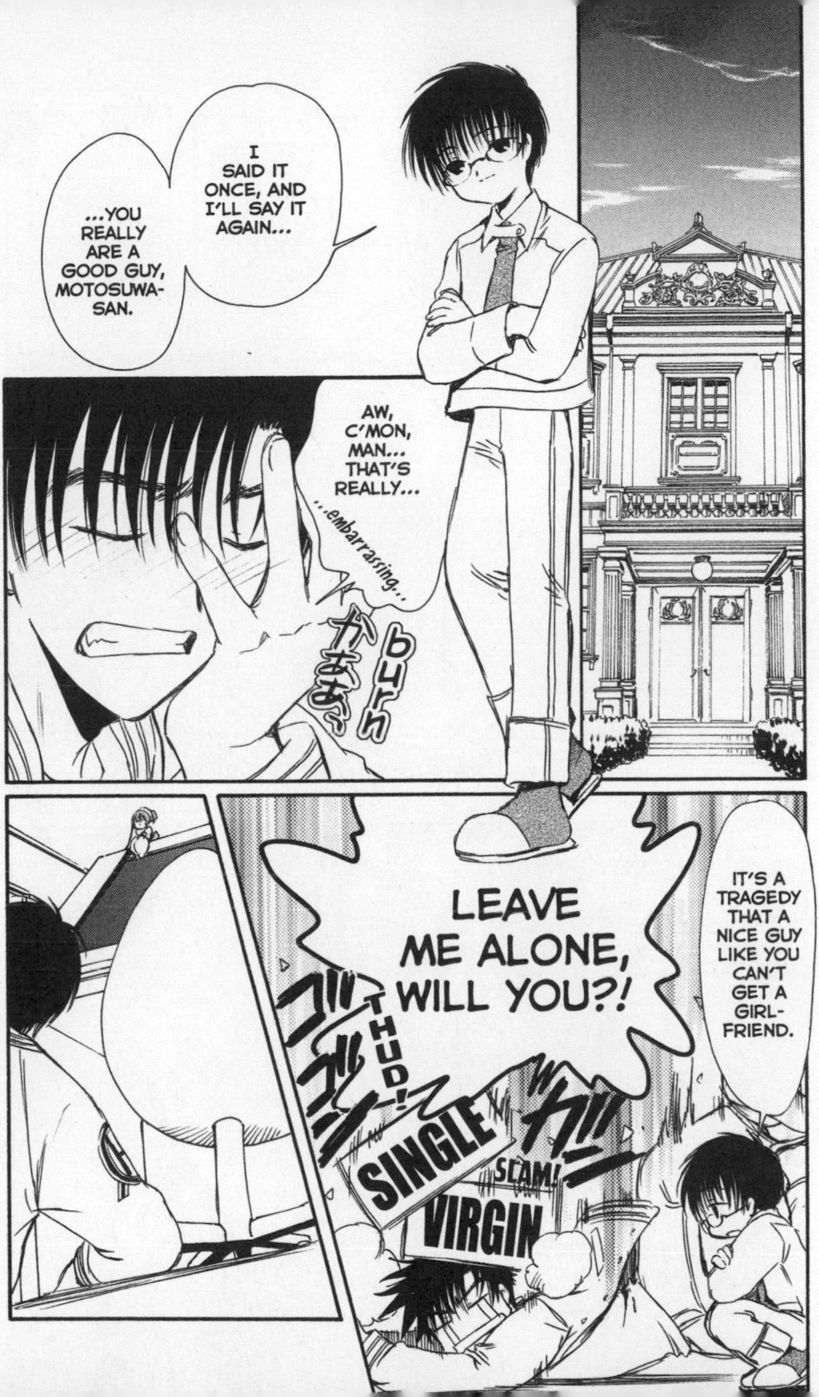
I SAID IT ONCE, AND I'LL SAY IT AGAIN...
...YOU REALLY ARE A GOOD GUY, MOTOSUWA-SAN.
AW, C'MON, MAN... THAT'S REALLY...
...embarrassing...
burn
IT'S A TRAGEDY THAT A NICE GUY LIKE YOU CAN'T GET A GIRLFRIEND.
LEAVE ME ALONE, WILL YOU?!
THUD!
SINGLE
SLAM!
VIRGIN

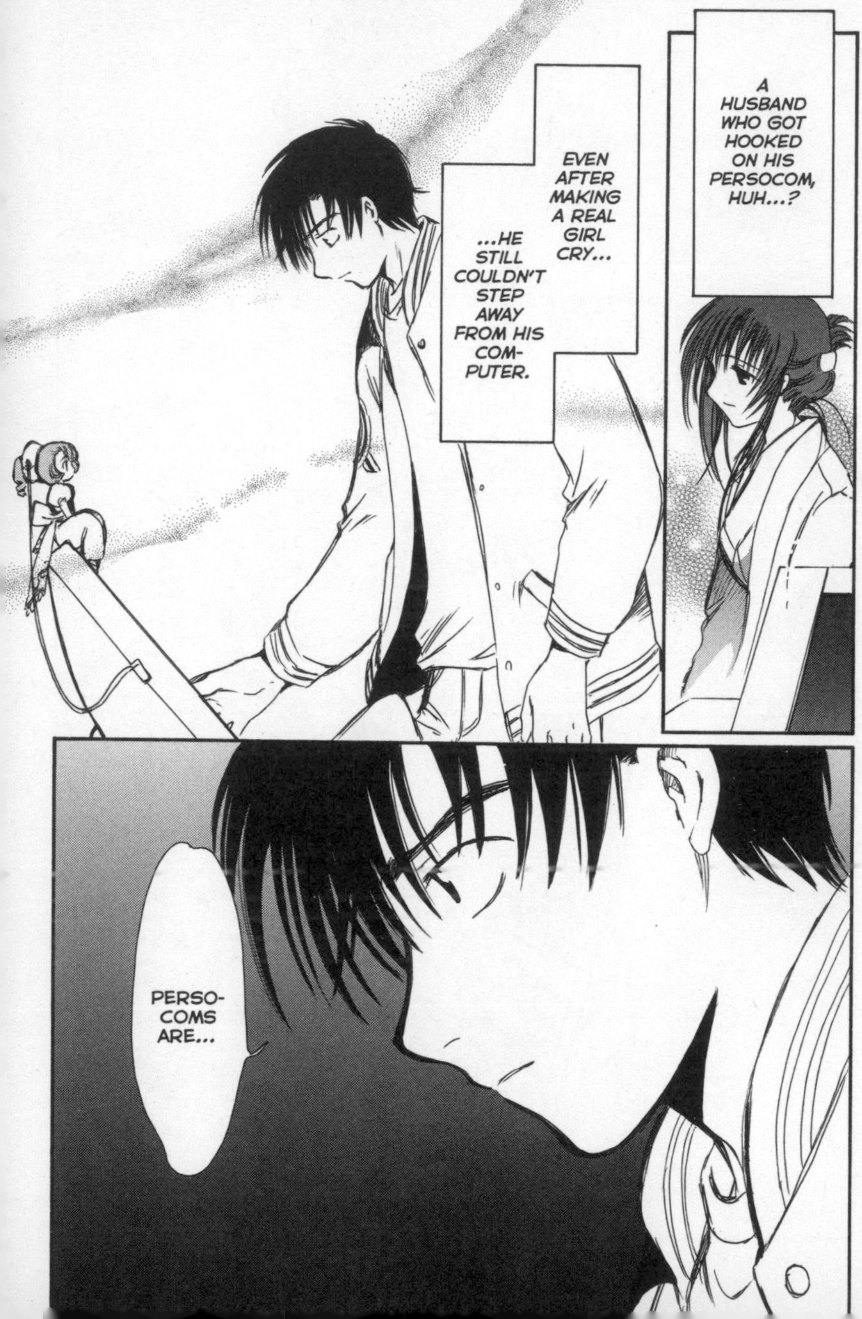
A HUSBAND WHO GOT HOOKED ON HIS PERSOCOM, HUH...?
EVEN AFTER MAKING A REAL GIRL CRY...
...HE STILL COULDN'T STEP AWAY FROM HIS COM-PUTER.
PERSO-COMS ARE...

Chobits
ちょびっツ

◀ **chapter 29** ▶

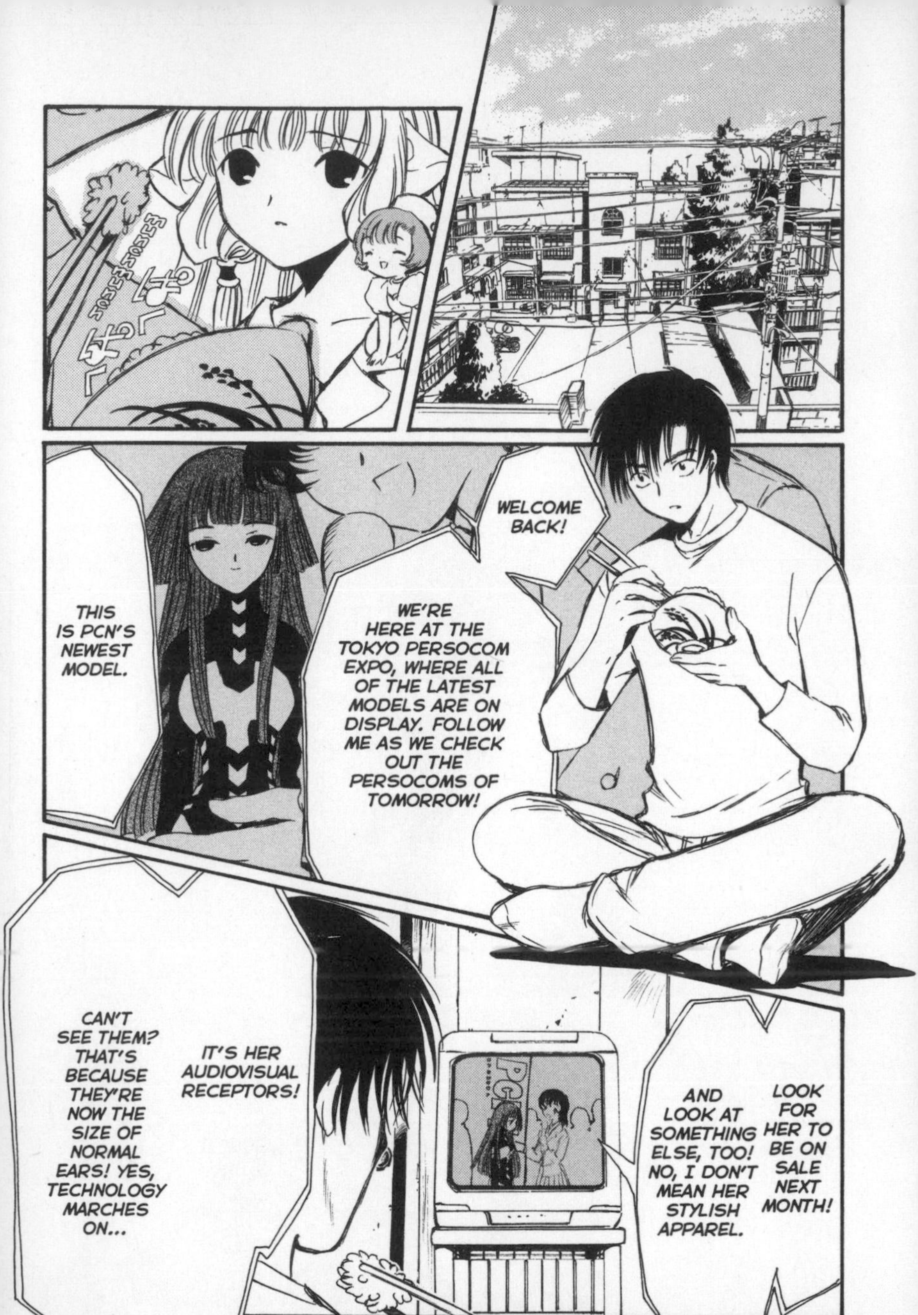
WELCOME BACK!
WE'RE HERE AT THE TOKYO PERSOCOM EXPO, WHERE ALL OF THE LATEST MODELS ARE ON DISPLAY. FOLLOW ME AS WE CHECK OUT THE PERSOCOMS OF TOMORROW!
THIS IS PCN'S NEWEST MODEL.
LOOK FOR HER TO BE ON SALE NEXT MONTH!
AND LOOK AT SOMETHING ELSE, TOO! NO, I DON'T MEAN HER STYLISH APPAREL.
IT'S HER AUDIOVISUAL RECEPTORS!
CAN'T SEE THEM? THAT'S BECAUSE THEY'RE NOW THE SIZE OF NORMAL EARS! YES, TECHNOLOGY MARCHES ON...

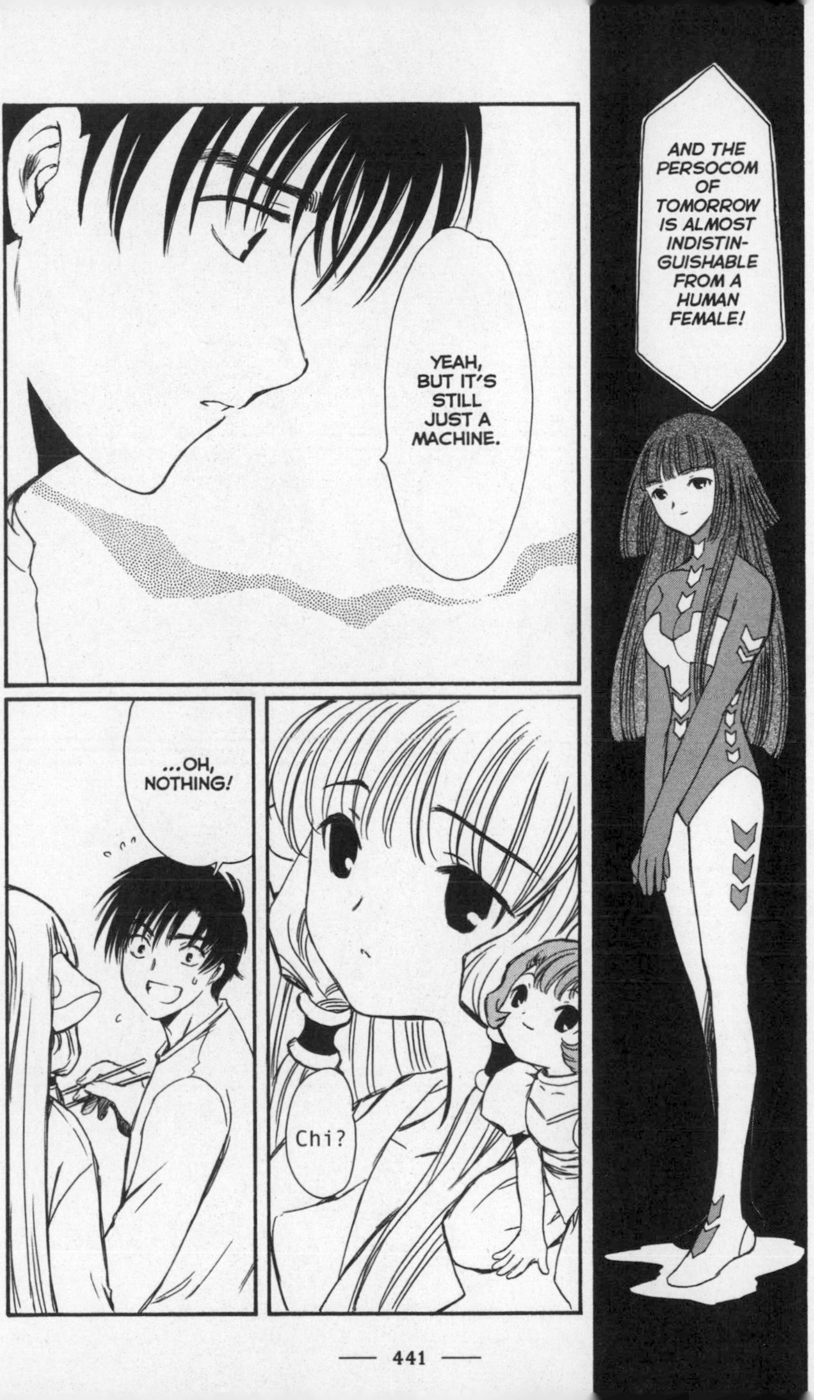
AND THE PERSOCOM OF TOMORROW IS ALMOST INDISTIN-GUISHABLE FROM A HUMAN FEMALE!
YEAH, BUT IT'S STILL JUST A MACHINE.
Chi?
...OH, NOTHING!

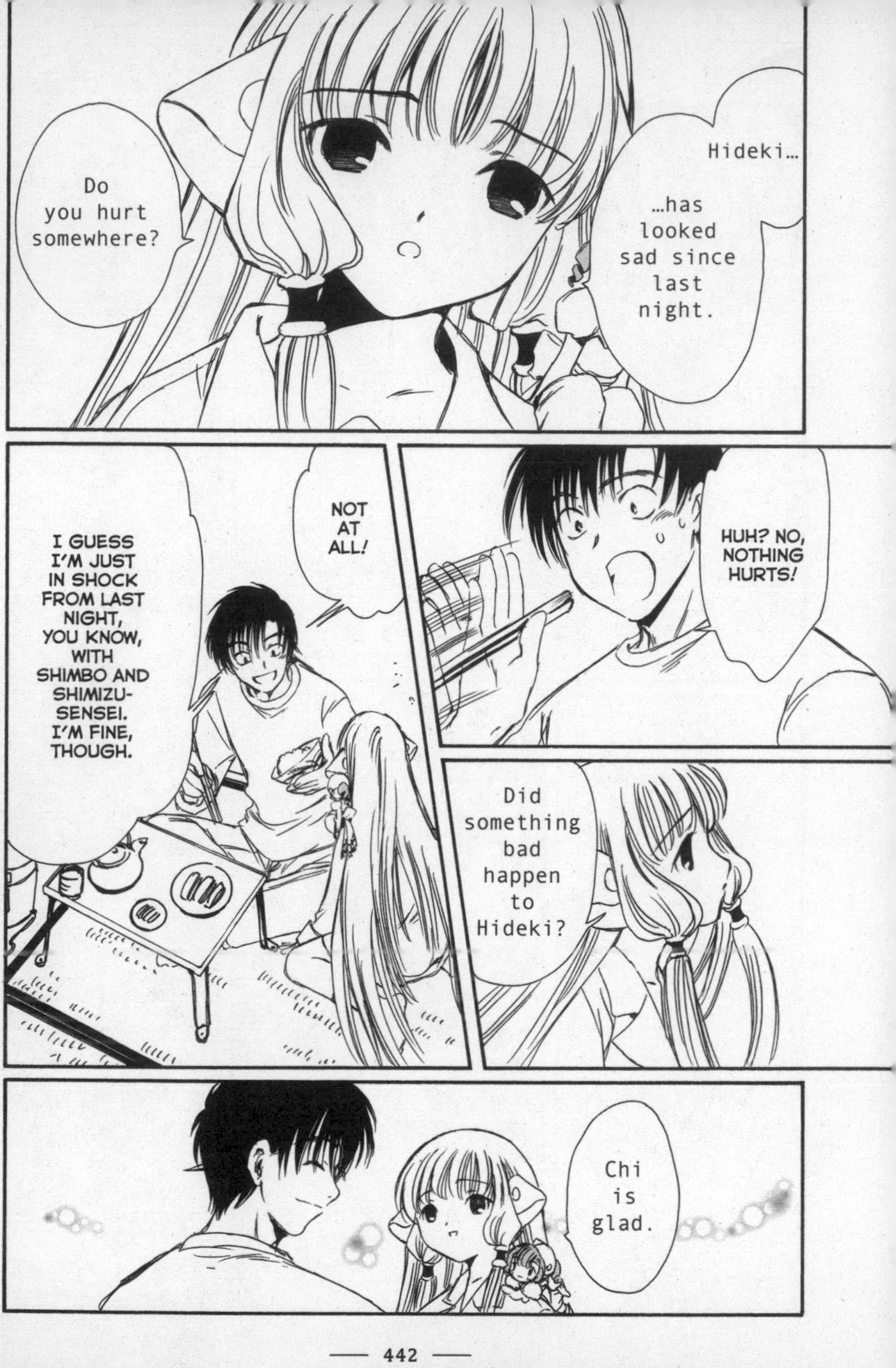
Hideki…
…has looked sad since last night.
Do you hurt somewhere?
HUH? NO, NOTHING HURTS!
Did something bad happen to Hideki?
NOT AT ALL!
I GUESS I'M JUST IN SHOCK FROM LAST NIGHT, YOU KNOW, WITH SHIMBO AND SHIMIZU-SENSEI. I'M FINE, THOUGH.
Chi is glad.

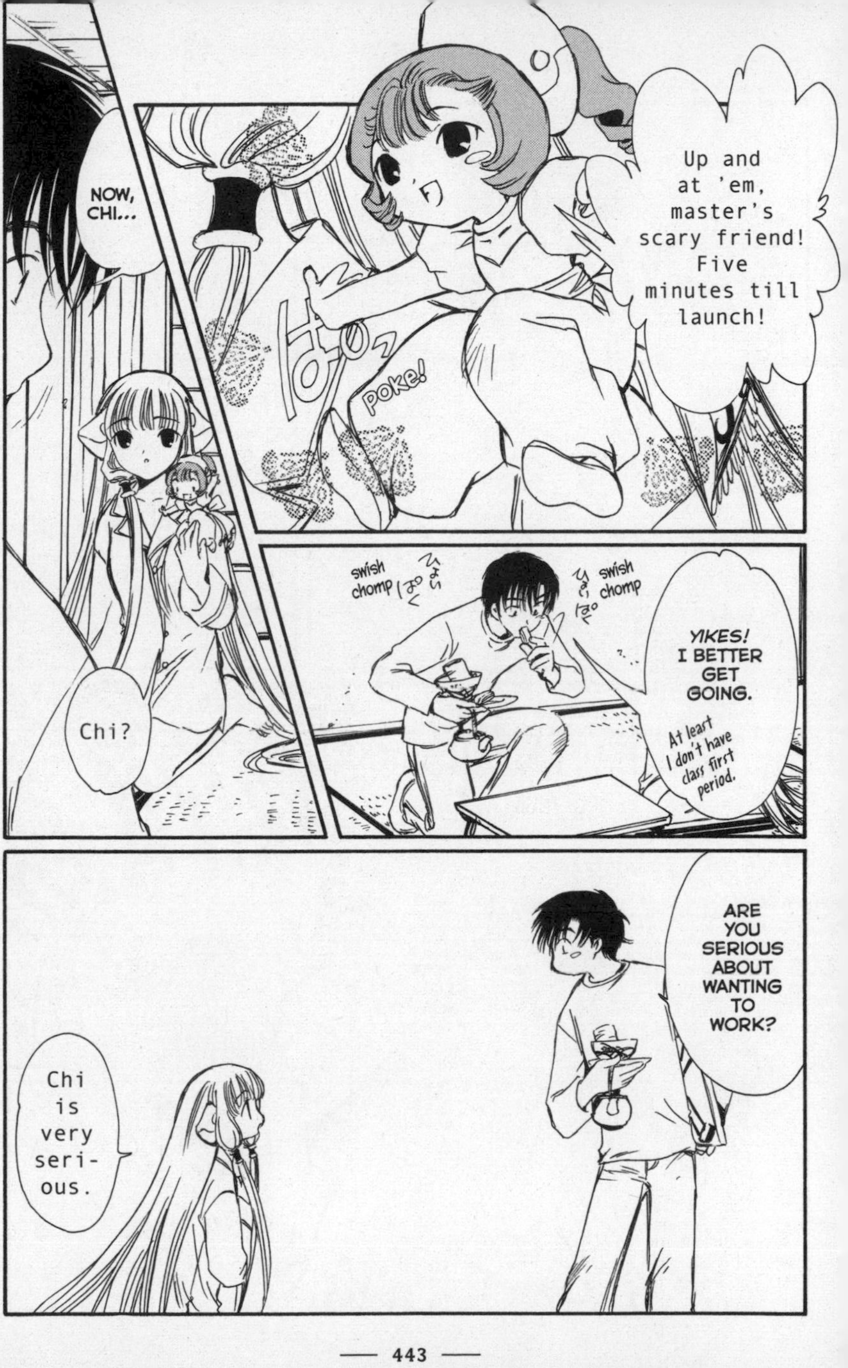
Up and at 'em, master's scary friend! Five minutes till launch!
poke!
swish chomp
swish chomp
YIKES! I BETTER GET GOING.
At least I don't have class first period.
NOW, CHI...
Chi?
ARE YOU SERIOUS ABOUT WANTING TO WORK?
Chi is very seri-ous.

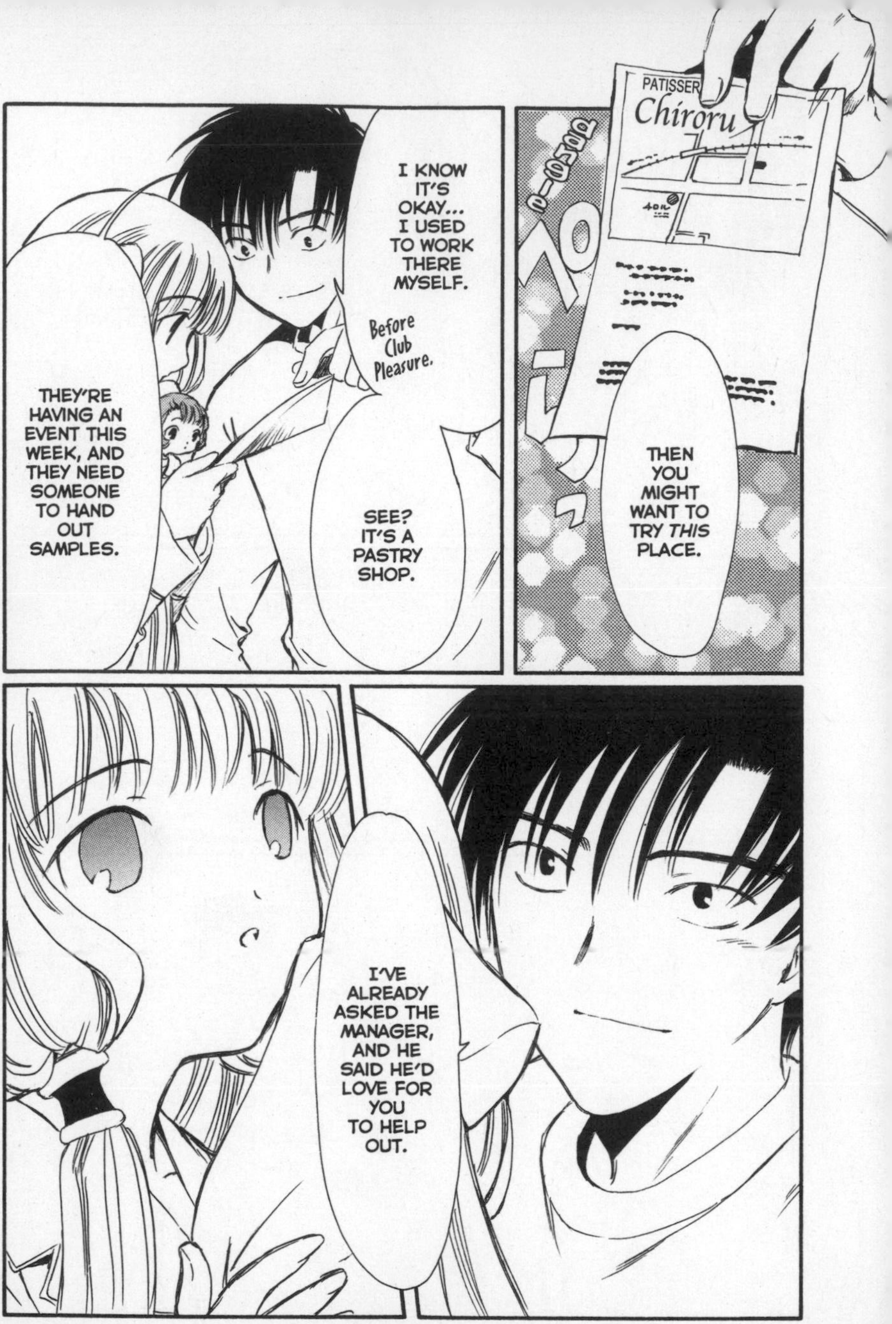
PATISSER
Chiroru
THEN YOU MIGHT WANT TO TRY *THIS* PLACE.
SEE? IT'S A PASTRY SHOP.
THEY'RE HAVING AN EVENT THIS WEEK, AND THEY NEED SOMEONE TO HAND OUT SAMPLES.
I KNOW IT'S OKAY... I USED TO WORK THERE MYSELF.
Before Club Pleasure.
I'VE ALREADY ASKED THE MANAGER, AND HE SAID HE'D LOVE FOR YOU TO HELP OUT.

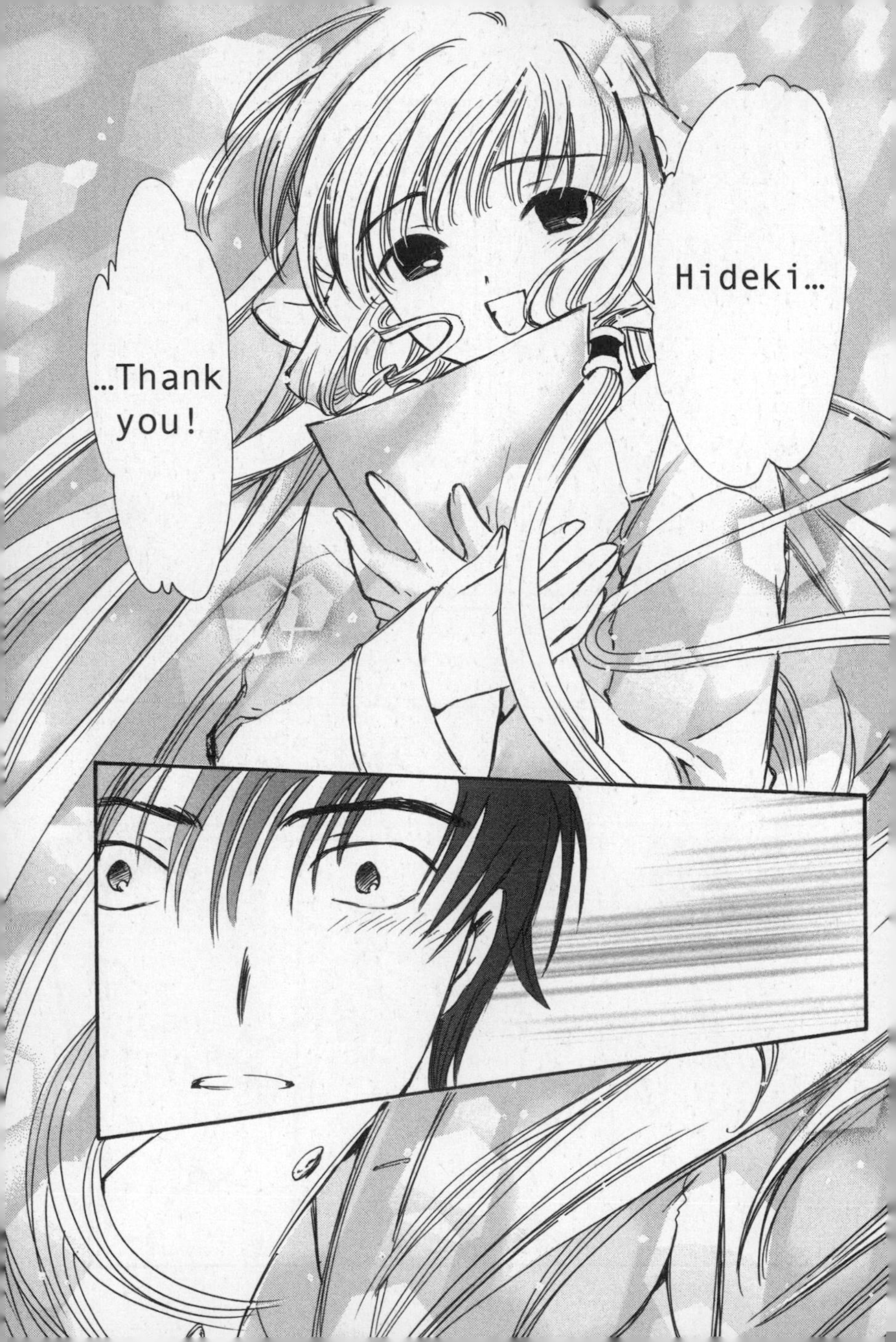
Hideki…
…Thank you!

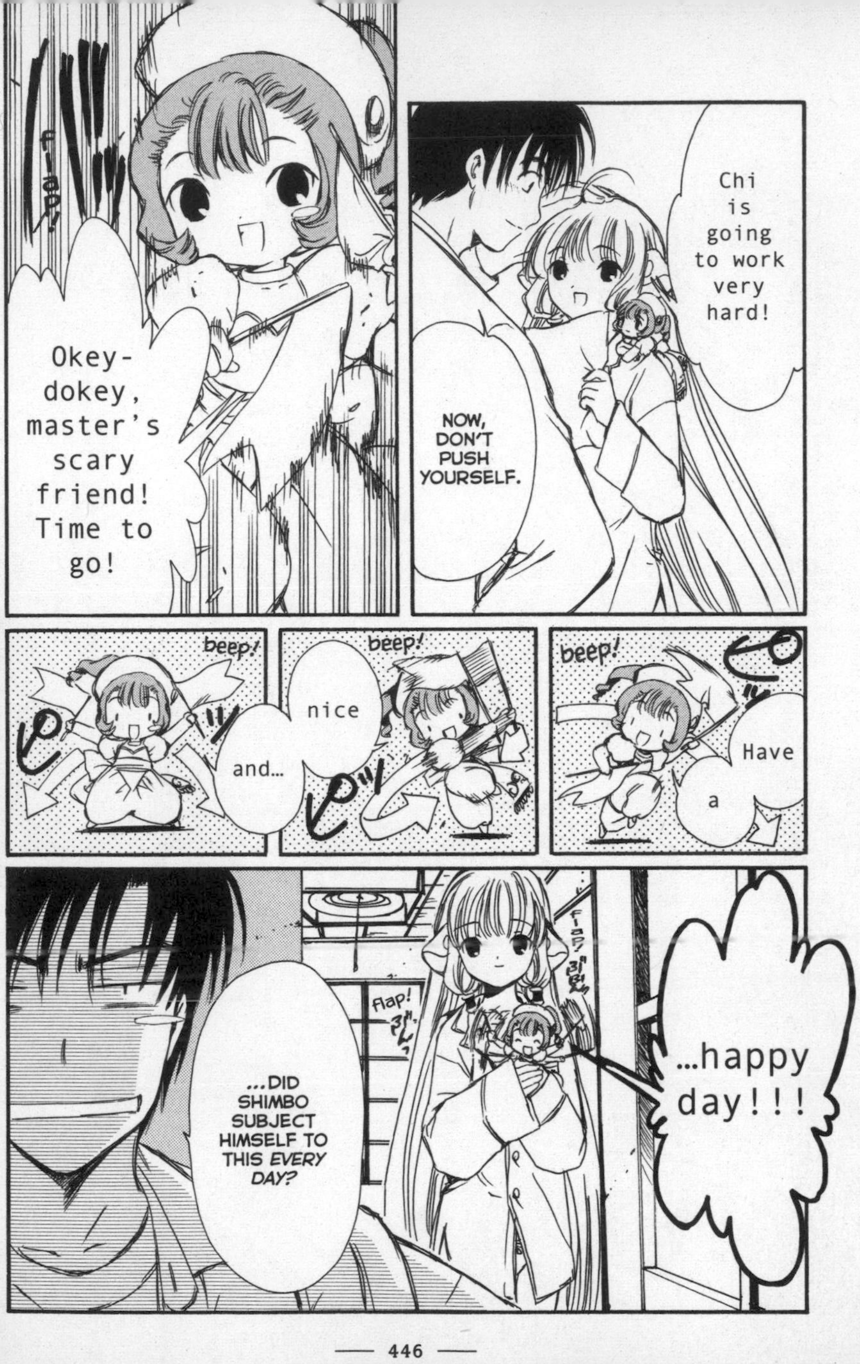
Chi is going to work very hard!
NOW, DON'T PUSH YOURSELF.
flap!
Okey-dokey, master's scary friend! Time to go!
beep!
Have a
beep!
nice
beep!
and...
...happy day!!!
flap!
flap!
...DID SHIMBO SUBJECT HIMSELF TO THIS EVERY DAY?

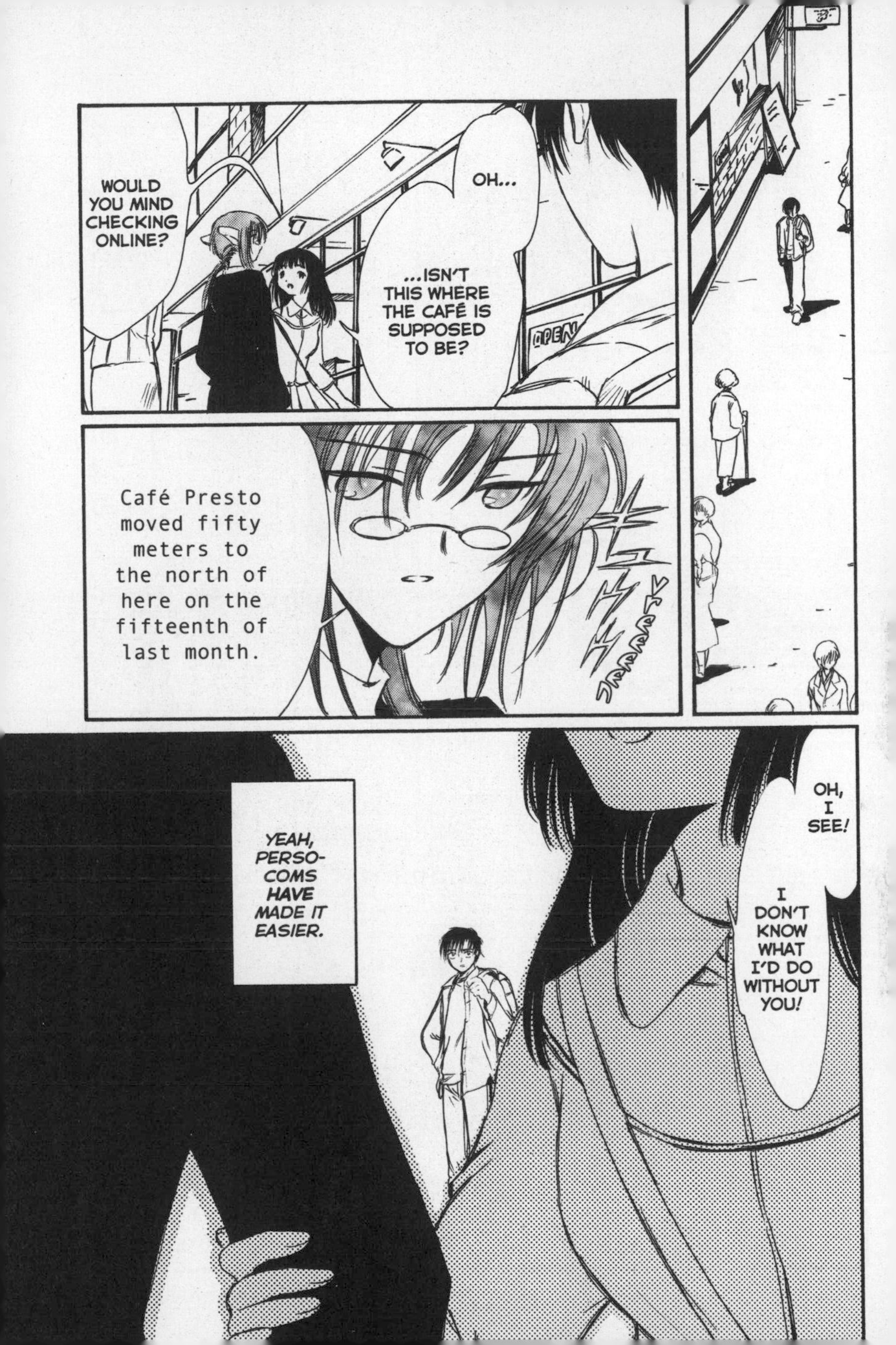
OH...
...ISN'T THIS WHERE THE CAFÉ IS SUPPOSED TO BE?
WOULD YOU MIND CHECKING ONLINE?
OPEN
Café Presto moved fifty meters to the north of here on the fifteenth of last month.
OH, I SEE!
I DON'T KNOW WHAT I'D DO WITHOUT YOU!
YEAH, PERSOCOMS HAVE MADE IT EASIER.

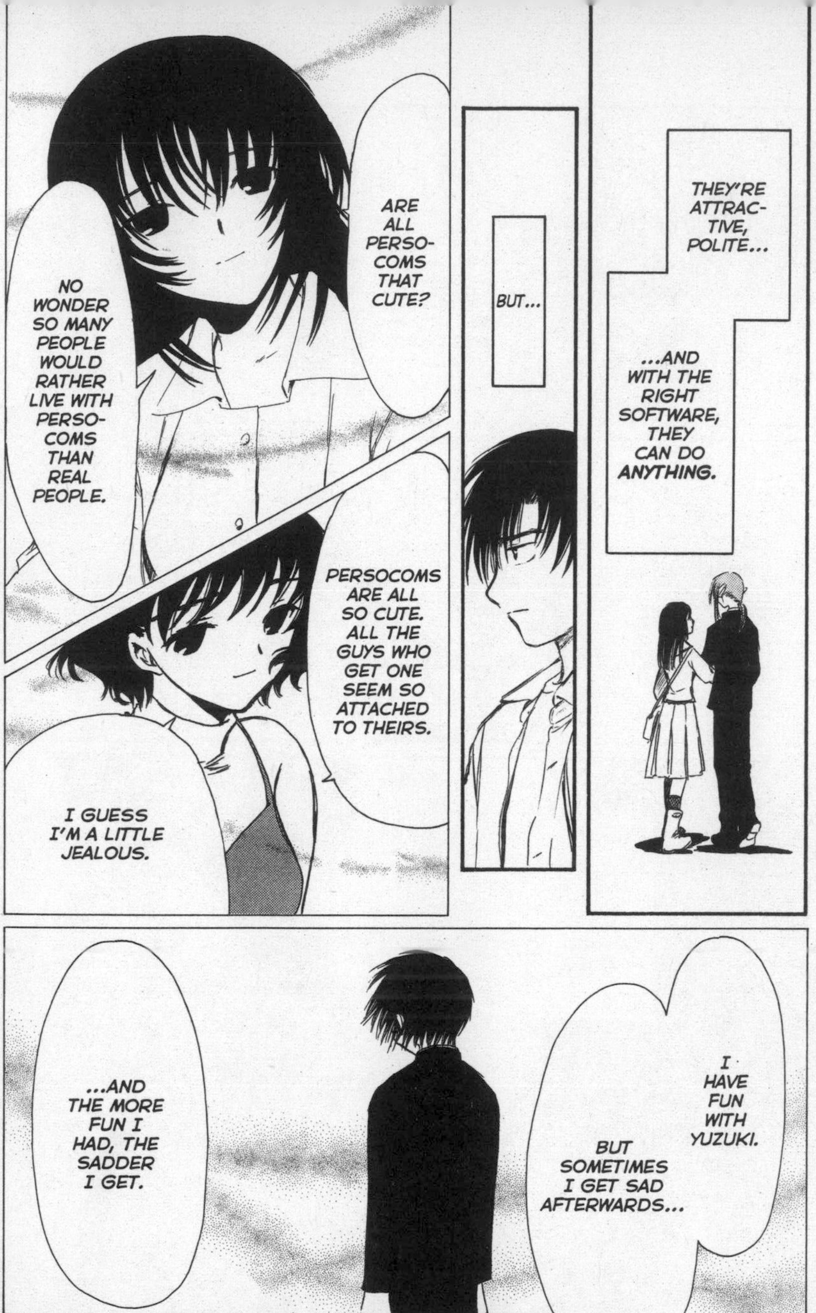
THEY'RE ATTRACTIVE, POLITE...
...AND WITH THE RIGHT SOFTWARE, THEY CAN DO **ANYTHING.**
BUT...
ARE ALL PERSOCOMS THAT CUTE?
NO WONDER SO MANY PEOPLE WOULD RATHER LIVE WITH PERSOCOMS THAN REAL PEOPLE.
PERSOCOMS ARE ALL SO CUTE. ALL THE GUYS WHO GET ONE SEEM SO ATTACHED TO THEIRS.
I GUESS I'M A LITTLE JEALOUS.
I HAVE FUN WITH YUZUKI.
BUT SOMETIMES I GET SAD AFTERWARDS...
...AND THE MORE FUN I HAD, THE SADDER I GET.

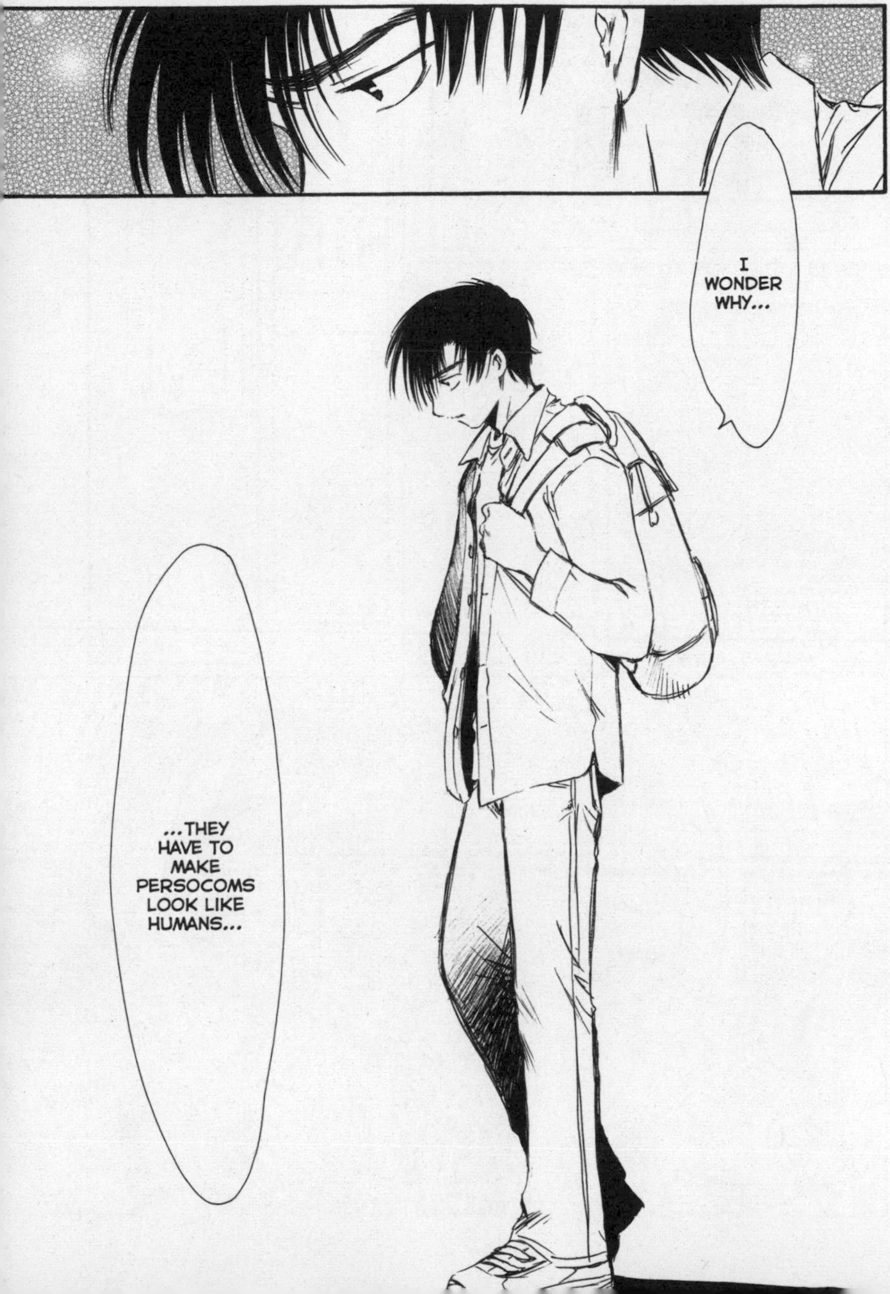
I WONDER WHY...
...THEY HAVE TO MAKE PERSOCOMS LOOK LIKE HUMANS...

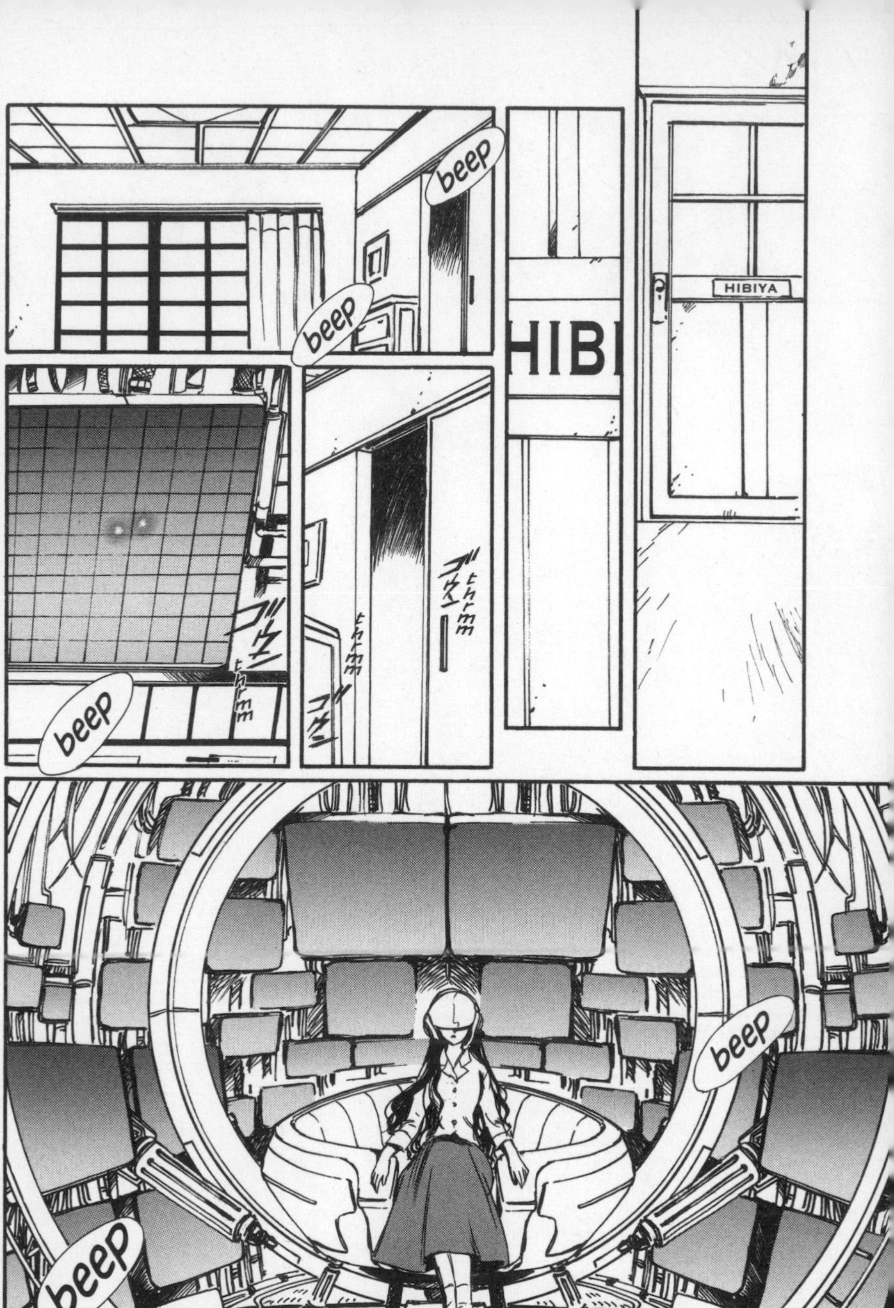
HIBIYA
HIBI
beep
beep
thrm
thrm
thrm
beep
beep
beep

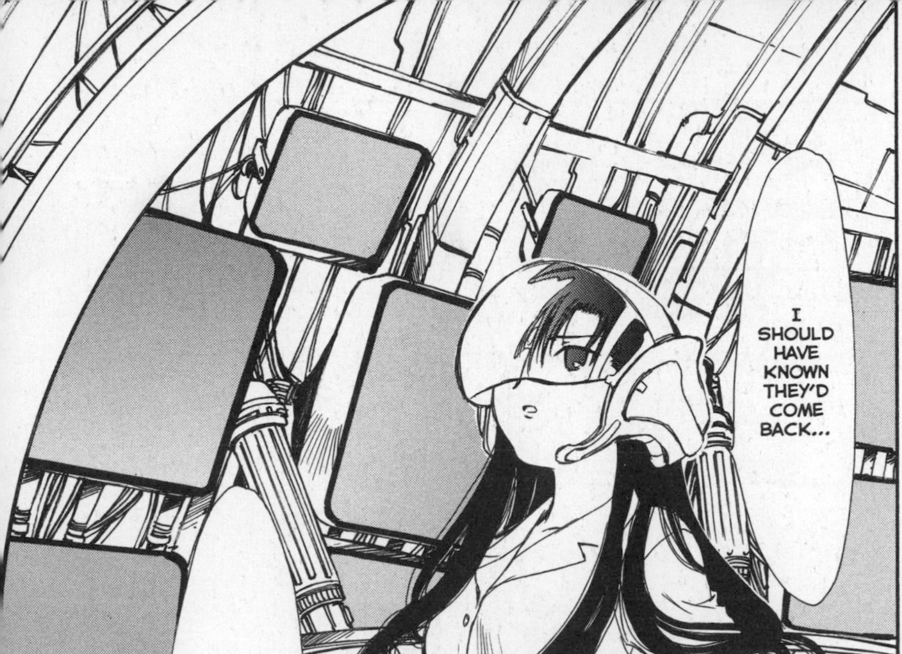
I SHOULD HAVE KNOWN THEY'D COME BACK...
...THOSE KIDS...

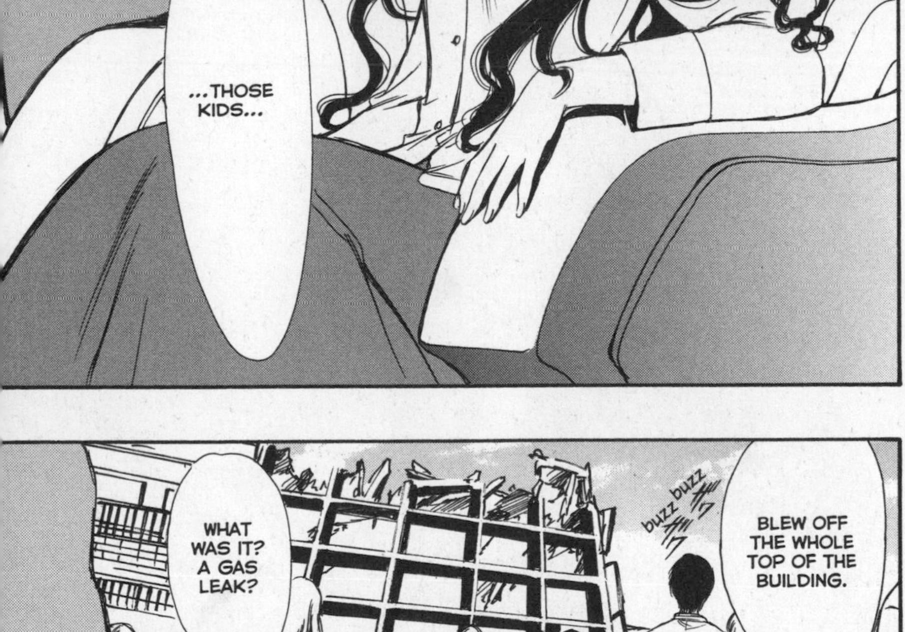
BLEW OFF THE WHOLE TOP OF THE BUILDING.
buzz buzz
WHAT WAS IT? A GAS LEAK?

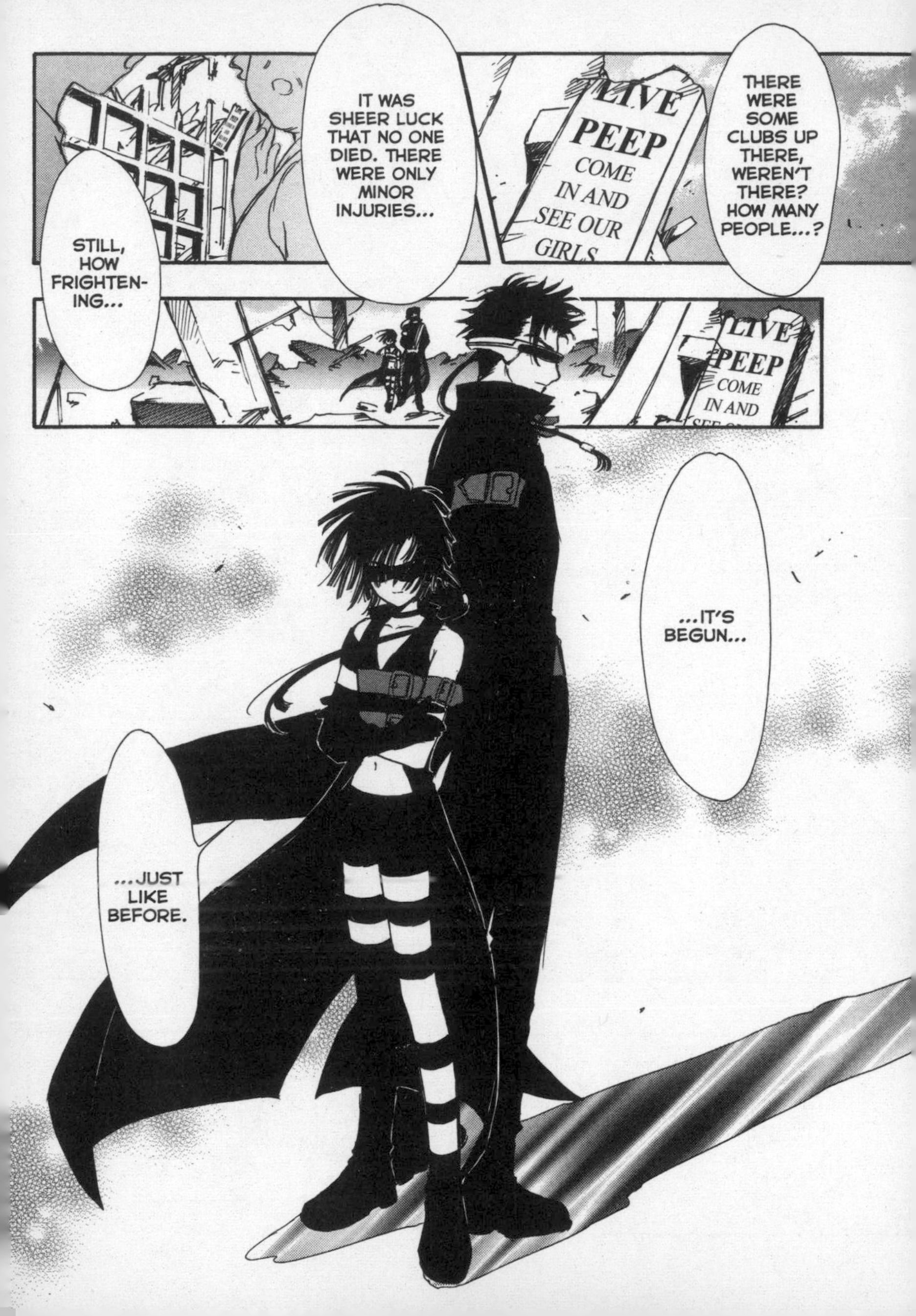
LIVE PEEP COME IN AND SEE OUR GIRLS
THERE WERE SOME CLUBS UP THERE, WEREN'T THERE? HOW MANY PEOPLE...?
IT WAS SHEER LUCK THAT NO ONE DIED. THERE WERE ONLY MINOR INJURIES...
STILL, HOW FRIGHTEN-ING...
...IT'S BEGUN...
...JUST LIKE BEFORE.

Chobits
ちょびっツ

◀ chapter 30 ▶

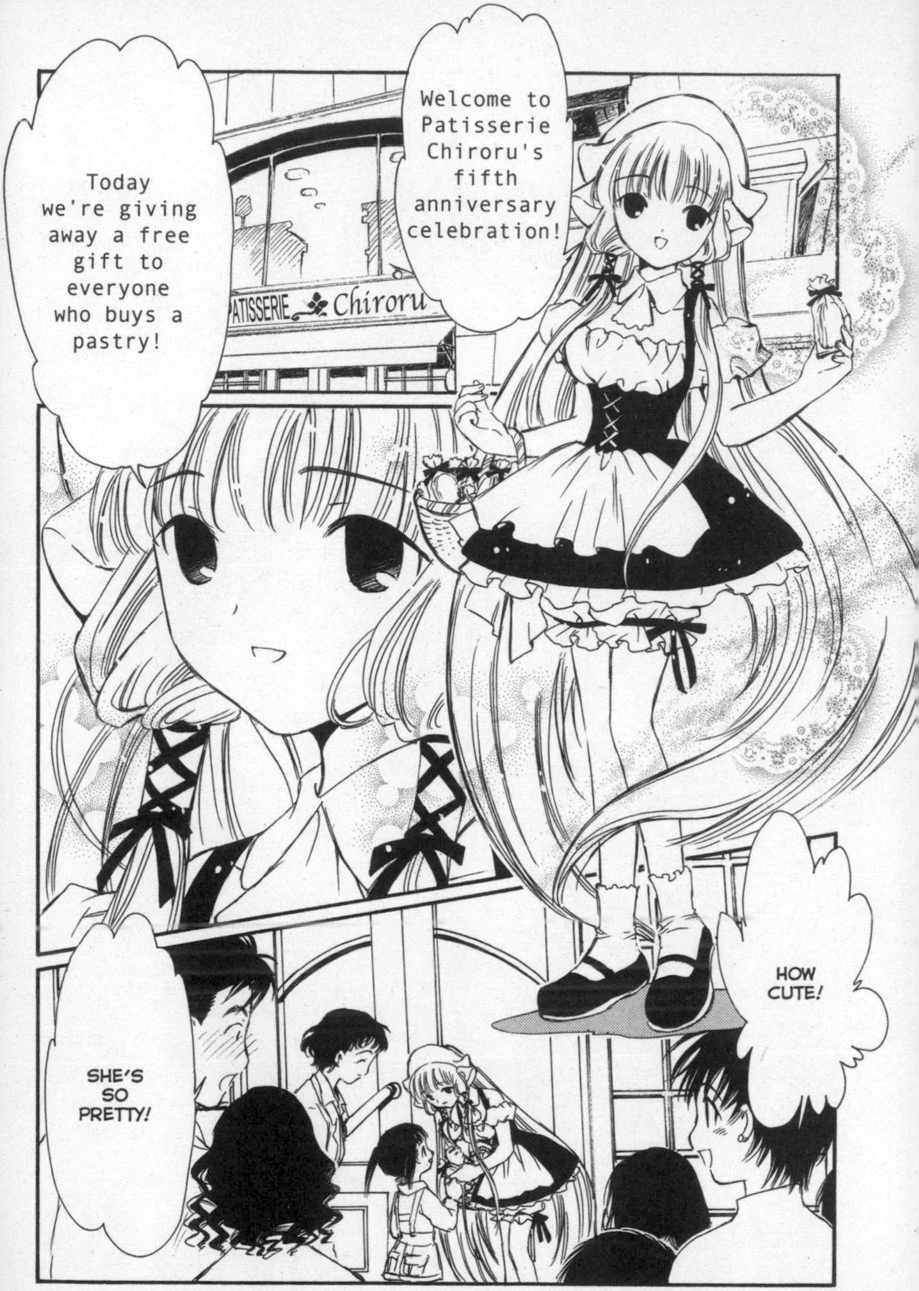
Welcome to Patisserie Chiroru's fifth anniversary celebration!
Today we're giving away a free gift to everyone who buys a pastry!
PATISSERIE Chiroru
HOW CUTE!
SHE'S SO PRETTY!

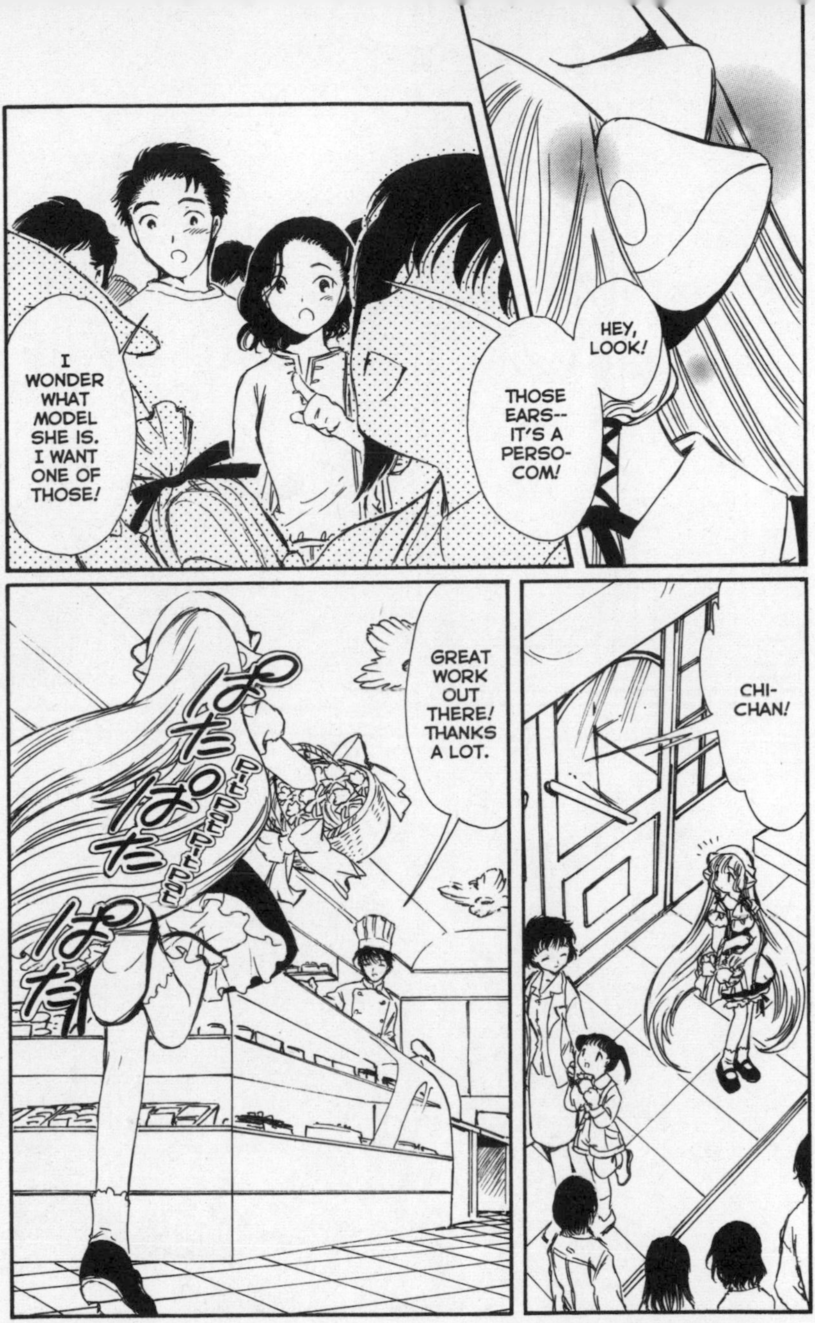
HEY, LOOK!
THOSE EARS-- IT'S A PERSO-COM!
I WONDER WHAT MODEL SHE IS. I WANT ONE OF THOSE!
CHI-CHAN!
GREAT WORK OUT THERE! THANKS A LOT.
ぱたぱたぱたぱた
pit pat pit pat

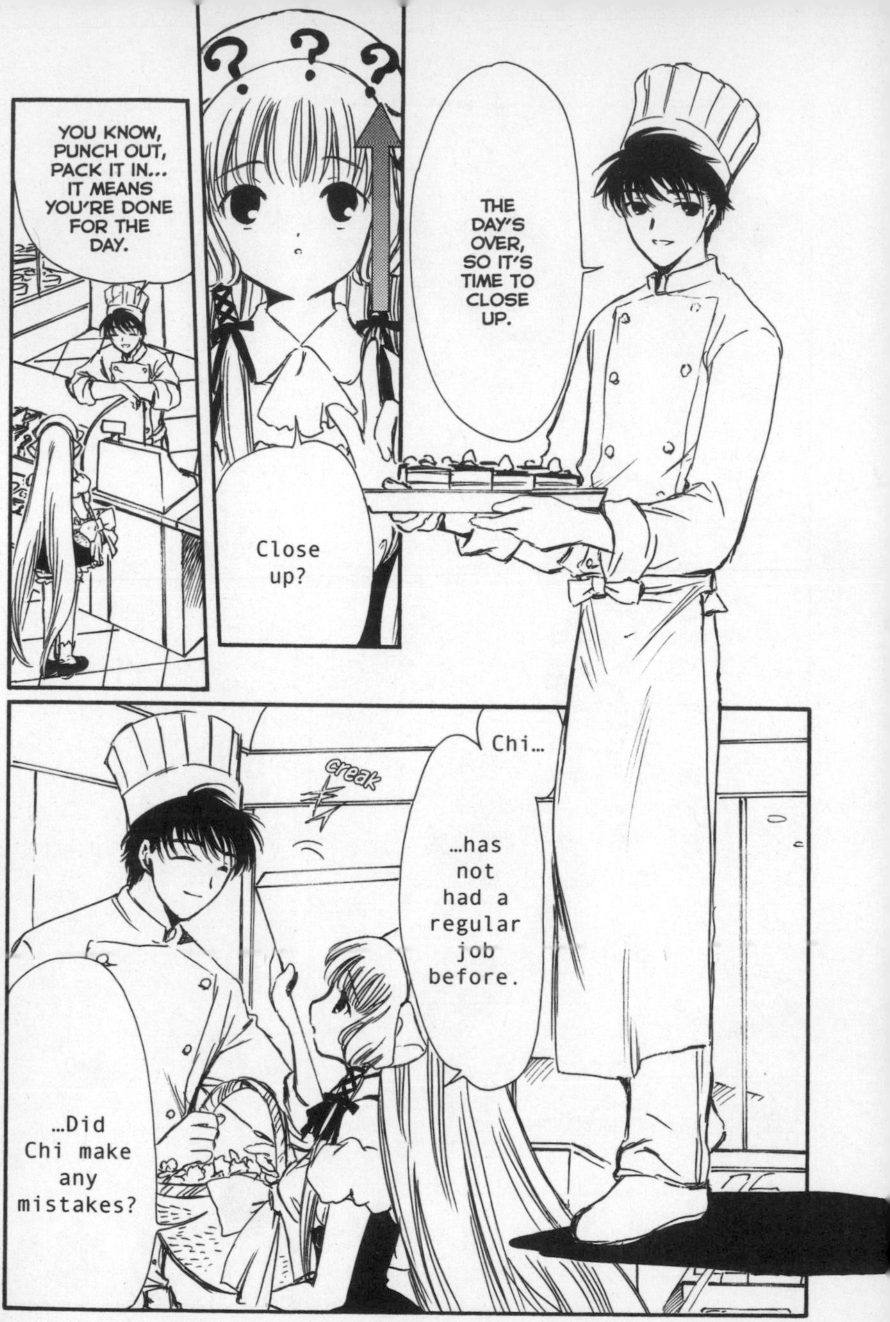
THE DAY'S OVER, SO IT'S TIME TO CLOSE UP.
Close up?
YOU KNOW, PUNCH OUT, PACK IT IN... IT MEANS YOU'RE DONE FOR THE DAY.
creak
Chi...
...has not had a regular job before.
...Did Chi make any mistakes?

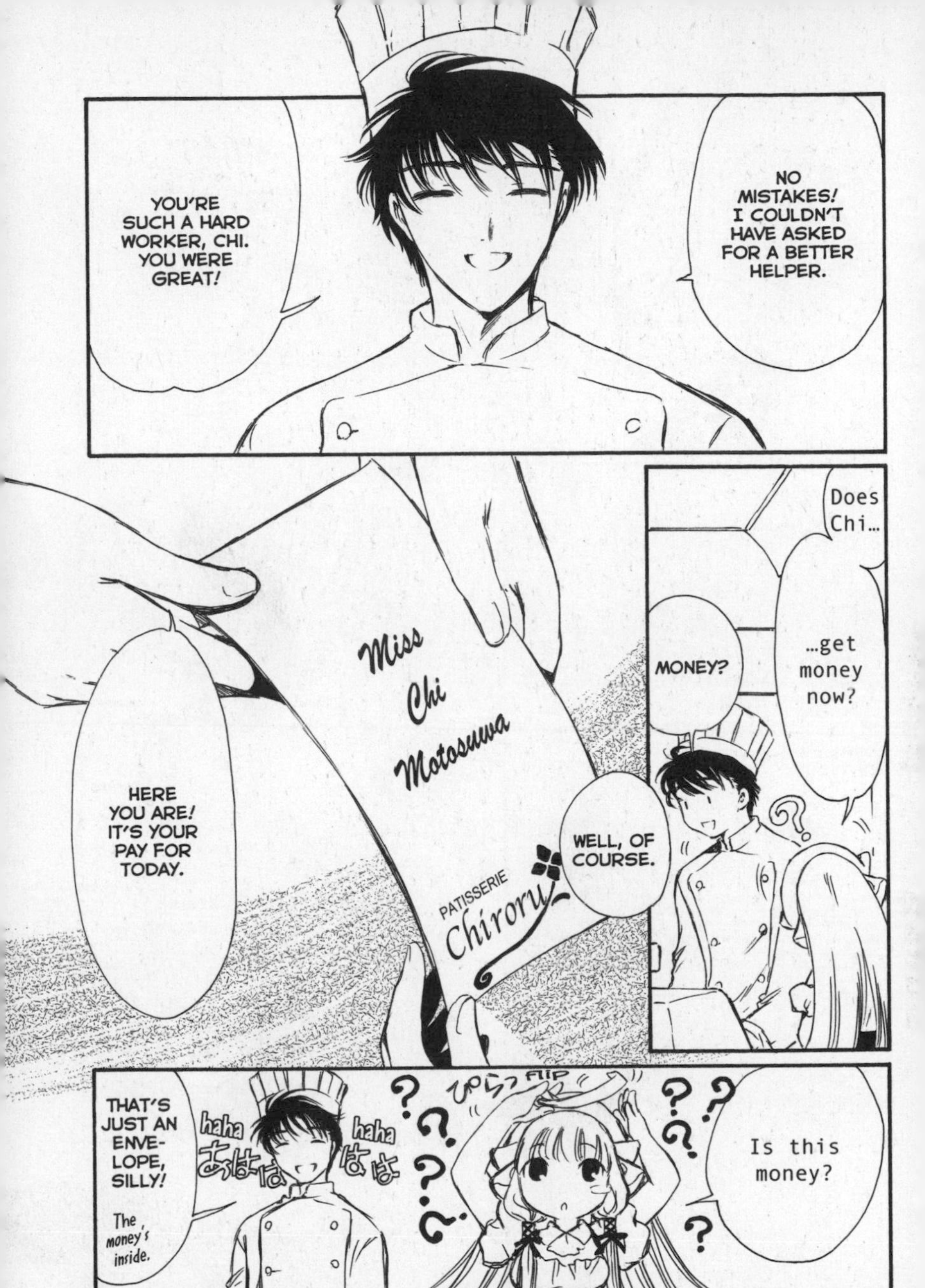
NO MISTAKES! I COULDN'T HAVE ASKED FOR A BETTER HELPER.
YOU'RE SUCH A HARD WORKER, CHI. YOU WERE GREAT!
Does Chi…
…get money now?
MONEY?
WELL, OF COURSE.
Miss Chi Motosuwa
PATISSERIE Chiroru
HERE YOU ARE! IT'S YOUR PAY FOR TODAY.
Is this money?
ぴらっ flip
haha あはは
haha はは
THAT'S JUST AN ENVE-LOPE, SILLY!
The money's inside.

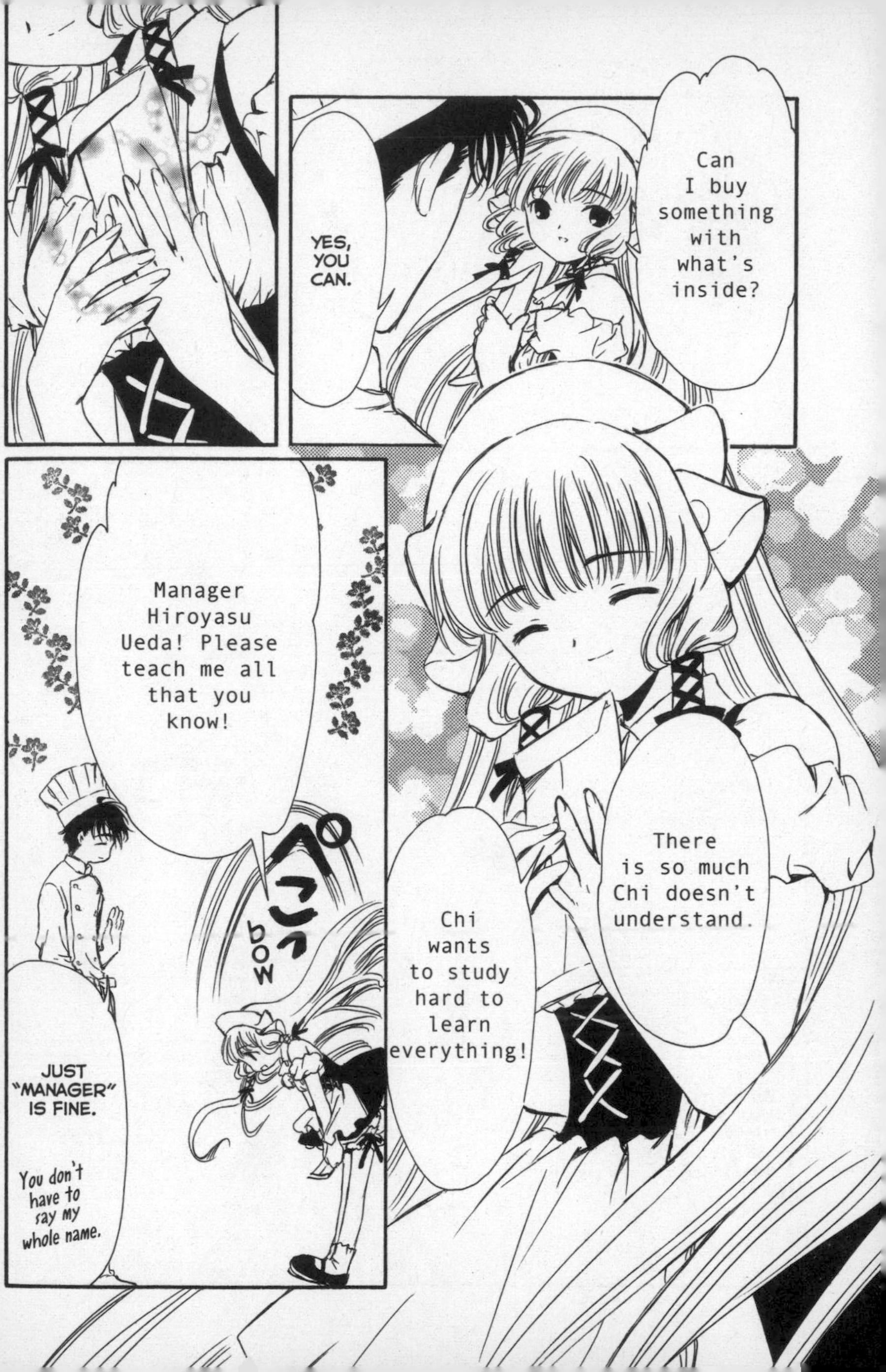
Can I buy something with what's inside?
YES, YOU CAN.
There is so much Chi doesn't understand.
Chi wants to study hard to learn everything!
Manager Hiroyasu Ueda! Please teach me all that you know!
ぺこっ
bow
JUST "MANAGER" IS FINE.
You don't have to say my whole name.

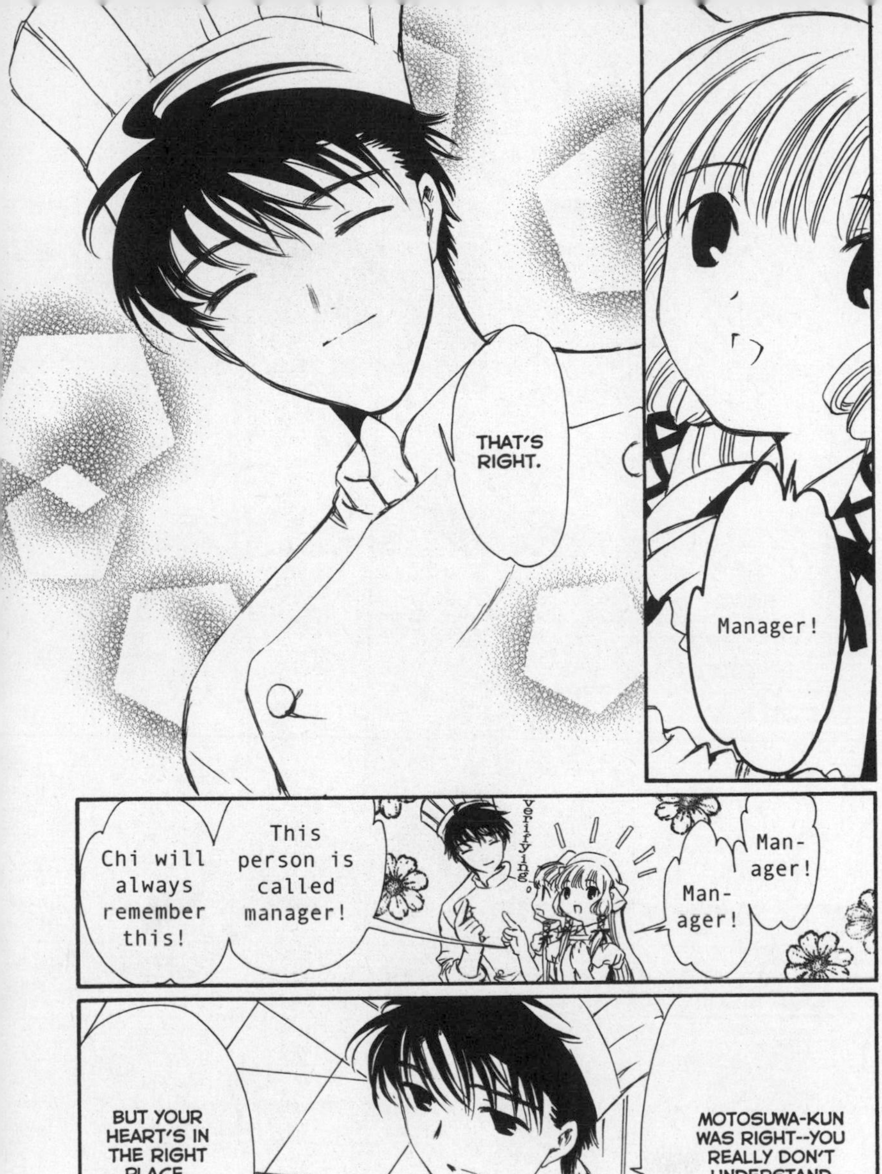
Manager!
THAT'S RIGHT.
Man-ager!
Man-ager!
verifying.
This person is called manager!
Chi will always remember this!
MOTOSUWA-KUN WAS RIGHT--YOU REALLY DON'T UNDERSTAND EVERYDAY BEHAVIOR.
BUT YOUR HEART'S IN THE RIGHT PLACE. YOU'RE A GOOD GIRL, CHI.

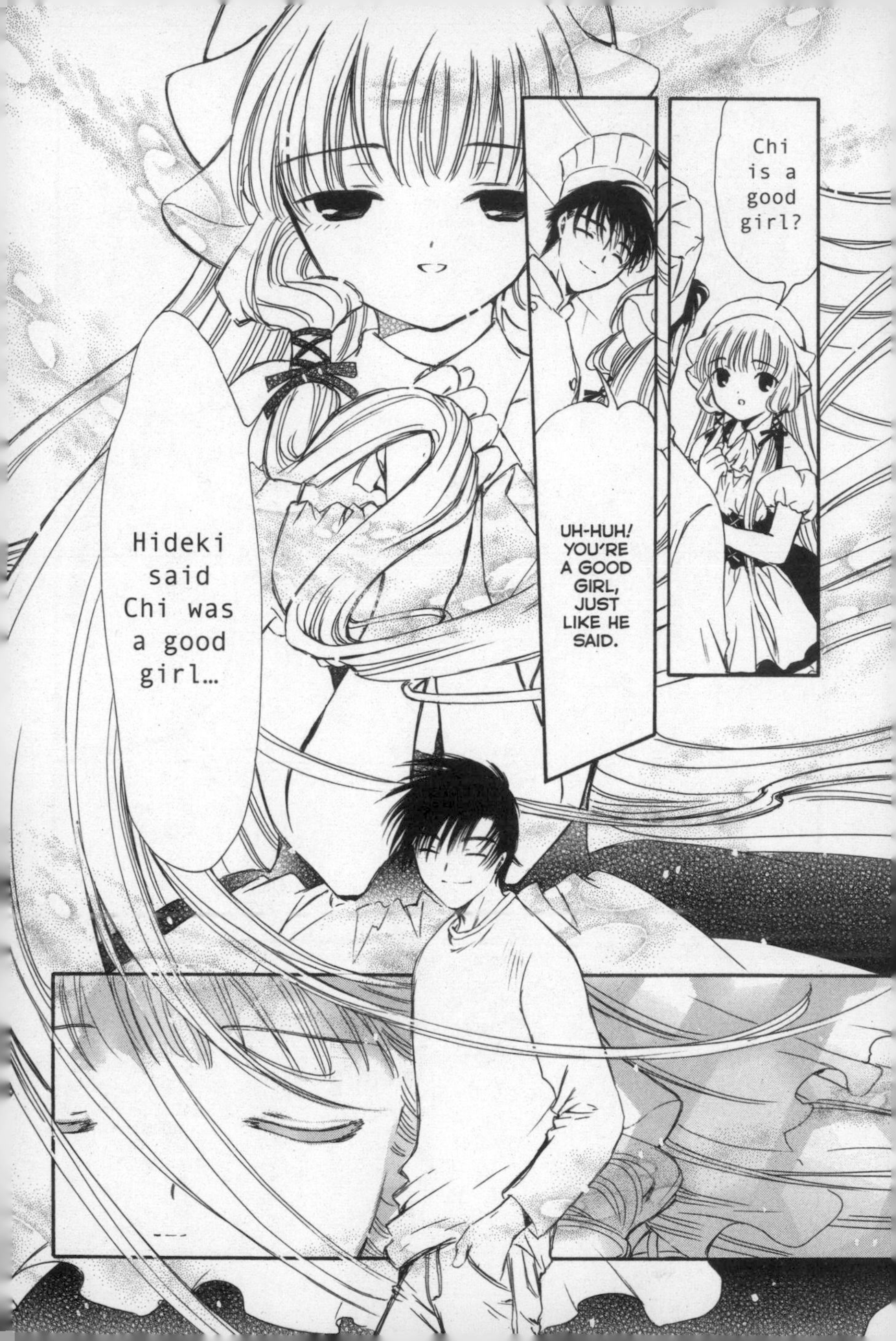
Chi is a good girl?
UH-HUH! YOU'RE A GOOD GIRL, JUST LIKE HE SAID.
Hideki said Chi was a good girl...

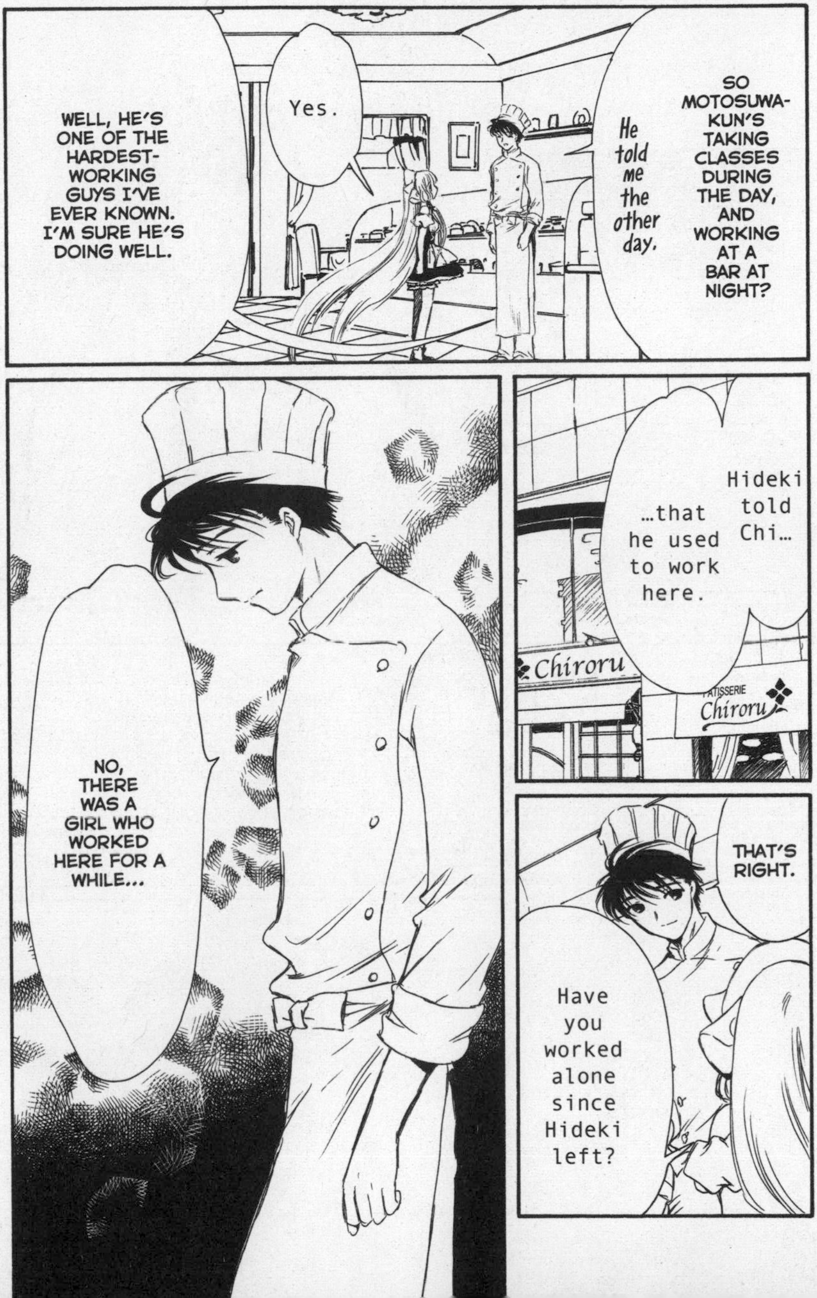
SO MOTOSUWA-KUN'S TAKING CLASSES DURING THE DAY, AND WORKING AT A BAR AT NIGHT?
He told me the other day.
Yes.
WELL, HE'S ONE OF THE HARDEST-WORKING GUYS I'VE EVER KNOWN. I'M SURE HE'S DOING WELL.
Hideki told Chi…
…that he used to work here.
Chiroru
PATISSERIE Chiroru
THAT'S RIGHT.
Have you worked alone since Hideki left?
NO, THERE WAS A GIRL WHO WORKED HERE FOR A WHILE…

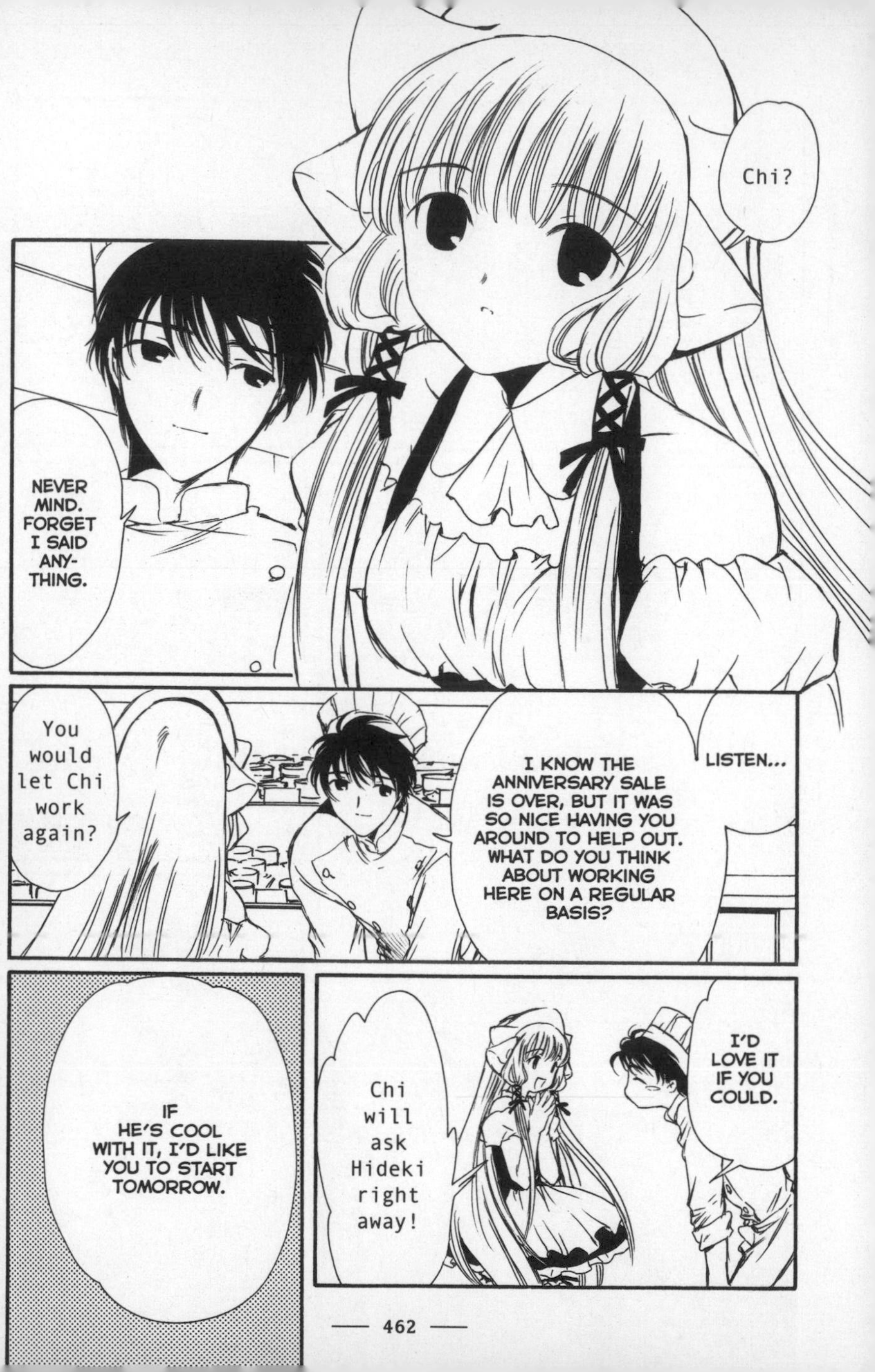
Chi?
NEVER MIND. FORGET I SAID ANY-THING.
LISTEN...
I KNOW THE ANNIVERSARY SALE IS OVER, BUT IT WAS SO NICE HAVING YOU AROUND TO HELP OUT. WHAT DO YOU THINK ABOUT WORKING HERE ON A REGULAR BASIS?
You would let Chi work again?
I'D LOVE IT IF YOU COULD.
Chi will ask Hideki right away!
IF HE'S COOL WITH IT, I'D LIKE YOU TO START TOMORROW.

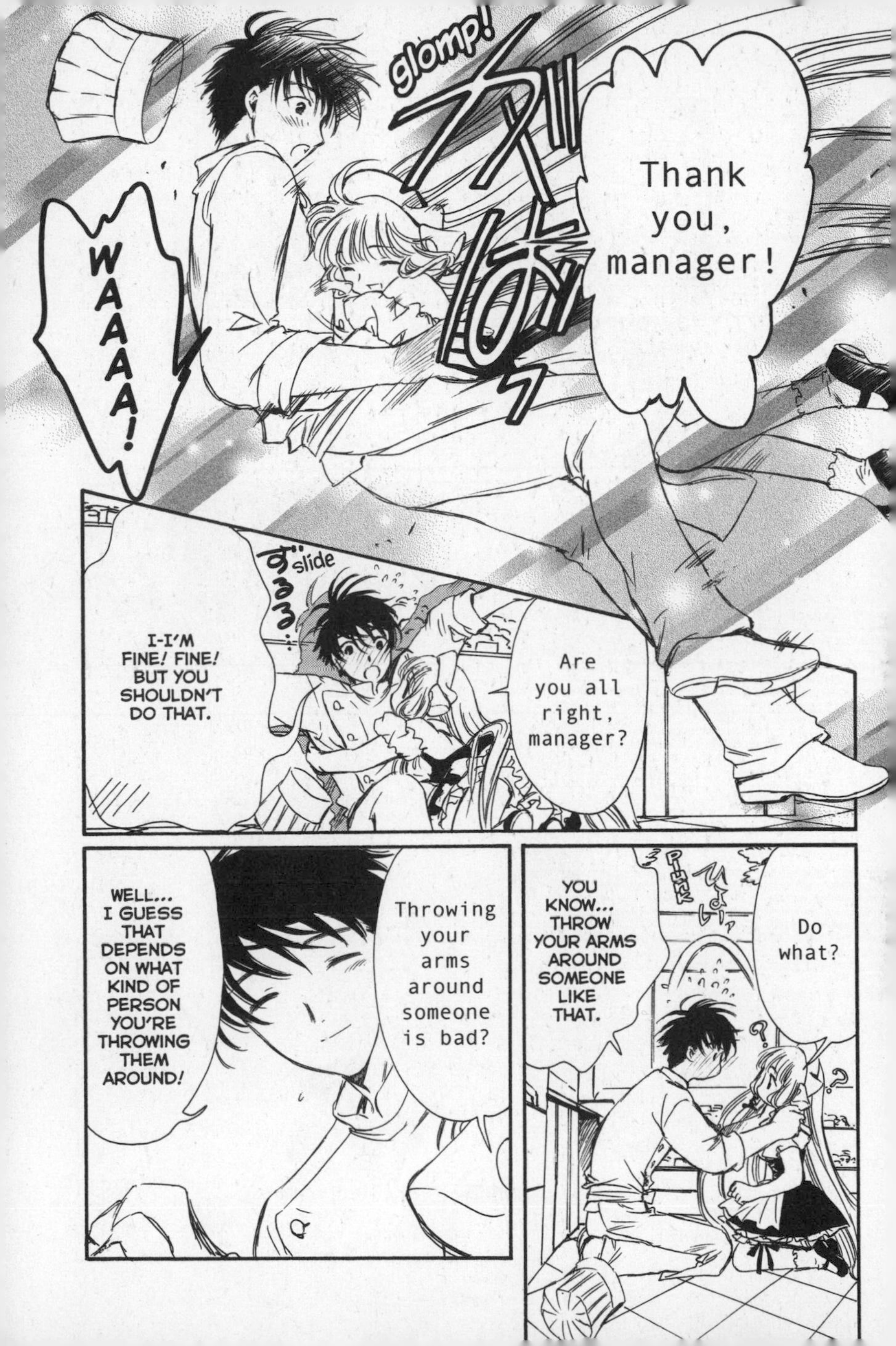
Thank you, manager!
glomp!
WAAAAA!
Are you all right, manager?
slide
I-I'M FINE! FINE! BUT YOU SHOULDN'T DO THAT.
Do what?
YOU KNOW... THROW YOUR ARMS AROUND SOMEONE LIKE THAT.
Throwing your arms around someone is bad?
WELL... I GUESS THAT DEPENDS ON WHAT KIND OF PERSON YOU'RE THROWING THEM AROUND!

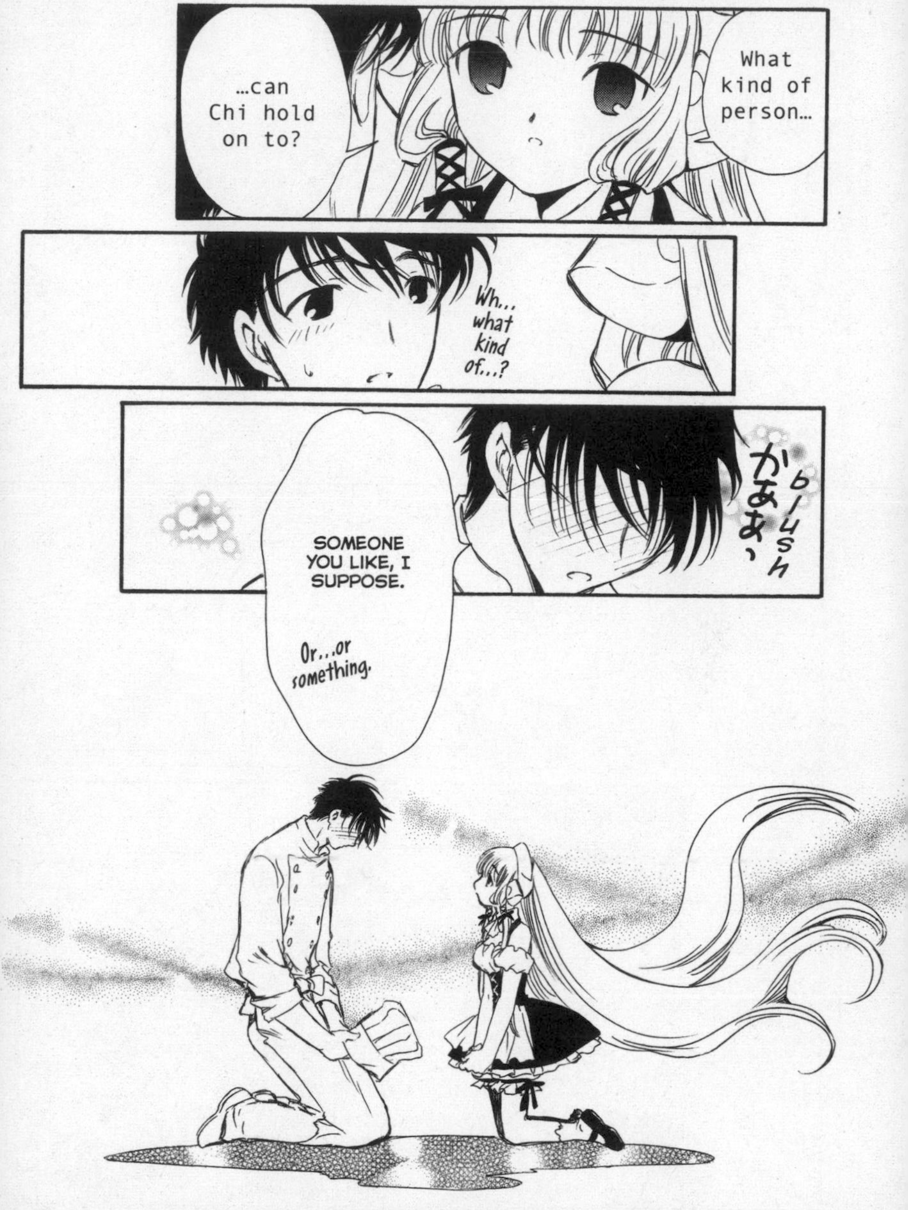
What kind of person…
…can Chi hold on to?
Wh… what kind of…?
かあぁ、
blush
SOMEONE YOU LIKE, I SUPPOSE.
Or…or something.

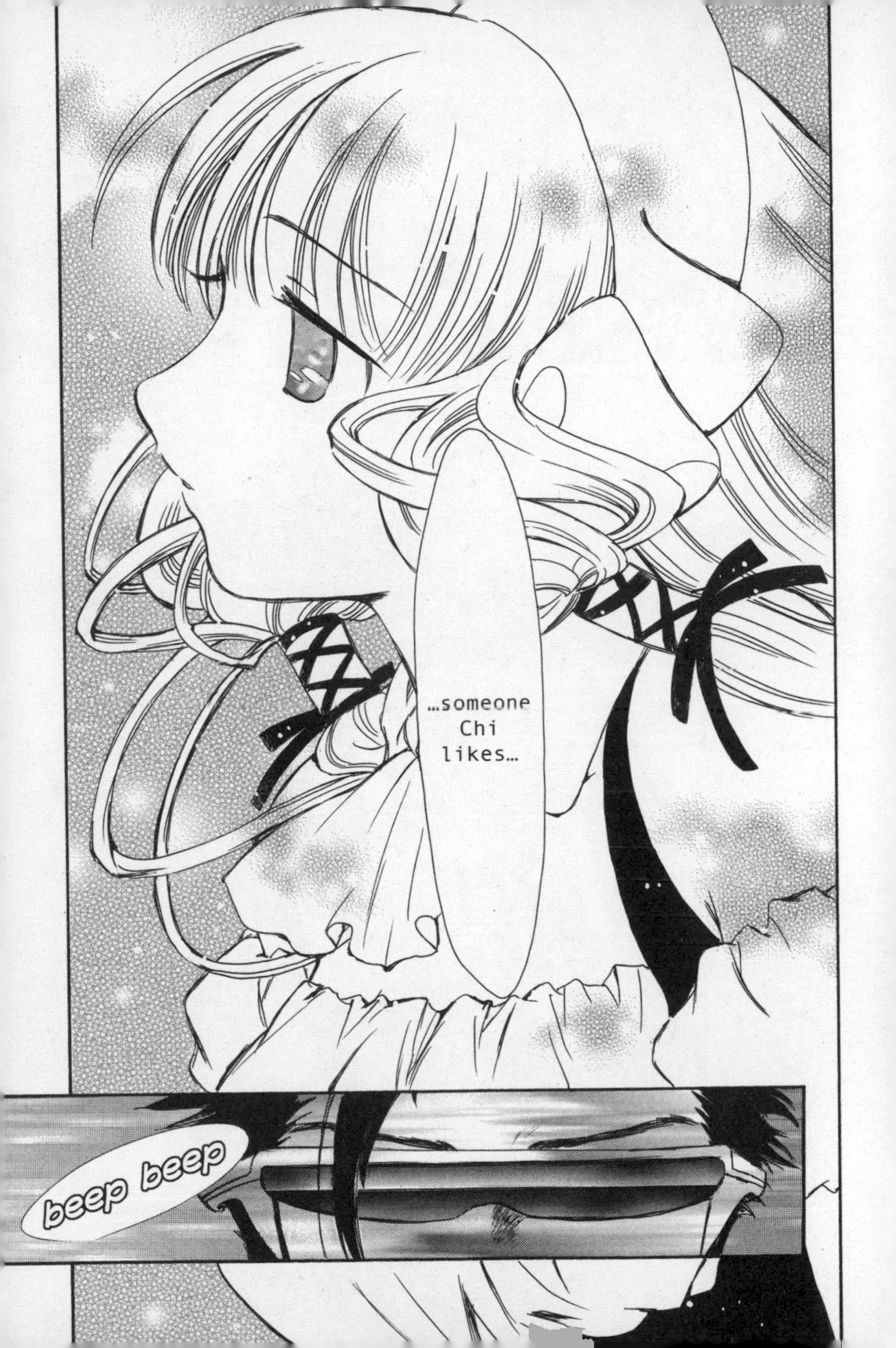
…someone Chi likes…
beep beep

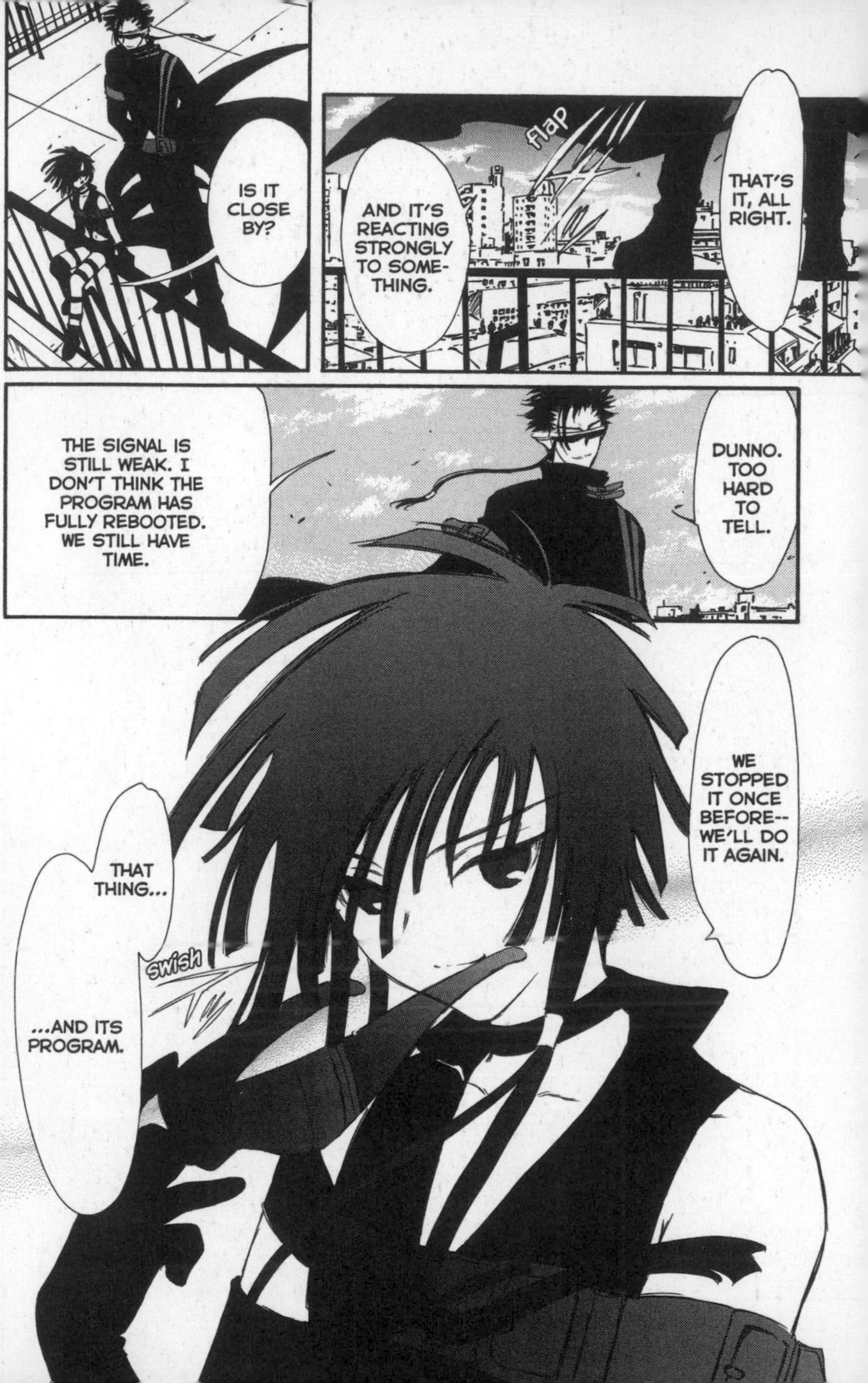
THAT'S IT, ALL RIGHT.
FLAP
AND IT'S REACTING STRONGLY TO SOME-THING.
IS IT CLOSE BY?
DUNNO. TOO HARD TO TELL.
THE SIGNAL IS STILL WEAK. I DON'T THINK THE PROGRAM HAS FULLY REBOOTED. WE STILL HAVE TIME.
WE STOPPED IT ONCE BEFORE-- WE'LL DO IT AGAIN.
THAT THING...
SWISH
...AND ITS PROGRAM.

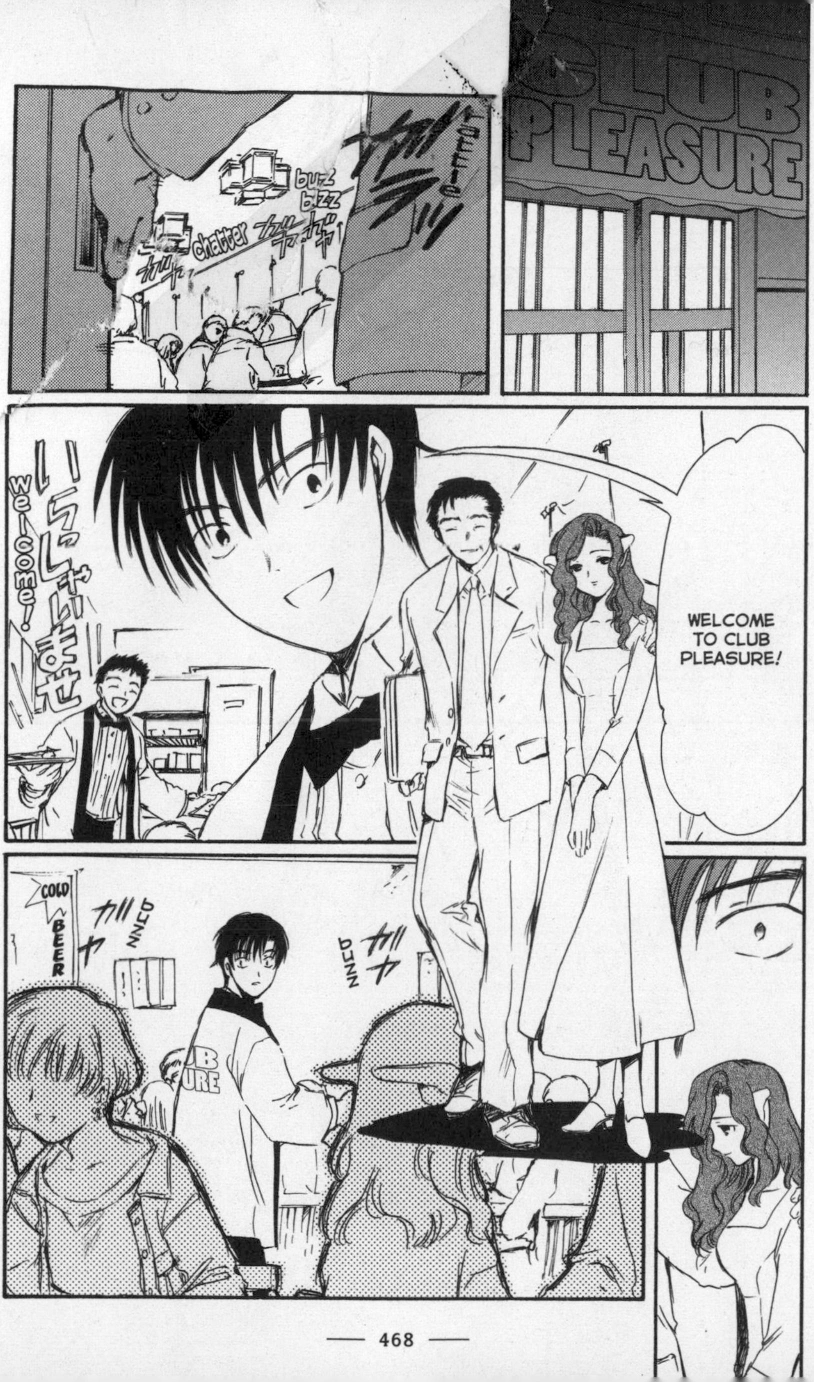
CLUB PLEASURE
buzz bzz
chatter
WELCOME TO CLUB PLEASURE!
いらっしゃいませ
welcome!
COLD BEER
BUZZ
BUZZ

Chobits
ちょびっツ

◀ **chapter 31** ▶

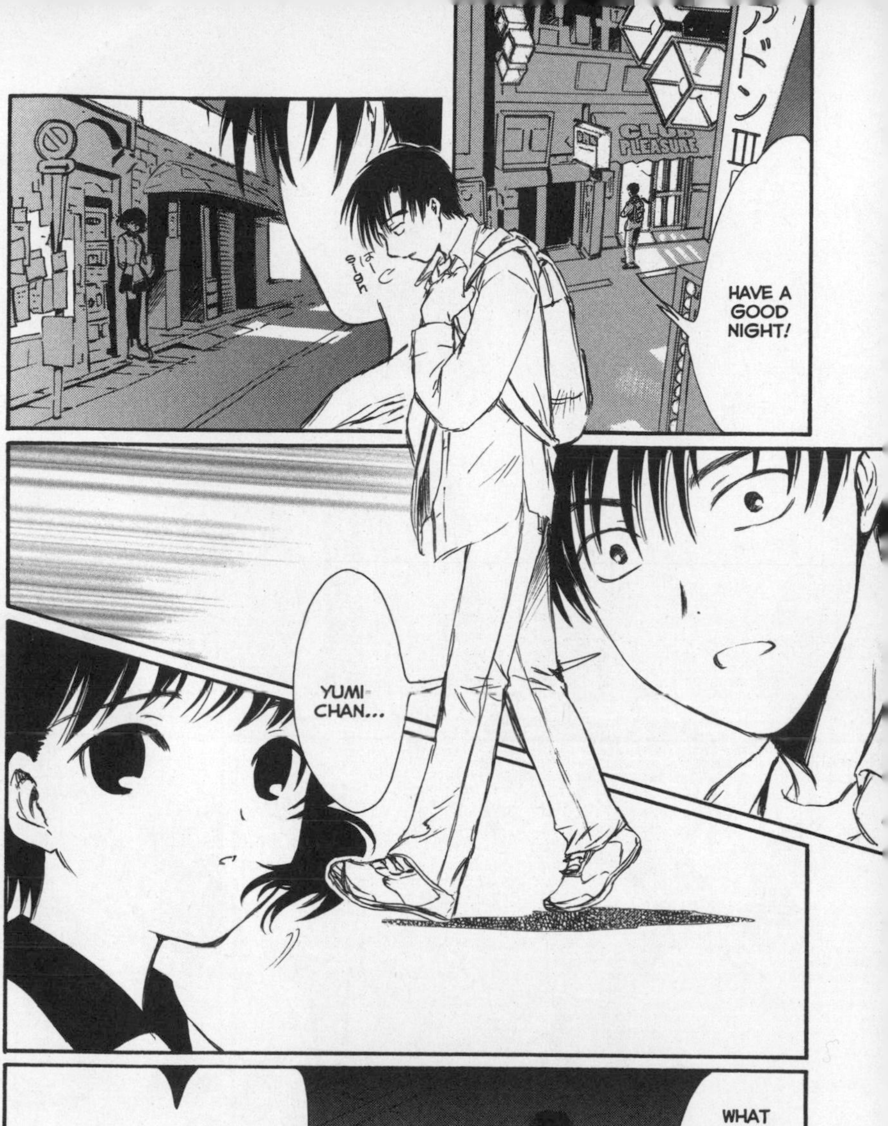
CLUB PLEASURE
HAVE A GOOD NIGHT!
sigh
YUMI-CHAN...
WHAT ARE YOU DOING HERE SO LATE? DIDN'T YOU GET OFF AT EIGHT?
YES, BUT...
...YOU JUST SEEMED SO DOWN TODAY.

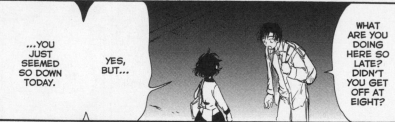

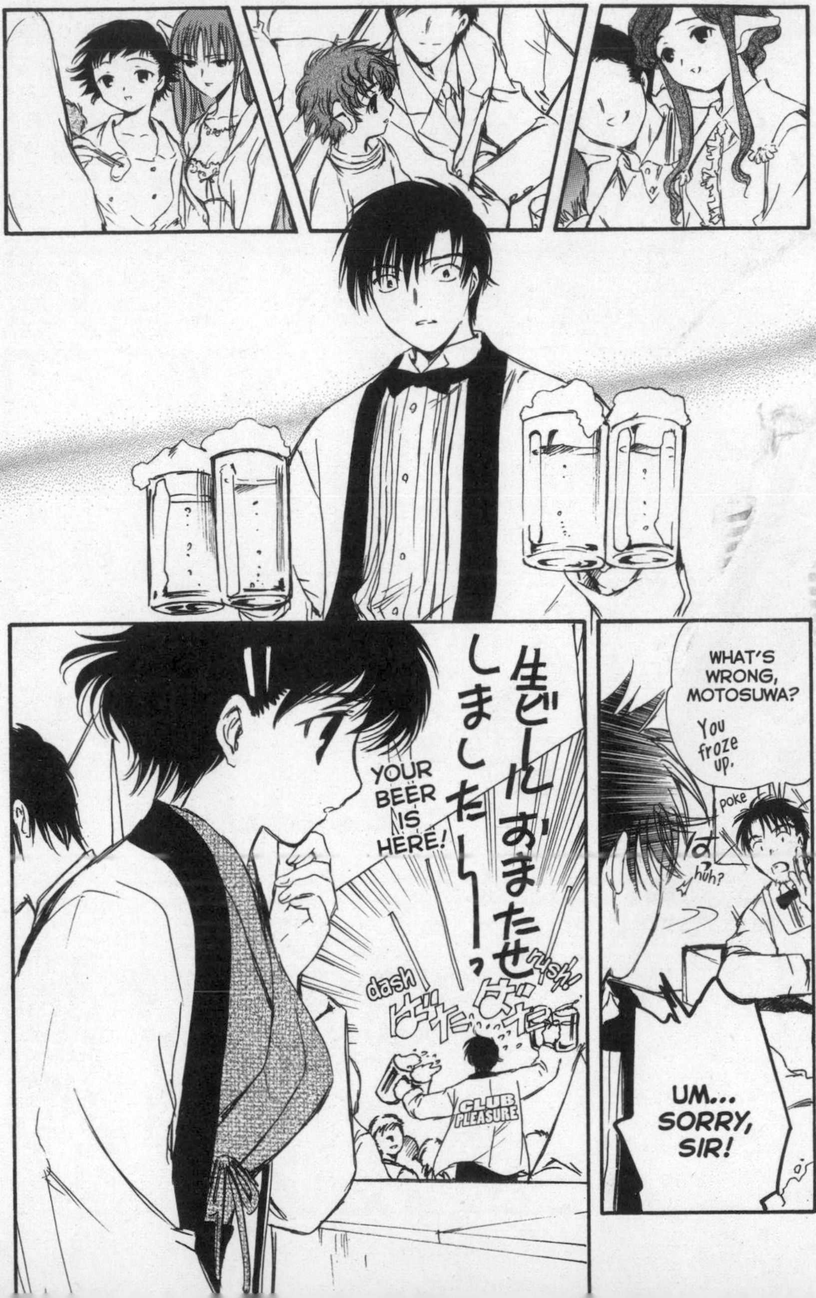
WHAT'S WRONG, MOTOSUWA?
You froze up.
poke
は
huh?
UM... SORRY, SIR!
生ビールおまたせしました~っ
YOUR BEER IS HERE!
rush!
dash
ばたばた
CLUB PLEASURE

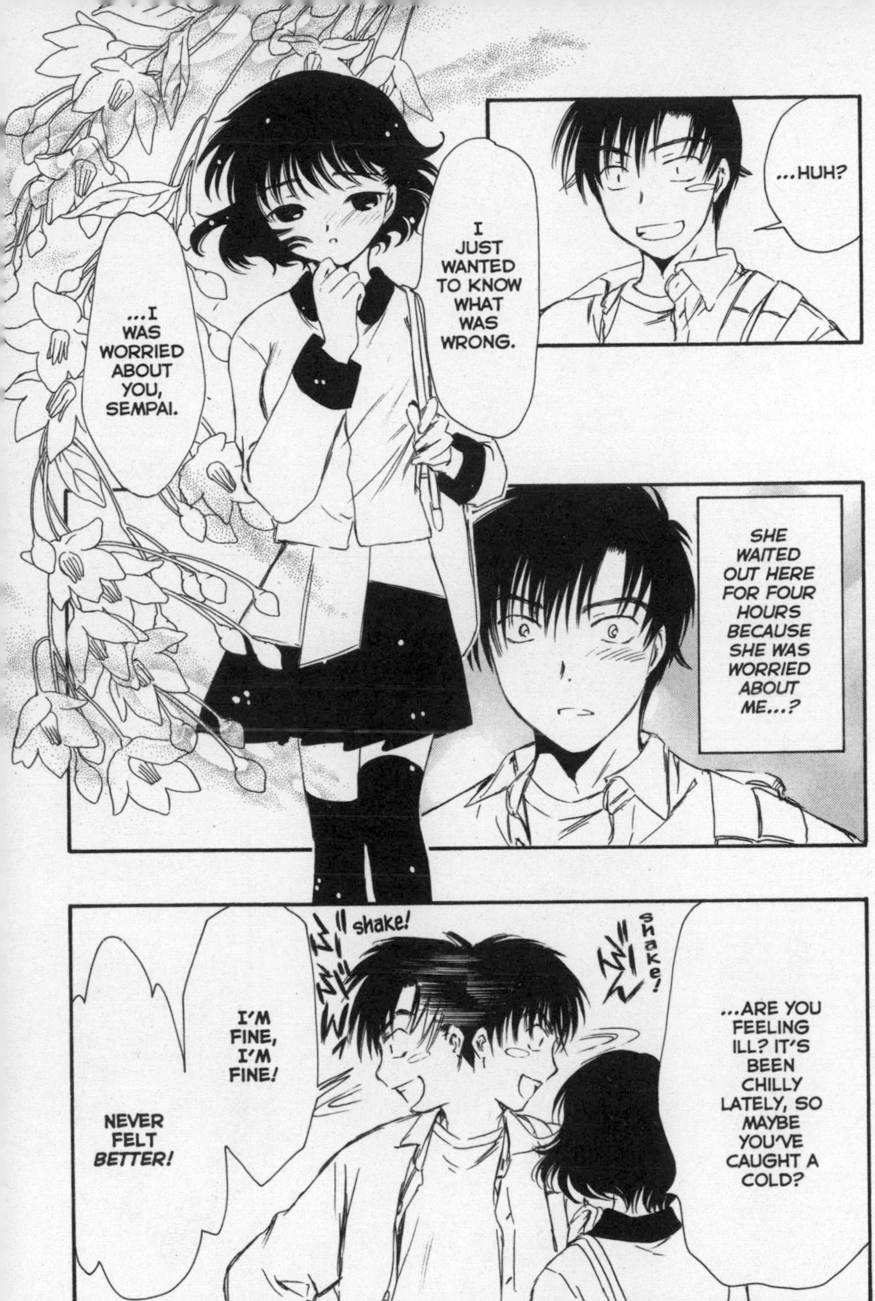
...HUH?
I JUST WANTED TO KNOW WHAT WAS WRONG.
...I WAS WORRIED ABOUT YOU, SEMPAI.
SHE WAITED OUT HERE FOR FOUR HOURS BECAUSE SHE WAS WORRIED ABOUT ME...?
shake!
shake!
...ARE YOU FEELING ILL? IT'S BEEN CHILLY LATELY, SO MAYBE YOU'VE CAUGHT A COLD?
I'M FINE, I'M FINE!
NEVER FELT *BETTER!*

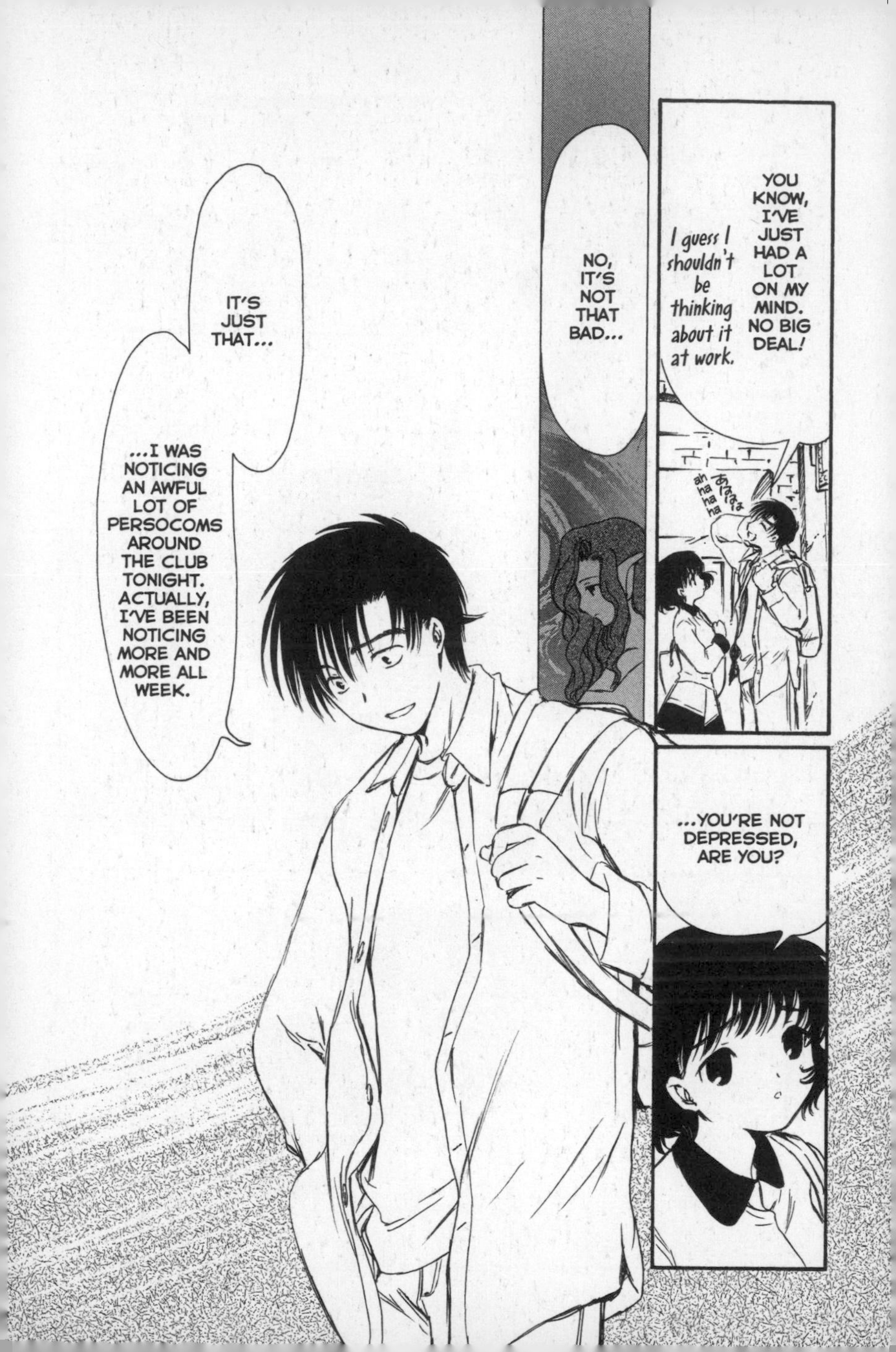
YOU KNOW, I'VE JUST HAD A LOT ON MY MIND. NO BIG DEAL!
I guess I shouldn't be thinking about it at work.
あははは
ah ha ha ha
...YOU'RE NOT DEPRESSED, ARE YOU?
NO, IT'S NOT THAT BAD...
IT'S JUST THAT...
...I WAS NOTICING AN AWFUL LOT OF PERSOCOMS AROUND THE CLUB TONIGHT. ACTUALLY, I'VE BEEN NOTICING MORE AND MORE ALL WEEK.

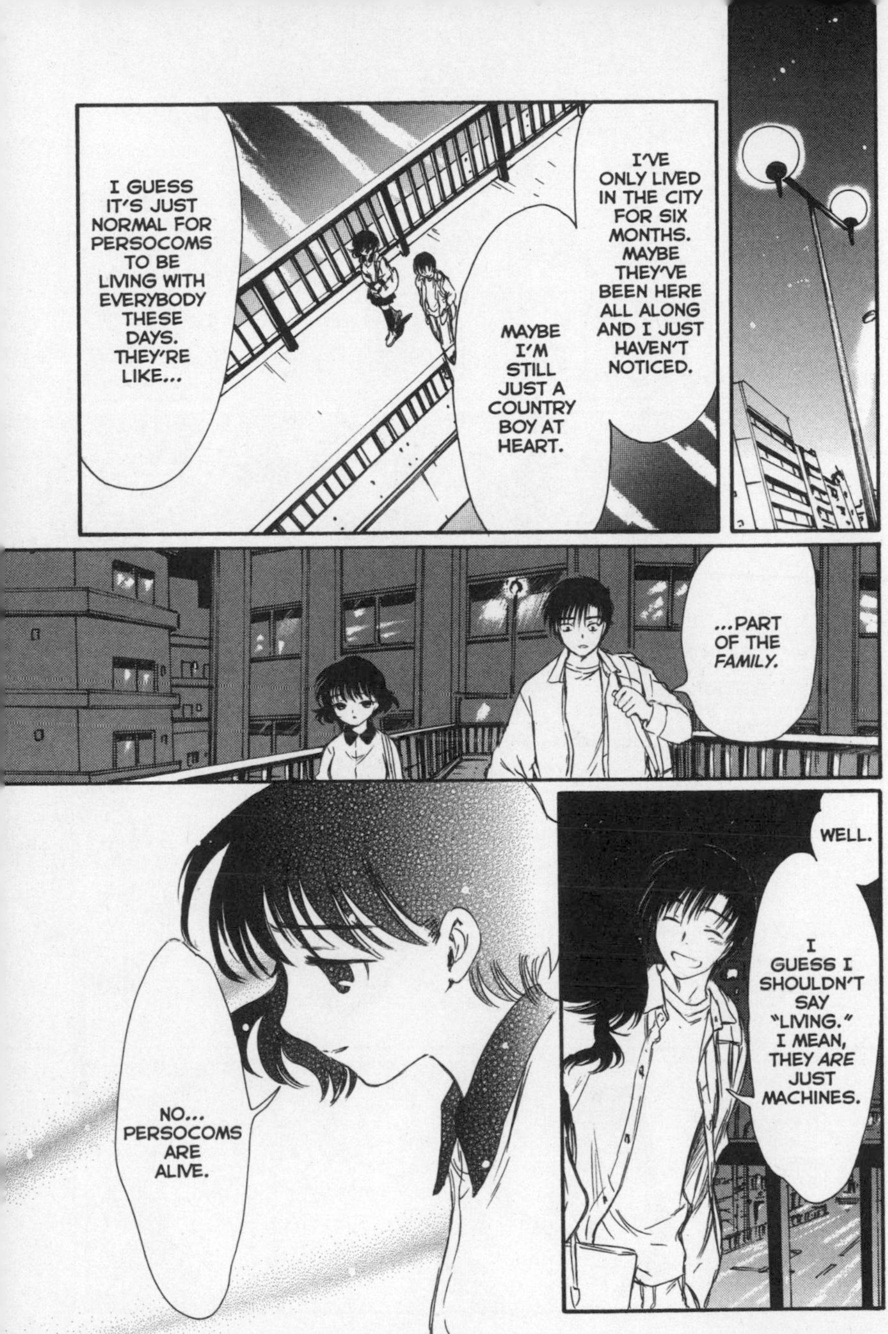
I'VE ONLY LIVED IN THE CITY FOR SIX MONTHS. MAYBE THEY'VE BEEN HERE ALL ALONG AND I JUST HAVEN'T NOTICED.
MAYBE I'M STILL JUST A COUNTRY BOY AT HEART.
I GUESS IT'S JUST NORMAL FOR PERSOCOMS TO BE LIVING WITH EVERYBODY THESE DAYS. THEY'RE LIKE...
...PART OF THE *FAMILY.*
WELL.
I GUESS I SHOULDN'T SAY "LIVING." I MEAN, THEY *ARE* JUST MACHINES.
NO... PERSOCOMS ARE ALIVE.

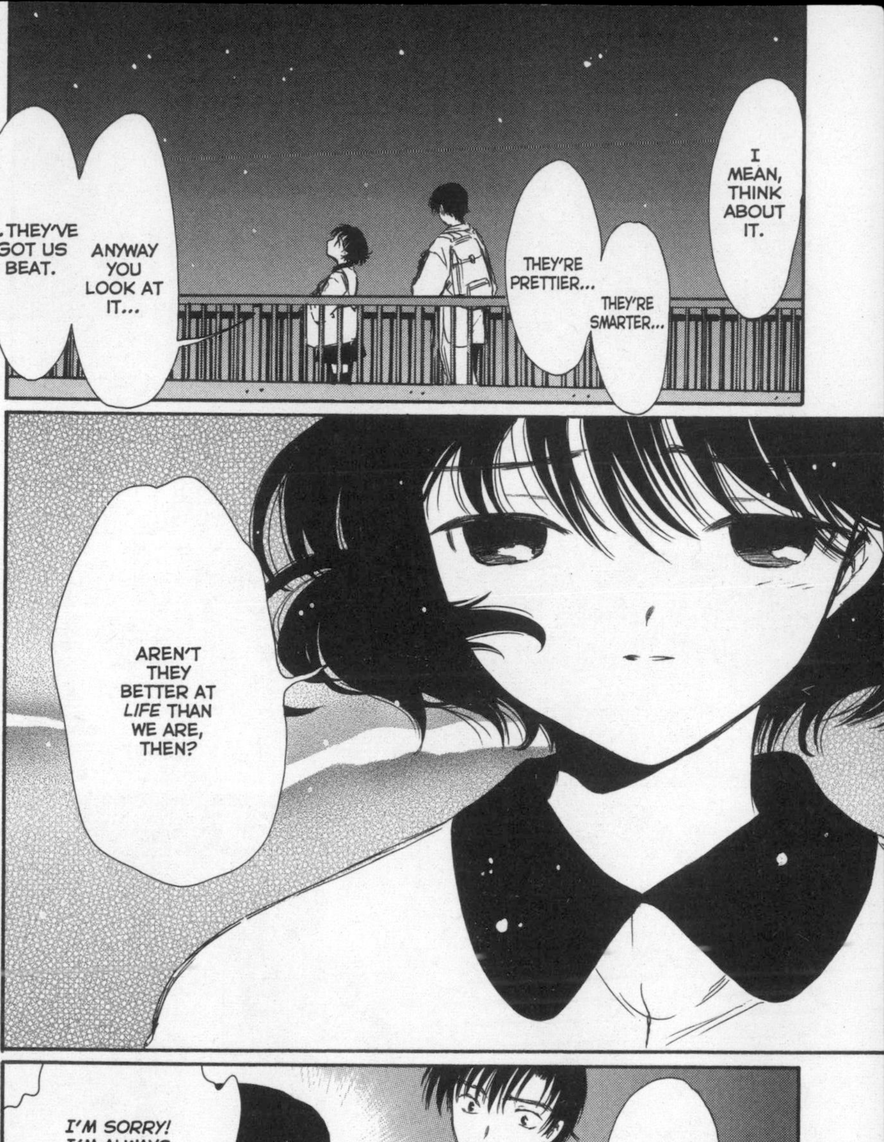
I MEAN, THINK ABOUT IT.
THEY'RE PRETTIER...
THEY'RE SMARTER...
ANYWAY YOU LOOK AT IT...
...THEY'VE GOT US BEAT.
AREN'T THEY BETTER AT *LIFE* THAN WE ARE, THEN?
YUMI-CHAN...
I'M SORRY! I'M ALWAYS GOING OFF LIKE THAT. YOU MUST THINK I'M REALLY WEIRD*!*

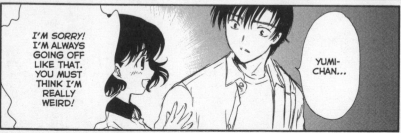

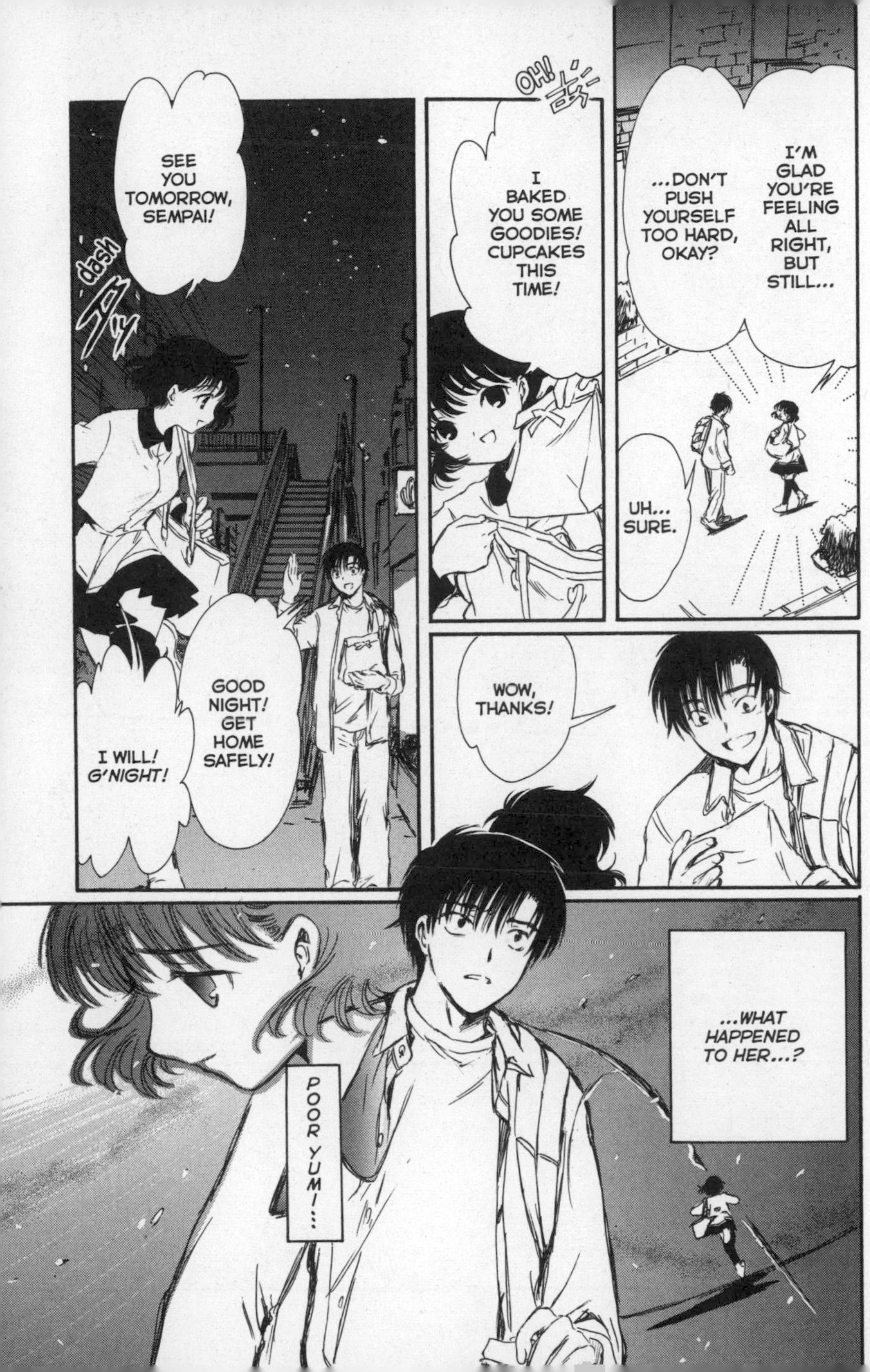
I'M GLAD YOU'RE FEELING ALL RIGHT, BUT STILL...
...DON'T PUSH YOURSELF TOO HARD, OKAY?
UH... SURE.
OH!
I BAKED YOU SOME GOODIES! CUPCAKES THIS TIME!
WOW, THANKS!
SEE YOU TOMORROW, SEMPAI!
dash
GOOD NIGHT! GET HOME SAFELY!
I WILL! G'NIGHT!
...WHAT HAPPENED TO HER...?
POOR YUMI!...

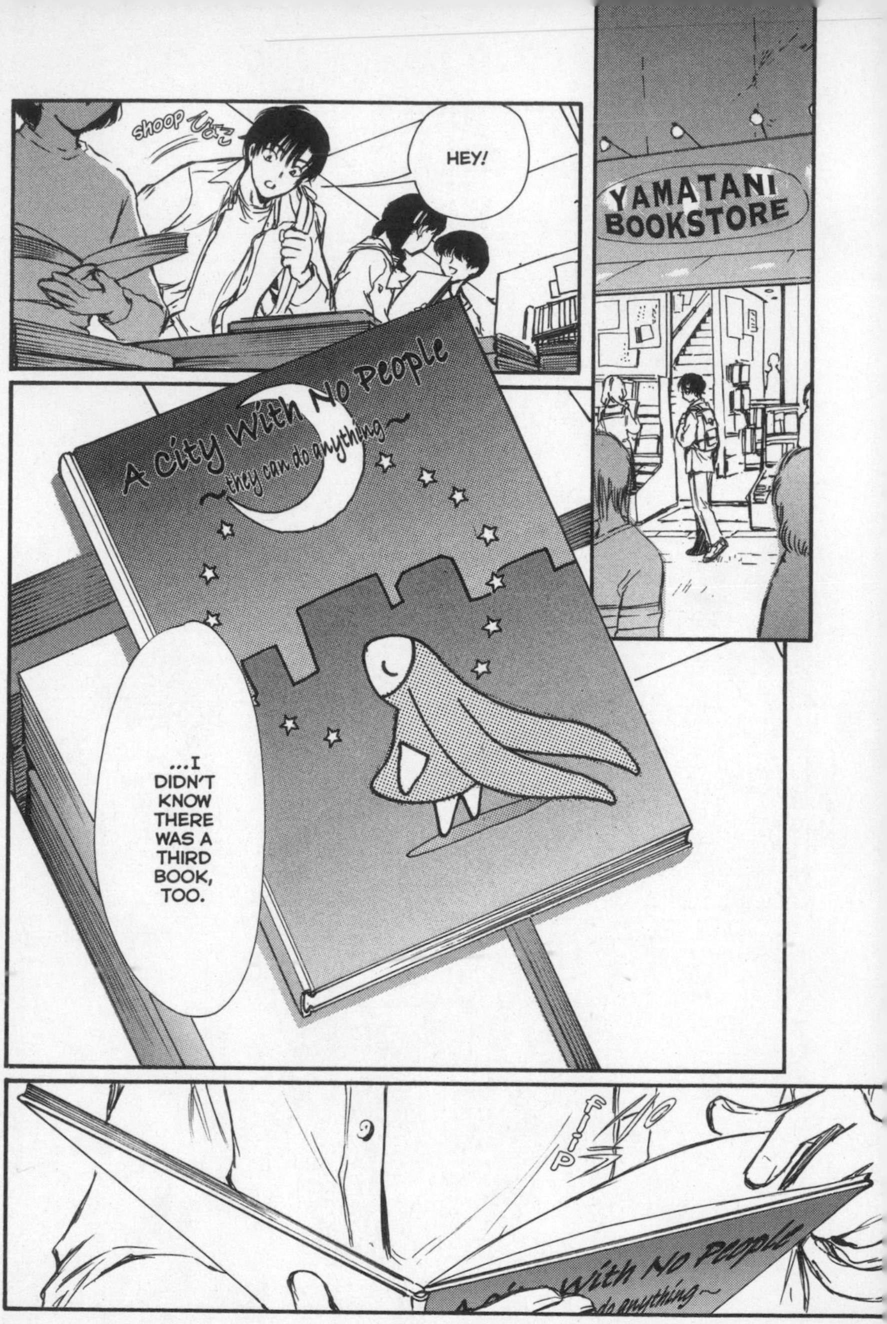
YAMATANI BOOKSTORE
shoop
HEY!
A City With No People
~they can do anything~
...I DIDN'T KNOW THERE WAS A THIRD BOOK, TOO.
flip

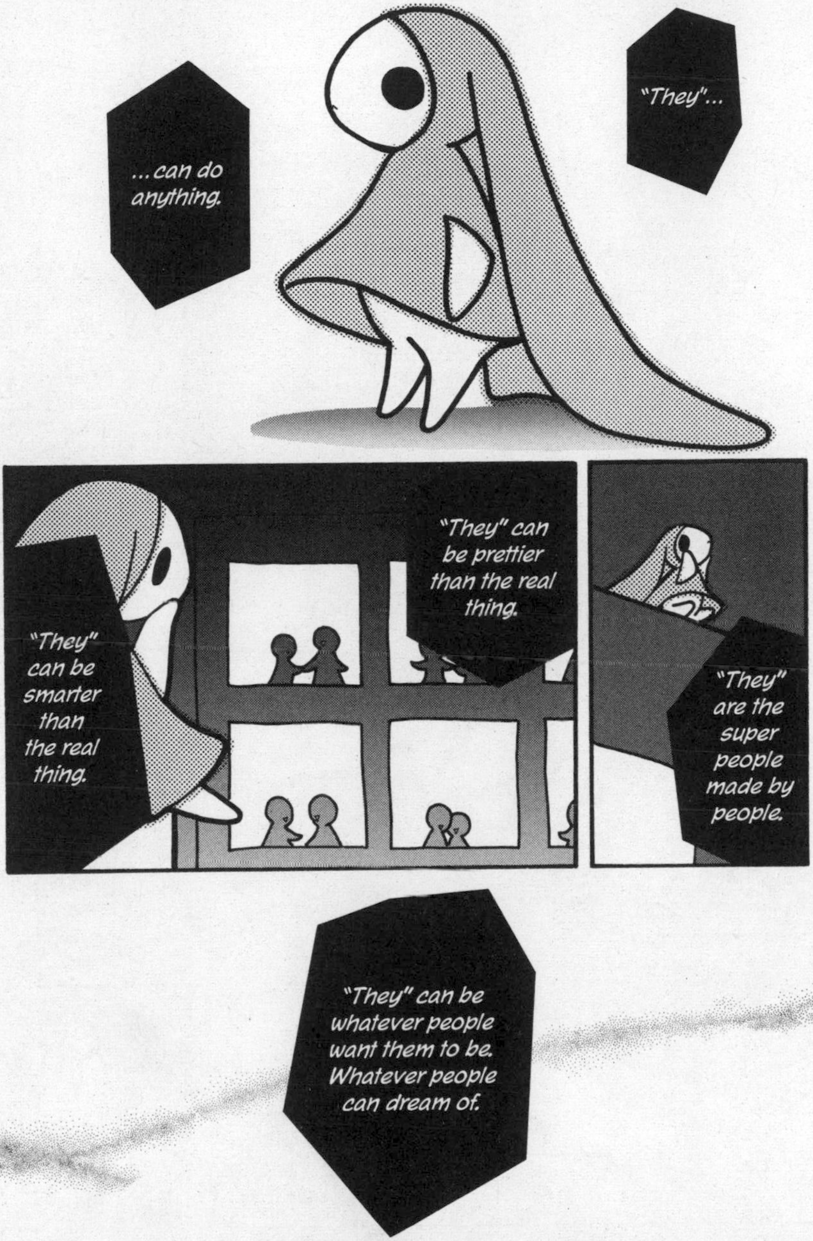
"They"...
...can do anything.
"They" are the super people made by people.
"They" can be prettier than the real thing.
"They" can be smarter than the real thing.
"They" can be whatever people want them to be. Whatever people can dream of.

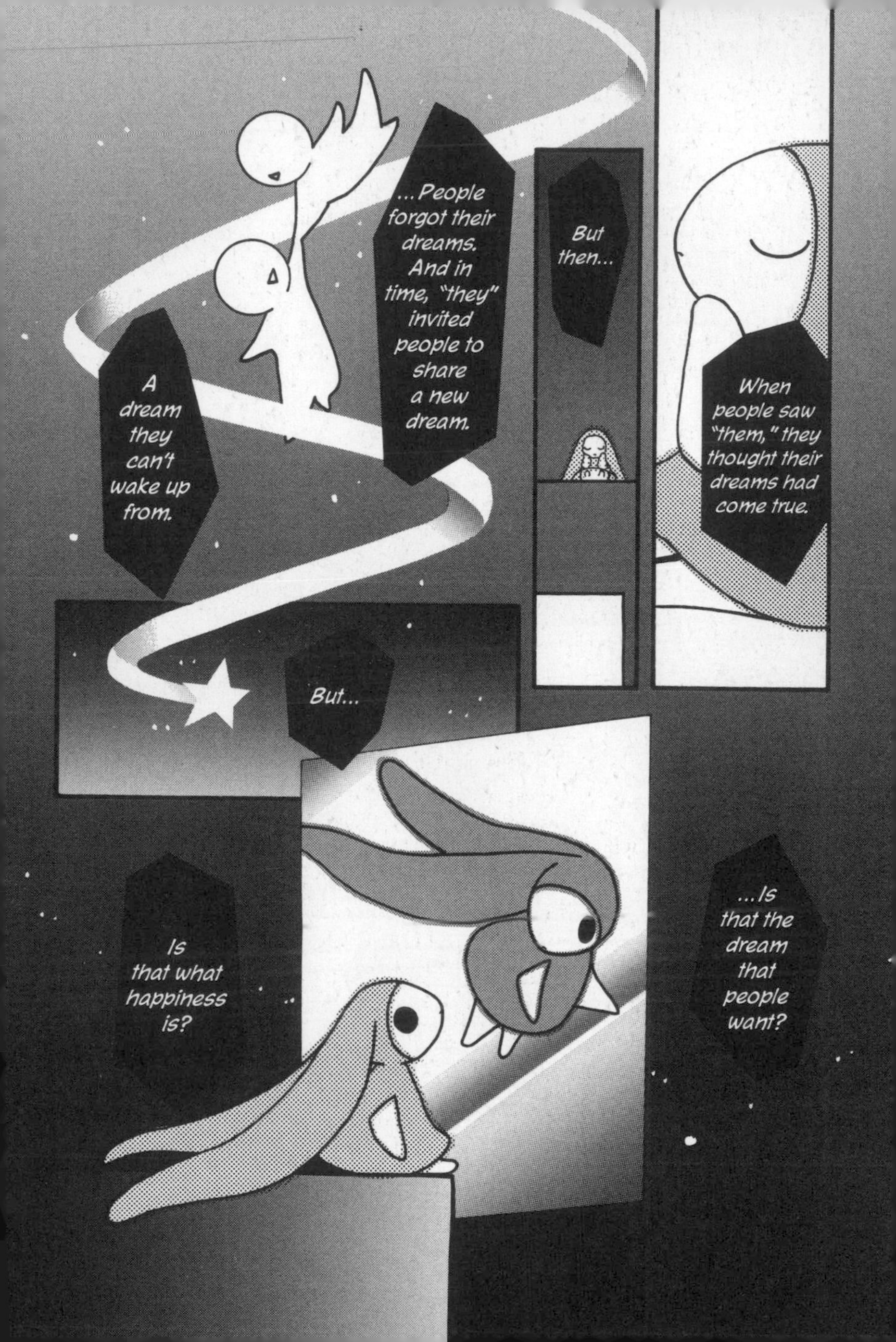
When people saw "them," they thought their dreams had come true.
But then...
...People forgot their dreams. And in time, "they" invited people to share a new dream.
A dream they can't wake up from.
But...
...Is that the dream that people want?
Is that what happiness is?

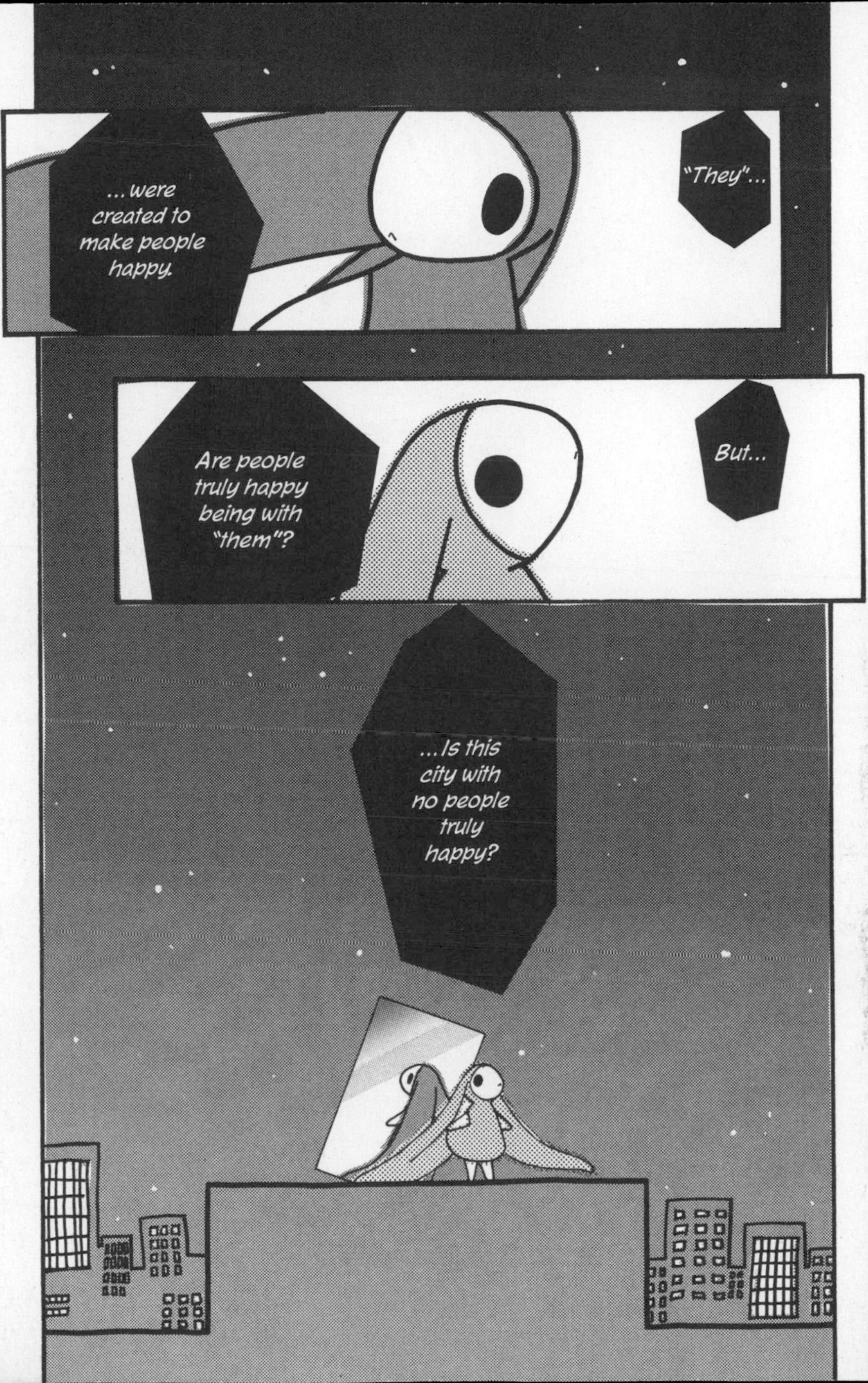
"They"...
...were created to make people happy.
But...
Are people truly happy being with "them"?
...Is this city with no people truly happy?

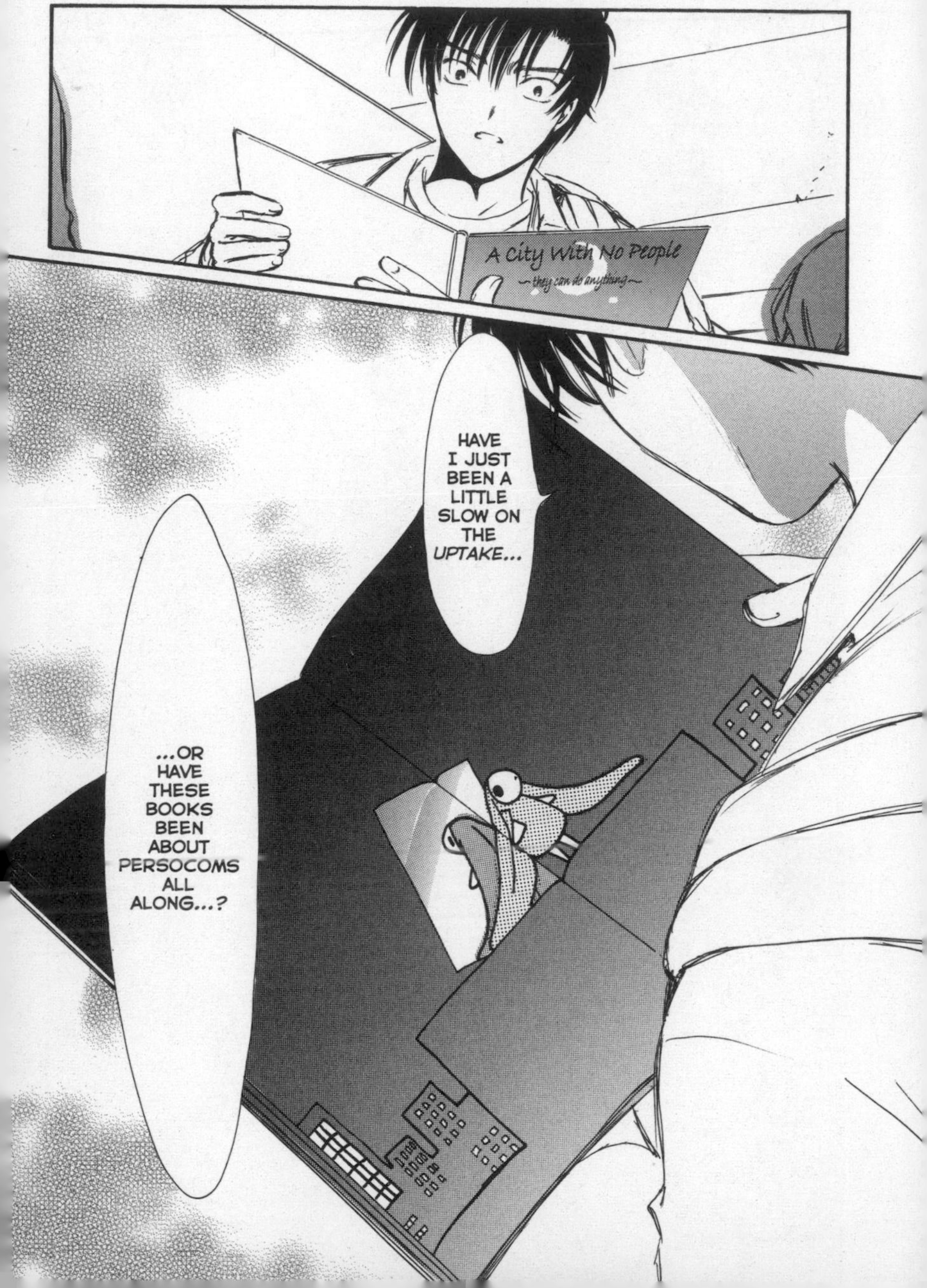
A City With No People
~they can do anything~
HAVE I JUST BEEN A LITTLE SLOW ON THE UPTAKE...
...OR HAVE THESE BOOKS BEEN ABOUT PERSOCOMS ALL ALONG...?

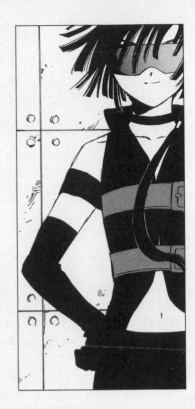

Chobits
ちょびっツ

◄ **chapter 32** ►

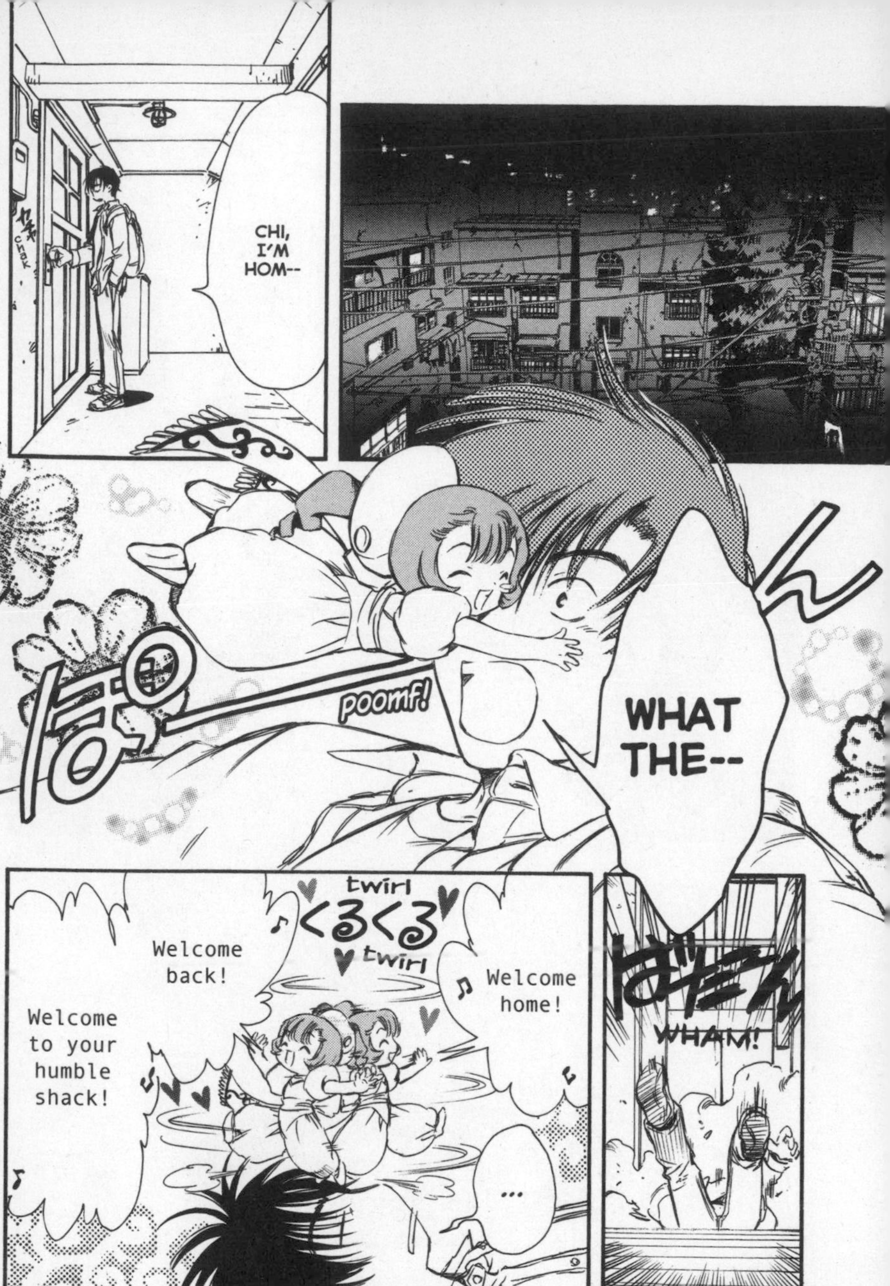

カチャ
chak
CHI, I'M HOM--
WHAT THE--
poomf!
ばたん
WHAM!
くるくる
twirl
twirl
Welcome home!
Welcome back!
Welcome to your humble shack!
...

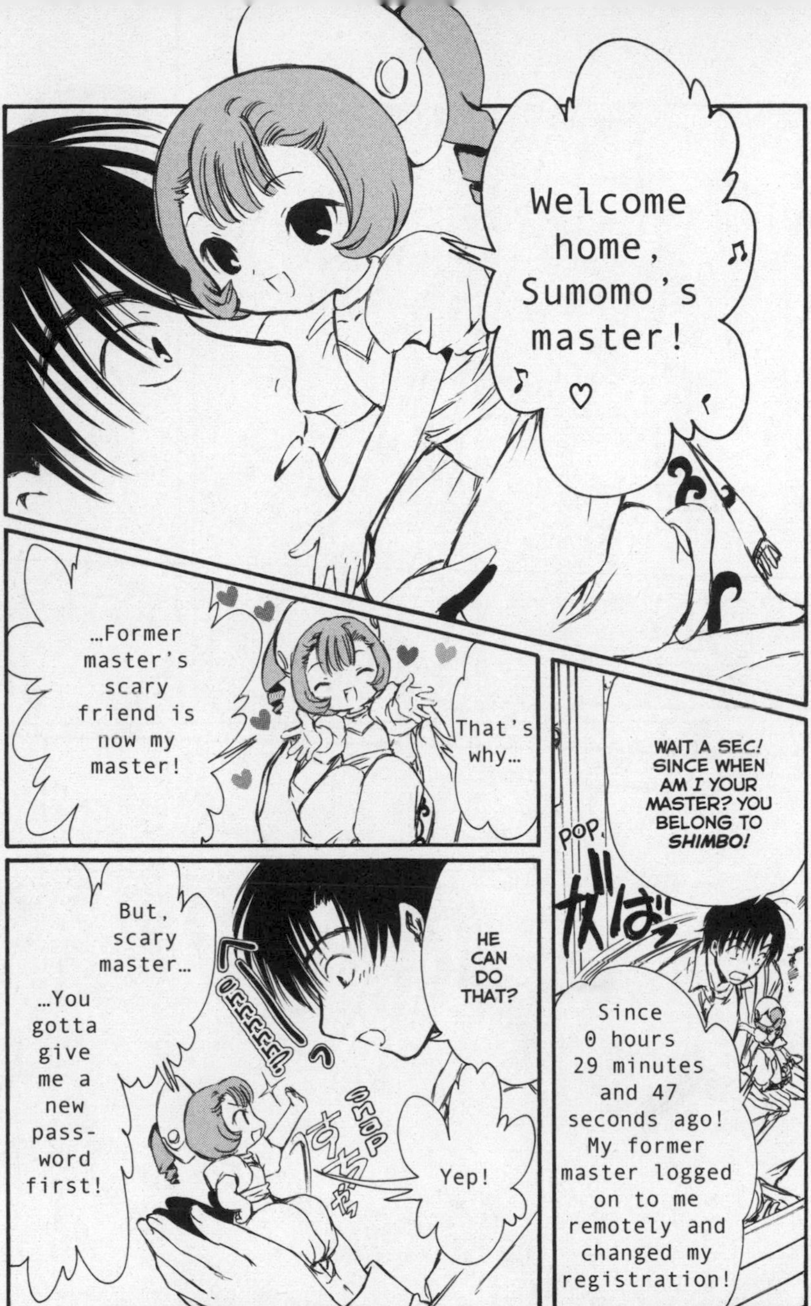
Welcome home, Sumomo's master! ♪ ♡
WAIT A SEC! SINCE WHEN AM I YOUR MASTER? YOU BELONG TO SHIMBO!
POP
Since 0 hours 29 minutes and 47 seconds ago! My former master logged on to me remotely and changed my registration!
That's why…
…Former master's scary friend is now my master!
HE CAN DO THAT?
Yep!
But, scary master…
…You gotta give me a new pass-word first!

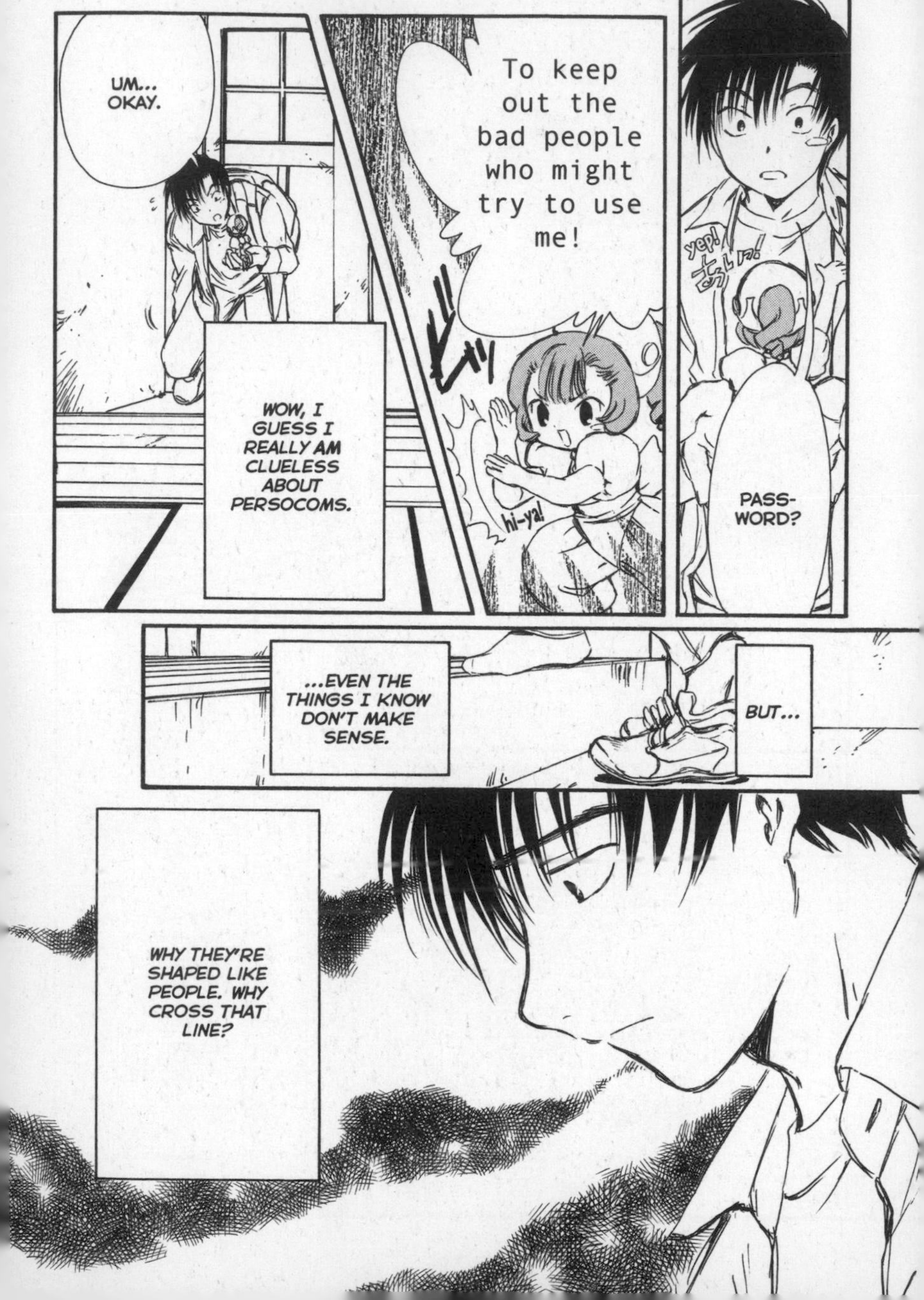
PASS-WORD?
yep!
To keep out the bad people who might try to use me!
hi-ya!
UM... OKAY.
WOW, I GUESS I REALLY AM CLUELESS ABOUT PERSOCOMS.
BUT...
...EVEN THE THINGS I KNOW DON'T MAKE SENSE.
WHY THEY'RE SHAPED LIKE PEOPLE. WHY CROSS THAT LINE?

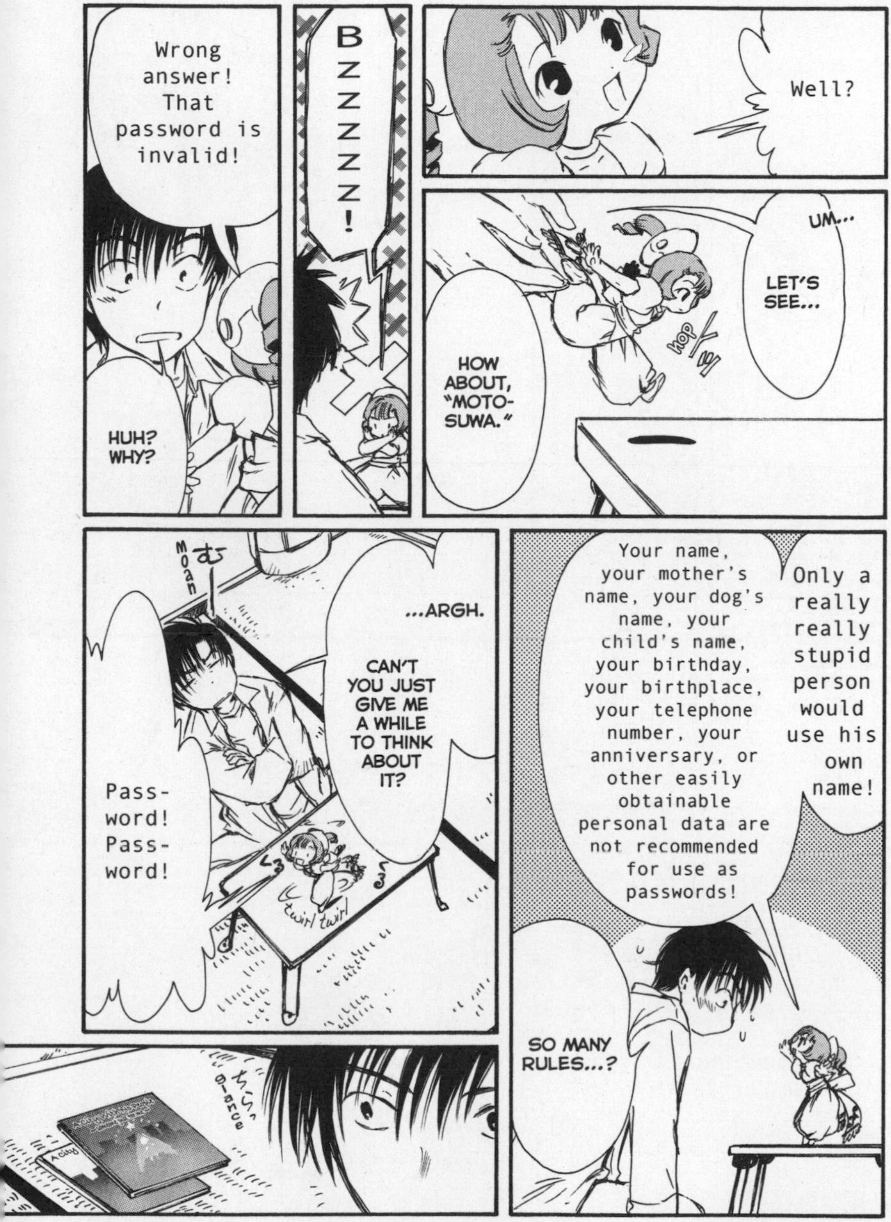
Well?
UM...
LET'S SEE...
hop
HOW ABOUT, "MOTO-SUWA."
BZZZZZZ!
Wrong answer! That password is invalid!
HUH? WHY?
Only a really really stupid person would use his own name!
Your name, your mother's name, your dog's name, your child's name, your birthday, your birthplace, your telephone number, your anniversary, or other easily obtainable personal data are not recommended for use as passwords!
SO MANY RULES...?
Moan
...ARGH.
CAN'T YOU JUST GIVE ME A WHILE TO THINK ABOUT IT?
Pass-word! Pass-word!
twirl twirl
glance

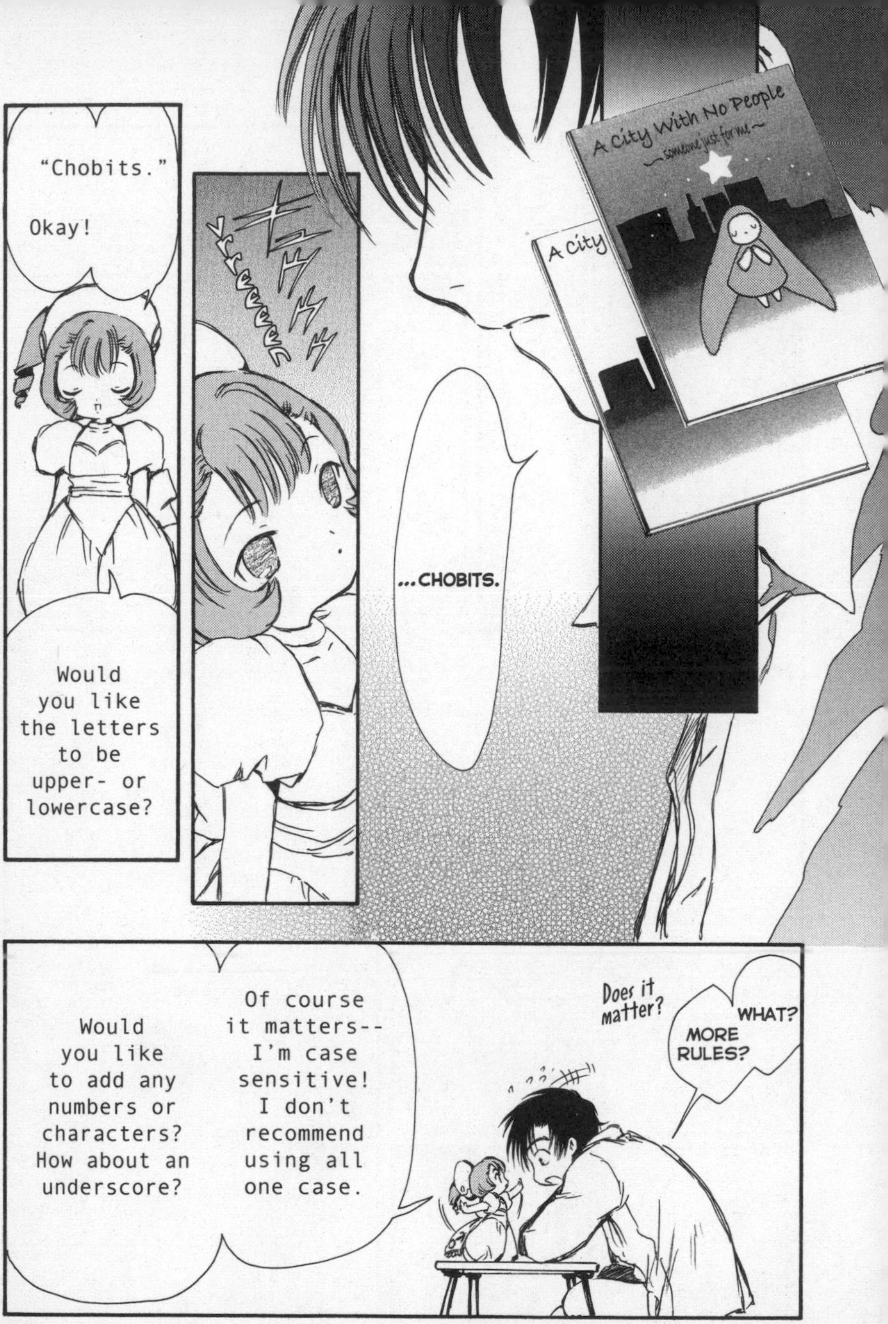
A City With No People
~someone just for me~
A City
...CHOBITS.
"Chobits."
Okay!
Would you like the letters to be upper- or lowercase?
Does it matter?
WHAT? MORE RULES?
Of course it matters-- I'm case sensitive! I don't recommend using all one case.
Would you like to add any numbers or characters? How about an underscore?

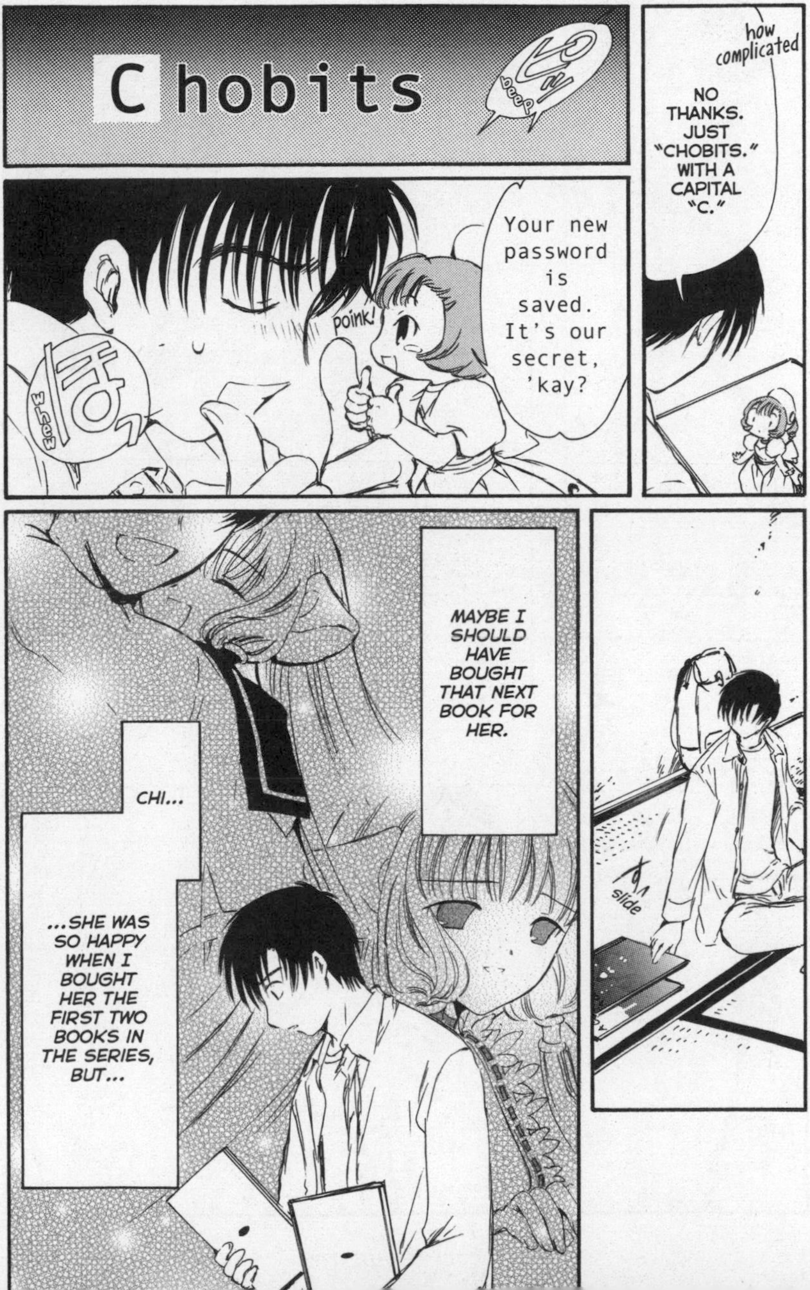

how complicated
NO THANKS. JUST "CHOBITS." WITH A CAPITAL "C."
beep
Chobits
Your new password is saved. It's our secret, 'kay?
poink!
whew
slide
MAYBE I SHOULD HAVE BOUGHT THAT NEXT BOOK FOR HER.
CHI...
...SHE WAS SO HAPPY WHEN I BOUGHT HER THE FIRST TWO BOOKS IN THE SERIES, BUT...

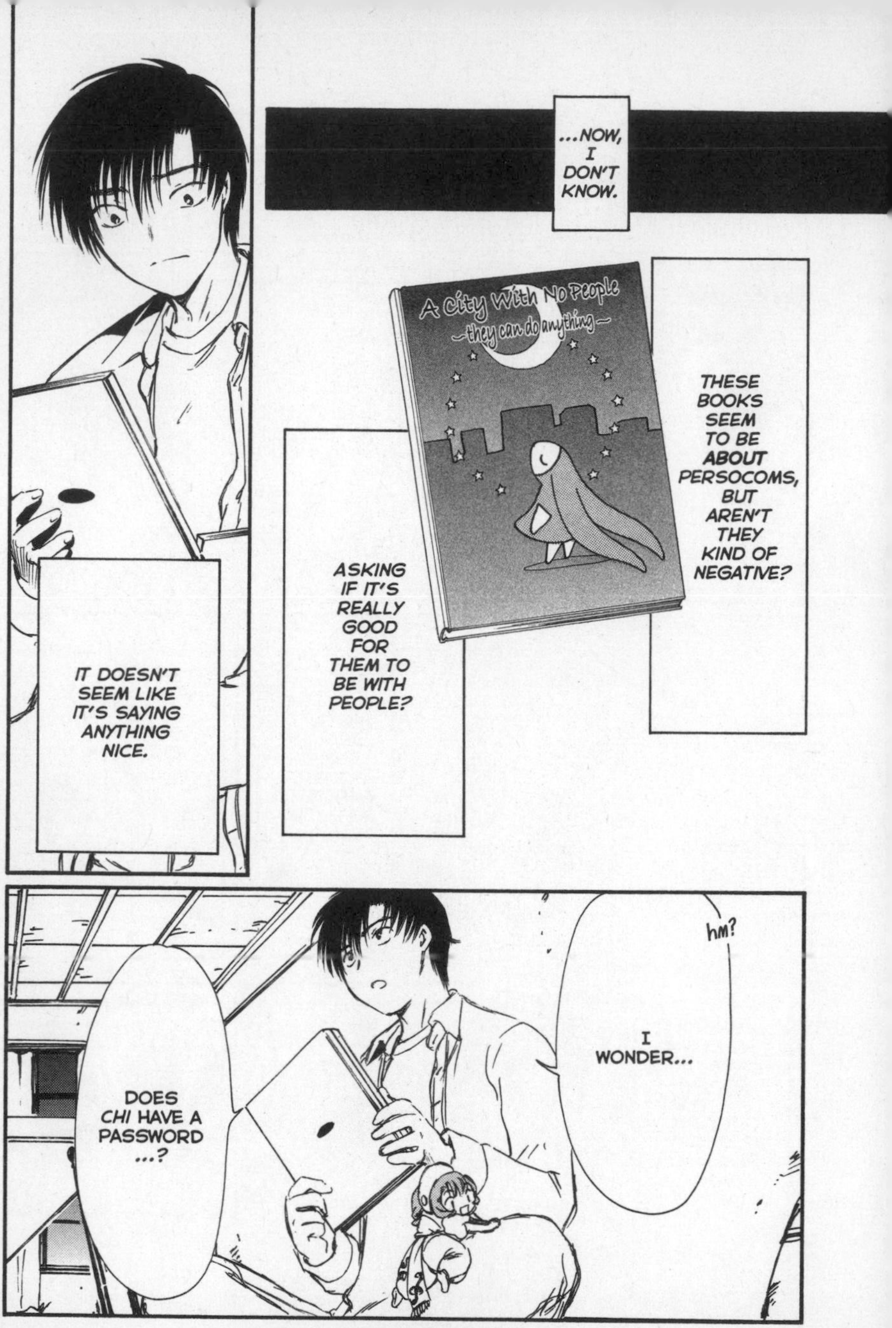
...NOW, I DON'T KNOW.
A City With No People
~they can do anything~
THESE BOOKS SEEM TO BE ABOUT PERSOCOMS, BUT AREN'T THEY KIND OF NEGATIVE?
ASKING IF IT'S REALLY GOOD FOR THEM TO BE WITH PEOPLE?
IT DOESN'T SEEM LIKE IT'S SAYING ANYTHING NICE.
hm?
I WONDER...
DOES CHI HAVE A PASSWORD ...?

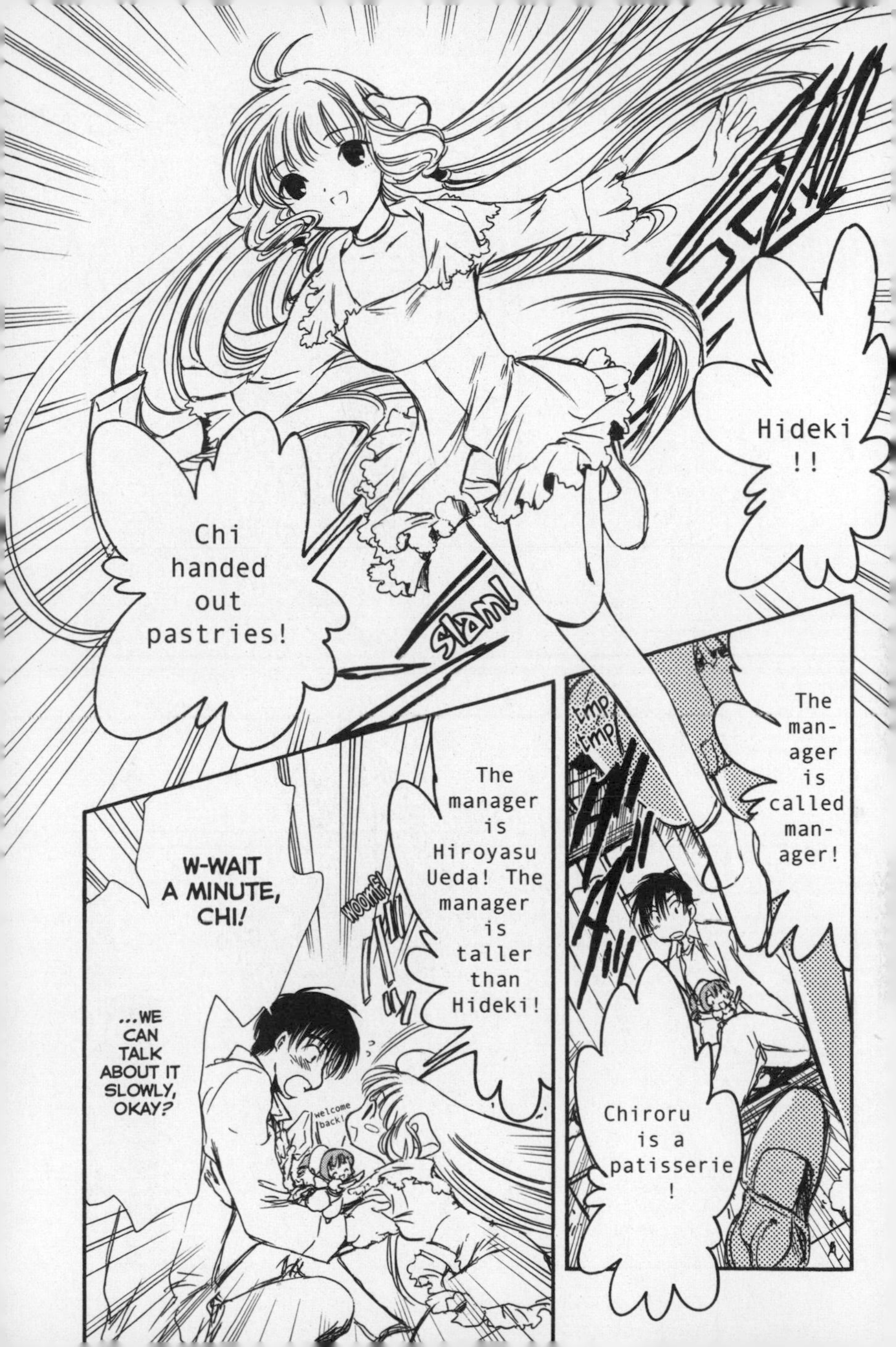
Hideki!!
Chi handed out pastries!
slam!
The manager is called manager!
tmp tmp
Chiroru is a patisserie!
The manager is Hiroyasu Ueda! The manager is taller than Hideki!
W-WAIT A MINUTE, CHI!
WOOMF!
welcome back!
...WE CAN TALK ABOUT IT SLOWLY, OKAY?

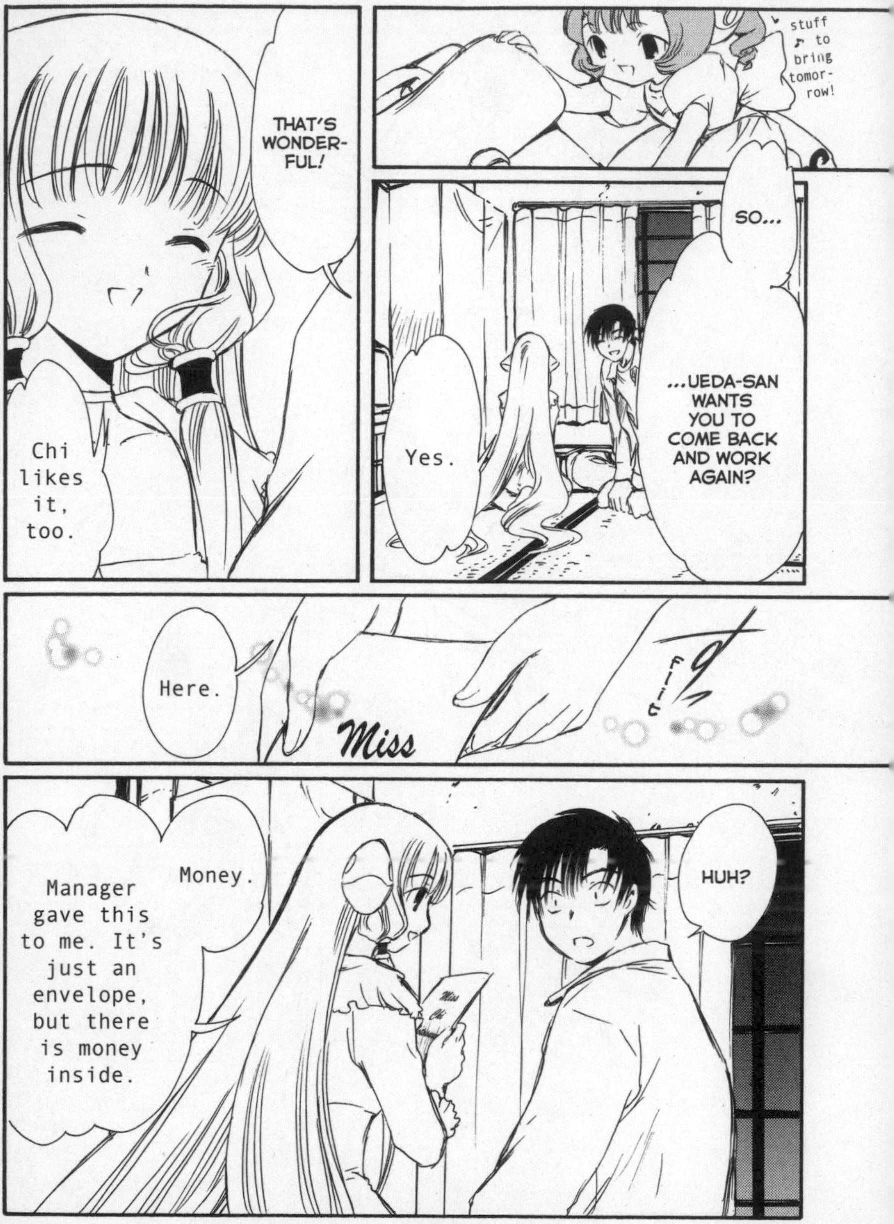
stuff to bring tomorrow!
SO...
...UEDA-SAN WANTS YOU TO COME BACK AND WORK AGAIN?
Yes.
THAT'S WONDERFUL!
Chi likes it, too.
Flit
Here.
Miss
HUH?
Money.
Manager gave this to me. It's just an envelope, but there is money inside.

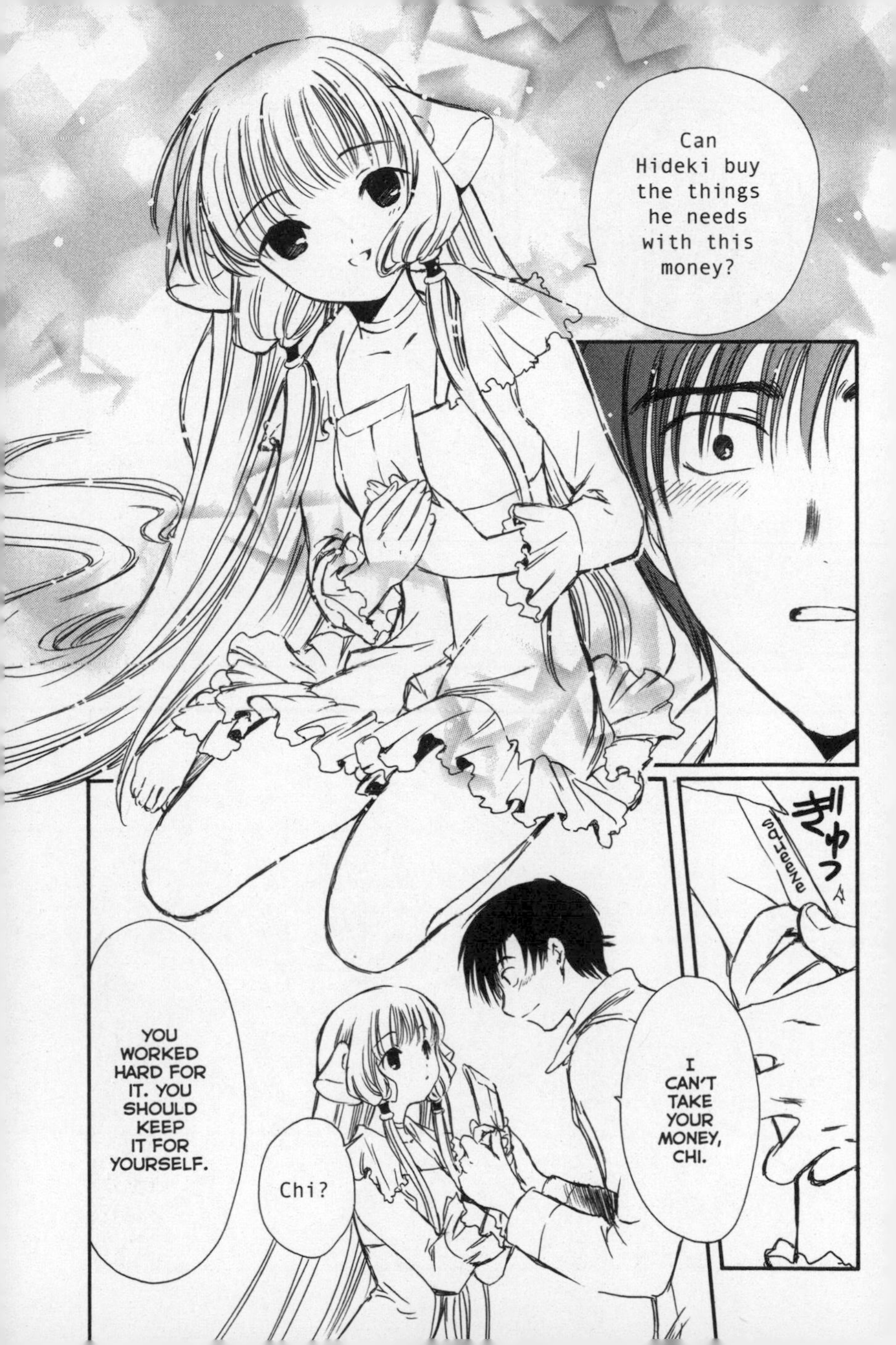
Can Hideki buy the things he needs with this money?
ぎゅっ
SQUEEZE
I CAN'T TAKE YOUR MONEY, CHI.
Chi?
YOU WORKED HARD FOR IT. YOU SHOULD KEEP IT FOR YOURSELF.

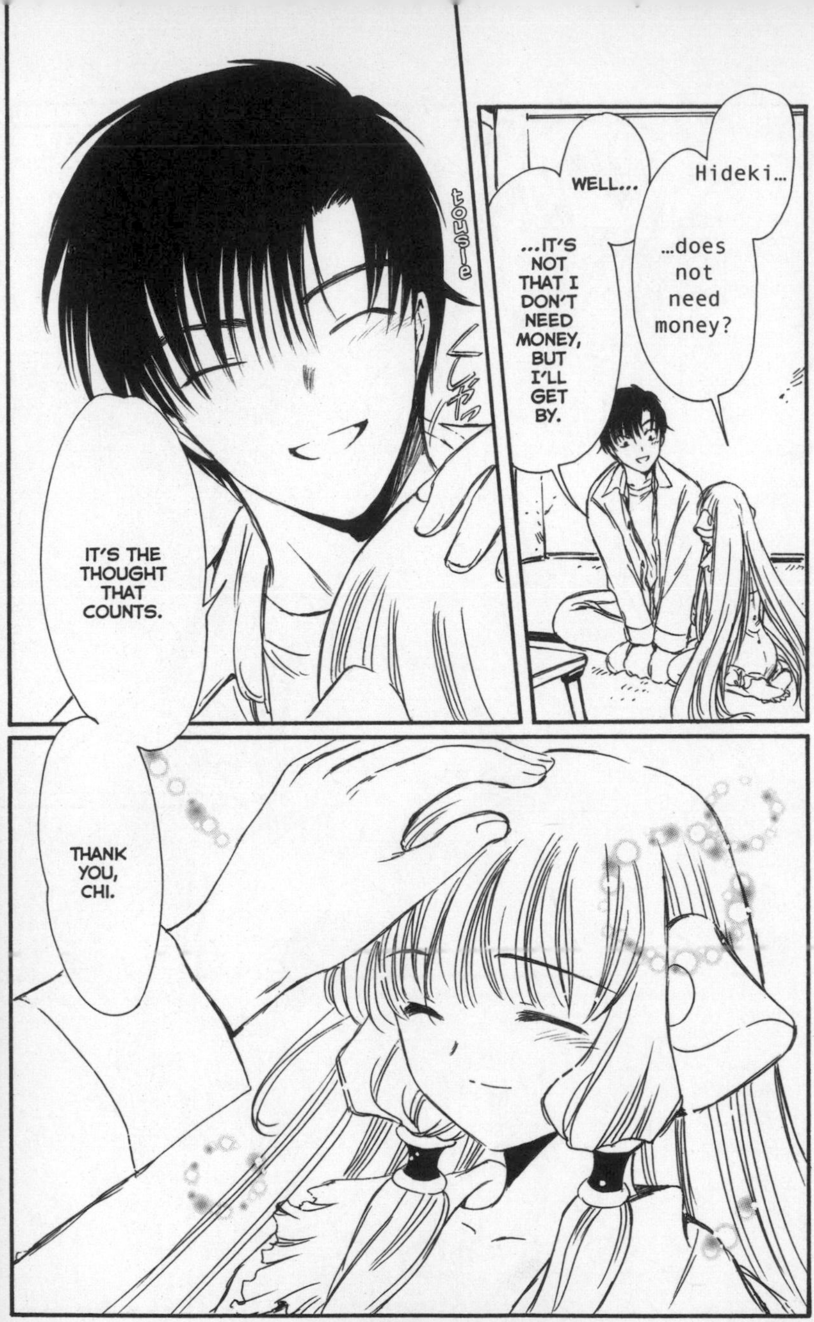
Hideki…
…does not need money?
WELL…
…IT'S NOT THAT I DON'T NEED MONEY, BUT I'LL GET BY.
tousle
IT'S THE THOUGHT THAT COUNTS.
THANK YOU, CHI.

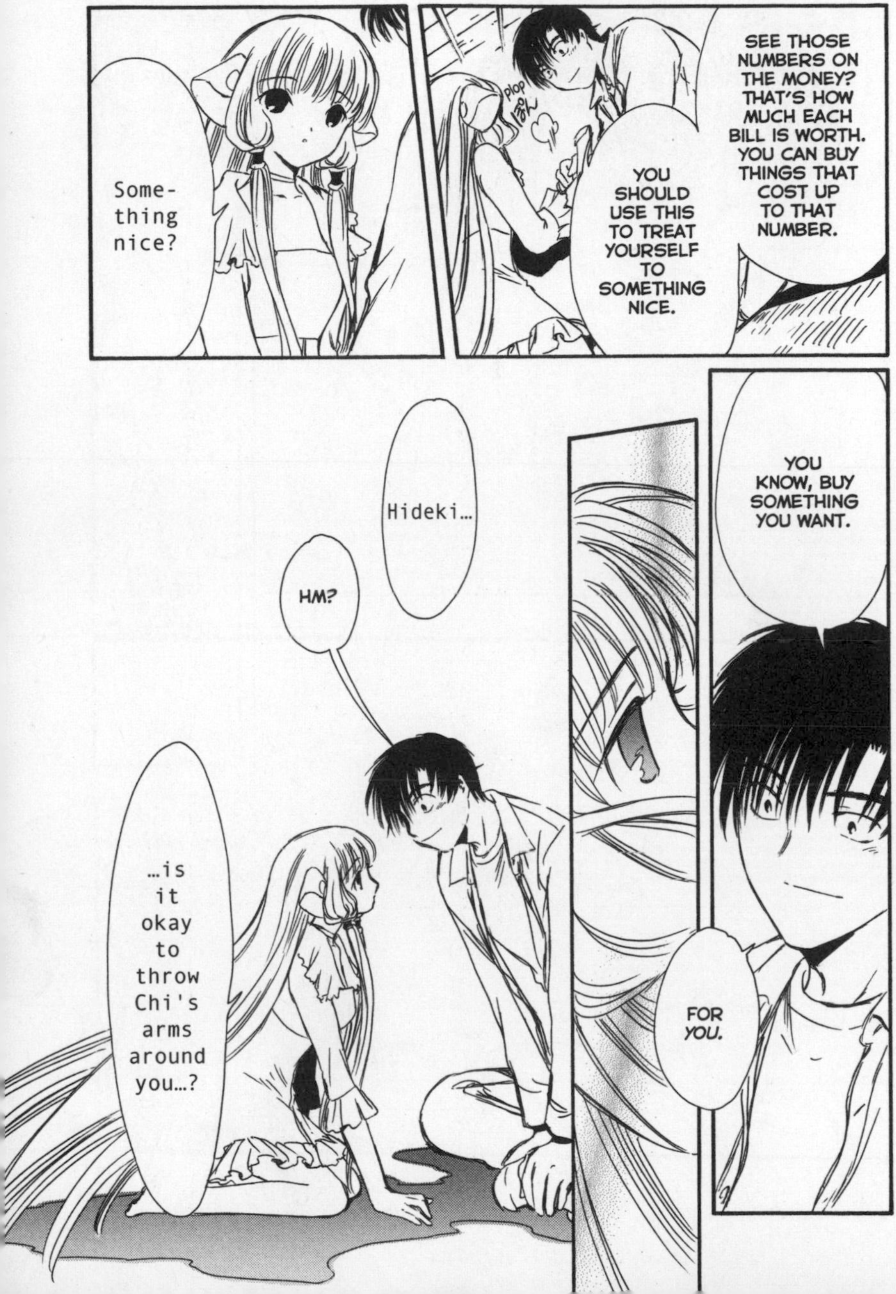
SEE THOSE NUMBERS ON THE MONEY? THAT'S HOW MUCH EACH BILL IS WORTH. YOU CAN BUY THINGS THAT COST UP TO THAT NUMBER.
YOU SHOULD USE THIS TO TREAT YOURSELF TO SOMETHING NICE.
plop
ぽん
Some-thing nice?
YOU KNOW, BUY SOMETHING YOU WANT.
FOR YOU.
Hideki…
HM?
…is it okay to throw Chi's arms around you…?

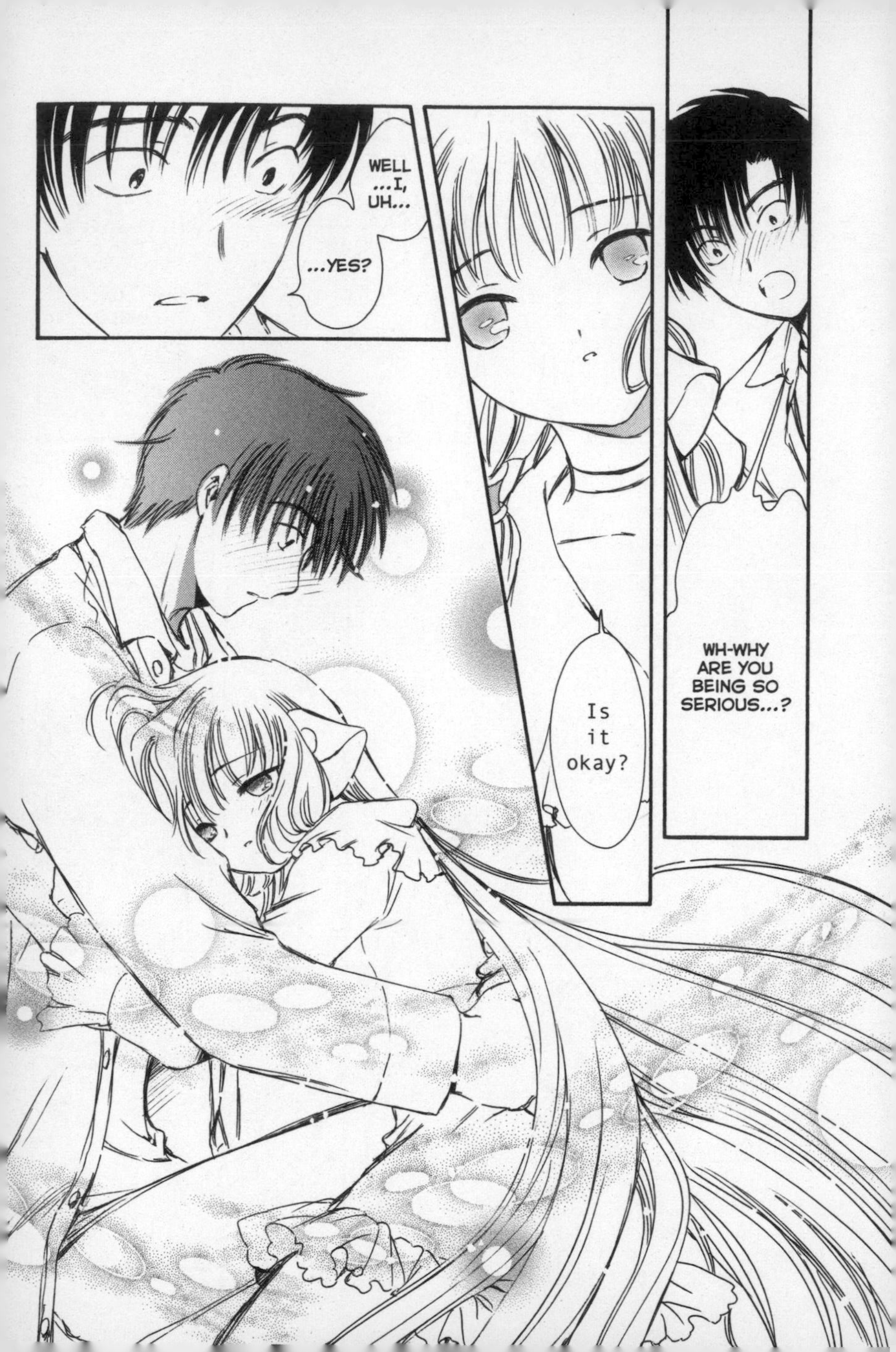
WH-WHY ARE YOU BEING SO SERIOUS...?
Is it okay?
WELL ...I, UH...
...YES?

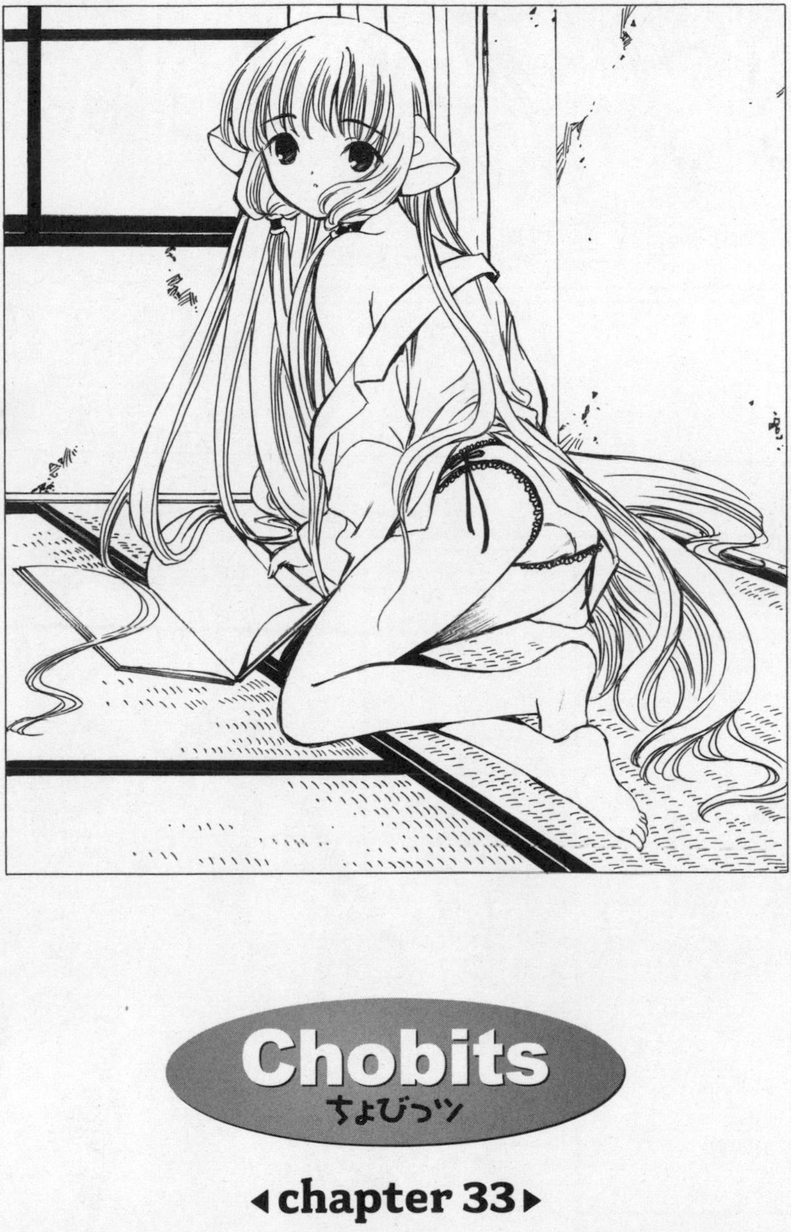

Chobits
ちょびっツ

◂chapter 33▸

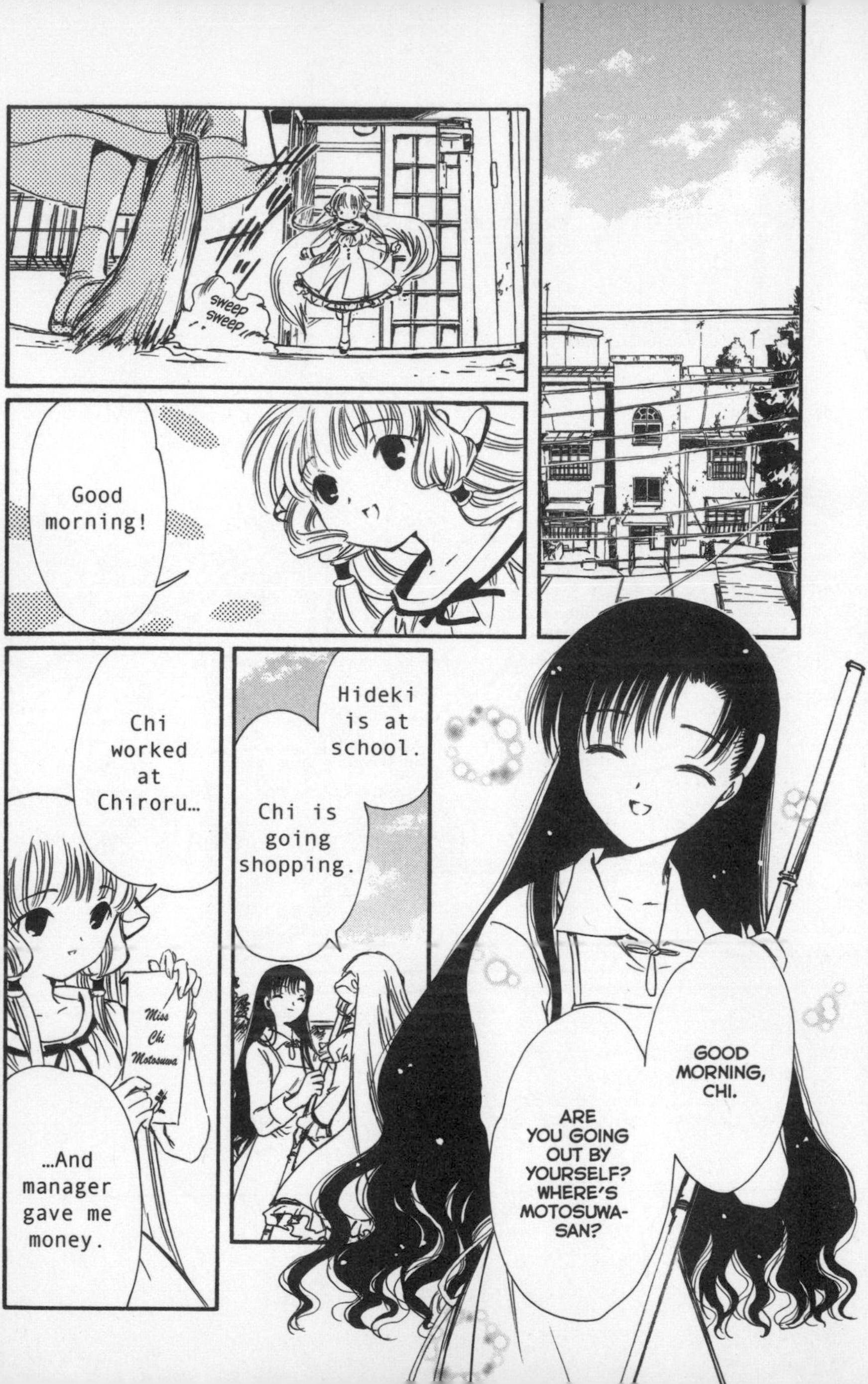
sweep sweep
Good morning!
GOOD MORNING, CHI.
ARE YOU GOING OUT BY YOURSELF? WHERE'S MOTOSUWA-SAN?
Hideki is at school.
Chi is going shopping.
Chi worked at Chiroru...
Miss Chi Motosuwa
...And manager gave me money.

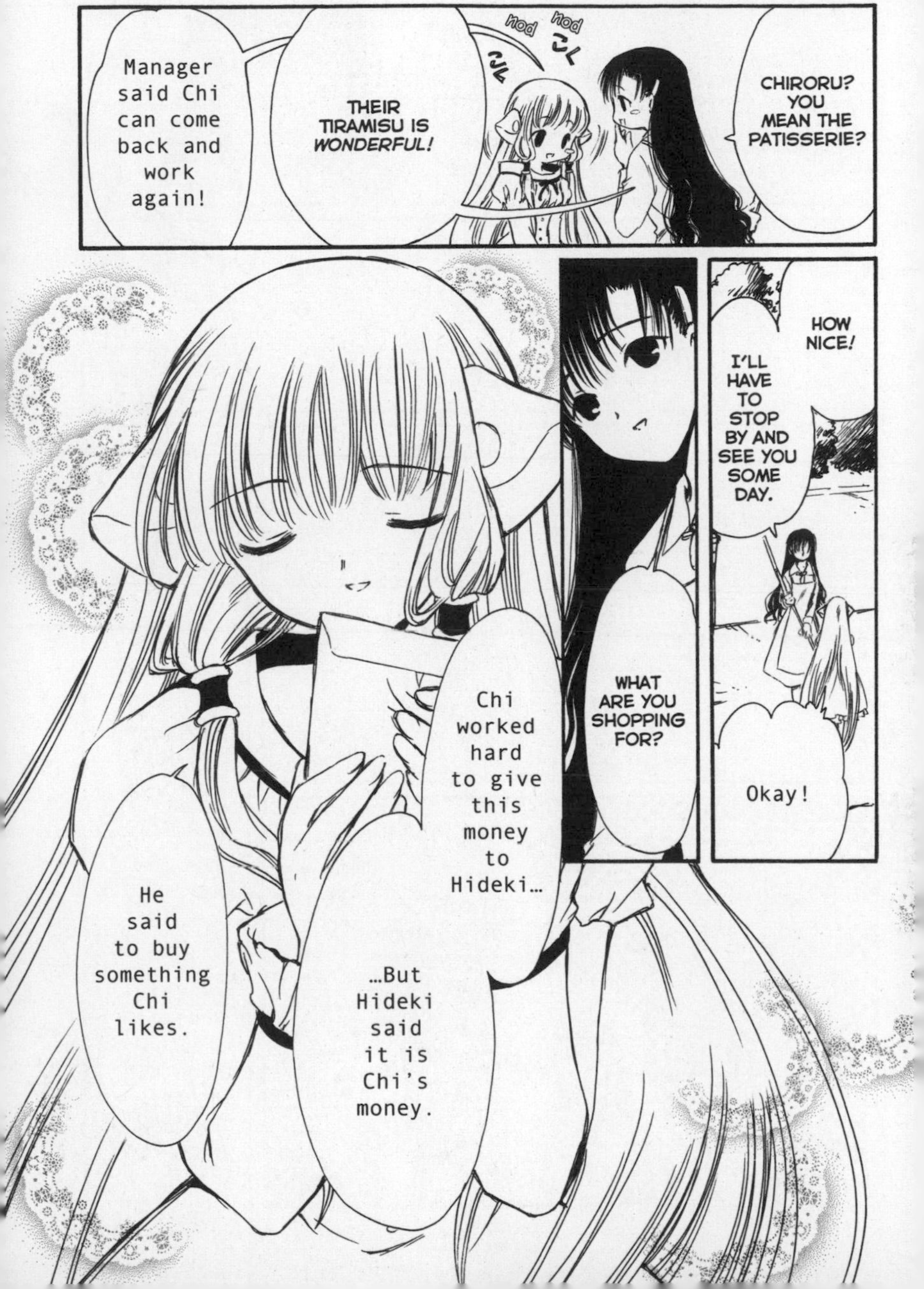
CHIRORU? YOU MEAN THE PATISSERIE?
nod
nod
THEIR TIRAMISU IS *WONDERFUL!*
Manager said Chi can come back and work again!
HOW NICE!
I'LL HAVE TO STOP BY AND SEE YOU SOME DAY.
Okay!
WHAT ARE YOU SHOPPING FOR?
Chi worked hard to give this money to Hideki…
…But Hideki said it is Chi's money.
He said to buy something Chi likes.

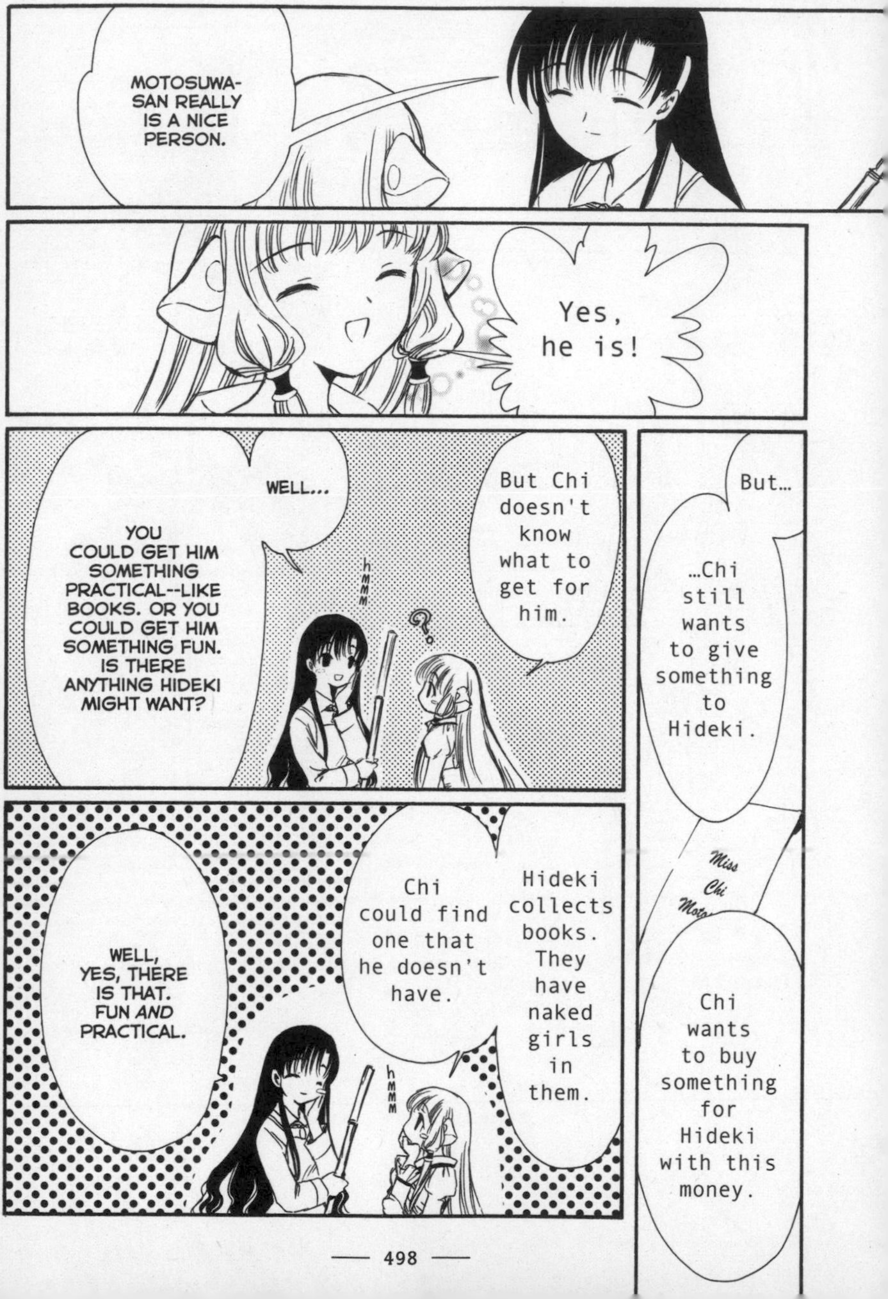
MOTOSUWA-SAN REALLY IS A NICE PERSON.
Yes, he is!
But...
...Chi still wants to give something to Hideki.
Miss Chi
Chi wants to buy something for Hideki with this money.
But Chi doesn't know what to get for him.
hmmm
WELL...
YOU COULD GET HIM SOMETHING PRACTICAL--LIKE BOOKS. OR YOU COULD GET HIM SOMETHING FUN. IS THERE ANYTHING HIDEKI MIGHT WANT?
Hideki collects books. They have naked girls in them.
Chi could find one that he doesn't have.
hmmm
WELL, YES, THERE IS THAT. FUN *AND* PRACTICAL.

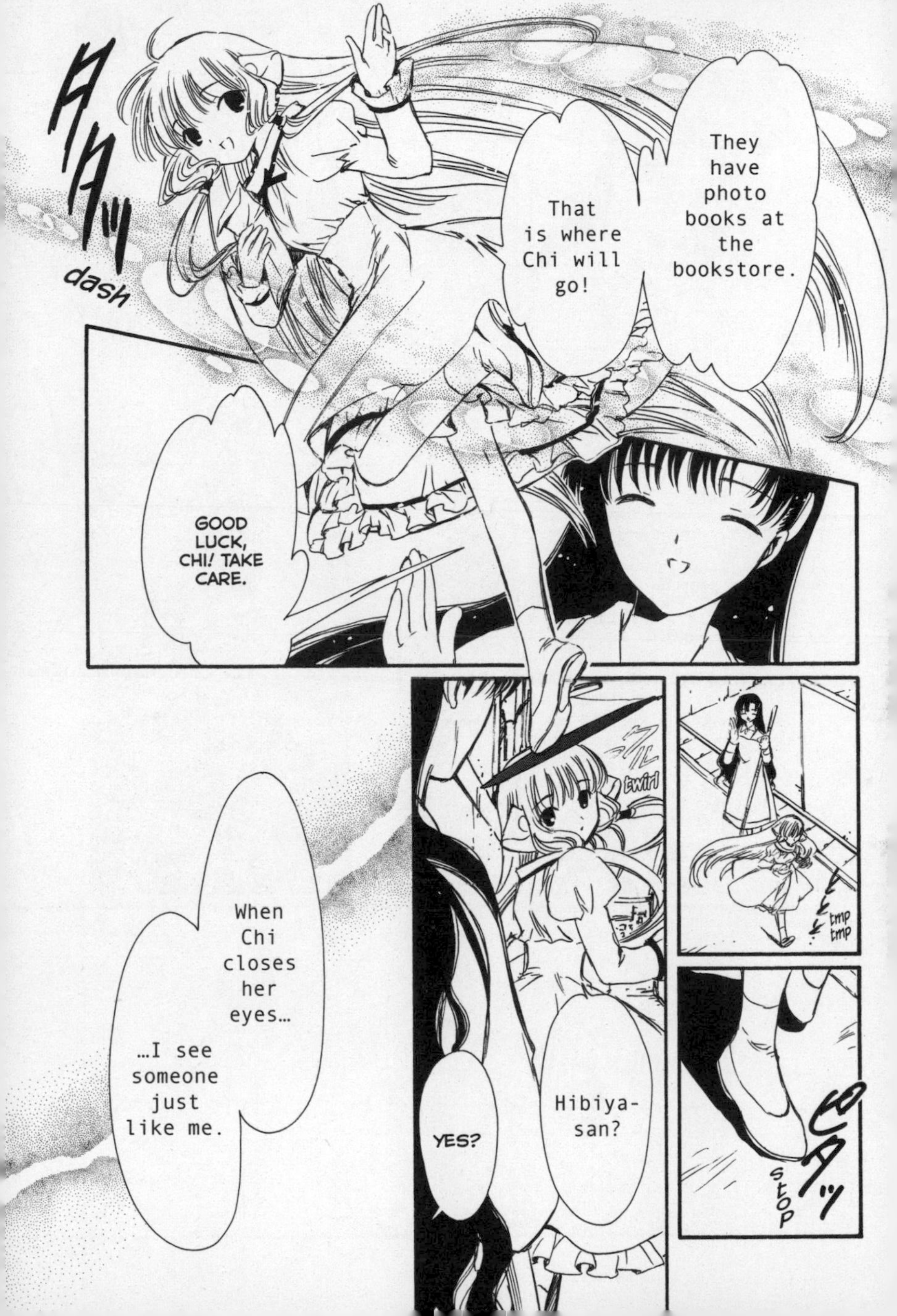

They have photo books at the bookstore.
That is where Chi will go!
dash
GOOD LUCK, CHI! TAKE CARE.
tmp tmp
stop
twirl
Hibiya-san?
YES?
When Chi closes her eyes…
…I see someone just like me.

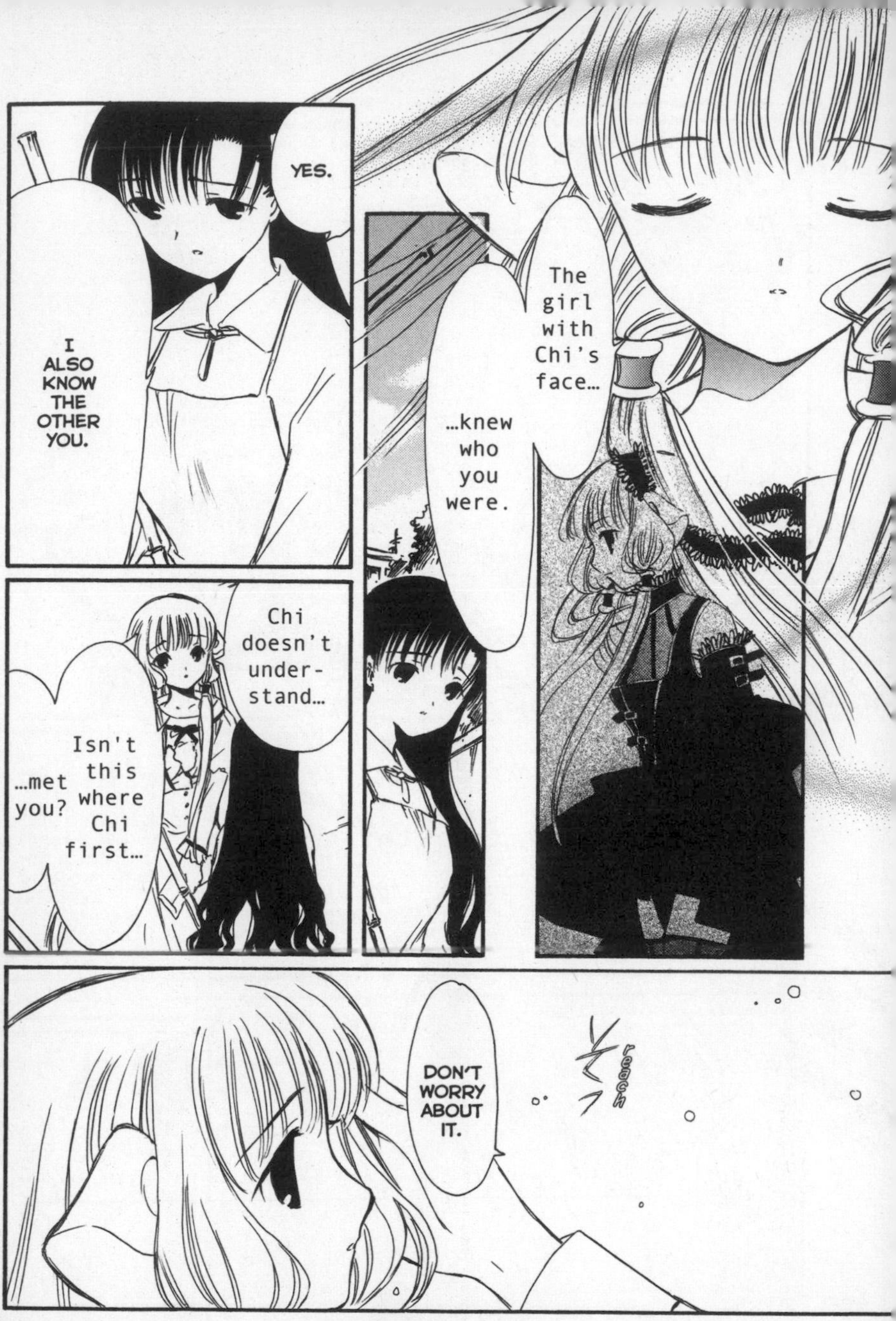
The girl with Chi's face...
...knew who you were.
YES.
I ALSO KNOW THE OTHER YOU.
Chi doesn't under-stand...
Isn't this where Chi first...
...met you?
reach
DON'T WORRY ABOUT IT.

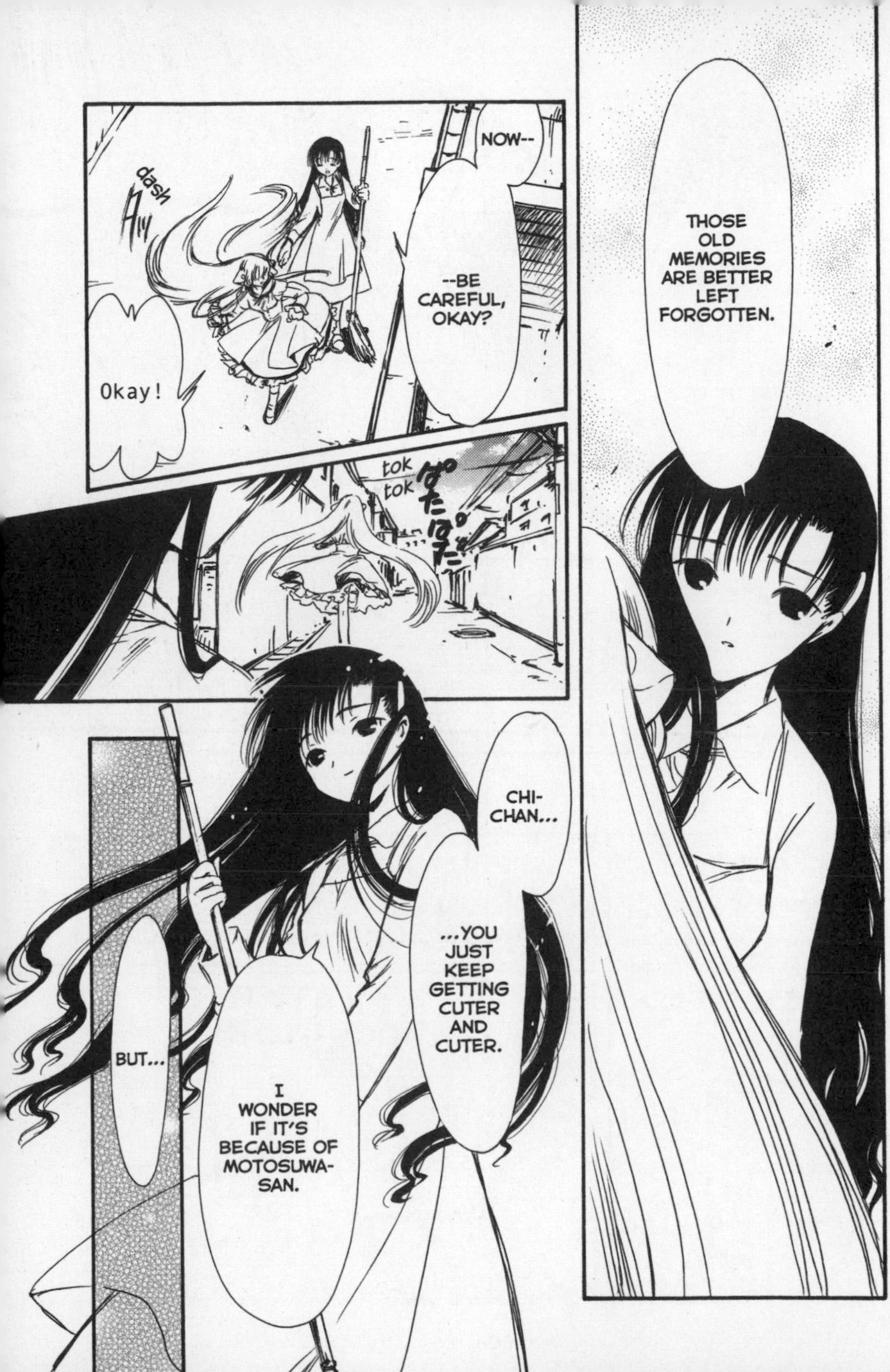
THOSE OLD MEMORIES ARE BETTER LEFT FORGOTTEN.
NOW--
--BE CAREFUL, OKAY?
dash
Okay!
tok tok
CHI-CHAN...
...YOU JUST KEEP GETTING CUTER AND CUTER.
I WONDER IF IT'S BECAUSE OF MOTOSUWA-SAN.
BUT...

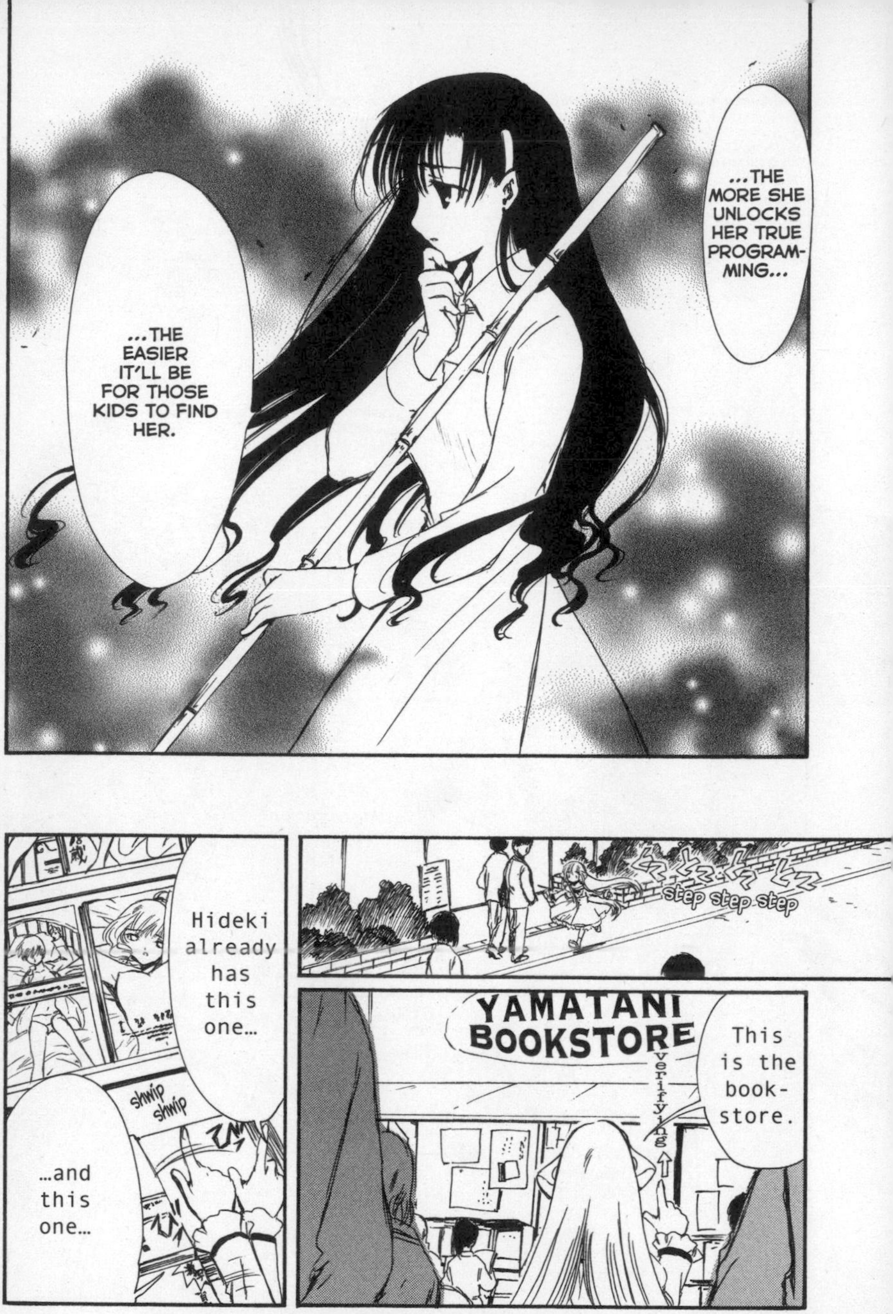

...THE MORE SHE UNLOCKS HER TRUE PROGRAMMING...
...THE EASIER IT'LL BE FOR THOSE KIDS TO FIND HER.
step step step
YAMATANI BOOKSTORE
This is the bookstore.
verifying
Hideki already has this one...
shwip shwip
...and this one...

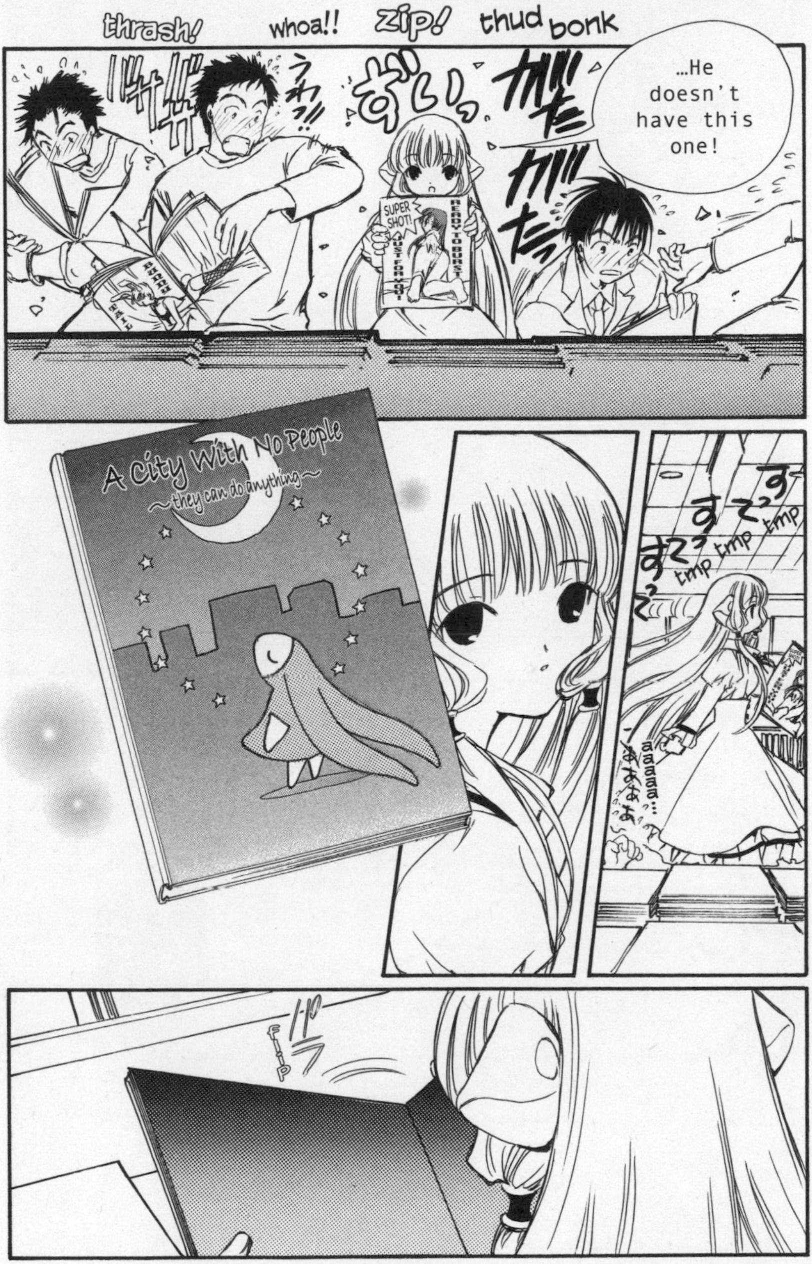
bonk
thud
…He doesn't have this one!
zip!
READY TO BURST
SUPER SHOT!
JUST FOR YOU!
whoa!!
thrash!
tmp tmp tmp
aaaaaa…
A City With No People
~they can do anything~
flip

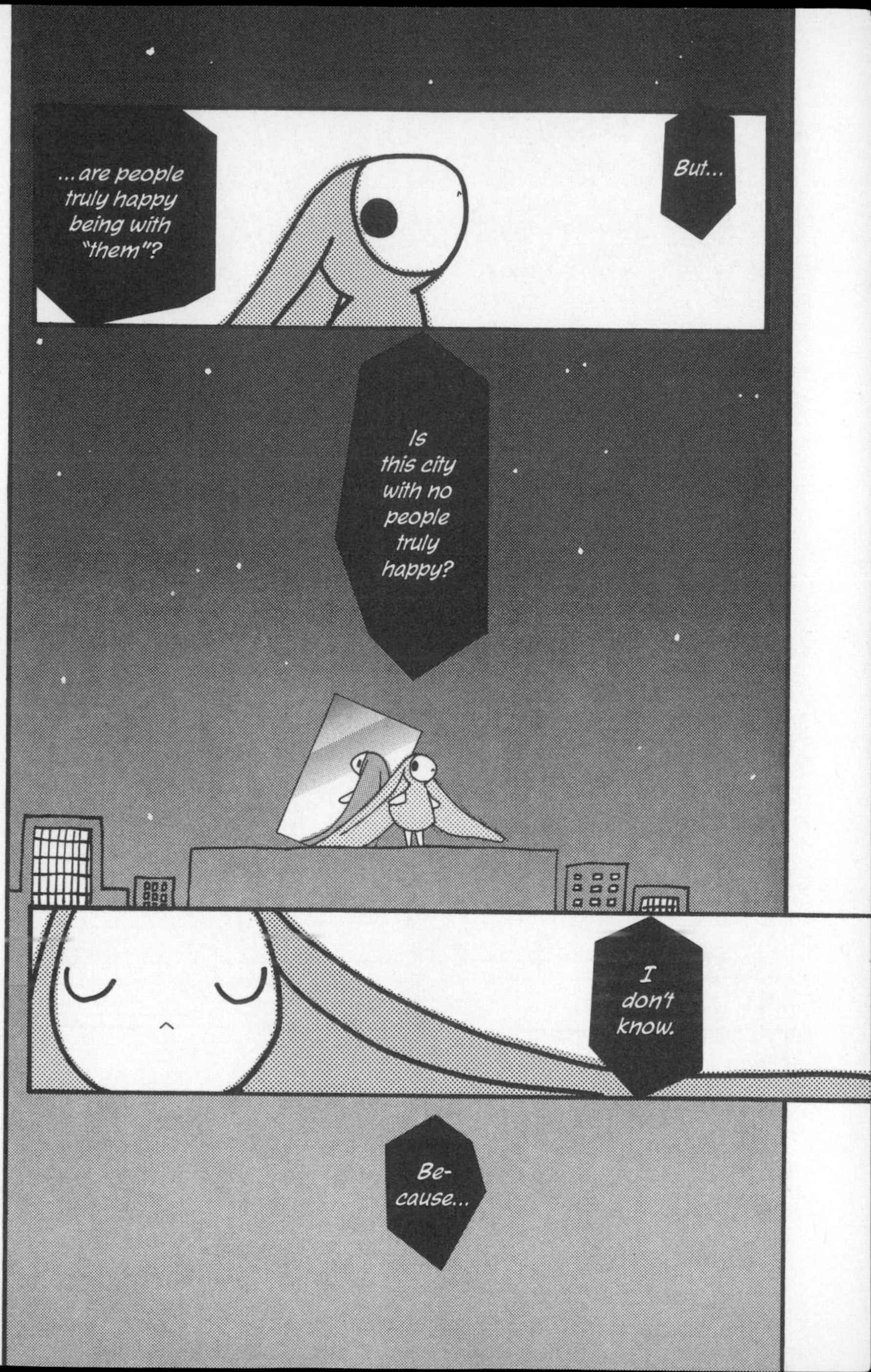
But...
...are people truly happy being with "them"?
Is this city with no people truly happy?
I don't know.
Be-cause...

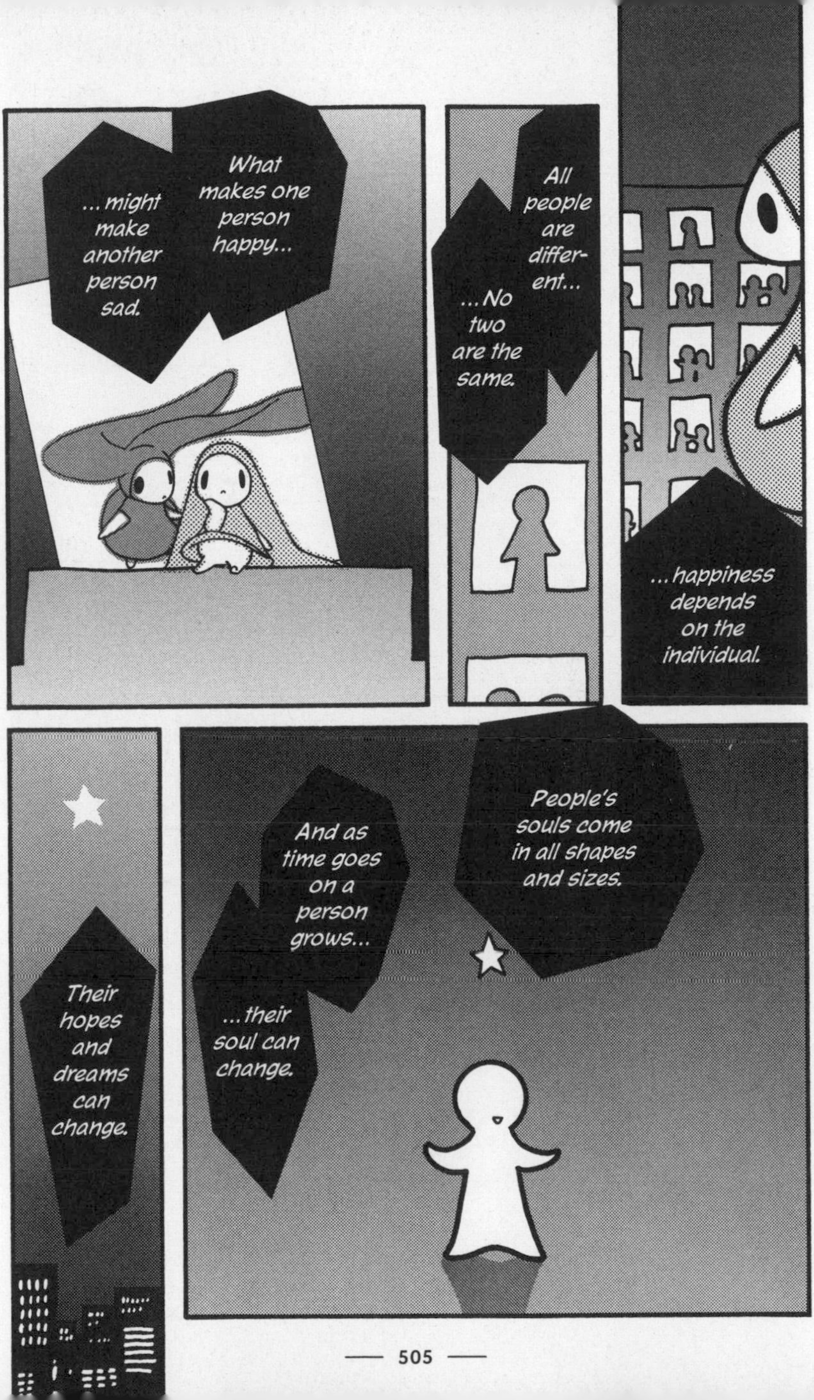
...happiness depends on the individual.
All people are differ-ent...
...No two are the same.
What makes one person happy...
...might make another person sad.
People's souls come in all shapes and sizes.
And as time goes on a person grows...
...their soul can change.
Their hopes and dreams can change.

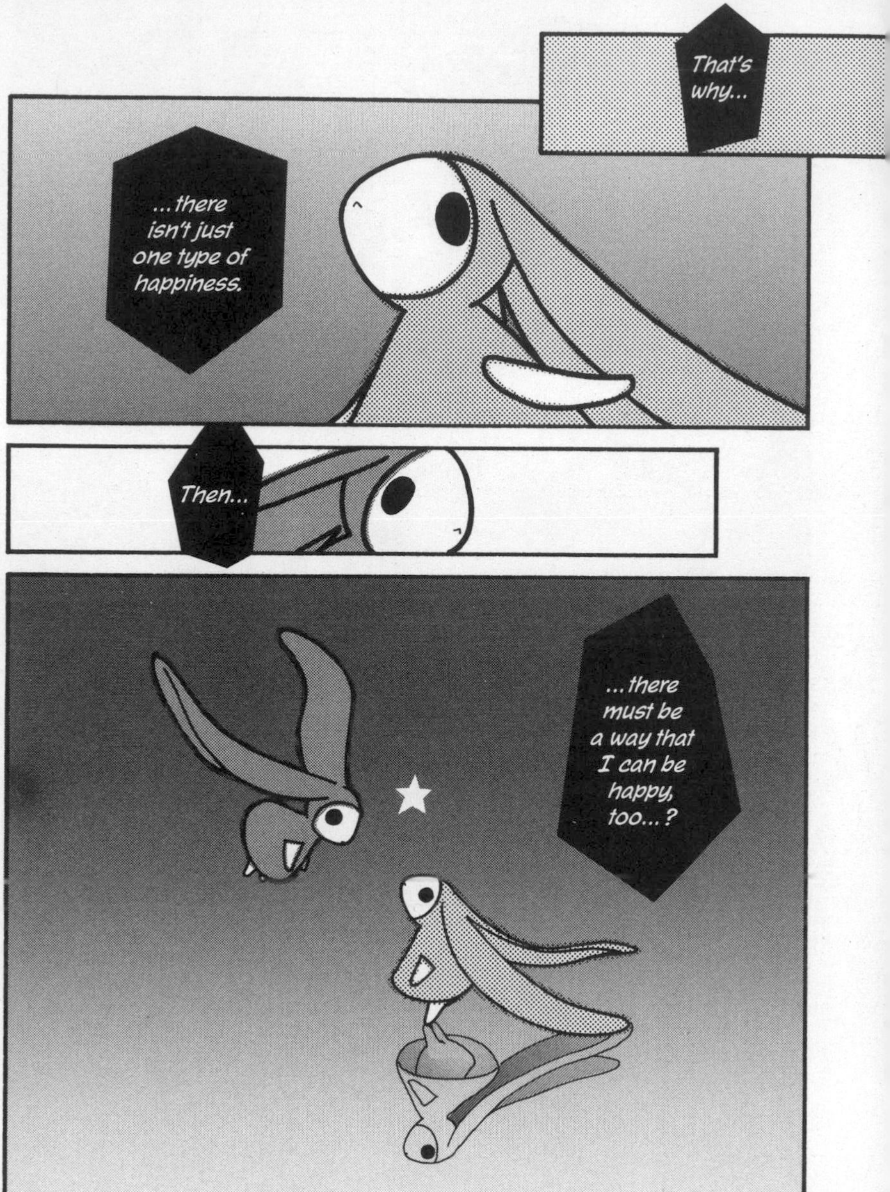
That's why...
...there isn't just one type of happiness.
Then...
...there must be a way that I can be happy, too...?

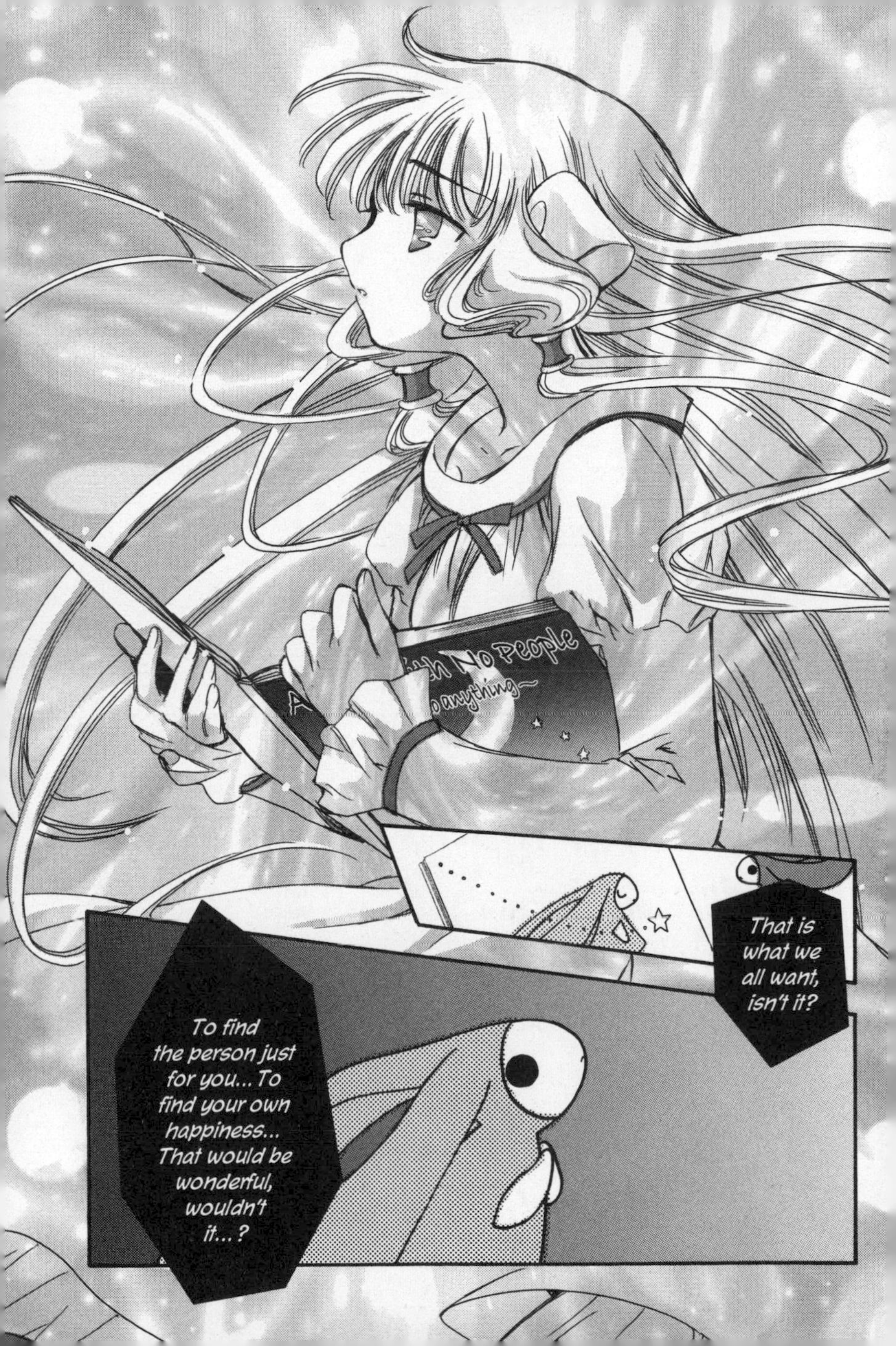
That is what we all want, isn't it?
To find the person just for you... To find your own happiness... That would be wonderful, wouldn't it...?

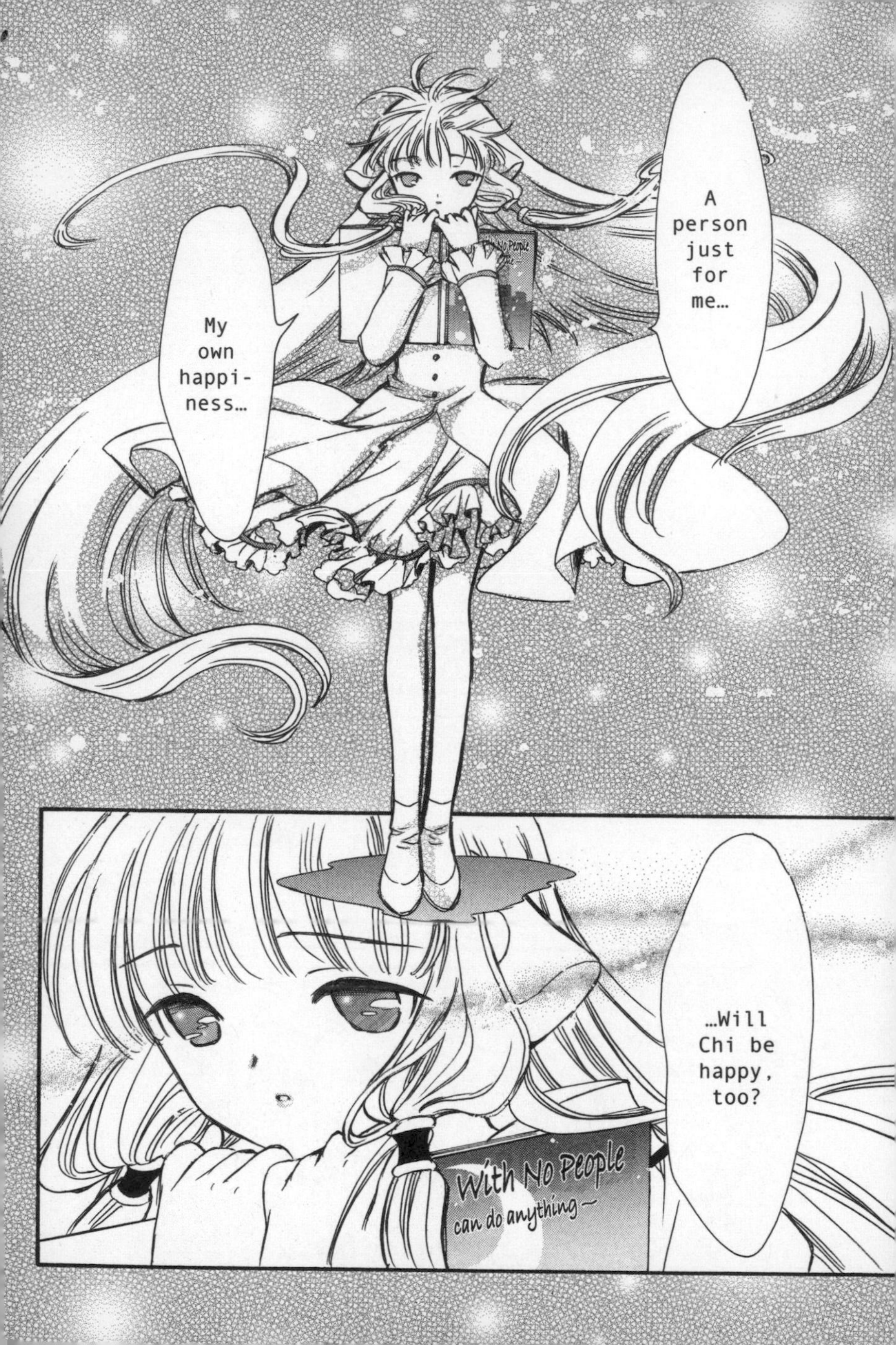
A person just for me…
My own happi-ness…
…Will Chi be happy, too?
With No People
can do anything~

Chobits

ちょびっツ

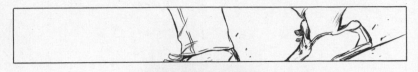

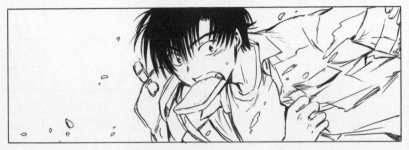

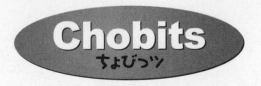

◂chapter 34▸

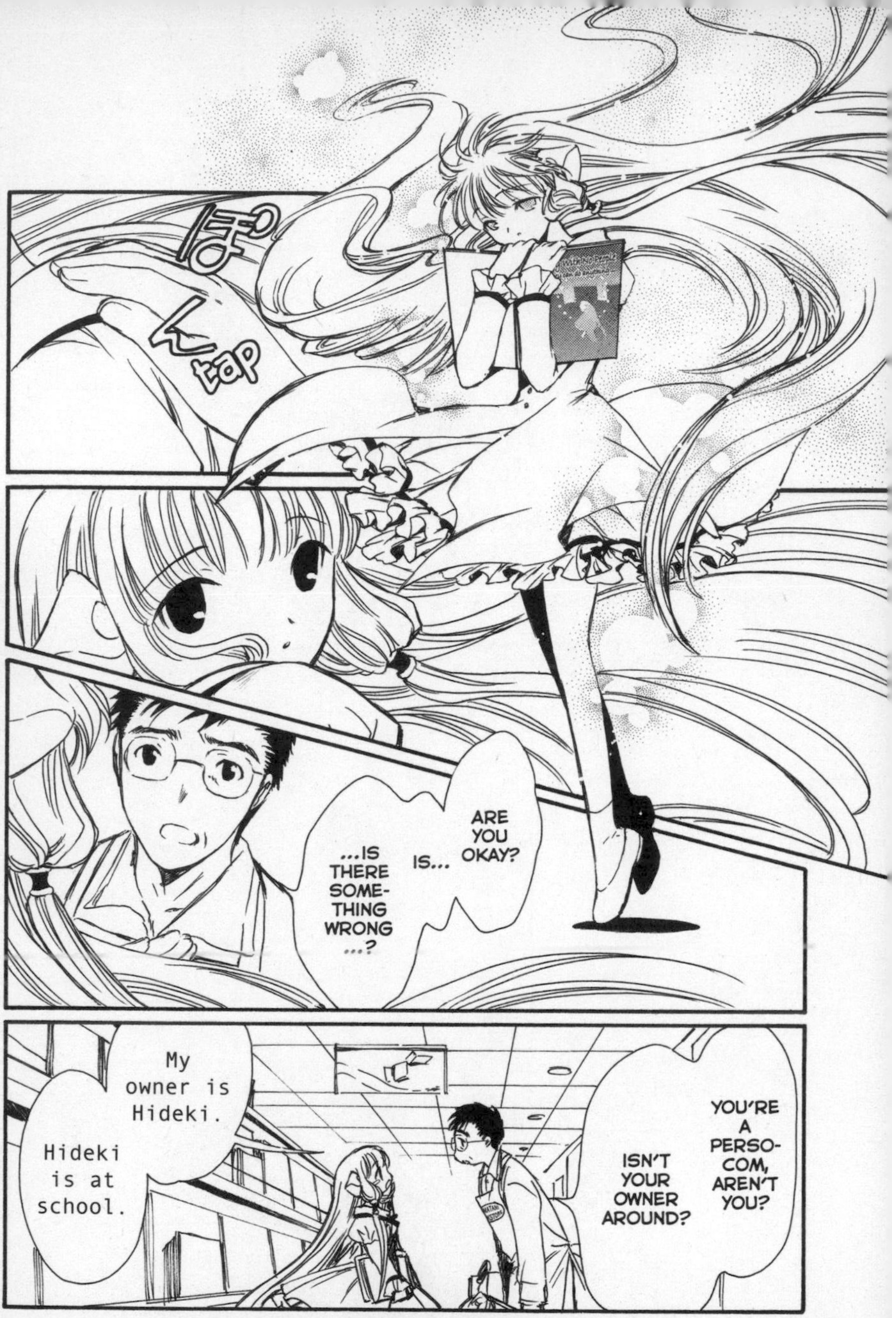
ぽん
tap
ARE YOU OKAY?
IS...
...IS THERE SOMETHING WRONG...?
YOU'RE A PERSOCOM, AREN'T YOU?
ISN'T YOUR OWNER AROUND?
My owner is Hideki.
Hideki is at school.

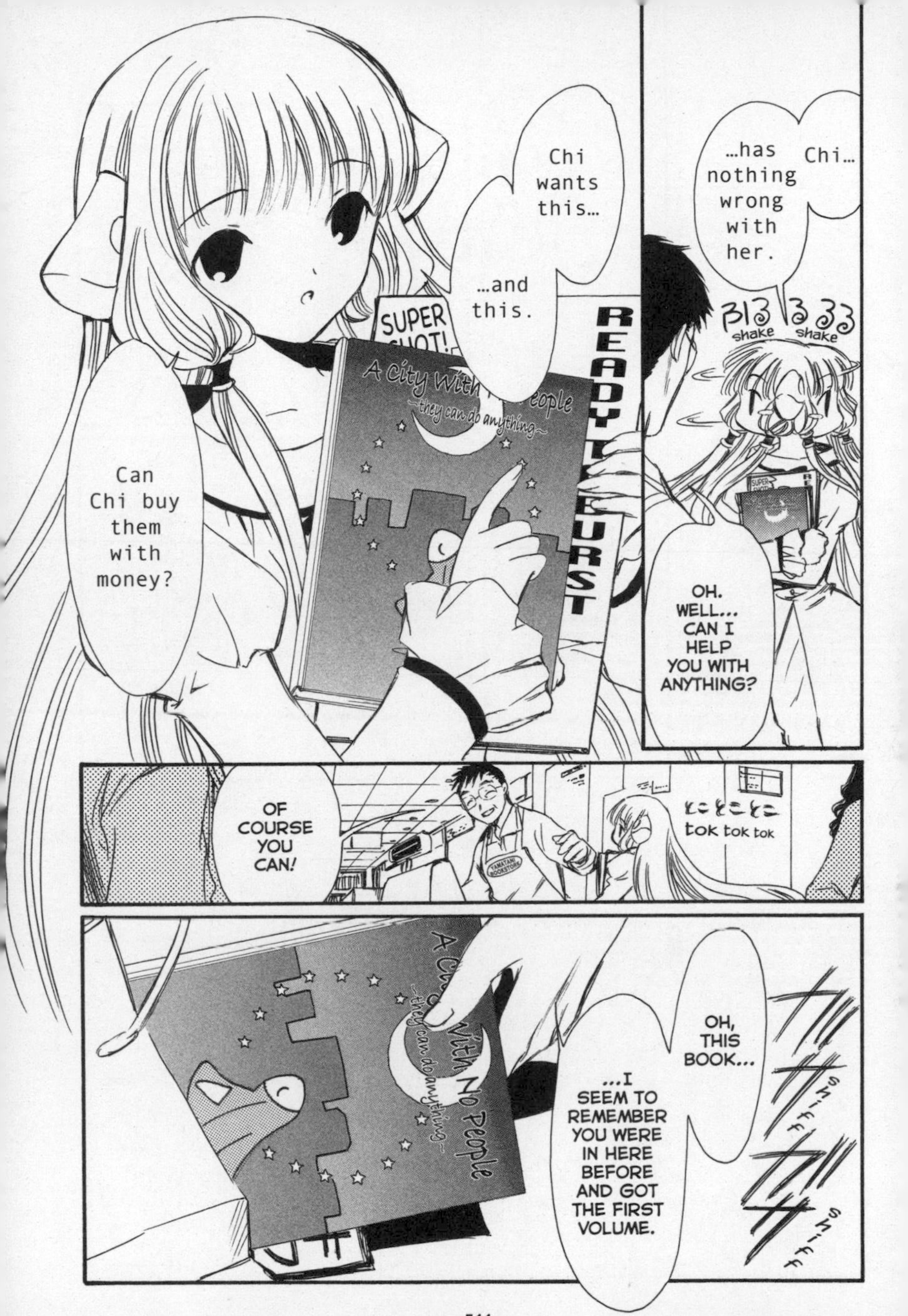

Chi…
…has nothing wrong with her.
shake shake
OH. WELL… CAN I HELP YOU WITH ANYTHING?
Chi wants this…
…and this.
SUPER SHOT!
~they can do anything~
Can Chi buy them with money?
tok tok tok
OF COURSE YOU CAN!
OH, THIS BOOK…
…I SEEM TO REMEMBER YOU WERE IN HERE BEFORE AND GOT THE FIRST VOLUME.

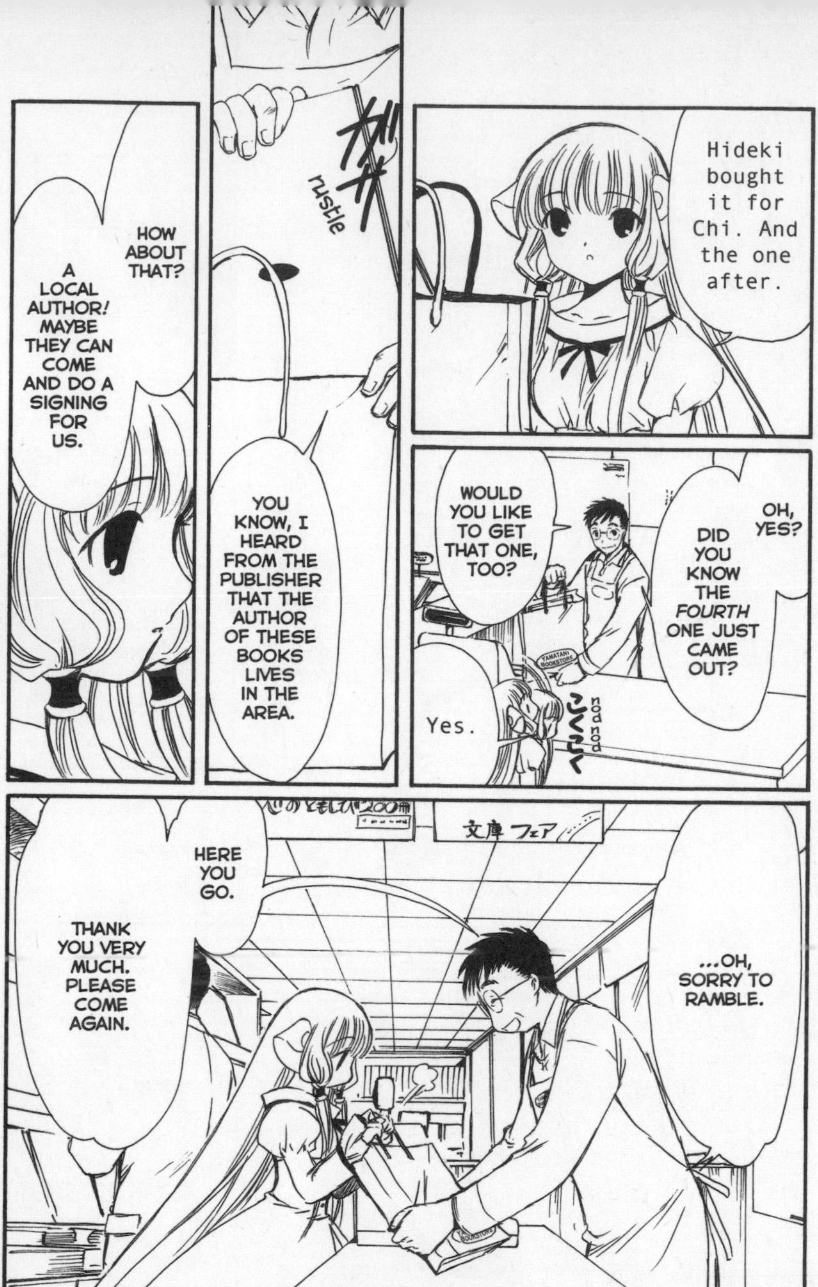
Hideki bought it for Chi. And the one after.
OH, YES?
DID YOU KNOW THE *FOURTH* ONE JUST CAME OUT?
WOULD YOU LIKE TO GET THAT ONE, TOO?
YAMATANI BOOKSTORE
nod nod
Yes.
rustle
YOU KNOW, I HEARD FROM THE PUBLISHER THAT THE AUTHOR OF THESE BOOKS LIVES IN THE AREA.
HOW ABOUT THAT?
A LOCAL AUTHOR! MAYBE THEY CAN COME AND DO A SIGNING FOR US.
文庫フェア
...OH, SORRY TO RAMBLE.
HERE YOU GO.
THANK YOU VERY MUCH. PLEASE COME AGAIN.

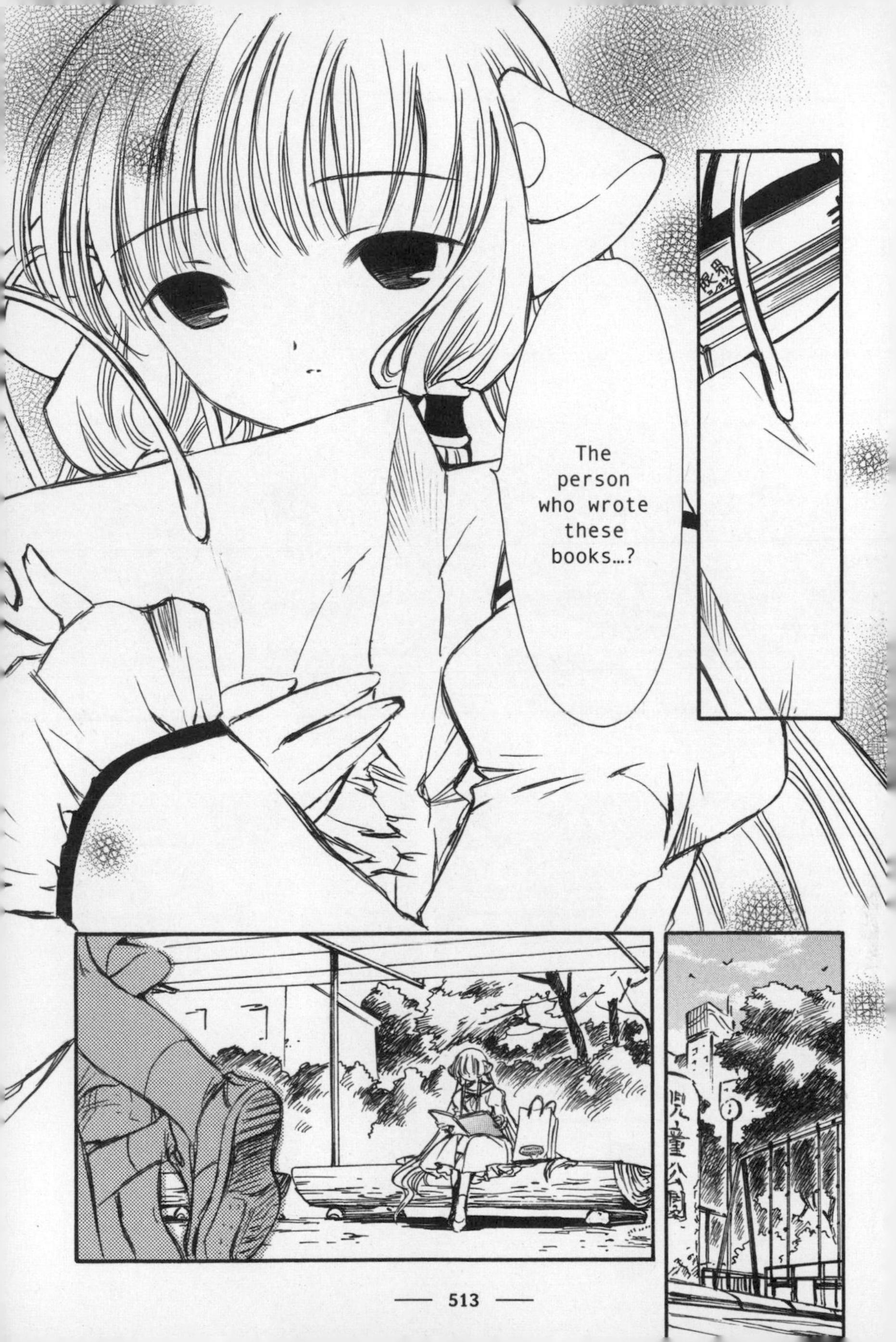
The person who wrote these books...?

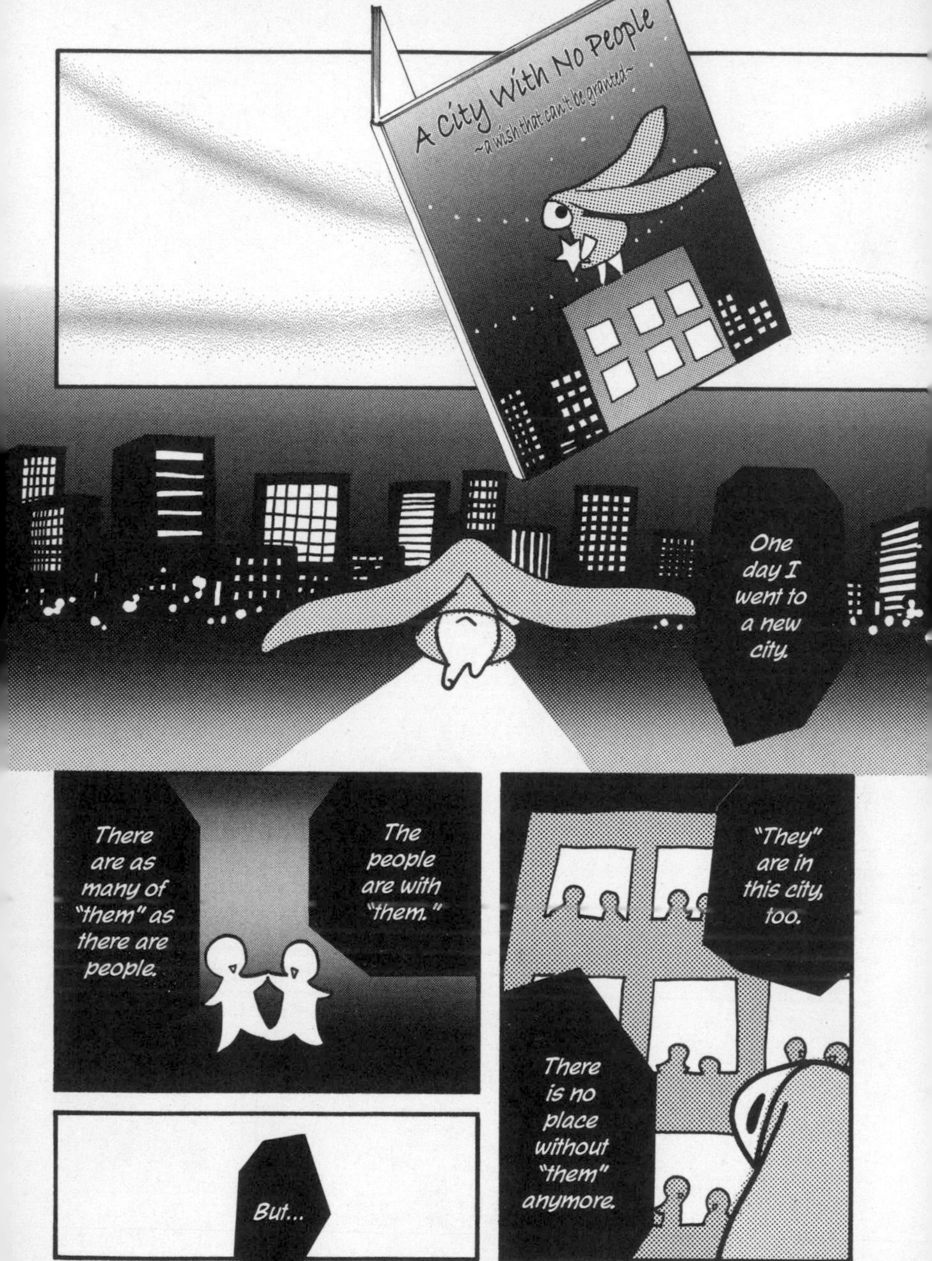
A City With No People
~a wish that can't be granted~
One day I went to a new city.
"They" are in this city, too.
There is no place without "them" anymore.
The people are with "them."
There are as many of "them" as there are people.
But...

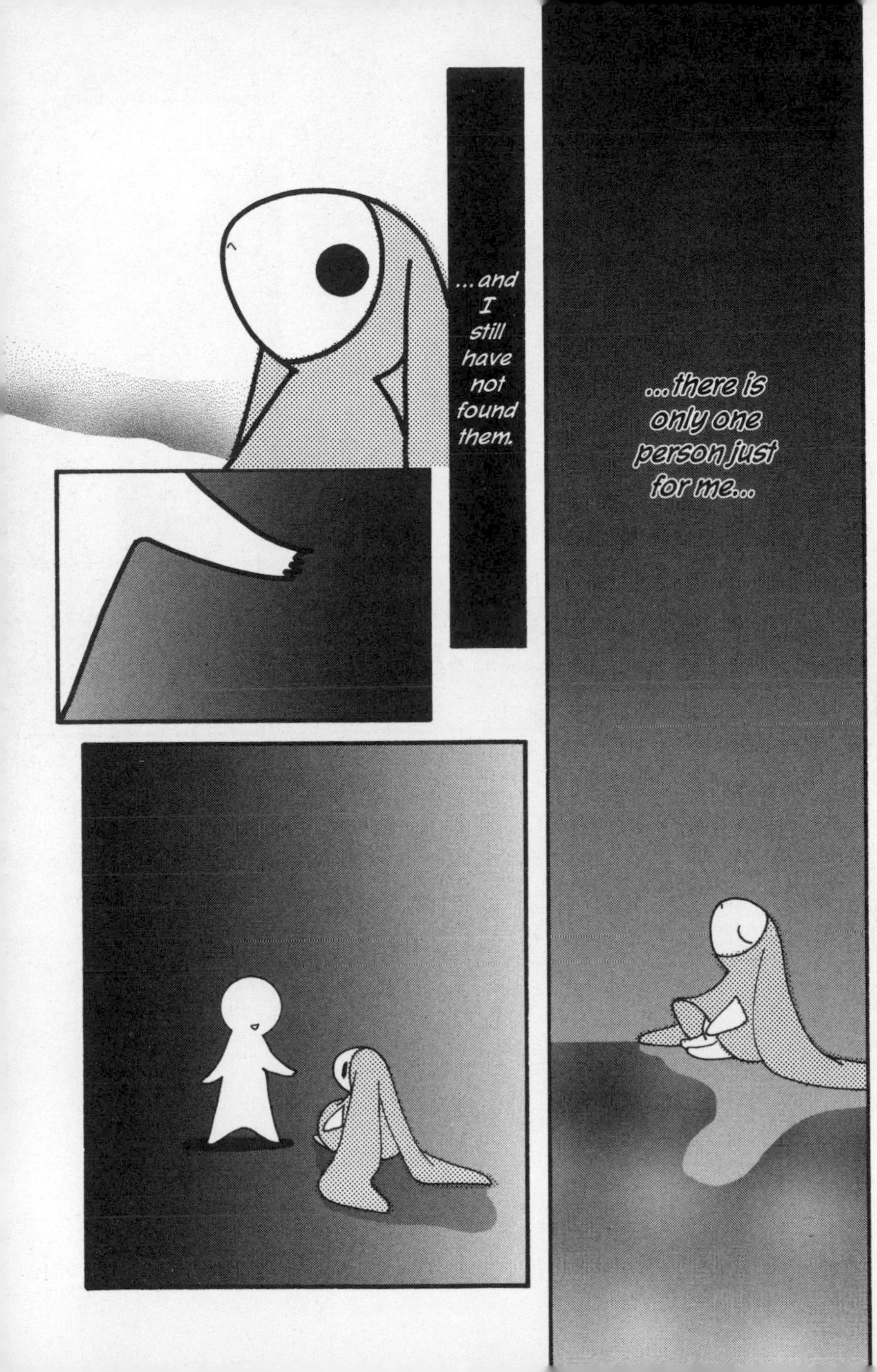
...there is only one person just for me...
...and I still have not found them.

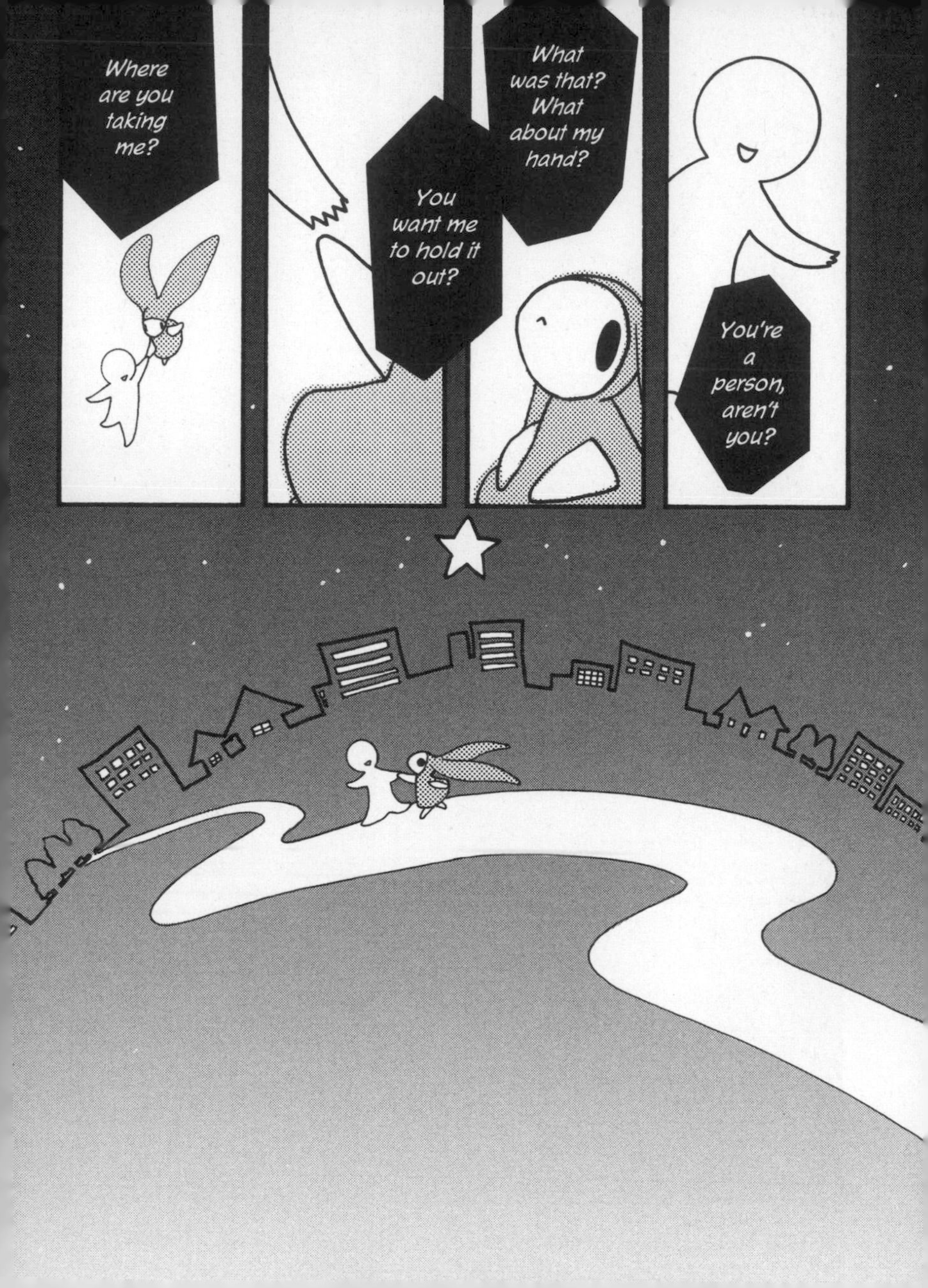
You're a person, aren't you?
What was that? What about my hand?
You want me to hold it out?
Where are you taking me?

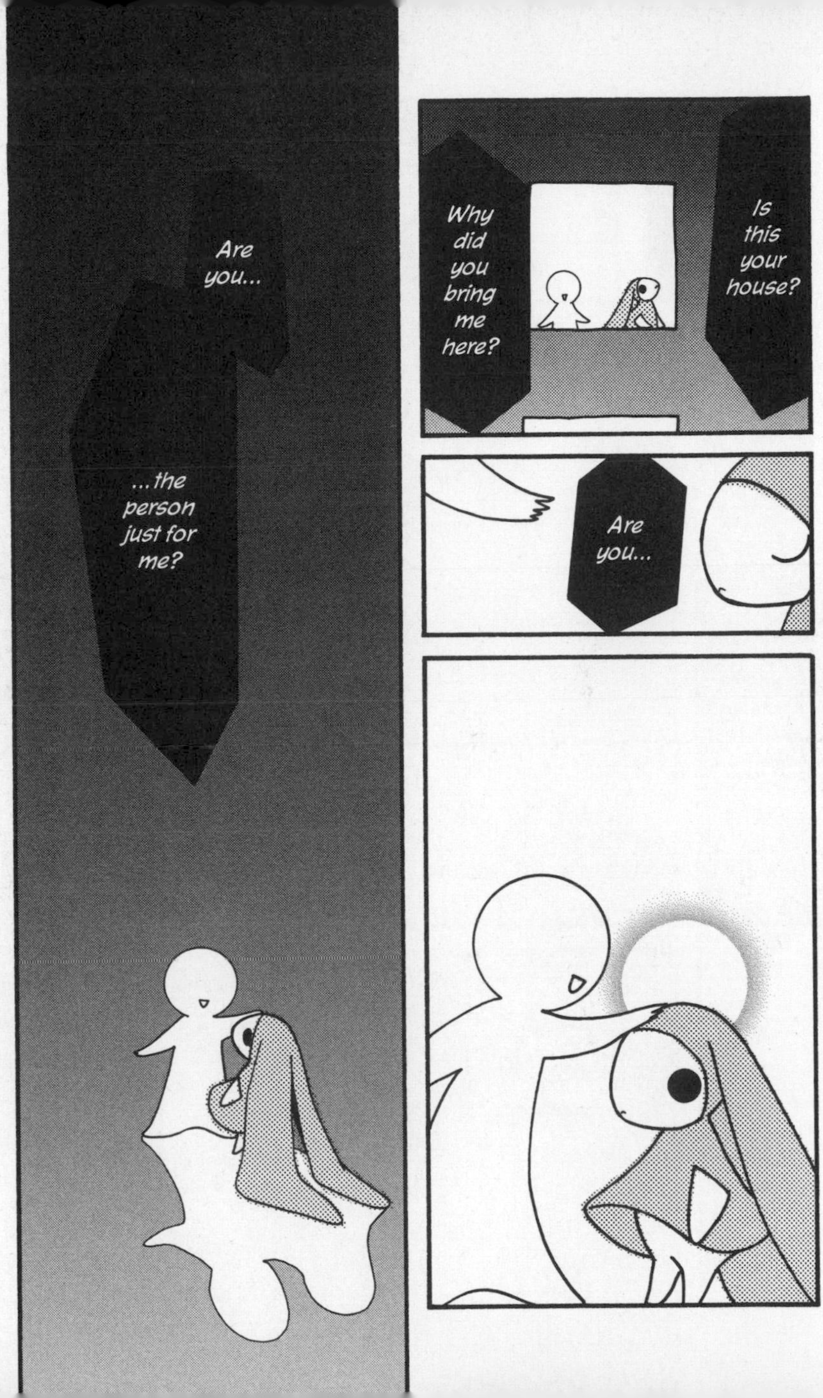
Is this your house?
Why did you bring me here?
Are you...
Are you...
...the person just for me?

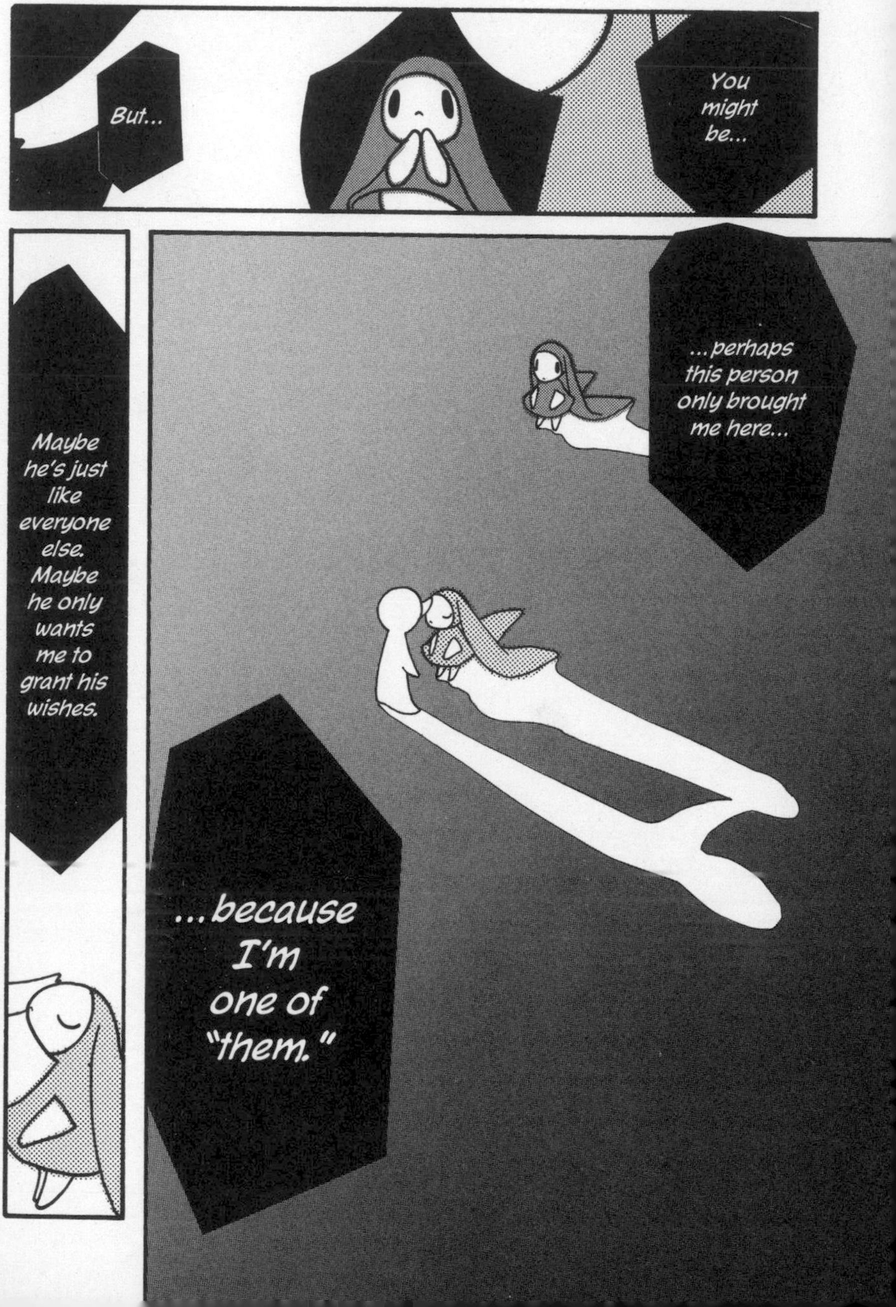
You might be...
But...
...perhaps this person only brought me here...
...because I'm one of "them."
Maybe he's just like everyone else. Maybe he only wants me to grant his wishes.

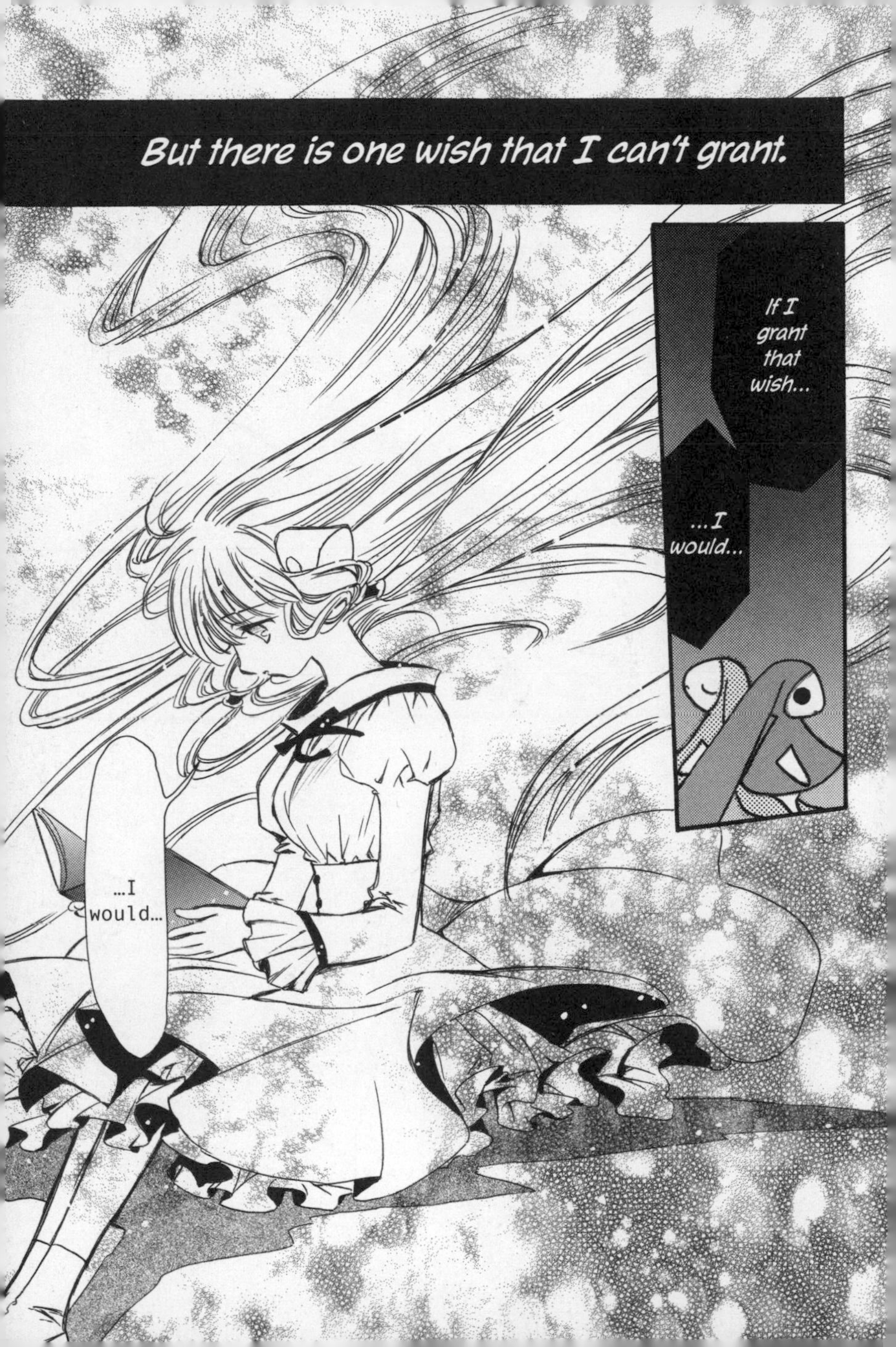
But there is one wish that I can't grant.
If I grant that wish...
...I would...
...I would...

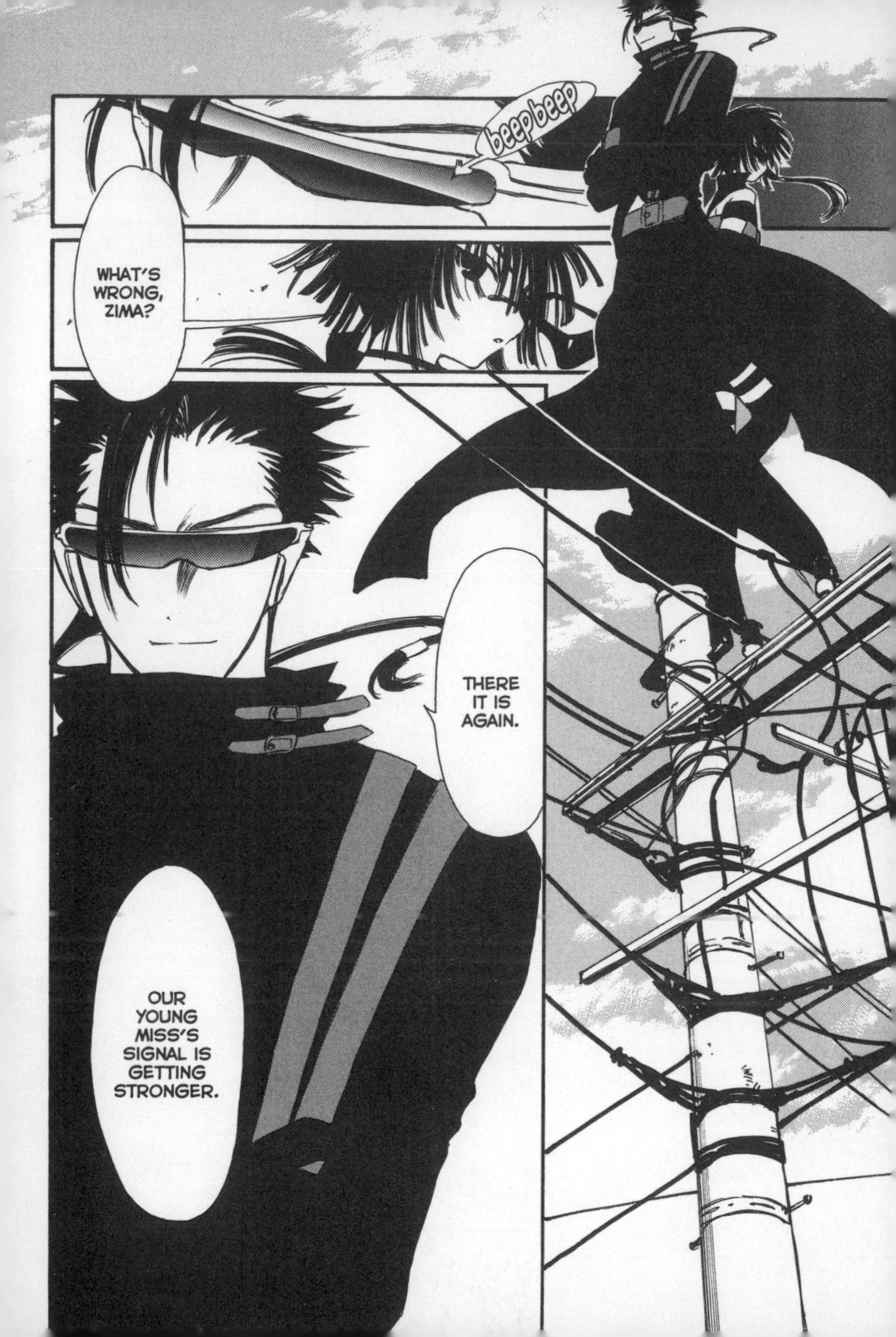
beep beep
WHAT'S WRONG, ZIMA?
THERE IT IS AGAIN.
OUR YOUNG MISS'S SIGNAL IS GETTING STRONGER.

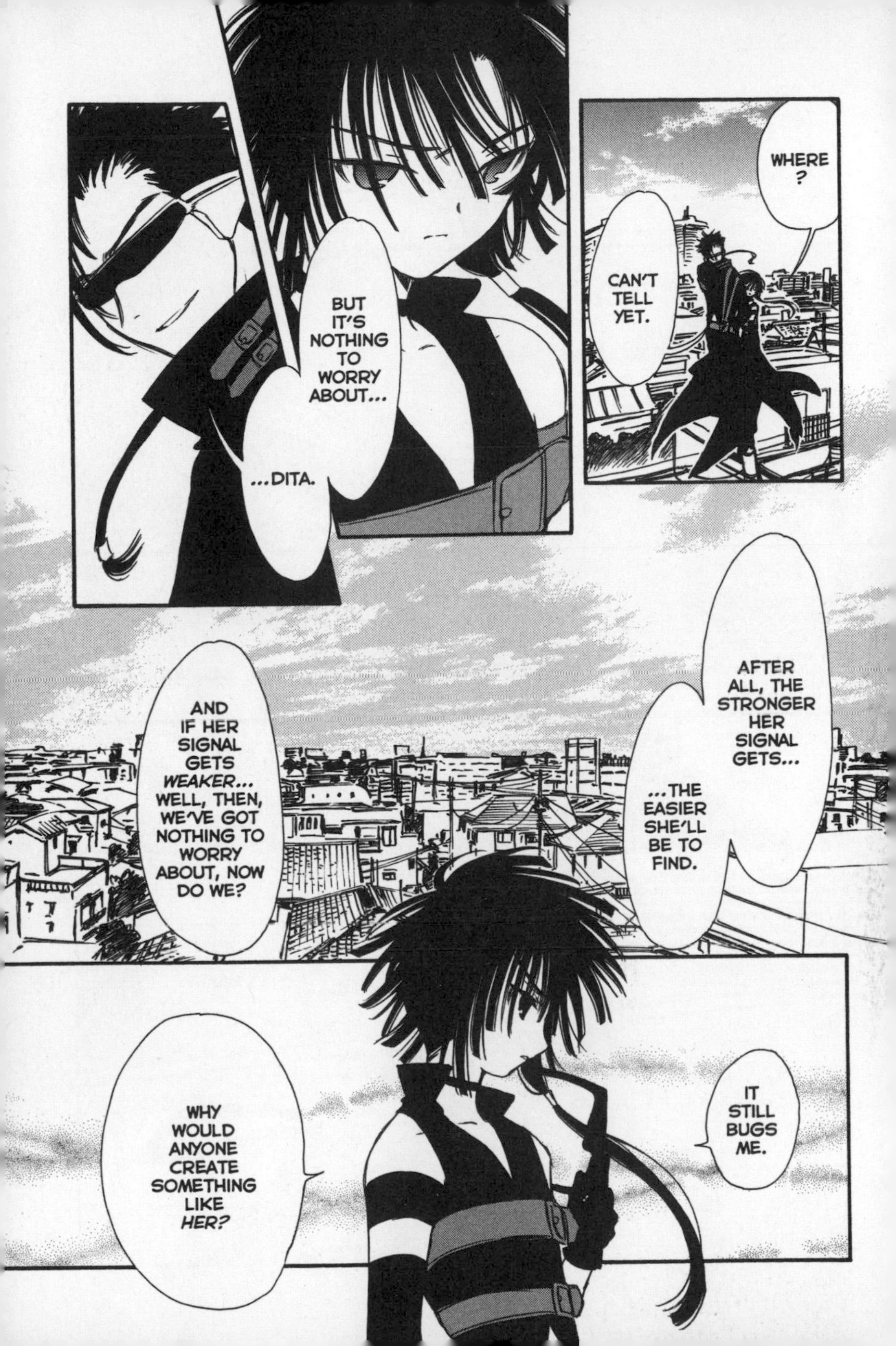
WHERE?
CAN'T TELL YET.
BUT IT'S NOTHING TO WORRY ABOUT...
...DITA.
AFTER ALL, THE STRONGER HER SIGNAL GETS...
...THE EASIER SHE'LL BE TO FIND.
AND IF HER SIGNAL GETS *WEAKER*... WELL, THEN, WE'VE GOT NOTHING TO WORRY ABOUT, NOW DO WE?
IT STILL BUGS ME.
WHY WOULD ANYONE CREATE SOMETHING LIKE *HER*?

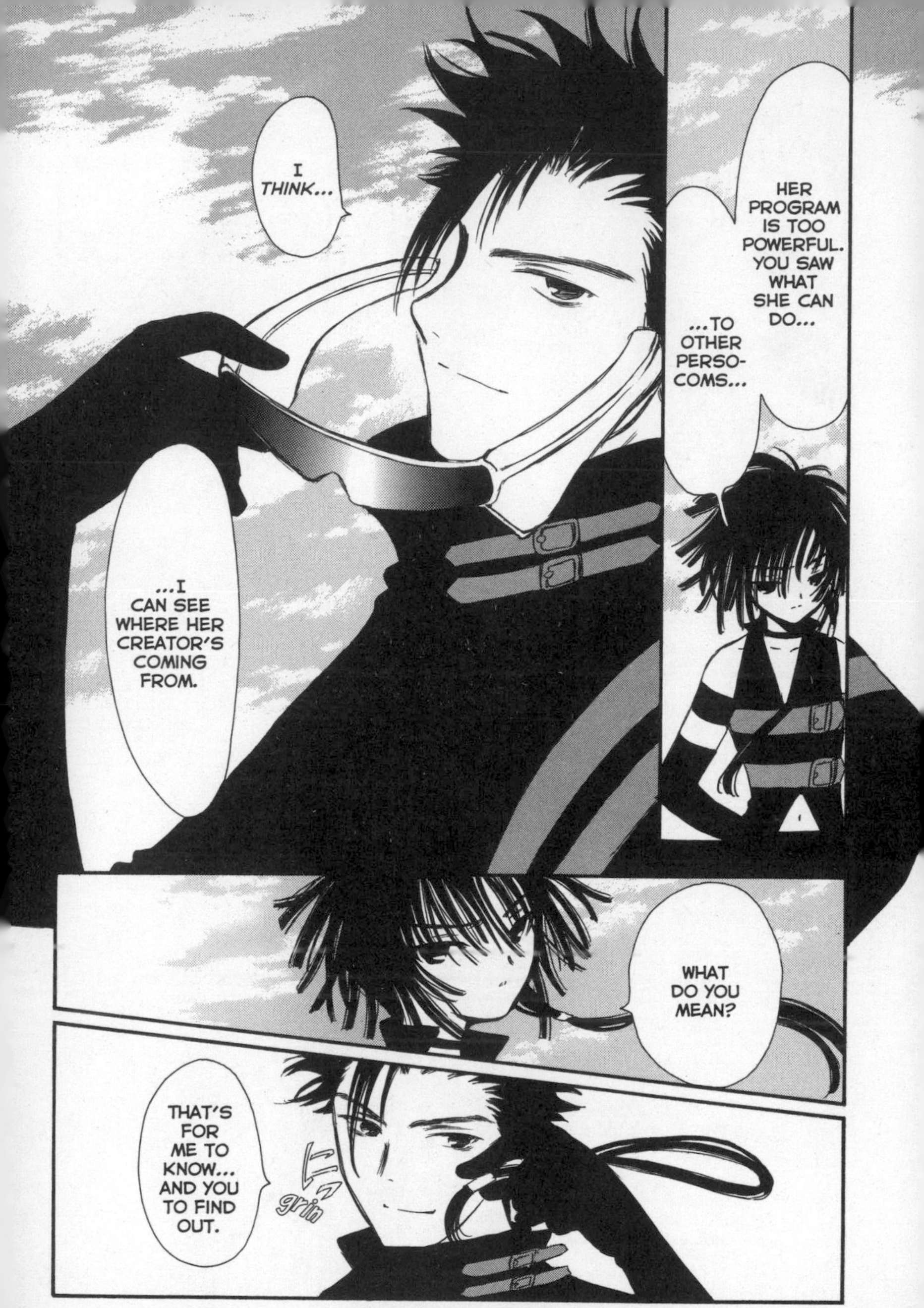

HER PROGRAM IS TOO POWERFUL. YOU SAW WHAT SHE CAN DO...
...TO OTHER PERSOCOMS...
I THINK...
...I CAN SEE WHERE HER CREATOR'S COMING FROM.
WHAT DO YOU MEAN?
THAT'S FOR ME TO KNOW... AND YOU TO FIND OUT.
grin

Chobits
ちょびっツ

◄ chapter 35 ►

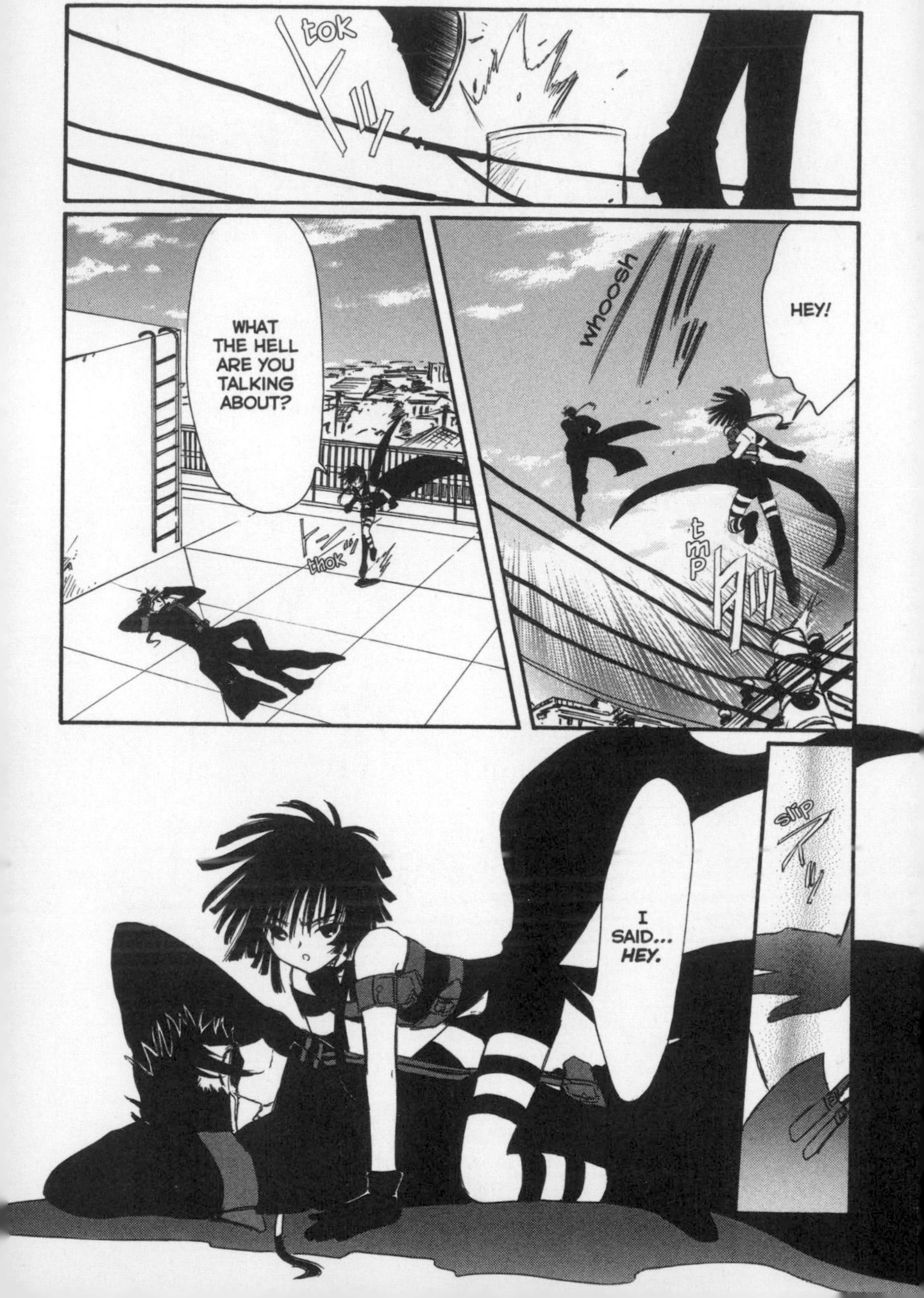
tok
HEY!
whoosh
tmp
WHAT THE HELL ARE YOU TALKING ABOUT?
thok
slip
I SAID... HEY.

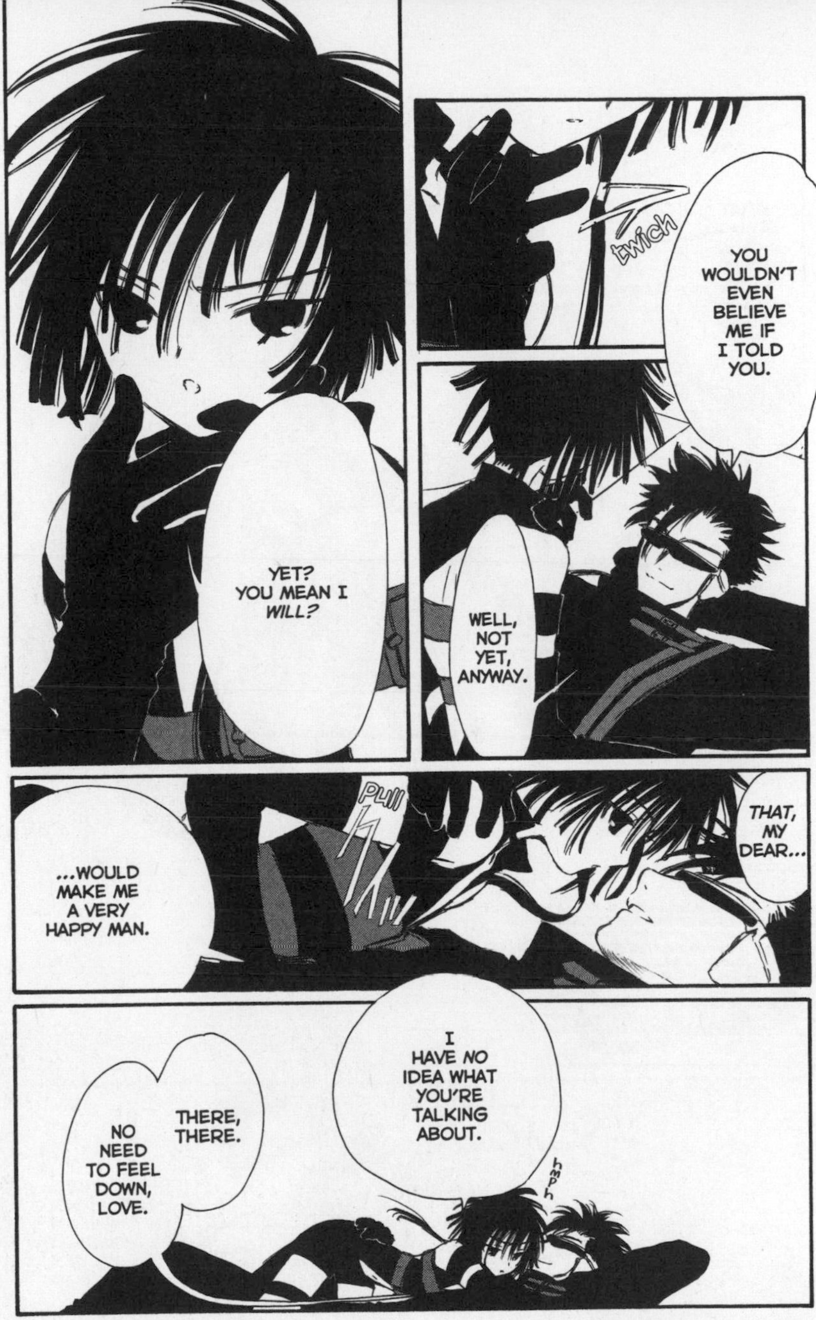
twich
YOU WOULDN'T EVEN BELIEVE ME IF I TOLD YOU.
WELL, NOT YET, ANYWAY.
YET? YOU MEAN I *WILL?*
THAT, MY DEAR...
PULL
...WOULD MAKE ME A VERY HAPPY MAN.
I HAVE *NO* IDEA WHAT YOU'RE TALKING ABOUT.
hmph
THERE, THERE.
NO NEED TO FEEL DOWN, LOVE.

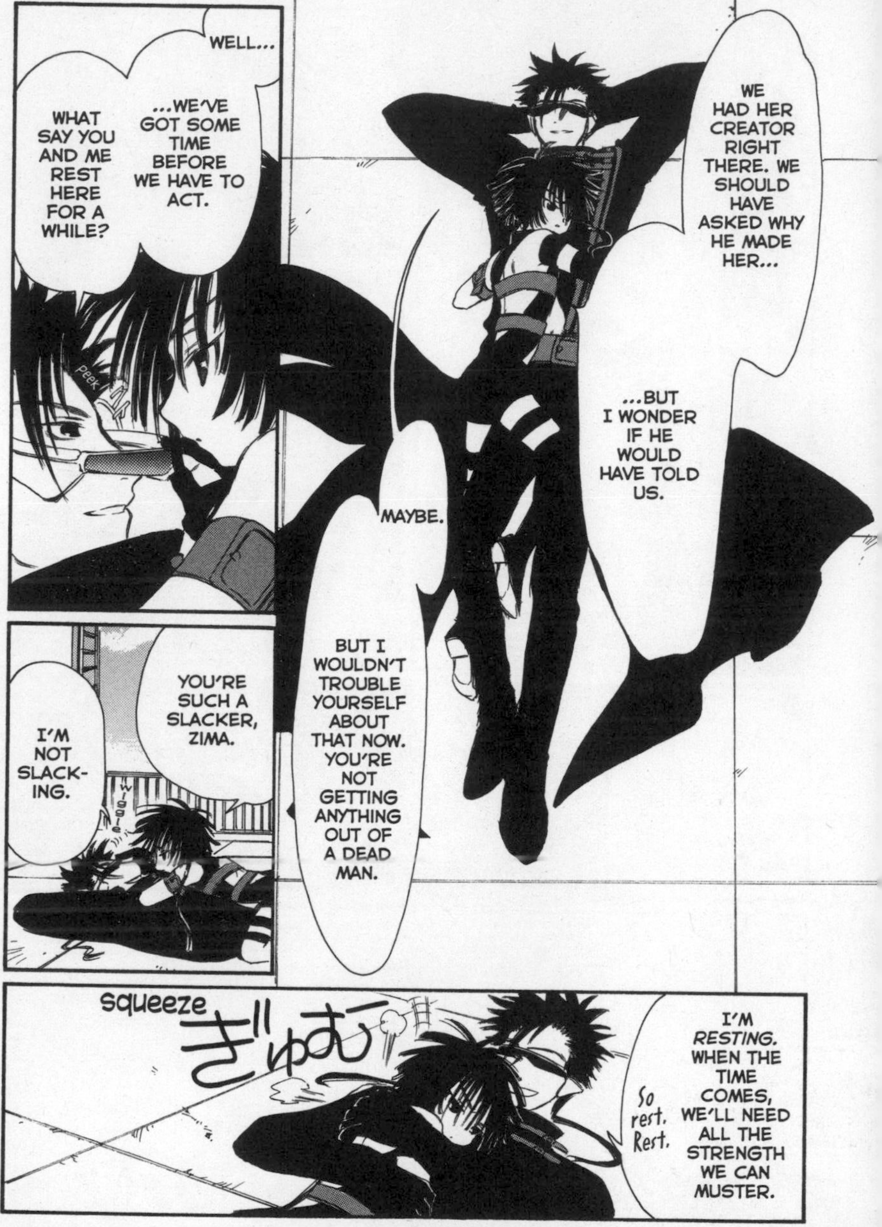

WE HAD HER CREATOR RIGHT THERE. WE SHOULD HAVE ASKED WHY HE MADE HER...
...BUT I WONDER IF HE WOULD HAVE TOLD US.
MAYBE.
BUT I WOULDN'T TROUBLE YOURSELF ABOUT THAT NOW. YOU'RE NOT GETTING ANYTHING OUT OF A DEAD MAN.
WELL...
...WE'VE GOT SOME TIME BEFORE WE HAVE TO ACT.
WHAT SAY YOU AND ME REST HERE FOR A WHILE?
peek
YOU'RE SUCH A SLACKER, ZIMA.
I'M NOT SLACKING.
wiggle
I'M *RESTING.* WHEN THE TIME COMES, WE'LL NEED ALL THE STRENGTH WE CAN MUSTER.
So rest. Rest.
squeeze
ぎゅむ～

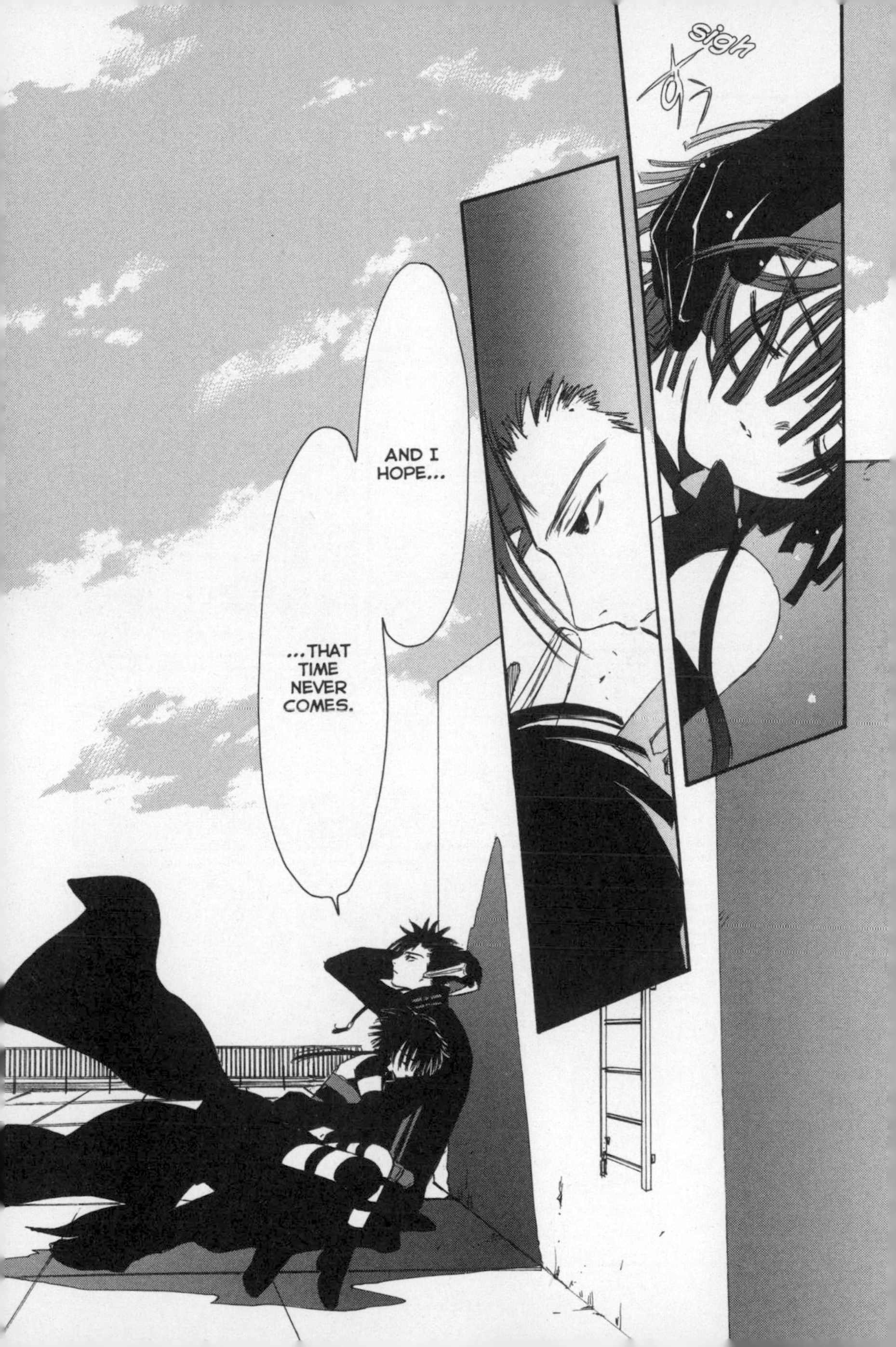
sigh
AND I HOPE...
...THAT TIME NEVER COMES.

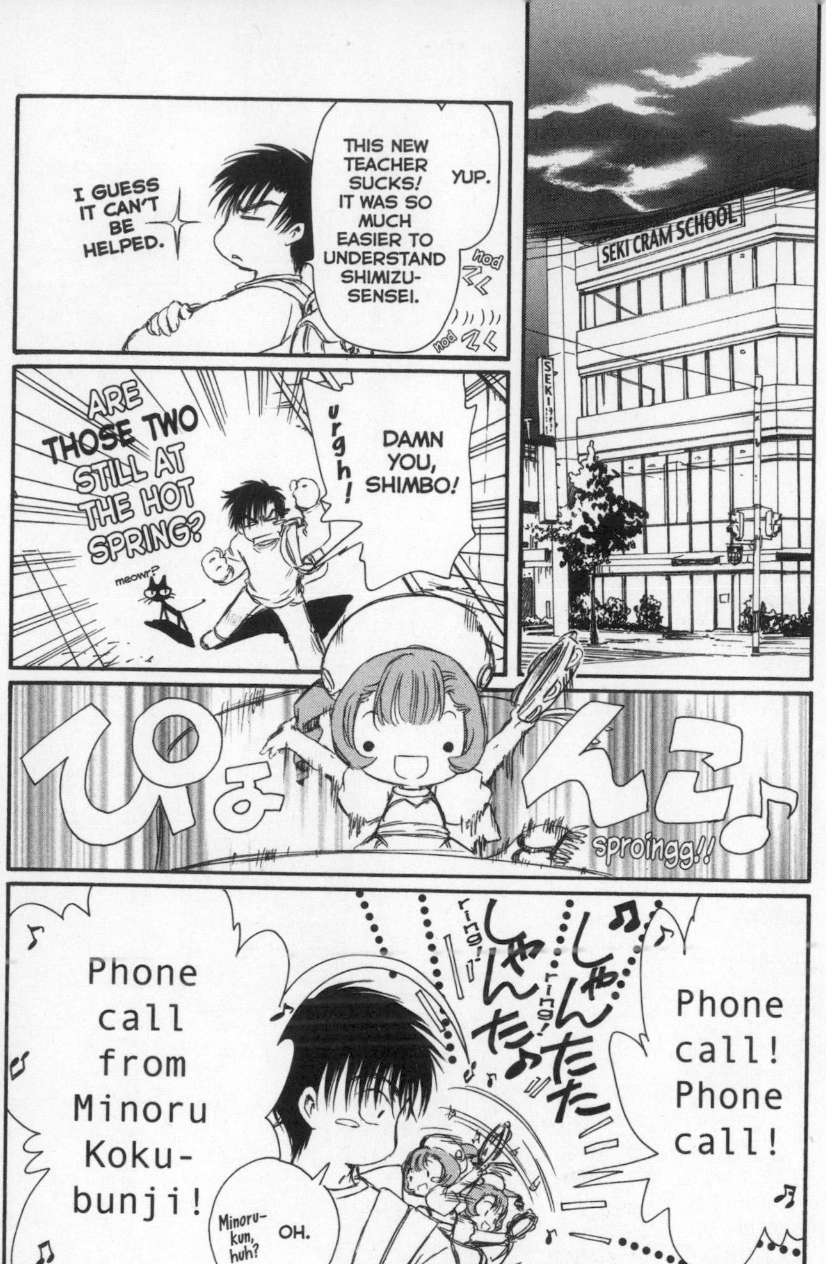
SEKI CRAM SCHOOL
SEKI
THIS NEW TEACHER SUCKS! IT WAS SO MUCH EASIER TO UNDERSTAND SHIMIZU-SENSEI.
YUP.
nod こく
nod こく
I GUESS IT CAN'T BE HELPED.
urgh!
DAMN YOU, SHIMBO!
ARE THOSE TWO STILL AT THE HOT SPRING?
meowr?
ぴょんこ♪
sproingg!!
Phone call! Phone call!
じゃんたた
ring! ring!
しゃんた♪
Phone call from Minoru Kokubunji!
OH.
Minoru-kun, huh?

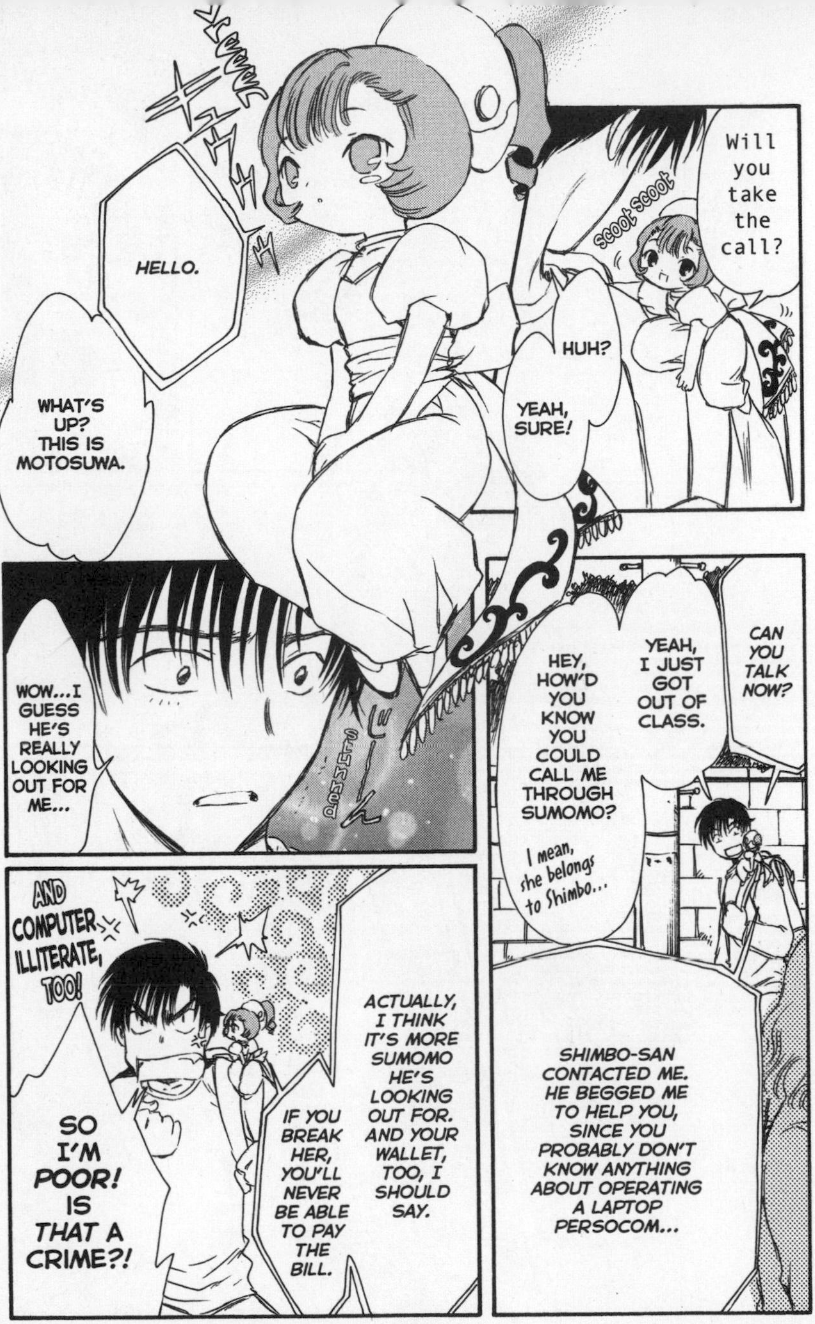
Will you take the call?
scoot scoot
HUH?
YEAH, SURE!
HELLO.
WHAT'S UP? THIS IS MOTOSUWA.
CAN YOU TALK NOW?
YEAH, I JUST GOT OUT OF CLASS.
HEY, HOW'D YOU KNOW YOU COULD CALL ME THROUGH SUMOMO?
I mean, she belongs to Shimbo...
WOW...I GUESS HE'S REALLY LOOKING OUT FOR ME...
SHIMBO-SAN CONTACTED ME. HE BEGGED ME TO HELP YOU, SINCE YOU PROBABLY DON'T KNOW ANYTHING ABOUT OPERATING A LAPTOP PERSOCOM...
ACTUALLY, I THINK IT'S MORE SUMOMO HE'S LOOKING OUT FOR. AND YOUR WALLET, TOO, I SHOULD SAY.
IF YOU BREAK HER, YOU'LL NEVER BE ABLE TO PAY THE BILL.
SO I'M POOR! IS THAT A CRIME?!
AND COMPUTER ILLITERATE, TOO!

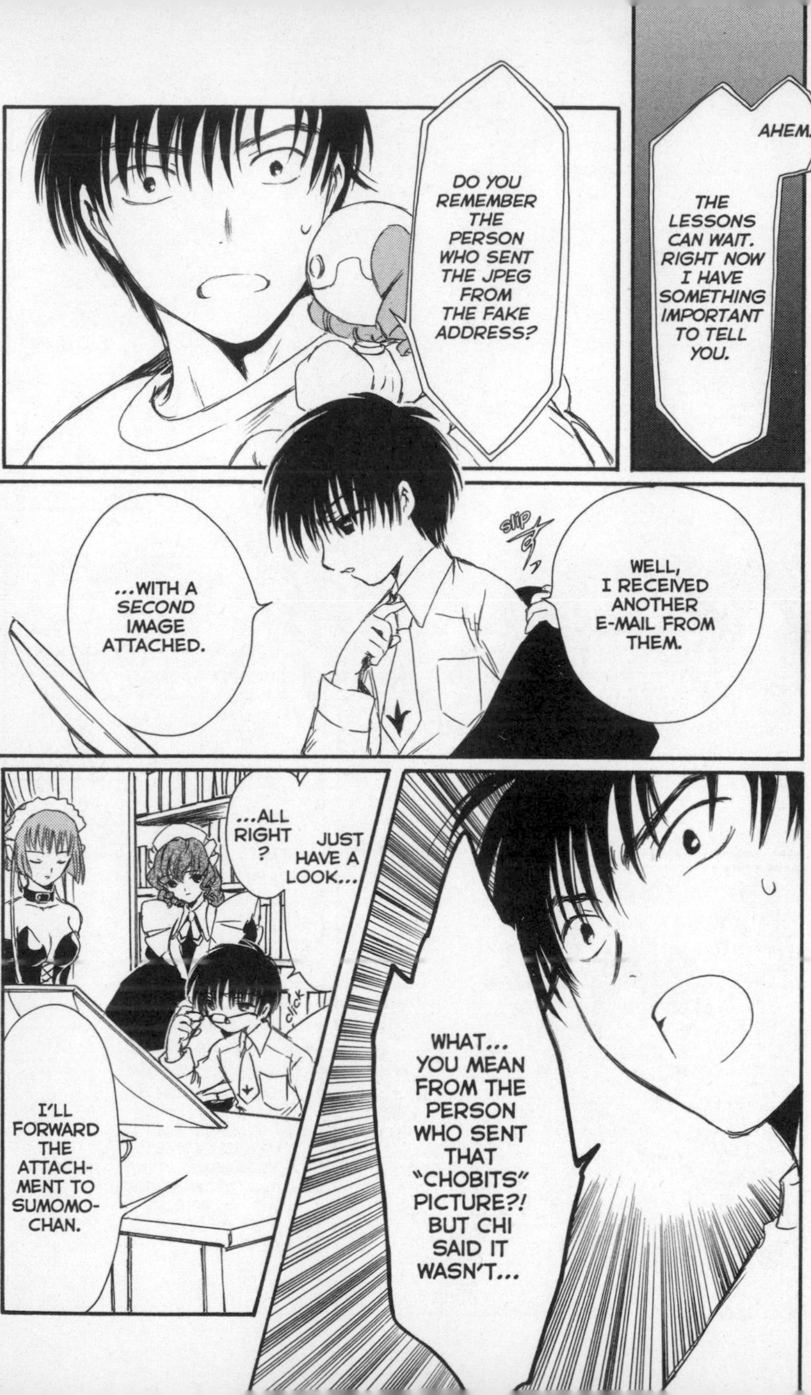
AHEM.
THE LESSONS CAN WAIT. RIGHT NOW I HAVE SOMETHING IMPORTANT TO TELL YOU.
DO YOU REMEMBER THE PERSON WHO SENT THE JPEG FROM THE FAKE ADDRESS?
slip
WELL, I RECEIVED ANOTHER E-MAIL FROM THEM.
...WITH A SECOND IMAGE ATTACHED.
WHAT... YOU MEAN FROM THE PERSON WHO SENT THAT "CHOBITS" PICTURE?! BUT CHI SAID IT WASN'T...
JUST HAVE A LOOK...
...ALL RIGHT?
click
I'LL FORWARD THE ATTACHMENT TO SUMOMO-CHAN.

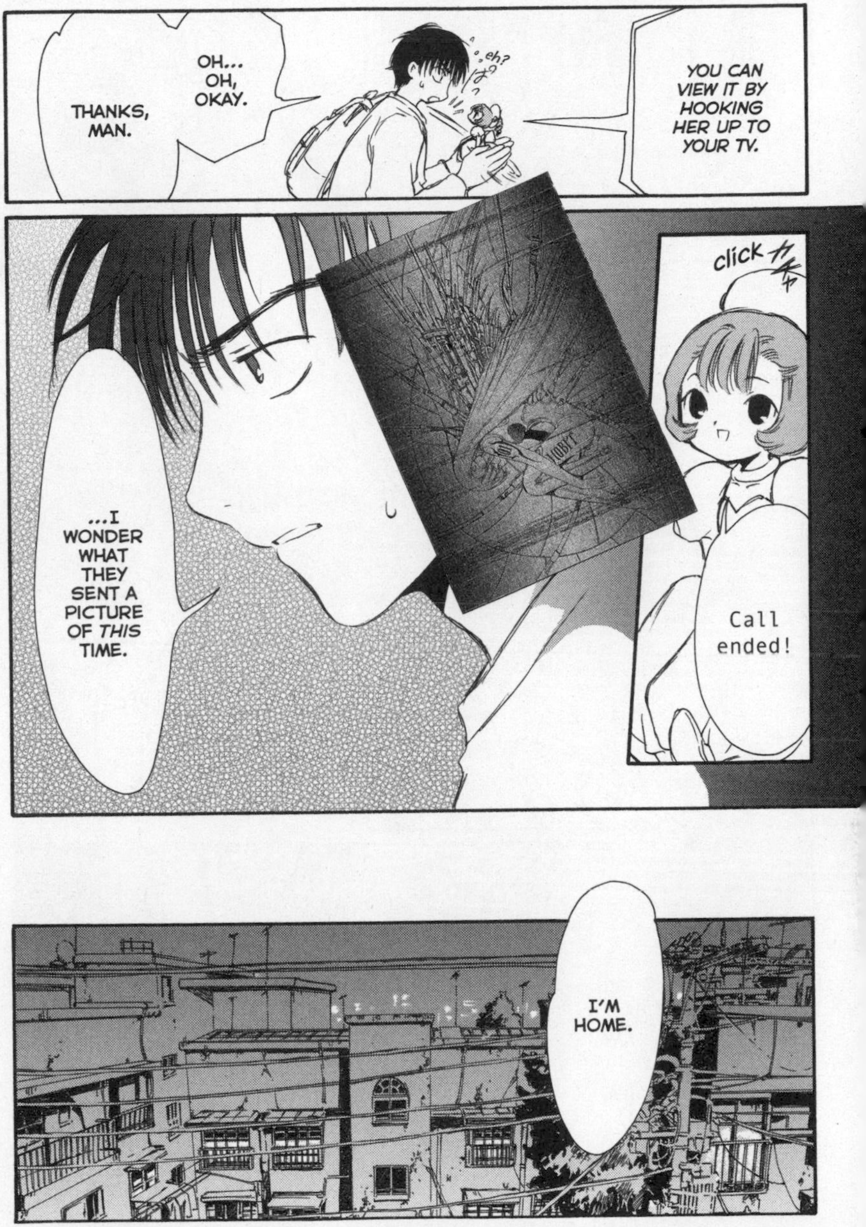
YOU CAN VIEW IT BY HOOKING HER UP TO YOUR TV.
eh?
OH... OH, OKAY.
THANKS, MAN.
click
Call ended!
...I WONDER WHAT THEY SENT A PICTURE OF *THIS* TIME.
I'M HOME.

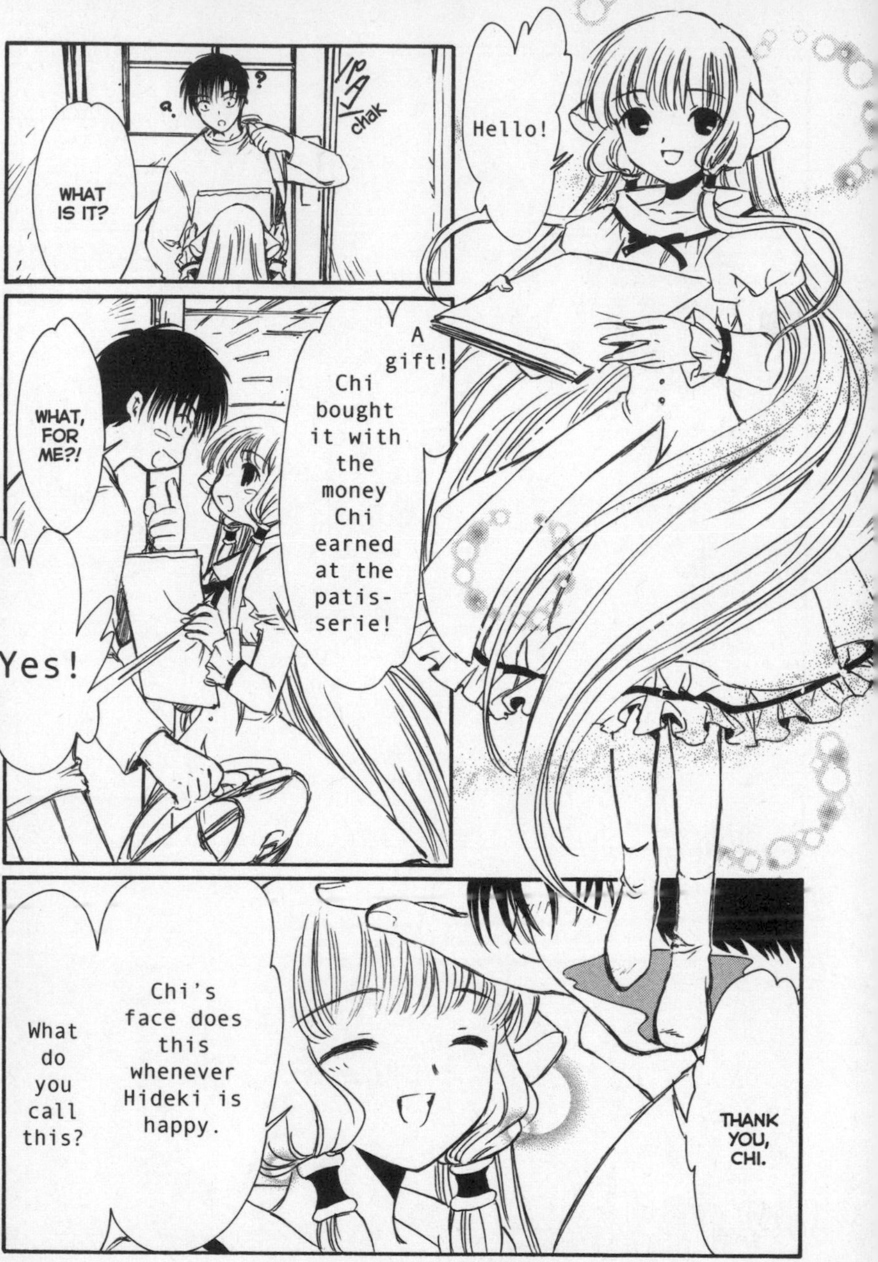
Hello!
chak
WHAT IS IT?
A gift! Chi bought it with the money Chi earned at the patis-serie!
WHAT, FOR ME?!
Yes!
THANK YOU, CHI.
Chi's face does this whenever Hideki is happy.
What do you call this?

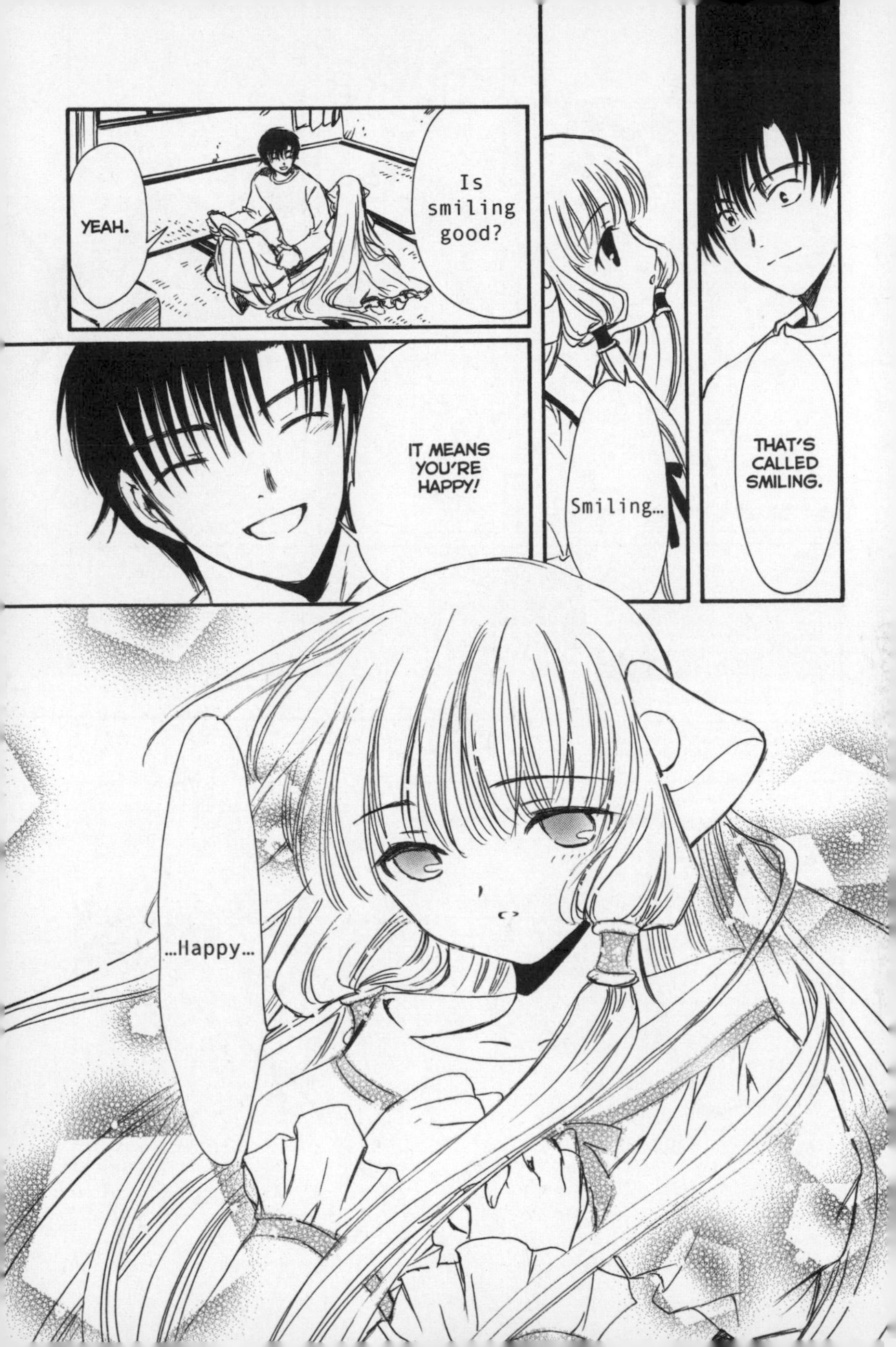
THAT'S CALLED SMILING.
Smiling...
Is smiling good?
YEAH.
IT MEANS YOU'RE HAPPY!
...Happy...

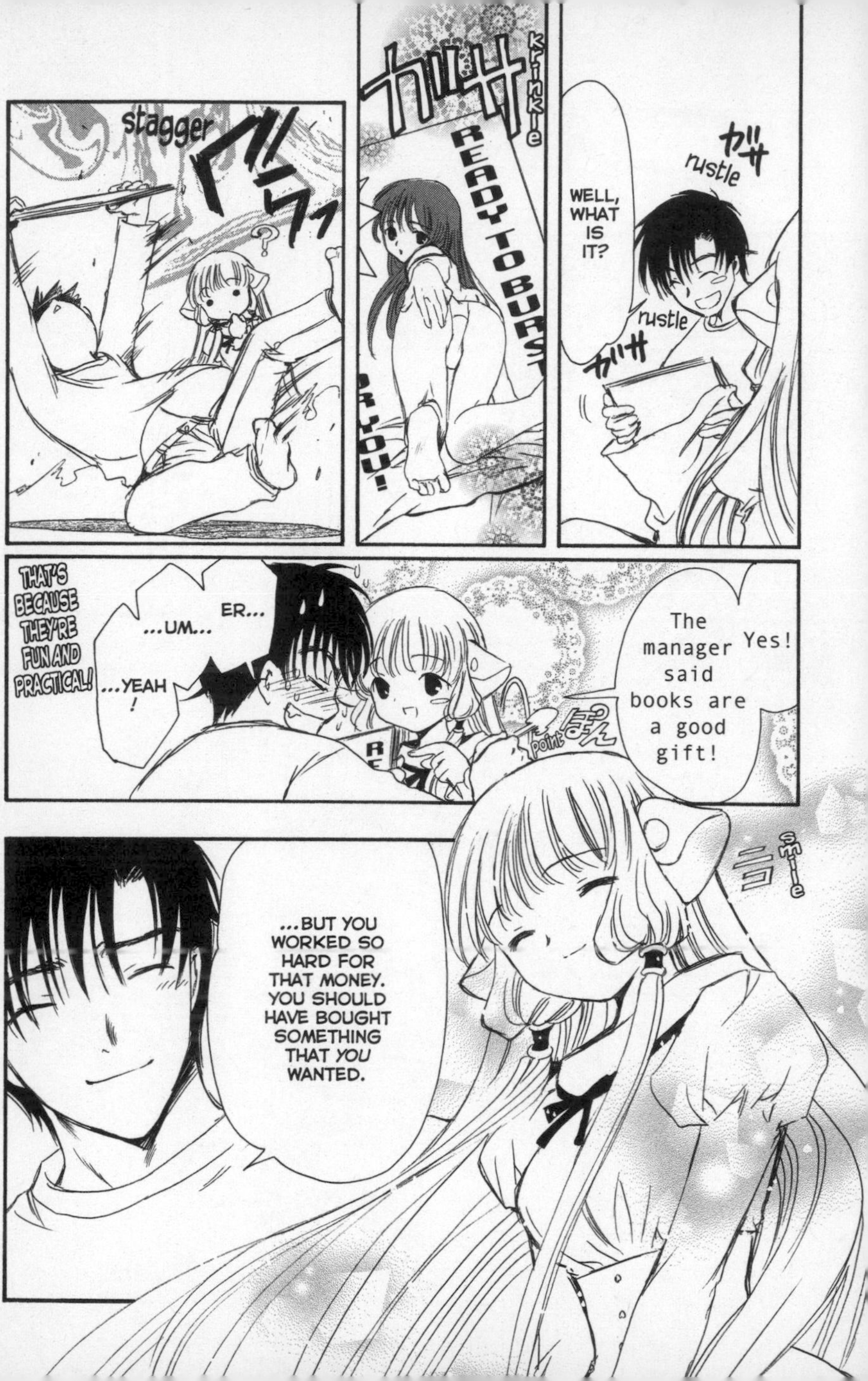
rustle
WELL, WHAT IS IT?
rustle
krinkle
READY TO BURST
OR YOU!
stagger
Yes! The manager said books are a good gift!
point
ER...
...UM...
...YEAH!
THAT'S BECAUSE THEY'RE FUN AND PRACTICAL!
smile
...BUT YOU WORKED SO HARD FOR THAT MONEY. YOU SHOULD HAVE BOUGHT SOMETHING THAT YOU WANTED.

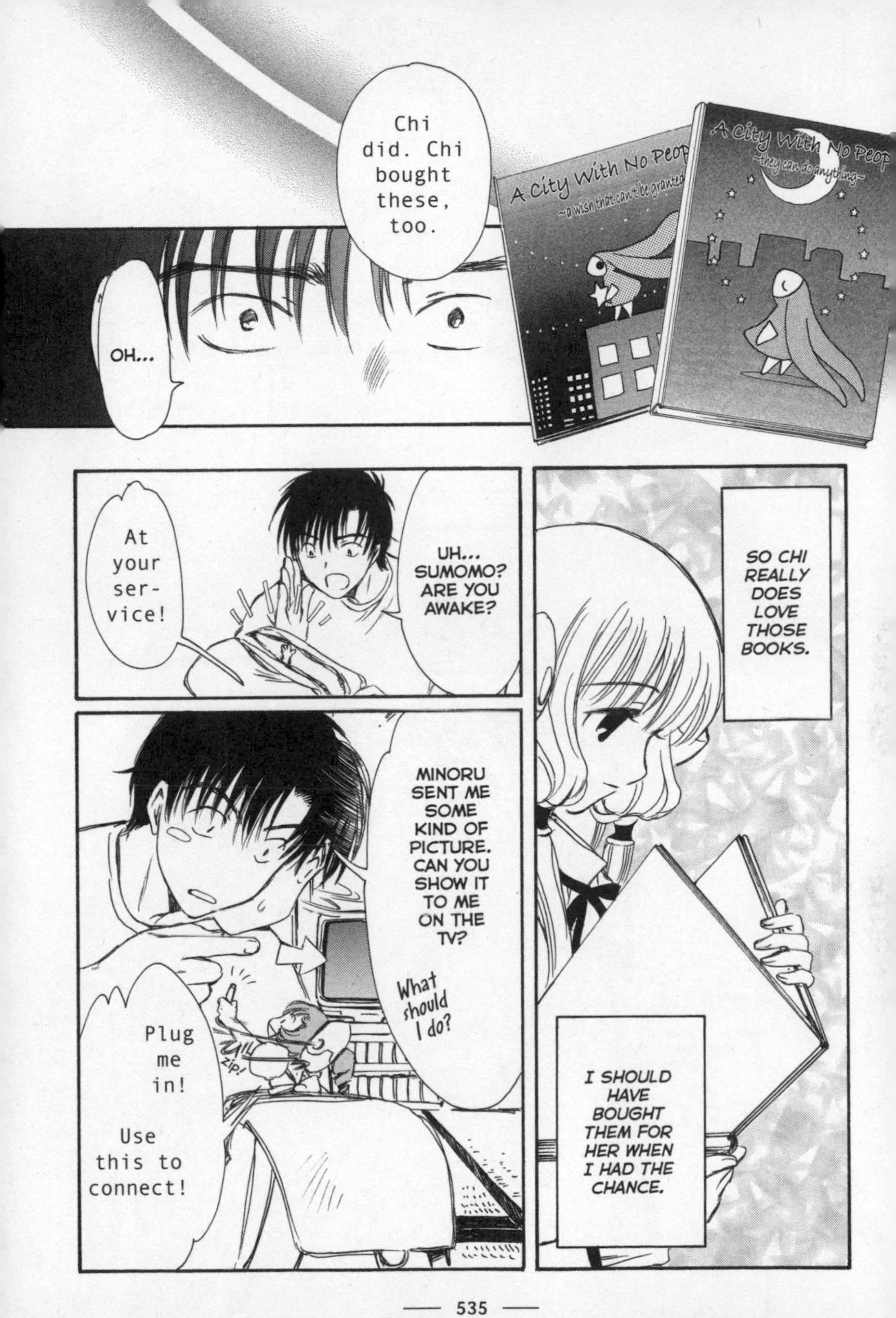

Chi did. Chi bought these, too.
A City With No Peop
~they can do anything~
A City With No Peop
~a wish that can't be granted
OH...
SO CHI REALLY DOES LOVE THOSE BOOKS.
I SHOULD HAVE BOUGHT THEM FOR HER WHEN I HAD THE CHANCE.
UH... SUMOMO? ARE YOU AWAKE?
At your ser-vice!
MINORU SENT ME SOME KIND OF PICTURE. CAN YOU SHOW IT TO ME ON THE TV?
What should I do?
Plug me in!
Use this to connect!
ZIP!

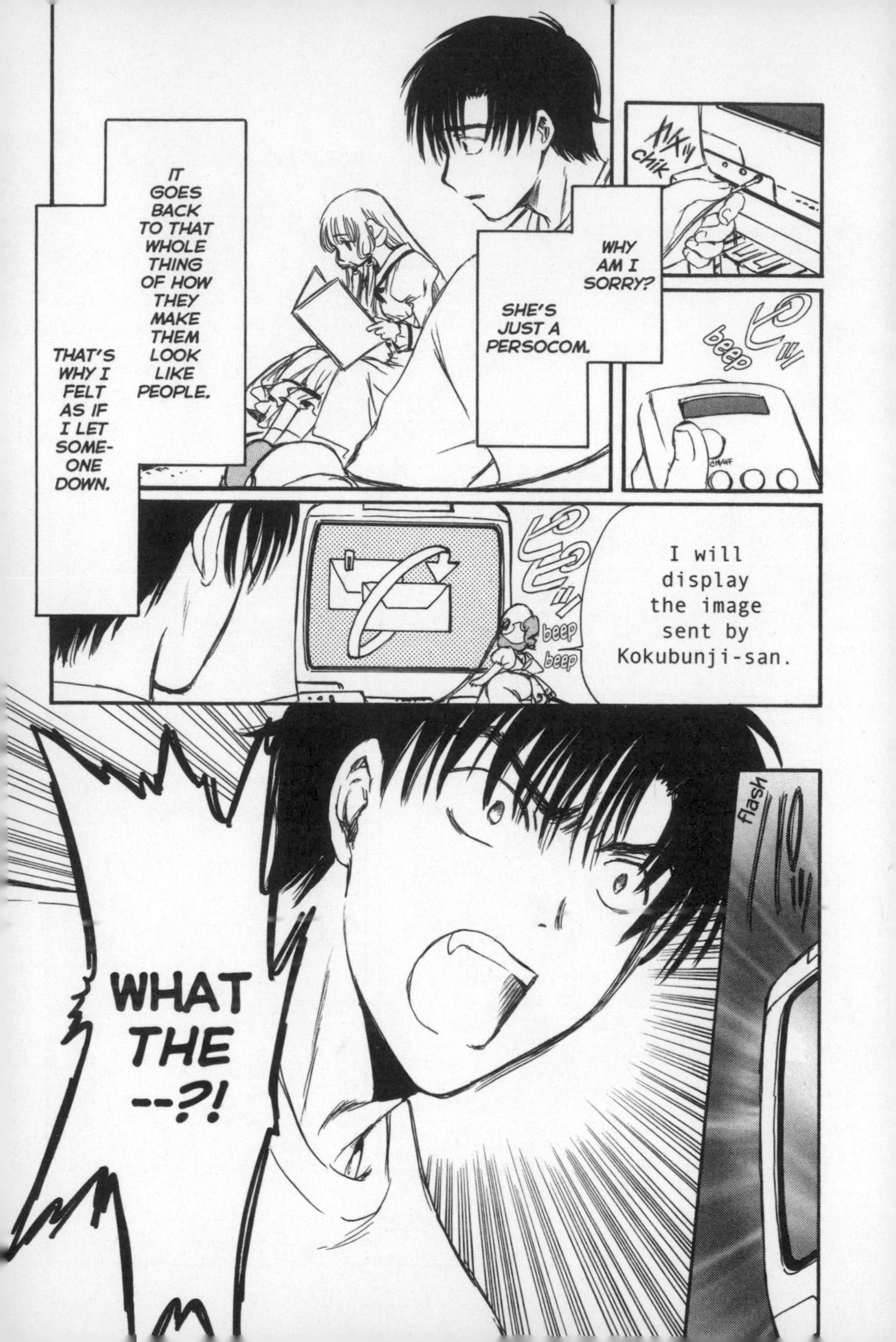
chik
beep
WHY AM I SORRY?
SHE'S JUST A PERSOCOM.
IT GOES BACK TO THAT WHOLE THING OF HOW THEY MAKE THEM LOOK LIKE PEOPLE.
THAT'S WHY I FELT AS IF I LET SOMEONE DOWN.
I will display the image sent by Kokubunji-san.
beep
beep
flash
WHAT THE --?!

Chobits
ちょびっツ

◀ **chapter 36** ▶

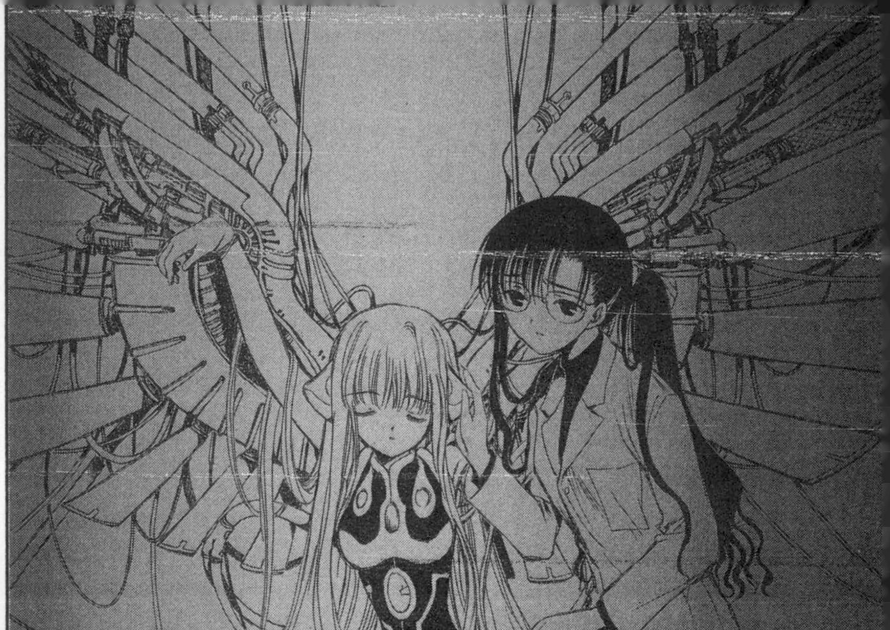

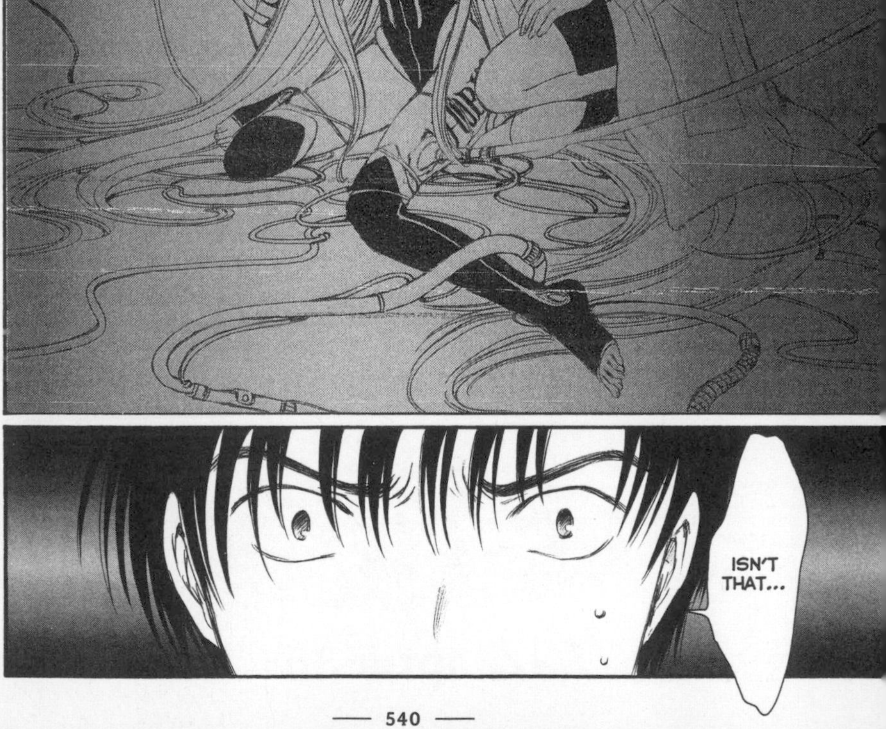
ISN'T THAT...

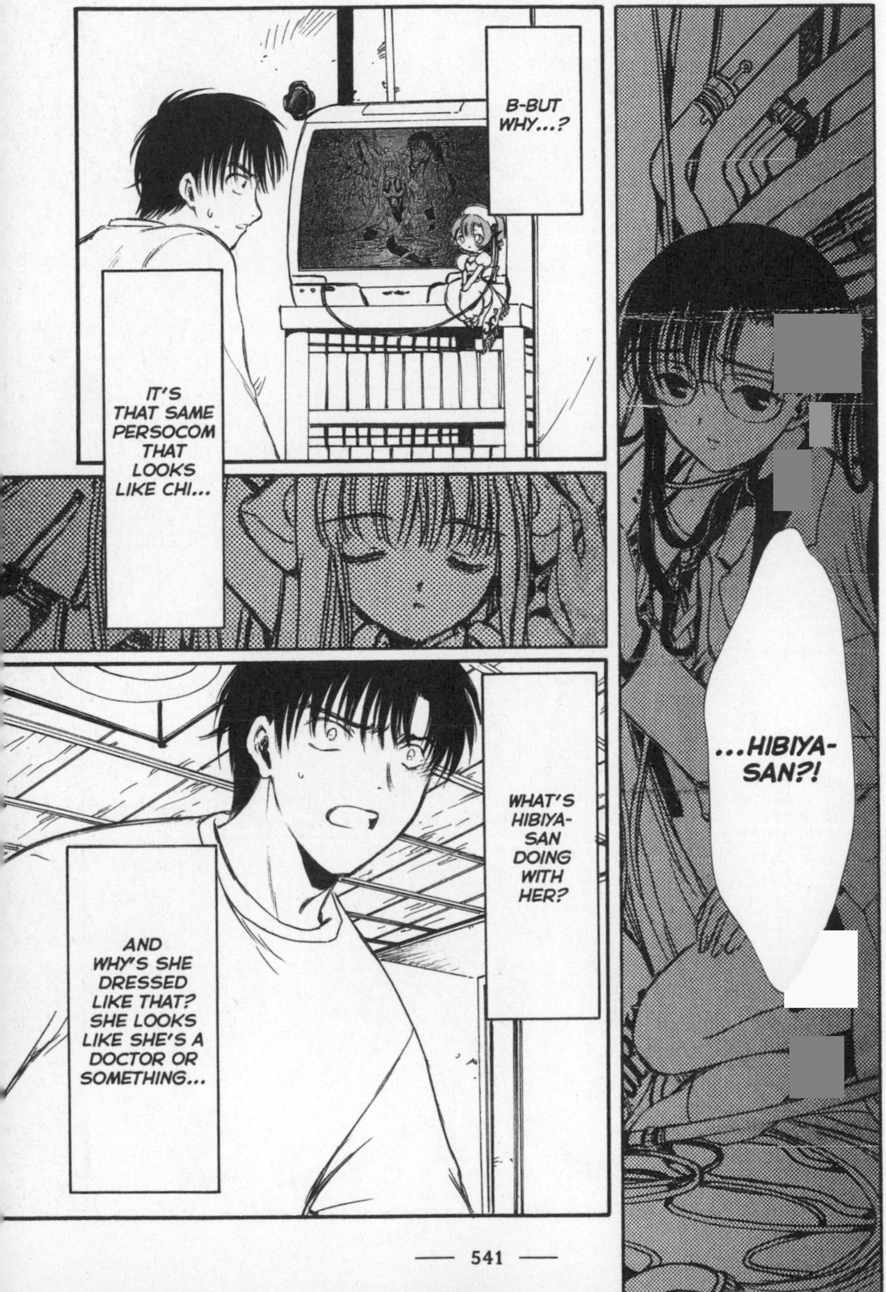

...HIBIYA-SAN?!
B-BUT WHY...?
IT'S THAT SAME PERSOCOM THAT LOOKS LIKE CHI...
WHAT'S HIBIYA-SAN DOING WITH HER?
AND WHY'S SHE DRESSED LIKE THAT? SHE LOOKS LIKE SHE'S A DOCTOR OR SOMETHING...

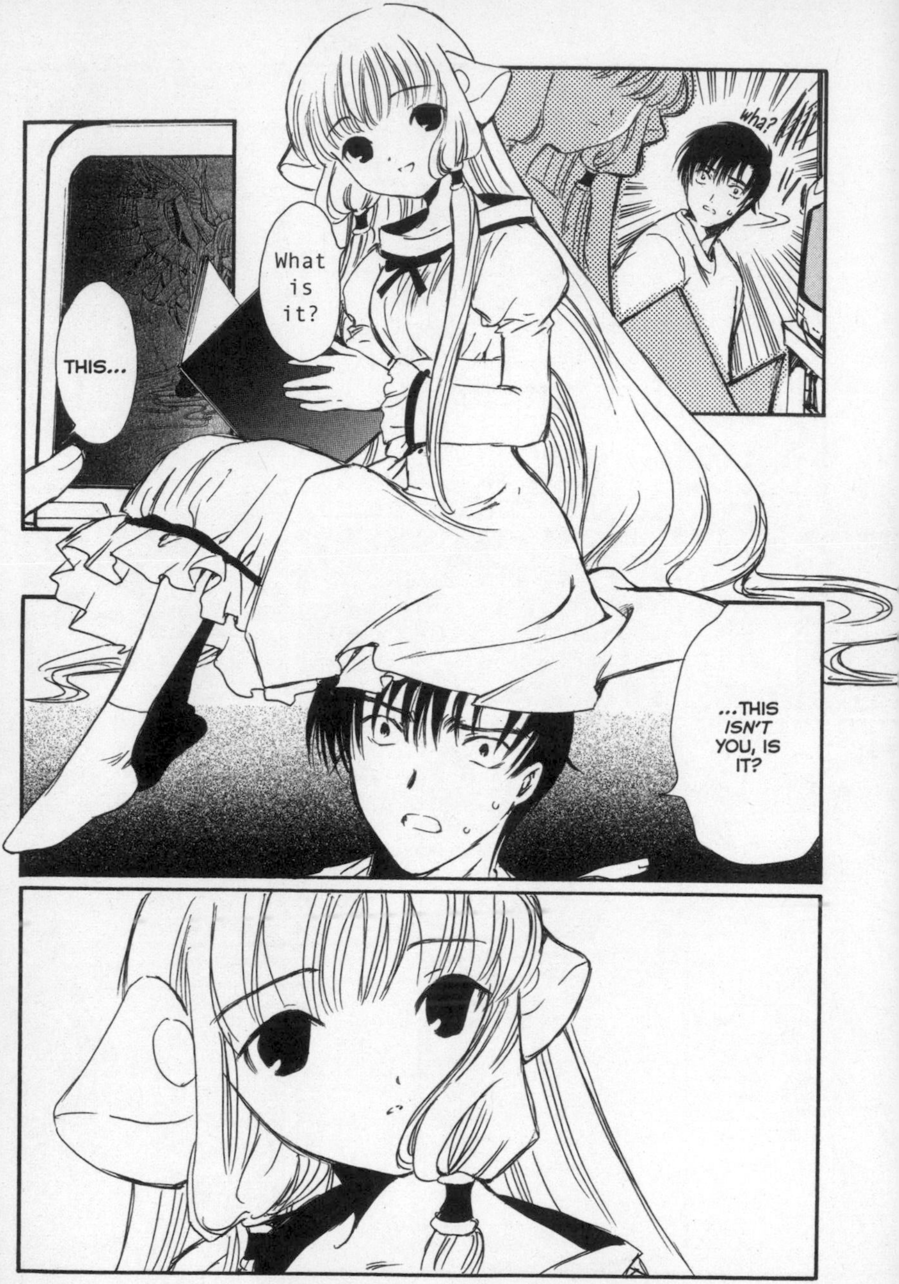
wha?
What is it?
THIS...
...THIS ISN'T YOU, IS IT?

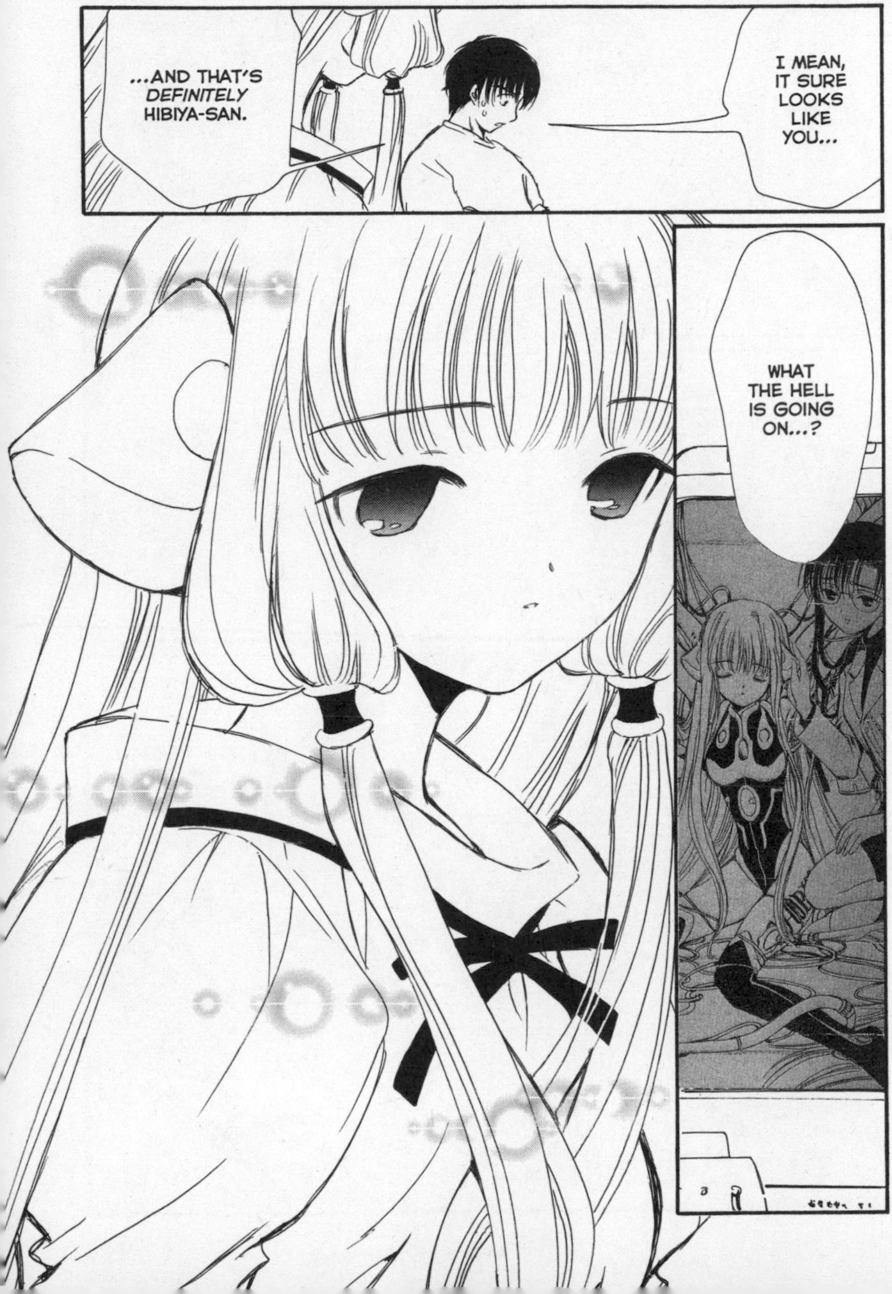
I MEAN, IT SURE LOOKS LIKE YOU...
...AND THAT'S *DEFINITELY* HIBIYA-SAN.
WHAT THE HELL IS GOING ON...?

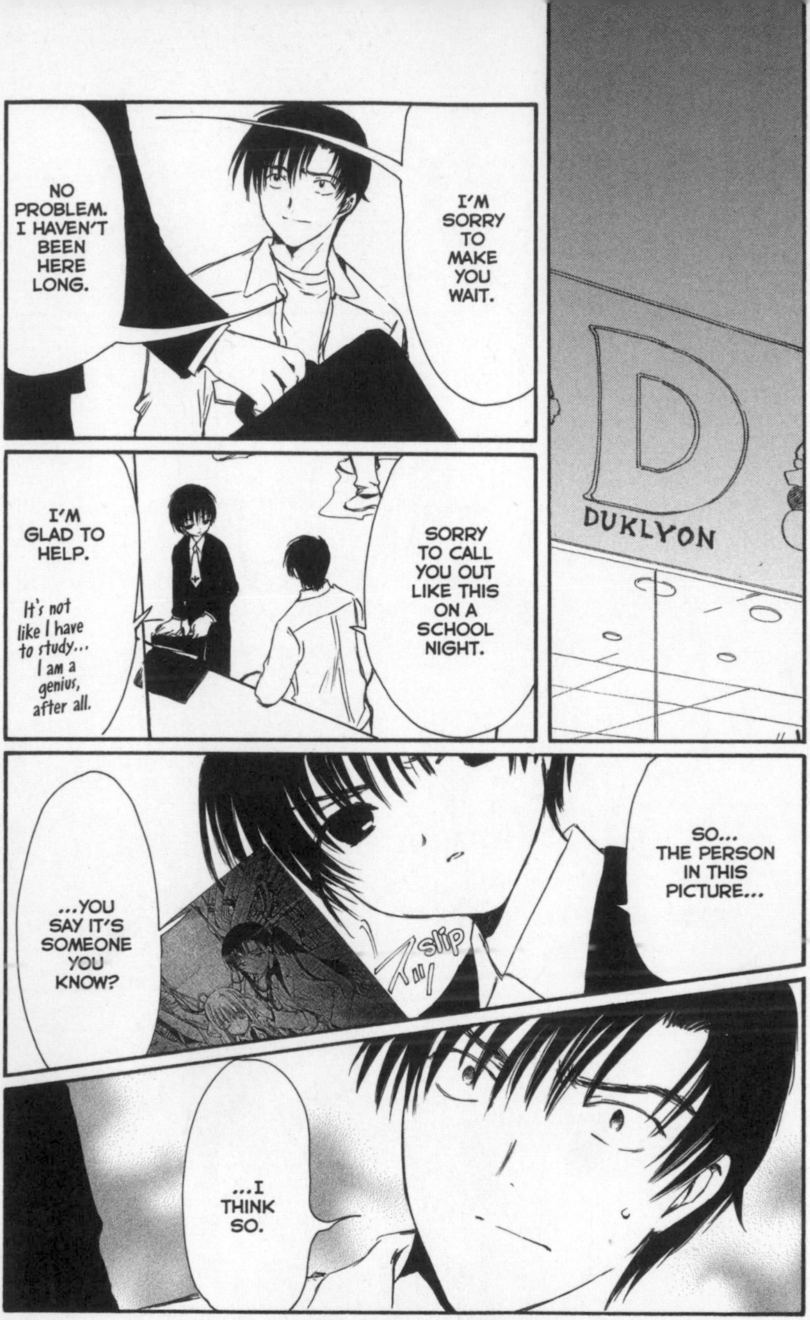
DUKLYON
I'M SORRY TO MAKE YOU WAIT.
NO PROBLEM. I HAVEN'T BEEN HERE LONG.
SORRY TO CALL YOU OUT LIKE THIS ON A SCHOOL NIGHT.
I'M GLAD TO HELP.
It's not like I have to study... I am a genius, after all.
SO... THE PERSON IN THIS PICTURE...
slip
...YOU SAY IT'S SOMEONE YOU KNOW?
...I THINK SO.

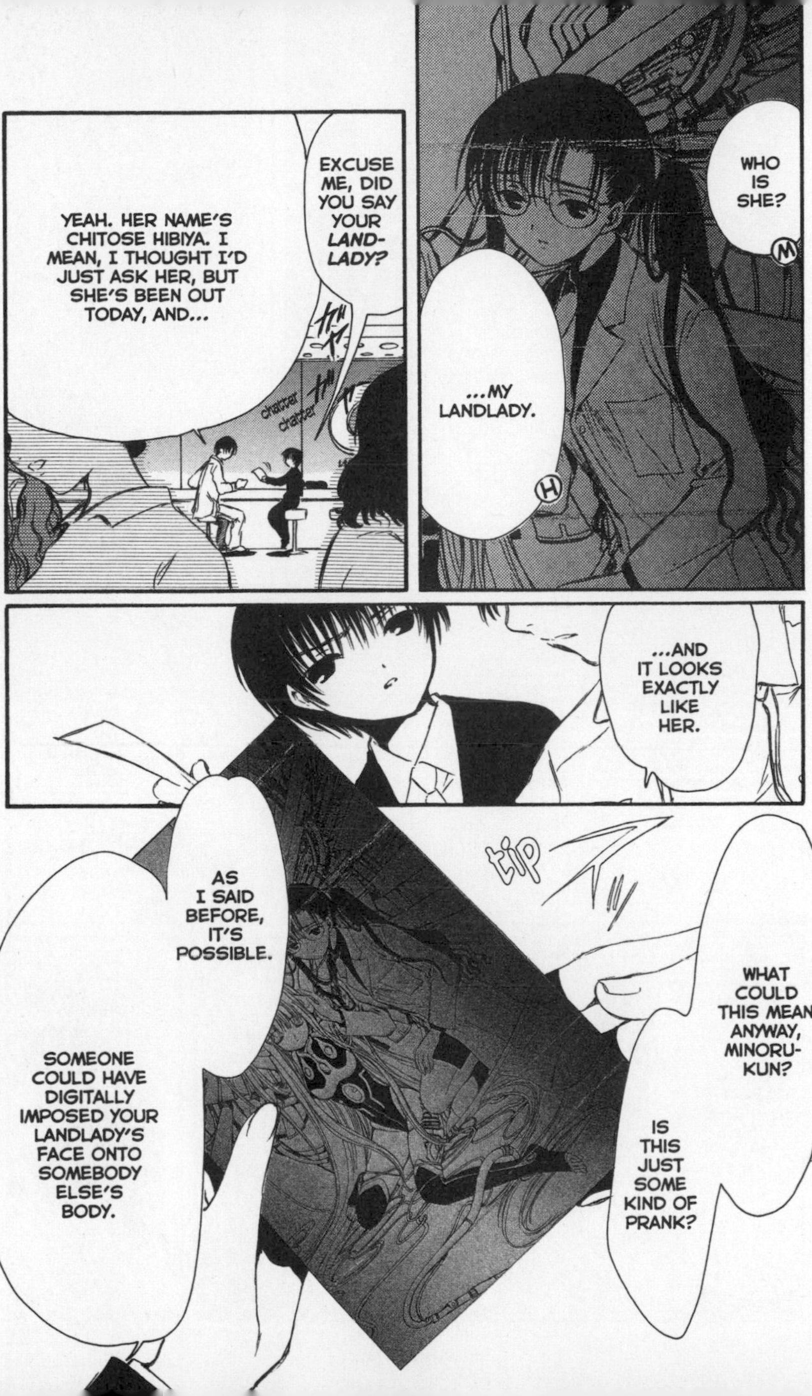
WHO IS SHE?
...MY LANDLADY.
EXCUSE ME, DID YOU SAY YOUR *LANDLADY?*
YEAH. HER NAME'S CHITOSE HIBIYA. I MEAN, I THOUGHT I'D JUST ASK HER, BUT SHE'S BEEN OUT TODAY, AND...
chatter chatter
...AND IT LOOKS EXACTLY LIKE HER.
tip
WHAT COULD THIS MEAN ANYWAY, MINORU-KUN?
IS THIS JUST SOME KIND OF PRANK?
AS I SAID BEFORE, IT'S POSSIBLE.
SOMEONE COULD HAVE DIGITALLY IMPOSED YOUR LANDLADY'S FACE ONTO SOMEBODY ELSE'S BODY.

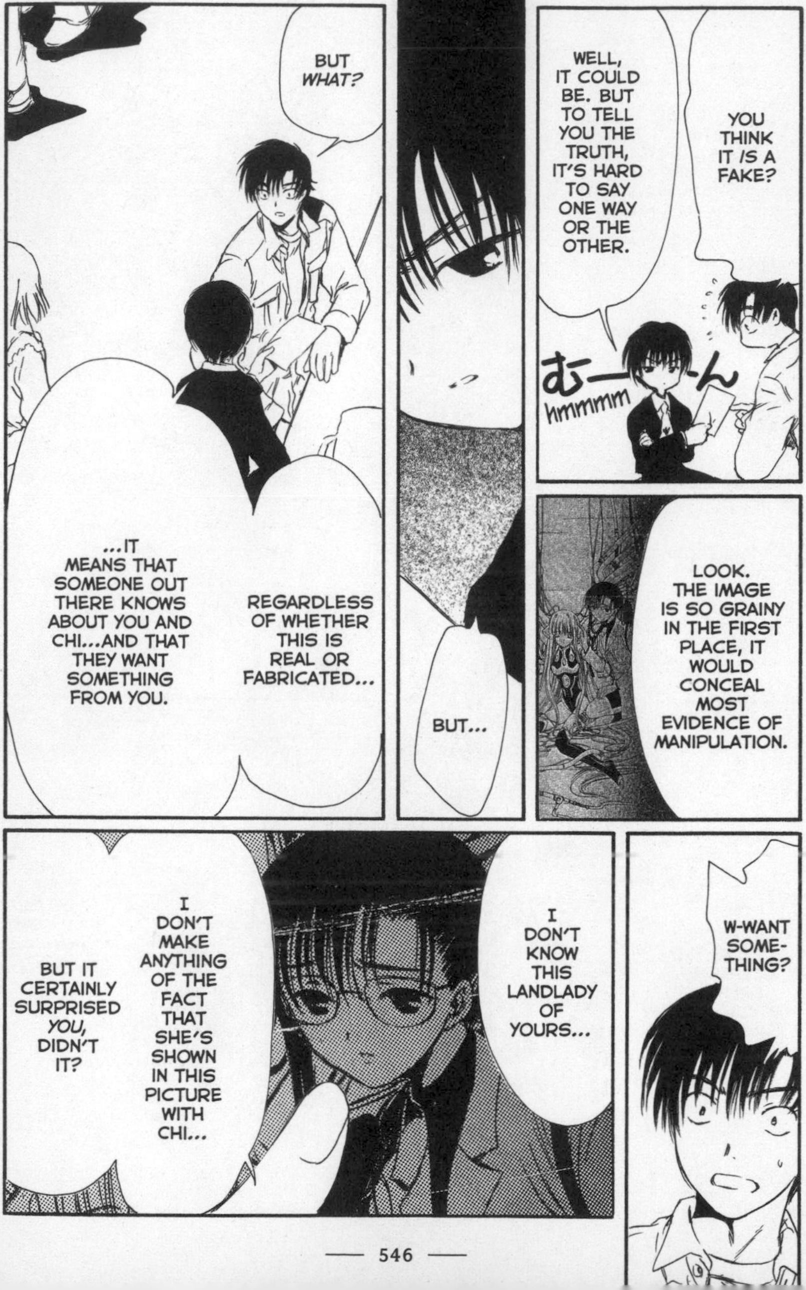
YOU THINK IT IS A FAKE?
WELL, IT COULD BE. BUT TO TELL YOU THE TRUTH, IT'S HARD TO SAY ONE WAY OR THE OTHER.
むーーん
hmmmm
LOOK. THE IMAGE IS SO GRAINY IN THE FIRST PLACE, IT WOULD CONCEAL MOST EVIDENCE OF MANIPULATION.
BUT...
BUT WHAT?
REGARDLESS OF WHETHER THIS IS REAL OR FABRICATED...
...IT MEANS THAT SOMEONE OUT THERE KNOWS ABOUT YOU AND CHI...AND THAT THEY WANT SOMETHING FROM YOU.
W-WANT SOME-THING?
I DON'T KNOW THIS LANDLADY OF YOURS...
I DON'T MAKE ANYTHING OF THE FACT THAT SHE'S SHOWN IN THIS PICTURE WITH CHI...
BUT IT CERTAINLY SURPRISED YOU, DIDN'T IT?

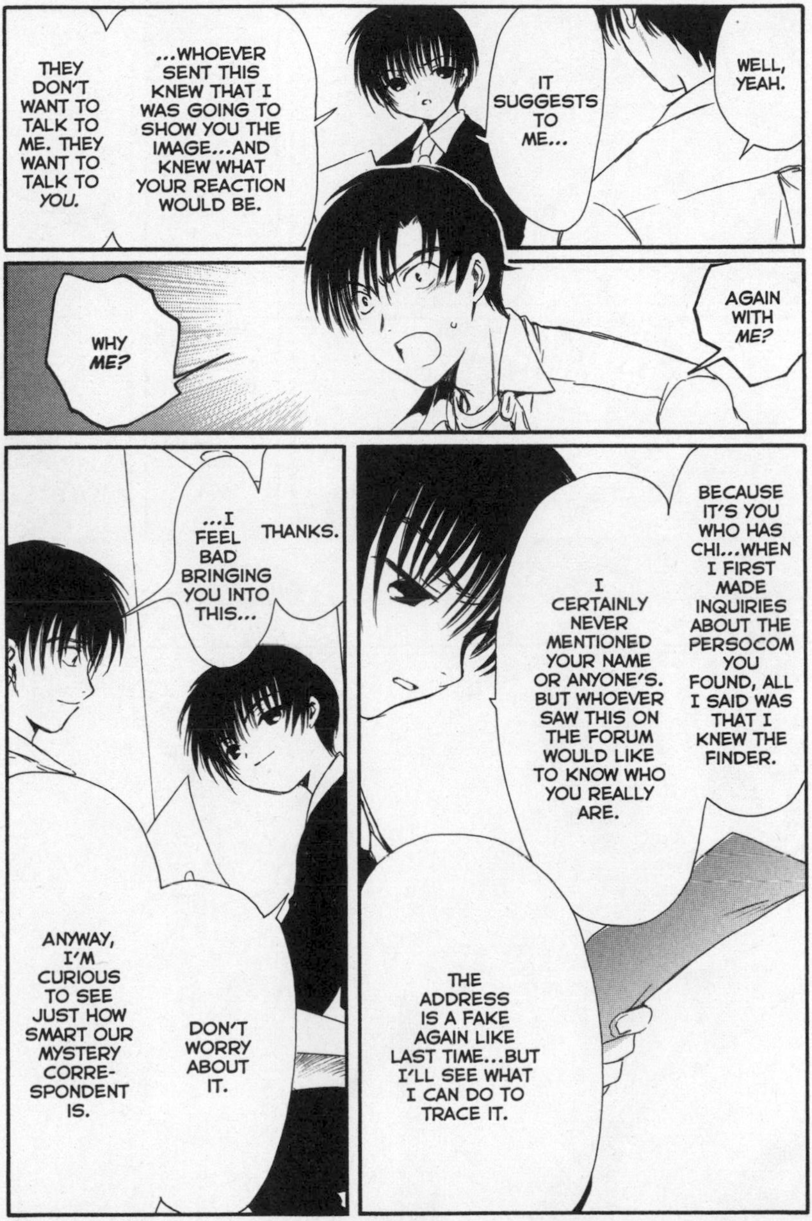
WELL, YEAH.
IT SUGGESTS TO ME...
...WHOEVER SENT THIS KNEW THAT I WAS GOING TO SHOW YOU THE IMAGE...AND KNEW WHAT YOUR REACTION WOULD BE.
THEY DON'T WANT TO TALK TO ME. THEY WANT TO TALK TO *YOU.*
AGAIN WITH *ME?*
WHY *ME?*
BECAUSE IT'S YOU WHO HAS CHI...WHEN I FIRST MADE INQUIRIES ABOUT THE PERSOCOM YOU FOUND, ALL I SAID WAS THAT I KNEW THE FINDER.
I CERTAINLY NEVER MENTIONED YOUR NAME OR ANYONE'S. BUT WHOEVER SAW THIS ON THE FORUM WOULD LIKE TO KNOW WHO YOU REALLY ARE.
THE ADDRESS IS A FAKE AGAIN LIKE LAST TIME...BUT I'LL SEE WHAT I CAN DO TO TRACE IT.
THANKS.
...I FEEL BAD BRINGING YOU INTO THIS...
DON'T WORRY ABOUT IT.
ANYWAY, I'M CURIOUS TO SEE JUST HOW SMART OUR MYSTERY CORRE-SPONDENT IS.

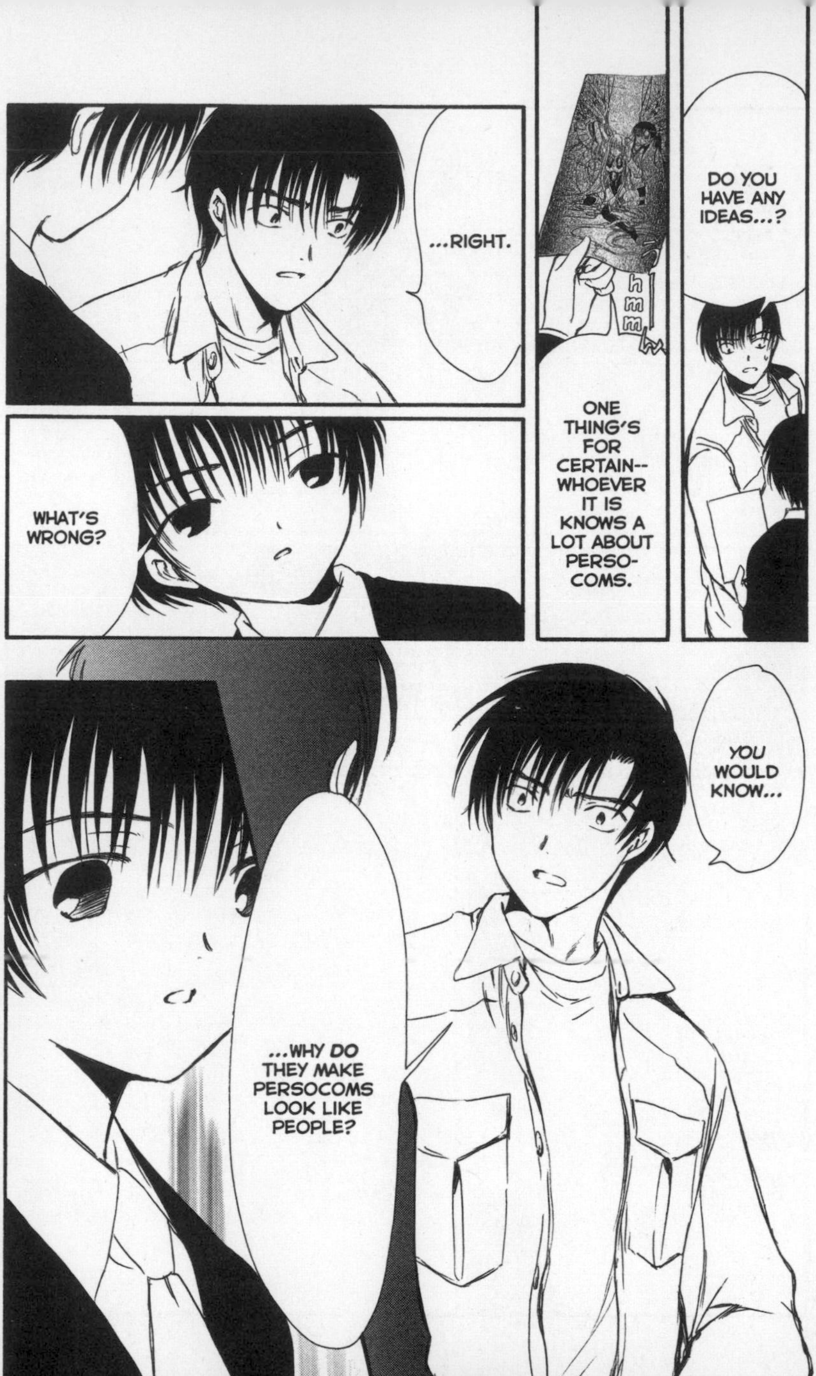
DO YOU HAVE ANY IDEAS...?
hmmm
ONE THING'S FOR CERTAIN--WHOEVER IT IS KNOWS A LOT ABOUT PERSO-COMS.
...RIGHT.
WHAT'S WRONG?
YOU WOULD KNOW...
...WHY *DO* THEY MAKE PERSOCOMS LOOK LIKE PEOPLE?

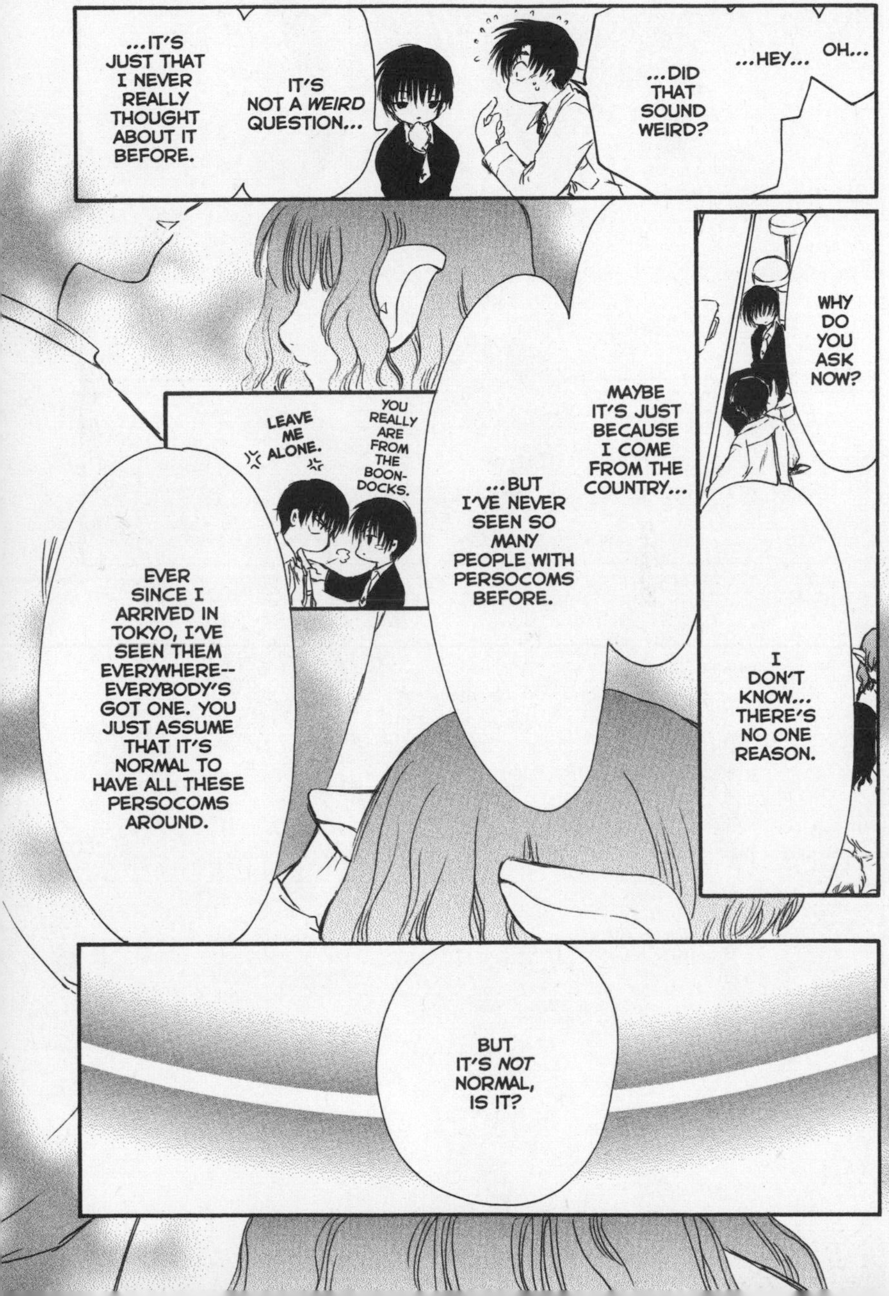

OH...
...HEY...
...DID THAT SOUND WEIRD?
IT'S NOT A *WEIRD* QUESTION...
...IT'S JUST THAT I NEVER REALLY THOUGHT ABOUT IT BEFORE.
WHY DO YOU ASK NOW?
I DON'T KNOW... THERE'S NO ONE REASON.
MAYBE IT'S JUST BECAUSE I COME FROM THE COUNTRY...
...BUT I'VE NEVER SEEN SO MANY PEOPLE WITH PERSOCOMS BEFORE.
YOU REALLY ARE FROM THE BOON-DOCKS.
LEAVE ME ALONE.
EVER SINCE I ARRIVED IN TOKYO, I'VE SEEN THEM EVERYWHERE-- EVERYBODY'S GOT ONE. YOU JUST ASSUME THAT IT'S NORMAL TO HAVE ALL THESE PERSOCOMS AROUND.
BUT IT'S *NOT* NORMAL, IS IT?

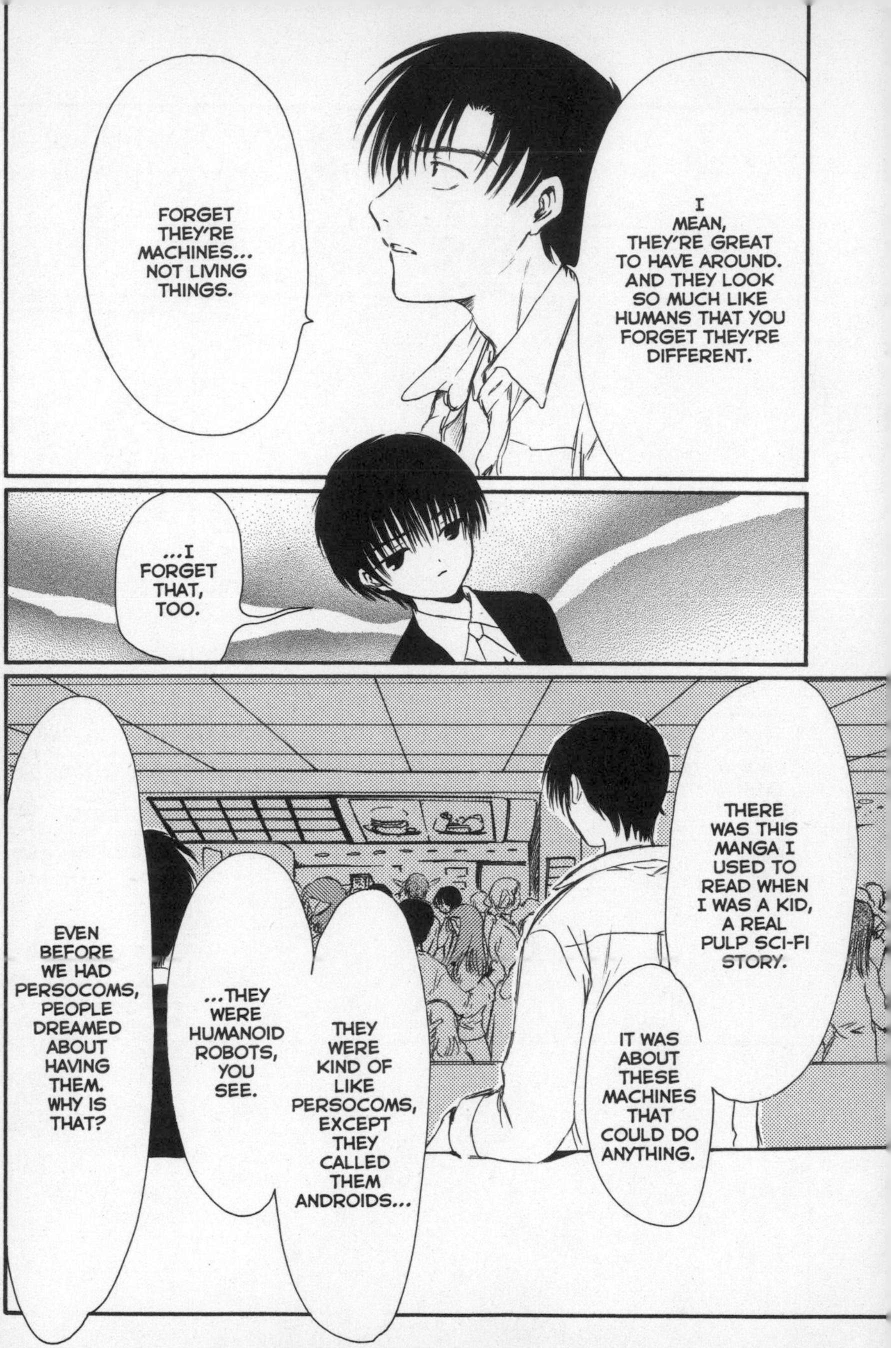
I MEAN, THEY'RE GREAT TO HAVE AROUND. AND THEY LOOK SO MUCH LIKE HUMANS THAT YOU FORGET THEY'RE DIFFERENT.
FORGET THEY'RE MACHINES... NOT LIVING THINGS.
...I FORGET THAT, TOO.
THERE WAS THIS MANGA I USED TO READ WHEN I WAS A KID, A REAL PULP SCI-FI STORY.
IT WAS ABOUT THESE MACHINES THAT COULD DO ANYTHING.
THEY WERE KIND OF LIKE PERSOCOMS, EXCEPT THEY CALLED THEM ANDROIDS...
...THEY WERE HUMANOID ROBOTS, YOU SEE.
EVEN BEFORE WE HAD PERSOCOMS, PEOPLE DREAMED ABOUT HAVING THEM. WHY IS THAT?

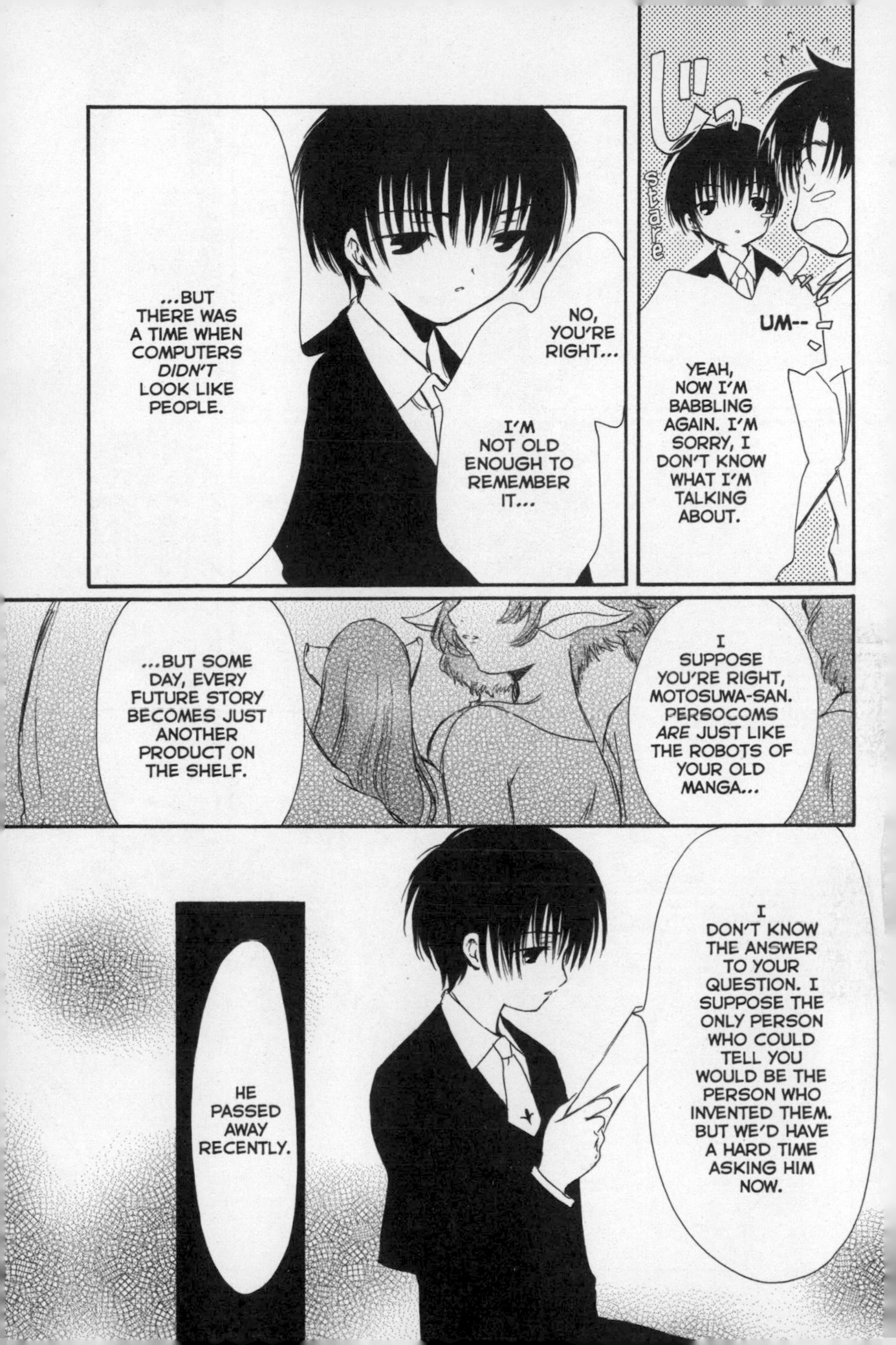
stare
UM--
YEAH, NOW I'M BABBLING AGAIN. I'M SORRY, I DON'T KNOW WHAT I'M TALKING ABOUT.
NO, YOU'RE RIGHT...
I'M NOT OLD ENOUGH TO REMEMBER IT...
...BUT THERE WAS A TIME WHEN COMPUTERS *DIDN'T* LOOK LIKE PEOPLE.
I SUPPOSE YOU'RE RIGHT, MOTOSUWA-SAN. PERSOCOMS *ARE* JUST LIKE THE ROBOTS OF YOUR OLD MANGA...
...BUT SOME DAY, EVERY FUTURE STORY BECOMES JUST ANOTHER PRODUCT ON THE SHELF.
I DON'T KNOW THE ANSWER TO YOUR QUESTION. I SUPPOSE THE ONLY PERSON WHO COULD TELL YOU WOULD BE THE PERSON WHO INVENTED THEM. BUT WE'D HAVE A HARD TIME ASKING HIM NOW.
HE PASSED AWAY RECENTLY.

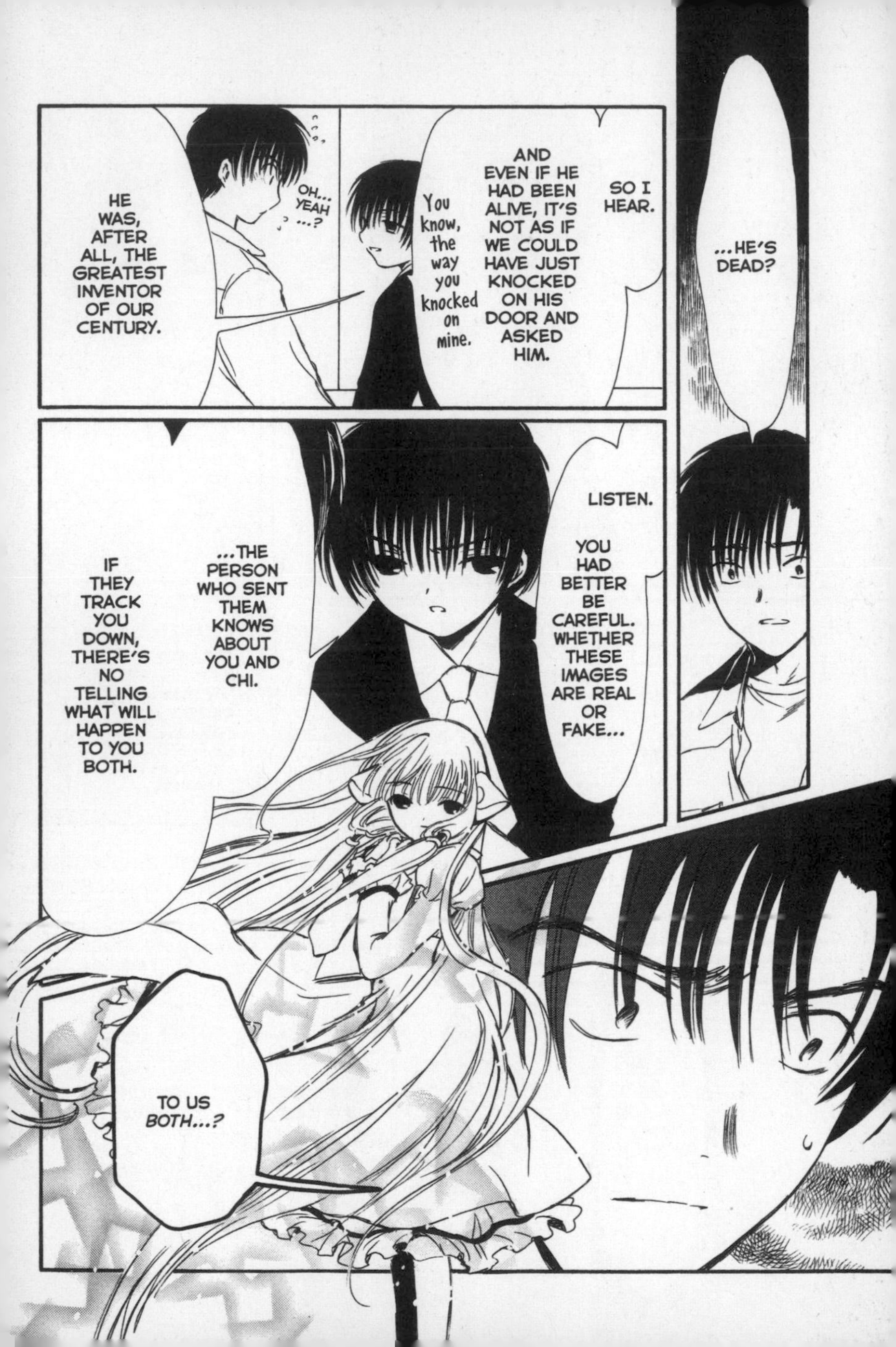
...HE'S DEAD?
SO I HEAR.
AND EVEN IF HE HAD BEEN ALIVE, IT'S NOT AS IF WE COULD HAVE JUST KNOCKED ON HIS DOOR AND ASKED HIM.
You know, the way you knocked on mine.
OH... YEAH ...?
HE WAS, AFTER ALL, THE GREATEST INVENTOR OF OUR CENTURY.
LISTEN.
YOU HAD BETTER BE CAREFUL. WHETHER THESE IMAGES ARE REAL OR FAKE...
...THE PERSON WHO SENT THEM KNOWS ABOUT YOU AND CHI.
IF THEY TRACK YOU DOWN, THERE'S NO TELLING WHAT WILL HAPPEN TO YOU BOTH.
TO US *BOTH*...?

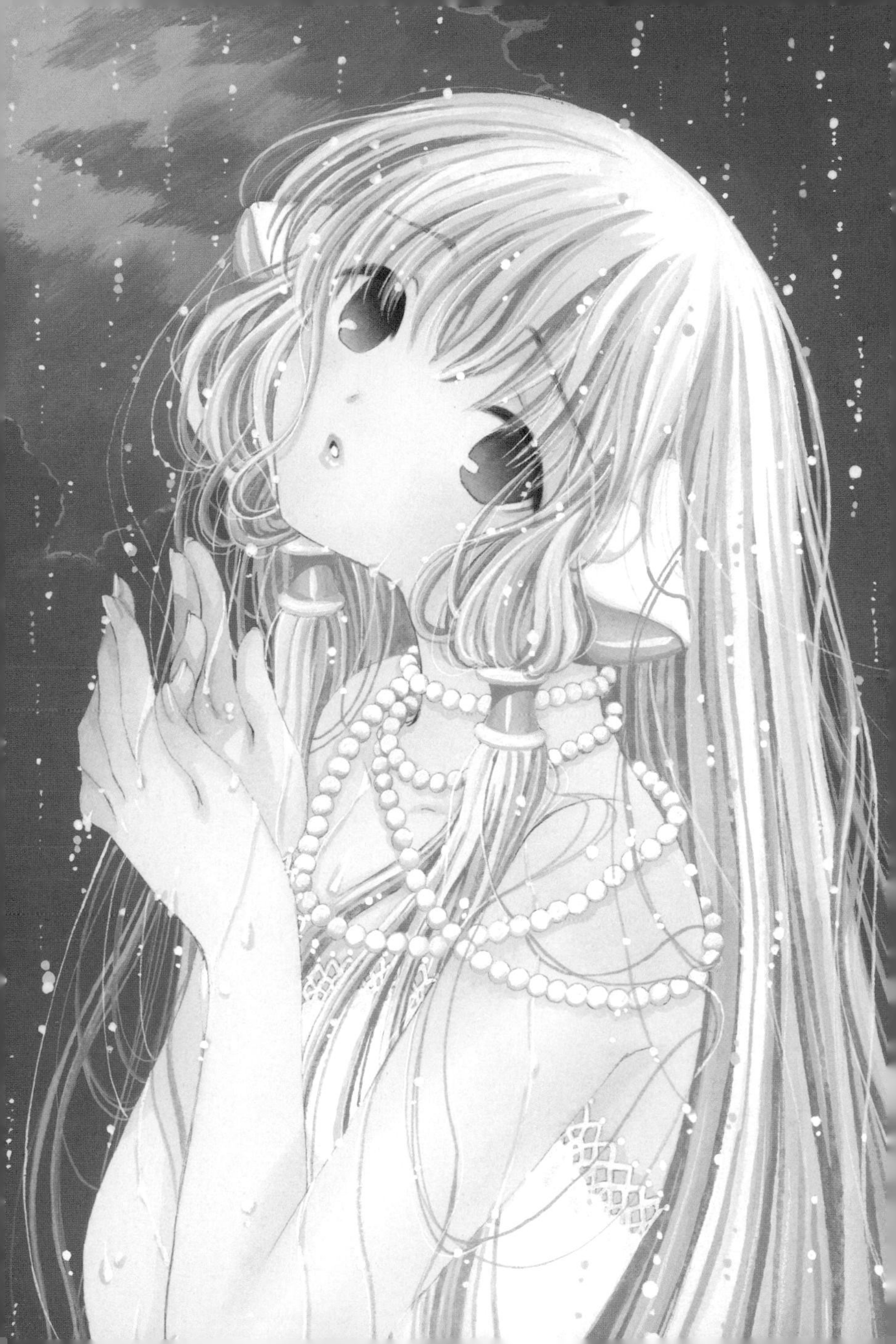

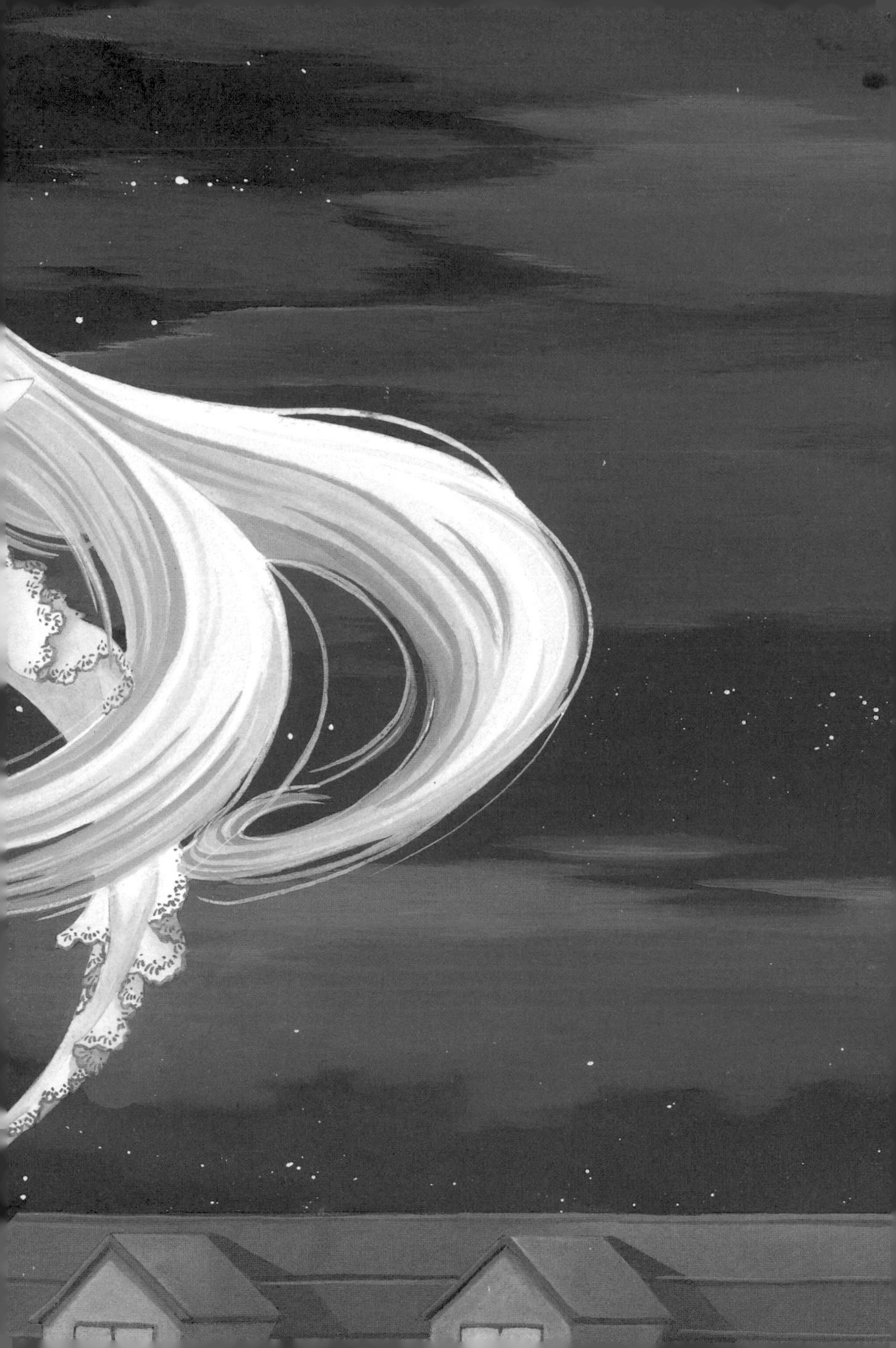

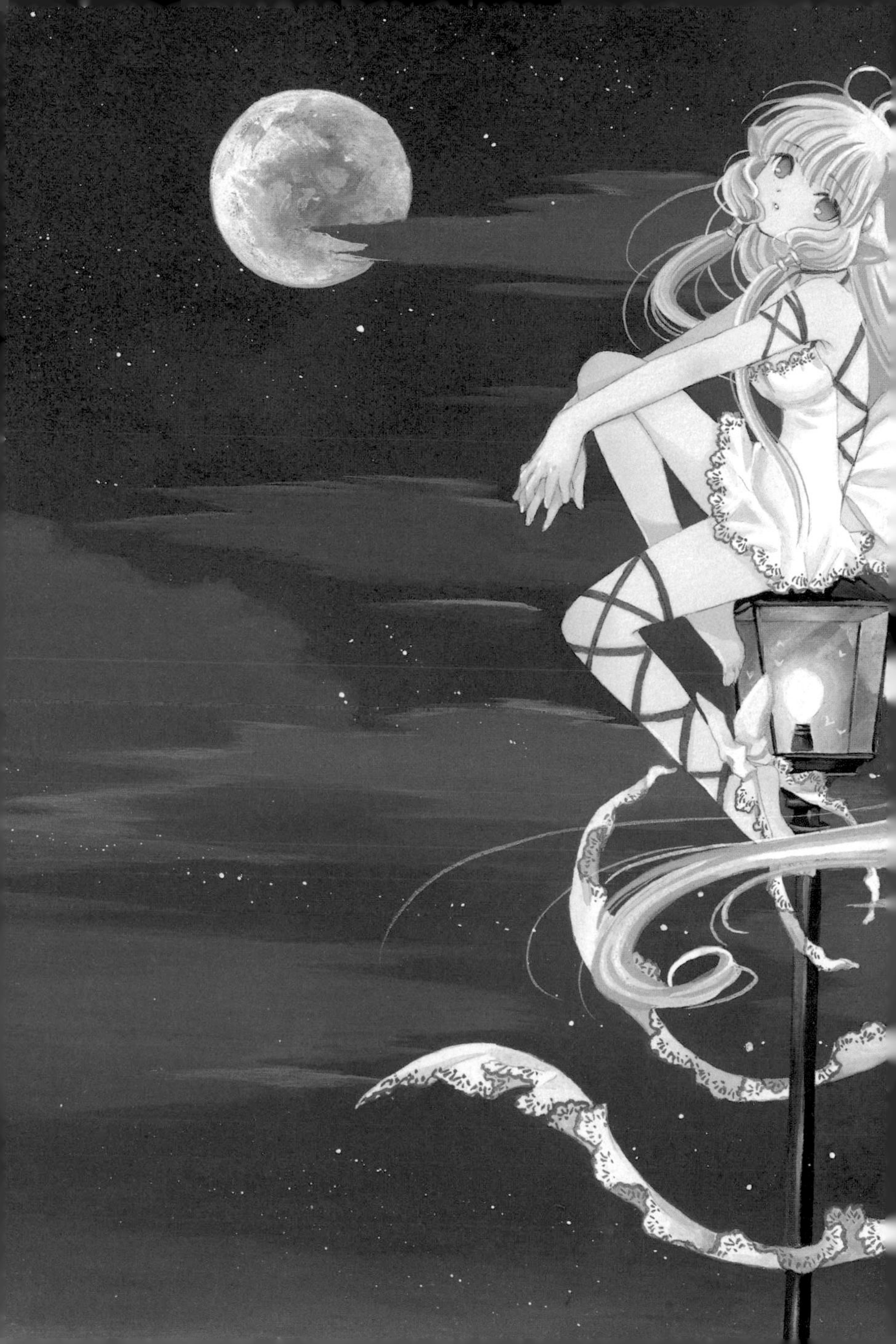

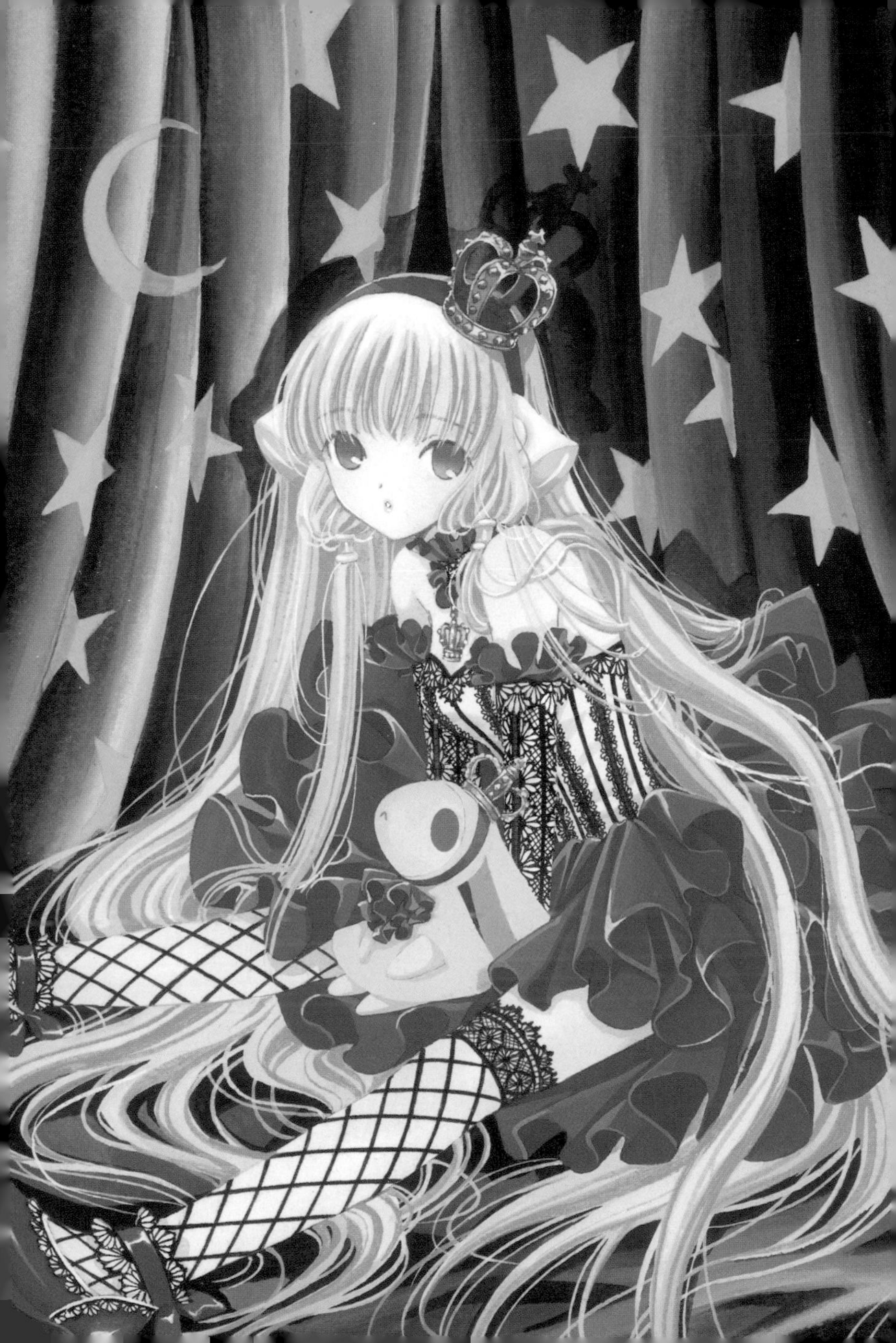

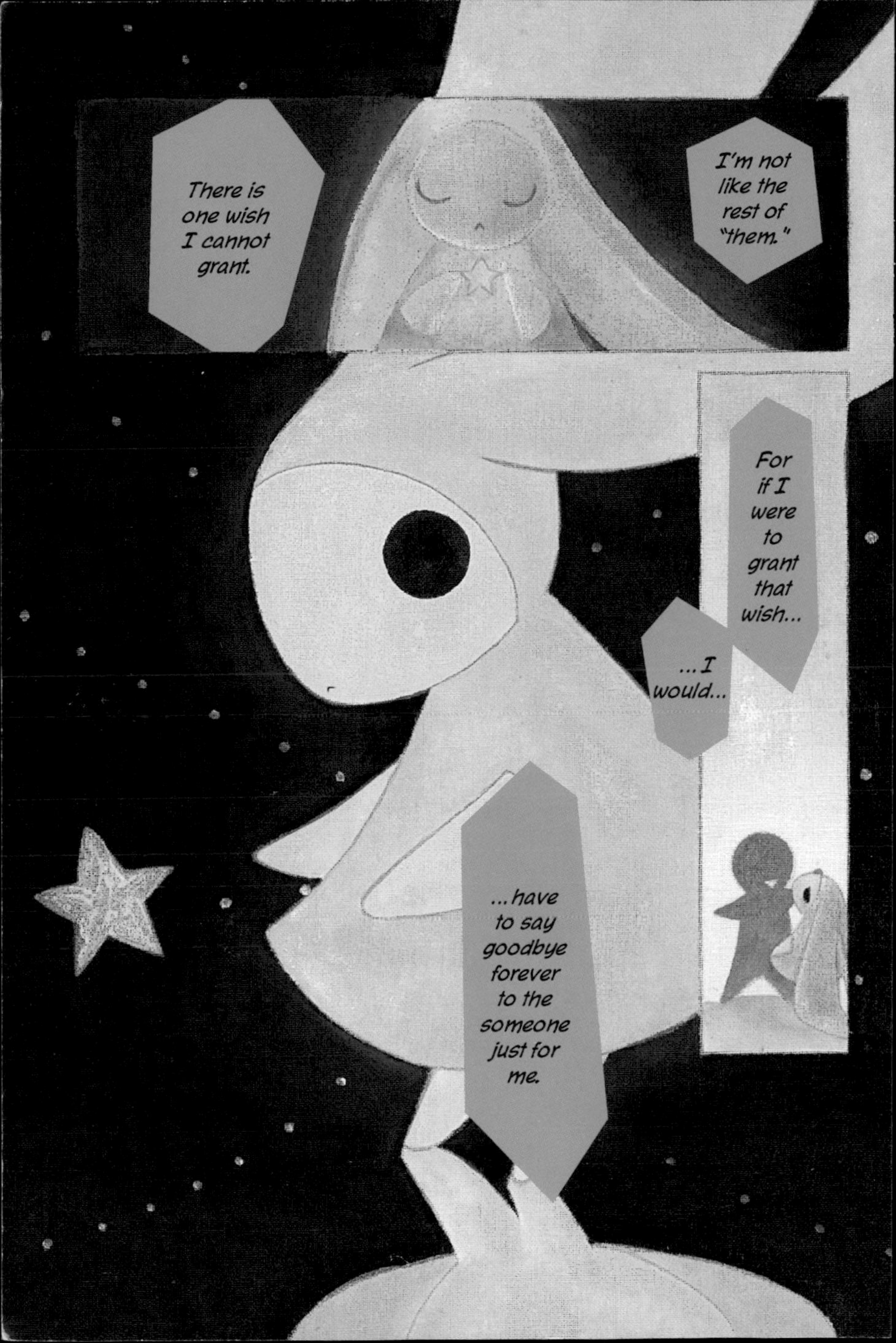
I'm not like the rest of "them."
There is one wish I cannot grant.
For if I were to grant that wish...
...I would...
...have to say goodbye forever to the someone just for me.

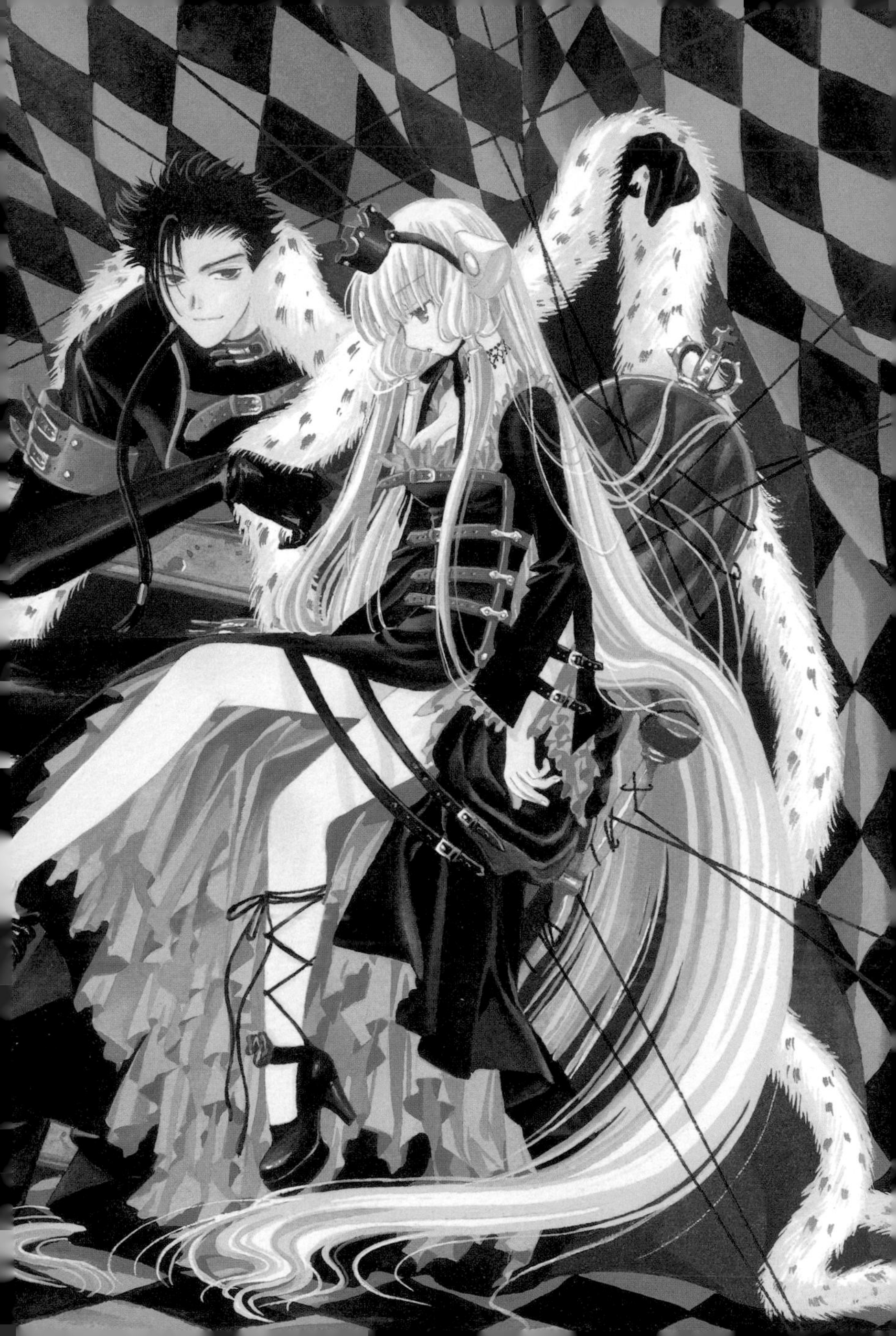

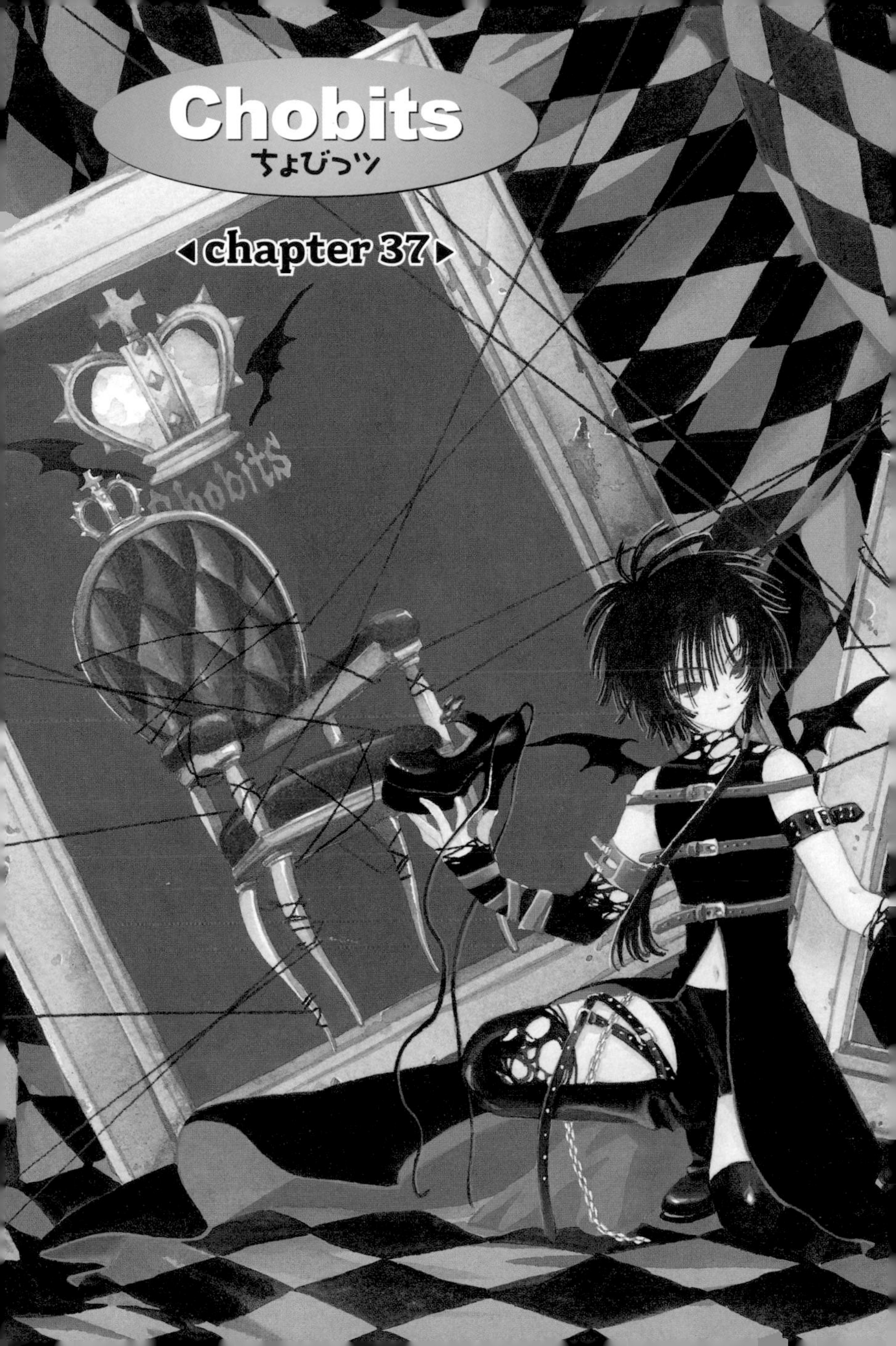
Chobits
ちょびっツ
chapter 37
Chobits

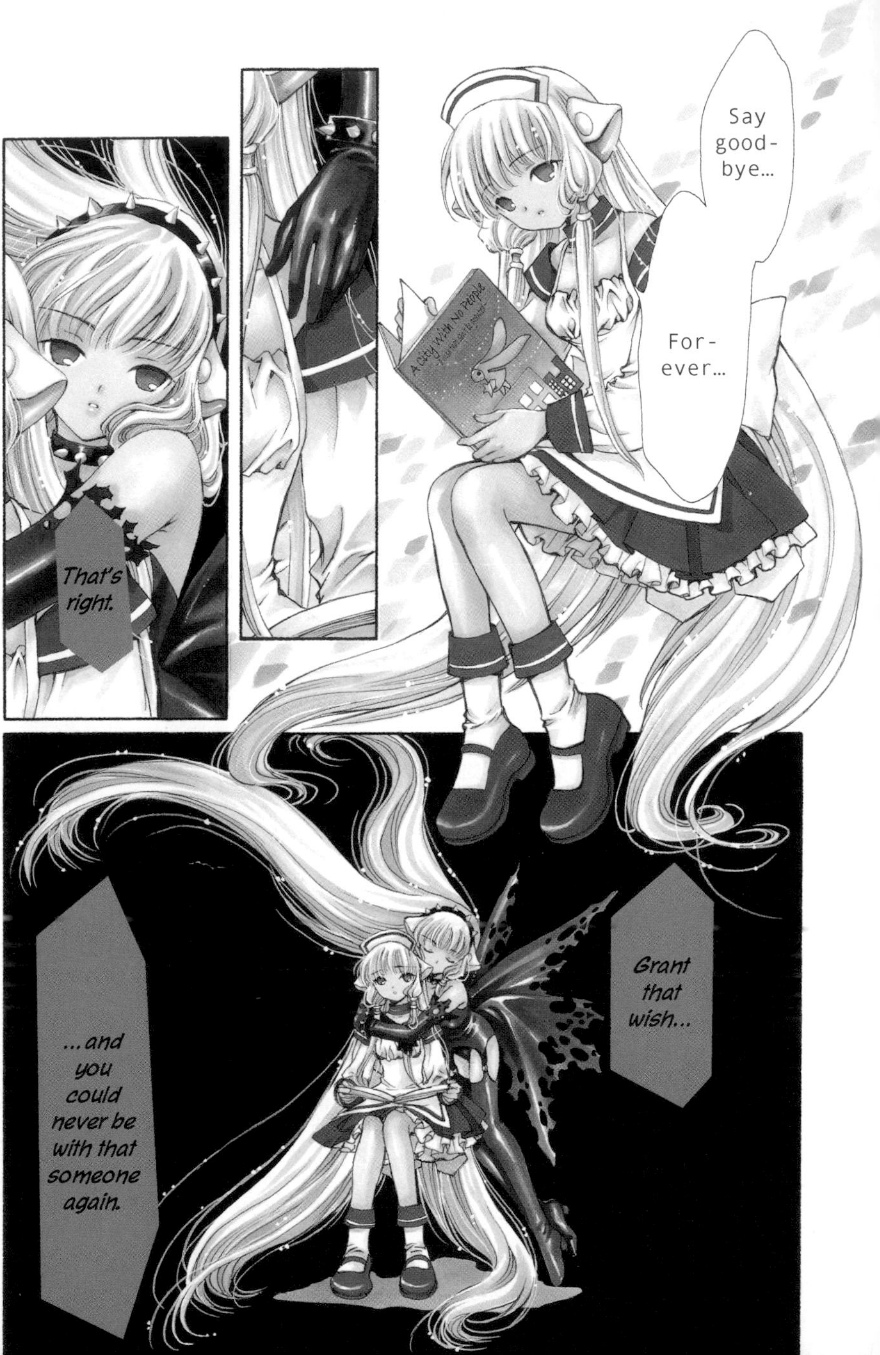
Say good-bye...
For-ever...
That's right.
Grant that wish...
...and you could never be with that someone again.

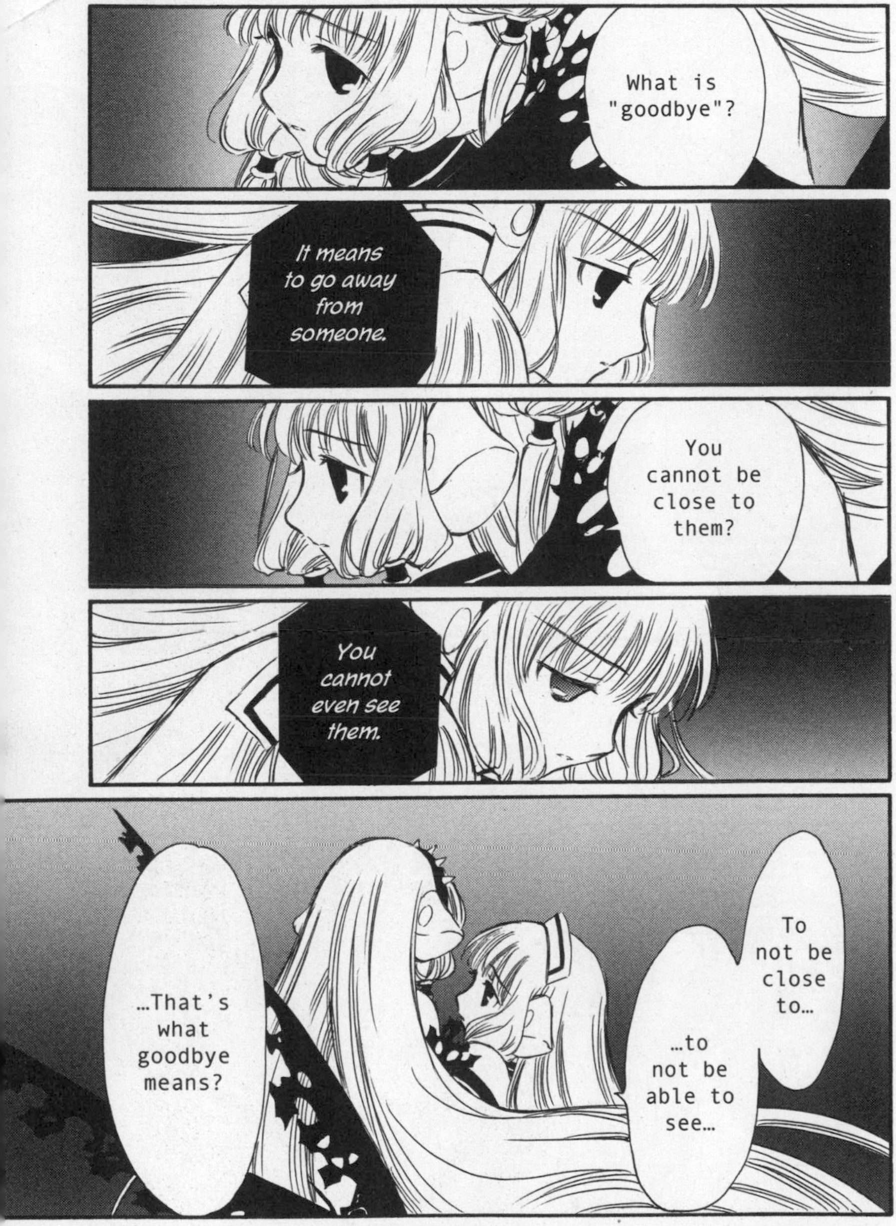
What is "goodbye"?
It means to go away from someone.
You cannot be close to them?
You cannot even see them.
To not be close to…
…to not be able to see…
…That's what goodbye means?

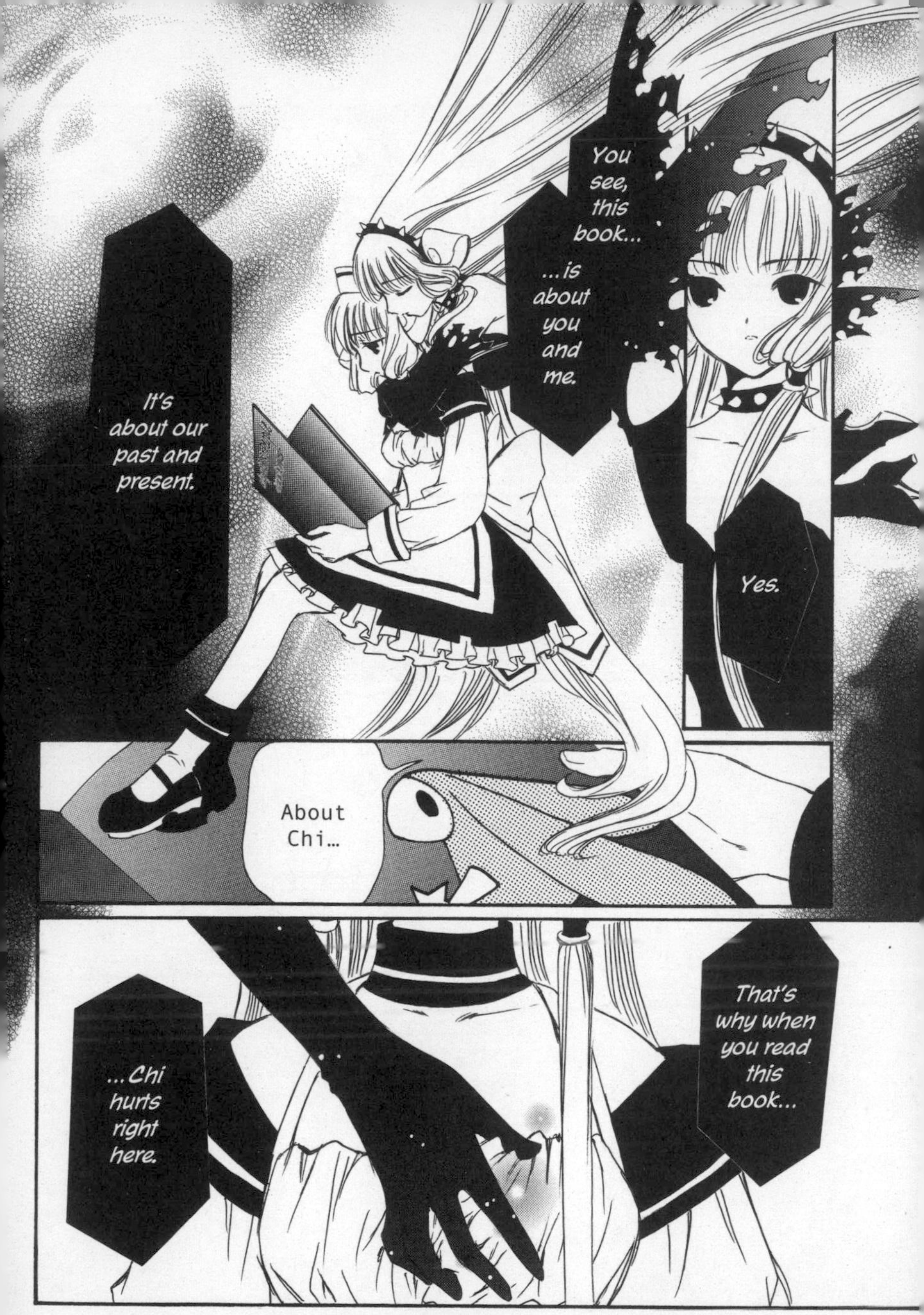
Yes.
You see, this book...
...is about you and me.
It's about our past and present.
About Chi...
That's why when you read this book...
...Chi hurts right here.

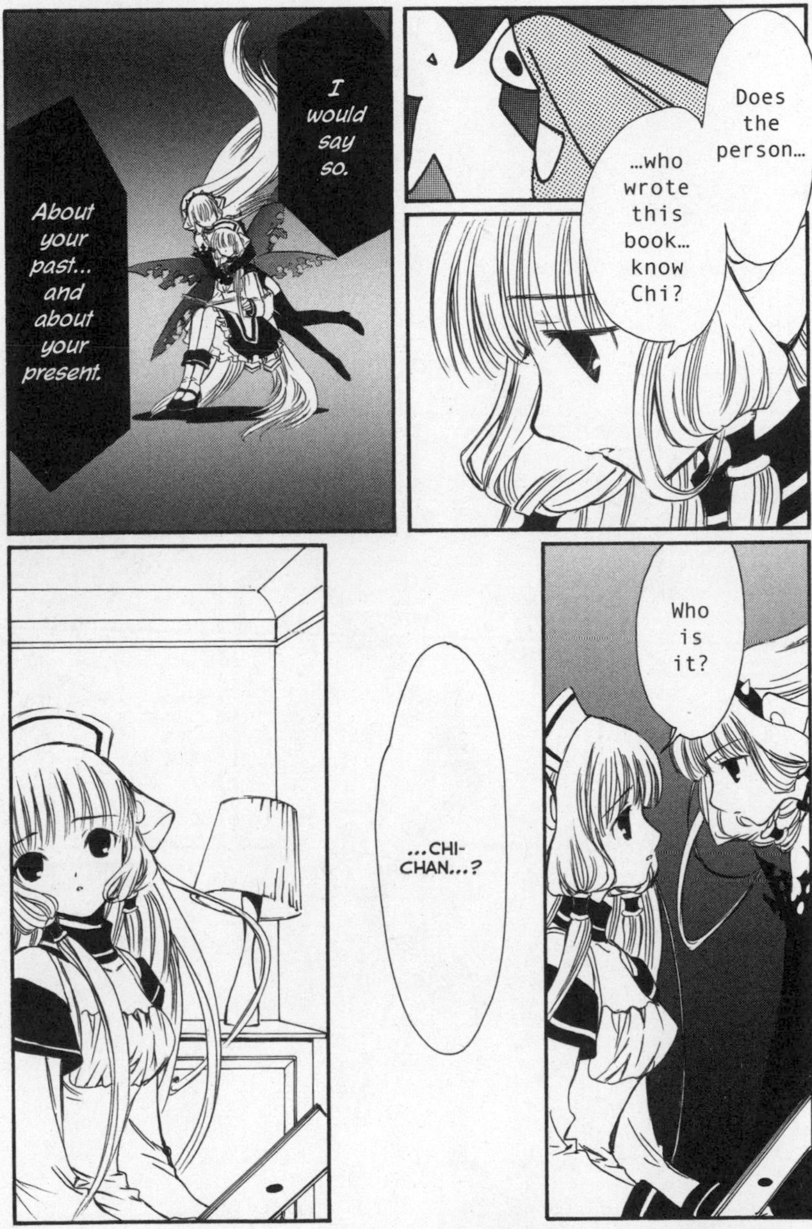
Does the person...
...who wrote this book... know Chi?
I would say so.
About your past... and about your present.
Who is it?
...CHI-CHAN...?

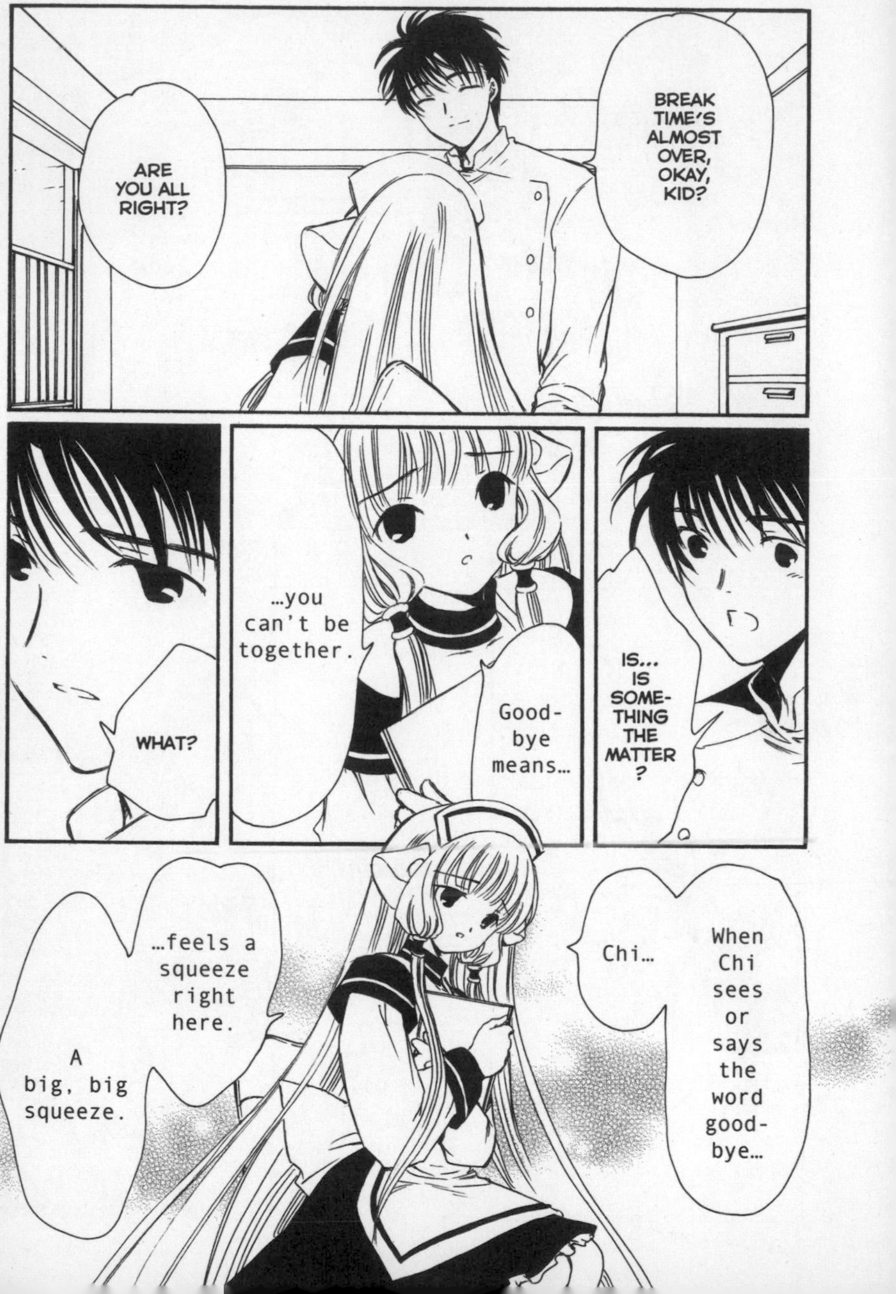
BREAK TIME'S ALMOST OVER, OKAY, KID?
ARE YOU ALL RIGHT?
IS... IS SOME-THING THE MATTER?
Good-bye means...
...you can't be together.
WHAT?
When Chi sees or says the word good-bye...
Chi...
...feels a squeeze right here.
A big, big squeeze.

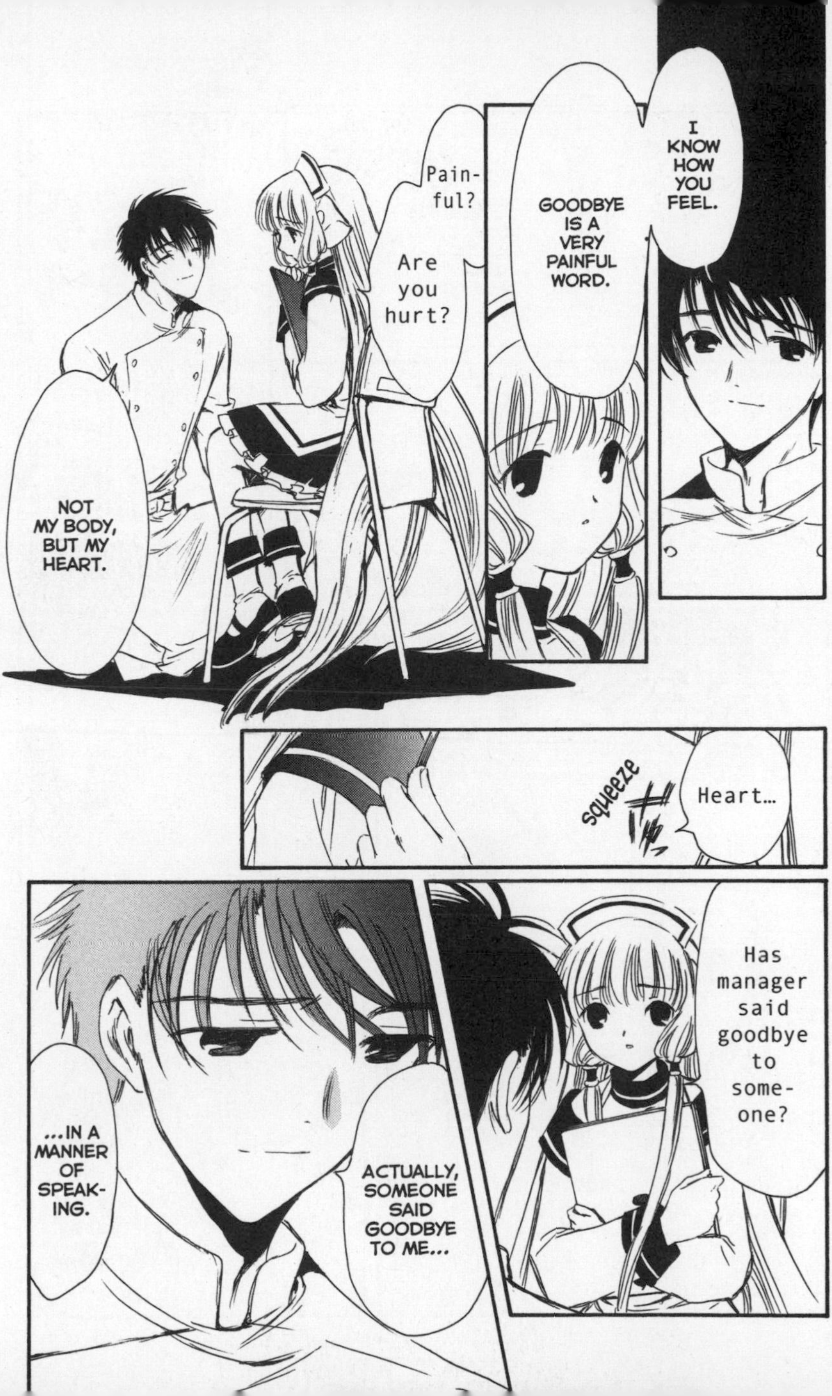
I KNOW HOW YOU FEEL.
GOODBYE IS A VERY PAINFUL WORD.
Pain-ful?
Are you hurt?
NOT MY BODY, BUT MY HEART.
Heart...
squeeze
Has manager said goodbye to some-one?
ACTUALLY, SOMEONE SAID GOODBYE TO ME...
...IN A MANNER OF SPEAK-ING.

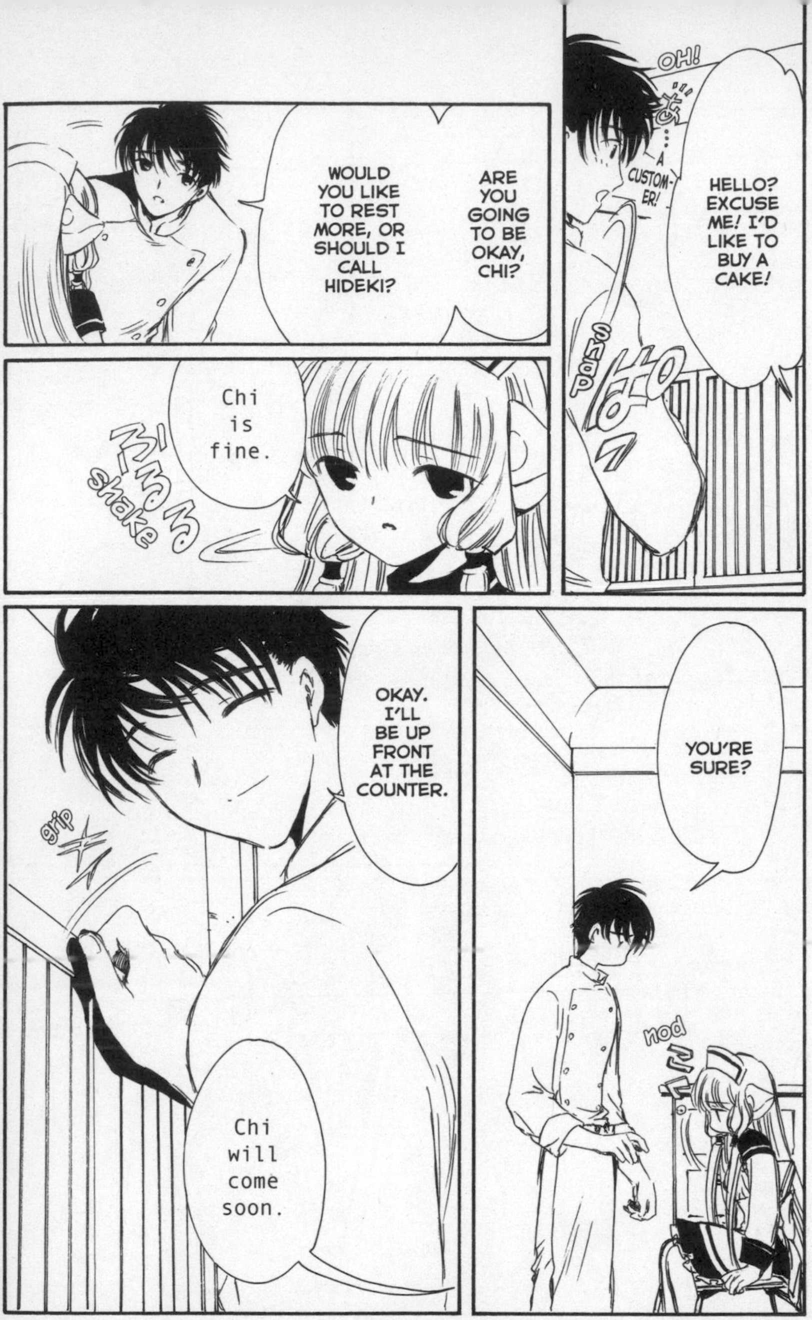
ARE YOU GOING TO BE OKAY, CHI?
WOULD YOU LIKE TO REST MORE, OR SHOULD I CALL HIDEKI?
Chi is fine.
ぷるる
shake
OH!
あ…
A CUSTOMER!
HELLO? EXCUSE ME! I'D LIKE TO BUY A CAKE!
はっ
snap
YOU'RE SURE?
こくん
nod
OKAY. I'LL BE UP FRONT AT THE COUNTER.
Chi will come soon.
grip

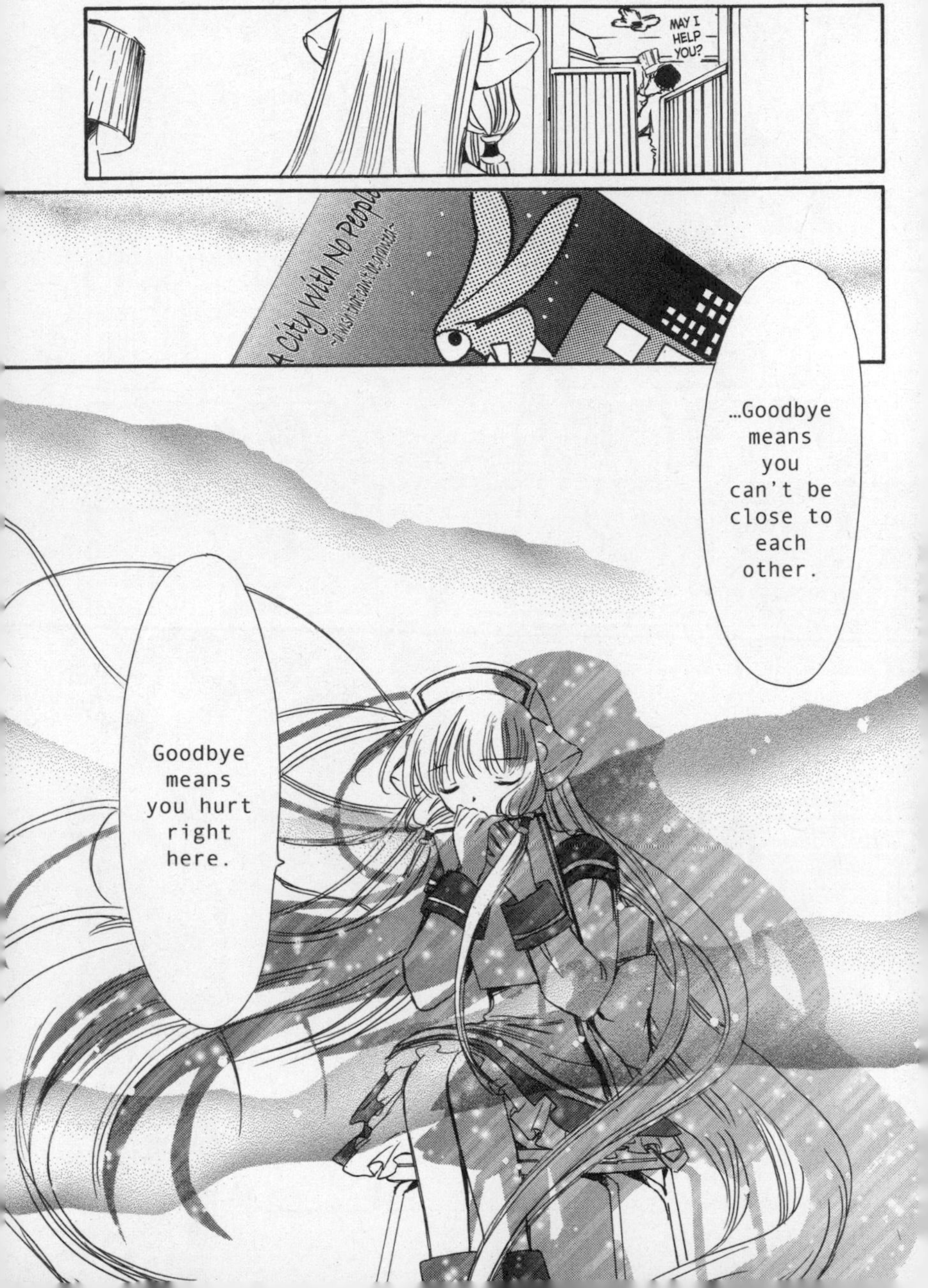
MAY I HELP YOU?
A city With No Peopl
~Wishes that can't be granted~
...Goodbye means you can't be close to each other.
Goodbye means you hurt right here.

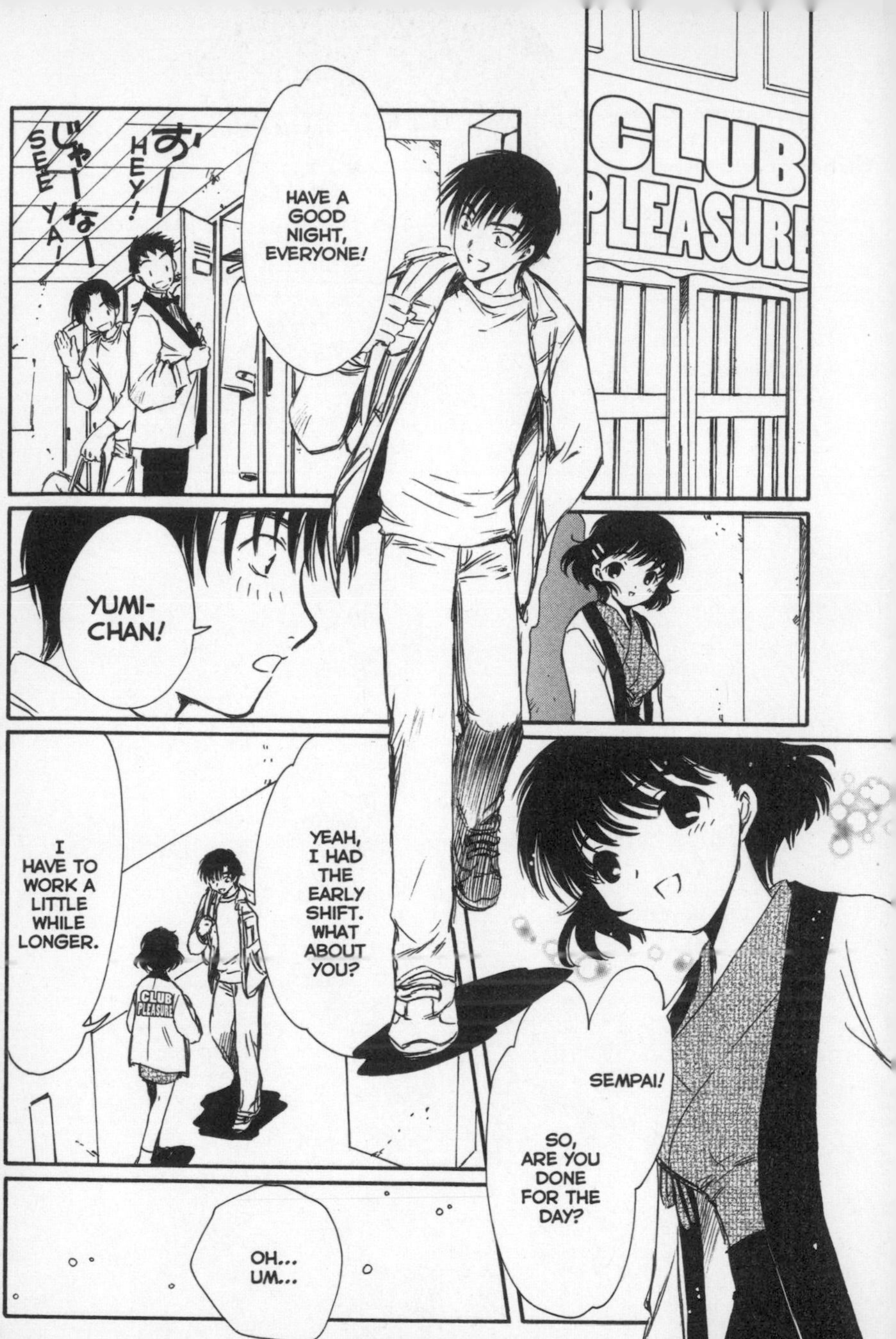
CLUB PLEASURE
HAVE A GOOD NIGHT, EVERYONE!
おー HEY!
じゃーなー SEE YA!
YUMI-CHAN!
SEMPAI!
SO, ARE YOU DONE FOR THE DAY?
YEAH, I HAD THE EARLY SHIFT. WHAT ABOUT YOU?
I HAVE TO WORK A LITTLE WHILE LONGER.
CLUB PLEASURE
OH... UM...
CLUB

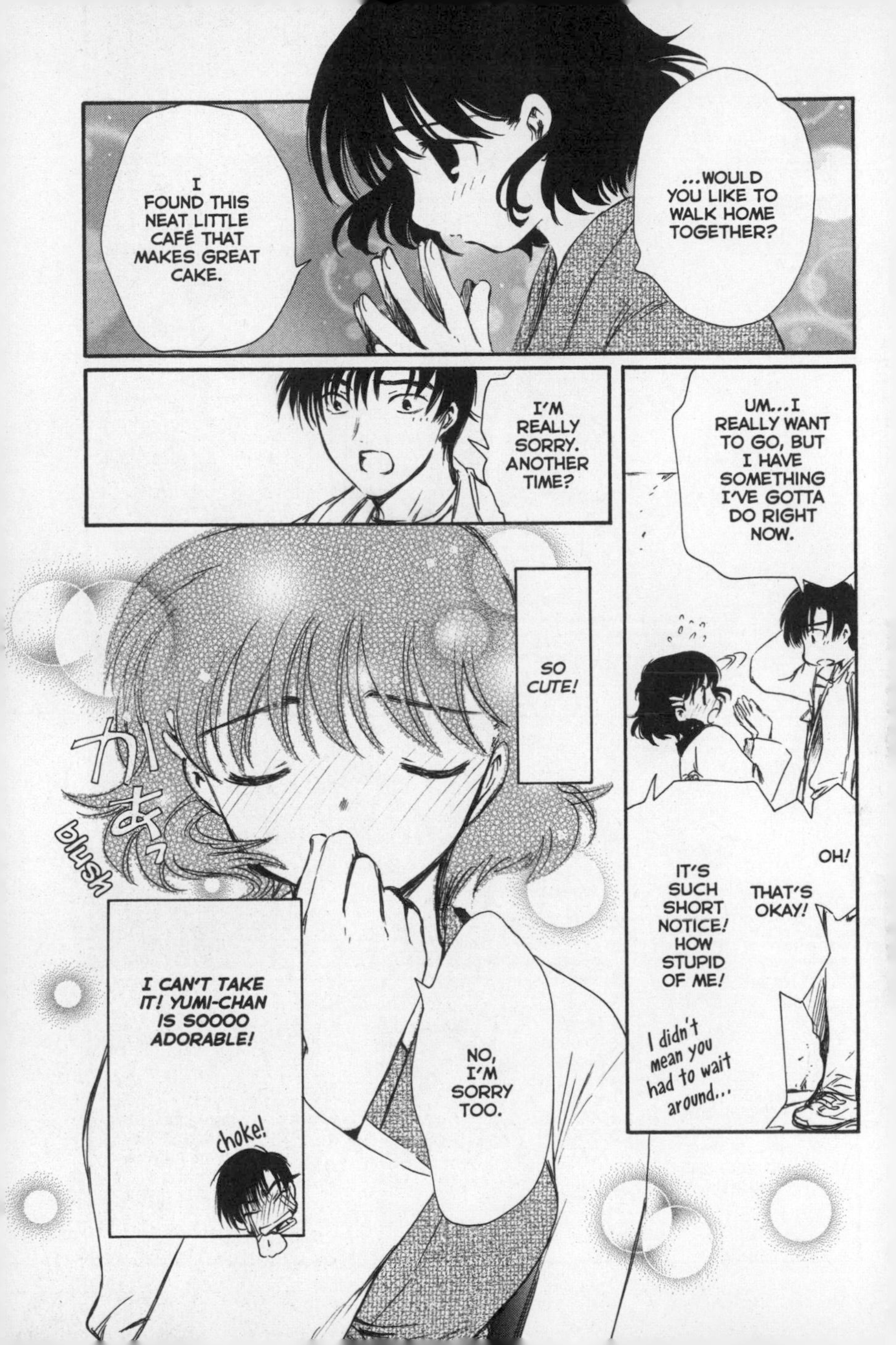
...WOULD YOU LIKE TO WALK HOME TOGETHER?
I FOUND THIS NEAT LITTLE CAFÉ THAT MAKES GREAT CAKE.
UM...I REALLY WANT TO GO, BUT I HAVE SOMETHING I'VE GOTTA DO RIGHT NOW.
OH!
THAT'S OKAY!
IT'S SUCH SHORT NOTICE! HOW STUPID OF ME!
I didn't mean you had to wait around...
I'M REALLY SORRY. ANOTHER TIME?
SO CUTE!
blush
I CAN'T TAKE IT! YUMI-CHAN IS SOOOO ADORABLE!
NO, I'M SORRY TOO.
choke!

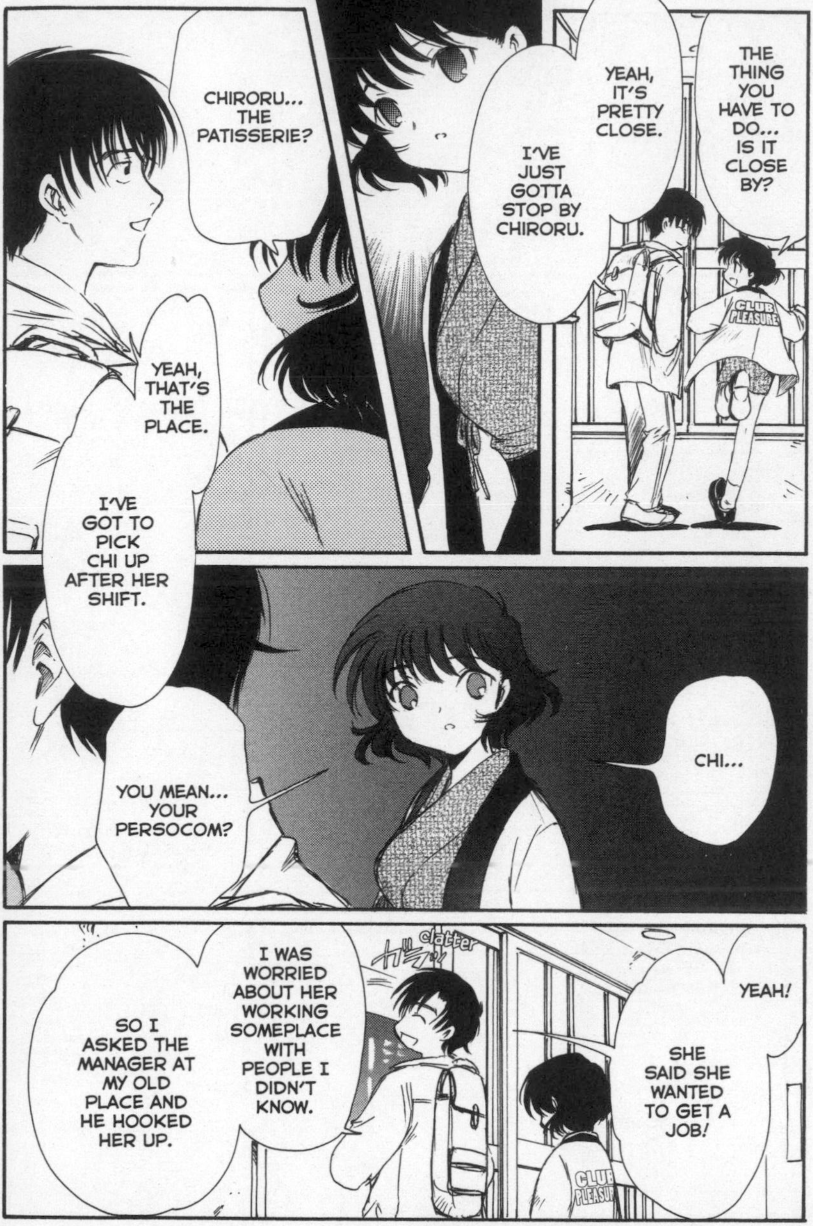
THE THING YOU HAVE TO DO... IS IT CLOSE BY?
YEAH, IT'S PRETTY CLOSE.
I'VE JUST GOTTA STOP BY CHIRORU.
CLUB PLEASURE
CHIRORU... THE PATISSERIE?
YEAH, THAT'S THE PLACE.
I'VE GOT TO PICK CHI UP AFTER HER SHIFT.
CHI...
YOU MEAN... YOUR PERSOCOM?
YEAH!
SHE SAID SHE WANTED TO GET A JOB!
clatter
I WAS WORRIED ABOUT HER WORKING SOMEPLACE WITH PEOPLE I DIDN'T KNOW.
SO I ASKED THE MANAGER AT MY OLD PLACE AND HE HOOKED HER UP.
CLUB PLEASURE

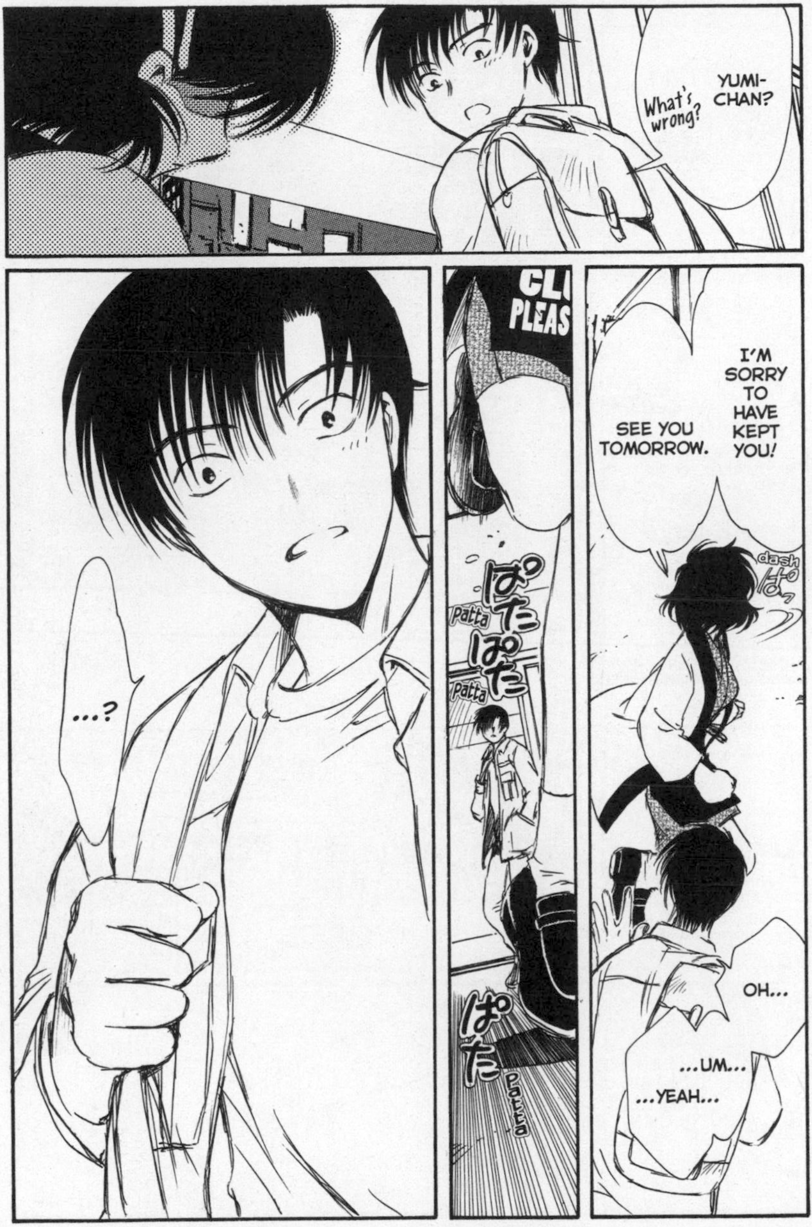
YUMI-CHAN?
What's wrong?
I'M SORRY TO HAVE KEPT YOU!
SEE YOU TOMORROW.
dash
ぱっ
OH...
...UM...
...YEAH...
ぱた
Patta
ぱた
Patta
ぱた
Patta
...?

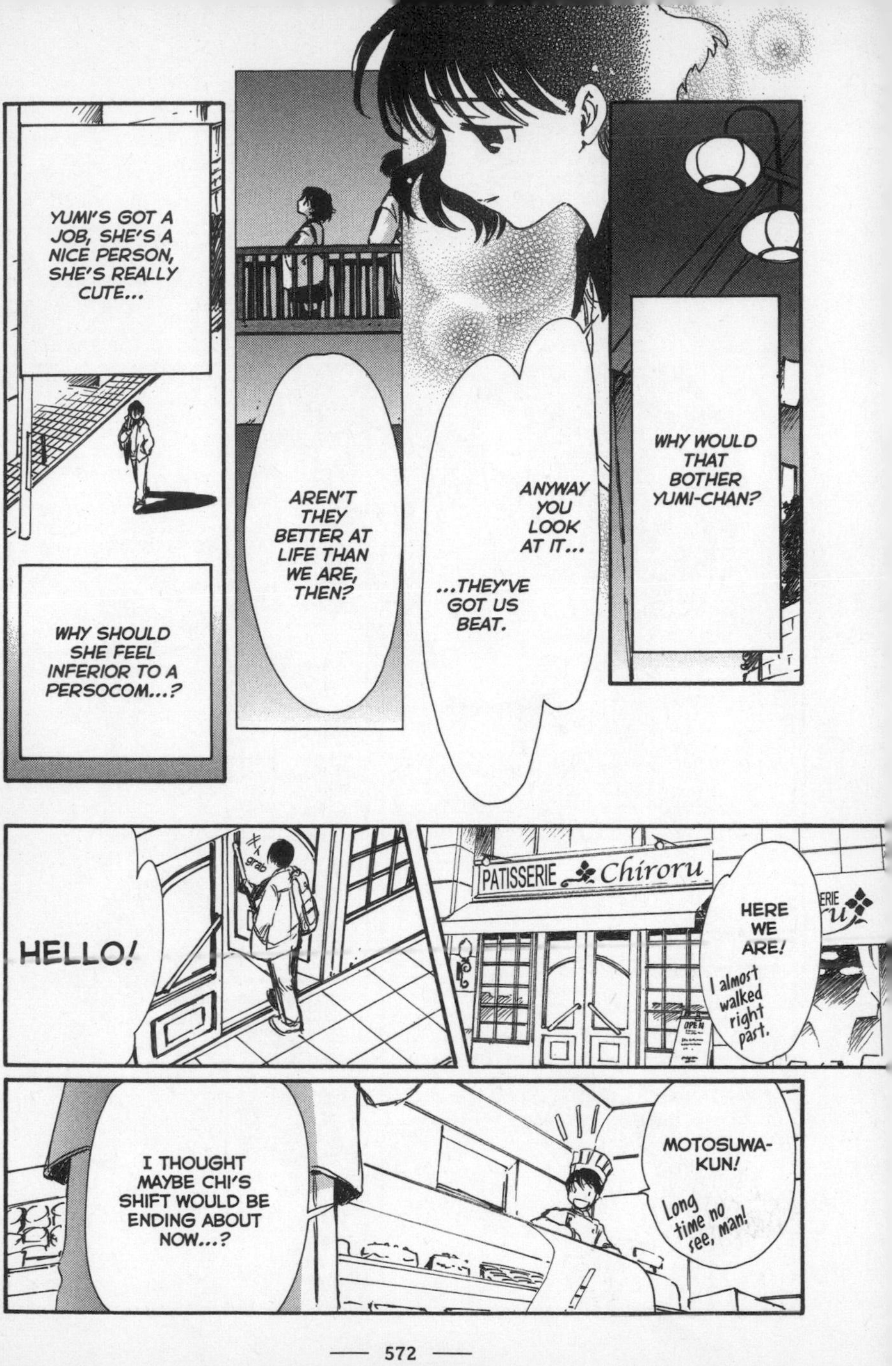
WHY WOULD THAT BOTHER YUMI-CHAN?
ANYWAY YOU LOOK AT IT...
...THEY'VE GOT US BEAT.
AREN'T THEY BETTER AT LIFE THAN WE ARE, THEN?
YUMI'S GOT A JOB, SHE'S A NICE PERSON, SHE'S REALLY CUTE...
WHY SHOULD SHE FEEL INFERIOR TO A PERSOCOM...?
PATISSERIE Chiroru
HERE WE ARE!
I almost walked right past.
grab
HELLO!
MOTOSUWA-KUN!
Long time no see, man!
I THOUGHT MAYBE CHI'S SHIFT WOULD BE ENDING ABOUT NOW...?

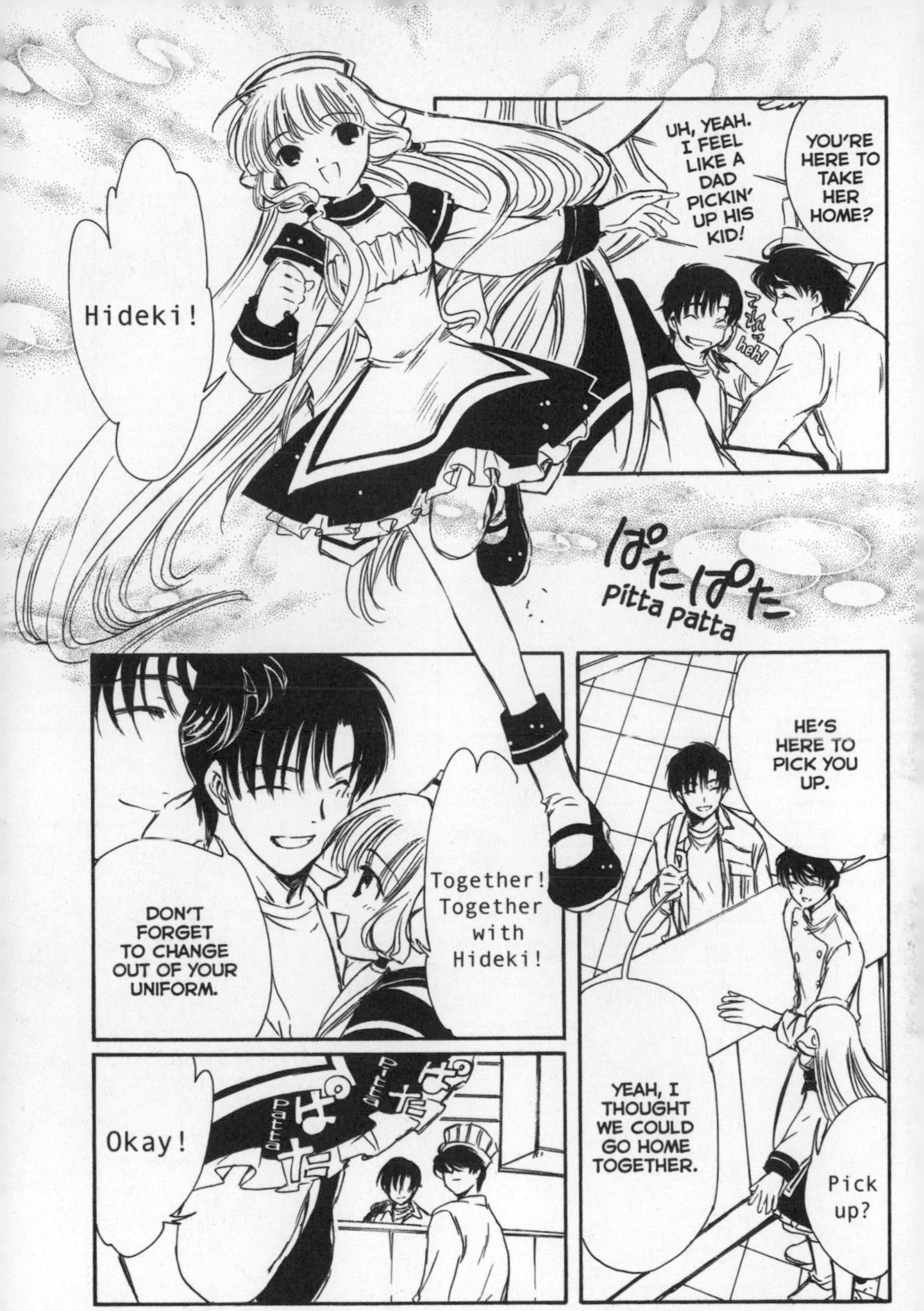

YOU'RE HERE TO TAKE HER HOME?
UH, YEAH. I FEEL LIKE A DAD PICKIN' UP HIS KID!
heh!
Hideki!
ぱたぱた
Pitta patta
HE'S HERE TO PICK YOU UP.
YEAH, I THOUGHT WE COULD GO HOME TOGETHER.
Pick up?
Together! Together with Hideki!
DON'T FORGET TO CHANGE OUT OF YOUR UNIFORM.
ぱた
pitta
ぱた
patta
Okay!

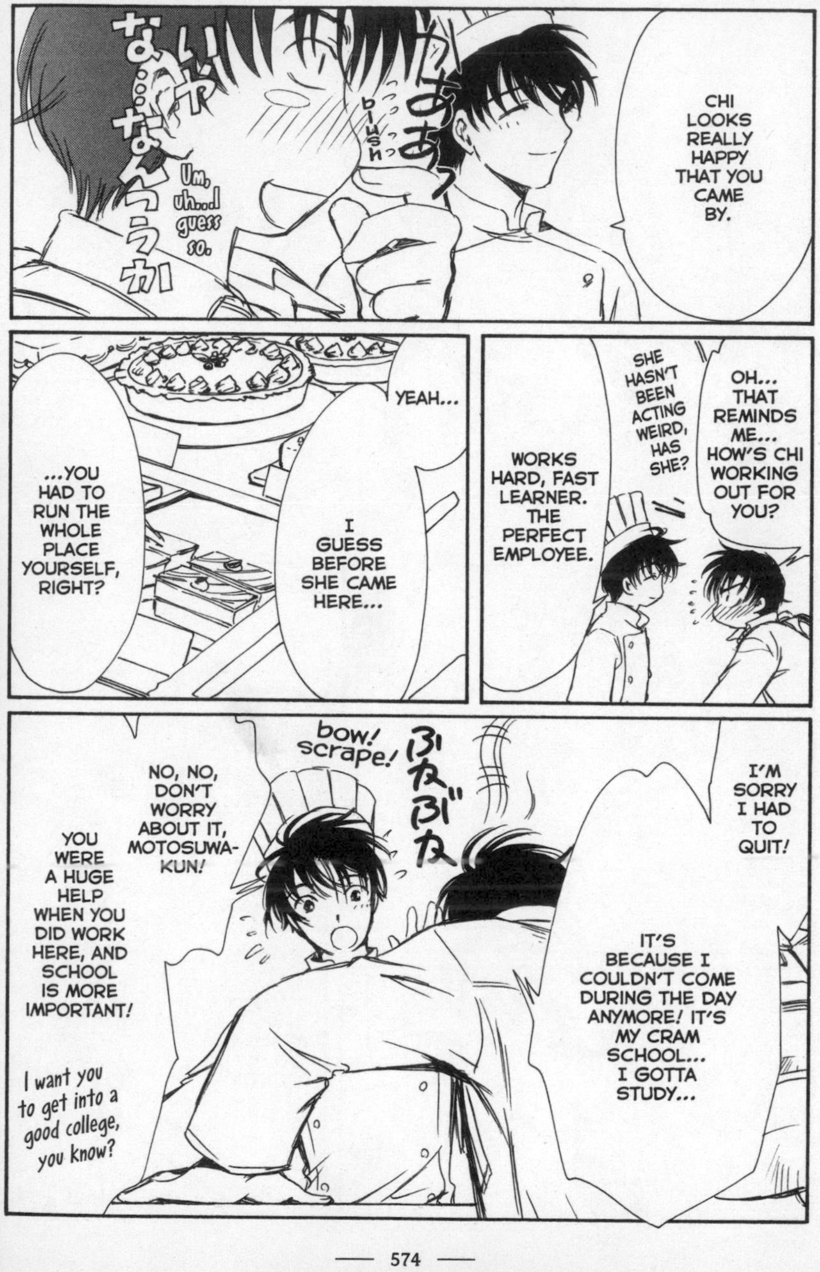
CHI LOOKS REALLY HAPPY THAT YOU CAME BY.
blush
Um, uh...I guess so.
OH... THAT REMINDS ME... HOW'S CHI WORKING OUT FOR YOU?
SHE HASN'T BEEN ACTING WEIRD, HAS SHE?
WORKS HARD, FAST LEARNER. THE PERFECT EMPLOYEE.
YEAH...
I GUESS BEFORE SHE CAME HERE...
...YOU HAD TO RUN THE WHOLE PLACE YOURSELF, RIGHT?
I'M SORRY I HAD TO QUIT!
IT'S BECAUSE I COULDN'T COME DURING THE DAY ANYMORE! IT'S MY CRAM SCHOOL... I GOTTA STUDY...
bow! scrape!
NO, NO, DON'T WORRY ABOUT IT, MOTOSUWA-KUN!
YOU WERE A HUGE HELP WHEN YOU DID WORK HERE, AND SCHOOL IS MORE IMPORTANT!
I want you to get into a good college, you know?

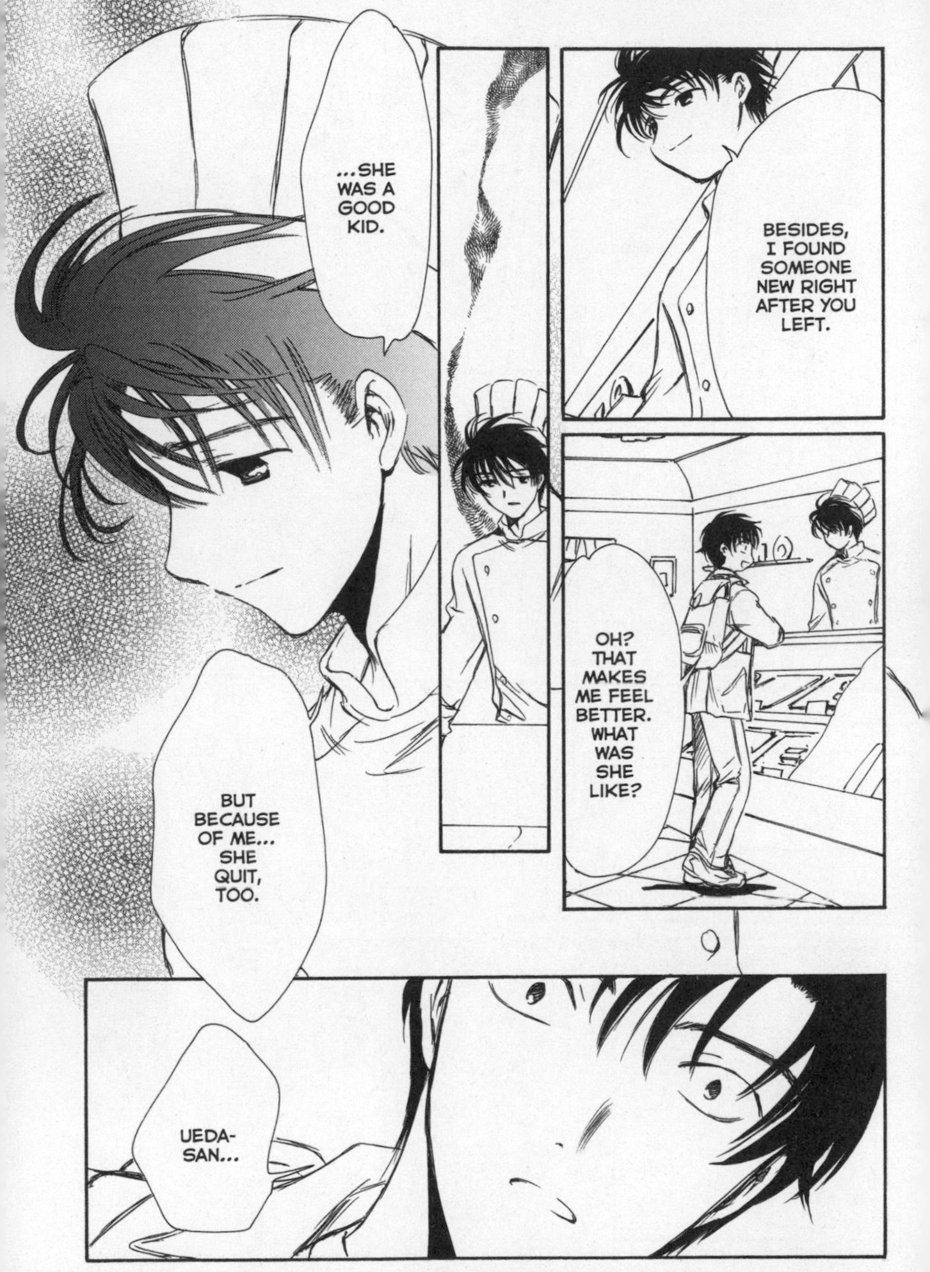
BESIDES, I FOUND SOMEONE NEW RIGHT AFTER YOU LEFT.
OH? THAT MAKES ME FEEL BETTER. WHAT WAS SHE LIKE?
...SHE WAS A GOOD KID.
BUT BECAUSE OF ME... SHE QUIT, TOO.
UEDA-SAN...

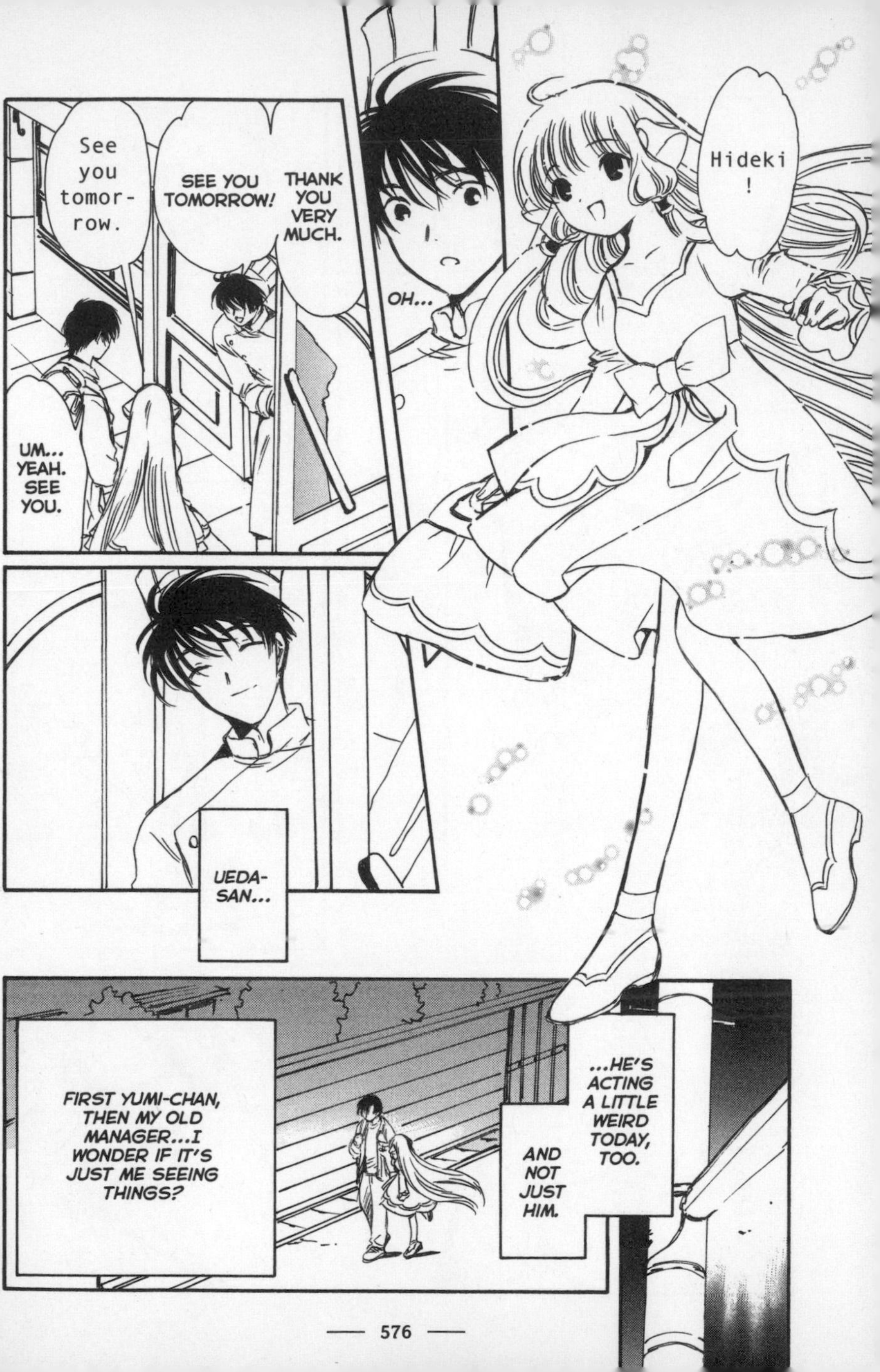
Hideki!
OH...
THANK YOU VERY MUCH.
SEE YOU TOMORROW!
See you tomorrow.
UM... YEAH. SEE YOU.
UEDA-SAN...
...HE'S ACTING A LITTLE WEIRD TODAY, TOO.
AND NOT JUST HIM.
FIRST YUMI-CHAN, THEN MY OLD MANAGER...I WONDER IF IT'S JUST ME SEEING THINGS?

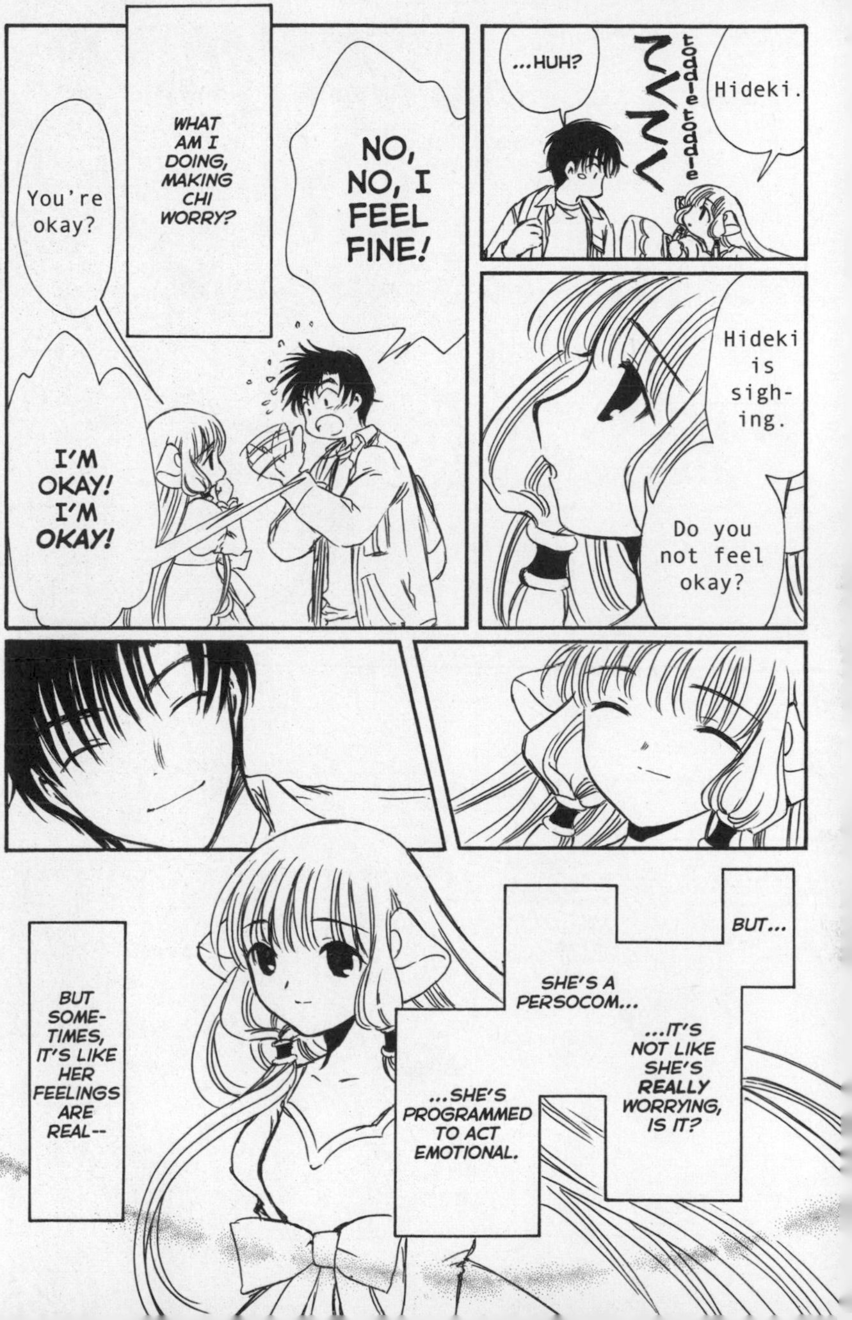
Hideki.
てくてく
toddle toddle
...HUH?
Hideki is sigh-ing.
Do you not feel okay?
NO, NO, I FEEL FINE!
WHAT AM I DOING, MAKING CHI WORRY?
You're okay?
I'M OKAY! I'M OKAY!
BUT...
SHE'S A PERSOCOM...
...IT'S NOT LIKE SHE'S REALLY WORRYING, IS IT?
...SHE'S PROGRAMMED TO ACT EMOTIONAL.
BUT SOME-TIMES, IT'S LIKE HER FEELINGS ARE REAL--

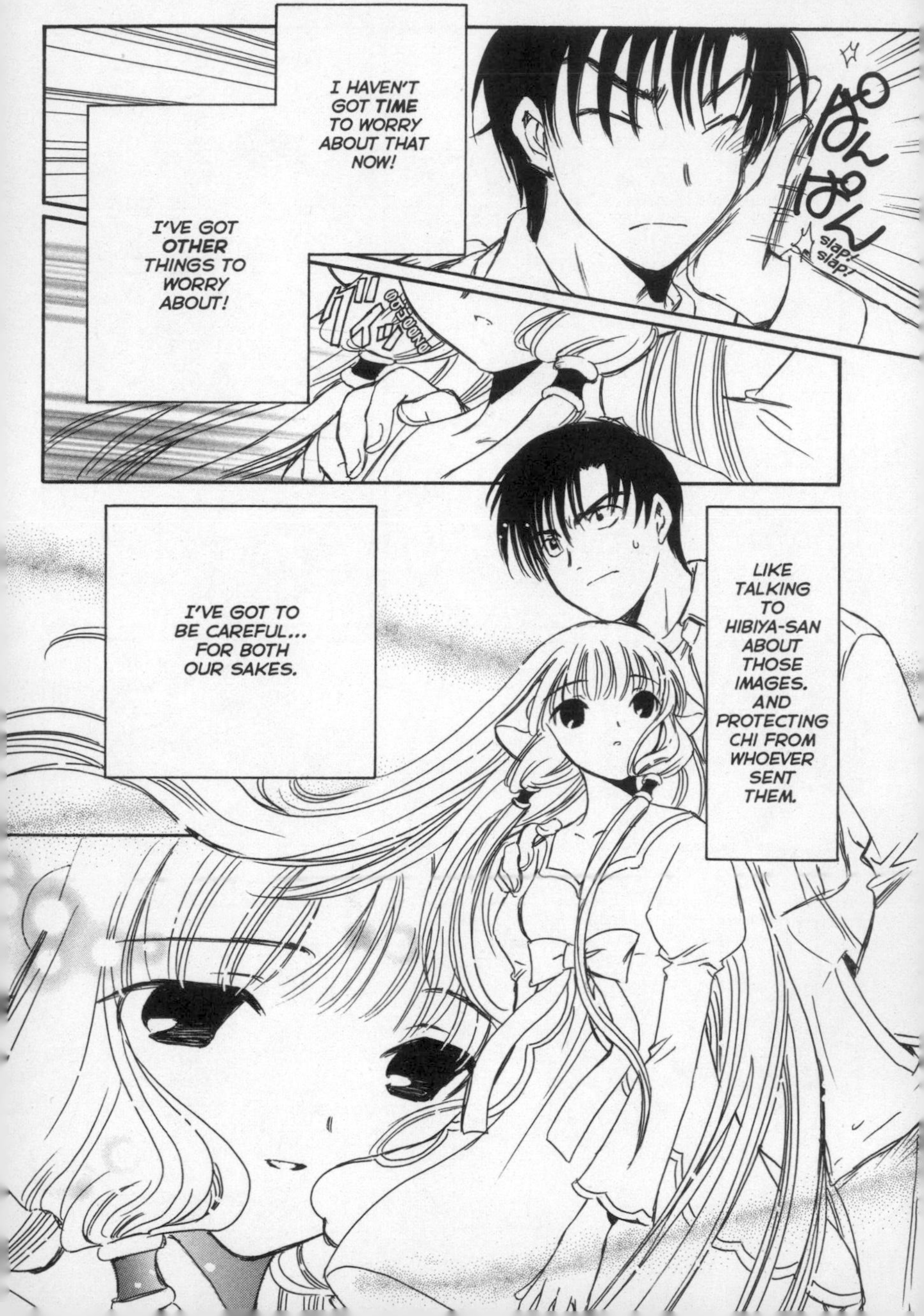
ぱんぱん
slap! slap!
I HAVEN'T GOT TIME TO WORRY ABOUT THAT NOW!
I'VE GOT OTHER THINGS TO WORRY ABOUT!
グイッ
LIKE TALKING TO HIBIYA-SAN ABOUT THOSE IMAGES. AND PROTECTING CHI FROM WHOEVER SENT THEM.
I'VE GOT TO BE CAREFUL... FOR BOTH OUR SAKES.

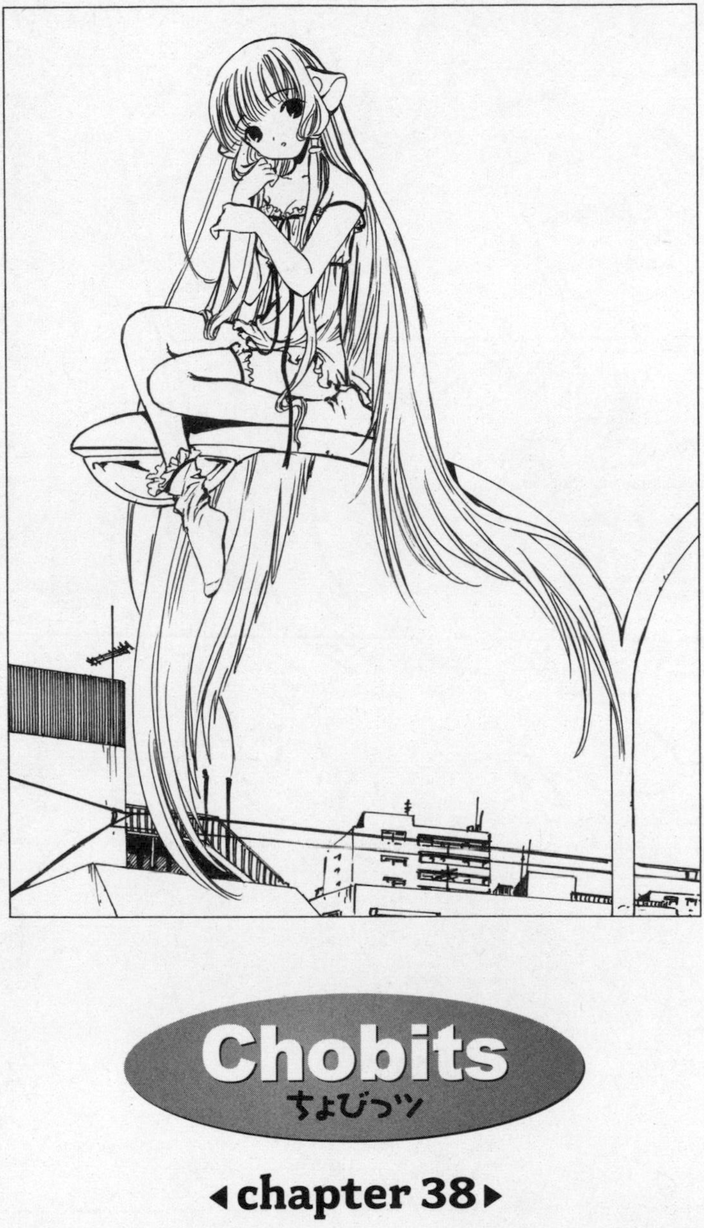

Chobits
ちょびっツ

◂chapter 38▸

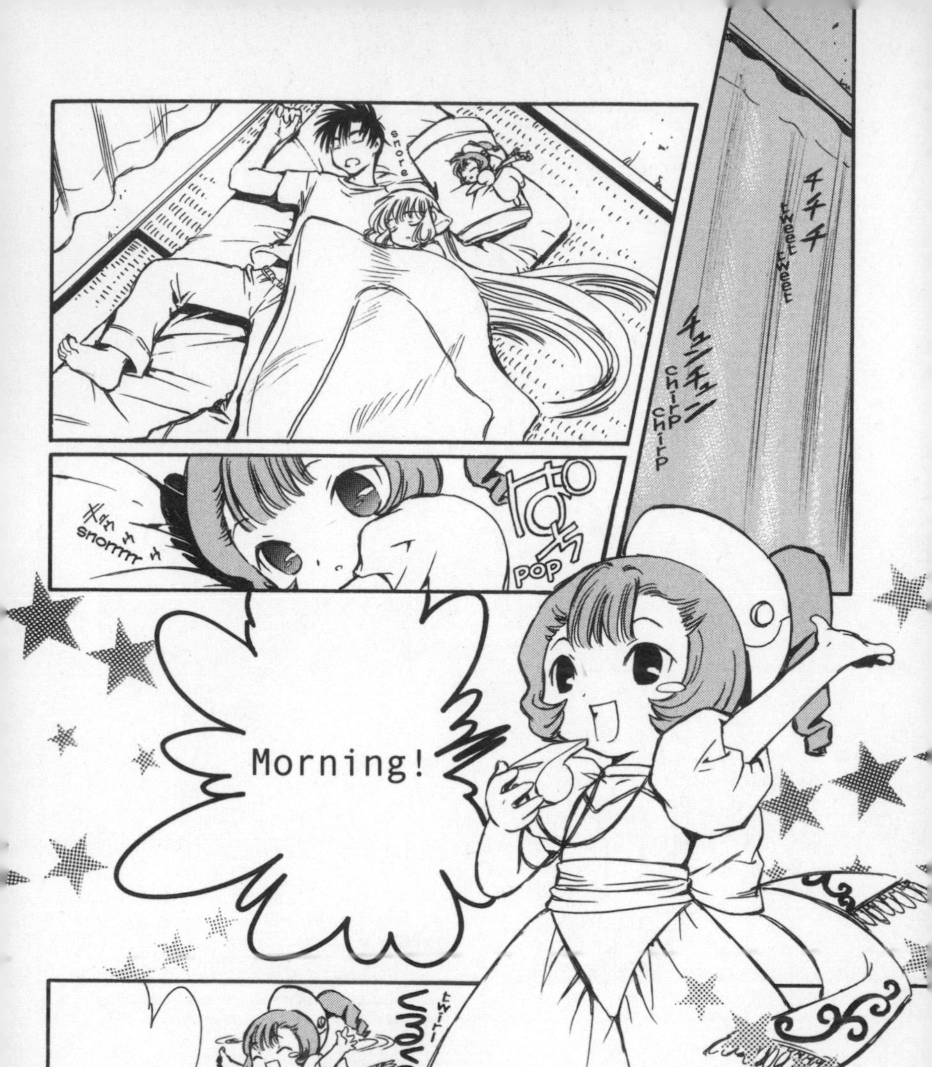
チチ
tweet tweet
チュンチュン
chirp chirp
snore
ぱち
pop
snorrrr
Morning!
twirl
Master! It's morning!

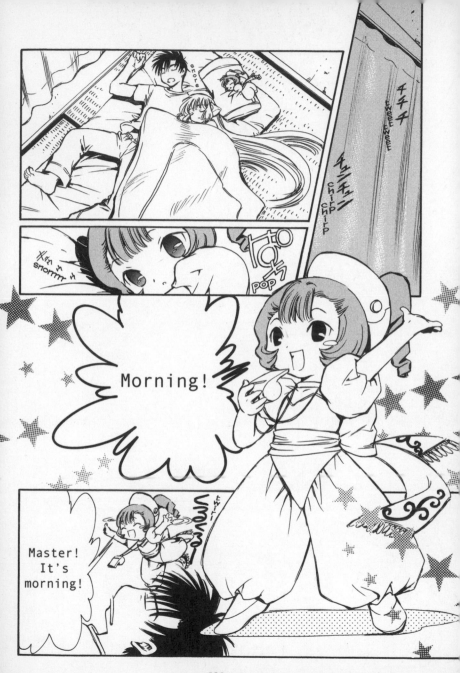

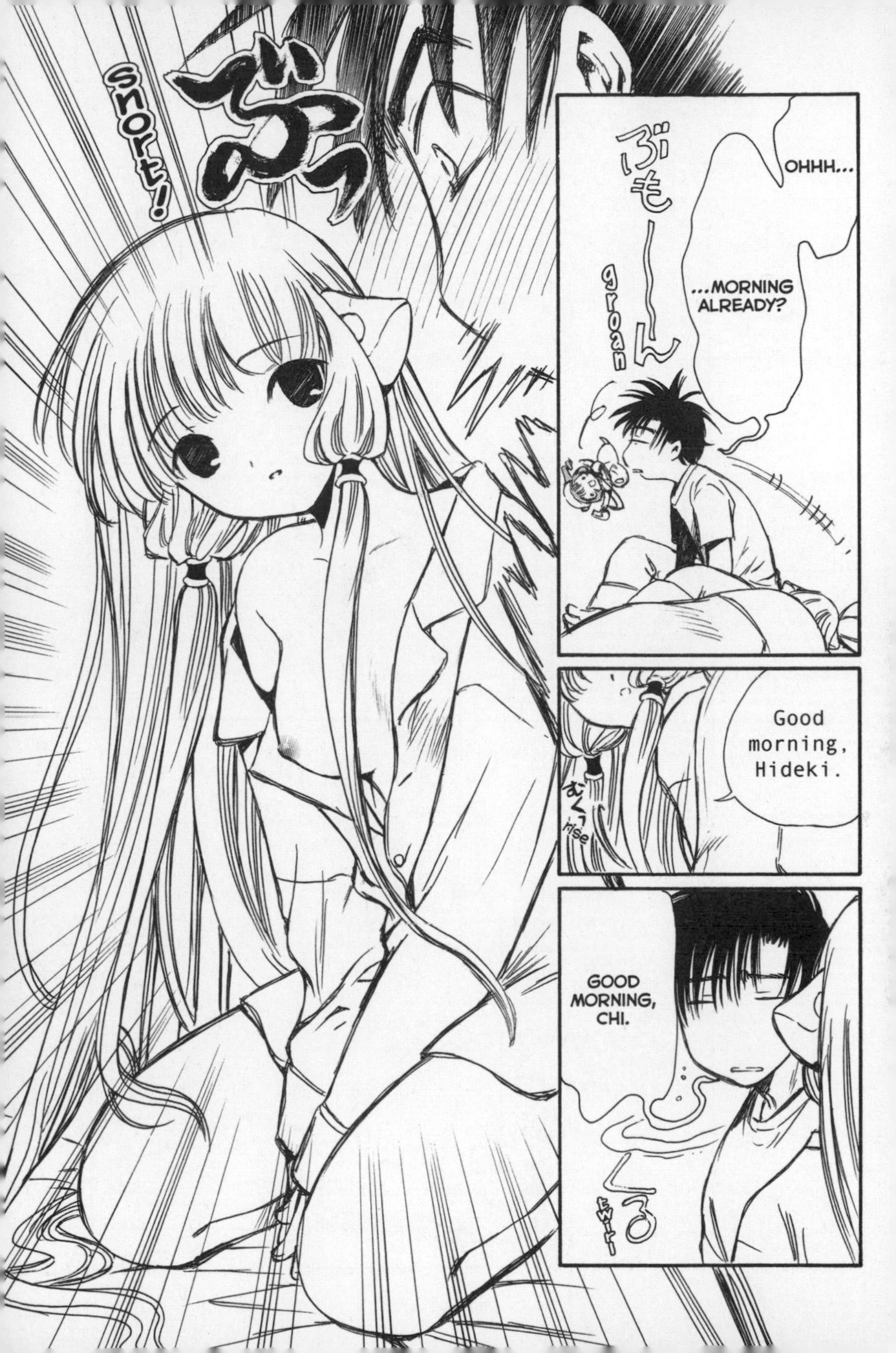
ぶもーーん
groan
OHHH...
...MORNING ALREADY?
むくっ
rise
Good morning, Hideki.
GOOD MORNING, CHI.
くる
twirl
ぶっ
Snort!

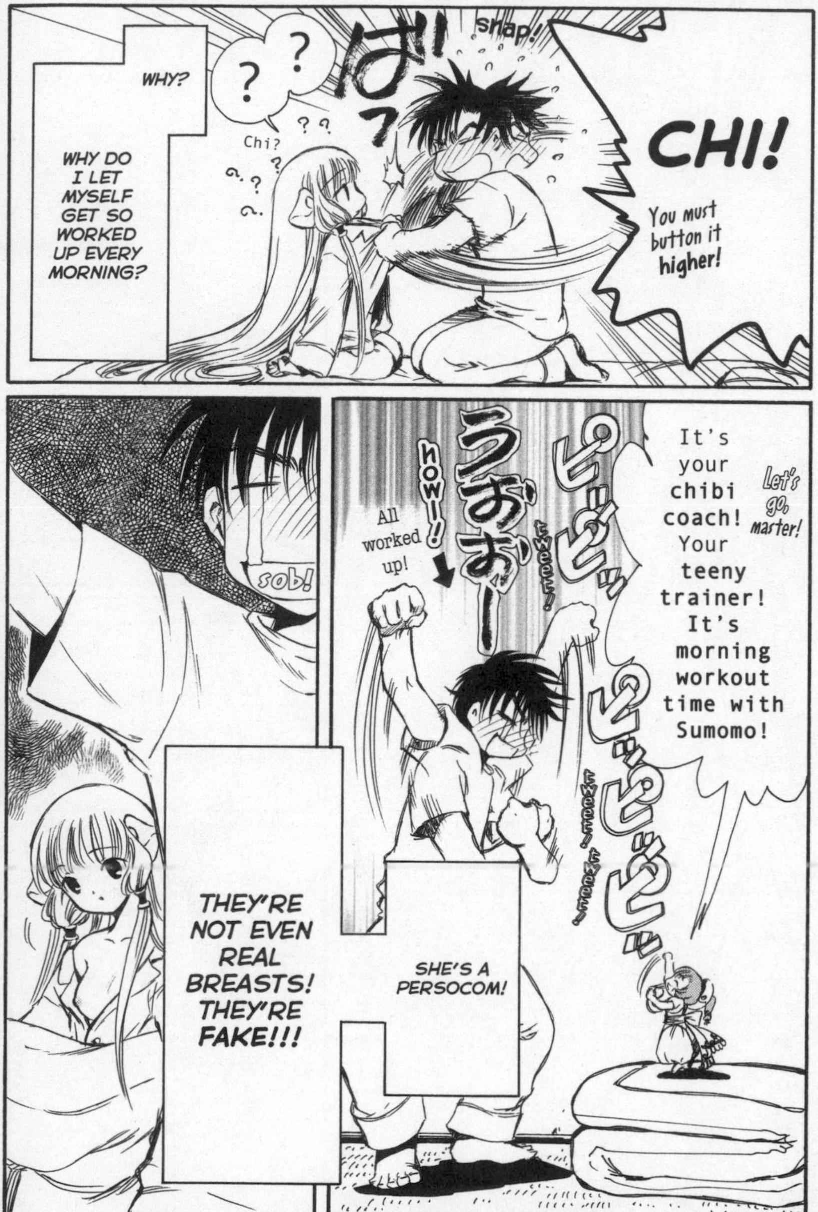
CHI!
You must button it higher!
snap!
ぱっ
? ?
Chi?
WHY?
WHY DO I LET MYSELF GET SO WORKED UP EVERY MORNING?
It's your chibi coach! Your teeny trainer! It's morning workout time with Sumomo!
Let's go, master!
ぴっぴっ
ぴっぴっぴっ
うおおー
now!
All worked up!
SHE'S A PERSOCOM!
sob!
THEY'RE NOT EVEN REAL BREASTS! THEY'RE FAKE!!!

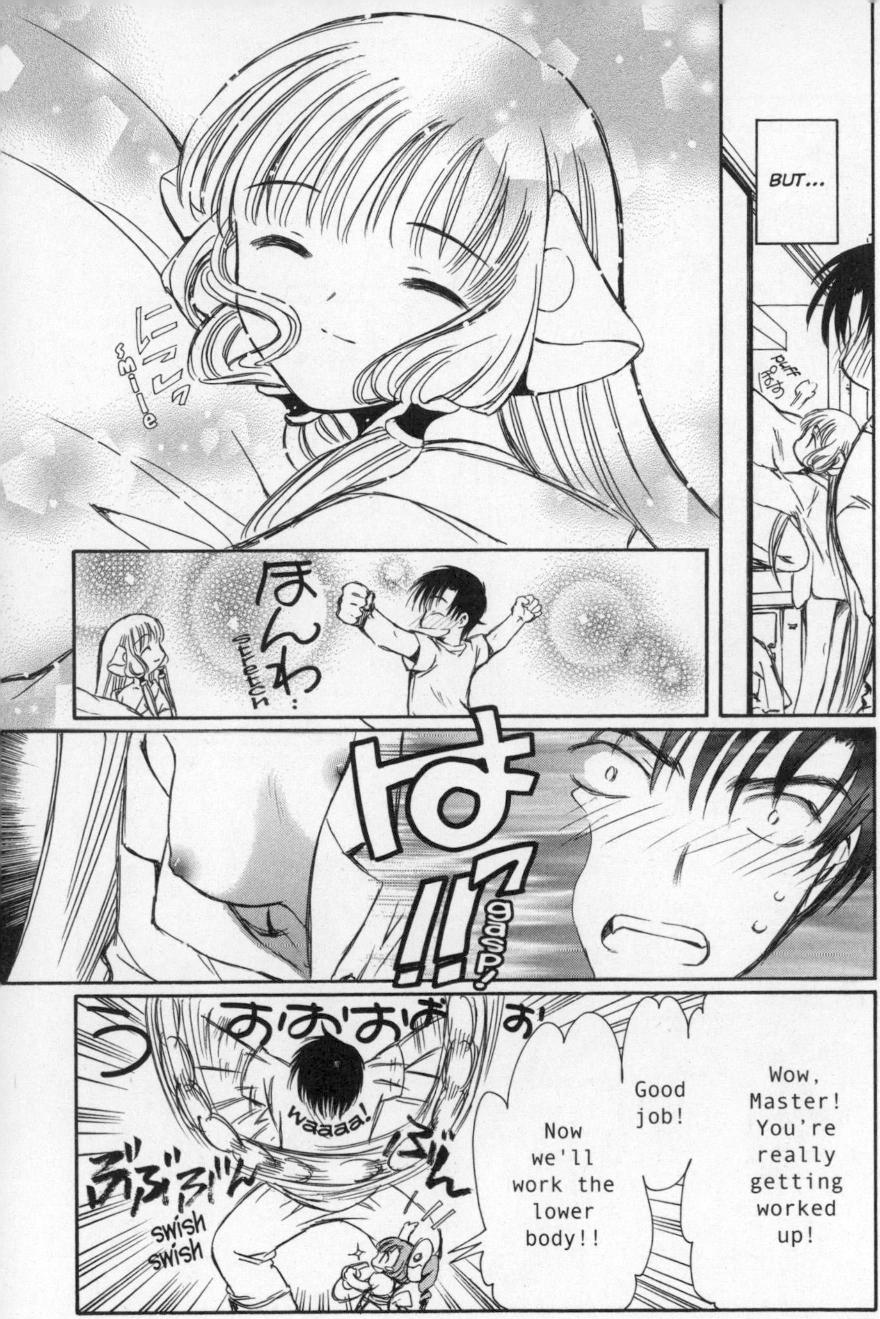
BUT...
puff
smile
stretch
gasp!
Wow, Master! You're really getting worked up!
Good job!
Now we'll work the lower body!!
waaaa!
swish swish

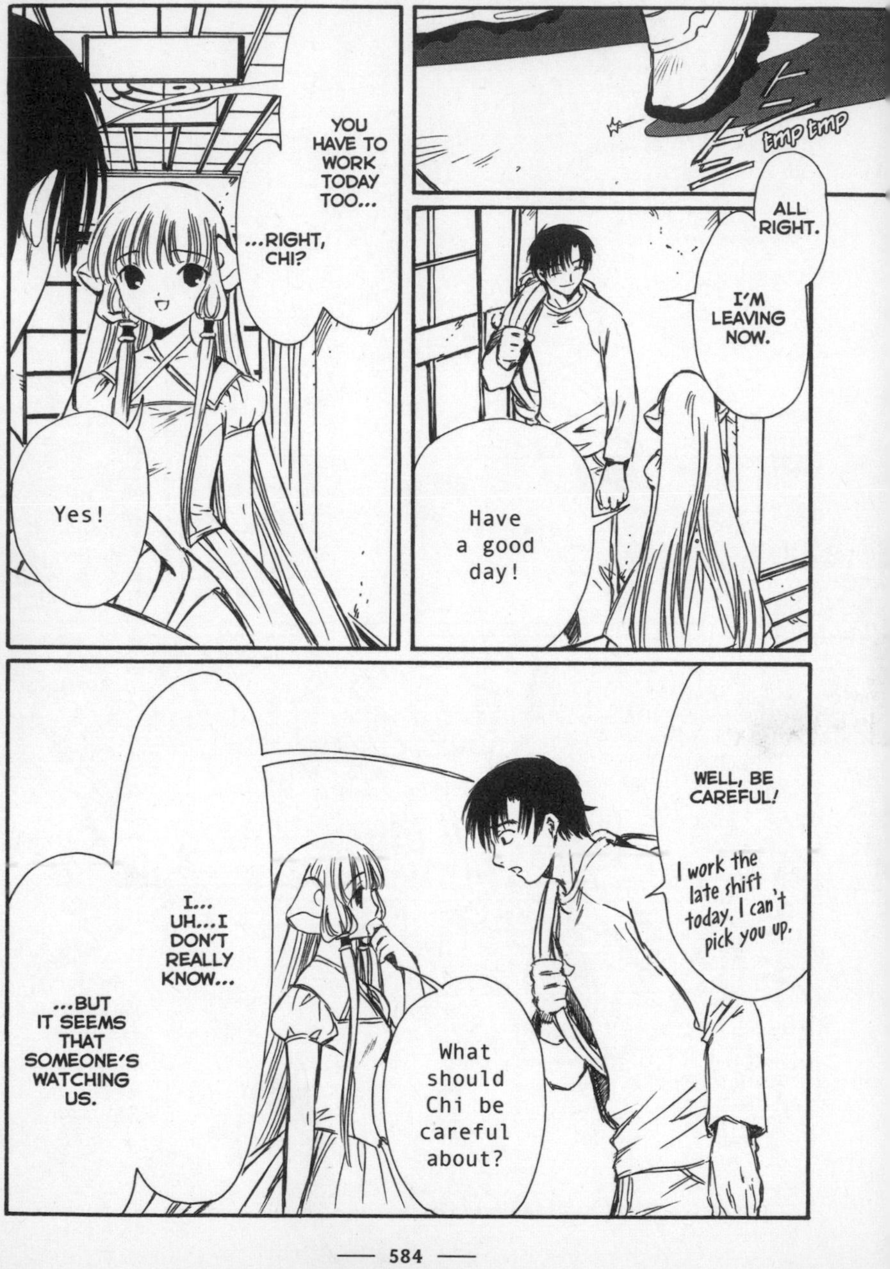
tmp tmp
ALL RIGHT.
I'M LEAVING NOW.
Have a good day!
YOU HAVE TO WORK TODAY TOO...
...RIGHT, CHI?
Yes!
WELL, BE CAREFUL!
I work the late shift today. I can't pick you up.
What should Chi be careful about?
I... UH...I DON'T REALLY KNOW...
...BUT IT SEEMS THAT SOMEONE'S WATCHING US.

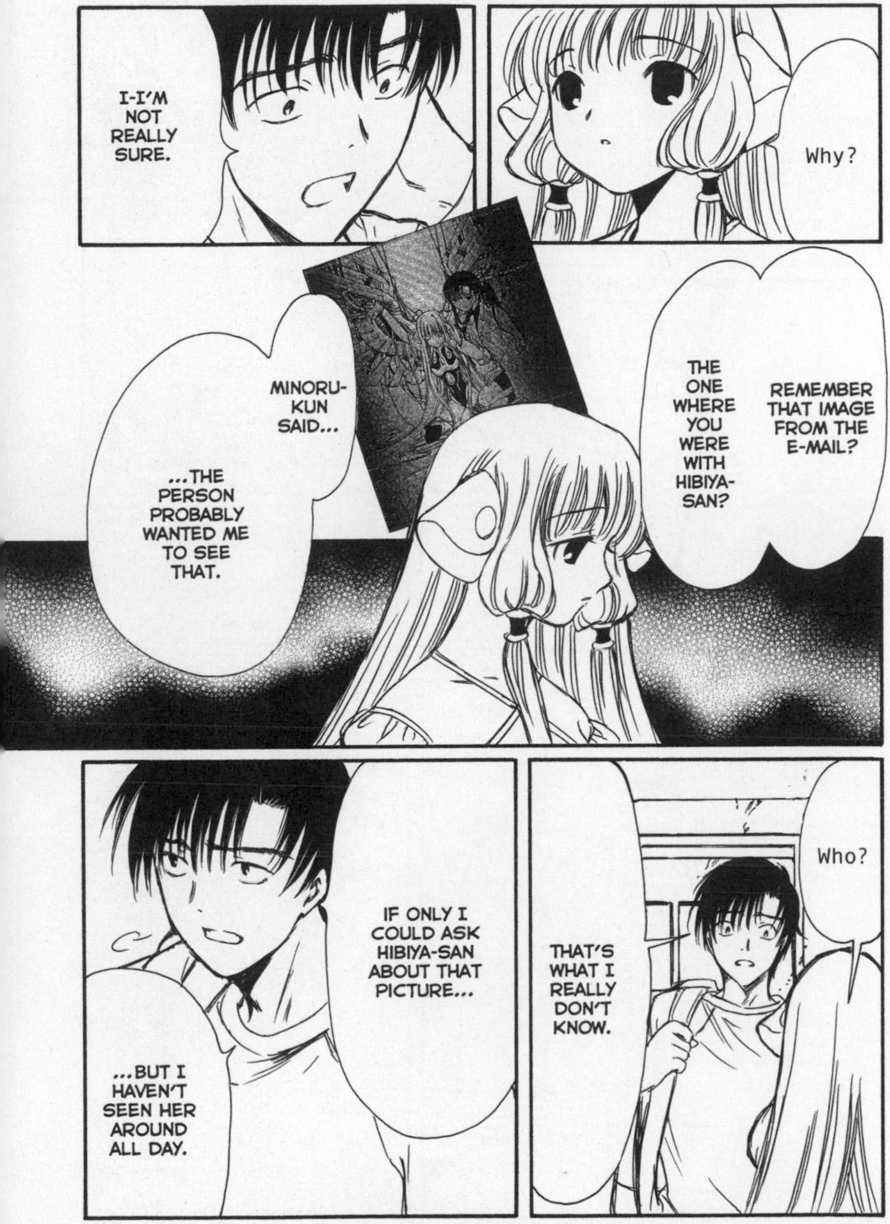
Why?
I-I'M NOT REALLY SURE.
REMEMBER THAT IMAGE FROM THE E-MAIL?
THE ONE WHERE YOU WERE WITH HIBIYA-SAN?
MINORU-KUN SAID...
...THE PERSON PROBABLY WANTED ME TO SEE THAT.
Who?
THAT'S WHAT I REALLY DON'T KNOW.
IF ONLY I COULD ASK HIBIYA-SAN ABOUT THAT PICTURE...
...BUT I HAVEN'T SEEN HER AROUND ALL DAY.

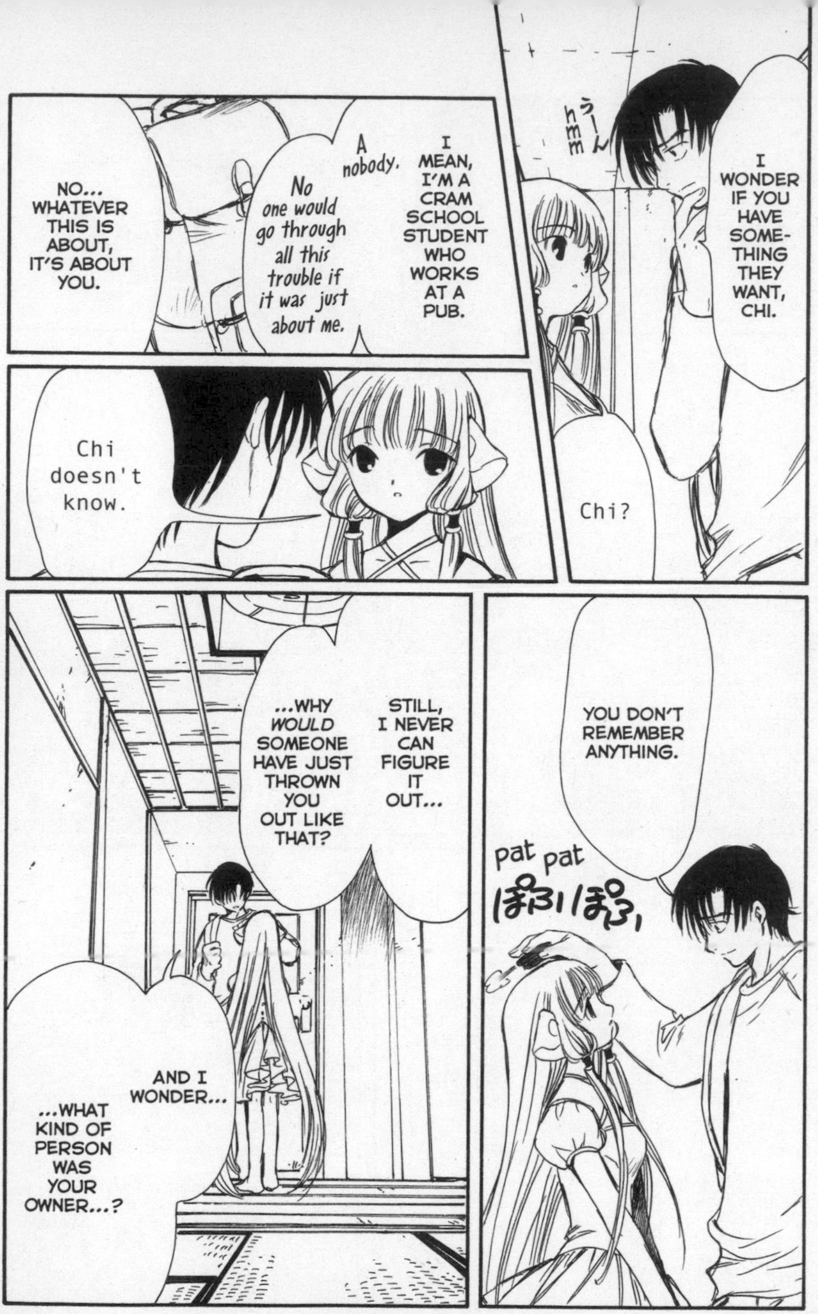
うーん hmm
I WONDER IF YOU HAVE SOMETHING THEY WANT, CHI.
Chi?
I MEAN, I'M A CRAM SCHOOL STUDENT WHO WORKS AT A PUB.
A nobody.
No one would go through all this trouble if it was just about me.
NO... WHATEVER THIS IS ABOUT, IT'S ABOUT YOU.
Chi doesn't know.
YOU DON'T REMEMBER ANYTHING.
pat pat ぽふぽふ
STILL, I NEVER CAN FIGURE IT OUT...
...WHY WOULD SOMEONE HAVE JUST THROWN YOU OUT LIKE THAT?
AND I WONDER...
...WHAT KIND OF PERSON WAS YOUR OWNER...?

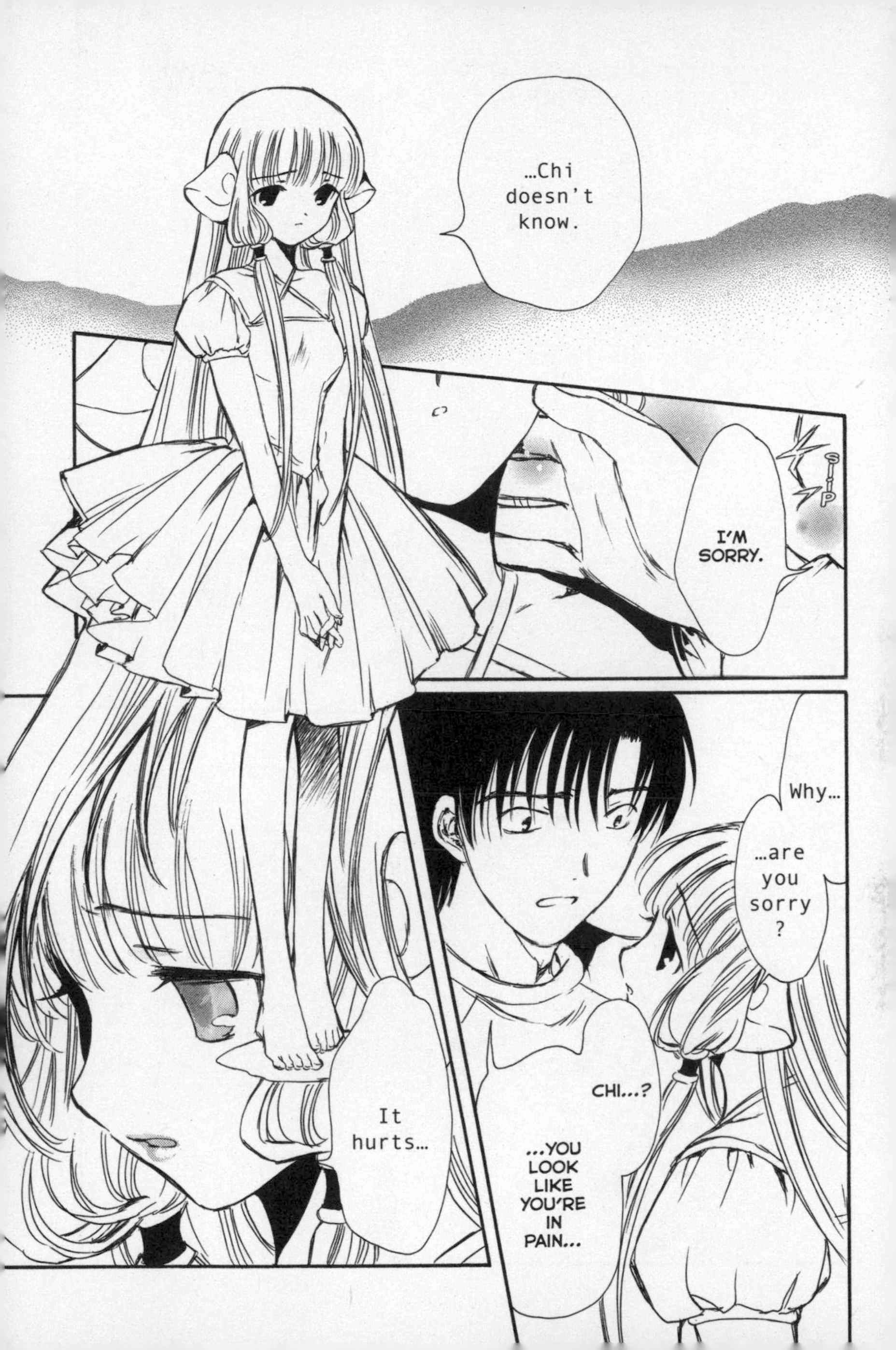
...Chi doesn't know.
SIP
I'M SORRY.
Why...
...are you sorry?
CHI...?
...YOU LOOK LIKE YOU'RE IN PAIN...
It hurts...

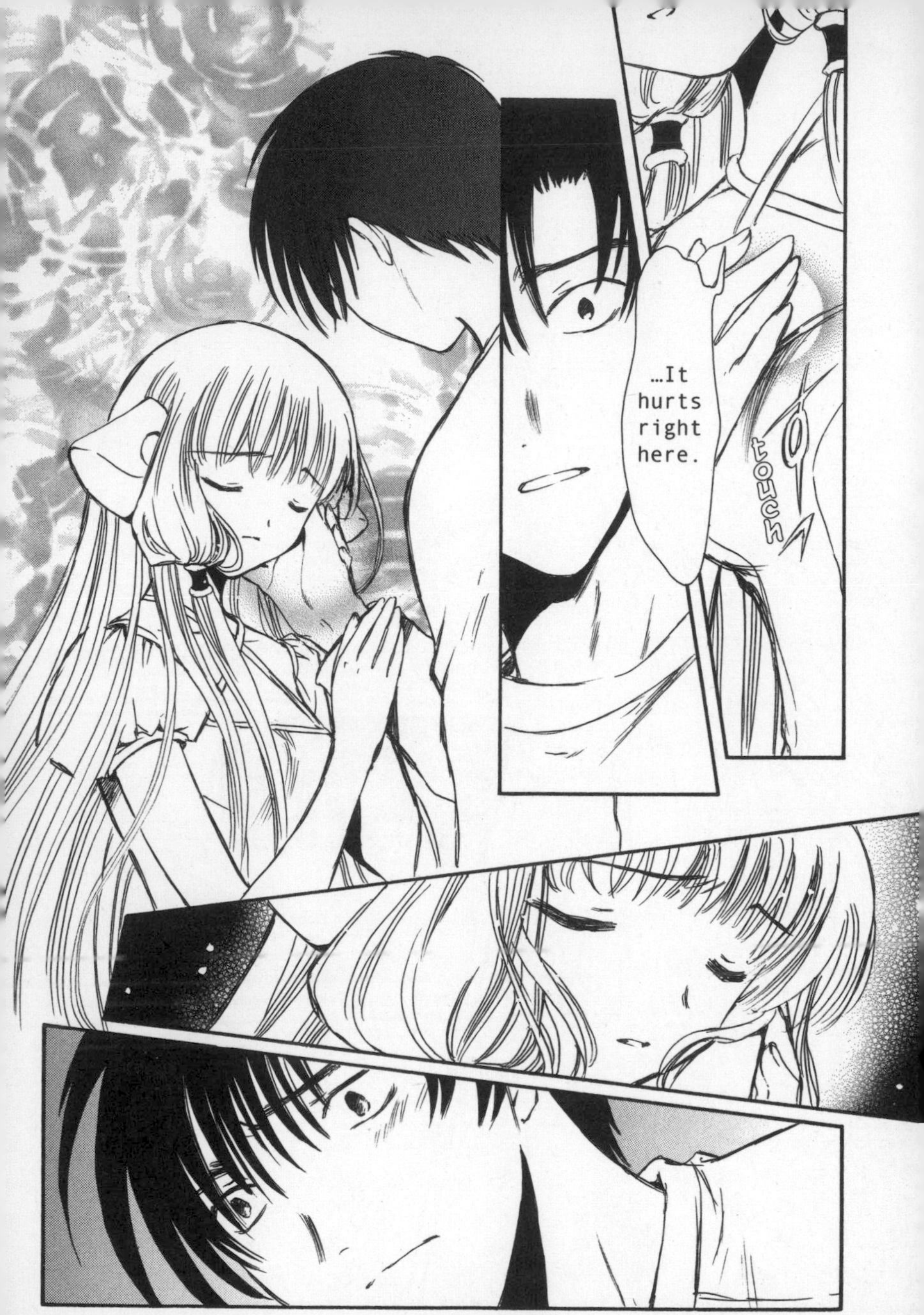
…It hurts right here.
touch

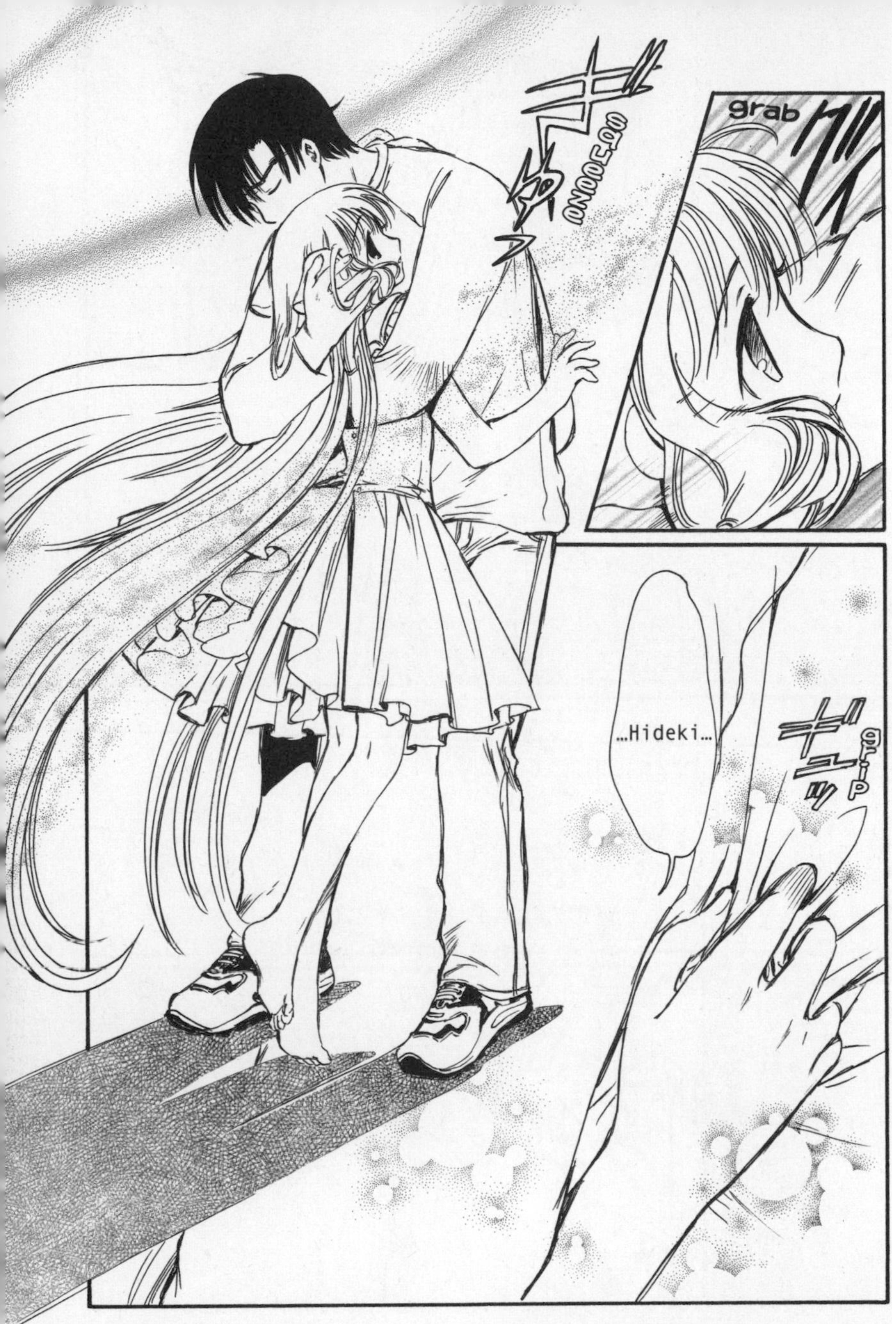
grab
grip
...Hideki...

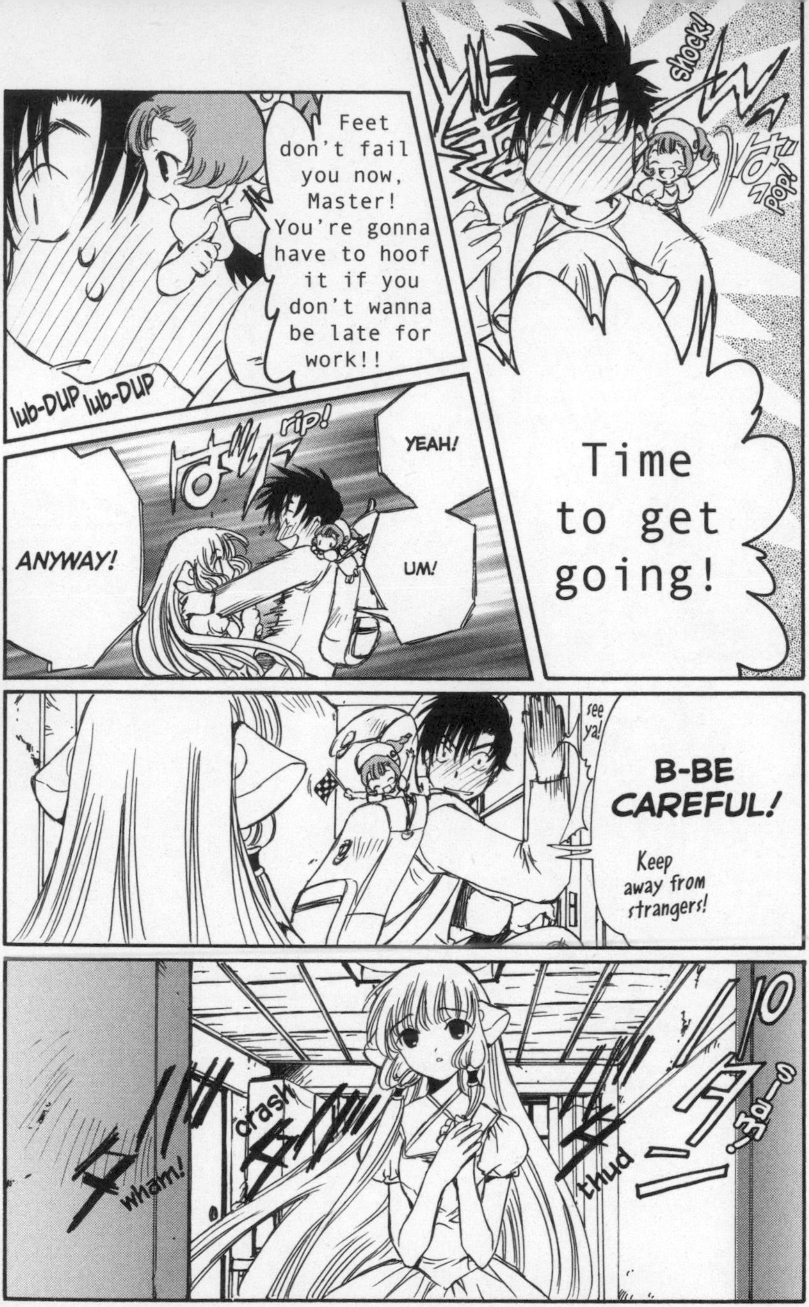

shock!
pop!
Time to get going!
Feet don't fail you now, Master! You're gonna have to hoof it if you don't wanna be late for work!!
lub-DUP lub-DUP
rip!
YEAH!
UM!
ANYWAY!
see ya!
B-BE CAREFUL!
Keep away from strangers!
thud
crash
wham!

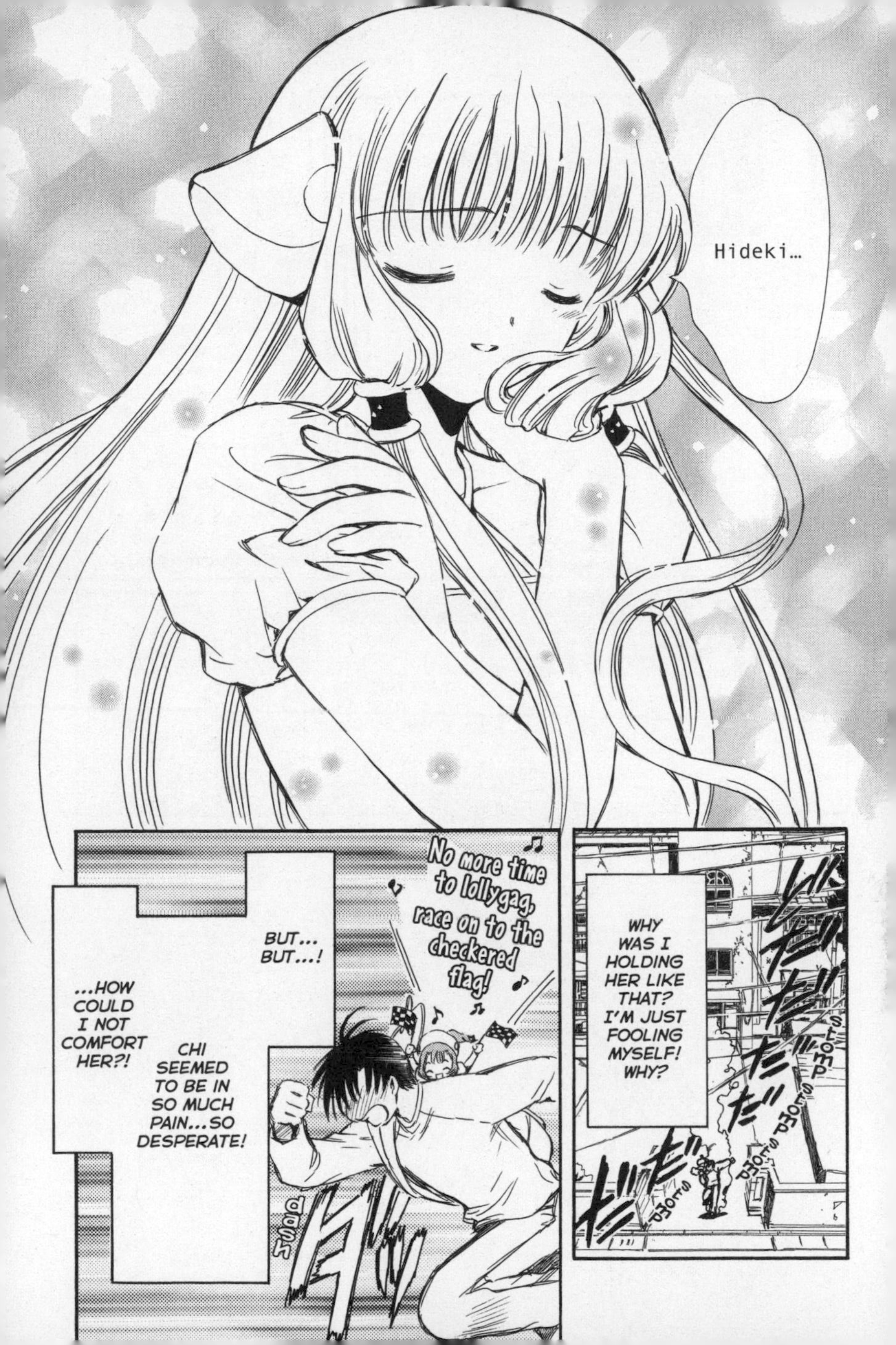
Hideki…
WHY WAS I HOLDING HER LIKE THAT? I'M JUST FOOLING MYSELF! WHY?
STOMP
No more time to lollygag, race on to the checkered flag!
BUT… BUT…!
…HOW COULD I NOT COMFORT HER?!
CHI SEEMED TO BE IN SO MUCH PAIN…SO DESPERATE!
OOPS

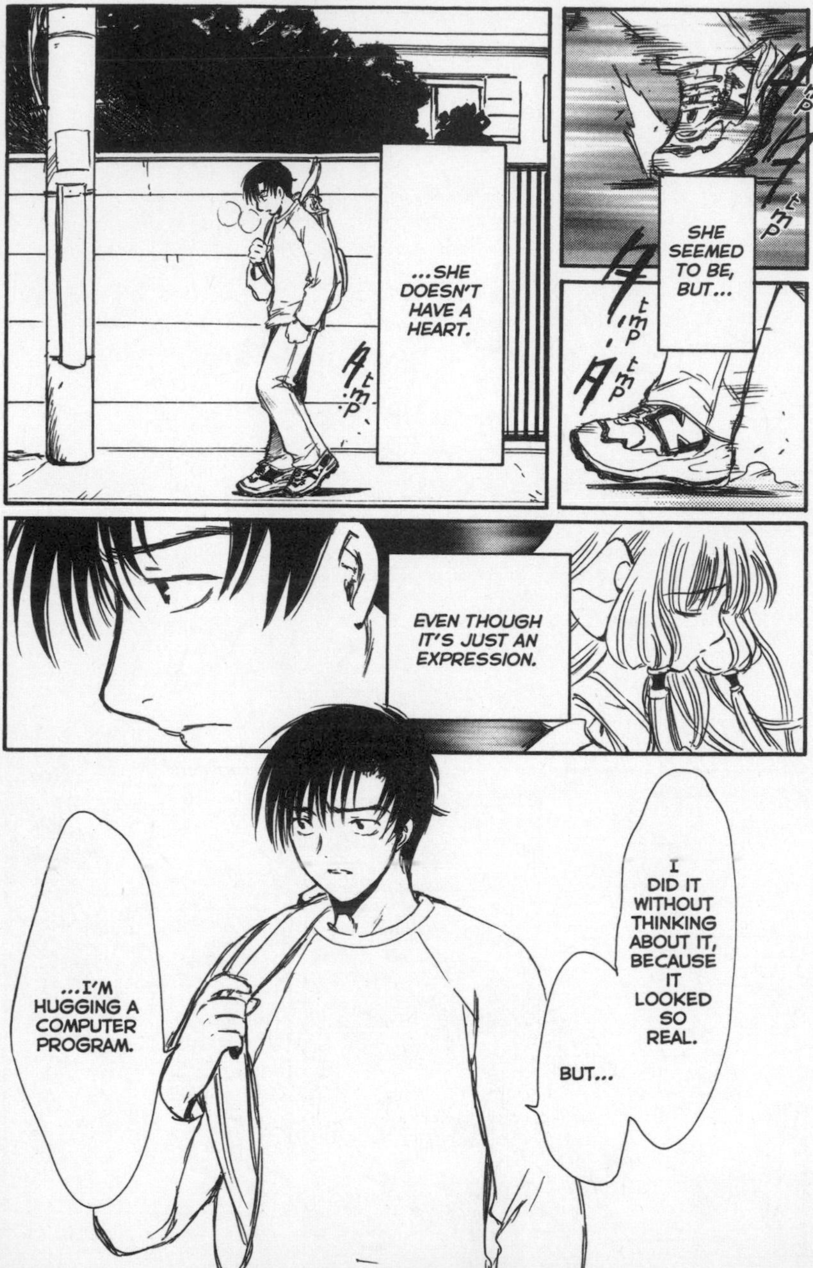
tmp
tmp
SHE SEEMED TO BE, BUT...
tmp
tmp
...SHE DOESN'T HAVE A HEART.
tmp
EVEN THOUGH IT'S JUST AN EXPRESSION.
I DID IT WITHOUT THINKING ABOUT IT, BECAUSE IT LOOKED SO REAL.
BUT...
...I'M HUGGING A COMPUTER PROGRAM.

Chobits

ちょびっツ

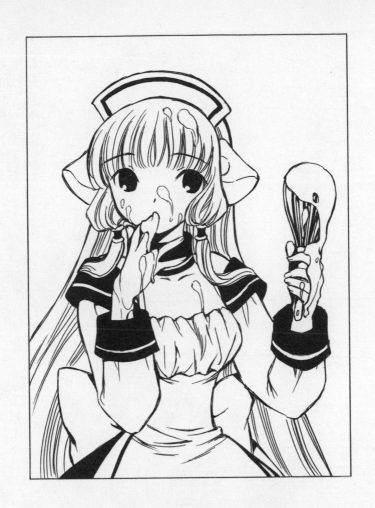

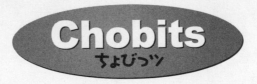

◂ chapter 39 ▸

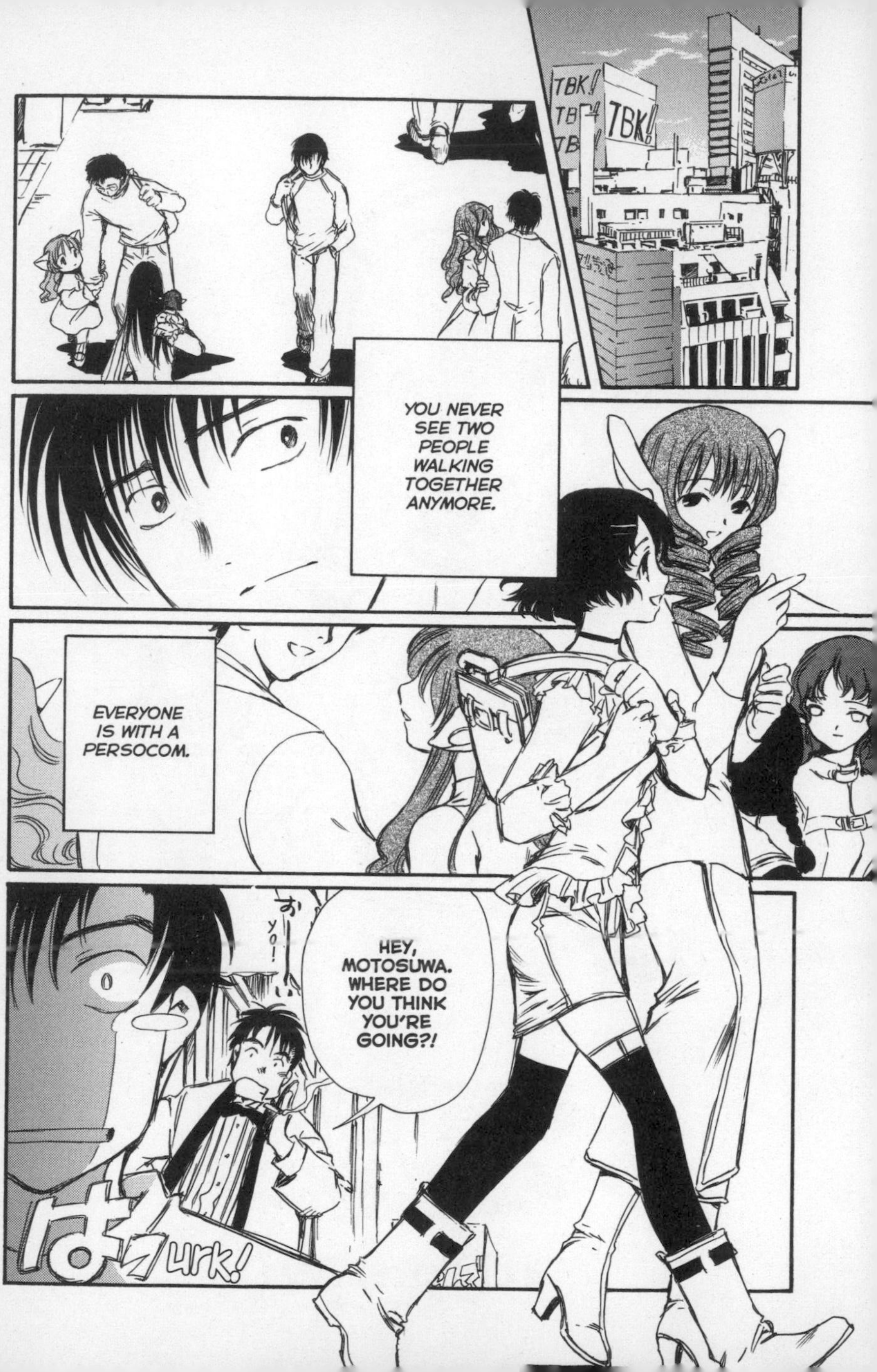
TBK!
YOU NEVER SEE TWO PEOPLE WALKING TOGETHER ANYMORE.
EVERYONE IS WITH A PERSOCOM.
yo!
HEY, MOTOSUWA. WHERE DO YOU THINK YOU'RE GOING?!
はっurk!

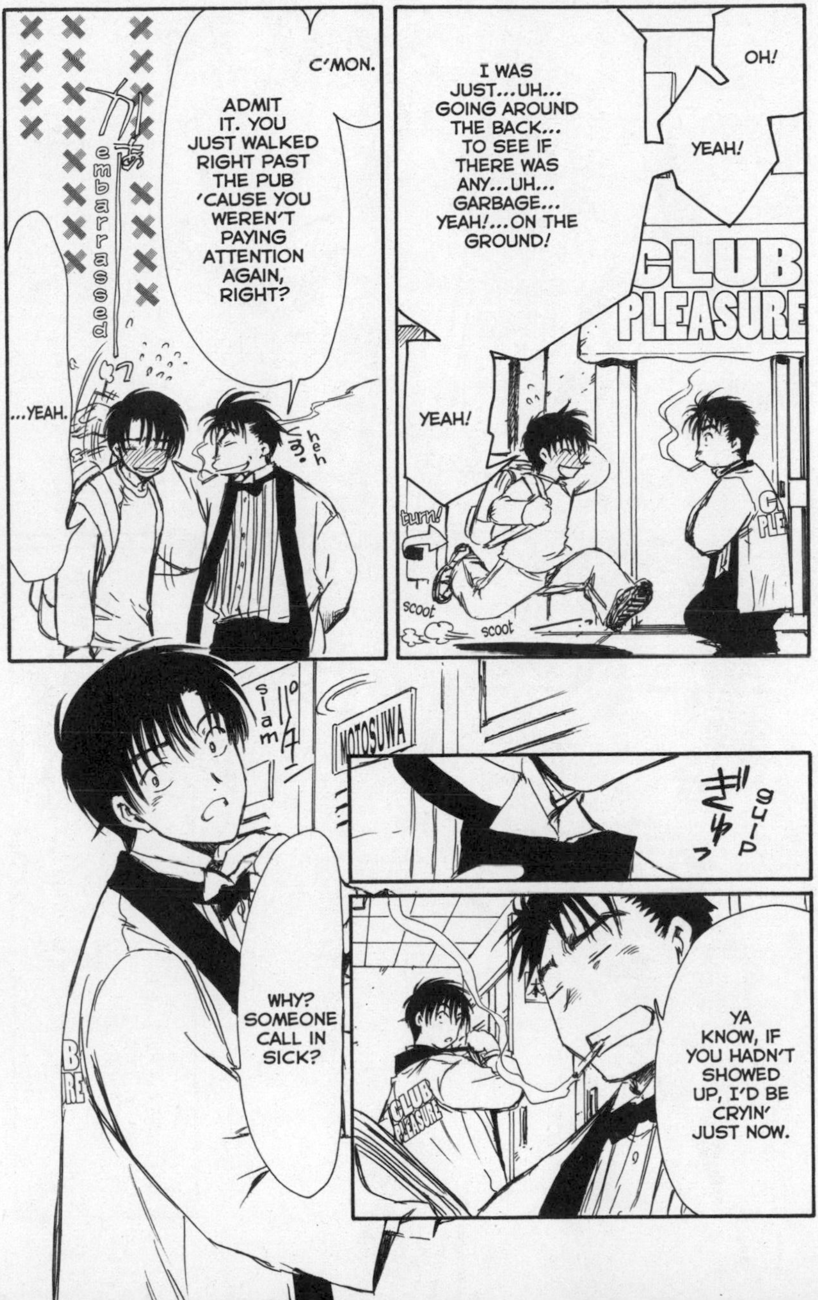
OH!
YEAH!
I WAS JUST...UH... GOING AROUND THE BACK... TO SEE IF THERE WAS ANY...UH... GARBAGE... YEAH!...ON THE GROUND!
CLUB PLEASURE
YEAH!
turn!
scoot
scoot
C'MON.
ADMIT IT. YOU JUST WALKED RIGHT PAST THE PUB 'CAUSE YOU WEREN'T PAYING ATTENTION AGAIN, RIGHT?
embarrassed
heh
...YEAH.
gulp
YA KNOW, IF YOU HADN'T SHOWED UP, I'D BE CRYIN' JUST NOW.
CLUB PLEASURE
slam
MOTOSUWA
WHY? SOMEONE CALL IN SICK?

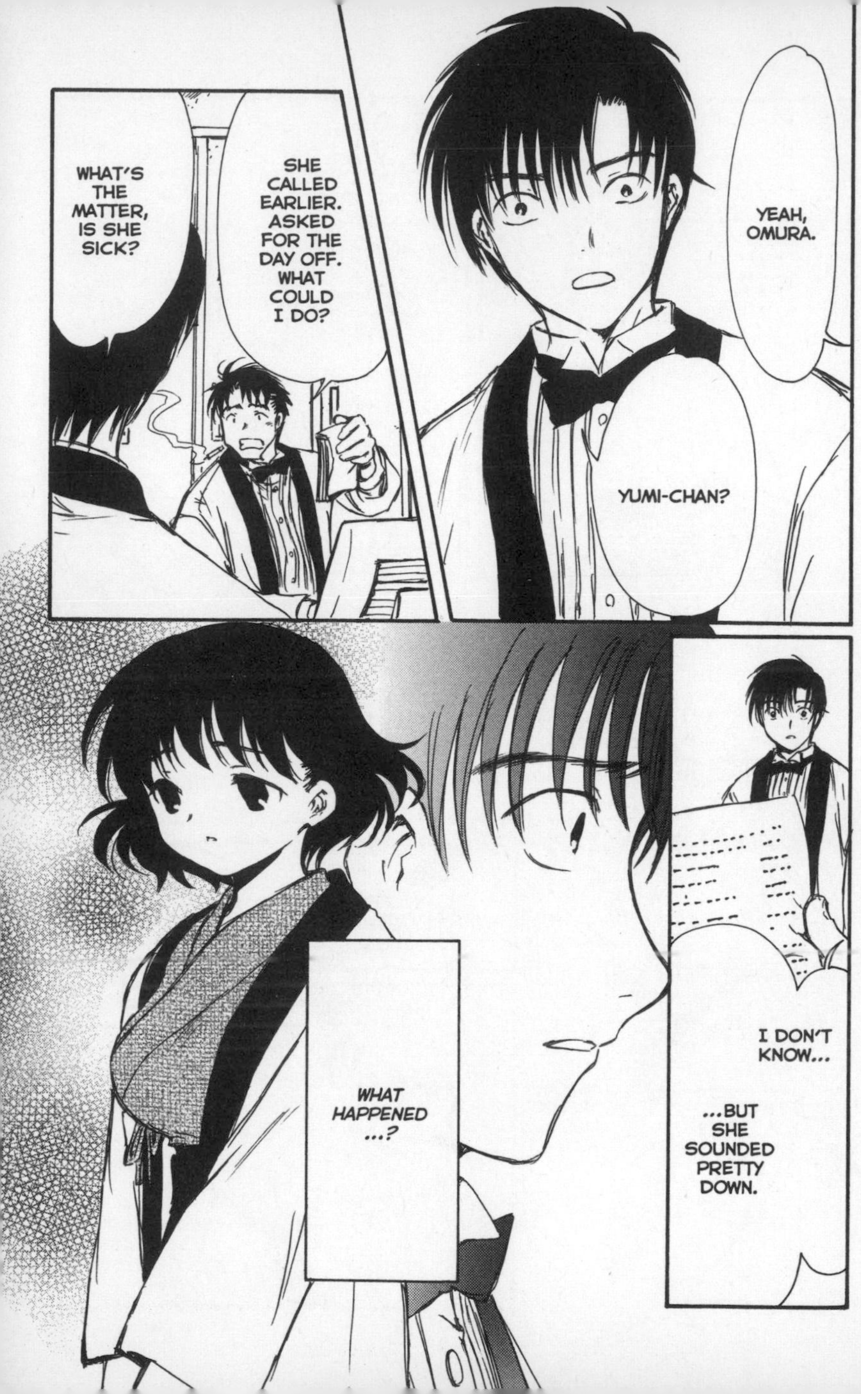
YEAH, OMURA.
YUMI-CHAN?
SHE CALLED EARLIER. ASKED FOR THE DAY OFF. WHAT COULD I DO?
WHAT'S THE MATTER, IS SHE SICK?
I DON'T KNOW...
...BUT SHE SOUNDED PRETTY DOWN.
WHAT HAPPENED ...?

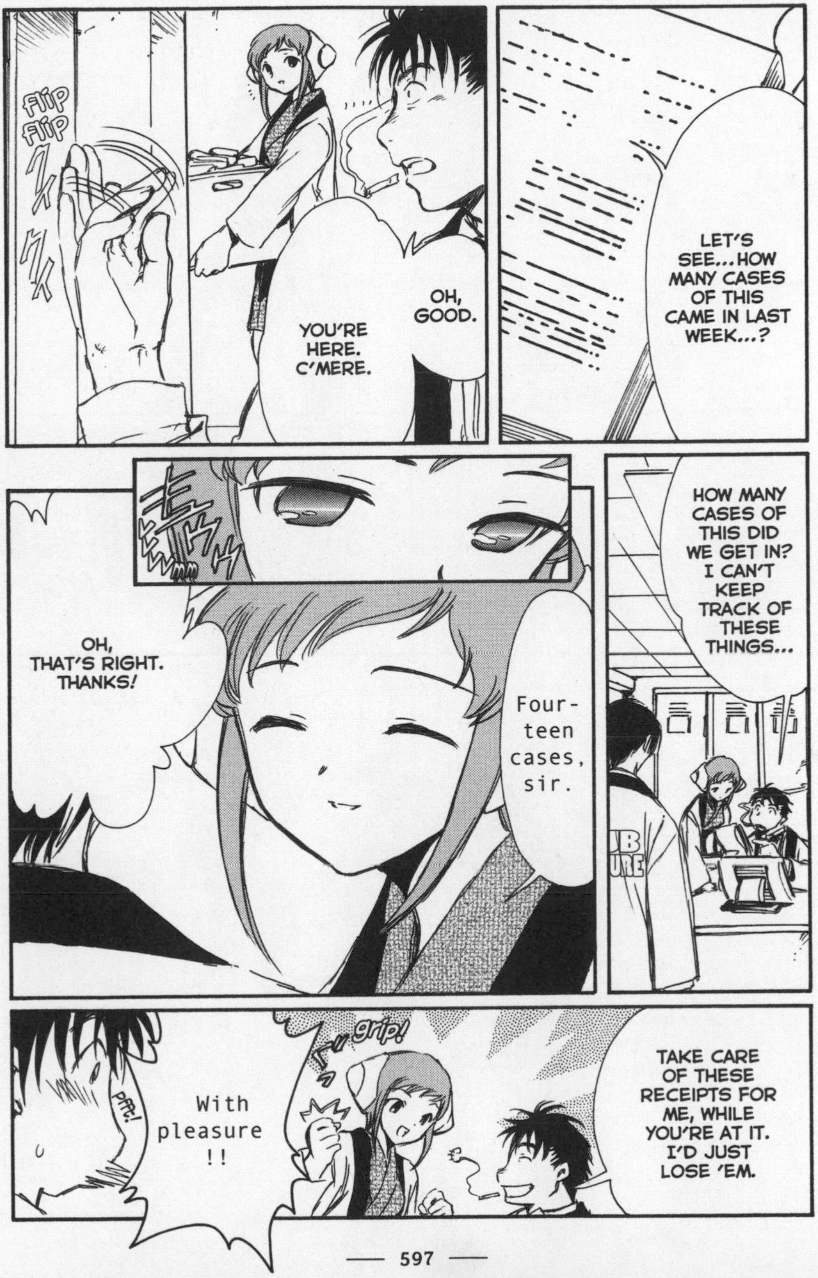
LET'S SEE...HOW MANY CASES OF THIS CAME IN LAST WEEK...?
flip flip
OH, GOOD.
YOU'RE HERE. C'MERE.
HOW MANY CASES OF THIS DID WE GET IN? I CAN'T KEEP TRACK OF THESE THINGS...
Four-teen cases, sir.
OH, THAT'S RIGHT. THANKS!
TAKE CARE OF THESE RECEIPTS FOR ME, WHILE YOU'RE AT IT. I'D JUST LOSE 'EM.
grip!
With pleasure !!
pfft!

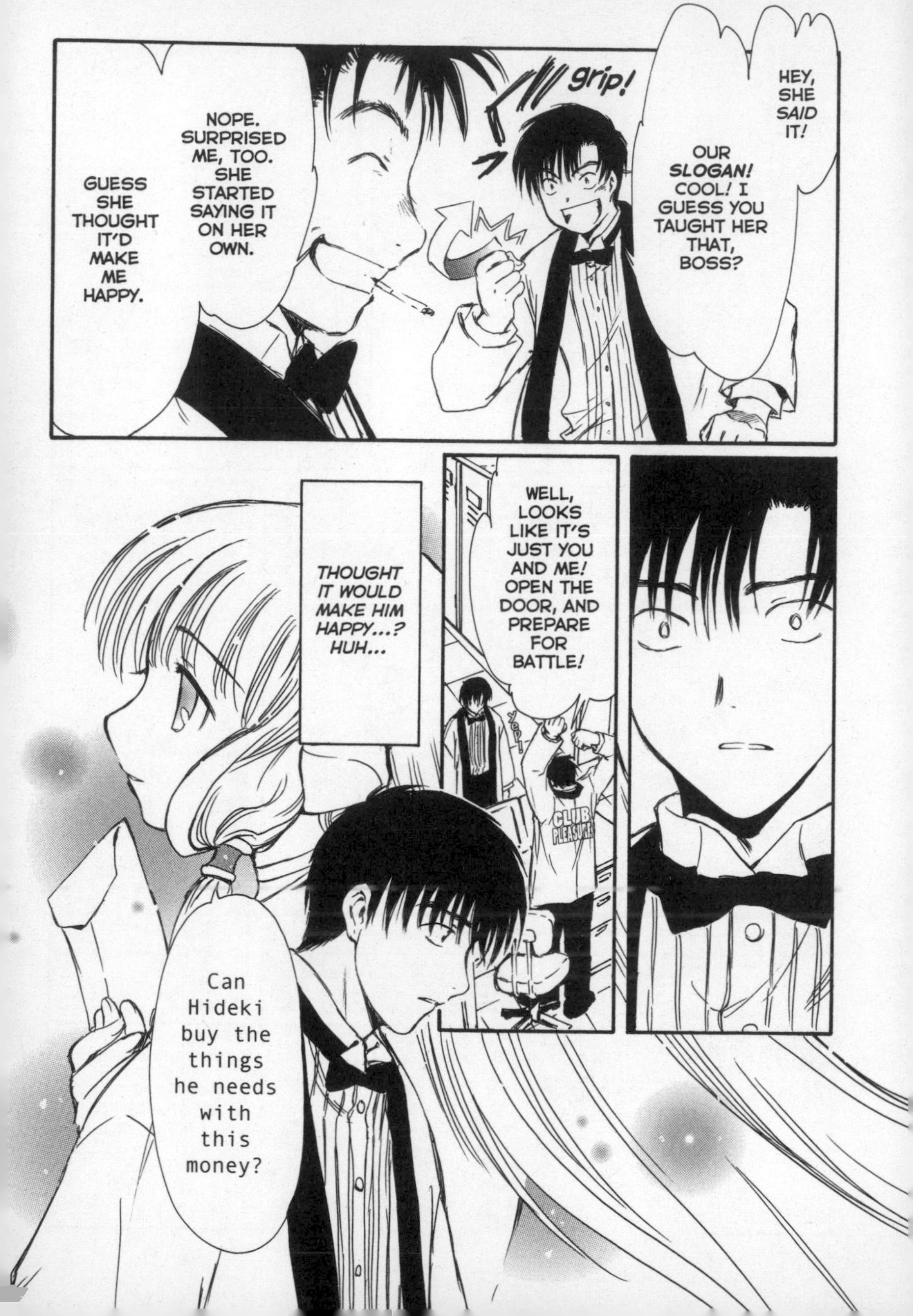
HEY, SHE SAID IT!
OUR SLOGAN! COOL! I GUESS YOU TAUGHT HER THAT, BOSS?
grip!
NOPE. SURPRISED ME, TOO. SHE STARTED SAYING IT ON HER OWN.
GUESS SHE THOUGHT IT'D MAKE ME HAPPY.
WELL, LOOKS LIKE IT'S JUST YOU AND ME! OPEN THE DOOR, AND PREPARE FOR BATTLE!
Yep!
CLUB PLEASURE
THOUGHT IT WOULD MAKE HIM HAPPY...? HUH...
Can Hideki buy the things he needs with this money?

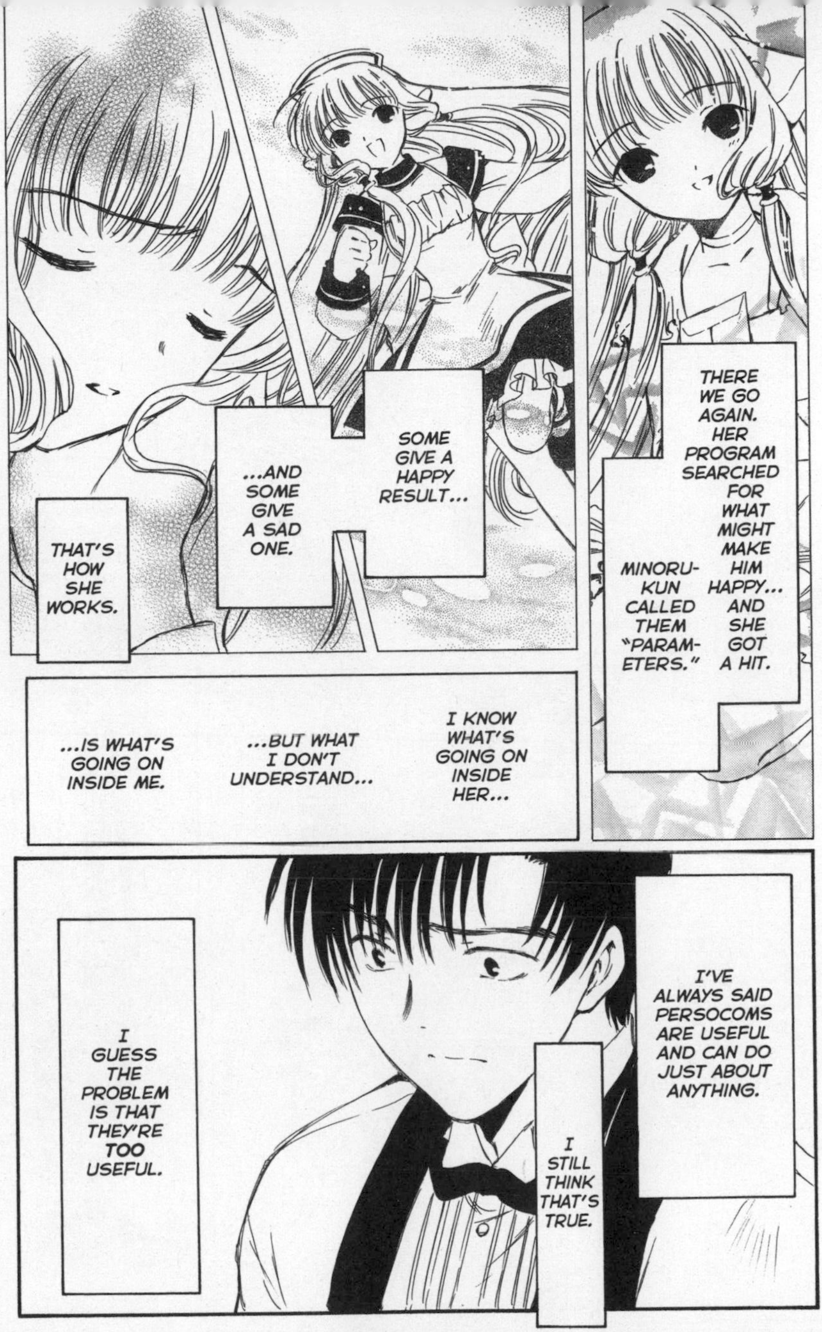
THERE WE GO AGAIN. HER PROGRAM SEARCHED FOR WHAT MIGHT MAKE HIM HAPPY... AND SHE GOT A HIT.
MINORU-KUN CALLED THEM "PARAMETERS."
SOME GIVE A HAPPY RESULT...
...AND SOME GIVE A SAD ONE.
THAT'S HOW SHE WORKS.
I KNOW WHAT'S GOING ON INSIDE HER...
...BUT WHAT I DON'T UNDERSTAND...
...IS WHAT'S GOING ON INSIDE ME.
I'VE ALWAYS SAID PERSOCOMS ARE USEFUL AND CAN DO JUST ABOUT ANYTHING.
I STILL THINK THAT'S TRUE.
I GUESS THE PROBLEM IS THAT THEY'RE TOO USEFUL.

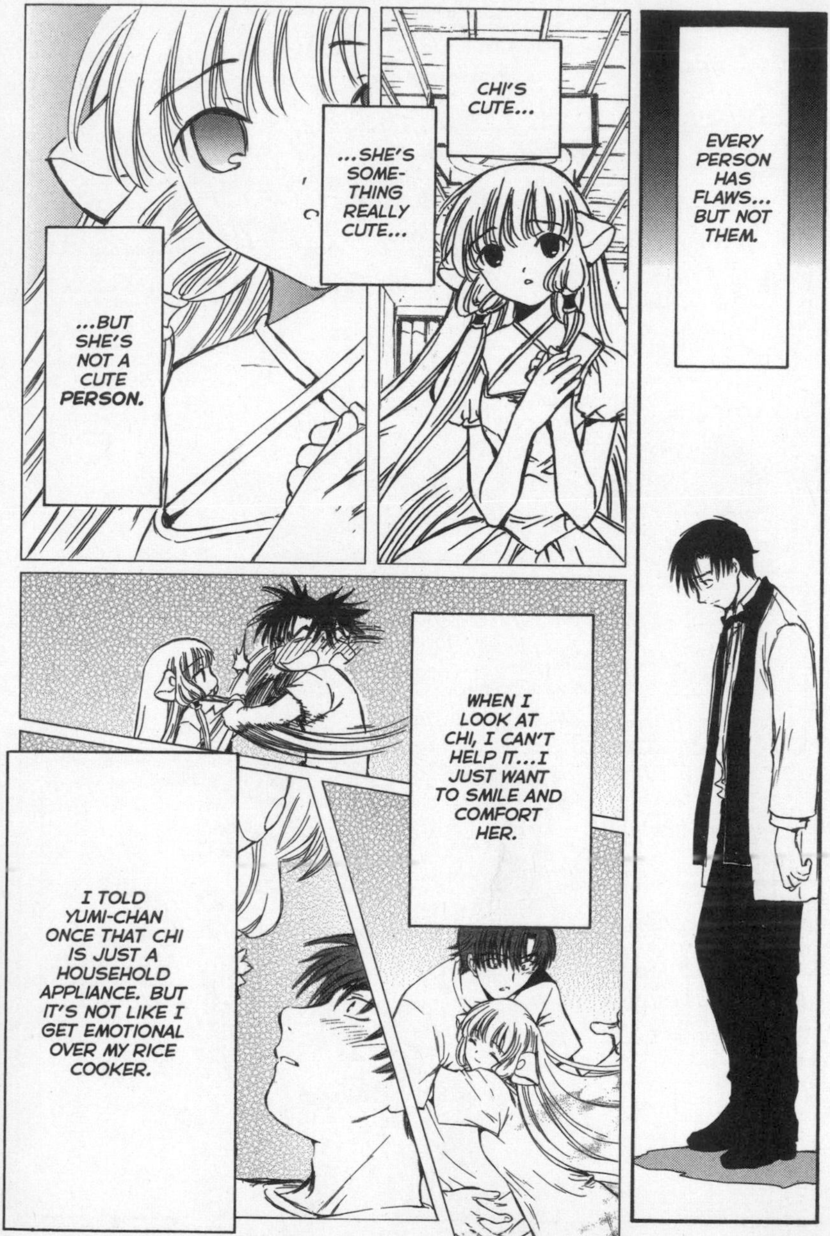
EVERY PERSON HAS FLAWS... BUT NOT THEM.
CHI'S CUTE...
...SHE'S SOMETHING REALLY CUTE...
...BUT SHE'S NOT A CUTE PERSON.
WHEN I LOOK AT CHI, I CAN'T HELP IT...I JUST WANT TO SMILE AND COMFORT HER.
I TOLD YUMI-CHAN ONCE THAT CHI IS JUST A HOUSEHOLD APPLIANCE. BUT IT'S NOT LIKE I GET EMOTIONAL OVER MY RICE COOKER.

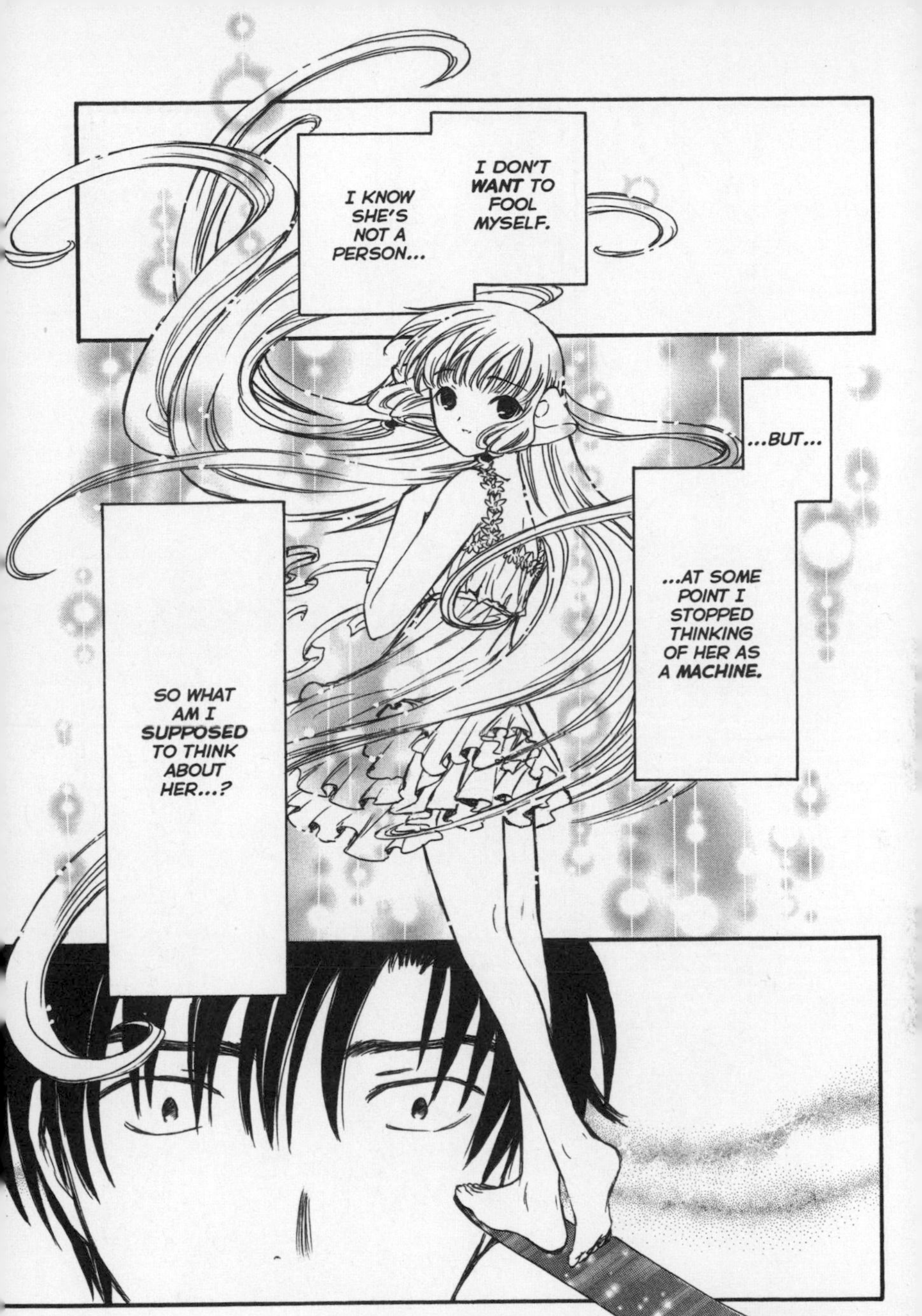
I DON'T WANT TO FOOL MYSELF.
I KNOW SHE'S NOT A PERSON...
...BUT...
...AT SOME POINT I STOPPED THINKING OF HER AS A MACHINE.
SO WHAT AM I SUPPOSED TO THINK ABOUT HER...?

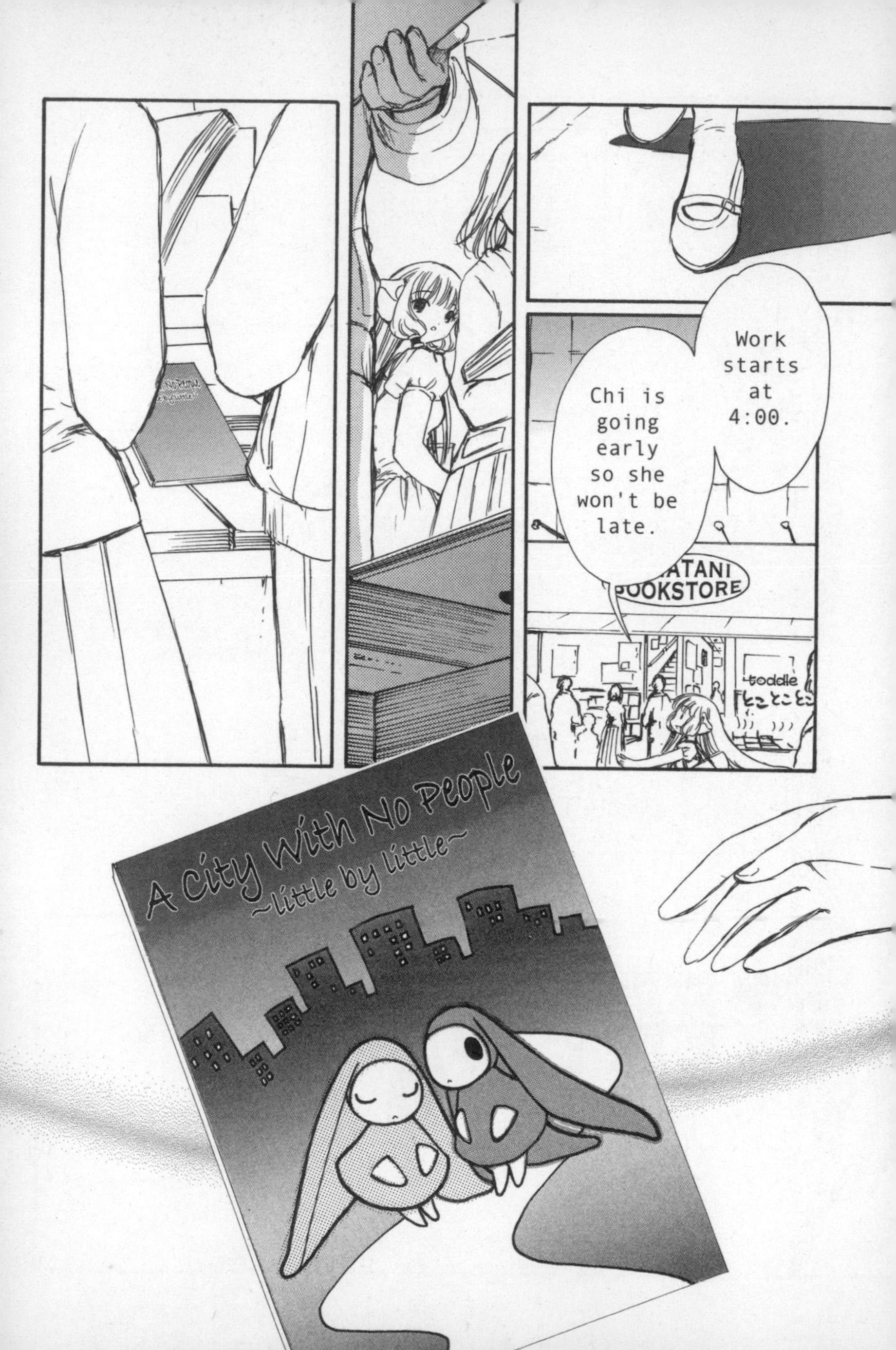
Work starts at 4:00.
Chi is going early so she won't be late.
toddle
A City With No People
~little by little~

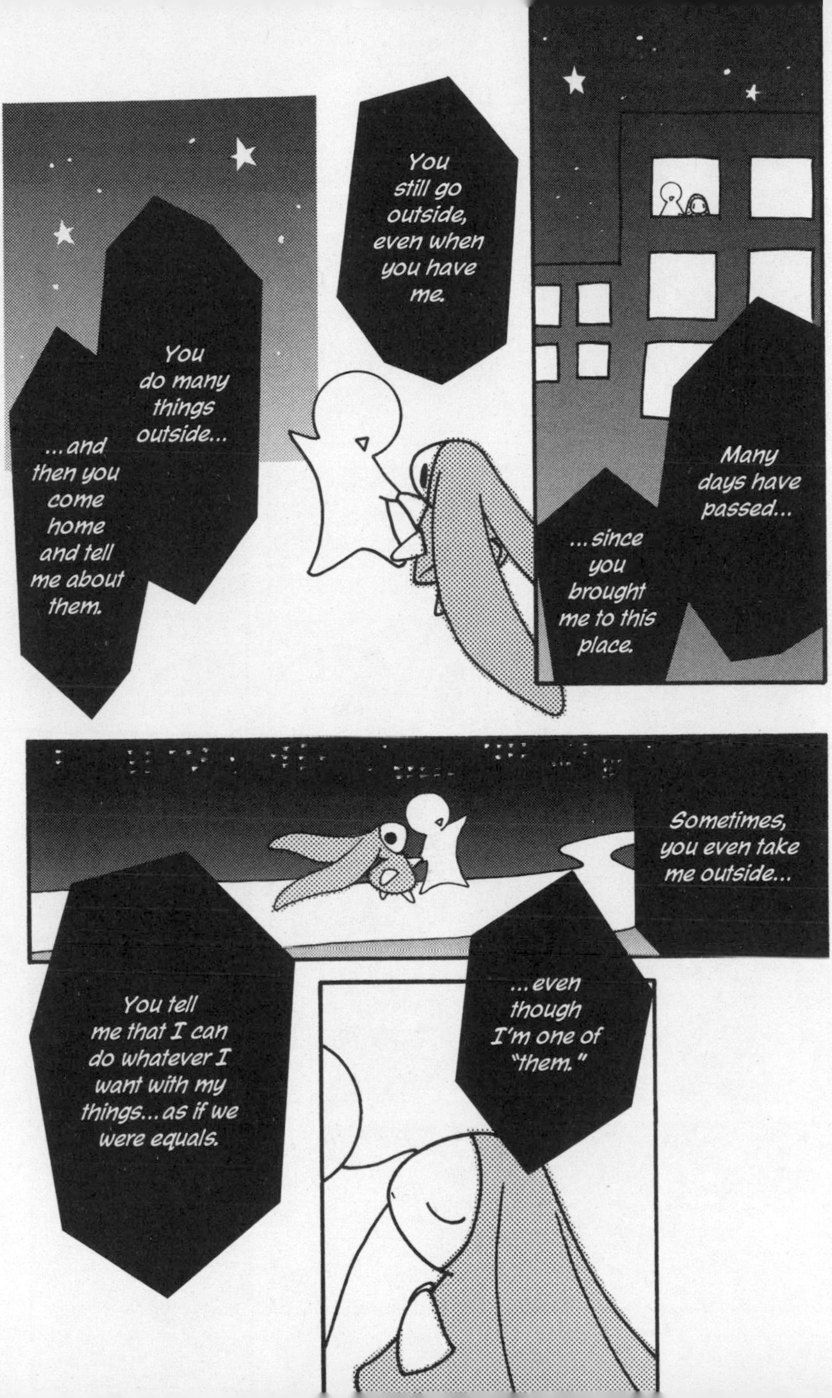
Many days have passed...
...since you brought me to this place.
You still go outside, even when you have me.
You do many things outside...
...and then you come home and tell me about them.
Sometimes, you even take me outside...
...even though I'm one of "them."
You tell me that I can do whatever I want with my things... as if we were equals.

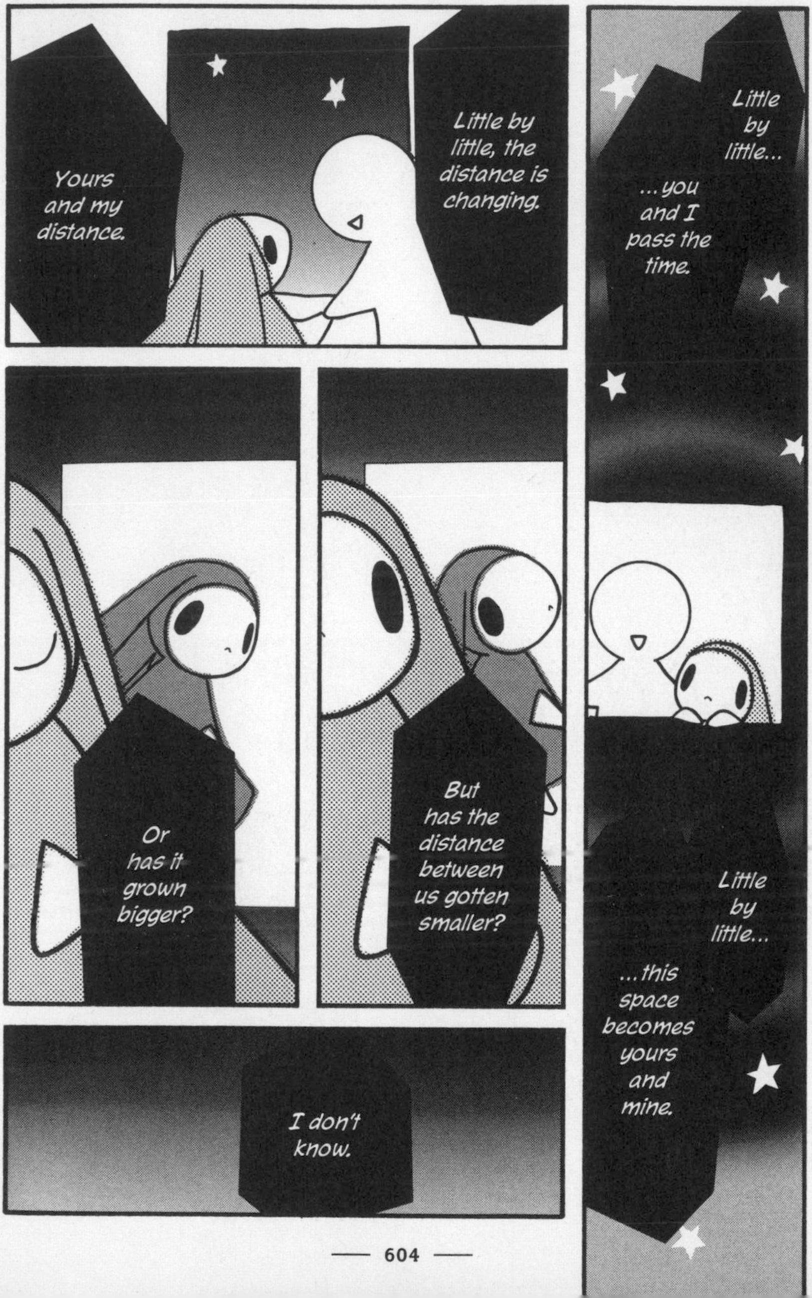
Little by little...
...you and I pass the time.
Little by little...
...this space becomes yours and mine.
Little by little, the distance is changing.
Yours and my distance.
But has the distance between us gotten smaller?
Or has it grown bigger?
I don't know.

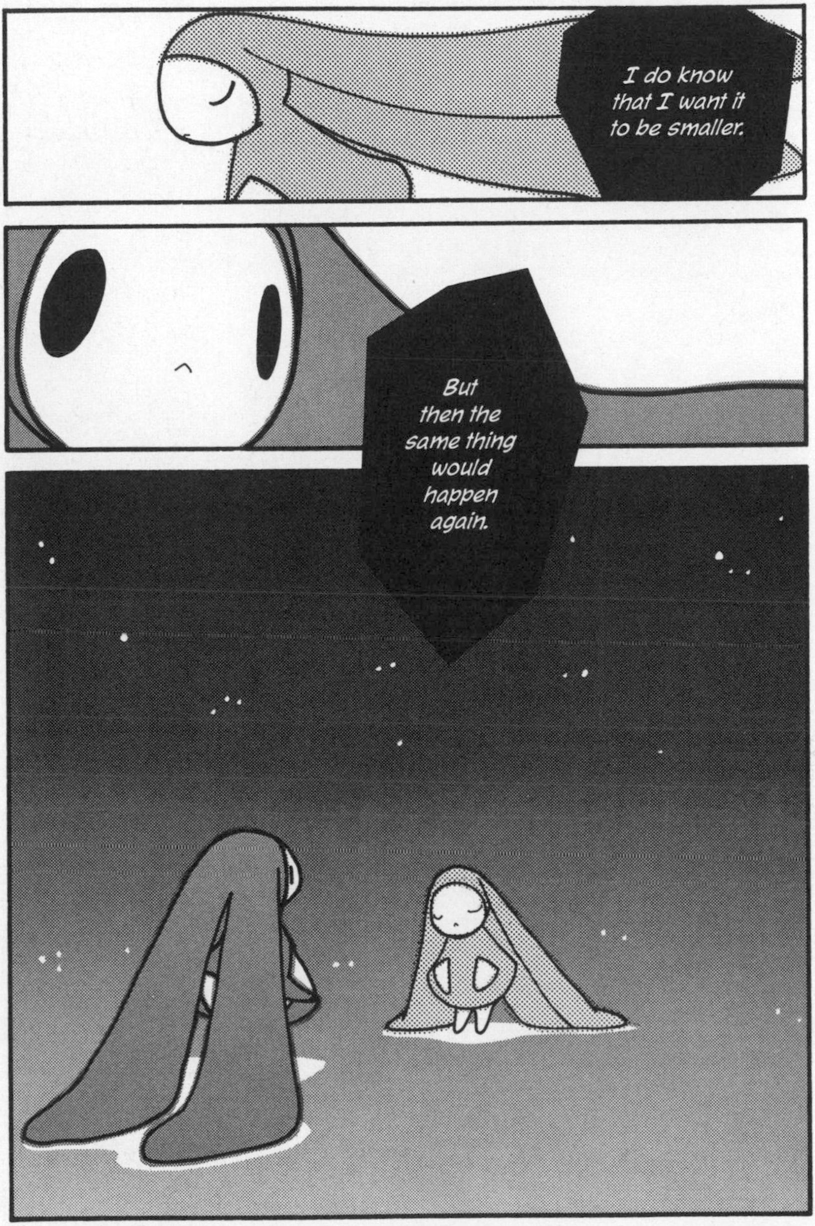
I do know that I want it to be smaller.
But then the same thing would happen again.

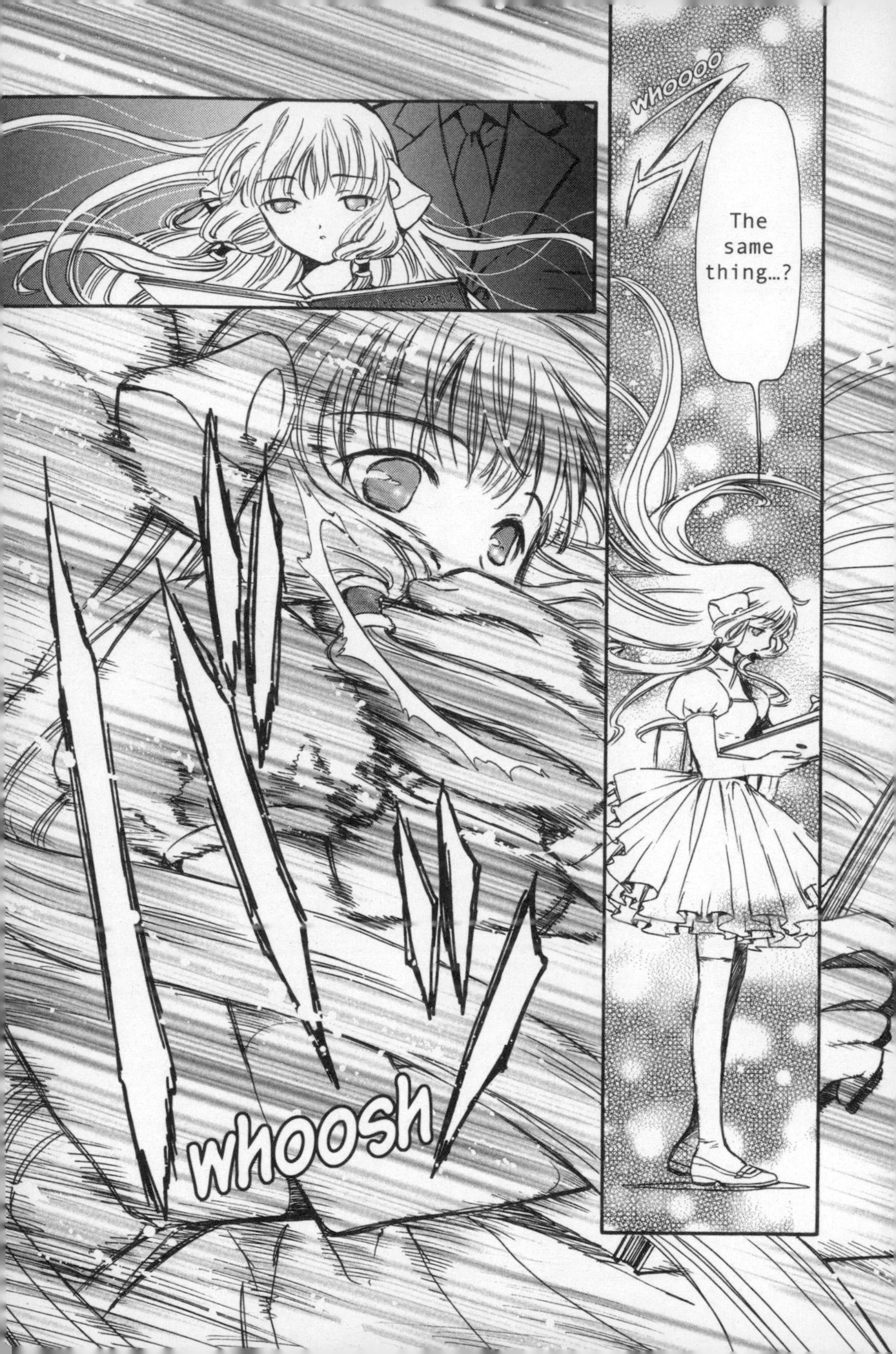
WHOOOO
The same thing…?
whoosh

Chobits

ちょびっツ

◀ chapter 40 ▶

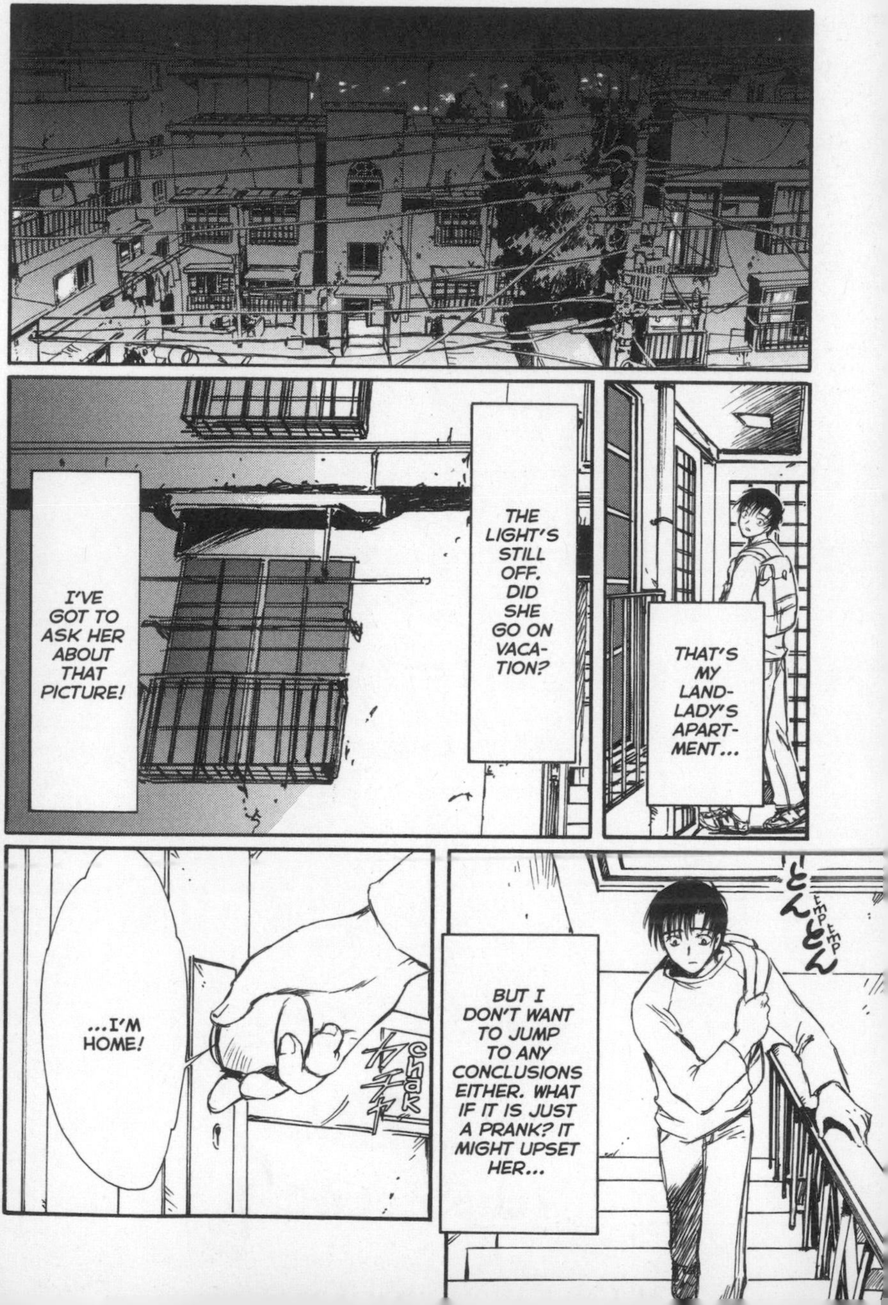
THAT'S MY LAND-LADY'S APART-MENT...
THE LIGHT'S STILL OFF. DID SHE GO ON VACA-TION?
I'VE GOT TO ASK HER ABOUT THAT PICTURE!
とんとん
TMP TMP
BUT I DON'T WANT TO JUMP TO ANY CONCLUSIONS EITHER. WHAT IF IT IS JUST A PRANK? IT MIGHT UPSET HER...
カチャ
chak
...I'M HOME!

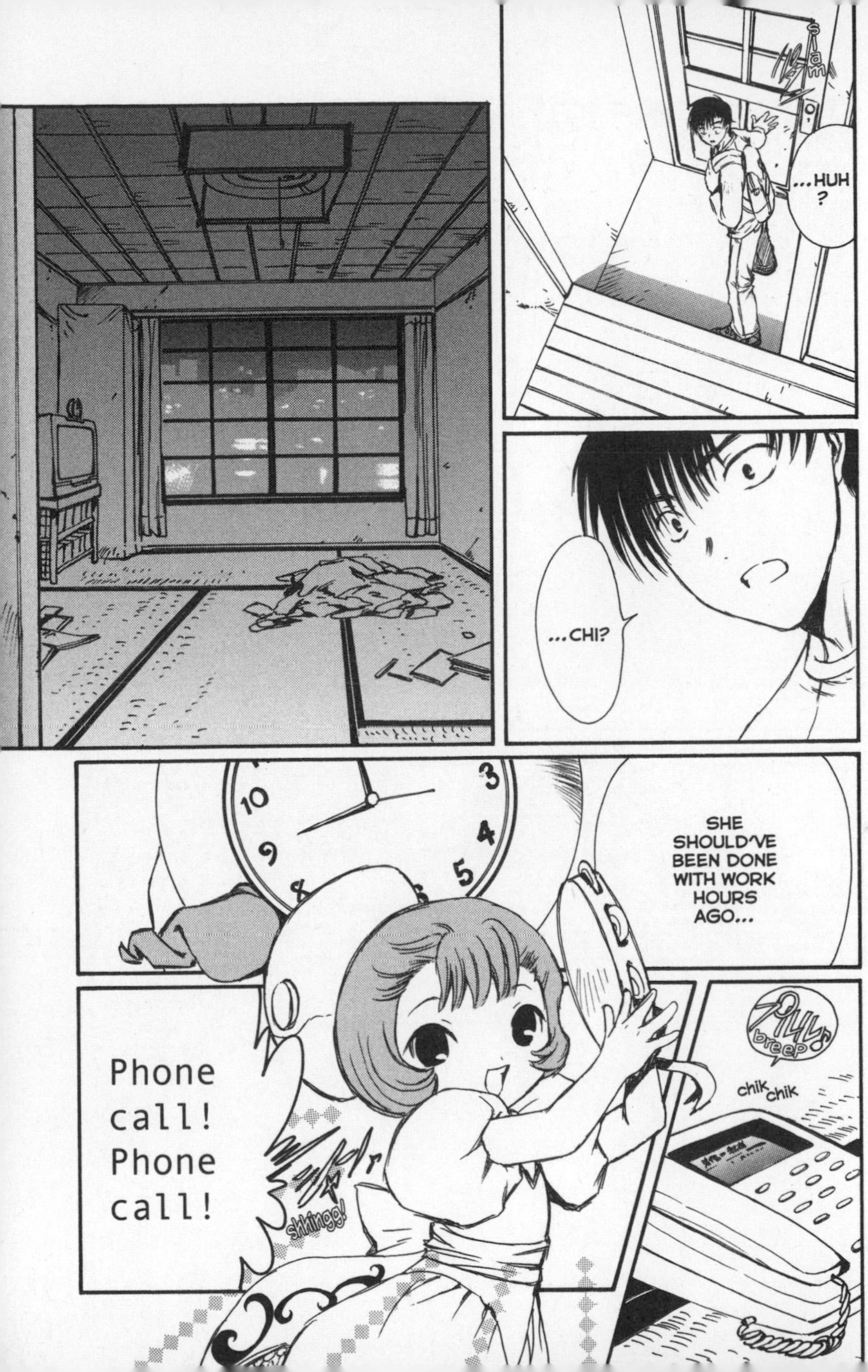
slam
...HUH?
...CHI?
SHE SHOULD'VE BEEN DONE WITH WORK HOURS AGO...
breep
chik chik
Phone call! Phone call!
shkingg!

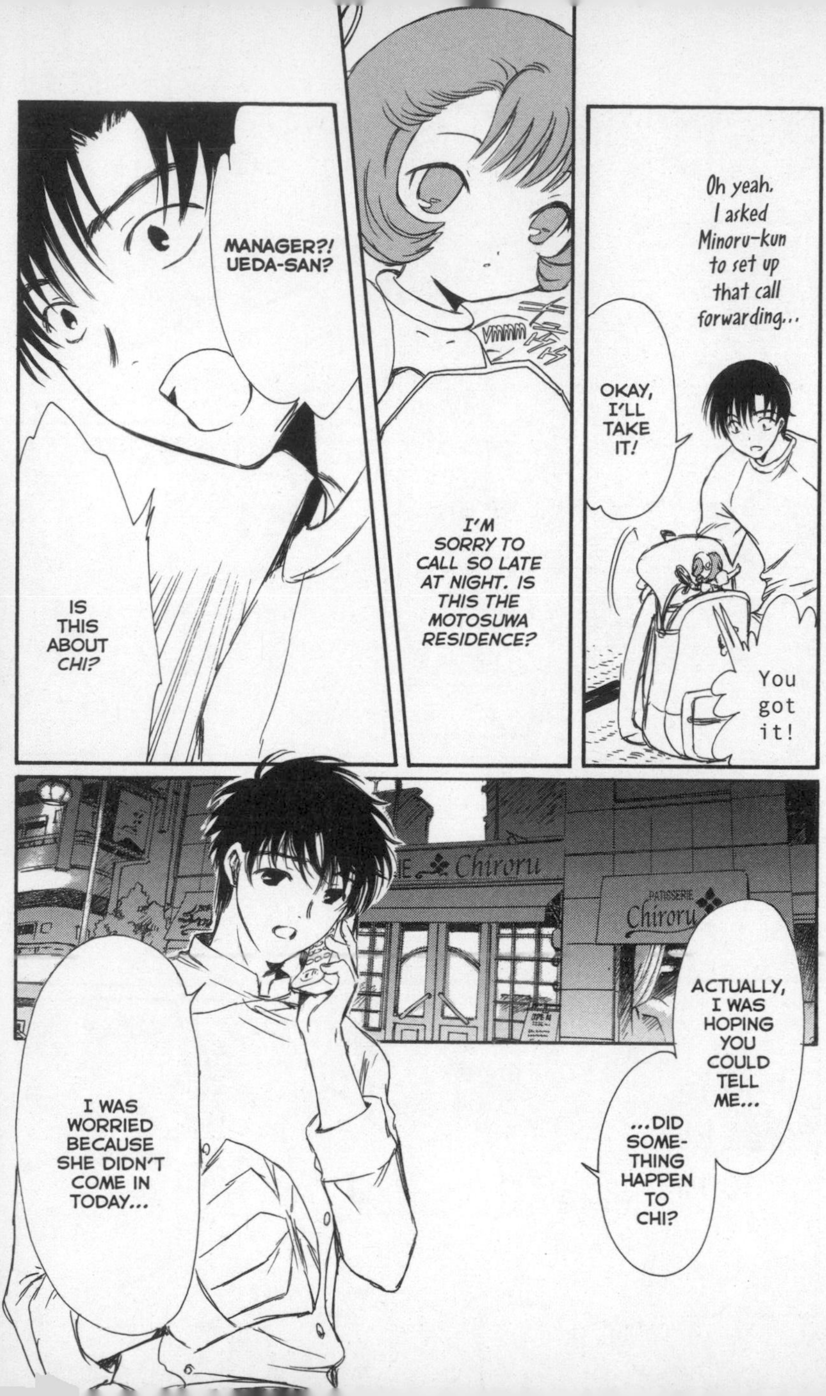
Oh yeah. I asked Minoru-kun to set up that call forwarding...
OKAY, I'LL TAKE IT!
You got it!
vmmm
I'M SORRY TO CALL SO LATE AT NIGHT. IS THIS THE MOTOSUWA RESIDENCE?
MANAGER?! UEDA-SAN?
IS THIS ABOUT CHI?
Chiroru
PATISSERIE Chiroru
ACTUALLY, I WAS HOPING YOU COULD TELL ME...
...DID SOME-THING HAPPEN TO CHI?
I WAS WORRIED BECAUSE SHE DIDN'T COME IN TODAY...

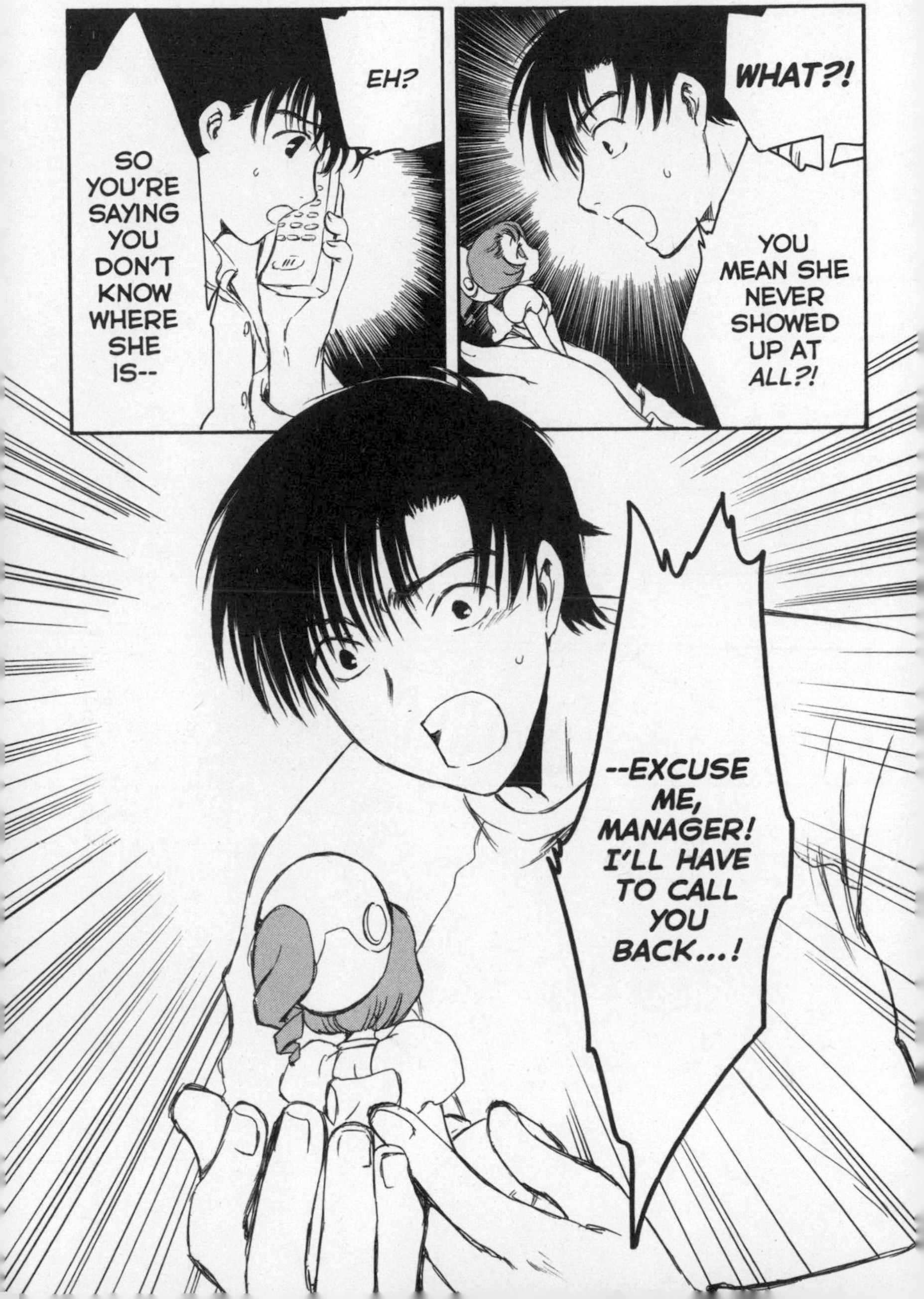
WHAT?!
YOU MEAN SHE NEVER SHOWED UP AT ALL?!
EH?
SO YOU'RE SAYING YOU DON'T KNOW WHERE SHE IS--
--EXCUSE ME, MANAGER! I'LL HAVE TO CALL YOU BACK...!

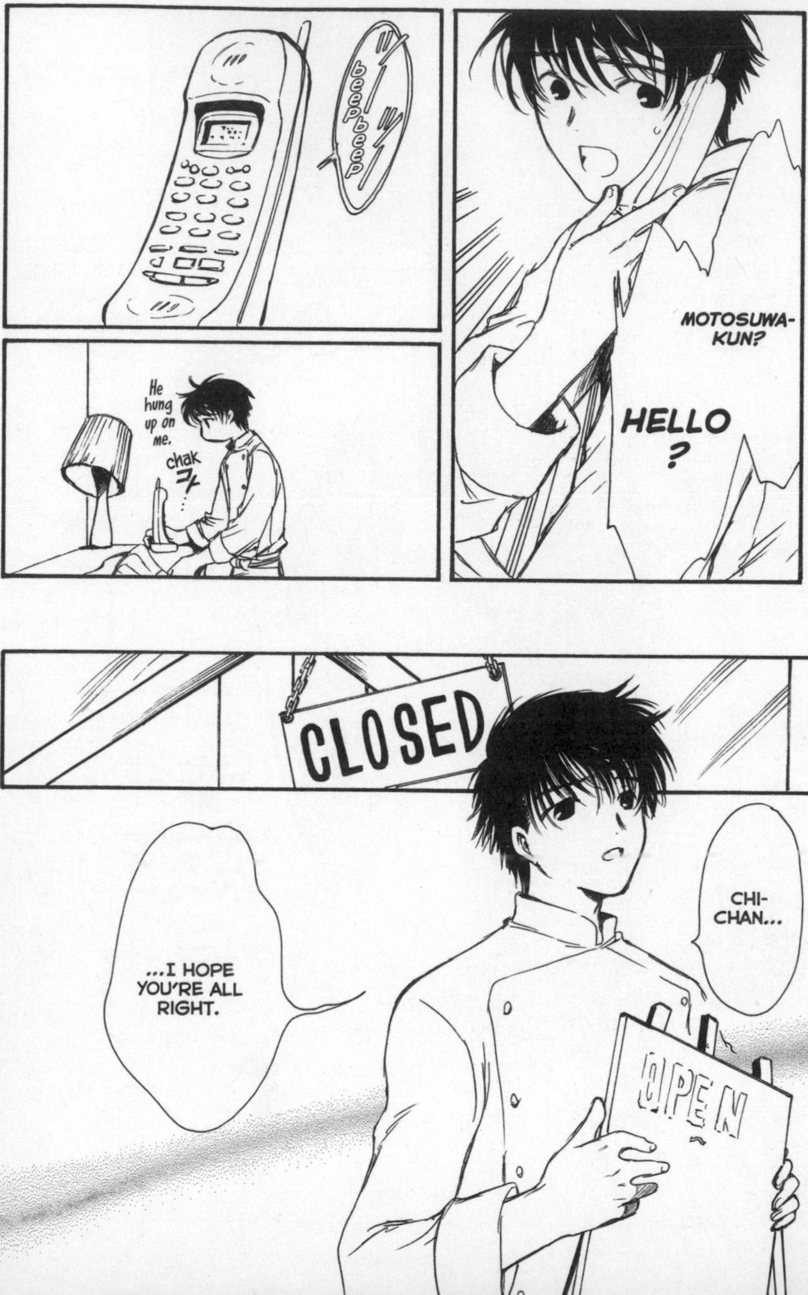
MOTOSUWA-KUN?
HELLO?
beepbeep
He hung up on me.
chak
CLOSED
CHI-CHAN...
...I HOPE YOU'RE ALL RIGHT.
OPEN

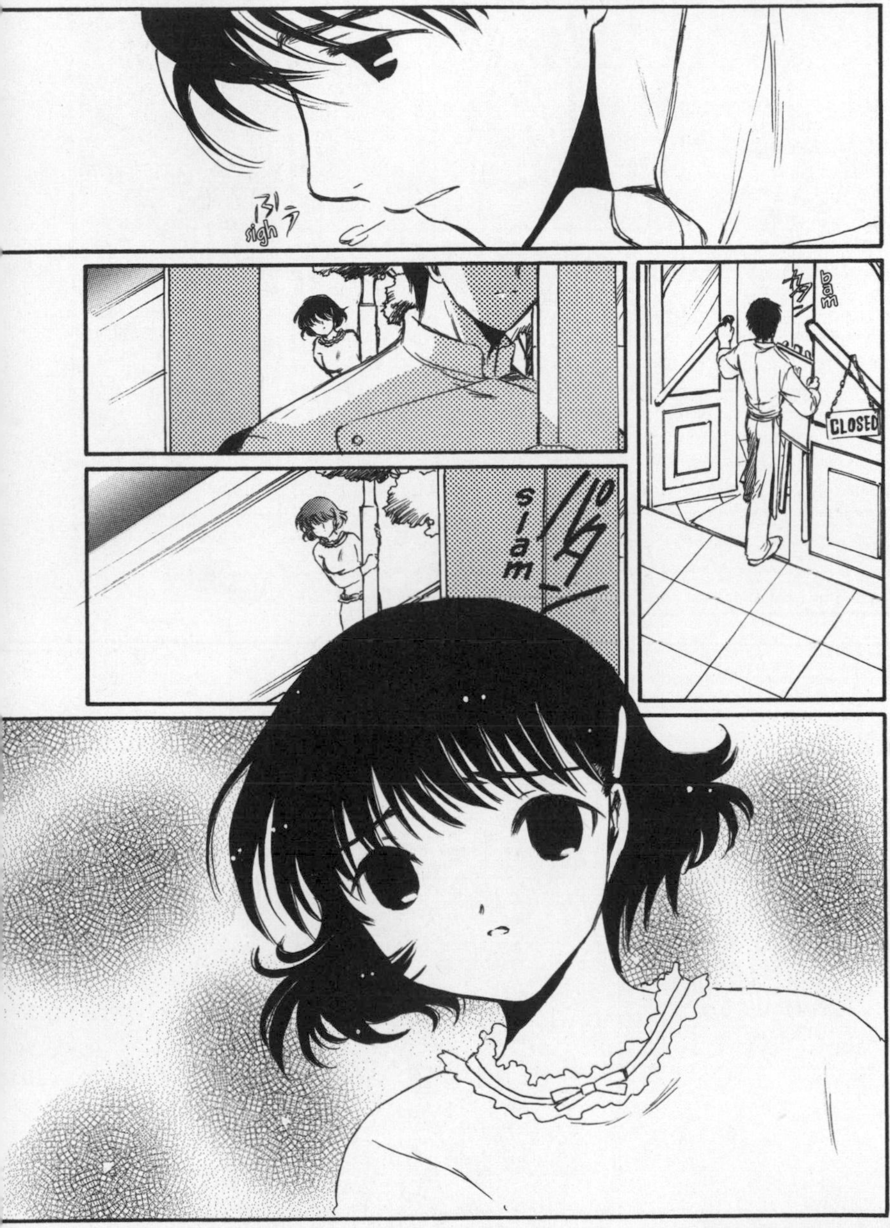
sigh
bam
CLOSED
slam

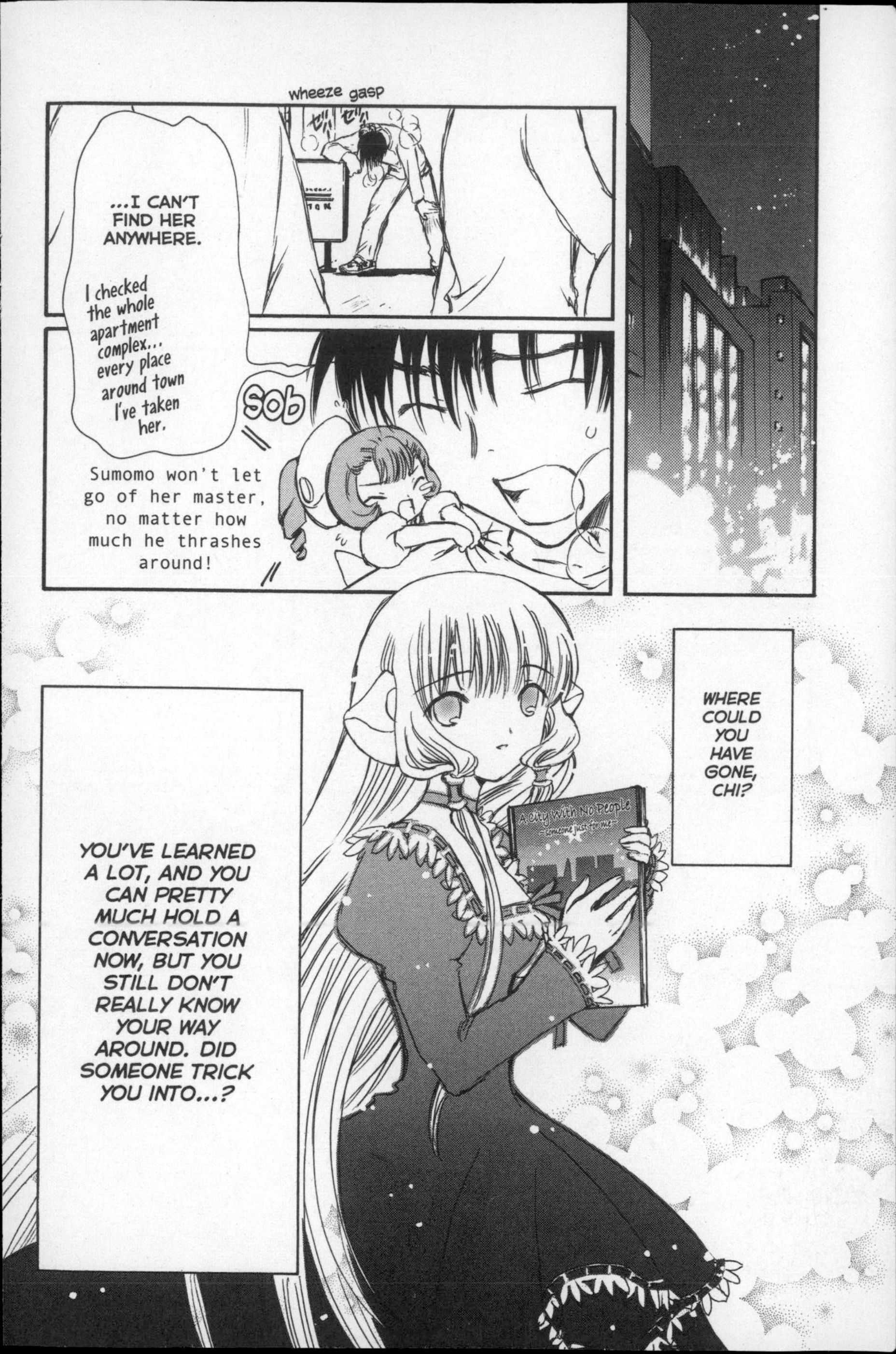
wheeze gasp
...I CAN'T FIND HER ANYWHERE.
I checked the whole apartment complex... every place around town I've taken her.
sob
Sumomo won't let go of her master, no matter how much he thrashes around!
WHERE COULD YOU HAVE GONE, CHI?
A City With No People
~someone just for me~
YOU'VE LEARNED A LOT, AND YOU CAN PRETTY MUCH HOLD A CONVERSATION NOW, BUT YOU STILL DON'T REALLY KNOW YOUR WAY AROUND. DID SOMEONE TRICK YOU INTO...?

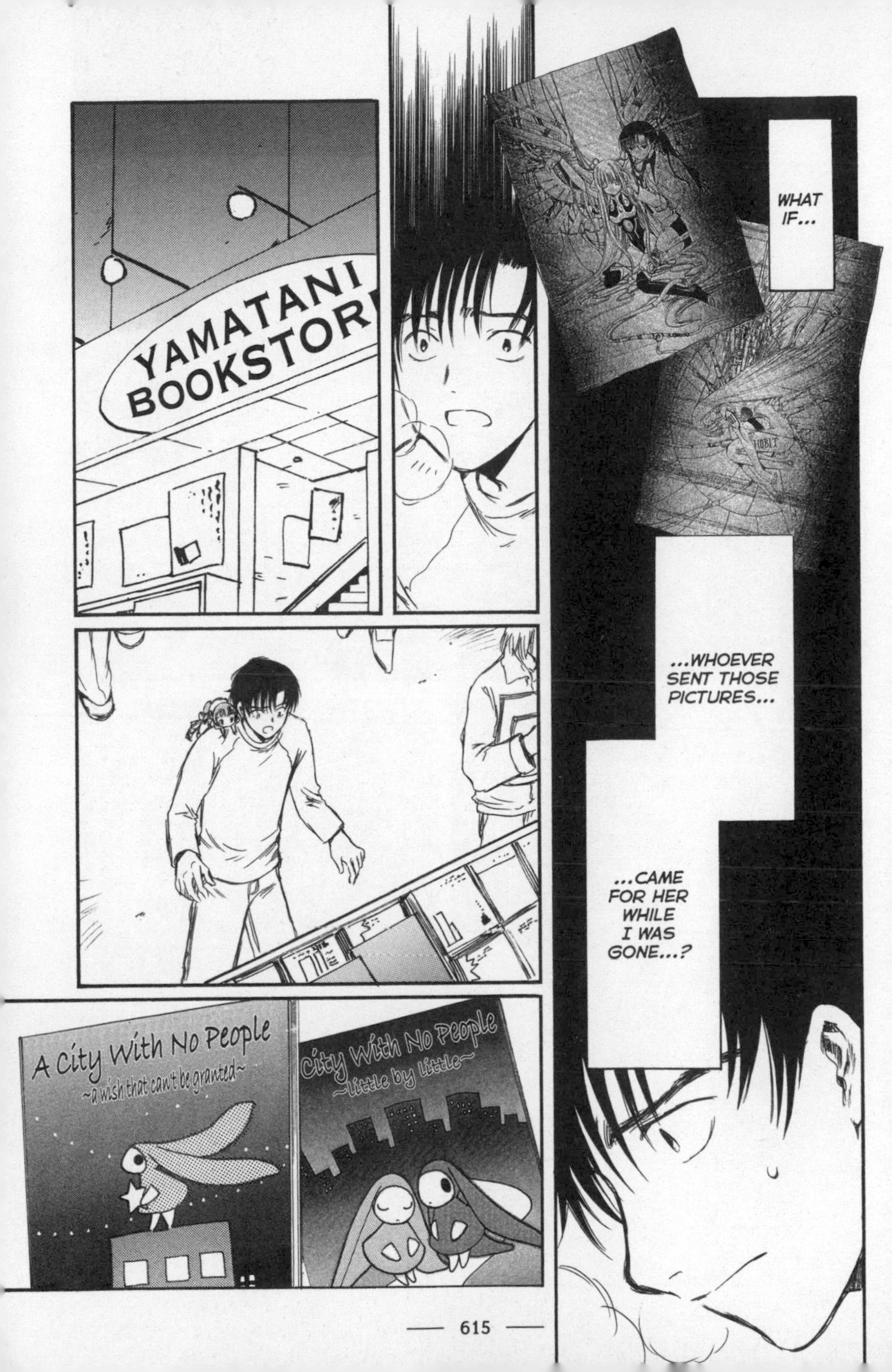
WHAT IF...
...WHOEVER SENT THOSE PICTURES...
...CAME FOR HER WHILE I WAS GONE...?
YAMATANI
BOOKSTOR
City With No People
~little by little~
A City With No People
~a wish that can't be granted~

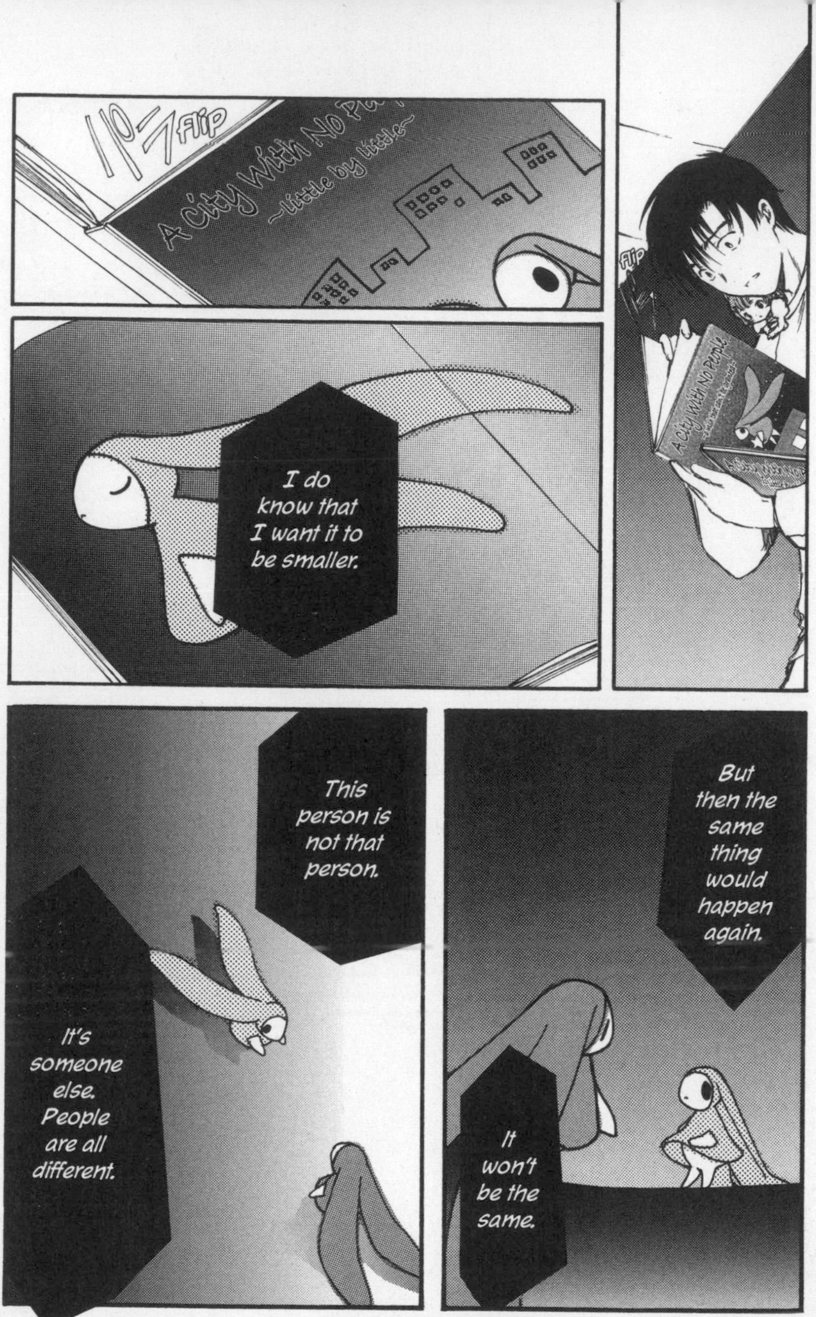
Flip
A City With No People
Flip
~little by little~
I do know that I want it to be smaller.
But then the same thing would happen again.
It won't be the same.
This person is not that person.
It's someone else. People are all different.

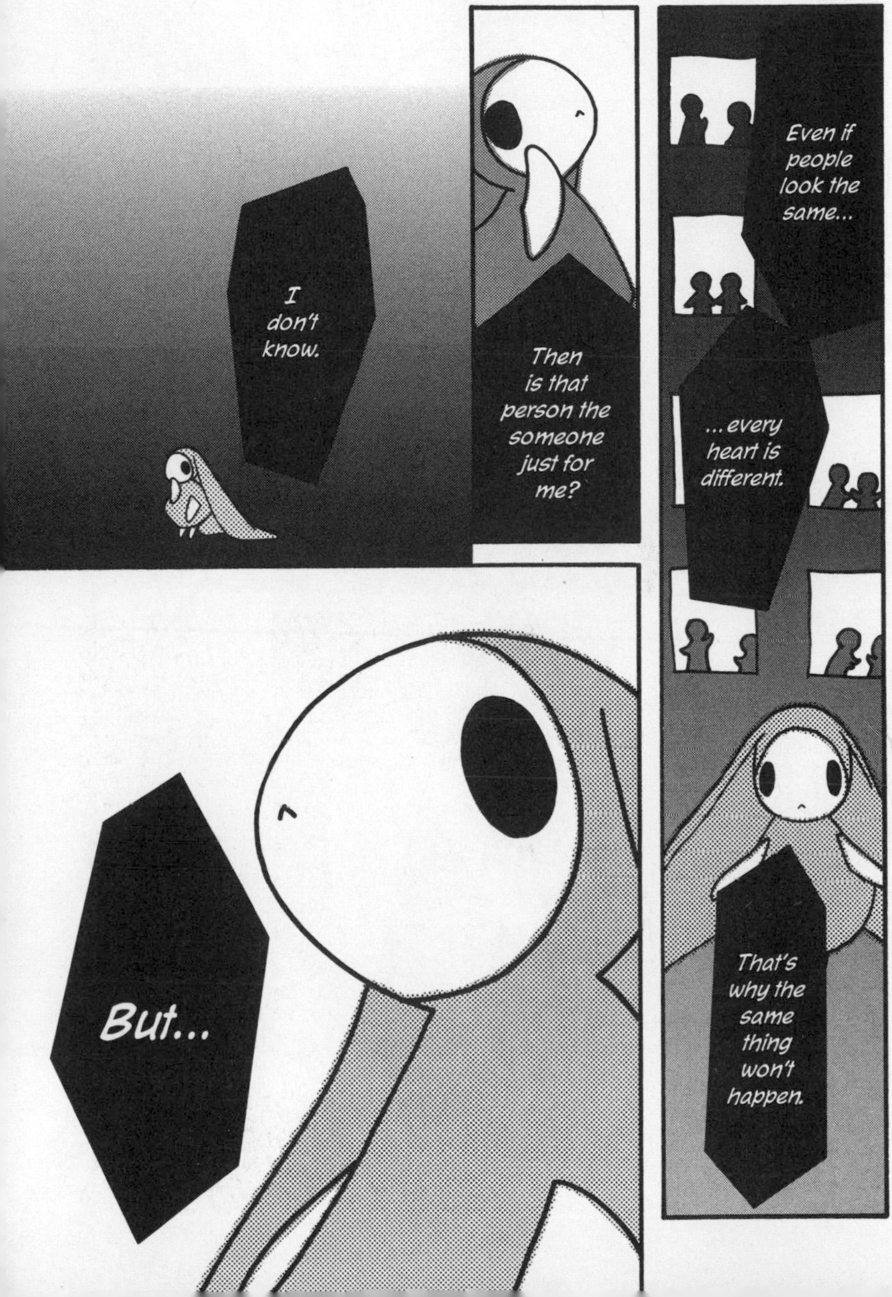
Even if people look the same...
...every heart is different.
That's why the same thing won't happen.
Then is that person the someone just for me?
I don't know.
But...

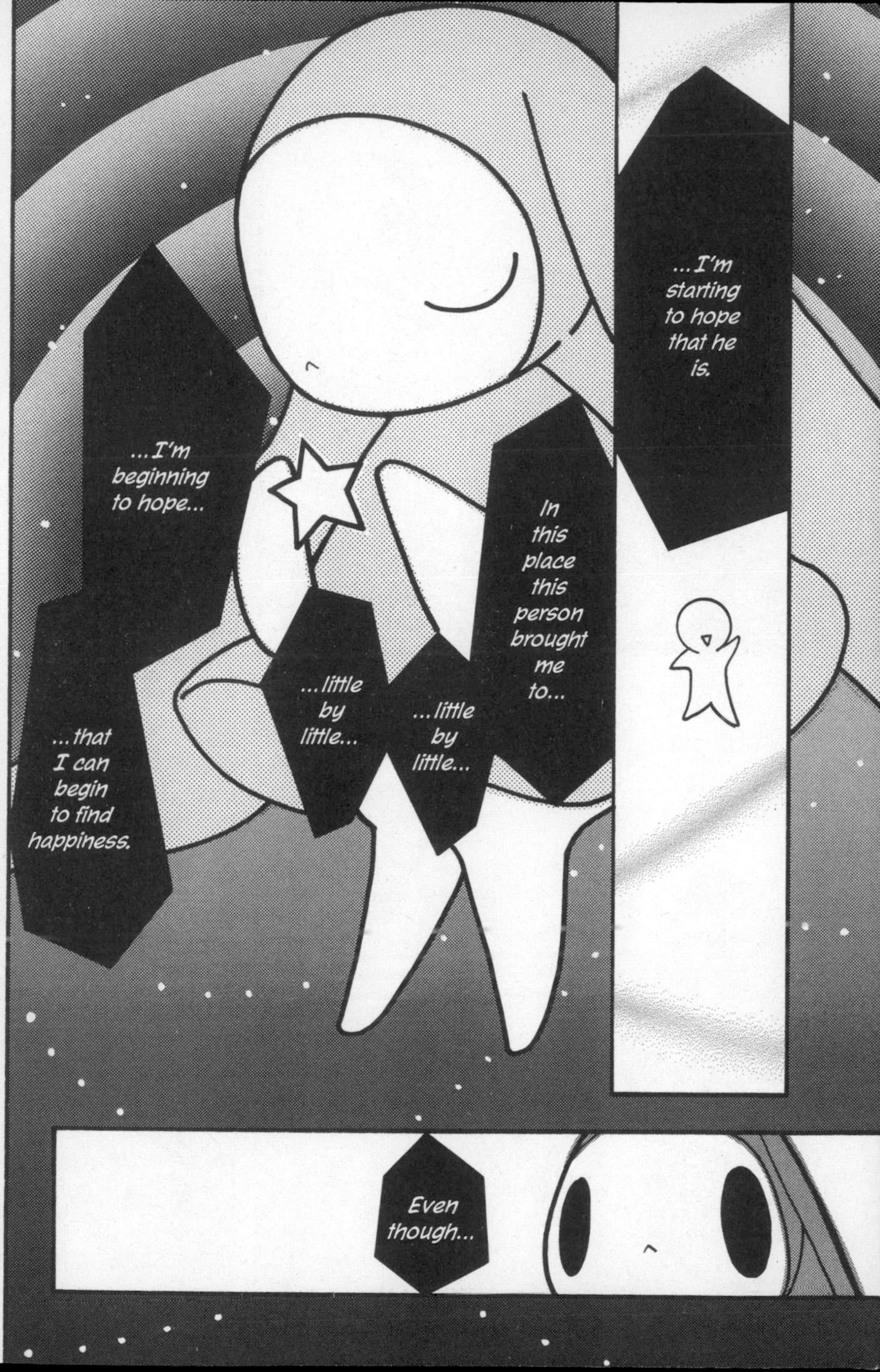
...I'm starting to hope that he is.
In this place this person brought me to...
...little by little...
...little by little...
...I'm beginning to hope...
...that I can begin to find happiness.
Even though...

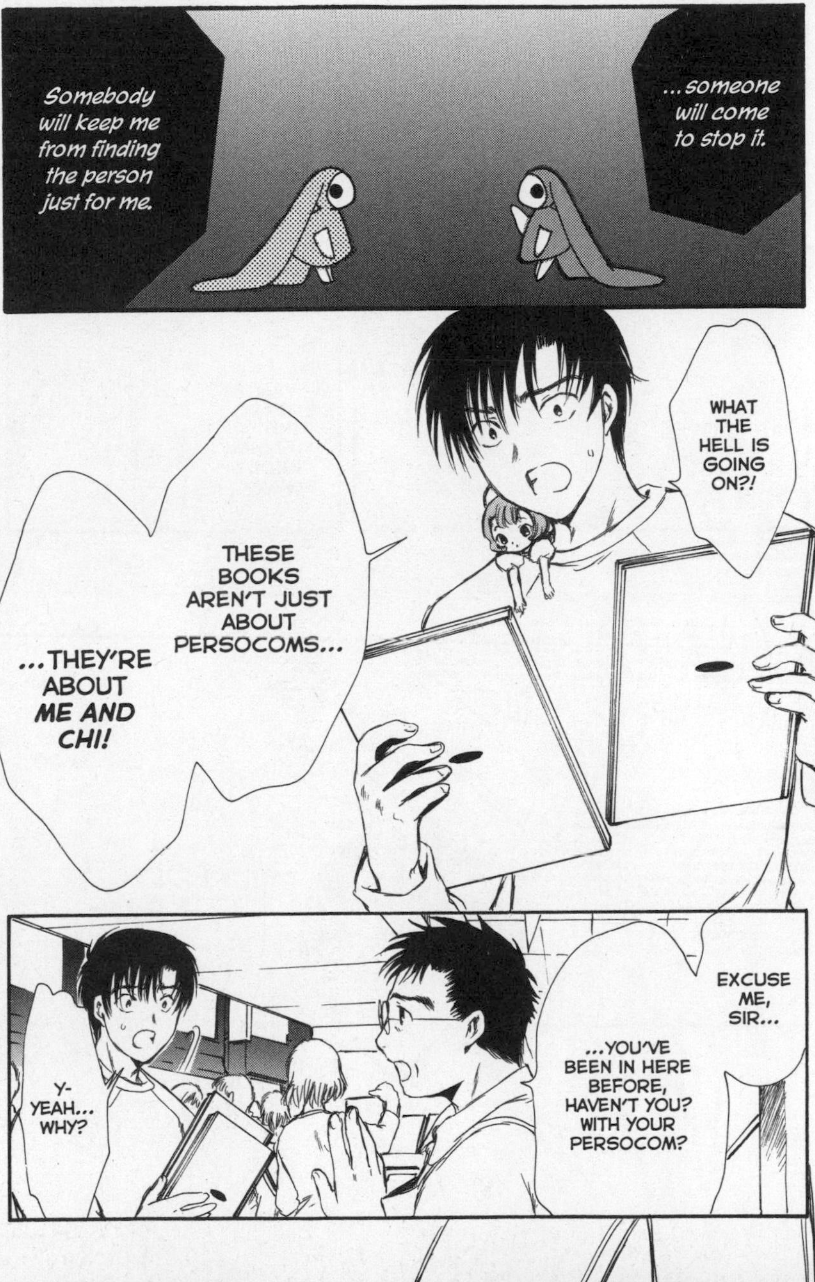
...someone will come to stop it.
Somebody will keep me from finding the person just for me.
WHAT THE HELL IS GOING ON?!
THESE BOOKS AREN'T JUST ABOUT PERSOCOMS...
...THEY'RE ABOUT ME AND CHI!
EXCUSE ME, SIR...
...YOU'VE BEEN IN HERE BEFORE, HAVEN'T YOU? WITH YOUR PERSOCOM?
Y-YEAH... WHY?

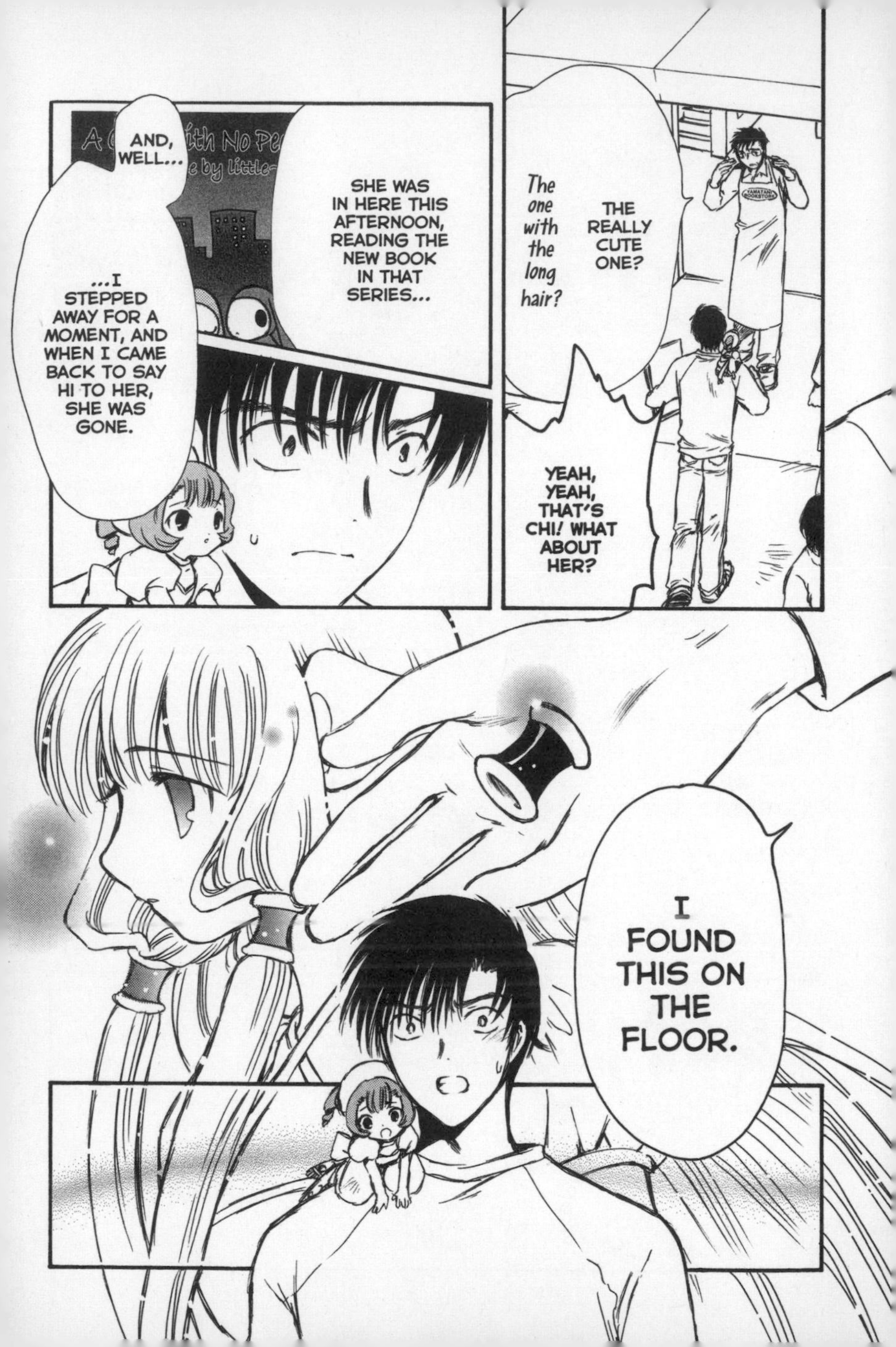
THE REALLY CUTE ONE?
The one with the long hair?
YEAH, YEAH, THAT'S CHI! WHAT ABOUT HER?
SHE WAS IN HERE THIS AFTERNOON, READING THE NEW BOOK IN THAT SERIES...
AND, WELL...
...I STEPPED AWAY FOR A MOMENT, AND WHEN I CAME BACK TO SAY HI TO HER, SHE WAS GONE.
I FOUND THIS ON THE FLOOR.

Chobits
ちょびッツ

◀chapter 41▶

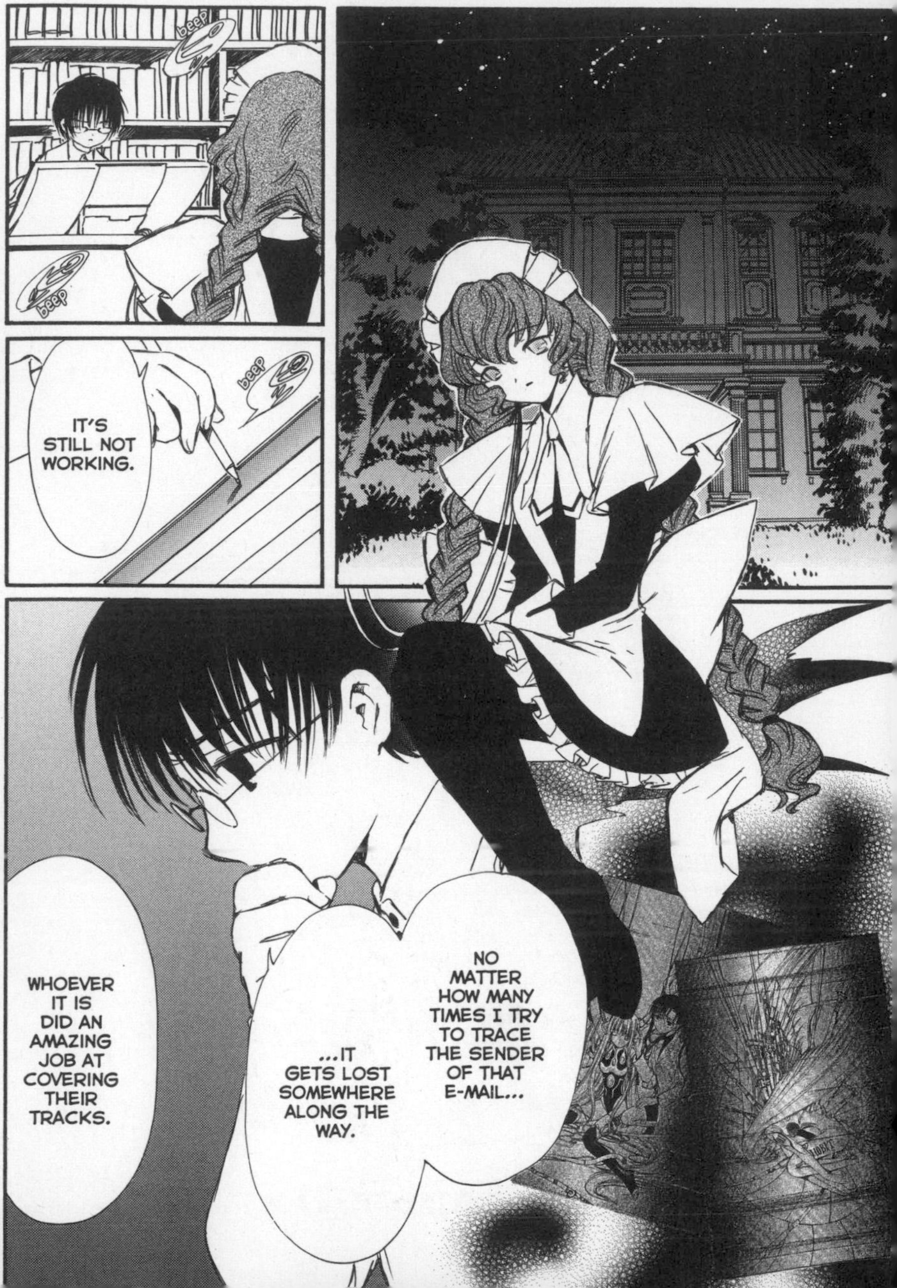
beep
beep
beep
IT'S STILL NOT WORKING.
NO MATTER HOW MANY TIMES I TRY TO TRACE THE SENDER OF THAT E-MAIL...
...IT GETS LOST SOMEWHERE ALONG THE WAY.
WHOEVER IT IS DID AN AMAZING JOB AT COVERING THEIR TRACKS.

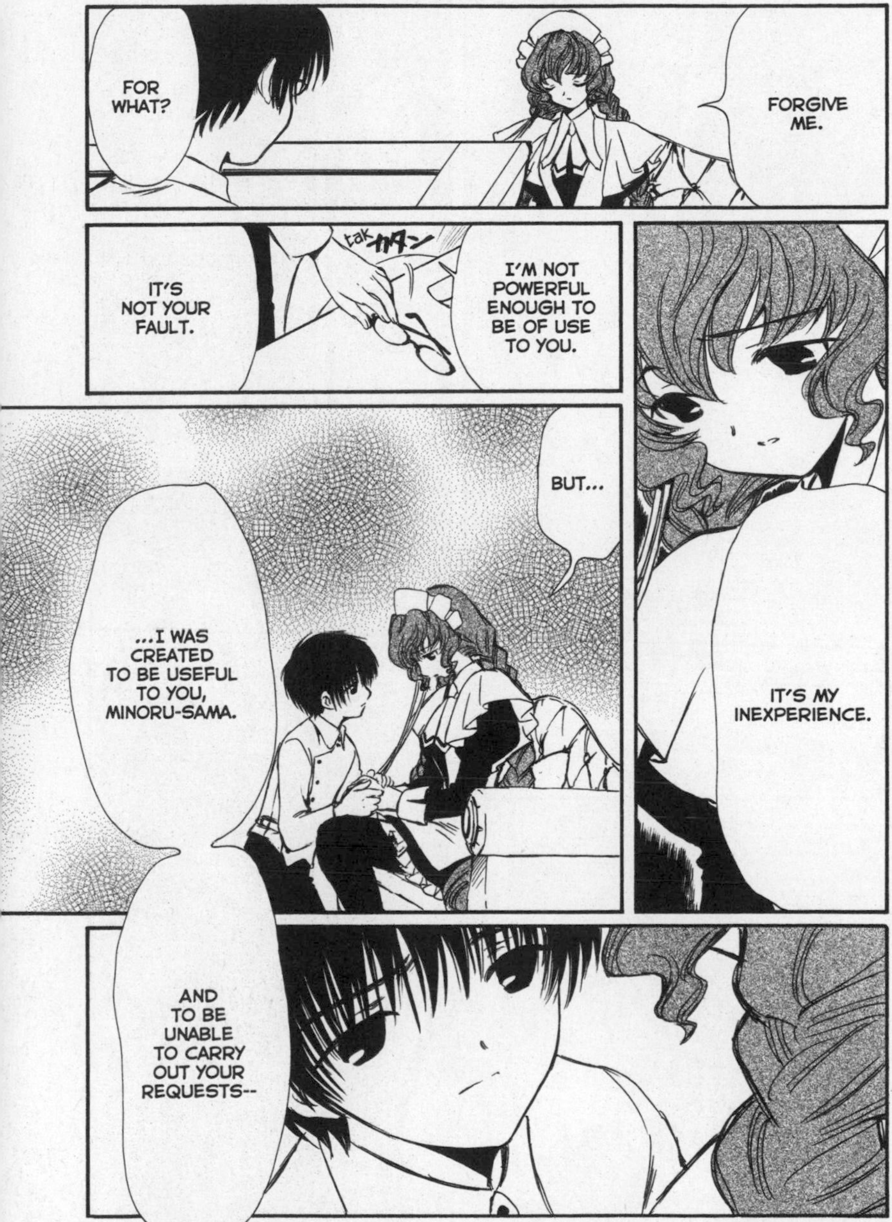

FORGIVE ME.
FOR WHAT?
IT'S MY INEXPERIENCE.
I'M NOT POWERFUL ENOUGH TO BE OF USE TO YOU.
tak カタン
IT'S NOT YOUR FAULT.
BUT...
...I WAS CREATED TO BE USEFUL TO YOU, MINORU-SAMA.
AND TO BE UNABLE TO CARRY OUT YOUR REQUESTS--

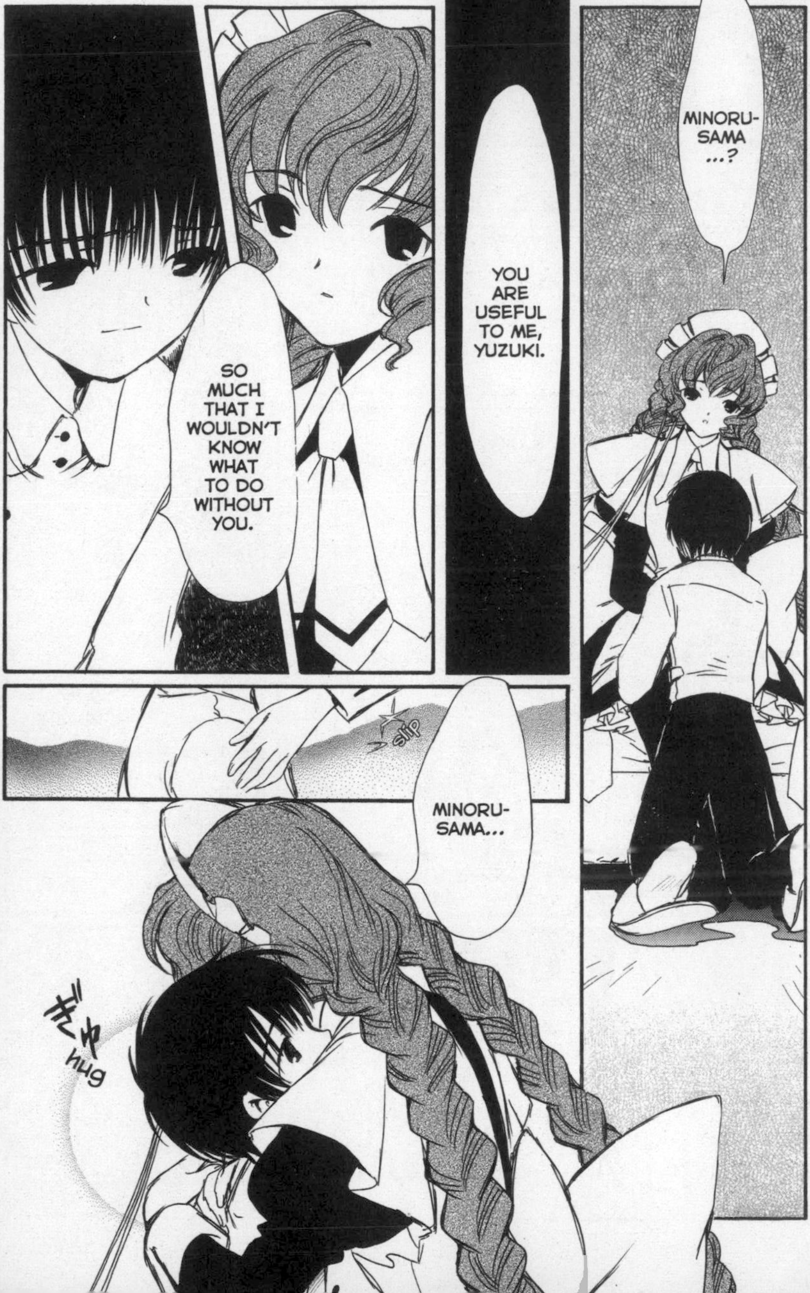
MINORU-SAMA ...?
YOU ARE USEFUL TO ME, YUZUKI.
SO MUCH THAT I WOULDN'T KNOW WHAT TO DO WITHOUT YOU.
slip
MINORU-SAMA...
ぎゅ
hug

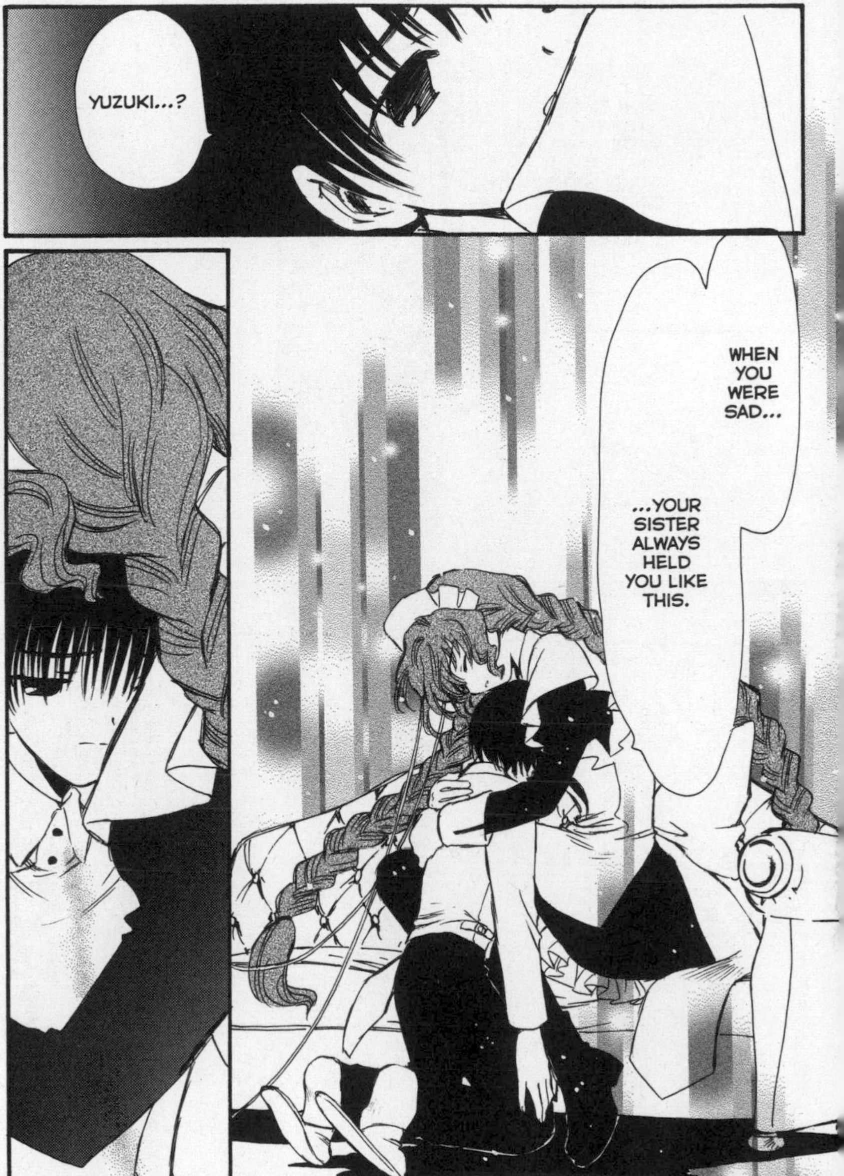
YUZUKI...?
WHEN YOU WERE SAD...
...YOUR SISTER ALWAYS HELD YOU LIKE THIS.

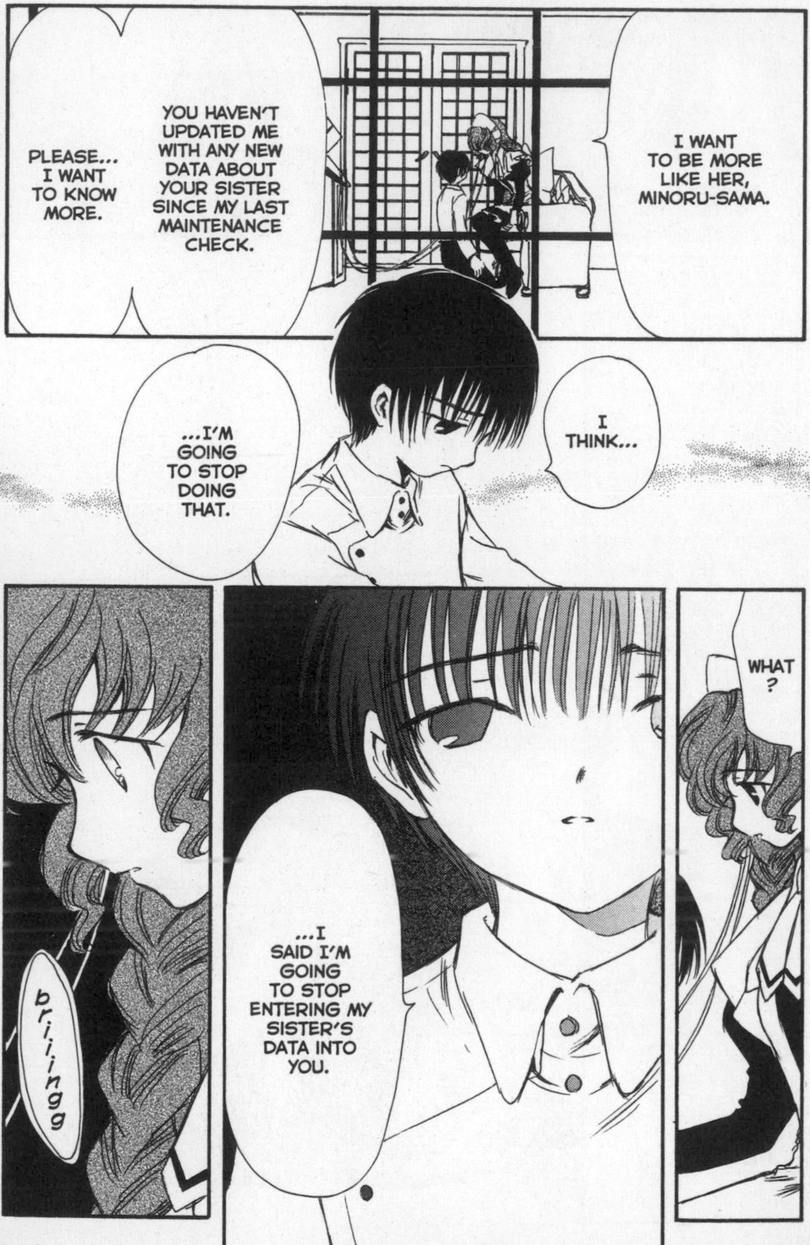
I WANT TO BE MORE LIKE HER, MINORU-SAMA.
YOU HAVEN'T UPDATED ME WITH ANY NEW DATA ABOUT YOUR SISTER SINCE MY LAST MAINTENANCE CHECK.
PLEASE... I WANT TO KNOW MORE.
I THINK...
...I'M GOING TO STOP DOING THAT.
WHAT?
...I SAID I'M GOING TO STOP ENTERING MY SISTER'S DATA INTO YOU.
briiingg

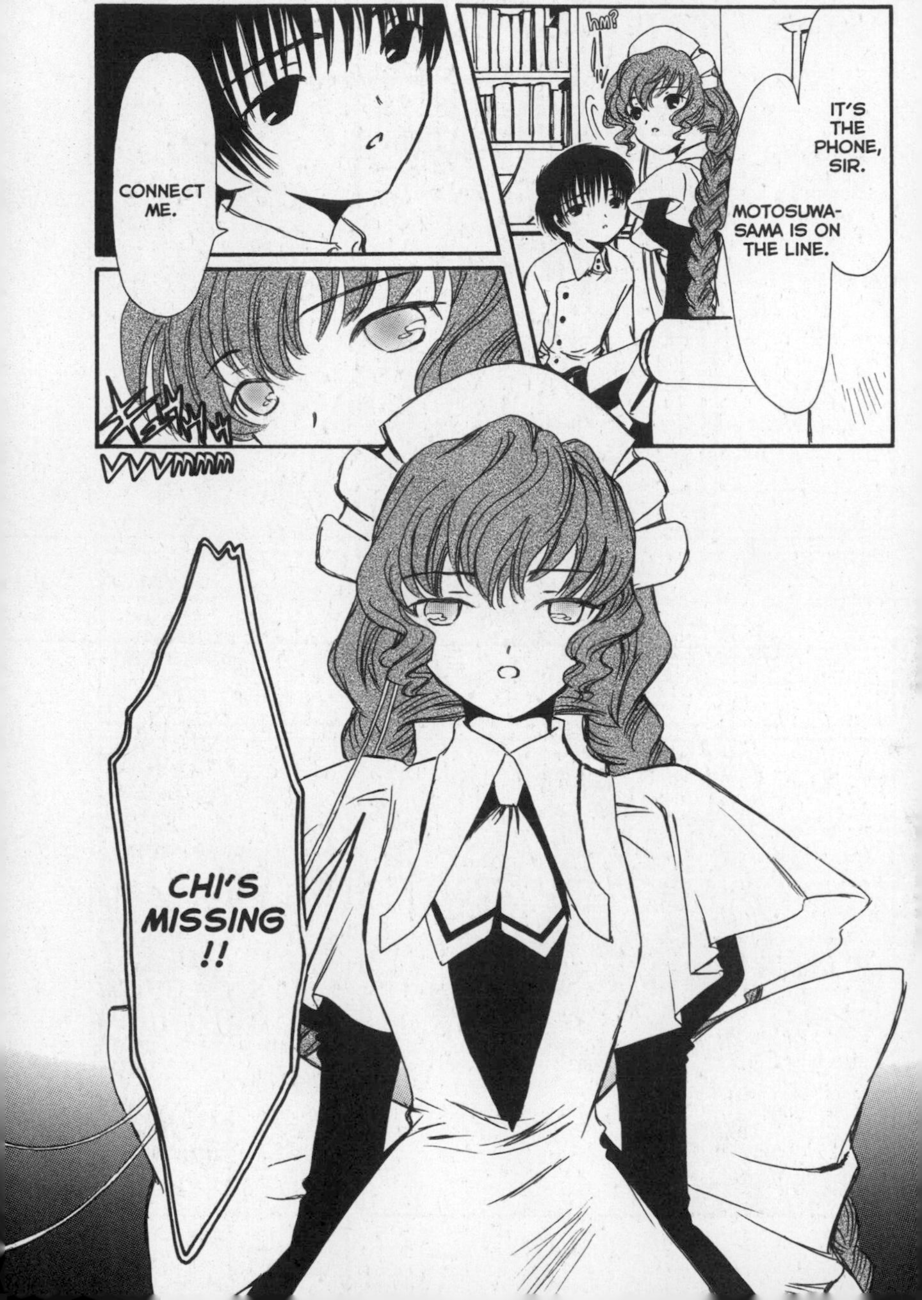
hm?
IT'S THE PHONE, SIR.
MOTOSUWA-SAMA IS ON THE LINE.
CONNECT ME.
VVVmmm
CHI'S MISSING !!

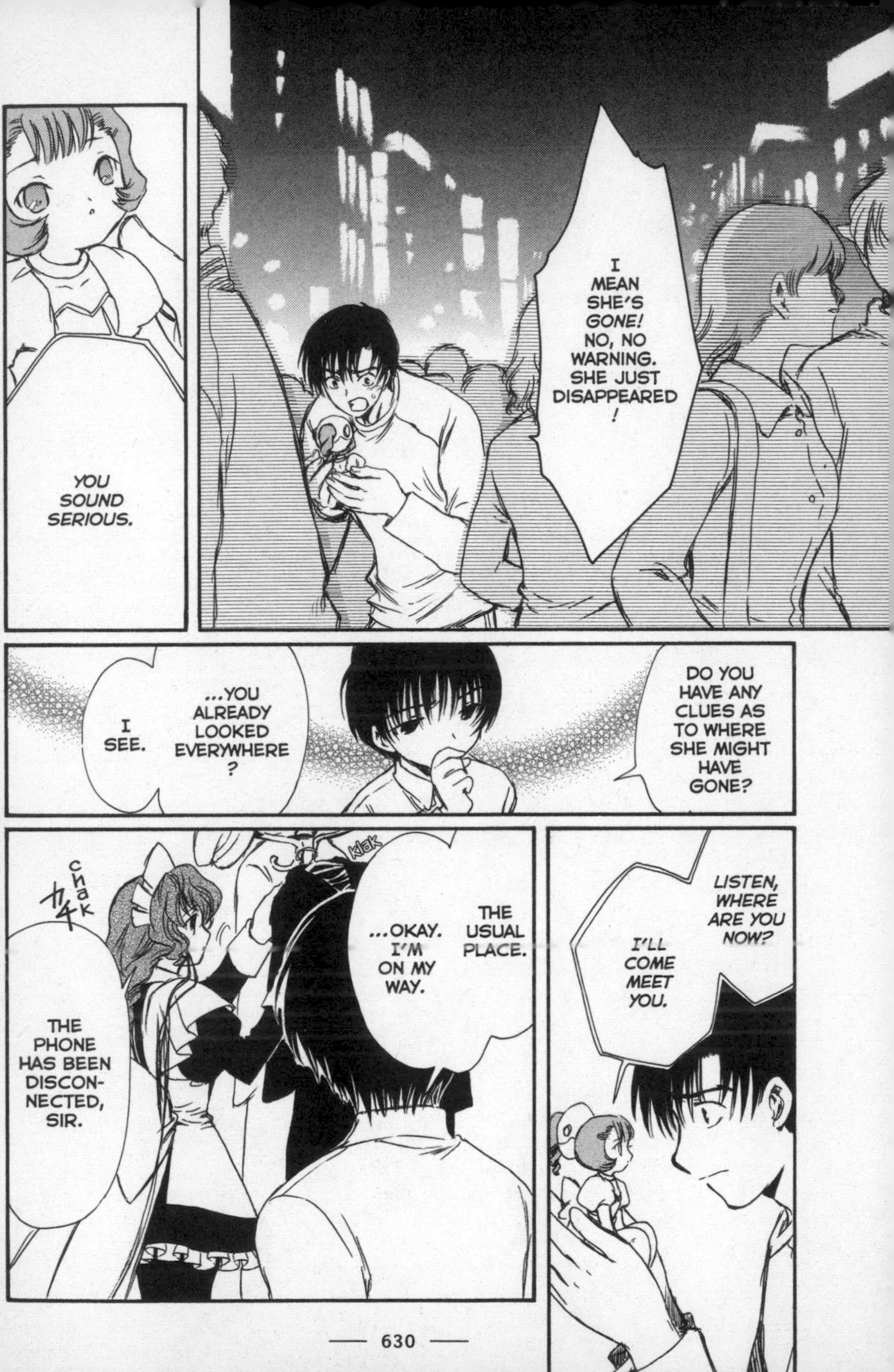
I MEAN SHE'S GONE! NO, NO WARNING. SHE JUST DISAPPEARED!
YOU SOUND SERIOUS.
DO YOU HAVE ANY CLUES AS TO WHERE SHE MIGHT HAVE GONE?
...YOU ALREADY LOOKED EVERYWHERE?
I SEE.
LISTEN, WHERE ARE YOU NOW?
I'LL COME MEET YOU.
THE USUAL PLACE.
...OKAY. I'M ON MY WAY.
klak
chak
カチ
THE PHONE HAS BEEN DISCONNECTED, SIR.

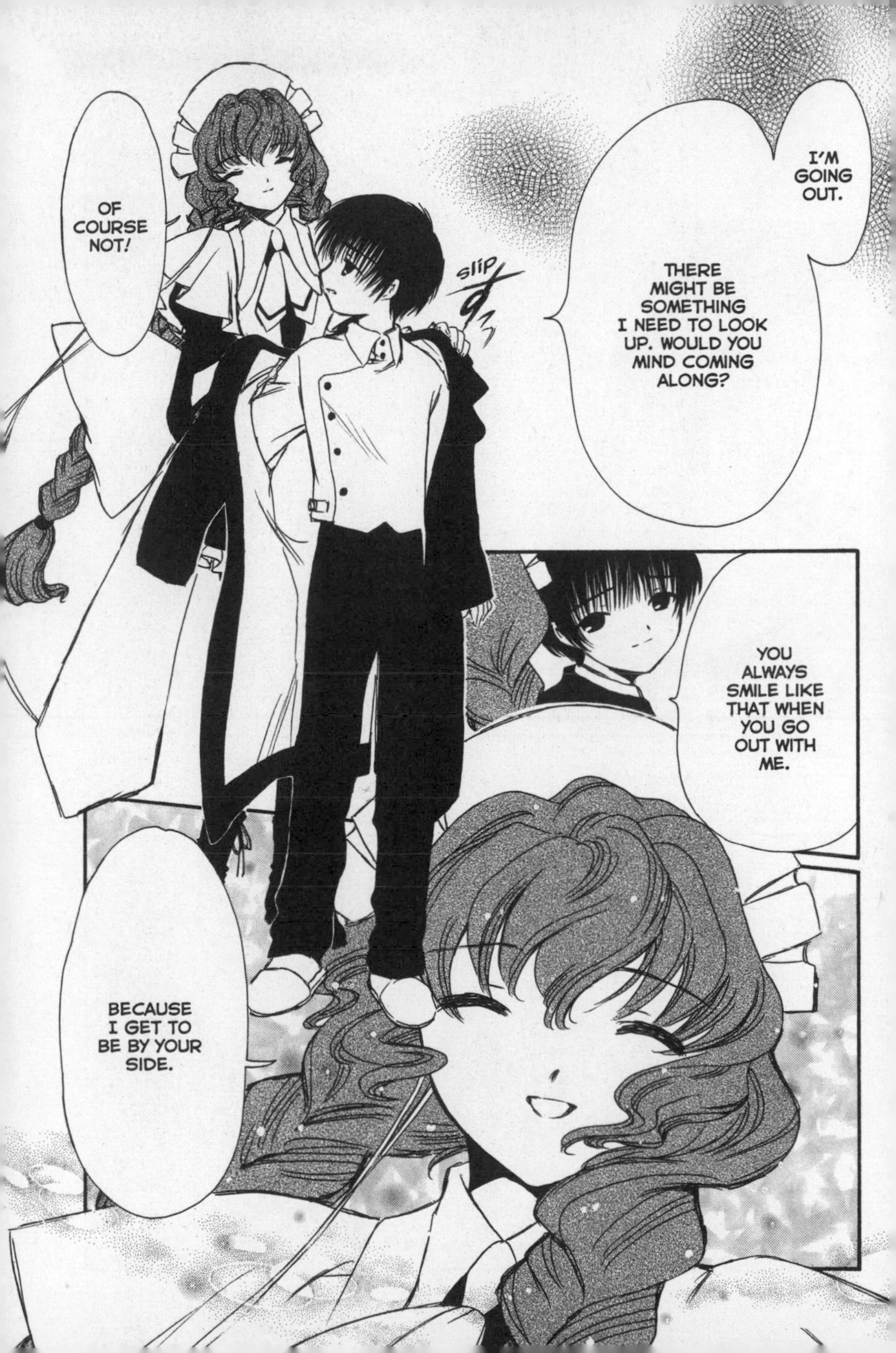
I'M GOING OUT.
THERE MIGHT BE SOMETHING I NEED TO LOOK UP. WOULD YOU MIND COMING ALONG?
slip
OF COURSE NOT!
YOU ALWAYS SMILE LIKE THAT WHEN YOU GO OUT WITH ME.
BECAUSE I GET TO BE BY YOUR SIDE.

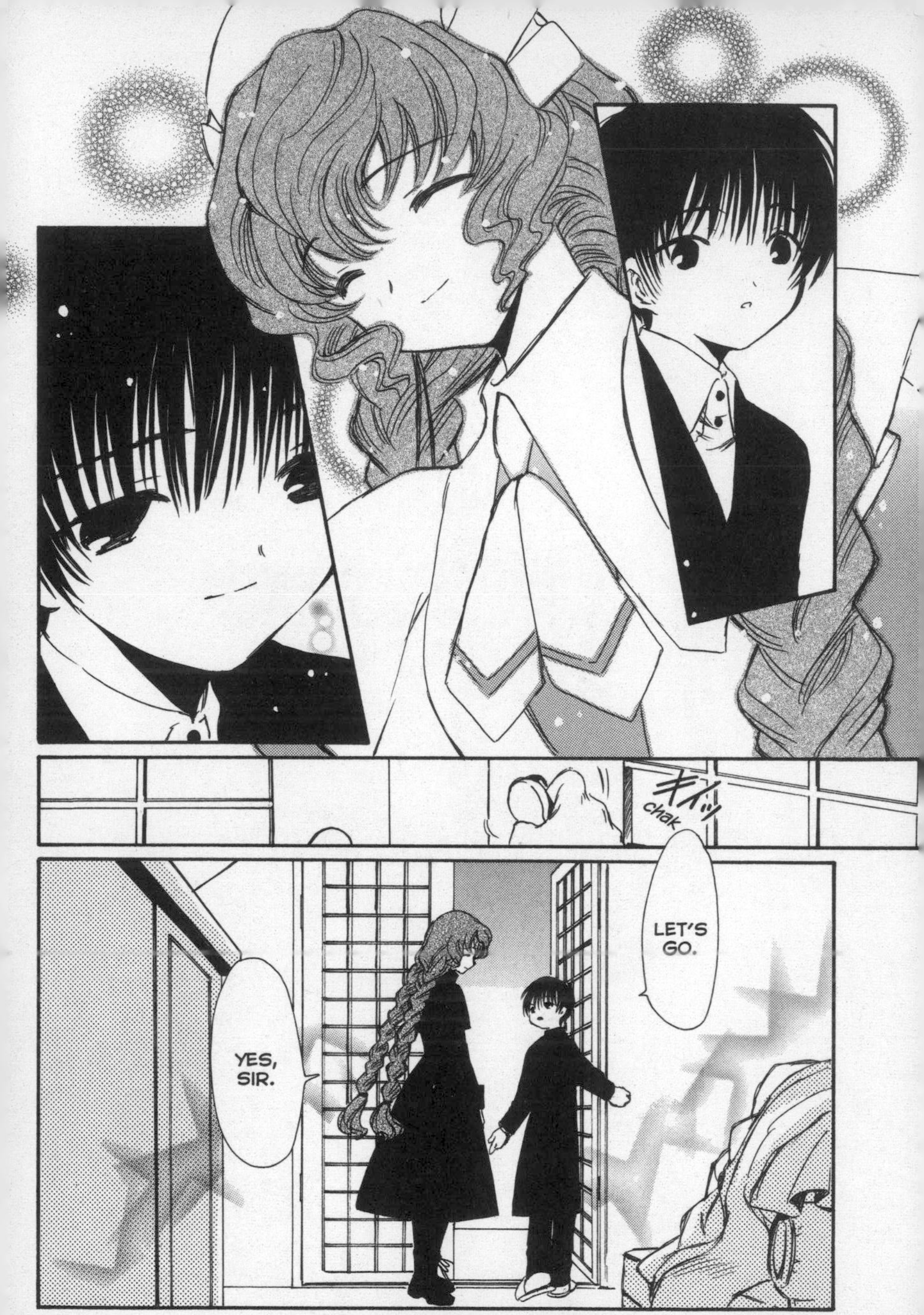
キィッ
chak
LET'S GO.
YES, SIR.

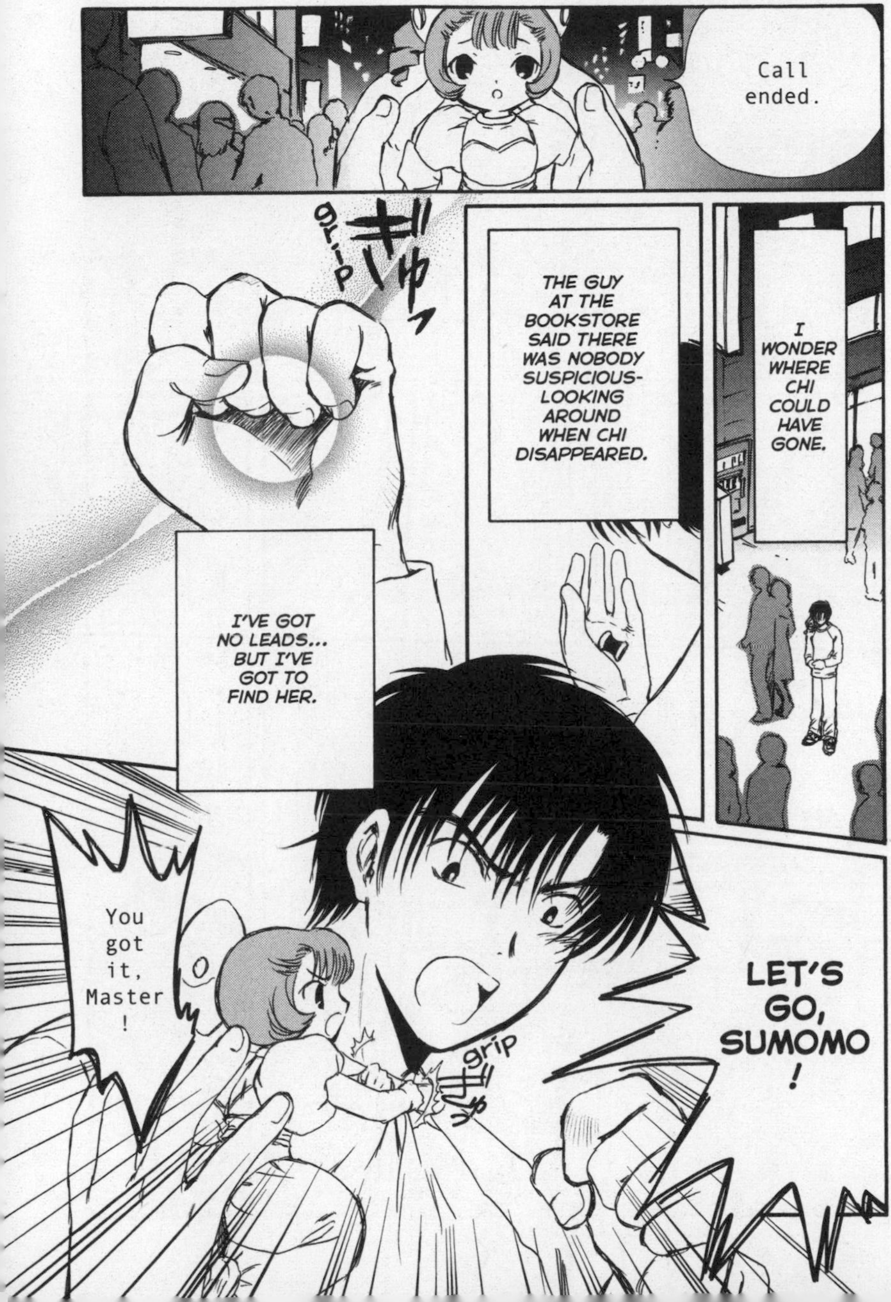
Call ended.
I WONDER WHERE CHI COULD HAVE GONE.
THE GUY AT THE BOOKSTORE SAID THERE WAS NOBODY SUSPICIOUS-LOOKING AROUND WHEN CHI DISAPPEARED.
grip
I'VE GOT NO LEADS... BUT I'VE GOT TO FIND HER.
LET'S GO, SUMOMO!
grip
You got it, Master!

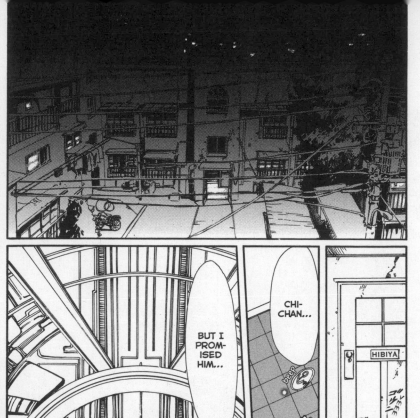

BUT I PROM-ISED HIM...

CHI-CHAN...

HIBIYA

...I WOULDN'T INTER-FERE.

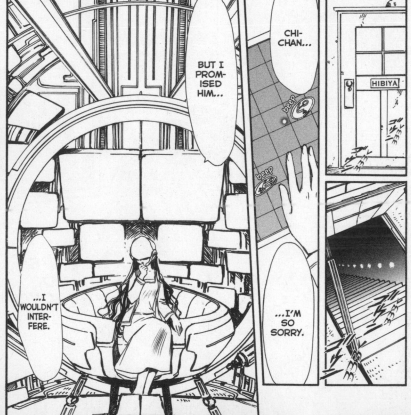

...I'M SO SORRY.

WELL,
WELL...NOW
THIS IS AN
INTERESTING
TURN.

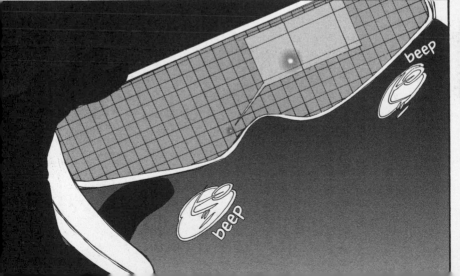

beep

beep

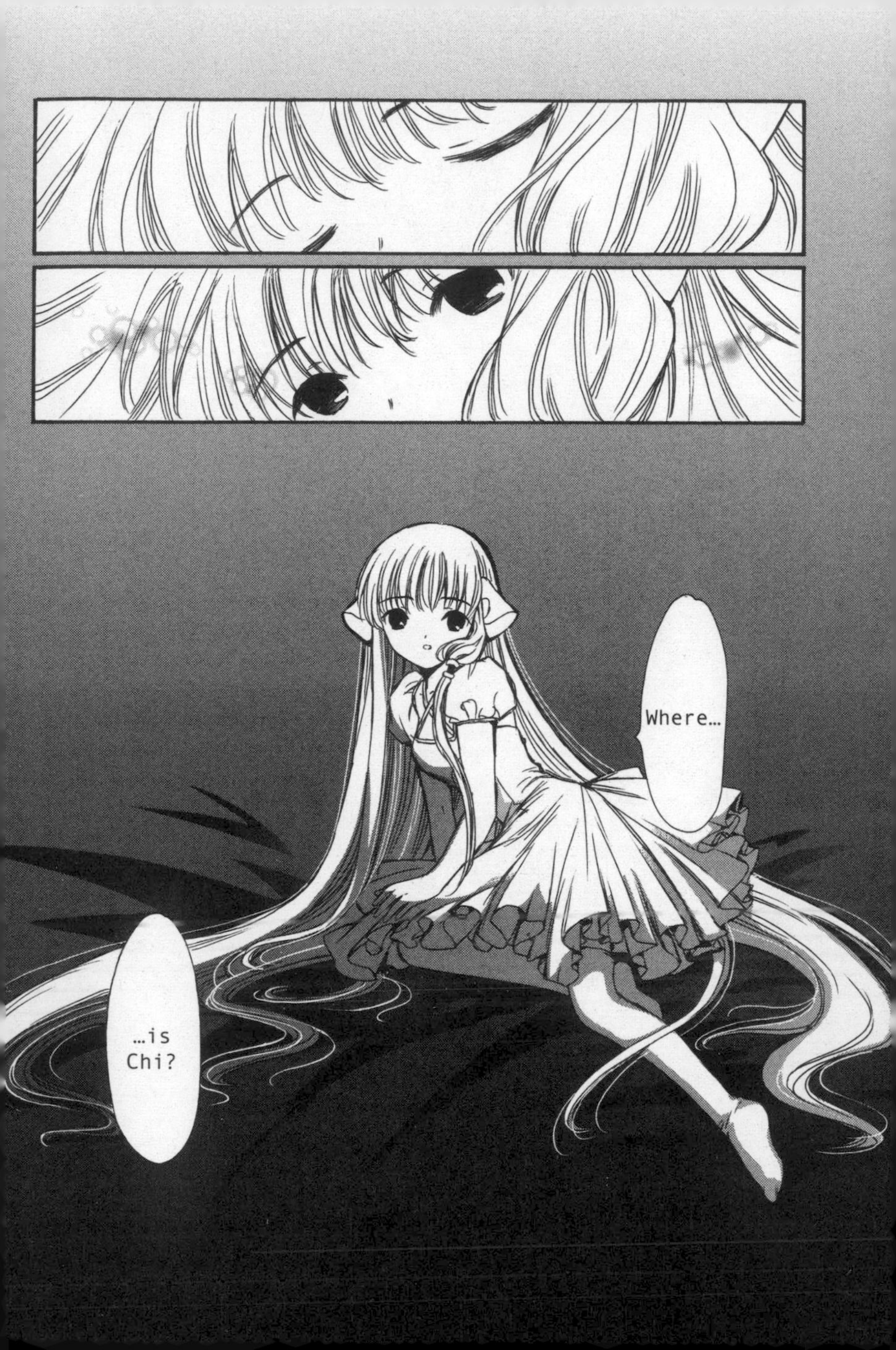
Where…
…is Chi?

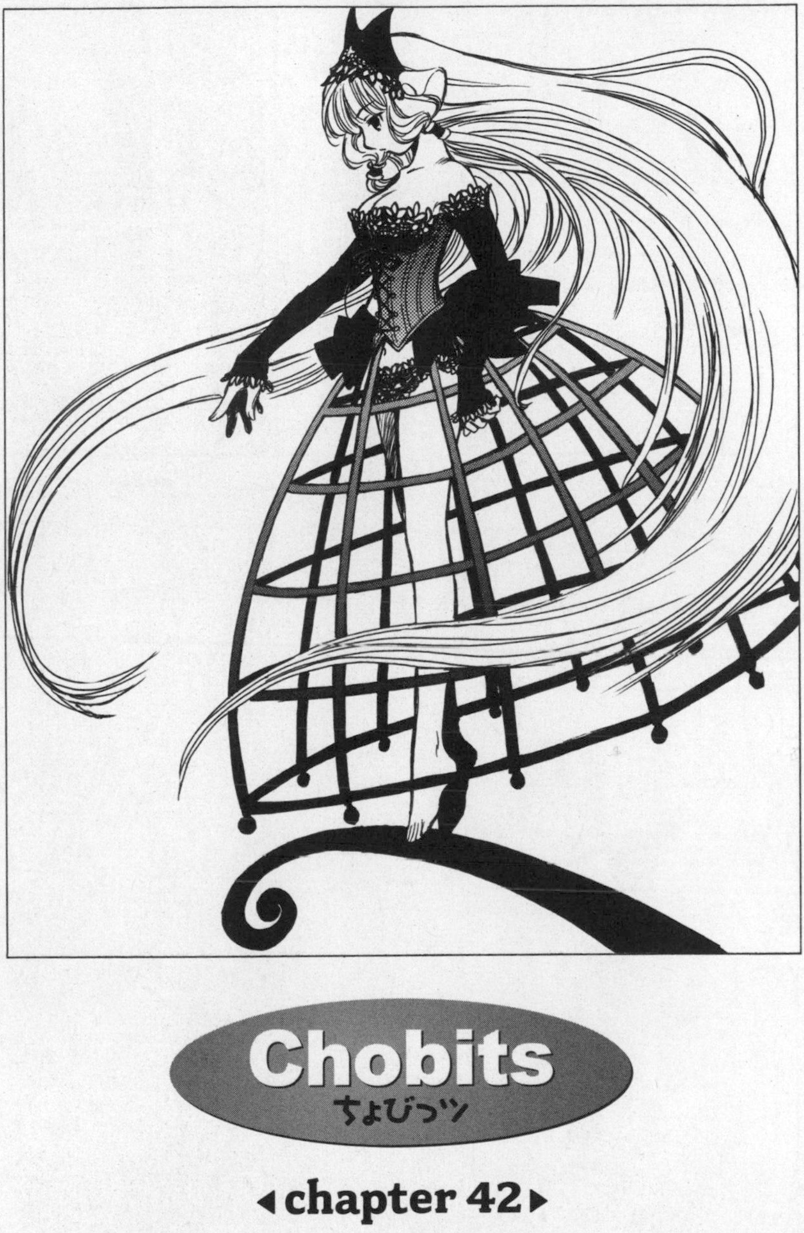

Chobits

ちょびっツ

chapter 42

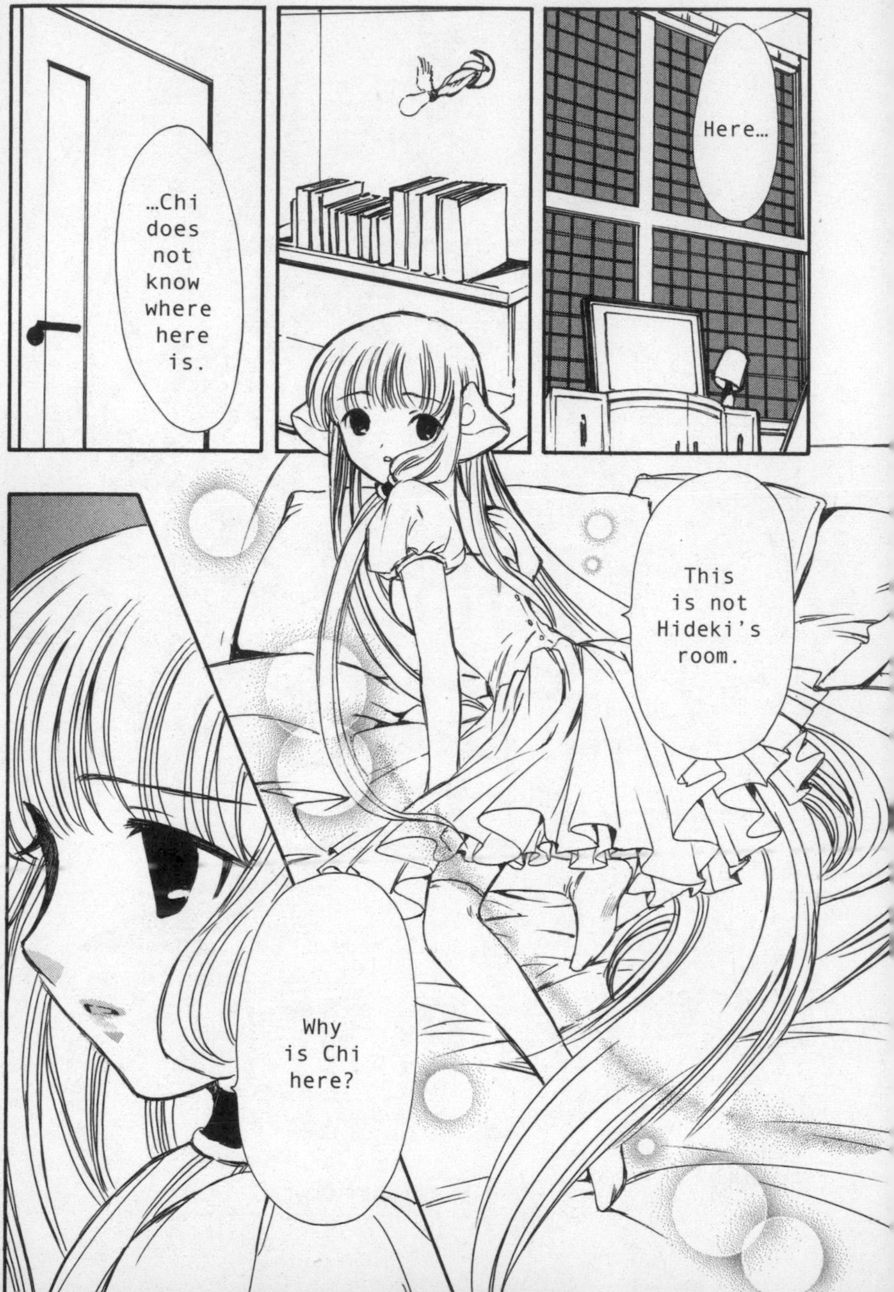
Here…
…Chi does not know where here is.
This is not Hideki's room.
Why is Chi here?

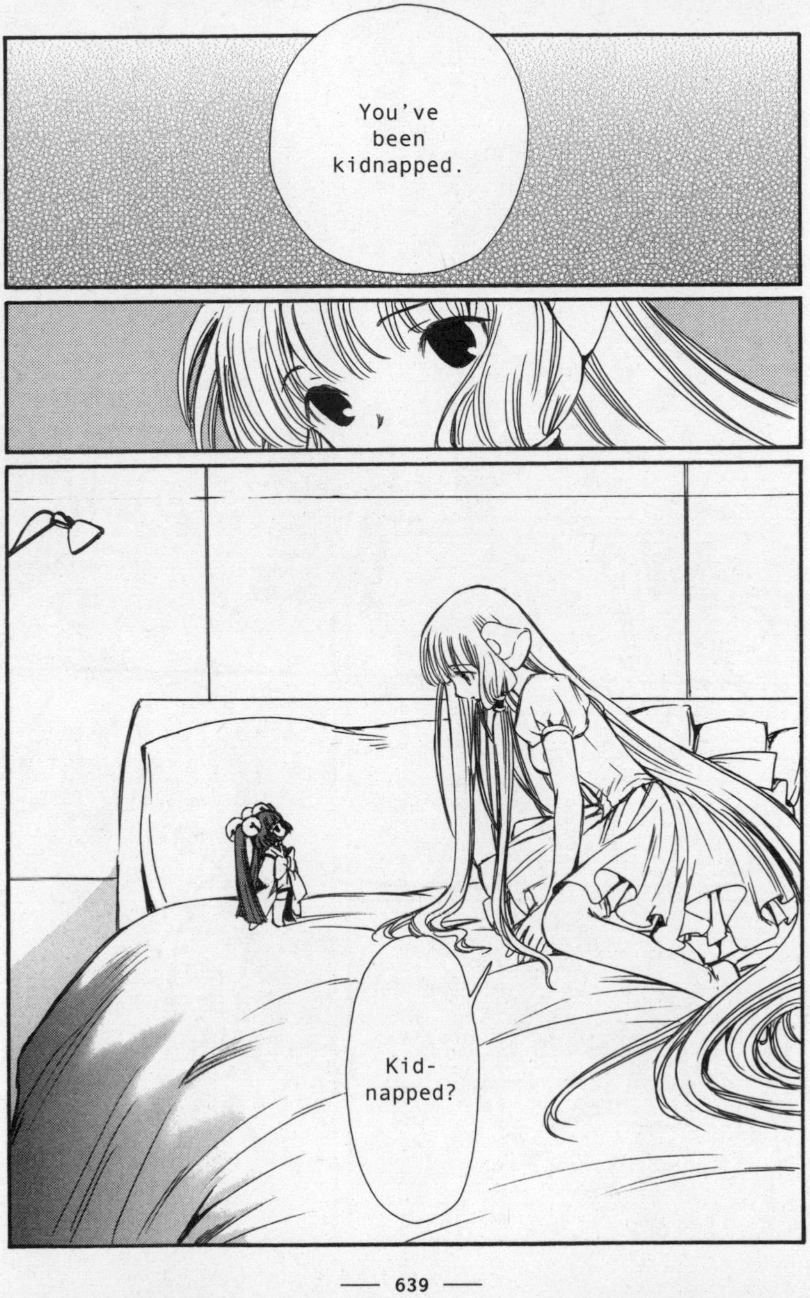
You've been kidnapped.
Kid-napped?

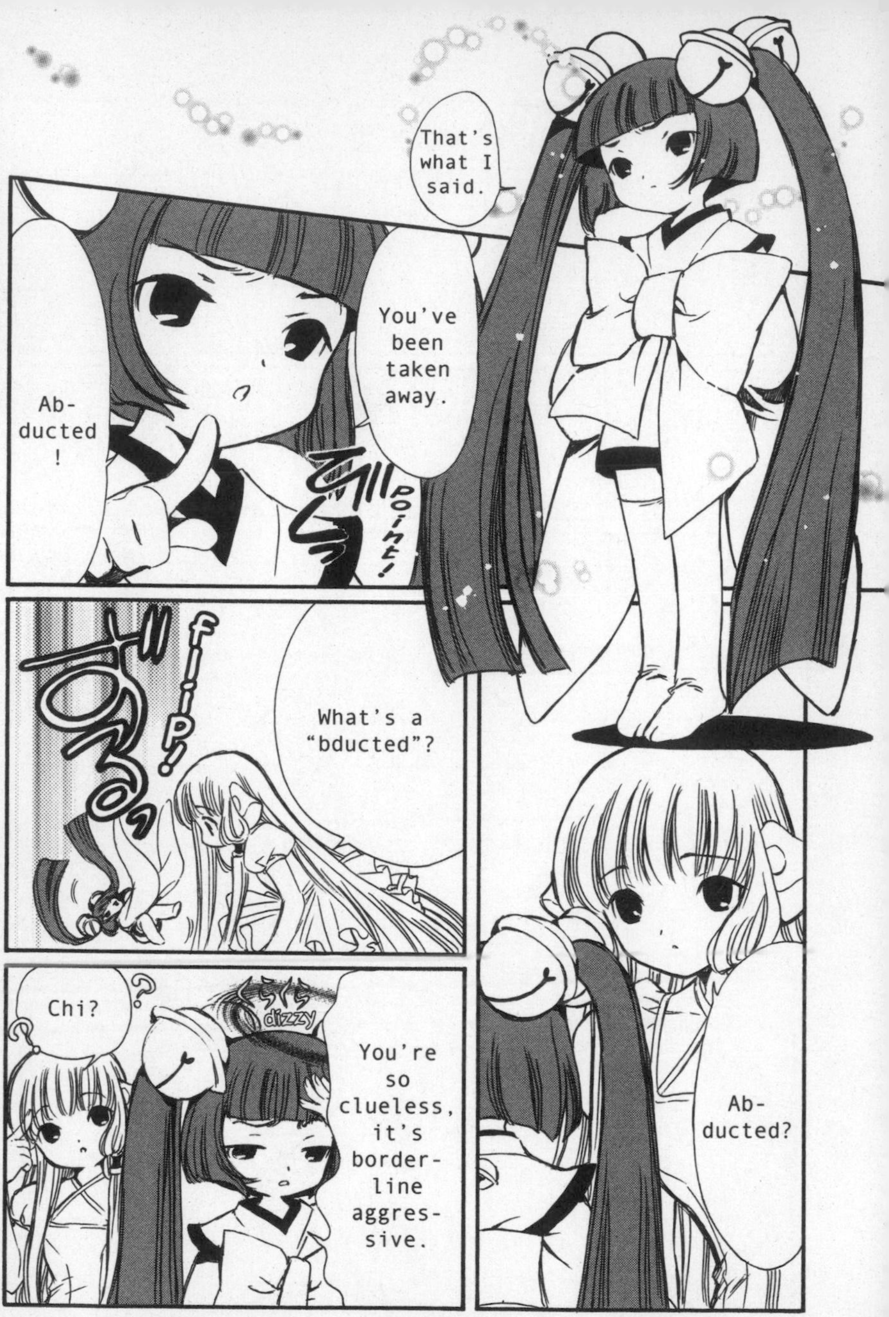

That's what I said.
You've been taken away.
point!
Ab-ducted!
Ab-ducted?
What's a "bducted"?
flip!
dizzy
You're so clueless, it's borderline aggressive.
Chi?

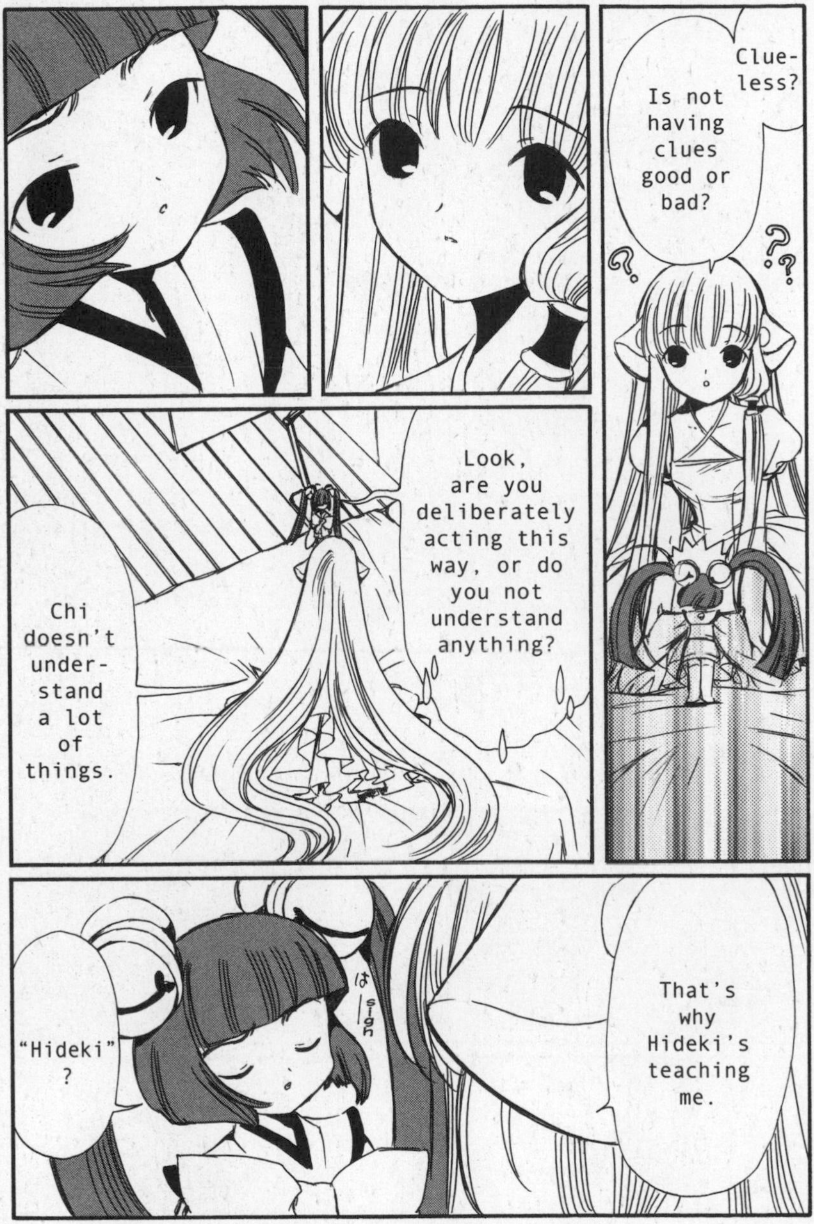
Clue-less?
Is not having clues good or bad?
Look, are you deliberately acting this way, or do you not understand anything?
Chi doesn't understand a lot of things.
That's why Hideki's teaching me.
は sigh
"Hideki"?

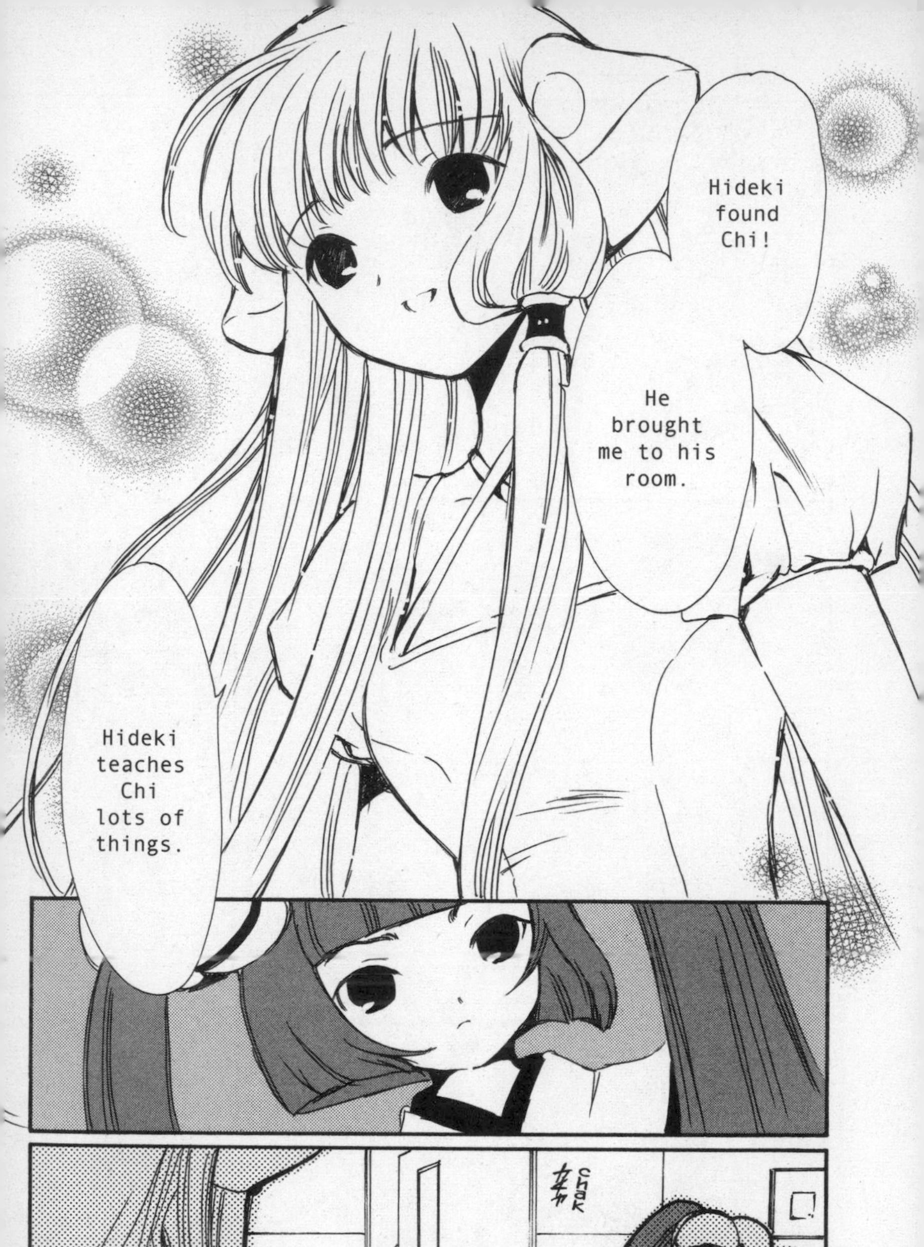
Hideki found Chi!
He brought me to his room.
Hideki teaches Chi lots of things.
chak

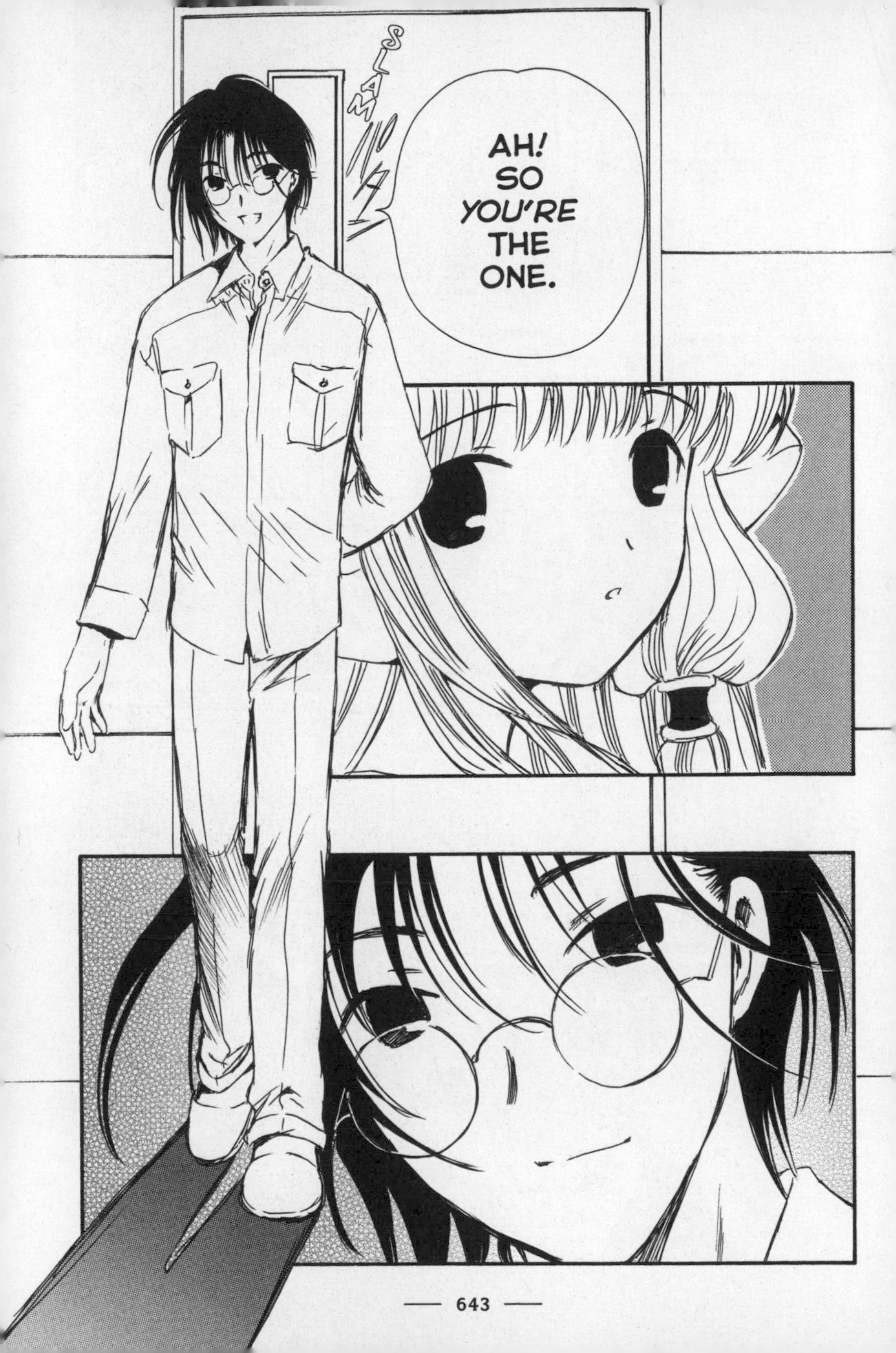
SLAM
AH! SO YOU'RE THE ONE.

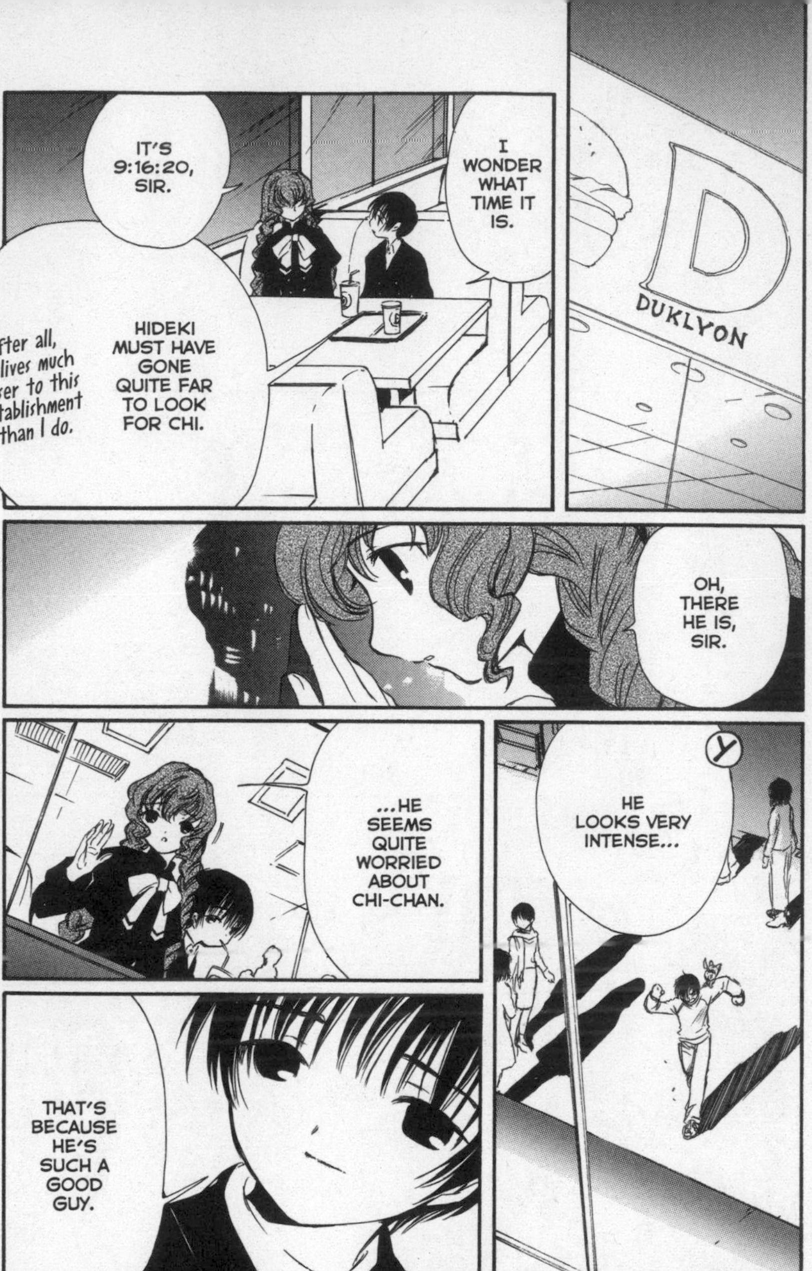
DUKLYON
I WONDER WHAT TIME IT IS.
IT'S 9:16:20, SIR.
HIDEKI MUST HAVE GONE QUITE FAR TO LOOK FOR CHI.
After all, he lives much closer to this establishment than I do.
OH, THERE HE IS, SIR.
HE LOOKS VERY INTENSE...
...HE SEEMS QUITE WORRIED ABOUT CHI-CHAN.
THAT'S BECAUSE HE'S SUCH A GOOD GUY.

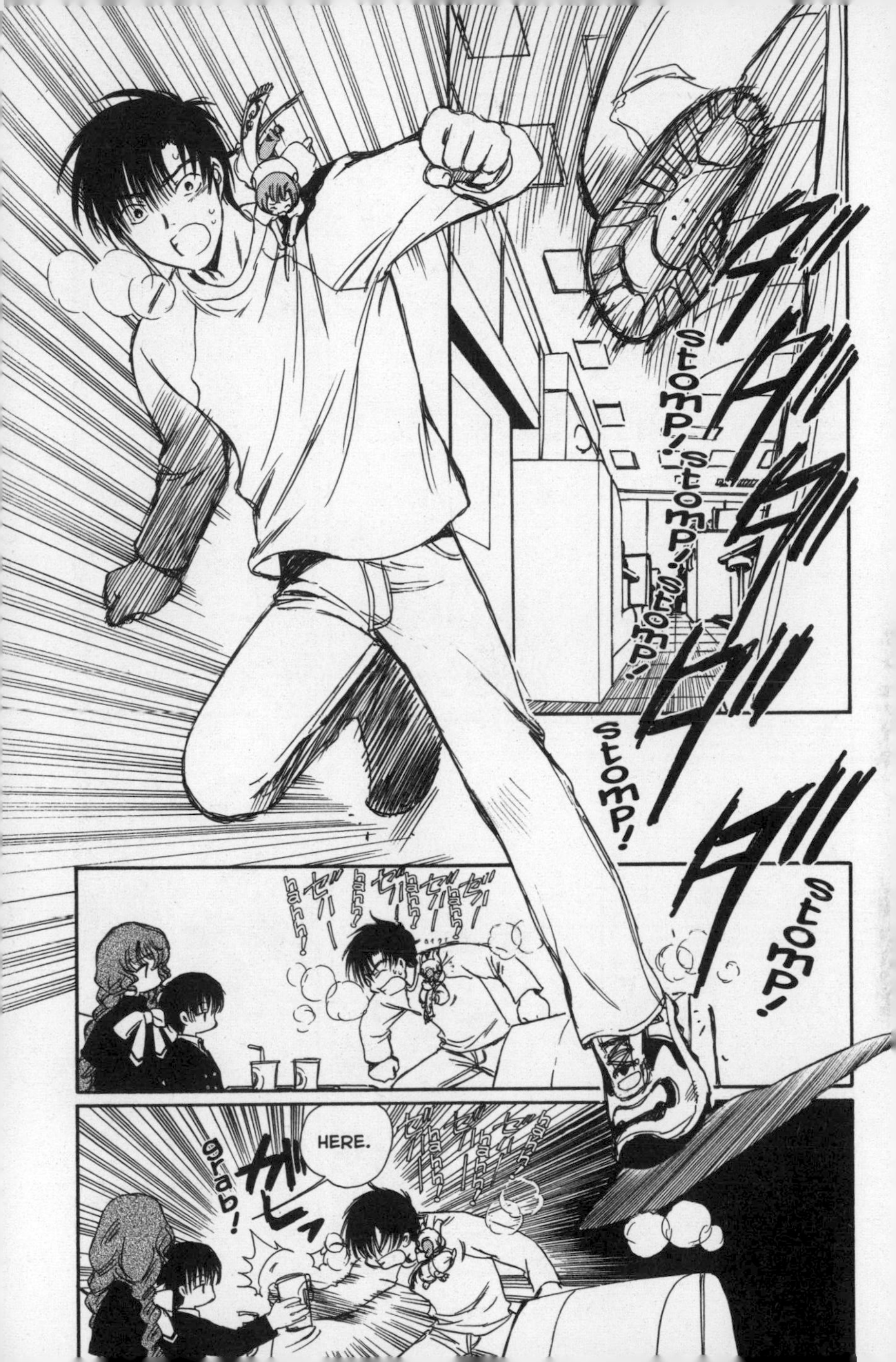
STOMP! STOMP! STOMP! STOMP!
STOMP!
STOMP!
hah! hah! hah! hah!
hah! hah! hah!
HERE.
grab!

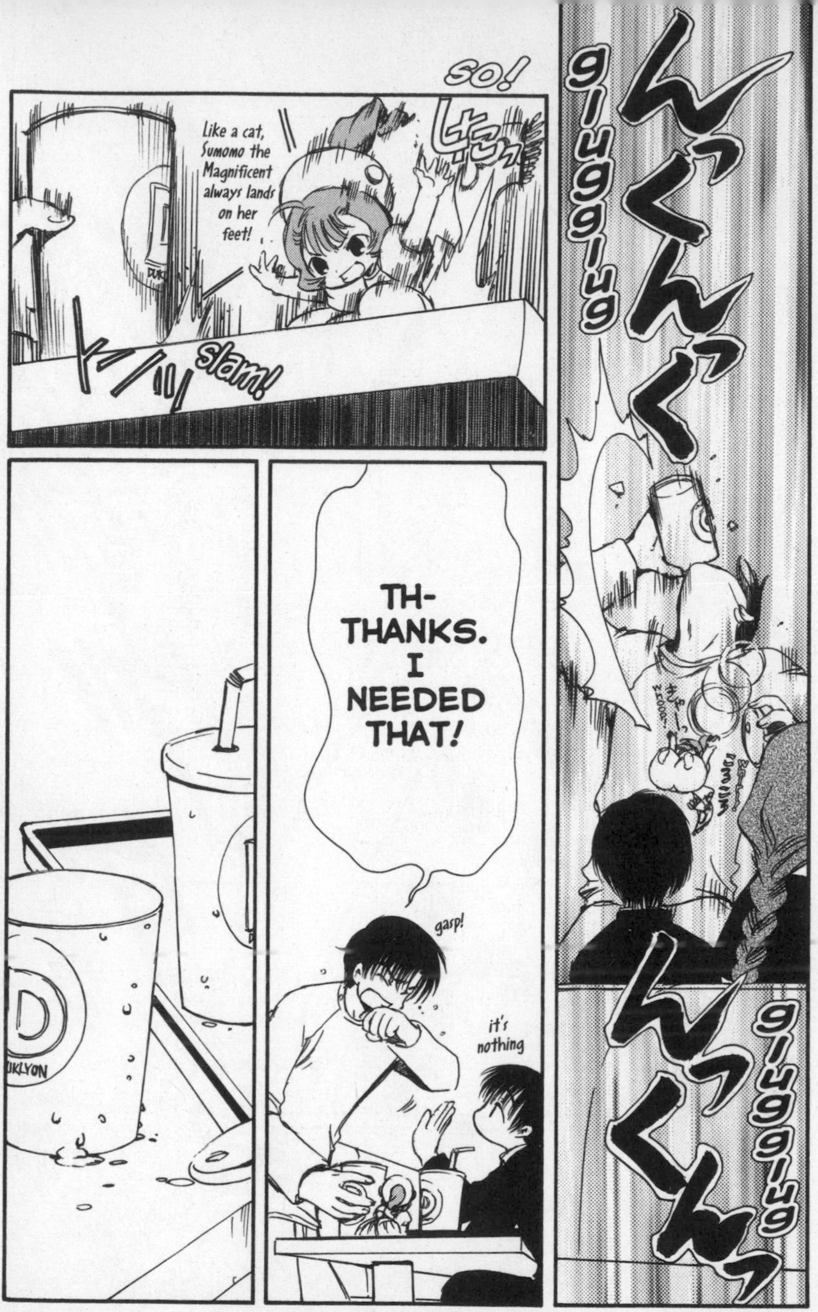
んっくんっく
glugglug
きゃーっ
WHOOP!
んっくんっくっ
gluggluglug
so!
しゅたっ
Like a cat, Sumomo the Magnificent always lands on her feet!
slam!
TH-THANKS. I NEEDED THAT!
gasp!
it's nothing

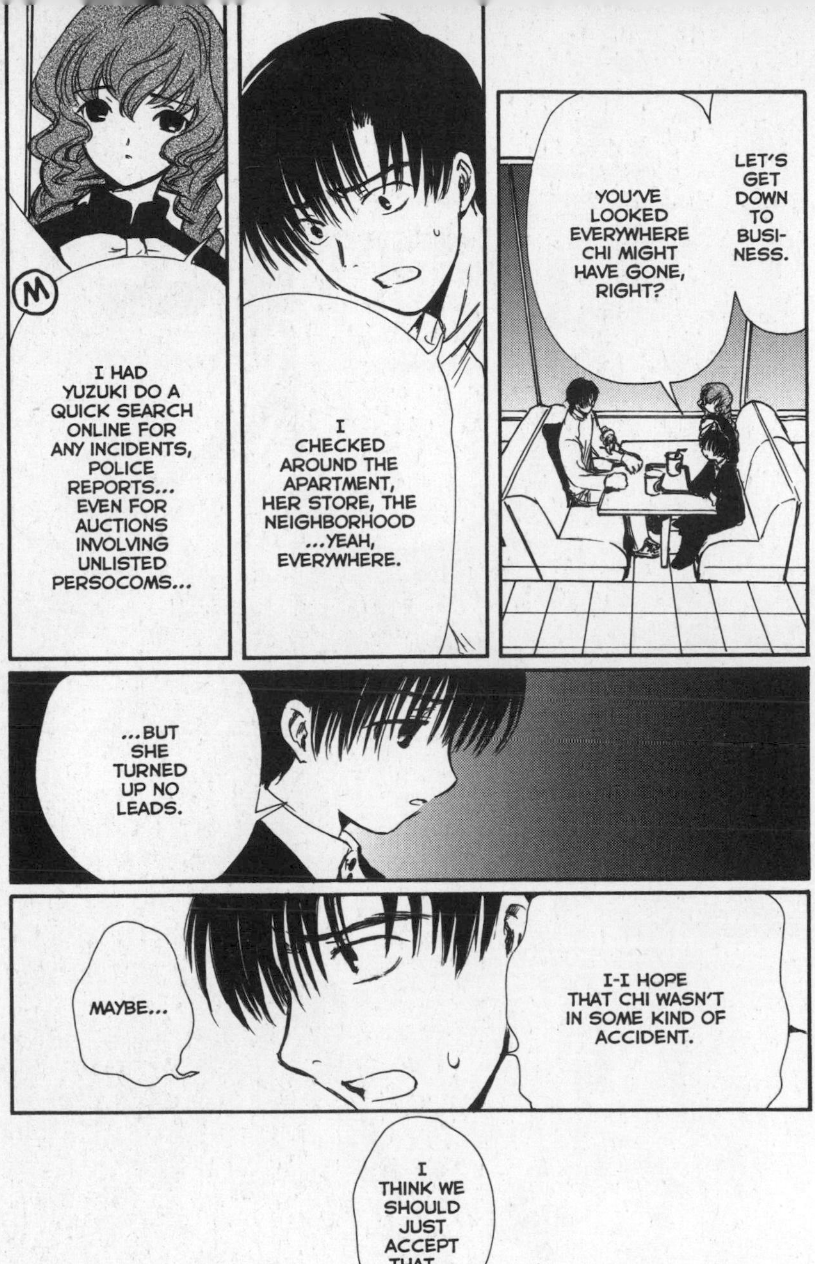
LET'S GET DOWN TO BUSINESS.
YOU'VE LOOKED EVERYWHERE CHI MIGHT HAVE GONE, RIGHT?
I CHECKED AROUND THE APARTMENT, HER STORE, THE NEIGHBORHOOD ...YEAH, EVERYWHERE.
I HAD YUZUKI DO A QUICK SEARCH ONLINE FOR ANY INCIDENTS, POLICE REPORTS... EVEN FOR AUCTIONS INVOLVING UNLISTED PERSOCOMS...
...BUT SHE TURNED UP NO LEADS.
I-I HOPE THAT CHI WASN'T IN SOME KIND OF ACCIDENT.
MAYBE...
I THINK WE SHOULD JUST ACCEPT THAT...

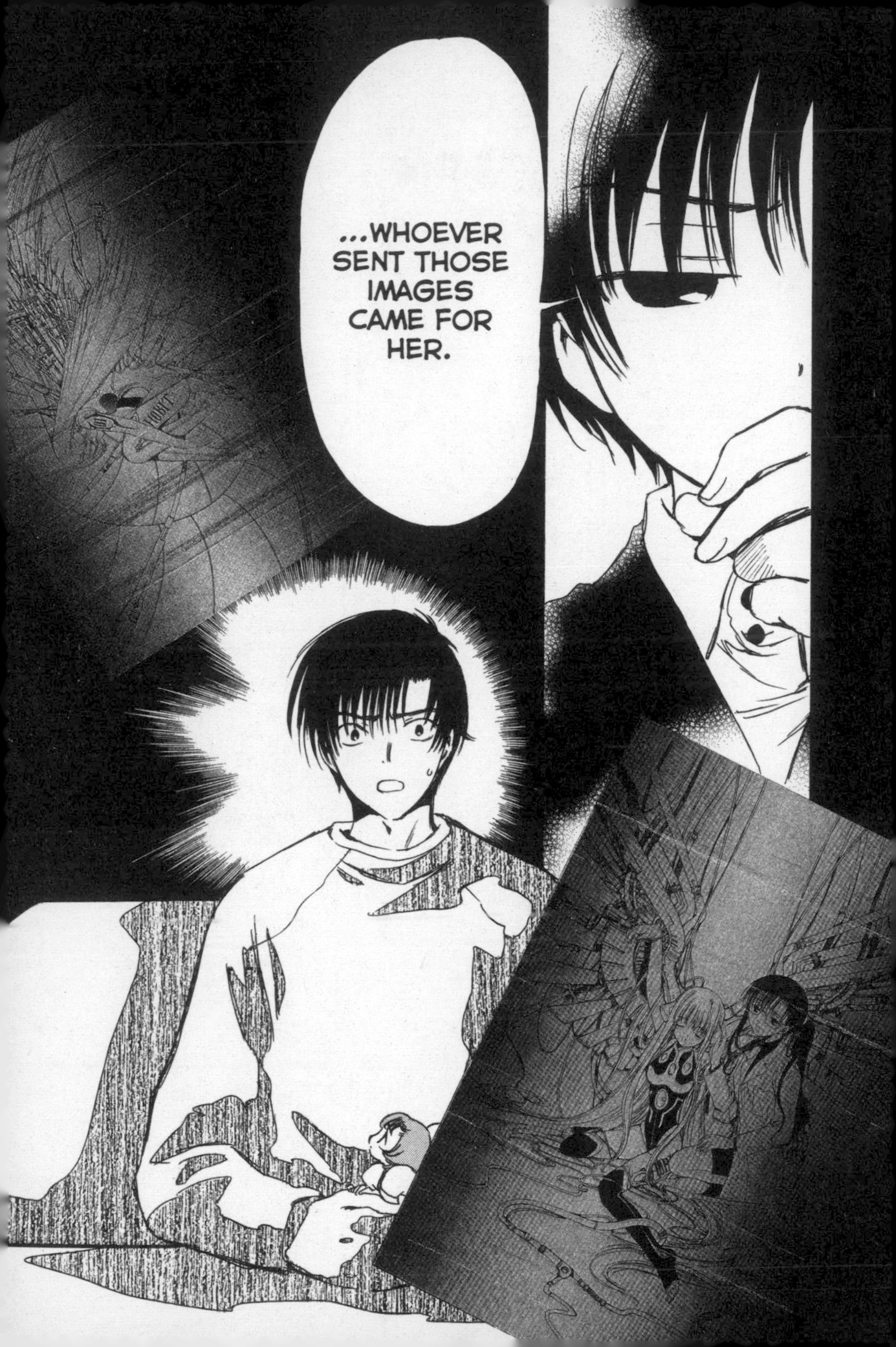
...WHOEVER SENT THOSE IMAGES CAME FOR HER.

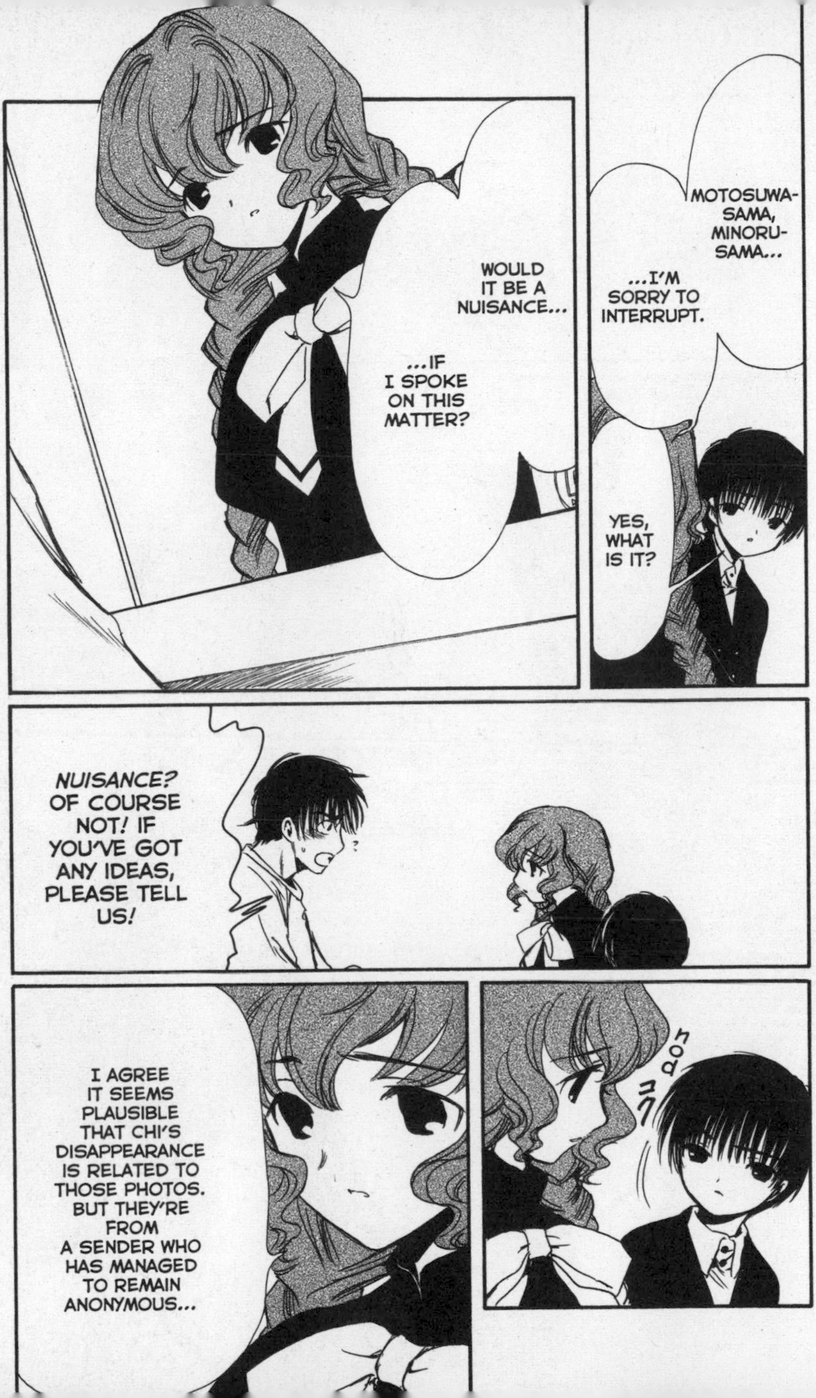
MOTOSUWA-SAMA, MINORU-SAMA...
...I'M SORRY TO INTERRUPT.
YES, WHAT IS IT?
WOULD IT BE A NUISANCE...
...IF I SPOKE ON THIS MATTER?
NUISANCE? OF COURSE NOT! IF YOU'VE GOT ANY IDEAS, PLEASE TELL US!
I AGREE IT SEEMS PLAUSIBLE THAT CHI'S DISAPPEARANCE IS RELATED TO THOSE PHOTOS. BUT THEY'RE FROM A SENDER WHO HAS MANAGED TO REMAIN ANONYMOUS...

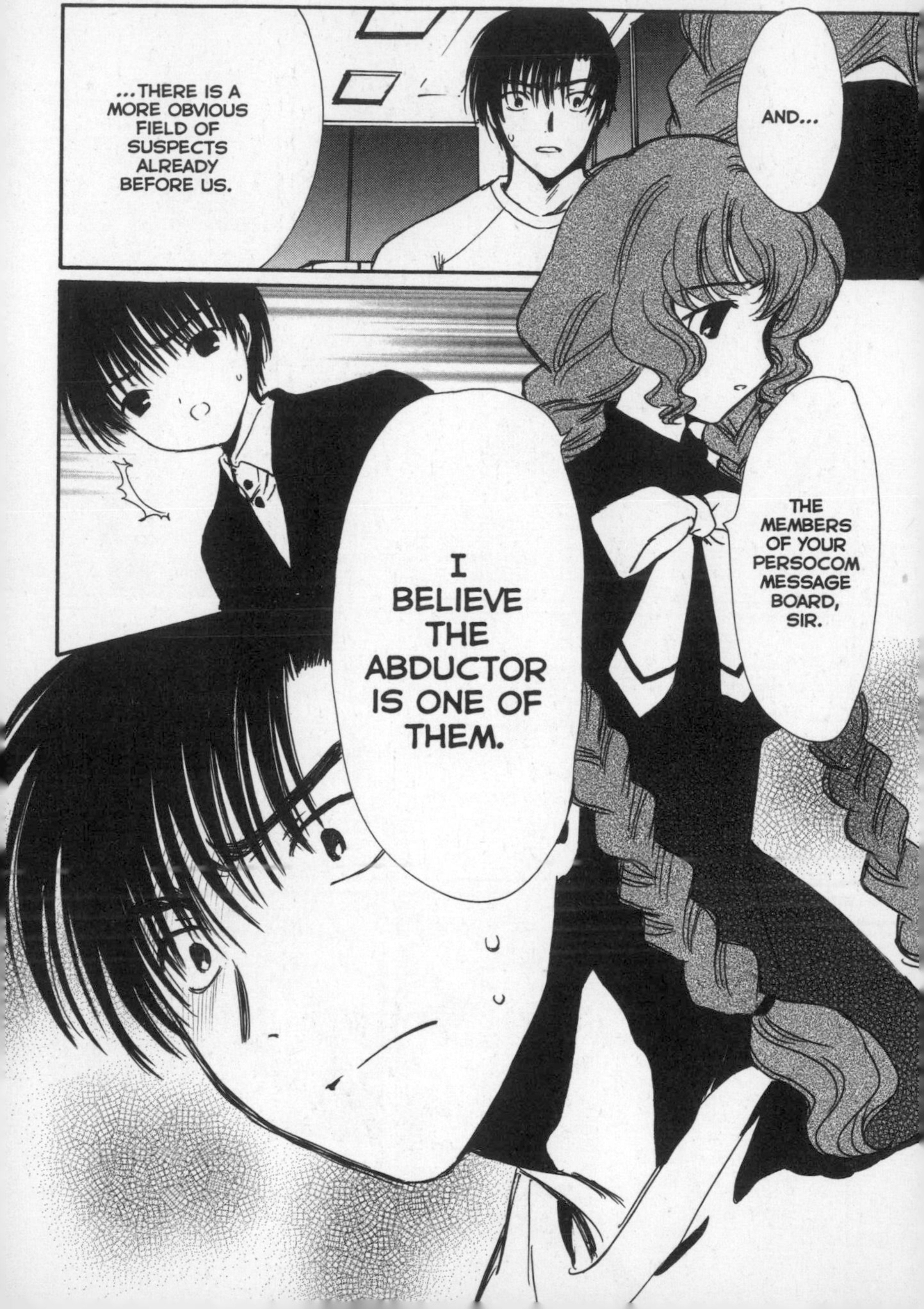
...THERE IS A MORE OBVIOUS FIELD OF SUSPECTS ALREADY BEFORE US.
AND...
THE MEMBERS OF YOUR PERSOCOM MESSAGE BOARD, SIR.
I BELIEVE THE ABDUCTOR IS ONE OF THEM.

Chobits
ちょびっツ

◀ chapter 43 ▶

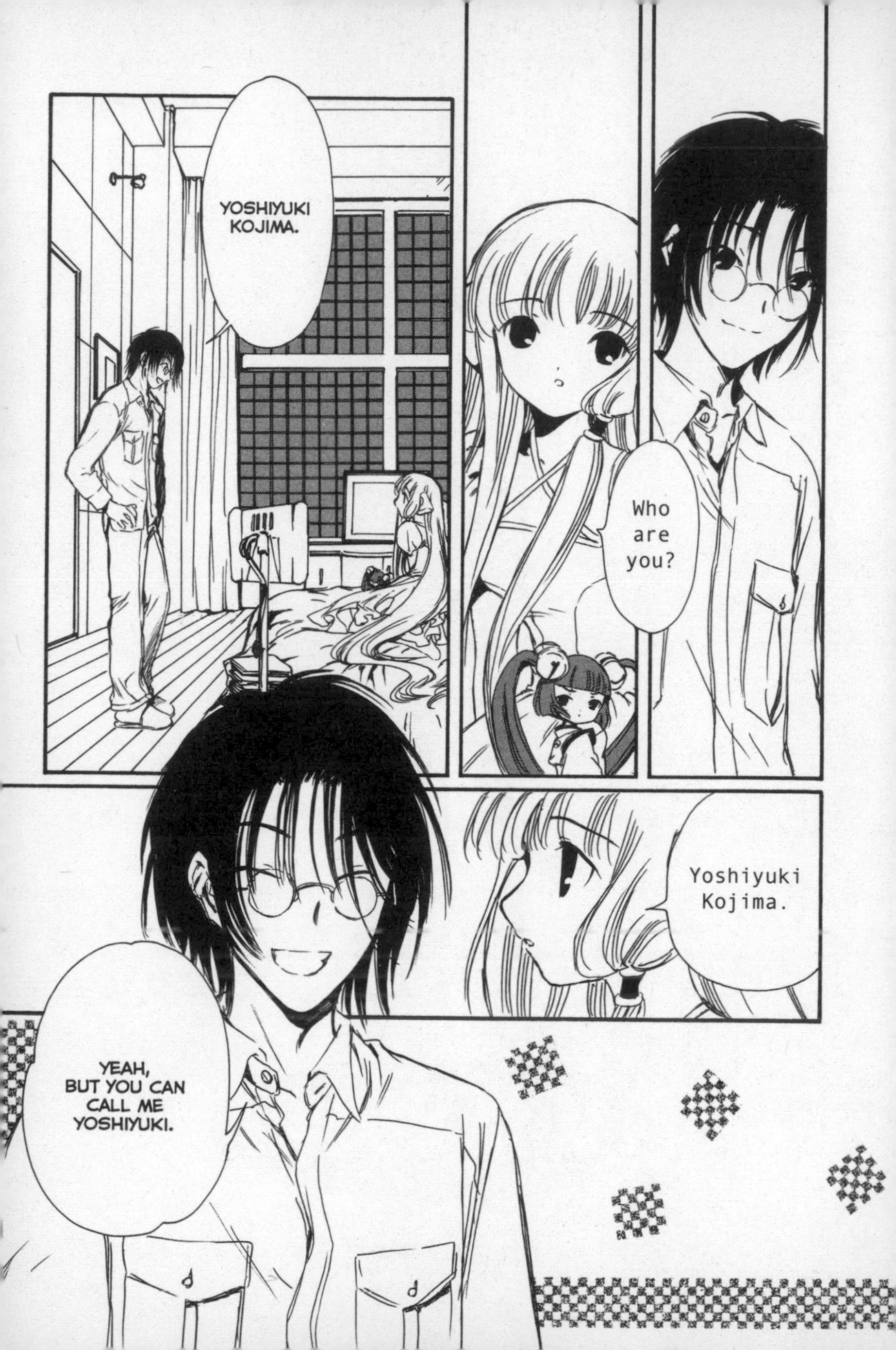
Who are you?
YOSHIYUKI KOJIMA.
Yoshiyuki Kojima.
YEAH, BUT YOU CAN CALL ME YOSHIYUKI.

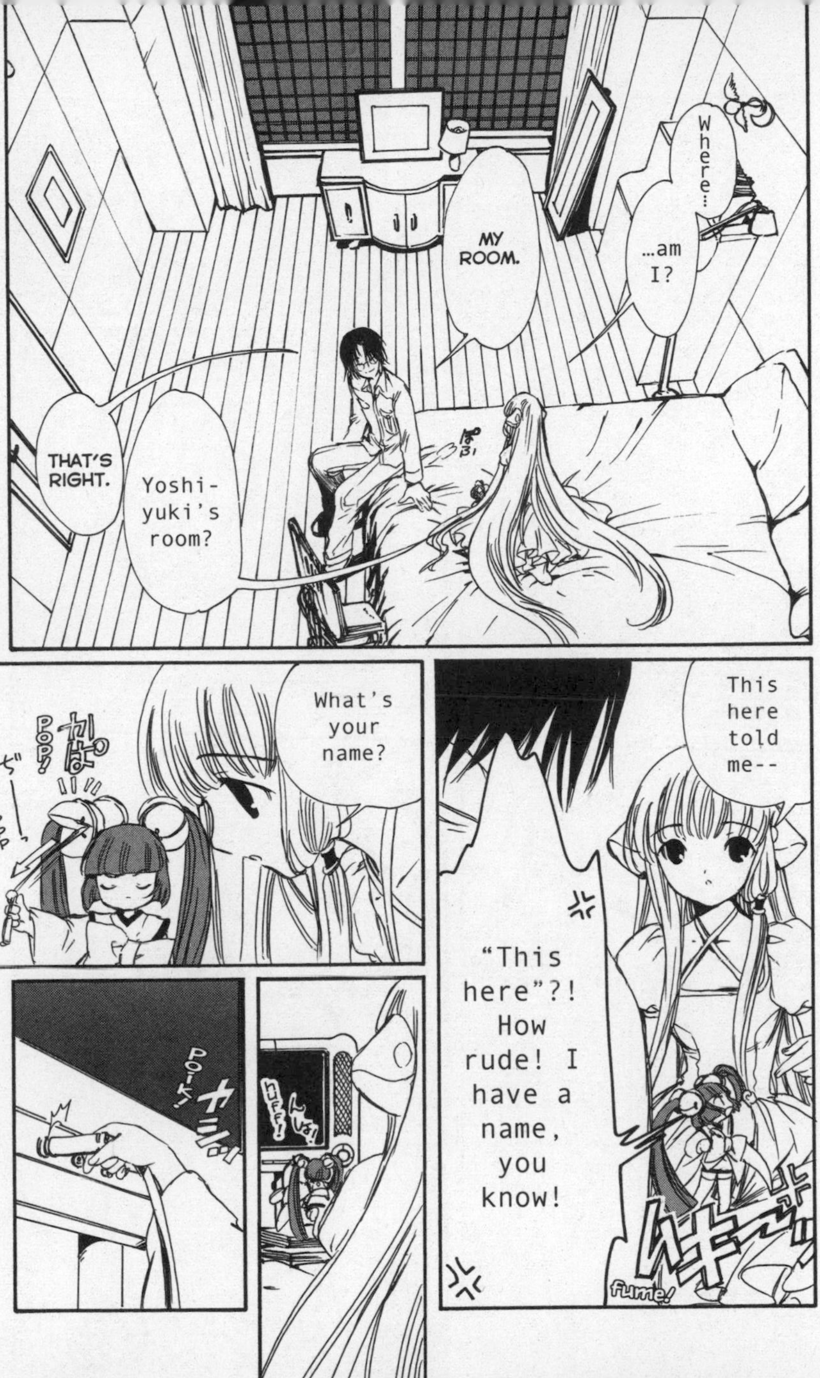

Where…
…am I?
MY ROOM.
Yoshi-yuki's room?
THAT'S RIGHT.
This here told me--
“This here”?! How rude! I have a name, you know!
fume!
What's your name?
POP!
ZZZIIPPP
HUFF!
POKE!

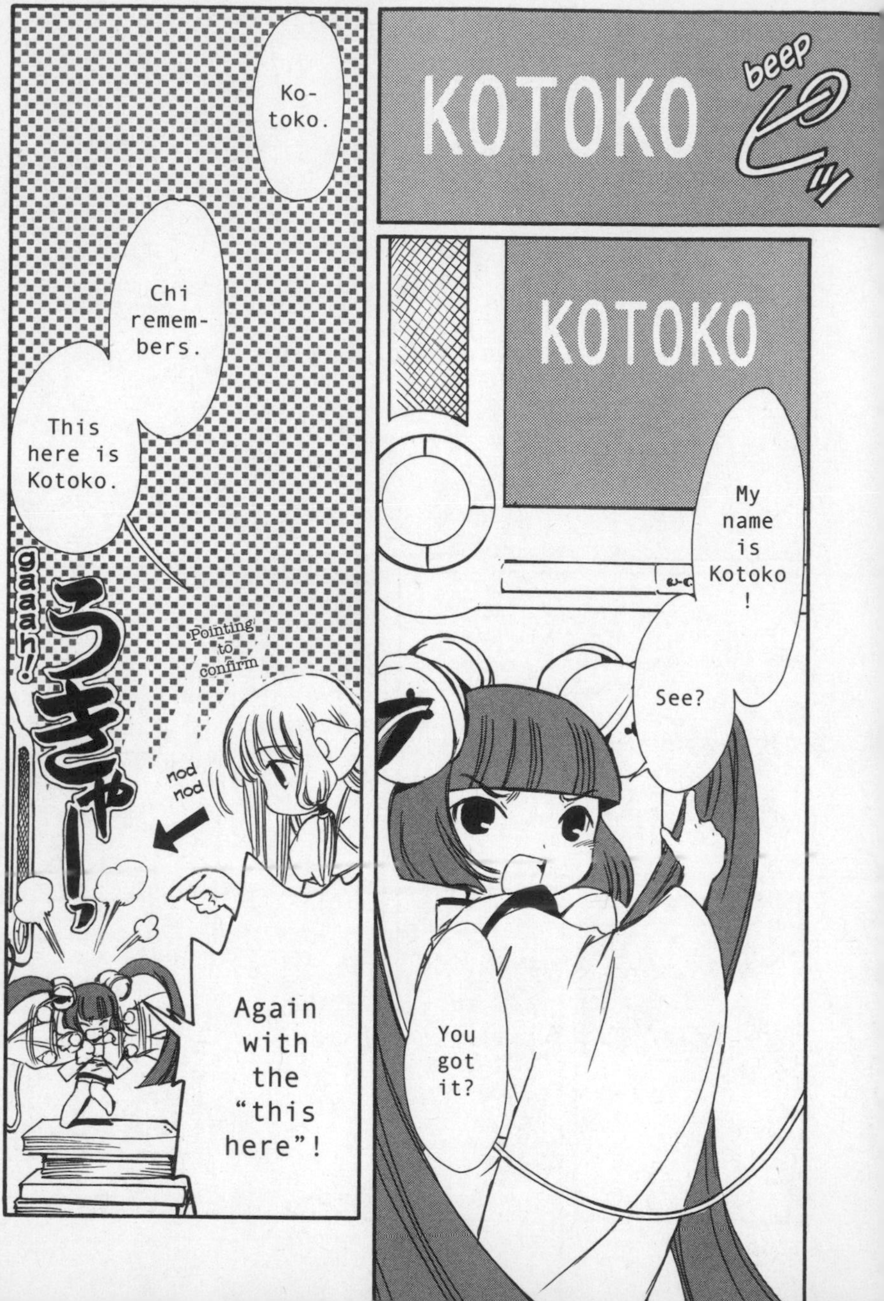
KOTOKO
beep ピッ
KOTOKO
My name is Kotoko!
See?
You got it?
Ko-toko.
Chi remem-bers.
This here is Kotoko.
Pointing to confirm
nod nod
gaaah! うきゃー
Again with the “this here”!

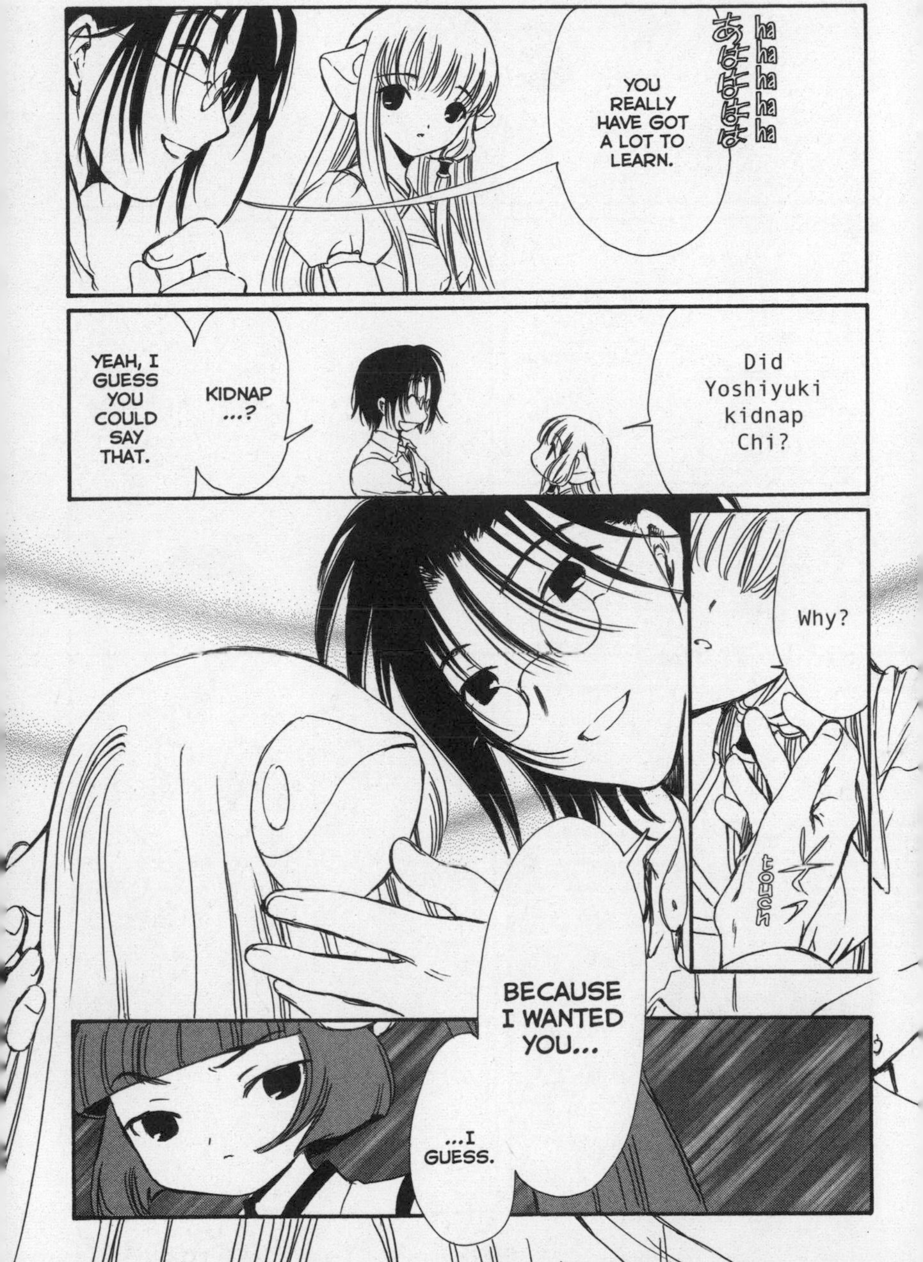
ha ha ha ha ha
YOU REALLY HAVE GOT A LOT TO LEARN.
Did Yoshiyuki kidnap Chi?
KIDNAP ...?
YEAH, I GUESS YOU COULD SAY THAT.
Why?
touch
BECAUSE I WANTED YOU...
...I GUESS.

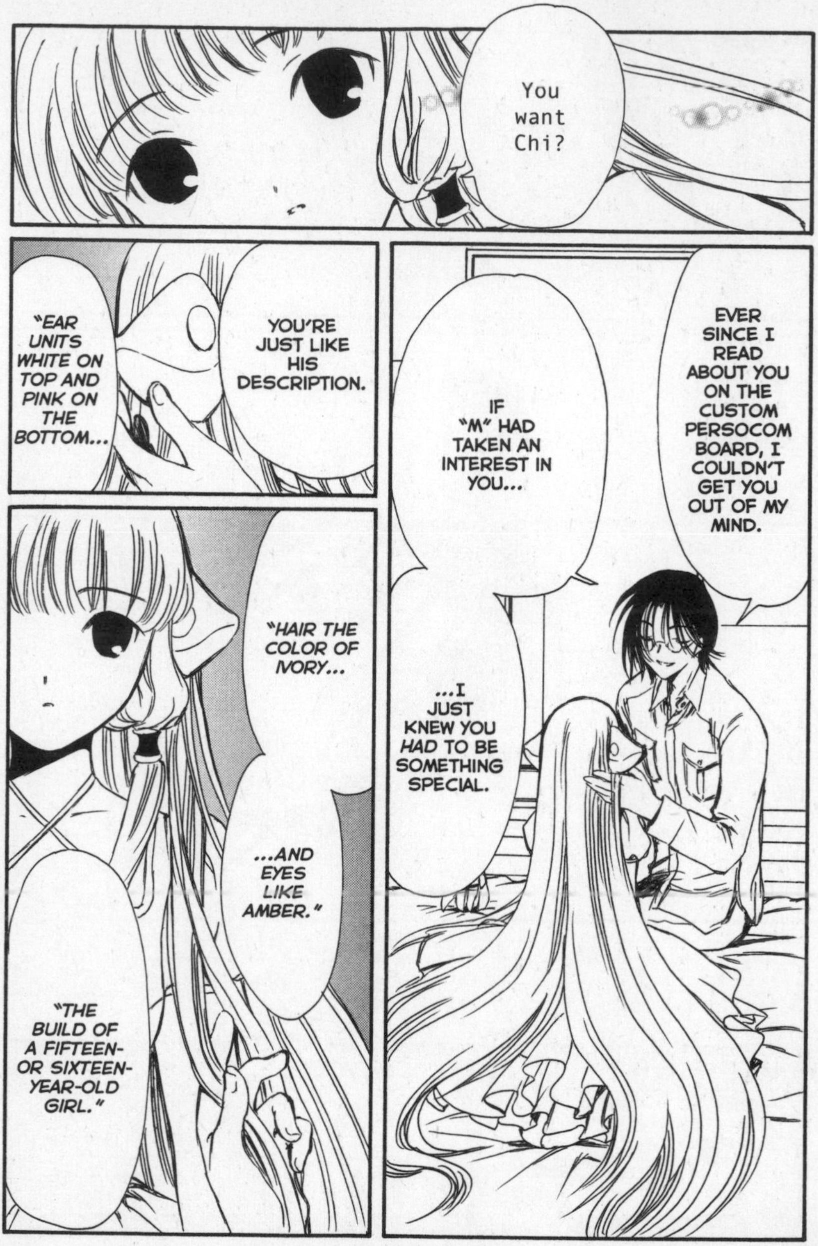
You want Chi?
EVER SINCE I READ ABOUT YOU ON THE CUSTOM PERSOCOM BOARD, I COULDN'T GET YOU OUT OF MY MIND.
IF "M" HAD TAKEN AN INTEREST IN YOU...
...I JUST KNEW YOU *HAD* TO BE SOMETHING SPECIAL.
YOU'RE JUST LIKE HIS DESCRIPTION.
"EAR UNITS WHITE ON TOP AND PINK ON THE BOTTOM...
"HAIR THE COLOR OF IVORY...
...AND EYES LIKE AMBER."
"THE BUILD OF A FIFTEEN- OR SIXTEEN-YEAR-OLD GIRL."

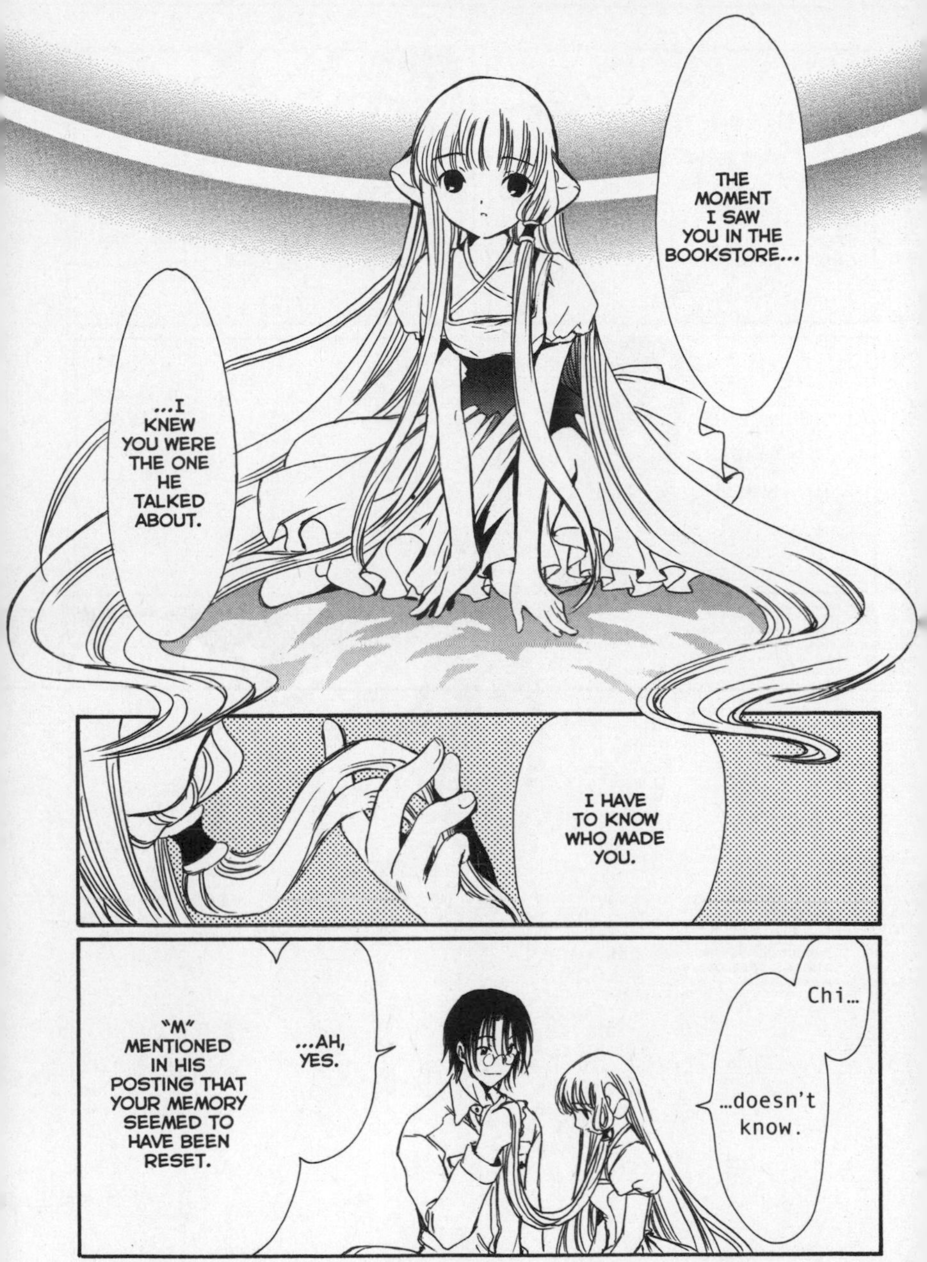
THE MOMENT I SAW YOU IN THE BOOKSTORE...
...I KNEW YOU WERE THE ONE HE TALKED ABOUT.
I HAVE TO KNOW WHO MADE YOU.
Chi...
...doesn't know.
...AH, YES.
"M" MENTIONED IN HIS POSTING THAT YOUR MEMORY SEEMED TO HAVE BEEN RESET.

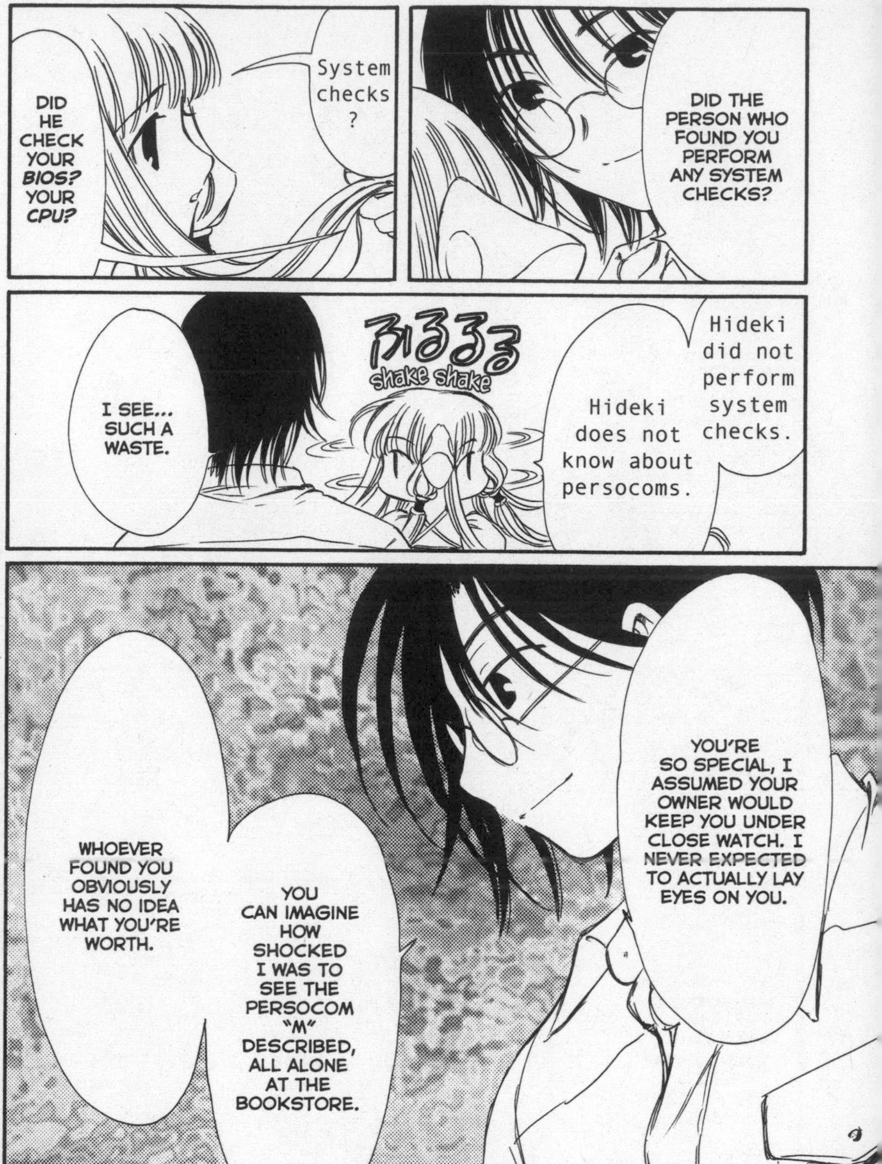
DID THE PERSON WHO FOUND YOU PERFORM ANY SYSTEM CHECKS?
System checks ?
DID HE CHECK YOUR *BIOS?* YOUR *CPU?*
Hideki did not perform system checks.
Hideki does not know about persocoms.
ふるるる
shake shake
I SEE... SUCH A WASTE.
YOU'RE SO SPECIAL, I ASSUMED YOUR OWNER WOULD KEEP YOU UNDER CLOSE WATCH. I NEVER EXPECTED TO ACTUALLY LAY EYES ON YOU.
YOU CAN IMAGINE HOW SHOCKED I WAS TO SEE THE PERSOCOM "M" DESCRIBED, ALL ALONE AT THE BOOKSTORE.
WHOEVER FOUND YOU OBVIOUSLY HAS NO IDEA WHAT YOU'RE WORTH.

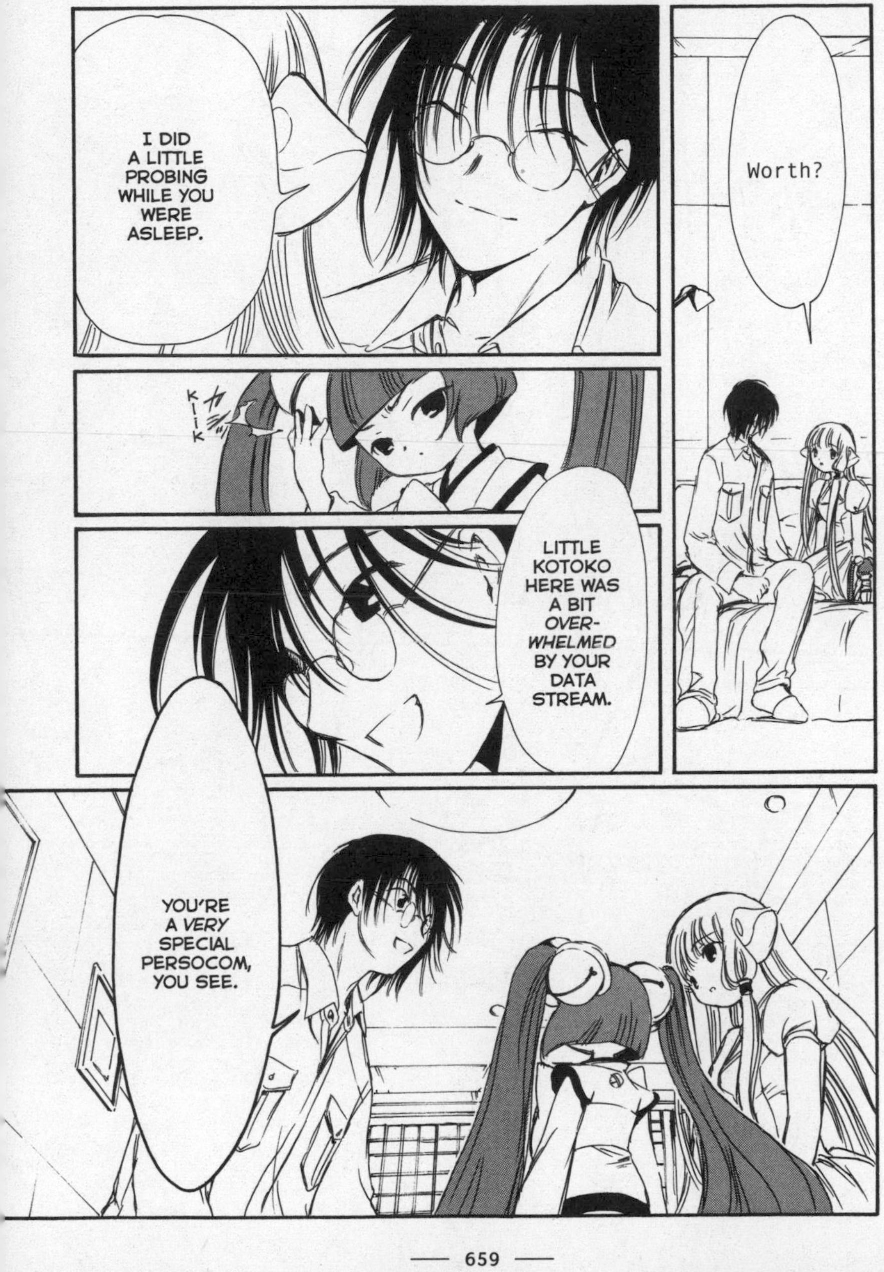
Worth?
I DID A LITTLE PROBING WHILE YOU WERE ASLEEP.
KLIK
LITTLE KOTOKO HERE WAS A BIT *OVERWHELMED* BY YOUR DATA STREAM.
YOU'RE A *VERY* SPECIAL PERSOCOM, YOU SEE.

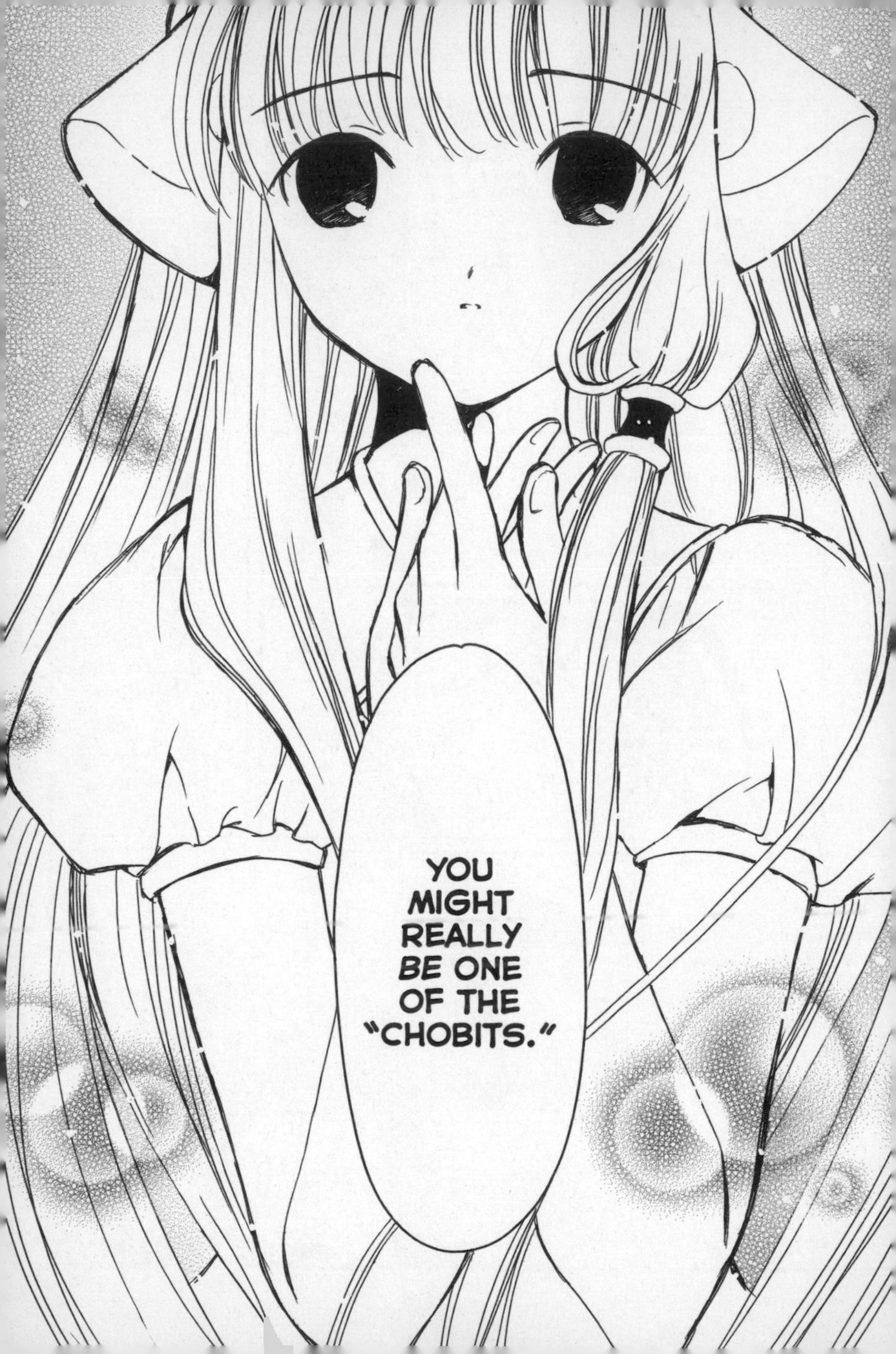
YOU MIGHT REALLY *BE* ONE OF THE "CHOBITS."

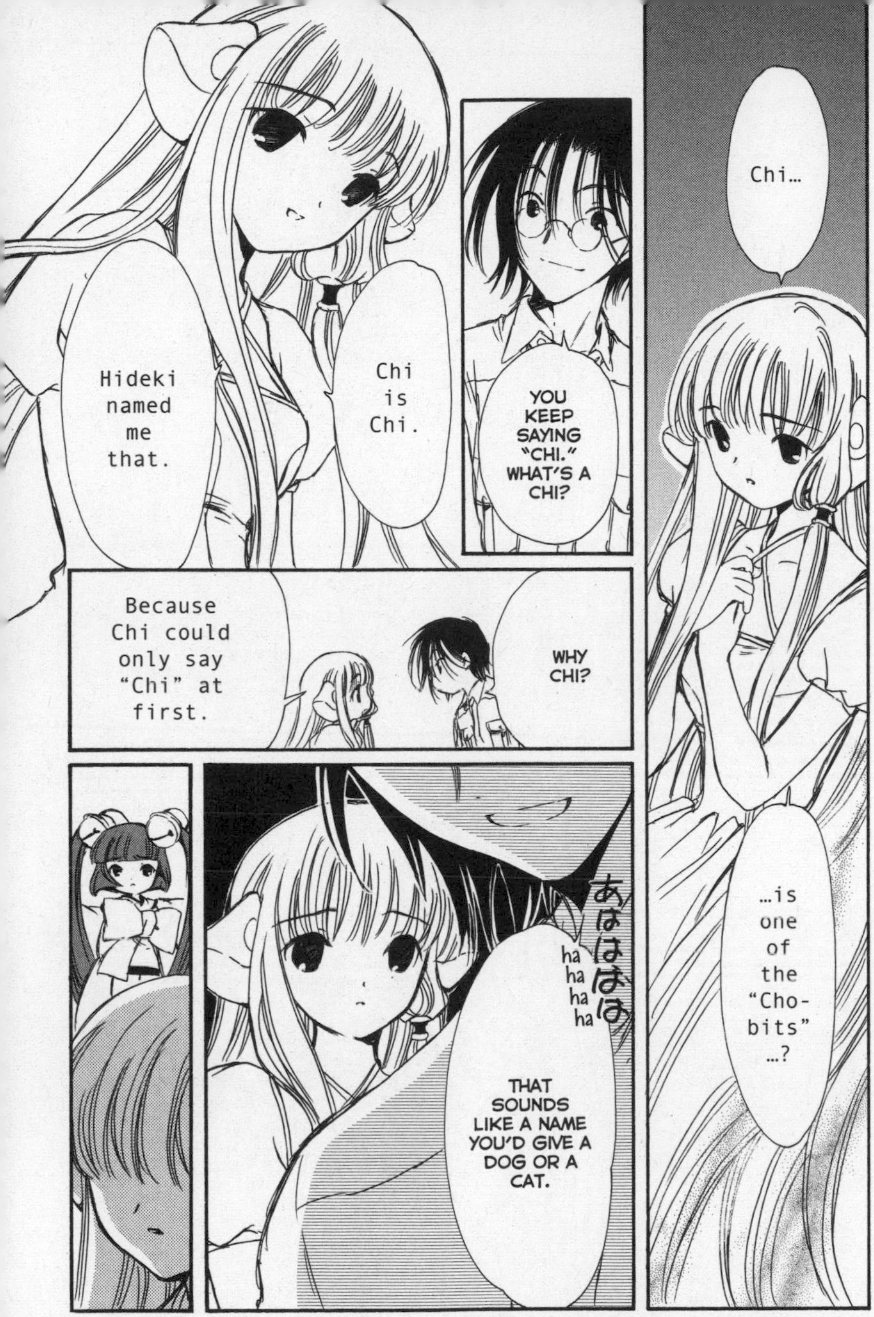
Chi…
…is one of the "Cho-bits" …?
YOU KEEP SAYING "CHI." WHAT'S A CHI?
Chi is Chi.
Hideki named me that.
WHY CHI?
Because Chi could only say "Chi" at first.
あははは
ha ha ha ha
THAT SOUNDS LIKE A NAME YOU'D GIVE A DOG OR A CAT.

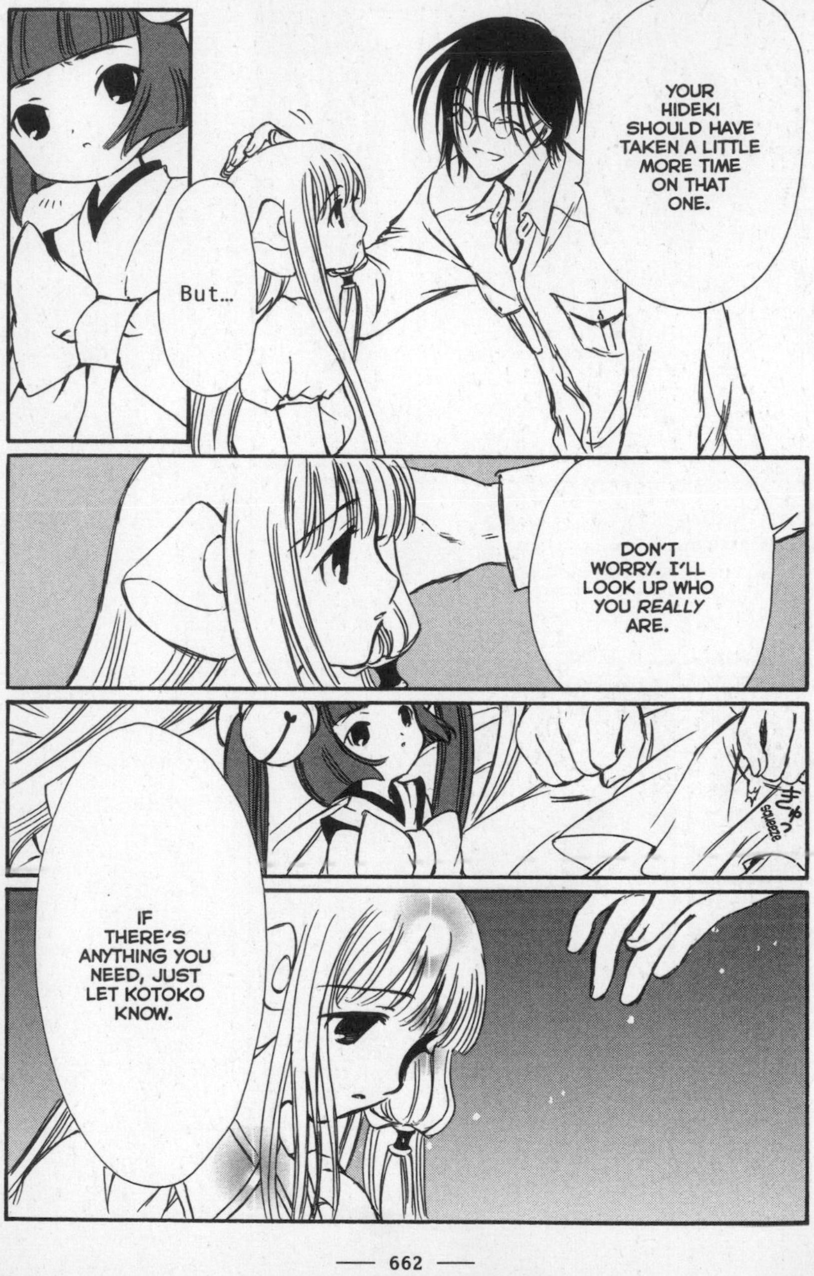
YOUR HIDEKI SHOULD HAVE TAKEN A LITTLE MORE TIME ON THAT ONE.
But...
DON'T WORRY. I'LL LOOK UP WHO YOU *REALLY* ARE.
きゅっ
squeeze
IF THERE'S ANYTHING YOU NEED, JUST LET KOTOKO KNOW.

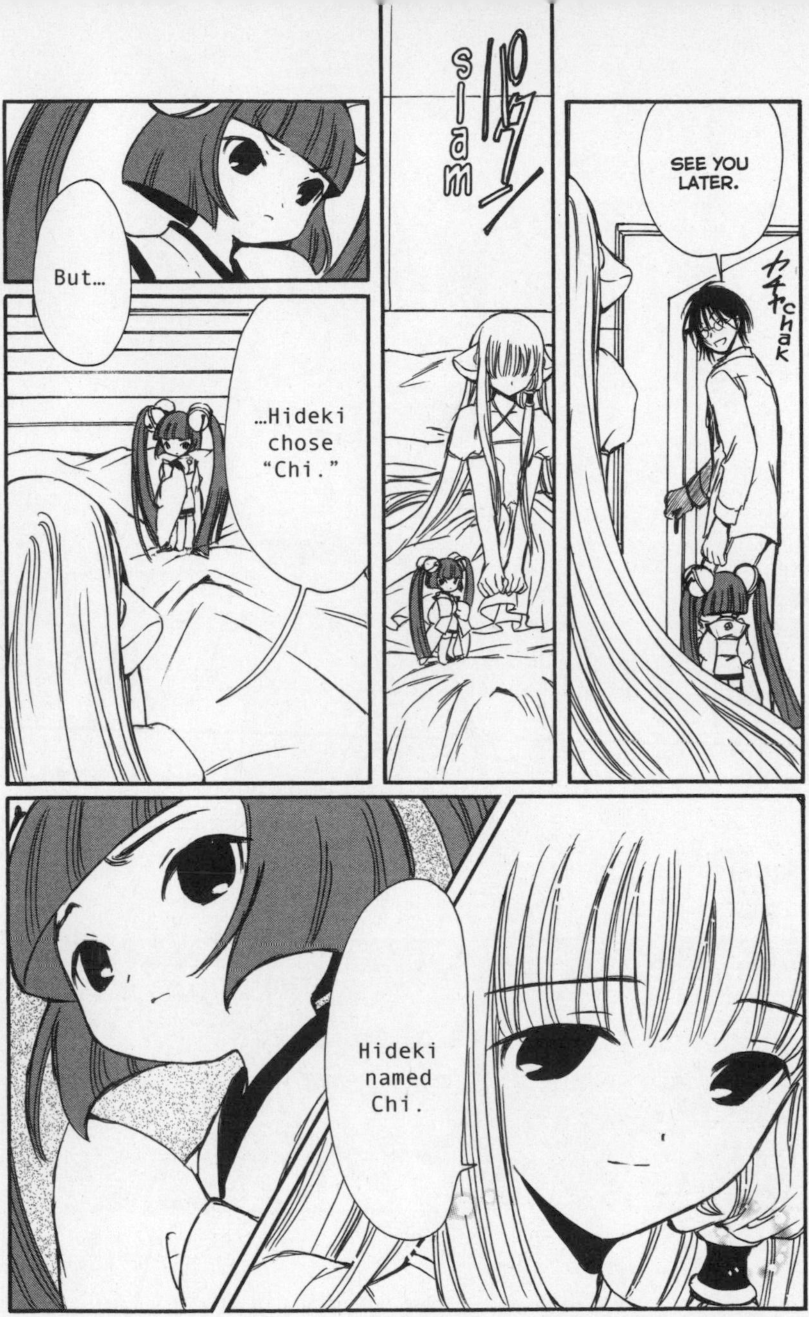
SEE YOU LATER.
chak
slam
But…
…Hideki chose "Chi."
Hideki named Chi.

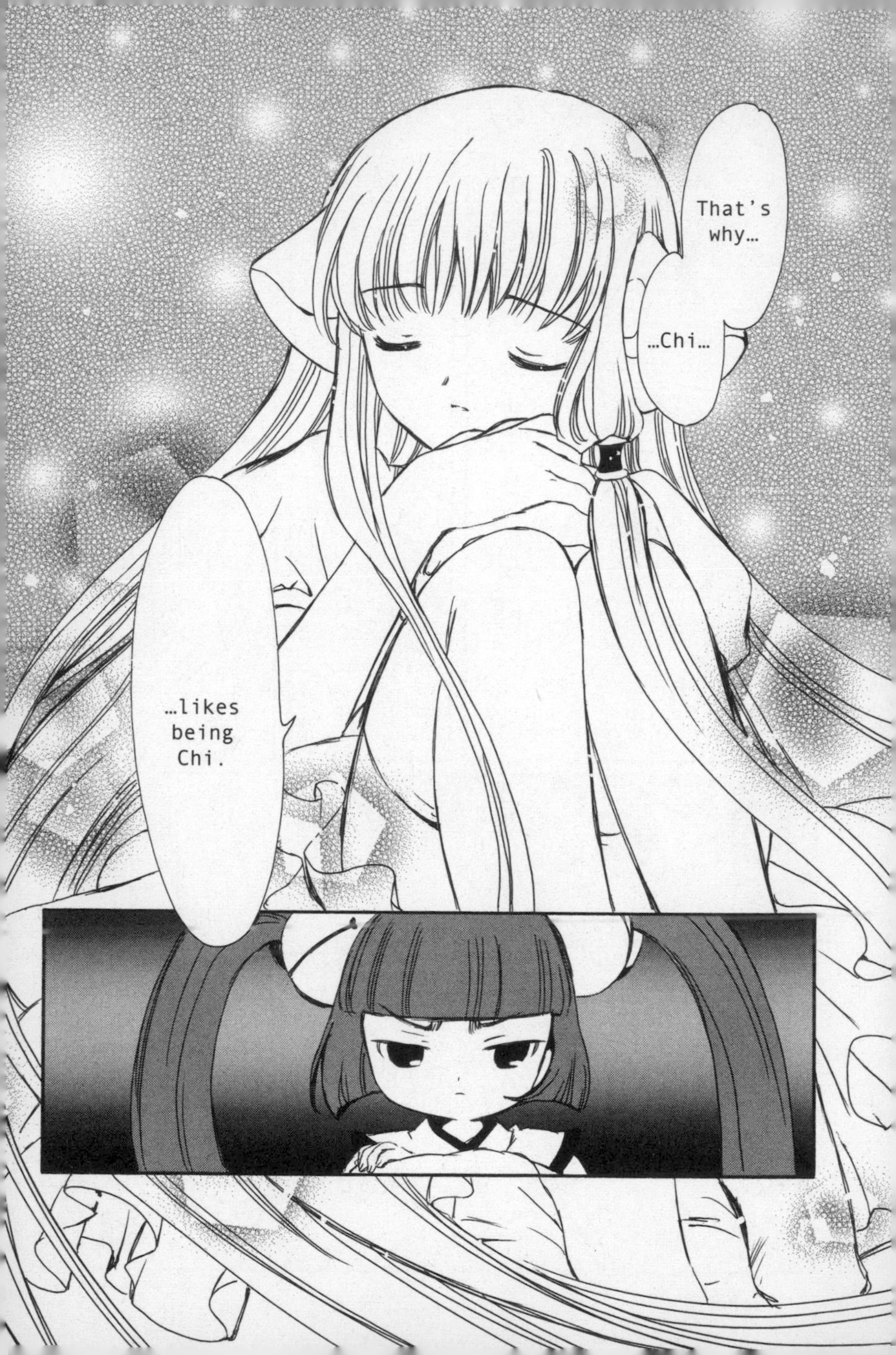
That's why…
…Chi…
…likes being Chi.

Chobits
ちょびッツ

◀ **chapter 44** ▶

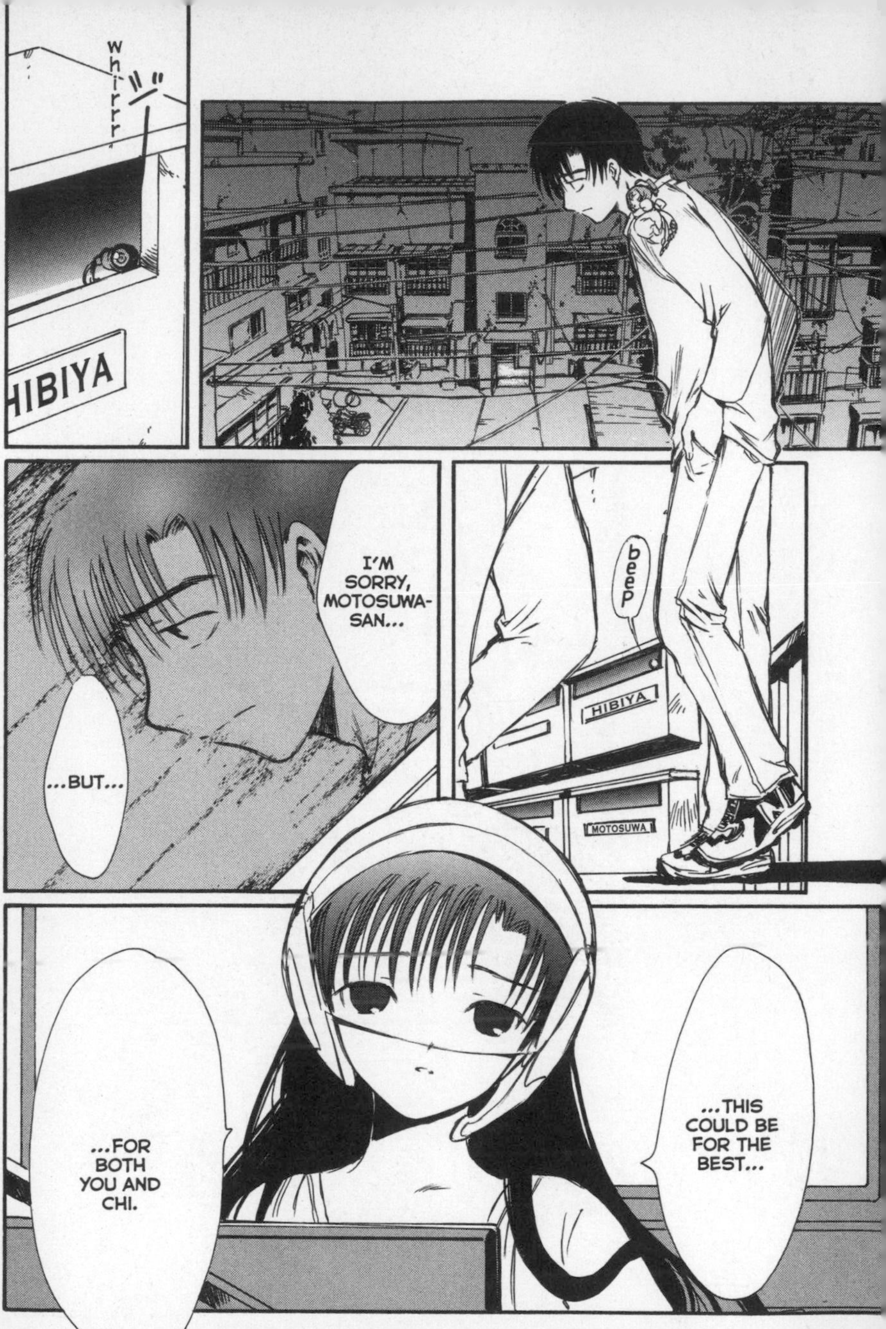
whirrr
HIBIYA
beep
HIBIYA
MOTOSUWA
I'M SORRY, MOTOSUWA-SAN...
...BUT...
...THIS COULD BE FOR THE BEST...
...FOR BOTH YOU AND CHI.

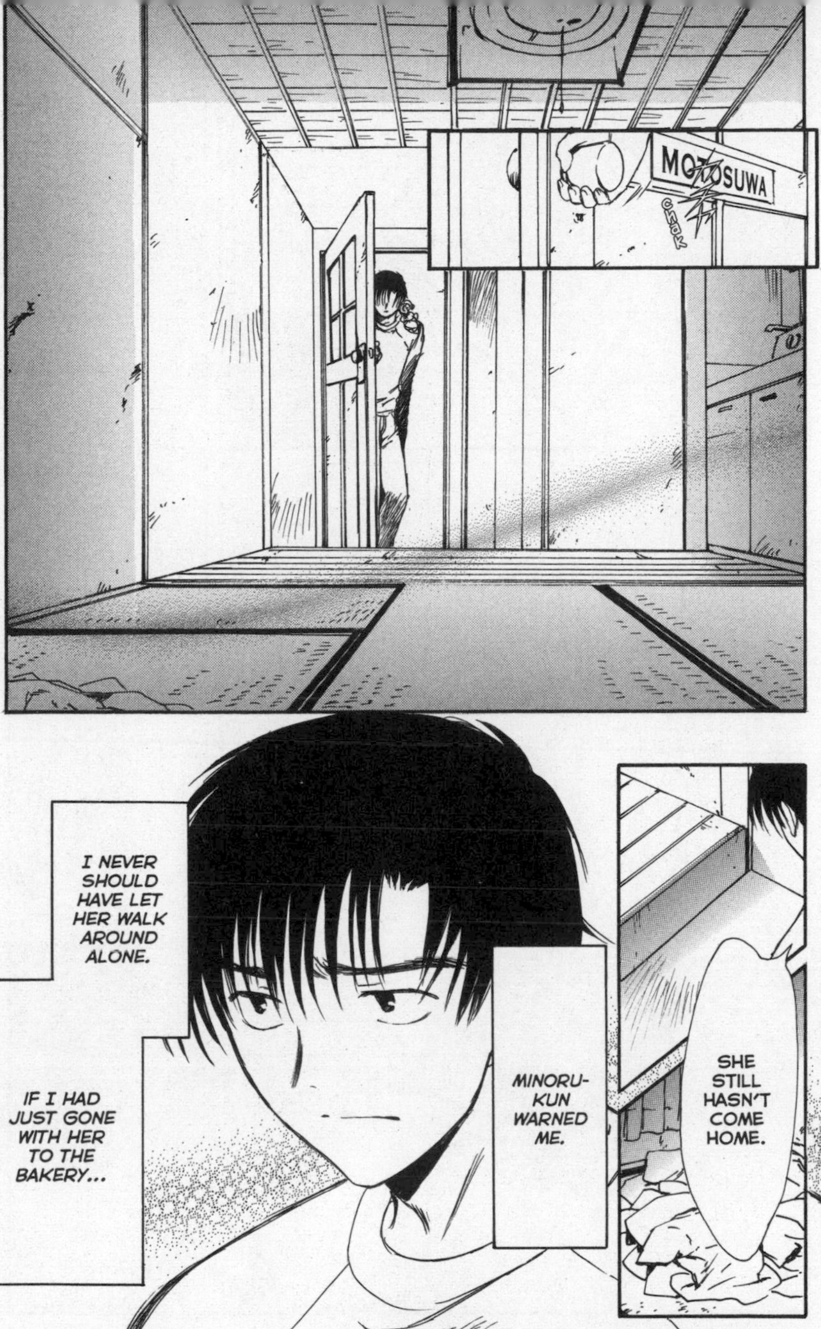
MOTOSUWA
CLICK
SHE STILL HASN'T COME HOME.
MINORU-KUN WARNED ME.
I NEVER SHOULD HAVE LET HER WALK AROUND ALONE.
IF I HAD JUST GONE WITH HER TO THE BAKERY...

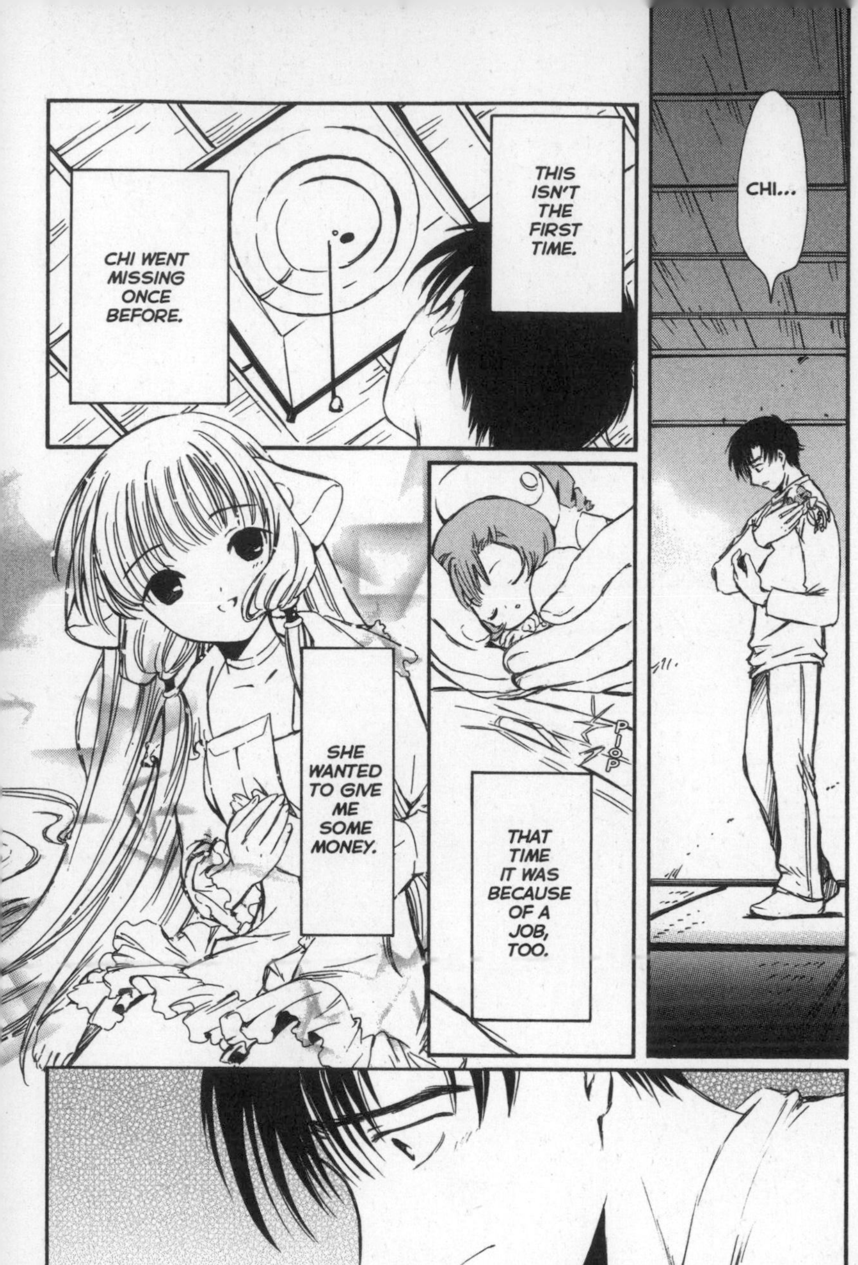
CHI...
THIS ISN'T THE FIRST TIME.
CHI WENT MISSING ONCE BEFORE.
PIP
THAT TIME IT WAS BECAUSE OF A JOB, TOO.
SHE WANTED TO GIVE ME SOME MONEY.

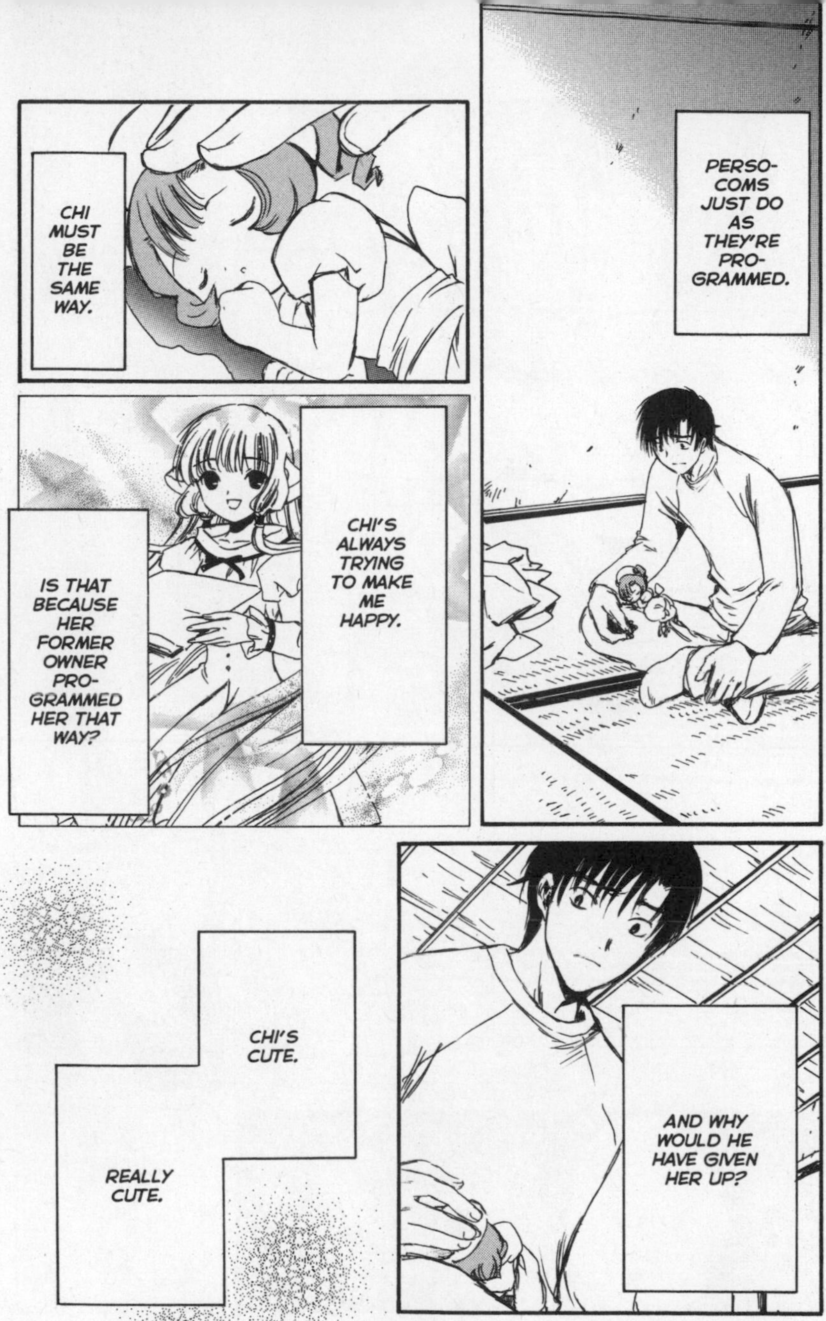
PERSO-COMS JUST DO AS THEY'RE PRO-GRAMMED.
CHI MUST BE THE SAME WAY.
CHI'S ALWAYS TRYING TO MAKE ME HAPPY.
IS THAT BECAUSE HER FORMER OWNER PRO-GRAMMED HER THAT WAY?
AND WHY WOULD HE HAVE GIVEN HER UP?
CHI'S CUTE.
REALLY CUTE.

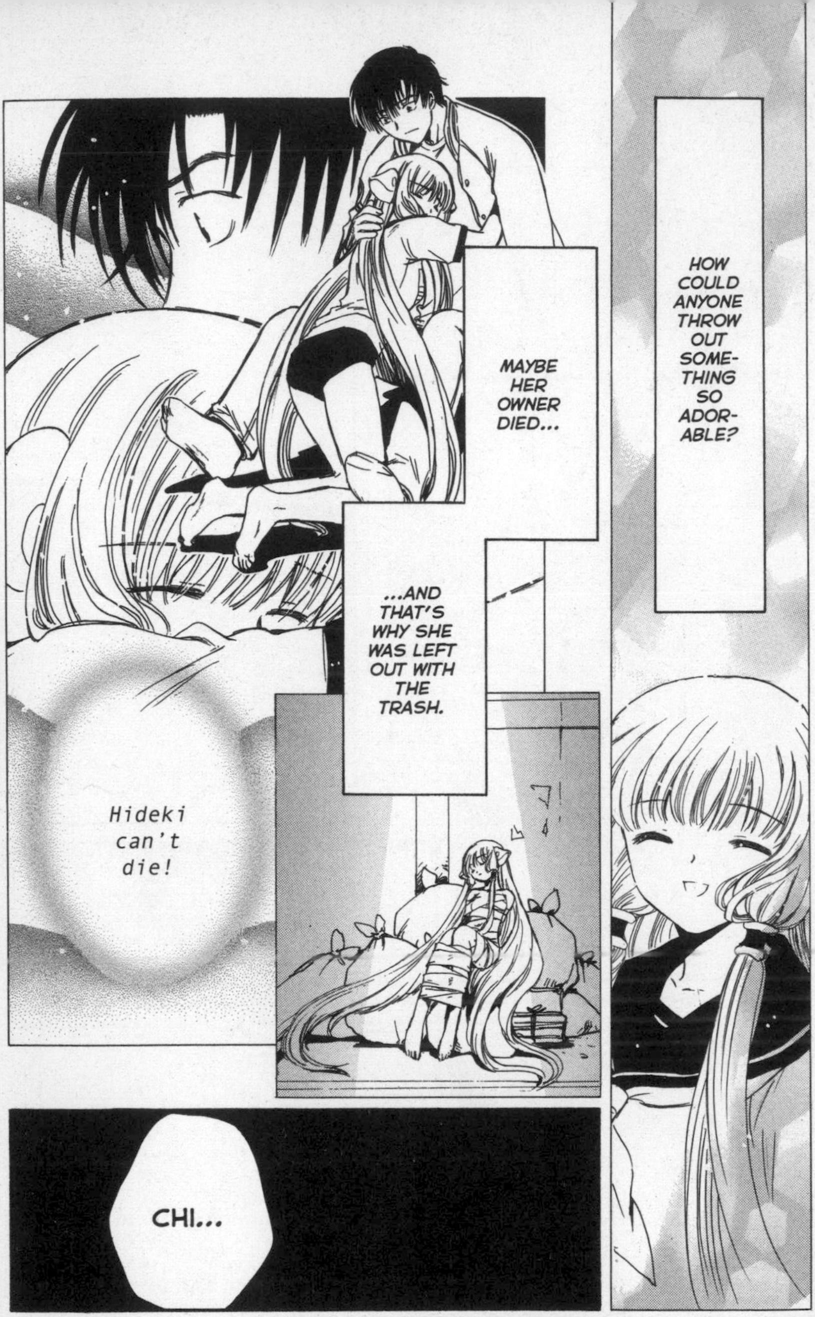
HOW COULD ANYONE THROW OUT SOMETHING SO ADORABLE?
MAYBE HER OWNER DIED...
...AND THAT'S WHY SHE WAS LEFT OUT WITH THE TRASH.
Hideki can't die!
CHI...

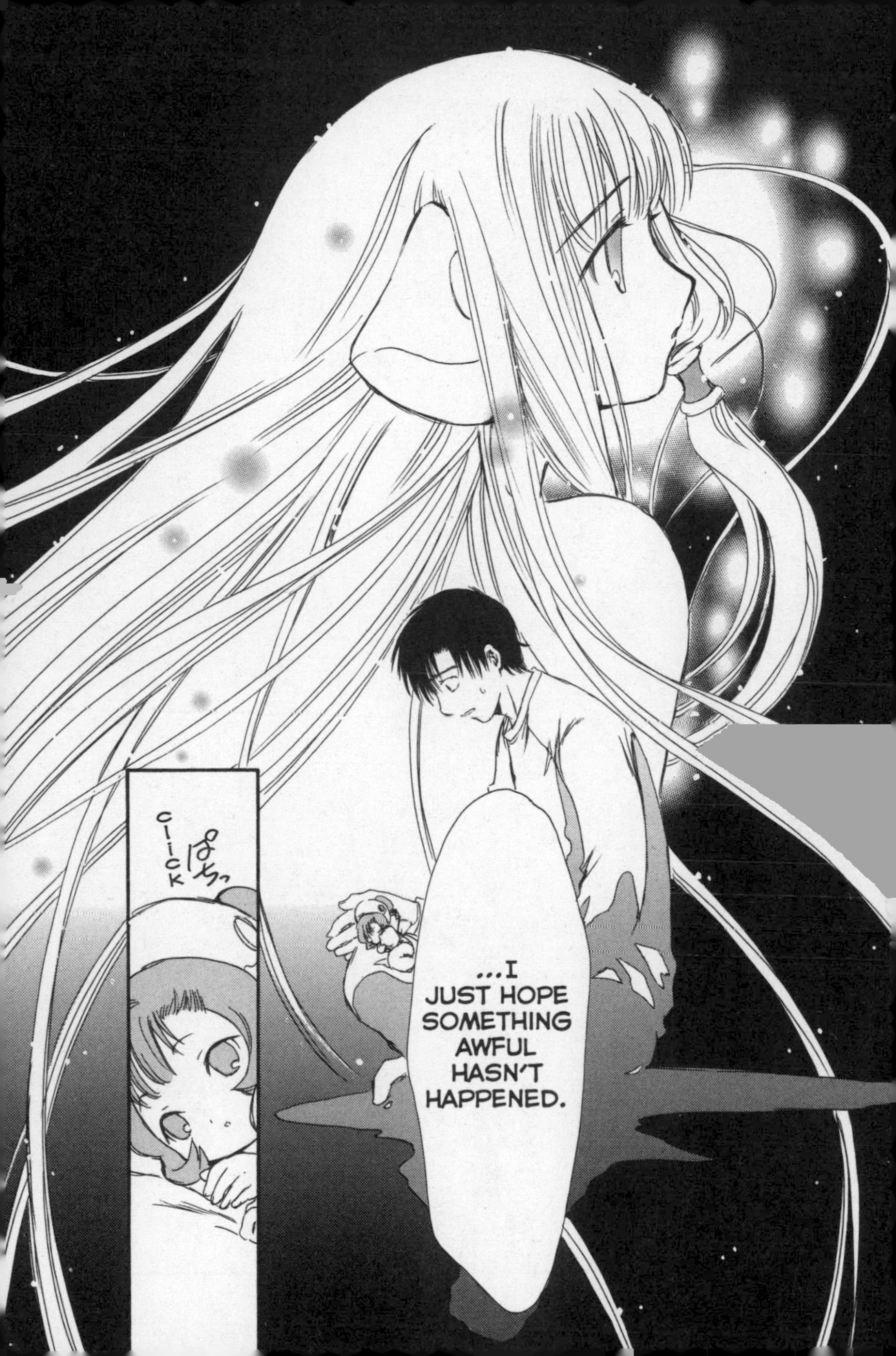
...I JUST HOPE SOMETHING AWFUL HASN'T HAPPENED.
ぱちっ
CLICK

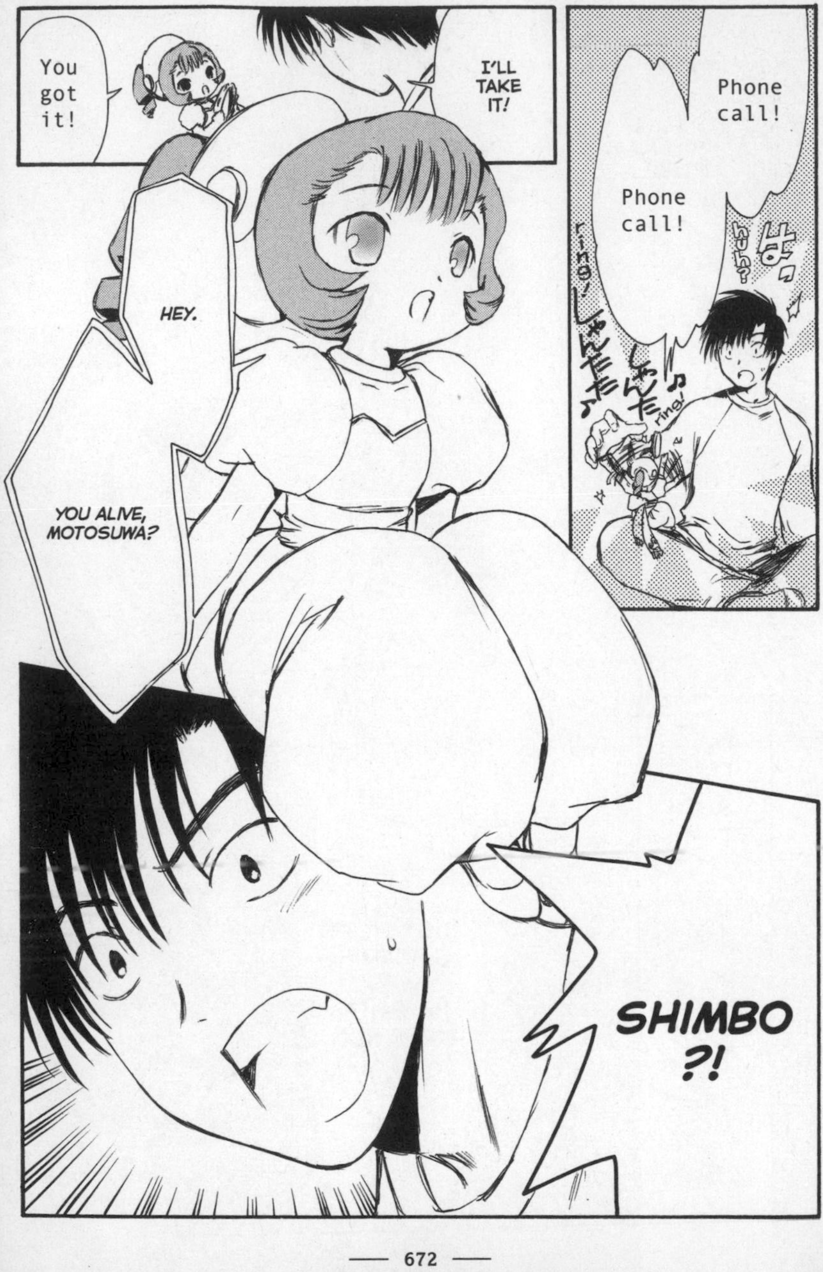
Phone call!
Phone call!
は、
huh?
しゃんた♪
ring!
しゃんた♪
ring!
I'LL TAKE IT!
You got it!
HEY.
YOU ALIVE, MOTOSUWA?
SHIMBO?!

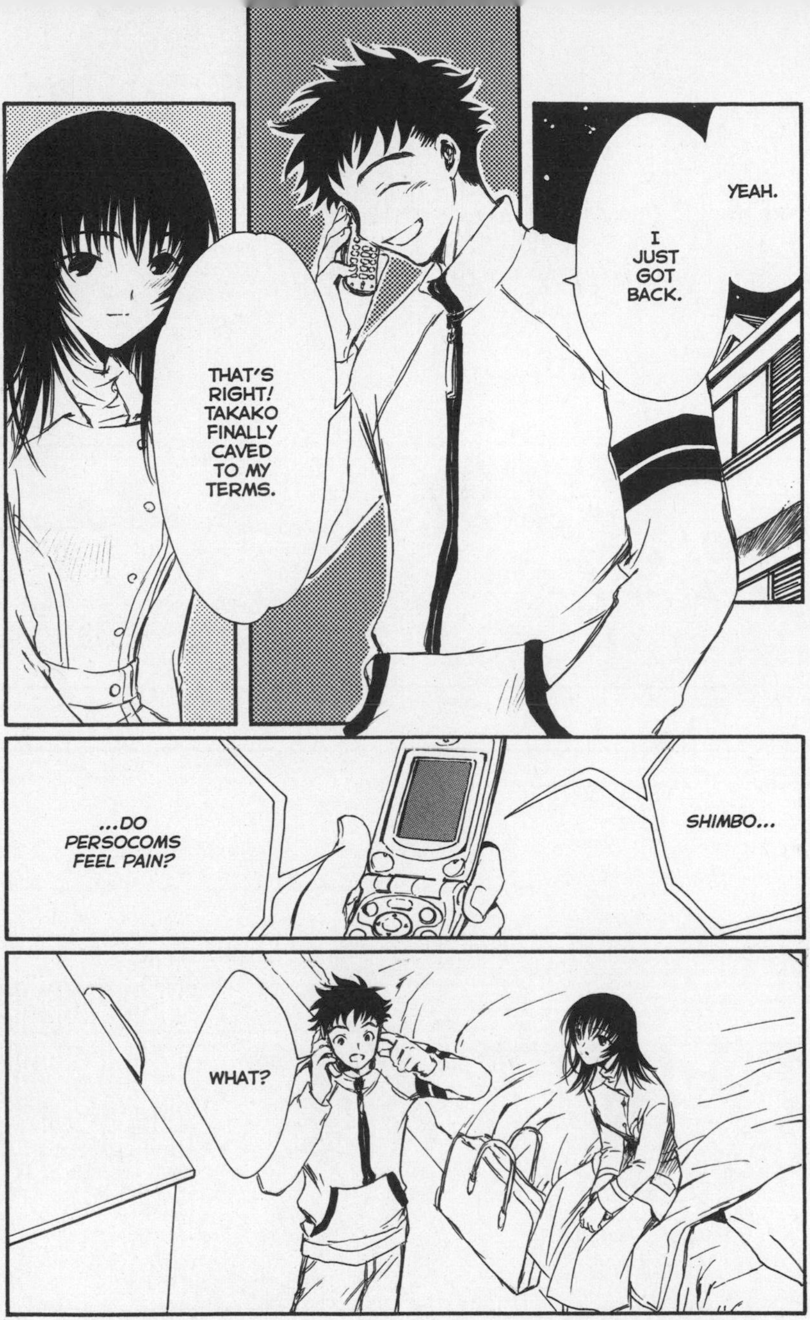
YEAH.
I JUST GOT BACK.
THAT'S RIGHT! TAKAKO FINALLY CAVED TO MY TERMS.
SHIMBO...
...DO PERSOCOMS FEEL PAIN?
WHAT?

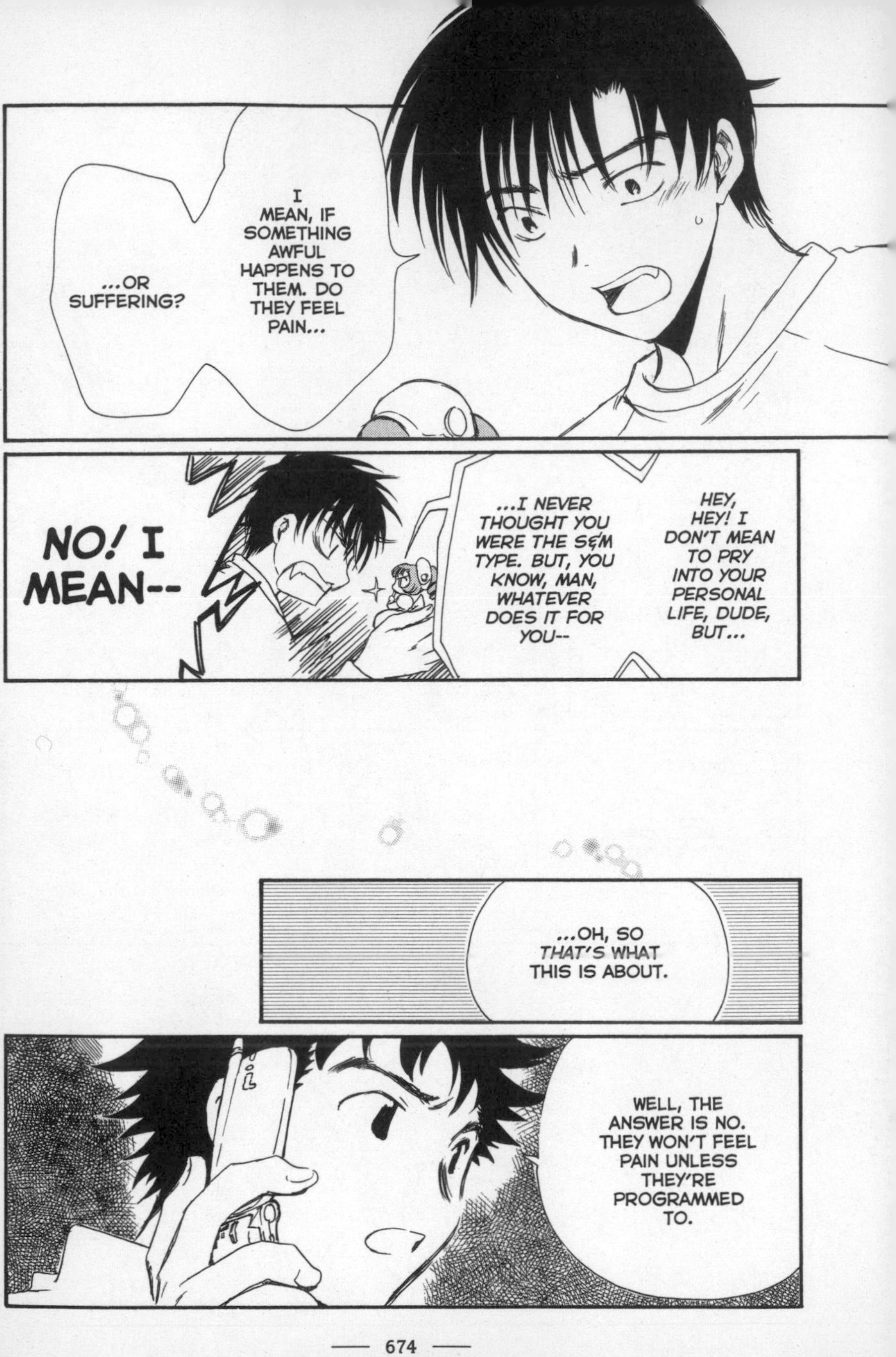
I MEAN, IF SOMETHING AWFUL HAPPENS TO THEM. DO THEY FEEL PAIN...
...OR SUFFERING?
HEY, HEY! I DON'T MEAN TO PRY INTO YOUR PERSONAL LIFE, DUDE, BUT...
...I NEVER THOUGHT YOU WERE THE S&M TYPE. BUT, YOU KNOW, MAN, WHATEVER DOES IT FOR YOU--
NO! I MEAN--
...OH, SO *THAT'S* WHAT THIS IS ABOUT.
WELL, THE ANSWER IS NO. THEY WON'T FEEL PAIN UNLESS THEY'RE PROGRAMMED TO.

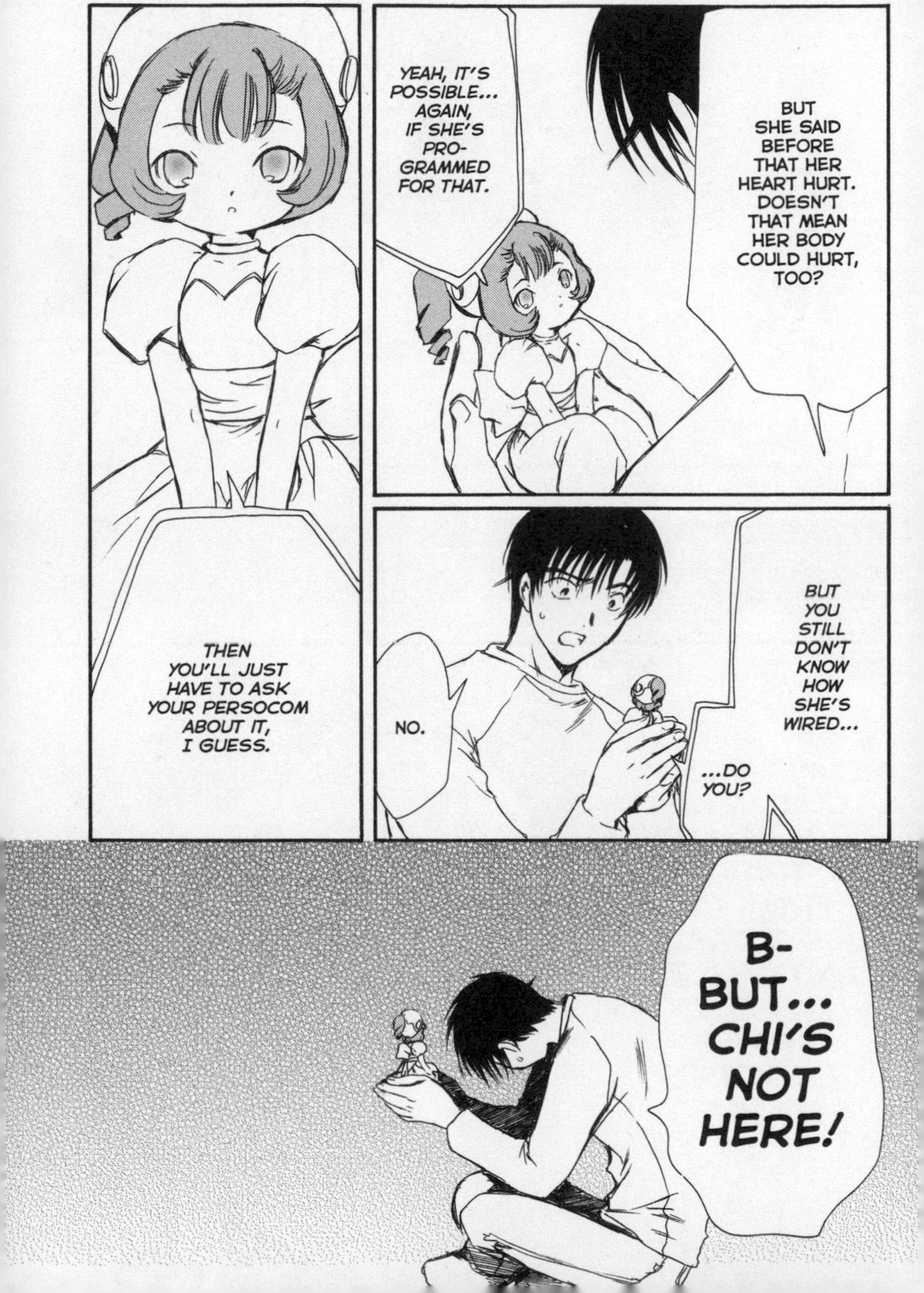
BUT SHE SAID BEFORE THAT HER HEART HURT. DOESN'T THAT MEAN HER BODY COULD HURT, TOO?
YEAH, IT'S POSSIBLE... AGAIN, IF SHE'S PRO-GRAMMED FOR THAT.
BUT YOU STILL DON'T KNOW HOW SHE'S WIRED...
...DO YOU?
NO.
THEN YOU'LL JUST HAVE TO ASK YOUR PERSOCOM ABOUT IT, I GUESS.
B-BUT... CHI'S NOT HERE!

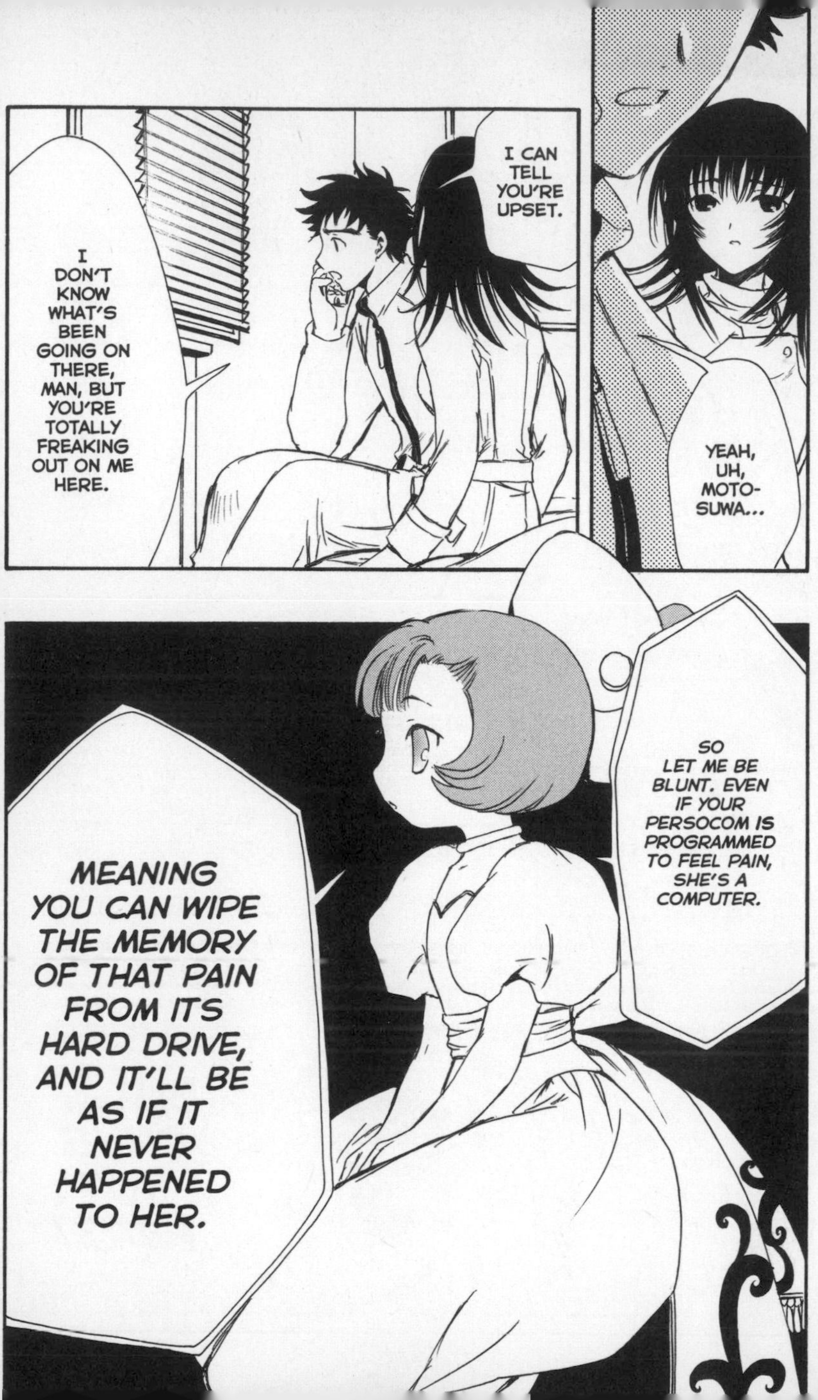
YEAH, UH, MOTO-SUWA...
I CAN TELL YOU'RE UPSET.
I DON'T KNOW WHAT'S BEEN GOING ON THERE, MAN, BUT YOU'RE TOTALLY FREAKING OUT ON ME HERE.
SO LET ME BE BLUNT. EVEN IF YOUR PERSOCOM IS PROGRAMMED TO FEEL PAIN, SHE'S A COMPUTER.
MEANING YOU CAN WIPE THE MEMORY OF THAT PAIN FROM ITS HARD DRIVE, AND IT'LL BE AS IF IT NEVER HAPPENED TO HER.

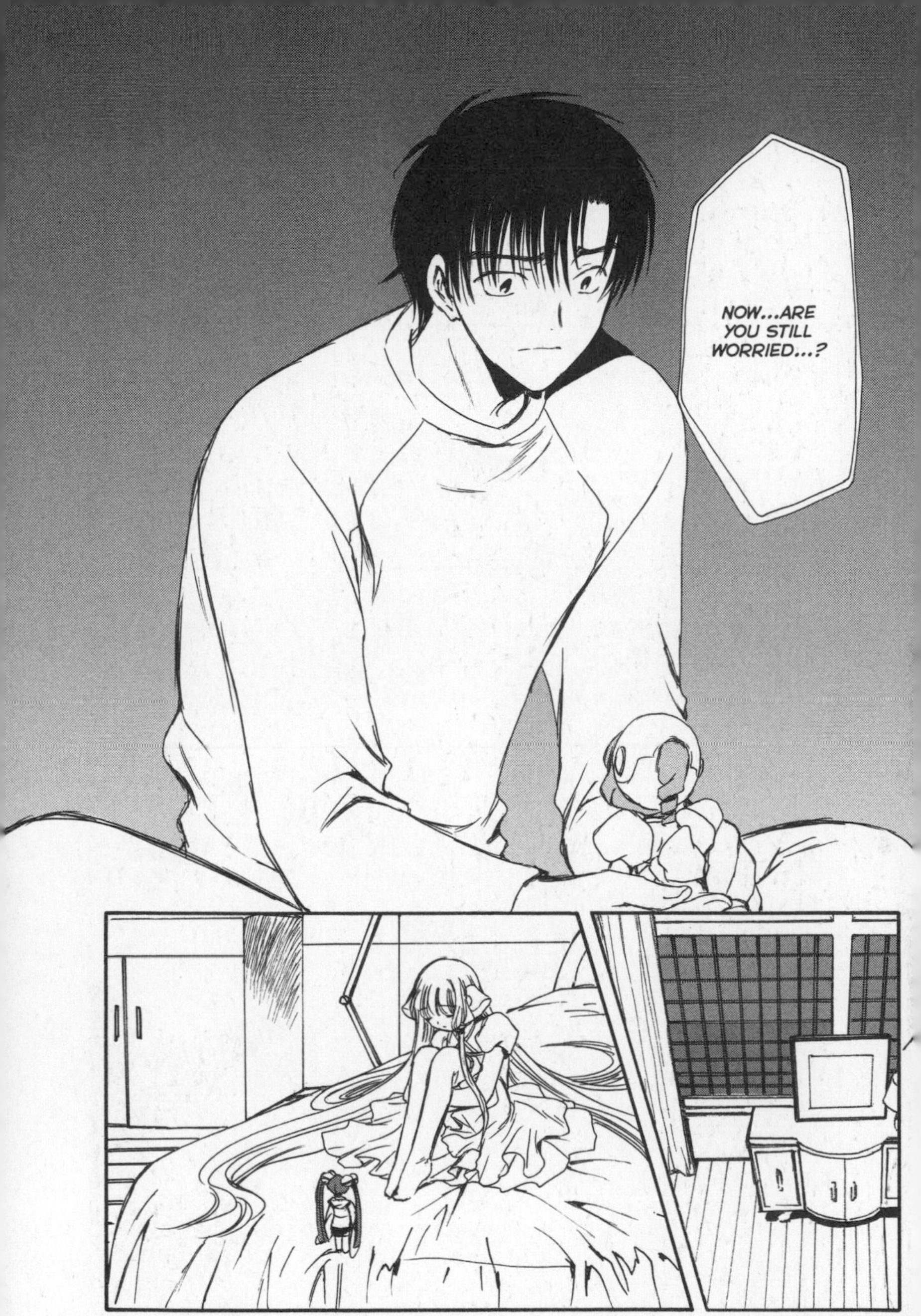
NOW...ARE YOU STILL WORRIED...?

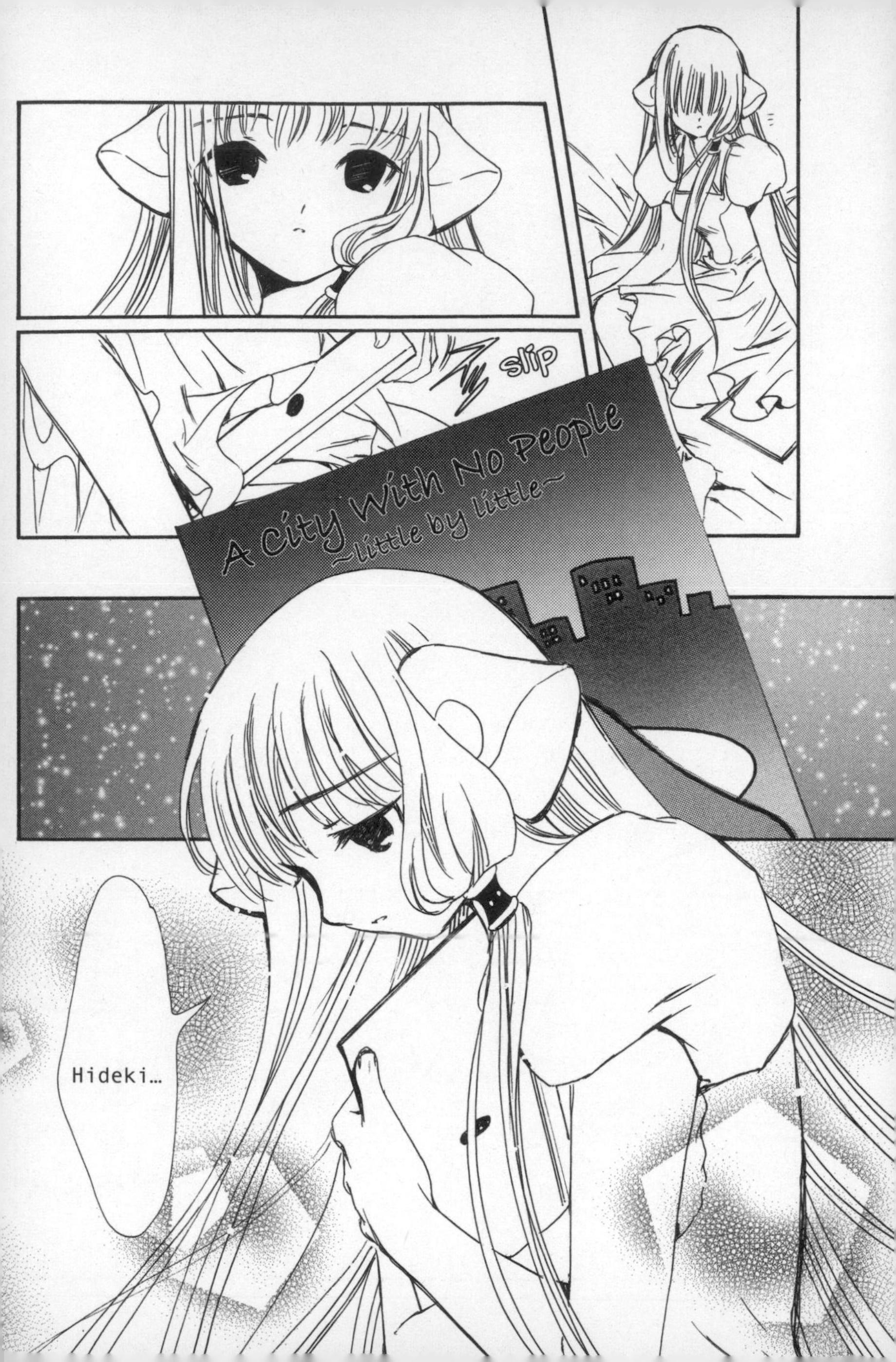
slip
A City With No People
~little by little~
Hideki...

Chobits
ちょびっツ

◂ chapter 45 ▸

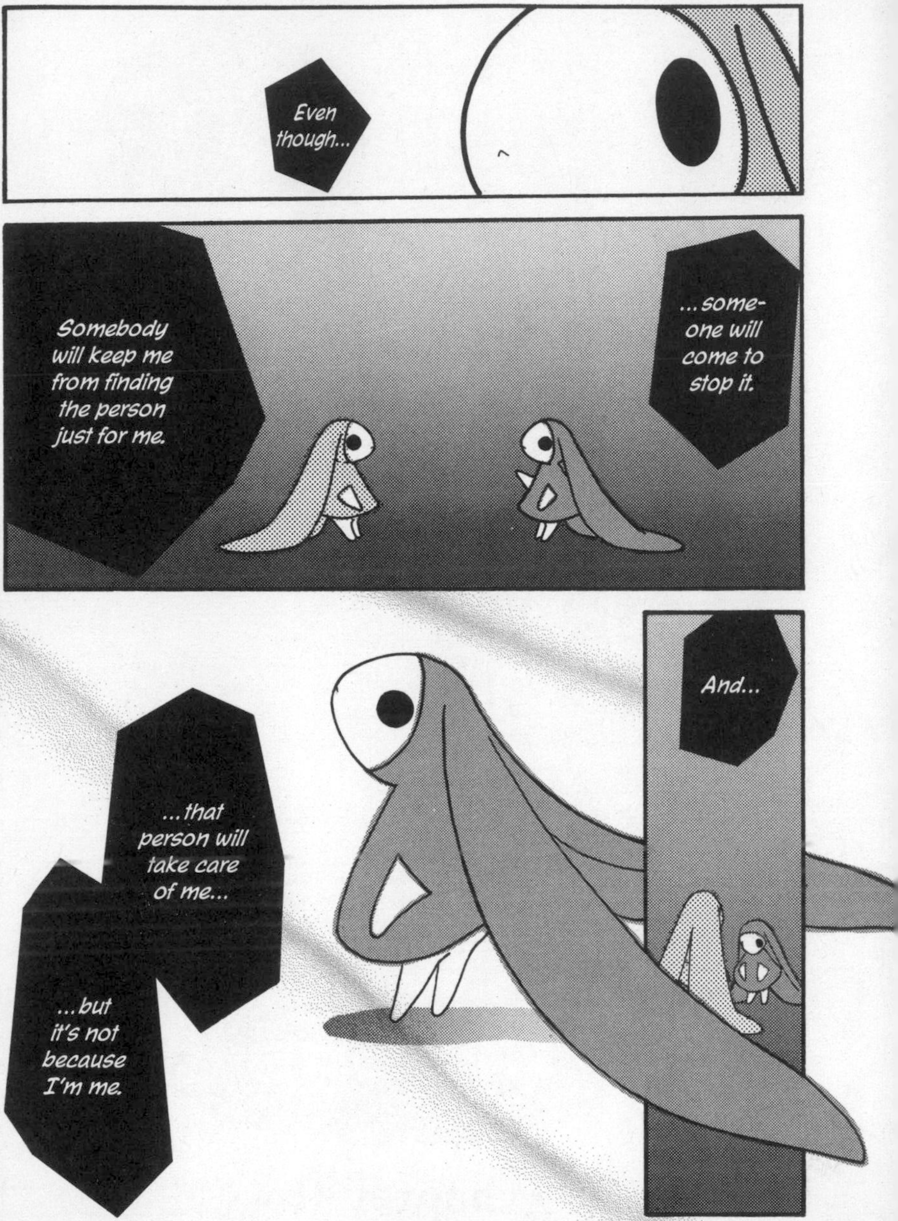
Even though...
...some-one will come to stop it.
Somebody will keep me from finding the person just for me.
And...
...that person will take care of me...
...but it's not because I'm me.

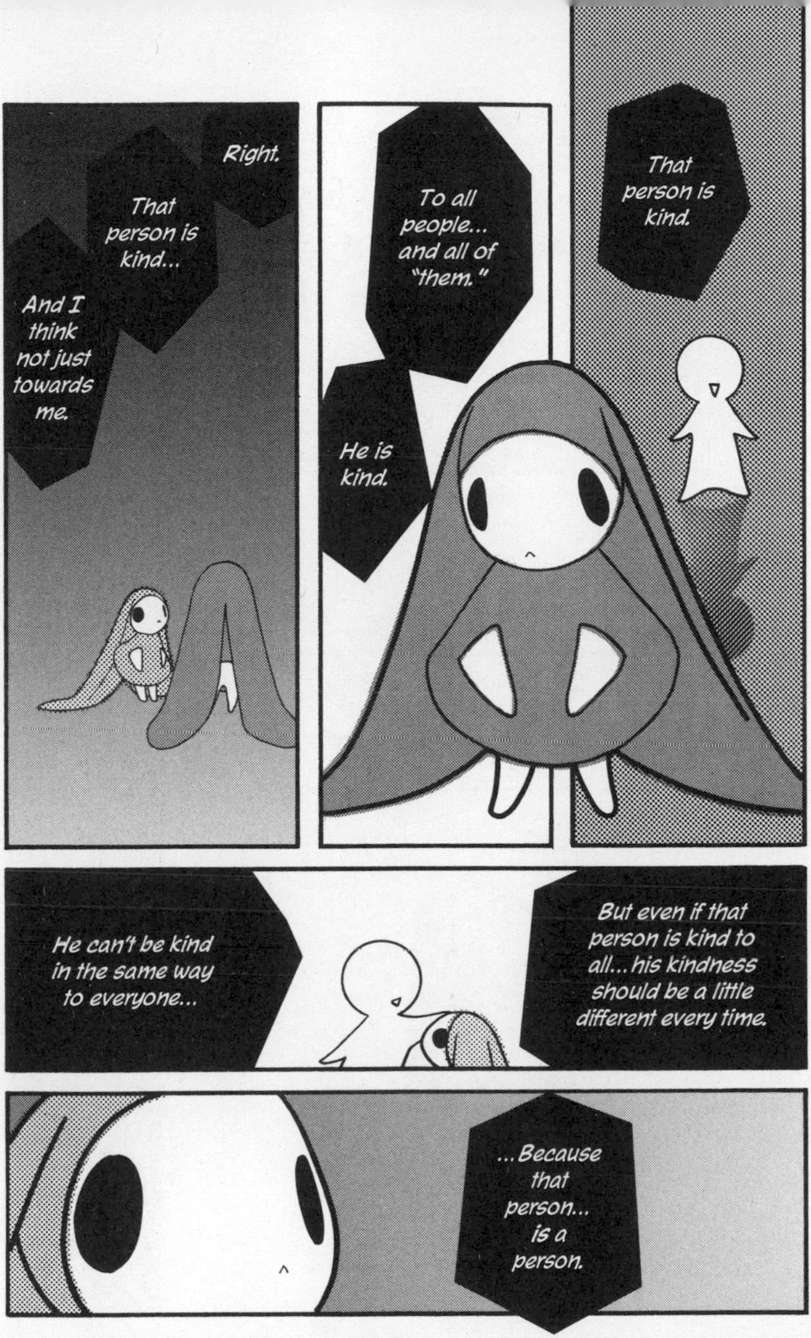
That person is kind.
To all people... and all of "them."
He is kind.
Right.
That person is kind...
And I think not just towards me.
But even if that person is kind to all... his kindness should be a little different every time.
He can't be kind in the same way to everyone...
...Because that person... is a person.

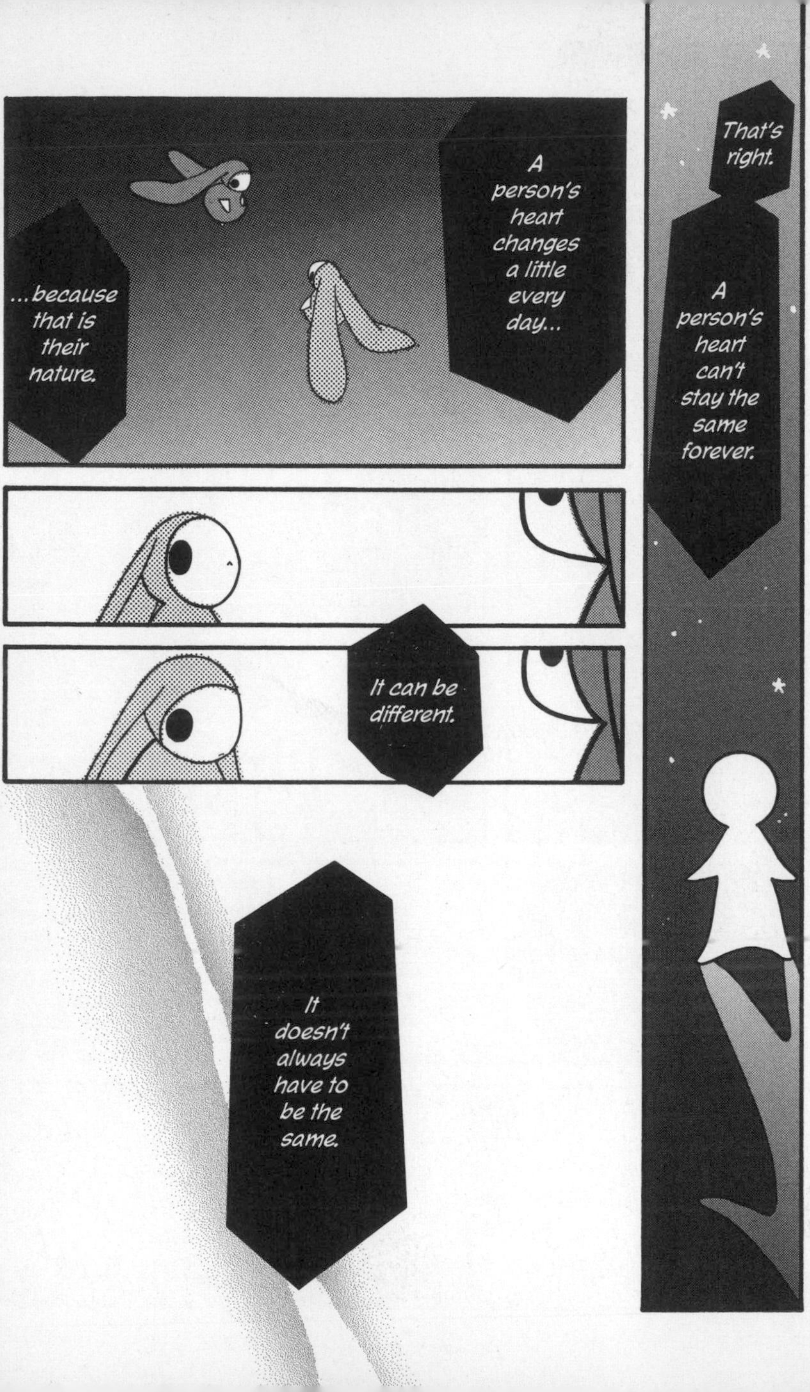
That's right.
A person's heart can't stay the same forever.
A person's heart changes a little every day...
...because that is their nature.
It can be different.
It doesn't always have to be the same.

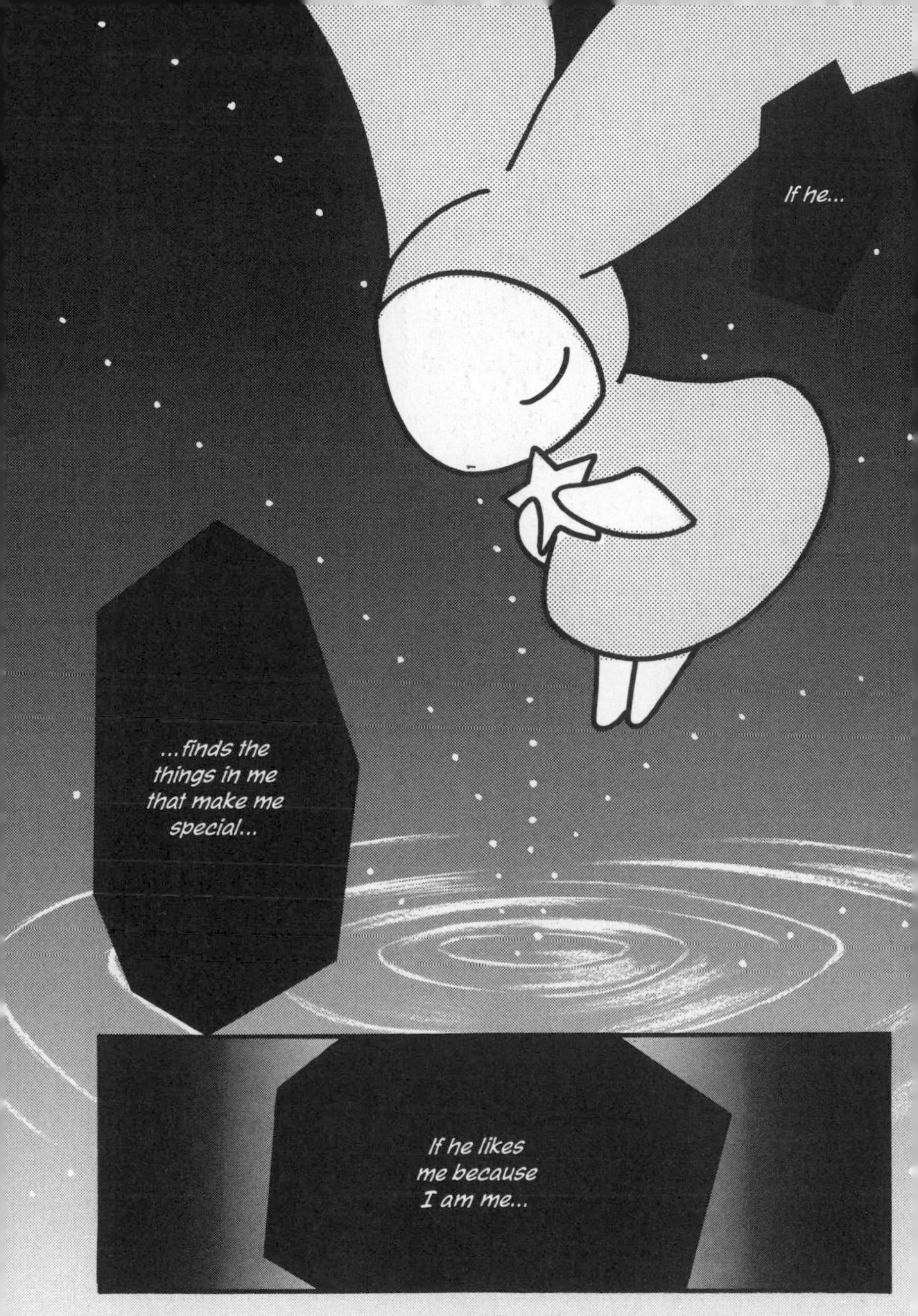
If he...
...finds the things in me that make me special...
If he likes me because I am me...

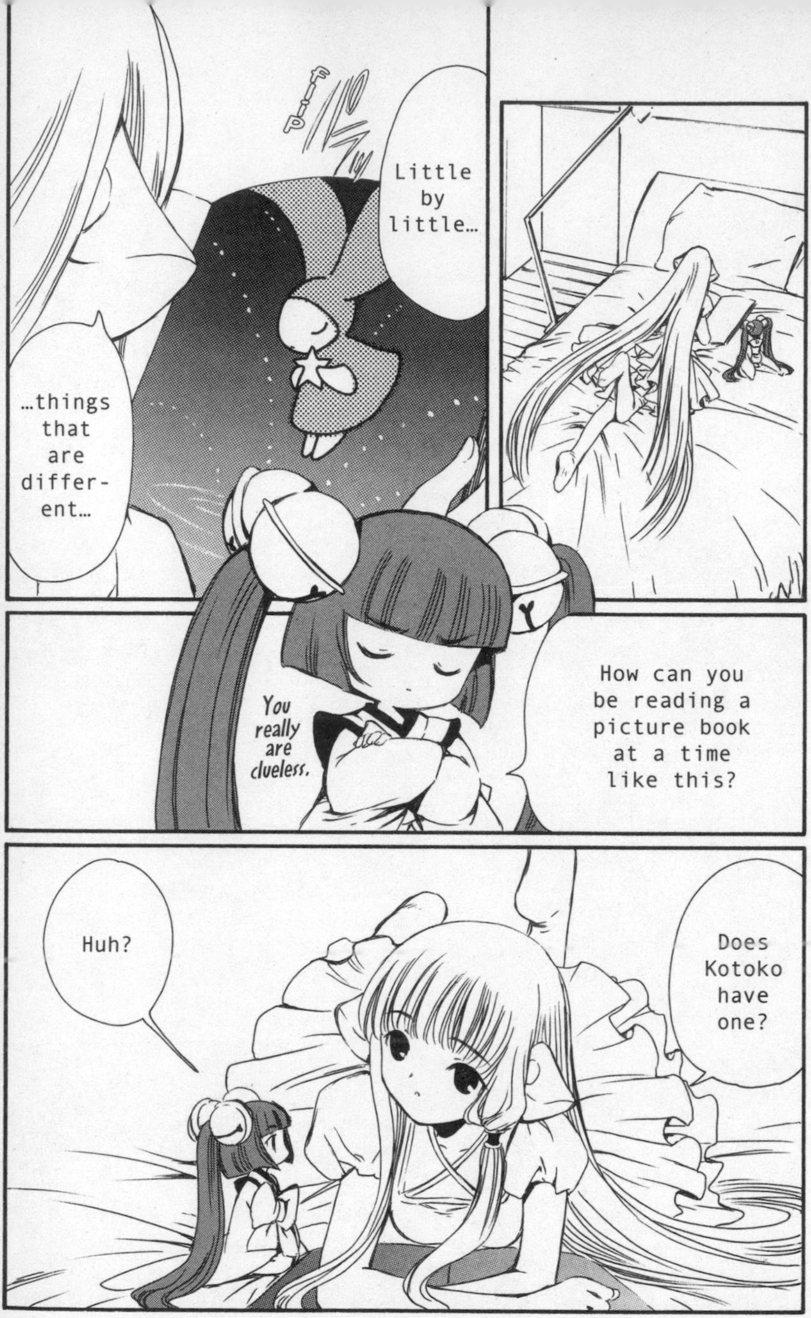
FLIP
Little by little...
...things that are different...
How can you be reading a picture book at a time like this?
You really are clueless.
Does Kotoko have one?
Huh?

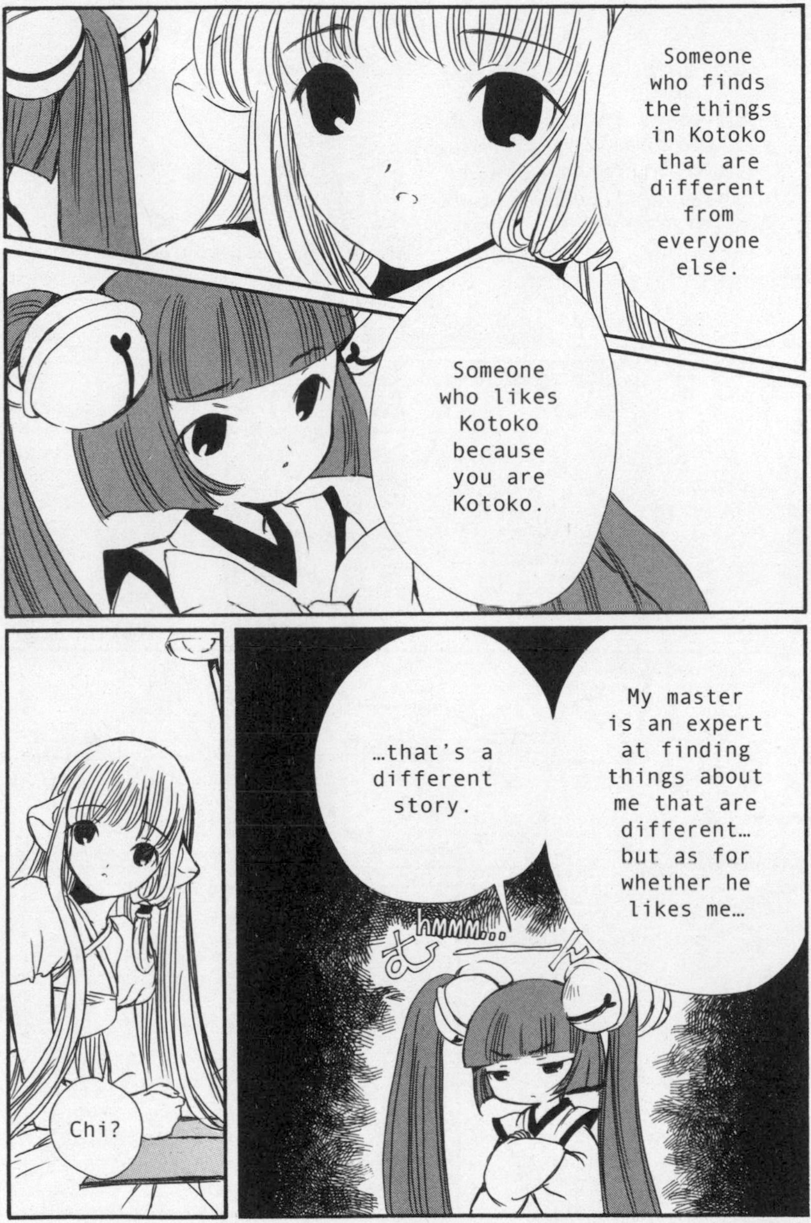
Someone who finds the things in Kotoko that are different from everyone else.
Someone who likes Kotoko because you are Kotoko.
My master is an expert at finding things about me that are different… but as for whether he likes me…
…that's a different story.
hmmm...
Chi?

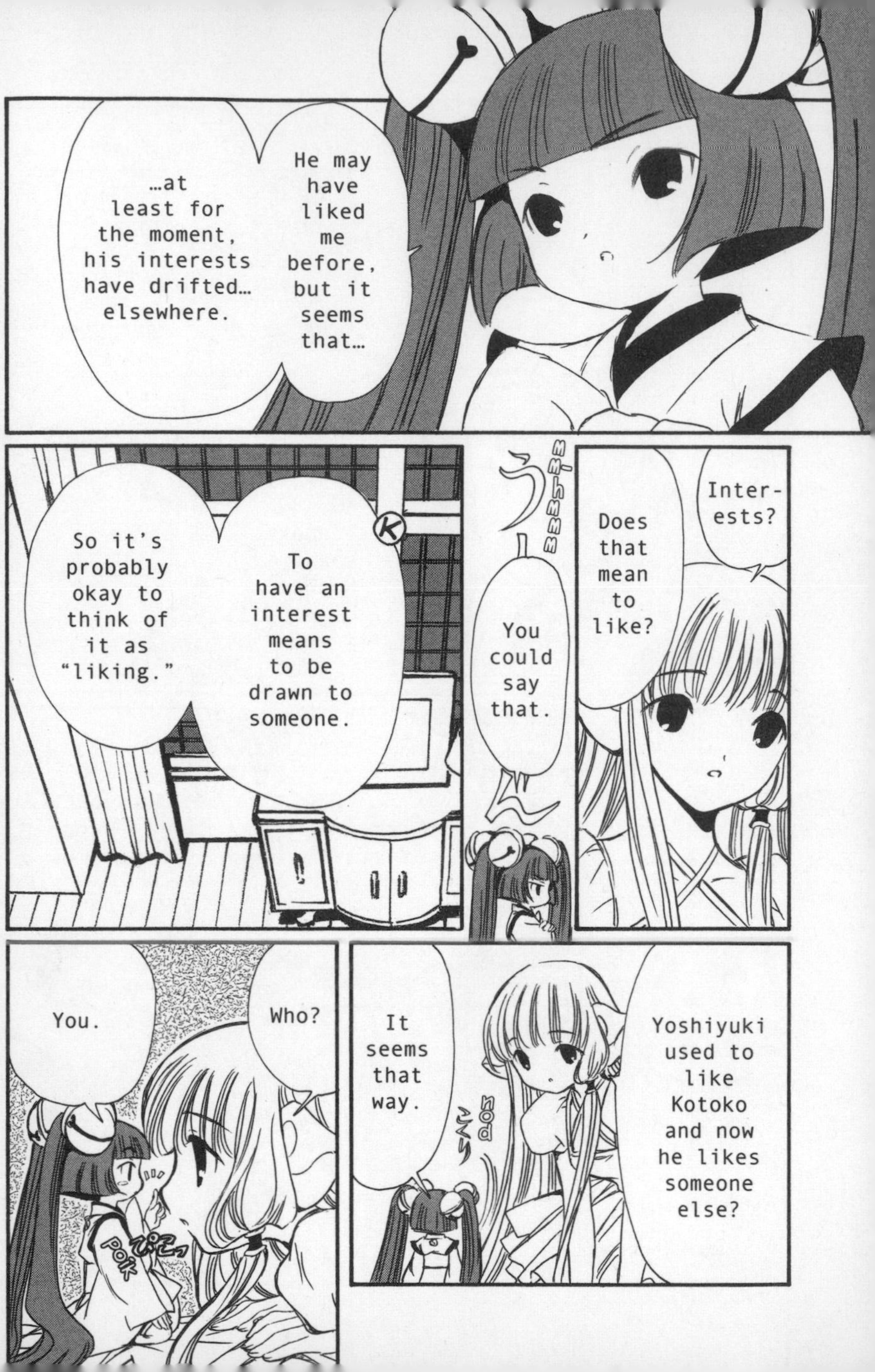
He may have liked me before, but it seems that…
…at least for the moment, his interests have drifted… elsewhere.
Inter-ests?
Does that mean to like?
Hmmm
You could say that.
To have an interest means to be drawn to someone.
So it's probably okay to think of it as "liking."
Yoshiyuki used to like Kotoko and now he likes someone else?
nod
It seems that way.
Who?
You.
POK

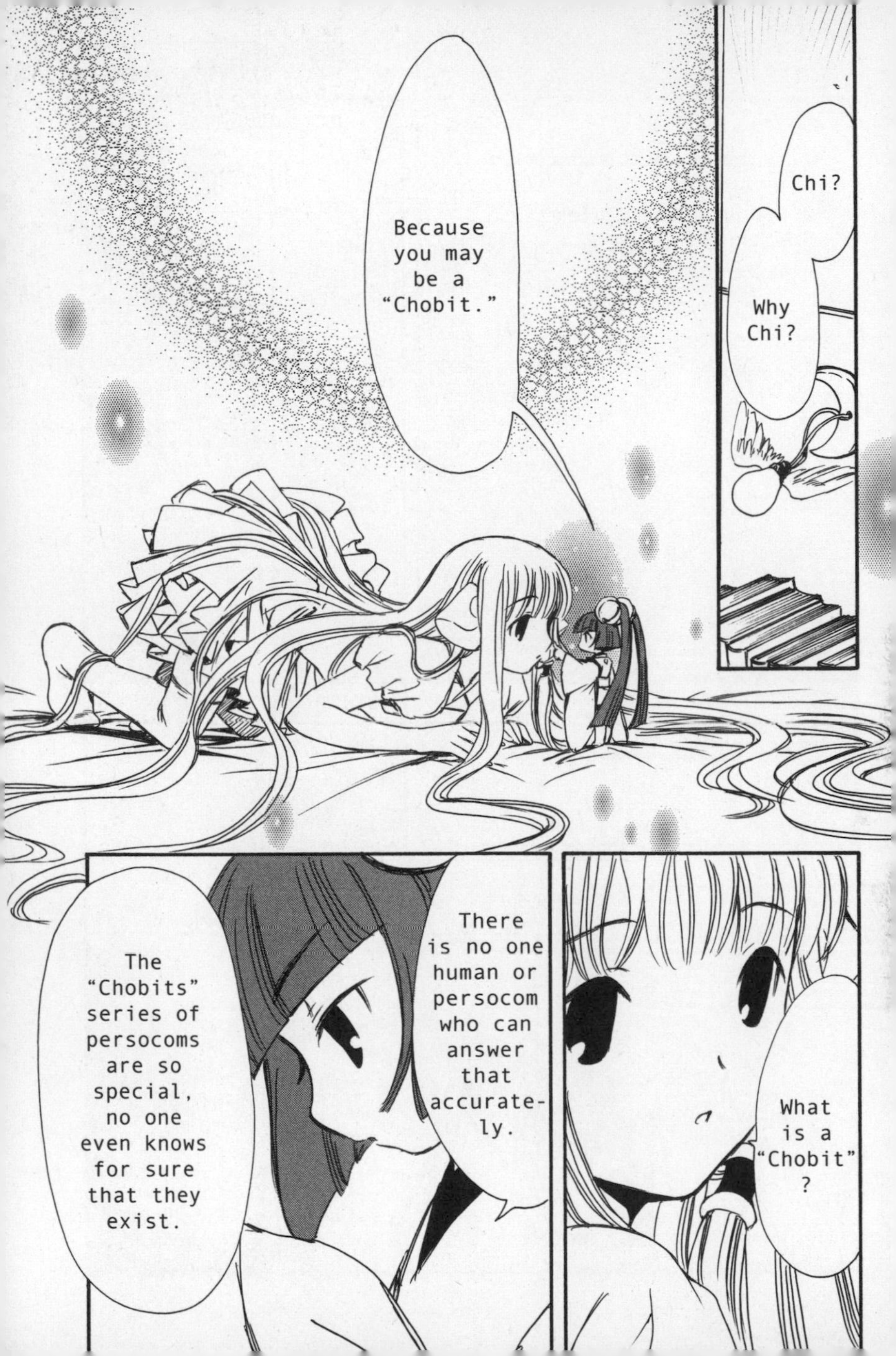
Chi?
Why Chi?
Because you may be a "Chobit."
What is a "Chobit" ?
There is no one human or persocom who can answer that accurate-ly.
The "Chobits" series of persocoms are so special, no one even knows for sure that they exist.

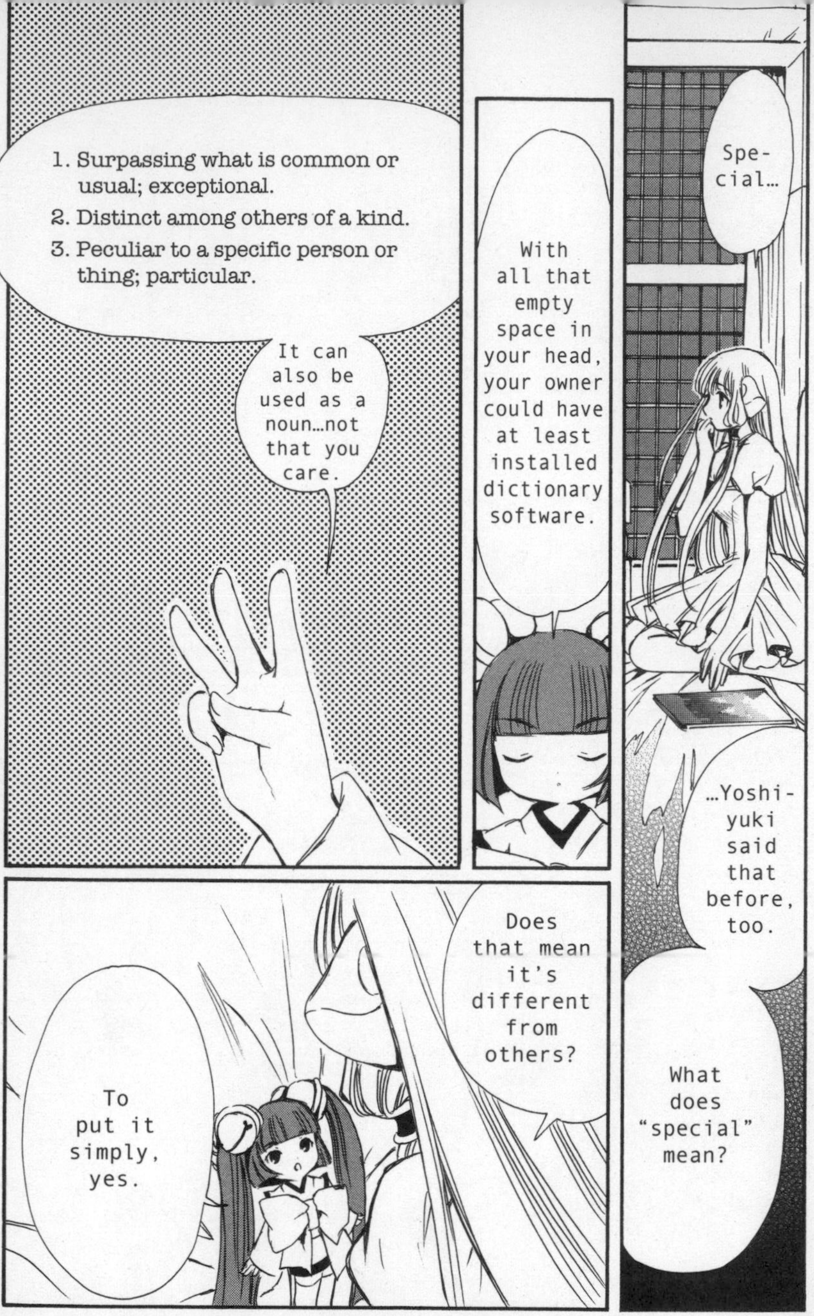

Spe-cial...
...Yoshi-yuki said that before, too.
What does "special" mean?
With all that empty space in your head, your owner could have at least installed dictionary software.
1. Surpassing what is common or usual; exceptional.
2. Distinct among others of a kind.
3. Peculiar to a specific person or thing; particular.
It can also be used as a noun...not that you care.
Does that mean it's different from others?
To put it simply, yes.

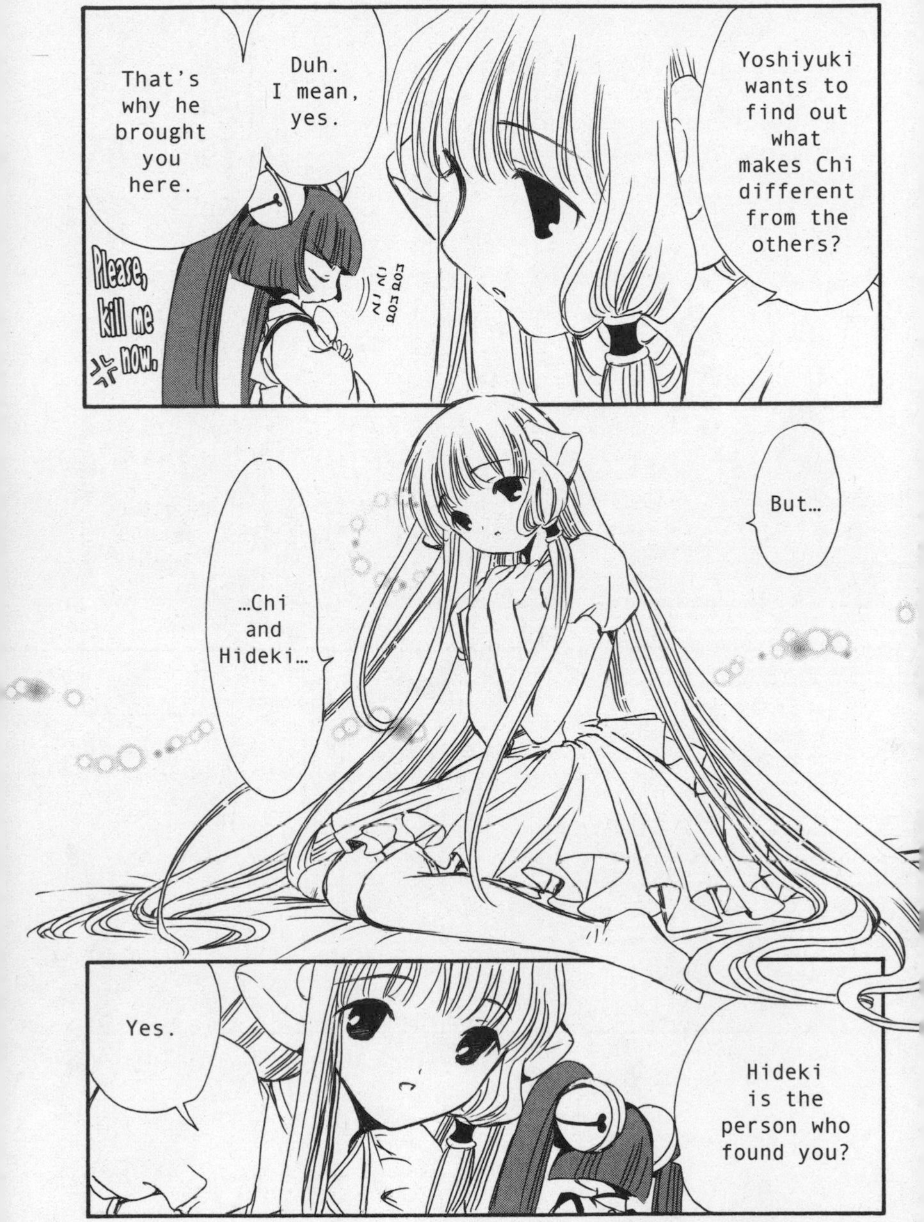
Yoshiyuki wants to find out what makes Chi different from the others?
Duh. I mean, yes.
That's why he brought you here.
Please, kill me now.
But...
...Chi and Hideki...
Hideki is the person who found you?
Yes.

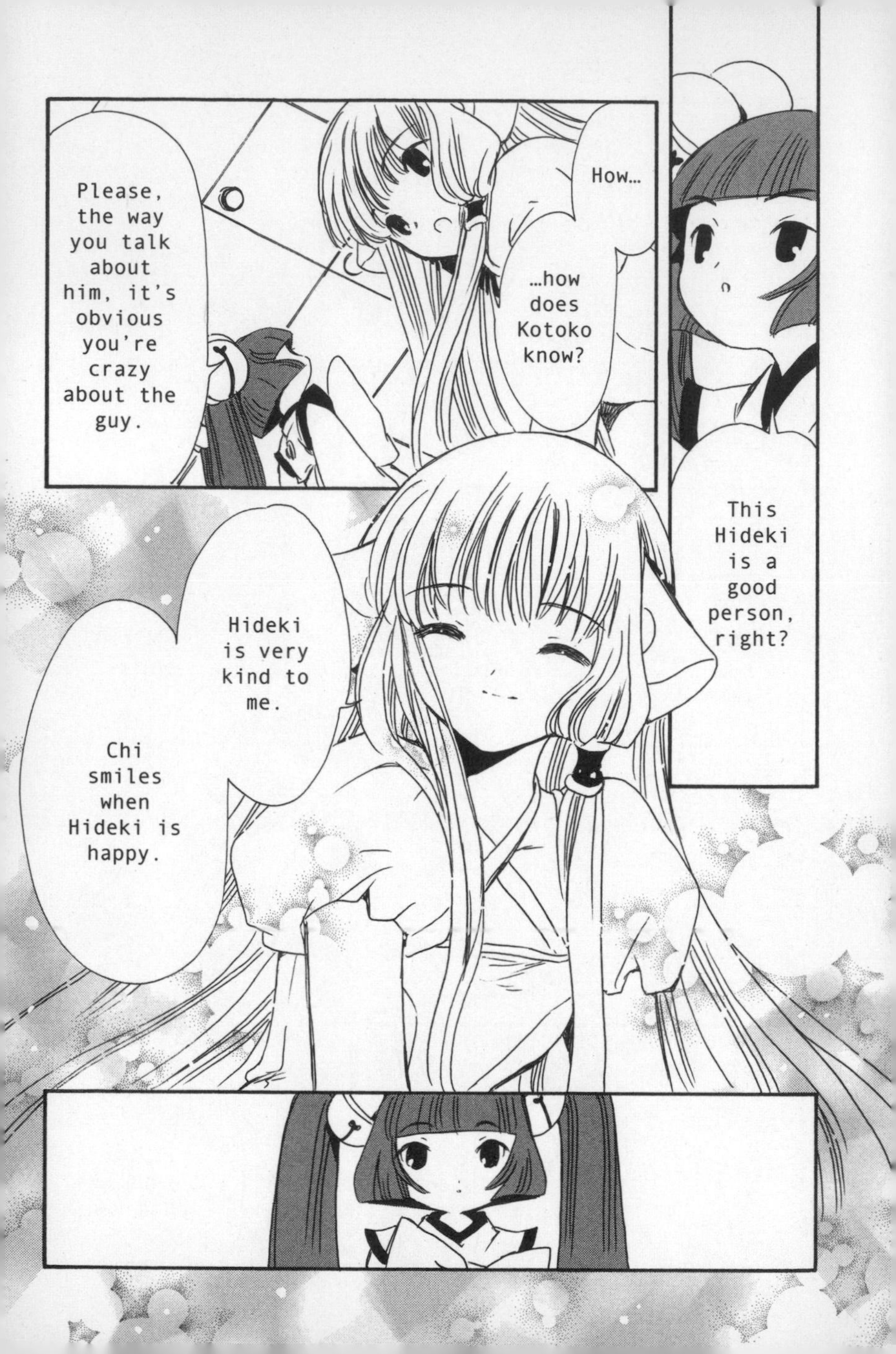
This Hideki is a good person, right?
How…
…how does Kotoko know?
Please, the way you talk about him, it's obvious you're crazy about the guy.
Hideki is very kind to me.
Chi smiles when Hideki is happy.

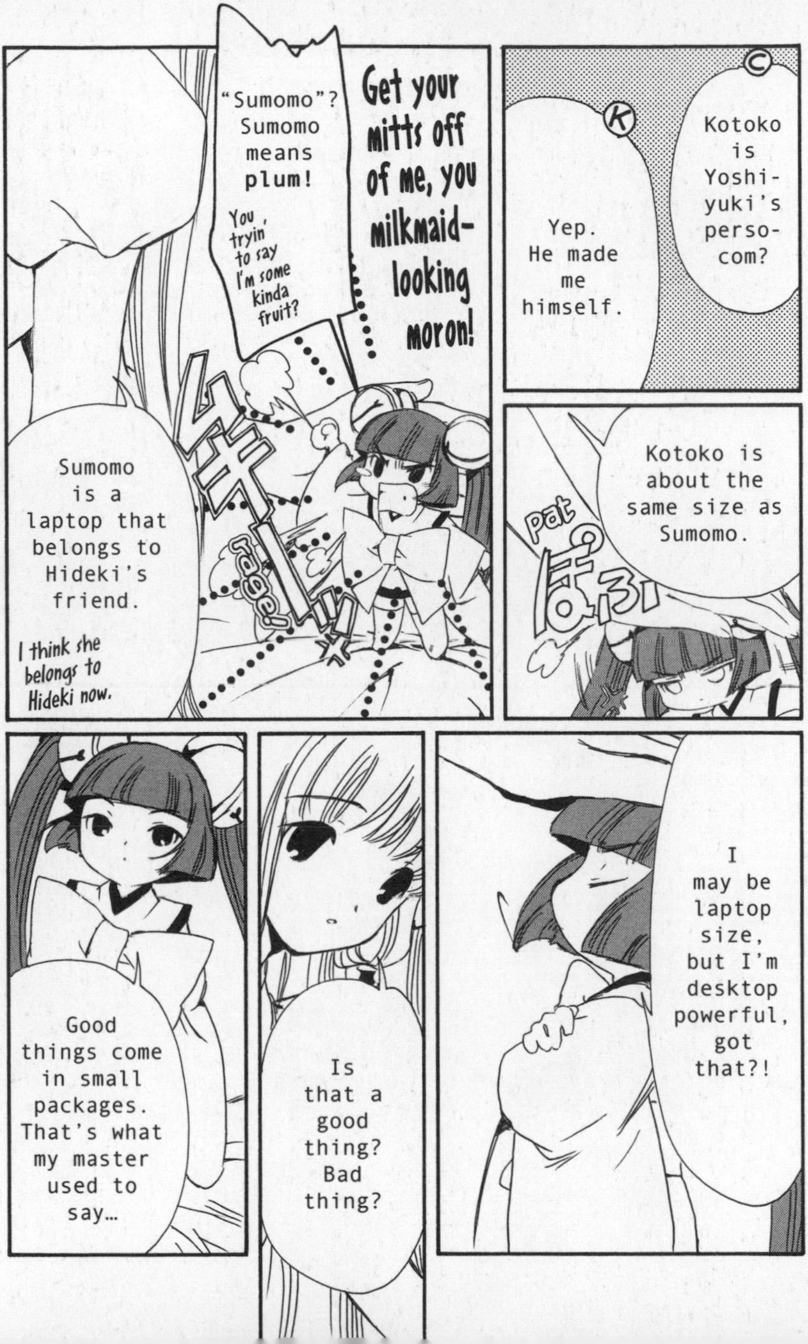
Kotoko is Yoshiyuki's persocom?
Yep. He made me himself.
Kotoko is about the same size as Sumomo.
pat
"Sumomo"? Sumomo means plum!
You tryin' to say I'm some kinda fruit?
Get your mitts off of me, you milkmaid-looking moron!
rage!
Sumomo is a laptop that belongs to Hideki's friend.
I think she belongs to Hideki now.
I may be laptop size, but I'm desktop powerful, got that?!
Is that a good thing? Bad thing?
Good things come in small packages. That's what my master used to say…

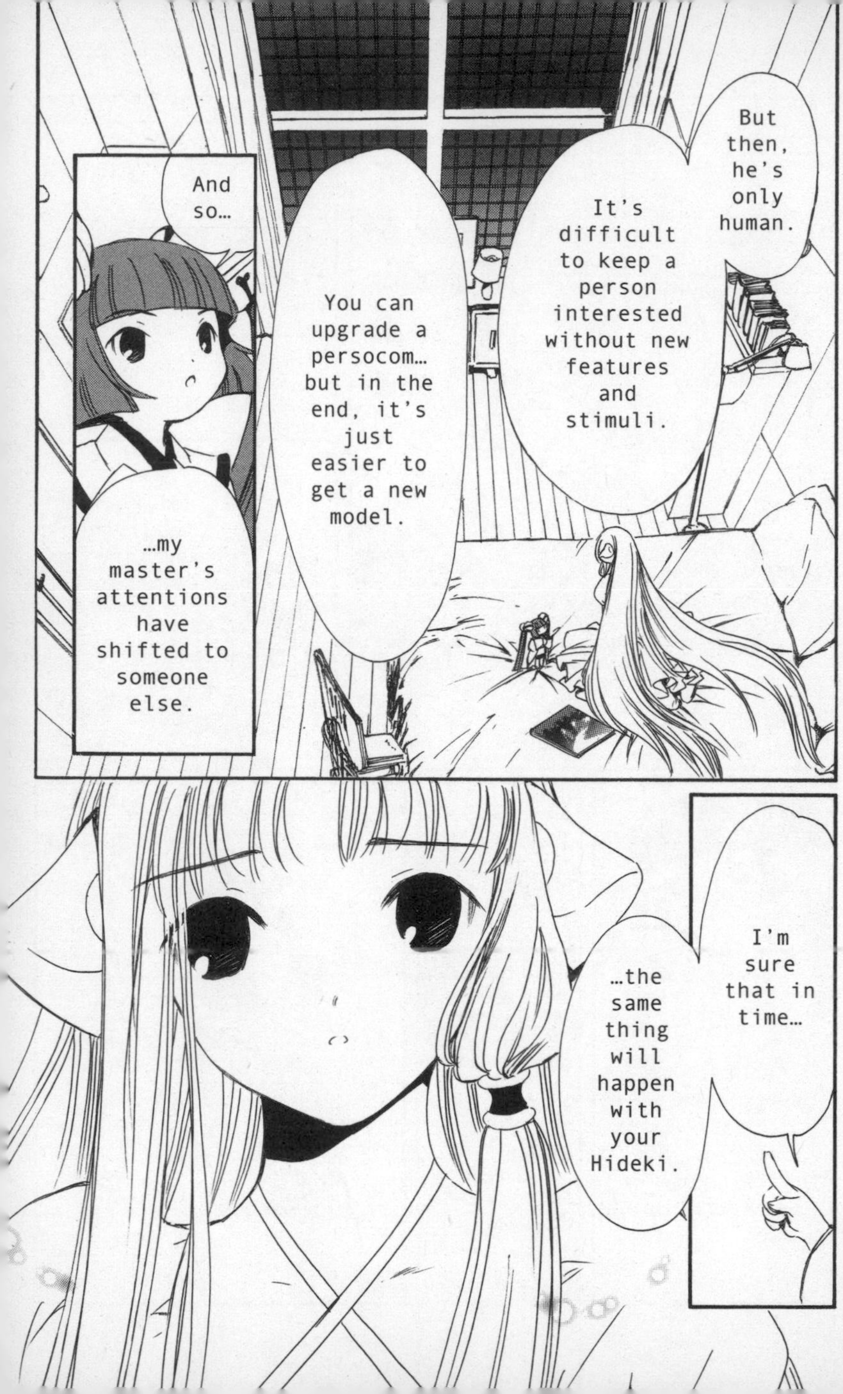

But then, he's only human.
It's difficult to keep a person interested without new features and stimuli.
You can upgrade a persocom… but in the end, it's just easier to get a new model.
And so…
…my master's attentions have shifted to someone else.
I'm sure that in time…
…the same thing will happen with your Hideki.

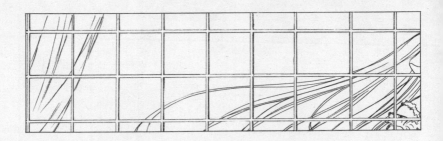

Chobits
ちょびっツ

◀ **chapter 46** ▶

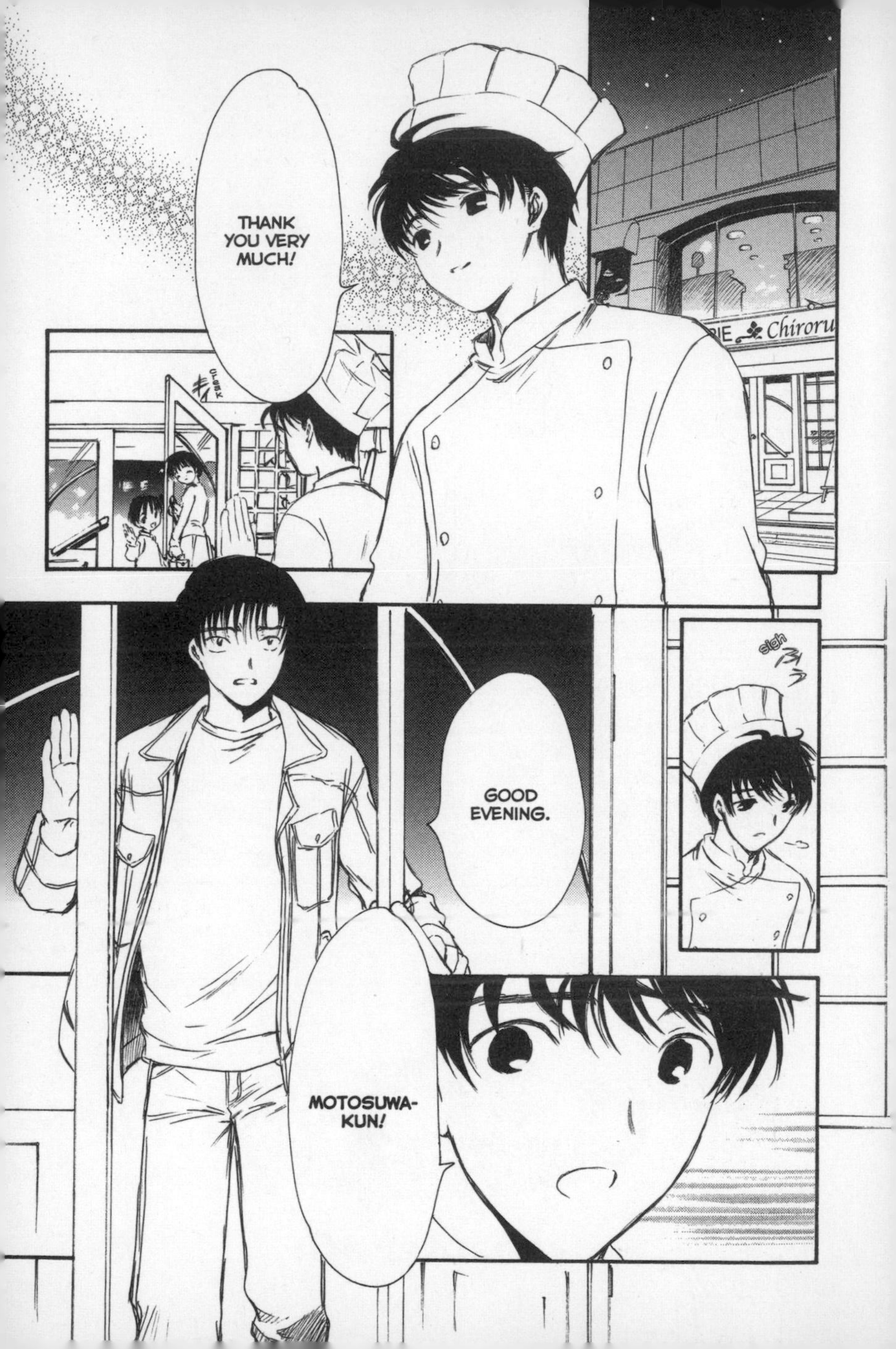
RIE Chiroru
THANK YOU VERY MUCH!
キイ
creak
sigh
GOOD EVENING.
MOTOSUWA-KUN!

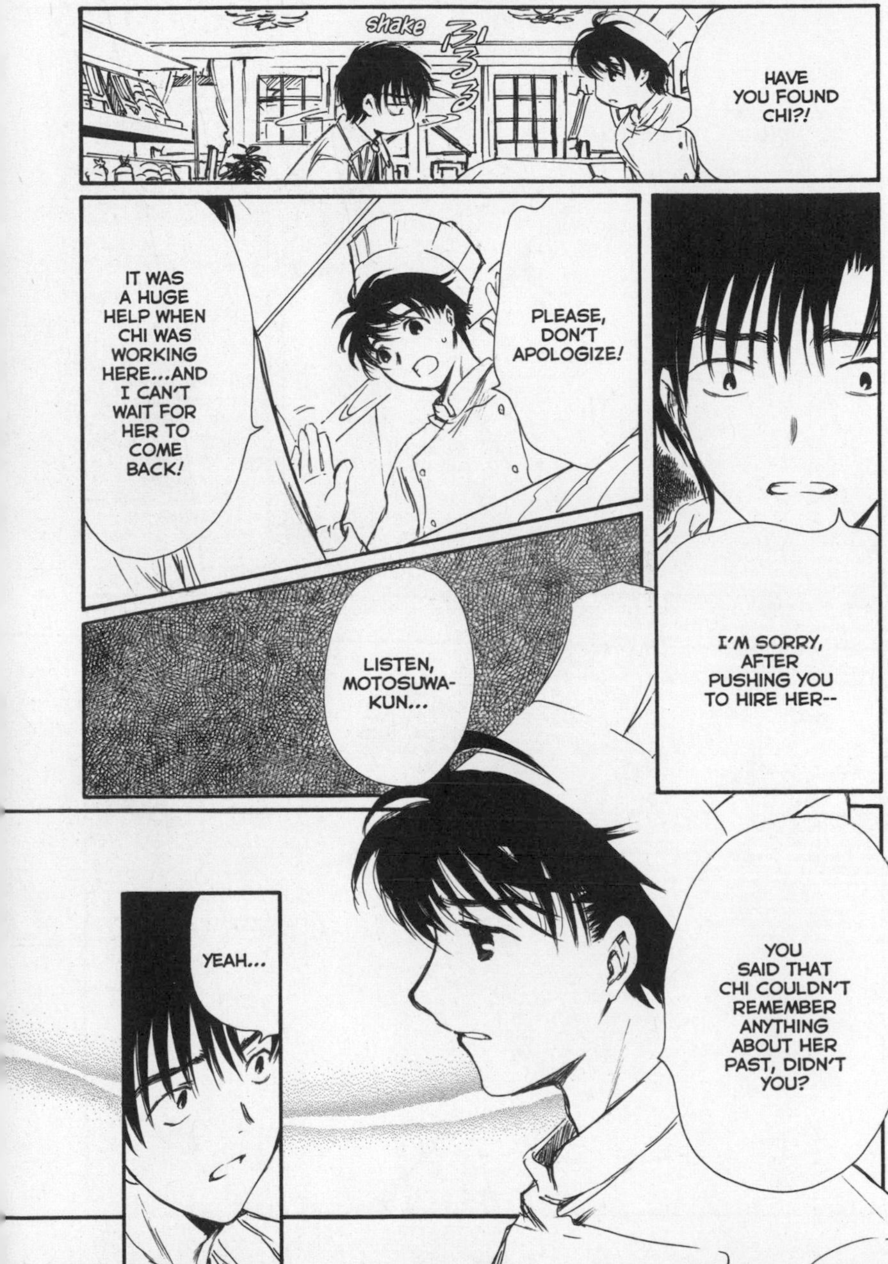
HAVE YOU FOUND CHI?!
shake
I'M SORRY, AFTER PUSHING YOU TO HIRE HER--
PLEASE, DON'T APOLOGIZE!
IT WAS A HUGE HELP WHEN CHI WAS WORKING HERE...AND I CAN'T WAIT FOR HER TO COME BACK!
LISTEN, MOTOSUWA-KUN...
YOU SAID THAT CHI COULDN'T REMEMBER ANYTHING ABOUT HER PAST, DIDN'T YOU?
YEAH...

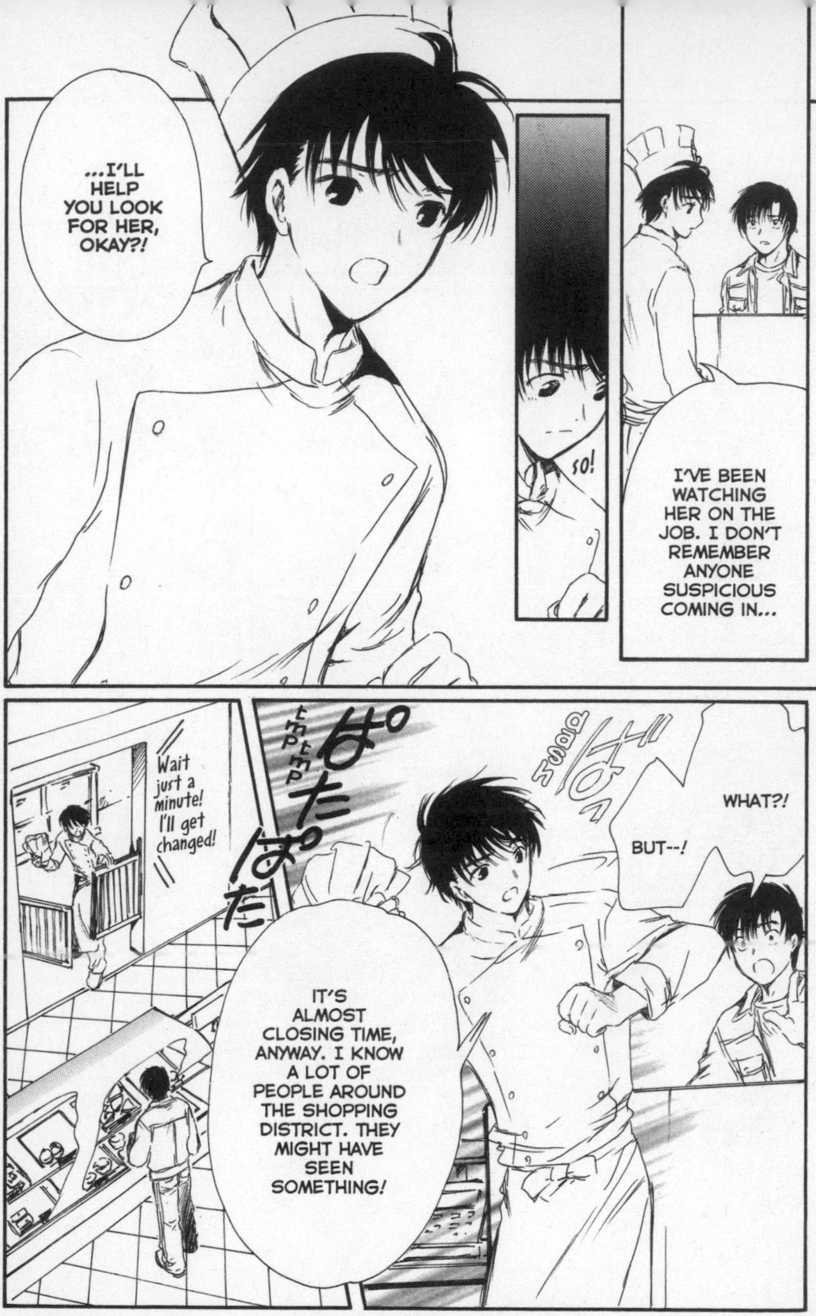
I'VE BEEN WATCHING HER ON THE JOB. I DON'T REMEMBER ANYONE SUSPICIOUS COMING IN...
so!
...I'LL HELP YOU LOOK FOR HER, OKAY?!
WHAT?!
BUT--!
gasp
IT'S ALMOST CLOSING TIME, ANYWAY. I KNOW A LOT OF PEOPLE AROUND THE SHOPPING DISTRICT. THEY MIGHT HAVE SEEN SOMETHING!
ぱたぱた
tmp tmp
Wait just a minute! I'll get changed!

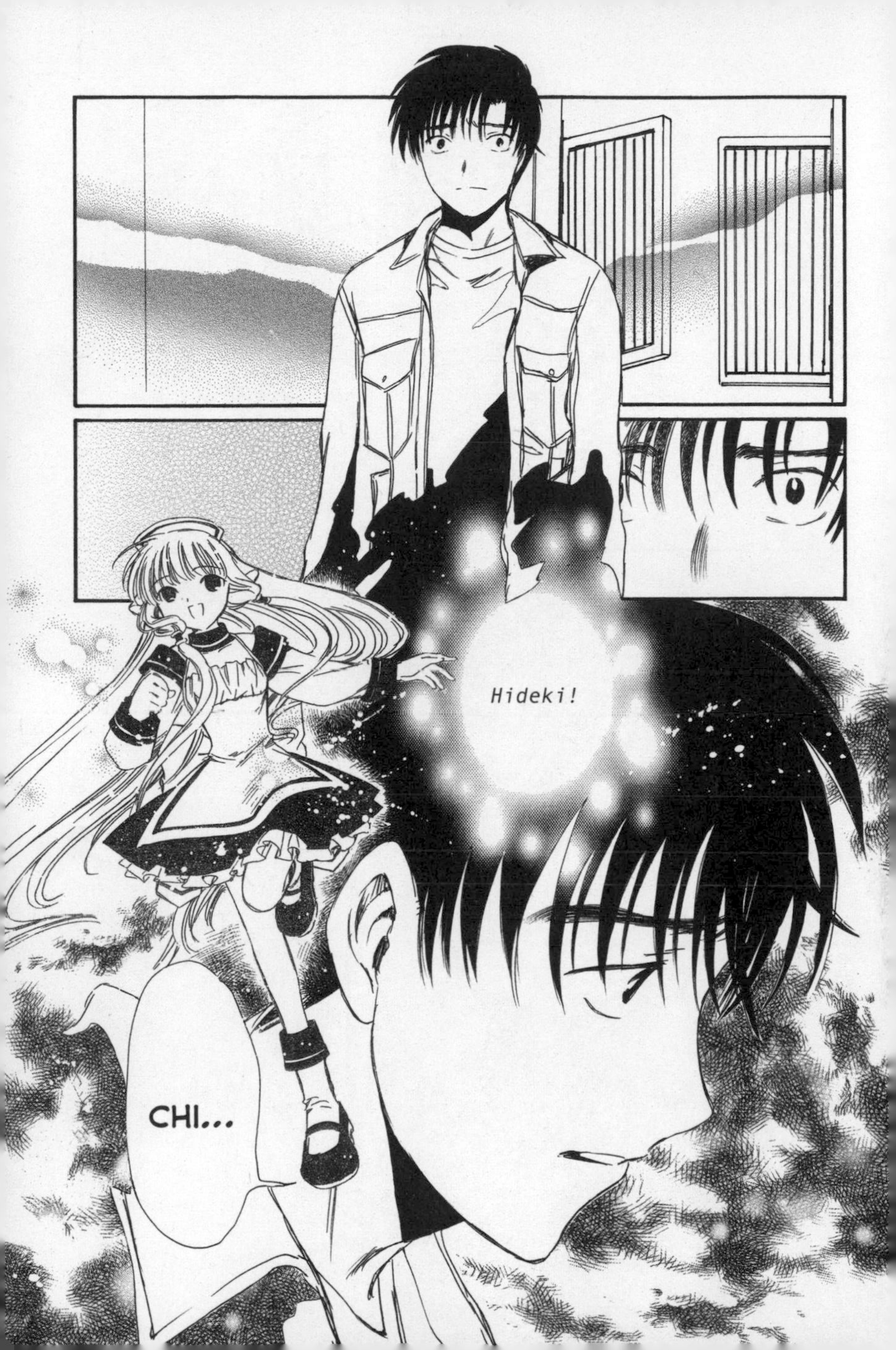
Hideki!
CHI...

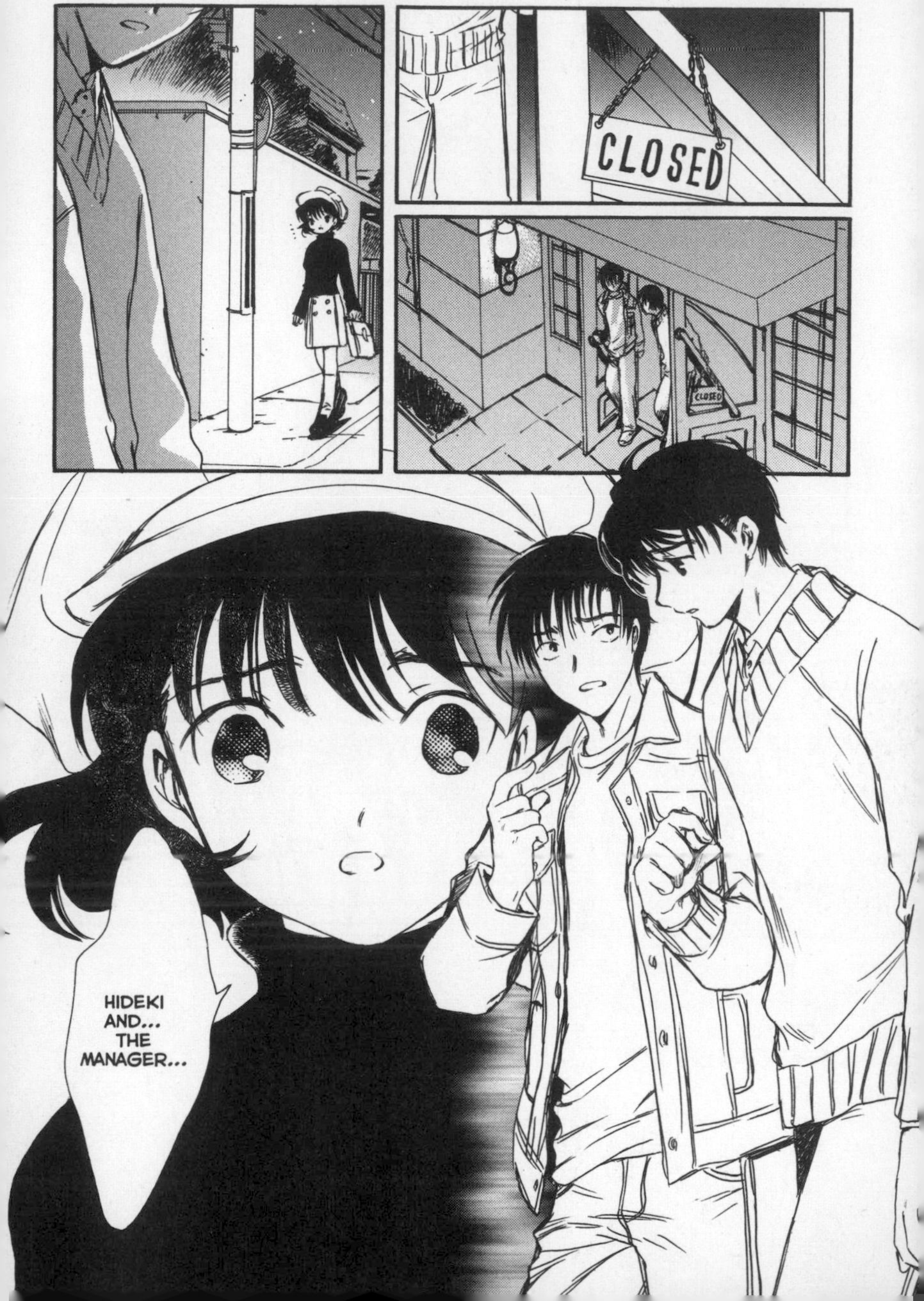
CLOSED
CLOSED
HIDEKI AND... THE MANAGER...

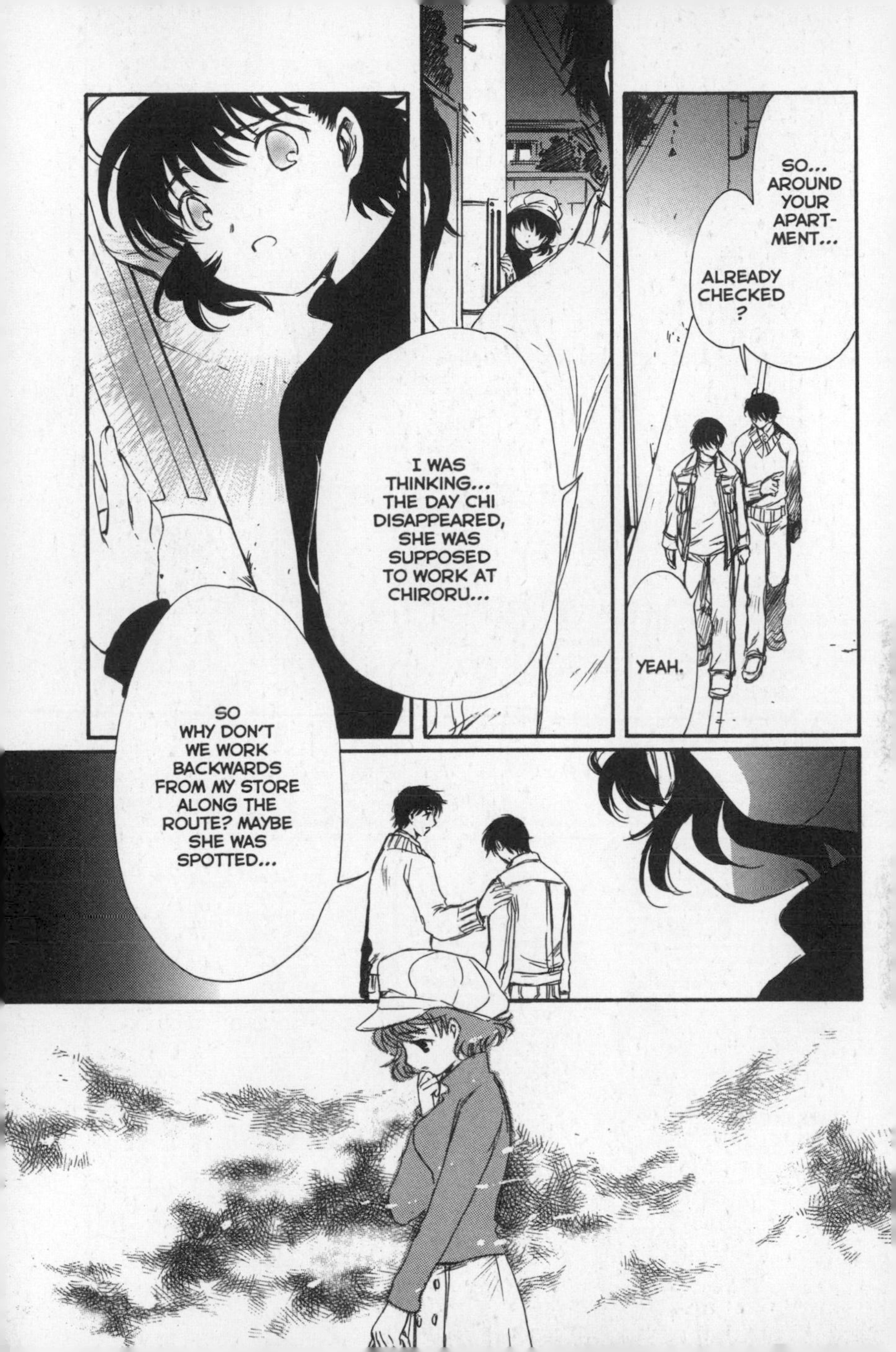
SO... AROUND YOUR APARTMENT... ALREADY CHECKED?
YEAH.
I WAS THINKING... THE DAY CHI DISAPPEARED, SHE WAS SUPPOSED TO WORK AT CHIRORU...
SO WHY DON'T WE WORK BACKWARDS FROM MY STORE ALONG THE ROUTE? MAYBE SHE WAS SPOTTED...

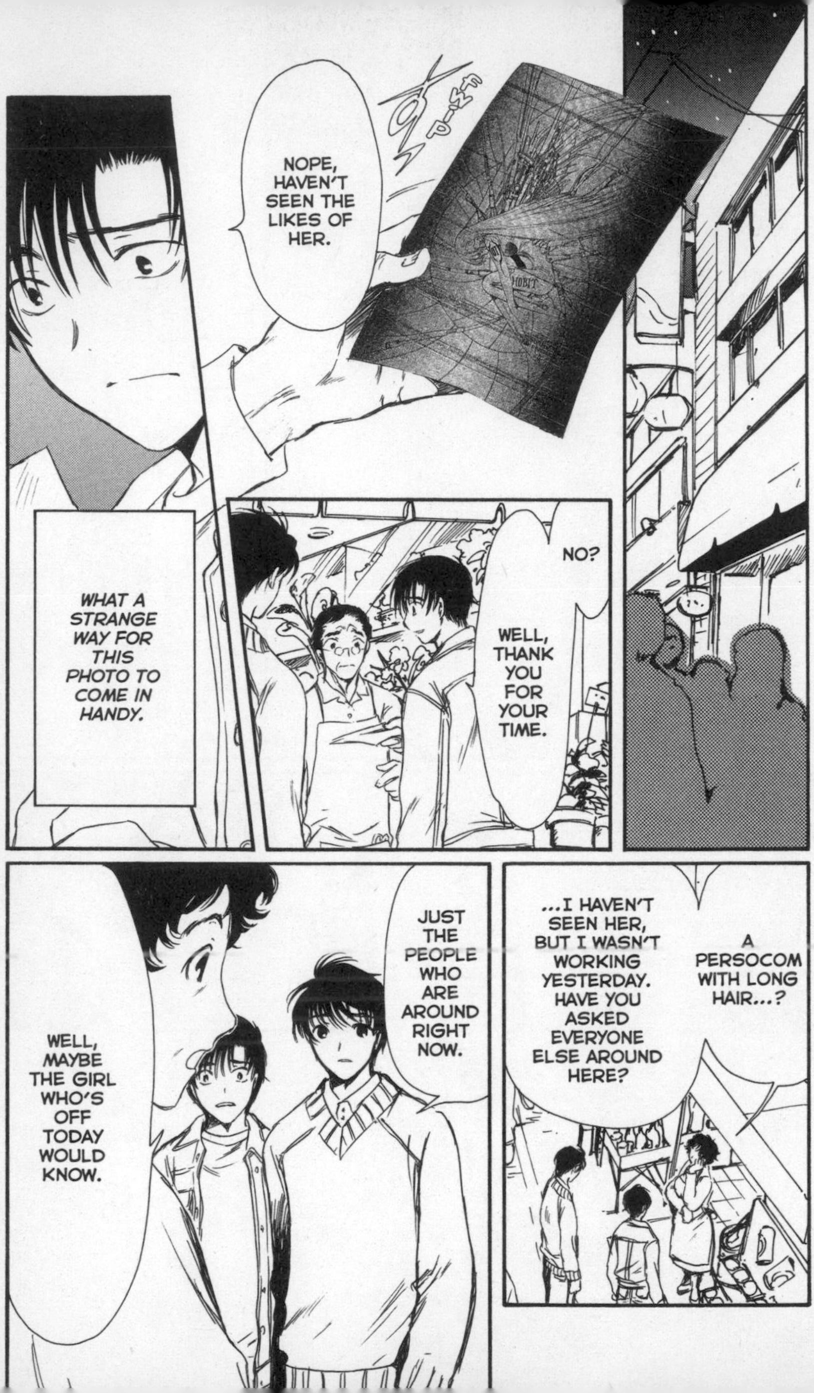
FLIP
NOPE, HAVEN'T SEEN THE LIKES OF HER.
NO?
WELL, THANK YOU FOR YOUR TIME.
WHAT A STRANGE WAY FOR THIS PHOTO TO COME IN HANDY.
A PERSOCOM WITH LONG HAIR...?
...I HAVEN'T SEEN HER, BUT I WASN'T WORKING YESTERDAY. HAVE YOU ASKED EVERYONE ELSE AROUND HERE?
JUST THE PEOPLE WHO ARE AROUND RIGHT NOW.
WELL, MAYBE THE GIRL WHO'S OFF TODAY WOULD KNOW.

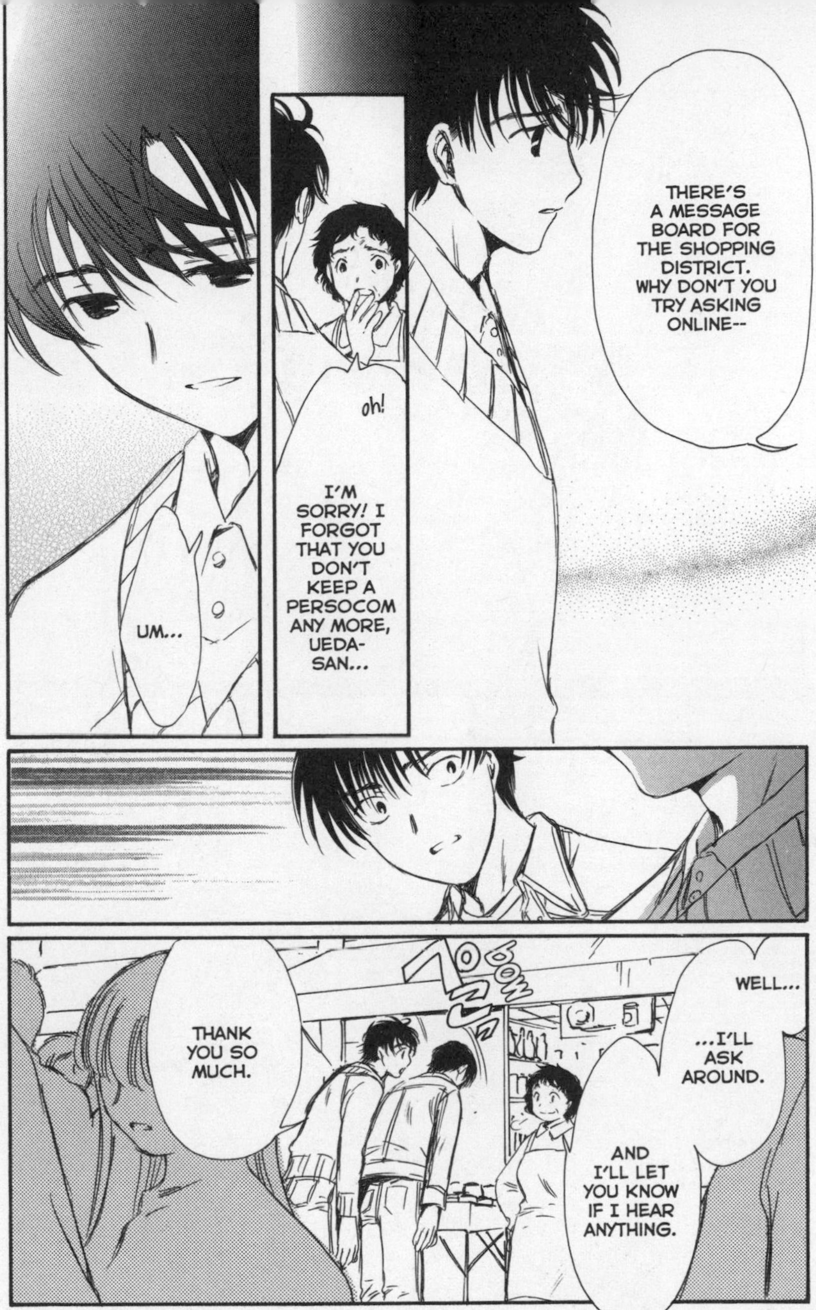
THERE'S A MESSAGE BOARD FOR THE SHOPPING DISTRICT. WHY DON'T YOU TRY ASKING ONLINE--
oh!
I'M SORRY! I FORGOT THAT YOU DON'T KEEP A PERSOCOM ANY MORE, UEDA-SAN...
UM...
WELL...
...I'LL ASK AROUND.
AND I'LL LET YOU KNOW IF I HEAR ANYTHING.
THANK YOU SO MUCH.

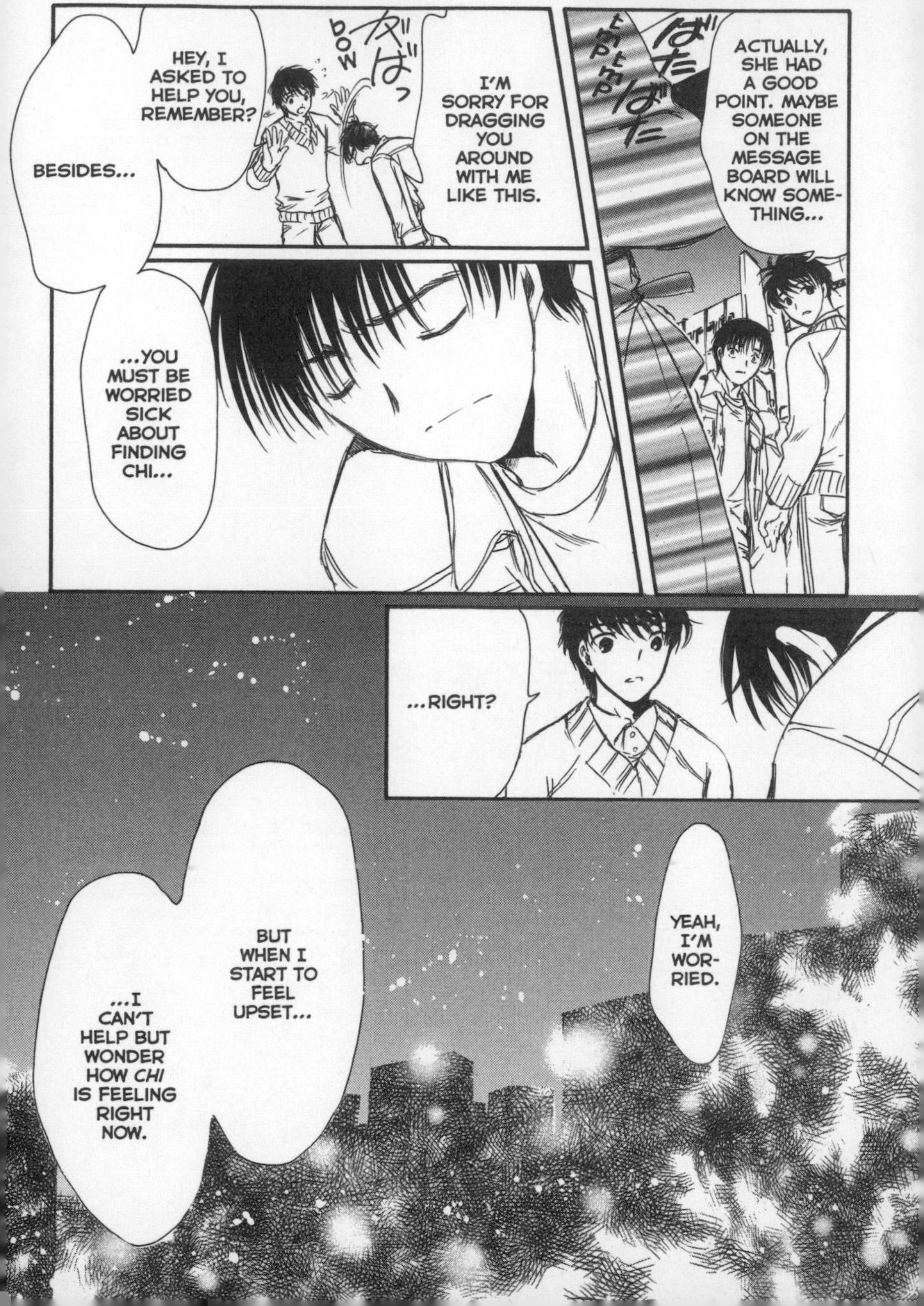
ばたばた
ACTUALLY, SHE HAD A GOOD POINT. MAYBE SOMEONE ON THE MESSAGE BOARD WILL KNOW SOMETHING...
I'M SORRY FOR DRAGGING YOU AROUND WITH ME LIKE THIS.
がばっ
BOW
HEY, I ASKED TO HELP YOU, REMEMBER?
BESIDES...
...YOU MUST BE WORRIED SICK ABOUT FINDING CHI...
...RIGHT?
YEAH, I'M WORRIED.
BUT WHEN I START TO FEEL UPSET...
...I CAN'T HELP BUT WONDER HOW *CHI* IS FEELING RIGHT NOW.

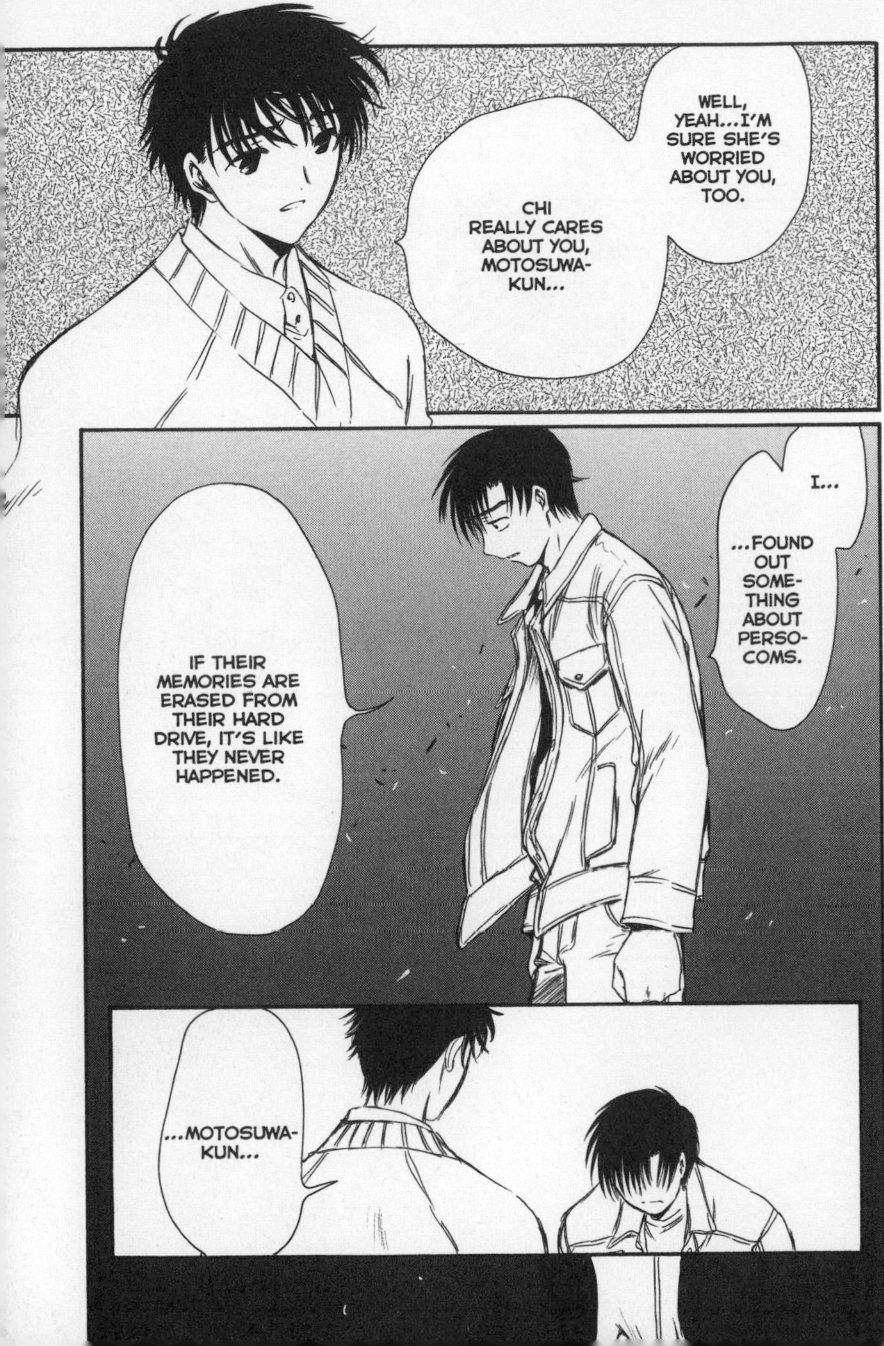
WELL, YEAH...I'M SURE SHE'S WORRIED ABOUT YOU, TOO.
CHI REALLY CARES ABOUT YOU, MOTOSUWA-KUN...
I...
...FOUND OUT SOMETHING ABOUT PERSOCOMS.
IF THEIR MEMORIES ARE ERASED FROM THEIR HARD DRIVE, IT'S LIKE THEY NEVER HAPPENED.
...MOTOSUWA-KUN...

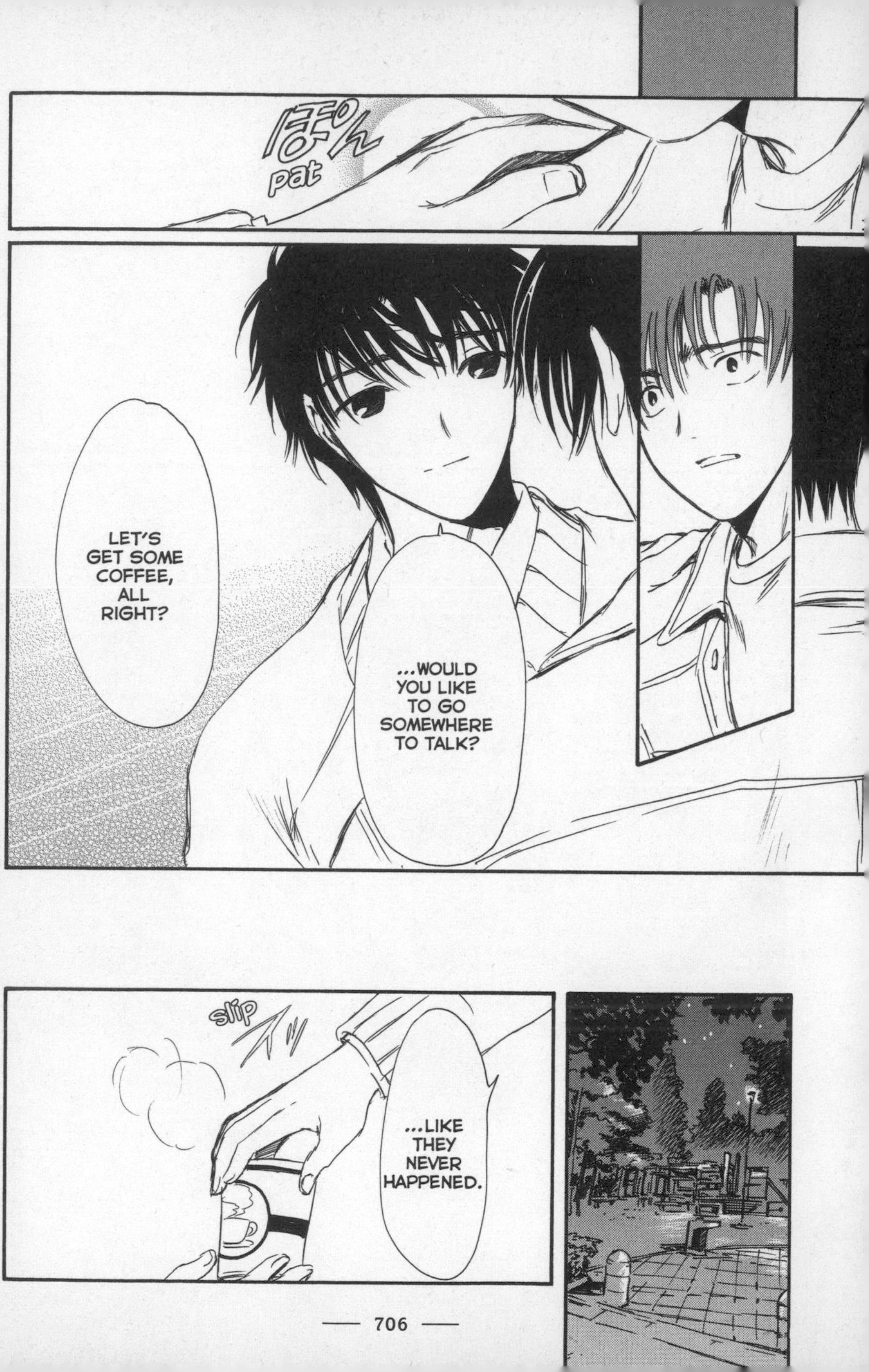

ぽん
pat
...WOULD YOU LIKE TO GO SOMEWHERE TO TALK?
LET'S GET SOME COFFEE, ALL RIGHT?
ズッ
slip
...LIKE THEY NEVER HAPPENED.

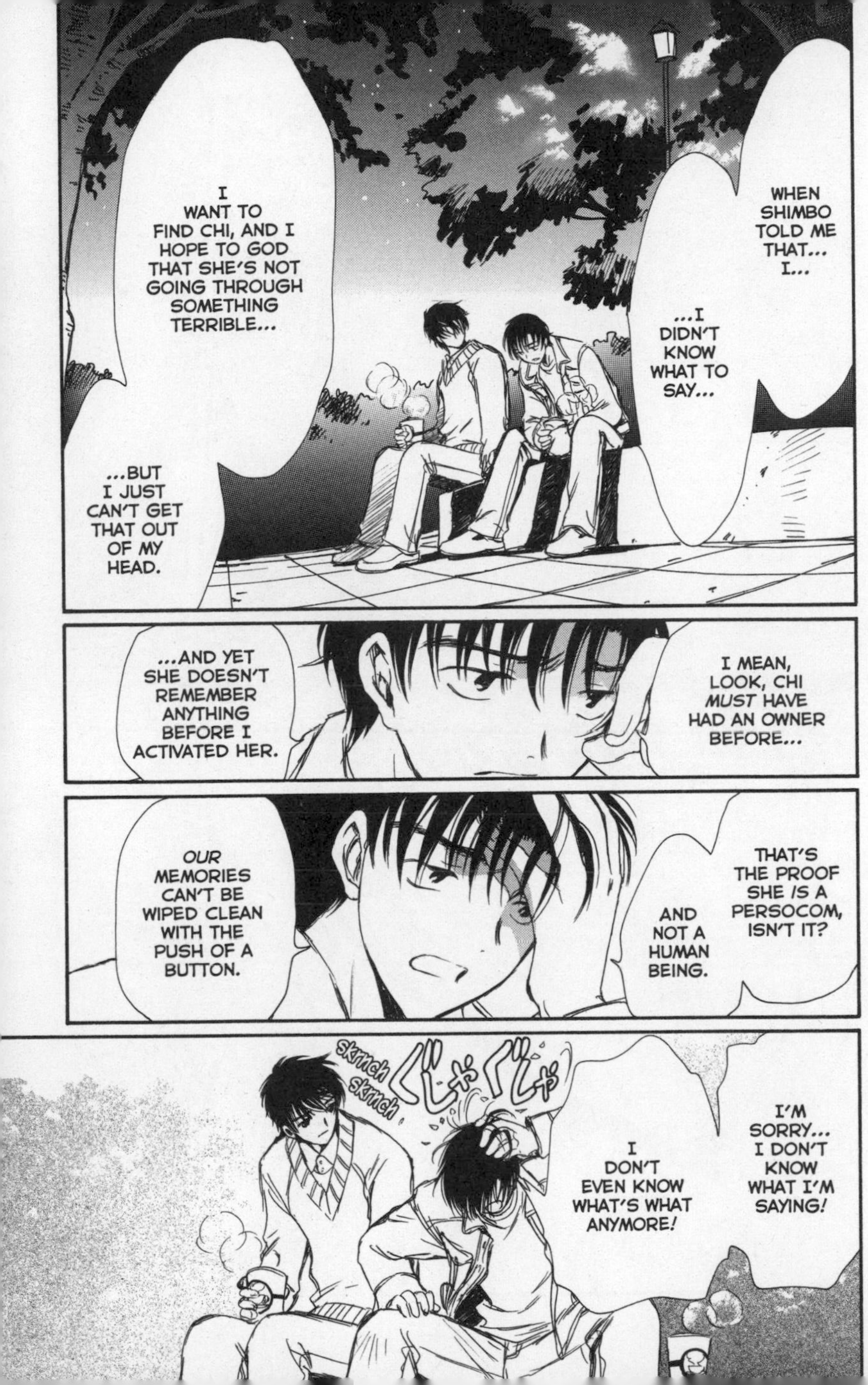

WHEN SHIMBO TOLD ME THAT... I...
...I DIDN'T KNOW WHAT TO SAY...
I WANT TO FIND CHI, AND I HOPE TO GOD THAT SHE'S NOT GOING THROUGH SOMETHING TERRIBLE...
...BUT I JUST CAN'T GET THAT OUT OF MY HEAD.
I MEAN, LOOK, CHI *MUST* HAVE HAD AN OWNER BEFORE...
...AND YET SHE DOESN'T REMEMBER ANYTHING BEFORE I ACTIVATED HER.
THAT'S THE PROOF SHE *IS* A PERSOCOM,
AND NOT A HUMAN BEING.
OUR MEMORIES CAN'T BE WIPED CLEAN WITH THE PUSH OF A BUTTON.
I'M SORRY... I DON'T KNOW WHAT I'M SAYING!
skrnch skrnch
ぐしゃぐしゃ
I DON'T EVEN KNOW WHAT'S WHAT ANYMORE!

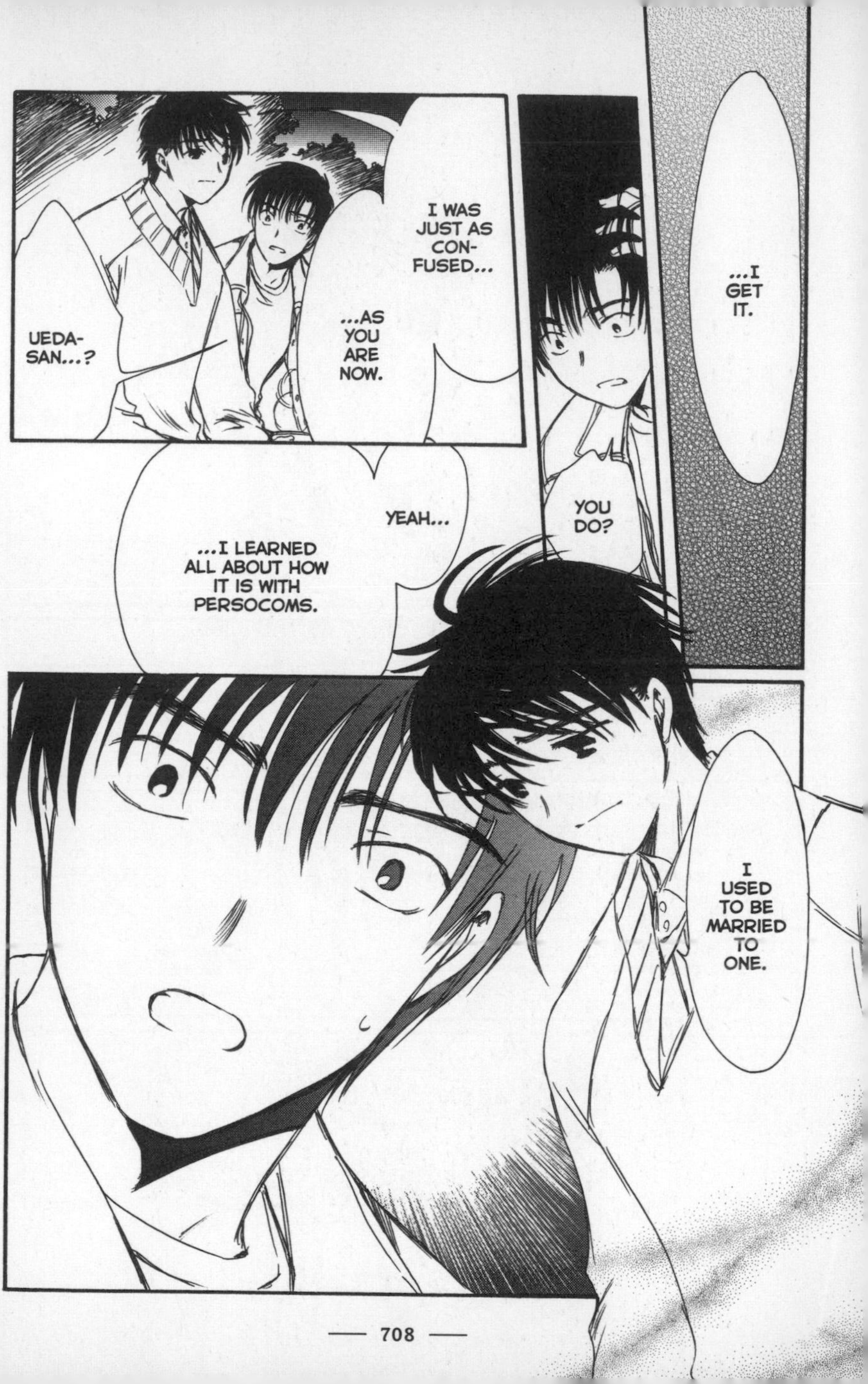
...I GET IT.
YOU DO?
YEAH...
...I LEARNED ALL ABOUT HOW IT IS WITH PERSOCOMS.
I WAS JUST AS CON-FUSED...
...AS YOU ARE NOW.
UEDA-SAN...?
I USED TO BE MARRIED TO ONE.

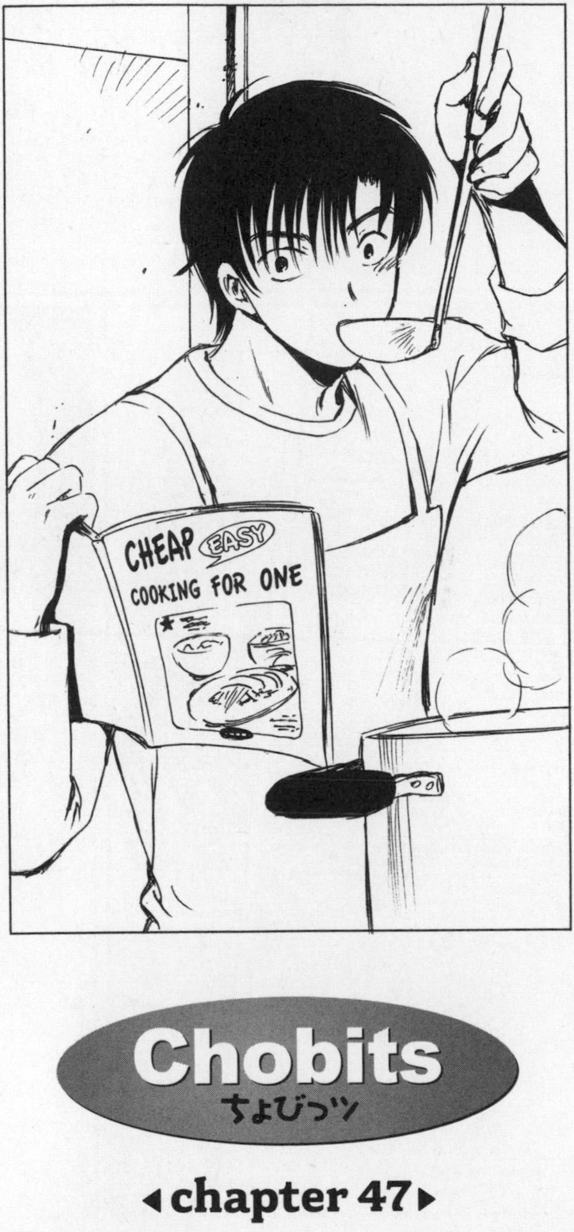
CHEAP
EASY
COOKING FOR ONE

Chobits

ちょびっツ

◂chapter 47▸

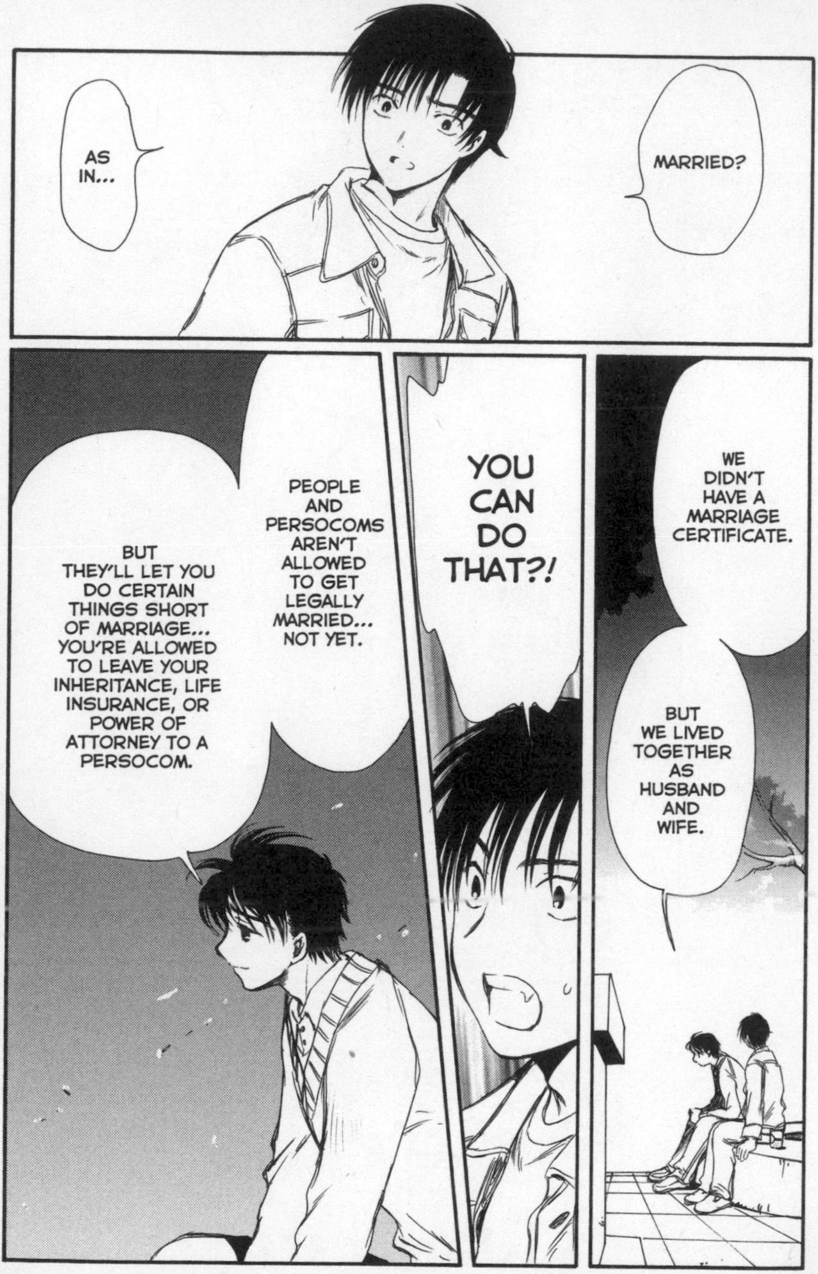
AS IN...
MARRIED?
WE DIDN'T HAVE A MARRIAGE CERTIFICATE.
BUT WE LIVED TOGETHER AS HUSBAND AND WIFE.
YOU CAN DO THAT?!
PEOPLE AND PERSOCOMS AREN'T ALLOWED TO GET LEGALLY MARRIED... NOT YET.
BUT THEY'LL LET YOU DO CERTAIN THINGS SHORT OF MARRIAGE... YOU'RE ALLOWED TO LEAVE YOUR INHERITANCE, LIFE INSURANCE, OR POWER OF ATTORNEY TO A PERSOCOM.

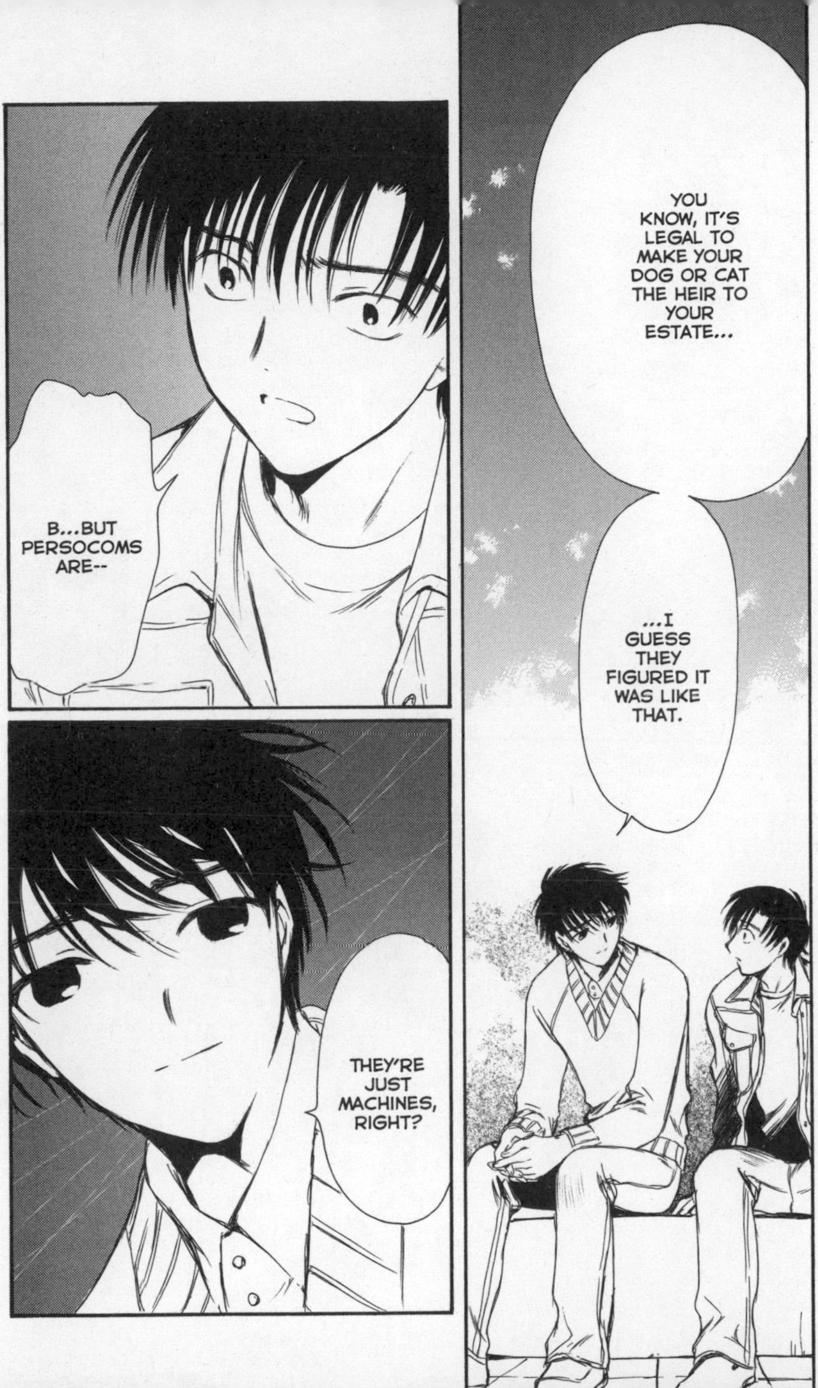
YOU KNOW, IT'S LEGAL TO MAKE YOUR DOG OR CAT THE HEIR TO YOUR ESTATE...
...I GUESS THEY FIGURED IT WAS LIKE THAT.
B...BUT PERSOCOMS ARE--
THEY'RE JUST MACHINES, RIGHT?

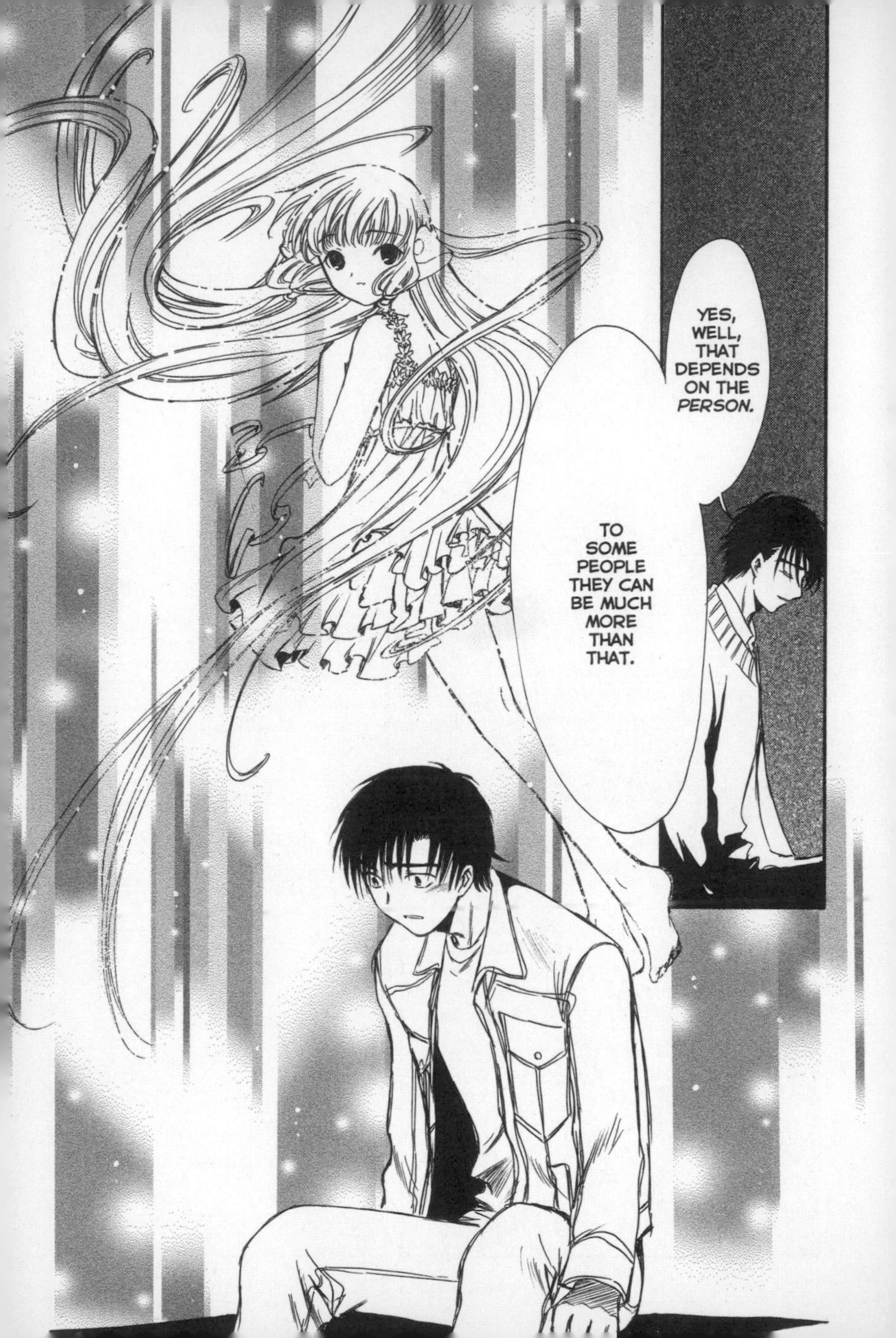
YES, WELL, THAT DEPENDS ON THE *PERSON.*
TO SOME PEOPLE THEY CAN BE MUCH MORE THAN THAT.

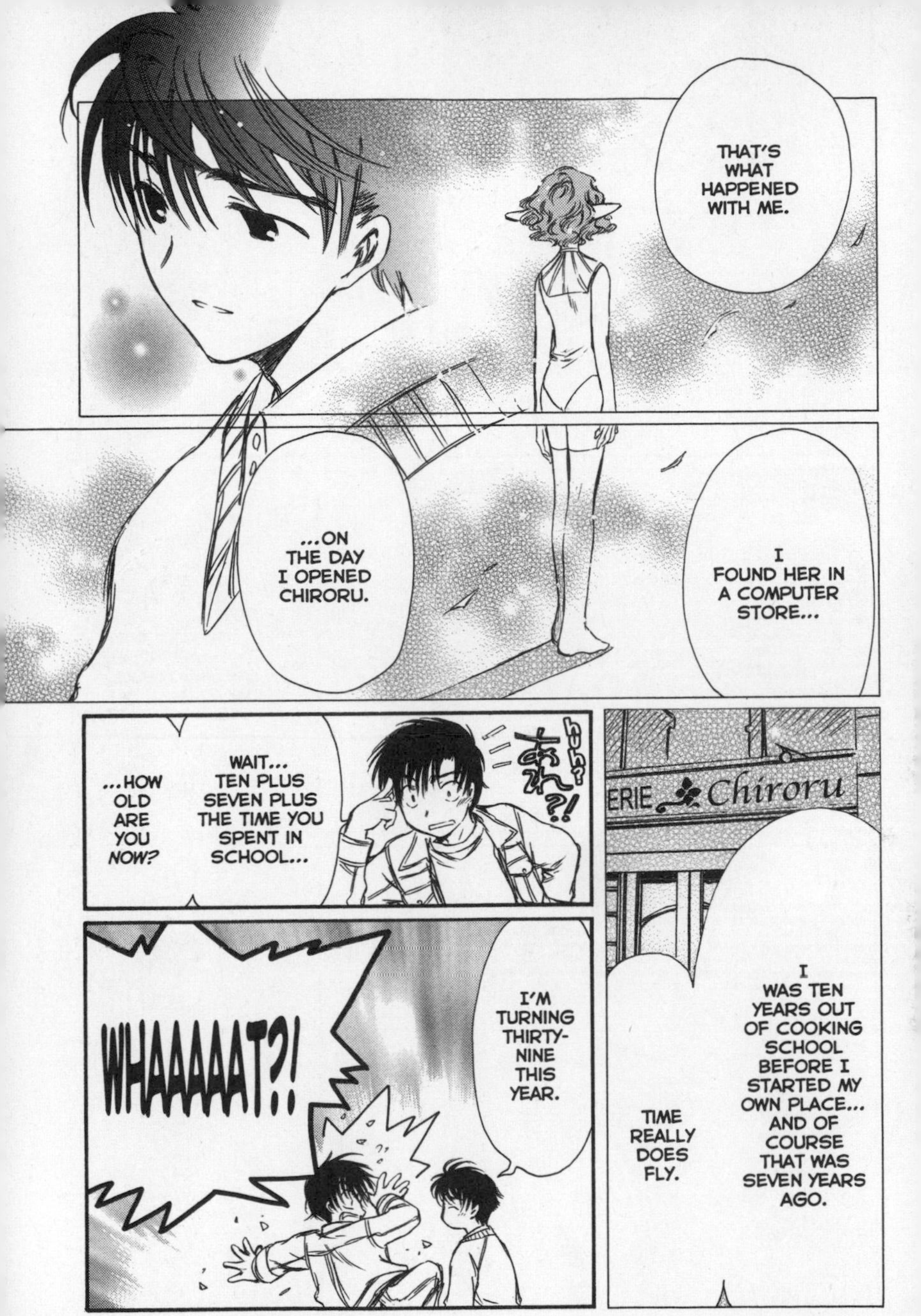
THAT'S WHAT HAPPENED WITH ME.
I FOUND HER IN A COMPUTER STORE...
...ON THE DAY I OPENED CHIRORU.
ERIE Chiroru
I WAS TEN YEARS OUT OF COOKING SCHOOL BEFORE I STARTED MY OWN PLACE... AND OF COURSE THAT WAS SEVEN YEARS AGO.
TIME REALLY DOES FLY.
huh?
あれ?!
WAIT... TEN PLUS SEVEN PLUS THE TIME YOU SPENT IN SCHOOL...
...HOW OLD ARE YOU *NOW?*
I'M TURNING THIRTY-NINE THIS YEAR.
WHAAAAAT?!

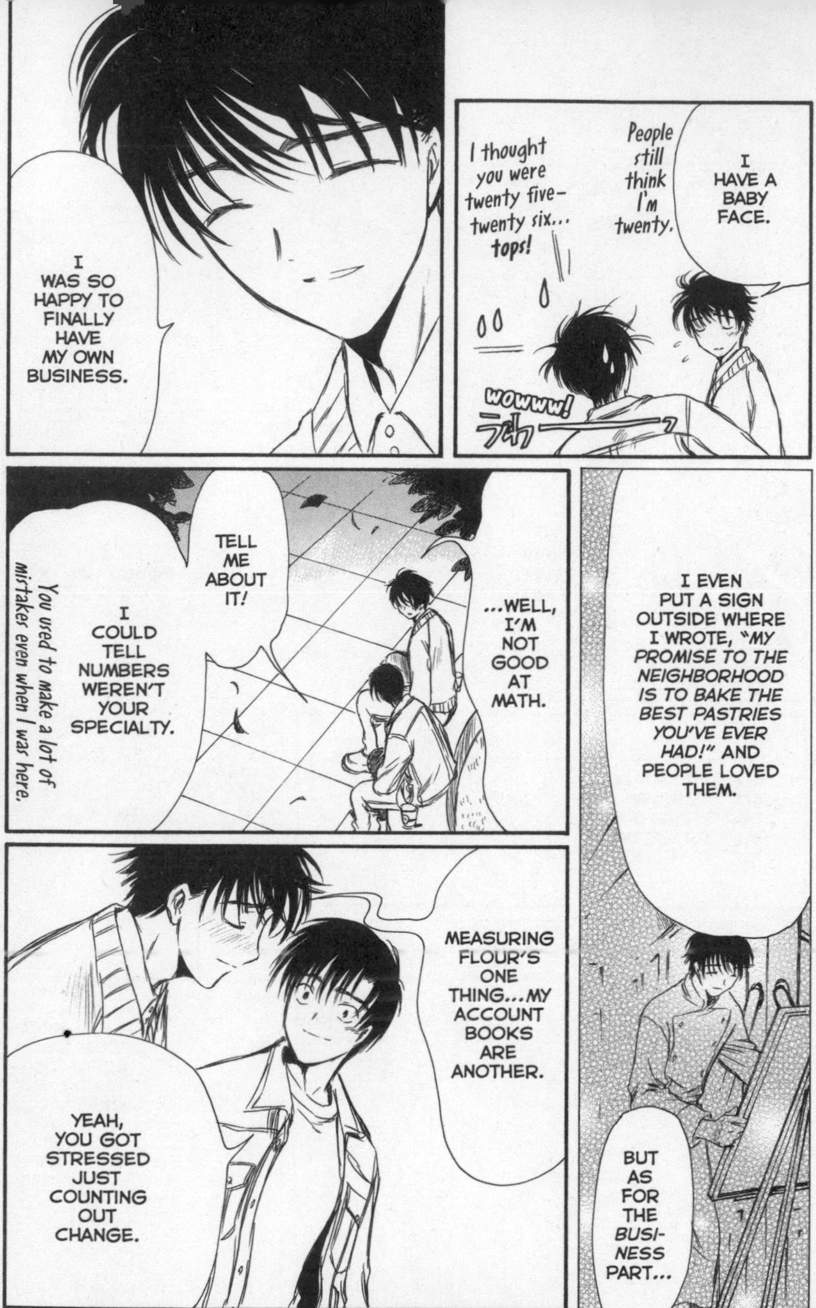
I HAVE A BABY FACE.
People still think I'm twenty.
I thought you were twenty five-twenty six... **tops!**
WOWWW!
I WAS SO HAPPY TO FINALLY HAVE MY OWN BUSINESS.
I EVEN PUT A SIGN OUTSIDE WHERE I WROTE, "*MY PROMISE TO THE NEIGHBORHOOD IS TO BAKE THE BEST PASTRIES YOU'VE EVER HAD!*" AND PEOPLE LOVED THEM.
BUT AS FOR THE *BUSINESS* PART...
...WELL, I'M NOT GOOD AT MATH.
TELL ME ABOUT IT!
I COULD TELL NUMBERS WEREN'T YOUR SPECIALTY.
You used to make a lot of mistakes even when I was here.
MEASURING FLOUR'S ONE THING... MY ACCOUNT BOOKS ARE ANOTHER.
YEAH, YOU GOT STRESSED JUST COUNTING OUT CHANGE.

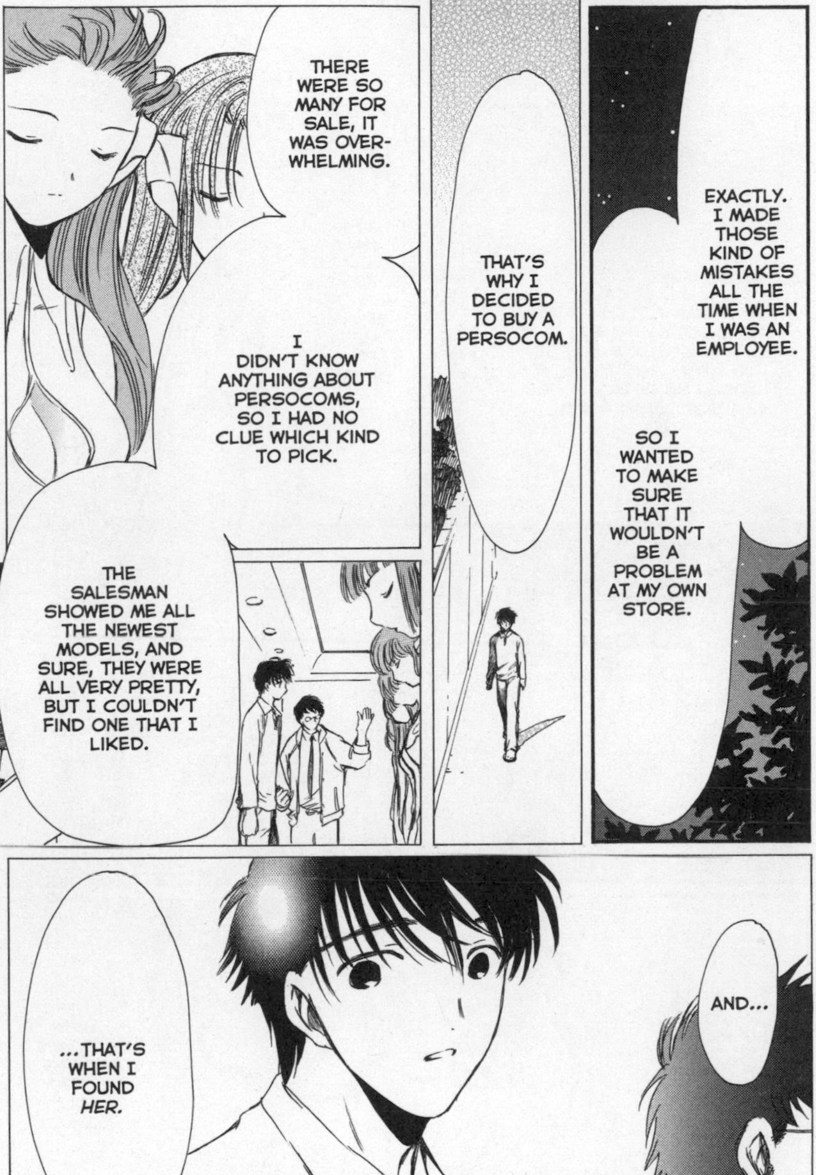

EXACTLY. I MADE THOSE KIND OF MISTAKES ALL THE TIME WHEN I WAS AN EMPLOYEE.
SO I WANTED TO MAKE SURE THAT IT WOULDN'T BE A PROBLEM AT MY OWN STORE.
THAT'S WHY I DECIDED TO BUY A PERSOCOM.
THERE WERE SO MANY FOR SALE, IT WAS OVER-WHELMING.
I DIDN'T KNOW ANYTHING ABOUT PERSOCOMS, SO I HAD NO CLUE WHICH KIND TO PICK.
THE SALESMAN SHOWED ME ALL THE NEWEST MODELS, AND SURE, THEY WERE ALL VERY PRETTY, BUT I COULDN'T FIND ONE THAT I LIKED.
AND...
...THAT'S WHEN I FOUND *HER*.

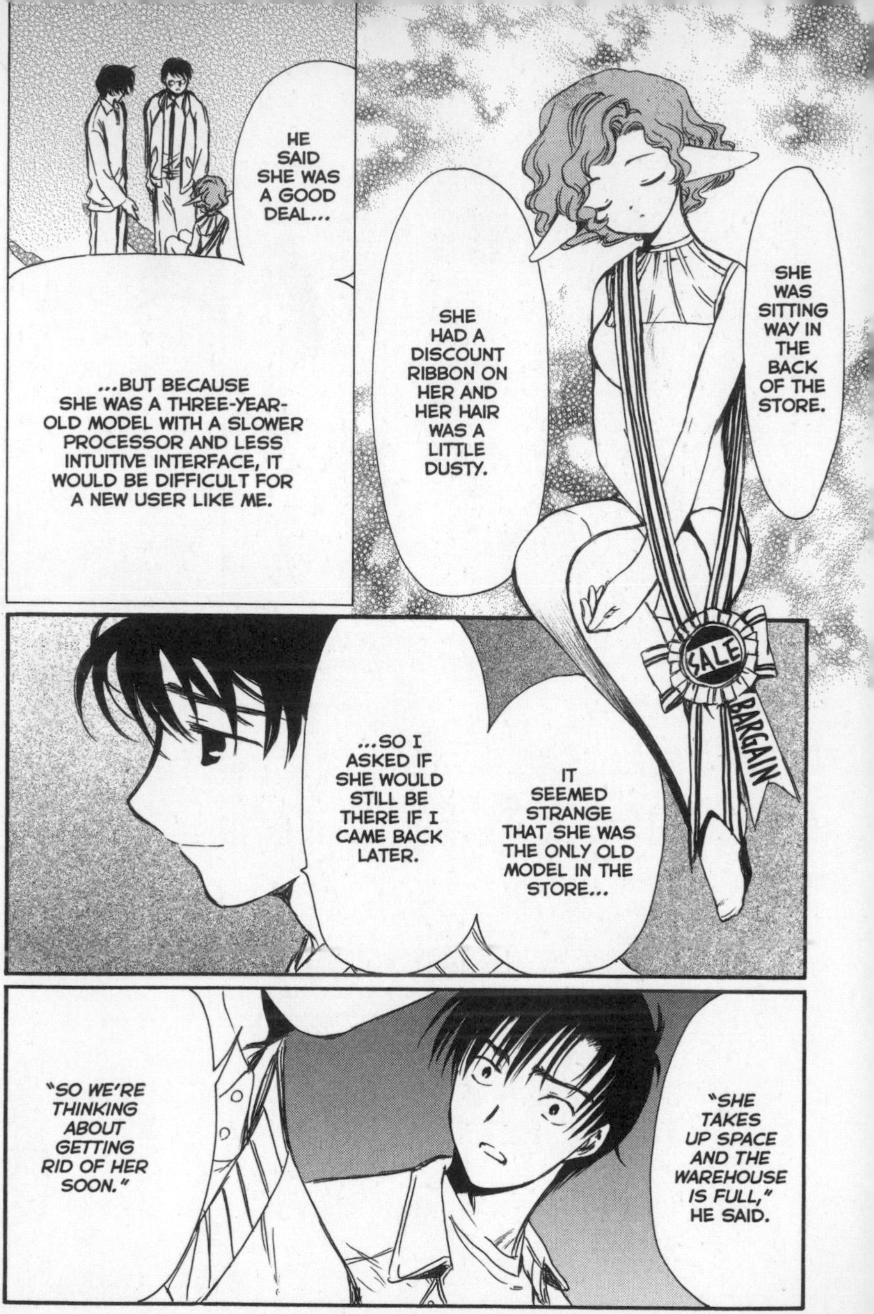
SHE WAS SITTING WAY IN THE BACK OF THE STORE.
SHE HAD A DISCOUNT RIBBON ON HER AND HER HAIR WAS A LITTLE DUSTY.
SALE
BARGAIN
HE SAID SHE WAS A GOOD DEAL...
...BUT BECAUSE SHE WAS A THREE-YEAR-OLD MODEL WITH A SLOWER PROCESSOR AND LESS INTUITIVE INTERFACE, IT WOULD BE DIFFICULT FOR A NEW USER LIKE ME.
IT SEEMED STRANGE THAT SHE WAS THE ONLY OLD MODEL IN THE STORE...
...SO I ASKED IF SHE WOULD STILL BE THERE IF I CAME BACK LATER.
"SHE TAKES UP SPACE AND THE WAREHOUSE IS FULL," HE SAID.
"SO WE'RE THINKING ABOUT GETTING RID OF HER SOON."

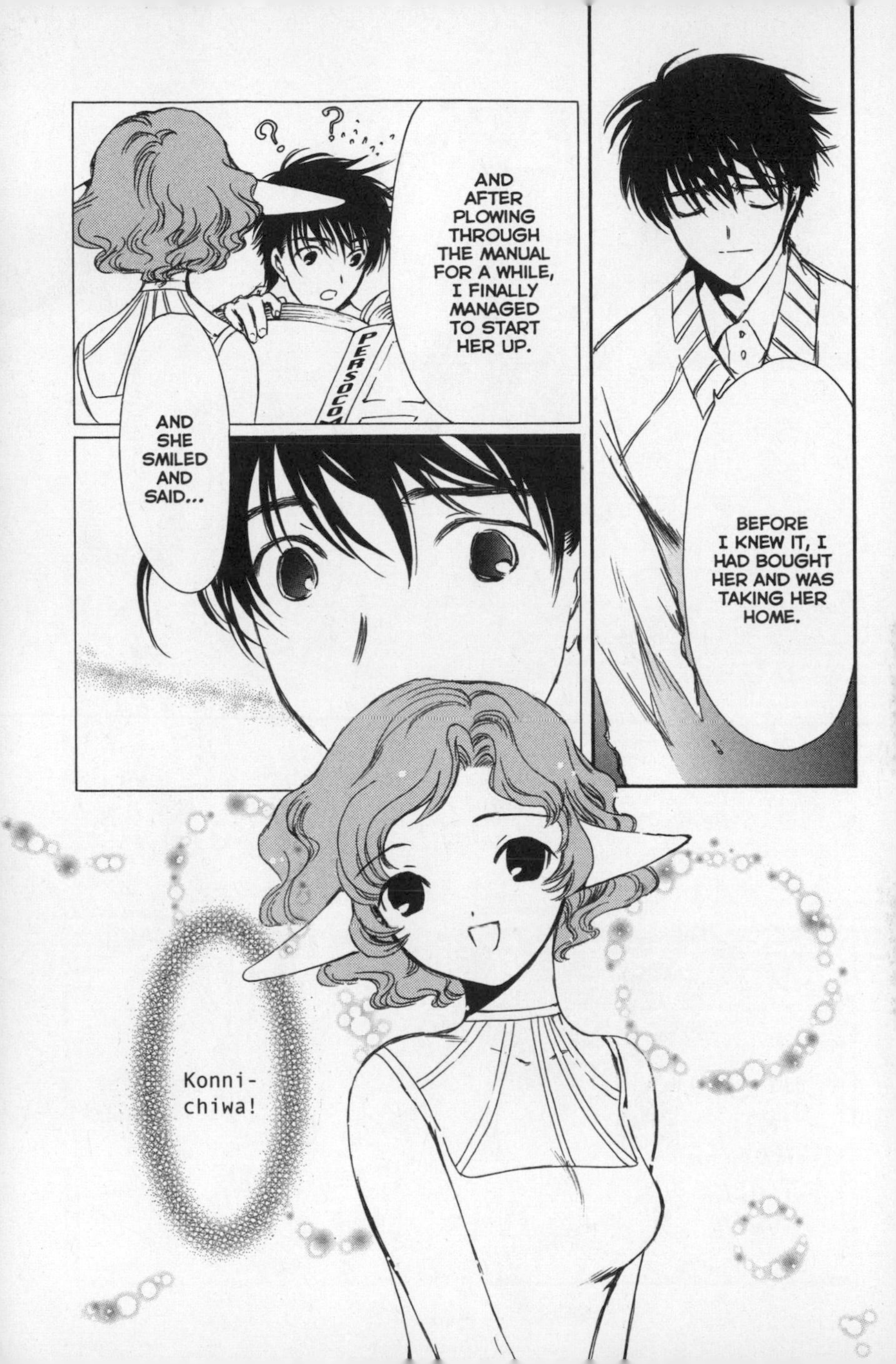
BEFORE I KNEW IT, I HAD BOUGHT HER AND WAS TAKING HER HOME.
AND AFTER PLOWING THROUGH THE MANUAL FOR A WHILE, I FINALLY MANAGED TO START HER UP.
PERSOCOM
AND SHE SMILED AND SAID...
Konni-chiwa!

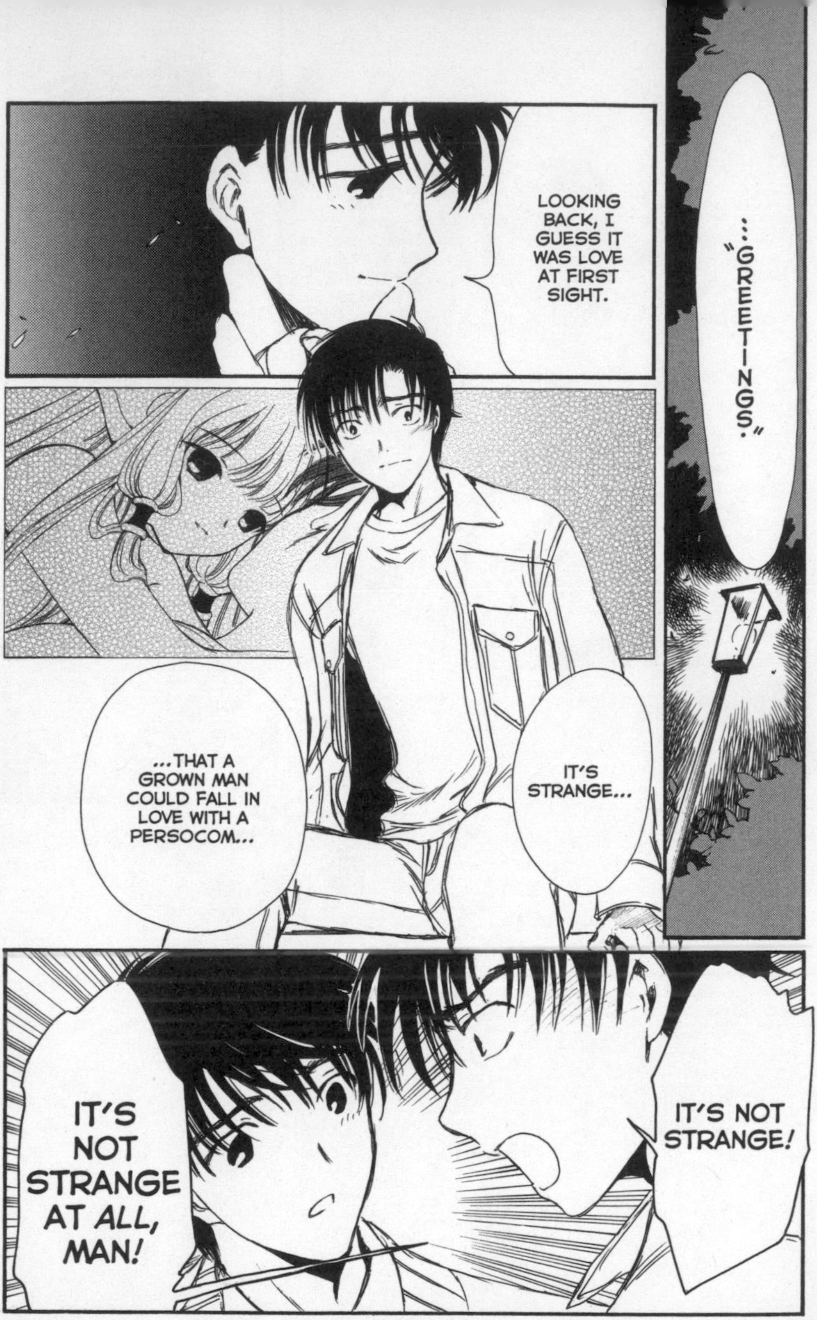

"...GREETINGS."
LOOKING BACK, I GUESS IT WAS LOVE AT FIRST SIGHT.
IT'S STRANGE...
...THAT A GROWN MAN COULD FALL IN LOVE WITH A PERSOCOM...
IT'S NOT STRANGE!
IT'S NOT STRANGE AT *ALL*, MAN!

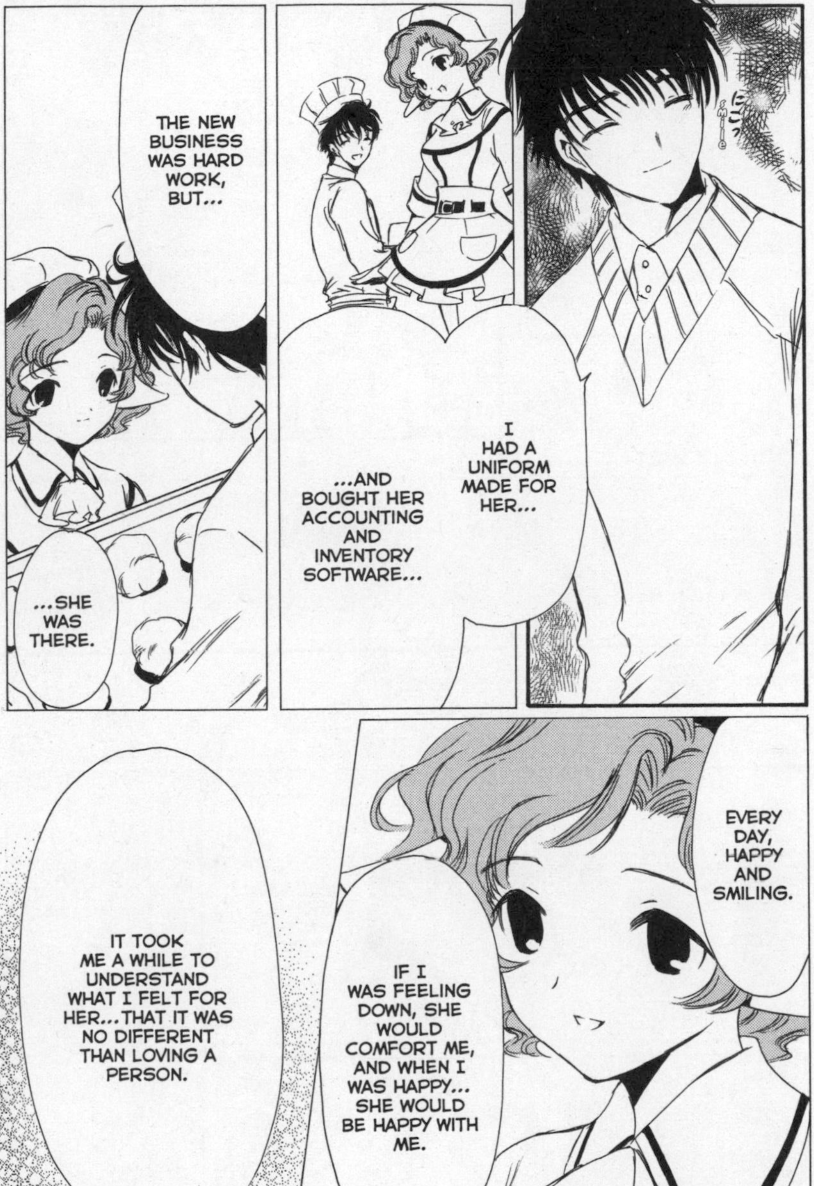
smile
I HAD A UNIFORM MADE FOR HER...
...AND BOUGHT HER ACCOUNTING AND INVENTORY SOFTWARE...
THE NEW BUSINESS WAS HARD WORK, BUT...
...SHE WAS THERE.
EVERY DAY, HAPPY AND SMILING.
IF I WAS FEELING DOWN, SHE WOULD COMFORT ME, AND WHEN I WAS HAPPY... SHE WOULD BE HAPPY WITH ME.
IT TOOK ME A WHILE TO UNDERSTAND WHAT I FELT FOR HER... THAT IT WAS NO DIFFERENT THAN LOVING A PERSON.

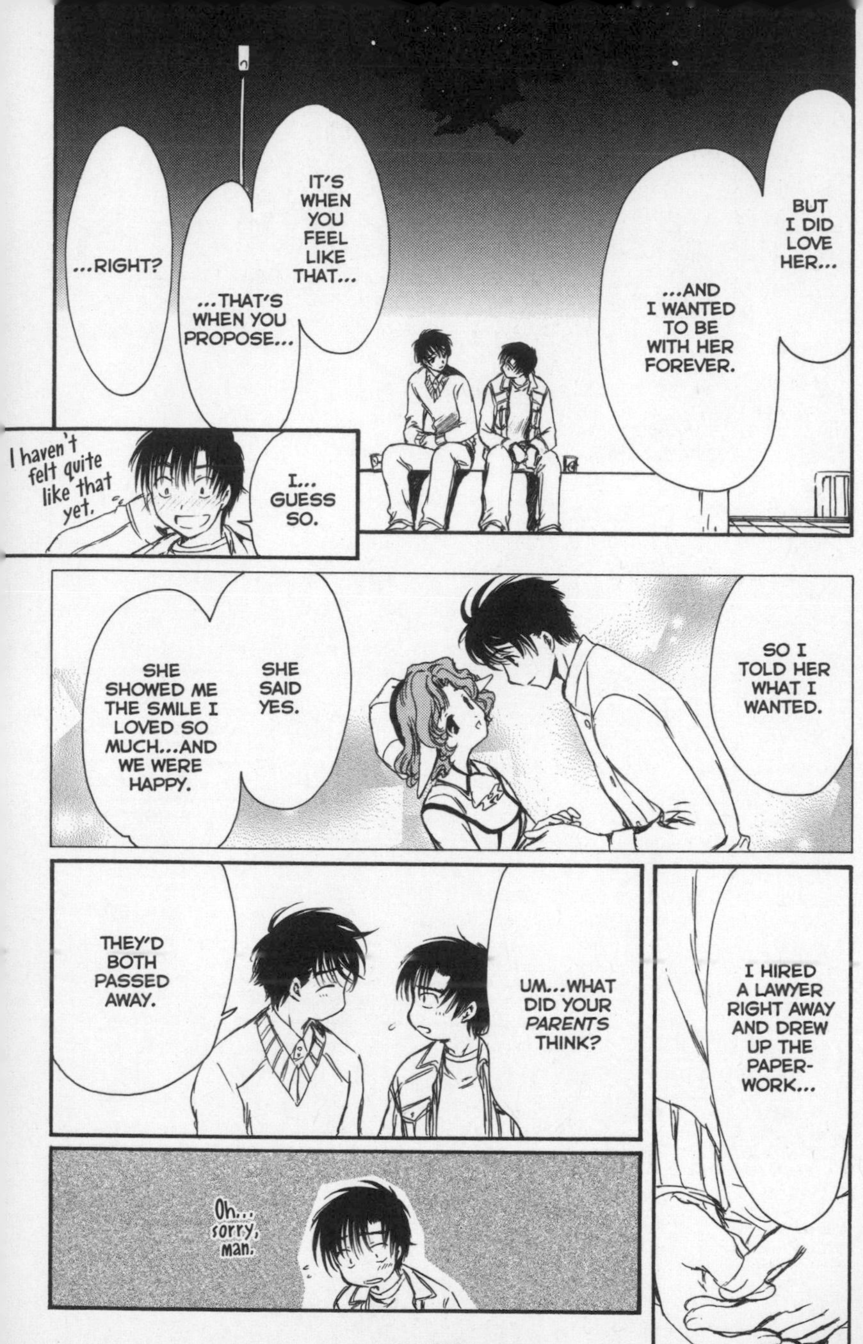
BUT I DID LOVE HER...
...AND I WANTED TO BE WITH HER FOREVER.
IT'S WHEN YOU FEEL LIKE THAT...
...THAT'S WHEN YOU PROPOSE...
...RIGHT?
I... GUESS SO.
I haven't felt quite like that yet.
SO I TOLD HER WHAT I WANTED.
SHE SAID YES.
SHE SHOWED ME THE SMILE I LOVED SO MUCH...AND WE WERE HAPPY.
I HIRED A LAWYER RIGHT AWAY AND DREW UP THE PAPER-WORK...
UM...WHAT DID YOUR *PARENTS* THINK?
THEY'D BOTH PASSED AWAY.
Oh... sorry, man.

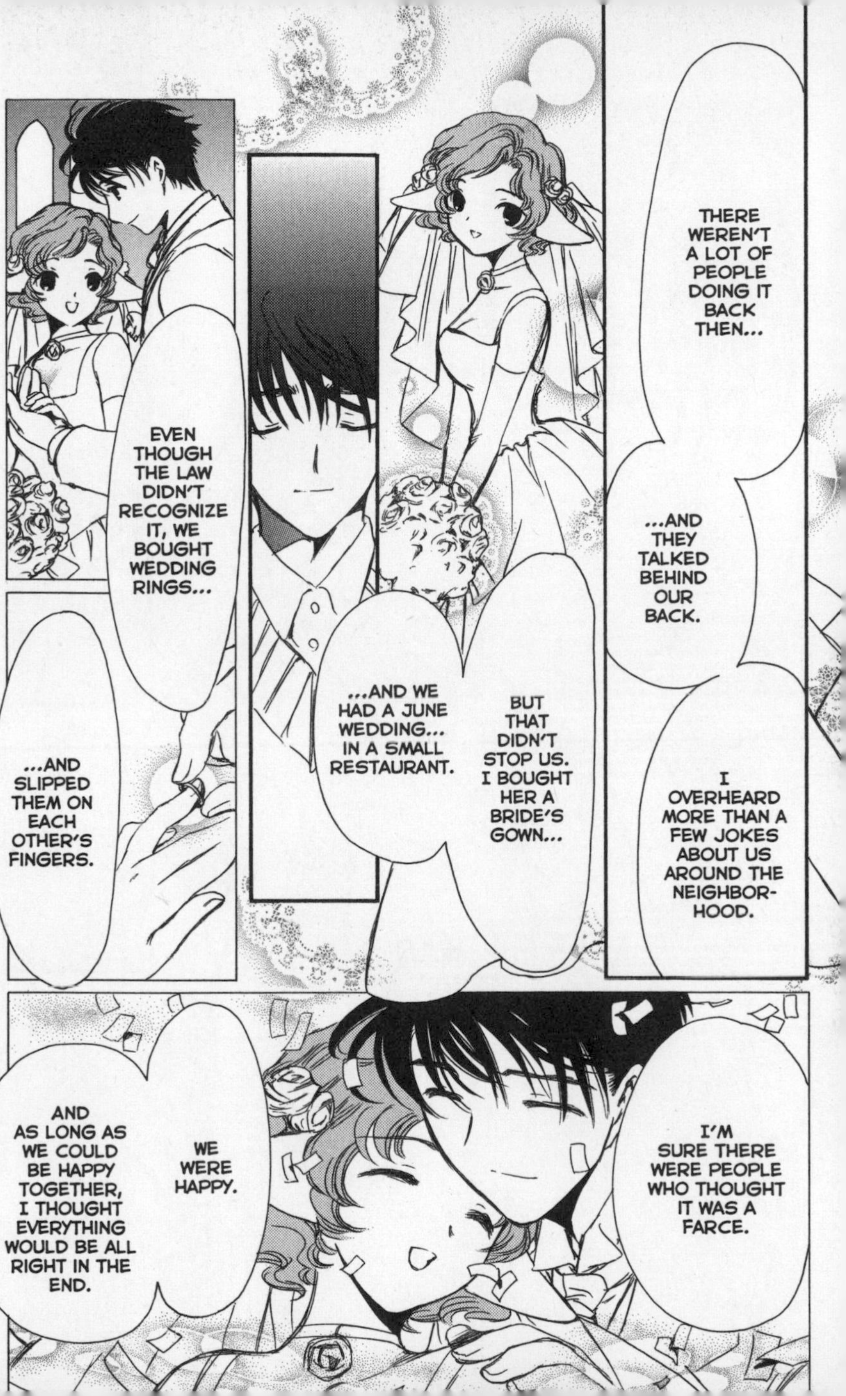
THERE WEREN'T A LOT OF PEOPLE DOING IT BACK THEN...
...AND THEY TALKED BEHIND OUR BACK.
I OVERHEARD MORE THAN A FEW JOKES ABOUT US AROUND THE NEIGHBOR-HOOD.
BUT THAT DIDN'T STOP US. I BOUGHT HER A BRIDE'S GOWN...
...AND WE HAD A JUNE WEDDING... IN A SMALL RESTAURANT.
EVEN THOUGH THE LAW DIDN'T RECOGNIZE IT, WE BOUGHT WEDDING RINGS...
...AND SLIPPED THEM ON EACH OTHER'S FINGERS.
I'M SURE THERE WERE PEOPLE WHO THOUGHT IT WAS A FARCE.
WE WERE HAPPY.
AND AS LONG AS WE COULD BE HAPPY TOGETHER, I THOUGHT EVERYTHING WOULD BE ALL RIGHT IN THE END.

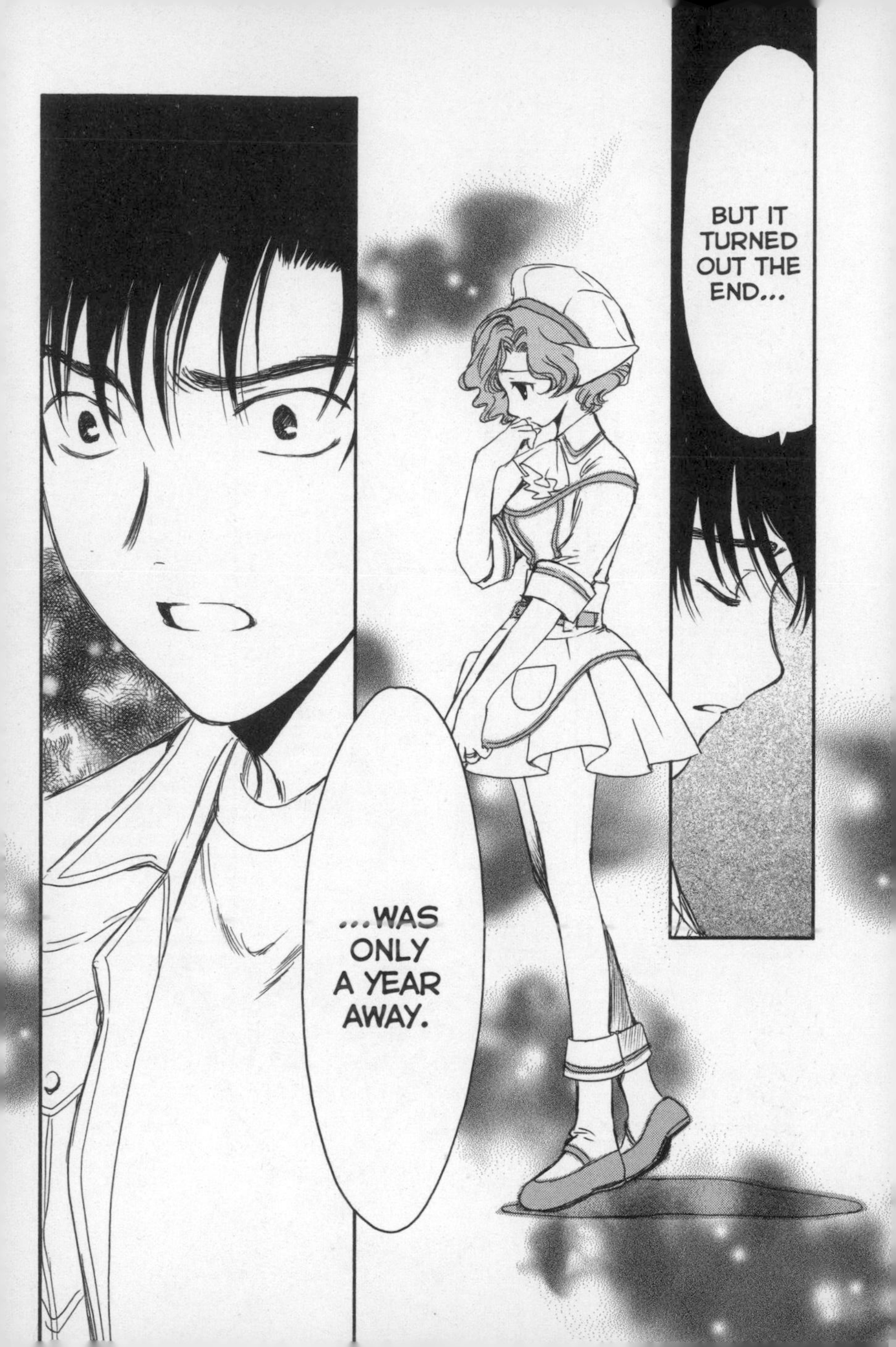
BUT IT TURNED OUT THE END...
...WAS ONLY A YEAR AWAY.

Chobits
ちょびっツ

◀ **chapter 48** ▶

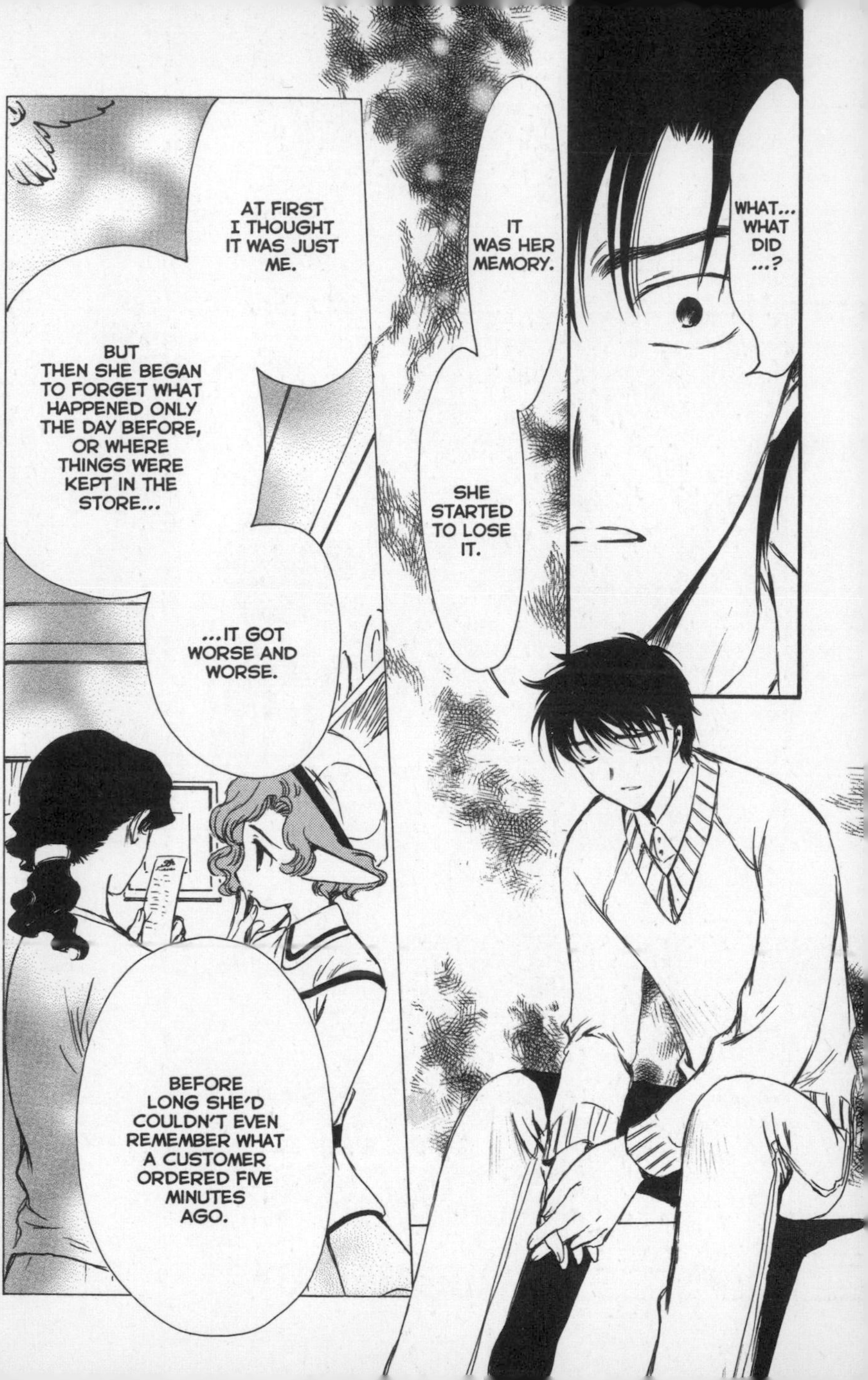
WHAT... WHAT DID ...?
IT WAS HER MEMORY.
SHE STARTED TO LOSE IT.
AT FIRST I THOUGHT IT WAS JUST ME.
BUT THEN SHE BEGAN TO FORGET WHAT HAPPENED ONLY THE DAY BEFORE, OR WHERE THINGS WERE KEPT IN THE STORE...
...IT GOT WORSE AND WORSE.
BEFORE LONG SHE'D COULDN'T EVEN REMEMBER WHAT A CUSTOMER ORDERED FIVE MINUTES AGO.

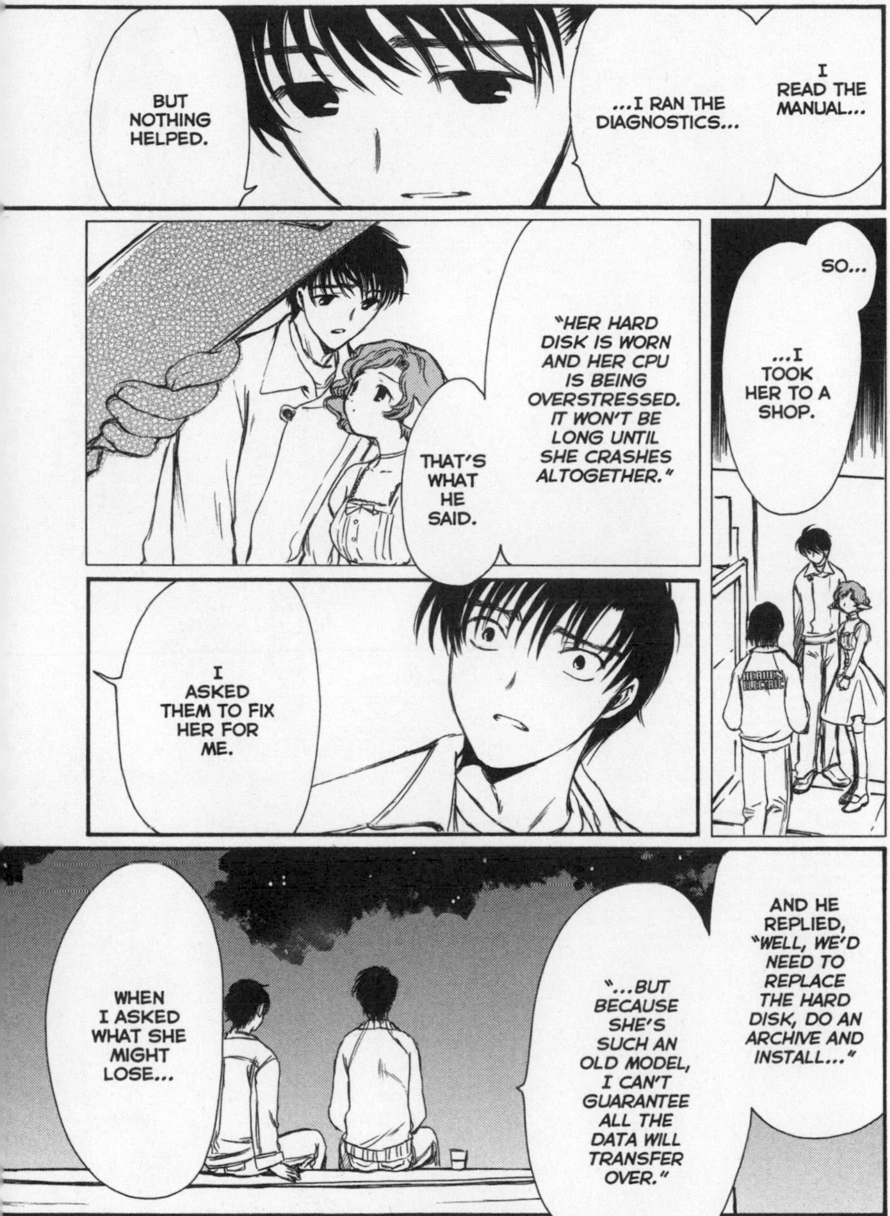
I READ THE MANUAL...
...I RAN THE DIAGNOSTICS...
BUT NOTHING HELPED.
SO...
...I TOOK HER TO A SHOP.
"HER HARD DISK IS WORN AND HER CPU IS BEING OVERSTRESSED. IT WON'T BE LONG UNTIL SHE CRASHES ALTOGETHER."
THAT'S WHAT HE SAID.
I ASKED THEM TO FIX HER FOR ME.
AND HE REPLIED, "WELL, WE'D NEED TO REPLACE THE HARD DISK, DO AN ARCHIVE AND INSTALL..."
"...BUT BECAUSE SHE'S SUCH AN OLD MODEL, I CAN'T GUARANTEE ALL THE DATA WILL TRANSFER OVER."
WHEN I ASKED WHAT SHE MIGHT LOSE...

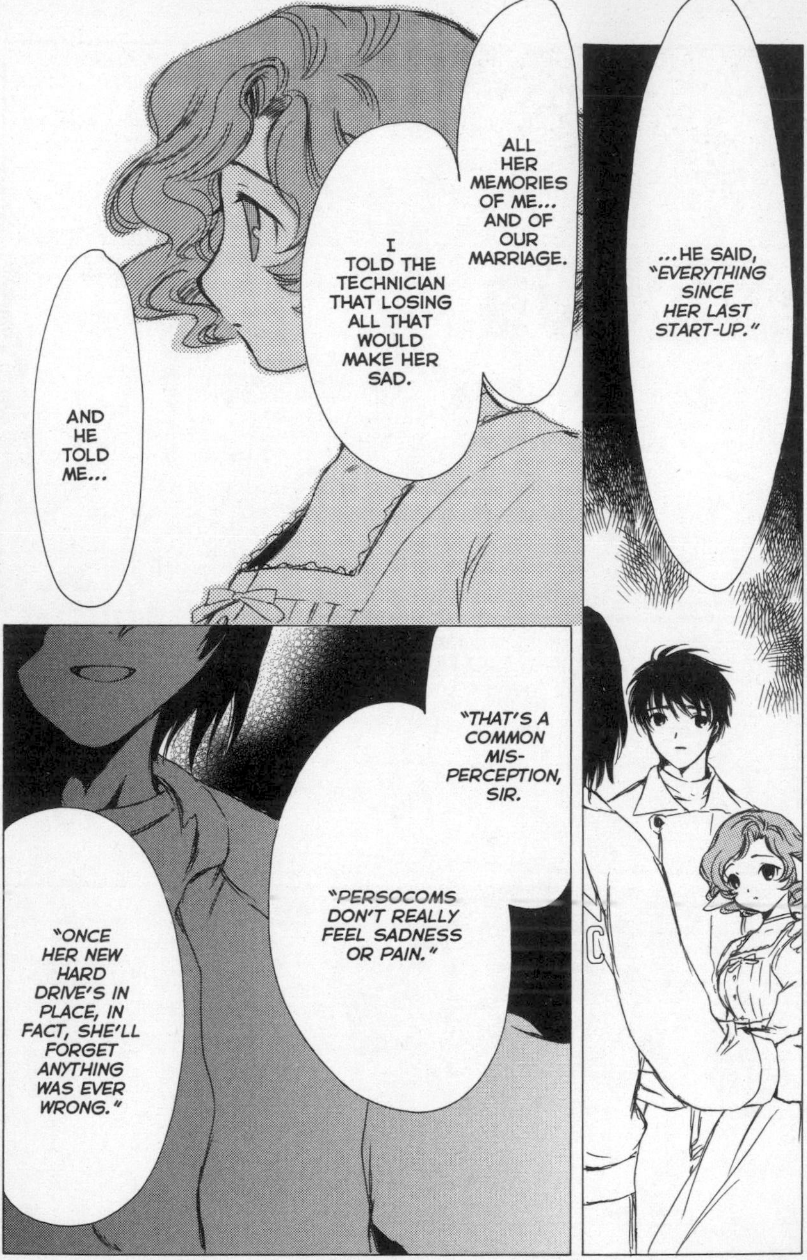
...HE SAID, "EVERYTHING SINCE HER LAST START-UP."
ALL HER MEMORIES OF ME... AND OF OUR MARRIAGE.
I TOLD THE TECHNICIAN THAT LOSING ALL THAT WOULD MAKE HER SAD.
AND HE TOLD ME...
"THAT'S A COMMON MIS-PERCEPTION, SIR.
"PERSOCOMS DON'T REALLY FEEL SADNESS OR PAIN."
"ONCE HER NEW HARD DRIVE'S IN PLACE, IN FACT, SHE'LL FORGET ANYTHING WAS EVER WRONG."

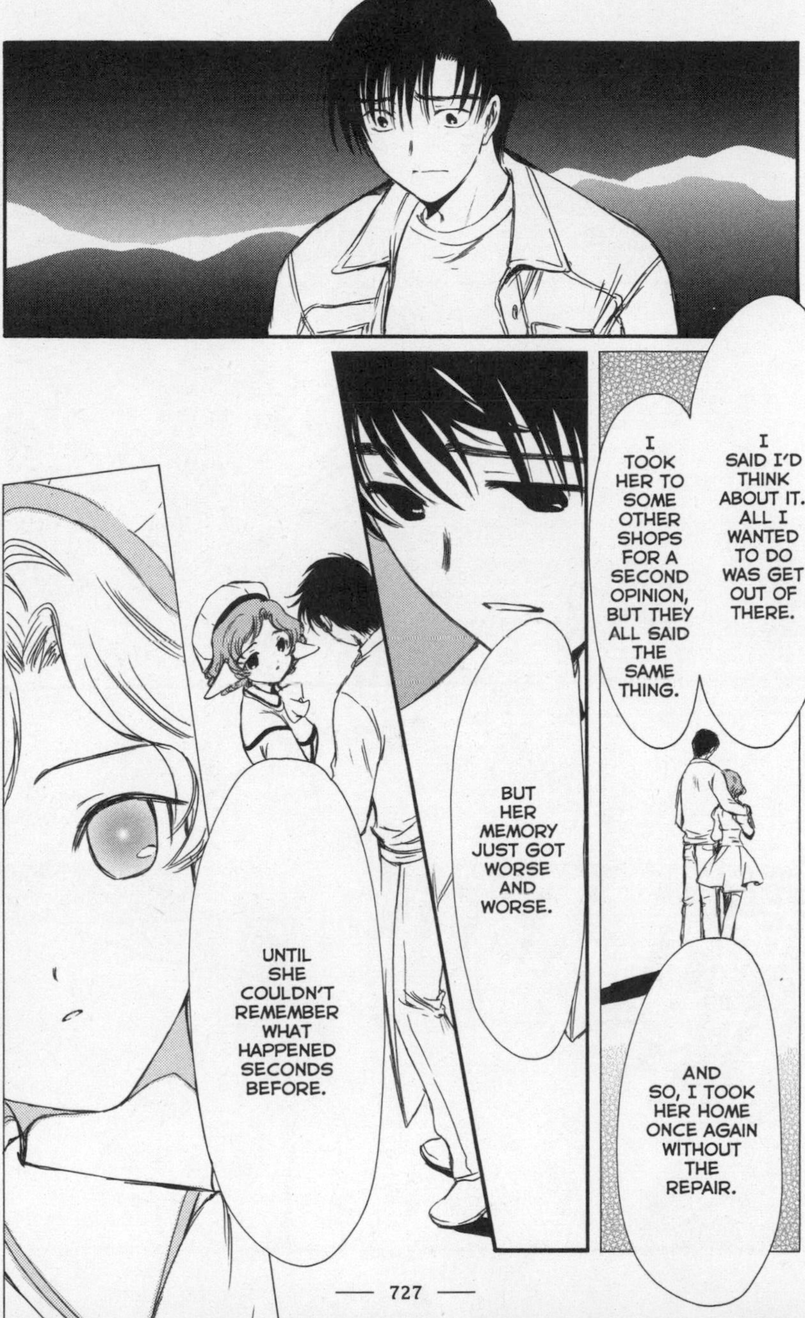
I SAID I'D THINK ABOUT IT. ALL I WANTED TO DO WAS GET OUT OF THERE.
I TOOK HER TO SOME OTHER SHOPS FOR A SECOND OPINION, BUT THEY ALL SAID THE SAME THING.
BUT HER MEMORY JUST GOT WORSE AND WORSE.
UNTIL SHE COULDN'T REMEMBER WHAT HAPPENED SECONDS BEFORE.
AND SO, I TOOK HER HOME ONCE AGAIN WITHOUT THE REPAIR.

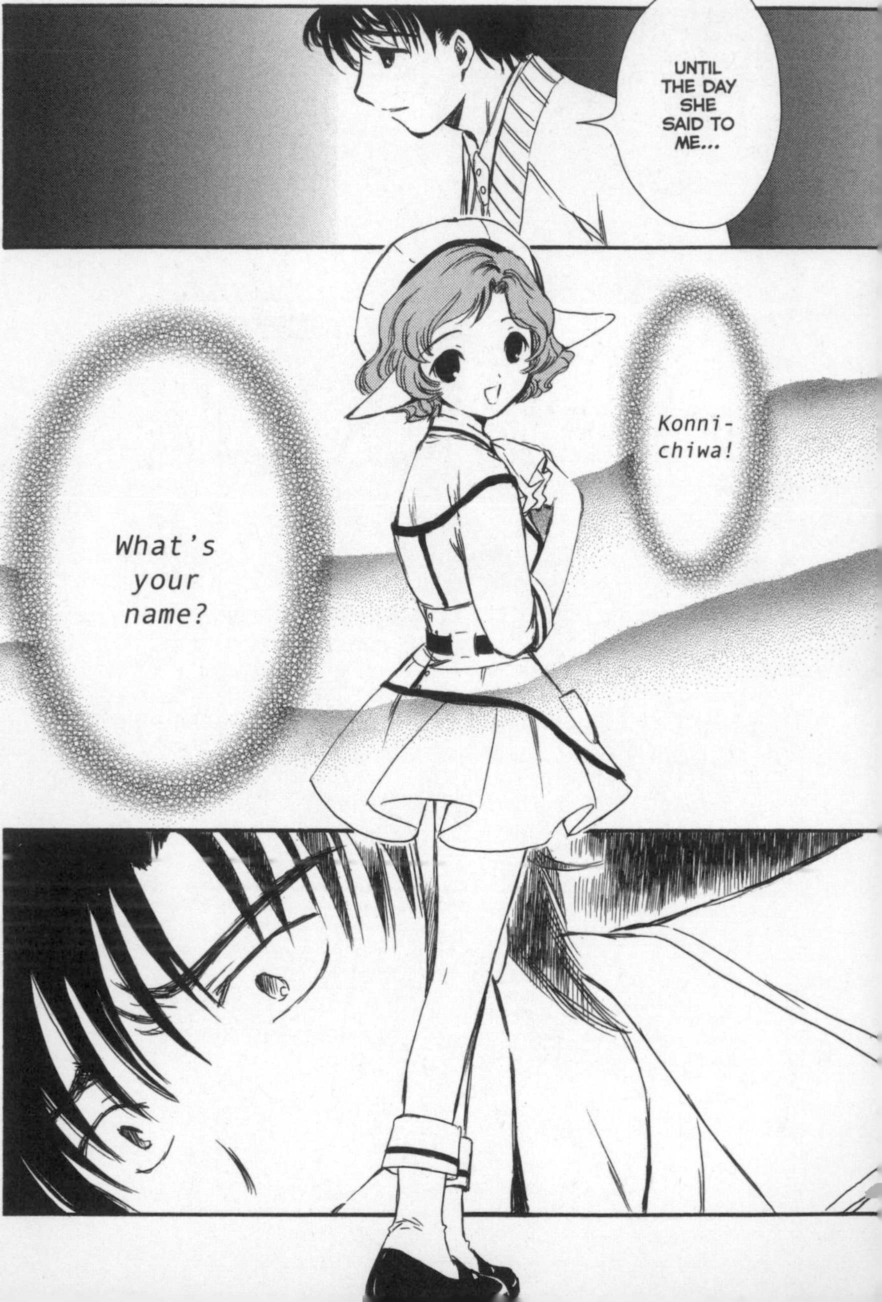
UNTIL THE DAY SHE SAID TO ME...
Konni-chiwa!
What's your name?

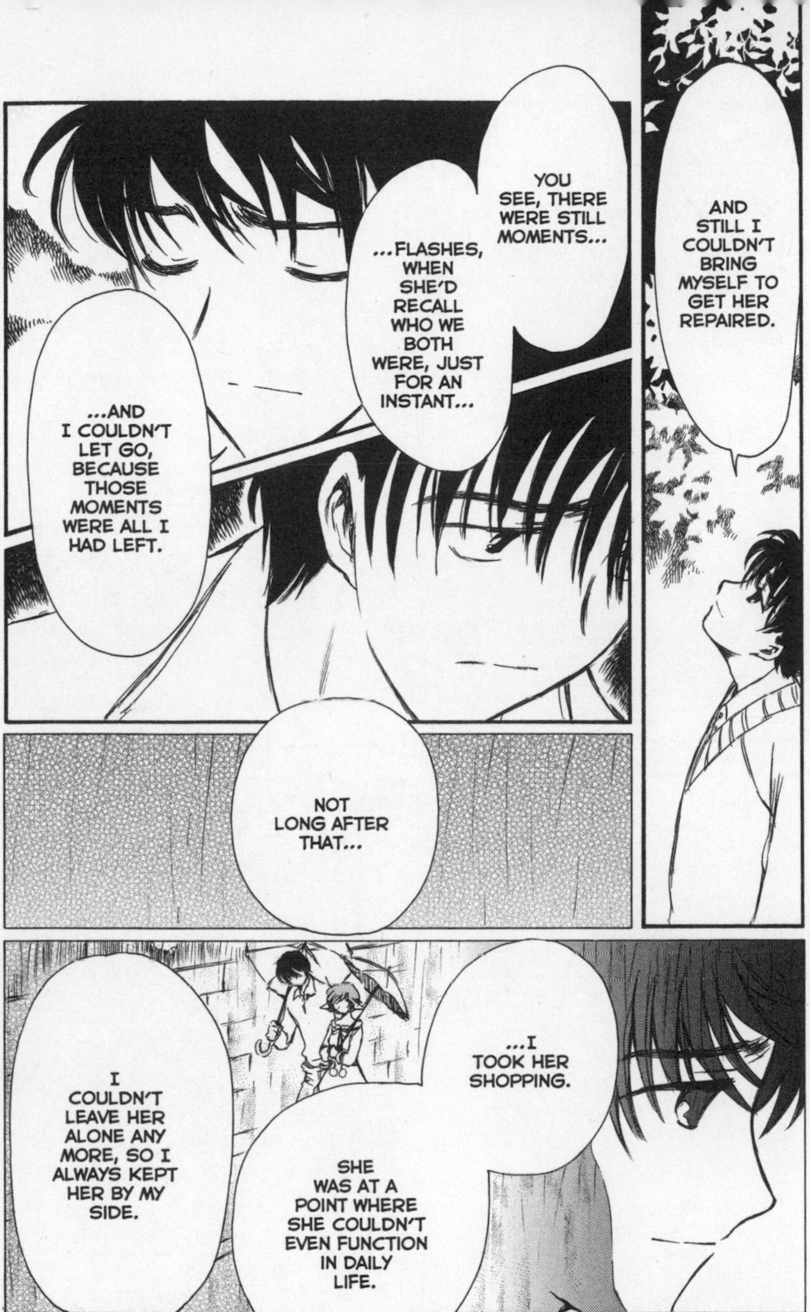
AND STILL I COULDN'T BRING MYSELF TO GET HER REPAIRED.
YOU SEE, THERE WERE STILL MOMENTS...
...FLASHES, WHEN SHE'D RECALL WHO WE BOTH WERE, JUST FOR AN INSTANT...
...AND I COULDN'T LET GO, BECAUSE THOSE MOMENTS WERE ALL I HAD LEFT.
NOT LONG AFTER THAT...
...I TOOK HER SHOPPING.
SHE WAS AT A POINT WHERE SHE COULDN'T EVEN FUNCTION IN DAILY LIFE.
I COULDN'T LEAVE HER ALONE ANY MORE, SO I ALWAYS KEPT HER BY MY SIDE.

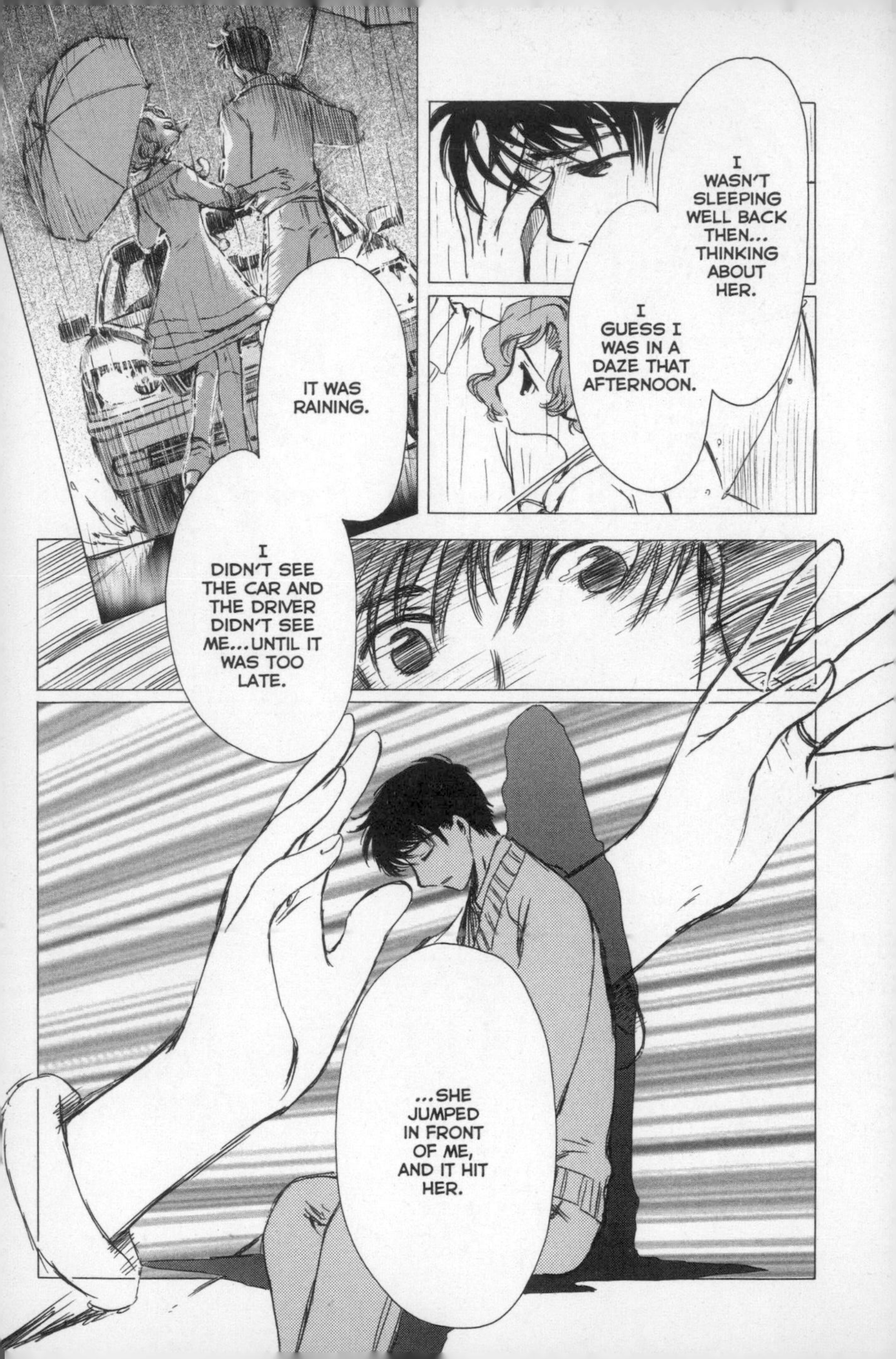
I WASN'T SLEEPING WELL BACK THEN... THINKING ABOUT HER.
I GUESS I WAS IN A DAZE THAT AFTERNOON.
IT WAS RAINING.
I DIDN'T SEE THE CAR AND THE DRIVER DIDN'T SEE ME...UNTIL IT WAS TOO LATE.
...SHE JUMPED IN FRONT OF ME, AND IT HIT HER.

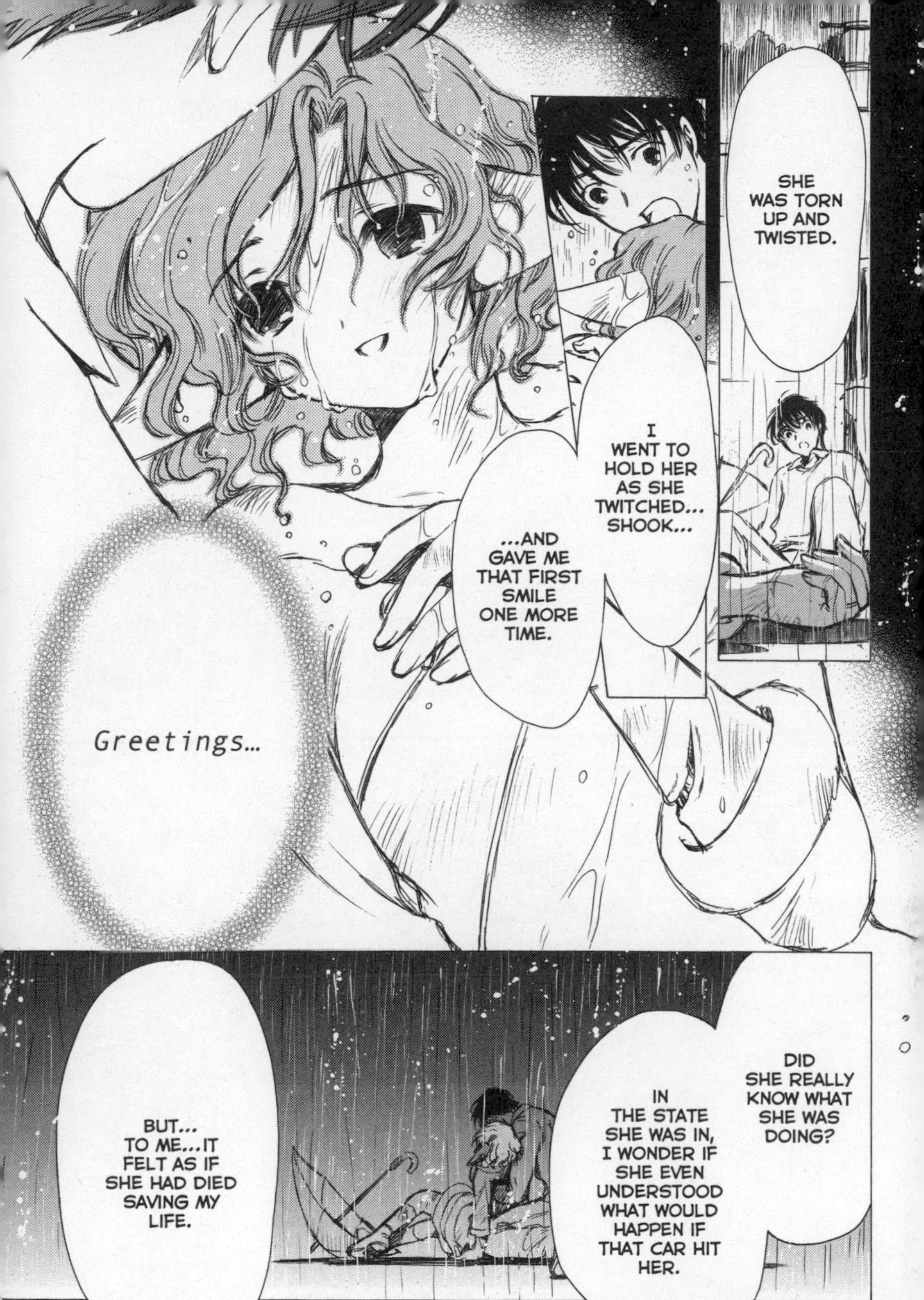
SHE WAS TORN UP AND TWISTED.
I WENT TO HOLD HER AS SHE TWITCHED... SHOOK...
...AND GAVE ME THAT FIRST SMILE ONE MORE TIME.
Greetings...
DID SHE REALLY KNOW WHAT SHE WAS DOING?
IN THE STATE SHE WAS IN, I WONDER IF SHE EVEN UNDERSTOOD WHAT WOULD HAPPEN IF THAT CAR HIT HER.
BUT... TO ME...IT FELT AS IF SHE HAD DIED SAVING MY LIFE.

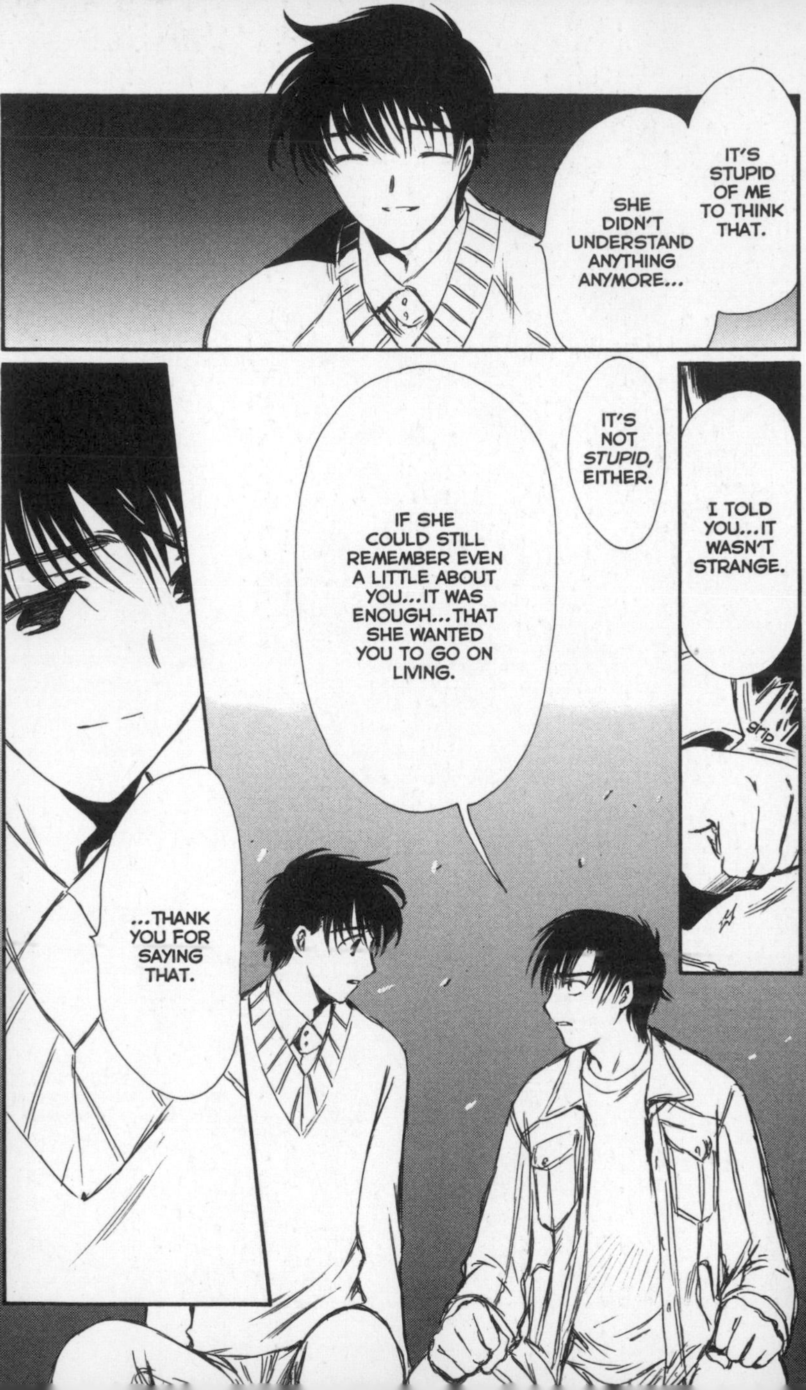
IT'S STUPID OF ME TO THINK THAT.
SHE DIDN'T UNDERSTAND ANYTHING ANYMORE...
I TOLD YOU...IT WASN'T STRANGE.
grip
IT'S NOT *STUPID*, EITHER.
IF SHE COULD STILL REMEMBER EVEN A LITTLE ABOUT YOU...IT WAS ENOUGH...THAT SHE WANTED YOU TO GO ON LIVING.
...THANK YOU FOR SAYING THAT.

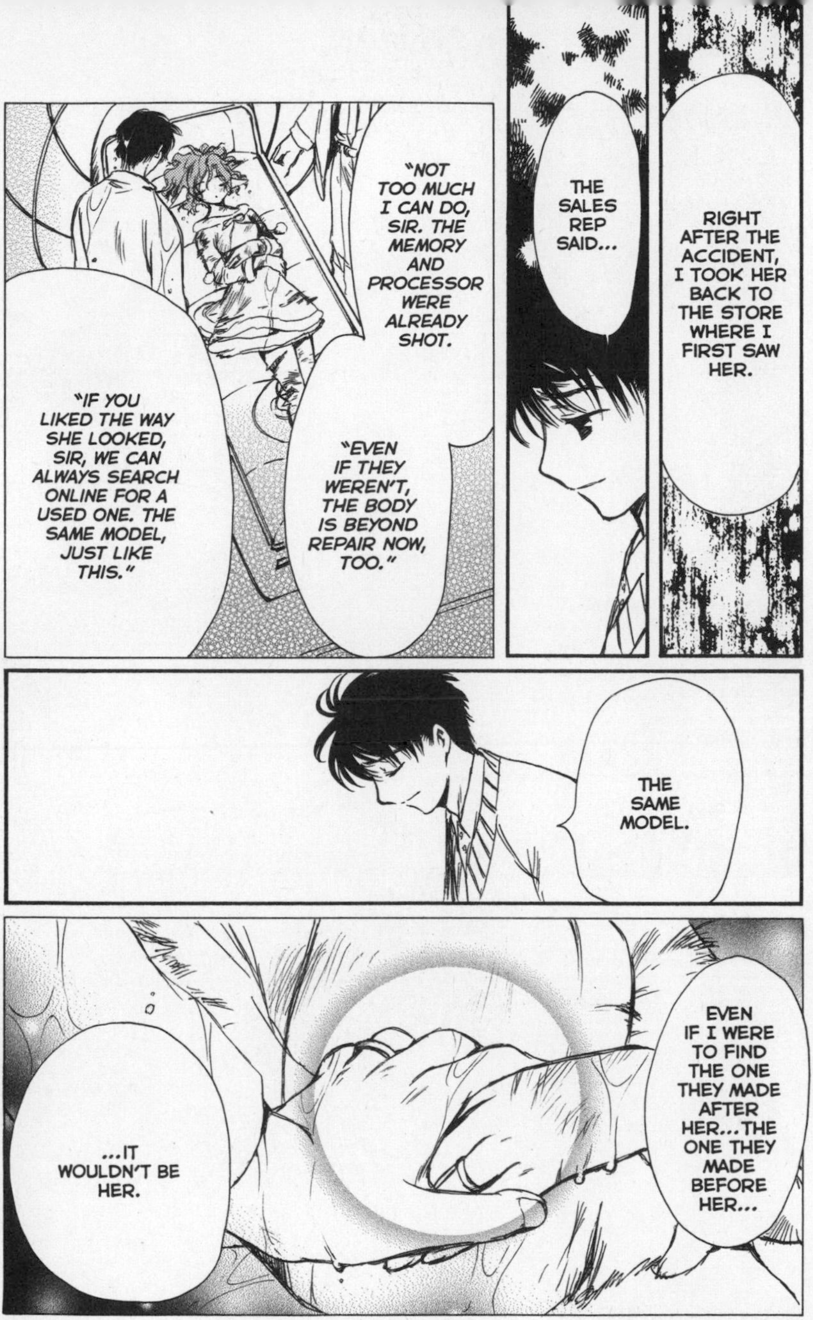
RIGHT AFTER THE ACCIDENT, I TOOK HER BACK TO THE STORE WHERE I FIRST SAW HER.
THE SALES REP SAID...
"NOT TOO MUCH I CAN DO, SIR. THE MEMORY AND PROCESSOR WERE ALREADY SHOT.
"EVEN IF THEY WEREN'T, THE BODY IS BEYOND REPAIR NOW, TOO."
"IF YOU LIKED THE WAY SHE LOOKED, SIR, WE CAN ALWAYS SEARCH ONLINE FOR A USED ONE. THE SAME MODEL, JUST LIKE THIS."
THE SAME MODEL.
EVEN IF I WERE TO FIND THE ONE THEY MADE AFTER HER...THE ONE THEY MADE BEFORE HER...
...IT WOULDN'T BE HER.

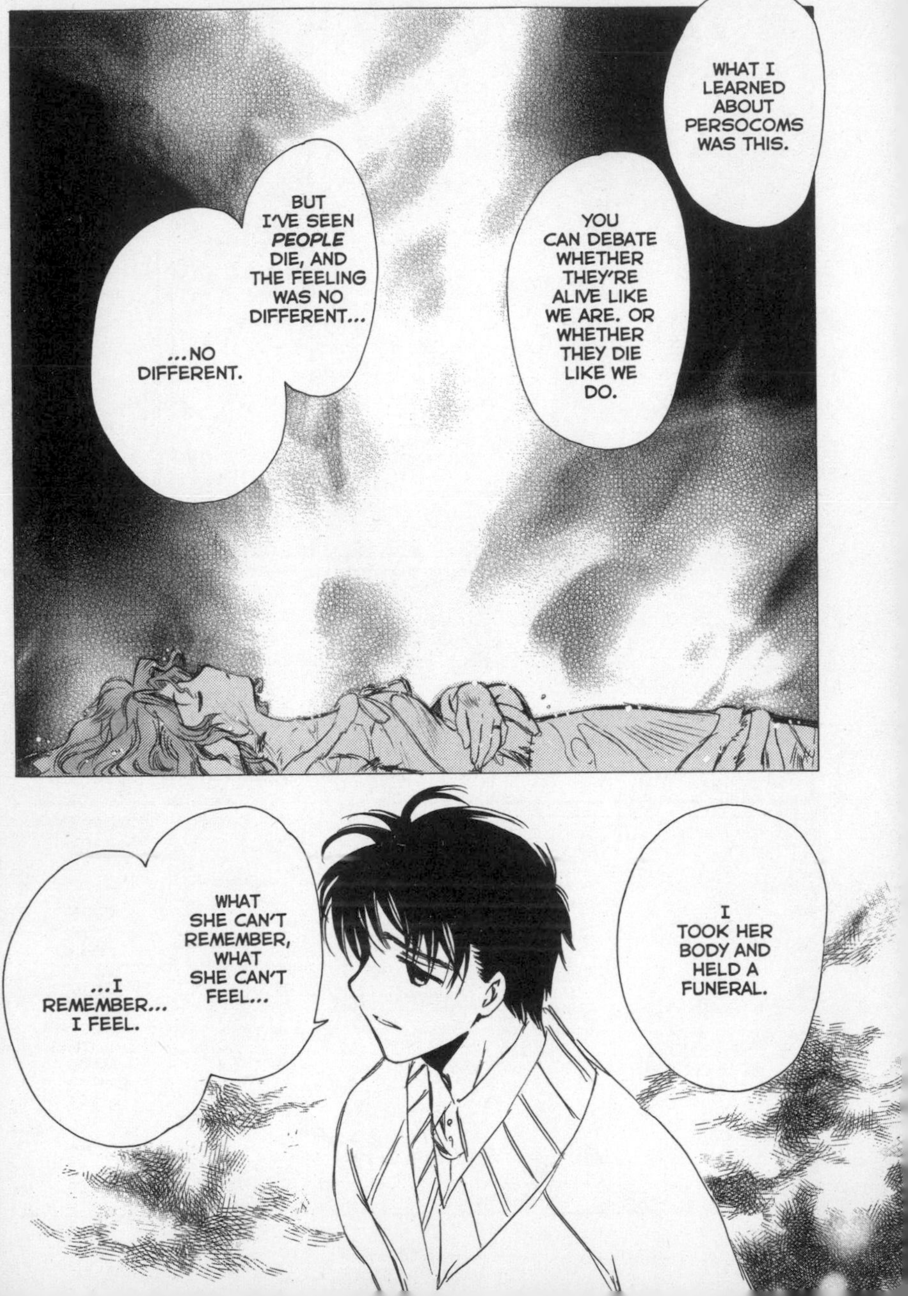
WHAT I LEARNED ABOUT PERSOCOMS WAS THIS.
YOU CAN DEBATE WHETHER THEY'RE ALIVE LIKE WE ARE. OR WHETHER THEY DIE LIKE WE DO.
BUT I'VE SEEN *PEOPLE* DIE, AND THE FEELING WAS NO DIFFERENT...
...NO DIFFERENT.
I TOOK HER BODY AND HELD A FUNERAL.
WHAT SHE CAN'T REMEMBER, WHAT SHE CAN'T FEEL...
...I REMEMBER... I FEEL.

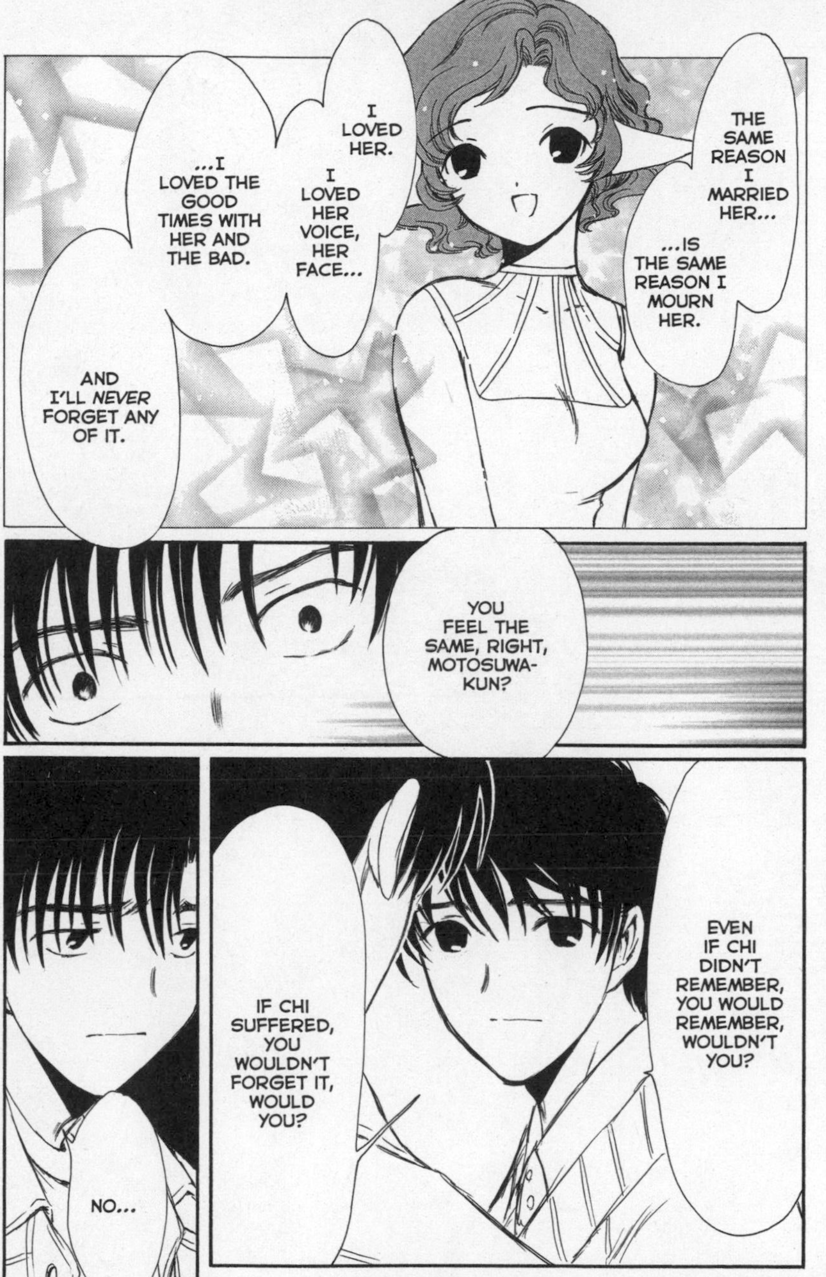
THE SAME REASON I MARRIED HER...
...IS THE SAME REASON I MOURN HER.
I LOVED HER.
I LOVED HER VOICE, HER FACE...
...I LOVED THE GOOD TIMES WITH HER AND THE BAD.
AND I'LL *NEVER* FORGET ANY OF IT.
YOU FEEL THE SAME, RIGHT, MOTOSUWA-KUN?
EVEN IF CHI DIDN'T REMEMBER, YOU WOULD REMEMBER, WOULDN'T YOU?
IF CHI SUFFERED, YOU WOULDN'T FORGET IT, WOULD YOU?
NO...

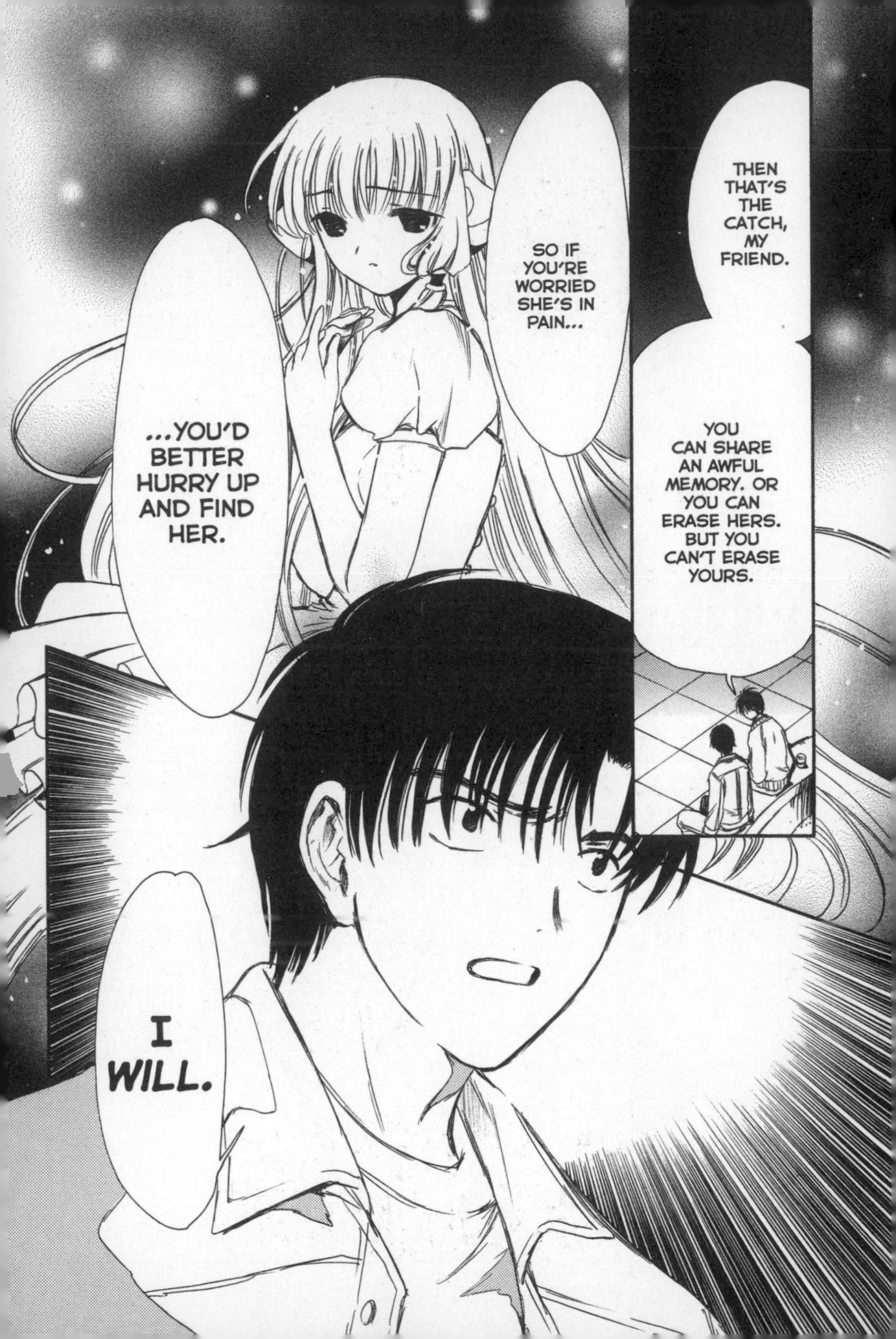
THEN THAT'S THE CATCH, MY FRIEND.
YOU CAN SHARE AN AWFUL MEMORY. OR YOU CAN ERASE HERS. BUT YOU CAN'T ERASE YOURS.
SO IF YOU'RE WORRIED SHE'S IN PAIN...
...YOU'D BETTER HURRY UP AND FIND HER.
I WILL.

IN *CHOBITS* BOOK 2!

As Hideki searches for the kid-napped Chi, he begins to think about what might be happening to her. He could erase her memories of it . . . but won't the memory still be real to him? And if *A City With No People* is really about his relationship with Chi . . . then who's writing the story? The conclusion of the *Chobits* saga is in book 2!

story+art **CLAMP**

SATSUKI IGARASHI
MOKONA
TSUBAKI NEKOI
NANASE OHKAWA

editor **CARL GUSTAV HORN**

original translation by **SHIRLEY KUBO**

lettering and retouch by **JOHN CLARK**

editorial assistant **ANNIE GULLION**

special thanks to **MICHAEL GOMBOS, KIYOKAZU FUJIMOTO, YOSHIE YOKOI,**

TERESA GRESHAM, and JAKE FORBES

designer **TINA ALESSI**

publisher **MIKE RICHARDSON**

English-language version produced by Dark Horse Comics

CHOBITS Book 1

© 2010 CLAMP. All rights reserved. Publication rights for this English edition arranged through Pyrotechnist, Ltd. All rights reserved. No portion of this publication may be reproduced or transmitted, in any form or by any means, without the express written permission of Dark Horse Comics, Inc. Names, characters, places, and incidents featured in this publication either are the product of the author's imagination or are used fictitiously. Any resemblance to actual persons (living or dead), events, institutions, or locales, without satiric intent, is coincidental. Dark Horse Manga™ is a trademark of Dark Horse Comics, Inc. All rights reserved.

Published by Dark Horse Manga, a division of Dark Horse Comics, Inc.
10956 SE Main Street | Milwaukie, OR 97222 | DarkHorse.com

To find a comics shop in your area, call the Comic Shop Locator Service toll-free at 1-888-266-4226.

First edition: March 2010
ISBN 978-1-59582-451-6

10 9 8 7 6
Printed in the United States of America

MIKE RICHARDSON President and Publisher NEIL HANKERSON Executive Vice President TOM WEDDLE Chief Financial Officer RANDY STRADLEY Vice President of Publishing MICHAEL MARTENS Vice President of Business Development ANITA NELSON Vice President of Marketing, Sales, and Licensing DAVID SCROGGY Vice President of Product Development DALE LAFOUNTAIN Vice President of Information Technology DARLENE VOGEL Director of Purchasing KEN LIZZI General Counsel DAVEY ESTRADA Editorial Director SCOTT ALLIE Senior Managing Editor CHRIS WARNER Senior Books Editor DIANA SCHUTZ Executive Editor CARY GRAZZINI Director of Design and Production LIA RIBACCHI Art Director CARA NIECE Director of Scheduling

A WORD ABOUT THE DIFFERENT DIALOGUE FONTS USED IN *CHOBITS*

In this omnibus edition of *Chobits*, rather than use the same font for all dialogue, we have done our best to examine the original Japanese edition of *Chobits* and take notice as to where and when CLAMP used different fonts for different characters, and then reflect those differences in this English-language edition.

For example, CLAMP had persocoms such as Chi and Sumomo speak in a distinct and more angular font, reflecting their machine nature (this font, by the way, is Andale Mono, and its use here was inspired by its appearance in the character profiles for the 2003 *Chobits Fan Book*). However, in the original Japanese, Yuzuki speaks in the same font as regular human beings do, which seems to reflect Minoru's attempt to make her as much like his idea of his late sister as possible (and perhaps, his skill as a programmer). Note that Sumomo sometimes speaks in "human" font when she's reading a person's message aloud.

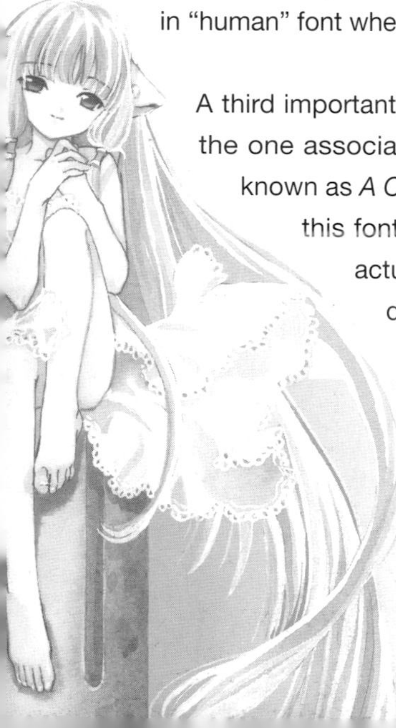

A third important font besides "persocom" and "human" is the one associated with the mysterious series of books known as *A City With No People*. You will recognize that this font appears not only when these books are actually being read, but also sometimes in the dreams and visions of the characters.

On the next six pages, please enjoy an extra bonus gallery of color Chobits *images, to go with the nine other bonus images elsewhere in book 1. And if fifteen isn't enough, we promise you over* forty pages *of bonus color in* Chobits *Book 2! See you then!*

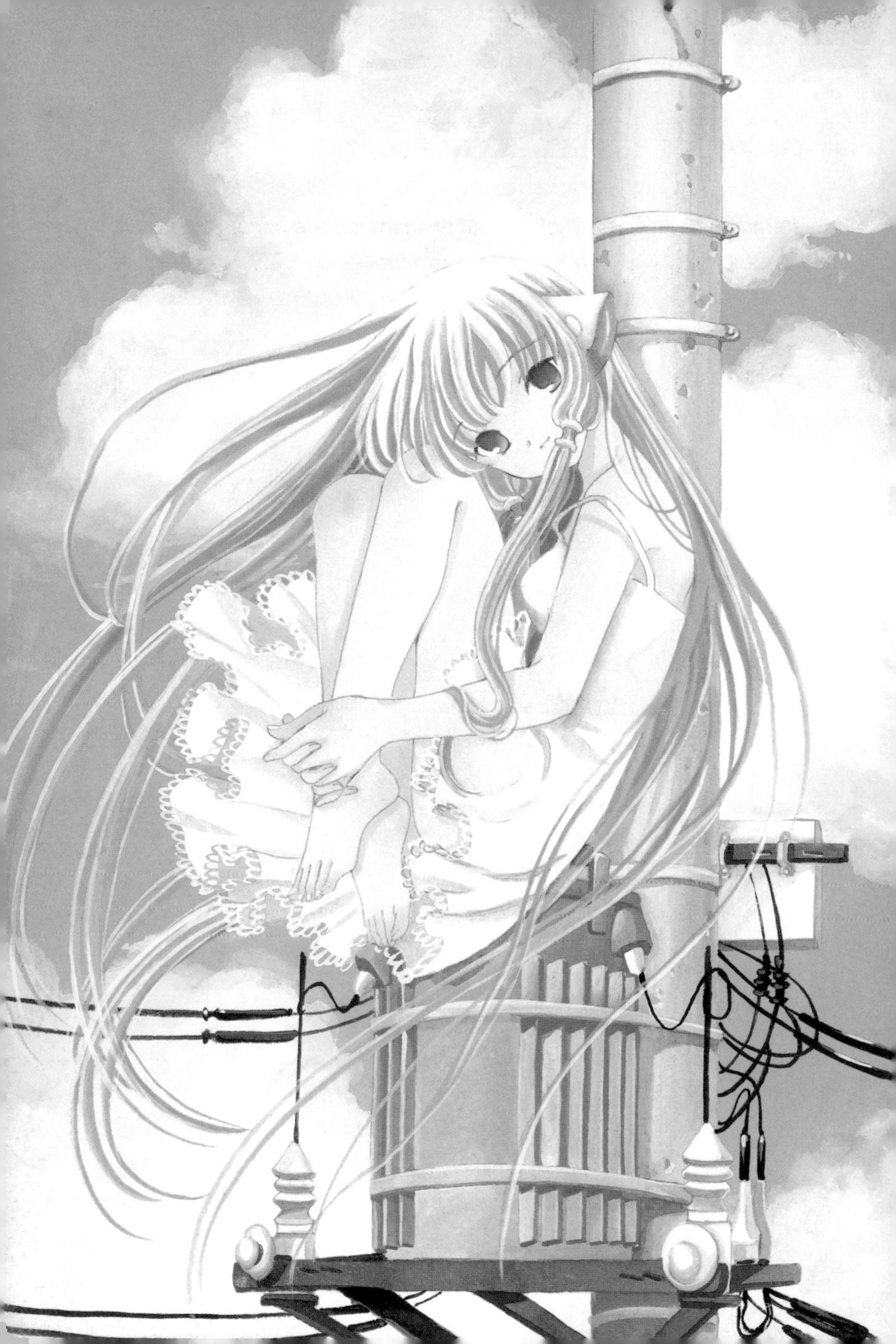

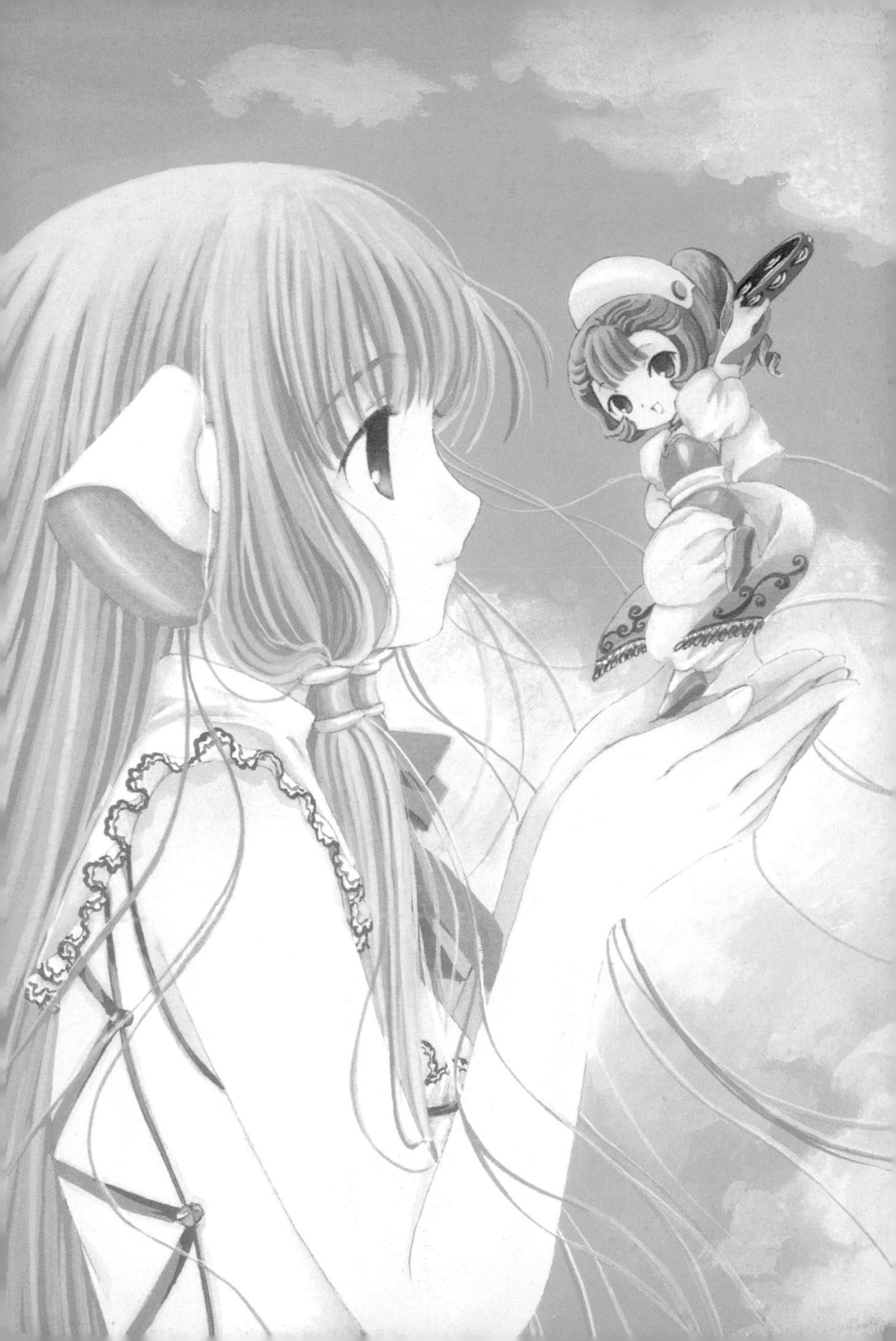

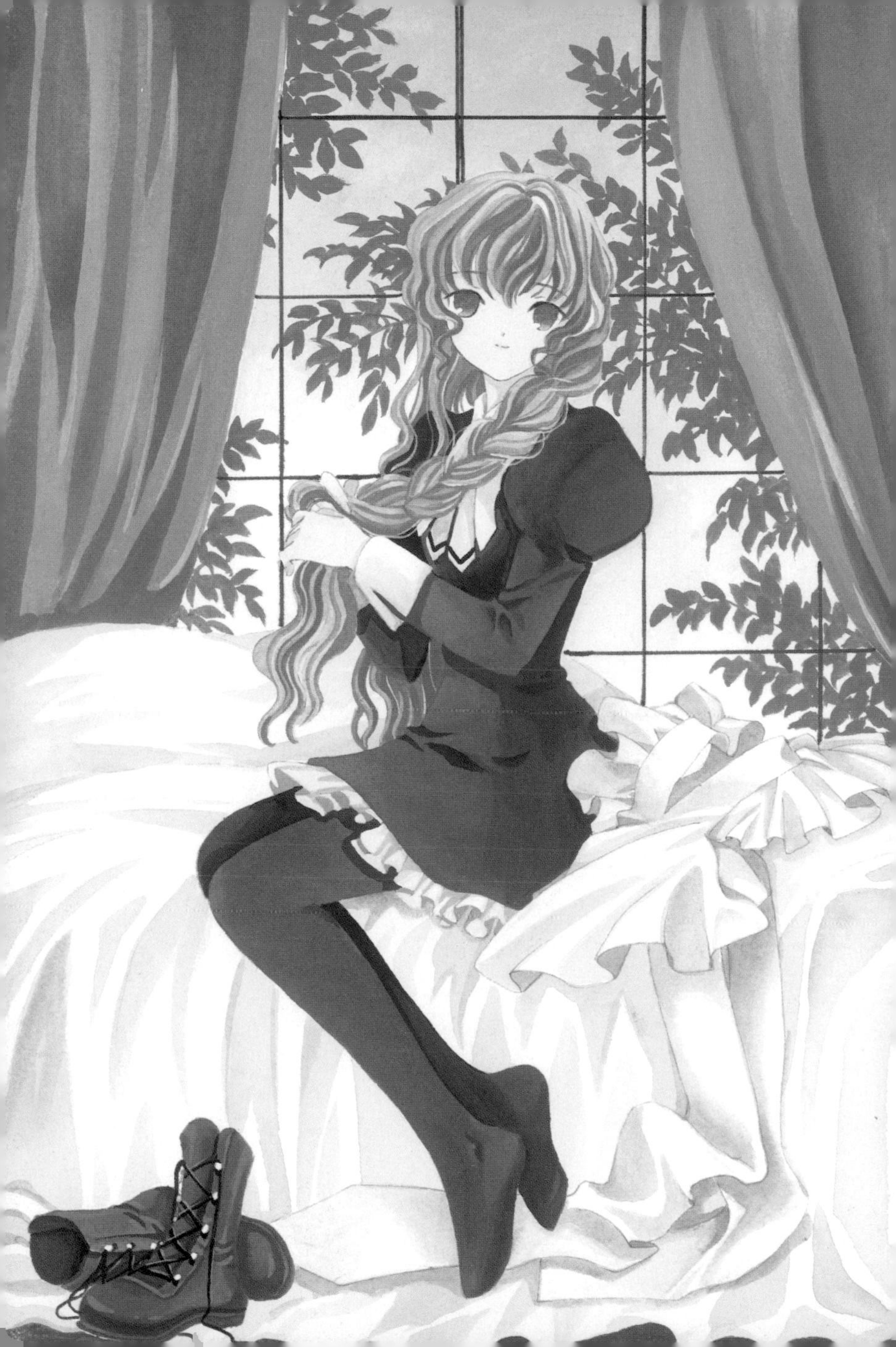

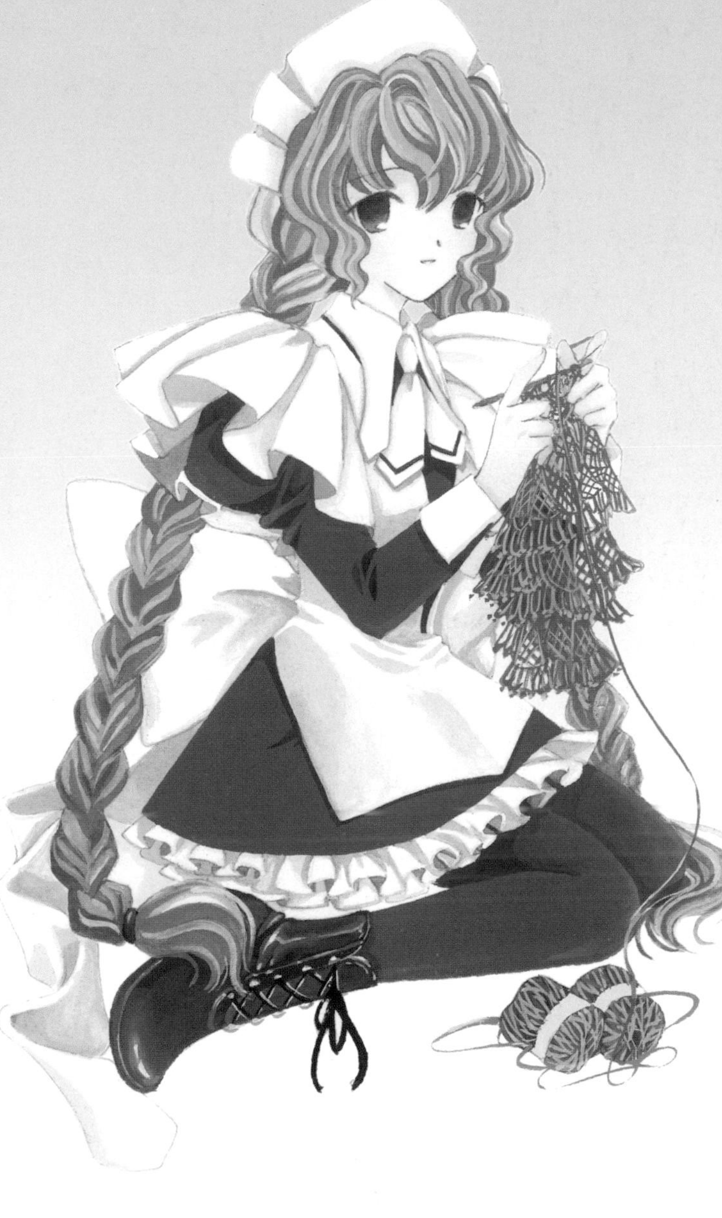

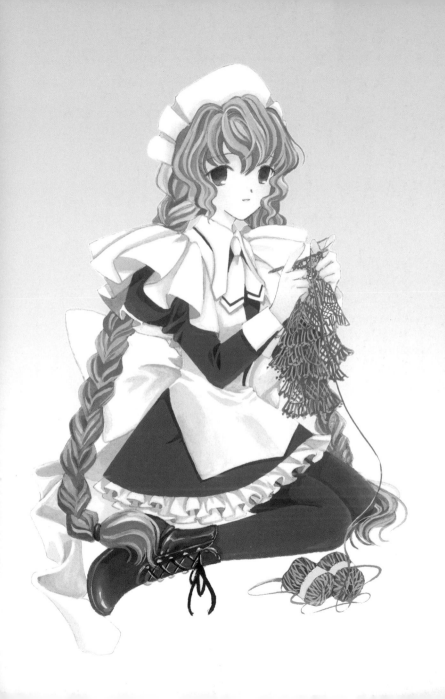

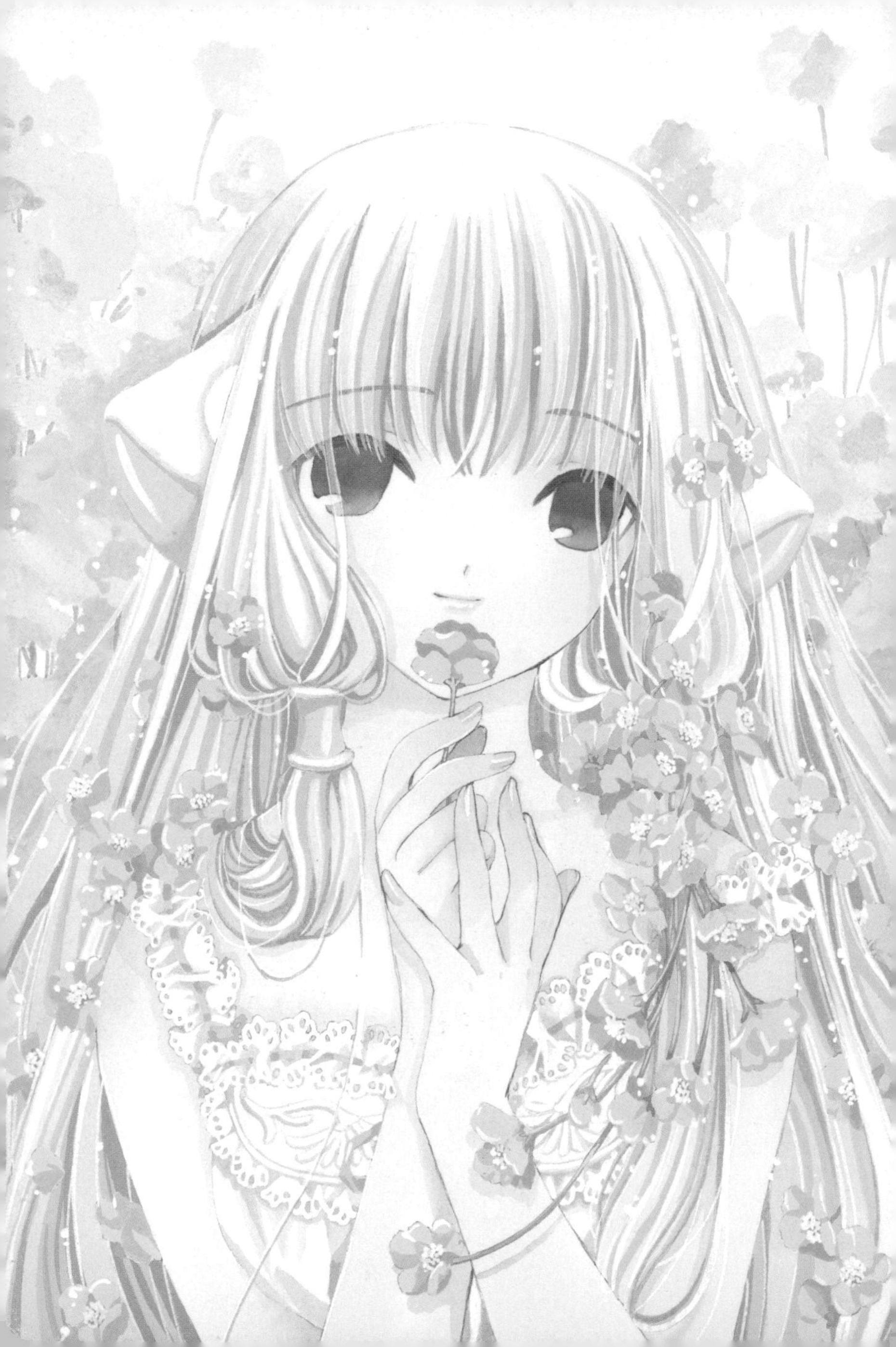

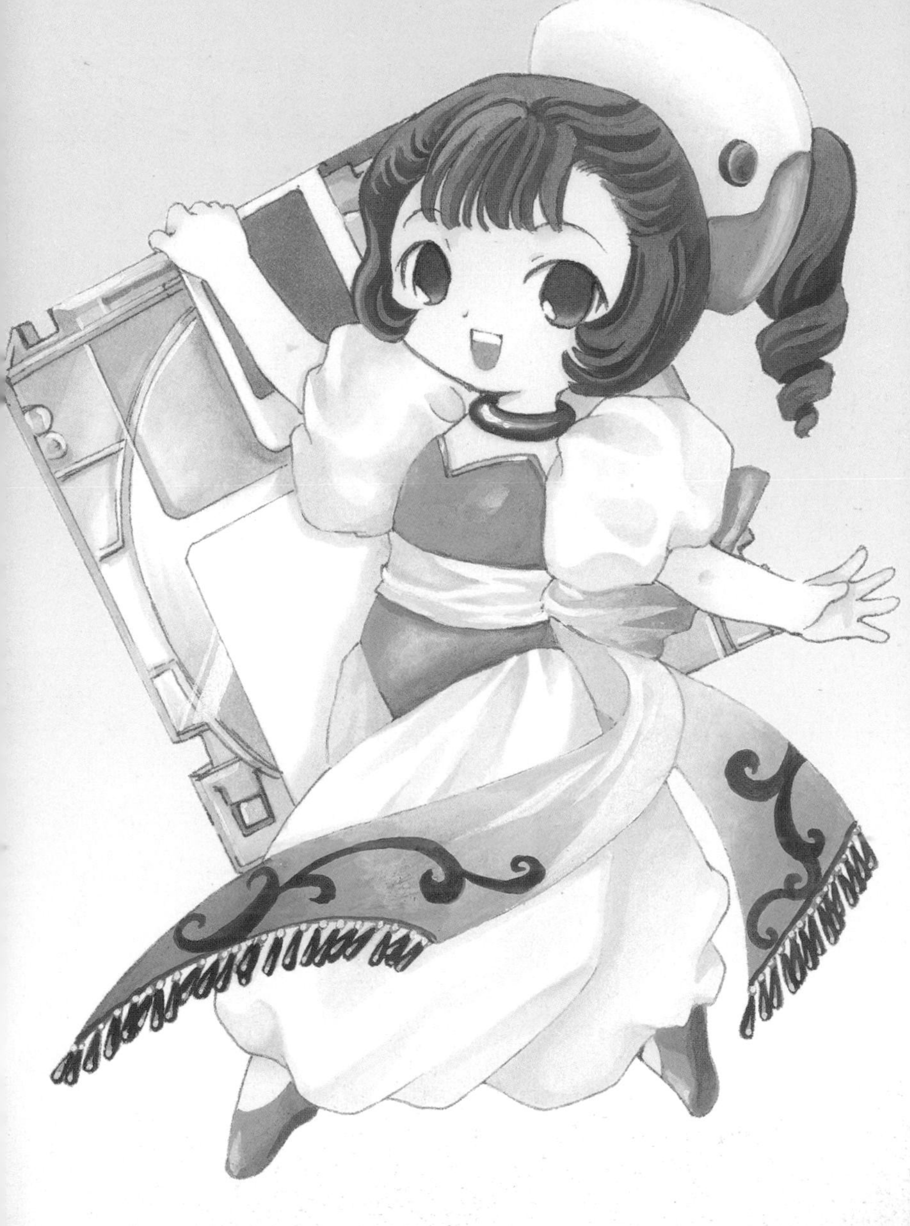

ANGELIC LAYER

Story and Art by
CLAMP

YOUNG TEEN MISAKI SUZUHARA has just arrived in Tokyo to attend the prestigious Eriol Academy. But what really excites her is Angelic Layer, the game where you control an Angel—a miniature robot fighter whose moves depend on your mind! Before she knows it, Misaki is an up-and-coming contender in Angelic Layer . . . and in way over her not-very-tall head! How far can enthusiasm take her in an arena full of much more experienced fighters . . . and a game full of secrets?

Don't miss the thrilling prequel to the acclaimed CLAMP manga *Chobits*! These omnibus-sized volumes feature not only the full story of *Angelic Layer* but also gorgeous, exclusive bonus color illustrations!

VOLUME ONE
978-1-61655-021-9

VOLUME TWO
978-1-61655-128-5

$19.99 each

AVAILABLE AT YOUR LOCAL COMICS SHOP OR BOOKSTORE
TO FIND A COMICS SHOP IN YOUR AREA, CALL 1-888-266-4226

For more information or to order direct:
On the web: DarkHorse.com ·E-mail: mailorder@darkhorse.com ·Phone: 1-800-862-0052
Mon.–Fri. 9 a.m. to 5 p.m. Pacific Time.

DARK HORSE MANGA
DarkHorse.com   Angelic Layer © CLAMP. (BL 7096)

Cardcaptor Sakura

カードキャプターさくら

MANGA BY
CLAMP

Fourth grader Sakura Kinomoto has found a strange book in her father's library—a book made by the wizard Clow to store dangerous spirits sealed within a set of magical cards. But when Sakura opens it up, there is nothing left inside but Kero-chan, the book's cute little guardian beast . . . who informs Sakura that since the Clow cards seem to have escaped while he was asleep, it's now her job to capture them!

With remastered image files straight from CLAMP, Dark Horse is proud to present *Cardcaptor Sakura* in omnibus form! Each book collects three volumes of the original twelve-volume series, and features thirty bonus color pages!

OMNIBUS BOOK 1
ISBN 978-1-59582-522-3

OMNIBUS BOOK 2
ISBN 978-1-59582-591-9

OMNIBUS BOOK 3
ISBN 978-1-59582-808-8

OMNIBUS BOOK 4
ISBN 978-1-59582-889-7

$19.99 each!

DARK
HORSE
MANGA
DarkHorse.com

AVAILABLE AT YOUR LOCAL COMICS SHOP OR BOOKSTORE!
To find a comics shop in your area, call 1-888-266-4226
For more information or to order direct: • On the web: DarkHorse.com
E-mail: mailorder@darkhorse.com • Phone: 1-800-862-0052 Mon.–Fri. 9 AM to 5 PM Pacific Time
Cardcaptor Sakura © 1996, 2011 by CLAMP. All rights reserved. English translation rights arranged with PYROTECHNIST CO. LTD., Tokyo. (BL 7085)

東京 TOKYO BABYLON

CLAMP

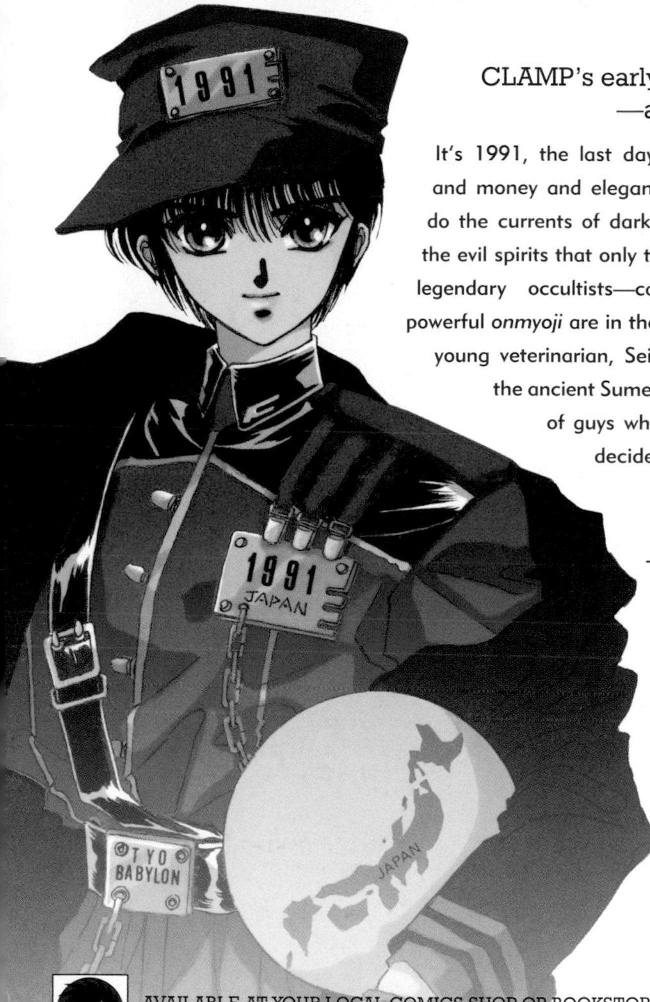
1991
1991
JAPAN
TYO
BABYLON
JAPAN

CLAMP's early epic of dangerous wor
—and dangerous attractio

It's 1991, the last days of Japan's bubble econom and money and elegance run through the streets. S do the currents of darkness beneath them, nourishin the evil spirits that only the arts of the *onmyoji*—Japan legendary occultists—can combat. The two mos powerful *onmyoji* are in the unlikely guises of a handsom young veterinarian, Seishiro, and the teenage heir t the ancient Sumeragi clan, Subaru—just a coupl of guys whom Subaru's sister Hokuto ha decided are destined to be together!

"Tokyo Babylon *is CLAMP*
first really great work.
—Manga: The Complete Guid

Each omnibus-size
volume features ove
a dozen full-colo
bonus pages

VOLUME ON
ISBN 978-1-61655-116-
$19.9

VOLUME TW
ISBN 978-1-61655-189-
$19.9

DARK HORSE MANGA
DarkHorse.com

AVAILABLE AT YOUR LOCAL COMICS SHOP OR BOOKSTORE!
To find a comics shop in your area, call 1-888-266-4226
For more information or to order direct: • On the web: DarkHorse.com
E-mail: mailorder@darkhorse.com • Phone: 1-800-862-0052 Mon.–Fri. 9 AM to 5 PM Pacific Time

CLAMP オキモノ キモノ
Mokona's
OKIMONO
KIMONO

CLAMP artist Mokona loves the art of traditional Japanese kimono. In fact, she designs kimono and kimono accessories herself and shares her love in *Okimono Kimono*, a fun and lavishly illustrated book full of drawings and photographs, interviews (including an interview with Onuki Ami of the J-pop duo Puffy AmiYumi), and exclusive short manga stories from the CLAMP artists!

From the creators of such titles as *Clover*, *Chobits*, *Cardcaptor Sakura*, *Magic Knight Rayearth*, and *Tsubasa*, *Okimono Kimono* is now available in English for the first time ever!

ISBN 978-1-59582-456-1

$12.99

AVAILABLE AT YOUR LOCAL COMICS SHOP OR BOOKSTORE
To find a comics shop in your area, call 1-888-266-4226
For more information or to order direct: • On the web: DarkHorse.com
E-mail: mailorder@darkhorse.com • Phone: 1-800-862-0052 Mon.–Fri. 9 AM to 5 PM Pacific Time.
CLAMP MOKONA NO OKIMONO KIMONO © 2007 CLAMP Mokona. Original Japanese edition published by Kawade Shabo Shinsha, Publishers. English translation copyright © 2010 Dark Horse Manga. Dark Horse Manga™ is a trademark of Dark Horse Comics, Inc. All rights reserved. (BL 7079)

DARK HORSE MANGA
DarkHorse.com

This is the back of the book!

This manga collection is translated into English, but arranged in right-to-left reading format to maintain the artwork's visual orientation as originally drawn and published in Japan. If you've never read comics this way before, take a look at the diagram below to give yourself an idea of how to go about it. Basically, you'll be starting in the upper right-hand corner, and will read each word balloon and panel moving right-to-left. It may take a little getting used to, but you should get the hang of it very quickly. Have fun! If this is the millionth manga you've read this way, never mind. ^_^

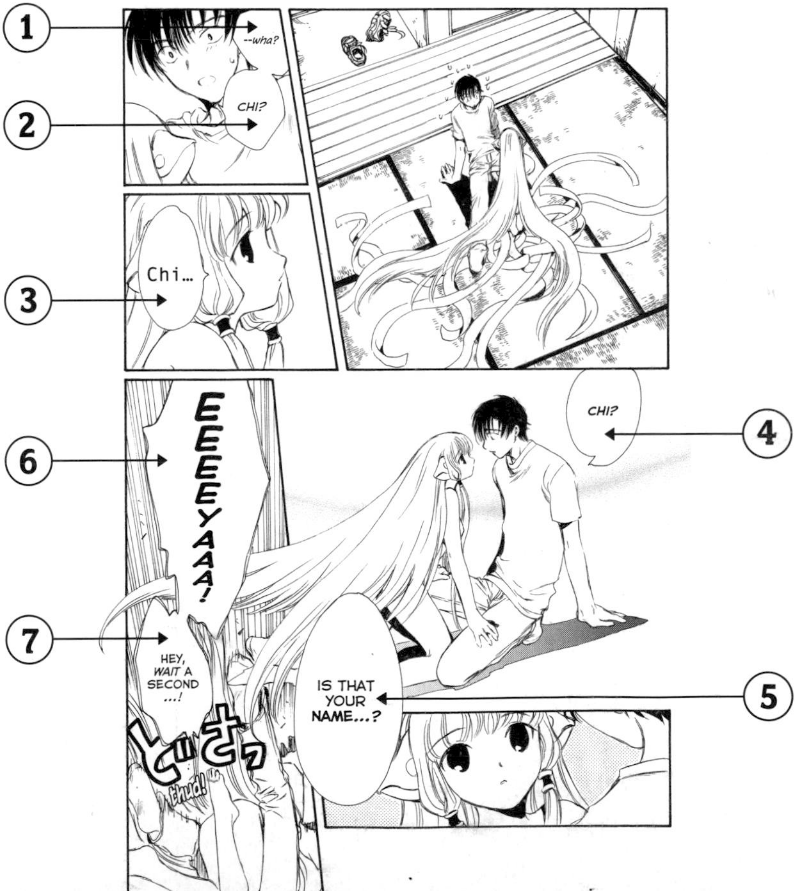
1
--wha?
2
CHI?
3
Chi…
4
CHI?
5
IS THAT YOUR NAME…?
6
EEEEEYAAA!
7
HEY, WAIT A SECOND …!
thud!

MANGA

VISIT THE MANGA ZONE ON DARKHORSE.COM TO EXPLORE GREAT FEATURES LIKE:

+ EXCLUSIVE CONTENT FROM EDITORS ON UPCOMING PROJECTS!

+ DOWNLOADABLE, EXCLUSIVE DESKTOPS!

+ ONLINE PREVIEWS, GAMES, AND OTHER FEATURES

+ MESSAGE BOARDS!

+ UP-TO-DATE INFORMATION ON THE LATEST RELEASES

+ LINKS TO OTHER COOL MANGA SITES!

Visit **DARKHORSE.COM** for more details!

© 2011 respective licensors. Dark Horse Comics® and the Dark Horse logo are trademarks of Dark Horse Comics, Inc., registered in various categories and countries. All rights reserved.